CRIMINOLOGY

13TH EDITION

THEORIES, PATTERNS, AND TYPOLOGIES

LARRY J. SIEGEL

University of Massachusetts, Lowell

CENGAGE
Learning®

Australia • Brazil • Mexico • Singapore • United Kingdom • United States

Criminology: Theories, Patterns, and Typologies, **Thirteenth Edition**
Larry J. Siegel

Senior Product Director: Marta Lee-Perriard

Senior Product Manager: Carolyn Henderson Meier

Senior Content Developer: Shelley Murphy

Product Assistant: Timothy Kappler

Marketing Director: Mark Linton

Senior Content Project Manager: Christy Frame

Senior Art Director: Helen Bruno

Senior Manufacturing Planner: Judy Inouye

Production Service: Linda Jupiter Productions

Photo Development Editor: Kim Adams Fox

Photo Researcher: Ugine Vinnarasi, Lumina Datamatics

Text Researcher: Ramya Selvaraj, Lumina Datamatics

Copy Editor: Lunaea Weatherstone

Proofreader: Susan Gall

Indexer: Janet Perlman

Text Designer: Debby Dutton

Cover Designer: Irene Morris Design

Cover Image: Mary DeLave

Compositor: MPS Limited

For product information and technology assistance, contact us at **Cengage Learning Customer & Sales Support, 1-800-354-9706.**

For permission to use material from this text or product, submit all requests online at **www.cengage.com/permissions.** Further permissions questions can be e-mailed to **permissionrequest@cengage.com.**

Unless otherwise noted, all content is © Cengage Learning

Library of Congress Control Number: 2016947586

Student Edition:
ISBN: 978-1-337-09184-8

Loose-leaf Edition:
ISBN: 978-1-337-09264-7

Cengage Learning
20 Channel Center Street
Boston, MA 02210
USA

Cengage Learning is a leading provider of customized learning solutions with employees residing in nearly 40 different countries and sales in more than 125 countries around the world. Find your local representative at **www.cengage.com.**

Cengage Learning products are represented in Canada by Nelson Education, Ltd.

To learn more about Cengage Learning Solutions, visit **www.cengage.com.**

Purchase any of our products at your local college store or at our preferred online store **www.cengagebrain.com.**

Printed in the United States of America
Print Number: 01   Print Year: 2016

This book is dedicated to my children, Eric, Julie, Rachel, and Andrew; my grandchildren, Jack, Brooke, and Kayla Jean; my sons-in-law, Jason Macy and Patrick Stephens; and my wife, partner, and best friend, Therese J. Libby.

ABOUT THE AUTHOR

Larry J. Siegel was born in the Bronx, New York. While living on Jerome Avenue and attending City College (CCNY) in the 1960s, he was swept up in the social and political currents of the time. He became intrigued with the influence contemporary culture had on individual behavior: did people shape society or did society shape people? He applied his interest in social forces and human behavior to the study of crime and justice. After graduating from CCNY, he attended the newly opened program in criminal justice at the State University of New York at Albany, where he earned both his M.A. and Ph.D. degrees. After completing his graduate work, Dr. Siegel began his teaching career at Northeastern University, where he was a faculty member for nine years. After leaving Northeastern, he held teaching positions at the University of Nebraska, Omaha, and Saint Anselm College in New Hampshire, and the School of Criminology and Justice Studies at the University of Massachusetts, Lowell, where he taught for 27 years; he is now a professor emeritus, still teaching online courses in criminology and criminal justice.

Dr. Siegel has written extensively in the area of crime and justice, including books on juvenile law, delinquency, criminology, criminal justice, and criminal procedure. He is a court-certified expert on police conduct and has testified in numerous legal cases. The father of four and grandfather of three, Larry Siegel now resides in Naples, Florida, with his wife, Terry, and their two dogs, Watson and Cody.

Terry and Larry Siegel at their daughter's wedding dinner.

Lois Fichner-Rathus

BRIEF CONTENTS

FEATURES

Criminology in Action

CONTENTS

Preface   xix

PART ONE | CONCEPTS OF CRIME, LAW, AND CRIMINOLOGY   1

CHAPTER 1
Crime and Criminology   3

CHAPTER 2
The Nature and Extent of Crime   27

PART TWO | THEORIES OF CRIME CAUSATION   99

CHAPTER 9

Developmental Theories:
Life Course, Latent Trait,
and Trajectory 305

PART | CRIME
THREE | TYPOLOGIES 343

CHAPTER 10

Interpersonal Violence 345

CHAPTER 11

Political Crime and Terrorism   393

CHAPTER 12

Property Crime   431

CHAPTER 13

Enterprise Crime: White-Collar, Green, and Transnational Organized Crime   461

CHAPTER 14

Public Order Crime: Sex and Substance Abuse   503

PREFACE

In 2007, Christine Belford and David Matusiewicz divorced, and Christine was awarded custody of their three young daughters. Instead of letting it all go, David Matusiewicz hatched a plot to stalk and harass his ex-wife even while he was doing time in prison for kidnapping the children during the divorce proceedings. Matusiewicz, a Delaware-based optometrist, enlisted the help of his mother, father, and sister, who together waged an elaborate, years-long online campaign against Christine Belford, during which they made charges that she endangered the lives of her daughters. The family employed a network of supporters whom they duped into helping them uncover information about Belford's life. By posting false allegations on websites and YouTube, they convinced people that she was a child abuser. The family also hired a private investigator to spy on Belford, who began to fear for her life.

In early 2013, David Matusiewicz, released from prison and on probation in Texas, requested a hearing regarding his child support arrearage and returned to Delaware with his parents, Lenore and Thomas Matusiewicz. On February 11, David and Thomas entered the courthouse shortly after 8 A.M.; the car they left in a nearby parking garage was later found to contain weapons, ammunition, a bulletproof vest, an electric shock device, recent photographs of the three children, and restraints in three different sizes. David passed through security and went upstairs; his father waited in the lobby, where he shot and killed Christine Belford and a friend, Laura Mulford, as they entered. He then took his own life after a shootout with police.

The three surviving family members—David, Lenore, and sister Amy Gonzalez—were the first people ever convicted on charges of cyberstalking resulting in death, a violation contained in the federal Violence Against Women Act.

Police seal off and guard the New Castle County (Delaware) Courthouse after three people were killed in the aftermath of a bitter divorce case.

Joseph Kaczmarek/AP Images

On February 18, 2016, they were each sentenced to life in prison for their crimes.

This tragic case is just one of many murderous incidents that have shaken the American public. It is not surprising that many Americans are concerned about crime and worried about becoming victims of violent crime themselves. We alter our behavior to limit the risk of victimization and question whether legal punishment alone can control criminal offenders. We watch movies and TV shows about the FBI, local police departments, and law firms and their clients. We are shocked when the news media offers graphic accounts of school shootings, police brutality, and sexual assaults.

I, too, have had a lifelong interest in crime, law, and justice. What causes people like the Matusiewicz family to first harass and then kill the mother of their children/grandchildren/nieces? Was their behavior the result of diseased minds and/or damaged personalities? If you believe that it is, how could four members of the same family be so similarly afflicted? Could their murderous rampage have been predicted and prevented? And what should be done with people who commit such horrendous crimes? Is it moral to execute someone even if they have taken another person's life? Should all the members of the family be considered guilty of murder even though only one pulled the trigger?

Goals of This Book

For almost 50 years, I have channeled my fascination with issues related to crime and justice into a career as a student and teacher of criminology. My goal in writing this text is to help students develop the same enthusiasm for criminology that has sustained me during my student days and teaching career. What could be more important or interesting than a field of study that deals with such wide-ranging topics as the motivation for mass murder, cybercrime, the effects of violent media on young people, drug abuse, and robbery? Criminology is a dynamic field, changing constantly with the release of major research studies, Supreme Court rulings, and governmental policy. Its dynamism and diversity make it an engrossing area of study.

One reason why the study of criminology is so important is that debates continue over the nature and extent of crime and the causes and prevention of criminality. Some view criminals as society's victims who are forced to violate the law because of poverty and lack of opportunity. Others view aggressive, antisocial behavior as a product of mental and physical abnormalities, present at birth or soon after, that are stable over the life course. Still another view is that crime is a function of the rational choice of greedy, selfish people who can be deterred from engaging in criminal behavior only by the threat of harsh punishments. It all comes down to this: Why do people do the things they do? How can we explain the intricacies and diversity of human behavior?

Because interest in crime and justice is so great and so timely, this text is designed to review these ongoing issues and cover the field of criminology in an organized and comprehensive manner. It is meant as a broad overview of the field, an introduction to whet the reader's appetite and encourage further and more in-depth exploration. I try to present how the academic study of criminology intersects with real-world issues.

Diversity is a key issue in criminology and a topic that has important real-world consequences. Therefore the text attempts to integrate issues of racial, ethnic, gender, and cultural diversity throughout.

My primary goals in writing this text were as follows:

1. To separate the facts from the fiction about crime and criminality
2. To provide students with a thorough knowledge of criminology and show its diversity and intellectual content
3. To be as thorough and up-to-date as possible
4. To be objective and unbiased
5. To describe current theories, crime types, and methods of social control, and to analyze their strengths and weaknesses
6. To show how criminological thought has influenced social policy

Features

- **Policy and Practice in Criminology** These boxes show how criminological ideas and research can be put into action through policies and practices of the criminal justice system. For example, in Chapter 8, the Policy and Practice feature discusses the Center for Restorative

Justice (CRJ) in Vermont, a nonprofit community justice agency that for more than 30 years has provided a variety of restorative justice programming and services ranging from drug abuse prevention for kids to reentry support for adults released from incarceration.

- **Race, Culture, Gender, and Criminology** These box features cover issues of racial, sexual, and cultural diversity. In Chapter 10, for example, a feature entitled "Honor Killing" looks at murders provoked by the belief that a family's honor has been threatened by a woman or girl's sexual misconduct. The United Nations estimates that 5,000 of these so-called honor killings occur annually; in some Palestinian territories, the number of killings has more than doubled in the past few years.

- **Criminology in Action** Throughout the book, every attempt is made to access the most current research and scholarship available. Most people who use the book have told me that this is one of its strongest features. I have attempted to present current research in a balanced fashion, even though this approach can be frustrating to students. It is comforting to reach an unequivocal conclusion about an important topic, but sometimes that simply is not possible. In an effort to be objective and fair, I have presented each side of important criminological debates in full. The boxed features titled Criminology in Action review critically important research topics in criminology. In Chapter 10, the feature titled "Violence and Human Nature" reviews a book by sociologist Randall Collins, *Violence: A Micro-sociological Theory*, which proposes that humans are inherently passive and violence is a function of social interaction. Most humans shirk from violent encounters and even those who talk aggressively are fearful and tense during violent encounters. Humans typically resort to violence only when they have overwhelming superiority over their opponents in terms of arms and numbers.

- **Profiles in Crime** These features are designed to present to students actual crimes that help illustrate the position or views within the chapter. In Chapter 15, this feature focuses on the Lost Boy case, an investigation into a transnational online forum where men with a sexual interest in young boys traded child pornography.

- **Famous Criminologists** are chapter inserts that spotlight some of the key thinkers and criminological theorists (past and present) in the discipline, showing their individual contributions to the field of criminology.

- **Thinking Like a Criminologist: An Ethical Dilemma** It is important for students to think critically about law and justice and to develop a critical perspective toward the social and legal institutions entrusted with crime control. Throughout the book, students are asked to critique research highlighted in boxed material and to think "outside the box," as it were. To aid in this task, each chapter contains a brief section called Thinking Like a Criminologist: An Ethical Dilemma, which presents a scenario that can be analyzed with the help of material found in the chapter. The chapter also includes critical thinking questions to guide classroom interaction.

- **Connections** are short inserts that help link the material to other areas covered in the book. A Connections insert in Chapter 15 points out how the ability to access pornographic material over the Internet has helped expand the sale of sexually related material (covered in Chapter 14). Most Connections boxes include **Ask Yourself . . .** which poses a scholarly question based on the material found at both sources. The Connections box in Chapter 15 poses this question: Considering that distributing pornography and kiddie porn is an international problem, should an independent law enforcement agency be created to enforce laws across borders? What might be a problem with creating an international agency?
- **Learning Objectives** spell out what students should learn in each chapter and are reinforced via a direct link to the end-of-chapter summary as well as all of the text's ancillary materials.
- Chapter **Outlines** provide a road map to coverage and serve as a useful review tool.
- A **running glossary** in the margins ensures that students understand words and concepts as they are introduced.

In sum, the text has been carefully structured to cover relevant material in a comprehensive, balanced, and objective fashion. Every attempt has been made to make the presentation of material interesting and contemporary. No single political or theoretical position dominates the text; instead, the many diverse views that are contained within criminology and characterize its interdisciplinary nature are presented. While the text includes analysis of the most important scholarly works and scientific research reports, it also includes a great deal of topical information on recent cases and events such as the Pulse nightclub shooting in Orlando, Florida, and the story of Owen Labrie and the St. Paul's School rape case.

Topic Areas

Criminology: TPT is a thorough introduction to this fascinating field and is intended for students in introductory courses in criminology. It is divided into three main sections or topic areas.

Part One provides a framework for studying criminology. The first chapter defines the field and discusses its most basic concepts: the definition of crime, the component areas of criminology, the history of criminology, the concept of criminal law, and the ethical issues that arise in this field. Chapter 2 covers criminological research methods, as well as the nature, extent, and patterns of crime. Chapter 3 is devoted to the concept of victimization, including the nature of victims, theories of victimization, and programs designed to help crime victims.

Part Two contains six chapters that cover criminological theory: Why do people behave the way they do? Why do they commit crimes? These views focus on choice (Chapter 4), biological and psychological traits (Chapter 5), social structure and culture (Chapter 6), social process and socialization (Chapter 7), social conflict (Chapter 8), and human development (Chapter 9).

Part Three is devoted to the major forms of criminal behavior. The chapters in this section cover violent crime (Chapter 10), political crime and terrorism (Chapter 11), theft offenses (Chapter12), enterprise crimes, including white-collar and transnational organized crime (Chapter 13) public order crimes, including sex offenses and substance abuse (Chapter 14), and cybercrime (Chapter 15).

Chapter-by-Chapter Changes in the 13th Edition

- **Chapter 1** now begins with a vignette on Syed Rizwan Farook and Tashfeen Malik, two lone-wolf terrorists who attacked a holiday party being held for employees at the San Bernardino County Department of Public Health. The case of *Glossip v. Gross* is analyzed, showing how Justices Breyer and Ginsburg relied on social science research by socio-legal scholar Samuel Gross and his colleagues in their decision making. It covers research evaluating the effect of sex offender registration in the state of Florida. There is a new section on legalizing marijuana. A number of states have now legalized the personal use of marijuana while others have legalized it for medical purposes.
- **Chapter 2** begins with a vignette on Dylann Roof, who killed nine African American parishioners in the Emanuel African Methodist Episcopal Church in Charleston, South Carolina. Roof was an avowed racist who committed the murders in order to spark a race war. All crime data in the chapter have been updated and now include 2015 data showing that the number of murders has risen sharply. Other updated sections include data on why people do not report crime and on the NIBRS program. A research study is reviewed in which one group of subjects was paid to be "honest and thoughtful" while another group was merely paid to participate. There are new sections on interview data, including analysis of research showing that sexual assault and its related trauma can disrupt survivors' employment in several ways. New data are supplied on the association between abortion and crime that question the association between these two controversial issues. The section "International Crime Trends" has been thoroughly updated. The future trends section has been revised. Research is reviewed that shows that while the vast majority of a city's homicides are committed with guns,

most guns used in crime are quite old, with a median age of more than 10 years. A new section on co-offending and crime covers the view that crime tends to be a group activity.

- **Chapter 3** begins with a story about the theft of a 300-year-old Stradivarius violin valued at more than $5 million. There is updated material on determining the true cost of victimization using complex mathematical models. There is new research on how robberies occurring in "semi-public" places, such as bars and restaurants, are less likely to result in injury than those in more secluded areas. The latest data available from the National Center for Educational Statistics on victimization in schools are presented. Other research focuses on how racial stereotypes affect criminal decision making and shape offenders' decisions. There is a section on "Victim Characteristics" that suggests that some people may invite or precipitate victimization because there is an element in their personality that incites attacks. Another new section looks at victim disability. The association between a criminal lifestyle and victimization is covered, including gang membership's impact on victimization risk. A Policy and Practice in Criminology box covers advocacy for the victims of intimate partner violence.

- **Chapter 4** begins with the story of how 13 co-conspirators were sent to prison after being convicted on charges relating to setting up a criminal enterprise designed to steal trucks, disassemble them in a chop shop, and sell them as scrap metal. A new Criminology in Action feature, "Human Agency, Personal Assessment, Crime, and Desistance," covers the central roles human agency and personal assessments play in the decision to commit crime. Another new Criminology in Action, "How Auto Thieves Plan Their Crimes," looks at the decision-making process of auto thieves, a group especially concerned about the reaction of their victims/targets. Another section on "Rational Thieves" shows how robbers and burglars display rationality in their choice of targets. A study of piracy found that when a ship's crew takes protective measures, the likelihood that a pirate attack will be successful is significantly reduced. Recent evidence is presented indicating that adding to police patrol forces does in fact help reduce crime rates.

- **Chapter 5** begins with a new vignette that covers the life of Chris Harper-Mercer, the man who opened fire at Umpqua Community College on October 1, 2015, killing nine people and wounding seven others. Data are presented from a Boston study of high school students that found adolescents who drank more than five cans of soft drinks per week were significantly more likely to carry weapons and to engage in violence with peers, family members, and intimate partners. The argument that social environment plays a more critical role in shaping behavior than genes and heredity is presented. There is a Profiles in Crime feature on Adam Lanza and the Newtown massacre. Research is presented showing that there are different types of psychopaths/sociopaths who fall along a continuum of critical behavior and personality traits, such as instability, inhibition, and attachment.

- **Chapter 6** begins with a vignette on Mara Salvatrucha 13 (MS-13) and their violent crimes in the Atlanta area, including the murder of one man and the shootings of two others, one of whom was a 14-year-old boy. A Criminology in Action feature called "*Labor's Love Lost*" reviews the book of the same name by Andrew Cherlin, which provides an explanation of the toll income and educational inequality takes on society. There are new data on income inequality: the 80 richest people on the planet have the same amount of wealth as the poorest 3.5 billion people combined. The groundbreaking book *Divergent Social Worlds* shows how among urban dwellers more than two-thirds of all whites, half of all African Americans, and one-third of Latinos live in segregated local neighborhoods. A new section is devoted to the "broken windows" model and how policing programs have been designed to reduce social disorder by concentrating on lifestyle crimes such as panhandling, loitering, and vandalism.

- **Chapter 7** returns to the story of Ethan Couch, the "affluenza" teen who made headlines again in 2015 when he violated his probation agreement and fled the country. There is a section on the family stress model, which shows that living in a disadvantaged neighborhood places terrific strain on family functioning, especially in single-parent families that experience social isolation from relatives. There is new research on children of incarcerated parents, who are more likely to act out and engage in expressive crimes of violence. A Criminology in Action feature looks at white-collar neutralization techniques. The long-term effects of stigma were observed in a recent study that found that students who are punished for behavioral problems by being suspended or expelled from school are more likely to be involved in the criminal justice system later in life. The toll the War on Drugs takes on African American drug offenders further illustrates the powerful effect stigma has on people's lives.

- **Chapter 8** opens with a vignette on the 2016 presidential primary campaign as an example of how conflict shapes society. There is a Profiles in Crime feature on Russian state-organized crime. A section called "Being Victimized" shows how sexual and other victimization of girls is a function of male socialization. A Policy and Practice in Criminology feature on the Center for Restorative Justice (CRJ) describes a nonprofit community justice agency that, for more than 30 years, has helped people in Vermont.

- **Chapter 9** begins with a vignette on the horrific Petit home invasion and murders by career criminals Steven Hayes and Joshua Komisarjevsky. The section "Why

Does Marriage Work?" describes new research findings that the seeds of marital success are planted early in childhood: kids who grow up with warm, nurturing parents are the ones most likely to have positive romantic relationships and later intact marriages. Another new section covers social schematic theory (SST). A new section called "Learning or Biology?" looks at whether there is a genetic/biosocial component to the development of impulsivity. Research shows that antisocial behavior runs in families and that having criminal relatives is a significant predictor of future misbehaviors. A new section on first offenders looks at why some offenders start early, others late, and some not at all.

■ **Chapter 10** opens with a vignette about a Dominican street gang in Lawrence, Massachusetts, known as the Joloperros and their "perfect" illegal enterprise: kidnap drug dealers, bookmakers, and money launderers, steal their cash and drugs, and then hold them for ransom. A Criminology in Action box called "Mass Shooters: Why Do Some Live and Why Do Some Die?" illustrates research on crime typologies. Another Criminology in Action feature, "Violence and Human Nature," looks at *Violence: A Micro-sociological Theory*, by sociologist Randall Collins, who proposes a theory of violence that argues that humans are inherently passive and violence is a function of social interaction. New research shows while most drug market participants do not routinely use firearms to commit crimes, those who were under the influence at the time they committed their crime were also the ones most likely to be carrying weapons. Active shooter incidents is another new topic. The chapter contains the latest data from the Department of Health and Human Services (DHHS) on the extent of child maltreatment. New hate crime data are included as well as the latest on workplace violence. The section on stalking has been expanded; all 50 states and the federal government now have stalking statutes that cover a wide range of criminal behavior.

■ **Chapter 11** begins with a vignette on WikiLeaks and how Chelsea Manning revealed information that showed us "the true human cost of our wars in Iraq and Afghanistan." A Profiles in Crime box features Edward Snowden. There is coverage of officials in the small town of Cudahy, California, who took part in widespread corruption scheme that included accepting cash bribes, abusing drugs at city hall, and throwing out absentee ballots that favored election challengers. A section called "How Common Is Voter Fraud?" finds that while *claims* of voter fraud are common, actual cases in the United States are relatively rare. There is a section on economic espionage cases aimed at U.S. companies, and another on the latest data in terrorism trends and casualties. A Criminology in Action feature covers the Islamic State of Iraq and the Levant (ISIL). A new section on lone-actor terrorists looks at people—such as the Boston Marathon bombers—who use violence to achieve some political or social goal and who do not receive orders, direction, support, or aid from any outside group. A section on the U.S. Freedom Act looks at how the law changed when the Patriot Act ended in 2015.

■ **Chapter 12** opens with a vignette on the infamous Pharmacy Burglars ring, which was responsible for more than 125 burglaries and attempted burglaries of pharmacies in New York City. The chapter looks at how in the Internet age some fences have begun to sell their merchandise online on a variety of merchandising websites. E-fencers like to sell at a discount small items in bulk—razor blades, makeup, skincare products, baby formula, over-the-counter medications, and the like. The section on which cars are stolen most often has been updated.

■ **Chapter 13** starts with the story of Allison Layton, who owned a California company called Miracles Egg Donation that was supposed to help women who wanted children, but ended up stealing her victims' hopes and dreams as well as their money. A section on investment swindles covers a $40 million Ponzi scheme by Keith Franklin Simmons, a North Carolina businessman looking for a way to make easy money. There is a new section on telemarketing swindles. A Profiles in Crime feature, "Aubrey Lee Price: Religious Swindler," looks at the career of a formerly devout Christian minister and trusted financial adviser, who was sentenced to 30 years in prison for bank fraud, embezzlement, and other crimes. There are sections on political corruption, including that of Sheldon Silver, speaker of New York State's assembly and one of the state's most powerful politicians, who was convicted of numerous charges of influence peddling. A Profiles in Crime box called "Mafia Looters" reviews a recent New Jersey case involving the Lucchese crime family that proves traditional organized crime can still be a potent threat.

■ **Chapter 14** begins with a vignette on MyRedBook, a website that hosted advertisements posted by prostitutes containing explicit photos, graphic descriptions of sexual services offered, and rates for the sexual services. There is an update on banned books. A section on the same-sex marriage crusade has been updated to reflect sweeping legal changes. The history of prostitution includes material on Jane Addams, one of the most famous and influential social reformers of the early twentieth century, who described accounts of victims of white slavery during her work at Hull House, a Chicago refuge for the needy. The newest data on drug abuse from the Monitoring the Future survey and other data sources are provided.

■ **Chapter 15** opens with a vignette about business e-mail compromise, a growing financial fraud that has resulted in actual and attempted losses of more than a billion dollars to businesses worldwide. A Profiles in Crime feature covers the Lost Boy case, which involved an online bulletin board where men with a sexual interest in young boys traded child pornography. A new section covers

Internet extortion. Other new sections cover overpayment fraud and recovery/impersonation schemes. The most recent data on cyberbullying, compiled by the National Center for Education Statistics, are presented. There is a discussion of the NSA's PRISM program, which extracts information from the servers of major American Internet companies. A Policy and Practice in Criminology feature reviews terrorism on the Net.

Supplements

MINDTAP® FOR CRIMINAL JUSTICE

The most applied learning experience available, MindTap is dedicated to preparing students to make the kinds of reasoned decisions they will have to as criminal justice professionals faced with real-world challenges. Available for virtually every Criminal Justice course, MindTap offers customizable content, course analytics, an e-reader, and more—all within your current learning management system. With its rich array of assets—video cases, interactive visual summaries, decision-making scenarios, quizzes, and writing skill builders—MindTap is perfectly suited to today's Criminal Justice students, engaging them, guiding them toward mastery of basic concepts, and advancing their critical thinking abilities.

INSTRUCTOR'S MANUAL WITH LESSON PLANS

The manual includes learning objectives, key terms, a detailed chapter outline, a chapter summary, lesson plans, discussion topics, student activities, "What If" scenarios, media tools, and sample syllabi. The learning objectives are correlated with the discussion topics, student activities, and media tools.

DOWNLOADABLE WORD TEST BANK

The enhanced test bank includes a variety of questions per chapter—a combination of multiple-choice, true/false, completion, essay, and critical thinking formats, with a full answer key. The test bank is coded to the learning objectives that appear in the main text and identifies where in the text (by section) the answer appears. Finally, each question in the test bank has been carefully reviewed by experienced criminal justice instructors for quality, accuracy, and content

coverage, so instructors can be sure they are working with an assessment and grading resource of the highest caliber.

CENGAGE LEARNING TESTING

Powered by Cognero, the accompanying assessment tool is a flexible, online system that allows you to:

- import, edit, and manipulate test bank content from the text's test bank or elsewhere, including your own favorite test questions
- create ideal assessments with your choice of 15 question types (including true/false, multiple choice, opinion scale/Likert, and essay)
- create multiple test versions in an instant using drop-down menus and familiar, intuitive tools that take you through content creation and management with ease
- deliver tests from your LMS, your classroom, or wherever you want—plus, import and export content into other systems as needed.

ONLINE POWERPOINT LECTURES

Helping you make your lectures more engaging while effectively reaching your visually oriented students, these handy Microsoft PowerPoint® slides outline the chapters of the main text in a classroom-ready presentation. The PowerPoint® slides reflect the content and organization of the new edition of the text and feature some additional examples and real-world cases for application and discussion.

Acknowledgments

My colleagues at Cengage Learning have done their typically outstanding job of aiding me in the preparation of this text and putting up with my yearly angst. Carolyn Henderson Meier, my wonderful product manager, helped guide this project from start to finish. Shelley Murphy is an honorary co-author, content developer, and dear friend. Kim Adams Fox and Lumina Datamatics did an outstanding job on photo research. Linda Jupiter, the book's production editor, is another close confidant and friend. I really appreciate the help of Lunaea Weatherstone, copy editor extraordinaire and my personal life coach. The sensational Christy Frame is an extraordinary content project manager, and Mark Linton, the marketing manager, is fantastic as always.

PART ONE | CONCEPTS OF CRIME, LAW, AND CRIMINOLOGY

CHAPTER 1
CRIME AND CRIMINOLOGY

CHAPTER 2
THE NATURE AND EXTENT OF CRIME

CHAPTER 3
VICTIMS AND VICTIMIZATION

Concern about crime and justice has been an important part of the human condition for more than 5,000 years, since the first criminal codes were set down in the Middle East. Although criminology—the scientific study of crime—is considered a modern science, it has existed for more than 200 years. The first section of the text covers some of the basic questions in criminology: How is crime defined? How much crime is there, and what are the trends and patterns in the crime rate? How many people fall victim to crime, and who is likely to become a crime victim? How did our system of criminal law develop, and what are the basic elements of crimes? What is the science of criminology all about?

These are some of the core issues that will be addressed in the first three chapters of this text. Chapter 1 introduces students to the field of criminology: its nature, area of study, methodologies, and its historical development. Chapter 2 focuses on the acquisition of crime data, crime rate trends, and observable patterns within the crime rate. Chapter 3 is devoted to victims and victimization. Topics include the effects of victimization, the cause of victimization, and efforts to help crime victims.

Photographs of victims of the San Bernardino terrorist attack.

SIERRA CLAYBORN

TIN NGUYEN

Sun Jul 27 19:28:11 CDT 2014

Tashfeen Malik (left) and Syed Farook

LEARNING OBJECTIVES

L01 Explain what is meant by the term *criminology*

L02 Identify the difference between crime and deviance

L03 Recognize the concept of "criminology in action" and articulate what criminologists do

L04 Discuss the three most prominent views of the meaning of "crime"

L05 Outline the development of criminal law

L06 Analyze the different categories of law

L07 Articulate the relationship between the criminal law and the U.S. Constitution

L08 Synthesize the different purposes of criminal law

L09 Compare and contrast the elements of the criminal law

L010 Summarize the main ethical issues in criminology

1 CRIME AND CRIMINOLOGY

On December 2, 2015, Syed Rizwan Farook and Tashfeen Malik attacked a holiday party being held for employees at the San Bernardino County Department of Public Health and killed 14 people; 22 others were seriously injured in the attack. Farook, who worked for the health department, was an American-born citizen of Pakistani descent, while Malik, his wife, was Pakistani-born and a lawful permanent resident. They had a 6-month-old daughter. After the shooting, the couple fled the scene in a rented SUV and were killed in a shootout with pursuing police.[1]

Farook and Malik are considered homegrown violent extremists, inspired by but not directed by a foreign group; they were not part of any known terrorist cell. Farook had visited Pakistan in 2014 and returned with Malik, who traveled on a Pakistani passport with a fiancée visa; they also visited Saudi Arabia. Although they had visited the Middle East, their radicalization is believed to have been via the Internet. After they returned from abroad, the couple was able to stockpile weapons, thousands of rounds of ammunition, and bomb-making equipment in their home in Redlands, California.

While the San Bernardino attack was horrific, it was soon supplanted in the national conscience on June 12, 2016, by the massacre committed at the Pulse nightclub in Orlando, Florida, by Omar Mir Seddique Mateen, a New York-born son of Afghan immigrants. Mateen, who pledged his allegiance to ISIL during the attack, was killed by police after murdering 49 people and wounding more than 50 others. The Orlando attack will be reviewed in more detail in Chapter 11.

The San Bernardino attack, the Orlando massacre, and the Boston Marathon bombing, and other high-profile criminal incidents have spurred interest in **criminology**, an academic discipline that uses the scientific method to study the nature, extent, cause, and control of criminal behavior. The subject matter of criminology ranges from explaining and understanding terrorist activity such as the San Bernardino shootings to preventing white-collar fraud, from drug legalization to cyberbullying. What motivates people like Syed Rizwan Farook and Tashfeen Malik to turn on co-workers and people they knew in the name of jihad? Or was that their real motive? Was their crime a matter of rational choice and decision making or the outcome of delusional thinking and mental illness?

Regardless of which areas of human behavior they study, **criminologists**, unlike political figures and media commentators—whose opinions about crime may be colored by personal experiences, biases, and election concerns—remain objective, unbiased, and impartial about the behaviors they study, even if it involves horrendous acts such as the marathon bombing.

This text analyzes criminology and its major subareas of inquiry. It focuses on the nature and extent of crime, the causes of crime, and patterns of criminal behavior. This chapter introduces and defines criminology: What are its goals? How do criminologists define crime? How do they conduct research? What ethical issues face those wishing to conduct criminological research?

What Is Criminology?

 Explain what is meant by the term *criminology*

Criminology is the scientific approach to studying criminal behavior. In their classic definition, preeminent criminologists Edwin Sutherland and Donald Cressey state:

criminology The scientific study of the nature, extent, cause, and control of criminal behavior.

criminologists Researchers who use scientific methods to study the nature, extent, cause, and control of criminal behavior.

scientific method Using verifiable principles and procedures for the systematic acquisition of knowledge; typically involves formulating a problem, creating a hypothesis, and collecting data through observation and experiment to verify the hypothesis.

Criminology is the body of knowledge regarding crime as a social phenomenon. It includes within its scope the processes of making laws, of breaking laws, and of reacting toward the breaking of laws. . . . The objective of criminology is the development of a body of general and verified principles and of other types of knowledge regarding this process of law, crime, and treatment.[2]

Sutherland and Cressey's definition includes some of the most important areas of interest to criminologists:

- *Crime is a social phenomenon.* Although some criminologists believe that individual traits and characteristics may play some role in the cause of criminals' antisocial behavior, most believe that social factors are at the root cause of crime. Even the most disturbed people are influenced by their environment and their social interactions and personal relationships.
- *The processes of making laws.* Sutherland and Cressey's definition recognizes the association between crime and the criminal law and shows how the law defines crime. How and why laws are created and why some are strengthened and others eliminated is of great interest to criminologists.
- *Breaking laws and reacting toward the breaking of laws.* At its core, the purpose of criminology is to understand both the onset of crime and the most effective methods for its elimination. Why do people commit illegal acts, and what can be done to convince them—and others who are contemplating crime—that it is in their best interests to turn their back on criminality? These concepts are naturally bound together: it is impossible to effectively control crime unless we understand its cause.
- *Development of a body of general and verified principles.* Sutherland and Cressey recognize that criminology is a social science and criminologists must use the **scientific method** when conducting research. Criminologists are required to employ valid and reliable experimental designs and sophisticated data analysis techniques or else lose standing in the academic community.

Criminology today is a unique and independent field of study. It has a major national organization—the American Society of Criminology—and numerous graduate programs award the Ph.D. degree in criminology. Nevertheless, it is often confused with two other areas of study, criminal justice and deviant behavior. What are the similarities and differences in these allied fields of scientific inquiry?

CRIMINOLOGY AND CRIMINAL JUSTICE

Although the terms *criminology* and **criminal justice** may seem similar, and people often confuse the two or lump them together, there are major differences between these fields of study. Criminology explains the etiology (origin), extent, and nature of crime in society. Criminal justice refers to the study of the agencies of social control—police, courts, and corrections—that arrest, prosecute, convict, and treat criminal offenders.

Since both fields are crime-related, they do overlap. Some criminologists devote their research to **justice** and social control. Their research focuses on how the agencies of justice operate, how they influence crime and criminals, and how justice policies shape crime rates and trends. Conversely, criminal justice experts often want to design effective programs of crime prevention or rehabilitation and to do so must develop an understanding of the nature of crime and its causation. It is common, therefore, for criminal justice programs to feature courses on criminology and for criminology courses to evaluate the agencies of justice.

The line that separates deviant behavior from the conventional is often quite blurry. Vincent Graham, a center manager, helps Mark Paquette, a patient, at the River Rock Medical Marijuana Center in Denver, Colorado. When Colorado legalized the sale of marijuana, a former deviant behavior that had become criminal was now quite normative. Colorado has experienced a spurt in tax revenue as people are buying weed in droves.

Matthew Staver/*New York Times*/Redux

CRIMINOLOGY AND DEVIANT BEHAVIOR

L02 Identify the difference between crime and deviance

Criminology is also related to the study of **deviant behaviors**—those actions that depart from social norms, values, and beliefs. Included within the broad spectrum of deviant acts are behaviors ranging from violent crimes to joining a nudist colony. The two fields of study are independent because significant distinctions can be made between crime and deviance: many crimes are not unusual or deviant; many deviant acts are neither illegal nor criminal.

Take, for instance, substance abuse. Selling or possessing recreational drugs, such as marijuana, may be illegal in most states and in the federal criminal code, but can it actually be considered deviant? A significant percentage of the population have used or are using drugs; more than half of all high school students have tried drugs before they graduate, and a number of states have legalized the sale and possession of marijuana. For some people smoking marijuana is a routine activity. Therefore, it is erroneous to argue that all crimes are deviant behaviors that depart from the norms of society.

Similarly, many deviant acts are not criminal even though they may be both disturbing and shocking to the conscience. Suppose a passerby witnesses someone floundering in the ocean and makes no rescue attempt. Most people would condemn the onlooker's coldhearted behavior as callous, immoral, and deviant. However, no legal action could be taken since a private citizen is not required by law

to risk his or her own life to save another's. There is no legal requirement that a person rush into a burning building, brave a flood, feed someone who is hungry, or jump into the ocean to save someone from harm. People who let others burn, drown, or starve are not held in high esteem, but according to the law, they are not criminals.

In sum, criminologists are concerned with the concept of deviance and its relationship to criminality, whereas those who study deviant behaviors often want to understand and/or identify the line that separates criminal from merely unusual behaviors. The shifting definition of deviant behavior is closely associated with our concepts of crime. The relationships among criminology, criminal justice, and the study of deviance are illustrated in Concept Summary 1.1.

criminal justice The field of study that focuses on law enforcement, the legal system, corrections, and other agencies of justice involved in the apprehension, prosecution, defense, sentencing, incarceration, and supervision of those suspected of or charged with criminal offenses.

justice The quality of being fair under the law. Justice is defined by the relationship that exists between the individual and the state; justice demands that the state treats every person as equally as possible without regard to his or her gender, religion, race, or any other personal status.

deviant behavior Behavior that departs from the social norm.

The principal purpose of the Office of National Drug Control Policy (ONDCP) is to establish policies, priorities, and objectives for the nation's drug control program, the goals of which are to reduce illicit drug use, manufacturing, and trafficking; reduce drug-related crime and violence; and reduce drug-related health consequences. For more information about the United States' program for controlling drugs, visit the ONDCP website at **http://www.whitehouse.gov/ondcp/**.

A number of states have now legalized marijuana for personal or medical use. Compare the laws of states such as Colorado that allow personal use with those such as Kansas and Alabama where it remains illegal to use or possess.

CONCEPT SUMMARY 1.1
Criminology, Criminal Justice, and Deviance

Criminology
Criminology explores the etiology (origin), extent, and nature of crime in society. Criminologists are concerned with identifying the nature, extent, and cause of crime.

Criminal Justice
Criminal justice refers to the agencies of social control that handle criminal offenders. Criminal justice scholars engage in describing, analyzing, and explaining operations of the agencies of justice, specifically the police departments, courts, and correctional facilities. They seek more effective methods of crime control and offender rehabilitation.

Criminology and Criminal Justice: Overlapping Areas of Concern
Criminal justice experts cannot begin to design effective programs of crime prevention or rehabilitation without understanding the nature and cause of crime. They require accurate criminal statistics and data to test the effectiveness of crime control and prevention programs.

Deviant Behavior
The study of deviant behavior refers to behavior that departs from social norms. Included within the broad spectrum of deviant acts are behaviors ranging from violent crimes to joining a nudist colony. Not all crimes are deviant or unusual acts, and not all deviant acts are illegal.

Crime and Deviance: Overlapping Areas of Concern
Under what circumstances do deviant behaviors become crimes? When does sexually oriented material cross the line from merely suggestive to obscene and therefore illegal? If an illegal act becomes a norm, should society reevaluate its criminal status? There is still debate over the legalization and/or decriminalization of abortion, recreational drug use, possession of handguns, and assisted suicide.

What Criminologists Do: Criminology in Action

L03 Recognize the concept of "criminology in action" and articulate what criminologists do

Regardless of their theoretical orientation, criminologists are devoted to the study of crime and criminal behavior. As two noted criminologists, Marvin Wolfgang and Franco Ferracuti, put it: "A criminologist is one whose professional training, occupational role, and pecuniary reward are primarily concentrated on a scientific approach to, and study and analysis of, the phenomenon of crime and criminal behavior."[3]

Criminology in action refers to the efforts of criminologists to use their insight, training, and experience to understand human behavior and predict its occurrence. Because criminologists have been trained in diverse fields, several subareas reflecting different orientations and perspectives are now contained within the broader area of criminology. Criminologists may specialize in a subarea in the same way that psychologists might specialize in a subfield of psychology, such as cognition, development, perception, personality, psychopathology, or sexuality. What are some of the specific goals and areas of study on which criminologists focus their attention?

CRIMINAL STATISTICS AND CRIME MEASUREMENT

The subarea of criminal statistics and crime measurement involves devising valid and reliable measures designed to calculate the amount and trends of criminal activity: How much crime occurs annually? Who commits it? When and where does it occur? Which crimes are the most serious? Criminologists:

- Formulate techniques for collecting and analyzing institutional (police, court, and correctional agency) records and data.
- Develop survey instruments to measure criminal activity not reported to the police by victims. These instruments can be used to estimate the percentage of people who commit crimes but escape detection by the justice system.
- Identify the victims of crime and create surveys designed to have victims report loss and injury that may not have been reported to the police.
- Develop data that can be used to test crime theory. Measuring community-level crime rates can help prove whether ecological factors, such as neighborhood poverty and unemployment rates, are related to crime rates.

Those criminologists who devote themselves to criminal statistics engage in a number of different tasks, including:

- Devising accurate methods of collecting crime data
- Using these tested methods to measure the amount and trends of criminal activity

Research shows that if people see their peers or friends committing crime or engaging in deviance, they are more likely to join in themselves.

Joel Gordon/Peer Pressure

- Using valid crime data to determine who commits crime and where it occurs
- Measuring the effect of social policy and social trends on crime rate changes
- Using crime data to design crime prevention programs and then measuring their effectiveness

The media love to sensationalize crime and report on lurid cases of murder and rape. The general public is influenced by these stories, becoming fearful and altering their behavior to avoid victimization.[4] These news accounts proclaiming crime waves are often driven by the need to pull in website readers or increase TV viewership. There is nothing like an impending crime wave or serial killer on the loose to boost readership or viewership. Media accounts therefore can be biased and inaccurate, and it is up to criminologists to set the record straight. Criminologists try to create valid and reliable measurements of criminal behavior. They create techniques to access the records of police and court agencies and use sophisticated statistical methods to understand underlying patterns and trends. They develop survey instruments and then use them with large samples to determine the actual number of crimes being committed and the number of victims who suffer criminal violations: how many people are victims of crime, and what percentage reports the crime to police.

Criminologists are also interested in helping agents of the criminal justice system develop effective crime control policies that rely on accurate measurement of crime rates. By using advanced statistical techniques to calculate where crime will take place, police departments can allocate patrol officers based on these predictions.[5]

The development of valid methods to measure crime and the accuracy of crime data are crucial aspects of the criminological enterprise. Without valid and reliable crime data

sources, efforts to conduct research on crime and create criminological theories would be futile. It is also important to determine why crime rates vary across and within regions in order to gauge the association between social and economic forces and criminal activity.

Today, about 9 million serious crimes are reported to police, a drop of more than 4 million reported crimes since the 1991 peak, and this despite a boost of about 50 million in the general population. Are the crime trends and patterns experienced in the United States unique or do they occur in other cultures as well?

SOCIO-LEGAL STUDIES

Socio-legal studies is a subarea of criminology concerned with the role social forces play in shaping criminal law and, concomitantly, the role of criminal law in shaping society. Socio-legal studies involves linking the study of law with such core social issues as social change and stability, order and disorder, the nation-state and capitalism, racial discrimination, income inequality, and justice. Research on socio-legal issues involves methodologically sophisticated empirical investigations as the central means of studying the dynamics of law in society.[6]

Criminologists interested in the interrelationship between law and society focus on such socio-legal topics as:

- The history of legal change and development
- How social forces shape the definition and content of the law
- The impact of legal change on society
- The relationship between law and social control
- The effect of criminalization/legalization on behaviors

Very often the content of the law and the focus of criminological inquiry are highly integrated, making socio-legal research quite relevant. Take for instance the crime of obscenity. Typically, there is no uniform standard of what is considered obscene; material that to some people is lewd and offensive may be considered a work of art by others. Nonetheless, anti-porn crusaders have had a long history of trying to curb the manufacture and distribution of sexually related material. In 1969 in the case of *Stanley v. Georgia*, the Supreme Court ruled that a person can legally possess, read, and view adult material in the privacy of their home.[7] Despite this legal green light, criminologists have conducted research aimed at determining whether viewing pornography is harmful. Are people who view pornography more

criminology in action Efforts of criminologists to use their knowledge, training, insight, and experience to understand human behavior and predict its occurrence.

Do Sex Offender Registration Laws Really Work?

Criminologists interested in legal studies also evaluate the impact new laws have on society after they have been in effect for a while. Take for instance the practice of sex offender registration, which requires convicted sex offenders to register with local law enforcement agencies when they move into a community. These are often called Megan's Laws in memory of 7-year-old Megan Kanka, killed in 1994 by sex offender Jesse Timmendequas, who had moved unannounced into her New Jersey neighborhood. Megan's Laws require law enforcement authorities to make information available to the public regarding registered sex offenders, including the offender's name, picture, address, incarceration date, and nature of crime. The information can be published in newspapers or put on a sex offender website.

In *Connecticut Dept. of Public Safety v. Doe* (2003), the U.S. Supreme Court upheld the legality of sex offender registration when it ruled that persons con-victed of sexual offenses may be required to register with a state's Department of Public Safety and then be listed on a sex offender registry on the Internet contain-ing registrants' names, addresses, photo-graphs, and descriptions. In a 9–0 opinion upholding the plan, the Court reasoned that, because the law was based on the fact that a defendant had been convicted of a sex offense, disclosing his or her name on the registry without a hearing did not violate due process.

But while sex offender registration laws may be constitutional and pervasive (they are used in all 50 states), appeal to politicians who may be swayed by media crusades against child molesters (i.e., "To Catch a Predator" on *Dateline NBC*), and appease the public's desire to "do something" about child predators, do they actually work? One problem is that they may stigmatize already troubled people and interfere with the treatment pro-cess. It is routine to have sex offenders be put on registration lists for 25 years to life, despite empirical evidence that risk of recidivism declines with increased offense-free time spent in the community. Long periods of registration create an inefficient distribution of resources without contributing meaningfully to community safety.

These negative outcomes might be overlooked if they actually deterred future sex offenses and reduced the incidence of predatory acts against children. To answer this question, a number of research stud-ies have sought to evaluate the impact of sex offender registration. Criminologists Kristen Zgoba and Karen Bachar con-ducted an in-depth study of the effective-ness of New Jersey's registration law and found that while expensive to maintain, the system did not produce effective results. Sex offense rates in New Jersey were in a steep decline before the sys-tem was installed and the rate of decline actually slowed down after 1995 when the law took effect. Zgoba and Bachar's data show that the greatest rate of decline in sex offending occurred prior to the pas-sage and implementation of Megan's Law.

likely to commit violent crime than nonwatchers?[8] Because criminologists have found evidence of a link between watch-ing obscenity and violence toward women, efforts continue to be made to control its creation and dissemination.[9]

The Supreme Court routinely uses and cites research findings by legal scholars and criminologists before it ren-ders an opinion.[10] Social science evidence is routinely used in death penalty cases. In their opinion in the case of *Glossip v. Gross,* Justices Breyer and Ginsburg relied on social science research by socio-legal scholar Samuel Gross and his colleagues showing that there is a greater likelihood of an initial wrongful conviction in a death penalty case.[11] Why is this so? Because capital cases typically involve horrendous murders and are thus accompanied by intense community pressure on police, prosecutors, and jurors to secure a con-viction. This pressure creates a greater likelihood of convict-ing the wrong person.[12] Here a legal opinion was informed by social science research. The Policy and Practice feature shows how criminologists take on the task of scientifically reviewing the effectiveness of a critical legal change.

THEORY CONSTRUCTION AND TESTING

Social theory can be defined as a systematic set of interre-lated statements or principles that explain some aspect of social life. At their core, theories should serve as models or frameworks for understanding human behavior and the forces that shape its content and direction.

Because, ideally, theories are based on verified *social facts*—readily observed phenomena that can be

CONNECTIONS

The impact of pornography on violence and legal efforts to control adult material will be discussed further in Chapter 14.

ASK YOURSELF . . .

Should sexually oriented material involving adults be subject to government control or is this a matter guaranteed by the First Amendment right to free speech?

Passage and implementation of Megan's Law did not reduce the number of rearrests for sex offenses, nor did it have any demonstrable effect on the time between when sex offenders were released from prison and the time they were rearrested for any new offense, such as a drug, theft, or another sex offense.

In a more recent study, Zgoba, working with Jill Levenson, evaluated the effect of sex offender registration in Florida. They found that sex offenders were less likely to recidivate than offenders in most other categories of crime, such as robbery or drug sales. Comparing the repeat arrest rates before and after implementation of sex offender registration laws in 1997, Zgoba and Levenson found that there was a statistically significant increase. Obviously, instituting sex offender registration in Florida did not have the desired effect policy makers intended.

Sex offender registration also has little effect on the recidivism rates of parolees. Levenson and her associates investigated the relationship between failure to register (FTR) as a sex offender and subsequent recidivism with a sample of 3,000 people convicted of sexually related crimes. Levenson found that there was no significant difference in the proportion of sexual recidivists and non-recidivists with registration violations nor did FTR predict sexual recidivism. And when there was recidivism, there was no significant difference in time to recidivism when comparing those who failed to register (2.9 years) with compliant registrants (2.8 years).

These results challenge the effectiveness of sex offender registration laws. Rather than deter crime, sex offender laws may merely cause sex offenders to be more cautious while giving parents a false sense of security. Offenders may target victims in other states or communities where they are not registered and parents are less cautious. And many of these laws restrict where offenders can live, pushing them into rural areas where social services are meager, thereby disrupting their chances of treatment and rehabilitation.

 CRITICAL THINKING

1. Considering the findings of Zgoba, Bachar, and Levenson, would you advocate abandoning sex offender registration laws because they are ineffective? Or might there be other reasons to keep them active?
2. What other laws do you think should be the topic of careful scientific inquiry to see if they actually work as advertised?

SOURCES: Jill S. Levenson and Kristen M. Zgoba, "Community Protection Policies and Repeat Sexual Offenses in Florida" *International Journal of Offender Therapy and Comparative Criminology*, first published online March 10, 2015; Jill S. Levenson, "An Evidence-Based Perspective on Sexual Offender Registration and Residential Restrictions," in Amy Phenix and Harry M. Hoberman, *Sexual Offending: Predisposing Antecedents, Assessments and Management* (New York: Springer Verlag, 2015): 861–870; Andrew Harris, Scott Walfield, Ryan Shields, and Elizabeth Letourneau, "Collateral Consequences of Juvenile Sex Offender Registration and Notification: Results from a Survey of Treatment Providers," *Sexual Abuse*, published online March 1, 2015; Kelly Socia, "The Policy Implications of Residency Restrictions on Sex Offender Housing in Upstate New York," *Criminology and Public Policy* 10 (2011): 351–389; Wesley Jennings, Kristen Zgoba, and Richard Tewksbury, "Comparative Longitudinal Analysis of Recidivism Trajectories and Collateral Consequences for Sex and Non-Sex Offenders Released Since the Implementation of Sex Offender Registration and Community Notification," *Journal of Crime and Justice* 35 (2012): 356–364; Jill Levenson, Elizabeth Letourneau, Kevin Armstrong, and Kristen Zgoba, "Failure to Register as a Sex Offender: Is It Associated with Recidivism?" *Justice Quarterly* 27 (2010): 305–331; *Connecticut Dept. of Public Safety v. Doe*, 538 U.S. 1 (2003); Kristen Zgoba and Karen Bachar, "Sex Offender Registration and Notification: Research Finds Limited Effects in New Jersey," *National Institute of Justice*, April 2009, http://www.ncjrs.gov/pdffiles1/nij/225402.pdf (accessed April 2016).

consistently quantified and measured—criminological theorists use the scientific method to test their theories. They gather data, derive hypotheses—testable expectations of behavior that can be derived from the theory—and then test them using valid empirical research methods. Social learning theory (see Chapter 7) states that people learn behavior by observing how other people act. Adolescent behavior is controlled by the influence of parents, peers, and neighbors. If this statement is accurate, then logically there should be a significant association between peer influence and behavior.

To test this theory, criminologists might conduct an experiment to see if peers who engage in and espouse deviant attitudes actually influence behavior.

CRIMINAL BEHAVIOR SYSTEMS AND CRIME TYPOLOGIES

Criminologists who study criminal behavior systems and crime typologies focus their research on specific criminal types and patterns: violent crime, theft crime, public order crime, and organized crime. Numerous attempts have been made to describe and understand particular crime types. Marvin Wolfgang's famous 1958 study, *Patterns in Criminal Homicide*—considered a landmark analysis of the nature of homicide and the relationship between victim and offender—found that victims often precipitate the incident that results in their death.[13] Edwin Sutherland's analysis of business-related offenses helped coin a new phrase—white-collar crime—to describe economic crime activities.

Criminologists also conduct research on the links between different types of crime and criminals. This is known as a **crime typology**. Some typologies focus on the criminal, suggesting the existence of offender groups, such

crime typology The study of criminal behavior involving research on the links between different types of crime and criminals. Because people often disagree about types of crimes and criminal motivation, no standard exists within the field. Some typologies focus on the criminal, suggesting the existence of offender groups, such as professional criminals, psychotic criminals, occasional criminals, and so on. Others focus on the crimes, clustering them into categories such as property crimes, sex crimes, and so on.

American Homicide

04

In *American Homicide*, social historian Randolph Roth charts changes in the homicide rate in the United States from colonial times to the present. Using a variety of data sources, including court records, newspaper accounts, vital records, and attitudes expressed in diaries and letters, he finds that murder rates are closely correlated with four distinct socio-cultural factors: political instability; a loss of government legitimacy; a lack of civility among members of society caused by racial, religious, or political conflict; and a loss of confidence in those who hold power.

Roth argues that the United States has a unique culture and the level of interpersonal violence is much higher than in comparable Western nations. These differences were not always present. During the seventeenth century, murder rates were very high, but by the mid-eighteenth century they declined and the nation was relatively nonhomicidal. After the Revolutionary War, murder rates soared as the newly formed United States struggled to absorb British loyalists. While murder rates remained high in the Georgia–South Carolina backcountry, where the revolution was a genuine civil war, they held steady or fell in the Shenandoah Valley of Virginia, which enjoyed political stability under patriot control throughout the revolution, and where support for the war effort and

the new federal government was stronger than anywhere else in the South.

Murder rates eventually declined, and by the early nineteenth century, rates in the North and parts of the South were extremely low. But the homicide rate rose substantially across the United States from the late 1840s through the mid-1870s due to the social conflict that grew up around the slavery issue; at the same time, homicide rates in most other Western nations held steady or fell. The end of the Civil War did not end the bitterness many Southerners felt toward the government, and consequently there was a dramatic rise in homicides in the rural South.

Homicide rates rose during the Depression and Prohibition eras in the early twentieth century, but fell during the 1930s when Franklin Roosevelt was elected president and Americans had increased faith in their nation and its leadership. The establishment of government legitimacy through the New Deal, World War II, and the Cold War appeared to have reduced homicide rates through the 1950s; the crisis of government legitimacy in the 1960s and 1970s (especially among African Americans) may have contributed to soaring homicide rates.

In sum, Roth argues that American homicide rates are not related to social factors such as poverty and drug abuse, unemployment, alcohol, race, or ethnicity,

but instead are controlled by the feelings that people have toward their government, the degree to which they identify with members of their own communities, and the opportunities they have to earn respect without resorting to violence. If an individual feels secure in his social standing, it's easier to get over life's disappointments. But for a person who feels alienated from the American Dream, even the smallest insult can provoke a murderous rage. To reduce homicide rates, we must learn to trust one another and the government too.

CRITICAL THINKING

Roth says, "State breakdowns and political crises of legitimacy produce surges in nondomestic homicides; the restoration of order and legitimacy produces declines in homicides." Do you agree that homicides involving strangers are a function of the political and social world in which we live? Or is it more personal and a function of intense and immediate interpersonal conflict? How does a political crisis affect someone who robs a liquor store and shoots the owner?

SOURCE: Randolph Roth, *American Homicide* (Cambridge, MA: Belknap Press of the Harvard University Press, 2009).

as professional criminals, psychotic criminals, amateur criminals, and so on. Others focus on the crimes, clustering them into categories such as property crimes, sex crimes, and so on. While 50 years ago they might have focused their attention on rape, murder, and burglary, they now may be looking at stalking, cybercrime, terrorism, and hate crimes. A number of criminologists are now doing research on terrorism, trying to determine if there is such a thing as a "terrorist personality." Among the findings:

- Mental illness is not a critical factor in explaining terrorist behavior.
- Most terrorists are not "psychopaths." There is no pathology that explains all terrorists or their crimes.

- There is no "terrorist personality," nor is there any accurate profile—psychologically or otherwise—of the terrorist.
- Histories of childhood abuse and trauma and themes of perceived injustice and humiliation often are prominent in terrorist biographies, but do not really help to explain terrorism.[14]

Research on criminal behavior systems and crime types is important because it enables criminologists to understand why people commit specific sorts of crime, and using this information, gives them the tools to devise crime reduction strategies. The Criminology in Action feature entitled "American Homicide" illustrates this area of research.

PUNISHMENT, PENOLOGY, AND SOCIAL CONTROL

Criminologists also are involved in creating effective crime policies, developing methods of social control, and the correction and control of known criminal offenders; it is this segment of criminology that overlaps criminal justice. Criminologists conduct research that is designed to evaluate justice initiatives in order to determine their efficiency, effectiveness, and impact. Take for instance this important legal issue: should capital punishment continue to be employed or is its use simply too risky? To explore this issue, Samuel Gross and his colleagues looked at death row inmates who were later found to be innocent. The sample of 340 death row inmates (327 men and 13 women), exonerated after having served years in prison, indicated that about half (144 people) were cleared by DNA evidence. Collectively, they had spent more than 3,400 years in prison for crimes they did not commit—an average of more than 10 years each. Gross and his colleagues found that exonerations from death row are more than 25 times more frequent than exonerations for other prisoners convicted of murder, and more than 100 times more frequent than for all imprisoned felons.[15] How many wrongful convictions might be uncovered if all criminal convictions were given the same degree of scrutiny as death penalty cases? The Gross research illustrates how important it is to evaluate penal measures in order to determine their effectiveness and reliability.

VICTIMOLOGY: VICTIMS AND VICTIMIZATION

In two classic criminological studies, one by Hans von Hentig and the other by Stephen Schafer, the critical role of the victim in the criminal process was first identified. These authors were the first to suggest that victim behavior is often a key determinant of crime and that victims' actions may actually precipitate crime. Both men believe that the study of crime is not complete unless the victim's role is considered.[16] For those studying the role of the victim in crime, these areas are of particular interest:

- Using victim surveys to measure the nature and extent of criminal behavior not reported to the police
- Calculating the actual costs of crime to victims
- Measuring the factors that increase the likelihood of becoming a crime victim
- Studying the role of the victim in causing or precipitating crime
- Designing services for the victims of crime, such as counseling and compensation programs

The study of victims and victimization has uncovered some startling results. For one thing, criminals have been found to be at greater risk for victimization than noncriminals.[17] Rather than being the passive receptors of criminal acts who are in the "wrong place at the wrong time," crime victims may engage in high-risk lifestyles that increase their own chance of victimization and make them highly vulnerable to crime.

The various elements of criminology in action are summarized in Concept Summary 1.2.

CONNECTIONS

In recent years, criminologists have devoted ever-increasing attention to the victim's role in the criminal process. It has been suggested that a person's lifestyle and behavior may actually increase the risk that he or she will become a crime victim. Some have suggested that living in a high-crime neighborhood increases risk; others point at the problems caused by associating with dangerous peers and companions. For a discussion of victimization risk, see Chapter 3.

ASK YOURSELF . . .

Does living in a college environment increase victimization risk? What can be done to make it safer? Are there places in your hometown that you avoid to reduce the risk of becoming a crime victim? Do you believe that crime victims are people in "the wrong place at the wrong time"?

CONCEPT SUMMARY 1.2
Criminology in Action

These subareas constitute the discipline of criminology:

Criminal Statistics and Research Methodology
Gathering valid crime data. Devising new research methods; measuring crime patterns and trends.

The Sociology of Law/Law and Society
Determining the origin of law. Measuring the forces that can change laws and society.

Theory Construction and Testing
Predicting individual behavior. Understanding the cause of crime rates and trends.

Criminal Behavior Systems and Crime Typologies
Determining the nature and cause of specific crime patterns. Studying violence, theft, organized, white-collar, and public order crimes.

Penology and Social Control
Studying the correction and control of criminal behavior. Using scientific methods to assess the effectiveness of crime control and offender treatment programs.

Victimology/Victims and Victimization
Studying the nature and cause of victimization. Aiding crime victims; understanding the nature and extent of victimization; developing theories of victimization risk.

How Criminologists View Crime

 L04 Discuss the three most prominent views of the meaning of "crime"

Professional criminologists usually align themselves with one of several schools of thought or perspectives in their field. Each perspective maintains its own view of what constitutes criminal behavior and what causes people to engage in criminality. This diversity of thought is not unique to criminology; biologists, psychologists, sociologists, historians, economists, and natural scientists disagree among themselves about critical issues in their fields. Considering the multidisciplinary nature of the field of criminology, fundamental issues such as the nature and definition of crime itself are cause for disagreement among criminologists.

A criminologist's choice of orientation or perspective depends, in part, on his or her definition of crime. This section discusses the three most common concepts of crime used by criminologists.

THE CONSENSUS VIEW OF CRIME

According to the **consensus view**, crimes are behaviors believed to be repugnant to all elements of society. The substantive criminal law, which is the written code that defines crimes and their punishments, reflects the values, beliefs, and opinions of society's mainstream. The term *consensus* is used because it implies that there is general agreement among a majority of citizens on what behaviors should be outlawed by the criminal law and henceforth viewed as crimes. As the eminent criminologists Edwin Sutherland and Donald Cressey put it:

> Criminal behavior is behavior in violation of the criminal law.... [I]t is not a crime unless it is prohibited by the criminal law [which] is defined conventionally as a body of specific rules regarding human conduct which have been promulgated by political authority, which apply uniformly to all members of the classes to which the rules refer, and which are enforced by punishment administered by the state.[18]

This approach to crime implies that it is a function of the beliefs, morality, and rules established by the existing legal power structure. According to Sutherland and Cressey's statement, criminal law is applied "uniformly to all members of the classes to which the rules refer." This statement reveals the authors' faith in the concept of an "ideal legal system" that deals adequately with all classes and types of people. Laws prohibiting theft and violence may be directed at the neediest members of society, whereas laws that sanction economic acts such as insider trading, embezzlement, and corporate price-fixing are aimed at controlling the wealthiest. The reach of the criminal law is not restricted to any single element of society.

Social Harm The consensus view of crime links illegal behavior to the concept of **social harm**. Though people generally enjoy a great deal of latitude in their behavior, it is agreed that behaviors that are harmful to other people and society in general must be controlled. Social harm is what sets strange, unusual, or deviant behavior—or any other action that departs from social norms—apart from criminal behaviors.[19]

This position is not without controversy. Although it is clear that rape, robbery, and murder are inherently harmful and their control justified, behaviors such as drug use and prostitution are more problematic because the harm they inflict is only on those who are willing participants. According to the consensus view, society is justified in controlling these so-called victimless crimes because public opinion holds that they undermine the social fabric and threaten the general well-being of society. Society has a duty to protect all its members—even those who choose to engage in high-risk behaviors.

THE CONFLICT VIEW OF CRIME

The **conflict view** depicts society as a collection of diverse groups—business owners, workers, professionals, students—who are in constant and continuing conflict.

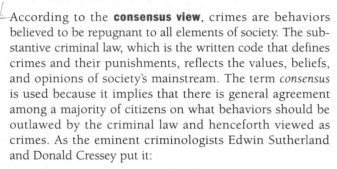

consensus view The belief that the majority of citizens in a society share common ideals and work toward a common good and that crimes are acts that are outlawed because they conflict with the rules of the majority and are harmful to society.

social harm A view that behaviors harmful to other people and society in general must be controlled. These acts are usually outlawed, but some acts that cause enormous amounts of social harm are perfectly legal, such as the consumption of tobacco and alcohol.

conflict view The view that human behavior is shaped by interpersonal conflict and that those who maintain social power will use it to further their own needs.

CONNECTIONS

The associations among crime, social harm, and morality are best illustrated in efforts to criminalize acts considered dangerous to the public welfare because they involve behaviors that offend existing social values. These so-called public order crimes include pornography, prostitution, and drug use. Though "victims" are often willing participants, some people believe it is society's duty to save them from themselves. To read more about crime, morality, and social harm, see Chapter 14.

ASK YOURSELF . . .

Should victimless crimes such as drug abuse be decriminalized? Or would that simply lead to more people using drugs on a regular basis like they do with cigarettes and alcohol now?

Groups able to assert their political power use the law and the criminal justice system to advance their economic and social position. Criminal laws, therefore, are viewed as acts created to protect the haves from the have-nots. Critical criminologists often compare and contrast the harsh penalties exacted on the poor for their "street crimes" (burglary, robbery, and larceny) with the minor penalties the wealthy receive for their white-collar crimes (securities violations and other illegal business practices), though the latter may cause considerably more social harm. While the poor go to prison for minor law violations, the wealthy are given lenient sentences for even the most serious breaches of law. Rather than being class neutral, criminal law reflects and protects established economic, racial, gendered, and political power and privilege.

Crime, according to this definition, is a political concept designed to protect the power and position of the upper classes at the expense of the poor. Even crimes prohibiting violent acts, such as armed robbery, rape, and murder, may have political undertones. Banning violent acts ensures domestic tranquility and guarantees that the anger of the poor and disenfranchised classes will not be directed at their wealthy capitalist exploiters. According to this conflict view of crime, "real" crimes would include the following acts:

- Violations of human rights due to racism, sexism, and imperialism
- Unsafe working conditions
- Inadequate child care
- Inadequate opportunities for employment and education
- Substandard housing and medical care
- Crimes of economic and political domination
- Pollution of the environment
- Price-fixing
- Police brutality
- Assassinations and war-making
- Violations of human dignity
- Denial of physical needs and necessities, and impediments to self-determination
- Deprivation of adequate food
- Blocked opportunities to participate in political decision making

THE INTERACTIONIST VIEW OF CRIME

The **interactionist view** of crime traces its antecedents to the symbolic interaction school of sociology, first popularized by pioneering sociologists George Herbert Mead, Charles Horton Cooley, and W. I. Thomas.[20] They created a school of thought that explains social behavior in terms of how people interact with each other via symbols. How people

communicate and interact with each other depends on how they interpret factors such as language, actions, physical status. A person might interpret someone approaching with a raised fist as a threat or a victory sign depending on the context. Sometimes the meaning of symbols change: having a visible tattoo once symbolized rebellion, now it's normative and stylish.

According to this perspective, there is no objective reality. People, institutions, and events are viewed subjectively and labeled either good or evil according to the interpretation of the evaluator. Take for instance how people react to the book and film *Fifty Shades of Grey*. Some readers/viewers consider it to be obscene, degrading, and distasteful while others view the same book and film as inoffensive, romantic, and provocative. The same interactions help define crime:

- The content of the criminal law and consequently the definition of crime often depend on human interaction and perceptions. Marijuana is now legal in some jurisdictions (Colorado and Washington among others) and illegal in others.
- Deciding whether an individual act is considered a crime is also a function of interaction and labeling. When a heated argument in a local tavern results in the death of one of the participants, a jury may be asked to decide whether the death was an intentional act—first-degree

interactionist view The view that one's perception of reality is significantly influenced by one's interpretations of the reactions of others to similar events and stimuli.

According to the interactionist view of crime, the definition of criminality is created by those holding social and economic power, so-called moral entrepreneurs. Leonardo DiCaprio starred in the 2013 film *The Wolf of Wall Street*, which focused on the greed and illegal behavior of stock market guru Jordan Belfort, who went to prison for his shady deals. His behavior was defined as criminal by those in power; he saw himself as a savvy businessman.

Paramount Pictures/Everett Collection

murder—or a lesser crime such as criminally negligent homicide. They may also find the death was legally justified, a result of self-defense, or merely an accidental fatality. Each person on the jury may have his or her own interpretation of what took place: whether the act is labeled a crime and the actor a criminal depends on the juror's personal interpretation of events.

■ If the act is labeled a crime and the perpetrator a criminal, the decision to punish is also highly subjective and dependent on social interaction. One person is viewed as an unrepentant hardcore offender and sent to a maximum security prison. Another, who has committed essentially the same crime, is considered remorseful and repentant and given probation in the community. Though their acts are similar, the treatment they receive is quite different.

In a classic statement, sociologist Howard Becker argued, "The deviant is one to whom that label has successfully been applied; deviant behavior is behavior people so labeled."[21] According to the interactionist view, the definition of crime reflects the preferences and opinions of people who hold social power in a particular legal jurisdiction. These **moral entrepreneurs** wage campaigns (moral crusades) to control behaviors they view as immoral and wrong (e.g., abortion) or, conversely, to legalize or decriminalize behaviors they consider harmless social eccentricities (e.g., smoking pot). Those who hold social and legal power control the definition of the law. Because drug use offends their moral sense, it is currently illegal to purchase cocaine and hashish, while liquor and cigarettes are sold openly, even though far more people die of alcoholism and smoking than from drug abuse each year.[22] Even the definition of serious violent offenses, such as rape and murder, depends on the prevailing moral values of those who shape the content of the criminal law. Florida has implemented a "stand your ground law" that legalizes the killing of an unarmed thief or intruder; in other states, shooting an unarmed person might be considered murder. Fifty years ago, a man could not be prosecuted for raping his wife; today, every state criminalizes marital rape. In sum, the definition of crime is more reflective of prevailing moral values than of any objective standard of right and wrong.

The interactionist view of crime is similar in some ways to the conflict perspective; both suggest that behavior is outlawed and considered criminal when it offends people who hold social, economic, and political power. However, unlike the conflict view, the interactionist perspective does not attribute capitalist economic and political motives to the process of defining crime. Laws against pornography,

---

moral entrepreneurs Interest groups that attempt to control social life and the legal order in such a way as to promote their own personal set of moral values. People who use their influence to shape the legal process in ways they see fit.

CONCEPT SUMMARY 1.3
The Definition of Crime

The definition of crime affects how criminologists view the cause and control of illegal behavior and shapes their research orientation.

Conflict View
■ The law is a tool of the ruling class.
■ Crime is a politically defined concept.
■ "Real crimes" are not outlawed.
■ The law is used to control the underclass.

Consensus View
■ The law defines crime.
■ The law reflects public opinion.
■ Agreement exists on outlawed behavior.
■ Laws apply to all citizens equally.

Interactionist View
■ Moral entrepreneurs define crime.
■ Crimes are illegal because society defines them that way.
■ The definition of crime evolves according to the moral standards of those in power.

---

prostitution, and drugs are believed to be motivated more by moral crusades than by economic values.

The three main views of crime are summarized in Concept Summary 1.3.

DEFINING CRIME

It is possible to take elements from each school of thought to formulate an integrated definition of crime, such as this one:

> Crime is a violation of societal rules of behavior as interpreted and expressed by a criminal legal code created by people holding social and political power. Individuals who violate these rules are subject to sanctions by state authority, social stigma, and loss of status.

This definition combines the consensus position that the criminal law defines crimes with the conflict perspective's emphasis on political power and control and the interactionist concept of labeling and stigma. Thus crime, as defined here, is a political, social, and economic function of modern life.

Crime and the Law

No matter which definition of crime we embrace, criminal behavior is tied to the law. It is therefore important for all criminologists to have some understanding of the development of law, its objectives, its elements, and how it has evolved.

A BRIEF HISTORY OF THE LAW

L05 Outline the development of criminal law

The concept of criminal law has been recognized for more than 3,000 years. Hammurabi (1792–1750 BCE), the sixth king of Babylon, created the most famous set of written laws of the ancient world, known today as the Code of Hammurabi. Preserved on basalt rock columns, the code established a system of crime and punishment based on physical retaliation ("an eye for an eye"). The severity of punishment depended on class standing: if convicted of an unprovoked assault, a slave would be killed, whereas a freeman might lose a limb.

More familiar is the Mosaic Code of the Israelites (1200 BCE). According to tradition, God entered into a covenant or contract with the tribes of Israel in which they agreed to obey his law (the 613 laws of the Old Testament, including the Ten Commandments), as presented to them by Moses, in return for God's special care and protection. The Mosaic Code is not only the foundation of Judeo-Christian moral teachings but also a basis for the U.S. legal system. Prohibitions against murder, theft, and perjury preceded by several thousand years the same laws found in the modern United States.

Though ancient formal legal codes were lost during the Dark Ages, early German and Anglo-Saxon societies developed legal systems featuring monetary compensation for criminal violations. Guilt was determined by two methods. One was compurgation, in which the accused person swore an oath of innocence with the backing of 12 to 25 oath helpers, who would attest to his or her character and claims of innocence. The second was trial by ordeal, which was based on the principle that divine forces would not allow an innocent person to be harmed. It involved such measures as having the accused place his or her hand in boiling water or hold a hot iron. If the wound healed, the person was found innocent; if the wound did not heal, the accused was deemed guilty. Another version, trial by combat, allowed the accused to challenge his accuser to a duel, with the outcome determining the legitimacy of the accusation. Punishments included public flogging, branding, beheading, and burning.

COMMON LAW

After the Norman conquest of England in 1066, royal judges began to travel throughout the land, holding court in each shire several times a year. When court was in session, the royal administrator, or judge, would summon a number of citizens who would, on their oath, tell of the crimes and serious breaches of the peace that had occurred since the judge's last visit. The royal judge would then decide what to do in each case, using local custom and rules of conduct as his guide. Courts were bound to follow the law established in previous cases unless a higher authority, such as the king or the pope, overruled the law.

The present English system of law came into existence during the reign of Henry II (1154–1189), when royal judges began to publish their decisions in local cases. Judges began to use these written decisions as a basis for their decision making, and eventually a fixed body of legal rules and principles was established. If a new rule was successfully applied in a number of different cases, it would become a precedent. These precedents would then be commonly applied in all similar cases—hence the term **common law**. Crimes such as murder, burglary, arson, and rape are common-law crimes whose elements were initially defined by judges. They are referred to as **mala in se**, inherently evil and depraved. When the situation required it, the English Parliament enacted legislation to supplement the judge-made common law. These were referred to as statutory or **mala prohibitum** crimes, which reflected existing social conditions. English common law evolved constantly to fit specific incidents that the judges encountered. In the *Carriers* case (1473), an English court ruled that a merchant who had been hired to transport merchandise was guilty of larceny (theft) if he kept the goods for his own purposes.[23] Before the *Carriers* case, it was not considered a crime under the common law when people kept something that was voluntarily placed in their possession, even if the rightful owner had only given them temporary custody of the merchandise. Breaking with legal tradition, the court acknowledged that the commercial system could not be maintained unless the laws of theft were expanded. The definition of larceny was altered in order to meet the needs of a growing free enterprise economic system. The definition of theft was changed to include the taking of goods not only by force or stealth but also by embezzlement and fraud.

THE LAW IN CONTEMPORARY SOCIETY

L06 Analyze the different categories of law

In contemporary U.S. society, the law governs almost all phases of human enterprise, including commerce, family life, property transfer, and the regulation of interpersonal conflict. It contains elements that control personal

---

common law Early English law, developed by judges, that incorporated Anglo-Saxon tribal custom, feudal rules and practices, and the everyday rules of behavior of local villages. Common law became the standardized law of the land in England and eventually formed the basis of the criminal law in the United States.

mala in se Acts that are outlawed because they violate basic moral values, such as rape, murder, assault, and robbery.

mala prohibitum Acts that are outlawed because they clash with current norms and public opinion, such as tax, traffic, and drug laws.

relationships between individuals and public relationships between individuals and the government. The former is known as *civil law*, and the latter is called *criminal law*. The law then can generally be divided into four broad categories:

- *Substantive criminal law*. The branch of the law that defines crimes and their punishment is known as **substantive criminal law**. It involves such issues as the mental and physical elements of crime, crime categories, and criminal defenses.
- *Procedural criminal law*. Those laws that set out the basic rules of practice in the criminal justice system are **procedural criminal laws**. Some elements of the law of criminal procedure are the rules of evidence, the law of arrest, the law of search and seizure, questions of appeal, jury selection, and the right to counsel.
- *Civil law*. The set of rules governing relations between private parties, including both individuals and organizations (such as business enterprises or corporations), is known as **civil law**. The civil law is used to resolve, control, and shape such personal interactions as contracts, wills and trusts, property ownership, and commerce. Contained within the civil law is tort law, discussed in Exhibit 1.1.
- *Public or administrative law*. The branch of law that deals with the government and its relationships with individuals or other governments is known as **public law**. It governs the administration and regulation of city, county, state, and federal government agencies.

The four categories of the law can be interrelated. A crime victim may file a tort action against a criminal defendant and sue for damages in a civil court. Under tort law, a crime victim may sue even if the defendant is found not guilty because the evidentiary standard in a civil action is less than is needed for a criminal conviction (preponderance of the evidence versus beyond a reasonable doubt). In some instances, the government has the option to pursue a legal matter through the

---

EXHIBIT 1.1

Types of Torts

- *Intentional torts* are injuries that the person knew or should have known would occur through his or her actions—a person attacks and injures another (assault and battery) after a dispute.
- *Negligent torts* are injuries caused because a person's actions were unreasonably unsafe or careless—a traffic accident is caused by a reckless driver.
- *Strict liability torts* are injuries that occur because a particular action causes damage prohibited by statute—a victim is injured because a manufacturer made a defective product.

SOURCE: © Cengage Learning

---

criminal process, file a tort action, or bring the matter before an administrative court. White-collar crimes often involve criminal, administrative, and civil penalties.

SHAPING THE CRIMINAL LAW

Before the American Revolution, the colonies, then under British rule, were subject to the common law. After the colonies won their independence, state legislatures standardized common-law crimes such as murder, burglary, arson, and rape by putting them into statutory form in criminal codes. As in England, whenever common law proved inadequate to deal with changing social and moral issues, the states and Congress supplemented it with legislative statutes. Similarly, statutes prohibiting such offenses as the sale and possession of narcotics or the pirating of DVDs have been passed to control human behavior unknown at the time the common law was formulated. Today, criminal behavior is defined primarily by statute. With few exceptions, crimes are removed, added, or modified by the legislature of a particular jurisdiction.

The content of the law may also be shaped by judicial decision making. A criminal statute may be no longer enforceable when an appellate judge rules that it is vague, deals with an act no longer of interest to the public, or is an unfair exercise of state control over an individual. Conversely, a judicial ruling may expand the scope of an existing criminal law, thereby allowing control over behaviors that heretofore were beyond its reach. In a famous 1990 case, 2 Live Crew (a prominent rap group made up of Luther Campbell, Christopher Wong Won, Mark Ross, and David Hobbs) found its sales restricted in Florida as police began arresting children under 18 for purchasing the band's sexually explicit CD *As Nasty as They Want to Be*. The hit single "Me So Horny" was banned from local radio stations. Prosecutors tried but failed to get a conviction after group members were arrested at a concert. If members of the Crew had in fact been found guilty and the conviction had been upheld by the state's highest appellate court, obscenity laws would have been expanded to cover people singing (or rapping) objectionable music lyrics.

L07 Articulate the relationship between the criminal law and the U.S. Constitution

Constitutional Limits Regardless of its source, all criminal law in the United States must conform to the rules and dictates of the U.S. Constitution.[24] Any criminal law that even appears to conflict with the various provisions and articles of the Constitution must reflect a compelling need to protect public safety or morals.[25]

Criminal laws have been interpreted as violating constitutional principles if they are too vague or too broad to give clear meaning of their intent. A law forbidding adults to engage in "immoral behavior" could not be enforced because it does not use clear and precise language or give adequate notice as to which conduct is forbidden.[26] The Constitution also prohibits laws that make a person's status a crime. Becoming or being a heroin addict is not a crime, although laws can forbid the sale, possession, and manufacture of heroin.

The Constitution limits laws that are overly cruel and/or capricious. Whereas the use of the death penalty may be constitutionally approved, capital punishment would be forbidden if it were used for lesser crimes such as rape or employed in a random, haphazard fashion.[27] Cruel ways of executing criminals that cause excessive pain are likewise forbidden. One method used to avoid "cruelty" is lethal injection. In the 2008 case *Baze and Bowling v. Rees*, the Court upheld the use of lethal injection unless there is a "substantial risk of serious harm" that the drugs will not work effectively.[28]

THE SUBSTANTIVE CRIMINAL LAW

L08 Synthesize the different purposes of criminal law

The substantive criminal law defines crime and punishment. Each state and the federal government have their own substantive criminal code, developed over many generations and incorporating moral beliefs, social values, and political, economic, and other societal concerns.

Criminal laws are divided into felonies and misdemeanors. The distinction is based on seriousness: a **felony** is a serious offense; a **misdemeanor** is a minor or petty crime. Crimes such as murder, rape, and burglary are felonies; they are punished with long prison sentences or even death.

The substantive criminal law sets out crime and punishment. Here, Charles Severance appears in Fairfax (Virginia) County Circuit Court on September 17, 2015. Severance, 55, was convicted in the fatal shootings of music teacher Ruthanne Lodato, regional transportation planner Ronald Kirby, and real estate agent Nancy Dunning. Prosecutors said bitterness over a child custody battle he lost and a general hatred of the elite motivated him to shoot the victims—all apparently strangers to him—in daylight attacks at their homes. At his sentencing hearing, Severance rambled, citing the Book of Common Prayer, Henry VIII, Elizabeth, and "the 37th article of religion." "It is lawful to wear weapons," he concluded. Then he went silent. He was given three life terms plus 48 years.

Washington Post/Getty Images

Crimes such as unarmed assault and battery, petty larceny, and disturbing the peace are misdemeanors; they are punished with a fine or a period of incarceration in a county jail.

Regardless of their classification, acts prohibited by the criminal law constitute behaviors considered unacceptable and impermissible by those in power. People who engage in these acts are eligible for severe sanctions. By outlawing these behaviors, the government expects to achieve a number of social goals:

- *Enforcing social control.* Those who hold political power rely on criminal law to formally prohibit behaviors believed to threaten societal well-being or to challenge their authority. U.S. criminal law incorporates centuries-old prohibitions against the following behaviors harmful to others: taking another person's possessions, physically harming another person, damaging another person's property, and cheating another person out of his or her possessions. Similarly, the law prohibits actions that challenge the legitimacy of the government, such as planning its overthrow, collaborating with its enemies, and so on.

felony A serious offense, such as rape, murder, robbery, or burglary, that is punishable by a prison sentence or, in the case of first-degree murder, by capital punishment.

misdemeanor A minor or petty crime, typically punished by a fine, community sentence, or a jail term.

- *Discouraging private revenge.* By punishing people who infringe on the rights, property, and freedom of others, the law shifts the burden of revenge from the individual to the state. As famed jurist and Supreme Court Judge Oliver Wendell Holmes stated, this prevents "the greater evil of private retribution."[29] Although state retaliation may offend the sensibilities of many citizens, it is greatly preferable to a system in which people would have to seek justice for themselves.

- *Expressing public opinion and morality.* Criminal law reflects constantly changing public opinions and moral values. *Mala in se* crimes, such as murder and forcible rape, are almost universally prohibited; however, the prohibition of legislatively created *mala prohibitum* crimes, such as traffic offenses and gambling violations, changes according to social conditions and attitudes. Criminal law is used to codify these changes.

- *Deterring criminal behavior.* Criminal law has a social control function. It can control, restrain, and direct human behavior through its sanctioning power. The threat of punishment associated with violating the law is designed to prevent crimes before they occur. During the Middle Ages, public executions drove this point home. Today, criminal law's impact is felt through news accounts of long prison sentences and an occasional execution.

- *Punishing wrongdoing.* The deterrent power of criminal law is tied to the authority it gives the state to sanction or punish offenders. Those who violate criminal law are subject to physical coercion and punishment.

- *Maintaining social order.* All legal systems are designed to support and maintain the boundaries of the social system they serve. In medieval England, the law protected the feudal system by defining an orderly system of property transfer and ownership. Laws in some socialist nations protect the primacy of the state by strictly curtailing profiteering and individual enterprise. Our own capitalist system is also supported and sustained by criminal law. In a sense, the content of criminal law is more a reflection of the needs of those who control the existing economic and political system than a representation of some idealized moral code.

- *Providing restoration.* Victims deserve restitution or compensation for their pain and loss. The criminal law can be used to restore to victims what they have lost. Because we believe in equity and justice, it is only fair that the guilty help repair the harm they have caused others by their crimes. Punishments such as fines, forfeiture, and restitution are connected to this legal goal.

THE ELEMENTS OF CRIMINAL LAW

L09 Compare and contrast the elements of the criminal law

Although each state and the federal government have unique methods of defining crime, there are significant uniformities and similarities that shape the essence of almost all criminal law codes. Although the laws of California, Texas, and Maine may all be somewhat different, the underlying concepts that guide and shape their legal systems are universal. The question remains: regardless of jurisdictional boundaries, what is the legal definition of a crime and how does the criminal law deal with it?

Legal Definition of a Crime   Today, in all jurisdictions, the legal definition of a crime involves the elements of the criminal acts that must be proven in a court of law if the defendant is to be found guilty.[30] For the most part, common criminal acts have both mental and physical elements, both of which must be present if the act is to be considered a legal crime. In order for a crime to occur, the state must show that the accused committed the guilty act, or *actus reus*, and had the *mens rea*, or criminal intent, to commit the act. The *actus reus* may be an aggressive act, such as taking someone's money, burning a building, or shooting someone; or it may be a failure to act when there is a legal duty to do so, such as a parent neglecting to seek medical attention for a sick child. The *mens rea* (guilty mind) refers to an individual's state of mind at the time of the act or, more specifically, the person's intent to commit the crime.

Actus Reus   To satisfy the requirements of *actus reus*, guilty actions must be voluntary. Even though an act may cause harm or damage, it is not considered a crime if it was done by accident or was an involuntary act. It would not be a crime if a motorist obeying all the traffic laws hit a child who ran into the street. If the same motorist were drinking or speeding, then his action would be considered a vehicular crime because it was a product of negligence. Similarly, it would not be considered a crime if a babysitter accidentally dropped a child and the child died. However, it would be considered manslaughter if the sitter threw the child down in anger or frustration and the blow caused the child's death. In some circumstances of *actus reus*, the use of words is considered criminal. In the crime of sedition, the words of disloyalty constitute the *actus reus*. If a person falsely yells "fire" in a crowded theater and people are injured in the rush to exit, that person is held responsible for the injuries because the use of the word in that situation constitutes an illegal act.

Typically, the law does not require people to aid others in distress, such as entering a burning building to rescue people trapped by a fire. However, failure to act is considered a crime in certain instances:

- *Relationship of the parties based on status.* Some people are bound by relationship to give aid. These relationships include parent/child and husband/wife. If a husband finds his wife unconscious because she took an overdose of sleeping pills, he is obligated to save her life by seeking medical aid. If he fails to do so and she dies, he can be held responsible for her death.

- *Imposition by statute.* Some states have passed laws requiring people to give aid. A person who observes a broken-down automobile in the desert but fails to stop and help the other parties involved may be committing a crime.

- *Contractual relationships.* These relationships include lifeguard and swimmer, doctor and patient, and babysitter or au pair and child. Because lifeguards have been hired to ensure the safety of swimmers, they have a legal duty to come to the aid of drowning persons. If a lifeguard knows a swimmer is in danger and does nothing about it and the swimmer drowns, the lifeguard is legally responsible for the swimmer's death.

Mens Rea   In most situations, for an act to constitute a crime, it must be done with criminal intent, or *mens rea* (guilty mind). Intent, in the legal sense, can mean carrying out an act intentionally, knowingly, and willingly. However, the definition also encompasses situations in which recklessness or negligence establishes the required criminal intent. Criminal intent exists if the results of an action, although originally unintended, are certain to occur. When Timothy McVeigh planted a bomb in front of the Murrah Federal Building in Oklahoma City, he did not intend to kill any particular person in the building. Yet the law would hold that McVeigh or any other person would be substantially certain that people in the building would be killed in the blast, and McVeigh therefore had the criminal intent to commit murder.

Strict Liability   Though common-law crimes require that both the *actus reus* and the *mens rea* must be present before a person can be convicted of a crime, several crimes defined by statute do not require *mens rea*. In these cases, the person accused is guilty simply by doing what the statute prohibits; intent does not enter the picture. These strict liability crimes, or public welfare offenses, include violations of health and safety regulations, traffic laws, and narcotic control laws. A person stopped for speeding is guilty of breaking the traffic laws regardless of whether he or she intended to go over the speed limit or did it by accident. The underlying purpose of these laws is to protect the public; therefore, intent is not required.

CRIMINAL DEFENSES

When people defend themselves against criminal charges, they must refute one or more of the elements of the crime of which they have been accused. A number of different approaches can be taken to create this defense.

First, defendants may deny the *actus reus* by arguing that they were falsely accused and that the real culprit has yet to be identified. Second, defendants may claim that although they engaged in the criminal act of which they are accused, they lacked the *mens rea* (intent) needed to be found guilty of the crime.

If a person whose mental state is impaired commits a criminal act, it is possible for the person to excuse his or her criminal actions by claiming that he or she lacked the capacity to form sufficient intent to be held criminally responsible. Insanity, intoxication, and ignorance are types of excuse

defenses. A defendant might argue that because he suffered from a mental impairment that prevented him from understanding the harmfulness of his acts, he lacked sufficient *mens rea* to be found guilty as charged.

Another type of defense is justification. Here the individual usually admits committing the criminal act but maintains that he or she should not be held criminally liable because the act was justified. Among the justification defenses are necessity, duress, self-defense, and entrapment. A battered wife who kills her mate might argue that she acted out of duress; her crime was committed to save her own life.

Persons standing trial for criminal offenses may thus defend themselves by claiming that they did not commit the act in question, that their actions were justified under the circumstances, or that their behavior can be excused by their lack of *mens rea*. If either the physical or mental elements of a crime cannot be proven, then the defendant cannot be convicted.

THE EVOLUTION OF CRIMINAL LAW

The criminal law is constantly evolving in an effort to reflect social and economic conditions. Sometimes legal changes are prompted by highly publicized cases that generate fear and concern. A number of highly publicized cases of celebrity stalking, including Robert John Bardo's fatal shooting of actress Rebecca Schaeffer on July 18, 1989, prompted every state to enact **stalking statutes** that prohibit acts typically defined as "the willful, malicious, and repeated following and harassing of another person."[31] Public outcry in California (and the nation) following Richard Allen Davis's abduction and murder of 12-year-old Polly Klaas prompted passage of a number of laws designed to control sexual predators, including the "three strikes law" which provides a life sentence for anyone convicted of three violent or serious felonies listed under California Penal Code section 1192.[32] Another California statute, the sexual predator law, which took effect on January 1, 1996, allows people convicted of sexually violent crimes against two or more victims to be committed to a mental institution after their prison terms have been served.[33]

The criminal law may also change because of shifts in culture and social conventions, reflecting a newfound tolerance of behavior condemned only a few years before. In an important 2003 case, *Lawrence v. Texas*, the Supreme Court declared that laws banning sodomy (a sexual act deemed to be "unnatural" or immoral) were unconstitutional because they violated the due process rights of citizens because of their sexual orientation. In its decision, the Court said:

> Although the laws involved . . . here . . . do not more than prohibit a particular sexual act, their penalties and purposes have more far-reaching consequences,

stalking statutes Laws that prohibit "the willful, malicious, and repeated following and harassing of another person."

touching upon the most private human conduct, sexual behavior, and in the most private of places, the home. They seek to control a personal relationship that, whether or not entitled to formal recognition in the law, is within the liberty of persons to choose without being punished as criminals. The liberty protected by the Constitution allows homosexual persons the right to choose to enter upon relationships in the confines of their homes and their own private lives and still retain their dignity as free persons.

As a result of the decision, all sodomy laws in the United States are now unconstitutional and therefore unenforceable.[34]

What are some of the new laws that are being created and old ones that have been eliminated?

Stalking Laws Stalking laws were originally formulated to protect women terrorized by former husbands and boyfriends, although celebrities are often plagued by stalkers as well. In celebrity cases, these laws often apply to stalkers who are strangers or casual acquaintances of their victims.

Assisted Suicide Some laws are created when public opinion turns against a previously legal practice. Physician-assisted suicide became the subject of a national debate when Dr. Jack Kevorkian began practicing what he called *obitiatry*, helping people take their own lives.[35] In an attempt to stop Kevorkian, Michigan passed a statutory ban on assisted suicide, reflecting what lawmakers believed to be prevailing public opinion.[36] Kevorkian was convicted of second-degree homicide and served more than eight years in prison. In June 2007, he was released on parole due to good behavior; he died in 2011 at age 83. Forty-five states (including Michigan) and the District of Columbia now disallow assisted suicide either by statute or common law.[37]

Registering Sex Offenders Some legal changes have been prompted by public outrage over a particularly heinous crime, such as the murder of Megan Kanka, a 7-year-old New Jersey girl who was raped and murdered by her neighbor, convicted sex offender Jesse Timmendequas. Because residents were unaware that a sex offender was living in their midst, the murder subsequently led to the passage of Megan's Law, which requires law enforcement to disclose details relating to the location of registered sex offenders.[38]

- *Sex offender registration.* A revision of the 1994 Jacob Wetterling Act, which had required the states to register individuals convicted of sex crimes against children, also established a community notification system.
- *Community notification.* States were compelled to make private and personal information on registered sex offenders available to the public.

Variations of Megan's Law have been adopted by all 50 states. Although civil libertarians have expressed concern that notification laws may interfere with an offender's post-release privacy rights, when DNA collection is included in the law, it helps reduce false accusations and convictions.[39]

Clarifying Rape Sometimes laws are changed to clarify the definition of crime and to quell public debate over the boundaries of the law. When does bad behavior cross the line into criminality, and when does it remain merely bad behavior? An example of the former can be found in changes to the law of rape.

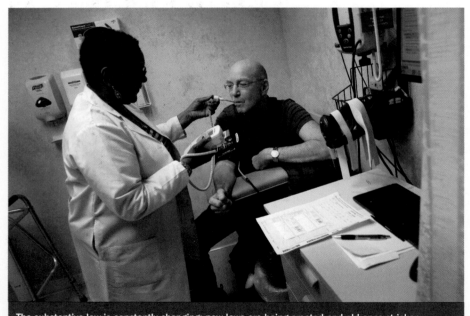

The substantive law is constantly changing; new laws are being created and old ones stricken from the criminal code. One new area of the law involves the right to take one's own life, an act that is a crime in most states. Here, Youssef Cohen gets checked by a nurse before undergoing cancer treatment in New York City. Cohen, 68, has an incurable cancer called mesothelioma and is advocating for the right to choose how and when he will die, proposed in New York State's End of Life Options Act, currently before the state legislature. Cohen is a professor of political science at New York University, on sabbatical due to his illness. He had his first bout with cancer in 2012 and has since undergone chemotherapy, surgery, and radiation. He is currently taking immunotherapy infusions of the drug Keytruda in a final effort to fight the disease. The national right-to-die movement is also known as "death with dignity"—or called "physician-assisted suicide" by opponents. If New York does not pass its legislation in time for Cohen's death, he and his wife say they are prepared to move to Oregon, the first state to make death with dignity legal, in order to ensure that he dies without suffering. Death with dignity is now completely legal in California, Oregon, Washington, and Vermont; more than a dozen other states are considering passing similar statutes.

John Moore/Getty Images

In a number of states, including California, it is now considered rape if the victim consents to sex, the sex act begins, the victim changes his or her mind during the act and tells his or her partner to stop, and the partner refuses and continues. The fact that the victim initially consented to and participated in a sexual act does not bar him or her from withdrawing that consent. However, the victim must communicate the withdrawal of consent in such a manner that the accused knew or reasonably should have known that the consent was withdrawn. Before the legal change, such a circumstance was not considered rape but merely aggressive sex.[40]

Controlling Technology   Changing technology and the ever-increasing role of technology in people's daily lives will require modifications of the criminal law. Such technologies as automatic teller machines and cell phones have already spawned a new generation of criminal acts involving theft of access numbers and software piracy. A modification to Virginia's Computer Crimes Act that took effect in 2005 makes *phishing*—sending out bulk email messages designed to trick consumers into revealing bank account passwords, Social Security numbers, and other personal information—a felony. Those convicted of selling the data or using the data to commit another crime, such as identity theft, now face twice the prison time.

Protecting the Environment   In response to the concerns of environmentalists, the federal government has passed numerous acts designed to protect the nation's well-being. The Environmental Protection Agency has successfully prosecuted significant violations of these and other new laws, including data fraud cases (e.g., private laboratories submitting false environmental data to state and federal environmental agencies); indiscriminate hazardous waste dumping that resulted in serious injuries and death; industrywide ocean dumping by cruise ships; oil spills that caused significant damage to waterways, wetlands, and beaches; and illegal handling of hazardous substances such as pesticides and asbestos that exposed children, the poor, and other especially vulnerable groups to potentially serious illness.[41]

CONNECTIONS

Cyberlaw and cybercrime will be covered in greater detail in Chapter 15. This is an emerging area of criminology presenting new challenges in both defining what is a crime and how cyberlaws can be enforced.

ASK YOURSELF . . .

Do you think people are turning from traditional crimes like larceny and burglary to cybercrime, helping to explain the decade-long drop in these crimes?

Legalizing Marijuana   A number of states have now legalized the personal use of marijuana while others have legalized it for medical purposes. In Colorado, an adult 21 years of age or older can now legally possess one ounce of marijuana. In addition to buds (flowers), many types of concentrated and edible forms of marijuana can be legally purchased and consumed so long as it is not in an open and public place (if caught in public, a fine will be issued). Nonresidents are allowed to purchase no more than a quarter-ounce (7 grams) in a single transaction, a restriction designed to prevent visitors from going from one retail store to another and stockpiling marijuana for export.[42] Colorado is not alone: at this writing, 23 states and Washington, D.C., have legalized marijuana use in some form, most for medical purposes. Recreational marijuana use is fully legal in Colorado, Alaska, Oregon, Washington, and the District of Columbia.

While providing medical marijuana has strong public support, the federal government still criminalizes any use of marijuana, and federal agents can arrest users even if they have prescriptions from doctors in states where medical marijuana is legal. The Supreme Court ruled in *Gonzales v. Raich* that the federal government can prosecute medical marijuana patients, even in states with compassionate use laws.[43] The Court ruled that under the Commerce Clause of the U.S. Constitution, which allows the U.S. Congress "To regulate Commerce . . . among the several States," Congress may ban the use of cannabis even where states approve its use for medicinal purposes. The reasoning: because of high demand, marijuana grown for medical reasons would find its way into the hands of ordinary drug users. So while the law may change on a local or state level, federal rules take precedent.

Responding to Terrorism   The criminal law has also undergone extensive change in both substance and procedure in the aftermath of the September 11, 2001, terrorist attacks.

Following the attacks, Congress passed the USA Patriot Act that gave government law enforcement agencies greater power to monitor suspected terrorists and access their electronic communications. In 2015, the USA Freedom Act replaced the Patriot Act. Both of these legal changes will be discussed in more detail in Chapter 11.

Ethical Issues in Criminology

L010 Summarize the main ethical issues in criminology

A critical issue facing students of criminology involves recognizing the field's political and social consequences. All too often, criminologists forget the social responsibility they bear as experts in the area of crime and justice. When government agencies request their views of issues, their pronouncements and opinions become the basis for sweeping social policy. The lives of millions of people can be influenced by criminological research data.

Debates over gun control, capital punishment, and mandatory sentences are ongoing and contentious. Some criminologists have successfully argued for social service, treatment, and rehabilitation programs to reduce the crime rate, but others consider them a waste of time, suggesting instead that a massive prison construction program coupled with tough criminal sentences can bring the crime rate down. By accepting their roles as experts on law-violating behavior, criminologists place themselves in a position of power; the potential consequences of their actions are enormous. Therefore, they must be aware of the ethics of their profession and be prepared to defend their work in the light of public scrutiny. Major ethical issues include these:

- What to study?
- Who to study?
- How to study?

WHAT TO STUDY?

Under ideal circumstances, when criminologists choose a subject for study, they are guided by their own scholarly interests, pressing social needs, the availability of accurate data, and other similar concerns. Nonetheless, in recent years, a great influx of government and institutional funding has influenced the direction of criminological inquiry. Major sources of monetary support include the Justice Department's National Institute of Justice, the National Science Foundation, and the National Institute of Mental Health. Private foundations, such as the Edna McConnell Clark Foundation, have also played an important role in supporting criminological research.

Though the availability of research money has spurred criminological inquiry, it has also influenced the direction research has taken. State and federal governments provide a significant percentage of available research funds, and they may also dictate the areas that can be studied. In recent years, the federal government has spent millions of dollars funding long-term cohort studies of criminal careers. Consequently, academic research has recently focused on criminal careers. Other areas of inquiry may be ignored because there is simply not enough funding to pay for or sponsor the research.

A potential conflict of interest may arise when the institution funding research is itself one of the principal subjects of the research project. Governments may be reluctant to fund research on fraud and abuse of power by government officials. They may also exert a not-so-subtle influence on the criminologists seeking research funding: if criminologists are too critical of the government's efforts to reduce or counteract crime, perhaps they will be barred from receiving further financial help. This situation is even more acute when we consider that criminologists typically work for universities or public agencies and are under pressure to bring in a steady flow of research funds or to maintain the continued viability of their agency. Even when criminologists maintain discretion of choice, the direction of their efforts may not be truly objective. The objectivity of research may be questioned if studies are funded by organizations that have a vested interest in the outcome of the research. A study on the effectiveness of the defensive use of handguns to stop crime may be tainted if the funding for the project comes from a gun manufacturer whose sales may be affected by the research findings. Efforts to show that private prisons are more effective than state correctional facilities might be tainted if the researchers received a research grant from a corporation that maintains private prisons.

WHO TO STUDY?

A second major ethical issue in criminology concerns who will be the subject of inquiries and study. Too often, criminologists focus their attention on the poor and minorities while ignoring the middle-class criminal who may be committing white-collar crime, organized crime, or government crime. Critics have charged that by "unmasking" the poor and desperate, criminologists have justified any harsh measures taken against them. A few social scientists have suggested that criminals have lower intelligence quotients than the average citizen, and that because minority group members have lower than average IQ scores, their crime rates are high.[44] This was the conclusion reached in *The Bell Curve*, a popular though highly controversial book written by Richard Herrnstein and Charles Murray.[45] Although such research is often methodologically unsound, it brings to light the tendency of criminologists to focus on one element of the community while ignoring others. The question that remains is whether it is ethical for criminologists to publish biased or subjective research findings, paving the way for injustice.

HOW TO STUDY?

Ethics are once again questioned in cases where subjects are misled about the purpose of the research. When white and African American individuals are asked to participate in a survey of their behavior or an IQ test, they are rarely told in advance that the data they provide may later be used to prove the existence of significant racial differences in their self-reported crime rates. Should subjects be told about the true purpose of a survey? Would such disclosures make meaningful research impossible? How far should criminologists go when collecting data? Is it ever permissible to deceive subjects to collect data? Criminologists must take extreme care when they select subjects for their research studies to ensure that they are selected in an unbiased and random manner.[46]

When criminological research efforts involve experimentation and treatment, care must be taken to protect those subjects who have been chosen for experimental and control groups. It may be unethical to provide a special treatment program for one group while depriving others of the same opportunity. Conversely, criminologists must be careful to protect subjects from experiments that may actually cause them harm. An examination of the highly publicized Scared Straight program, which brought youngsters into contact with hardcore prison inmates who gave them graphic insights into prison life (to scare them out of a life of crime), discovered that the young subjects may have been harmed by their experience. Rather than being frightened into conformity, subjects actually increased their criminal behavior.[47]

SUMMARY

LO1 Explain what is meant by the term *criminology*

Criminology is the scientific approach to the study of criminal behavior and society's reaction to law violations and violators. It is an academic discipline that uses the scientific method to study the nature, extent, cause, and control of criminal behavior. Criminology is an interdisciplinary science. Criminologists hold degrees in a variety of fields, most commonly sociology, but also criminal justice, political science, psychology, economics, engineering, and the natural sciences. Criminology is a fascinating field, encompassing a wide variety of topics that have both practical application and theoretical importance.

LO2 Identify the difference between crime and deviance

Criminologists devote themselves to measuring, understanding, and controlling crime and deviance. Deviance includes a broad spectrum of behaviors that differ from the norm, ranging from the most socially harmful to the relatively inoffensive. Criminologists are often concerned with the concept of deviance and its relationship to criminality.

LO3 Recognize the concept of "criminology in action" and articulate what criminologists do

Criminology in action refers to the efforts of criminologists to use their insight, training, and experience to understand human behavior and predict its occurrence. The various subareas included within the scholarly discipline of criminology, taken as a whole, define the field of study. The subarea of criminal statistics/crime measurement involves calculating the amount of, and trends in, criminal activity. Sociology of law/law and society/socio-legal studies is a subarea of criminology concerned with the role that social forces play in shaping criminal law and the role of criminal law in shaping society. Criminologists also explore the causes of crime. Another subarea of criminology involves research on specific criminal types and patterns: violent crime, theft crime, public order crime, organized crime, and so on. The study of penology, correction, and sentencing involves the treatment of known criminal offenders. Criminologists recognize that the victim plays a critical role in the criminal process and that the victim's behavior is often a key determinant of crime.

LO4 Discuss the three most prominent views of the meaning of "crime"

According to the consensus view, crimes are behaviors that all elements of society consider repugnant. This view holds that the majority of citizens in a society share common values and agree on what behaviors should be defined as criminal. The conflict view depicts criminal behavior as being defined by those in power to protect and advance their own self-interest. According to the interactionist view, those with social power are able to impose their values on society as a whole, and these values then define criminal behavior.

LO5 Outline the development of criminal law

The criminal law used in U.S. jurisdictions traces its origin to the English system. At first the law of precedent was used to decide conflicts on a case-by-case basis during the Middle Ages. Judges began to use these written decisions as a basis for their decision making, and eventually a fixed body of legal rules and principles was established. If a new rule was successfully applied in a number of different cases, it would become a precedent. These precedents would then be commonly applied in all similar cases—hence the term *common law*. In the U.S. legal system, lawmakers have codified common-law crimes into state and federal penal codes.

LO6 Analyze the different categories of law

Substantive criminal law involves such issues as the mental and physical elements of crime, crime categories, and criminal defenses. Procedural criminal law sets out the basic rules of practice in the criminal justice system. It includes the rules of evidence, the law of arrest, the law of search and seizure, questions of appeal, jury selection, and the right to counsel. The civil law governs relations between private parties, including both individuals and organizations (such as business enterprises and/or corporations), and is used to resolve, control, and shape such personal interactions as contracts, wills and trusts, property ownership, personal disputes (torts), and commerce. Administrative laws are enforced by governmental agencies such as the IRS or EPA.

L07 Articulate the relationship between the criminal law and the U.S. Constitution

All criminal law in the United States must conform to the rules and dictates of the U.S. Constitution. Criminal laws have been interpreted as violating constitutional principles if they are too vague or too broad to give clear meaning of their intent. The Constitution also prohibits laws that make a person's status a crime. The Constitution limits laws that are overly cruel or capricious.

L08 Synthesize the different purposes of criminal law

The criminal law serves several important purposes. It represents public opinion and moral values. It enforces social controls. It deters criminal behavior and wrongdoing. It punishes transgressors. It creates equity and abrogates the need for private retribution.

L09 Compare and contrast the elements of the criminal law

The criminal law contains two main elements: the criminal act (*actus reas*) and the mental intent to commit that act (*mens rea*). In most instances, both must be present before an act can be considered a crime. A criminal defense can be either (a) to deny the act took place or to claim that the accused did not commit the act or (b) to deny intent, claiming the act was justified because it was committed in self-defense or should be excused because it was a product of mental illness or intoxication. Some crimes are strict liability—they do not require intent; the mere act is sufficient to be considered criminal.

L010 Summarize the main ethical issues in criminology

Ethical issues arise when information-gathering methods appear biased or exclusionary. These issues may cause serious consequences because research findings can significantly affect individuals and groups. Criminologists must be concerned about the topics they study. Another ethical issue in criminology revolves around the selection of research subjects. A third area of concern involves the methods used in conducting research.

CRITICAL THINKING QUESTIONS

1. Some criminologists believe that the threat of punishment is sufficient to control crime. Are there other forms of social control? Aside from the threat of legal punishments, what else controls your own behavior?

2. Would it be ethical for a criminologist to observe a teenage gang by "hanging" with them, drinking alcohol with underage minors, and watching as they steal cars? Should the criminologist report that behavior to the police?

3. Can you identify behaviors that are deviant but not criminal? S What about crimes that are illegal but not deviant? 2

5 crimes

4. Do you agree that some of the most damaging acts in society are not punished as crimes? If so, what are they?

5. Should the concept of *mens rea* or the "guilty mind" be eliminated from the criminal law and replaced with a strict liability standard? (If you do the crime, you do the time, regardless of what you were thinking at the time.)

6. If you could change the criminal law, what behaviors would you legalize? What would you criminalize? Would you want to legalize drug use? What might be the consequences of your actions? In other words, are there any hidden drawbacks or benefits?

KEY TERMS

criminology (4)
criminologists (4)
scientific method (4)
criminal justice (4)
justice (5)
deviant behavior (5)

criminology in action (6)
crime typology (9)
consensus view (12)
social harm (12)
conflict view (12)
interactionist view (13)

moral entrepreneurs (14)
common law (15)
mala in se (15)
mala prohibitum (15)
substantive criminal law (16)
procedural criminal law (16)

civil law (16)
public (or administrative) law (16)
felony (17)
misdemeanor (17)
stalking statutes (19)

NOTES

All sites accessed in 2016.

1. CNN, "San Bernardino Shooting," http://www.cnn.com/specials/san-bernardino-shooting/.
2. Edwin Sutherland and Donald Cressey, *Principles of Criminology*, 6th ed. (Philadelphia: J. B. Lippincott, 1960), p. 3.
3. Marvin Wolfgang and Franco Ferracuti, *The Subculture of Violence* (London: Social Science Paperbacks, 1967), p. 20.
4. Mirka Smolej and Janne Kivivuori, "The Relation Between Crime News and Fear of Violence," *Journal of Scandinavian Studies in Criminology and Crime Prevention* 7 (2006): 211–227.
5. Jacqueline Cohen, Wilpen Gorr, and Andreas Olligschlaeger, "Leading Indicators and Spatial Interactions: A Crime-Forecasting Model for Proactive Police Deployment," *Geographical Analysis* 39 (2007): 105–127.
6. The Sociology of Law Section of the American Sociological Association, http://www.departments.bucknell.edu/soc_anthro/soclaw/textfiles/Purpose_soclaw.txt.
7. *Stanley v. Georgia*, 394 U.S. 557, 89 S. Ct. 1243, 22 L. Ed. 2d 542, 1969 U.S.
8. Megan Lim, Elise Carrotte, and Margaret Hellard, "The Impact of Pornography on Gender-Based Violence, Sexual Health and Well-Being: What Do We Know?" *Journal of Epidemiology and Community Health,* published online May 28, 2015.
9. Walter S. DeKeseredy and Marilyn Corsianos, *Violence Against Women in Pornography* (London: Routledge, 2015).
10. Rosemary Erickson and Rita Simon, *The Use of Social Science Data in Supreme Court Decisions* (Champaign: University of Illinois Press, 1998).
11. *Glossip v. Gross*, 576 U.S. ___ (2015).
12. Samuel Gross, Kristen Jacoby, Daniel Matheson, Nicholas Montgomery, and Sujata Patil, "Exonerations in the United States 1989 Through 2003," *Journal of Criminal Law and Criminology* 95 (2005): 523–560, at 531–533.
13. Marvin Wolfgang, *Patterns in Criminal Homicide* (Philadelphia: University of Pennsylvania Press, 1958).
14. John Horgan, *The Psychology of Terrorism*, 2nd ed. (New York: Taylor and Francis, 2014); Randy Borum, *Psychology of Terrorism* (Tampa: University of South Florida, 2004), http://www.ncjrs.gov/pdffiles1/nij/grants/208552.pdf.
15. Gross et al., "Exonerations in the United States 1989 Through 2003."
16. Hans von Hentig, *The Criminal and His Victim* (New Haven: Yale University Press, 1948); Stephen Schafer, *The Victim and His Criminal* (New York: Random House, 1968).
17. Linda Teplin, Gary McClelland, Karen Abram, and Darinka Mileusnic, "Early Violent Death Among Delinquent Youth: A Prospective Longitudinal Study," *Pediatrics* 115 (2005): 1586–1593.
18. Sutherland and Cressey, *Criminology*, 6th ed., p. 8.
19. Charles McCaghy, *Deviant Behavior* (New York: MacMillan, 1976), pp. 2–3.
20. See Herbert Blumer, *Symbolic Interactionism* (Englewood Cliffs, NJ: Prentice Hall, 1969).
21. Howard Becker, *Outsiders: Studies in the Sociology of Deviance* (New York: Free Press, 1963), p. 9.
22. The National Council on Alcoholism and Drug Dependence, http://www.ncadd.org/.
23. *Carriers case*, 13 Edward IV 9.pL.5 (1473).
24. See John Weaver, *Warren—The Man, the Court, the Era* (Boston: Little, Brown, 1967); see also "We the People," *Time*, July 6, 1987, p. 6.
25. *Kansas v. Hendricks*, 117 S.Ct. 2072 (1997); *Chicago v. Morales*, 119 S.Ct. 246 (1999).
26. *City of Chicago v. Morales et al.*, 527 U.S. 41 (1999).
27. Daniel Suleiman, "The Capital Punishment Exception: A Case for Constitutionalizing the Substantive Criminal Law," *Columbia Law Review* 104 (2004): 426–458.
28. *Baze and Bowling v. Rees*, 553 U.S. 35 (2008).
29. Oliver Wendell Holmes, *The Common Law*, ed. Mark De Wolf (Boston: Little, Brown, 1881), p. 36.
30. The following is based on Joshua Dressler, *Cases and Materials on Criminal Law* (American Casebook Series) (Eagan, MN: West Publishing, 2003); Joel Samaha, *Criminal Law* (Belmont, CA: Wadsworth Publishing, 2001).
31. National Institute of Justice, *Project to Develop a Model Anti-Stalking Statute* (Washington, DC: National Institute of Justice, 1994).
32. Lisa Stolzenberg and Stewart D'Alessio, "'Three Strikes and You're Out': The Impact of California's New Mandatory Sentencing Law on Serious Crime Rates," *Crime and Delinquency* 43 (1997): 457–469.
33. Associated Press, "Judge Upholds State's Sexual Predator Law," *Bakersfield Californian*, October 2, 1996.
34. *Lawrence et al. v. Texas*, No. 02-102. June 26, 2003.
35. Marvin Zalman, John Strate, Denis Hunter, and James Sellars, "Michigan Assisted Suicide Three-Ring Circus: The Intersection of Law and Politics," *Ohio Northern Law Review* 23 (1997): 863–903.
36. 1992 P.A. 270, as amended by 1993 P.A.3, M.C. L. ss. 752.1021 to 752.1027.
37. Michigan Code of Criminal Procedure, "Assisting a Suicide," Section 750.329a.
38. William Glaberson, "Man at Heart of Megan's Law Convicted of Her Grisly Murder," *New York Times*, May 31, 1997, http://www.nytimes.com/1997/05/31/nyregion/man-at-heart-of-megan-s-law-convicted-of-her-grisly-murder.html.
39. Sarah Welchans, "Megan's Law: Evaluations of Sexual Offender Registries," *Criminal Justice Policy Review* 16 (2005): 123–140.
40. Matthew Lyon, "No Means No? Withdrawal of Consent During Intercourse and the Continuing Evolution of the Definition of Rape," *Journal of Criminal Law and Criminology* 95 (2004): 277–314.
41. Environmental Protection Agency, Criminal Enforcement, https://www.epa.gov/enforcement/criminal-enforcement/.
42. Colorado Pot Guide, Marijuana Laws in Colorado, 2016 https://www.coloradopotguide.com/marijuana-laws-in-colorado/.
43. *Gonzales v. Raich*, 545 U.S. 1, 2005.
44. See Michael Hindelang and Travis Hirschi, "Intelligence and Delinquency: A Revisionist Review," *American Sociological Review* 42 (1977): 471–486.
45. Richard Herrnstein and Charles Murray, *The Bell Curve* (New York: Free Press, 1994).
46. Victor Boruch, Timothy Victor, and Joe Cecil, "Resolving Ethical and Legal Problems in Randomized Experiments," *Crime and Delinquency* 46 (2000): 330–353.
47. Anthony Petrosino, Carolyn Turpin-Petrosino, and James Finckenauer, "Well-Meaning Programs Can Have Harmful Effects! Lessons from Experiments of Programs Such as Scared Straight," *Crime and Delinquency* 46 (2000): 354–379.

$1.25 · NYDailyNews.com   SPORTS FINAL   Morning shower, 85/67. Friday, June 19, 2015

DAILY NEWS
NEW YORK'S HOMETOWN NEWSPAPER

Twisted killer Dylann Roof in custody after 14-hour manhunt.

America's disease
Racist S.C. church shooter captured

GUN VIOLENCE STRIKES NATION AGAIN — PAGES 2,3,4,5,6,7 AND EDITORIAL

New York Daily News/Getty Images

LEARNING OBJECTIVES

LO1 Compare and contrast the most widely used forms of crime data collection

LO2 Articulate the problems associated with collecting the official crime data

LO3 Identify recent trends in the crime rate

LO4 Discuss the factors that influence crime rate trends

LO5 Assess how crime rates reflect different ecological conditions

LO6 Debate the association between social class and crime

LO7 Clarify what is meant by the term *aging out process*

LO8 Describe the gender and racial patterns in crime

LO9 Describe the pioneering research on chronic offending by Wolfgang, Figlio, and Sellin

LO10 Evaluate the suspected causes of chronicity

2 THE NATURE AND EXTENT OF CRIME

On June 17, 2015, Dylann Roof killed nine African American parishioners, including the senior pastor, Clementa Pinckney, in the Emanuel African Methodist Church in Charleston, South Carolina. When he was captured in North Carolina, authorities quickly learned that Roof was an avowed racist who committed the murders in order to spark a race war. He had posted photos on the Web showing him posing with symbols of racial hatred, white supremacy, and Nazism. Efforts were soon made to understand Roof's motive for committing this shocking crime. There was talk that his father was verbally and physically abusive to the family. Dylann routinely smoked marijuana and exhibited obsessive behavior traits. He was a high school dropout who spent his time taking drugs, drinking, and playing video games. He was socially isolated and cut off from his family. Despite this conjecture, his racist attitudes, identification with white supremacy, and advocacy of racial segregation seemed to be the triggers that prompted his murderous outburst. "I have no choice," he posted on the Internet. "I am not in the position to, alone, go into the ghetto and fight. I chose Charleston because it is [the] most historic city in my state, and at one time had the highest ratio of blacks to whites in the country." He goes on to say "someone has to have the bravery to take it to the real world, and I guess that has to be me." His ranting was similar to what can be found on white supremacist websites.[1] His own website, called "The Last Rhodesian," contained photos of him wearing a jacket with the flags of apartheid-era South Africa and Rhodesia. Other photos showed Roof holding a gun in one hand and a Confederate flag in the other, standing on and burning American flags, and posing in front of historic slave cabins and cemeteries, as well as South Carolina's Museum and Library of Confederate History.[2] In the aftermath of his crime, South Carolina passed legislation ordering the removal of the Confederate battle flag from the state capitol building. Protestors had argued that the flag was a symbol of racism and white supremacy that shouldn't remain on the capitol grounds after the Charleston massacre.

When stories such as the Charleston killings are splashed across the media and rehashed on nightly talk shows, they help convince most Americans that we live in an extremely violent society. If a misguided, troubled young man like Dylann Roof can buy a .45 Glock automatic and kill people in a church after a prayer session, is anyone safe? Roof told authorities he almost did not start shooting because people were so nice to him in the hour he spent in the church. When people read headlines about a violent attack such as Roof's they begin to fear crime and take steps to protect themselves, perhaps avoiding public places and staying at home in the evening. More than one-third of Americans say they are afraid to walk alone in their neighborhood at night.[3] Even though the crime rate has dropped considerably for more than a decade, about 70 percent of Americans still believe it is more dangerous today than it was a year ago.[4]

Are Americans justified in their fear of violent crime? Should they barricade themselves behind armed guards? Are crime rates actually rising or falling? Where do most crimes occur and who commits them? To answer these and similar questions, criminologists have devised elaborate methods of crime data collection and analysis. Without accurate data on the nature and extent of crime, it would not be possible to formulate theories that explain the onset of crime or to devise social policies that facilitate its control or elimination. Valid and reliable data are also critical for such criminological tasks as assessing the nature and extent of crime, tracking changes in the crime rate, and measuring the individual and social factors that may influence criminality.

In this chapter, we review how crime data are collected on criminal offenders and offenses and what this information tells us about crime patterns and trends. We also examine the concept of criminal careers and discover what available crime data can tell us about the onset, continuation, and termination of criminality.

Primary Sources of Crime Data

L01 Compare and contrast the most widely used forms of crime data collection

The primary sources of crime data include official records and large-scale survey data collected, compiled, and analyzed by government agencies such as the Bureau of Justice Statistics and the Federal Bureau of Investigation (FBI). Criminologists use the data collected by these government agencies to measure the nature and extent of criminal behavior and the personality, attitudes, and background of criminal offenders. It is important to understand how these data are collected to gain insight into how professional criminologists approach various problems and questions in their field.

OFFICIAL RECORDS: THE UNIFORM CRIME REPORT

What is commonly called "official" crime data is that collected from local law enforcement agencies by the FBI and published yearly in their **Uniform Crime Report (UCR)**.[5]

> The Bureau of Justice Statistics website is one of the most important sources of crime data. Become familiar with their annual collections on law enforcement, court processing, and correctional populations, among other topics. Access the BJS site at **http://www.bjs.gov/**.
> **As an exercise, find out how many local police departments there are in the United States.**

The UCR, the best known and most widely cited source of official criminal statistics, includes both crimes reported to local law enforcement departments and the number of arrests made by police agencies. The FBI receives and compiles records from more than 17,000 police departments serving a majority of the U.S. population. Its major unit of analysis involves **index crimes** or **Part I crimes**: murder and nonnegligent manslaughter, forcible rape, robbery, aggravated assault, burglary, larceny, arson, and motor vehicle theft. Exhibit 2.1 defines these crimes; note that the definition of rape was changed in 2012. The revised definition now includes any gender of victim or perpetrator, and includes instances in which the victim is incapable of giving consent because of temporary or permanent mental or physical incapacity, including due to the influence of drugs or alcohol or because of age. The ability of the victim to give consent must be determined in accordance with state statute. Physical resistance from the victim is not required to demonstrate lack of consent.[6]

The FBI tallies and annually publishes the number of reported offenses by city, county, standard metropolitan statistical area, and geographical divisions of the United States. In addition to recording crimes reported to the police, the UCR also collects data on the number and characteristics (age, race, and gender) of individuals who have been arrested for committing a crime. Included in the arrest data are people who are suspected of committing Part I crimes and people who have been arrested for all other crimes,

Uniform Crime Report (UCR) Large database, compiled by the Federal Bureau of Investigation, of crimes reported and arrests made each year throughout the United States.

index crimes The eight crimes that, because of their seriousness and frequency, the FBI reports the incidence of in the annual Uniform Crime Report. Index crimes include murder, rape, assault, robbery, burglary, arson, larceny, and motor vehicle theft.

Part I crimes Another term for index crimes; eight categories of serious, frequent crimes.

EXHIBIT 2.1

Part I (Index) Crime Offenses

CRIMINAL HOMICIDE

Murder and Nonnegligent Manslaughter The willful (nonnegligent) killing of one human being by another. Deaths caused by negligence, attempts to kill, assaults to kill, suicides, accidental deaths, and justifiable homicides are excluded. Justifiable homicides are limited to (a) the killing of a felon by a law enforcement officer in the line of duty and (b) the killing of a felon, during the commission of a felony, by a private citizen.

Manslaughter by Negligence The killing of another person through gross negligence. Traffic fatalities are excluded. Although manslaughter by negligence is a Part I crime, it is not included in the crime index.

RAPE

The penetration, no matter how slight, of the vagina or anus with any body part or object, or oral penetration by a sex organ of another person, without the consent of the victim. Included are rapes by force and attempts or assaults to rape. The FBI has used this definition since 2013; the old definition ("The carnal knowledge of a female forcibly and against her will") is included in some legacy data.

ROBBERY

The taking or attempting to take anything of value from the care, custody, or control of a person or persons by force or threat of force or violence or by putting the victim in fear.

AGGRAVATED ASSAULT

An unlawful attack by one person upon another for the purpose of inflicting severe or aggravated bodily injury. This type of assault usually is accompanied by the use of a weapon or by means likely to produce death or great bodily harm. Simple assaults are excluded.

BURGLARY/BREAKING OR ENTERING

The unlawful entry of a structure to commit a felony or a theft. Attempted forcible entry is included.

LARCENY/THEFT (EXCEPT MOTOR VEHICLE THEFT)

The unlawful taking, carrying, leading, or riding away of property from the possession or constructive possession of another. Examples are thefts of bicycles or automobile accessories, shoplifting, pocket picking, or the stealing of any property or article that is not taken by force and violence or by fraud. Attempted larcenies are included. Embezzlement, con games, forgery, worthless checks, and so on are excluded.

MOTOR VEHICLE THEFT

The theft or attempted theft of a motor vehicle. A motor vehicle is self-propelled and runs on the surface and not on rails. Specifically excluded from this category are motorboats, construction equipment, airplanes, and farming equipment.

ARSON

Any willful or malicious burning or attempt to burn, with or without intent to defraud, a dwelling house, public building, motor vehicle, or aircraft, personal property of another, or the like.

SOURCE: FBI, Uniform Crime Report, *Crime in the United States, 2014.*

---

known collectively as **Part II crimes**. This latter group includes such criminal acts as sex crimes, drug trafficking, and vandalism.

COMPILING THE UNIFORM CRIME REPORT

 Articulate the problems associated with collecting the official crime data

The methods used to compile the UCR are quite complex. Each month law enforcement agencies report the number of index crimes known to them. These data are collected from records of all crime complaints that victims, officers who discovered the infractions, or other sources reported to these agencies.

Whenever criminal complaints are found through investigation to be unfounded or false, they are eliminated from the actual count. However, the number of actual offenses known is reported to the FBI whether or not anyone is arrested for the crime, the stolen property is recovered, or prosecution ensues.

The UCR uses three methods to express crime data. First, the number of crimes reported to the police is expressed as raw figures. In 2014, an estimated 1,165,383 violent crimes occurred nationwide. Second, crime rates per 100,000 people are computed: in 2014, an estimated 365 violent crimes took place per 100,000 inhabitants. This is the equation used:

$$\frac{\text{Number of Reported Crimes}}{\text{Total U.S. Population}} \times 100,000 = \text{Rate per } 100,000$$

Third, the FBI computes changes in rate of crime and the number of crimes over time. Preliminary 2015 data show that the number of murders may have risen sharply, increasing more than 6 percent during the period January to June 2014–2015.[7]

Part II crimes All crimes other than index and minor traffic offenses. The FBI records annual arrest information for Part II offenses.

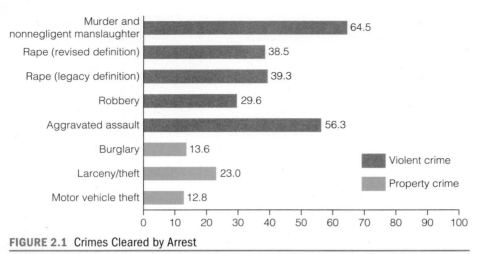

FIGURE 2.1 Crimes Cleared by Arrest

SOURCE: FBI, *Crime in the United States, 2014*, https://www.fbi.gov/about-us/cjis/ucr/crime-in-the-u.s/2014/crime-in-the-u.s.-2014/offenses-known-to-law-enforcement/clearances/main (accessed April 2016).

Clearance Rates In addition, each month law enforcement agencies report how many crimes are **cleared**. Crimes are cleared in two ways: (1) when at least one person is arrested, charged, and turned over to the court for prosecution; or (2) by exceptional means, when some element beyond police control precludes the physical arrest of an offender (e.g., the offender leaves the country). Data on the number of clearances involving the arrest of only juvenile offenders, data on the value of property stolen and recovered in connection with Part I offenses, and detailed information pertaining to criminal homicide are also reported.

Traditionally, about half of all violent crime and 20 percent of property crimes are cleared by arrest each year. Not surprisingly, as Figure 2.1 shows, the most serious crimes such as murder and rape are cleared at much higher rates than less serious property crimes such as larceny. What factors account for this clearance rate differential?

- The media gives more attention to serious violent crimes, and as a result local and state police departments are more likely to devote time and spend more resources in their investigations.
- There is more likely to be a prior association between victims of violent/serious crimes and their attackers, a fact that aids police investigations.
- Even if they did not know one another beforehand, violent crime victims and offenders interact so that identification is facilitated.

cleared crimes Crimes are cleared in two ways: when at least one person is arrested, charged, and turned over to the court for prosecution; or by exceptional means, when some element beyond police control precludes the physical arrest of an offender (for example, the offender leaves the country).

- Serious violent crimes often produce physical evidence—blood, body fluids, fingerprints—that can be used to identify suspects.

ARE THE UNIFORM CRIME REPORTS VALID?

Despite criminologists' continued reliance on the UCR, its accuracy has been suspect. The three main areas of concern are inconsistent reporting practices, law enforcement reporting practices, and methodological issues.

Inconsistent Reporting Less than half of all violent crimes and only one-third of property crimes are reported to the police.[8] The reasons for not reporting vary:

- *Confidence in law enforcement.* Some victims do not trust the police or have confidence in their ability to solve crimes. Cities in which people believe the police can help them are more likely to report crime.[9]
- *Insurance.* Victims without property insurance believe it is useless to report theft.
- *Reprisal.* Some victims fail to report because they fear reprisals from an offender's friends or family or, in the case of family violence, from their spouse, boyfriend, or girlfriend.[10]
- *Not important enough.* The more serious the crime and the greater the loss, the more likely citizens will report crime to police.[11] Some victims believe that the incident was "a private matter," that "nothing could be done," or that the victimization was "not important enough." If they are injured, especially if a weapon was involved, they are more likely to consider the incident serious and report it to the police. If the crime was completed, and the criminal got away with their wallet, purse, car, or package, reporting is more likely to occur.

- *Dirty hands.* People who are themselves involved in criminal activities and have "dirty hands" are less likely to report crime than those whose "hands are clean." The dirty hands may not be related to criminal activity: people who cheat on their spouse, drink excessively, or have other skeletons in the closet are less likely to call the police than their less deviant peers.

Those who do report crime are more likely to do so if they perceive social support from family, friends, and social service agencies. Crimes involving strangers are more likely to be reported than those involving friends and relatives. One exception to this rule: if the crime was committed by an ex-husband or ex-wife, the police are more likely to be called than if it was committed by a stranger.[12] Crimes involving multiple offenders are also more likely to come to the attention of police than those with a single perpetrator.[13]

Law Enforcement Reporting Practices   The way police departments record and report criminal and delinquent activity also affects the validity of UCR statistics. Some police departments define crimes loosely—reporting a trespass as a burglary or an assault on a woman as an attempted rape—whereas others pay strict attention to FBI guidelines. These reporting practices may help explain interjurisdictional differences in crime.[14] Changes in reporting can shape the crime trends reported in the UCR.[15] So what may be viewed as a significant change in crime rates may in fact represent a change in victims' behavior more than in criminals' behavior. Arson is seriously underreported because many fire departments do not report to the FBI, and those that do define many fires that may well have been set by arsonists as "accidental" or "spontaneous."[16]

Some local police departments make systematic errors in UCR reporting. They may count an arrest only after a formal booking procedure, although the UCR requires arrests to be counted if the suspect is released without a formal charge.

More serious allegations claim that in some cases police officials may deliberately alter reported crimes to improve their department's public image. Police administrators interested in lowering the crime rate may falsify crime reports by classifying a burglary as a nonreportable trespass. John Eterno and Eli Silverman studied reporting practices in New York City and found that police commanders, under intense pressure to reduce crime by hard-charging police commissioners, manipulated crime statistics in order to show success.[17] How did they cheat? One method was to check eBay and other websites to find prices for items that had been reported stolen that were actually lower than the value provided by the crime victim. They would then use the lower values to reduce felony grand larcenies (crimes that are in the UCR) to misdemeanor petit larcenies that go unrecorded. Some commanders reported sending officers to crime scenes to persuade victims not to file complaints or to alter crimes so they did not have to be reported to the FBI.

While it is possible that the New York police administrators were under more pressure to reduce crime than their counterparts around the country, the fact that members of the largest police department in the United States may have fudged UCR data is disturbing.

Crime rates also may be altered based on the way law enforcement agencies process UCR data. As the number of employees assigned to dispatching, record keeping, and criminal incident reporting increases, so too will national crime rates. What appears to be a rising crime rate may be simply an artifact of improved police record-keeping ability.

Methodological Issues   Methodological issues also contribute to questions pertaining to the UCR's validity. The most frequent issues include the following:

- No federal crimes are reported.
- Reports are voluntary and vary in accuracy and completeness.
- Not all police departments submit reports.
- The FBI uses estimates in its total crime projections.
- According to the "Hierarchy Rule," in a multiple-offense incident, only the most serious crime is counted. Thus if an armed bank robber commits a robbery, assaults a patron as he flees, steals a car to get away, and damages property during a police chase, only the robbery is reported because it is the most serious offense. Consequently, many lesser crimes go unreported.
- Each act is listed as a single offense for some crimes but not for others. If a man robbed six people in a bar, the offense is listed as one robbery, but if he assaulted or murdered them, it would be listed as six assaults or six murders.
- Incomplete acts are lumped together with completed ones.
- Important differences exist between the FBI's definition of certain crimes and those used in a number of states.

In addition to these issues, the complex scoring procedure used in the UCR program means that many serious crimes are not counted. While each of these problems create serious validity issues, they are present every time the UCR is collected. However, the crime reports remain a highly useful tool to compare year to year trends in the crime rate. They are also a significant tool to compare regional differences in the crime rate.[18]

THE NATIONAL INCIDENT-BASED REPORTING SYSTEM (NIBRS)

Clearly, there must be a more reliable source for crime statistics than the UCR as it stands today. Beginning in 1982, a five-year redesign effort was undertaken to provide more comprehensive and detailed crime statistics. The effort resulted in the **National Incident-Based Reporting System (NIBRS)**, a program that collects data on each reported crime incident. Instead of submitting statements of the kinds of crime that individual citizens report to the police and summary statements of resulting arrests, the new program requires local police agencies to provide at least a brief account of each incident and arrest, including the incident, victim, and offender information. Under NIBRS, law enforcement authorities provide information to the FBI on each criminal incident involving one or more of 46 specific offenses, including the 8 Part I crimes, that occur in their jurisdiction; arrest information on the 46 offenses plus 11 lesser offenses is also provided in NIBRS. These expanded crime categories include numerous additional crimes, such as blackmail, embezzlement, drug offenses, and bribery; this allows a national database on the nature of crime, victims, and criminals to be developed. Other collected information includes statistics gathered by federal law enforcement agencies, as well as data on hate or bias crimes. When fully implemented, NIBRS will provide:

- Expansion of the number of offense categories included
- Detail on individual crime incidents (offenses, offenders, victims, property, and arrests)
- Linkage between arrests and clearances to specific incidents or offenses
- Inclusion of all offenses in an incident rather than only the most serious offense
- The ability to distinguish between attempted and completed crimes
- Linkages between offense, offender, victim, property, and arrestee variables that permit examination of interrelationships[19]

Today, 6,520 law enforcement agencies, representing coverage of more than 93 million U.S. inhabitants, submit NIBRS data. While not yet nationally representative, this coverage represents 35 percent of all law enforcement agencies that participate in the UCR program.[20] When fully implemented and adopted across the nation, NIBRS should bring about greater uniformity in cross-jurisdictional reporting and

improve the accuracy of official crime data. Whether it can capture cases missing in the UCR remains to be seen.[21]

 For more information about NIBRS, visit **http:// www.bjs.gov/index.cfm?ty=dcdetail&iid=301.** **In what ways would knowledge and information about individual crimes help criminologists?**

SURVEY RESEARCH

The second primary source of crime/victimization measurement is through surveys in which people are asked about their attitudes, beliefs, values, and characteristics, as well as their experiences with crime and victimization. Surveys typically involve **sampling**, which refers to the process of selecting for study a limited number of subjects who are representative of entire groups sharing similar characteristics, called the **population**. To understand the social forces that produce crime, a criminologist might interview a sample of 3,000 prison inmates drawn from the population of more than 2 million inmates in the United States; in this case, the sample represents the entire population of U.S. inmates. It is assumed that the characteristics of people or events in a carefully selected sample will be quite similar to those of the population at large. If the sampling was done correctly, the responses of the 3,000 inmates should represent the entire population of inmates.

In some circumstances, criminologists may want the survey to be representative of all members of society; this is referred to as a **cross-sectional survey**. A survey of all students who attend the local public high school would be considered a cross-sectional survey since all members of the community, both rich and poor, male and female, go to high school. Cross-sectional surveys are a useful and cost-effective technique for measuring the characteristics of large numbers of people:

- Because questions and methods are standardized for all subjects, uniformity is unaffected by the perceptions or biases of the person gathering the data.
- Carefully drawn samples enable researchers to generalize their findings from small groups to large populations.
- Though surveys measure subjects at a single point in their life span, questions can elicit information on subjects' past behavior as well as expectations of future behaviors.[22]

 A number of academic institutes are devoted to survey research, including the Princeton University Survey Research Center (SRC). Visit them at **http://www.princeton.edu/~psrc/.** **Do a self-report survey in class: By a show of hands, how many students have *never* committed a crime—never taken drugs, gambled, shoplifted, engaged in underage drinking? What does this tell you about the true amount of crime in society?**

National Incident-Based Reporting System (NIBRS) A program that requires local police agencies to provide a brief account of each incident and arrest within 22 crime patterns, including incident, victim, and offender information.

sampling Selecting a limited number of people for study as representative of a larger group.

population All people who share a particular personal characteristic, such as all high school students or all police officers.

cross-sectional survey Survey data derived from all age, race, gender, and income segments of the population measured simultaneously. Because people from every age group are represented, age-specific crime rates can be determined. Proponents believe this is a sufficient substitute for the more expensive longitudinal approach that follows a group of subjects over time to measure crime rate changes.

THE NATIONAL CRIME VICTIMIZATION SURVEY (NCVS)

Because more than half of all victims do not report their experiences to the police, the UCR cannot measure all the annual criminal activity. To address the nonreporting issue, the federal government's Bureau of Justice Statistics sponsors the **National Crime Victimization Survey (NCVS)**, a comprehensive, nationwide survey of victimization in the United States. Begun in 1973, the NCVS provides a detailed picture of crime incidents, victims, and trends.[23] It provides information about victims (age, sex, race, ethnicity, marital status, income, and educational level), offenders (sex, race, approximate age, and victim–offender relationship), and the crimes (time and place of occurrence, use of weapons, nature of injury, and economic consequences). Questions also cover the experiences of victims with the criminal justice system, self-protective measures used by victims, and possible substance abuse by offenders. Supplements are added periodically to the survey to obtain detailed information on topics such as school crime.

How the NCVS Is Conducted   The NCVS is administered to persons age 12 or older from a nationally representative sample of households, defined as a group of members who all reside at a sampled address. Persons are considered household members when the sampled address is their usual place of residence at the time of the interview and when they have no usual place of residence elsewhere. Once selected, households remain in the sample for three years, and eligible persons in these households are interviewed every six months either in person or over the phone for a total of seven interviews. In the most recent survey, about 90,000 households were selected and more than 158,000 persons age 12 or older were interviewed for the NCVS. Each household was interviewed twice during the year. The response rate was 87 percent for households and 87 percent for eligible persons. Since the NCVS relies on a sample rather than a census of the entire U.S. population, the data is weighted to reflect population totals and to compensate for survey nonresponse and other aspects of the sample design.

Since its inception, the survey has undergone a number of significant modifications. In 1993, it was redesigned

CONNECTIONS

Victim surveys provide information not only about criminal incidents that have occurred, but also about the individuals who are most at risk of falling victim to crime, and where and when they are most likely to become victimized. Data from recent NCVS surveys will be used in Chapter 3 to draw a portrait of the nature and extent of victimization in the United States.

ASK YOURSELF . . .

If you were contacted by the NCVS, would you be willing to share information on your personal victimizations?

to provide detailed information on the frequency and nature of the crimes of rape, sexual assault, personal robbery, aggravated and simple assault, household burglary, theft, and motor vehicle theft. In 2006, significant methodological changes were made, including a new sampling method, a change in the method of handling first-time interviews with households, and a change in the method of interviewing. Some selected areas were dropped from the sample while others were added. Finally, computer-assisted personal interviewing (CAPI) replaced paper and pencil interviewing (PAPI).

NCVS: Advantages and Problems   The greatest advantage of the NCVS over official data sources such as the UCR is that it can estimate the total amount of annual crimes and not only those that are reported to police, which means that the NCVS data provide a more complete picture of the nation's crime problem. Also, because some crimes are significantly underreported, the NCVS is an indispensable measure of their occurrence. Take for example the crimes of rape and sexual assault, crimes which are traditionally underreported. The UCR shows that in 2014 slightly more than 84,000 rapes occurred, as compared to the 284,000 rapes and sexual assaults found by the NCVS. In addition, the NCVS helps us understand why crimes are not reported to police and whether the type and nature of the criminal event influence whether the police will ever know it occurred. With the crime of rape, research shows that victims are much more likely to report rape if it is accompanied by another crime such as robbery than they are if it is a stand-alone event. Official data alone cannot provide that type of information.[24]

While its utility and importance are unquestioned, the NCVS may suffer from some methodological problems. As a result, its findings must be interpreted with caution. Among the potential problems are the following:

- Overreporting due to victims' misinterpretation of events. A lost wallet may be reported as stolen, or an open door may be viewed as a burglary attempt.
- Underreporting due to the embarrassment of reporting crime to interviewers, fear of getting in trouble, or simply forgetting an incident.
- Inability to record the personal criminal activity of those interviewed, such as drug use or gambling; murder is also not included, for obvious reasons.
- Sampling errors, which produce a group of respondents who do not represent the nation as a whole.
- Inadequate question format that invalidates responses. Some groups, such as adolescents, may be particularly susceptible to error because of question format.[25]

National Crime Victimization Survey (NCVS) The ongoing victimization study conducted jointly by the Justice Department and the U.S. Census Bureau that surveys victims about their experiences with law violation.

While these issues are critical, there is no substitute available that provides national information on crime and victimization with extensive detail on victims and the social context of the criminal event.

SELF-REPORT SURVEYS

While the NCVS is designed to measure victimization directly and criminal activity indirectly, participants in **self-report surveys** are asked to describe, in detail, their recent and lifetime participation in criminal activity. Self-reports are generally given anonymously in groups, so that the people being surveyed are assured that their responses will remain private and confidential. Secrecy and anonymity are essential to maintain the honesty and validity of responses. Since identity is guarded, self-report surveys can be used to assess the "dark figures of crime," offenses that would never otherwise be counted in the official crime data. Self-reports have been used to measure trends and patterns in teen substance abuse, something that official data would never be able to assess.

Self-report survey questions might ask:

- How many times in the past year have you taken something worth more than $50?
- How many times in the past year did you hurt someone so badly that he or she needed medical care?
- How many times in the past year did you vandalize or damage school property?
- How many times in the past year did you use marijuana?

---

self-report survey A research approach that requires subjects to reveal their own participation in delinquent or criminal acts.

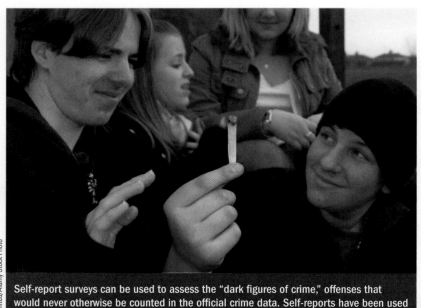

Self-report surveys can be used to assess the "dark figures of crime," offenses that would never otherwise be counted in the official crime data. Self-reports have been used to measure trends and patterns in teen substance abuse, something that official data would never be able to assess.

While most self-report studies have focused on juvenile delinquency and youth crime, they can also be used to examine the offense histories of select groups such as prison inmates, drug users, and even police officers.[26]

In addition to crime-related items, most self-report surveys contain questions about attitudes, values, and behaviors. There may be questions about participants' substance abuse history, arrest history, and their family relations, such as "Did your parents ever strike you with an implement such as a belt?" By correlating the responses, criminologists are able to analyze the relationship between personal factors and criminal behaviors. Statistical analysis of the responses can be used to determine whether people who report being abused as children are more likely to use drugs as adults.

One of the most important sources of self-report data is the Monitoring the Future (MTF) study, which researchers at the University of Michigan Institute for Social Research (ISR) have been conducting annually since 1978. This national survey typically involves more than 2,500 high school seniors.[27] The MTF is considered the national standard to measure substance abuse trends among American teens.

Visit the Monitoring the Future website, **http://www.monitoringthefuture.org/**.

Do you believe that people answering self-report studies are truthful? Are you concerned that they fail to report their criminal activity or that the teenage subjects exaggerate in order to be "cool"?

The MTF data indicate that the number of people who break the law is far greater than the number projected by official statistics. Almost everyone questioned is found to have violated a law at some time, including truancy, alcohol abuse, false ID use, shoplifting or larceny under $50, fighting, marijuana use, or damage to the property of others. Furthermore, self-reports dispute the notion that criminals and delinquents specialize in one type of crime or another; offenders seem to engage in a mixed bag of crime and deviance.[28]

Validity of Self-Reports Critics of self-report studies frequently suggest that it is unreasonable to expect people to candidly admit illegal acts. This is especially true of those with official records, who may be engaging in the most criminality. At the same time, some people may exaggerate their criminal acts, forget some of them, or be confused about what is being asked. Some surveys contain an overabundance of trivial offenses, such as shoplifting small items or using false identification to obtain alcohol, often lumped together with serious crimes to form a total crime index. Consequently, comparisons between groups can be highly misleading.

The "missing cases" phenomenon is also a concern. Even if 90 percent of a school population voluntarily participate in a self-report study, researchers can never be sure whether the few who refuse to participate or are absent that day comprise a significant portion of the school's population of persistent high-rate offenders. Research indicates that offenders with the most extensive prior criminality are also the most likely "to be poor historians of their own crime commission rates."[29] It is also unlikely that the most serious chronic offenders in the teenage population are willing to cooperate with criminologists administering self-report tests.[30]

Institutionalized youths, who are not generally represented in the self-report surveys, are not only more delinquent than the general youth population but are also considerably more misbehaving than the most delinquent youths identified in the typical self-report survey.[31] Consequently, self-reports may measure only nonserious, occasional delinquents while ignoring hardcore chronic offenders who may be institutionalized and unavailable for self-reports.

There is also concern that the way self-reports are administered may change their outcomes. One study in which researchers actually paid one group of subjects to be "honest and thoughtful" and compared them with those who were merely paid to participate found important differences between the two groups. Those who were paid to tell the truth reported a greater willingness to offend and lower estimates of perceived risk for drinking and driving and cheating on exams.[32] This outcome suggests that the way a survey is administered and who the administrator is may shape responses. Can we really be sure unpaid participants are telling the truth?

To address these criticisms, various techniques have been used to verify self-report data. The "known group" method compares people known to be offenders with those who are not, to see whether the former report more crime, which they should. Research shows that when people are asked whether they have ever been arrested or sent to court,

their responses accurately reflect their true-life experiences.[33] In addition, responses to self-reports are consistent over time: people who either exaggerate or understate their criminal activities in youth also do so as adults.[34]

There is also evidence that reporting accuracy differs among racial, ethnic, and gender groups. It is possible that some groups are more worried about image than others and less willing to report crime, deviance, and/or victimization for fear that it would make them or their group look bad. Take these cases, for instance:

- Research shows that girls are usually more willing than boys to disclose drug use, with the exception of Latina girls, who significantly underreport their drug usage. Such gender- and ethnic-based differences in reporting might provide a skewed and inaccurate portrait of criminal and/or delinquent activity—in this case, the self-report data would falsely show that Latina girls use fewer drugs than other females.[35]
- African Americans have been found to be less willing to report traffic stops than Caucasians, a phenomenon that prevents accurate assessments of **racial profiling** by police. Because of this reluctance to report stops that have occurred, it is possible that the "driving while black" phenomenon is actually more frequent than research surveys indicate.[36]

Self-reports also contain other problems that cloud their validity. Asking subjects about their past behavior may capture more serious crimes but miss minor criminal acts—that is, people remember armed robberies and rapes better than they do minor assaults and altercations.[37] In addition, some classes of offenders, such as substance abusers, may have a tough time accounting for their prior misbehavior.[38]

EVALUATING THE PRIMARY SOURCES OF CRIME DATA

The UCR, NCVS, and self-reports are the standard sources of data used by criminologists to track trends and patterns in the crime rate. Each has its own strengths and weaknesses.

- The UCR contains information on the number and characteristics of people arrested, information that the other data sources lack; it also provides unique data on homicide rates and trends.[39] However, UCR data omit many criminal incidents victims choose not to report to police, and it is subject to the reporting caprices of individual police departments.
- The NCVS includes unreported crime and important information on the personal characteristics of victims. While highly important, NCVS data consist of estimates made from relatively limited samples of the total U.S. population, so that even narrow fluctuations in the rates

CONNECTIONS

Criminologists suspect that a few high-rate offenders are responsible for a disproportionate share of all serious crime. Results would be badly skewed if even a few of these chronic offenders were absent or refused to participate in school-wide self-report surveys. For more on chronic offenders, see the sections at the end of this chapter. Self-report data are used to track the development of criminal careers, a topic that is discussed in great detail in Chapter 9.

ASK YOURSELF . . .

How might errors in self-reporting skew perceptions of the nature and extent of delinquent and/or criminal involvement?

racial profiling Selecting suspects on the basis of their ethnic or racial background.

of some crimes can have a major impact on findings. It also relies on personal recollections that may be inaccurate. The NCVS does not include data on important crime patterns, including murder and drug abuse.

■ Self-report surveys provide unique information on the personal characteristics of offenders—such as their attitudes, values, beliefs, personal history, and psychological profiles—that is unavailable from any other source. Yet, at their core, self-reports rely on the honesty of criminal offenders and drug abusers, a population not generally known for accuracy and integrity.

Although their tallies of crimes are certainly not in synch, the crime patterns and trends the three sources provide are often quite similar (see Concept Summary 2.1).[40]

CONCEPT SUMMARY 2.1
Data Collection Methods

Uniform Crime Report
■ Data are collected from records from police departments across the nation, crimes reported to police, and arrests.
■ Strengths of the UCR are that it measures homicides and arrests, and it is a consistent, national sample.
■ Weaknesses of the UCR are that it omits crimes not reported to police, omits most drug usage, and contains reporting errors.

National Crime Victimization Survey
■ Data are collected from a large national survey.
■ Strengths of the NCVS are that it includes crimes not reported to the police, uses careful sampling techniques, and is a yearly survey.
■ Weaknesses of the NCVS are that it relies on victims' memory and honesty, and it omits substance abuse.

Self-Report Surveys
■ Data are collected from local surveys.
■ Strengths of self-report surveys are that they include unreported crimes, they can be used to measure substance abuse, and they often include questions that can assess an offender's personal history information, values, attitudes, and beliefs.
■ Weaknesses of self-report surveys are that they rely on the honesty of offenders and they omit offenders who refuse or are unable to participate and who may be the most deviant.

---

cohort A sample of subjects whose behavior is followed over a period of time.

retrospective cohort study A study that uses an intact cohort of known offenders and looks back into their early life experiences by checking their educational, family, police, and hospital records.

Each of the sources of crime data agree about the personal characteristics of serious criminals (age and gender) and where and when crime occurs (urban areas, nighttime, and summer months). In addition, the problems inherent in each source are consistent over time. Therefore, even if the data sources are incapable of providing an exact, precise, and valid count of crime at any given time, they are reliable indicators of changes and fluctuations in yearly crime rates.

Secondary Sources of Crime Data

In addition to these main sources of crime data, a number of other techniques are used by criminologists to gather data on specific crime problems and trends, to examine the lives of criminal offenders, and to assess the effectiveness of crime control efforts.

COHORT RESEARCH

Cohort research involves observing a group of people who share a like characteristic over time. Researchers might select all girls born in Albany, New York, in 1970 and then follow their behavior patterns for 20 years. The research data might include their school experiences, arrests, hospitalizations, and information about their family life (divorces, parental relations). The subjects might be given repeated intelligence and physical exams; their diets might be monitored.

Data may be collected directly from the subjects during interviews and meetings with family members. Criminologists might also examine records of social organizations, such as hospitals, schools, welfare departments, courts, police departments, and prisons. School records contain data on students' academic performance, attendance, intelligence, disciplinary problems, and teacher ratings. Hospitals record incidents of drug use and suspicious wounds, which may be indicative of child abuse. Police files contain reports of criminal activity, arrest data, personal information on suspects, victim reports, and actions taken by police officers. Court records enable researchers to compare the personal characteristics of offenders with the outcomes of their court appearances, conviction rates, and types of sentence. Prison records contain information on inmates' personal characteristics, adjustment problems, disciplinary records, rehabilitation efforts, and length of sentence served. If the cohort is carefully drawn, it may be possible to determine which life experiences produce criminal careers.

Because it is extremely difficult, expensive, and time-consuming to follow a cohort over time, another approach is to take an intact cohort from the past and collect data from their educational, family, police, and hospital records. This format is known as a **retrospective cohort study**.[41] For example, a cohort of girls who were in grade school in 1970 could be selected from school attendance records.

A criminologist might then acquire their police and court records over the following four decades to determine (a) which ones developed a criminal record and (b) whether school achievement predicts adult criminality.

EXPERIMENTAL RESEARCH

Sometimes criminologists are able to conduct controlled experiments to collect data on the cause of crime. They may wish to directly test whether (a) watching a violent TV show will (b) cause viewers to act aggressively. This test requires experimental research. To conduct experimental research, criminologists manipulate or intervene in the lives of their subjects to see the outcome or the effect of the intervention. True experiments usually have three elements: (1) random selection of subjects, (2) a control or comparison group, and (3) an experimental condition. Using this approach to find out the effects of viewing violent media content, a criminologist might have one group of randomly chosen subjects watch an extremely violent and gory film (*Resident Evil* or *World War Z*) while another randomly selected group viewed something more mellow (*The Lego Movie* or *Toy Story*). If the subjects who watched the violent film were significantly more aggressive than those who watched the nonviolent film, an association between media content and behavior would be supported. The fact that both groups were randomly selected would prevent some preexisting condition from invalidating the results of the experiment. The Criminology in Action feature describes an experimental approach to criminological research.

Quasi-experiments   Because it is sometimes impossible to randomly select subjects or manipulate conditions, criminologists may be forced to rely on what is known as a *quasi-experimental design*. A criminologist may want to measure whether kids who were abused as children are more likely to become violent as adults. Of course, it is impossible to randomly select youth, assign them to two independent groups, and then purposely abuse members of one group in order to gauge their reactions. To get around this dilemma, a criminologist may select a group of adults who years earlier had been identified by school or medical authorities as being abused and then compare them with a control group who, though similar in every other respect, were never so identified. Even if a difference could be found in current behavior, it would still be impossible to know for certain whether the earlier child abuse was the source of adult violence or some other factor was the actual cause. It is possible that child abuse victims self-medicate with drugs and alcohol, and substance abuse—not child abuse—is the true cause of future antisocial behavior.

Despite the need for them, true criminological experiments using all the elements of the scientific method are relatively rare because they are difficult and expensive to conduct; they involve manipulating subjects' lives, which can cause ethical and legal roadblocks; and they require long follow-up periods to verify results.

OBSERVATIONAL AND INTERVIEW RESEARCH

Sometimes criminologists focus their research on relatively few subjects, interviewing them in depth or observing them as they go about their activities. One recent interview study assessed the economic impact of sexual assaults, using data from 27 qualitative interviews with rape survivors. Rebecca Loya found that the aftermath of sexual assault and its related trauma can disrupt survivors' employment in several ways, including forcing victims to take time off or diminishing their job performance, resulting in job loss and inability to find work. These disruptive employment consequences can have long-term implications for survivors' economic well-being over the life course. So rather than

Measuring the Effect of Deviant Peers

Criminologists Ray Paternoster, Jean Marie McGloin, Holly Nguyen, and Kyle J. Thomas conducted an interesting and informative experiment to measure whether peers influence behavior choices. They set up an experiment at a local university that was allegedly designed to measure short-term memory. The experimenter read a list of 20 words, which the subjects would be asked to recall at the end of the experiment; they were told they would receive $1 for each word they recalled correctly, for a maximum possible payment of $20. The participants were also asked to complete a short online survey about their background (demographic information), self-perceived memory ability, and other factors. Participants were told that they had eight minutes to answer the survey questions on the computer and that if they finished before then, they should simply sit quietly and wait so that every person waited the same amount of time before recalling the words. The experimenter left the room, and when he returned he told the subjects how to enter the words online. The experimenter then appeared to be shocked as he noticed four "junk web links" located at the bottom of the recall page. The experimenter clicked on the links and announced that they opened up lists of the words to be recalled (i.e., each of the four links opened a page of 5 words, giving participants access to all 20 words).

The experimenter said the presence of the links was a software error and the partic-ipants should ignore the links when recalling the words. He then told the participants that he was going to leave the room to speak with a technician about removing the links. All subjects were well aware that there was an opportunity to cheat on this task.

Unknown to the participants, a hired actor was also in the room who looked and acted like the other students (he was a student at another university). In some cases, the peer confederate completed the memory task without cheating and said nothing. In the experimental condition, once the experimenter left the room to talk to the technician, the peer confederate addressed the other subjects in the room using the following script:

> That guy was right—you can totally see the words if you click the links. Screw it. I'm using the lists. I thought we were guaranteed the 20 dollars—now we have to remember all the words? That's ridiculous. I am doing it.

The confederate then openly and clearly cheated on the task by clicking on all four links and using them to fill in the word recall list.

When the experimenter came back, he told the group that because of the need to fix the software glitch, there was no time to count the number of correct words for each subject in order to determine payment, so everyone would receive the $20 compensation.

Despite the fact the peer deviance was committed by a stranger offering a verbal intention and justification for cheating that lasted less than 15 seconds, his behavior significantly increased the probability of subjects engaging in deviance. While none of the control subjects cheated, 38 percent of the participants exposed to the cheating peer chose to do so!

This experiment lends significant support to both the influence of peers and the theory of differential association: people exposed to positive attitudes toward deviant behavior are more likely to adapt similar behaviors themselves. And remember, the actor was merely a peer and not a close friend. Had a best friend approved cheating, for a longer duration than 15 seconds, we can only imagine what the outcome would have been.

 CRITICAL THINKING

Would you be influenced by someone loudly proclaiming it is okay to cheat on a test if an instructor left the room? Be honest now, would another student whom you hardly knew influence your behavior? What if everyone around you started to cheat?

SOURCE: Ray Paternoster, Jean Marie McGloin, Holly Nguyen, and Kyle J. Thomas, "The Causal Impact of Exposure to Deviant Peers: An Experimental Investigation," *Journal of Research in Crime and Delinquency* 50 (2013): 476–503.

being only a physical attack, sexual assault can also be considered an economic crime.[42] Interviews have not only been used in the United States, they are a staple of criminological research around the world. In one recent (2015) effort, 30 Spanish mothers were interviewed to assess the impact of intimate partner violence (IPV) on their children. The interviews showed that, as might be expected, IPV has damaging effects on a child's well-being and development. The mothers told how as a result of their exposure to violence, children often develop psychological, social, and school problems. IPV teaches them to be aggressive and they sometimes direct their hostile feelings toward their mothers.

Thus, IPV results in double victimization: from partners and from children. While some children are capable of mature response to IPV, others aren't and create an atmosphere that inhibits the treatment process.[43]

Another common criminological method is to observe criminals firsthand to gain insight into their motives and activities. This may involve going into the field and participating in group activities; this was done in sociologist William Whyte's famous study of a Boston gang, *Street Corner Society*.[44] Other observers conduct field studies but remain in the background, observing but not being part of the ongoing activity.[45]

META-ANALYSIS AND SYSTEMATIC REVIEW

Meta-analysis involves gathering data from a number of previous studies. Compatible information and data are extracted and pooled together. When analyzed, the grouped data from several different studies provide a more powerful and valid indicator of relationships than the results provided from a single study. A **systematic review** is another widely accepted means of evaluating the effectiveness of public policy interventions. It involves collecting the findings from previously conducted scientific studies that address a particular problem, appraising and synthesizing the evidence, and using the collective evidence to address a particular scientific question.

Through these well-proven techniques, criminologists can identify what is known and what is not known about a particular problem and use the findings as a first step for carrying out new research. Criminologists David Farrington and Brandon Welsh used a systematic review and a meta-analysis to study the effects of street lighting on crime.[46] After identifying and analyzing 13 relevant studies, Farrington and Welsh found evidence showing that neighborhoods that improve their street lighting do in fact experience a reduction in crime rates. Their findings should come as no great surprise: it seems logical that well-lit streets would have fewer robberies and thefts because (a) criminals could not conceal their efforts under the cover of darkness and (b) potential victims could take evasive action if they saw a suspicious-looking person lurking about. The meta-analysis also produced an unusual finding: improving lighting caused the crime rate to go down during the day just as much as it did during the night! Obviously, the crime-reducing effect of streetlights had little to do with illuminating the streets. Farrington and Welsh speculate that improved street lighting increases community pride and solidarity, and the result of this newfound community solidarity is a lowered crime rate, during both the day and evening.

DATA MINING

Data mining uses multiple advanced computational methods, including artificial intelligence (the use of computers to perform logical functions), to analyze large data sets usually involving one or more data sources. The goal is to identify significant and recognizable patterns, trends, and relationships that are not easily detected through traditional analytical techniques alone. Criminologists then use this

Criminologists have been conducting observational and interview studies for many years. Here, Nathan Leopold (right), a thrill-slayer who served 28 years in prison for the 1924 murder of a 14-year-old boy, talks with Professor William Byron, Northwestern University sociologist and criminologist, a few months before Leopold was granted parole from the Stateville Penitentiary in Joliet, Illinois, March 13, 1953.

AP Images/Ed Maloney

information for various purposes, such as the prediction of future events or behaviors.

Data mining has been employed to help police departments allocate resources to combat crime based on offense patterns. To determine if such a pattern exists, data mining is used with a variety of sources, including calls for service data, crime or incident reports, witness statements, suspect interviews, tip information, telephone toll analysis, and Internet activity. This approach has resulted in the development of what is now called **predictive policing**, a technique that relies on data mining's ability to direct proactive or "risk-based" deployment of police resources. Proactive policing makes use of highly sophisticated data analysis techniques, using available information and geospatial technologies, to improve public safety. It is aimed at moving law enforcement from merely reacting to crimes into the realm of predicting

meta-analysis A research technique that uses the grouped data from several different studies.

systematic review A research technique that involves collecting the findings from previously conducted studies, appraising and synthesizing the evidence, and using the collective evidence to address a particular scientific question.

predictive policing A technique that relies on data mining's ability to predict future crime using large data sets and geospatial technologies.

what and where crime is likely to occur and informing police executives on how to deploy resources accordingly.[47] Predictive policing uses computer models to anticipate likely criminal events and suggest the most efficient and effective actions to prevent crime before it occurs. Predictions are based upon analysis of prior crime incident data, and incorporating situational factors such as demographic trends, parolee population locations, and economic trends. Research shows that the technique can predict up to twice as much crime compared to less sophisticated techniques, such as having an in-house crime analyst direct patrol allocation. In sum, dynamic police patrol allocation using data mining techniques to predict where crime will occur can disrupt opportunities for crime and lead to real crime reductions.[48]

CRIME MAPPING

Criminologists use crime maps to create graphic representations of the spatial geography of crime. Computerized crime maps allow criminologists to analyze and correlate a wide array of data to create immediate, detailed visuals of crime patterns. The most simple maps display crime locations or concentrations and can be used, for example, to help law enforcement agencies increase the effectiveness of their patrol efforts. More complex maps can be used to chart trends in criminal activity. For example, criminologists can determine if certain neighborhoods in a city have significantly higher crime rates than others—so-called hot spots of crime.[49] Figure 2.2 illustrates a crime map generated in Providence, Rhode Island.

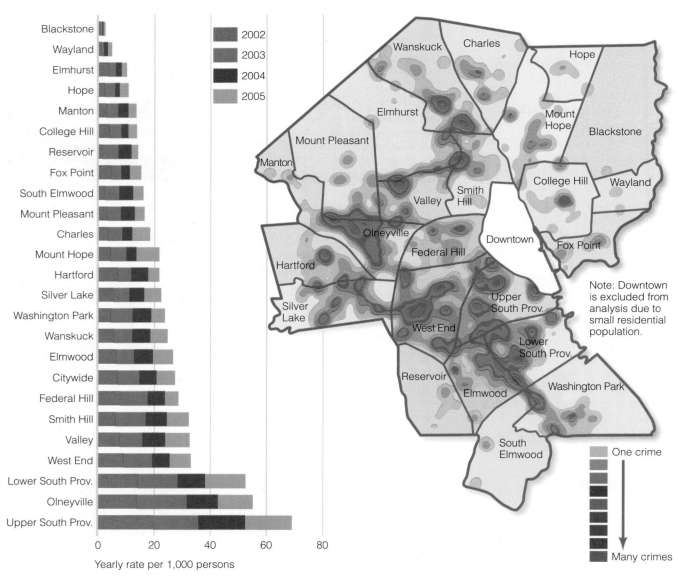

FIGURE 2.2 Police Crime Map: Providence, Rhode Island

SOURCE: © Cengage Learning

Crime Trends

L03 Identify recent trends in the crime rate

Crime is not new to this century. Studies have indicated that a gradual increase in the crime rate, especially in violent crime, occurred from 1830 to 1860. Following the Civil War, this rate increased significantly for about 15 years. Then, from 1880 up to the time of the first World War, with the possible exception of the years immediately preceding and following the war, the number of reported crimes decreased. After a period of readjustment, the crime rate steadily declined until the Depression (about 1930), when another crime wave was recorded. As measured by the UCR, crime rates increased gradually following the 1930s until the 1960s, when the growth rate became much greater. The homicide rate, which had actually declined from the 1930s to the 1960s, also began a sharp increase that continued through the 1970s.[50]

OFFICIAL CRIME TRENDS

By 1992, police recorded about 14.6 million crimes. Since then, the number of crimes has been in decline; in 2014, about 10 million crimes were reported to the police, a drop of more than 4 million recorded crimes from the peak despite an increasing national population. Both violent and property crimes have been in steep decline.

As Tables 2.1 and 2.2 show, the number and rate of violent and property crimes have declined significantly during the past two decades despite the fact that the population has increased by more than 50 million people!

VICTIMIZATION TRENDS

The number of victimizations reported to the NCVS has also shown a significant downturn. At its peak in 1993, more than 40 million victimizations were reported to the NCVS, including more than 10 million violent crimes. By 2014, that number was cut by more than 50 percent (20.7 million total victimizations).[51] As Figure 2.3 shows, the victimization rate for violence has dropped by almost 80 percent from the peak, while property crime victimization has been reduced by more than two-thirds.

TRENDS IN SELF-REPORTING

Self-report results appear to be more stable than the UCR and NCVS data indicate. When the results of recent self-report surveys are compared with various studies conducted over a 20-year period, a uniform pattern emerges. The use of drugs and alcohol increased markedly in the 1970s, leveled off in the 1980s, increased until the mid-1990s, and has been in decline ever since. Theft, violence, and damage-related crimes seem more stable. Although a self-reported crime wave has not occurred, neither has there been any visible reduction in self-reported criminality. Findings from the most recent MTF survey are shown in Table 2.3.[52]

As Table 2.3 shows, a surprising number of teenagers report involvement in serious criminal behavior. About 13 percent reported hurting someone badly enough that the victim needed medical care (6 percent said they did it more than once); about 25 percent reported stealing something worth less than $50, and another 9 percent stole something worth more than $50; 24 percent reported shoplifting one or more times; 11 percent damaged school property, 5 percent more than once.

If the MTF data are accurate, the crime problem is much greater than official statistics would lead us to believe. There are approximately 40 million youths between the ages of 10 and 18. Extrapolating from the MTF findings, this group accounts for more than 100 percent of all the theft offenses reported in the UCR. About 3 percent of high school students said they had used force to steal (which is the legal

TABLE 2.1			
Number of Violent Crimes and Violence Rates			
YEAR	POPULATION	NUMBER OF VIOLENT CRIMES	RATE PER 100,000
1992	255,029,699	1,932,274	757
2000	281,421,906	1,425,486	506
2004	293,656,842	1,360,088	463
2009	307,006,550	1,318,398	429
2012	312,780,968	1,214,462	365
2014	320,050,716	1,165,383	365

SOURCE: FBI, *Uniform Crime Reports, 2014,* https://www.fbi.gov/about-us/cjis/ucr/crime-in-the-u.s/2014/crime-in-the-u.s.-2014/offenses-known-to-law-enforcement/violent-crime (accessed April 2016).

TABLE 2.2			
Number of Property Crimes and Property Crime Rates			
YEAR	POPULATION	NUMBER OF PROPERTY CRIMES	RATE PER 100,000
1992	255,029,699	12,505,917	2,903
2000	281,421,906	10,182,584	3,618
2004	293,656,842	10,319,386	3,514
2009	307,006,550	9,320,971	3,036
2012	312,780,968	8,975,438	2,859
2014	320,050,716	8,277,829	2,596

SOURCE: FBI, *Uniform Crime Reports, 2014,* https://www.fbi.gov/about-us/cjis/ucr/crime-in-the-u.s/2014/crime-in-the-u.s.-2014/offenses-known-to-law-enforcement/property-crime/property-crime (accessed April 2016).

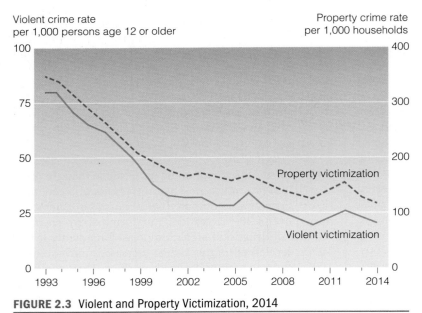

Violent crime rate per 1,000 persons age 12 or older

Property crime rate per 1,000 households

FIGURE 2.3 Violent and Property Victimization, 2014

SOURCE: Bureau of Justice Statistics, National Crime Victimization Survey.

TABLE 2.3

Monitoring the Future Survey of Criminal Activity of High School Seniors

	PERCENTAGE ENGAGING IN OFFENSES	
TYPE OF DELINQUENCY	COMMITTED ONCE	COMMITTED TWO OR MORE TIMES
Set fire on purpose	1	2
Damaged school property	6	5
Damaged work property	2	2
Auto theft	2	2
Auto part theft	2	2
Break and enter	11	13
Theft, less than $50	11	14
Theft, more than $50	4	5
Shoplifted	10	14
Gang or group fight	9	8
Hurt someone badly enough to require medical care	7	6
Used force or a weapon to steal	1	2
Hit teacher or supervisor	1	2
Participated in serious fight	7	5

SOURCE: Monitoring the Future, 2015, University of Michigan Institute for Social Research.

definition of a robbery). Two-thirds of them said they committed this crime more than once in a year. At this rate, high school students alone commit more than 1.56 million robberies per year. In comparison, the UCR now tallies about 325,000 robberies for all age groups yearly. While official data show that the overall crime rate is in decline, the MTF surveys indicate that, with a few exceptions, self-reported participation in theft, violence, and damage-related crimes seems to be more stable than the trends reported in the UCR arrest data.[53]

What factors influence these trends, either causing an upward spiral or a downtrend in the crime rate? This topic is the subject of the Criminology in Action feature.

INTERNATIONAL CRIME TRENDS

There has been a marked decline in overall U.S. crime rates, which are now below those of other industrial nations, including England and Wales, Denmark, and Finland.[54] Making international comparisons is often difficult because the legal definitions of crime vary from country to country. There are also differences in the way crime is measured. In the United States, crime may be measured by counting criminal acts reported to the police or by using victim surveys, whereas in many European countries, the number of cases solved by the police is used as the measure of crime. Despite these problems, valid comparisons can still be made about crime across different countries using a number of reliable data sources.

Countries with the highest crime and victimization rate are Ireland, England and Wales, New Zealand, and Iceland. Lowest overall victimization rates are found in Spain, Japan, Hungary, and Portugal. Some cities have much higher crime rates than others. The cities in developed countries with the lowest victimization rates are Hong Kong, Lisbon, Budapest, Athens, and Madrid; the highest victimization rates are found in London and Tallinn, Estonia. Where crime has been reduced, the downward trend is most pronounced in property crimes such as vehicle-related crimes (bicycle theft, thefts from cars, and joyriding) and burglary. One reason is that people around the world are taking precautions to prevent crime. Improved security may well have been one of the main forces behind the universal drop in crimes such as joyriding and household burglary.

Homicide   The global average homicide rate is about 6 per 100,000 population. Southern Africa and Central America have rates over four times higher than that (more than 24 victims per 100,000 population), making them the subregions with the highest homicide rates on record, followed by South America, Central Africa, and the Caribbean (between 16 and 23 homicides per 100,000 population). Subregions with very low homicide rates include Eastern Asia, Southern Europe, and Western Europe. Homicide levels in some countries, such as Brazil, are now stabilizing, and those in South Africa, Russia, and Central Asia are actually decreasing.

Rape and Sexual Assault   Southern Africa, Oceania, and North America have the highest recorded rape rates, Asia the lowest. Violence against women is related to economic hardship and the social status of women. Rates are high in poor nations in which women are oppressed. Where women are more emancipated, the rates of violence against women are lower.

For many women, sexual violence starts in childhood and adolescence and may occur in the home, school, and community. Studies conducted in a wide variety of nations ranging from Cameroon to New Zealand found high rates of reported forced sexual initiation. In some nations, as many as 50 percent of adolescent women and 20 percent of adolescent men report sexual coercion at the hands of family members, teachers, boyfriends, or strangers.

Sexual violence has significant health consequences, including suicide, stress, mental illnesses, unwanted pregnancies, sexually transmitted diseases, HIV/AIDS, self-inflicted injuries, and (in the case of child sexual abuse) adoption of high-risk behaviors such as multiple sexual partners and drug use.

Human Trafficking   Trafficking in persons affects virtually every country in every region of the world. Most trafficking is intraregional, meaning that the origin and the destination of the trafficked victim are within the same region of the world. However, in the rich countries of the Middle East, Western Europe, and North America, trafficking victims may be imported from East and South Asia and sub-Saharan Africa. Richer countries attract victims from a variety of origins, including from other continents, whereas less affluent countries are mainly affected by domestic or subregional trafficking.

The most common form of human trafficking is sexual exploitation. The victims of sexual exploitation are predominantly women and girls. The second most common form of human trafficking is forced labor, although this may be a misrepresentation because forced labor is less frequently detected and reported than trafficking for sexual exploitation. Trafficking for exploitation that is neither sexual nor forced labor, including trafficking of children for armed combat or for petty crime or forced begging, is also increasing.

Worldwide, almost 20 percent of all trafficking victims are children. However, in some parts of Africa and Asia, children are the majority (up to 100 percent in parts of West Africa). Although trafficking seems to imply people moving across continents, most exploitation takes place close to home. Data show intraregional and domestic trafficking are the major forms of trafficking in persons.

Child Abuse   According to the World Health Organization more than 50,000 children are murdered worldwide each year. Between 80 and 93 percent of children suffer some form of physical punishment in their homes; a third are punished using implements. International studies reveal that approximately 20 percent of women and 5 to 10 percent of men report being sexually abused as children, while 25 to 50 percent of all children report being physically abused. Additionally, many children are subject to emotional abuse (sometimes referred to as psychological abuse) and to neglect.

Drug Crimes   Drug use continues to exact a significant toll around the world on both human lives and economic productivity. More than 180,000 drug-related deaths now occur each year; a mortality rate of 40 deaths per million among the population ages 15 to 64. Globally, it is estimated that between 160 million and 325 million people used marijuana, opium, cocaine, or amphetamine at least once in the previous year. About 40 million people can be considered drug dependent.

Today, there is an annual flow of up to 450 tons of heroin into the global heroin market. Of that total, opium from Myanmar and the Lao People's Democratic Republic yields some 50 tons, while the rest, some 380 tons of heroin and morphine, is produced in Afghanistan. While approximately 5 tons are consumed and seized in Afghanistan, the remaining bulk of 375 tons is trafficked worldwide. The most common route is through Iran via Pakistan, Turkey, Greece, and Bulgaria, then across southeastern Europe to the Western European market, with an annual market value of some $20 billion. The northern route runs mainly through Tajikistan and Kyrgyzstan (or Uzbekistan or Turkmenistan)

Factors That Influence Crime Trends

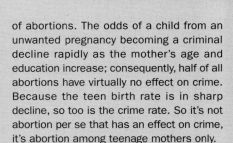

04

Crime experts have identified a variety of social, economic, personal, and demographic factors that influence crime rate trends. Although crime experts are still uncertain about how these factors impact these trends, directional change seems to be associated with changes in crime rates.

Age Structure

As a general rule, the crime rate follows the proportion of teens in the population: more kids, more crime! Crime rates skyrocketed in the 1960s when the baby boomers became teens and the 13 to 19 population grew rapidly. Crime rate drops since 1993 can be explained in part by an aging society: the elderly commit relatively few crimes. However, the age–crime relationship may be mitigated by social factors: areas where youth are alienated and disengaged have higher crime rates than communities whose youth population are involved with prosocial institutions such as school or church. So while young people are more likely to get in trouble with the law than their elders, not all do and those who don't are the ones who have successful involvement with supportive social institutions.

Immigration

The prevailing view of criminologists is that immigration has a suppressor effect on crime: immigrants are less crime prone than the general population, so that as the number of immigrants increases per capita crime rates decline. During the past two decades, cities with the largest increases in immigration have experienced the largest decreases in crime rates, especially homicides and robberies. The effect seems greatest in communities with high preexisting murder rates: when immigrants arrive, homicide rates experience a significant decline.

Two factors mitigate the positive effect of immigration on the crime rate. First, crime reporting is lower in communities with large immigrant populations, and immigrants themselves seem loath to report crimes. One reason is that many come from nations where police are mistrusted and feared.[53] A second issue is that the immigrant effect may be short-lived: by the second generation, children of immigrants have begun to catch up and their crime rates begin to resemble that of the native-born population.

Economy

The general public believes that crime rates increase as the economy turns down and unemployment rises. However, there is little correlation between these indicators of economic prosperity and crime rates. Unemployed people do not suddenly join gangs or commit armed robberies. Criminals are usually unemployed or underemployed and therefore not affected by short-term economic conditions.

Crime rates may, however, be influenced by other types of economic factors. The decline in the burglary rate over the past decade may be explained in part by the abundance and subsequent decline in price of commonly stolen merchandise such as iPads, laptops, cell phones, flat screen TVs, and digital cameras. On the other hand, new targets may increase crime rates; subway crime increased in New York when thieves began targeting people carrying iPads and expensive cell phones such as the iPhone.

Abortion

There is evidence that the recent drop in the crime rate is linked to the availability of legalized abortion. In 1973, *Roe v. Wade* legalized abortion nationwide, and the drop in the crime rate began approximately 18 years later, in 1991. According to John Donohue and Steven Levitt's widely cited research, crime rates began to decline when the first groups of potential offenders affected by the abortion decision began reaching the peak age of criminal activity. Donohue and Levitt posit that the link between crime rates and abortion is the result of two mechanisms: (1) selective abortion on the part of women most at risk to have children who would engage in criminal activity as they matured and (2) because fewer women were bringing unwanted pregnancies to term, more services would be available for other children in need.

Recently, Gary Shoesmith reanalyzed the data on abortion and crime while disaggregating the data by age, education, and state of residence. His findings question Donohue and Levitt's conclusion that "unwantedness leads to high crime." Shoesmith concludes that the association between abortion and crime only applies to teen mothers and not older women, who now account for more than 80 percent

of abortions. The odds of a child from an unwanted pregnancy becoming a criminal decline rapidly as the mother's age and education increase; consequently, half of all abortions have virtually no effect on crime. Because the teen birth rate is in sharp decline, so too is the crime rate. So it's not abortion per se that has an effect on crime, it's abortion among teenage mothers only.

The abortion–crime association is still being debated. And due to its controversial nature it will most likely be a research topic for quite some time.

Gun Availability

The availability of firearms may influence the crime rate: as the number of guns in the population increases, so do violent crime rates. Handguns are especially dangerous if they fall into the hands of teens. Surveys of high school students indicate that between 6 and 10 percent carry guns at least some of the time. Guns also cause escalation in the seriousness of crime. As the number of gun-toting students increases, so too does the seriousness of violent crime as a schoolyard fight turns into murder.

Gangs

Another factor that affects crime rates is the explosive growth in teenage gangs. Surveys indicate that there are about 800,000 gang members in the United States. Data collected by the National Youth Gang Center show that gang members are responsible for a large proportion of all violent offenses committed during the adolescent years.

Boys who are members of gangs are far more likely to possess guns than non-gang members; criminal activity increases when kids join gangs. Gangs involved in the urban drug trade recruit juveniles because they work cheaply, are immune from heavy criminal penalties, and are daring and willing to take risks. Arming themselves for protection, these drug-dealing children present a menace to their community, which persuades non–gang-affiliated neighborhood adolescents to arm themselves for protection. The result is an arms race that produces an increasing spiral of violence. As gangs become more organized, so too does their level of violence and drug dealing. Without gang influence, the crime rate might be much lower.

Drug Use

The presence of drug users in the population impacts crime rates. Drug users routinely commit property crimes to feed their habits; recreational drug users frequently commit crimes to buy marijuana and methamphetamines. Substance abusers also commit violent crimes. Some experts tie increases in the violent crime rate between 1985 and 1993 to the crack epidemic, which swept the nation's largest cities, and to drug-trafficking gangs that fought over drug turf. These well-armed gangs did not hesitate to use violence to control territory, intimidate rivals, and increase market share. As the crack epidemic subsided, so too did the violence rates in New York City and other metropolitan areas where crack use was rampant. A sudden increase in drug use, on the other hand, may be a harbinger of future increases in the crime rate, especially if guns are easily obtained and fall into the hands of gang members.

Media

Some experts argue that violent media can influence the direction of crime rates. As the availability of media with a violent theme skyrocketed with the introduction of home video players, DVDs, cable TV, computer and video games, and so on, so too did teen violence rates. Efforts to curb violence on TV may help account for a declining crime rate.

Medical Technology

Some crime experts believe that the presence and quality of health care can have a significant impact on murder rates. Murder rates might be up to five times higher than they are today without medical breakthroughs in treating victims of violence developed over the past 40 years. The big breakthrough occurred in the 1970s when technology developed to treat injured soldiers in Vietnam was applied to trauma care in the nation's hospitals. Since then, fluctuations in the murder rate can be linked to the level and availability of emergency medical services.

Justice Policy

Some law enforcement experts have suggested that a reduction in crime rates may be attributed to adding large numbers of police officers and using them in aggressive police practices that target "quality of life" crimes such as panhandling, graffiti, petty drug dealing, and loitering. By showing that even the smallest infractions will be dealt with seriously, aggressive police departments may be able to discourage potential criminals from committing more serious crimes. Cities employing aggressive, focused police work may be able to lower homicide rates in the area.

It is also possible that tough laws imposing lengthy prison terms on drug dealers and repeat offenders can affect crime rates. The fear of punishment may inhibit some would-be criminals and place a significant number of potentially high-rate offenders behind bars, lowering crime rates. As the nation's prison population expanded, the crime rate has fallen.

However, justice policy can sometimes backfire and actually lift crime rates. Take for instance the long-term effect of incarceration. The imprisonment boom has resulted in more than 2 million people behind bars. While this policy may take some dangerous offenders off the street, eventually most get out. About 600,000 inmates are now being released each year, and many return to their communities without marketable skills or resources. The number of releasees will rise for the foreseeable future as more and more sentences bestowed during the high-crime-rate 1990s are completed. The recidivism rate of paroled inmates is quite high, averaging about 40 percent for those released from federal penitentiaries and 67 percent for those released from state custody. Inmates reentering society may have a significant effect on local crime rates.

Social and Cultural Change

International scholar Martin Kilias notes that crime trends can be influenced by sudden "breaches"—that is, new opportunities for offending that open as a result of changes in the technological or social environment. As an example he shows that violence among men has decreased since 1850 in some countries because the concept of "honor" has lost most of its importance. There is evidence, he finds, that it was common in the past for a small argument to end in a duel or at least a brawl if a person's personal or family honor was impugned or questioned. Today, honor-based killings can still be found, such as in areas of Turkey where any critical remark about a person's reputation is dealt with by aggression against the source of "rumors."

While maintaining honor and saving face are still important factors in contemporary society, other cultural macro-level conditions such as the number of single-parent families, high school dropout rates, racial conflict, and the prevalence of teen pregnancies also exert a powerful influence on crime rates. High levels of race- and ethnicity-based income inequality have been shown to have an impact on crime rates. Areas where there is both within and between group inequality expe-rience more violent crimes than neighbor-hoods in which most residents are doing equally well.

 CRITICAL THINKING

Can you think of some other factors that may increase or reduce crime rates? Take for instance the justice policy that has created a culture of mass incarceration. Do such policies actually decrease crime rates or is that an illusion?

SOURCES: Richard B. Felson and Jeremy Staff, "Committing Economic Crime for Drug Money," *Crime and Delinquency*, first published online June 26, 2015; Gary L. Shoesmith, "Crime, Teenage Abortion, and Unwantedness," *Crime and Delinquency*, first published online November 18, 2015; Graham Ousey and Charis Kubrin, "Immigration and the Changing Nature of Homicide in US Cities, 1980-2010," *Journal of Quantitative Criminology* 30 (2014): 453-483; Bianca Bersani, "A Game of Catch-Up? The Offending Experience of Second-Generation Immigrants," *Crime and Delinquency* 60 (2014): 60-84; David Weisburd, Cody Telep, and Brian Lawton, "Could Innovations in Policing Have Contributed to the New York City Crime Drop Even in a Period of Declining Police Strength? The Case of Stop, Question and Frisk as a Hot Spots Policing Strategy," *Justice Quarterly* 31 (2014): 129-153; Richard Rosenfeld and Robert Fornango, "The Impact of Police Stops on Precinct Robbery and Burglary Rates in New York City, 2003-2010," *Justice Quarterly* 31 (2014): 96-122; Patricia L. McCall, Kenneth Land, Cindy Brooks Dollar, and Karen F. Parker, "The Age Structure-Crime Rate Relationship: Solving a Long-Standing Puzzle," *Journal of Quantitative Criminology* 29 (2013): 167-190; Tim Wadsworth, "Is Immigration Responsible for the Crime Drop? An Assessment of the Influence of Immigration on Changes in Violent Crime Between 1990 and 2000," *Social Science Quarterly* 91 (2010): 531-553; Amy Anderson and Lorine Hughes, "Exposure to Situations Conducive to Delinquent Behavior: The Effects of Time Use, Income, and Transportation," *Journal of Research in Crime and Delinquency* 46 (2009): 5-34; Ramiro Martinez Jr. and Matthew Amie Nielsen, "Segmented Assimilation, Local Context and Determinants of Drug Violence in Miami and San Diego: Does Ethnicity and Immigration Matter?" *International Migration Review* 38 (2004): 131-157; Richard Rosenfeld, Robert Fornango, and Andres Rengifo, "The Impact of Order-Maintenance Policing on New York City Homicide and Robbery Rates: 1988-2001," *Criminology* 45 (2007): 355-384; National Youth Gang Center, "What Proportion of Serious and Violent Crime Is Attributable to Gang Members?" http://www.nationalgangcenter .gov/About/FAQ#R50 (accessed April 2016); Martin Killias, "The Opening and Closing of Breaches: A Theory on Crime Waves, Law Creation and Crime Prevention," *European Journal of Criminology* 3 (2006): 11-31; Alfred Blumstein, "The Crime Drop in America: An Exploration of Some Recent Crime Trends," *Journal of Scandinavian Studies in Criminology and Crime Prevention* 7 (2006): 17-35; Brad Bushman and Craig Anderson, "Media Violence and the American Public," *American Psychologist* 56 (2001): 477-489; John J. Donohue and Steven D. Levitt, "The Impact of Legalized Abortion on Crime," *Quarterly Journal of Economics* 116 (2001): 379-420.

to Kazakhstan and the Russian Federation. The size of that market is estimated to total $13 billion per year. There are about 17 million opiate users in the world, and another 17 million who use cocaine.

WHAT THE FUTURE HOLDS

 L04 Discuss the factors that influence crime rate trends

It is risky to speculate about the future of crime trends because current conditions can change rapidly. Preliminary UCR data covering the first six months of 2015 indicate that while property crimes continue to slide, murder actually increased by more than 6 percent from the preceding year. The increase has been most pronounced in larger metropolitan areas where the number of murders increased more than 10 percent in a single year! The incidence of rape also showed a significant increase over the previous year (calculated using both the older or legacy definition and the current one). Using the revised definition, big cities experienced an 8 percent change in the number of rapes.

It's too early to tell whether this spike in homicide is a temporary blip or a harbinger of consistent increase. Nonetheless, the recent uptick in the murder rate has police officials worried. Murders seem to be spiking in Chicago, Baltimore, Milwaukee, and other major cities. While some blame easy access to guns as the culprit, others point to what has become known as the "Ferguson Effect": the suggestion that police officers may be reluctant to take aggressive action in the aftermath of the protests that followed the shooting of Michael Brown by a police officer in Ferguson, Missouri. However, it's unlikely that the Brown shooting alone could have influenced police responses and the crime rate; murders were ticking up in many large cities before the shooting occurred on August 9, 2014.[55]

It's also possible that crime rates may rise in the future because of limited economic opportunities. Globalization and the outsourcing of manufacturing jobs may cause the current generation of teens and young adults to lose hope of ever gaining meaningful, high-paid employment. While the unemployment rate has recently fallen, income inequality remains a significant social problem. Today 3 million workers are still being paid the minimum wage of $7.25 per hour (though efforts are under way to increase that rate).[56] Most of these jobs offer no room for growth or promotion. As high-paid job opportunities disappear, young men and women may seek alternative sources of income and prestige. Gang membership may increase and those involved in gangs may remain in them longer. However, even if teens commit more crime in the future, their contribution may be offset by the aging of the population, which will produce a large number of senior citizens and elderly, a group with a relatively low crime rate.[57]

There is, of course, no telling what changes are in store that may influence crime rates. Technological developments such as e-commerce on the Internet have created new classes of crime that are not recorded by any of the traditional methods of crime measurement. It's possible that some crimes such as fraud, larceny, prostitution, obscenity, vandalism, stalking, and harassment have become cybercrimes, falling under the radar of official crime data. The number of people arrested for prostitution has declined almost 20 percent during the past decade. It's possible that (a) there are simply fewer prostitutes, (b) police are less likely to arrest prostitutes than they were a decade ago, or (c) prostitution is booming, but because it's being conducted via the Internet, prostitutes are now better equipped to avoid detection.

Crime Patterns

Criminologists look for stable crime rate patterns to gain insight into the nature of crime. The cause of crime may be better understood by examining the rate. If, for example, criminal statistics consistently show that crime rates are higher in poor neighborhoods in large urban areas, then the cause of crime may be related to poverty and neighborhood decline. If, in contrast, crime rates are spread evenly across society, and rates are equal in poor and affluent neighborhoods, this would provide little evidence that crime has an economic basis. Instead, crime might be linked to socialization, personality, intelligence, or some other trait unrelated to class position or income. In this section, we examine traits and patterns that may influence the crime rate.

THE ECOLOGY OF CRIME

 L05 Assess how crime rates reflect different ecological conditions

Patterns in the crime rate seem to be linked to temporal and ecological factors. Some of the most important of these are discussed here.

Place, Time, Season, Climate There are distinct temporal and ecological patterns in the crime rate.[58] Metropolitan areas are more crime prone than suburban or rural areas. But even in large cities not all areas and neighborhoods have similar crime rates. Most reported crimes occur in confined geographical areas: there are stable block-by-block and neighborhood-by-neighborhood differences in the crime rate. These concentrated areas may contain ecological features such as housing projects that experience a disproportionate share of crime incidents. Crime-prone neighborhoods making up less than 10 percent of a city's area may experience more than 50 percent of the city's crime.[59]

There are also seasonal differences. Crime rates are highest during the warm summer months of July and August.

During the summer, teenagers, who usually have the highest crime levels, are out of school and have greater opportunity to commit crime. People spend more time outdoors during warm weather, making themselves easier targets. Similarly, homes are left vacant more often during the summer, making them more vulnerable to property crimes. Two exceptions to this trend are murders and robberies, which occur frequently in December and January (although rates are also high during the summer). One reason: robberies are more likely to take place when it gets dark out, something that occurs earlier in these winter months (in the United States and Europe, at least).[60]

Crime rates also may be higher on the first day of the month than at any other time. Government welfare and Social Security checks arrive at this time, and with them come increases in such activities as breaking into mailboxes and accosting recipients on the streets. Also, people may have more disposable income at this time, and the availability of extra money may relate to behaviors associated with crime such as drinking, partying, gambling, and so on.[61]

Time of day is also an issue. Some crimes are more likely to take place at night while others are more common during daytime; others are time resistant and take place at any hour of the day. Take robbery for instance. Robbers target corner stores and fast-food restaurants at any time since these establishments may do business around the clock. In contrast, robbers who target check cashing stores strike later in the day, after people have gotten paid and need cash. Robberies

Crime is more common in some areas at certain times of the year. While crime rates decline in the winter, crime does not disappear when it gets cold outside. Here, a man stands in front of an Electromania store in Newark, New Jersey, after it was hit during an early morning robbery on January 3, 2014. The thieves, according to Mohammed Mallouk, son of the owner, used a pickup truck to ram through the entrance of the store before taking off with merchandise in a snowstorm. It wasn't the first time the store had been robbed in such fashion—in 2013 a robber did the same thing during another snowstorm.

AP Images/Julio Cortez

in public parks occur at times when people engage in recreational activities. ATMs are open all day, but robbers seem to prefer times when people feel comfortable walking away with cash, during the morning and daytime hours; potential victims may take more precautions at night.[62]

Temperature Weather effects (such as temperature swings) may have an impact on violent crime rates. Traditionally, the association between temperature and crime was thought to resemble an inverted U-shaped curve: crime rates increase with rising temperatures and then begin to decline at some point (85 degrees) when it may be too hot for any physical exertion.[63] However, criminologists continue to debate this issue:

- Some believe that crime rates rise with temperature (i.e., the hotter the day, the higher the crime rate).[64]
- Others have found evidence that the curvilinear model is correct.[65]
- Some research shows that a rising temperature will cause some crimes to continually increase (e.g., domestic assault), while others (e.g., rape) will decline after temperatures rise to an extremely high level.[66]

If in fact there is an association between temperature and crime, how can it be explained? The relationship may be due to the stress and tension caused by extreme temperatures. The human body generates stress hormones (adrenaline and testosterone) in response to excessive heat;

CONNECTIONS

The rationality of robbers will be revisited in Chapters 4 and 10. The fact that robbers take into account the likelihood of success and the potential for a big score in their decision making supports the view that robbery is a function of rational planning and choice.

ASK YOURSELF . . .

If robbery is rational, what steps might you take to lower your risk of being robbed?

hormonal activity has been linked to aggression.[67] One way to combat the temperature–crime association: turn off your air conditioner! James Rotton and Ellen Cohn found that assaults in air-conditioned settings increased as the temperature rose; assaults in non-air-conditioned settings declined after peaking at moderately high temperatures.[68]

Regional Differences   While large urban areas have by far the highest violence rates, there are some exceptions to this pattern. Low-population resort areas with large transient or seasonal populations typically have higher crime rates than the norm; this phenomenon has been observed in the United States and abroad.[69] Typically, the western and southern states have had consistently higher crime rates than the Midwest and Northeast. This pattern has convinced some criminologists that regional cultural values influence crime rates; others believe that regional differences can be explained by economic differences.

USE OF FIREARMS

Firearms play a dominant role in criminal activity. According to the UCR, about two-thirds of all murders and 40 percent of robberies involve firearms; most of these weapons are handguns. Because of these findings, there is an ongoing debate over gun control. Internationally respected criminologists have argued that the proliferation of handguns and the high rate of lethal violence they cause are the most significant factors separating the crime problem in the United States from the rest of the developed world.[70]

In contrast, some criminologists believe that personal gun use can actually be a deterrent to crime while not causing an increase in the murder rate. Gary Kleck, probably the most widely known scholar on this issue, recently reviewed the existing literature and concluded that higher gun ownership rates do not cause higher crime rates, including homicide rates.[71] In a classic study, Gary Kleck and Marc Gertz claimed that as many as 400,000 people per year use guns in situations in which they later claim that the guns "almost certainly" saved lives. Even if these estimates are off by a factor of 10, it means that armed citizens may save 40,000 lives annually. Although Kleck and Gertz recognize that guns are involved in murders, suicides, and accidents, which claim more than 30,000 lives per year, they believe their benefit as a crime prevention device should not be overlooked.[72]

While gun control remains a heated national debate, evidence out of Chicago underlines the difficulty of keeping guns out of the hands of criminals. Research by Philip Cook and his associates found that while the vast majority of the city's homicides are committed with guns, most guns used in crime are quite old, with a median age of over 10 years. They conclude that guns used in crime have gone through a series of transactions before being acquired by the current owner. It is very rare for guns used in crime to be purchased new from a gun dealer in a documented sale; new guns were used less than 2 percent of the time. Most of these guns came from out

Handguns are involved in most murders, and efforts to control the illegal sale of guns have been challenging. One method is to file suit against gun shops that sell to unqualified people. With a picture of his son behind him, retired Chicago police officer Thomas Wortham III fights back tears at a press conference where it was announced that a lawsuit had been filed by the Brady Center to Prevent Gun Violence on behalf of the Wortham family against Ed's Pawn Shop and Salvage Yard in Byhalia, Mississippi. The suit claimed that Wortham's son, Chicago police officer and Iraq War veteran Thomas Wortham IV, was killed by a gun wrongfully sold to a straw purchaser at the pawn shop. Wortham IV was shot outside his parents' home when four reported gang members tried to rob him of his motorcycle.

Scott Olson/Getty Images

of state; 60 percent of the new guns were likewise imported. Cook concludes that licensed dealers may play only a very small direct role in arming gang members, and other intermediaries—including straw purchasers, brokers, and traffickers who remain outside the law—are far more important.[73]

SOCIAL CLASS, SOCIOECONOMIC CONDITIONS, AND CRIME

L06 Debate the association between social class and crime

It makes sense that crime is inherently a lower-class phenomenon. After all, people at the lowest rungs of the social structure have the greatest incentive to commit crimes, and people who are undergoing financial difficulties are the ones most likely to become their targets.[74] It seems logical that people who are outside the economic mainstream and therefore are unable to obtain desired goods and services legally will resort to illegal activities—such as selling narcotics—to obtain a share of the American Dream: if you can't afford a car, steal it; if you cannot afford designer clothes, become a drug dealer. **Instrumental crimes** are those committed by indigent people to compensate for the lack of legitimate economic opportunity. People living in poverty are also believed to engage in disproportionate amounts of **expressive crimes**, such as rape and assault, as a result of their frustration with what they believe to be an unfair and unjust society. Boiling with anger over social issues such as **income inequality**, they express their rage through irrational crimes that bring them no economic gain.[75]

When measured with UCR data, official statistics indicate that crime rates in inner-city, high-poverty areas are generally higher than those in suburban or wealthier areas. Surveys of prison inmates consistently show that prisoners were members of the lower class and unemployed or underemployed in the years before their incarceration. These are empirical indicators of a class–crime connection.

While the association between class and crime seems logical, it is not accepted by all criminologists. An alternative explanation is that the relationship between official crime and social class is a function of law enforcement practices, not actual criminal behavior patterns. Police may devote more resources to poor areas, and consequently apprehension rates may be higher there. Similarly, police may be more likely to formally arrest and prosecute lower-class citizens, especially racial and ethnic minorities, while giving those in the middle and upper classes more lenient treatment, such as handling their law violations with a warning. Consequently, police bias and use of discretion in making arrests may account for the lower class's overrepresentation in official statistics and the prison population. This explanation is supported by self-report data that do not find a direct relationship between social class and crime.[76] The conclusion: if the poor have more extensive criminal records than the wealthy, this difference is attributable to differential law enforcement and not to class-based behavior differences. That is, police may be more likely to arrest lower-class offenders and treat the affluent more leniently.[77]

Evaluating the Class–Crime Association

While the true relationship between class and crime is difficult to determine, the weight of recent evidence seems to suggest that serious, official crime such as rape, murder, and burglary is more prevalent among the lower classes and that lower-class communities have higher crime rates than more affluent neighborhoods. Less serious and self-reported crime is spread more evenly throughout the social structure.[78] Neighborhoods experiencing income inequality and resource deprivation have crime rates significantly higher than those that can provide equal or more economic opportunities to their citizens.[79]

Crime and Unemployment   It stands to reason that if there is a relationship between crime and socioeconomic status, then crime rates should correlate with

instrumental crimes Offenses designed to improve the financial or social position of the criminal.

expressive crimes Crimes that have no purpose except to accomplish the behavior at hand, such as shooting someone.

income inequality The unequal distribution of household or individual income across the various participants in an economy.

The association between class and crime is not clear: most poor people are not criminals and some very rich people break the law. Nonetheless, crime rates are higher in lower-class communities and people may be influenced by their environment. Here, Reggy Colby, age 30 and a recovering heroin addict, digs through the trash looking for food on August 21, 2013, in Camden, New Jersey. Colby got out of jail two days before, where he was forced to get clean while serving a 30-day sentence for stealing food. Colby says he grew up in a *Leave It to Beaver* home in Cherry Hill, an affluent city nearby, and studied architecture in college before dropping out. After leaving school he moved to Florida, where he married and had a daughter. He joined the army in 2007, trained as a field artillery specialist, and served in Afghanistan in 2009 through 2010, until he was injured by an improvised explosive device, which peppered his body with shrapnel. It was while recovering from his injuries that he became addicted to heroin, a drug he had also tried as a teen. Since becoming addicted, he has been dishonorably discharged from the army, divorced, estranged from his daughter, and has become homeless in Camden. "As a kid I was terrified to come to Camden. I was so scared—I never thought I would be out here, never . . . it's just like, what . . . happened."

unemployment rates, peaking during tough economic times when people are out of work and the poor are hard-pressed to find jobs.

While this association seems logical, there is a great deal of conflicting research, some of which shows that aggregate crime rates and aggregate unemployment rates are only weakly related: crime rates sometimes rise during periods of economic prosperity and fall during periods of economic decline.[80] In contrast, other research links unemployment rates to higher rates of economic crimes, especially when the state does not provide sufficient economic support such as welfare and unemployment benefits.[81]

There are five diverging views on the association between the economy and crime rates:

- *Bad economy means higher crime rates.* When the economy turns down, people who are underemployed or unemployed will become motivated to commit property crimes to obtain desperately needed resources.
- *Good economy means higher crime rates.* A good economy requires that more people be hired, including teens. Students with after-school jobs are more likely to engage in antisocial activities. High teenage employment will actually increase the overall crime rate.[82] A good economy means that people can buy valuable goods which make tempting targets.
- *Good economy means lower crime rates.* When people perceive that the economy is doing well, and there is positive consumer sentiment, the rate of property crimes such as burglary, larceny, and motor vehicle theft declines; why steal when you can get a good job and buy what you need without the risk of crime?[83]
- *Bad economy means lower crime rates.* During an economic downturn, unemployed parents are at home to supervise children and guard their possessions. When people are unemployed, they have less money on hand and purchase fewer things worth stealing. They may even sell their valuables to raise cash, reducing suitable targets for burglars and thieves.
- *Crime and the economy are unrelated.* It is also possible that the state of the economy and crime rates are unrelated. It seems unlikely that middle-class workers will suddenly join gangs or become bank robbers when they lose their jobs. Unemployed people are neither likely to stick up gas stations, banks, and drug stores, nor are they more likely to engage in nonviolent property crimes, including shoplifting, residential burglary, theft of motor vehicle parts, and theft of automobiles, trucks, and motorcycles.[84]

One reason for all this confusion may simply be methodological: measuring the associations among variables such as jobs, the economy, and crime is often quite difficult. There are significant economic differences at the state, county, community, and neighborhood level. While people in one area of the city are doing quite well, their neighbors living in another part of town may be suffering unemployment. Crime rates may even vary by street, an association that is difficult to detect.

Long-Term Trends   It is also possible that the association between crime and the economy is not immediate. Just because unemployment is high does not mean that crime rates are also on the increase. Criminologist Shawn Bushway has shown that crime rates go up and down in long, slow trajectories that vary considerably from period to period. These trajectories may be influenced by changes in the economic structure of society. Since 1960, women have joined the workforce in large numbers, union influence has shrunk, manufacturing has moved overseas, and computers and the Internet have changed the way that resources are created and distributed. As manufacturing has moved overseas, less-educated, untrained male workers have been frozen out of the job market. These workers may find themselves competing in illegal markets: selling drugs may be more profitable than working in a fast-food restaurant. Similarly, people may find prostitution and/or sex work more lucrative relative to minimum-wage jobs in the legitimate market. When the economy turns, drug dealers do not suddenly quit the trade and get a job with GE or IBM. Bushway finds that labor markets, rather than unemployment rates, are the economic engine that shapes the crime rate and creates incentives for individuals to participate in illegal activities.[85]

So the association between economic factors and crime is quite complex and cannot be explained with a simple linear relationship (i.e., the higher the unemployment rate, the more crime).[86] Class and economic conditions may affect some crimes and some people differently than they affect others. Some subgroups in the population (e.g., women, African Americans) seem more deeply influenced by economic factors than others (e.g., men, whites).[87]

CONNECTIONS

If class and crime are related, then crime is primarily a lower-class phenomenon. This view is discussed in Chapter 6. If, however, crime and economic conditions are unrelated, then the causes of crime must be found in factors experienced by members of all social classes—psychological impairment, family conflict, peer pressure, school failure, and so on. Theories that view crime as a function of problems experienced by individuals in all social classes are reviewed in Chapters 4 and 5. And theories that combine both individual and social causes are discussed in Chapter 9.

ASK YOURSELF . . .

Before reading further, what is your take on crime? Is it a social problem, an individual problem, or a combination of both?

AGE AND CRIME

There is general agreement that age is inversely related to criminality. Criminologists Travis Hirschi and Michael Gottfredson state, "Age is everywhere correlated with crime. Its effects on crime do not depend on other demographic correlates of crime."[88] In other words, regardless of economic status, marital status, race, sex, and so on, younger people commit crime more often than their older peers.

Crime is a young person's game. Adolescents, especially those who are destined to become high rate offenders, begin committing crime in their childhood, rapidly increase their offending activities in late adolescence, and then begin a slowdown in adulthood. These early starters tend to commit more crime and are more likely to continue to be involved in criminality over a longer period of time.[89]

Crime is attractive to young people because it brings social benefits. Kids who assume an outlaw persona find that their antisocial acts bring them increased social status among peers who admire their risk-taking behaviors. Young criminals may be looking for an avenue of behavior that improves their peer group standing.[90] Hence, they commit more crime in adolescence.

The elderly are particularly resistant to the temptations of crime; they make up more than 14 percent of the population and less than 1 percent of arrests. Elderly males 65 and over are predominantly arrested for alcohol-related matters (e.g., public drunkenness and drunk driving) and elderly females for larceny (e.g., shoplifting). The elderly crime rate has remained stable for the past 20 years, but because the over-65 population is increasing and will continue to increase as the baby boomers come of age, the number of elderly involved with the criminal justice system will surely follow suit.[91]

There are a few crime patterns in which adults offend at a higher rate than juveniles and teenagers—for example, adults use cocaine and heroin considerably more than adolescents.[92] But for the most part, the statement "crime declines with age" has repeatedly been shown to be accurate.

CONNECTIONS

Hirschi and Gottfredson have used their views on the age-crime relationship as a basis for their General Theory of Crime. This important theory holds that the factors that produce crime change little after birth and that the association between crime and age is constant. For more on this view, see the section on the General Theory of Crime in Chapter 9.

ASK YOURSELF . . .

Why do you think crime rates drop with age? Isn't it true that the economic, social, and emotional problems that cause crime in adolescence are still present in adulthood?

 L07 Clarify what is meant by the term *aging out process*

Aging Out of Crime   Most kids who commit crime as teens discontinue their illegal activities as they mature. **Aging out** of crime may be a function of the natural history of the human life cycle.[93] Deviance in adolescence is fueled by the need for money and sex and reinforced by close relationships with peers who defy conventional morality. At the same time, teenagers are becoming independent from parents and other adults who enforce conventional standards of morality and behavior. They have a new sense of energy and strength and are involved with peers who are similarly vigorous and frustrated.

In adulthood, people strengthen their ability to delay gratification and forgo the immediate gains that law violations bring. They also start wanting to take responsibility for their behavior and to adhere to conventional mores.[94] Getting married, raising a family, and creating long-term family ties provide the stability that helps people desist from crime.[95]

CO-OFFENDING AND CRIME

It is generally accepted that crime tends to be a group activity and that adolescents, in particular, are overwhelmingly likely to commit crime in groups. Peer support encourages offending in adolescence.[96] Rather than being shunned by their peers, antisocial adolescents enjoy increased social status among peers who admire their risk-taking behaviors.[97] Of course, not all offenders enjoy being part of a group or gang; many are lone wolves who shun peer involvement.[98] But crime, especially among the young, appears to be a group activity.

Because co-offending requires offenders to cooperate with one another in a risky endeavor, it is more likely to occur in communities that contain a supply of appropriate criminal associates who can keep their mouths shut and never cooperate with police. Co-offending is more prevalent in neighborhoods that are less disadvantaged, more stable, and contain more people who can be trusted. Ironically, this means that efforts to improve neighborhood stability and cohesiveness may also help produce an environment that encourages group offending.[99] Does it pay to offend in groups or are you better off as a lone wolf? Recent research by Marie Skubak Tillyer and Rob Tillyer analyzed NIBRS data to determine whether co-offending in robberies actually works. Their findings are somewhat surprising: co-offending results in significantly less property value stolen

aging out The process by which individuals reduce the frequency of their offending behavior as they age. It is also known as spontaneous remission, because people are believed to spontaneously reduce the rate of their criminal behavior as they mature. Aging out is thought to occur among all groups of offenders.

per offender, while increasing the likelihood of an incident resulting in an arrest. One reason for the greater apprehension risk: the more robbers, the more likely the victim will recognize someone he or she knows. Why do robbers commit crime in groups if co-offending produces lower gain and greater pain? Committing crime in groups helps to control offender fear during the incident while increasing peer group respect. Working in a group also may facilitate opportunities for more frequent offending, thus leading to higher overall profits for the offender. So in the final tally, working in a group may produce higher overall profit even if it does require more work.[100]

GENDER AND CRIME

 Describe the gender and racial patterns in crime

Male crime rates are much higher than those of females. Victims report that their assailant was male in more than 80 percent of all violent personal crimes. The most recent (2014) Uniform Crime Report statistics indicate that more than 73 percent of the persons arrested were males. They accounted for almost 80 percent of persons arrested for violent crime and 62 percent of persons arrested for property crime; murder arrests are 7 males to 1 female. MTF data also show that young men commit more serious crimes, such as robbery, assault, and burglary, than their female peers.

Even though gender differences in the crime rate have persisted over time, there seems little question that females are now involved in more crime than ever before and that there are more similarities than differences between male and female offenders.[101]

Explaining Gender Differences in the Crime Rate
Early criminologists pointed to emotional, physical, and psychological differences between males and females to explain the differences in crime rates. Cesare Lombroso's 1895 book *The Female Offender* argued that a small group of female criminals lacked "typical" female traits of "piety, maternity, undeveloped intelligence, and weakness."[102] In physical appearance as well as in their emotional makeup, delinquent females appeared closer to men than to other women. Lombroso's theory became known as the **masculinity hypothesis**; in essence, a few "masculine" females were responsible for the handful of crimes women commit.

Another early view of female crime focused on the supposed dynamics of sexual relationships. Female criminals were viewed as either sexually controlling or sexually

masculinity hypothesis The view that women who commit crimes have biological and psychological traits similar to those of men.

chivalry hypothesis The idea that low female crime and delinquency rates are a reflection of the leniency with which police treat female offenders.

CONNECTIONS

Gender differences in the crime rate have been linked to hormones that cause areas of the brain to become less sensitive to environmental stimuli. Gender differences in biochemical makeup result in males being more likely to seek high levels of stimulation and to tolerate more pain in the process. Chapter 5 discusses the biosocial causes of crime and reviews this issue in greater detail.

ASK YOURSELF . . .
Why do you think males are more involved in criminal activity than females?

naive, either manipulating men for profit or being manipulated by them. The female's criminality was often masked because criminal justice authorities were reluctant to take action against a woman.[103] This perspective is known as the **chivalry hypothesis**, which holds that much female criminality is hidden because of the culture's generally protective and benevolent attitude toward women.[104] In other words, police are less likely to arrest, juries are less likely to convict, and judges are less likely to incarcerate female offenders.

Although these early writings are no longer taken seriously, some criminologists still believe that gender-based traits are a key determinant of crime rate differences. Among the suspected differences include physical strength and hormonal influences. According to this view, male sex hormones (androgens) account for more aggressive male behavior, and gender-related hormonal differences explain the gender gap in the crime rate.[105]

Socialization and Development   Although there are few gender-based differences in aggression during the first few years of life, girls are socialized to be less aggressive than boys and are supervised more closely by parents.[106] Differences in aggression become noticeable between ages 3 and 6 when children are first socialized into organized peer groups such as the daycare center or school. Males are more likely to display physical aggression while girls display relational aggression—excluding disliked peers from playgroups, gossiping, and interfering with social relationships.

Males are taught to be more aggressive and assertive and are less likely to form attachments to others. They often view their aggression as a gender-appropriate means to gain status and power, either by joining deviant groups and gangs or engaging in sports. Even in the middle-class suburbs, they may seek approval by knocking down or running through peers on the playing field, while females literally cheer them on. The male search for social approval through aggressive behavior may make them more susceptible to criminality, especially when the chosen form of aggression is antisocial or illegal. Jean Bottcher found that young boys perceive their roles as being more dominant than young girls.[107] Male perceptions of power, their ability to have freedom and hang with their friends, helped explain the gender differences in crime and delinquency.

In contrast, girls are encouraged to care about other people and avoid harming them; their need for sensitivity and understanding may help counterbalance the effects of poverty and family problems. And because they are more verbally proficient, many females may develop social skills that help them deal with conflict without resorting to violence. Females are taught to be less aggressive and to view belligerence as a lack of self-control—a conclusion that is unlikely to be reached by a male.

Girls learn—directly or indirectly—to respond to provocation by feeling anxious and depressed, whereas boys are encouraged to retaliate. Overall, when they are provoked, females are much more likely to feel distressed than males—experiencing sadness, anxiety, and uneasiness. Although females may get angry as often as males, many have been taught to blame themselves for harboring such negative feelings. Females are therefore much more likely than males to respond to anger with feelings of depression, anxiety, fear, and shame. Although females are socialized to fear that their anger will harm valued relationships, males react with "moral outrage," looking to blame others for their discomfort.[108]

Cognitive Differences   Psychologists note significant cognitive differences between boys and girls that may impact on their antisocial behaviors. Girls have been found to be superior to boys in verbal ability, while boys test higher in visual-spatial performance. Girls acquire language faster, learning to speak earlier and faster with better pronunciation. Girls are far less likely to have reading problems than boys, while boys do much better on standardized math tests. (This difference is attributed by some experts to boys receiving more attention from math teachers.) In most cases these cognitive differences are small, narrowing, and usually attributed to cultural expectations. When given training, girls demonstrate an ability to increase their visual-spatial skills to the point where their abilities become indistinguishable from the ability of boys.

Cognitive differences may contribute to behavioral variations. Even at an early age, girls are found to be more empathic than boys—that is, more capable of understanding and relating to the feelings of others.[109] Empathy for others may help shield girls from antisocial acts because they are more likely to understand a victim's suffering. Girls are more concerned with relationship and feeling issues, and they are less interested than boys are in competing for material success. Boys who are not tough and aggressive are labeled sissies and cry babies. In contrast, girls are given different messages; they are expected to form closer bonds with their friends and share feelings. Their superior verbal skills may allow girls to talk rather than fight. When faced with conflict, women might be more likely to attempt to negotiate rather than to either respond passively or to

physically resist, especially when they perceive increased threat of harm or death.[110]

Feminist Views   In the 1970s, **liberal feminist theory** focused attention on the social and economic role of women in society and its relationship to female crime rates.[111] This view suggested that the traditionally lower crime rate for women could be explained by their "second-class" economic and social position. As women's social roles changed and their lifestyles became more like men's, it was believed that their crime rates would converge. Criminologists, responding to this research, began to refer to the "new female criminal." The rapid increase in the female crime rate, especially in what had traditionally been male-oriented crimes (such as burglary and larceny), supports the feminist view. In addition, self-report studies seem to indicate that (a) the pattern of female criminality, if not its frequency, is quite similar to that of male criminality, and (b) the factors that predispose male criminals to crime have an equal impact on female criminals.[112]

RACE AND CRIME

Official crime data indicate that minority group members are involved in a disproportionate share of criminal activity. African Americans make up about 12 percent of the general population, yet they account for almost 38 percent of Part I violent crime arrests and 28 percent of property crime arrests. They also are responsible for a disproportionate number of Part II arrests (except for alcohol-related arrests for crimes such as DWI). Self-report studies using large samples also show that about 30 percent of black males have experienced at least one arrest by age 18

liberal feminist theory Theory suggesting that the traditionally lower crime rate for women can be explained by their second-class economic and social position. As women's social roles have changed and their lifestyles have become more like those of men, it is believed that their crime rates will converge.

CONNECTIONS

Critical criminologists view gender inequality as stemming from the unequal power of men and women in a capitalist society and the exploitation of females by fathers and husbands. This perspective is considered more fully in Chapter 8.

ASK YOURSELF . . .

As gender differences in socialization evaporate, should crime rate differences also disappear? Or do you think gender differences in crime and violence are a function of biological and not social factors?

(versus about 22 percent for white males), and by age 23 almost 50 percent of black males have been arrested (versus about 38 percent for white males).[113]

Are these data a reflection of true racial differences in the crime rate, or do they reflect racial bias in the justice process? We can evaluate this issue by comparing racial differences in self-report data with those found in official delinquency records. Charges of racial discrimination in the justice process would be substantiated if whites and blacks self-reported equal numbers of crimes, but minorities were arrested and prosecuted far more often.

Early efforts by noted criminologists found virtually no relationship between race and self-reported delinquency, a finding that supported racial bias in the arrest decision process.[114] Other, more recent self-report studies that use large national samples of youths have also found little evidence of racial disparity in self-reported crimes committed.[115] These and other self-report studies seem to indicate that the delinquent behavior rates of black and white teenagers are generally similar and that differences in arrest statistics may indicate a differential selection policy by police.[116] Suspects who are poor, minority, or male are more likely to be formally arrested than suspects who are white, affluent, or female.[117]

racial profiling Police-initiated action directed at a suspect or group of suspects based solely on race.

System Bias   Race-based differences in the crime rate can be explained in part as an effect of unequal or biased treatment by the justice system. Racial differences in the arrest rate may be an artifact of institutional bias found in the justice system and not actual differences in criminal activity: police are more likely to stop, search, and arrest racial minorities than they are members of the white majority. Institutional bias creates a vicious cycle: because they are targeted more frequently, young black men are more likely to possess a criminal record; having a criminal record is associated with repeat stops and searches.[118]

Racial Profiling   Evidence of racial bias in the arrest process can be found in the use of racial profiling to stop African Americans and search their cars without probable cause or reasonable suspicion.[119] Police officers, some social commentators note, have created a new form of traffic offense called DWB, "driving while black."[120] National surveys of driving practices show that young black and Latino males are in fact more likely to be stopped by police and suffer citations, searches, and arrests, as well as be the target of force even though they are no more likely to be in the possession of illegal contraband than white drivers.[121]

The fact that police unfairly target African Americans is so widely accepted that the term **racial profiling** is now routinely used to describe the stop and search of minority citizens if they seem "out of place" (i.e., driving in a white neighborhood).[122] Tammy Rinehart Kochel and her associates recently found significant evidence that minority suspects are more likely to be arrested than white suspects when stopped by police for the same behaviors.[123] Racial profiling may be more common in communities where there are relatively few racial minorities. In racially segregated neighborhoods and communities, police may be suspicious of people based on their race if it is inconsistent with the neighborhood racial composition.[124]

Racial profiling creates a cycle of hostility: young black men see their experience with police as unfair or degrading; they approach future encounters with preexisting hostility; police take this as a sign that young black men pose a special danger; they respond with harsh treatment; a never-ending cycle of mutual mistrust is created.[125]

The relationship between the police and the African American community has come under increasing public scrutiny since the shooting of Michael Brown in the city of Ferguson, Missouri. The incident spurred the creation of the Black Lives Matter movement. Here, Ferguson police search a vehicle while the occupants, two African American males, stand with their hands on the trunk of the car. After the car was searched the occupants were released. The Ferguson police chief resigned after the Justice Department released a report citing the police department for racially biased and exploitative practices.

Scott Olson/Getty Images

Race-based differences are not confined to the arrest process. A significant body of research shows that bias can be found across the entire justice process.[126] Black and Latino adults are less likely than whites to receive bail in cases of violent crime.[127] African Americans, especially those who are indigent or unemployed, receive longer prison sentences than whites with the same employment status. Recent research conducted in New York City found that when compared to whites, black and Latino defendants were more likely than white defendants to be detained, to be incarcerated, and if sent to prison to receive especially punitive outcomes, especially if they were convicted of violent crimes. In contrast, Asians received the most lenient treatment in the justice process.[128]

Racial Threat Hypothesis Why does profiling exist? According to the **racial threat hypothesis** as the percentage of minorities in the population increases, so too does the amount of social control that police direct at minority group members.[129] The source of racial threat begins when residents overestimate the proportion of minorities living in their neighborhood, which can lead to false perceptions and increased racist attitudes.[130] When fear grips an area, police are more likely to aggressively patrol minority areas; suspect, search, and arrest minority group members; and make arrests for minor infractions, helping to raise the minority crime rate.[131] As perceptions of racial threat increases, so too does the demand for greater law enforcement protection.[132] The result is a stepped-up effort to control and punish minority citizens, which segregates minorities from the economic mainstream and reinforces the physical and social isolation of the barrio.[133]

The Race, Culture, Gender, and Criminology feature discusses the associations between the threat of arrest, incarceration, poverty, and culture in the minority community.

As adults, minority group members, especially those who are indigent or unemployed, continue to receive disparate treatment. Black and Latino adults are less likely to receive bail in violent crime cases than whites, and consequently more likely to be kept in detention pending trial.[134] They also receive longer prison sentences than whites who commit similar crimes and have similar criminal histories. Take for instance the use of habitual offender statutes that provide very long sentences for a second or third conviction ("three strikes and you're out"). Matthew Crow and Kathrine Johnson looked at the use of habitual sentencing practices in Florida and reached the conclusion that race and ethnicity still matter: minority drug and violent offenders are viewed as particular threats to dominant, mainstream values and are more likely to be charged as habitual offenders than are European Americans.[135] Nor is this solely a state court problem. After reviewing sentences in the federal court system, Jill Doerner and Stephen Demuth found that particularly harsh punishments are focused disproportionately on the youngest Hispanic and black male defendants. Young Hispanic male defendants have the highest odds of incarceration, and young black male defendants receive the longest sentences.[136] Yet when African Americans are victims of crime, their predicaments receive less public concern and media attention than that afforded white victims.[137] Murders involving whites (and females) are much more likely to be punished with death than those whose victims are black males, a fact not lost on the minority population.[138]

Disparities in justice policy result in the widely disproportionate makeup of the prison population. The percentage of minority men and women who are behind bars is far higher than the percentage of European Americans. It is not surprising that African Americans of all social classes hold negative attitudes toward the justice system and view it as an arbitrary and unfair institution.[139]

CULTURAL BIAS

Another explanation of racial differences in the crime rate rests on the legacy of racial discrimination based on personality and behavior.[140] The fact that U.S. culture influences African American crime rates is underscored by the fact that black violence rates are much lower in other nations—both those that are predominantly white, such as Canada, and those that are predominantly black, such as Nigeria.[141]

Some criminologists view black crime as a function of socialization in a society where the black family was torn apart and black culture destroyed in such a way that recovery has proven impossible. Early experiences, beginning with slavery, have left a wound that has been deepened by racism and lack of opportunity.[142] Children of the slave society were thrust into a system of forced dependency and ambivalence and antagonism toward one's self and group.

In an important work, *All God's Children: The Bosket Family and the American Tradition of Violence,* crime reporter Fox Butterfield chronicles the history of the Boskets, a black family, through five generations.[143] He focuses on Willie Bosket, who is charming, captivating, and brilliant. He is also one of the worst criminals in the New York State penal system. By the time he was in his teens, he had committed more than 200 armed robberies and 25 stabbings. Butterfield shows how the early struggles in the South, with its violent slave culture, led directly to Willie Bosket's rage and violence on the streets of New York City. Beginning in South Carolina in the 1700s, the southern slave society was a place where white notions of honor demanded immediate retaliation for the smallest slight. According to Butterfield, contemporary black violence is a tradition inherited from white southern violence. The need for respect has turned into a cultural mandate that can provoke retaliation at the slightest hint of insult.

> **racial threat hypothesis** The belief that as the percentage of minorities in the population increases, so too does the amount of social control that police direct at minority group members.

On the Run

When sociologist Alice Goffman was an undergraduate at the University of Pennsylvania, she tutored a high school student named Aisha. She later met Aisha's brother Ronny, age 15, when he came home from a juvenile detention center, and Ronny introduced her to Mike, who was 21, and then Mike's best friend Chuck, age 18, who also came home from county jail. Chuck, Mike, and Ronny were part of a loose group of about 15 young men who grew up around 6th Street in Philadelphia, most of whom were unemployed and trying to make it outside of the formal economy. Some worked as low-level crack dealers; others sold marijuana, "wet" (PCP and/or embalming fluid), or pills like Xanax. Some of the men occasionally made money by robbing other drug dealers. One earned his keep by exotic dancing and offering sex to women.

Goffman spent six years documenting the police stops, searches, raids, and beatings that young men in the neighborhood are forced to endure after they get ensnared in the justice system. Through her connections to these young people, Goffman was able to draw an understanding of life in the Philadelphia underclass, the burdens faced by the urban poor, and the role of law enforcement in everyday life. On 6th Street, the constant threat of arrest and incarceration shaped behavior and values and became an integral part of everyday behavior.

In these neighborhoods, children learn at an early age to watch out for the police and to prepare to run when they see them in the neighborhood. The first topic of the day focused on who had been taken into custody the night before and who had outrun the cops and gotten away. The young men discussed how the police identified and located the people they were looking for, what the charges were likely to be, what physical harm had been done to the man as he was caught and arrested, and what property the police had taken and what had been wrecked or lost during the chase.

In the 6th Street neighborhood, a significant portion of the young men were "on the run," some because they were suspects in actual street crimes, but most because there were outstanding arrest warrants for minor infractions such as shoplifting or possession of recreational drugs. Young men were constantly worried that they would be picked up by the police and taken into custody even when they did not have a warrant out for their arrest. Those on probation or parole, on house arrest, or going through a trial expressed concern that they would soon be picked up and taken into custody for some violation that would "come up in the system." People on the run made a concerted effort to thwart their discovery and apprehension.

Goffman found that once a man finds that he may be stopped by the police and taken into custody, he discovers that people, places, and relations he formerly relied on, and that are integral to maintaining a respectable identity, get redefined as paths to confinement. Public places and institutions are seen as threatening. When Alex and his girlfriend, Donna, both age 22, drove to the hospital for the birth of their son, two police officers came into the room and arrested Alex for violating parole. After Alex was arrested, other young men expressed hesitation to go to the hospital when their babies were born. Equally scary was a job in the legitimate economy where the police knew your schedule in advance and traps could be set, resulting in arrest and confinement.

People learn to avoid calling upon the justice system for help, especially if they have a criminal record. Goffman noted numerous instances in which members of the group contacted the police when they were injured, robbed, or threatened. These men were either in good standing with the courts or had no pending legal constraints. She did not observe any

ECONOMIC AND SOCIAL DISPARITY

Racial and ethnic differentials in crime rates may also be tied to economic and social disparity. Racial and ethnic minorities are often forced to live in high-crime areas where the risk of victimization is significant. People who witness violent crime and are victimized may themselves engage in violence.[144]

Racial and ethnic minorities face a greater degree of social isolation and economic deprivation than the white majority, a condition that has been linked by empirical research to high violence rates.[145] Not helping the situation is the fact that during tough economic times, blacks and whites may find themselves competing for shrinking job opportunities. As economic competition between the races grows, interracial homicides do likewise; economic and political rivalries lead to greater levels of interracial violence.[146]

Even during times of economic growth, lower-class African Americans are left out of the economic mainstream, a fact that meets with a growing sense of frustration and failure.[147] As a result of being shut out of educational and economic opportunities enjoyed by the rest of society, this population may be prone to the lure of illegitimate gain and criminality. African Americans living in lower-class inner-city areas may be disproportionately violent because they are exposed to more violence in their daily lives than other racial and economic groups.[148] Many black youths are forced to attend essentially segregated schools that are underfunded and deteriorated, a condition that elevates the likelihood of their being incarcerated in adulthood.[149]

Family Dissolution   Family dissolution in the minority community may be tied to low employment rates among

person with a warrant call the police or voluntarily make use of the courts during the six years she spent there. Young men with warrants seemed to see the authorities only as a threat to their safety. This has two important implications:

- Because they steer clear of the law, young men with criminal records are vulnerable to criminals looking for an easy score.
- Because they cannot call the police, wanted people are more likely to use violence to protect themselves or to get back at others. This kind of self-help crime is typically carried out when the police and the courts are unavailable because people have warrants out for their arrest and may be held in custody if they contact the authorities.

Like going to the hospital or using the police and the courts, even more intimate relations—friends, family, and romantic partners—may pose a threat and thus have to be avoided or at least carefully navigated. In some instances, the police are used as agents of social control and as a form of direct retaliation. When Michelle, age 16, got pregnant, she claimed that 17-year-old Reggie was the father. Reggie denied he had gotten her pregnant until he was in jail and was forced to admit he was the father of Michelle and her aunt.

While family members, partners, or friends of a wanted man occasionally call the police on him to control his behavior or to punish him for a perceived wrong, close kin or girlfriends also link young men to the police because the police compel them to do so. It is common practice for the police to put pressure on friends, girlfriends, and family members to provide information, particularly when these people have their own warrants, are serving probation or parole, or have a pending trial. Family members and friends who are not themselves caught up in the justice system may be threatened with eviction or with having their children taken away.

In this world, maintaining a secret and unpredictable routine decreases the chance of arrest: it is easier for the police to find a person through his last known address if he comes home at around the same time to the same house every day. Finding a person at work is easier if he works a regular shift in the same place every day. Cultivating secrecy and unpredictability, then, serves as a general strategy to avoid confinement. The "secret life" also provides an excuse for failure: "I could not lead a respectable life because it would lead me to jail." This explains social and economic failure in a culturally acceptable manner.

The presence of the criminal justice system in the lives of the poor, Goffman found, cannot simply be measured by the number of people sent to prison or the number who return home with felony convictions. The rise in imprisonment has fostered a climate of fear and suspicion in poor communities—a climate in which family members and friends are pressured to inform on one another and young men live as suspects and fugitives, with the daily fear of confinement. One strategy for coping with these risks is to avoid dangerous places, people, and interactions entirely. A young man thus does not attend the birth of his child or seek medical help when he is badly beaten. He avoids the police and the courts, even if it means using violence when he is injured or becoming the target of others who are looking for someone to rob. A second strategy is to cultivate unpredictability—to remain secretive and to work outside the economic mainstream. To ensure that those close to him will not inform on him, a young man comes and goes in irregular and unpredictable ways, remaining elusive and untrusting, sleeping in different beds, and deceiving those close to him about his life. Considering this burden, is it surprising that young men raised in this environment find themselves on the run and outside the law?

 CRITICAL THINKING

Goffman paints a pretty bleak picture of underclass life and the social forces that shape its existence. Should the United States intervene in other countries in attempts at "nation building" or to develop democracy abroad in third-world nations when there are so many problems here at home?

SOURCE: Alice Goffman, *Fugitive Life in an American City* (Chicago: University of Chicago Press, 2014); "On the Run: Wanted Men in a Philadelphia Ghetto," *American Sociological Review* 74 (2009): 339–357.

CONNECTIONS

The concept of relative deprivation refers to the fact that people compare their success to those with whom they are in immediate contact. Even if conditions improve, they still may feel as if they are falling behind. A sense of relative deprivation, discussed in Chapter 6, may lead to criminal activity.

ASK YOURSELF . . .

Which do you think has a greater impact on behavior, actual or relative deprivation?

African American males, which places a strain on marriages. The relatively large number of single-female-headed households in these communities may be tied to the high mortality rate among African American males, caused by disease and violence.[150] When families are weakened or disrupted, their social control is compromised. It is not surprising, then, that divorce and separation rates are significantly associated with homicide rates in the African American community.[151]

Is Convergence Possible? Race differences in family structure, economic status, education achievement, and other social factors persist. Does that mean that racial differences in the crime rate will persist, or is convergence possible? One argument is that if and when economic conditions improve in the minority community, differences in crime rates will eventually disappear.[152] Another view is that the trend toward residential integration, under way since 1980, may also help reduce crime rate differentials.[153] An important study by Gary LaFree and his associates tracked race-specific homicide arrest differences in 80 large U.S. cities from 1960 to 2000, and found substantial convergence in black/white homicide arrest rates over time.[154]

Homicide rate differences narrowed in cities with a growing black population and also where there was little race-based difference in the number of intact families. In other words, where the percentage of families led by a single parent were equal in the black and white communities, crime rates went down. Conversely, homicide ratios expanded in cities where African Americans were involved in more drug-related crimes than whites. This finding indicates that crime rate convergence may be linked to social factors. Positive factors, such as equality in family structure, will reduce race-based differences; negative factors, such as drug use differentials, will enhance race-based differences. In sum, the weight of the evidence shows that although there is little difference in the self-reported crime rates of racial groups, Hispanics and African Americans are more likely to be arrested for serious violent crimes. The causes of minority crime have been linked to poverty, racism, hopelessness, lack of opportunity, and urban problems experienced by all too many minority citizens.

IMMIGRATION AND CRIME

There is a prevailing view that illegal immigrants are dangerous and violent people and that areas that house illegal immigrants experience a spike in their crime rates. How true is this perception? In reality, immigrants are far less likely than the average U.S. native to commit crime. Significantly lower rates of incarceration and institutionalization among foreign-born adults suggest that long-standing fears of immigration as a threat to public safety are unjustified. One study in California found:

- People born outside the United States make up about 35 percent of California's adult population but represent about 17 percent of the state prison population.
- U.S.-born adult men are incarcerated in state prisons at rates up to 3.3 times higher than foreign-born men.
- Among men ages 18 to 40—the age group most likely to commit crime—those born in the United States are 10 times more likely than immigrants to be in county jail or state prison.
- Noncitizen men from Mexico ages 18 to 40—a group disproportionately likely to have entered the United States illegally—are more than 8 times *less* likely than U.S.-born men in the same age group to be in a correctional setting (0.48 percent versus 4.2 percent).[155]

career criminal A person who repeatedly violates the law and organizes his or her lifestyle around criminality.

chronic offender According to Wolfgang, a delinquent offender who is arrested five or more times before he or she is 18 stands a good chance of becoming an adult criminal; such offenders are responsible for more than half of all serious crimes.

The findings are striking because immigrants in California are more likely than the U.S.-born to be young and male and to have low levels of education—all characteristics associated with higher rates of crime and incarceration. Yet the report shows that institutionalization rates of young male immigrants with less than a high school diploma are extremely low, particularly when compared with U.S.-born men with low levels of education.

The California report is not unique. A number of research studies have concluded that immigrants have lower crime rates than the norm. Ramiro Martínez's study of homicide rates in Texas found that counties on the Mexican border had significantly *lower* homicide rates than nonborder counties, and Texas counties with *higher* levels of immigration concentration had lower levels of homicide. Not only are Latino homicide rates lower in these areas, so are those of non-Latino whites and blacks. No compelling support was found for the claim that border areas are more violent due to proximity or immigration.[156]

The low rates of criminal involvement by immigrants may be due in part to current U.S. immigration policy, which screens immigrants for criminal history and assigns extra penalties to noncitizens who commit crimes. While some research efforts question whether the arrival of immigrants suppresses crime rates, the prevailing wisdom is: more immigrants, less crime.[157]

CHRONIC OFFENDERS/CRIMINAL CAREERS

L09 Describe the pioneering research on chronic offending by Wolfgang, Figlio, and Sellin

Crime data show that most offenders commit a single criminal act and upon arrest discontinue their antisocial activity. Others commit a few less serious crimes. A small group of criminal offenders, however, account for a majority of all criminal offenses. These persistent offenders are referred to as **career criminals** or **chronic offenders**. The concept of the chronic or career offender is most closely associated with the research efforts of Marvin Wolfgang, Robert Figlio, and Thorsten Sellin.[158] In their landmark 1972 study, *Delinquency in a Birth Cohort*, they used official records to follow the criminal careers of a cohort of 9,945 boys born in Philadelphia in 1945 from the time of their birth until they reached 18 years of age in 1963. Official police records were used to identify delinquents. About one-third of the boys (3,475) had some police contact. The remaining two-thirds (6,470) had none. Each delinquent was given a seriousness weight score for every delinquent act.[159] The weighting of delinquent acts allowed the researchers to differentiate between a simple assault requiring no medical attention for the victim and serious battery in which the victim needed hospitalization. The best-known discovery of Wolfgang and his associates was that of the so-called chronic offender. The cohort data indicated that 54 percent (1,862) of the sample's delinquent youths were repeat offenders, whereas the remaining

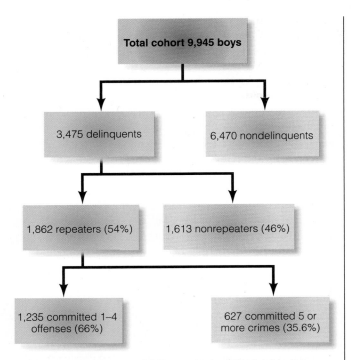

Total cohort 9,945 boys

3,475 delinquents   6,470 nondelinquents

1,862 repeaters (54%)   1,613 nonrepeaters (46%)

1,235 committed 1–4 offenses (66%)   627 committed 5 or more crimes (35.6%)

FIGURE 2.4 Distribution of Offenses in the Philadelphia Cohort

SOURCE: Marvin Wolfgang, Robert Figlio, and Thorsten Sellin, *Delinquency in a Birth Cohort* (Chicago: University of Chicago Press, 1972). Reprinted with permission of University of Chicago Press.

46 percent (1,613) were one-time offenders. The repeaters could be further categorized as nonchronic recidivists and chronic recidivists. The former consisted of 1,235 youths who had been arrested more than once but fewer than five times and who made up 35.6 percent of all delinquents. The latter were a group of 627 boys arrested five times or more, who accounted for 18 percent of the delinquents and 6 percent of the total sample of 9,945. (See Figure 2.4.)

The chronic offenders (known today as "the chronic 6 percent") were involved in the most dramatic amounts of delinquent behavior: they were responsible for 5,305 offenses, or 51.9 percent of all the offenses committed by the cohort. Even more striking was the involvement of chronic offenders in serious criminal acts. Of the entire sample, the chronic 6 percent committed 71 percent of the homicides, 73 percent of the rapes, 82 percent of the robberies, and 69 percent of the aggravated assaults.

Wolfgang and his associates found that arrests and court experience did little to deter the chronic offender. In fact, punishment was inversely related to chronic offending: the more stringent the sanction chronic offenders received, the more likely they would be to engage in repeated criminal behavior.

In a second cohort study, Wolfgang and his associates selected a new, larger birth cohort, born in Philadelphia in 1958, which contained both male and female subjects.[160] Although the proportion of delinquent youths was about the same as that in the 1945 cohort, they again found a

similar pattern of chronic offending. Chronic female delinquency was relatively rare—only 1 percent of the females in the survey were chronic offenders. Wolfgang's pioneering effort to identify the chronic career offender has been replicated by a number of other researchers in a variety of locations in the United States.[161] The chronic offender has also been found abroad.[162]

L010 Evaluate the suspected causes of chronicity

What Causes Chronicity? As might be expected, kids who have been exposed to a variety of personal and social problems at an early age are the most at risk to repeat offending, a concept referred to as **early onset**. One important study of delinquent offenders in Orange County, California, conducted by Michael Schumacher and Gwen Kurz, found several factors (see Exhibit 2.2) that characterized the chronic

early onset A term that refers to the assumption that a criminal career begins early in life and that people who are deviant at a very young age are the ones most likely to persist in crime.

EXHIBIT 2.2

Characteristics That Predict Chronic Offending

SCHOOL BEHAVIOR/PERFORMANCE FACTORS

- Attendance problems (truancy or a pattern of skipping school)
- Behavior problems (recent suspensions or expulsion)
- Poor grades (failing two or more classes)

FAMILY PROBLEM FACTORS

- Poor parental supervision and control
- Significant family problems (illness, substance abuse, discord)
- Criminal family members
- Documented child abuse, neglect, or family violence

SUBSTANCE ABUSE FACTOR

- Alcohol or drug use (by minors in any way but experimentation)

DELINQUENCY FACTORS

- Stealing pattern of behavior
- Runaway pattern of behavior
- Gang member or associate

SOURCE: Michael Schumacher and Gwen Kurz, *The 8% Solution: Preventing Serious Repeat Juvenile Crime* (Thousand Oaks, CA: Sage, 1999).

It is evident that chronic offenders suffer from a profusion of social problems. Some criminologists believe that accumulating a significant variety of these social deficits is the key to understanding criminal development. For more on this topic, see the discussion on problem behavior syndrome in Chapter 9.

ASK YOURSELF . . .

Make a list of all the social problems that you believe contribute to crime and then compare what you wrote to other students in class.

offender, including problems in the home and at school.[163] Other research studies have found that early involvement in criminal activity (getting arrested before age 15), relatively low intellectual development, and parental drug involvement were key predictive factors for chronicity.[164] Offenders who accumulate large debts, use drugs, and resort to violence are more likely to persist.[165] In contrast, those who spend time in a juvenile facility and later in an adult prison are more likely to desist.[166]

Persistence: The Continuity of Crime   One of the most important findings from the cohort studies is that persistent juvenile offenders are the ones most likely to continue their criminal careers into adulthood.[167] Paul Tracy and Kimberly Kempf-Leonard followed up all subjects in the second 1958 cohort and found that two-thirds of delinquent offenders desisted from crime, but those who started their delinquent careers early and who committed serious violent crimes throughout adolescence were the most likely to persist as adults.[168] This phenomenon is referred to as **persistence** or the **continuity of crime**.[169]

Children who are found to be disruptive and antisocial as early as age 5 or 6 are the most likely to exhibit stable, long-term patterns of disruptive behavior throughout adolescence.[170] They have measurable behavior problems in areas such as learning and motor skills, cognitive abilities, family relations, and other areas of social, psychological, and physical functioning.[171] Youthful offenders who persist are more likely to abuse alcohol, get into trouble while in military service, become economically dependent, have lower aspirations, get divorced or separated, and have a

persistence   The idea that those who started their delinquent careers early and who committed serious violent crimes throughout adolescence are the most likely to persist as adults.

continuity of crime   The view that crime begins early in life and continues throughout the life course. Thus, the best predictor of future criminality is past criminality.

weak employment record. They do not specialize in one type of crime; rather, they engage in a variety of criminal acts, including theft, use of drugs, and violent offenses.

Implications of the Chronic Offender Concept   The findings of the cohort studies and the discovery of the chronic offender revitalized criminological theory. If relatively few offenders become chronic, persistent criminals, then perhaps they possess some individual trait that is responsible for their behavior. Most people exposed to troublesome social conditions, such as poverty, do not become chronic offenders, so it is unlikely that social conditions alone can cause chronic offending. Traditional theories of criminal behavior have failed to distinguish between chronic and occasional offenders. They concentrate more on explaining why people begin to commit crime and pay scant attention to why people stop offending. The discovery of the chronic offender 40 years ago forced criminologists to consider such issues as persistence and desistance in their

THINKING LIKE A CRIMINOLOGIST

An Ethical Dilemma

Does Tough Love Work?

The planning director for the State Department of Juvenile Justice has asked for your advice on how to reduce the threat of chronic offenders. Some of the more conservative members of her staff seem to believe that these kids need a strict dose of rough justice if they are to be turned away from a life of crime. They believe juvenile delinquents who are punished harshly are less likely to recidivate than youths who receive lesser punishments, such as community corrections or probation. In addition, they believe that hardcore, violent offenders deserve to be punished; excessive concern for offenders and not their acts ignores the rights of victims and society in general.

The planning director is unsure whether such an approach is ethical. Is it ethical to use tough punishment with kids, as it may produce deviant identities that lock kids into a criminal way of life? She is concerned that a strategy stressing punishment is not only unethical, but it will have relatively little impact on chronic offenders and, if anything, may cause escalation in serious criminal behaviors.

The director has asked you for your professional advice on this ethical dilemma. Write a two-page memorandum: On the one hand, the system must be sensitive to the adverse effects of stigma and labeling. On the other hand, the need for control and deterrence must not be ignored. Is it possible to reconcile these two opposing views?

explanations of crime; more recent theories account for not only the onset of criminality but also its termination.

The chronic offender has become a central focus of crime control policy. Apprehension and punishment seem to have little effect on the offending behavior of chronic offenders, and most repeat their criminal acts after their correctional release. Because chronic offenders rarely learn from their mistakes, sentencing policies designed to incapacitate chronic offenders for long periods of time without hope of probation or parole have been established. Incapacitation rather than rehabilitation is the goal. Among the policies spurred by the chronic offender concept are mandatory sentences for violent or drug-related crimes, "**three strikes**" policies, which require people convicted of a third felony offense to serve a mandatory life sentence, and "truth in sentencing" policies, which require that convicted felons spend a significant portion of their sentence behind bars. Whether such policies can reduce crime rates or are merely "get tough" measures designed to placate conservative voters remains to be seen.

> **three strikes** Policies whereby people convicted of three felony offenses receive a mandatory life sentence.

SUMMARY

L01 Compare and contrast the most widely used forms of crime data collection

The Federal Bureau of Investigation collects data from local law enforcement agencies and publishes that information yearly in its Uniform Crime Report (UCR). The National Incident-Based Reporting System (NIBRS) is a program that collects data on each reported crime incident. The National Crime Victimization Survey (NCVS) is a nationwide survey of victimization in the United States. Self-report surveys ask people to describe, in detail, their recent and lifetime participation in criminal activity. Other forms of crime data come from mapping, data mining, experiments, and examining records from hospitals and schools.

L02 Articulate the problems associated with collecting the official crime data

Many serious crimes are not reported to police and therefore are not counted by the UCR. Police may misrepresent crimes to lower or raise crime rates. There are also unintentional mistakes. Methodological issues such as counting only the most serious crime can invalidate counts.

L03 Identify recent trends in the crime rate

Official crime rates peaked in 1991 when police recorded almost 15 million crimes. Since then, the number of crimes has been in decline. About 10 million crimes were reported in 2014, a drop of 4 million reported crimes since the 1991 peak, despite an increase of about 50 million in the general population. NCVS data show that criminal victimizations have declined significantly during the past 30 years. Self-report trends are more stable. While crime rates have been down for the past two decades, there was a troubling increase in the murder rate during the first six months of 2015.

L04 Discuss the factors that influence crime rates

The age composition of the population, the number of immigrants, the availability of legalized abortion, the number of guns, drug use, availability of emergency medical services, numbers of police officers, the state of the economy, cultural change, and criminal opportunities all influence crime rates.

L05 Assess how crime rates reflect different ecological conditions

Patterns in the crime rate seem to be linked to temporal and ecological factors. Most reported crimes occur during July and August. Large urban areas have by far the highest rates of violent crimes, and rural areas have the lowest per capita. But even in large cities some neighborhoods have much higher crime rates than others; there may be block by block differences. The West and South have higher crime rates than the North and Midwest.

L06 Debate the association between social class and crime

People living in poverty engage in disproportionate amounts of expressive crimes, such as rape and assault. Crime rates in inner-city, high-poverty areas are generally higher than those in suburban or wealthier areas. However, the association between unemployment and crime is less clear. Crime rates sometimes drop during periods of high unemployment, perhaps because parents are unemployed and remain home where they can supervise their children during their crime-prone years.

L07 Clarify what is meant by the term *aging-out process*

Regardless of economic status, marital status, race, sex, and other factors, people tend to commit less crime as they age, and this relationship has been stable over time. Changes in biological and social factors help explain the aging-out process.

L08 Describe the gender and racial patterns in crime

Male crime rates are higher than those of females, especially violent crime rates. Gender differences in the crime rate have persisted over time, but there is little question that females are now involved in more crime than ever before and that there

are more similarities than differences between male and female offenders. Official crime data indicate that minority group members are involved in a disproportionate share of criminal activity. Racial and ethnic differentials in crime rates may be tied to economic and social disparity, institutional and structural racism, and other factors.

 L09 **Describe the pioneering research on chronic offending by Wolfgang, Figlio, and Sellin**

The concept of the chronic or career offender is most closely associated with the research efforts of Marvin Wolfgang, Robert Figlio, and Thorsten Sellin. Chronic offenders are involved in significant amounts of delinquent behavior and tend later to become adult criminals. Unlike most offenders, they do not age out of crime.

L010 **Evaluate the suspected causes of chronicity**

Kids who have been exposed to a variety of personal and social problems at an early age are the most at risk to repeat offending. Chronic offenders often have problems in the home and at school, relatively low intellectual development, and parental drug involvement.

CRITICAL THINKING QUESTIONS

1. Would you answer honestly if a national crime survey asked you about your criminal behavior, including drinking and drug use? If not, why not? If you would not answer honestly, do you question the accuracy of self-report surveys?

2. How would you explain gender differences in the crime rate? Why do you think males are more violent than females?

3. Assuming that males are more violent than females, does that mean crime has a biological rather than a social basis (because males and females share a similar environment)?

4. The UCR reports that crime rates are higher in large cities than in small towns. What does that tell us about the effects of violent TV and films and rap music on teenage behavior?

5. What social and environmental factors do you believe influence the crime rate? Do you think a national emergency would increase or decrease crime rates?

6. Considering what you learned about crime rates, what would you do to be as safe as possible and avoid the chance of becoming a crime victim?

KEY TERMS

Uniform Crime Report (UCR) (28)
index crimes (28)
Part I crimes (28)
Part II crimes (29)
cleared crimes (30)
National Incident-Based Reporting System (NIBRS) (32)

sampling (32)
population (32)
cross-sectional survey (32)
National Crime Victimization Survey (NCVS) (33)
self-report survey (34)
racial profiling (35)
cohort (36)
retrospective cohort study (36)

meta-analysis (39)
systematic review (39)
predictive policing (39)
instrumental crimes (49)
expressive crimes (49)
income inequality (49)
aging out (51)
masculinity hypothesis (52)
chivalry hypothesis (52)

liberal feminist theory (53)
racial profiling (54)
racial threat hypothesis (55)
career criminal (58)
chronic offender (58)
early onset (59)
persistence (60)
continuity of crime (60)
three strikes (61)

NOTES

All URLs accessed in 2016.
1. Matt Pearce, "What Happens When a Millennial Goes Fascist? He Starts Up a Neo-Nazi Site," *Los Angeles Times*, June 24, 2015, http://www.latimes.com/nation/la-na-daily-stormer-interview-20150624-story.html.
2. Ray Sanchez and Ed Payne, "Charleston Church Shooting: Who Is Dylann Roof?" CNN, June 23, 2015, http://www.cnn.com/2015/06/19/us/charleston-church-shooting-suspect/.
3. Andrew Dugan, "In U.S., 37% Do Not Feel Safe Walking at Night Near Home," http://www.gallup.com/poll/179558/not-feel-safe-walking-night-near-home.aspx.
4. Gallup Poll, "Crime, 2015," http://www.gallup.com/poll/1603/Crime.aspx.
5. Federal Bureau of Investigation, *Crime in the United States, 2014*, https://www.fbi.gov/about-us/cjis/ucr/crime-in-the-u.s/2014/crime-in-the-u.s.-2014.
6. FBI, "U.S. Department of Justice Attorney General Eric Holder Announces Revisions to the Uniform Crime Report's Definition of Rape; Data Reported on Rape Will Better Reflect State Criminal Codes, Victim Experiences," January 6, 2012, http://www.fbi.gov/news/pressrel/press-releases/attorney-general-eric-holder-announces-revisions

-to-the-uniform-crime-reports-definition-of-rape.

7. FBI, *Preliminary Semiannual Uniform Crime Report*, January–June 2015, https://www.fbi.gov/about-us/cjis/ucr/crime-in-the-u.s/2015/preliminary-semiannual-uniform-crime-report-januaryjune-2015/tables/table-1.

8. Jennifer Truman, Lynn Langton, and Michael Planty, *Criminal Victimization, 2012* (Washington, DC: Bureau of Justice Statistics, 2013), http://www.bjs.gov/content/pub/pdf/cv12.pdf.

9. Min Xie, "Area Differences and Time Trends in Crime Reporting: Comparing New York with Other Metropolitan Areas," *Justice Quarterly* 31 (2014): 43–73.

10. Richard Felson, Steven Messner, Anthony Hoskin, and Glenn Deane, "Reasons for Reporting and Not Reporting Domestic Violence to the Police," *Criminology* 40 (2002): 617–648.

11. Bradford W. Reyns and Ryan Randa, "Victim Reporting Behaviors Following Identity Theft Victimization: Results from the National Crime Victimization Survey," *Crime and Delinquency*, first published online December 18, 2015.

12. Andrew Karmen, *Crime Victims: An Introduction to Victimology* (Belmont, CA: Cengage, 2012).

13. Heather Zaykowski, "Reconceptualizing Victimization and Victimization Responses," *Crime and Delinquency* 61 (2015): 271–296.

14. Duncan Chappell, Gilbert Geis, Stephen Schafer, and Larry Siegel, "Forcible Rape: A Comparative Study of Offenses Known to the Police in Boston and Los Angeles," in *Studies in the Sociology of Sex*, ed. James Henslin (New York: Appleton Century Crofts, 1971), pp. 169–193.

15. Eric Baumer and Janet Lauritsen, "Reporting Crime to the Police, 1973–2005: A Multivariate Analysis of Long-Term Trends in the National Crime Survey (NCVS)," *Criminology* 48 (2010): 131–185.

16. Patrick Jackson, "Assessing the Validity of Official Data on Arson," *Criminology* 26 (1988): 181–195.

17. John Eterno and Eli B. Silverman, *The Crime Numbers Game: Management by Manipulation* (Boca Raton, FL: CRC Press, 2012).

18. FBI, *UCR Handbook* (Washington, DC: U.S. Government Printing Office, 1998), p. 33.

19. National Archive of Criminal Justice Data, *National Incident-Based Reporting System Resource Guide*, http://www.icpsr.umich.edu/NACJD/NIBRS/.

20. "FBI Releases 2014 Crime Statistics from the National Incident-Based Reporting System," December 14, 2015, https://www.fbi.gov/about-us/cjis/ucr/nibrs/2014/resource-pages/summary-of-nibrs-2014_final.pdf.

21. Lynn Addington, "The Effect of NIBRS Reporting on Item Missing Data in Murder Cases," *Homicide Studies* 8 (2004): 193–213.

22. Michael Gottfredson and Travis Hirschi, "The Methodological Adequacy of Longitudinal Research on Crime," *Criminology* 25 (1987): 581–614.

23. FBI, "The Nation's Two Crime Measures," https://www.fbi.gov/about-us/cjis/ucr/crime-in-the-u.s/2011/crime-in-the-u.s.-2011/crime-measures.

24. Lynn A. Addington and Callie Marie Rennison, "Rape Co-occurrence: Do Additional Crimes Affect Victim Reporting and Police Clearance of Rape?" *Journal of Quantitative Criminology* 24 (2008): 205–226.

25. L. Edward Wells and Joseph Rankin, "Juvenile Victimization: Convergent Validation of Alternative Measurements," *Journal of Research in Crime and Delinquency* 32 (1995): 287–307.

26. Saul Kassin, Richard Leo, Christian Meissner, Kimberly Richman, Lori Colwell, Amy-May Leach, and Dana La Fon, "Police Interviewing and Interrogation: A Self-Report Survey of Police Practices and Beliefs," *Law and Human Behavior* 31 (2007): 381–400.

27. Lloyd Johnston, Patrick O'Malley, Jerald Bachman, et al., *Monitoring the Future, 2014*, http://www.monitoringthefuture.org/.

28. D. Wayne Osgood, Lloyd Johnston, Patrick O'Malley, and Jerald Bachman, "The Generality of Deviance in Late Adolescence and Early Adulthood," *American Sociological Review* 53 (1988): 81–93.

29. Leonore Simon, "Validity and Reliability of Violent Juveniles: A Comparison of Juvenile Self-Reports with Adult Self-Reports Incarcerated in Adult Prisons," paper presented at the annual meeting of the American Society of Criminology, Boston, November 1995, p. 26.

30. Stephen Cernkovich, Peggy Giordano, and Meredith Pugh, "Chronic Offenders: The Missing Cases in Self-Report Delinquency Research," *Journal of Criminal Law and Criminology* 76 (1985): 705–732.

31. Terence Thornberry, Beth Bjerregaard, and William Miles, "The Consequences of Respondent Attrition in Panel Studies: A Simulation Based on the Rochester Youth Development Study," *Journal of Quantitative Criminology* 9 (1993): 127–158.

32. Thomas A. Loughran, Ray Paternoster, and Kyle J. Thomas, "Incentivizing Responses to Self-report Questions in Perceptual Deterrence Studies: An Investigation of the Validity of Deterrence Theory Using Bayesian Truth Serum," *Journal of Quantitative Criminology* 30 (2014): 677–707.

33. Alex Piquero, Carol Schubert, and Robert Brame, "Comparing Official and Self-Report Records of Offending Across Gender and Race/Ethnicity in a Longitudinal Study of Serious Youthful Offenders," *Journal of Research in Crime and Delinquency* 51 (2014): 526–556.

34. Amanda. Emmert, Arna Carlock, Alan Lizotte, and Marvin Krohn, "Predicting Adult Under- and Over-Reporting of Self-Reported Arrests From Discrepancies in Adolescent Self-Reports of Arrests: A Research Note," *Crime and Delinquency*, first published online March 12, 2015.

35. Julia Yun Soo Kim, Michael Fendrich, and Joseph S. Wislar, "The Validity of Juvenile Arrestees' Drug Use Reporting: A Gender Comparison," *Journal of Research in Crime and Delinquency* 37 (2000): 419–432.

36. Donald Tomaskovic-Devey, Cynthia Pfaff Wright, Ronald Czaja, and Kirk Miller, "Self-Reports of Police Speeding Stops by Race: Results from the North Carolina Reverse Record Check Survey," *Journal of Quantitative Criminology* 22 (2006): 279–297.

37. Jennifer Roberts, Edward Mulvey, Julie Horney, John Lewis, and Michael Arter, "A Test of Two Methods of Recall for Violent Events," *Journal of Quantitative Criminology* 21 (2005): 175–193.

38. Lila Kazemian and David Farrington, "Comparing the Validity of Prospective, Retrospective, and Official Onset for Different Offending Categories," *Journal of Quantitative Criminology* 21 (2005): 127–147.

39. Barbara Warner and Brandi Wilson Coomer, "Neighborhood Drug Arrest Rates: Are They a Meaningful Indicator of Drug Activity? A Research Note," *Journal of Research in Crime and Delinquency* 40 (2003): 123–139.

40. Alfred Blumstein, Jacqueline Cohen, and Richard Rosenfeld, "Trend and Deviation in Crime Rates: A Comparison of UCR and NCVS Data for Burglary and Robbery," *Criminology* 29 (1991): 237–248. See also Michael Hindelang, Travis Hirschi, and Joseph Weis, *Measuring Delinquency* (Beverly Hills: Sage, 1981).

41. See, generally, David Farrington, Lloyd Ohlin, and James Q. Wilson, *Understanding and Controlling Crime* (New York: Springer-Verlag, 1986), pp. 11–18.

42. Rebecca Loya, "Rape as an Economic Crime: The Impact of Sexual Violence on Survivors' Employment and Economic Wellbeing," *Journal of Interpersonal Violence* 30 (2015): 2793–2813.

43. Ainhoa Izaguirre and Esther Calvete, "Children Who Are Exposed to Intimate Partner Violence: Interviewing Mothers to Understand Its Impact on Children," *Child Abuse and Neglect* 48 (2015): 58–67.

44. William F. Whyte, *Street Corner Society* (Chicago: University of Chicago Press, 1955).

45. Herman Schwendinger and Julia Schwendinger, *Adolescent Subcultures and Delinquency* (New York: Praeger, 1985).

46. David Farrington and Brandon Welsh, "Improved Street Lighting and Crime Prevention," *Justice Quarterly* 19 (2002): 313–343.

47. National Institute of Justice, "Predictive Policing," http://www.nij.gov/topics/law-enforcement/strategies/predictive-policing/.

48. G. O. Mohler, M. B. Short, Sean Malinowski, Mark Johnson, G. E. Tita, Andrea L. Bertozzi,

and P. J. Brantingham, "Randomized Controlled Field Trials of Predictive Policing," *Journal of the American Statistical Association* 110 (2015): 1399–1411.

49. Jerry Ratcliffe, "Aoristic Signatures and the Spatio-Temporal Analysis of High Volume Crime Patterns," *Journal of Quantitative Criminology* 18 (2002): 23–43.

50. Clarence Schrag, *Crime and Justice: American Style* (Washington, DC: U.S. Government Printing Office, 1971), p. 17.

51. Jennifer Truman and Lynn Langton, *Criminal Victimization, 2014* (Washington, DC: Bureau of Justice Statistics, 2015). Victim data in this chapter come from this source.

52. Lloyd Johnston, Patrick O'Malley, and Jerald Bachman, *Monitoring the Future, 8* (Ann Arbor, MI: Institute for Social Research, 2011), http://www.monitoringthefuture.org/.

53. Carmen Gutierrez and David S. Kirk, "Silence Speaks: The Relationship Between Immigration and the Underreporting of Crime," *Crime and Delinquency*, first published online September 23, 2015.

54. Data in this section come from United Nations Office on Drugs and Crime, *Drug Trafficking, 2016*, https://www.unodc.org/unodc/en/drug-trafficking/; Office on Drugs and Crime, *Global Report on Trafficking in Persons, 2014*, http://www.unodc.org/documents/data-and-analysis/glotip/GLOTIP_2014_full_report.pdf; United Nations, *Global Studies on Homicide, 2013*, http://www.unodc.org/gsh/; Stefan Harrendorf, Markku Heiskanen, and Steven Malby, eds., *International Statistics on Crime and Justice*, European Institute for Crime Prevention and Control, Affiliated with the United Nations, http://www.heuni.fi/Oikeapalsta/Search/1266333832841; UN World Health Organization, *Child Maltreatment, 2014*, http://www.who.int/mediacentre/factsheets/fs150/en/.

55. Monica Davey and Mitch Smith, "Murder Rates Rising Sharply in Many U.S. Cities," *New York Times*, August 31, 2015, http://www.nytimes.com/2015/09/01/us/murder-rates-rising-sharply-in-many-us-cities.html.

56. Bureau of Labor Statistics, "Characteristics of Minimum Wage Workers, 2014," http://www.bls.gov/opub/reports/cps/characteristics-of-minimum-wage-workers-2014.pdf.

57. Steven Levitt, "The Limited Role of Changing Age Structure in Explaining Aggregate Crime Rates," *Criminology* 37 (1999): 581–599.

58. Timothy Hart and Terance Miethe, "Configural Behavior Settings of Crime Event Locations: Toward an Alternative Conceptualization of Criminogenic Microenvironments," *Journal of Research in Crime and Delinquency* 52 (2015): 373–402.

59. David Weisburd, "The Law of Crime Concentration and the Criminology of Place," *Criminology* 53 (2015): 133–157.

60. Lisa Tompson and Kate Bowers, "A Stab in the Dark? A Research Note on Temporal Patterns of Street Robbery," *Journal of Research in Crime and Delinquency* 50 (2013): 616–631.

61. Ellen Cohn, "The Effect of Weather and Temporal Variations on Calls for Police Service," *American Journal of Police* 15 (1996): 23–43.

62. Cory Haberman and Jerry Ratcliffe, "Testing for Temporally Differentiated Relationships Among Potentially Criminogenic Places and Census Block Street Robbery Counts," *Criminology* 53 (2015): 457–483.

63. R. A. Baron, "Aggression as a Function of Ambient Temperature and Prior Anger Arousal," *Journal of Personality and Social Psychology* 21 (1972): 183–189.

64. Brad Bushman, Morgan Wang, and Craig Anderson, "Is the Curve Relating Temperature to Aggression Linear or Curvilinear? Assaults and Temperature in Minneapolis Reexamined," *Journal of Personality and Social Psychology* 89 (2005): 62–66.

65. Paul Bell, "Reanalysis and Perspective in the Heat-Aggression Debate," *Journal of Personality and Social Psychology* 89 (2005): 71–73.

66. Ellen Cohn, "The Prediction of Police Calls for Service: The Influence of Weather and Temporal Variables on Rape and Domestic Violence," *Journal of Environmental Psychology* 13 (1993): 71–83.

67. John Simister and Cary Cooper, "Thermal Stress in the U.S.A.: Effects on Violence and on Employee Behaviour," *Stress and Health* 21 (2005): 3–15.

68. James Rotton and Ellen Cohn, "Outdoor Temperature, Climate Control, and Criminal Assault," *Environment and Behavior* 36 (2004): 276–306.

69. Daniel Montolio and Simón Planells-Struse, "Does Tourism Boost Criminal Activity? Evidence from a Top Touristic Country," *Crime and Delinquency*, first published online October 28, 2013.

70. Franklin Zimring and Gordon Hawkins, *Crime Is Not the Problem: Lethal Violence in America* (New York: Oxford University Press, 1997).

71. Gary Kleck, "The Impact of Gun Ownership Rates on Crime Rates: A Methodological Review of the Evidence," *Journal of Criminal Justice* 43 (2015): 40–48.

72. Gary Kleck and Marc Gertz, "Armed Resistance to Crime: The Prevalence and Nature of Self-Defense with a Gun," *Journal of Criminal Law and Criminology* 86 (1995): 219–249; Gary Kleck and Jongyeon Tark, "Resisting Crime: The Effects of Victim Action on the Outcomes of Crimes," *Criminology* 42 (2005): 861–909.

73. Philip J Cook, Richard J. Harris, Jens Ludwig, and Harold A. Pollack, "Some Sources of Crime Guns in Chicago: Dirty Dealers, Straw Purchasers, and Traffickers," *Journal of Criminal Law and Criminology* 104 (2015): 717–760.

74. Felipe Estrada and Anders Nilsson, "Segregation and Victimization: Neighbourhood Resources, Individual Risk Factors and Exposure to Property Crime," *European Journal of Criminology* 5 (2008): 193–216.

75. Aki Roberts and Dale Willits, "Income Inequality and Homicide in the United States: Consistency Across Different Income Inequality Measures and Disaggregated Homicide Types," *Homicide Studies* 19 (2015): 28–57.

76. James Short and F. Ivan Nye, "Extent of Unrecorded Juvenile Delinquency, Tentative Conclusions," *Journal of Criminal Law, Criminology, and Police Science* 49 (1958): 296–302.

77. Charles Tittle, Wayne Villemez, and Douglas Smith, "The Myth of Social Class and Criminality: An Empirical Assessment of the Empirical Evidence," *American Sociological Review* 43 (1978): 643–656.

78. Judith Blau and Peter Blau, "The Cost of Inequality: Metropolitan Structure and Violent Crime," *American Sociological Review* 147 (1982): 114–129; Richard Block, "Community Environment and Violent Crime," *Criminology* 17 (1979): 46–57; Robert Sampson, "Structural Sources of Variation in Race-Age-Specific Rates of Offending Across Major U.S. Cities," *Criminology* 23 (1985): 647–673.

79. John R. Hipp and Adam Boessen, "Egohoods as Waves Washing Across the City: A New Measure of Neighborhoods," *Criminology* 51 (2013): 287–327; Ramiro Martínez, Jacob Stowell, and Jeffrey Cancino, "A Tale of Two Border Cities: Community Context, Ethnicity, and Homicide," *Social Science Quarterly* 89 (2008): 1–16.

80. Steven Messner, Lawrence Raffalovich, and Richard McMillan, "Economic Deprivation and Changes in Homicide Arrest Rates for White and Black Youths, 1967–1998: A National Time Series Analysis," *Criminology* 39 (2001): 591–614.

81. Mikko Aaltonen, John M. Macdonald, Pekka Martikainen, and Janne Kivivuor, "Examining The Generality of the Unemployment–Crime Association," *Criminology* 51 (2013): 561–594.

82. Robert Apel, Shawn Bushway, Robert Brame, Amelia M. Haviland, Daniel S. Nagin, and Ray Paternoster, "Unpacking the Relationship Between Adolescent Employment and Antisocial Behavior: A Matched Samples Comparison," *Criminology* 45 (2007): 67–97.

83. Richard Rosenfeld and Robert Fornango, "The Impact of Economic Conditions on Robbery and Property Crime: The Role of Consumer Sentiment," *Criminology* 45 (2007): 735–769.

84. Gary Kleck and Ted Chiricos, "Unemployment and Property Crime: A

Target-Specific Assessment of Opportunity and Motivation as Mediating Factors," *Criminology* 40 (2002): 649–680.

85. Shawn Bushway, "Economy and Crime," *The Criminologist* 35 (2010): 1–5.

86. Douglas Smith and Laura Davidson, "Interfacing Indicators and Constructs in Criminological Research: A Note on the Comparability of Self-Report Violence Data for Race and Sex Groups," *Criminology* 24 (1986): 473–488.

87. R. Gregory Dunaway, Francis Cullen, Velmer Burton, and T. David Evans, "The Myth of Social Class and Crime Revisited: An Examination of Class and Adult Criminality," *Criminology* 38 (2000): 589–632.

88. Travis Hirschi and Michael Gottfredson, "Age and the Explanation of Crime," *American Journal of Sociology* 89 (1983): 552–584, at 581.

89. Misaki Natsuaki, Xiaojia Ge, and Ernst Wenk, "Continuity and Changes in the Developmental Trajectories of Criminal Career: Examining the Roles of Timing of First Arrest and High School Graduation," *Journal of Youth and Adolescence* 37 (2008): 431–444.

90. Derek Kreager, "When It's Good to Be 'Bad': Violence and Adolescent Peer Acceptance," *Criminology* 45 (2007): 893–923.

91. Ronald Aday and Jennifer Krabill, "Aging Offenders in the Criminal Justice System," *Marquette Elder's Advisor* 7 (2006): 237–258.

92. Wanda Leal and Carrie Mier, "What's Age Got to Do With It? Comparing Juveniles and Adults on Drugs and Crime," *Crime and Delinquency*, first published online November 18, 2015.

93. James Q. Wilson and Richard Herrnstein, *Crime and Human Nature* (New York: Simon and Schuster, 1985), pp. 126–147.

94. Ibid., p. 219.

95. Ryan King, Michael Massoglia, and Ross MacMillan, "The Context of Marriage and Crime: Gender, the Propensity to Marry, and Offending in Early Adulthood," *Criminology* 45 (2007): 33–65.

96. Franklin Zimring and Hannah Laqueur, "Kids, Groups, and Crime: In Defense of Conventional Wisdom," *Journal of Research in Crime and Delinquency* 52 (2015) 403–413.

97. Kreager, "When It's Good to Be 'Bad': Violence and Adolescent Peer Acceptance."

98. Lisa Stolzenberg and Stewart D'Alessio, "Co-offending and the Age-Crime Curve," *Journal of Research in Crime and Delinquency* 45 (2008): 65–86.

99. David R. Schaefer, Nancy Rodriguez, and Scott H. Decker, "The Role of Neighborhood Context in Youth Co-offending," *Criminology* 52 (2014): 117–139.

100. Marie Skubak Tillyer and Rob Tillyer, "Maybe I Should Do This Alone: A Comparison of Solo and Co-offending Robbery Outcomes," *Justice Quarterly* 32 (2015): 1064–1088.

101. Paul Tracy, Kimberly Kempf-Leonard, and Stephanie Abramoske-James, "Gender Differences in Delinquency and Juvenile Justice Processing: Evidence from National Data," *Crime and Delinquency* 55 (2009): 171–215.

102. Cesare Lombroso, *The Female Offender* (New York: Appleton, 1920), p. 122.

103. Otto Pollack, *The Criminality of Women* (Philadelphia: University of Pennsylvania, 1950).

104. For a review of this issue, see Darrell Steffensmeier, "Assessing the Impact of the Women's Movement on Sex-Based Differences in the Handling of Adult Criminal Defendants," *Crime and Delinquency* 26 (1980): 344–357.

105. Alan Booth and D. Wayne Osgood, "The Influence of Testosterone on Deviance in Adulthood: Assessing and Explaining the Relationship," *Criminology* 31 (1993): 93–118.

106. This section relies on the following sources: Kristen Kling, Janet Shibley Hyde, Carolin Showers, and Brenda Buswell, "Gender Differences in Self-Esteem: A Meta Analysis," *Psychological Bulletin* 125 (1999): 470–500; Anne Campbell, *Men, Women and Aggression* (New York: Basic Books, 1993); Ann Beutel and Margaret Mooney Marini, "Gender and Values," *American Sociological Review* 60 (1995): 436–448; John Gibbs, Velmer Burton, Francis Cullen, T. David Evans, Leanne Fiftal Alarid, and R. Gregory Dunaway, "Gender, Self-Control, and Crime," *Journal of Research in Crime and Delinquency* 35 (1998): 123–147.

107. Jean Bottcher, "Social Practices of Gender: How Gender Relates to Delinquency in the Everyday Lives of High-Risk Youths," *Criminology* 39 (2001): 893–932.

108. Daniel Mears, Matthew Ploeger, and Mark Warr, "Explaining the Gender Gap in Delinquency: Peer Influence and Moral Evaluations of Behavior," *Journal of Research in Crime and Delinquency* 35 (1998): 251–266.

109. Lisa Broidy, Elizabeth Cauffman, and Dorothy Espelage, "Sex Differences in Empathy and Its Relation to Juvenile Offending," *Violence and Victims* 18 (2003): 503–516.

110. Debra Kaysen, Miranda Morris, Shireen Rizvi, and Patricia Resick, "Peritraumatic Responses and Their Relationship to Perceptions of Threat in Female Crime Victims," *Violence Against Women* 11 (2005): 1515–1535.

111. Freda Adler, *Sisters in Crime* (New York: McGraw-Hill, 1975); Rita James Simon, *The Contemporary Woman and Crime* (Washington, DC: U.S. Government Printing Office, 1975).

112. David Rowe, Alexander Vazsonyi, and Daniel Flannery, "Sex Differences in Crime: Do Mean and Within-Sex Variation Have Similar Causes?" *Journal of Research in Crime*

and Delinquency 32 (1995): 84–100; Michael Hindelang, "Age, Sex, and the Versatility of Delinquency Involvements," *Social Forces* 14 (1971): 525–534; Martin Gold, *Delinquent Behavior in an American City* (Belmont, CA: Brooks/Cole, 1970); Gary Jensen and Raymond Eve, "Sex Differences in Delinquency: An Examination of Popular Sociological Explanations," *Criminology* 13 (1976): 427–448.

113. Robert Brame, Shawn Bushway, Ray Paternoster, and Michael G. Turner, "Demographic Patterns of Cumulative Arrest Prevalence by Ages 18 and 23," *Crime and Delinquency* 60 (2014): 471–486.

114. Leroy Gould, "Who Defines Delinquency: A Comparison of Self-Report and Officially Reported Indices of Delinquency for Three Racial Groups," *Social Problems* 16 (1969): 325–336; Harwin Voss, "Ethnic Differentials in Delinquency in Honolulu," *Journal of Criminal Law, Criminology, and Police Science* 54 (1963): 322–327; Ronald Akers, Marvin Krohn, Marcia Radosevich, and Lonn Lanza-Kaduce, "Social Characteristics and Self-Reported Delinquency," in *Sociology of Delinquency*, ed. Gary Jensen (Beverly Hills: Sage, 1981), pp. 48–62.

115. David Huizinga and Delbert Elliott, "Juvenile Offenders: Prevalence, Offender Incidence, and Arrest Rates by Race," *Crime and Delinquency* 33 (1987): 206–223. See also Dale Dannefer and Russell Schutt, "Race and Juvenile Justice Processing in Court and Police Agencies," *American Journal of Sociology* 87 (1982): 1113–1132.

116. Paul Tracy, "Race and Class Differences in Official and Self-Reported Delinquency," in *From Boy to Man, from Delinquency to Crime*, ed. Marvin Wolfgang, Terence Thornberry, and Robert Figlio (Chicago: University of Chicago Press, 1987), p. 120.

117. Miriam Sealock and Sally Simpson, "Unraveling Bias in Arrest Decisions: The Role of Juvenile Offender Type-Scripts," *Justice Quarterly* 15 (1998): 427–457.

118. Rob Tillyer, "Opening the Black Box of Officer Decision-Making: An Examination of Race, Criminal History, and Discretionary Searches," *Justice Quarterly* 31 (2014): 961–986.

119. Billy Close and Patrick L. Mason, "Searching for Efficient Enforcement: Officer Char-acteristics and Racially Biased Policing," *Review of Law and Economics* 3 (2007): 263–321.

120. Nicola Persico and Petra Todd, "The Hit Rates Test for Racial Bias in Motor-Vehicle Searches," *Justice Quarterly* 25 (2008): 37–53.

121. Robin Shepard Engel and Jennifer Calnon, "Examining the Influence of Drivers' Characteristics During Traffic Stops with Police: Results from a National Survey," *Justice Quarterly* 21 (2004): 49–90.

122. Leo Carroll and M. Lilliana Gonzalez. "Out of Place: Racial Stereotypes and the Ecology of Frisks and Searches Following Traffic Stops," *Journal of Research in Crime and Delinquency* 51 (2014): 559–584.

123. Tammy Rinehart Kochel, David Wilson, and Stephen Mastrofski, "Effect of Suspect Race on Officers' Arrest Decisions," *Criminology* 49 (2011): 473–512.

124. Kenneth Novak and Mitchell Chamlin, "Racial Threat, Suspicion, and Police Behavior: The Impact of Race and Place in Traffic Enforcement," *Crime and Delinquency* 58 (2012): 275–300.

125. Richard Rosenfeld, Jeff Rojek, and Scott Decker, "Age Matters: Race Differences in Police Searches of Young and Older Male Drivers," *Journal of Research in Crime and Delinquency* 49 (2011): 31–55.

126. Karen Parker, Brian Stults, and Stephen Rice, "Racial Threat, Concentrated Disadvantage and Social Control: Considering the Macro-Level Sources of Variation in Arrests," *Criminology* 43 (2005): 1111–1134; Lisa Stolzenberg, J. Stewart D'Alessio, and David Eitle, "A Multilevel Test of Racial Threat Theory," *Criminology* 42 (2004): 673–698.

127. Traci Schlesinger, "Racial and Ethnic Disparity in Pretrial Criminal Processing," *Justice Quarterly* 22 (2005): 170–192.

128. Besiki Kutateladze, Nancy Andiloro, Brian Johnson, and Cassia Spohn, "Cumulative Disadvantage: Examining Racial and Ethnic Disparity in Prosecution and Sentencing," *Criminology* 52 (2014): 514–551.

129. Hurbert Blalock, Jr., *Toward a Theory of Minority-Group Relations* (New York: Capricorn Books, 1967).

130. Rebecca Wickes, John R. Hipp, Renee Zahnow, and Lorraine Mazerolle, "'Seeing' Minorities and Perceptions of Disorder: Explicating the Mediating and Moderating Mechanisms of Social Cohesion," *Criminology* 51 (2013): 519–560.

131. Engel and Calnon, "Examining the Influence of Drivers' Characteristics During Traffic Stops with Police."

132. Malcolm Holmes, Brad Smith, Adrienne Freng, and Ed Muñoz, "Minority Threat, Crime Control, and Police Resource Allocation in the Southwestern United States," *Crime and Delinquency* 54 (2008): 128–152.

133. Bradley Keen and David Jacobs, "Racial Threat, Partisan Politics, and Racial Disparities in Prison Admissions," *Criminology* 47 (2009): 209–238.

134. Michael Leiber and Kristan Fox, "Race and the Impact of Detention on Juvenile Justice Decision Making," *Crime and Delinquency* 51 (2005): 470–497; Traci Schlesinger, "Racial and Ethnic Disparity in Pretrial Criminal Processing," *Justice Quarterly* 22 (2005): 170–192.

135. Matthew Crow and Kathrine Johnson, "Race, Ethnicity, and Habitual-Offender Sentencing: A Multilevel Analysis of Individual and Contextual Threat," *Criminal Justice Policy Review* 19 (2008): 63–83.

136. Jill Doerner and Stephen Demuth, "The Independent and Joint Effects of Race/ Ethnicity, Gender, and Age on Sentencing Outcomes in U.S. Federal Courts," *Justice Quarterly* 27 (2010): 1–27.

137. Alexander Weiss and Steven Chermak, "The News Value of African-American Victims: An Examination of the Media's Presentation of Homicide," *Journal of Crime and Justice* 21 (1998): 71–84.

138. Jefferson Holcomb, Marian Williams, and Stephen Demuth, "White Female Victims and Death Penalty Disparity Research," *Justice Quarterly* 21 (2004): 877–902.

139. Ronald Weitzer and Steven Tuch, "Race, Class, and Perceptions of Discrimination by the Police," *Crime and Delinquency* 45 (1999): 494–507.

140. Barry Sample and Michael Philip, "Perspectives on Race and Crime in Research and Planning," in *The Criminal Justice System and Blacks*, ed. Daniel Georges-Abeyie (New York: Clark Boardman Callaghan, 1984), pp. 21–36.

141. Ruth Peterson, Lauren Krivo, and Mark Harris, "Disadvantage and Neighborhood Violent Crime: Do Local Institutions Matter?" *Journal of Research in Crime and Delinquency* 37 (2000): 31–63.

142. James Comer, "Black Violence and Public Policy," in *American Violence and Public Policy*, ed. Lynn Curtis (New Haven, CT: Yale University Press, 1985), pp. 63–86.

143. Fox Butterfield, *All God's Children: The Bosket Family and the American Tradition of Violence* (New York: Avon, 1996).

144. Joanne Kaufman, "Explaining the Race/ Ethnicity–Violence Relationship: Neighborhood Context and Social Psychological Processes," *Justice Quarterly* 22 (2005): 224–251.

145. Karen Parker and Patricia McCall, "Structural Conditions and Racial Homicide Patterns: A Look at the Multiple Disadvantages in Urban Areas," *Criminology* 37 (1999): 447–469.

146. David Jacobs and Katherine Woods, "Interracial Conflict and Interracial Homicide: Do Political and Economic Rivalries Explain White Killings of Blacks or Black Killings of Whites?" *American Journal of Sociology* 105 (1999): 157–190.

147. Melvin Thomas, "Race, Class and Personal Income: An Empirical Test of the Declining Significance of Race Thesis, 1968–1988," *Social Problems* 40 (1993): 328–339.

148. Mallie Paschall, Robert Flewelling, and Susan Ennett, "Racial Differences in Violent Behavior Among Young Adults: Moderating and Confounding Effects," *Journal of Research in Crime and Delinquency* 35 (1998): 148–165.

149. Gary LaFree and Richard Arum, "The Impact of Racially Inclusive Schooling on Adult Incarceration Rates Among U.S. Cohorts of African Americans and Whites Since 1930," *Criminology* 44 (2006): 73–103.

150. R. Kelly Raley, "A Shortage of Marriageable Men? A Note on the Role of Cohabitation in Black–White Differences in Marriage Rates," *American Sociological Review* 61 (1996): 973–983.

151. Julie Phillips, "Variation in African-American Homicide Rates: An Assessment of Potential Explanations," *Criminology* 35 (1997): 527–559.

152. Roy Austin, "Progress Toward Racial Equality and Reduction of Black Criminal Violence," *Journal of Criminal Justice* 15 (1987): 437–459.

153. Reynolds Farley and William Frey, "Changes in the Segregation of Whites from Blacks During the 1980s: Small Steps Toward a More Integrated Society," *American Sociological Review* 59 (1994): 23–45.

154. Gary LaFree, Eric Baumer, and Robert O'Brien, "Still Separate and Unequal? A City-Level Analysis of the Black–White Gap in Homicide Arrests Since 1960," *American Sociological Review* 75 (2010): 75–100.

155. Kristin F. Butcher and Anne Morrison Piehl, "Crime, Corrections, and California: What Does Immigration Have to Do with It?" Public Policy Institute of California, 2008, http://www.ppic.org/main/publication .asp?i=776.

156. Ramiro Martínez, Jr., "Crime and Immigration," *The Criminologist* 35 (2010): 16–17.

157. Patrick Schnapp, "Identifying the Effect of Immigration on Homicide Rates in U.S. Cities: An Instrumental Variables Approach," *Homicide Studies* 19 (2015): 103–122.

158. Marvin Wolfgang, Robert Figlio, and Thorsten Sellin, *Delinquency in a Birth Cohort* (Chicago: University of Chicago Press, 1972).

159. See Thorsten Sellin and Marvin Wolfgang, *The Measurement of Delinquency* (New York: Wiley, 1964), p. 120.

160. Marvin Wolfgang, "Delinquency in Two Birth Cohorts," in *Perspective Studies of Crime and Delinquency*, ed. Katherine Teilmann van Dusen and Sarnoff Mednick (Boston: Kluwer-Nijhoff, 1983), pp. 7–17.

161. Lyle Shannon, *Criminal Career Opportunity* (New York: Human Sciences Press, 1988).

162. D. J. West and David P. Farrington, *The Delinquent Way of Life* (London: Hienemann, 1977).

163. Michael Schumacher and Gwen Kurz, *The 8% Solution: Preventing Serious Repeat Juvenile Crime* (Thousand Oaks, CA: Sage, 1999).

164. Peter Jones, Philip Harris, James Fader, and Lori Grubstein, "Identifying Chronic Juvenile Offenders," *Justice Quarterly* 18 (2001): 478–507.

165. Lila Kazemian and Marc LeBlanc, "Differential Cost Avoidance and Successful Criminal Careers," *Crime and Delinquency* 53 (2007): 38–63.

166. Rudy Haapanen, Lee Britton, and Tim Croisdale, "Persistent Criminality and Career Length," *Crime and Delinquency* 53 (2007): 133–155.

167. See, generally, Wolfgang, Thornberry, and Figlio, eds., *From Boy to Man, from Delinquency to Crime.*

168. Paul Tracy and Kimberly Kempf-Leonard, *Continuity and Discontinuity in Criminal Careers* (New York: Plenum Press, 1996).

169. Kimberly Kempf-Leonard, Paul Tracy, and James Howell, "Serious, Violent, and Chronic Juvenile Offenders: The Relationship of Delinquency Career Types to Adult Criminality," *Justice Quarterly* 18 (2001): 449–478.

170. R. Tremblay, R. Loeber, C. Gagnon, P. Charlebois, S. Larivee, and M. LeBlanc, "Disruptive Boys with Stable and Unstable High Fighting Behavior Patterns During Junior Elementary School," *Journal of Abnormal Child Psychology* 19 (1991): 285–300.

171. Jennifer White, Terrie Moffitt, Felton Earls, Lee Robins, and Phil Silva, "How Early Can We Tell? Predictors of Childhood Conduct Disorder and Adolescent Delinquency," *Criminology* 28 (1990): 507–535.

AP Images/*Milwaukee Journal-Sentinel,* Mark Hoffman

LEARNING OBJECTIVES

LO1 Discuss the greatest problems faced by crime victims

LO2 Clarify the term *cycle of violence*

LO3 Analyze the victim's role in the crime process

LO4 Assess the ecology of victimization risk

LO5 Describe the victim's household

LO6 Categorize the most dominant victim characteristics

LO7 Explain the concept of repeat victimization

LO8 Compare and contrast the most important theories of victimization

LO9 Assess programs dedicated to caring for the victim

LO10 Articulate why there is a need for victims' rights

3 VICTIMS AND VICTIMIZATION

When Milwaukee Symphony Orchestra concertmaster Frank Almond emerged from a back door of a concert hall at Wisconsin Lutheran College in 2014, he was carrying a 300-year-old Stradivarius violin valued at more than $5 million.[1] The "Lipinski Strad" was made by Antonio Stradivari in 1715 and later named for the Polish violinist Karol Lipinski, who used the violin in concerts. As Almond walked to his car, a man approached, pulled a taser from his coat, and fired. While Almond was temporarily incapacitated by the stun gun, the thief grabbed the Lipinski and fled to a waiting vehicle. Hours later, Milwaukee Police Department officers found the violin case discarded by the side of the road.

Aware of the value and cultural significance of the violin—and that time was of the essence—the Milwaukee Police Department swiftly marshaled its forces and, with FBI assistance, began searching for leads outside of Wisconsin. Using evidence found at the crime scene, the police were able to trace the taser from the manufacturer to the purchaser—a Milwaukee barber who sold it to someone else. But who was this taser-carrying culprit? Police then received a tip (a $100,000 reward had been offered) implicating Milwaukee resident Salah Salahaydn in the robbery. Within a week, Salahaydn was arrested and charged, and a few days later led investigators to a Milwaukee home where the violin was found stored in a crawl space into the attic.

This crime was not one of impulse. Salahaydn told investigators that he had conducted extensive surveillance on Almond and knew where he and his family lived. He told an acquaintance such a robbery would be his dream crime because of the instrument's value and the ease of grabbing it from a musician walking down the street.

At his trial in May 2014, Salahaydn told Milwaukee County Circuit Judge Dennis Moroney that he had wanted to sell the violin and use the proceeds to buy a 36-unit apartment building he used to manage. Salahadyn said he felt gentrification had unfairly forced the eviction of poorer and older tenants, whom he wanted to help move back.

This was not his first art-related crime: 20 years before, he was convicted of receiving stolen property after he tried to sell a $25,000 sculpture back to the gallery from which it was taken. After pleading guilty to the violin theft, Salahaydn was sentenced to seven years in prison.

While the theft of a $5 million violin is certainly not routine, almost 700,000 robbery victimizations occur each year. Why do people become victims, the targets of predatory criminals? Is it simply bad luck, being in the wrong place at the wrong time, or do victims somehow contribute to their own mistreatment? Should Frank Almond have taken greater precautions instead of walking around alone at night with a $5 million violin under his arm? Or is this unfairly blaming the victim? The crime also shows the chances of becoming a crime victim is not a random event: people who are suitable targets, who flaunt easily transportable yet extremely valuable items, who put themselves in harm's way, are much more likely to become crime victims than those who lock themselves away in a secure environment.

Criminologists who focus their attention on crime victims refer to themselves as **victimologists**. This chapter examines victims and their relationship to the criminal process. We begin with discussion of the problems of victims and the costs of victimization. The nature and extent of **victimization** and the relationship between victims and criminal offenders are then reviewed. Finally, the various theories of victimization and how society has responded to the needs of victims are covered in some detail.

Problems of Crime Victims

L01 Discuss the greatest problems faced by crime victims

The National Crime Victimization Survey (NCVS) indicates that 20 million theft and violence victimizations occur each year.[2] And while this number has declined considerably during the past 20 years, it still means that more than 12 *percent of all the households in America experience theft sometime during the year and about 20 in every 1,000 citizens are raped, robbed, or assaulted.* These data are especially disturbing considering that becoming a victim of these violent acts can not only be immediately devastating but also have considerable long-term consequences and costs, ranging from damaged property to mental anguish.[3] What are the main effects of these millions of annual victimizations?

ECONOMIC COSTS

Victimization brings with it a bevy of economic costs (see Exhibit 3.1). When the costs of goods taken during property crimes is added to productivity losses caused by injury, pain, and emotional trauma, the cost of victimization is estimated to be in the hundreds of billions of dollars.

A number of different methods have been developed to measure the cost of victimization to American society and how that cost influences the average American. Mark Cohen pioneered these efforts by focusing on the total costs of a criminal act rather than the out-of-pocket expenses incurred by victims. He instead used complex mathematical models to estimate the additional cost of such intangibles as pain, suffering, and fear caused by crime. He also used the device of calculating what a jury would award in personal injury and accident cases to estimate monetary values for pain, suffering,

---

CONNECTIONS

Chapter 12 reviews research on common property theft. Most are spontaneous acts committed by amateurs and the rest are carefully planned schemes developed by professional criminals. Salah Salahaydn seems to fall somewhere in between, not a professional criminal but a calculating amateur.

ASK YOURSELF . . .

Can something be done to convince people like Salah Salahaydn that "crime does not pay"?

---

victimologists People who study the victim's role in criminal transactions.

victimization (by the justice system) While the crime is still fresh in their minds, victims may find that the police interrogation following the crime is handled callously, with innuendos or insinuations that they were somehow at fault. Victims have difficulty learning what is going on in the case; property is often kept for a long time as evidence and may never be returned. Some rape victims report that the treatment they receive from legal, medical, and mental health services is so destructive that they cannot help but feel "re-raped."

EXHIBIT 3.1

Costs Associated with Victimization

VICTIM COSTS
Personal economic losses, including medical care costs, lost earnings, and property loss/damage.

CRIMINAL JUSTICE SYSTEM COSTS
Local, state, and federal government funds spent on police protection and investigations; legal and adjudication services, such as prosecution, public defenders, and trial costs; and the cost of both community and secure corrections programs, including counseling and other programs.

CRIME CAREER COSTS
Opportunity costs associated with the criminal's choice to engage in illegal rather than legal and productive activities, including funds spent on supporting their families.

INTANGIBLE COSTS
Indirect losses suffered by crime victims, including pain and suffering, decreased quality of life, and psychological distress.

SOURCE: Kathryn McCollister, Michael T. French, and Hai Fang, "The Cost of Crime to Society: New Crime-Specific Estimates for Policy and Program Evaluation," *Drug and Alcohol Dependence* 108 (2010): 98–109.

and fear associated with crime. By one estimate he calculated just the personal costs of crime to be $90 billion per year.[4] Cohen suggests that the typical career criminal causes $1.3 to $1.5 million in external costs; a heavy drug user, $370,000 to $970,000; and a crime-committing dropout, $243,000 to $388,000. Eliminating duplication between crimes committed by individuals (for example, those who are both heavy drug users and career criminals) results in an overall estimate of lifetime cost for each chronic offender at between $1.7 and $2.3 million. This means that a treatment program for youth that costs $10 million annually will pay for itself if it can "save" five or six youthful offenders each year.

Cohen's efforts have prompted other criminologists to estimate the economic costs of criminal victimization. Kathryn McCollister and her associates employed complex statistical analysis to determine how much an individual crime might cost society; their calculations included intangible, tangible, criminal justice system, and other costs. The crimes they could put a figure on included:

- Murder: $8,982,907 (range = $4,144,677 to $11,350,687)
- Rape/sexual assault: $240,776 (range = $80,403 to $369,739)
- Robbery: $42,310 (range = $18,591 to $280,237)
- Household burglary: $6,462 (range = $1,974 to $30,197)
- Stolen property: $7,974 (range = $151 to $22,739)

According to McCollister, the cost to society of an average murder is almost $9 million. Considering that about 14,000 Americans are the victims of murder each year, murder alone has costs of about $126 million.[5]

Total Impact Another way of gauging the cost of victimization is to measure the total impact all crimes have on the economic well-being of society. Economist David Anderson estimates that the annual cost of crime increased from $2.4 trillion in the mid-1990s to more than $3 trillion today, despite the fact that crime has undergone a significant drop. The total cost of crime during the past decade is what the government spent on both the wars in Afghanistan and Iraq, plus American military aid to Pakistan!

Driving the price of crime up are such costs as lost productivity, the value of items taken from victims, private security, fences, alarm systems, computer security software, safe deposit boxes, insurance, safety lighting, lethal and nonlethal weapons, martial arts courses, and other goods and services. The per capita cost for every American citizen is approximately $5,300 per year.

Some crimes are particularly costly. While murder may be the most costly crime, rape adds $20 billion to the total. Heroin abuse costs the nation another $20 billion per year, including the medical complications of heroin addiction, primarily treatment for HIV/AIDS and psychiatric care, as well as paying for incarceration, policing, legal adjudication, and the cost to crime victims. There is also the cost of lost productivity—heroin addicts are less than half as likely to have a full-time job as compared with the national average—and the treatment of heroin addiction in clinics and hospitals.[6]

Despite these efforts, the many intangibles involved in determining the "value" of a crime make it most difficult to calculate the true cost of victimization. Take for instance the decline in value of a home that has been the scene of a crime. The impact of a high-profile murder on real estate can be particularly devastating. The Brentwood, California, home where Nicole Brown Simpson (ex-wife of O. J. Simpson) and her friend Ron Goldman were murdered in 1994 hit the market the following year with a $795,000 price tag; it sat for more than two years before selling for $595,000.[7] A high-profile crime can affect the value of all homes in the neighborhood.

Attempts to accurately monetize victimization were recently criticized by noted legal scholar Michael Tonry, who reminds us that most such efforts ignore the social costs of punishment that are levied on offenders and their families.[8] Even if imprisoning a chronic offender saves millions of dollars in victim costs, it simultaneously places an economic burden on his family who thereafter may need government assistance and welfare. Since there is a significant correlation between parental incarceration and children's delinquency, incarcerating parents may actually create more victimization than it saves; parental absence due to incarceration has a greater effect on kids than parental separation due to illness, death, or divorce.[9] While these factors may add to the true cost of victimization, they negate or neutralize the economic benefits accrued from incarcerating criminals.

INDIVIDUAL COSTS

In addition to these societal costs, victims may suffer long-term losses in earnings and occupational attainment. Some victims are physically disabled as a result of serious wounds sustained during episodes of random violence, including a growing number who suffer paralyzing spinal cord injuries. If victims have no insurance, the long-term effects of the crime may have devastating financial as well as emotional and physical consequences.[10]

Vicarious Fear Even if people are not personally victimized, those who observe or are exposed to violence on a routine basis become fearful.[11] Hearing about another's victimization may make people timid and cautious.[12] If they don't fear for themselves, they become concerned for others—their wives or husbands, children, elderly parents, and siblings.[13] Not only are people likely to move out of their neighborhood if they become crime victims, but they are also likely to relocate if they hear that a friend or neighbor has suffered a break-in or burglary.[14]

Vicarious fear is escalated by lurid news accounts of crime and violence.[15] For example, news stories about serial killers on a rampage can cause a chill felt throughout the city. People who read or hear about serial killers experience an increase in their fear of crime that prompts them to protect themselves and their family by implementing some sort of protective measure, such as carrying mace or pepper spray or adding a security device to their home.[16]

Suffering Stress   Victims may suffer stress and anxiety long after the incident is over and the justice process has been completed. **Posttraumatic stress disorder (PTSD)**—a condition whose symptoms include depression, anxiety, and self-destructive behavior—is a common problem, especially when the victim does not receive adequate support from family and friends.[17] To shield themselves, some victims deny the attack occurred or question whether they were "really raped." But denial only goes so far and does not shield victims from the long-term effects of sexual assault.[18]

Men may be particularly susceptible to post-rape PTSD, believing that their situation is both unique and somehow "unmanly." Knowing the effect of a sexual assault on men, rape has become an interrogation tool in some theaters of war; sexual assault was routinely used during the civil war in Yugoslavia to terrorize male prisoners.[19]

Adolescent Stress   Younger victims are also more prone to suffer stress and PTSD.[20] Kids who have either witnessed child abuse at home or personally experienced abuse are the most likely to experience negative personal outcomes.[21] People who have traumatic sexual experiences in childhood later suffer psychological deficits.[22] A history of childhood trauma, including rape and molestation, is significantly associated with visual, auditory, and tactile hallucinations.[23]

Many young victims run away to escape their environment, which puts them at risk for juvenile arrest and involvement with the justice system.[24] Others suffer post-traumatic mental problems, including acute stress disorders, depression, eating disorders, nightmares, anxiety, suicidal ideation, and other psychological problems.[25]

Victimization in childhood has long-term consequences: it may lead to despair, depression, and even homelessness in adulthood. Children who are psychologically, sexually, or physically abused are more likely to suffer low self-esteem and be more suicidal as adults.[26] They are also placed at greater risk to be re-abused as adults than those who escaped childhood victimization.[27] The re-abused

carry higher risks for psychological and physical problems, ranging from sexual promiscuity to increased HIV infection rates.[28]

Leana Bouffard and Maria Koeppel studied the long-term effects of childhood victimization and found that individuals who are victimized before the age of 12, especially those who experienced repeated bullying, are more susceptible to a number of physical and mental health issues, such as negative self-perceptions and obsessive thoughts, smoking, subsequent victimization experiences, and homelessness.[29] Another study of homeless women found that they were much more likely than other women to report childhood physical abuse, childhood sexual abuse, adult physical assault, previous sexual assault in adulthood, and a history of mental health problems.[30]

Relationship Stress   The stress encountered in childhood endures into adulthood, especially for those who are the victim of intimate partner violence (IPV). People who were abused as youth are more likely to become involved in abusive relationships as they mature. Early victimization has what is referred to as a "transformative effect," making childhood victims extremely vulnerable to IPV when they form co-residential romantic unions.[31]

Numerous research efforts show that people who suffer IPV experience an extremely high prevalence of psychological problems, including but not limited to depression, generalized anxiety disorder (GAD), panic disorder, substance use disorders, borderline personality disorder, antisocial personality disorder, posttraumatic stress disorder, anxiety disorder, and **obsessive-compulsive disorder** (an extreme preoccupation with certain thoughts and compulsive performance of certain behaviors).[32] One reason may be that abusive partners are as likely to mistreat their victims psychologically with threats and intimidation as they are to use physical force; psychological abuse can lead to depression and other long-term disabilities.[33]

Fear   People who live in crime-ridden neighborhoods develop an overwhelming sense of fear.[34] Those who have actually experienced crime are the most fearful, dreading the fact that they may be victimized again.[35]

Many people fear crime, especially the elderly, the poor, and minority group members.[36] Their fear is escalated by lurid news accounts of crime and violence.[37] While hearing about crime causes fear, those who experience it are even more likely to be fearful and change their behaviors.[38] Victims of violent crime are the most deeply affected, fearing a repeat of their attack. Many go through a fundamental life change, viewing the world more suspiciously and as a less safe, controllable, and meaningful place. Some develop a generalized fear of crime and worry about being revictimized.

Those who experience one type of crime may fear another: if they have been assaulted, they may develop fears that their house will be burglarized.[39] These people are

---

posttraumatic stress disorder (PTSD) Psychological reaction to a highly stressful event; symptoms may include depression, anxiety, flashbacks, and recurring nightmares.

obsessive-compulsive disorder An extreme preoccupation with certain thoughts and compulsive performance of certain behaviors.

more likely to suffer psychological stress for extended periods of time.[40]

There are gender differences in the fear of crime, and women are more fearful than men, especially those living in crime-ridden communities.[41] In a moving book, *Aftermath: Violence and the Remaking of a Self*, rape victim Susan Brison recounts the difficult time she had recovering from her ordeal. The trauma disrupted her memory, cutting off events that happened before the rape from those that occurred afterward, and eliminated her ability to conceive of a happy or productive future. Although sympathizers encouraged her to forget the past, she found that confronting it could be therapeutic.[42]

In some instances fear can be a good thing. Research shows that people who experience victimization and fear its consequences are less likely to engage in criminal activity. In contrast, those experiencing violence and surviving its consequences may embolden some victims and contribute to their perception that offending is not dangerous; this group is the one most likely to engage in violence themselves.[43]

Victims experience fear and anxiety long after the criminal incident occurred. Sometimes the support of others can help the healing experience begin. Kristina Ponischil is shown here in 2012 on the campus of the University of Washington in Seattle, where she works as a researcher. For months after Ponischil was raped at a party in her off-campus apartment, her life at Western Washington University was hell. Police wouldn't act. Despite a restraining order, she kept running into her assailant on campus, prompting panic attacks. But if the criminal justice system let Ponischil down, Western Washington did not, offering her the support she needed and suspending her assailant, removing him from campus until she graduated in 2009. "I was able to start healing," she said. "When I was constantly afraid, there was no healing. It was just constant fear."

AP Images/Elaine Thompson

 The National Organization for Victim Assistance is a private, nonprofit organization of victim and witness assistance programs and practitioners, criminal justice agencies and professionals, mental health professionals, researchers, former victims and survivors, and others committed to the recognition and implementation of victim rights and services. For more information, visit **http://www.trynova.org/.** In addition, visit the National Advocate Credentialing Program (NACP) at **http://www.trynova.org /help-crime-victim/nacp/.** The NACP, developed through the cooperative effort of multiple national and state victim assistance organizations, was launched in 2003 as the first voluntary credentialing program available to crime victim advocates nationwide.

What does it take to become a victim advocate?

THE CYCLE OF VIOLENCE

L02 Clarify the term *cycle of violence*

Victimization also increases the chance of getting involved in antisocial behavior; violence begets violence.[44] According to the **cycle of violence** phenomenon, people who are the victims of violence and abuse in adolescence are more likely to later engage in violent behavior as adults; victims of sexual abuse may often grow up to be sexual offenders themselves.[45] They are also more likely to smoke, drink, and take drugs than nonabused youth.[46] As adults, people who are the victims of violence are also quite likely to later become perpetrators.[47]

 The mission of the National Center for Victims of Crime is to help victims of crime rebuild their lives: "We are dedicated to serving individuals, families, and communities harmed by crime." The NCVC released *Taking Action: An Advocate's Guide to Assisting Victims of Financial Fraud* to provide those who serve the more than 30 million Americans who are victims of financial fraud every year with an important tool to aid their clients. Learn more by visiting **http://www.victimsofcrime.org/.**

Should people who make foolish investments be compensated or should "the buyer beware"?

cycle of violence The idea that victims of crime, especially childhood abuse, are more likely to commit crimes themselves.

L03 Analyze the victim's role in the crime process

The Link Between Victimization and Crime How can this association between victimization and crime be explained? There are actually a number of proposed linkages:

- *Victimization causes social problems.* People who are crime victims experience long-term negative consequences, including problems with unemployment and developing personal relationships, factors related to criminality. Some young victims may run away from home, taking to the streets and increasing their risk of becoming a crime victim again.[48]
- *Victimization causes stress and anger.* Victimization may produce anger, stress, and strain. Known offenders report significant amounts of posttraumatic stress disorder as a result of prior victimization, which may in part explain their violent and criminal behaviors.[49] Victims, especially those who lack self-control, may try to cope with this stress by self-medicating, drinking, or taking drugs, a form of behavior highly correlated with future criminality.[50]
- *Victimization prompts revenge.* Victims may seek revenge against the people who harmed them or whom they believe are at fault for their problems. In some cases, these feelings become generalized to others who share the same characteristics of their attackers (e.g., men, Hispanics).[51] As a result, their reactions become displaced, and they may lash out at people who are not their attackers. They may take drastic measures, fearing revictimization, and arm themselves for self-protection.[52] In some cultures, retaliation is an expected and accepted response to victimization.[53]

Spurious and/or Nonlinear Relationship While some victims engage in antisocial behaviors, others do not. Victims and criminals are actually two separate groups linked together because both have the same lifestyle and live in the same neighborhoods, making it seem they are one and the same. The personal traits that produce violent criminals may not be the same ones that produce victims.[54] It is also possible that while there is some overlap, the association between victimization and crime fluctuates over time. Younger victims are more likely to respond with antisocial activities after an attack.[55]

The Nature of Victimization

How many crime victims are there in the United States, and what are the trends and patterns in victimization? As noted earlier, 20 million criminal victimizations now occur each year.[56] While this total is significant, it represents almost a 20-year decline in criminal victimization from a peak of more than 40 million reported victimizations in 1995.

While the number and rate of victimizations have declined, patterns in the victimization survey findings are stable and repetitive, suggesting that victimization is not random but is a function of personal and ecological factors. The stability of these patterns allows us to make judgments about the nature of victimization; policies can then be created in an effort to reduce the victimization rate. Who are victims? Where does victimization take place? What is the relationship between victims and criminals? The following sections discuss some of the most important victimization patterns and trends.

THE SOCIAL ECOLOGY OF VICTIMIZATION

L04 Assess the ecology of victimization risk

Violent victimization is more likely to take place in an open, public area (such as a street, a park, or a field), in a school building, or at a commercial establishment such as a tavern during the daytime or early evening hours than in a private home during the morning or late evening hours. The more serious violent crimes, such as rape and aggravated assault, typically take place after 6 P.M.

Approximately two-thirds of rapes and sexual assaults occur at night—6 P.M. to 6 A.M. Less serious forms of violence, such as unarmed robberies and personal larcenies like purse snatching, are more likely to occur during the daytime. Neighborhood characteristics affect the chances of victimization. Those living in the central city have significantly higher rates of theft and violence than suburbanites; people living in rural areas have a victimization rate almost half that of city dwellers. The risk of murder for both men and women is significantly higher in disorganized inner-city areas where gangs flourish and drug trafficking is commonplace.

Time and place also influence the risk of injury. Recent research by Marie Skubak Tillyer and Rob Tillyer found robberies occurring in "semi-public" places, such as bars and restaurants, were less likely to result in injury than those in more secluded areas; semi-public areas offer a degree of place management that reduces injury severity. Similarly, robberies that took place during daytime hours were also associated with a lower risk of victim injury than nighttime attacks; the likelihood of third-party intervention was greater during daylight hours.[57]

School Victimization Schools, unfortunately, are the locale of a great deal of victimization because they are populated by one of the most dangerous segments of society, teenage males. The latest data available from the National Center for Educational Statistics found that among students ages 12 to 18, there were about 1,421,000 nonfatal victimizations at school, which included 454,900 theft victimizations and 966,000 violent victimizations (simple assault and serious violent victimizations).[58] Twenty students died in schools, 15 from homicide, 5 from suicide.

Why are so many school children vulnerable to victimization? During before-school and after-school activities, adult supervision is minimal, and hallways and locker rooms are typically left unattended. Kids who participate in school sports may leave their valuables in locker rooms that make attractive targets; others may congregate in unguarded places, making them attractive targets for predators who come on school grounds.[59] So, ironically, while for most people and most crimes summer is the most dangerous season, for adolescents victimization actually peaks in the fall when the school year begins and declines in the summer after the school year ends.[60]

THE VICTIM'S HOUSEHOLD

 Describe the victim's household

The NCVS tells us that within the United States, larger homes, African American homes, urban homes, and those in the West are the most vulnerable to crime. In contrast, rural homes, white homes, and those in the Northeast are the least likely to contain crime victims or be the target of theft offenses, such as burglary or larceny. People who own their homes are less vulnerable than renters.

Recent population movement and changes may account for decreases in crime victimization. U.S. residents have become extremely mobile, moving from urban areas to suburban and rural areas. In addition, family size has been reduced; more people than ever before are living in single-person homes (about one-quarter of the population). It is possible that the decline in household victimization rates during the past decades can be explained by the fact that smaller households in less populated areas have a lower victimization risk.

VICTIM CHARACTERISTICS

 Categorize the most dominant victim characteristics

Social and demographic characteristics also distinguish victims and nonvictims. The most important of these factors are gender, age, social status, marital status, and race and ethnicity.

Gender Gender affects victimization risk. Except for the crimes of rape and sexual assault, males are more likely than females to be the victims of violent crime. Men are almost twice as likely as women to experience robbery. Women, however, are six times more likely than men to be victims of rape, domestic violence, and sexual assault. Although males

Unfortunately, schools are the location of a great deal of crime, including tragic incidents of school shootings, the most deadly being the killings at Sandy Hook Elementary School in Newtown, Connecticut, on December 14, 2012. Here, a young girl is given a blanket after being evacuated from the site of that school shooting. Twenty-six teachers, workers, and children were killed when a young man named Adam Lanza opened fire in the school. Lanza committed suicide as police closed in.

Michelle Mcloughlin/Reuters

are more likely to be victimized than females, the gender differences in the victimization rate have narrowed significantly over time.

When men are the aggressors, injuries are more severe. Female aggressors tend to engage in verbal rather than physical abuse. Violence is more severe when perpetrated by males versus females as indicated by higher injury rates and greater victim fear.[61]

One significant gender difference is that women are much more likely to be victimized by someone they know or with whom they live. Of those offenders victimizing females, about two-thirds are someone the victim knew or was related to. In contrast, fewer than half of male victims were attacked by a friend, relative, or acquaintance.

While women are more likely to be the target of domestic assaults, intimate partner violence seems to be declining. One reason may be an increasing amount of economic and political opportunities for women: research shows that economic inequality is significantly related to female victimization rates. As more laws or acts favorable to women are passed and more economic opportunities become available, the lower their rates of violent victimization.[62]

Age Victim data reveal that young people face a much greater victimization risk than do older persons. Even the youngest kids are not immune and are as likely to experience serious child abuse as their older siblings.[63]

Victim risk diminishes rapidly after age 25: teens 16 to 19 suffer 45 violent crimes per 1,000, whereas people over 65 experience only 2 per 1,000. Teens and young adults experience the highest rates of violent crime. Violent crime rates declined in recent years for most age groups.

Although the elderly are less likely to become crime victims than the young, they are most often the victims of a narrow band of criminal activities from which the young are more immune. Frauds and scams, purse snatching, pocket picking, stealing checks from the mail, and committing crimes in long-term care settings claim more older than younger victims. The elderly are especially susceptible to fraud schemes because they have insurance, pension plans, proceeds from the sale of homes, and money from Social Security and savings that make them attractive financial targets. Because many elderly live by themselves and are lonely, they remain more susceptible to telephone and mail fraud. Unfortunately, once victimized, the elderly have more limited opportunities either to recover their lost money or to earn enough to replace what they have lost.[64]

The New York State Office of Victim Services (OVS) helps people in a number of ways to cope with victimization from a crime. Go to their website at **http://www.ovs.ny.gov/** and read "A Guide to Crime Victim Compensation in New York State," "Frequently Asked Questions," and "Our Claim Application and Instructions."

Elder abuse is a particularly important issue because of shifts in the U.S. population. Currently, there are about 40 million people in the United States over age 65 and the U.S. Census Bureau predicts that by 2050 the population over age 65 will reach 70 million people, and older people will make up more than 20 percent of the population (up from 12 percent in 1990). The saliency of elder abuse is underscored by reports from the National Center on Elder Abuse that between 8 and 10 percent of elderly people experience abuse each year. Despite the fact that an overwhelming number of cases of abuse, neglect, and exploitation go undetected and untreated each year, there is still an increasing trend in the reporting of elder abuse. Another growing problem: financial exploitation, which may be higher than rates of emotional, physical, and sexual abuse or neglect.[65]

What causes people to abuse the elderly? Some of the most significant views of elder abuse are set out in Exhibit 3.2.

Social Status   The poorest Americans are also the most likely victims of violent and property crime. For example, homeless people, who are among the poorest individuals in America, suffer very high rates of assault.[66] This association occurs across all gender, age, and racial groups. Although

elder abuse A disturbing form of domestic violence by children and other relatives with whom elderly people live.

EXHIBIT 3.2

What Causes Elder Abuse?

- The *caregiver stress view* asserts that parents experiencing stress are more likely to maltreat their children. In the context of elder maltreatment, maltreatment occurs when family members caring for an impaired older adult are unable to adequately manage their caregiving responsibilities. The elderly victim is typically described as highly dependent on the caregiver, who becomes overwhelmed, frustrated, and abusive because of the continuous caregiving demands posed by the elderly person.

- The *social learning view* holds that elder abuse results from the abusive individual learning to use violence to either resolve conflicts or obtain a desired outcome.

- The *social exchange view* is rooted in psychology and economics. It conceptualizes social behavior as involving negotiated exchanges of material and nonmaterial goods and services. When the sociodynamic balance in a relationship is upset or perceived to have been upset, the disadvantaged party will use violence to restore balance. People who abuse elders perceive themselves as not receiving their fair share from their relationship with the elderly person or other family members, and their resort to violence is an effort to restore or obtain deserved equilibrium.

- The *background-situational view* asserts that relationship discord results from a combination of contextual factors (e.g., a history of family violence) and situational factors (e.g., a lack of relationship satisfaction), which primes a person's acceptance of violence as a conflict resolution strategy. Elder abuse occurs when the abusive individual is the spouse or intimate partner of the victim, but it might also apply when the abusive individual is a codependent adult child or caregiver of the elderly person.

- The *power and control view* highlights an abusive individual's use of a pattern of coercive tactics to gain and maintain power and control during the course of a relationship with another person. It has been used to explain spousal abuse among elderly couples, although it could be applied as well when such traits describe an adult child or caregiver who has assumed, perhaps grudgingly, responsibility for the elderly person.

- The *ecological model* explains human behavior by including a range of potential influences on this process, including the impact of individual, relationship, community, and societal influences.

- In the *biopsychosocial model*, elder maltreatment can be attributed to the characteristics of both the elderly person and the abusive individual, both of whom are embedded in a larger sociocultural context (family and friends); their status inequality, relationship type, and power and exchange dynamics all help explain the outcome of their interactions.

SOURCE: Shelley Jackson and Thomas Hafemeister, *Understanding Elder Abuse*, National Institute of Justice, 2013, https://www.ncjrs.gov /pdffiles1/nij/241731.pdf (accessed April 2016).

the poor are more likely to suffer violent crimes, the wealthy are more likely targets of personal theft crimes such as pocket picking and purse snatching. Perhaps the affluent—sporting more expensive attire and driving better cars—attract the attention of thieves.

Marital Status   Johnny Brickman Wall, a Salt Lake City pediatrician, was convicted in 2015 of killing his cancer researcher ex-wife amid a bitter custody dispute. He was sentenced to 15-to-life in prison for attacking the 49-year-old woman with a knife, dosing her with the anti-anxiety drug Xanax, and drowning her in her bathtub.[67] The Wall case is certainly not unusual, considering that divorce claims about half of all first marriages and domestic violence is a significant social problem. Considering this turmoil, one might expect that married people have a greater chance of violent victimization than single people. But the data show quite the opposite effect: never-married males and females are victimized more often than married people. Widows and widowers have the lowest victimization risk. This association between marital status and victimization is probably influenced by age, gender, and lifestyle:

- Adolescents and teens, who have the highest victimization risk, are too young to have been married.
- Young single people go out in public more often and sometimes interact with high-risk peers, increasing their exposure to victimization.
- Widows and widowers suffer much lower victimization rates because they are older, interact with older people, and are more likely to stay home at night and to avoid public places.

Not all married people are the same and those who marry young are much more likely to be the victim of intimate partner violence.[68] One reason may be that early marriage is positively associated with divorce, and the problems that promote divorce are also highly correlated with victimization.

Race and Ethnicity   African Americans and ethnic minorities are more likely than whites to be victims of violent crime. What factors explain racial differences in the victimization rates? Because of income inequality, racial and minority group members are often forced to live in deteriorated urban areas beset by alcohol and drug abuse, poverty, racial discrimination, and violence. Consequently, their lifestyle places them in the most at-risk population group.

Another problem: When minority group members are victimized, their attackers are more likely to use weapons. Criminologist Mark Berg speculates that racial stereotypes affect criminal decision making and shape offenders' decisions about how to incapacitate a potential target. Criminals believe African American men are tough and not willing to back down or surrender their valuables without a fight. When African Americans are targeted, the use of a weapon increases their chances of injury.[69]

L07   Explain the concept of repeat victimization

Repeat Victimization   Individuals who have been crime victims have a significantly higher chance of future victimization than people who have not been victims.[70] Repeat victimization can involve people: some individuals are victimization prone, targeted over and over. One reason may be lifestyle. When Marie Skubak Tillyer and her associates studied repeat sexual assault victimization among high school students, they found that chronic victims were impulsive kids who hung out with antisocial peers and who were involved in unsupervised social activities.[71]

Repeat victimization can also involve place: some locations are repeatedly targeted. In fact, those places that have experienced victimization in the past are the ones most likely to experience it again in the future.[72] People who specialize in one type of crime (e.g., burglary) are more likely to choose the same target over and over again, especially if it is nearby and convenient. Why travel when you can burglarize a building close to home, especially if you got away with it the first time?[73]

What factors predict **chronic victimization**? Most repeat victimizations occur soon after a previous crime has occurred, suggesting that repeat victims share some personal characteristic that makes them a magnet for predators.[74] Predators have specific targets: children who are shy, physically weak, or socially isolated may be prone to being bullied in the schoolyard.[75] David Finkelhor and Nancy Asigian have found that three specific types of characteristics increase the potential for victimization:

- *Target vulnerability.* The victims' physical weakness or psychological distress renders them incapable of resisting or deterring crime and makes them easy targets.

chronic victimization   Those who have been crime victims maintain a significantly higher chance of future victimization than people who have remained nonvictims. Most repeat victimizations occur soon after a previous crime has occurred, suggesting that repeat victims share some personal characteristic that makes them a magnet for predators.

- *Target gratifiability.* Some victims have some quality, possession, skill, or attribute that an offender wants to obtain, use, have access to, or manipulate. Having attractive possessions such as a leather coat may make one vulnerable to predatory crime.
- *Target antagonism.* Some characteristics increase risk because they arouse anger, jealousy, or destructive impulses in potential offenders. Being gay or effeminate, for example, may bring on undeserved attacks in the street; being argumentative and alcoholic may provoke barroom assaults.[76]

Repeat victimization may occur when the victim does not take defensive action. If an abusive husband finds out that his battered wife will not call the police, he repeatedly victimizes her; if a hate crime is committed and the police do not respond to reported offenses, the perpetrators learn they have little to fear from the law.[77] Women who fight back and/or use self-protective action during the first incident of sexual battering reduce their likelihood of being a recurrent victim.[78]

Of course, not all victims are repeaters. Some take defensive measures to lessen their chance of future victimizations. They may change their lifestyle, take fewer risks, and cut back on associating with dangerous people; once burnt, twice shy.[79] Those victims who have enough self-control to make lifestyle changes are the ones the least likely to become chronic victims.[80]

victim precipitation theory The idea that the victim's behavior was the spark that ignited the subsequent offense, such as when the victim abused the offender verbally or physically.

Most murder victims knew their attackers, who were friends, relatives, acquaintances, or romantic partners. In a highly publicized case, Bob Bashara is shown here talking to the judge during his trial on April 12, 2016 in Detroit. A jury convicted Bashara of first-degree murder in the 2012 death of his wife, Jane Bashara, whose body was found strangled in her Mercedes-Benz in a Detroit alley.

VICTIMS AND THEIR CRIMINALS

The victim data also tell us something about the relationship between victims and criminals. Males are more likely to be violently victimized by a stranger, and females are more likely to be victimized by a friend, an acquaintance, or an intimate.

Victims report that most crimes are committed by a single offender over age 20. Crime tends to be intraracial: black offenders victimize blacks, and whites victimize whites. However, because the country's population is predominantly white, it stands to reason that criminals of all races will be more likely to target white victims. Victims report that substance abuse is involved in about one-third of violent crime incidents.[81]

Although many violent crimes are committed by strangers, a surprising number of violent crimes are committed by relatives or acquaintances of the victims. In fact, more than half of all nonfatal personal crimes are committed by people who are described as being known to the victim. Women are especially vulnerable to people they know. More than 60 percent of rape or sexual assault victims state the offender was an intimate, a relative, a friend, or an acquaintance. Women are more likely than men to be robbed by a friend or acquaintance; most males report that the people who robbed them were strangers.

Theories of Victimization

 L08 Compare and contrast the most important theories of victimization

For many years, while criminological theory focused on the actions of the criminal offender, the role of the victim was virtually ignored. This orientation began to change when such scholars as Stephen Schafer and Hans Van Hentig began to realize that the victim is not a passive target in crime, but someone whose behavior can influence his or her own fate, someone who "shapes and molds the criminal."[82] These early works helped focus attention on the role of the victim in the crime problem and led to further research efforts that have sharpened the image of the crime victim. Today, a number of different theories attempt to explain the causes of victimization; the most important are discussed here.

VICTIM PRECIPITATION THEORY

According to **victim precipitation theory**, some people may actually initiate the confrontation that eventually leads to their injury or death. Victim precipitation can be either active or passive.

Active precipitation occurs when victims act provocatively, use threats or fighting words, or even attack first.[83] In 1971, Menachem Amir suggested that female rape victims often contribute to their attacks by dressing provocatively or pursuing a relationship with the rapist.[84] Amir's findings are considered highly controversial. In recent years, there has been a great deal of change in the way rape victims are perceived, and state criminal laws have been revised to offer greater protection to victims. Nonetheless, rape myths still exist (for example, that women make false reports of rape when they later regret consensual sexual activity). It is still not unusual for courts to exonerate defendants in rape cases unless there is overwhelming proof that the victim did not consent to sexual intimacy.[85]

Passive precipitation occurs when the victim exhibits some personal characteristic that unknowingly either threatens or encourages the attacker. Although the victim may never have met the attacker or even know of his or her existence, the attacker feels menaced and acts accordingly.[86] In some instances, the crime can occur because of personal conflict—for example, when two people compete over a job, promotion, love interest, or some other scarce and coveted commodity. A woman may become the target of domestic violence when she increases her job status and her success results in a backlash from a jealous spouse or partner.[87]

Passive precipitation may also occur when the victim belongs to a group whose mere presence threatens the attacker's reputation, status, or economic well-being. For example, hate-crime violence may be precipitated by immigrant group members arriving in the community to compete for jobs and housing. Research indicates that passive precipitation is related to power: if the target group can establish themselves economically or gain political power in the community, their vulnerability will diminish. They are still a potential threat, but they become too formidable a target to attack; they are no longer passive precipitators.[88] By implication, economic power reduces victimization risk.

Victim Personality   One reason some people may invite or precipitate victimization is because there is an element in their personality that incites attacks.[89] Depression and anxiety have been linked to victimization. Perhaps criminals single out people who lack confidence and seem anxious and depressed; they may be considered easy targets unlikely to fight back.

A number of research efforts have found that both male and female victims have an impulsive personality and low self-control.[90] People who are impulsive and lack self-control are less likely to have a high tolerance for frustration and a physical rather than mental orientation; they are less likely to practice risk avoidance. It is possible that impulsive people are not only antagonistic and therefore more likely to become targets, but they also are risk takers who get involved in dangerous situations and fail to take precautions.[91]

Victim Disability   Not only do criminals seek out people with personality deficits, but those with physical disabilities are also more at risk. The rate of violent victimization for persons with disabilities (36 per 1,000) is more than twice the rate for persons without disabilities (14 per 1,000), adjusting for age since persons with disabilities—hearing, vision, cognitive, ambulatory, self-care, or independent living limitations—are generally older. In a single year (2013), persons with disabilities experienced about 1.3 million violent victimizations. Rates of serious violent victimization—rape, sexual assault, robbery, or aggravated assault—were more than three times higher for persons with disabilities (14 per 1,000) than the age-adjusted rate for persons without disabilities (4 per 1,000). When surveyed, people with disabilities believed they were purposively targeted because of their physical status.[92]

LIFESTYLE THEORY

People may become crime victims because their risky lifestyle increases their exposure to criminal offenders.[93] Victimization risk is increased by such behaviors as associating with young men, going out in public places late at night, and living in an urban area. Conversely, one's chances of victimization can be reduced by staying home at night, moving to a rural area, staying out of public places, earning more money, and getting married. The basis of **lifestyle theory** is that victimization is not a random occurrence but rather a function of the victim's lifestyle.

People who belong to groups that have an extremely risky life—homeless, runaways, drug users—are at high risk for victimization; the more time they are exposed to street life, the greater their risk of becoming crime victims.[94] When Kimberly Tyler and Morgan Beal interviewed more than 100 homeless youth in midwestern cities, they found that personal and behavioral characteristics helped put them in danger for physical and sexual abuse. Those who ran away at an earlier age, slept on the street, panhandled, and hung out with deviant peers rather than protective family members were the ones most likely to suffer physical victimization. Sexual victimization risk was elevated if the homeless youth was a female, had an unkempt and disheveled appearance, and had friends who were willing to trade sex for money.[95] Tyler and Beal's research shows that lifestyle promotes victimization.

active precipitation The view that the source of many criminal incidents is the aggressive or provocative behavior of victims.

passive precipitation The view that some people become victims because of personal and social characteristics that make them attractive targets for predatory criminals.

lifestyle theory People may become crime victims because their lifestyle increases their exposure to criminal offenders.

The college lifestyle is associated with victimization risk, and sexual assault on campus remains a significant social problem. Universities are searching for ways to protect students and help them seek justice. Jessica Ladd, shown here, is the founder of Sexual Health Innovations, whose Callisto service lets college students anonymously record details of sexual assaults and report them later. Callisto's hypothesis is that some students will be more likely initially to document a sexual assault on a third-party site than to report it to school officials on the phone or in person.

rate than women in the general population.[100] Fisher and her colleagues found that 90 percent of the victims knew the person who sexually victimized them. Most often this was a boyfriend, ex-boyfriend, classmate, friend, acquaintance, or coworker; college professors were not identified as committing any rapes or sexual coercions. The vast majority of sexual victimizations occurred in the evening (after 6 P.M.), typically (60 percent) in the students' living quarters; many were connected to drinking. Other common crime scenes were other living quarters on campus and fraternity houses (about 10 percent). Off-campus sexual victimizations, especially rapes, also occurred in residences. Incidents where women were threatened or touched also took place in settings such as bars, dance clubs or nightclubs, and work settings. Research confirms that young women who involve themselves in substance abuse and come into contact with men who are also substance abusers increase the likelihood that they will be sexual assault victims.[101]

Others are exposed to risk because of their status. Teenage males have an extremely high victimization risk because their lifestyle places them at risk both at school and once they leave the school grounds.[96] They spend a great deal of time hanging out with friends and pursuing recreational fun.[97] Their friends may give them a false ID so they can go drinking in the neighborhood bar, or they may hang out in taverns at night, which places them at risk because many fights and assaults occur in places that serve liquor.

College Lifestyle On January 25, 2015, Florida State University agreed to pay $950,000 to settle a lawsuit filed by former student Erica Kinsman, who in 2012 accused former FSU quarterback Jameis Winston of rape. Although the university did not admit to liability in the matter, they did agree to create five years of sexual assault awareness programs and to publish annual reports on those programs. Winston himself was never criminally charged in the case, in part because the police investigation was not thorough enough to allow the DA to press charges. The victim will receive $250,000; her lawyers get the rest. Winston is now the quarterback for the Tampa Bay Buccaneers, with a four-year $25 million contract.[98]

The Florida State rape accusation is certainly not unique. College students maintain a high-risk lifestyle—partying, staying out late at night, taking recreational drugs—that makes them victimization prone.[99] Bonnie Fisher and her colleagues surveyed thousands of college students and found that college women face the risk of sexual assault at a higher

The Office for Victims of Crime (OVC) was established by the 1984 Victims of Crime Act (VOCA) to oversee diverse programs that benefit victims of crime. The OVC provides substantial funding to state victim assistance and compensation programs and supports training designed to educate criminal justice and allied professionals regarding the rights and needs of crime victims. Learn more about assistance to victims of crime by visiting **http://www.ovc.gov/**.

Every month, the OVC Web Forum presents a special topic led by a guest host. Read one of their sessions, "Integrating Crime Victims' Issues into College and University Curricula," at the OVC site.

CONNECTIONS

The topic of campus rape is discussed in more detail in Chapter 10. While a significant number of college women, more than 20 percent, are sexually assaulted while in school, a great number of these crimes are not reported to authorities and all too often little is done to investigate the incident.

ASK YOURSELF . . .

What steps should college administrators take to reduce the incidence of campus rape?

Criminal Lifestyle   Not surprisingly, getting involved in criminality also increases the chance of victimization. There is evidence that the association between offending and personal victimization begins early in life and can be both direct and indirect.

- *Direct influence.* Kids who are delinquent risk being victimized from angry targets seeking retaliation or from bystanders acting as good Samaritans.
- *Indirect influence.* People who engage in criminal activities also associate with risk-taking peers and engage in risky behaviors. They consume alcohol, congregate with peers in the absence of authority figures, and hang out at night in public places. These unsafe behaviors all increase victimization risk.[102]

The perils of a deviant lifestyle do not end in adolescence; they haunt risk takers throughout their life. Kids with a history of family violence and involvement in crime increase their chances of becoming the victims of homicide as adults.[103] Kids who take drugs and carry weapons in their adolescence maintain a greater chance of being shot and killed as adults.[104]

The association between a criminal lifestyle and victimization risk may at first seem puzzling: why would someone target dangerous people, many of whom go around armed? While one might not think that hardcore criminals are at risk, there are actually groups of criminal offenders who specialize in preying on fellow criminals. Drug dealers make a tempting target. After all, they have a ready supply of cash and are unlikely to call the cops! If they want to avoid being a target, drug dealers better go around armed, use highly aggressive tactics, and be prepared to do violence themselves.[105]

Gang Lifestyle   Gang boys are a group with an extremely high risk for victimization. The gang lifestyle—engaging in serious crime and delinquency, carrying guns, selling drugs, retaliating against perceived slights or disrespect—typifies behaviors that significantly increase the chances of becoming a victim of violent crimes. Protecting the gang's turf and engaging in retaliatory vendettas to maintain the gang's reputation also increase the risk of personal victimization.[106] Gang boys are much more likely to own guns and associate with violent peers than nonmembers.[107] Those who choose aggressive or violent friends are more likely to begin engaging in antisocial behavior themselves and suffer psychological deficits.[108] Experiencing victimization brings on retaliation, creating a never-ending cycle of violence begetting even more violence.[109]

Gang membership's impact on victimization risk is reinforced by recent research conducted by Andrew Papachristos and his associates.[110] Using data from Newark, New Jersey, Papachristos discovered that about one-third of the city's gunshot victims were members of a social network that contained less than 4 percent of the city's total population. Gun violence clustered in groups that have gang members in the network. Ganging significantly elevated the likelihood of being the target of gun violence.

DEVIANT PLACE THEORY

According to **deviant place theory**, the greater their exposure to dangerous places, the more likely people will become victims of crime and violence.[111] Victims do not encourage crime but are victim prone because they reside in socially disorganized high-crime areas where they have the greatest risk of coming into contact with criminal offenders, irrespective of their own behavior or lifestyle.[112] The more often victims visit high crime areas, the more likely they will be victimized.[113] Neighborhood crime levels, then, may be more important for determining the chances of victimization than individual characteristics. Consequently, there may be little reason for residents in lower-class areas to alter their lifestyle or take safety precautions because personal behavior choices do not influence the likelihood of victimization.[114]

Deviant places are poor, densely populated, highly transient neighborhoods in which commercial and residential property exist side by side.[115] The commercial property provides criminals with easy targets for theft crimes, such as shoplifting and larceny. Successful people stay out of these stigmatized areas; they are homes for "demoralized kinds of people" who are easy targets for crime: the homeless, the addicted, the intellectually disabled, and the elderly poor.[116] People who live in more affluent areas and take safety precautions significantly lower their chances of becoming crime victims; the effect of safety precautions is less pronounced in poor areas. Residents of poor areas have a much greater risk of becoming victims because they live near many motivated offenders. Sociologist William Julius Wilson has described how people who can afford to leave dangerous areas do so. He suggests that affluent people realize that criminal victimization can be avoided by moving to an area with greater law enforcement and lower crime rates. Because there are significant interracial income differences, white residents are able to flee inner-city high-crime areas, leaving members of racial minorities behind to suffer high victimization rates.[117]

ROUTINE ACTIVITIES THEORY

Routine activities theory was first articulated in a series of papers by Lawrence Cohen and Marcus Felson.[118] They concluded that the volume and distribution of predatory crime

deviant place theory People become victims because they reside in socially disorganized, high-crime areas where they have the greatest risk of coming into contact with criminal offenders.

routine activities theory The view that the volume and distribution of predatory crime are closely related to the interaction of suitable targets, motivated offenders, and capable guardians.

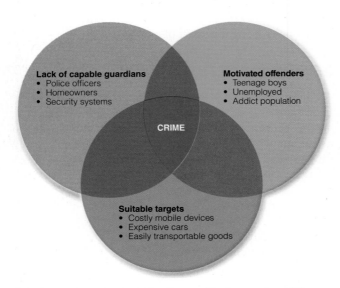

FIGURE 3.1 Routine Activities Theory: The Interaction of Three Factors

SOURCE: © Cengage Learning

(violent crimes against a person and crimes in which an offender attempts to steal an object directly) are closely related to the interaction of three variables that reflect the routine activities of the typical American lifestyle (see Figure 3.1):

- The availability of **suitable targets**, such as homes containing easily salable goods
- The absence of **capable guardians**, such as police, homeowners, neighbors, friends, parents, and relatives
- The presence of **motivated offenders**, such as a large number of unemployed and unsupervised teenagers

The presence of these components increases the likelihood that a predatory crime will take place. Targets are more likely to be victimized if they are poorly guarded and exposed to a large group of motivated offenders, such as teenage boys.[119] As targets increase in value and availability, so too should crime rates. Conversely, as the resale value of formerly pricey goods such as iPads and smart phones declines, so too should burglary rates.[120]

Increasing the number of motivated offenders and placing them in close proximity to valuable goods will increase

suitable target According to routine activities theory, a target for crime that is relatively valuable, easily transportable, and not capably guarded.

capable guardians Effective deterrents to crime, such as police or watchful neighbors.

motivated offenders The potential offenders in a population. According to rational choice theory, crime rates will vary according to the number of motivated offenders.

victimization levels. Even after-school programs, designed to reduce criminal activity, may produce higher crime rates because they lump together motivated offenders—teen boys—with vulnerable victims (other teen boys).[121] Young women who drink to excess in bars and frat houses may elevate their risk of rape because (a) they are perceived as easy targets, and (b) their attackers can rationalize the attack because they view intoxication as a sign of immorality ("She's loose, so I didn't think she'd care").[122] Conversely, people can reduce their chances of victimization if they adopt a lifestyle that limits their exposure to danger: by getting married, having children, and moving to a small town.[123]

Guardianship   Even the most motivated offenders may ignore valuable targets if they are well guarded. Despite containing valuable commodities, private homes and/or public businesses may be considered off-limits by seasoned criminals if they are well protected by capable guardians and efficient security systems.[124]

Criminals are also aware of police guardianship. In order to convince them that crime does not pay, more cops can be put on the street. Proactive, aggressive law enforcement officers who quickly get to the scene of the crime help deter criminal activities.[125]

Hot Spots   Motivated people—such as teenage males, drug users, and unemployed adults—are the ones most likely to commit crime. If they congregate in a particular neighborhood, it becomes a "hot spot" for crime and violence. People who live in these hot spots elevate their chances of victimization. For example, people who live in public housing projects may have high victimization rates because their fellow residents, mostly indigent, are extremely motivated to commit crime.[126] Yet motivated criminals must have the opportunity to find suitable undefended targets before they commit crime. Even the most desperate criminal might hesitate to attack a well-defended target, whereas a group of teens might rip off an unoccupied home on the spur of the moment.[127] In hot spots for crime, therefore, an undefended yet attractive target becomes an irresistible objective for motivated criminals. Hot spots may be chosen because of routine activities. Motivated offenders may choose them simply because they pass them by as they pursue other activities such as shopping and because they do not want to go too far out of their way to commit crimes.[128]

Support for Routine Activities Theory   Research supports many facets of routine activities theory (see the Criminology in Action feature). Cohen and Felson themselves found that crime rates increased between 1960 and 1980 because the number of adult caregivers at home during the day (guardians) decreased as a result of increased female participation in the workforce. While mothers are at work and children in day care, homes are left unguarded. Similarly, with the growth of

CRIMINOLOGY IN ACTION

Crime and Everyday Life

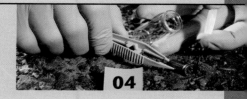

04

According to Marcus Felson, crime trends are a function of routine social conditions found in everyday life. Crime began to increase in the United States as the country changed from a nation of small villages and towns to one of large urban environments. Metropolitan areas provide a critical population mass, predatory criminals are better able to hide and evade apprehension. Criminals can blend into the crowd, disperse their loot, and make a quick escape using the public transportation system.

As the population became more urban, the middle class, fearing criminal victimization, fled to the suburbs. Rather than being safe from crime, the suburbs produced a unique set of routine activities that promote victimization risk. In many families, both parents are likely to commute to work, leaving teens unsupervised. Affluent kids own or drive cars, date, and socialize with peers in unsupervised settings, all behaviors that are related to both crime and victimization.

The downtown shopping district was replaced by the suburban shopping mall. Here, strangers converge in large numbers and youths hang out. The interior is filled with people, so drug deals can be concealed in the pedestrian flow. Stores have attractively displayed goods, encouraging shoplifting and employee pilferage. Substantial numbers of cars are parked in areas that make larceny and car theft virtually undetectable. Cars that carry away stolen merchandise have an undistinguished appearance: who notices people placing items in a car in a shopping mall lot? Also, shoppers can be attacked in parking lots as they walk in isolation to and from their cars. As car ownership increases, teens have greater access to transportation outside parental control. So while victimization rates in urban areas are still higher, routine activities in the suburbs may also produce the risk of victimization. Felson has set out the factors that increase the likelihood of victimization as the features of metropolitan living have spread to the suburbs:

- It has become more difficult to protect people from criminal entry because homes have been dispersed over larger areas, huge parking lots have been created, and building heights lowered.
- By spreading people and vehicles over larger areas as they travel and park, people are more exposed to attack.
- There are fewer people in each household and consequently less interpersonal and intrafamily supervision.

- As shopping, work, and socializing are spread farther from home, people are forced to leave their immediate neighborhood, and, as strangers, they become more vulnerable to attack.
- By spreading vast quantities of retail goods throughout huge stores and malls, with fewer employees to watch over them, the divergent metropolis creates a retail environment that invites people of all ages to shoplift.
- Commuting to the inner city for work requires that millions of dollars' worth of vehicles be left in parking lots without supervision.

 CRITICAL THINKING

Does routine activities theory merely describe why people become victims rather than get at the heart of the matter? Why are there motivated offenders? If people are motivated to commit crime, where does their motivation come from?

SOURCE: Marcus Felson and Mary Eckert, *Crime and Everyday Life: Insights and Implications for Society*, 5th ed. (Thousand Oaks, CA: Sage, 2009).

suburbia and the decline of the traditional neighborhood, the number of such familiar guardians as family, neighbors, and friends diminished.[129] Steven Messner and his associates found that as adult unemployment rates *increase*, juvenile homicide arrest rates *decrease*. One possible reason for this phenomenon: juvenile arrests may decrease because unemployed adults are at home to supervise their children and make sure they do not get in trouble or join gangs.[130] The availability and cost of easily transportable goods has also been shown to influence victimization rates: as the costs of goods such as cell phones and camcorders declined, so too did burglary rates.[131]

Routine Activities and Lifestyle Routine activities theory and the lifestyle approach have a number of similarities.

They both assume that a person's living arrangements can affect victim risk and that people who live in unguarded areas are at the mercy of motivated offenders. These two theories both rely on four basic concepts: (1) proximity to criminals, (2) time of exposure to criminals, (3) target attractiveness, and (4) guardianship.[132]

Based on the same basic concepts, these theories share five predictions: People increase their victimization risk if they (1) live in high-crime areas, (2) go out late at night, (3) carry valuables such as an expensive watch, (4) engage in risky behavior such as drinking alcohol, and (5) are without friends or family to watch or help them.[133]

The various theories of victimization are summarized in Concept Summary 3.1.

	MAJOR PREMISE	STRENGTHS OF THE THEORY	RESEARCH FOCUS OF THE THEORY
Victim precipitation	The major premise of victim precipitation theory is that victims trigger criminal acts by their provocative behavior. Active precipitation involves fighting words or gestures. Passive precipitation occurs when victims unknowingly threaten their attacker.	The strength of the theory is that it explains multiple victimizations: if people precipitate crime, it follows that they will become repeat victims if their behavior persists over time.	The research focuses of the theory are the victim's role, crime provocation, and the victim–offender relationship.
Lifestyle	The major premise of lifestyle theory is that victimization risk is increased when people have a high-risk lifestyle. Placing oneself at risk by going out to dangerous places results in increased victimization.	The strength of the theory is that it explains victimization patterns in the social structure. Males, young people, and the poor have high victimization rates because they have a higher-risk lifestyle than females, the elderly, and the affluent.	The research focuses of the theory are personal activities, peer relations, place of crime, and type of crime.
Deviant place	The major premise of deviant place theory is that victims do not encourage crime but are victim prone because they reside in socially disorganized high-crime areas where they have the greatest risk of coming into contact with criminal offenders, irrespective of their own behavior or lifestyle.	The strength of the theory is that it shows why people with conventional lifestyles become crime victims in high-risk areas. Victimization is a function of place and location, not lifestyle and risk taking.	The research focus of the theory is victimization in high-crime, disorganized neighborhoods.
Routine activities	The major premise of routine activities theory is that crime rates can be explained by the availability of suitable targets, the absence of capable guardians, and the presence of motivated offenders.	The strengths of the theory are that it can explain crime rates and trends, it shows how victim behavior can influence criminal opportunity, and it suggests that victimization risk can be reduced by increasing guardianship and/or reducing target vulnerability.	The research focuses of the theory are opportunity to commit crime, effect of police and guardians, population shifts, and crime rates.

Caring for the Victim

 L09 Assess programs dedicated to caring for the victim

National victim surveys indicate that almost every American age 12 and over will one day become the victim of a common-law crime, such as larceny or burglary, and in the aftermath suffer financial problems, mental stress, and physical hardship. Surveys show that more than 75 percent of the general public has been victimized by crime at least once in their life; as many as 25 percent of the victims develop posttraumatic stress disorder, and their symptoms last for more than a decade after the crime occurred. The effects of childhood victimization are long term, affecting people over the life course.[134] The long-term effects of sexual victimization can include years of problem avoidance, social withdrawal, and self-criticism. Helping these victims adjust and improve their coping techniques can be essential to their recovery.[135] Law enforcement agencies, courts, and correctional and human service systems have come to realize that due process and human rights exist for both the defendant and the victim of criminal behavior.

THE GOVERNMENT'S RESPONSE TO VICTIMIZATION

Because of public concern over violent personal crime, President Ronald Reagan created a Task Force on Victims of Crime in 1982.[136] This group suggested that a balance be achieved between recognizing the victim's rights and providing the defendant with due process. Recommendations included providing witnesses and victims with protection from intimidation, requiring restitution in criminal cases, developing guidelines for fair treatment of crime victims and witnesses, and expanding programs of victim compensation.[137] Consequently, the Omnibus Victim and Witness Protection Act was passed, which required the use of victim impact statements at sentencing in federal criminal cases, greater protection for witnesses, more stringent bail laws, and the use of restitution in criminal cases.

In 1984, the Comprehensive Crime Control Act and the Victims of Crime Act authorized federal funding for state victim compensation and assistance projects.[138] With these acts, the federal government began to address the plight of the victim and make victim assistance an even greater concern of the public and the justice system. In 2004, the Justice for All Act modified existing federal law and created a new set of rights for victims. Part of this act, the Crime Victims' Rights Act, sets out these rights, including the right to be protected from the accused in their case and to be informed of their release (see Exhibit 3.3).[139]

Due to this recognition of the needs of victims, an estimated 2,000 **victim-witness assistance programs** have developed around the United States.[140] Victim-witness assistance programs are organized on a variety of governmental levels and serve a variety of clients. We will look at the most prominent forms of victim services operating in the United States.[141]

Victim compensation programs help ease the cost incurred from a criminal act. But what about people who are victimized while in other states? Should they be compensated also? Here, Boston Marathon bombing survivor Heather Abbott walks out of her home in Newport, Rhode Island. On April 12, 2016, the state senate voted 38–0 to allow Rhode Island victims of terror attacks to receive compensation money even if the attack happened outside the state. The bill is a response to the bureaucratic struggles encountered by Abbott when she applied for the state's crime victim compensation fund after the 2013 attack in Boston.

AP Images/Elise Amendola

EXHIBIT 3.3

The Rights Established Under the Crime Victims' Rights Act of 2004

The Crime Victims' Rights Act of 2004, 18 U.S.C. § 3771, provides that officers and employees of the Department of Justice shall make their best efforts to see that crime victims are notified of, and accorded, the following rights:

- The right to be reasonably protected from the accused
- The right to reasonable, accurate, and timely notice of any public court proceeding, or any parole proceeding, involving the crime or of any release or escape of the accused
- The right not to be excluded from any such public court proceeding, unless the court, after receiving clear and convincing evidence, determines that testimony by the victim would be materially altered if the victim heard other testimony at that proceeding
- The right to be reasonably heard at any public proceeding in the district court involving release, plea, sentencing, or any parole proceeding
- The reasonable right to confer with the attorney for the government in the case
- The right to full and timely restitution as provided by law
- The right to proceedings free from unreasonable delay
- The right to be treated with fairness and with respect for the victim's dignity and privacy

SOURCE: The Justice for All Act of 2004, 18 U.S.C. § 3771, http://www.ojp.usdoj.gov/ovc/publications/factshts/justforall/fs000311.pdf (accessed April 2016).

Victim Compensation In order to help victims survive their ordeal, state governments have set up **victim compensation** programs to help pay for damages associated with the crime. Rarely are two compensation schemes alike, however, and many state programs suffer from lack of both adequate funding and proper organization within the criminal justice system. Compensation may be made for medical bills, loss of wages, loss of future earnings, and counseling. In the case of death, the victim's survivors can receive burial expenses and aid for loss of support.[142] Awards are typically in the $100 to $15,000 range. Occasionally, programs will provide emergency assistance to indigent victims until compensation is available. Emergency assistance may come in the form of food vouchers or replacement of prescription medicines. Three typical victim compensation programs are described in Exhibit 3.4.

victim-witness assistance programs Government programs that help crime victims and witnesses; may include compensation, court services, and/or crisis intervention.

victim compensation The victim ordinarily receives compensation from the state to pay for damages associated with the crime. Rarely are two compensation schemes alike, however, and many state programs suffer from lack of both adequate funding and proper organization within the criminal justice system. Compensation may be made for medical bills, loss of wages, loss of future earnings, and counseling. In the case of death, the victim's survivors can receive burial expenses and aid for loss of support.

EXHIBIT 3.4

State Victim Compensation Programs

- The Idaho Crime Victims Compensation Program (ICVC), which has collected restitution since 1998, regularly serves as a mentor to other states interested in building their capacity in this area. ICVC collects payments through its website; the program has implemented a monthly billing system. Offenders with outstanding payments due are notified and ordered to make a payment. The program is reporting success, particularly in collecting large sums from offenders who were not aware they owed restitution.

- The New Jersey Victims of Crime Compensation Office is helping protect the rights of victims by providing funding for legal representation in court, which ensures that victims' rights are respected in situations where the victim might be overwhelmed by unfamiliar legal requirements and procedures. Many states permit victims to hire an attorney to help them file claims, but the New Jersey compensation program provides for assistance in any legal matter related to the victimization associated with the claim. There is a $1,000 cap for these services; payment is deducted from the maximum claim benefit.

- The 17th Judicial District Crime Victim Compensation Program in Brighton, Colorado, is almost entirely paperless—increasing efficiency while going green. Files are scanned, queued until they are assigned to victim files, and managed from a central storage drive. Staff members send board members case summaries and relevant documents through an encrypted online document management system. In turn, board members use their district-issued tablets to access the software, review claims, and prepare for monthly board meetings.

SOURCE: Office for the Victims of Crime, "2013 OVC Report to the Nation," http://www.ovc.gov/pubs/reporttonation2013/voca_cn.html (accessed April 2016).

In 1984, the federal government created the Victims of Crime Act (VOCA), which grants money to state compensation boards derived from fines and penalties imposed on federal offenders. The money is distributed each year to the states to fund both their crime victim compensation programs and their victim assistance programs, such as rape crisis centers and domestic violence shelters. Victims of child abuse and victims of domestic violence receive most of the funds. VOCA money goes to support victims' medical expenses, gives them economic support for lost wages, helps to compensate for the death of loved ones, and provides mental health counseling.[143] To give some idea of how much funding is available, the Consolidated Appropriations Act, 2016, increases the cap on the Crime Victims Fund from $2.361 billion in 2015 to $3.042 billion in 2016. Included in this amount is a transfer of $379 million to the Office on Violence Against Women and $10 million to the Office of the Inspector General for "oversight and auditing purposes." Of the $2.65 billion remaining for programs authorized under the VOCA statute, about $2.26 billion will be available for state VOCA victim assistance grants, an increase of about $300 million over 2015 funding.[144]

Victim Advocates Ensuring victims' rights can involve an eclectic group of advocacy groups, some independent, others government sponsored, and some self-help. Advocates can be especially helpful when victims need to interact with the agencies of justice. Advocates lobby police departments to keep investigations open as well as request the return of recovered stolen property. They also work closely with police when victims are interviewed about violent crimes, helping them to deal with reliving traumatic events.

Police departments are now instituting training designed to prepare officers to work more effectively with victim advocates.[145] They can demand from prosecutors and judges protection from harassment and reprisals by, for example, making "no contact" a condition of bail. They can help victims make statements during sentencing hearings as well as probation and parole revocation procedures. Victim advocates can also interact with news media, making sure that reporting is accurate and that victim privacy is not violated.

Some programs assign advocates to help victims understand the operations of the justice system and guide them through the process. Victims of sexual assault may be assigned the assistance of a rape victim advocate to stand by their side as they negotiate the legal and medical systems that must process their case. Research shows that rape survivors who had the assistance of an advocate were significantly more likely to have police reports taken, were less likely to be treated negatively by police officers, and reported less distress from their medical contact experiences.[146]

Court advocates prepare victims and witnesses by explaining court procedures: how to be a witness, how bail works, and what to do if the defendant makes a threat. In some instances, victim aid is provided to surviving family members. In New Hampshire, all homicides, excluding negligent homicides, are prosecuted out of the Homicide Bureau of the Attorney General's Office, enabling a centralized victim services unit to be involved from the onset of the investigation. The office has victim-witness advocates who are on call 24 hours a day. When a homicide occurs, an advocate responds to the scene and is responsible for notifying the victim's family of the death of their loved one and for providing immediate crisis intervention and support to both family members and witnesses to the crime. From arranging for the cleanup of the homicide scene to informing the family on the results of the autopsy, to assisting them with funeral arrangements, the advocate provides each family extensive support and services at a difficult and extremely painful time.[147]

The Policy and Practice feature describes programs designed to help women who are victims of intimate partner violence.

Advocacy for the Victims of Intimate Partner Violence

Intimate partner violence involves the abuse of a woman by a male or female partner with whom she currently is or formerly was in an intimate relationship. Advocacy interventions for women who have experienced intimate partner violence aim to empower women and link them to helpful services in the community. The goals of advocacy interventions include helping abused women access necessary services, reducing or preventing incidents of abuse, and improving women's physical and psychological health.

Advocacy interventions are targeted at abused women who are still with their partners or who have left the abusive relationship. Although the interventions target women, services and support for any children involved in the abusive relationship may also be provided. Interventions may be primary, secondary, or tertiary. Primary interventions focus on preventing the onset of abuse. Secondary interventions focus on preventing further abuse, and tertiary interventions focus on dealing with the consequences of abuse once the abuse has ceased.

The core activities of advocacy interventions can vary from program to program and can include:

- Providing legal, housing, and financial advice
- Facilitating access to and use of community resources such as shelters, emergency housing, and psychological interventions
- Providing safety planning advice

In addition, advocates may provide ongoing support and informal counseling. The amount of time that advocacy is provided for abused women will vary, depending upon the specific needs of each woman. Short-term or crisis advocacy usually involves the advocate working with the woman for a short period of time (though she may be referred for additional services with a specialized agency). The duration of short-term advocacy interventions can range from 1 hour to about 12 hours, whereas long-term advocacy interventions, such as counseling services, can last as long as 12 months, if necessary. Advocacy interventions can take place within health care settings such as hospitals, but may also take place in other settings such as shelters.

Practice Theory

Advocacy interventions are based on the concept of empowerment. This includes talking with the abused woman about potential solutions (rather than being prescriptive and telling her what to do); helping her achieve goals she has set (rather than setting the goals for her); and helping her understand and make sense of the situation and how she responds. Advocates who work with abused women to identify their needs and connect them to resources in the community can include trained paraprofessionals, therapists, counselors, and social workers.

While evaluations of these programs are preliminary, they suggest that women who received advocacy interventions experienced significantly less physical abuse, compared with women in the control groups—a positive trend that substantiates the utility of advocacy.

SOURCES: National Institute of Justice, "Advocacy Interventions for Women Who Experience Intimate Partner Violence," https://www.crimesolutions.gov/PracticeDetails.aspx?ID=55 (accessed April 2016).

Helping Child Abuse Victims   One of the most significant problems court advocates must deal with is helping the victim of child abuse navigate a court hearing. Children get confused and frightened and may change their testimony. Much controversy has arisen over the accuracy of children's reports of physical and sexual abuse, resulting in hung juries. Prosecutors and experts have been accused of misleading children or eliciting incriminating testimony.

State jurisdictions have enacted legislation allowing videotaped statements or interviews with child witnesses to be admissible in court in order to spare child witnesses the trauma of testifying in open court. Most of the states now allow a child's testimony to be given on closed-circuit television (CCTV). The child can view the judge and attorneys, and the courtroom participants can observe the child. In addition to innovative methods of testimony, children in sexual abuse cases have been allowed to use anatomically correct dolls to demonstrate happenings that they cannot describe verbally. The Victims of Child Abuse Act of 1990 allows children to use these dolls when testifying in federal courts; currently nine states have passed similar legislation.[148] Other programs are designed to help very young children remember what happened and be able to tell authorities about their victimization.

Many victim programs also provide transportation to and from court, and advocates may remain in the courtroom during hearings to explain procedures and provide support. Court escorts are particularly important for elderly and disabled victims, victims of child abuse and assault, and victims who have been intimidated by friends or relatives of the defendant. These types of services may be having a positive effect since recent research shows that victims may now be less traumatized by a court hearing than previously believed.[149]

Public Education   More than half of all victim programs include public education to help familiarize the general public with their services and with other agencies that assist crime victims. In some instances, these are primary education programs, which teach methods of dealing with conflict without resorting to violence. For example, school-based programs present information on spousal and dating abuse followed by discussions of how to reduce violent incidents.[150]

Crisis Intervention   Most victim programs refer victims to specific services to help them recover from their ordeal, referred to as **crisis intervention**. Clients are commonly referred to the local network of public and private social service agencies that provide emergency and long-term assistance with transportation, medical care, shelter, food, and clothing. In addition, more than half of all victim programs provide crisis intervention for victims who feel isolated, vulnerable, and in need of immediate services. Some programs counsel at their offices; others visit victims in their homes, at the crime scene, or in the hospital. For example, the Good Samaritans program in Mobile County, Alabama, unites law enforcement and faith-based and community organizations to train and mobilize volunteers who can help crime victims. Good Samaritan volunteers provide services such as:

- Making repairs to a home after a break-in
- Conducting home safety inspections to prevent revictimization
- Accompanying victims to court
- Supplying "victim care kits" or other support[151]

VICTIM-OFFENDER RECONCILIATION PROGRAMS

Victim-offender reconciliation programs (VORPs) use mediators to facilitate face-to-face encounters between victims and their attackers. The aim is to engage in direct negotiations that lead to **restitution agreements** and, possibly, reconciliation between the two parties involved.[152] Hundreds of programs are currently in operation, and they handle thousands of cases per year. Designed at first to address routine misdemeanors such as petty theft and vandalism, programs now commonly hammer out restitution agreements in more serious incidents such as residential burglary and even attempted murder.

crisis intervention Emergency counseling for crime victims.

restitution agreements Conditions of probation in which the offenders repay society or the victims of crime for the trouble the offenders caused. Monetary restitution involves a direct payment to the victim as a form of compensation. Community service restitution may be used in victimless crimes and involves work in the community in lieu of more severe criminal penalties.

 Since 1982, the Victim Offender Reconciliation Program (VORP) has been bringing victims and offenders together in safe mediation or family group conference settings to permit the offender to take responsibility for his or her actions, to make things as right as possible with the victim, and to be clear about future intentions. VORP follows up to ensure that agreements are kept. Read about their history, programs, and training assistance at **http://vorp.org/**.

CONNECTIONS

Reconciliation programs are based on the concept of restorative justice, which rejects punitive correctional measures in favor of viewing crimes of violence and theft as interpersonal conflicts that need to be settled in the community through noncoercive means. See Chapter 8 for more on this approach.

ASK YOURSELF . . .

If you were a victim, would you be willing to meet and reconcile with the person who attacked you or stole your property?

Victim Impact Statements   Every state jurisdiction allows victims to make an impact statement before the sentencing judge. Victim impact information is part of the Federal Crime Act of 1994, in which Congress gave federal victims of violent crime or sexual assault the right to speak at sentencing. Through the Child Protection Act of 1990, child victims of federal crimes are allowed to submit victim impact statements that are "commensurate with their age and cognitive development," which can include drawings, models, etc.[153]

This gives the victim an opportunity to tell of his or her experiences and describe the ordeal. In the case of a murder trial, the surviving family can recount the effect the crime has had on their lives and well-being.[154]

The effect of victim impact statements on sentencing has been the topic of some debate. Some research finds that victim statements result in a higher rate of incarceration, but others find that the statements are insignificant.[155] One recent study by Joel Caplan found that the use of victim statements at parole hearings had little influence on the decision process, and inmate release was based more on factors such as measures of institutional behavior, crime severity, and criminal history.[156]

Those who favor the use of impact statements argue that because the victim is harmed by the crime, he or she has the right to influence the outcome of the case. After all, the public prosecutor is allowed to make sentencing recommendations because the public has been harmed by the crime. Logically, the harm suffered by the victim legitimizes his or her right to make sentencing recommendations.[157]

COMMUNITY ORGANIZATION

Citizens have been working independently and in cooperation with local police agencies in neighborhood patrol and block watch programs. These programs organize local citizens in urban areas to patrol neighborhoods, watch for suspicious people, help secure the neighborhood, lobby for improvements (such as increased lighting), report crime to police, put out community newsletters, conduct home security surveys, and serve as a source for crime information or tips.[158] Although such programs are welcome additions to police services, there is little evidence that they appreciably affect the crime rate. There is also concern that their effectiveness is spottier in low-income, high-crime areas, which need the most crime prevention assistance.[159] Block watches and neighborhood patrols seem more successful when they are part of general-purpose or multi-issue community groups rather than when they focus directly on crime problems.[160]

VICTIMS AND SELF-PROTECTION

Although the general public mostly approves of the police, fear of crime and concern about community safety have prompted some to become their own "police force," taking an active role in community protection and citizen crime control groups.[161] The more crime in an area, the greater the amount of fear and the more likely residents will be to engage in self-protective measures.[162]

Research indicates that a significant number of crimes may not be reported to police simply because victims prefer to take matters into their own hands.[163] One manifestation of this trend is the concept of **target hardening**, or making one's home and business crime proof through locks, bars, alarms, and other devices.[164] Other commonly used crime prevention techniques include a fence or barricade at the entrance; a doorkeeper, guard, or receptionist in an apartment building; an intercom or phone to gain access to the building; surveillance cameras; window bars; warning signs; and dogs chosen for their ability to guard the house. The use of these measures is inversely proportional to perception of neighborhood safety: people who fear crime are more likely to use crime prevention techniques. Although the true relationship is still unclear, there is mounting evidence that people who protect their homes are less likely to be victimized by property crimes.[165] One study conducted in the Philadelphia area found that people who install burglar alarms are less likely to suffer burglary than those who forgo similar preventive measures.[166]

Fighting Back Some people take self-protection to its ultimate end by preparing to fight back when criminals attack. How successful are victims when they resist? The research results are decidedly mixed. Some find that victims who fight back frustrate their attackers and prevent the crime from being completed; others find that forcefully resisting increases both the chance of the crime being completed and the likelihood of personal injury.[167]

What about the use of firearms for self-protection? Again, there is no clear-cut answer. Each year, millions of victims use guns for defensive purposes (a number that is not surprising considering that about one-third of U.S. households contain guns).[168] Gary Kleck has estimated that armed victims kill more attackers than police and the risk of collateral injury is relatively rare. In one study, conducted with colleague Jongyeon Tark, Kleck reviewed more than 27,000 contact crime incidents and found that when compared to nonresistance, self-protection significantly reduced the likelihood of property loss and injury and that the most forceful tactics, including resistance with a gun, appear to have the strongest effects in

target hardening Making one's home or business crime proof through the use of locks, bars, alarms, and other devices.

THINKING LIKE A CRIMINOLOGIST

An Ethical Dilemma

Stand Your Ground

The governor's council is sponsoring an open house debate on a proposed "stand your ground" law. More than 20 states have passed laws that allow crime victims to use deadly force in certain situations in which they might have formerly been charged with a crime. Some allow the use of deadly force when a person reasonably believes it necessary to prevent the commission of a "forcible felony," including carjacking, robbery, or assault, and the governor's council wants to follow suit.

The traditional "castle doctrine" requires that people could use deadly force only in their own home when they reasonably believed that their lives were in danger. The new law being proposed allows average citizens to use deadly force when they reasonably believe that their home or vehicle has been illegally invaded. Furthermore, under the new law, people have no duty to retreat and can meet force with force; they are granted immunity from prosecution if they can prove they were the target of a crime and feared that their life was in danger.

A number of controversial cases have put the "stand your ground" law under a legal microscope. Most notable was the killing of Trayvon Martin by George Zimmerman, who was acquitted after convincing a Florida jury that he feared for his life despite the fact that Martin was an unarmed teen. There is a question of ethics: Is it appropriate to allow someone to take a life for committing a crime that would not be subject to capital punishment? Why should a citizen be allowed to take a life if the state cannot?

Divide the class into two groups and have each prepare a "talking points" paper, one supporting the ethical value of the "stand your ground" concept and the other pointing out its flaws and limitations.

Jesse Timmendequas and Megan's Law

Richard and Maureen Kanka thought that their 7-year-old daughter Megan was safe in their quiet, suburban neighborhood in Hamilton Township, New Jersey. Then, on July 29, 1994, their lives were shattered when Megan went missing. Maureen Kanka searched the neighborhood and met 33-year-old Jesse Timmendequas, who lived across the street. Timmendequas told her that he had seen Megan earlier that evening while he was working on his car. The police were called in and soon focused their attention on Timmendequas's house when they learned that he and two other residents were convicted sex offenders who had met at a treatment center and decided to live together upon their release. Timmendequas, who appeared extremely nervous when questioned, was asked to accompany police back to their headquarters, where he confessed to luring Megan into his home by inviting her to see a puppy, then raping her and strangling her to death.

Timmendequas had served six years in prison for aggravated assault and attempted sexual assault on another child. The fact that a known sex offender was living anonymously in the Kankas' neighborhood turned Megan's death into a national crusade to develop laws that require sex offenders to register with local police

when they move into a neighborhood and require local authorities to provide community notification of the sex offender's presence. New York State's Sex Offender Registration Act is typical of these efforts, commonly known as Megan's Law. Becoming effective on January 21, 1996, the statute requires that sex offenders in New York are classified by the risk of reoffense. A court determines whether an offender is a level 1 (low risk), 2 (moderate risk), or 3 (high risk). The court also determines whether an offender should be given the designation of a sexual predator, sexually violent offender, or predicate sex offender. Offenders are required to be registered for 20 years or life. Level 1 offenders with no designation must register for 20 years. Level 1 offenders with a designation, as well as level 2 and level 3 offenders regardless of whether they have a designation, must register for life. Local law enforcement agencies are notified whenever a sex offender moves into their jurisdiction. That agency may notify schools and other "entities with vulnerable populations" about the presence of a level 2 or level 3 offender if the offender poses a threat to public safety. The act established a toll-free telephone information line that citizens can call to inquire whether a person is listed in the registry and access information on sex offenders living in their

neighborhoods. On the federal level, the Jacob Wetterling Crimes Against Children Law, passed in May 1996, requires states to pass some version of Megan's Law or lose federal aid. At least 47 states plus the District of Columbia have complied. Jesse Timmendequas was sentenced to death on June 20, 1997; his sentence was commuted to life without parole when New Jersey abolished the death penalty in 2007.

 CRITICAL THINKING

The case of Megan Kanka illustrates both the risk children face from sexual predators and the efforts being made by the justice system to limit that risk. To some civil liberty groups, such as the American Civil Liberties Union, registration laws go too far because they will not prevent sex offenders from committing crimes and because they victimize rehabilitated ex-offenders and their families. Should the rights of the victim take precedent over the privacy of the offender?

SOURCE: New York State Sex Offender Registry and the Sex Offender Registration Act (SORA), http://www.criminaljustice.ny.gov /nsor/ (accessed April 2016), New York State Correction Law Article 6-C (Section 168 et seq.).

---

reducing the risk of injury. Importantly, the research indicated that resistance did not contribute to injury in any meaningful way. The conclusion: it is better to fight than flee.[169]

VICTIMS' RIGHTS

 Articulate why there is a need for victims' rights

More than 30 years ago, legal scholar Frank Carrington suggested that crime victims have legal rights that should assure them of basic services from the government.[170] According to Carrington, just as the defendant has the right to counsel and a fair trial, society is also obliged to ensure basic rights for law-abiding citizens. These rights range from adequate

protection from violent crimes to victim compensation and assistance from the criminal justice system.

Because of the influence of victims' rights advocates, every state now has a set of legal rights for crime victims in its code of laws, often called a Victims' Bill of Rights.[171] These generally include the right:

- To be notified of proceedings and the status of the defendant
- To be present at criminal justice proceedings
- To make a statement at sentencing and to receive restitution from a convicted offender
- To be consulted before a case is dismissed or a plea agreement is entered

- To a speedy trial
- To keep the victim's contact information confidential

Not only has the victims' rights movement caught on in the United States, it has also had an impact in Europe. The European Union member nations have agreed in principle to a set of rules that creates minimum standards for the protection of victims of crime. These guarantee that all victims should:

- Be treated with respect
- Have their entitlement to a real and appropriate role in criminal proceedings recognized
- Have the right to be heard during proceedings and to supply evidence
- Receive information on: the type of support available; where and how to report an offense; criminal proceedings and their role in them; access to protection and advice; entitlement to compensation; and, if they wish, the outcomes of their complaints, including sentencing and release of the offender
- Have communication safeguards: that is, member states should take measures to minimize communication difficulties in criminal proceedings

- Have access to free legal advice concerning their role in the proceedings and, where appropriate, legal aid
- Receive payment of expenses incurred as a result of participation in criminal proceedings
- Receive reasonable protection, including protection of privacy
- Receive compensation in the course of criminal proceedings
- Receive penal mediation in the course of criminal proceedings where appropriate
- Benefit from various measures to minimize the difficulties faced where victims are residents in another member state, especially when organizing criminal proceedings[172]

A final, albeit controversial, element of the victims' rights movement is the development of offender registration laws that require that the name and sometimes addresses of known sex offenders be posted by law enforcement agencies. Though almost every state has adopted sex offender registration, as you may recall (Chapter 1), these measures have not proven effective.[173] Sex offender registration is indelibly linked to the death of Megan Kanka, an incident described in the Profiles in Crime feature "Jesse Timmendequas and Megan's Law."

SUMMARY

(L01) Discuss the greatest problems faced by crime victims

The costs of victimization can include such things as damaged property, pain and suffering to victims, and the involvement of the police and other agencies of the justice system. The pain and suffering inflicted on an individual can result in the need for long-term medical care and counseling, the loss of wages from not being able to go to work, and reduced quality of life from debilitating injuries and/or fear of being victimized again.

(L02) Know what is meant by the term *cycle of violence*

People who are crime victims may be more likely to commit crime themselves. Some may seek revenge against the people who harmed them. The abuse–crime phenomenon is referred to as the cycle of violence.

(L03) Analyze the victim's role in the crime process

There is an association between crime and victimization, but the linkage is a matter of some debate. One view is the people who are crime victims experience long-term negative consequences that lead them to commit crime. It is also possible that victimization may produce anger, stress, and strain that result in their involvement in antisocial behavior. Victims may seek revenge against the people who harmed them or whom they believe are at fault for their problems. It is also possible that both criminals and victims tend to have the same lifestyle and live in the same neighborhoods, making it seem they are one and the same.

(L04) Assess the ecology of victimization risk

Victimization is more likely to take place in an open, public area, such as a street, a park, or a field. The more serious violent crimes, such as rape and aggravated assault, typically take place after 6 P.M. Those living in the central city have significantly higher rates of theft and violence victimizations than suburbanites; people living in rural areas have a victimization rate almost half that of city dwellers. Schools unfortunately are the site of a great deal of victimization because they are populated by one of the most dangerous segments of society, teenage males.

(L05) Describe the victim's household

The NCVS tells us that within the United States, larger, African American, western, and urban homes are the most vulnerable to crime. In contrast, rural, European American homes in the Northeast are the least likely to contain crime victims or be the target of theft offenses, such as burglary and larceny. People who own their homes are less vulnerable than renters.

(L06) Categorize the most dominant victim characteristics

Except for the crimes of rape and sexual assault, males are more likely than females to be the victims of violent crime. Victim data reveal that young people face a much greater victimization risk than older persons. The poorest Americans are the most likely to be victims of violent and property crime. This association occurs across all gender, age, and racial groups. African Americans are about twice as likely as European Americans to be victims of violent crime. Never-married males and females are victimized more often than married people.

 Explain the concept of repeat victimization

Individuals who have been crime victims have a significantly higher chance of future victimization than people who have remained nonvictims. Households that have experienced victimization in the past are the ones most likely to experience it again in the future. One reason: some victims' physical weakness or psychological distress renders them incapable of resisting or deterring crime and makes them easy targets.

L08 **Compare and contrast the most important theories of victimization**

According to victim precipitation theory, some people may actually initiate the confrontation that eventually leads to their injury or death. Victim precipitation can be either active or passive. Some criminologists believe that people may become crime victims because their lifestyle increases their exposure to criminal offenders. People who have high-risk lifestyles—drinking, taking drugs, getting involved in crime—have a much greater chance of victimization. According to deviant place theory, the greater their exposure to dangerous places, the more likely people are to become victims of crime and violence. Deviant places are poor, densely populated, highly transient neighborhoods in which commercial and residential properties exist side by side. Routine activities theory links victimization to the availability of suitable targets, the absence of capable guardians, and the presence of motivated offenders.

 Assess programs dedicated to caring for the victim

Victim-witness assistance programs are government programs that help crime victims and witnesses; they may include compensation, court services, and/or crisis intervention. Such programs often include victim compensation—financial aid awarded to crime victims to repay them for their loss and injuries; this assistance may cover medical bills, loss of wages, loss of future earnings, and/or counseling. Some programs assign counselors to victims to serve as advocates to help them understand the operation of the justice system and guide them through the process. Every state jurisdiction allows victims to make an impact statement before the sentencing judge. Most victim programs refer victims to specific services to help them recover from their ordeal.

 Articulate why there is a need for victims' rights

Every state now has a set of legal rights for crime victims in its code of laws, often called a Victims' Bill of Rights. These generally include the victim's right to be notified of proceedings and the status of the defendant, to be present at criminal justice proceedings and to make statements at trials, to receive restitution from a convicted offender, and to be consulted about trial procedures, such as when a plea is offered.

CRITICAL THINKING QUESTIONS

1. Considering what you learned in this chapter about crime victimization, what measures can you take to better protect yourself from crime?
2. Do you agree with the assessment that schools are some of the most dangerous locations in the community? Did you find your high school to be a dangerous environment?
3. Does a person bear some of the responsibility for his or her victimization if the person maintains a lifestyle that contributes to the chances of becoming a crime victim? In other words, should we "blame the victim"?
4. Have you ever experienced someone "precipitating" crime? If so, did you do anything to help the situation?
5. Are potential victims justified in using deadly force if they believe their life is in danger even if their assailant is unarmed?

KEY TERMS

victimologists (70)
victimization (70)
posttraumatic stress disorder (PTSD) (72)
obsessive-compulsive disorder (72)

cycle of violence (73)
elder abuse (76)
chronic victimization (77)
victim precipitation theory (78)
active precipitation (79)
passive precipitation (79)

lifestyle theory (79)
deviant place theory (81)
routine activities theory (81)
suitable target (82)
capable guardians (82)
motivated offenders (82)

victim-witness assistance programs (85)
victim compensation (85)
crisis intervention (88)
restitution agreements (88)
target hardening (89)

NOTES

All URLs accessed in 2016.

1. Federal Bureau of Investigation, "Art Crime: The Case of the Stolen Stradivarius," January 23, 2015, https://www.fbi.gov/news/stories/2015/january/the-case-of-the-stolen-stradivarius/the-case-of-the-stolen-stradivarius.

2. Jennifer Truman and Lynn Langton, Bureau of Justice Statistics, *Criminal Victimization, 2014,* http://www.bjs.gov/content/pub/pdf/cv14.pdf.

3. Arthur Lurigio, "Are All Victims Alike? The Adverse, Generalized, and Differential Impact of Crime," *Crime and Delinquency* 33 (1987): 452–467.

4. Mark Cohen, *The Costs of Crime and Justice* (New York: Routledge, 2005); Ted Miller, Mark Cohen, and Brian Wiersema, *Victim Costs and Consequences: A New Look* (Washington, DC: U.S. Department of Justice, 1996).

5. Kathryn McCollister, Michael T. French, and Hai Fang, "The Cost of Crime to Society: New Crime-Specific Estimates for Policy and Program Evaluation," *Drug and Alcohol Dependence* 108 (2010): 98–109.

6. National Institute of Drug Abuse, "Heroin," https://www.drugabuse.gov/publications/research-reports/heroin/letter-director.

7. Sheree Curry, "Fate of a Murder House," AOL Real Estate, February 11, 2010, https://wonderland1981.wordpress.com/2013/10/22/fate-of-a-murder-house/.

8. Michael Tonry, "The Fog Around Cost-of-Crime Studies May Finally Be Clearing, Prisoners and Their Kids Suffer Too," *Criminology and Public Policy* 14 (2015): 653–671.

9. Joseph Murray and David Farrington, "Parental Imprisonment: Effects on Boys' Antisocial Behaviour and Delinquency Through the Life-Course," *Journal of Child Psychology and Psychiatry* 46 (2005): 1269–1278.

10. James Anderson, Terry Grandison, and Laronistine Dyson, "Victims of Random Violence and the Public Health Implication: A Health Care or Criminal Justice Issue?" *Journal of Criminal Justice* 24 (1996): 379–393.

11. Chris Gibson, Zara Morris, and Kevin Beaver, "Secondary Exposure to Violence During Childhood and Adolescence: Does Neighborhood Context Matter?" *Justice Quarterly* 26 (2009): 30–57.

12. Susan Popkin, Victoria Gwlasda, Dennis Rosenbaum, Jean Amendolla, Wendell Johnson, and Lynn Olson, "Combating Crime in Public Housing: A Qualitative and Quantitative Longitudinal Analysis of the Chicago Housing Authority's Anti-Drug Initiative," *Justice Quarterly* 16 (1999): 519–557.

13. Karen Snedker, "Altruistic and Vicarious Fear of Crime: Fear for Others and Gendered Social Roles," *Sociological Forum* 21 (2006): 163–195.

14. Min Xie and David McDowall, "Escaping Crime: The Effects of Direct and Indirect Victimization on Moving," *Criminology* 46 (2008): 809–840.

15. Mirka Smolej and Janne Kivivuori, "The Relation Between Crime News and Fear of Violence," *Journal of Scandinavian Studies in Criminology and Crime Prevention* 7 (2006): 211–227.

16. Matthew Lee and Erica DeHart, "The Influence of a Serial Killer on Changes in Fear of Crime and the Use of Protective Measures: A Survey-Based Case Study of Baton Rouge," *Deviant Behavior* 28 (2007): 1–28.

17. Angela Scarpa, Sara Chiara Haden, and Jimmy Hurley, "Community Violence Victimization and Symptoms of Post-traumatic Stress Disorder: The Moderating Effects of Coping and Social Support," *Journal of Interpersonal Violence* 21 (2006): 446–469.

18. Heather Littleton and Craig Henderson, "If She Is Not a Victim, Does That Mean She Was Not Traumatized? Evaluation of Predictors of PTSD Symptomatology Among College Rape Victims," *Violence Against Women* 15 (2009): 148–167.

19. Mladen Loncar, Neven Henigsberg, and Pero Hrabac, "Mental Health Consequences in Men Exposed to Sexual Abuse During the War in Croatia and Bosnia," *Journal of Interpersonal Violence* 25 (2010): 191–203.

20. David Finkelhor, Heather Turner, and Richard Ormrod, "Kid's Stuff: The Nature and Impact of Peer and Sibling Violence on Younger and Older Children," *Child Abuse and Neglect* 30 (2006): 1401–1421; Dean Kilpatrick, Benjamin Saunders, and Daniel Smith, *Youth Victimization: Prevalence and Implications* (Washington, DC: National Institute of Justice, 2003); Catherine Grus, "Child Abuse: Correlations with Hostile Attributions," *Journal of Developmental and Behavioral Pediatrics* 24 (2003): 296–298.

21. Noora Ilonen, Minna Piispa, Kirsi Peltonen, and Mikko Oranen, "Exposure to Parental Violence and Outcomes of Child Psychosocial Adjustment," *Violence and Victims* 28 (2013): 3–15.

22. Kim Logio, "Gender, Race, Childhood Abuse, and Body Image Among Adolescents," *Violence Against Women* 9 (2003): 931–955.

23. Mark Shevlin, Martin Dorahy, and Gary Adamson, "Childhood Traumas and Hallucinations: An Analysis of the National Comorbidity Survey," *Journal of Psychiatric Research* 41 (2007): 222–228.

24. Jeanne Kaufman and Cathy Spatz Widom, "Childhood Victimization, Running Away, and Delinquency," *Journal of Research in Crime and Delinquency* 36 (1999): 347–370.

25. N. N. Sarkar and Rina Sarkar, "Sexual Assault on Woman: Its Impact on Her Life and Living in Society," *Sexual and Relationship Therapy* 20 (2005): 407–419.

26. Michael Wiederman, Randy Sansone, and Lori Sansone, "History of Trauma and Attempted Suicide Among Women in a Primary Care Setting," *Violence and Victims* 13 (1998): 3–11; Susan Leslie Bryant and Lillian Range, "Suicidality in College Women Who Were Sexually and Physically Abused and Physically Punished by Parents," *Violence and Victims* 10 (1995): 195–215; William Downs and Brenda Miller, "Relationships Between Experiences of Parental Violence During Childhood and Women's Self-Esteem," *Violence and Victims* 13 (1998): 63–78; Sally Davies-Netley, Michael Hurlburt, and Richard Hough, "Childhood Abuse as a Precursor to Homelessness for Homeless Women with Severe Mental Illness," *Violence and Victims* 11 (1996): 129–142.

27. Jane Siegel and Linda Williams, "Risk Factors for Sexual Victimization of Women," *Violence Against Women* 9 (2003): 902–930.

28. Michael Miner, Jill Klotz Flitter, and Beatrice Robinson, "Association of Sexual Revictimization with Sexuality and Psychological Function," *Journal of Interpersonal Violence* 21 (2006): 503–524.

29. Leana Bouffard and Maria Koeppel, "Understanding the Potential Long-Term Physical and Mental Health Consequences of Early Experiences of Victimization," *Justice Quarterly,* first published online October 22, 2012.

30. Lana Stermac and Emily Paradis, "Homeless Women and Victimization: Abuse and Mental Health History Among Homeless Rape Survivors," *Resources for Feminist Research* 28 (2001): 65–81.

31. Danielle Kuhl, David Warner, and Tara Warner, "Intimate Partner Violence Risk Among Victims of Youth Violence: Are Early Unions Bad, Beneficial, or Benign?" *Criminology* 53 (2015): 427–456.

32. Gregory Stuart, Todd M. Moore, Kristina Coop Gordon, Susan Ramsey, and Christopher Kahler, "Psychopathology in Women Arrested for Domestic Violence," *Journal of Interpersonal Violence* 21 (2006): 376–389; Caron Zlotnick, Dawn Johnson, and Robert Kohn, "Intimate Partner Violence and Long-Term Psychosocial Functioning in a National Sample of American Women," *Journal of Interpersonal Violence* 21 (2006): 262–275.

33. K. Daniel O'Leary, "Psychological Abuse: A Variable Deserving Critical Attention in Domestic Violence," *Violence and Victims* 14 (1999): 1–21.

34. Jihong Solomon Zhao, Brian Lawton, and Dennis Longmire, "An Examination of the Micro-Level Crime–Fear of Crime Link," *Crime and Delinquency* 61 (2015): 19–44.

35. Ron Acierno, Alyssa Rheingold, Heidi Resnick, and Dean Kilpatrick, "Predictors of Fear of Crime in Older Adults," *Journal of Anxiety Disorders* 18 (2004): 385–396.

36. Ibid.

37. Smolej and Kivivuori, "The Relation Between Crime News and Fear of Violence."

38. Fawn T. Ngo and Raymond Paternoster, "Toward an Understanding of the Emotional and Behavioral Reactions to Stalking: A Partial Test of General Strain Theory," *Crime and Delinquency*, first published online November 7, 2013.

39. Pamela Wilcox Rountree, "A Reexamination of the Crime–Fear Linkage," *Journal of Research in Crime and Delinquency* 35 (1998): 341–372.

40. Robert Davis, Bruce Taylor, and Arthur Lurigio, "Adjusting to Criminal Victimization: The Correlates of Postcrime Distress," *Violence and Victimization* 11 (1996): 21–34.

41. Karen A. Snedker, "Neighborhood Conditions and Fear of Crime: A Reconsideration of Sex Differences," *Crime and Delinquency* 61 (2015): 45–70.

42. Susan Brison, *Aftermath: Violence and the Remaking of a Self* (Princeton, NJ: Princeton University Press, 2001).

43. Tyler Frederick, Bill McCarthy, and John Hagan, "Perceived Danger and Offending: Exploring the Links Between Violent Victimization and Street Crime," *Violence and Victims* 28 (2013): 16–35.

44. Alex R. Piquero, John MacDonald, Adam Dobrin, Leah E. Daigle, and Francis T. Cullen, "Self-Control, Violent Offending, and Homicide Victimization: Assessing the General Theory of Crime," *Journal of Quantitative Criminology* 25 (2005): 55–71.

45. Cathy Spatz Widom, *The Cycle of Violence* (Washington, DC: National Institute of Justice, 1992), p. 1; Amy Reckdenwald, Christina Mancini, and Eric Beauregard, "The Cycle of Violence: Examining the Impact of Maltreatment Early in Life on Adult Offending," *Violence and Victims* 28 (2013): 466–482.

46. Timothy Ireland and Cathy Spatz Widom, *Childhood Victimization and Risk for Alcohol and Drug Arrests* (Washington, DC: National Institute of Justice, 1995).

47. Marie Skubak Tillyer, and Emily M. Wright, "Intimate Partner Violence and the Victim-Offender Overlap" *Journal of Research in Crime and Delinquency*, first published online April 29, 2013.

48. Min Jung Kim, Emiko Tajima, Todd I. Herrenkohl, and Bu Huang, "Early Child Maltreatment, Runaway Youths, and Risk of Delinquency and Victimization in Adolescence: A Mediational Model," *Social Work Research* 33 (2009): 19–28.

49. Brigette Erwin, Elana Newman, Robert McMackin, Carlo Morrissey, and Danny Kaloupek, "PTSD, Malevolent Environment, and Criminality Among Criminally Involved Male Adolescents," *Criminal Justice and Behavior* 27 (2000): 196–215.

50. Jillian J. Turanovic and Travis C. Pratt, "The Consequences of Maladaptive Coping: Integrating General Strain and Self-Control Theories to Specify a Causal Pathway Between Victimization and Offending," *Journal of Quantitative Criminology* 29 (2013): 321–345.

51. Ulrich Orth, Leo Montada, and Andreas Maercker, "Feelings of Revenge, Retaliation Motive, and Posttraumatic Stress Reactions in Crime Victims," *Journal of Interpersonal Violence* 21 (2006): 229–243.

52. Chris Melde, Finn-Aage Esbensen, and Terrance Taylor, "'May Piece Be with You': A Typological Examination of the Fear and Victimization Hypothesis of Adolescent Weapon Carrying," *Justice Quarterly* 26 (2009): 348–376.

53. Charis Kubrin and Ronald Weitzer, "Retaliatory Homicide: Concentrated Disadvantage and Neighborhood Culture," *Social Problems* 50 (2003): 157–180.

54. Christopher Schreck, Eric Stewart, and D. Wayne Osgood, "A Reappraisal of the Overlap of Violent Offenders and Victims," *Criminology* 46 (2008): 872–906.

55. Christopher Schreck, Mark Berg, Graham Ousey, Eric Stewart, and J. Mitchell Miller, "Does the Nature of the Victimization–Offending Association Fluctuate Over the Life Course? An Examination of Adolescence and Early Adulthood," *Crime and Delinquency*, first published online December 18, 2015.

56. Truman and Langton, *Criminal Victimization, 2014.*

57. Marie Skubak Tillyer and Rob Tillyer, "Violence in Context: A Multilevel Analysis of Victim Injury in Robbery Incidents," *Justice Quarterly* 31 (2014): 767–791.

58. Simone Robers, Anlan Zhang, Rachel Morgan, and Lauren Musu-Gillette, *Indicators of School Crime and Safety: 2014*, National Center for Education Statistics, U.S. Department of Education, and Bureau of Justice Statistics, Office of Justice Programs, U.S. Department of Justice, 2015, http://www.bjs.gov/content/pub/pdf/iscs14.pdf.

59. Pamela Wilcox, Marie Skubak Tillyer, and Bonnie S. Fisher, "Gendered Opportunity? School-Based Adolescent Victimization," *Journal of Research in Crime and Delinquency* 46 (2009): 245–269.

60. Kristin Carbone-Lopez and Janet Lauritsen, "Seasonal Variation in Violent Victimization: Opportunity and the Annual Rhythm of the School Calendar," *Journal of Quantitative Criminology* 29 (2013): 399–422.

61. Sherry Hamby, David Finkelhor, and Heather Turner, "Perpetrator and Victim Gender Patterns for 21 Forms of Youth Victimization in the National Survey of Children's Exposure to Violence," *Violence and Victims* 28 (2013): 915–939.

62. Victoria Titterington, "A Retrospective Investigation of Gender Inequality and Female Homicide Victimization," *Sociological Spectrum* 26 (2006): 205–231.

63. David Finkelhor, Heather Turner, and Richard Ormrod, "Kid's Stuff: The Nature and Impact of Peer and Sibling Violence on Younger and Older Children," *Child Abuse and Neglect* 30 (2006): 1401–1421.

64. Lamar Jordan, "Law Enforcement and the Elderly: A Concern for the 21st Century," *FBI Law Enforcement Bulletin* 71 (2002): 20–24.

65. Data from the National Center for Elder Abuse, 2015, http://www.ncea.aoa.gov /Library/Data/index.aspx#population.

66. Tracy Dietz and James Wright, "Age and Gender Differences and Predictors of Victimization of the Older Homeless," *Journal of Elder Abuse and Neglect* 17 (2005): 37–59.

67. CBS News, *Crimesider*, "Utah Pediatrician Sentenced in Ex-wife's Death," July 8, 2015, http://www.cbsnews.com/news/utah -pediatrician-sentenced-in-ex-wifes-death/.

68. Danielle Kuhl, David Warner, and Andrew Wilczak, "Adolescent Violent Victimization and Precocious Union Formation," *Criminology* 50 (2012): 1089–1127.

69. Mark T. Berg, "Accounting for Racial Disparities in the Nature of Violent Victimization," *Journal of Quantitative Criminology* 30 (2014): 629–650.

70. Karin Wittebrood and Paul Nieuwbeerta, "Criminal Victimization During One's Life Course: The Effects of Previous Victimization and Patterns of Routine Activities," *Journal of Research in Crime and Delinquency* 37 (2000): 91–122; Janet Lauritsen and Kenna Davis Quinet, "Repeat Victimizations Among Adolescents and Young Adults," *Journal of Quantitative Criminology* 11 (1995): 143–163.

71. Marie Skubak Tillyer, Brooke Miller Gialopsos, and Pamela Wilcox, "The Short-Term Repeat Sexual Victimization of Adolescents in School," *Crime and Delinquency*, first published online September 9, 2013.

72. Denise Osborn, Dan Ellingworth, Tim Hope, and Alan Trickett, "Are Repeatedly Victimized Households Different?" *Journal of Quantitative Criminology* 12 (1996): 223–245.

73. Marre Lammers, Barbara Menting, Stijn Ruiter, and Wim Bernasco, "Biting Once, Twice: The Influence of Prior on Subsequent Crime Location Choice," *Criminology* 53 (2015): 309–329.

74. Graham Farrell, "Predicting and Preventing Revictimization," in *Crime and Justice: An Annual Review of Research*, Vol. 20, ed. Michael Tonry and David Farrington (Chicago: University of Chicago Press, 1995), pp. 61–126.

75. Ibid., p. 61.

76. David Finkelhor and Nancy Asigian, "Risk Factors for Youth Victimization: Beyond a Lifestyles/Routine Activities Theory Approach," *Violence and Victimization* 11 (1996): 3–19.

77. Graham Farrell, Coretta Phillips, and Ken Pease, "Like Taking Candy: Why Does Repeat Victimization Occur?" *British Journal of Criminology* 35 (1995): 384–399.

78. Bonnie S. Fisher, Leah E. Daigle, and Francis T. Cullen, "What Distinguishes Single from Recurrent Sexual Victims? The Role of Lifestyle-Routine Activities and First-Incident Characteristics," *Justice Quarterly* 27 (2010): 102–129.

79. Graham C. Ousey, Pamela Wilcox, and Bonnie S. Fisher, "Something Old, Something New: Revisiting Competing Hypotheses of the Victimization–Offending Relationship Among Adolescents," *Journal of Quantitative Criminology*, published online July 2010.

80. Jillian Turanovic and Travis Pratt, "'Can't Stop, Won't Stop': Self-Control, Risky Lifestyles, and Repeat Victimization," *Journal of Quantitative Criminology* 30 (2014): 29–56.

81. Christopher Innes and Lawrence Greenfeld, *Violent State Prisoners and Their Victims* (Washington, DC: Bureau of Justice Statistics, 1990).

82. Hans von Hentig, *The Criminal and His Victim: Studies in the Sociobiology of Crime* (New Haven: Yale University Press, 1948), p. 384; Stephen Schafer, *Victimology: The Victim and His Criminal* (Virginia: Reston, 1977).

83. Marvin Wolfgang, *Patterns of Criminal Homicide* (Philadelphia: University of Pennsylvania Press, 1958).

84. Menachem Amir, *Patterns in Forcible Rape* (Chicago: University of Chicago Press, 1971).

85. Rose Corrigan, *Up Against a Wall: Rape Reform and the Failure of Success* (New York: New York University Press, 2013); Sokratis Dinos, Nina Burrowes, Karen Hammond, and Christina Cunliffe, "A Systematic Review of Juries' Assessment of Rape Victims: Do Rape Myths Impact on Juror Decision-Making?" *International Journal of Law, Crime and Justice* 43 (2015): 36–49.

86. Martin Daly and Margo Wilson, *Homicide* (New York: Aldine de Gruyter, 1988).

87. Edem Avakame, "Female's Labor Force Participation and Intimate Femicide: An Empirical Assessment of the Backlash Hypothesis," *Violence and Victim* 14 (1999): 277–283.

88. Rosemary Gartner and Bill McCarthy, "The Social Distribution of Femicide in Urban Canada, 1921–1988," *Law and Society Review* 25 (1991): 287–311.

89. Jean-Louis van Gelder, Margit Averdijk, Manuel Eisner, and Denis Ribaud, "Unpacking the Victim-Offender Overlap: On Role Differentiation and Socio-psychological Characteristics," *Journal of Quantitative Criminology* 31 (2015): 653–675.

90. Jeffrey Ward, Kathleen Fox, Marie Skubak Tillyer, and Jodi Lane, "Gender, Low Self-Control, and Violent Victimization," *Deviant Behavior* 36 (2015): 113–129.

91. Christopher Schreck, Eric Stewart, and Bonnie Fisher, "Self-Control, Victimization, and Their Influence on Risky Lifestyles: A Longitudinal Analysis Using Panel Data," *Journal of Quantitative Criminology* 22 (2006): 319–340.

92. Bureau of Justice Statistics, "Crime Against Persons with Disabilities, 2009–2013, Statistical Tables," May 2015, http://www.bjs.gov/content/pub/pdf/capd0913st_sum.pdf.

93. Jillian Turanovic, Michael Reisig, and Travis Pratt, "Risky Lifestyles, Low Self-control, and Violent Victimization Across Gendered Pathways to Crime" *Journal of Quantitative Criminology* 31 (2015): 183–206.

94. Dan Hoyt, Kimberly Ryan, and Mari Cauce, "Personal Victimization in a High-Risk Environment: Homeless and Runaway Adolescents," *Journal of Research in Crime and Delinquency* 36 (1999): 371–392.

95. Kimberly Tyler and Morgan Beal, "The High-Risk Environment of Homeless Young Adults: Consequences for Physical and Sexual Victimization," *Violence and Victims* 25 (2010): 101–115.

96. See, generally, Gary Gottfredson and Denise Gottfredson, *Victimization in Schools* (New York: Plenum Press, 1985).

97. Gary Jensen and David Brownfield, "Gender, Lifestyles, and Victimization: Beyond Routine Activity Theory," *Violence and Victims* 1 (1986): 85–99.

98. Marc Tracyjan, "Florida State Settles Suit Over Jameis Winston Rape Inquiry," *New York Times*, January 25, 2016.

99. Bonnie Fisher, John Sloan, Francis Cullen, and Chunmeng Lu, "Crime in the Ivory Tower: The Level and Sources of Student Victimization," *Criminology* 36 (1998): 671–710.

100. Bonnie Fisher, Francis Cullen, and Michael Turner, *The Sexual Victimization of College Women* (Washington, DC: National Institute of Justice, 2001).

101. Elizabeth Reed, Hortensia Amaro, Atsushi Matsumoto, and Debra Kaysen, "The Relation Between Interpersonal Violence and Substance Use Among a Sample of University Students: Examination of the Role of Victim and Perpetrator Substance Use," *Addictive Behaviors* 34 (2009): 316–318.

102. Marget Averdijk and Wim Bernasco, "Testing the Situational Explanation of Victimization Among Adolescents," *Journal of Research in Crime and Delinquency* 52 (2015): 151–180.

103. Michael Ezell and Emily Tanner-Smith, "Examining the Role of Lifestyle and Criminal History Variables on the Risk of Homicide Victimization," *Homicide Studies* 13 (2009): 144–173; Rolf Loeber, Mary DeLamatre, George Tita, Jacqueline Cohen, Magda Stouthamer-Loeber, and David Farrington, "Gun Injury and Mortality: The Delinquent Backgrounds of Juvenile Offenders," *Violence and Victim* 14 (1999): 339–351; Adam Dobrin, "The Risk of Offending on Homicide Victimization: A Case Control Study," *Journal of Research in Crime and Delinquency* 38 (2001): 154–173.

104. Loeber et al., "Gun Injury and Mortality"; Dobrin, "The Risk of Offending on Homicide Victimization."

105. Mark Berg and Rolf Loeber, "Violent Conduct and Victimization Risk in the Urban Illicit Drug Economy: A Prospective Examination," *Justice Quarterly* 32 (2015): 32–55.

106. James Howell, "Youth Gang Homicides: A Literature Review," *Crime and Delinquency* 45 (1999): 208–241.

107. Alan Lizotte and David Sheppard, *Gun Use by Male Juveniles* (Washington, DC: Office of Juvenile Justice and Delinquency Prevention, 2001); Daneen Deptula and Robert Cohen, "Aggressive, Rejected, and Delinquent Children and Adolescents: A Comparison of Their Friendships," *Aggression and Violent Behavior* 9 (2004): 75–104.

108. Sylvie Mrug, Betsy Hoza, and William Bukowski, "Choosing or Being Chosen by Aggressive-Disruptive Peers: Do They Contribute to Children's Externalizing and Internalizing Problems?" *Journal of Abnormal Child Psychology* 32 (2004): 53–66.

109. Daniel Neller, Robert Denney, Christina Pietz, and R. Paul Thomlinson, "Testing the Trauma Model of Violence," *Journal of Family Violence* 20 (2005): 151–159.

110. Andrew Papachristos, Anthony Braga, Eric Piza, and Leigh Grossman, "The Company You Keep? The Spillover Effects of Gang Membership on Individual Gunshot Victimization in a Co-offending Network," *Criminology* 53 (2015): 624–650.

111. Maryse Richards, Reed Larson, and Bobbi Viegas Miller, "Risky and Protective Contexts and Exposure to Violence in Urban African American Young Adolescents," *Journal of Clinical Child and Adolescent Psychology* 33 (2004): 138–148.

112. James Garofalo, "Reassessing the Lifestyle Model of Criminal Victimization," in *Positive Criminology*, ed. Michael Gottfredson and Travis Hirschi (Newbury Park, CA: Sage, 1987), pp. 23–42.

113. Richards, Larson, and Miller, "Risky and Protective Contexts and Exposure to Violence in Urban African American Young Adolescents."

114. Terance Miethe and David McDowall, "Contextual Effects in Models of Criminal Victimization," *Social Forces* 71 (1993): 741–759.

115. Rodney Stark, "Deviant Places: A Theory of the Ecology of Crime," *Criminology* 25 (1987): 893–911.

116. Ibid., p. 902.

117. William Julius Wilson, *The Truly Disadvantaged* (Chicago: University of Chicago Press, 1990); see also Allen Liska and Paul Bellair, "Violent-Crime Rates and Racial Composition: Convergence Over Time," *American Journal of Sociology* 101 (1995): 578–610.

118. Lawrence Cohen and Marcus Felson, "Social Change and Crime Rate Trends: A Routine Activities Approach," *American Sociological Review* 44 (1979): 588–608.

119. Teresa LaGrange, "The Impact of Neighborhoods, Schools, and Malls on the Spatial Distribution of Property Damage," *Journal of Research in Crime and Delinquency* 36 (1999): 393–422.

120. Melanie Wellsmith and Amy Burrell, "The Influence of Purchase Price and Ownership Levels on Theft Targets: The Example of Domestic Burglary," *British Journal of Criminology* 45 (2005): 741–764.

121. Denise Gottfredson and David Soulé, "The Timing of Property Crime, Violent Crime, and Substance Use Among Juveniles," *Journal of Research in Crime and Delinquency* 42 (2005): 110–120.

122. Georgina Hammock and Deborah Richardson, "Perceptions of Rape: The Influence of Closeness of Relationship, Intoxication, and Sex of Participant," *Violence and Victimization* 12 (1997): 237–247.

123. Wittebrood and Nieuwbeerta, "Criminal Victimization During One's Life Course," pp. 112–113.

124. Brandon Welsh and David Farrington, "Surveillance for Crime Prevention in Public Space: Results and Policy Choices in Britain and America," *Criminology and Public Policy* 3 (2004): 701–730.

125. Richard Timothy Coupe and Laurence Blake, "The Effects of Patrol Workloads and Response Strength on Arrests at Burglary Emergencies," *Journal of Criminal Justice* 33 (2005): 239–255.

126. Don Weatherburn, Bronwyn Lind, and Simon Ku, "'Hotbeds of Crime?' Crime and Public Housing in Urban Sydney," *Crime and Delinquency* 45 (1999): 256–271.

127. Andy Hochstetler, "Opportunities and Decisions: Interactional Dynamics in Robbery and Burglary Groups," *Criminology* 39 (2001): 737–763.

128. Richard Felson, "Routine Activities and Involvement in Violence as Actor, Witness, or Target," *Violence and Victimization* 12 (1997): 209–223.

129. Lawrence Cohen, Marcus Felson, and Kenneth Land, "Property Crime Rates in the United States: A Macrodynamic Analysis, 1947–1977, with Ex-ante Forecasts for the Mid-1980s," *American Journal of Sociology* 86 (1980): 90–118.

130. Steven Messner, Lawrence Raffalovich, and Richard McMillan, "Economic Deprivation and Changes in Homicide Arrest Rates for White and Black Youths, 1967–1998: A National Time Series Analysis," *Criminology* 39 (2001): 591–614.

131. Melanie Wellsmith and Amy Burrell, "The Influence of Purchase Price and Ownership Levels on Theft Targets: The Example of Domestic Burglary," *British Journal of Criminology* 45 (2005): 741–764.

132. Terance Miethe and Robert Meier, *Crime and Its Social Context: Toward an Integrated Theory of Offenders, Victims, and Situations* (Albany, NY: State University of New York Press, 1994).

133. Felson, "Routine Activities and Involvement in Violence as Actor, Witness, or Target."

134. Madhur Kulkarni, Nnamdi Pole, and Christine Timko, "Childhood Victimization, Negative Mood Regulation, and Adult PTSD Severity," *Psychological Trauma: Theory, Research, Practice, and Policy* 5 (2013): 359–365.

135. Cassidy Gutner, Shireen Rizvi, Candice Monson, and Patricia Resick, "Changes in Coping Strategies, Relationship to the Perpetrator, and Posttraumatic Distress in Female Crime Victims," *Journal of Traumatic Stress* 19 (2006): 813–823.

136. U.S. Department of Justice, *Report of the President's Task Force on Victims of Crime* (Washington, DC: U.S. Government Printing Office, 1983).

137. Ibid., pp. 2–10; "Review on Victims/ Witnesses of Crime," *Massachusetts Lawyers Weekly*, April 25, 1983, p. 26.

138. Robert Davis, *Crime Victims: Learning How to Help Them* (Washington, DC: National Institute of Justice, 1987).

139. Michael M. O'Hear, "Punishment, Democracy, and Victims," *Federal Sentencing Reporter* 19 (2006): 1.

140. Peter Finn and Beverly Lee, *Establishing a Victim-Witness Assistance Program* (Washington, DC: U.S. Government Printing Office, 1988).

141. This section leans heavily on Albert Roberts, "Delivery of Services to Crime Victims: A National Survey," *American Journal of Orthopsychiatry* 6 (1991):

128–137; see also Albert Roberts, *Helping Crime Victims: Research, Policy, and Practice* (Newbury Park, CA: Sage, 1990).

142. Ibid.

143. National Association of Crime Victim Compensation Boards, http://www.nacvcb.org.

144. National Association of VOCA Assistance Administrators, http://www.navaa.org/.

145. Karen Rich and Patrick Seffrin, "Police Officers' Collaboration with Rape Victim Advocates: Barriers and Facilitators," *Violence and Victims* 28 (2013): 681–696.

146. Rebecca Campbell, "Rape Survivors' Experiences with the Legal and Medical Systems: Do Rape Victim Advocates Make a Difference?" *Violence Against Women* 12 (2006): 30–45.

147. New Hampshire Department of Justice, Office of Victim/Witness Assistance http://doj.nh.gov/criminal/victim-assistance/.

148. National District Attorneys Association, "Anatomical Dolls and Diagrams," http://www.ndaajustice.org/pdf/Anatomical_Dolls_11_7_2014.pdf.

149. Ulrich Orth and Andreas Maercker, "Do Trials of Perpetrators Retraumatize Crime Victims?" *Journal of Interpersonal Violence* 19 (2004): 212–228.

150. Pater Jaffe, Marlies Sudermann, Deborah Reitzel, and Steve Killip, "An Evaluation of a Secondary School Primary Prevention Program on Violence in Intimate Relationships," *Violence and Victims* 7 (1992): 129–145.

151. Good Samaritans Program, http://www.ojp.usdoj.gov/ovc/publications/infores/Good_Samaritans/.

152. Andrew Karmen, "Victim–Offender Reconciliation Programs: Pro and Con," *Perspectives of the American Probation and Parole Association* 20 (1996): 11–14.

153. Information provided by the National Center for Victims of Crime, http://www.victimsofcrime.org/.

154. Rachelle Hong, "Nothing to Fear: Establishing an Equality of Rights for Crime Victims Through the Victims' Rights Amendment," *Notre Dame Journal of Legal Ethics and Public Policy* (2002): 207–225; see also *Payne v. Tennessee*, 111 S.Ct. 2597, 115 L.Ed.2d 720 (1991).

155. Robert Davis and Barbara Smith, "The Effects of Victim Impact Statements on Sentencing Decisions: A Test in an Urban Setting," *Justice Quarterly* 11 (1994): 453–469; Edna Erez and Pamela Tontodonato, "The Effect of Victim Participation in Sentencing on Sentence Outcome," *Criminology* 28 (1990): 451–474.

156. Joel Caplan, "Parole Release Decisions: Impact of Positive and Negative Victim and Nonvictim Input on a Representative Sample of Parole-Eligible Inmates," *Violence and Victims* 25 (2010): 224–242.

157. Douglas E. Beloof, "Constitutional Implications of Crime Victims as

Participants," *Cornell Law Review* 88 (2003): 282–305.

158. James Garofalo and Maureen McLeod, *Improving the Use and Effectiveness of Neighborhood Watch Programs* (Washington, DC: National Institute of Justice, 1988).

159. Peter Finn, *Block Watches Help Crime Victims in Philadelphia* (Washington, DC: National Institute of Justice, 1986).

160. Ibid.

161. Sara Flaherty and Austin Flaherty, *Victims and Victims' Risk* (New York: Chelsea House, 1998).

162. Pamela Wilcox Rountree and Kenneth Land, "Burglary Victimization, Perceptions of Crime Risk, and Routine Activities: A Multilevel Analysis Across Seattle Neighborhoods and Census Tracts," *Journal of Research in Crime and Delinquency* 33 (1996): 1147–1180.

163. Leslie Kennedy, "Going It Alone: Unreported Crime and Individual Self-Help," *Journal of Criminal Justice* 16 (1988): 403–413.

164. Ronald Clarke, "Situational Crime Prevention: Its Theoretical Basis and Practical Scope," in *Annual Review of Criminal Justice Research*, ed. Michael Tonry and Norval Morris (Chicago: University of Chicago Press, 1983).

165. See, generally, Dennis P. Rosenbaum, Arthur J. Lurigio, and Robert C. Davis, *The Prevention of Crime: Social and Situational Strategies* (Belmont, CA: Wadsworth, 1998).

166. Andrew Buck, Simon Hakim, and George Rengert, "Burglar Alarms and the Choice Behavior of Burglars," *Journal of Criminal Justice* 21 (1993): 497–507; for an opposing view, see James Lynch and David Cantor, "Ecological and Behavioral Influences on Property Victimization at Home: Implications for Opportunity Theory," *Journal of Research in Crime and Delinquency* 29 (1992): 335–362.

167. Ráchael Powers, "Consequences of Using Self-Protective Behaviors in Nonsexual Assaults: The Differential Risk of Completion and Injury by Victim Sex," *Violence and Victims* 30 (2015): 846–869.

168. Gary Kleck, "Defensive Gun Use Is Not a Myth," *Politico*, February 17, 2015, http://www.politico.com/magazine/story/2015/02/defensive-gun-ownership-gary-kleck-response-115082.html; Gary Kleck, *Targeting Guns: Firearms and Their Control* (Hawthorne, NY: Aldine de Gruyter, 1997); Gary Kleck and Marc Gertz, "Armed Resistance to Crime: The Prevalence and Nature of Self-Defense with a Gun," *Journal of Criminal Law and Criminology* 86 (1995): 150–187; Gary Kleck, *Point Blank: Guns and Violence in America* (Hawthorne, NY: Aldine de Gruyter, 1991).

169. Jongyeon Tark and Gary Kleck, "Resisting Rape: The Effects of Victim Self-Protection on Rape Completion and Injury," *Violence Against Women* 20 (2014): 270–292; Jongyeon Tark and Gary Kleck, "Resisting Crime: The Effects of Victim Action on the Outcomes of Crimes," *Criminology* 42 (2004): 861–909.

170. See Frank Carrington, "Victim's Rights Litigation: A Wave of the Future," in *Perspectives on Crime Victims*, ed. Burt Galaway and Joe Hudson (St. Louis: Mosby, 1981).

171. National Center for Victims of Crime, http://www.victimsofcrime.org/.

172. "Council Framework Decision of 15 March 2001 on the Standing of Victims in Criminal Proceedings," http://eur-lex.europa.eu/LexUriServ/LexUriServ.do?uri=OJ:L:2001:082:0001:0004:EN:PDF; "Proposal for a Council Directive on Compensation to Crime Victims," http://ec.europa.eu/civiljustice/comp_crime_victim/comp_crime_victim_ec_en.htm.

173. U.S. Department of Justice, Dru Sjodin National Sex Offender Public Registry, http://www.nsopr.gov.

PART TWO | THEORIES OF CRIME CAUSATION

An important goal of criminologists is to create valid and accurate theories of crime causation. A theory can be defined as an abstract statement that explains why certain phenomena or things do (or do not) happen. A valid theory must (a) have the ability to predict future occurrences or observations of the phenomenon in question and (b) have the ability to be validated or tested through experiment or some other form of empirical observation. So, if a theory states that watching violent TV shows leads to aggressive behavior, it can be considered valid only if careful and empirically sound tests can prove that kids who watch a lot of violent TV in the present will become violent sometime in the future.

Criminologists have sought to collect vital facts about crime and interpret them in a scientifically meaningful fashion. By developing empirically verifiable statements, or hypotheses, and organizing them into theories of crime causation, they hope to identify the causes of crime.

Since the late nineteenth century, criminological theory has pointed to various underlying causes of crime. The earliest theories generally attributed crime to a single underlying cause: atypical body build, genetic abnormality, insanity, physical anomalies, socialization, or poverty. More recent theoretical efforts are more dynamic, incorporating multiple personal and social factors into a complex web to explain the onset, continuation, and eventual desistance from a criminal career.

In this section, theories of crime causation are grouped into six chapters. Chapters 4 and 5 focus on theories that view crime as based on individual traits. They hold that crime is either a free will choice made by an individual, a function of personal psychological or biological abnormality, or both. Chapters 6, 7, and 8 investigate theories based in sociology and political economy. These theories portray crime as a function of the structure, process, and conflicts of social living. Chapter 9 is devoted to theories that combine or integrate a number of concepts that explain criminal behavior over the life course, otherwise known as developmental views of crime.

LEARNING OBJECTIVES

LO1 Describe the development of rational choice theory

LO2 Discuss the most important concepts of rational choice theory

LO3 Analyze the process in which offenders structure criminality

LO4 Depict in your own words how criminals structure crime

LO5 Clarify the arguments that crime is rational

LO6 Identify the elements of the CRAVED model of crime choice

LO7 Assess the validity of situational crime prevention techniques for reducing crime

LO8 Categorize the elements of general deterrence

LO9 Articulate the basic concepts of specific deterrence

LO10 Critique the incapacitation strategy to reduce crime

4 RATIONAL CHOICE THEORY

n 2015, Michael Wymer was sentenced to 27 years in prison after being convicted, along with 13 co-conspirators—including his son, two brothers, and two nephews—of charges relating to setting up a criminal enterprise designed to steal trucks, disassemble them in his chop shop in Toledo, Ohio, and sell them as scrap metal.

Wymer's scheme was quite complex. He and his fellow conspirators would travel outside of the Toledo area—including to Michigan and Indiana—to steal trucks so they could avoid detection by one single jurisdiction. They would go "shop" for semi-trucks and trailers at truck stops or other locations that were fairly close to interstate highways. If they were traveling in Wymer's personally owned semi-truck (minus a trailer), they would back the truck onto the trailer they wanted and then tow it away. If in the car, one or two of the thieves would break into an empty semi-truck with an attached trailer, manipulate the ignition to get it started, and drive the entire vehicle onto the closest interstate highway.

The Wymer team preferred items that could be chopped into scrap metal—so they stole things like motorcycles, all-terrain vehicles, copper wire, spools of metal, even actual loads of scrap metal. How did they know what the trucks were hauling? By breaking into the trailers and taking a look.

Once back in Toledo with the stolen property, Wymer would take the truck to one of his two chop shop locations, where he had everything he needed—from heavy moving equipment and floor jacks to blow torches and chain saws. He would remove and sell parts from the truck and then "chop" the rest of the truck, the trailer, and the trailer's contents into scrap metal within a couple of hours. He would then load the material into one of his trucks and transport it to various businesses and/or recycling companies interested in buying scrap metal. Video surveillance cameras were used to keep an eye on his chop shop locations. Adding to the evidence was video footage from cameras placed by Wymer himself inside his chop shops to keep an eye on his merchandise. All the evidence needed to convict was on film![1]

Wymer's 27-year sentence most likely means that the 56-year-old will never be free again. One reason for the harsh sentence: Wymer had served previous prison time for operating a chop shop, and resumed the business almost as soon as he was released. At his sentencing hearing, Judge James Carr told Wymer, "If I have ever seen a career criminal, you are it. And I want to see to it that your career ends today and you can never resume it."[2]

he Wymer case clearly illustrates that the decision to commit crimes involves rational actions and planned decision making, designed to maximize profits and avoid detection. Rather than being unthinking and spontaneous, most crimes involve thought and planning. Law violators such as Wymer carefully plan their activities, buy the proper equipment, try to avoid detection, and then attempt to squirrel away their criminal profits in some hidden bank account. Some criminologists go as far as suggesting that the source of all criminal violations—even those that seem at first glance unplanned and spontaneous, such as vandalizing property or getting involved in a brawl—rests upon at least some sort of rational decision making with a clear motivation: greed, revenge, need, anger, lust, jealousy, thrill-seeking, or vanity. But the final decision to commit a crime is only made after the likely offender carefully weighs the potential benefits and consequences of their planned action and decides that the benefits of crime are greater than its consequences:

- The jealous suitor concludes that the risk of punishment is worth the satisfaction of punching a rival in the nose.
- The greedy shopper considers the chance of apprehension by store detectives so small that she takes a "five-finger discount" on a new sweater.
- The drug dealer concludes that the huge profit from a single shipment of cocaine far outweighs the possible costs of apprehension.
- The schoolyard bully carefully selects his next victim—someone who is weak, unpopular, and probably won't fight back.
- The college student downloads a program that allows her to illegally copy music onto her iPod.

But can all crimes be a function of planning and calculation? While we can easily assume that calculating thieves such as Michael Wymer use planning, organization, and rational decision making when they commit their crimes, is it possible that serial rapists and mass killers are equally thoughtful and cunning? Can their actions be considered calculated and shrewd or random and senseless? Would they assault or attack someone much larger and muscular who would fight back and injure them severely? Or is the decision to attack someone made after calculating the costs and benefits of the confrontation?

Some criminologists believe that most (if not all) criminal behavior, no matter how destructive or seemingly irresponsible, is actually a matter of thought and decision making. As a group, they are referred to as rational choice theorists. This chapter reviews the philosophical underpinnings of rational choice theory, tracing it back to the classical school of criminology.

We then turn to more recent theoretical models that flow from the concept of choice. These models hold that because criminals are rational, their behavior can be controlled or deterred by the fear of punishment; desistance can be explained by a growing and intense fear of criminal sanctions. While this seems logical, many criminals like Michael Wymer have been punished in the past but soon return to a criminal way of life. Is it possible that severe sanctions, even a stay in prison, do little to deter people from criminal careers? To help answer this question, this chapter reviews methods of crime control based on rational choice, including situational crime control, general deterrence, specific deterrence, and incapacitation. Finally, the chapter briefly reviews how choice theory has influenced criminal justice policy.

The Development of Rational Choice

L01 Describe the development of rational choice theory

During the early Middle Ages (1200–1400), superstition and fear of satanic possession dominated thinking. People who violated social norms or religious practices were believed to be witches or possessed by demons and not rational decision makers. St. Thomas Aquinas (1225–1274) argued that there was a God-given "natural law" that was based on people's natural tendency to do good. People who were evil were manifesting original sin and a fall from grace, similar to that experienced by Adam and Eve when they were expelled from the Garden of Eden.

The prescribed method for dealing with the possessed was burning at the stake, a practice that survived into the seventeenth century. Beginning in the mid-thirteenth century, the jurisdiction of central governments reached a significantly broader range of social behaviors. Human problems and conflicts began to be dealt with in a formalized and legal manner.[3] Nonetheless, superstition and harsh punishments did not end quickly. The authorities were on guard against Satan's offspring, who engaged in acts ranging from witchcraft to robbery. Between 1581 and 1590, Nicholas Remy, head of the Inquisition in the French province of Lorraine, ordered 900 sorcerers and witches burned to death; likewise, Peter Binsfield, the bishop of the German city of Trier, ordered the death of 6,500 people. An estimated 100,000 people were prosecuted throughout Europe for witchcraft during the sixteenth and seventeenth centuries. It was also commonly believed that some families produced offspring who were unsound or unstable and that social misfits were inherently damaged by reason of their "inferior blood."[4] It was common practice to use cruel tortures to extract confessions, and those convicted of violent or theft crimes suffered extremely harsh penalties, including whipping, branding, maiming, and execution. Almost all felons were punished with death; the law made little distinction between thieves and murderers.

This rather fantastical vision of deviant behavior and its control began to wane as new insights were developed about human nature and behavior during the Renaissance. One influential authority, philosopher Thomas Hobbes (1588–1678), suggested the existence of a "social contract" between people and the state: people naturally pursue their own self-interests but are rational enough to realize that selfishness will produce social chaos, so they agree to give up their own selfish interests as long as everyone else does the same thing. Not all agree to the social contract, and therefore the state became empowered with the right to use force to maintain the contract.

DEVELOPMENT OF CLASSICAL CRIMINOLOGY

During the eighteenth-century **Enlightenment** period, social philosophers such as Jeremy Bentham (1748–1833) began to embrace the view that human behavior was a result of rational thought processes.

According to Bentham's "utilitarian calculus," people choose to act when, after weighing costs and benefits, they believe that their actions will bring them an increase in pleasure and a reduction of pain. It stands to reason that criminal behavior could be eliminated or controlled if would-be law violators could be convinced that the pain of punishment exceeds the benefits of crime.[5] The purpose of law is to produce and support the total happiness of the community it serves. Because punishment is in itself harmful, its existence is justified only if it promises to prevent greater evil than it creates. Punishment, therefore, has four main objectives:

1. To prevent all criminal offenses
2. When it cannot prevent a crime, to convince the offender to commit a less serious crime
3. To ensure that a criminal uses no more force than is necessary
4. To prevent crime as cheaply as possible[6]

CESARE BECCARIA

The development of rational classical criminology is most closely identified with the thoughts of Italian social philosopher Cesare Beccaria (1738–1794) and his famous treatise "On Crimes and Punishment" in which he called for fair and certain punishment to deter crime. Beccaria believed people are egotistical and self-centered, and therefore they must be motivated by the fear of punishment, which provides a tangible motive for them to obey the law and suppress the "despotic spirit" that resides in every person.[7] He suggested that (a) people choose all behavior, including criminal behavior; (b) their choices are designed to bring them pleasure and reduce pain; (c) criminal choices can be controlled by fear of punishment; and (d) the *more severe, certain, and swift the punishment*, the greater its ability to control criminal behavior.

According to Beccaria, punishment must be proportional to the seriousness of crime; if not, people would be encouraged to commit more serious offenses. If robbery, rape, and murder were all punished by death, robbers or rapists would have little reason to refrain from killing their victims to eliminate them as witnesses to the crime. Today, this is referred to as the concept of **marginal deterrence**—if petty offenses were subject to the same punishment as more serious crimes, offenders would choose the more serious crime because the resulting punishment would be about the same.[8]

Beccaria also suggested that the extremely harsh punishments of the day and routine use of torture were inappropriate and excessive. To deter crime, the pain of punishment must be administered in a fair, balanced, and proportionate amount, just enough to counterbalance the pleasure obtained from crime. Beccaria stated his famous theorem like this:

> In order for punishment not to be in every instance, an act of violence of one or many against a private citizen, it must be essentially public, prompt, necessary, the least possible in the given circumstances, proportionate to the crimes, and dictated by the laws.[9]

To read more about Beccaria, go to **http://www .iep.utm.edu/beccaria/**.
How have Beccaria's ideas influenced contemporary criminal law in the United States?

CLASSICAL CRIMINOLOGY

The writings of Beccaria and his followers form the core of what today is referred to as **classical criminology**. As originally conceived in the eighteenth century, classical criminology theory had several basic elements:

- In every society, people have free will to choose criminal or lawful solutions to meet their needs or settle their problems.
- Criminal solutions can be very attractive because for little effort they hold the promise of a huge payoff.

Enlightenment A philosophical, intellectual, and cultural movement of the seventeenth and eighteenth centuries that stressed reason, logic, criticism, education, and freedom of thought over dogma and superstition.

marginal deterrence The concept that a penalty for a crime may prompt commission of a marginally more severe crime because that crime receives the same magnitude of punishment as the original one.

classical criminology Eighteenth-century social thinkers believed that criminals choose to commit crime and that crime can be controlled by judicious punishment.

- A person will choose not to commit crime only if he or she believes that the pain of expected punishment is greater than the promise of reward. This is the principle of deterrence.
- In order to be an effective crime deterrent, punishment must be severe, certain, and swift enough to convince potential criminals that "crime does not pay."

The classical perspective influenced penal practices for more than 200 years. The law was made proportionate to crime so that the most serious offenses earned the harshest punishments. Executions were still widely used but slowly began to be employed for only the most serious crimes. The catchphrase was "let the punishment fit the crime."

Beccaria's ideas and writings inspired social thinkers to believe that criminals choose to commit crime and that crime can be controlled by judicious punishment. His vision was widely accepted throughout Europe and the United States.[10]

This vision was embraced by France's post-revolutionary Constituent Assembly (1789) in its Declaration of the Rights of Man:

> [T]he law has the right to prohibit only actions harmful to society. . . . The law shall inflict only such punishments as are strictly and clearly necessary . . . no person shall be punished except by virtue of a law enacted and promulgated previous to the crime and applicable to its terms.

Similarly, a prohibition against cruel and unusual punishment was incorporated in the Eighth Amendment to the U.S. Constitution.

Beccaria's writings have been credited as the basis of the elimination of torture and severe punishment in the nineteenth century. The practice of incarcerating criminals and structuring prison sentences to fit the severity of crime was a reflection of his classical criminology.

By the end of the nineteenth century, the popularity of the classical approach began to decline, and by the middle of the twentieth century, this perspective was neglected by mainstream criminologists. During this period, criminologists focused on internal and external factors—poverty, IQ, education, home life—which were believed to be the true causes of criminality. Because these conditions could not be easily manipulated, the concept of punishing people for behaviors beyond their control seemed both foolish and cruel. Although classical principles still controlled the way police, courts, and correctional agencies operated, most criminologists rejected classical criminology as an explanation of criminal behavior.

CONTEMPORARY CHOICE THEORY EMERGES

Beginning in the mid-1970s, there was renewed interest in the classical approach to crime. First, the rehabilitation of known criminals came under attack. According to liberal criminology, if crime was caused by some social or psychological problem, such as poverty, then crime rates could be reduced by providing good jobs and economic opportunities. Despite some notable efforts to provide such opportunities, a number of national surveys (the best known being Robert Martinson's "What Works?") failed to find examples of rehabilitation programs that prevented future criminal activity.[11] A well-publicized book, *Beyond Probation*, by Charles Murray and Louis Cox, went as far as suggesting that punishment-oriented programs could suppress future criminality much more effectively than those that relied on rehabilitation and treatment efforts.[12]

A significant increase in the reported crime rate, as well as serious disturbances in the nation's prisons, frightened the general public. The media depicted criminals as callous and dangerous rather than as needy people deserving of public sympathy. Some criminologists began to suggest that it made more sense to frighten these cold calculators with severe punishments than to waste public funds by futilely trying to improve entrenched social conditions linked to crime, such as poverty.[13]

Thinking About Crime In the 1970s, a number of criminologists began producing books and monographs expounding the theme that criminals are rational actors who plan their crimes, fear punishment, and deserve to be penalized for their misdeeds. In a 1975 book that came to symbolize renewed interest in classical views, *Thinking About Crime*, political scientist James Q. Wilson debunked the view that crime was a function of external forces, such as poverty, that could be altered by government programs. Instead, he argued, efforts should be made to reduce criminal opportunity by deterring would-be offenders and incarcerating known criminals. People who are likely to commit crime, he maintained, lack inhibition against misconduct, value the excitement and thrills of breaking the law, have a low stake in conformity, and are willing to take greater chances than the average person. If they could be convinced that their actions will bring severe punishment, only the totally irrational would be willing to engage in crime.[14] Wilson made this famous observation:

> Wicked people exist. Nothing avails except to set them apart from innocent people. And many people, neither wicked nor innocent, but watchful, dissembling, and calculating of their chances, ponder our reaction to wickedness as a clue to what they might profitably do.[15]

Here Wilson is saying that unless we react forcefully to crime, those "sitting on the fence" will get a clear message—crime pays.

 To read a famous talk given by James Wilson, "Two Nations," the 1997 Francis Boyer lecture delivered at the annual dinner of the American Enterprise Institute, visit **https://www.aei.org/publication /two-nations-3/**.
Wilson says "Religion, independent of social class, reduces deviance." Do you agree?

Impact on Crime Control   Wilson's book was part of the conservative shift in U.S. crime control policy in the 1980s that led to tough new laws creating mandatory prison sentences for many different crimes, including drug dealing. There was a prison construction boom and the nation's prison population skyrocketed.[16] A disproportionate number of young minority men were locked up for drug law violations; more than half of the prison population is now African American or Hispanic.[17] The "get tough" attitude was buoyed by the fact that as the prison population grew to new heights, the crime rate has been in a steep decline. To some this meant that a "lock 'em up" correctional policy can produce markedly lower crime rates. To others, it was an abandonment of the liberal rehabilitation and treatment philosophy.[18]

 Even if the death penalty were an effective deterrent, some critics believe it presents ethical problems that make its use morally dubious. For more information about what the American Civil Liberties Union has to say, visit **https://www.aclu.org/issues /capital-punishment**.
Do you agree with the ACLU positions on capital punishment?

The Concepts of Rational Choice

 LO2 Discuss the most important concepts of rational choice theory

From these roots, a more contemporary version of classical theory has evolved, referred to as **rational choice theory**. It is based on the premise that criminal decision making is rational and coherent, not spontaneous or impulsive.[19] The decision to commit crime is shaped by human emotions and thought processes, influenced by social relationships, individual traits and capabilities, and environmental characteristics. So this new version of rational choice theory assumes that human behavior is both "willful and determined."[20]

According to the contemporary rational choice approach, law-violating behavior occurs when an offender decides to risk breaking the law after considering both personal factors (i.e., the need for money, revenge, thrills, and entertainment) and situational factors (i.e., how well a target is protected and the efficiency of the local police force). People who believe that the risks of crime outweigh the rewards may decide to go straight. If they think they are likely to be arrested and punished, they are more likely to seek treatment and turn their lives around than risk criminal activities.[21]

WHY CRIME?

The core premise of rational choice theory is that people will choose crime if the circumstances are right: great reward with little risk. Though the consequences can be painful, costly, and embarrassing, for some people choosing crime is actually an easy decision to make. Take adolescents, who regularly violate the law. The criminal lifestyle fits well with this group, whose members routinely organize their lives around risk taking and partying. Crimes can provide money for drugs and alcohol and serve as an ideal method for displaying courage and fearlessness to one's running mates. Rather than creating overwhelming social problems, a criminal way of life can be extremely beneficial, helping kids overcome the problems and stress they face in their daily lives.

Crime also can help some people, especially teens, achieve a sense of control or mastery over their environment. Adolescents in particular may find themselves feeling out of control because society limits their opportunities and resources.[22] Antisocial behavior gives them the opportunity to exert control over their own lives and destinies by helping

rational choice theory The view that crime is a function of a decision-making process in which the potential offender weighs the potential costs and benefits of an illegal act.

them avoid situations they find uncomfortable or repellant (e.g., running away from an abusive home) and can help them obtain resources for desired activities and commodities (e.g., stealing or selling drugs to buy stylish outfits).[23] Crime may also help them boost their self-esteem by attacking perceived enemies (e.g., they vandalize the property of an adult who has called the cops on them). Drinking and drug taking may help some kids ward off depression and compensate for a lack of positive experiences; they learn how to self-medicate. Some, angry at their mistreatment, may turn to violence to satisfy a desire for revenge or retaliation.[24]

Engaging in risky behavior helps some people feel alive and competent. Some turn to substance abuse to increase their sense of personal power, to become more assertive, and reduce tension and anxiety.[25] Others embrace a deviant lifestyle to compensate for their feelings of powerlessness or ordinariness. There is also evidence that antisocial acts can provide positive solutions to problems. Violent kids may have learned that being aggressive with others is a good means to control the situation and get what they want; counterattacks may be one means of controlling people who are treating them poorly.[26] So while most of us see crime as a poor choice that can result in many unhappy and unwanted consequences, for some people choosing crime can bring desired social, economic, and psychic benefits; it can be a good choice despite its consequences.

CHOOSING CRIME

Even those who decide to enter a criminal way of life do not commit crime all the time. People who commit crime go to school, church, or work; they have family time, engage in romances, play sports, and go to movies. Why do they choose to commit a particular crime at a particular time?

Before choosing to commit a crime, **reasoning criminals** evaluate the risk of apprehension, the seriousness of expected punishment, the potential value of the criminal enterprise, and their immediate need for criminal gain; their behavior is systematic and selective. Burglars choose targets based on their value, novelty, and resale potential. A piece of electronic gear such as the newest iPhone or iPad may be a prime target because it has not yet saturated the market and still retains high value.[27]

---

reasoning criminal According to the rational choice approach, law-violating behavior occurs when an offender decides to risk breaking the law after considering both personal factors (such as the need for money, revenge, thrills, and entertainment) and situational factors (how well a target is protected and the efficiency of the local police force).

human agency A person's ability to intentionally make choices based on free will.

Risk evaluations may cover a wide range of topics: What's the chance of getting caught? How difficult will it be to commit the crime? Is the profit worth the effort? Should I risk committing crime in my own neighborhood where I know the territory, or is it worth traveling to a strange place in order to increase my profits?[28]

People who decide to get involved in crime weigh up the chances of arrest (based on their past experiences), plus the subjective psychic rewards of crime, including the excitement and social status it brings and perceived opportunities for easy gains. If the rewards are great, the perceived risk small, and the excitement high, the likelihood of committing additional crimes increases.[29] Successful thieves say they will do it again in the future; past experience has taught them the rewards of illegal behavior.[30] The decision to commit crime is shaped by **human agency**, a topic covered in the Criminology in Action feature entitled "Human Agency, Personal Assessment, Crime, and Desistance."

Criminals, then, are people who share the same ambitions as conventional citizens but have decided to cut corners and use illegal means to achieve their goals. Many criminal offenders retain conventional American values of striving for success, material attainment, and hard work.[31] Even drug dealers express motivations not dissimilar from the average citizen: they are upwardly mobile, scrambling around to obtain their "piece of the pie."[32] If they commit crime, it is because they have chosen an illegal path to obtain the goals that might otherwise have been out of reach.

Choosing Noncrime Considering its benefits, why do most at-risk people choose not to commit crime? While crime may provide short-run solutions that are appealing to adolescents, it becomes less attractive as a long-term answer to personal problems. The decision to forgo crime and seek other means to solve problems may occur when those who contemplate crime realize that risks outweigh rewards:

- They stand a good chance of being caught and punished.
- They begin to fear the consequences of punishment.
- They learn that crime rarely pays as well as they thought.
- They risk losing the respect of their peers, damaging their reputations, and experiencing feelings of guilt or shame.[33]
- They grasp the fact that the risk of apprehension outweighs the profit and/or pleasure of crime.[34]

These issues escalate as people mature and begin to appreciate the dangers of using crime to solve problems.[35] Going to a drunken frat party may sound appealing to sophomores who want to improve their social life, but the risks involved to safety and reputation make such parties off limits as people grow older. As people mature, their thinking extends farther into the future, and risky behavior is a threat to long-range plans.

04

Human Agency, Personal Assessment, Crime, and Desistance

Recently, criminologists Robert Agnew and Steven Messner recognized the central role human agency and personal assessments make in the decision to commit crime. After carefully reviewing the literature, they conclude that human agency—the ability to intentionally make choices that are not fully determined by forces beyond the individual's control—plays a major role in shaping personal assessments.

So, given the same set of prior conditions, one person may choose crime to get what they want while another person relies on more conventional and law abiding solutions.

People also use human agency to assess their life experiences and immediate personal situation. Crime becomes a reasonable alternative when, after making these assessments:

- They come to believe that crime pays. Offenders believe that crime is the best and maybe the only way for them to get ahead financially and that it provides emotional benefits as well, such as satisfaction and excitement.
- They believe that conventional success, such as decent jobs and respectable status, is beyond reach.
- Crime is considered something necessary and/or expected. There is no guilt for crimes because crime is considered acceptable, attractive, and desirable.
- They assess that their bond to conventional society is severed beyond

repair and that consequently they have little to lose by committing crime.
- They decide to adopt identities favorable to crime, although they do not necessarily think of themselves as "criminals." They may view themselves as thieves, hustlers, gangstas, gang bangers, thugs, crazy, wild, outlaws, hardmen, badasses, real men, and/or other identities conducive to crime. Choosing a "bad identity" involves an emphasis on masculinity, as defined by physical and emotional toughness.

Assessments are also made when an offender decides to desist. Agnew and Messner find that offenders desist following major life changes or turning points during the life course, such as getting married or finding a good job. These changes in life circumstances are most likely to lead to desistance when they are associated with or prompt "cognitive shifts" (or "cognitive transformations" or the adoption of "redemption scripts"). These shifts correspond with reassessing one's life and circumstances. Crime is no longer as attractive as it used to be. Criminal identities, such as gangsta or playa, no longer seem compatible with the current lifestyle. Thereafter the person chooses another persona—devoted husband, good father, enterprising worker—that is incompatible with crime. Here we can see how change in life circumstances may bring about personal reassessment, cognitive change, and desistance from crime. Why

do some people choose to remain chronic offenders even if their life circumstances change? They can but decide not to take that step toward cognitive transformations. Individuals must take the initiative to reassess their lives and make a commitment to stop offending: self-efficacy, or the perceived ability to stop offending, is a key trait of desisters.

The decision to commit crime and the decision to stop rest on the general assessment of life circumstances. Because different people assess their lives differently, the concept of assessment can help explain why given the same set of circumstances one person will choose crime while another remains law abiding and conventional.

🔎 CRITICAL THINKING

Cognitive shifts occur when people reassess their life circumstances: something happens, something changes, and suddenly their current path no longer seems relevant. Has that ever happened to you? Has something suddenly knocked you off your game and changed your life?

SOURCES: Robert Agnew and Steven F. Messner, "General Assessments and Thresholds for Chronic Offending: An Enriched Paradigm for Explaining Crime," *Criminology* 53 (2015): 571–596.

OFFENSE AND OFFENDER

Rational choice theorists view crime as both offense- and offender-specific.[36] That a crime is **offense-specific** means that offenders will react selectively to the characteristics of an individual criminal act. Take for instance the decision to commit a burglary. The thought process might include:

- Evaluating the target yield
- Probability of security devices

- Police patrol effectiveness
- Ease of escape
- Effort needed to dispose of stolen merchandise
- Presence of occupants
- Neighbors who might notice a break-in

offense-specific crime The idea that offenders react selectively to the characteristics of particular crimes.

- Presence of guard dogs
- Presence of escape routes
- Entry points and exits

The fact that a crime is **offender-specific** means that criminals are not robots who engage in unthinking, unplanned random acts of antisocial behavior. Before deciding to commit crime, individuals must decide whether they have the prerequisites to commit a successful criminal act. This might include evaluation of:

- Whether they possess the necessary skills to commit the crime

offender-specific crime The idea that offenders evaluate their skills, motives, needs, and fears before deciding to commit crime.

criminality A personal trait of the individual as distinct from a "crime," which is an event.

- Their immediate need for money or other valuables
- Whether legitimate financial alternatives to crime exist, such as a high-paying job
- Whether they have available resources to commit the crime
- Their fear of expected apprehension and punishment
- Availability of alternative criminal acts, such as selling drugs
- Physical ability, including health, strength, and dexterity

Note the distinction made here between crime and criminality.[37] Crime is an event; **criminality** is a personal trait. Professional criminals do not commit crime all the time, and even ordinary citizens may, on occasion, violate the law. Some people considered high risk because they are indigent or disturbed may never violate the law, whereas others who are seemingly affluent and well adjusted may risk criminal behavior given enough provocation and/or opportunity. What conditions promote crime and enhance criminality?

STRUCTURING CRIMINALITY

 L03 Analyze the process in which offenders structure criminality

The decision to commit crime is shaped by both personal factors and situational conditions. Time, place, audience, guardianship, and other factors all play a role in criminal decision making.

Analysis of the situational factors that draw people into criminal events have identified peers and guardianship, thrills and excitement, economic opportunity, learning and experience, and knowledge of criminal techniques as being among the most important.

Peers and Guardianship   Guardianship plays an important role in criminal decision making. Monitoring by parents reduces the likelihood kids will commit crime; hanging out with adolescent friends increases the risk.[38] Kids are more likely to choose crime when they are drinking with their buddies, in a public space, without adult supervision. In the absence of peer support and the presence of adult supervision, that choice is less likely to occur.[39]

Differences in guardianship and peer relations help explain gender differences in the crime rate. Adolescent girls are more likely to experience direct and indirect supervision in their social activities, including their parents insisting on knowing where they are, with whom they are socializing, and where and how the socializing is taking place—for example, a friend's parents must be home. Adolescent boys are given more freedom to socialize as they wish.[40] Because of this control, girls are more likely to socialize at home than their male peers, a restriction that limits their opportunities for deviance.

Rational choice theorists view the offense and offenders as separate elements in a criminal event. Under some circumstances anyone may commit crime and in others even highly motivated offenders will refrain from criminal acts. Why does someone like Alexis Wright, 30, here leaving the Cumberland County Courthouse, a Zumba fitness instructor in Portland, Maine, engage in prostitution? Was there another path she might have traveled? Why people choose crime is a question that rational choice theorists seek to answer.

AP Images/Robert F. Bukaty

Because they are less likely to be monitored, adolescent males are free to roam public places where they find more opportunities to engage in delinquent behavior. When girls do go out, they tend to gather in places like shopping malls, where there are security guards and cameras that monitor behavior and limit criminal choice.

Excitement and Thrills Some criminal offenders may engage in illegal behavior because they love the excitement and thrills that crime can provide. In his highly influential work *Seductions of Crime*, sociologist Jack Katz argues that there are immediate benefits to criminality that "seduce" people into a life of crime.[41] For some people, shoplifting and vandalism are attractive because getting away with crime is a thrilling demonstration of personal competence; Katz calls this "sneaky thrills." The need for excitement may counter fear of apprehension and punishment. In fact, some offenders will deliberately seek out especially risky situations because of the added "thrill." The need for excitement is a significant predictor of criminal choice.[42]

Economic Opportunity Perceptions of economic opportunity influence the decision to commit crime. Some people may engage in criminal activity simply because they need the money to support their lifestyle and perceive few other potential income sources. Sociologists Melissa Thompson and Christopher Uggen found that people who begin taking hard drugs also increase their involvement in crime, taking in from $500 to $700 per month. Once they become cocaine and heroin users, the benefits of other criminal enterprises become overwhelmingly attractive: How else can a drug user earn enough to support his or her habit?[43]

Crime also becomes attractive when an individual is convinced that it will result in excessive profits with few costs. Criminals are motivated to commit crime when they know people who have made big scores and begin to believe they can gain economic freedom via crime.[44] They are likely to desist if they begin to believe that their future criminal earnings will be relatively low and that attractive and legal opportunities to generate income are available.[45]

How much do you have to earn before crime is considered an economically viable alternative? Thompson and Uggen found that the typical drug dealer earned less than $800 profit per month; those committing predatory offenses such as burglary and robbery earned an average of $1,087. The real winners were criminals who sold drugs and also committed predatory crimes; they averaged $1,723 per month from illegal sources.[46] But even the most "successful" criminals earned less than $24,000. This is not enough to justify the dangerous risks of a criminal career; it's not surprising then that most criminals eventually desist from crime—it just does not pay (enough).

Learning and Experience Learning and experience may be important elements in structuring the choice of crime.[47] Career criminals may learn the limitations of their powers;

CONNECTIONS

The role of economic needs in the motivation of white-collar criminals is discussed in Chapter 13. Research shows that even consistently law-abiding people may turn to criminal solutions when faced with overwhelming economic needs. They make the rational decision to commit crimes to solve some economic crisis.

ASK YOURSELF . . .

Do you believe that a law-abiding citizen would suddenly become a thief if they faced a severe economic hardship? Are there circumstances where you might commit crime to solve an economic problem?

they know when to take a chance and when to be cautious. Experienced criminals may turn from a life of crime when they develop a belief that the risk of crime is greater than its potential profit.[48] Patricia Morgan and Karen Ann Joe's three-city study (San Francisco, San Diego, and Honolulu) of female drug abusers found that experience helped dealers avoid detection. One dealer, earning $50,000 per year, explained her strategy this way:

> I stayed within my goals, basically . . . I don't go around doing stupid things. I don't walk around telling people I have drugs for sale. I don't have people sitting out in front of my house. I don't have traffic in and out of my house . . . I control the people I sell to.[49]

Here we see how experience in the profession shapes criminal decision making.

Knowledge of Criminal Techniques Criminals report learning techniques that help them avoid detection, a sure sign of rational thinking and planning. Some are specialists who learn to be professional car thieves or bad-check artists. Others are generalists who sell drugs one day and commit burglaries the next. In his studies of drug dealers, criminologist Bruce Jacobs found that crack dealers learn how to stash crack cocaine in some undisclosed location so they are not forced to carry large amounts of product on their persons. Dealers carefully evaluate the security of their sales area before setting up shop.[50] Most consider the middle of a long block the best place for drug deals because they can see everything in both directions; police raids can be spotted before they develop.[51] If a buyer seems dangerous or unreliable, the dealer requires that they do business in spaces between apartment buildings or in back lots. Although dealers lose the tactical edge of being on a public street, they gain a measure of protection because their associates can watch over the deal and come to the rescue if the buyer tries to "pull something."[52]

When Jacobs, along with Jody Miller, studied female crack dealers, they discovered a variety of defensive moves used by the dealers to avoid detection.[53] One of these techniques, called stashing, involved learning how to hide drugs on their person, in the street, or at home. One dealer told Jacobs and Miller how she hid drugs in the empty shaft of a curtain rod; another wore hollow earmuffs to hide crack. Because only female officers may conduct body cavity searches on women, the dealers often had time to get rid of their drugs before they got to the station house. Dealers are aware of legal definitions of possession. One said she stashed her drugs 250 feet from her home because that was beyond the distance (150 feet) police considered a person legally to be in "constructive possession" of drugs.

Criminals who learn the proper techniques may be able to prolong their criminal careers. Jacobs found that these offenders use specific techniques to avoid being apprehended by police. They play what they call the "peep game" before dealing drugs, scoping out the territory to make sure the turf is free from anything out of place that could be a potential threat (such as police officers or rival gang members).[54]

Drug dealers told Jacobs that they also carefully consider whether they should deal alone or in groups; large groups draw more attention from police but can offer more protection. Drug-dealing gangs and groups can help divert the attention of police: if their drug dealing is noticed by detectives, a dealer can slyly walk away or dispose of evidence while confederates distract the cops.[55]

STRUCTURING CRIME

LO4 Depict in your own words how criminals structure crime

Criminal decision making is not only based on an assessment of personal needs and capabilities but also on a rational assessment of the criminal event. Decisions must be made about what, where, when, and whom to target.

CONNECTIONS

Rational choice theory dovetails with routine activities theory, which you learned about in Chapter 3. Although not identical, these approaches both claim that crime rates are a normal product of criminal opportunity. Both suggest that criminals consider such elements as guardianship and target attractiveness before they decide to commit crimes. The routine activities and rational choice views also agree that criminal opportunity is a key element in the criminal process. The overlap between these two viewpoints may help criminologists suggest means for effective crime control.

ASK YOURSELF . . .

If criminals are rational decision makers, what can you do to reduce your chances of becoming a victim of burglary? Do you think buying a dog might help?

Choosing the Type of Crime The choice of crime may be dictated by market conditions. Generalists may alter their criminal behavior according to shifting opportunity structures: they may rob the elderly on the first of the month when they know that Social Security checks have been cashed, switch over to shoplifting if a new fence moves into the neighborhood, and, if a supply becomes available, sell a truckload of hijacked cigarettes to neighborhood convenience stores. Crack users choose robbery over burglary: they need to make quick cash to purchase drugs and are in no position to plan a burglary and take the time to sell their loot; hitting someone with a lead pipe and taking their wallet is faster and provides instant funds.[56]

Choosing the Time and Place of Crime There is also evidence that criminal choice is structured by the time and place. Interviews with burglars show that they prefer "working" between 9 A.M. and 11 A.M. and in mid-afternoon, when parents are either at work or dropping off or picking up kids at school.[57] Burglars avoid Saturdays because most families are at home; Sunday morning during church hours is considered a prime time for weekend burglaries.[58] Some find out which families have star high school athletes because those that do are sure to be at the weekend game, leaving their houses unguarded.[59]

The place of crime is also carefully chosen. Because criminals often go on foot or use public transportation, they are unlikely to travel long distances to commit crimes and are more likely to drift toward the center of a city than move toward outlying areas.[60] Some may occasionally commute to distant locations to commit crimes if they believe the payoff is greater, but most prefer to stay in their own neighborhood where they are familiar with the terrain.[61] They will only travel to unfamiliar areas if they believe the new location contains a worthy target and lax law enforcement. They may be encouraged to travel when the police are cracking down in their own neighborhood and the "heat is on."[62] Predatory criminals are in fact aware of law enforcement capabilities and consider them closely before deciding to commit crimes. Communities with the reputation of employing aggressive crime-fighting cops are less likely to attract potential offenders than areas perceived to have passive law enforcers.[63]

Selecting the Target of Crime Criminals may also be well aware of target vulnerability. When they choose targets, they may shy off if they sense danger. In a series of interviews with career property offenders, Kenneth Tunnell found that burglars avoid targets if they feel there are police in the area or if "nosy neighbors" might be suspicious and cause trouble.[64] Paul Bellair found that robbery levels are relatively low in neighborhoods where residents keep a watchful eye on their neighbors' property.[65]

Predatory criminals seek out easy targets who can't or won't fight back and avoid those who seem menacing and dangerous. Not surprisingly, they tend to shy away from potential victims whom they believe are armed and dangerous.[66] The search for suitable victims may bring them in contact with people who themselves engage in deviant or antisocial behaviors.[67] Perhaps predatory criminals sense that people with "dirty hands" make suitable targets because they are unlikely to want to call the police or get entangled with the law.

In some instances, however, targets are chosen in order to send a message rather than to generate capital. Bruce Jacobs and Richard Wright used in-depth interviews with street robbers who target drug dealers and found that their crimes are a response to one of three types of violations:[68]

- *Market-related* violations emerge from "professional" disputes over territory.
- *Status-based* violations involve violence that starts when someone challenges the robber's character or manhood.
- *Personalistic* violations occur when the robber believes someone is acting like a punk and needs to be taught a lesson.

Robbery in this instance is an instrument used to settle scores, display dominance, and stifle potential rivals. Retaliation certainly is rational in the sense that actors who lack legitimate access to the law and who prize respect above everything else will often choose to resolve their grievances through a rough and ready brand of self-help.

Is Crime Rational?

 L05 Clarify the arguments that crime is rational

It is relatively easy to show that some crimes are the product of rational, objective thought, especially when they involve an ongoing criminal conspiracy centered on economic gain. When prominent bankers in the savings and loan industry were indicted for criminal fraud, their elaborate financial schemes exhibited not only signs of rationality but brilliant, though flawed, financial expertise.[69] The stock market manipulations of Wall Street executives, the drug dealings of international cartels, and the gambling operations of organized crime bosses all demonstrate a reasoned analysis of market conditions, interests, and risks. Even small-time wheeler-dealers, such as the female drug dealers discussed earlier in the chapter, are guided by their rational assessment of the likelihood of apprehension and take pains to avoid detection. But what about common crimes of theft and violence? Are these rational acts or unplanned, haphazard, and spontaneous?

IS THEFT RATIONAL?

Some common theft-related crimes—larcenies, shoplifting, auto theft, purse snatchings—seem more likely to be random acts of criminal opportunity than well-thought-out conspiracies. However, there is evidence that even these

seemingly unplanned events may be the product of careful risk assessment, including environmental, social, and structural factors.

Professional shoplifters, referred to as **boosters**, use complex methods in order to avoid detection. They steal with the intention of reselling stolen merchandise online or reselling it to professional fences, another group of criminals who use cunning and rational decision making in their daily activities. Fences may buy the stolen goods and then resell them to the merchants who were the original target of the professional shoplifters!

Another group of criminals, professional burglars, seem to carefully choose the neighborhood location of their crimes.[70] They seem to avoid areas where residents protect their homes with alarms, locks, and other methods of "target hardening" or where residents watch out for one another and try to control unrest or instability in their communities.[71] Most burglars prefer to commit crimes in **permeable neighborhoods**, those with a greater than usual number of access streets from traffic arteries into the neighborhood.[72] These areas are chosen for theft and break-ins because they are familiar and well traveled, they appear more open and vulnerable, and they offer more potential escape routes.[73] Burglars appear to monitor car and pedestrian traffic and avoid selecting targets on heavily traveled streets.[74] Corner homes, usually near traffic lights or stop signs, are the ones most likely to be burglarized: stop signs give criminals a legitimate reason to stop their cars and look for an attractive target.[75] Secluded homes, such as those at the end of a cul-de-sac or surrounded by wooded areas, also make suitable targets.[76]

Burglars are choosy when they select targets. They avoid freestanding buildings because they can more easily be surrounded by police; they like to select targets that are known to do a primarily cash business, such as bars, supermarkets, and restaurants.[77] Burglars also seem to know the market and target goods that are in demand.

Auto thieves are another group of criminals who use rational choice while planning crimes. The Criminology in Action feature "How Auto Thieves Plan Their Crimes" looks at how auto thieves plan their crimes.

IS DRUG USE RATIONAL?

Did Oscar-winning actor Philip Seymour Hoffman make an objective, rational choice to OD on heroin? Did rising young star Heath Ledger make a rational choice when he abused prescription drugs to the point that they killed him? And what about British singer Amy Winehouse, did she choose

boosters Professional shoplifters who steal with the intention of reselling stolen merchandise.

permeable neighborhood Areas with a greater than usual number of access streets from traffic arteries into the neighborhood.

How Auto Thieves Plan Their Crimes

04

Bruce Jacobs and Michael Cherbonneau recently studied the decision-making process of auto thieves, who as a group are especially concerned about the reaction of their victim/targets. Their data were drawn from in-depth, semi-structured interviews with 35 active offenders recruited from the streets of a large Midwestern city.

Jacobs and Cherbonneau found that two factors figured prominently in the offenders' decision making: the area around the target and the target itself. The first galvanized the offenders' attention to and management of informal social control. The second enjoined offenders to balance speed and stealth in breaching the target. They found that auto thieves could be deterred by the threat of confrontation and the self-defense measures taken by the car owners. While the wheels of justice may be slow, victim responses are immediate—and potent. Making a mistake in crime planning can produce severe reactions for even minor violations.

At the most basic level, fear of confrontation forced the offenders to gauge the coercive power of their victims and the likelihood that victims will use that power during an encounter. Offenders must "intuit" potential scenarios and plan accordingly. They must calculate whether the car's owner is absent, the likelihood of the owner's return, and what force the victim has at his or her disposal. These tasks require time, know-how, patience, and coolness under pressure. Offenders must figure out a way to make their behavior seem normal to observers, to hide their intentions from prying eyes, and to neutralize the desire of car owners to take action to protect their property.

In auto theft, such measures involve the maximization of stealth and speed during the theft. Stealth keeps victims unaware of the fact that a theft is occurring, while speed minimizes the duration of exposure within the actual offense. By adopting both strategies, offenders seek to reduce the perceived certainty of detection.

To meet these requirements, auto thieves avoid situations that would bring contact with victims or people who could potentially notify victims. Areas rich in natural surveillance produce a substantial risk of observation, and being observed is one step from being noticed. The mere prospect of being noticed gives auto thieves serious pause about targeting a vehicle with anyone around. One tactic is to carefully scope out an area on foot or in a drive-by to make sure there are no bystanders lurking about. If an offender were to see a driver exit a vehicle, the offender might wait to gauge whether a return was likely. Some use an "occupancy probe," knocking on the owner's door to see if he or she is home; others wait until

to drink herself to death? Or Michael Jackson, who died of acute propofol and benzodiazepine intoxication on June 25, 2009? Is it possible that these and other drug users, a group not usually associated with clear thinking, make rational choices? And some, like Prince, who died in 2016, may use opioid medication to treat chronic pain and may simply not realize the deadly effects of the drugs they are using.

Research does in fact show that from its onset drug use is controlled by rational decision making. Users report that they begin taking drugs when they believe that the benefits of substance abuse outweigh its costs (e.g., they believe that drugs will provide a fun, exciting, thrilling experience). Their entry into substance abuse is facilitated by their perception that valued friends and family members endorse and encourage drug use and abuse substances themselves.[78]

In adulthood, heavy drug users and dealers show signs of rationality and cunning in their daily activity, approaching drug dealing as a business proposition. Research conducted by Leanne Fiftal Alarid and her partners shows that women drawn into dealing drugs learn the trade in a businesslike manner. One young dealer told them how she learned the techniques of the trade from an older male partner:

> He taught me how to "recon" [reconstitute] cocaine, cutting and repacking a brick from 91 proof to 50 proof, just like a business. He treats me like an equal partner, and many of the friends are business associates. I am a catalyst. . . . I even get guys turned on to drugs.[79]

Note the business terminology used. This coke dealer could be talking about an IT training course at a major corporation! Nor are Alarid's research findings unique. When James Densley studied drug-dealing gangs in London, he found that they evolved from nonviolent, noncriminal peer groups into organized criminal enterprises.[80] Nothing was left to chance, one gang member, street name "Wolverine," explained to Denlsey:

> We was committing crimes so we sat down together, it was like a meeting, I suppose and we just gave each other names and it started like that. Because it was not like socializing, it was actually going out to commit crime and do stuff. We was premeditating what we was doing before it happened. Planning it up.

the early morning hours when most people are asleep.

Not all offenders count on such strategies; they use lookouts, co-offenders who provide a critical "heads-up" in the event the owner or related party is watching, approaching, or in danger of intervening. Lookouts allow thieves to make quick decisions without a lot of preparation. A thief named Will told Jacobs and Cherbonneau how he targeted a vehicle driven to a nightclub. After watching the owner go inside, Will had a co-offender follow the man into the club and keep an eye on his movements. If "he was going [to] walk off and leave," Will explained, "[My partner] was going [to] call . . . on the cell phone . . . I didn't want to be breaking somebody's car down and here he all of a sudden decides to go."

Female thieves may hook up with a car owner to catch them off guard. One told how she knocked out her target with sleeping pills and morphine (which she slipped into his drink during their date), and then took his car once he fell unconscious. "I knew that he wasn't gonna come out for a minute," she recalled. Although there is some risk of post-offense retaliation, most thieves were unconcerned, believing they could talk their way out of involvement if they were somehow tracked down.

Another concern was alarms. No matter how stealthy they were, it did not matter if a car alarm started blaring. One method was to break a window to gain access and get away quickly. Others looked for cars with open windows or ones that already had a broken window. The faster the thief broke into the vehicle, the faster the offense would be over, and the quicker he could escape. Some would purposely jostle the vehicles and then wait to see whether the owner came out if an alarm went off. If the owner did appear, the thieves would simply slink down the street as if uninvolved. Others felt the easiest way was to target vehicles left running in gas stations or convenience store parking lots. Although these open spaces afforded little concealment, speed of access and escape trumped the deterrent power of victim proximity: by the time the owner realized what happened, the crime would be over.

Despite all their precautions, auto thieves were afraid of run-ins with car owners. They were auto thieves, after all, not violent criminals. Some reported fear of getting shot by an irate owner and conclude that although sneaky property crimes such as auto theft were unlikely to land offenders in the crosshairs of an angry victim, the mere prospect encour-

aged offenders to apply confrontation avoidance measures at the front end of the offense. By reducing the certainty of detection, the offenders sought to short-circuit consequences that they anticipated would be both swift and severe.

Jacobs and Cherbonneau's research underscores both the rationality of crime and the fact that criminals can be deterred by the fear of informal sanctions—that is, victim retaliation. Even a crime of opportunity such as car theft requires careful planning, skill, and cognition if it is to be carried out with success.

 CRITICAL THINKING

After reading what Jacobs and Cherbonneau have to say about auto thieves' decision making, would you advise people to actively defend their vehicle or hand over the keys and hope that insurance will cover the loss?

SOURCE: Bruce Jacobs and Michael Cherbonneau, "Managing Victim Confrontation: Auto Theft and Informal Sanction Threats," *Justice Quarterly* 33 (2016): 21–44.

Densley found that that drug dealers learn special skills—how to seize territory, how to use violence, how to maintain secrecy, how to obtain intelligence—that enable them to successfully regulate and control the production and distribution of illegal drugs while maximizing their profits.

Drug dealers are infamous for overcharging customers and handing over less than has been paid for; after all, customers can't call the police or hire a lawyer to collect what they are owed. Drug dealers do not cheat every customer and seem to make rational decisions on whom to rip off. This is what Scott Jacques and his colleagues found when they interviewed 25 active dealers. They discovered that dealers typically target six types of customers: persons who are strangers, first-time, or irregular customers; those who do not have sufficient money on hand to make a purchase; buyers who are uninformed about the actual price of illegal drugs; those who seem unlikely to retaliate; those who are obnoxious and offensive; and hardcore addicts. Why are these groups targeted? Some of these types seem naïve and unlikely to be repeat customers. Others are drug addled and unaware they are getting ripped off and therefore unlikely to

seek vengeance. Some are annoying and deserving of being mistreated.[81]

IS VIOLENCE RATIONAL?

Is it possible that violent acts, through which the offender gains little material benefit, are the product of reasoned decision making? Yes, it is. There are a number of indicators that suggest violence has rational elements. When Trevor Bennett and Fiona Brookman conducted interviews with offenders with a history of violence, they found that some motivations were cultural, such as maintaining one's status and honor, and others might be visceral, such as excitement and getting a buzz from dangerous pursuits. However, there were also rational elements to violent acts, such as calculating whether they could win the battle. Put another way, violent repeaters don't start something they can't finish: if the target looks tough, they look for someone else to attack.[82]

Crime expert Richard Felson argues that violence is a matter of choice and serves specific goals:

- *Control.* The violent person may want to control his or her victim's behavior and life.

Shooting suspect Robert Lewis Dear appears before Judge Gilbert Martinez via video feed with public defender Dan King on November 30, 2015, in Colorado Springs, Colorado. Dear attacked a Planned Parenthood clinic in Colorado Springs on November 27, killing three people, including a police officer; nine others were injured. On May 11, 2016, after a number of hearings during which Dear told the judge that he believes the FBI cuts holes in his clothes and leaves feathers in his home, that Robin Williams told a joke about President Obama—the "antichrist"—and committed suicide two weeks later, and that President Obama will declare martial law and rebuild himself as the antichrist, Dear was found to be incompetent to stand trial due to mental defect. Can any mass murderer such as Dear truly be competent and rational?

Pool/Getty Images

to travel farther than juveniles, especially if they have driver's licenses![84]

Street robbers are likely to choose victims who are vulnerable, have low coercive power, and do not pose any threat.[85] They size up their prey and get ready to use violence if the target appears to be street wise. During the robbery, offenders are more likely to use physical force against a victim who resists; compliant victims are treated with greater restraint. Robbers therefore take a rational approach to sizing up and dealing with their victims.[86]

In a classic study, James Wright and Peter Rossi found that robbers avoid victims who may be armed and dangerous. About three-fifths of all felons interviewed were more afraid of armed victims than of police, about two-fifths had avoided a victim because they believed the victim was armed, and almost one-third reported that they had been scared off, wounded, or captured by armed victims.[87] It comes as no surprise that cities with higher than average gun-carrying rates generally have lower rates of unarmed robbery.[88]

Robbers also tend to pick the time and day of crimes carefully. When they rob a commercial establishment, they choose the time when there is the most cash on hand to increase their take from the crime. Robbery rates increase in the winter partly because the Christmas shopping season means more money in the cash registers of potential targets.[89] Targets are generally found close to robbers' homes or in areas in which they routinely travel. Familiarity with the area gives them ready knowledge of escape routes; this is referred to as their "awareness space."[90] A familiar location allows them to blend in, not look out of place, and not get lost when returning home with their loot.[91]

- *Retribution.* The perpetrator may want punish someone without calling the police or using the justice system to address his or her grievances. The person takes the law into his or her own hands.
- *Deterrence.* The attacker may want to stop someone from repeating acts that he or she considers hostile or provocative.
- *Reputation.* An attack may be motivated by the need to enhance reputation and create self-importance in the eyes of others.

Felson also recognizes that the violent act may have multiple goals. But in any case, even violence may be a product of rational decision making.[83]

Rational Thieves Robbers and burglars display rationality in their choice of targets. Burglars like to target residences close to where they live so they know the territory and have access to escape routes. Adult burglars are willing

Rational Killers? Hollywood likes to portray deranged people killing innocent victims at random, but people who carry guns and are ready to use them typically do so for more rational reasons. They may perceive that they live in a dangerous environment and carry a weapon for self-protection. Some are involved in dangerous illegal activities such as drug dealing and carry weapons as part of the job.[92] Even in apparently senseless killings among strangers, the conscious motive is typically revenge for a prior dispute or disagreement among the parties involved or their families.[93] Many homicides are motivated by offenders' desire to avoid retaliation from a victim they assaulted or to avoid future prosecutions by getting rid of witnesses.[94] Although some killings are the result of anger and aggression, others are the result of rational planning.

Even serial murderers, outwardly the most irrational of all offenders, tend to pick their targets with care. Most choose victims who are defenseless or who cannot count on police protection: prostitutes, gay men, hitchhikers, children, hospital patients, the elderly, and the homeless. Rarely do serial killers target weightlifters, martial arts experts, or any other potentially powerful group.[95]

Rational Sex Criminals? One might think that sex crimes are highly irrational, motivated by emotions and psychological maladies that defy rational planning. But sex criminals report using rational thought and planning when carrying out their crimes. Serial rapists rationally choose their targets. They travel, on average, three miles from their homes to commit their crimes in order to avoid victims who might recognize them later. The desire to avoid detection supersedes the wish to obtain a victim with little effort. Younger sex offenders create scripts that guide their interactions with victims. If they follow the script, they can commit their crimes and avoid detection. Before committing their crimes, the young sex offender will go through a series of steps, first finding their victims in institutional, domestic, or public places, gaining their victims' trust, and then formulating strategies to proceed to the best location for sexual contact. For that purpose, offenders will usually promise rewards or give inducements such as money, or even threaten or use violence to get their way.[96]

Child molesters/rapists report that they volunteer or seek employment in day care centers and other venues where victims can be found. They use their status to gain the trust of children and to be seen as nonthreatening to the child. Within the context of this work environment they can then use subtle strategies of manipulation, such as giving love and attention to suitable targets (e.g., spending a lot of time with them), so they can gradually desensitize the children and gain their cooperation in sexual activity (e.g., through nonsexual touching).[97] These efforts obviously display planning and rationality.

Is Hate Rational? Can hate crimes possibly be rational? Hard to believe, but when Ryan King and Gretchen Sutto examined the characteristics of an outbreak of hate crimes they found that three factors seem to trigger these events: an antecedent incident that leaves one group with a grievance against another, a definable target group held responsible for the deed, and publicity sufficient to make the event known to a broad public; all these are signs of rationality.[98] A lethal, highly publicized terror attack such as the bombing at the Boston Marathon in April 2013 might ignite a spate of hate crimes aimed at the Muslim community, which increase

Hate crimes seem inherently irrational, but attackers single out victims in a rational manner. Here, Elliot Morales waits in a New York courtroom as the jury deliberated his guilt in the May 2013 shooting death of Mark Carson, which came on the heels of a drunken, violent antigay tirade. According to the police who arrested him, minutes later Morales sat on the street in handcuffs laughing and boasting about the killing. On March 9, 2016, he was convicted of murder as a hate crime, which carries a prison term of life without parole.

almost immediately after the incident and then deescalate at an equally rapid pace. When anger and prejudice drive retaliatory hate crimes they dissipate quickly. Hate crimes, then, are not merely the product of a disturbed mind, but rather a calculated response to a concrete event whose impact is often fanned and inflamed by the media.

Eliminating Crime

For many people, crime is attractive; it brings rewards, excitement, prestige, or other desirable outcomes without lengthy work or effort.[99] Whether the motive is economic gain, revenge, or hedonism, crime has an allure that some people cannot resist.[100] Some law violators describe the adrenaline rush that comes from successfully executing illegal activities in dangerous situations as **edgework**, the "exhilarating, momentary integration of danger, risk, and skill" that motivates people to try a variety of dangerous criminal and noncriminal behaviors.[101] Crime is not some random act, but a means that can provide both pleasure and solutions to vexing personal problems. As Michael Gottfredson and Travis Hirschi put it, these criminals derive satisfaction from "money without work, sex without courtship, revenge without court delays."[102]

edgework The excitement or exhilaration of successfully executing illegal activities in dangerous situations.

Considering its allure, how can crime be prevented or eliminated? It seems logical that if crime is rational and people choose to commit crime after weighing its rewards and benefits and factoring in their needs and abilities, then it can be controlled or eradicated by convincing potential offenders that:

- Crime is a poor choice that will not bring them rewards, but instead lead to hardship and deprivation.
- Crime is not worth the effort. It is easier to work at a legitimate job than to evade police, outwit alarms, and avoid security.
- Crime brings pain that is not easily forgotten. People who experience the pains of punishment will not readily commit more crimes.

The following sections discuss each of these crime reduction or control strategies in some detail.

Situational Crime Prevention

 L06 Identify the elements of the CRAVED model of crime choice

Desperate people may contemplate crime, but only the truly irrational would attack a well-defended, inaccessible target and risk strict punishment. Criminals and terrorists seek out targets that are attractive yet vulnerable.[103] Crime prevention can be achieved by convincing people that a particular target is neither—not worth the effort, too hard a nut to crack—a practice known as **situational crime prevention**. According to this concept, in order to reduce criminal activity, planners must be aware of the characteristics of sites and situations that are at risk to crime; the things that draw or push people toward these sites and situations; what equips potential criminals to take advantage of illegal opportunities offered by these sites and situations; and what constitutes the immediate triggers for criminal actions.[104] Criminal acts will be avoided if (a) potential targets are guarded securely, (b) the means to commit crime are controlled, and (c) potential offenders are carefully monitored.

Situational crime prevention was first popularized in the United States in the early 1970s by Oscar Newman, who coined the term **defensible space**. This term signifies that crime can be prevented or displaced through the use of residential architectural designs that reduce criminal

opportunity, such as well-lit housing projects that maximize surveillance.[105] C. Ray Jeffery wrote *Crime Prevention Through Environmental Design*, which extended Newman's concepts and applied them to nonresidential areas, such as schools and factories.[106] According to this view, mechanisms such as security systems, deadbolt locks, high-intensity street lighting, and neighborhood watch patrols should reduce criminal opportunity.[107]

In 1992, Ronald Clarke published *Situational Crime Prevention*, which compiled the best-known strategies and tactics to reduce criminal incidents.[108] Clarke later formulated the CRAVED model of theft, which suggests that the appropriation of property is most likely to occur when the target is:

- *Concealable.* Merchandise that is easily hidden is more vulnerable to shoplifters than bulkier items. Things that are difficult to identify after being stolen are desirable. While it might be possible to identify a diamond ring, commodities such as copper tubing are easily concealable.
- *Removable.* Mobile items such as cars or bikes are desirable. A laptop makes a more appealing target than a desktop. Jewelry, cash, drugs, and the like are easy to carry and quite valuable on resale. Refrigerators may cost more, but you would need three people and a truck to remove them from a home.
- *Available.* Desirable objects that are widely available and easy to find are at high risk for theft. Cars actually become at greater risk as they get older because similar models need parts and car thieves can bring them to chop shops to be stripped. Older cars are also owned by people living in disorganized neighborhoods with motivated offenders and limited security.
- *Valuable.* Thieves will generally choose more expensive, in-demand goods that are easily sold. Some may want to keep valuable goods for themselves and target goods that will confer status, such as a Rolex.
- *Enjoyable.* Hot products tend to be enjoyable things to own or consume, such as the newest electronic gadget or flashy bling.
- *Disposable.* Thieves tend to target items that are easy to sell. Cartons of cigarettes can be resold at a discount to a convenience store. While more valuable, it's tougher to sell a Picasso print.[109]

Based on this research, criminologists have suggested using a number of situational crime prevention efforts that might reduce crime rates. One approach is not to target a specific crime but to create an environment that can reduce the overall crime rate by limiting the access to tempting targets for a highly motivated offender group (such as high school students).[110]

TARGETING SPECIFIC CRIMES

Situational crime prevention can also involve developing tactics to reduce or eliminate a specific crime problem (such as shoplifting in an urban mall or street-level drug dealing).

situational crime prevention A method of crime prevention that stresses tactics and strategies to eliminate or reduce particular crimes in narrow settings, such as reducing burglaries in a housing project by increasing lighting and installing security alarms.

defensible space The principle that crime prevention can be achieved through modifying the physical environment to reduce the opportunity individuals have to commit crime.

Typically, situational crime prevention efforts are divided into a number of strategies:[111]

- Increase the effort needed to commit crime
- Reduce the opportunity to commit crime
- Increase the risks of committing crime
- Reduce the rewards for committing crime
- Reduce provocation/induce guilt or shame for committing crime
- Reduce excuses for committing crime

Increase Effort   The harder it is to attack a target, the less likely it will be attacked! Some of the tactics to increase effort include target-hardening techniques such as putting unbreakable glass on storefronts, locking gates, and fencing yards. Some people go as far as living in gated communities, protected by guards and fences. Does it work? Research by Lynn Addington and Callie Marie Rennison shows that living in a gated community actually reduces the risk of being targeted by burglars.[112]

Technological advances can make it more difficult to commit crimes and easier to solve them once they occur. Having the owner's photo on credit cards should reduce the use of stolen cards. Using biometrics to identify individuals through facial analysis is becoming commonplace in high-risk environments such as airports. Fast and accurate identification enhances police officer safety, instantly detects wanted or identified criminals, secures facilities and information systems from unauthorized access, makes borders more secure, and prevents identity theft.[113] Another approach that is being developed is to be able to determine what segments in a person's DNA are responsible for physical appearance, including hair, eye, and skin pigmentation, as well as facial features. Once this technique is perfected, it will be possible to take a DNA sample left at a crime scene and develop a physical portrait of a suspect. Research has progressed significantly in the past decade and scientists can now use DNA to determine, with more than 75 percent probability, an individual's eye and hair color and ethnic heritage.[114]

Reduce Opportunities   Another way to increase effort is to reduce opportunities for criminal activity. At least 30 states and thousands of municipalities have passed laws preventing registered sex offenders from residing within a specific distance of schools, parks, day care centers, school bus stops, or other places commonly frequented by children; buffer zones typically range from 500 to 2,500 feet between the offender's home and designated locations. While aimed at reducing sex offending and reducing recidivism, there is scant evidence that such measures can be effective.[115]

Many cities have established curfew laws in an effort to limit the opportunity juveniles have to engage in antisocial behavior.[116] However, curfew laws have not met with universal success.[117] So another approach has been to involve kids in after-school programs that take up their time and reduce their opportunity to get in trouble. An example of this type of program is the Doorsteps Neighbourhood Program in Toronto, Ontario, which is designed to help children in high-risk areas complete their schoolwork as well as provide them with playtime that helps improve their literacy and communication skills. Children who are part of this program enter into routines that increase the effort they must make if they want to get involved in after-school crime and nuisance activities.[118]

Reduce Rewards   Target reduction strategies are designed to reduce the value of crime to the potential criminal. These include marking property so it is more difficult to sell when stolen and using caller ID to discourage obscene phone calls. Tracking systems, such as those made by the LoJack Corporation, help police locate and return stolen vehicles.[119]

Increase Risk   If criminals believe that committing crime is very risky, only the most foolhardy would attempt to commit criminal acts. Managing crime falls into the hands of people Marcus Felson calls **crime discouragers**.[120] These discouragers can be grouped into three categories: guardians, who monitor targets (such as store security guards); handlers, who monitor potential offenders (such as parole officers and parents); and managers, who monitor places (such as homeowners and doorway attendants). If crime discouragers do their job correctly, the potential criminal will be convinced that the risk of crime outweighs any potential gains.[121]

Crime discouragers have different levels of responsibility, ranging from highly personal involvement, such as the homeowner protecting her house and the parent controlling his children, to the most impersonal general involvement, such as a stranger who stops someone from shoplifting in the mall (see Exhibit 4.1).

Research indicates that crime discouragers can have an impact on crime rates. An evaluation of a police initiative in Oakland, California, found that an active working partnership with residents and businesspeople who have a stake in maintaining order in their places of work or residences can reduce levels of drug dealing while at the same time increasing civil behavior. Collective action and cooperation in solving problems were effective in controlling crime, whereas individual action (such as calling 911) seemed to have little effect.[122]

It may also be possible to raise the risks of committing crime by creating mechanical devices that increase the likelihood that a criminal will be observed and captured. One prominent approach is the installation of closed-circuit

crime discouragers Discouragers can be grouped into three categories: guardians, who monitor targets (such as store security guards); handlers, who monitor potential offenders (such as parole officers and parents); and managers, who monitor places (such as homeowners and doorway attendants).

EXHIBIT 4.1

Crime Discouragers

Level of Responsibility	Types of Supervisors and Objects of Supervision		
	Guardians (Monitoring Suitable Targets)	Handlers (Monitoring Likely Offenders)	Managers (Monitoring Amenable Places)
Personal (owners, family, friends)	Student keeps eye on own laptop	Parent makes sure child gets home from school	Homeowner monitors house
Assigned (employees with specific assignment)	Store clerk monitors iPhones	Police officer sends kids back to school	Concierge protects building
Diffuse (employees with general assignment)	Accountant notes shoplifting	School clerk discourages truancy	Hotel maid impairs trespasser
General (strangers, other citizens)	Bystander reports shoplifter	Stranger questions teens at mall	Customer observes parking garage

SOURCE: Adapted from *Crime and Place*, ed. John E. Eck and David Weisburd (Boulder, CO: Lynne Rienner Publishers, 2010).

television (CCTV) surveillance cameras and improved street lighting, techniques that are currently being used around the world. CCTV can deter would-be criminals who fear detection and apprehension while aiding police in the detection and apprehension of suspects, aid in the prosecution of alleged offenders, improve police officer safety and compliance with the law (cameras mounted on the dashboard of police cruisers to record police stops, searches, and so on), and aid in the detection and prevention of terrorist activities.[123] Nowhere is the popularity of CCTV more apparent than in Great Britain, where there are now estimated to be more than 4 million CCTV cameras, or 1 for every 14 citizens, in operation. Some cities in the United States have large numbers of security cameras: New York City has more than 4,000 cameras in Manhattan alone; Chicago's linked public and private security cameras number around 10,000.[124] Research shows that CCTV interventions (a) have a moderate but significant desirable effect on crime, (b) are most effective in reducing crime in car parks (parking lots), (c) are most effective in reducing vehicle crimes, and (d) are more effective in reducing crime in the United Kingdom than in other countries.[125]

Increase Shame   Crime may be reduced or prevented if we can communicate to people the wrongfulness of their behavior and how it is harmful to society. We may tell them to "say no to drugs" or that "users are losers." By making people aware of the shamefulness of their actions we hope to prevent their criminal activities even if chances of detection and punishment are slight.

Another method is to order people convicted of socially unacceptable crimes to advertise their guilt in the hope that they will be too ashamed to recidivate. "John lists" have been published to shame men involved in hiring prostitutes or other sex offenses.

Other methods of inducing guilt or shame might include such techniques as posting signs or warnings to embarrass potential offenders or creating mechanisms to identify perpetrators and/or publicize their crimes.[126] Megan's Laws require sex offender registration and notification systems. While these systems have been used for more than two decades, there is little evidence that they reduce sex crimes: research shows that sex offender registration does not have a statistically significant effect on the number of rapes reported at the state level.[127] One reason may be that instead of deterring crime, public disclosure resulting from community notification laws negatively impacts an offender's efforts at rehabilitation, resulting in further offending.[128]

Reduce Provocation   Some crimes, such as road rage, are the result of extreme provocation. It might be possible to reduce provocation by creating programs that reduce conflict. Posting guards outside of schools at recess might prevent childish taunts from escalating into full-blown brawls. Antibullying programs that have been implemented in schools are another method of reducing provocation.

Alcohol may act as a fuel that fans the flames, turning a disagreement into an assault. One way to reduce this sort of crime is to raise the price of beer, wine, and hard liquor through taxation, which has been shown to be effective.[129] Another approach: mandating an early closing time in local bars and pubs might limit assaults that result from late-night drinking and conflicts in pubs at closing time.

Remove Excuses   Crime may be reduced by making it difficult for people to excuse their criminal behavior by saying things like "I did not know that was illegal" or "I had no choice." Some municipalities have set up roadside displays that electronically flash cars' speed rate as they drive by, so that when stopped by police, drivers cannot say they did not know how fast they were going. Litter boxes, brightly displayed, can eliminate the claim that "I just did not know where to throw my trash." Reducing or eliminating excuses also makes it physically easy for people to comply with laws and regulations, thereby reducing the likelihood they will choose crime.

Integrated Situational Efforts   The interactive effect of a mix of situational techniques may have greater impact on crime elimination than any single technique acting independently.[130] When Jon Shane and Shannon Magnuson studied pirate attacks around the world they discovered data that support the interactive effect. They found that when a ship's crew takes protective measures that increase the perceived effort needed to commit piracy, the likelihood that a pirate attack will be successful is significantly reduced.[131] Successful attacks diminished when watchmen were present ready to raise an alarm. Attacks were further reduced by adding measures to increase the perceived effort: electric perimeter fencing, evasive maneuvering, and increasing ship speed. Piracy diminished as more situational techniques were added; situational crime prevention could explain a significant amount of the reasons for reduced pirate attacks.

SITUATIONAL CRIME PREVENTION: COSTS AND BENEFITS

 L07 Assess the validity of situational crime prevention techniques for reducing crime

Some attempts at situational crime prevention have proven highly successful while others have not met their goals. However, it is now apparent that the approach brings with it certain nontransparent or hidden costs and benefits that can either increase effectiveness or undermine success. Before the overall success of this approach can be evaluated, these costs and benefits must be considered. Among the hidden benefits of situational crime control efforts are:

- *Diffusion.* Sometimes efforts to prevent one crime help prevent another; in other instances, crime control efforts in one locale reduce crime in surrounding areas.[132] This effect is referred to as **diffusion of benefits**. Diffusion may be produced by two independent effects: We can see the effect of diffusion when video cameras set up in a mall to reduce shoplifting can also reduce vandalism. Police surveillance teams whose aim is to control trafficking in a known drug zone unintentionally reduce the incidence of prostitution and other public order crimes by scaring off would-be clients (drug users).[133] Intensive police patrols designed to target teen gangs in one area of town have been shown to help reduce crime in neighboring areas as well.[134]

- *Discouragement.* When protection efforts become effective, potential criminals may become discouraged. **Discouragement** may cause them to either leave the area or seek other methods of gaining financial rewards.

While there are hidden benefits to situational crime prevention, there may also be costs that limit their effectiveness:

- *Displacement.* A program that seems successful because it helps lower crime rates at specific locations or neighborhoods may simply be redirecting offenders to alternative targets; this is known as **displacement**, as crime is not prevented but deflected or displaced.[135] Beefed-up police patrols in one area may shift crimes to a more vulnerable neighborhood.[136]

- *Extinction.* Sometimes crime reduction programs may produce a short-term positive effect, but benefits dissipate as criminals adjust to new conditions. Would-be criminals learn to dismantle alarms or avoid patrols; they may try new offenses they had previously avoided. And elimination of one crime may encourage commission of another: if every residence in a neighborhood has a foolproof burglar alarm system, motivated offenders may be forced to turn to armed robbery, a riskier and more violent crime. A recent analysis of a program in Philadelphia that made use of foot patrols to lower crime rates in areas with high violence rates found that while the program produced statistically significantly less violent crime at first, the deterrent effects began to quickly slow down and eventually became extinct. It is possible that at first offenders may have overestimated the risk of apprehension but as time went on began to realize their mistake and resumed illegal activities; positive results were relatively short lived.[137]

- *Encouragement.* Crime reduction programs may boomerang and increase rather than decrease the potentiality for crime. Some situational efforts rely on increasing the risk of crime by installing street lighting, assuming that rational criminals will avoid areas where their criminal activities are more visible. Take for instance street lighting: many people believe that criminals will avoid a well-lit street. Such plans may backfire. Well-lit areas may bring a greater number of potential victims and potential offenders into the same physical space;

diffusion of benefits Efforts to prevent one crime help prevent another; in other instances, crime control efforts in one locale reduce crime in another area.

discouragement Crime control efforts targeting a particular locale help reduce crime in surrounding areas and populations.

displacement A program that helps lower crime rates at specific locations or neighborhoods may be redirecting offenders to alternative targets.

increased visibility may allow potential offenders to make better judgments of target vulnerability and attractiveness (e.g., they can spot people with jewelry and other valuables). Increased illumination may make it easier for offenders to commit crimes and to escape.[138]

Before the effectiveness of situational crime prevention can be accepted, these hidden costs and benefits must be weighed and balanced.

General Deterrence

L08 Categorize the elements of general deterrence

According to the rational choice view, motivated, rational people will violate the law if left free and unrestricted. **General deterrence** theory holds that crime can be controlled by the threat and/or application of criminal punishment. If people fear being apprehended and punished, being locked up in a harsh prison, or even sentenced to death, they will not risk breaking the law. An inverse relationship should then exist between crime rates and legal sanctions. If the punishment for a crime is increased and the effectiveness and efficiency of the criminal justice system improved, then the number of people willing to risk committing crime should decline.

The severity, certainty, and speed of punishment are interrelated. If a particular crime—say, robbery—is punished severely, but few robbers are ever caught or punished, the severity of punishment for robbery will probably not deter people from robbing. However, if the certainty of apprehension and conviction is increased by modern technology, more efficient police work, or some other factor, then even minor punishment might deter the potential robber.

The certainty of punishment seems to have a greater impact than its severity or speed. People will more likely be deterred from crime if they believe that they will get caught; what happens to them after apprehension seems to have less impact.[139] And there is research showing a robust

general deterrence A crime control policy that depends on the fear of criminal penalties. General deterrence measures, such as long prison sentences for violent crimes, are aimed at convincing the potential law violator that the pains associated with crime outweigh its benefits.

perceptual deterrence The theory that the perceived certainty, severity, and celerity of punishment are inversely related to the decisions by would-be offenders to commit crime, regardless of the actual likelihood of being apprehended and punished. People who believe they will be punished will be deterred even if the actual likelihood of punishment is insignificant.

deterrence theory The view that if the probability of arrest, conviction, and sanctioning increases, crime rates should decline.

association between police arrest data and crime rate levels: the more crimes that result in arrest, the lower the subsequent crime rate.[140]

Nonetheless, all three elements of the deterrence equation are important, and it would be a mistake to emphasize one at the expense of the others. If all resources were given to police agencies to increase the probability of arrest, crime rates might increase because there were insufficient funds for swift prosecution and effective correction.[141]

THE PERCEPTION OF PUNISHMENT AND DETERRENCE

The *perception of punishment* plays a major role in producing crime deterrence.[142] People who feel threatened, who believe they will get caught and punished, will be deterred from committing crime even if the true likelihood of detection and punishment is insignificant; this is referred to as **perceptual deterrence**.[143] Conversely, the *actual likelihood* of punishment will have little effect if potential criminals believe they can escape detection.[144]

Sometimes perceptual deterrence is achieved by passing strict laws accompanied by long prison terms. Take for instance white-collar criminals, who may feel shielded from punishment since they are typically educated, well-off people who move within respected circles of society. Passing strict punishments not only increases the perception of deterrence, but it also reminds judges not to let white-collar defendants use their social status and other resources to avoid the consequences of their violations.[145]

In addition to passing strict laws, what else can be done to increase the perception of punishment? Hiring more police officers and allocating them in ways that increase their visibility have been shown to deter potential offenders.[146] Even the most committed offenders (e.g., gang members, domestic terrorists) who fear legal punishments will forgo or reduce criminal activities if they believe they will be apprehended and punished.[147]

The perception of deterrence works for some people and some crimes more than others; deterrence is rarely an all or nothing proposition.[148] The most significant deterrent effects can be achieved on minor petty criminals, whereas more serious offenders such as murderers are harder to discourage.[149] People who have already experienced punishment in the past are more likely to overestimate the likelihood of future punishments.[150] People "learn from their mistakes," and those who are caught and punished will perceive greater risk than those who have escaped detection.[151]

CERTAINTY OF PUNISHMENT AND DETERRENCE

According to **deterrence theory**, crime and punishment are inversely related: as the probability of legal sanction increases, crime rates decline. If punishment were both certain and imminent, even the most motivated criminal would desist because the risks of crime outweigh its rewards.[152]

Unfortunately, punishment is not very certain. Only 10 percent of all serious offenses result in apprehension (half go unreported, and police make arrests in about 20 percent of reported crimes). As offenders are processed through all the stages of the criminal justice system, the odds of their receiving serious punishment diminish. As a result, some believe they will not be severely punished for their acts and consequently have little regard for the law's deterrent power. If, however, the certainty of punishment could be increased to a critical level, the so-called **tipping point**, then the deterrent effect would kick in and crime rates decline.[153]

One way of reaching the tipping point is to add police officers. As the number of active, aggressive, crime-fighting cops increases, so too do arrests and convictions, convincing would-be criminals that the risk of apprehension outweighs the benefits they can gain from crime.[154]

SEVERITY OF PUNISHMENT AND DETERRENCE

According to general deterrence theory, as the severity of punishment increases, crime rates should decrease. Does this equation hold water? The evidence is decidedly mixed. While some studies have found that increasing sanction levels can control common criminal behaviors, others have not achieved a positive result.[155]

Take the case of enhancing punishment in order to discourage people from using handguns. In this instance a state might add five years to a criminal sentence if a handgun was used during the commission of a crime. When Daniel Kessler and Steven Levitt evaluated the deterrent effect of California's sentencing enhancement act, they found that it did in fact lower crime rates.[156] While these findings are encouraging, optimism is tempered somewhat by the fact that during the same period gun crimes went down in other states, even those that did not enhance or increase their sentences![157]

It stands to reason that if severity of punishment can deter crime, then fear of the death penalty—the ultimate legal deterrent—should significantly reduce murder rates. What does the evidence show? Because this topic is so important, it is featured in the Criminology in Action feature, "Does the Death Penalty Discourage Murder?".

Shame and Humiliation   Fear of shame and embarrassment can be a powerful deterrent to crime. Those who fear being rejected by family and peers are reluctant to engage in deviant behavior.[158] These factors manifest themselves in two ways: (1) personal shame over violating the law and (2) the fear of public humiliation if the deviant behavior becomes public knowledge. People who say that their involvement in crime would cause them to feel ashamed are less likely to offend than people who deny fears of embarrassment.[159]

CONNECTIONS

Even if capital punishment proves to be a deterrent, many experts still question its morality, fairness, and legality. In Chapter 10, murder is discussed in some detail, and there is material that can help you decide whether the death penalty is an appropriate response to intentionally killing someone. Ironically, some people who commit the worst, most dreadful crimes avoid the death penalty by pleading guilty, while others who ask for a trial are sentenced to death for what appear to be less horrific acts.

ASK YOURSELF . . .

Is it fair to condemn someone to death for exercising their constitutional rights?

People who are afraid that significant others—such as parents, peers, neighbors, and teachers—will disapprove of their behavior are less likely to commit crime. The fear of exposure and consequent shaming also may vary according to the cohesiveness of community structure and the type of crime. **Informal sanctions** may be most effective in highly unified areas where everyone knows one another and the crime cannot be hidden from public view. The threat of informal sanctions seems to have the greatest influence on instrumental crimes, which involve planning, and not on impulsive or expressive criminal behaviors or those associated with substance abuse.[160]

While shame can be a potent deterrent, offenders also seem to be influenced by forgiveness and acceptance. They are less likely to repeat their criminal activity if victims are willing to grant them forgiveness.[161]

SPEED (CELERITY) OF PUNISHMENT AND DETERRENCE

The third leg of Beccaria's model of deterrence involves the celerity, or speed, of punishment: the faster punishment is applied and the more closely it is linked to the crime, the more likely it will serve as a deterrent.[162] Research indicates that the value of a given criminal sanction steadily decreases as the lag between crime and punishment lengthens. Because criminals discount punishments that trail behind their crimes, how and when punishment is applied can alter its effect. A criminal who is apprehended, tried, and convicted soon after committing a crime will be more

tipping point   The minimum amount of expected punishment necessary to produce a significant reduction in crime rates.

informal sanctions   Disapproval, stigma, or anger directed toward an offender by significant others (parents, peers, neighbors, teachers), resulting in shame, embarrassment, and loss of respect.

Does the Death Penalty Discourage Murder?

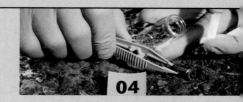

04

According to deterrence theory, the death penalty—the ultimate deterrent—should deter criminals from committing murder—the ultimate crime. A majority of Americans, even convicted criminals who are currently behind bars, approve of the death penalty. But is the public's approval warranted? Does the death penalty actually discourage murder?

Empirical research on the association between capital punishment and murder can be divided into three types: immediate impact studies, comparative research, and time-series studies.

- *Immediate impact.* If capital punishment is a deterrent, the reasoning goes, then its impact should be greatest after a well-publicized execution. However, most research has failed to find evidence that an execution produces an immediate decline in the murder rate; even highly publicized executions had little impact on the murder rate.
- *Comparative research.* It is also possible to compare murder rates in jurisdictions that have abolished the death penalty with the rates in jurisdictions that routinely employ the death penalty. Studies using this approach have found little difference between the murder rates of adjacent states, regardless of their use of the death penalty; capital punishment did not appear to affect the reported rate of homicide.
- *Time-series studies.* If capital punishment is a deterrent, then periods that have an upswing in executions should also experience a downturn in violent crime and murder. Most research efforts have failed to show such a relationship. Economic conditions, population density, and incarceration rates have a much greater impact on the murder rate than does the death penalty.

Rethinking the Deterrent Effect of Capital Punishment

Some recent studies have concluded that executing criminals may, in fact, bring the murder rate down. These newer studies, using sophisticated data analysis, have been able to uncover a more significant association—when a state routinely uses executions, the deterrent effect becomes significant.

These recent pro–death penalty studies are not without their detractors. Jeffrey Fagan, a highly regarded criminologist, finds fault with the methodology now being used, arguing that "this work fails the tests of rigorous replication and robustness analysis that are the hallmarks of good science." Fagan and his colleagues compared homicide rates in two Asian cities with vastly different execution risks. Singapore had at one time a surge in execution rate that made it the highest in the world, before significantly reducing the number of executions. Hong Kong, by contrast, has had no executions all. Nonetheless, homicide levels and trends are remarkably similar in these two cities, with neither the surge in Singapore executions nor the more recent steep drop producing any differential impact. By comparing two closely matched places with huge contrasts in actual execution but no differences in homicide trends, Fagan disputes the relative effectiveness of capital punishment as a crime deterrent.

Similarly, John Donohue and Justin Wolfers examined statistical studies that claimed to show a deterrent effect from the death penalty and found that they "are simply not credible." In fact, they reach an opposite conclusion: applying the death penalty actually *increases* the number of murders.

Rethinking the Death Penalty

The death penalty debate continues. Advocates argue that even if marginally deeply affected than one who experiences a significant delay between crime and punishment.[163]

Unfortunately, the American justice system is handcuffed by delaying tactics by trial lawyers. It is routine to request postponements for trial preparation, in the hope that delaying the trial will benefit their client: evidence may be lost, victims relocate, police officers retire, key witnesses die or change their minds about testifying. As a result, the criminal process can be delayed to a point where the connection between crime and punishment is broken. Take for instance how the death penalty is employed. More than 10 years typically elapse between the time a criminal is convicted for murder and his or her execution. Delay in its application may mitigate or neutralize the potential deterrent effect of capital punishment.

Not unexpectedly, the most experienced offenders, those who know the ins and outs of the system, are the hardest to deter: they know that crimes provide immediate gratification, whereas the threat of punishment is far in the future.[164] The threat of punishment may also be neutralized by the belief that even if caught criminals can avoid severe punishment by having a smart lawyer who can either get them off or reduce their sentence through plea negotiations.[165]

Restrictive/Partial Deterrence Deterrence measures may not eliminate crime but reduce or restrict its occurrence. Deterrence measures may not totally convince criminals that crime does not pay but might help increase their sensitivity to the risks involved in crime and thereby alter or shape their decision making.

effective, capital punishment ensures that convicted murderers never get the opportunity to kill again: about 9 percent of all inmates on death row have had prior convictions for homicide. Advocates note that the murder rate has been in dramatic decline since capital punishment has been reinstated, and the general public approves of its use as a deterrent to murder. Further, as Meredith Martin Rountree's research shows, more than 10 percent of inmates who have been executed hastened their executions by abandoning their appeals, many because they believed their execution was actually fair and justified. If so many death row inmates approve of the death penalty, how can its abolition be justified?

Far from being persuaded, abolitionists note that capital punishment has significant drawbacks. Since 1976, more than 100 people have been wrongfully convicted and sentenced to death in the United States only to be exonerated when new scientific evidence has proven their innocence; the possibility that an innocent person can be executed is real and frightening. In addition, as legal scholar David Baldus and his associates have found, racial bias may influence death penalty decisions in both civilian and military courts. People are more likely to be sentenced to death when a victim is white or in cases involving black criminals and white victims—a race-based outcome that tarnishes the validity of capital punishment.

CRITICAL THINKING

1. Even if it is effective, the death penalty is not without serious problems. When Geoffrey Rapp studied the effect of the death penalty on the safety of police officers, he found that the introduction of capital punishment actually created an extremely dangerous environment for law enforcement officers. Because the death penalty does not have a deterrent effect, criminals are more likely to kill police officers when the death penalty is in place. Tragically, the death penalty may lull officers into a false sense of security, causing them to let down their guard—killing fewer criminals but getting killed more often themselves. Given Rapp's findings, should we still maintain the death penalty?

2. Is it possible that the insignificant effects of the death penalty on murder rates is a function in the legal delays that prolong the sentence from being carried out, leaving killers on death row for many years, even decades, before they are executed? Would you recommend that the process be accelerated and executions carried out soon after guilt is established? Or is there a real purpose to delaying executions so that people on death row can exercise every avenue of appeal, making sure an innocent person is not wrongfully executed?

SOURCE: Jeffrey A. Fagan, "Capital Punishment: Deterrent Effects and Capital Costs," Columbia University School of Law, http://www.law.columbia.edu/law_school/communications/reports/summer06/capitalpunish; Franklin Zimring, Jeffrey Fagan, and David Johnson, "Executions, Deterrence and Homicide: A Tale of Two Cities," http://papers.ssrn.com/sol3/papers.cfm?abstract_id=1436993; Meredith Martin Rountree, "'I'll Make Them Shoot Me': Accounts of Death Row Prisoners Advocating for Execution," *Law and Society Review* 46 (2012): 589–622; David Baldus, Catherine Grosso, George Woodworth, and Richard Newell, "Racial Discrimination in the Administration of the Death Penalty: The Experience of the United States Armed Forces (1984–2005)," *Journal of Criminal Law and Criminology* 101 (2011): 1227–1335; Cass R. Sunstein and Adrian Vermeule, "Is Capital Punishment Morally Required? Acts, Omissions, and Lifetime Tradeoffs," *Stanford Law Review* 58 (2006): 703–750, at 749; Tomislav Kovandzic, Lynne Vieraitis, and Denise Paquette Boots, "Does the Death Penalty Save Lives? New Evidence from State Panel Data, 1977 to 2006," *Criminology and Public Policy* 8 (2009): 803–843; Jeffrey Fagan, "Death and Deterrence Redux: Science, Law and Causal Reasoning on Capital Punishment," *Ohio State Journal of Criminal Law* 4 (2006): 255–320; Joanna Shepherd, "Deterrence versus Brutalization: Capital Punishment's Differing Impacts Among States," *Michigan Law Review* 104 (2005): 203–253; John Donohue and Justin Wolfers, "Uses and Abuses of Empirical Evidence in the Death Penalty Debate," *Stanford Law Review* 58 (2005): 791–845; Geoffrey Rapp, "The Economics of Shootouts: Does the Passage of Capital Punishment Laws Protect or Endanger Police Officers?" *Albany Law Review* 65 (2002): 1051–1084. URLs accessed April 2016.

Criminologist Bruce Jacobs has identified the concept of **restrictive deterrence**, a phenomenon that occurs when deterrence measures convince would-be criminals that the risk of committing a particular crime is just too great. Potential criminals then find ways to adapt to this perceived threat:

- The offender reduces the number of crimes he or she commits during a particular period of time.
- The offender commits less serious crimes, assuming that even if he or she is apprehended, the punishment will not be as severe for a more minor infraction (thus, an offender shoplifts a $100 pair of jeans instead of robbing a convenience store for the same monetary reward).
- The offender takes actions to reduce the chance that he or she will be caught and to increase the chance that the contemplated offense will be undertaken without risk of

detection (e.g., wearing a disguise to avoid being identified by the victim).
- Recognizing danger, the offender commits the same crime at a different place or time.[166]

ANALYZING GENERAL DETERRENCE

While the threat of legal punishment should, on the face of it, deter lawbreakers through fear, the relationship between crime rates and deterrent measures is less than clear cut.

restrictive deterrence Convincing criminals that committing a serious crime is too risky and that other less-dangerous crimes or actions might be a better choice.

Despite efforts to punish criminals and make them fear to commit crime, there is little evidence that the fear of apprehension and punishment alone can reduce crime rates. How can this discrepancy be explained?

Rationality   Deterrence theory assumes a rational offender who weighs the costs and benefits of a criminal act before deciding on a course of action. In many instances, criminals are desperate people who suffer from personality disorders that impair their judgment and render them incapable of making truly rational decisions.[167] It is doubtful that any deterrent measure could have influenced an irrational Jared Loughner when he attempted to assassinate U.S. Representative Gabrielle Giffords or Adam Lanza when he killed children in a Newtown, Connecticut, school. Some criminals may be deranged, impulsive, and imprudent rather than reasoning and calculating.

Compulsion   Many offenders act compulsively and are therefore unlikely to be deterred by the future threat of punishment. Take for instance sex offenders, whose behavior is difficult to control. As you may recall, the evidence showing that sex offender lists can control crime has been spotty. Research shows that registration lists have little effectiveness as a crime control mechanism.[168]

We know that a relatively small group of chronic offenders commits a significant percentage of all serious crimes. Some psychologists believe this select group suffers from an innate or inherited emotional state that renders them both incapable of fearing punishment and less likely to appreciate the consequences of crime.[169] Their compulsive behavior and heightened emotional state negate the deterrent effect of the law.[170]

Need   Many offenders are members of the underclass—people cut off from society, lacking the education and skills they need to be in demand in the modern economy.[171] Such desperate people may not be deterred from crime by fear of punishment because, in reality, they have few other options for success. Among poor, high-risk groups, such as teens living in economically depressed neighborhoods, the threat of formal sanctions is irrelevant.[172] Young people in these areas have less to lose because their opportunities are few, and they have little attachment to social institutions such as school or family. In their environment, they see many people who appear relatively well off (such as the neighborhood drug dealer) committing crimes without getting caught or punished.[173]

Greed   Some may be immune to deterrent effects because they believe the profits from crime are worth the risk of punishment; it may be their only significant chance for gain and profit. The lure of criminal gains outweighs the fear of capture and punishment. Perceived risk of punishment may deter some potential and active criminal offenders, but only if they doubt that they can make a "big score" from committing a crime.[174]

Mark Kelly leans his head on the shoulder of his wife, former Congresswoman Gabby Giffords, as they attend a news conference asking Congress and the Senate to provide stricter gun control in the United States. Giffords and Kelly were joined by survivors of the Tucson shooting as they spoke outside the Safeway grocery store where the shooting happened in 2011. Six people were killed, including a 9-year-old girl. Can such shootings be prevented or deterred?

In 2012, Jared Lee Loughner was judged competent to stand trial for murder. He pleaded guilty and was sentenced to life plus 140 years in federal prison. Is someone like Loughner truly rational?

Greed may encourage some law violators to overestimate the rewards of crime that in reality are often quite meager. When Steven Levitt and Sudhir Alladi Venkatesh studied the financial rewards of being in a drug gang, they found that despite enormous risks to health, life, and freedom, average gang members earned only slightly more than what they could in the legitimate labor market.[175] Why then did they stay in the gang? Members believed that there was a strong potential for future riches if they stayed in the drug business and earned a "management" position (i.e., gang leaders earned a lot more). Deterrence is neutralized because the gang boys' greed causes them to overestimate the potential for future criminal gain versus the probability of apprehension and punishment.[176]

Specific Deterrence

L09 Articulate the basic concepts of specific deterrence

The theory of **specific deterrence** (also called special or particular deterrence) holds that after experiencing criminal sanctions that are swift, sure, and powerful, known criminals will never dare repeat their criminal acts. While general deterrence relies on the perception of future punishments, specific deterrence relies on its application:

- The drunk driver whose sentence is a substantial fine and a week in the county jail should be convinced that the price to be paid for drinking and driving is too great to consider future violations.
- The burglar who spends five years in a tough maximum security prison will find his enthusiasm for theft dampened.
- The tax cheat who is assessed triple damages will think twice before filing a false return.

In principle, punishment works if a connection can be established between the planned action and memories of its consequence; if these recollections are adequately intense, the action will be unlikely to occur again.[177] Yet the connection between experiencing punishment and fearing future punishment is not always as strong as expected.[178]

At first glance, specific deterrence does not seem to work because a majority of known criminals are not deterred by their punishment. Arrest and punishment seem to have little effect on experienced criminals and may even increase the likelihood that first-time offenders will commit new crimes.[179] A sentence to a juvenile justice facility does little to deter a persistent delinquent from becoming an adult criminal.[180] Most prison inmates had prior records of arrest and conviction before their current offenses.[181] About two-thirds of all convicted felons are rearrested within three years of their release from prison, and those who have been punished in the past are the most likely to recidivate.[182] Incarceration may sometimes slow down or delay recidivism in the short term, but the overall probability of rearrest does not change following incarceration.[183]

According to the theory of specific deterrence, the harsher the punishment, the less likely the chances of recidivism. But research shows that this is not always the case. Offenders sentenced to prison do not have lower rates of recidivism than those receiving more lenient community sentences for similar crimes. The effect of incarceration on rearrest appears to be minimal.[184] White-collar offenders who receive prison sentences are as likely to recidivate as those who receive community-based sanctions.[185]

CAN PUNISHMENT PRODUCE MORE CRIME?

In some instances, rather than reducing the frequency of crime, severe punishments may actually increase reoffending rates.[186] Some states are now employing high-security "supermax" prisons that use bare minimum treatment and 23-hours-a-day lockdown. Certainly, such a harsh regimen should deter future criminality. But a recent study in the state of Washington showed that upon release supermax prisoners had significantly higher felony recidivism rates when compared to a matched sample of traditional inmates.[187] There are a number of factors that might help explain why severe punishments promote rather than restrict criminality:

- Offenders may believe they have learned from their experiences, and now know how to beat the system and get away with crime.[188]
- Severely punished offenders may represent the "worst of the worst," who will offend again no matter what punishments they experience.[189]
- Punishment may bring defiance rather than deterrence. People who are harshly treated may want to show that they cannot be broken by the system. Punishment might be perceived to be capricious, unjust, or unfair, which causes sanctioned offenders to commit additional crimes as a way to lash out and retaliate.
- Harsh treatment labels and stigmatizes offenders, locking them into a criminal career.
- Criminals who are punished may also believe that the likelihood of getting caught twice for the same type of crime is remote: "Lightning never strikes twice in the same spot," they may reason; no one is that unlucky.[190]

One crime that is notorious for involving repeat incidents is domestic violence. Can punishment reduce repeat offending? This topic is discussed in the Policy and Practice in Criminology feature.

specific deterrence The view that if experienced punishment is severe enough, convicted offenders will be deterred from repeating their criminal activity.

Deterring Domestic Violence

One of the most famous efforts to determine the specific deterrent effect of punishment was the classic study by Lawrence Sherman and Richard Berk on the effects of arrest on domestic violence. Sherman and Berk had police officers in Minneapolis randomly assign one of three outcomes to domestic assault cases they encountered on their beats:

- Advice and mediation only
- Remove the assailant from the home for a period of eight hours
- Formally arrest the assailant

According to specific deterrence theory, a formal arrest should have a greater impact than advice and mediation, and in this case it did. Sherman and Berk found that when police took formal action (arrest), the chance of recidivism was substantially less than when less punitive measures, such as warning offenders or ordering offenders out of the house for a cooling-off period, were used. A six-month follow-up found that only 10 percent of those who were arrested repeated their violent behavior, while 19 percent of those advised and 24 percent of those sent away repeated their offenses. Sherman and Berk concluded that a formal arrest was the most effective means of controlling domestic violence, regardless of what happened to the offender in court, and the specific deterrent effect of arrest produced positive long-term outcomes.

The Minneapolis experiment deeply affected police operations around the nation. Atlanta, Chicago, Dallas, Denver, Detroit, Miami, New York, San Francisco, and Seattle, among other large cities, adopted policies encouraging arrests in domestic violence cases. A number of states adopted legislation mandating that police either take formal action in domestic abuse cases or explain in writing their failure to act. Nonetheless, replicating the Minneapolis experiment in five other locales—including Omaha, Nebraska, and Charlotte, North Carolina—failed to duplicate the original results. In these locales, formal arrest was not a greater deterrent to domestic abuse than warning or advising the assailant.

Subsequent efforts to link punishment and deterrence in domestic violence cases have also produced inconclusive results. Andrew Klein and Terri Tobin found that batterers in a Massachusetts district court were undeterred by arrest, prosecution, probation supervision, incarceration, and treatment. Although only a minority of the men in the study reabused (32 percent) or were arrested for any crime (43 percent) within a year of their first involvement with the justice system, over the next decade, the majority (60 percent) were involved in a second incident and almost three-fourths were rearrested for a domestic abuse or nondomestic abuse crime. The implications of the domestic violence research are that even if punishment can produce a short-term specific deterrent effect, it fails to produce longer-term behavior change.

CRITICAL THINKING

If the effect of arrest on spouse abuse is only short term, what else can be done to convince men not to batter? Is treatment rather than punishment a better approach? Or would arrest work if it were backed up by mandatory prison sentences? Maybe getting tough is still not tough enough.

SOURCE: Frank Sloan, Alyssa Platt, Lindsey Chepke, and Claire Blevins, "Deterring Domestic Violence: Do Criminal Sanctions Reduce Repeat Offenses?" *Journal of Risk and Uncertainty* 46 (2013): 51–80; Lawrence Sherman and Richard Berk, "The Specific Deterrent Effects of Arrest for Domestic Assault," *American Sociological Review* 49 (1984): 261–272; J. David Hirschel, Ira Hutchison, and Charles Dean, "The Failure of Arrest to Deter Spouse Abuse," *Journal of Research in Crime and Delinquency* 29 (1992): 7–33; Franklyn Dunford, David Huizinga, and Delbert Elliott, "The Role of Arrest in Domestic Assault: The Omaha Experiment," *Criminology* 28 (1990): 183–206. Andrew Klein and Terri Tobin, "A Longitudinal Study of Arrested Batterers, 1995–2005: Career Criminals," *Violence Against Women* 14 (2008): 136–157.

Incapacitation

 Critique the incapacitation strategy to reduce crime

It stands to reason that if more criminals are sent to prison, the crime rate should go down. Because most people age out of crime, the duration of a criminal career is limited. Placing offenders behind bars during their prime crime years

incapacitation effect The idea that keeping offenders in confinement will eliminate the risk of their committing further offenses.

should lessen their lifetime opportunity to commit crime. The shorter the span of opportunity, the fewer offenses they can commit during their lives; hence, crime is reduced. This theory, known as the **incapacitation effect**, seems logical, but does it work? The most recent data indicate that nationwide about 1.5 million people are in prison and another 750,000 are incarcerated in local jails.[191] Because the number of American adults is about 245 million, this means that one in every 100 adults is behind bars.[192] Advocates of incapacitation suggest that this growth in the prison/jail population is directly responsible for the decades-long decline in the crime rate: by putting dangerous felons under lock and key for longer periods of time, the opportunity they have to commit crime is significantly reduced and so too is the crime rate.

Belief that a strict incarceration policy can shape criminal choice and reduce crime rates has encouraged states to adopt tough sentencing laws such as the "three strikes and you're out" policy. This sentencing model mandates that people convicted of three felony offenses serve a mandatory life term without parole. Other states employ habitual offender laws that provide long (or life) sentences for repeat offenders. Those who advocate for these tough laws credit them with producing the two-decade crime drop in America.[193]

DOES INCARCERATION CONTROL CRIME?

The fact that crime rates have dropped while the prison population has boomed supports incapacitation as an effective crime control policy. This assumption seems logical considering how much crime chronic offenders commit each year and the fact that criminal opportunities are ended once they are behind bars. While it is difficult to measure precisely, there is at least some evidence that crime rates and incarceration rates are interrelated. Economist Steven Levitt concludes that each person put behind bars results in a decrease of 15 serious crimes per year. He argues that the social benefits associated with crime reduction equal or exceed the social and financial costs of incarceration.[194] Recent research by Benjamin Meade and his associates support Levitt's conclusion: inmates serving long sentences (five

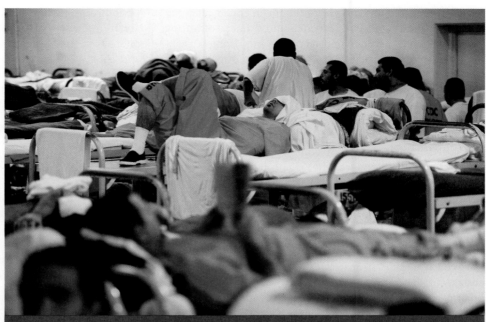

The downside of an incarceration policy: inmates at the California Institution for Men in Chino, California, which houses 5,500 inmates, sleep on double and triple bunk beds in a gymnasium that was modified to house 213 prisoners. A federal court ruling required that the California state prison system release 40,000 prisoners to cope with overcrowding so severe that it violated their human rights. More than 144,000 inmates are currently incarcerated in prisons that were designed to hold about 80,000.

Kevork Djansezian/Getty Images News/Getty Images

years or more) are less likely to recidivate once released than those serving shorter sentences.[195]

What are some of the limitations of incapacitation as an effective method of crime control?

- There is little evidence that incapacitating criminals will deter them from future criminality and even more reason to believe they may be more inclined to commit crimes upon release. The more prior incarceration experiences inmates have, the more likely they are to recidivate (and return to prison) within 12 months of their release.[196] Former inmates often suffer post-release personal and financial problems that cause them to commit more crimes than they might have had they not been sentenced to prison. The crimes that are "saved" while they serve time are more than made up for by the extra ones they commit because they are now "ex-cons."[197]

- By its nature, the prison experience exposes young, first-time offenders to higher-risk, more experienced inmates who can influence their lifestyle and help shape their attitudes. Novice inmates also run an increased risk of becoming infected with AIDS and other health hazards, and that exposure reduces their life chances after release.[198] The short-term crime reduction effect of incapacitating criminals is negated if the prison experience has the long-term effect of escalating frequency of criminal behavior upon release.

- The economics of crime suggest that if money can be made from criminal activity, there will always be

CONNECTIONS

Chapter 2 discussed the factors that control crime rates. If the crime rate drops as more people are sent to prison, it would appear that incapacitation works. However, crime rates may really be dropping because potential criminals now fear punishment and are being deterred from crime. What appears to be an incapacitation effect may actually be caused by perceptual deterrence.

ASK YOURSELF . . .

The crime rate has dropped while the prison population has skyrocketed. Is this an effect of incapacitation or might other factors be at work?

someone to take the place of the incarcerated offender. New criminals will be recruited and trained, offsetting any benefit accrued by incarceration. Imprisoning established offenders may likewise open new opportunities for competitors who were suppressed by more experienced criminals. Incarcerating gang members or organized crime figures may open crime and illegal drug markets to new groups and gangs who are even hungrier and more aggressive than the gangs they replaced.

- Most criminal offenses are committed by teens and very young adult offenders who are unlikely to be sent to prison for a single felony conviction. Aging criminals are already past the age when they are likely to commit crime. As a result, a strict incarceration policy may keep people in prison beyond the time they are a threat to society while a new cohort of high-risk adolescents is on the street.[199]

Even if incarceration could reduce the crime rate, the costs would be enormous. Are U.S. taxpayers willing to spend billions more on new prison construction and annual maintenance fees? A strict incarceration policy would result in a growing number of elderly inmates whose maintenance costs are far higher than those of younger inmates. The numbers of elderly inmates are already skyrocketing: there are now 240,000 elderly inmates behind bars, costing states about $70,000 per inmate annually to care for and maintain.[200] Most recently the Federal Bureau of Prisons (BOP) incarcerated 164,566 federal inmates, of which those age 50 and older were the fastest growing segment, increasing 25 percent since 2009, while the number of younger inmates actually decreased.[201]

- If incarceration were routinely used, the "value" of each commitment would be reduced. Locking up a murderer saves society millions in costs; locking up a shoplifter saves very little. The more incarceration is used, the less "bang for the buck."
- Eventually, most inmates return to society in a process referred to as reentry. In most states, prison inmates, especially those convicted of drug crimes, have come from comparatively few urban inner-city areas. Their return may contribute to family disruption, undermine social institutions, and create community disorganization. Rather than act as a crime suppressant, incarceration may have the long-term effect of accelerating crime rates.[202]
- The incarceration–crime rate relationship is not linear or predictable. There are times when a surge in incarceration coincided with a significant decline in crime rates (1991–2000); however, during other time periods, crime rate increases coincided with increasing incarceration rates (1984–1991).[203] Such findings weaken the argument that the key to lower crime rates is locking people up for long periods of time.

While the debate over the effectiveness of incapacitating criminals to reduce the crime rate rages on, there is no doubt that U.S. sentencing policies have embraced the practice of putting lots of people behind bars for very long periods of time. Prison sentences in the United States today are frequently two to three times the length for similar offenses in the United Kingdom, the Netherlands, France, and other industrialized nations.[204]

Concept Summary 4.1 outlines the various methods of crime control and their effects.

CONCEPT SUMMARY 4.1
Crime Control Strategies Based on Rational Choice

Situational Crime Prevention

- This strategy is aimed at convincing would-be criminals to avoid specific targets. It relies on the doctrine that crime can be avoided if motivated offenders are denied access to suitable targets.
- Operationalizations of this strategy are home security systems or guards, which broadcast the message that guardianship is great here, stay away; the potential reward is not worth the risk of apprehension.
- Problems with the strategy are the extinction of the effect and displacement of crime.

General Deterrence Strategies

- These strategies are aimed at making potential criminals fear the consequences of crime. The threat of punishment is meant to convince rational criminals that crime does not pay.
- Operationalizations of these strategies are the death penalty, mandatory sentences, and aggressive policing.
- Problems with these strategies are that criminals do not fear punishment and the certainty of arrest and punishment is low.

Specific Deterrence Strategy

- This strategy refers to punishing known criminals so severely that they will never be tempted to repeat their offenses. If crime is rational, then painful punishment should reduce its future allure.
- Operationalizations of this strategy are harsh prisons and stiff fines.
- A problem with this strategy is that punishment may increase reoffending rates rather than deter crime.

Incapacitation Strategies

- These strategies attempt to reduce crime rates by denying motivated offenders the opportunity to commit crime. If, despite the threat of law and punishment, some people still find crime attractive, then the only way to control their behavior is to incarcerate them for extended periods.
- Operationalizations of these strategies are long prison sentences, placing more people behind bars.
- A problem with these strategies is that people are kept in prison beyond the years they may commit crime. Minor, nondangerous offenders are also locked up, and this is a very costly strategy.

An Ethical Dilemma

No Frills

The governor is running for reelection on a law and order plank. He claims that prisons don't work because they are too lenient. He proposes ending hot meals, education programs, counseling, and phone privileges. Television and other recreation would be curtailed, as well as visitation. His reasoning is that if prison were just an awful experience, few inmates would risk returning and therefore would be afraid to commit new crimes.

Write a brief position paper giving your take on the plan. Would it work? Even if it did, are there ethical issues with the governor's proposed "no frills" approach? To paraphrase the decision in *Bell v. Wolfish*, prisons are places for punishment, but should they be punishing places?

Public Policy Implications of Choice Theory

From the origins of classical theory to the development of modern rational choice views, the belief that criminals choose to commit crime has influenced the relationships among law, punishment, and crime. Although research on the core principles of choice theory and deterrence theories produces mixed results, these models have had an important impact on crime prevention strategies.

POLICE AND DETERRENCE

While adding cops seems a logical way of deterring crime, this assumption has been questioned ever since the classic Kansas City patrol study found that crime rates were unaffected by merely increasing (or decreasing) the number of police on patrol. However, there has been some recent evidence indicating that adding to police patrol forces does in fact help reduce crime rates and that police are a more effective deterrent than toughening sentences or putting people in prison.[205]

The deterrent effect of police may be aided by the tactics they use to control crime. Focused crime-fighting initiatives, targeting specific crimes such as murder or robbery, are more effective than routine patrol. Some police departments have instituted **crackdowns**, sudden changes in police activity designed to increase the communicated threat or actual certainty of punishment. Lawrence Sherman found that while crackdowns initially deterred crime, crime rates returned to earlier levels once the crackdown ended.[206] While there is little evidence that crackdowns alone can deter crime, there is some support for an approach where police departments combine crackdowns with aggressive problem-solving and community improvement techniques, such as increasing lighting and cleaning vacant lots. Merely saturating an area with police may not deter crime, but focusing efforts on a particular problem area has a deterrent effect.

Another recent approach known as "pulling levers policing" or **focused deterrence** is about activating or pulling every deterrent "lever" available to reduce the targeted problem. If it is juvenile gang violence, responses may include shutting down drug markets, serving warrants, enforcing probation restrictions, and making disorder arrests. A major component of this approach is communicating direct and explicit messages to offenders about the responses they can expect if this behavior is not stopped. One of the most successful examples of this policing strategy is Boston's Operation Ceasefire, which employed a variety of law enforcement and social agencies, including probation and parole, the Bureau of Alcohol, Tobacco, Firearms, and Explosives (ATF), gang outreach and prevention street workers, local police, and the Drug Enforcement Administration (DEA).

The Ceasefire group delivered its message clearly to gang members: "We're ready, we're watching, we're waiting: Who wants to be next?" Careful evaluations using sophisticated matching group comparisons found that the program was an effective deterrent to gang crime.[207]

COURTS, SENTENCING, AND DETERRENCE

The fact that punishment may deter criminals from committing crime has shaped sentencing policy. A number of states have adopted draconian sentencing policies that require mandatory prison terms for specific crimes such as drug trafficking or the use of a firearm while committing a crime. Another deterrence strategy is the "three strikes and you're out" laws, which require the state courts to hand down mandatory periods of incarceration of up to life in prison to persons who have been convicted of a serious criminal offense on three or more separate occasions. While a policy of placing people convicted of a third felony behind bars for life is politically compelling, many criminologists believe these laws are ineffective and will create a growing population of expensive to maintain elderly inmates who committed relatively minor crimes.[208]

And despite the ongoing debate about its deterrent effect, the death penalty is still employed in a majority of states and by the federal government. Some advocates argue that the death penalty can effectively restrict criminality; at

crackdowns The concentration of police resources on particular problem areas, such as street-level drug dealing, to eradicate or displace criminal activity.

focused deterrence A policy that relies on pulling every deterrent "lever" available to reduce crime in the targeted problem.

least it ensures that convicted criminals never again get the opportunity to kill. Many observers are dismayed because people who are convicted of murder sometimes kill again when released on parole. About 9 percent of all inmates on death row have had prior convictions for homicide. Death penalty advocates argue that if these criminals had been executed for their first offenses, hundreds of people would be alive today.[208] And the recent evidence indicating that if used a lot capital punishment can reduce a state's murder rate has encouraged some members of the moral and legal community to suggest that capital punishment is justified because it is a life-saving social policy. Writing in the *Stanford Law Review*, Cass Sunstein and Adrian Vermeule conclude that "a government that settles upon a package of crime control policies that does *not* include capital punishment might well seem, at least prima facie, to be both violating the rights and reducing the welfare of its citizens—just as would a state that failed to enact simple environmental measures promising to save a great many lives."[209]

JUST DESERT

The concept of criminal choice has also prompted the creation of justice policies referred to as **just desert**. In his classic book *Doing Justice*, legal expert Andrew von Hirsch suggests that punishment, commensurate with the seriousness of the crime, is needed to preserve the social equity disturbed by crime.[210] As he puts it, those who violate others' rights deserve to be punished, but, to be fair, since punishment makes those punished suffer, it should only be sufficient to prevent more misery than it inflicts—no more, no less.[211] Punishing someone to deter others is wrong and unfair and so is punishing someone so they won't commit crime in the future, since the future is impossible to predict. People should be punished simply because they deserve to be; they are **blameworthy**.

> **just desert** The philosophy of justice that asserts that those who violate the rights of others deserve to be punished. The severity of punishment should be commensurate with the seriousness of the crime.
>
> **blameworthy** Basing punishment solely on whether a person is responsible for wrongdoing and deserving of censure or blame.

According to legal scholar Richard Frase, two basic elements determine an offender's degree of blameworthiness: the nature and seriousness of the harm caused or threatened by the crime, and the offender's degree of fault in committing the crime.[212] If an offender is blameworthy for what they did in the present, their punishment should only reflect the character of their present offense; people deserve to be punished for what they did, not for what others may do or what they may do in the future.

Assigning Blame   How do we determine how much punishment is fitting for a particular crime? In other words, how do we assess blame? According to Frase, in contemporary society, fault is measured by a number of factors: the offender's intent (e.g., deliberate wrongdoing is considered more serious than criminal negligence); his or her capacity to obey the law (e.g., blameworthiness is tempered by such conditions as mental disease or defect, chemical dependency, or situational factors such as threats or other strong inducements to commit the crime); the offender's motives for committing the crime (which may mitigate or aggravate culpability); and, for multidefendant crimes, the defendant's role in the offense as instigator, leader, follower, primary actor, or minor player.[213] According to Frase, fairness is brought to the justice process by assessing blame in a fair and even-handed manner: fairness to the victim and the victim's family (i.e., otherwise they might seek vengeance on their own), fairness to law-abiding persons (who refrained from committing this offense), and fairness to the defendant (who has a right to be punished in proportion to his blameworthiness).

In sum, the just desert model suggests that retribution justifies punishment because people deserve what they get for past deeds. Punishment based on deterrence or incapacitation is wrong because it involves an offender's future actions, which cannot accurately be predicted. Punishment should be the same for all people who commit the same crime. Criminal sentences based on individual needs or characteristics are inherently unfair because all people are equally blameworthy for their misdeeds. The influence of von Hirsch's views can be seen in sentencing models that give the same punishment to all people who commit the same type of crime.

SUMMARY

L01 **Describe the development of rational choice theory**

Rational choice theory has its roots in the classical school of criminology developed by the eighteenth-century Italian social thinker Cesare Beccaria. James Q. Wilson observed that people who are likely to commit crime are unafraid of breaking the law because they value the excitement and thrills of crime, have a low stake in conformity, and are willing to take greater chances than the average person.

L02 **Discuss the most important concepts of rational choice theory**

Law-violating behavior is the product of careful thought and planning. People who commit crime believe that the rewards of crime outweigh the risks. If they think they are likely to get arrested and punished, people will not risk criminal activities. Before choosing to commit a crime, reasoning criminals carefully select targets, and their behavior is systematic and selective. Rational choice theorists view crime as both offense- and offender-specific.

L03 Analyze the process in which offenders structure criminality

Criminals consider their needs and capabilities before committing crimes. One important decision that is made before someone enters a life of crime is the need for money. Personal experience may be an important element in structuring criminality. Before committing crimes, criminals report, they actually learn techniques to help them avoid detection while making profits.

L04 Depict in your own words how criminals structure crime

Criminals carefully choose where they will commit their crime. Evidence of rational choice may be found in the way criminals locate their targets. Rational choice involves both shaping criminality and structuring crime. If a target appears dangerous, criminals will choose another.

L05 Clarify the arguments that crime is rational

There is evidence that theft-related crimes are the product of careful risk assessment, including environmental, social, and structural factors. Target selection seems highly rational. Even drug use is controlled by rational decision making. Users report that they begin taking drugs when they believe the benefits of substance abuse outweigh its costs. Evidence confirms that even violent criminals select suitable targets by picking people who are vulnerable and lack adequate defenses. In some instances, targets are chosen in order to send a message rather than to generate capital.

L06 Identify the elements of the CRAVED model of crime choice

According to the CRAVED model of crime choice, the elements that encourage crime are targets that are easily hidden, portable, widely available and easy to find, valuable, enjoyable to own, and easy to sell.

L07 Assess the validity of situational crime prevention techniques for reducing crime

Situational crime prevention involves developing tactics to reduce or eliminate a specific crime problem. These include tactics to increase the effort required to commit crime, such as putting unbreakable glass on storefronts, locking gates, and fencing yards. It can also involve increasing the risks of crime through better security efforts. Reducing the rewards of crime is designed to lessen the value of crime to the potential criminal. Crime may be reduced or prevented if we can communicate to people the wrongfulness of their behavior and how it is harmful to society. Crime may be reduced by making it difficult for people to excuse their criminal behavior by saying things like "I didn't know that was illegal" or "I had no choice."

L08 Categorize the elements of general deterrence

As the fear of punishment increases, crime rates decrease. If the certainty of arrest, conviction, and sanctioning increases, crime rates should decline. The threat of severe punishment should also bring the crime rate down. The faster punishment is applied and the more closely it is linked to the crime, the more likely it will serve as a deterrent. Not only does the actual chance of punishment influence criminality, so too does the perception of punishment. People who perceive they will be punished for crimes will avoid doing those crimes.

L09 Articulate the basic concepts of specific deterrence

The theory of specific deterrence holds that criminal sanctions should be so powerful that known criminals will never repeat their criminal acts. Research on specific deterrence does not provide any clear-cut evidence that punishing criminals is an effective means of stopping them from committing future crimes. Punishment may bring defiance rather than deterrence. People who are harshly treated may want to show that they cannot be broken by the system. The stigma of harsh treatment labels people and helps lock offenders into a criminal career instead of convincing them to avoid one.

L010 Critique the incapacitation strategy to reduce crime

The more criminals are sent to prison, the more the crime rate should go down. Placing offenders behind bars during their prime crime years should reduce their lifetime opportunity to commit crime. The shorter the span of opportunity, the fewer offenses they can commit during their lives; hence, crime is reduced. However, there is little evidence that incapacitating criminals will deter them from future criminality and reason to believe they may be more inclined to commit even more crimes upon release.

CRITICAL THINKING QUESTIONS

1. Are criminals rational decision makers, or are they motivated by uncontrollable psychological and emotional drives?
2. Would you want to live in a society where crime rates are low because criminals are subjected to extremely harsh punishments, such as flogging?
3. If you were caught by the police while shoplifting, which would you be more afraid of: receiving criminal punishment or being ashamed to face your friends or relatives?
4. Is it possible to create a method of capital punishment that would actually deter murder by televising executions? What might be some of the negative consequences of such a policy?

KEY TERMS

Enlightenment (103)
marginal deterrence (103)
classical criminology (103)
rational choice theory (105)
reasoning criminal (106)
human agency (106)
offense-specific crime (107)
offender-specific crime (108)

criminality (108)
boosters (111)
permeable neighborhood (111)
edgework (115)
situational crime
  prevention (116)
defensible space (116)
crime discouragers (117)

diffusion of benefits (119)
discouragement (119)
displacement (119)
general deterrence (120)
perceptual deterrence (120)
deterrence theory (120)
tipping point (121)
informal sanctions (121)

restrictive deterrence (123)
specific deterrence (125)
incapacitation effect (126)
crackdowns (129)
focused deterrence (129)
just desert (130)
blameworthy (130)

NOTES

All URLs accessed in 2016.

1. United States Attorney's Office, Northern District of Ohio, "Toledo Man Sentenced to 27 Years in Prison for Operating Chop Shop, Eight Others Also Sent to Prison," http://www.justice.gov/usao-ndoh/pr/toledo -man-sentenced-27-years-prison-operating -chop-shop-0; FBI, "Multi-State Chop Shop Operation Disrupted: Criminal Enterprise Leader Among Those Convicted," June 23, 2015, https://www.fbi.gov/news/stories /2015/june/multi-state-chop-shop-operation -disrupted/.

2. Jennifer Feeha, "Chop-Shop Ringleader Sentenced to 27 Years, Theft Ring Stole, Cut Up Big Rigs," *The Blade*, May 5, 2015, http://www.toledoblade.com/news /2015/05/05/Chop-shop-ringleader -sentenced-to-27-years.html.

3. Alan Harding, *Medieval Law and the Foundations of the State* (New York: Oxford University Press, 2002).

4. Eugen Weber, *A Modern History of Europe* (New York: W. W. Norton, 1971), p. 398.

5. Jeremy Bentham, *A Fragment on Government and an Introduction to the Principle of Morals and Legislation* (1776), ed. Wilfred Harrison (Oxford: Basil Blackwell, 1967).

6. Ibid., p. xi.

7. Ibid.

8. George J. Stigler, "The Optimum Enforcement of Laws," *Journal of Political Economy* 78 (1970): 526–528.

9. Marvin Wolfgang, *Patterns in Criminal Homicide* (Philadelphia: University of Pennsylvania Press, 1958).

10. Bob Roshier, *Controlling Crime* (Chicago: Lyceum Books, 1989), p. 10.

11. Robert Martinson, "What Works? Questions and Answers about Prison Reform," *Public Interest* 35 (1974): 22–54.

12. Charles Murray and Louis Cox, *Beyond Probation* (Beverly Hills: Sage, 1979).

13. Ronald Bayer, "Crime, Punishment, and the Decline of Liberal Optimism," *Crime and Delinquency* 27 (1981): 190.

14. James Q. Wilson, *Thinking About Crime*, rev. ed. (New York: Vintage Books, 1983), p. 260.

15. Ibid., p. 128.

16. Michael Tonry, *Malign Neglect: Race, Crime and Punishment in America* (New York: Oxford University Press, 1995).

17. Ann Carson and Daniela Golinelli, *Prisoners in 2012—Advance Counts* (Washington, DC: Bureau of Justice Statistics, 2013), http:// www.bjs.gov/content/pub/ascii/p12ac.txt.

18. John Irwin and James Austin, *It's About Time: America's Imprisonment Binge* (Belmont, CA: Wadsworth, 1997).

19. See, generally, Derek Cornish and Ronald Clarke, eds., *The Reasoning Criminal: Rational Choice Perspectives on Offending* (New York: Springer Verlag, 1986); and Morgan Reynolds, *Crime by Choice: An Economic Analysis* (Dallas: Fisher Institute, 1985).

20. David A. Ward, Mark C. Stafford, and Louis N. Gray, "Rational Choice, Deterrence, and Theoretical Integration," *Journal of Applied Social Psychology* 36 (2006): 571–585.

21. Hung-en Sung and Linda Richter, "Rational Choice and Environmental Deterrence in the Retention of Mandated Drug Abuse Treatment Clients," *International Journal of Offender Therapy and Comparative Criminology* 51 (2007): 686–702.

22. Timothy Brezina, "Delinquent Problem-Solving: An Interpretive Framework for Criminological Theory and Research," *Journal of Research in Crime and Delinquency* 37 (2000): 3–30.

23. Bill McCarthy and John Hagan, "Mean Streets: The Theoretical Significance of Situational Delinquency Among Homeless Youths," *American Journal of Sociology* 3 (1992): 597–627.

24. Andy Hochstetler, "Opportunities and Decisions: Interactional Dynamics in Robbery and Burglary Groups," *Criminology* 39 (2001): 737–763.

25. Jeff Ferrell, "Criminological Verstehen: Inside the Immediacy of Crime," *Justice Quarterly* 14 (1997): 3–23.

26. Peter Wood, Walter Gove, James Wilson, and John Cochran, "Nonsocial Reinforcement and Habitual Criminal Conduct: An Extension of Learning," *Criminology* 35 (1997): 335–366.

27. Melanie Wellsmith and Amy Burrell, "The Influence of Purchase Price and Ownership Levels on Theft Targets: The Example of Domestic Burglary," *British Journal of Criminology* 45 (2005): 741–764.

28. Carlo Morselli and Marie-Noële Royer, "Criminal Mobility and Criminal Achievement," *Journal of Research in Crime and Delinquency* 45 (2008): 4–21.

29. Ross Matsueda, Derek Kreager, and David Huizinga, "Deterring Delinquents: A Rational Choice Model of Theft and Violence," *American Sociological Review* 71 (2006): 95–122.

30. Jeffrey Bouffard, "Predicting Differences in the Perceived Relevance of Crime's Costs and Benefits in a Test of Rational Choice Theory," *International Journal of Offender Therapy and Comparative Criminology* 51 (2007): 461–485.

31. Christopher Uggen and Melissa Thompson, "The Socioeconomic Determinants of Ill-Gotten Gains: Within-Person Changes in Drug Use and Illegal Earnings," *American Journal of Sociology* 109 (2003): 146–187.

32. Philippe Bourgois, *In Search of Respect: Selling Crack in El Barrio* (Cambridge: Cambridge University Press, 1995), p. 326.

33. Bouffard, "Predicting Differences in the Perceived Relevance of Crime's Costs and Benefits in a Test of Rational Choice Theory."

34. George Rengert and John Wasilchick, *Suburban Burglary: A Time and Place for Everything* (Springfield, IL: Charles C Thomas, 1985).

35. Christopher Birkbeck and Gary LaFree, "The Situational Analysis of Crime and Deviance," *American Review of Sociology* 19 (1993): 113–137.

36. Derek Cornish and Ronald Clarke, "Understanding Crime Displacement: An Application of Rational Choice Theory," *Criminology* 25 (1987): 933–947.

37. Michael Gottfredson and Travis Hirschi, *A General Theory of Crime* (Stanford, CA: Stanford University Press, 1990).

38. D. Wayne Osgood and Amy Anderson, "Unstructured Socializing and Rates of Delinquency," *Criminology* 42 (2004): 519–550.

39. Wim Bernasco, Stijn Ruiter, Gerben Bruinsma, Lieven Pauwels, and Frank Weerman, "Situational Causes of Offending: A Fixed-Effects Analysis of Space–Time Budget Data," *Criminology* 51 (2013): 895–926.

40. Megan Bears Augustyn and Jean Marie McGloin, "The Risk of Informal Socializing with Peers: Considering Gender Differences Across Predatory Delinquency and Substance Use," *Justice Quarterly* 30 (2013): 117–143.

41. Jack Katz, *The Seductions of Crime* (New York: Basic Books, 1988).

42. Holly Nguyen and Jean Marie McGloin, "Does Economic Adversity Breed Criminal Cooperation? Considering the Motivation Behind Group Crime," *Criminology* 51 (2013): 833–870.

43. Uggen and Thompson, "The Socioeconomic Determinants of Ill-Gotten Gains."

44. Pierre Tremblay and Carlo Morselli, "Patterns in Criminal Achievement: Wilson and Abrahamse Revisited," *Criminology* 38 (2000): 633–660.

45. Liliana Pezzin, "Earnings Prospects, Matching Effects, and the Decision to Terminate a Criminal Career," *Journal of Quantitative Criminology* 11 (1995): 29–50.

46. Melissa Thompson and Christopher Uggen, "Dealers, Thieves, and the Common Determinants of Drug and Nondrug Illegal Earnings," *Criminology* 59 (2012): 1057–1087.

47. Ronald Akers, "Rational Choice, Deterrence, and Social Learning Theory in Criminology: The Path Not Taken," *Journal of Criminal Law and Criminology* 81 (1990): 653–676.

48. Neal Shover, *Aging Criminals* (Beverly Hills: Sage, 1985).

49. Patricia Morgan and Karen Ann Joe, "Citizens and Outlaws: The Private Lives and Public Lifestyles of Women in the Illicit Drug Economy," *Journal of Drug Issues* 26 (1996): 125–142, at 132.

50. Bruce Jacobs, "Crack Dealers' Apprehension Avoidance Techniques: A Case of Restrictive Deterrence," *Justice Quarterly* 13 (1996): 359–381.

51. Ibid., p. 367.

52. Ibid., p. 372.

53. Bruce Jacobs and Jody Miller, "Crack Dealing, Gender, and Arrest Avoidance," *Social Problems* 45 (1998): 550–566.

54. Jacobs, "Crack Dealers' Apprehension Avoidance Techniques."

55. Ibid., p. 368.

56. Eric Baumer, Janet Lauritsen, Richard Rosenfeld, and Richard Wright, "The Influence of Crack Cocaine on Robbery, Burglary, and Homicide Rates: A Cross-City, Longitudinal Analysis," *Journal of Research in Crime and Delinquency* 35 (1998): 316–340.

57. George Rengert and John Wasilchick, *Space, Time, and Crime: Ethnographic Insights into Residential Burglary* (Washington, DC: National Institute of Justice, 1989); see also Rengert and Wasilchick, *Suburban Burglary.*

58. Paul Cromwell, James Olson, and D'Aunn Wester Avary, *Breaking and Entering, an Ethnographic Analysis of Burglary* (Newbury Park, CA: Sage, 1989), pp. 30–32.

59. Ibid., p. 24.

60. Michael Costanzo, William Halperin, and Nathan Gale, "Criminal Mobility and the Directional Component in Journeys to Crime," in *Metropolitan Crime Patterns*, ed. Robert Figlio, Simon Hakim, and George Rengert (Monsey, NY: Criminal Justice Press, 1986), pp. 73–95.

61. Morselli and Royer, "Criminal Mobility and Criminal Achievement."

62. Joseph Deutsch and Gil Epstein, "Changing a Decision Taken Under Uncertainty: The Case of the Criminal's Location Choice," *Urban Studies* 35 (1998): 1335–1344.

63. Robert Sampson and Jacqueline Cohen, "Deterrent Effects of the Police on Crime: A Replication and Theoretical Extension," *Law and Society Review* 22 (1988): 163–188.

64. Kenneth Tunnell, *Choosing Crime* (Chicago: Nelson-Hall, 1992), p. 105.

65. Paul Bellair, "Informal Surveillance and Street Crime: A Complex Relationship," *Criminology* 38 (2000): 137–167.

66. Gary Kleck and Don Kates, *Armed: New Perspectives on Guns* (Amherst, NY: Prometheus Books, 2001).

67. Elizabeth Ehrhardt Mustaine and Richard Tewksbury, "Predicting Risks of Larceny Theft Victimization: A Routine Activity Analysis Using Refined Lifestyle Measures," *Criminology* 36 (1998): 829–858.

68. Bruce A. Jacobs and Richard Wright, "Researching Drug Robbery," *Crime and Delinquency* 54 (2008): 511–531.

69. Associated Press, "Thrift Hearings Resume Today in Senate," *Boston Globe*, January 2, 1991, p. 10.

70. Ralph Taylor and Stephen Gottfredson, "Environmental Design, Crime, and Prevention: An Examination of Community Dynamics," in *Communities and Crime*, ed. Albert Reiss and Michael Tonry (Chicago: University of Chicago Press, 1986), pp. 387–416.

71. Pamela Wilcox, Tamara Madensen, and Marie Skubak Tillyer, "Guardianship in Context: Implications for Burglary Victimization Risk and Prevention," *Criminology* 45 (2007): 771–803.

72. Garland White, "Neighborhood Permeability and Burglary Rates," *Justice Quarterly* 7 (1990): 57–67.

73. Ibid., p. 65.

74. Matthew Robinson, "Lifestyles, Routine Activities, and Residential Burglary Victimization," *Journal of Criminal Justice* 22 (1999): 27–52.

75. Cromwell, Olson, and Avary, *Breaking and Entering.*

76. Andrew Buck, Simon Hakim, and George Rengert, "Burglar Alarms and the Choice Behavior of Burglars: A Suburban Phenomenon," *Journal of Criminal Justice* 21 (1993): 497–507.

77. John Gibbs and Peggy Shelly, "Life in the Fast Lane: A Retrospective View by Commercial Thieves," *Journal of Research in Crime and Delinquency* 19 (1982): 229–230.

78. John Petraitis, Brian Flay, and Todd Miller, "Reviewing Theories of Adolescent Substance Use: Organizing Pieces in the Puzzle," *Psychological Bulletin* 117 (1995): 67–86.

79. Leanne Fiftal Alarid, James Marquart, Velmer Burton, Francis Cullen, and Steven Cuvelier, "Women's Roles in Serious Offenses: A Study of Adult Felons," *Justice Quarterly* 13 (1996): 431–454, at 448.

80. James A. Densley, "It's Gang Life, but Not as We Know It: The Evolution of Gang Business," *Crime and Delinquency,* first published online April 4, 2012.

81. Scott Allen and Richard Wright, "Drug Dealers' Rational Choices on Which Customers to Rip-off," *International Journal of Drug Policy* 25 (2014): 251–256.

82. Trevor Bennett and Fiona Brookman, "The Role of Violence in Street Crime: A Qualitative Study of Violent Offenders," *International Journal of Offender Therapy and Comparative Criminology* 53 (2009): 617–633.

83. Richard B. Felson, *Violence and Gender Reexamined* (Washington, DC: American Psychological Association, 2002).

84. Michael Townsley, Daniel Birks, Wim Bernasco, Stijn Ruiter, Shane D. Johnson, and Gentry White, "Burglar Target Selection: A Cross-National Comparison," *Journal of Research in Crime and Delinquency* 52 (2015): 3–31.

85. Richard Felson and Steven Messner, "To Kill or Not to Kill? Lethal Outcomes in Injurious Attacks," *Criminology* 34 (1996): 519–545, at 541.

86. Marie Rosenkrantz Lindegaard, Wim Bernasco, and Scott Jacques, "Consequences of Expected and Observed Victim Resistance for Offender Violence During Robbery Events," *Journal of Research in Crime and Delinquency* 52 (2015): 32–61.

87. James Wright and Peter Rossi, *Armed and Considered Dangerous: A Survey of Felons and Their Firearms* (Hawthorne, NY: Aldine De Gruyter, 1983), pp. 141–159.

88. Gary Kleck and Marc Gertz, "Carry Guns for Protection: Results from the National Self-Defense Survey," *Journal of Research in Crime and Delinquency* 35 (1998): 193–224.

89. Peter van Koppen and Robert Jansen, "The Time to Rob: Variations in Time and Number of Commercial Robberies," *Journal of Research in Crime and Delinquency* 36 (1999): 7–29.

90. William Smith, Sharon Glave Frazee, and Elizabeth Davison, "Furthering the Integration of Routine Activity and Social Disorganization Theories: Small Units of Analysis and the Study of Street Robbery as a Diffusion Process," *Criminology* 38 (2000): 489–521.

91. Wim Bernasco and Paul Nieuwbeerta, "How Do Residential Burglars Select Target Areas? A New Approach to the Analysis of Criminal Location Choice," *British Journal of Criminology* 45 (2005): 296–315.

92. Alan Lizotte, Marvin Krohn, James Howell, Kimberly Tobin, and Gregory Howard, "Factors Influencing Gun Carrying Among Young Urban Males over the Adolescent–Young Adult Life Course," *Criminology* 38 (2000): 811–834.

93. Scott Decker, "Deviant Homicide: A New Look at the Role of Motives and Victim–Offender Relationships," *Journal of Research in Crime and Delinquency* 33 (1996): 427–449.

94. Felson and Messner, "To Kill or Not to Kill?"

95. Eric Hickey, *Serial Murderers and Their Victims* (Pacific Grove, CA: Brooks/Cole, 1991), p. 84.

96. Benoit Leclerc, Richard Wortley, and Stephen Smallbone, "Getting into the Script of Adult Child Sex Offenders and Mapping Out Situational Prevention Measures," *Journal of Research in Crime and Delinquency* 48 (2011): 209–237.

97. Benoit Leclerc, Jean Proulx, and André McKibben, "Modus Operandi of Sexual Offenders Working or Doing Voluntary Work with Children and Adolescents," *Journal of Sexual Aggression* 11 (2005): 187–195.

98. Ryan King and Gretchen Sutto, "High Times for Hate Crimes: Explaining the Temporal Clustering of Hate-Motivated Offending," *Criminology* 51 (2013): 871–894.

99. Christopher Birkbeck and Gary LaFree, "The Situational Analysis of Crime and Deviance," *American Review of Sociology* 19 (1993): 113–137; Karen Heimer and Ross Matsueda, "Role-Taking, Role Commitment, and Delinquency: A Theory of Differential Social Control," *American Sociological Review* 59 (1994): 400–437.

100. Peter Wood, Walter Gove, James Wilson, and John Cochran, "Nonsocial Reinforcement and Habitual Criminal Conduct: An Extension of Learning," *Criminology* 35 (1997): 335–366.

101. Ferrell, "Criminological Verstehen," p. 12.

102. Gottfredson and Hirschi, *A General Theory of Crime*.

103. Jeff Gruenewald, Kayla Allison-Gruenewald, and Brent R. Klein, "Assessing the Attractiveness and Vulnerability of Eco-Terrorism Targets: A Situational Crime Prevention Approach," *Studies in Conflict and Terrorism* 38 (2015): 433–455.

104. Patricia Brantingham, Paul Brantingham, and Wendy Taylor, "Situational Crime Prevention as a Key Component in Embedded Crime Prevention," *Canadian Journal of Criminology and Criminal Justice* 47 (2005): 271–292.

105. Oscar Newman, *Defensible Space: Crime Prevention Through Urban Design* (New York: Macmillan, 1973).

106. C. Ray Jeffery, *Crime Prevention Through Environmental Design* (Beverly Hills: Sage, 1971).

107. See also Pochara Theerathorn, "Architectural Style, Aesthetic Landscaping, Home Value, and Crime Prevention," *International Journal of Comparative and Applied Criminal Justice* 12 (1988): 269–277.

108. Ronald Clarke, *Situational Crime Prevention: Successful Case Studies* (Albany, NY: Harrow and Heston, 1992).

109. Gohar A. Petrossian and Ronald V. Clarke, "Explaining and Controlling Illegal Commercial Fishing, An Application of the CRAVED Theft Model," *British Journal of Criminology* 54 (2014): 73–90; Ronald Clarke, Rick Kemper, and Laura Wyckoff, "Controlling Cell Phone Fraud in the U.S.," *Security Journal* 14 (2001): 7–22.

110. Marcus Felson, "Routine Activities and Crime Prevention," in *National Council for Crime Prevention, Studies on Crime and Crime Prevention, Annual Review*, Vol. 1 (Stockholm: Scandinavian University Press, 1992), pp. 30–34.

111. Derek Cornish and Ronald Clarke, "Opportunities, Precipitators and Criminal Decisions: A Reply to Wortley's Critique of Situational Crime Prevention," *Crime Prevention Studies* 16 (2003): 41–96; Ronald Clarke and Ross Homel, "A Revised Classification of Situational Prevention Techniques," in *Crime Prevention at a Crossroads*, ed. Steven P. Lab (Cincinnati: Anderson Publishing, 1997).

112. Lynn A. Addington and Callie Marie Rennison, "Keeping the Barbarians Outside the Gate? Comparing Burglary Victimization in Gated and Non-Gated Communities," *Justice Quarterly* 32 (2015): 168–192.

113. National Institute of Justice, "Biometrics," 2016, http://www.nij.gov/topics/technology/biometrics/.

114. Jim Dawson, "Fighting Crime With Science," *NIJ Journal* 276 (2016), http://www.nij.gov/journals/276/Pages/fighting-crime-with-science.aspx.

115. Matt Nobles, Jill Levenson, and Tasha Youstin, "Effectiveness of Residence Restrictions in Preventing Sex Offense Recidivism," *Crime and Delinquency* 58 (2012): 491–513.

116. Eric Fritsch, Tory Caeti, and Robert Taylor, "Gang Suppression Through Saturation Patrol, Aggressive Curfew, and Truancy Enforcement: A Quasi-Experimental Test of the Dallas Anti-Gang Initiative," *Crime and Delinquency* 45 (1999): 122–139.

117. Kenneth Adams, "The Effectiveness of Juvenile Curfews at Crime Prevention," *Annals of the American Academy of Political and Social Science* 587 (2003): 136–159.

118. Brantingham, Brantingham, and Taylor, "Situational Crime Prevention as a Key Component in Embedded Crime Prevention."

119. http://www.lojack.com/.

120. Marcus Felson, "Those Who Discourage Crime," in *Crime and Place, Crime Prevention Studies*, Vol. 4, ed. John Eck and David Weisburd (New York: Criminal Justice Press, 1995), pp. 53–66; John Eck, "Drug Markets and Drug Places: A Case-Control Study of the Spatial Structure of Illicit Drug Dealing," Ph.D. dissertation, University of Maryland, College Park, 1994.

121. Eck, "Drug Markets and Drug Places," p. 29.

122. Lorraine Green Mazerolle, Colleen Kadleck, and Jan Roehl, "Controlling Drug and Disorder Problems: The Role of Place Managers," *Criminology* 36 (1998): 371–404.

123. Brandon Welsh, David Farrington, and Sema Taheri, "Effectiveness and Social Costs of Public Area Surveillance for Crime Prevention," *Annual Review of Law and Social Science* 11 (2015): 111–130.

124. Keith Proctor, "The Great Surveillance Boom," CNN News, April 26, 2013, http://fortune.com/2013/04/26/the-great-surveillance-boom/.

125. Welsh, Farrington, and Taheri, "Effectiveness and Social Costs of Public Area Surveillance for Crime Prevention"; Brandon C. Welsh and David P. Farrington, *Making Public Places Safer: Surveillance and Crime Prevention* (New York: Oxford University Press, 2008).

126. Ronald Clarke, "Deterring Obscene Phone Callers: The New Jersey Experience," *Situational Crime Prevention*, ed. Ronald Clarke (Albany, NY: Harrow and Heston, 1992), pp. 124–132.

127. Bob Edward Vásquez, Sean Maddan, and Jeffery T. Walker, "The Influence of Sex Offender Registration and Notification Laws in the United States: A Time-Series Analysis," *Crime and Delinquency* 54 (2008): 175–192.

128. Naomi J. Freeman, "The Public Safety Impact of Community Notification Laws: Rearrest of Convicted Sex Offenders," *Crime and Delinquency* 58 (2012): 539–564.

129. Philip Cook and Jens Ludwig, "The Economist's Guide to Crime Busting," *NIJ Journal* 270 (2012), http://nij.gov/nij/journals/270/economists-guide.htm.

130. Read Hayes, Daniel M. Downs, and Robert Blackwood, "Anti-theft Procedures and Fixtures: A Randomized Controlled Trial of Two Situational Crime Prevention Measures," *Journal of Experimental Criminology* 8 (2012): 1–15.

131. Jon Shane and Shannon Magnuson, "Successful and Unsuccessful Pirate Attacks Worldwide: A Situational Analysis," *Justice Quarterly*, first published online September 25, 2014.

132. Ronald Clarke and David Weisburd, "Diffusion of Crime Control Benefits: Observations of the Reverse of Displacement," in *Crime Prevention Studies*, Vol. 2, ed. Clarke.

133. David Weisburd and Lorraine Green, "Policing Drug Hot Spots: The Jersey City Drug Market Analysis Experiment," *Justice Quarterly* 12 (1995): 711–734.

134. Anthony Braga, Andrew Papachristos, and David M. Hureau, "The Effects of Hot Spots Policing on Crime: An Updated Systematic Review and Meta-Analysis," *Justice Quarterly*, first published online May 16, 2012.

135. Robert Barr and Ken Pease, "Crime Placement, Displacement, and Deflection," in *Crime and Justice, A Review of Research*, Vol. 12, ed. Michael Tonry and Norval Morris (Chicago: University of Chicago Press, 1990), pp. 277–319.

136. Bruce Taylor, Christopher Koper, and Daniel Woods, "A Randomized Control Trial of Different Policing Strategies at Hot Spots of Violent Crime," *Journal of Experimental Criminology* 7 (2011): 149–181.

137. Evan Sorg, Cory Haberman, Jerry Ratcliffe, and Elizabeth Groff, "Foot Patrol in Violent Crime Hot Spots: The Longitudinal Impact of Deterrence and Posttreatment Effects of Displacement," *Criminology* 51 (2013): 65–101.

138. Brandon Welsh and David Farrington, "Crime Prevention and Hard Technology: The Case of CCTV and Improved Street Lighting," in *The New Technology of Crime, Law, and Social Control*, ed. James Byrne and Donald Rebovich (Monsey, NY: Criminal Justice Press, 2007).

139. Daniel Nagin and Greg Pogarsky, "An Experimental Investigation of Deterrence: Cheating, Self-Serving Bias, and Impulsivity," *Criminology* 41 (2003): 167–195.

140. Hope Corman and Naci Mocan, "Alcohol Consumption, Deterrence and Crime in New York City," *Journal of Labor Research* 36 (2015): 103–128.

141. Silvia Mendes, "Certainty, Severity, and Their Relative Deterrent Effects: Questioning the Implications of the Role of Risk in Criminal Deterrence Policy," *Policy Studies Journal* 32 (2004): 59–74.

142. Robert Apel, Greg Pogarsky, and Leigh Bates, "The Sanctions–Perceptions Link in a Model of School-Based Deterrence," *Journal of Quantitative Criminology* 25 (2009): 201–226.

143. Etienne Blais and Jean-Luc Bacher, "Situational Deterrence and Claim Padding: Results from a Randomized Field Experiment," *Journal of Experimental Criminology* 3 (2007): 337–352.

144. Robert Bursik, Harold Grasmick, and Mitchell Chamlin, "The Effect of Longitudinal Arrest Patterns on the Development of Robbery Trends at the Neighborhood Level," *Criminology* 28 (1990): 431–450.

145. Peter Henning, "Deterrence Relevant in Sentencing White-Collar Defendants?" *Wayne Law Review* 61 (2015): 25–57.

146. Steven Durlauf and Daniel Nagin, "Imprisonment and Crime: Can Both Be Reduced?" *Criminology and Public Policy* 10 (2011): 13–54.

147. Jennifer Varriale Carson, "Counterterrorism and Radical Eco-Groups: A Context for Exploring the Series Hazard Model," *Journal of Quantitative Criminology*, first published online October 2013; Cheryl L. Maxson, Kristy N. Matsuda, and Karen Hennigan, "Deterrability Among Gang and Nongang Juvenile Offenders: Are Gang Members More (or Less) Deterrable than Other Juvenile Offenders?" *Crime and Delinquency* 57 (2011): 516–543.

148. Greg Pogarsky, "Identifying 'Deterrable' Offenders: Implications for Deterrence Research," *Justice Quarterly* 19 (2002): 431–452.

149. Dieter Dolling, Horst Entorf, Dieter Hermann, and Thomas Rupp, "Deterrence Effective? Results of a Meta-Analysis of Punishment," *European Journal on Criminal Policy and Research* 15 (2009): 201–224.

150. Thomas Loughran, Alex Piquero, Jeffrey Fagan, and Edward Mulvey, "Differential Deterrence: Studying Heterogeneity and Changes in Perceptual Deterrence Among Serious Youthful Offenders," *Crime and Delinquency* 58 (2012): 3–27.

151. Shamena Anwar and Thomas Loughran, "Testing a Bayesian Learning Theory of Deterrence Among Serious Juvenile Offenders," *Criminology* 49 (2011): 667–698.

152. R. Steven Daniels, Lorin Baumhover, William Formby, and Carolyn Clark-Daniels, "Police Discretion and Elder Mistreatment: A Nested Model of Observation, Reporting, and Satisfaction," *Journal of Criminal Justice* 27 (1999): 209–225.

153. Charles Tittle and Alan Rowe, "Certainty of Arrest and Crime Rates: A Further Test of the Deterrence Hypothesis," *Social Forces* 52 (1974): 455–462.

154. David Bayley, *Policing for the Future* (New York: Oxford, 1994).

155. Nagin and Pogarsky, "Integrating Celerity, Impulsivity, and Extralegal Sanction Threats into a Model of General Deterrence," pp. 884–885.

156. Daniel Kessler and Steven D. Levitt, "Using Sentence Enhancements to Distinguish Between Deterrence and Incapacitation," *Journal of Law and Economics* 42 (1999): 343–363.

157. Cheryl Marie Webster, Anthony Doob, and Franklin Zimring, "Proposition 8 and Crime Rates in California: The Case of the Disappearing Deterrent," *Criminology and Public Policy* 5 (2006): 417–448.

158. Donald Green, "Past Behavior as a Measure of Actual Future Behavior: An Unresolved Issue in Perceptual Deterrence Research," *Journal of Criminal Law and Criminology* 80 (1989): 781–804, at 803; Matthew Silberman, "Toward a Theory of Criminal Deterrence," *American Sociological Review* 41 (1976): 442–461; Linda Anderson, Theodore Chiricos, and Gordon Waldo, "Formal and Informal Sanctions: A Comparison of Deterrent Effects," *Social Problems* 25 (1977): 103–114. See also Maynard Erickson and Jack Gibbs, "Objective and Perceptual Properties of Legal Punishment and Deterrence Doctrine," *Social Problems* 25 (1978): 253–264; and Daniel Nagin and Raymond Paternoster, "Enduring Individual Differences and Rational Choice Theories of Crime," *Law and Society Review* 27 (1993): 467–485.

159. Harold Grasmick and Robert Bursik, "Conscience, Significant Others, and Rational Choices: Extending the Deterrence Model," *Law and Society Review* 24 (1990): 837–861, at 854.

160. Thomas Peete, Trudie Milner, and Michael Welch, "Levels of Social Integration in Group Contexts and the Effects of Informal Sanction Threat on Deviance," *Criminology* 32 (1994): 85–105.

161. Harry Wallace, Julie Juola Exline, and Roy Baumeister, "Interpersonal Consequences of Forgiveness: Does Forgiveness Deter or Encourage Repeat Offenses?" *Journal of Experimental Social Psychology* 44 (2008): 453–460.

162. Richard D. Clark, "Celerity and Specific Deterrence: A Look at the Evidence," *Canadian Journal of Criminology* 30 (1988): 109–122.

163. Yair Listokin, "Crime and (with a Lag) Punishment: The Implications of Discounting for Equitable Sentencing," *American Criminal Law Review* 44 (2007): 115–140.

164. Greg Pogarsky, KiDeuk Kim, and Ray Paternoster, "Perceptual Change in the National Youth Survey: Lessons for Deterrence Theory and Offender Decision-Making," *Justice Quarterly* 22 (2005): 1–29.

165. Charles N. W. Keckler, "*Life v. Death*: Who Should Capital Punishment Marginally Deter?" *Journal of Law, Economics and Policy* 2 (2006): 101–161.

166. Bruce A. Jacobs, "Deterrence and Deterrability," *Criminology* 48 (2010): 417–442.

167. James A. Swartz and Arthur J. Lurigio, "Serious Mental Illness and Arrest: The Generalized Mediating Effect of Substance Use," *Crime and Delinquency* 53 (2007): 581–604.

168. Cynthia Najdowski, Hayley Cleary, and Margaret Stevenson, "Adolescent Sex Offender Registration Policy: Perspectives on General Deterrence Potential from Criminology and Developmental Psychology," *Psychology, Public Policy, and Law*, September 7, 2015.

169. David Lykken, "Psychopathy, Sociopathy, and Crime," *Society* 34 (1996): 30–38.

170. George Lowenstein, Daniel Nagin, and Raymond Paternoster, "The Effect of Sexual Arousal on Expectations of Sexual Force-fulness," *Journal of Research in Crime and Delinquency* 34 (1997): 443–473.

171. Ken Auletta, *The Under Class* (New York: Random House, 1982).

172. Wanda Foglia, "Perceptual Deterrence and the Mediating Effect of Internalized Norms Among Inner-City Teenagers," *Journal of Research in Crime and Delinquency* 34 (1997), 414–442 ; Raymond Paternoster, "Decisions to Participate in and Desist from Four Types of Common Delinquency," *Law and Society Review* 23 (1989), 7–40; Raymond Paternoster, "Examining Three-Wave Deterrence Models: A Question of Temporal Order and Specification," *Journal of Criminal Law and Criminology* 79 (1988): 135–163; Raymond Paternoster, Linda Saltzman, Gordon Waldo, and Theodore Chiricos, "Estimating Perceptual Stability and Deterrent Effects: The Role of Perceived Legal Punishment in the Inhibition of Criminal Involvement," *Journal of Criminal Law and Criminology* 74 (1983): 270–297; M. William Minor and Joseph Harry, "Deterrent and Experiential Effects in Perceptual Deterrence Research: A Replication and Extension," *Journal of*

Research in Crime and Delinquency 19 (1982): 190–203; Lonn Lanza-Kaduce, "Perceptual Deterrence and Drinking and Driving Among College Students," *Criminology* 26 (1988): 321–341.

173. Foglia, "Perceptual Deterrence and the Mediating Effect of Internalized Norms Among Inner-City Teenagers," pp. 419–443.

174. Alex Piquero and George Rengert, "Studying Deterrence with Active Residential Burglars," *Justice Quarterly* 16 (1999): 451–462.

175. Steven Levitt and Sudhir Alladi Venkatesh, "An Economic Analysis of a Drug-Selling Gang's Finances," *NBER Working Papers* 6592 (Cambridge, MA: National Bureau of Economic Research, Inc., 1998).

176. Bill McCarthy, "New Economics of Sociological Criminology," *Annual Review of Sociology* (2002): 417–442.

177. James Q. Wilson and Richard Herrnstein, *Crime and Human Nature* (New York: Simon & Schuster, 1985), p. 494.

178. Alicia Sitren and Brandon Applegate, "Testing the Deterrent Effects of Personal and Vicarious Experience with Punishment and Punishment Avoidance," *Deviant Behavior* 28 (2007): 29–55.

179. Christina Dejong, "Survival Analysis and Specific Deterrence: Integrating Theoretical and Empirical Models of Recidivism," *Criminology* 35 (1997): 561–576.

180. Paul Tracy and Kimberly Kempf-Leonard, *Continuity and Discontinuity in Criminal Careers* (New York: Plenum Press, 1996).

181. Lawrence Greenfeld, *Examining Recidivism* (Washington, DC: U.S. Government Printing Office, 1985).

182. Allen Beck and Bernard Shipley, *Recidivism of Prisoners Released in 1983* (Washington, DC: Bureau of Justice Statistics, 1989).

183. Dejong, "Survival Analysis and Specific Deterrence," p. 573.

184. Daniel Nagin and G. Matthew Snodgrass, "The Effect of Incarceration on Re-offending: Evidence from a Natural Experiment in Pennsylvania," *Journal of Quantitative Criminology* December 29 (2013): 601–642.

185. David Weisburd, Elin Waring, and Ellen Chayet, "Specific Deterrence in a Sample of Offenders Convicted of White-Collar Crimes," *Criminology* 33 (1995): 587–607.

186. Dejong, "Survival Analysis and Specific Deterrence"; Raymond Paternoster and Alex Piquero, "Reconceptualizing Deterrence: An Empirical Test of Personal and Vicarious Experiences," *Journal of Research in Crime and Delinquency* 32 (1995): 251–258.

187. David Lovell, L. Clark Johnson, and Kevin Cain, "Recidivism of Supermax Prisoners in Washington State," *Crime and Delinquency* 53 (2007): 633–656.

188. Peter Wood, "Exploring the Positive Punishment Effect Among Incarcerated Adult Offenders," *American Journal of Criminal Justice* 31 (2007): 8–22.

189. Jacobs, "Deterrence and Deterrability."

190. Greg Pogarsky and Alex R. Piquero, "Can Punishment Encourage Offending? Investigating the 'Resetting' Effect," *Journal of Research in Crime and Delinquency* 40 (2003): 92–117.

191. Danielle Kaeble, Lauren Glaze, Anastasios Tsoutis, and Todd Minton, *Correctional Populations in the United States, 2014* (Washington, DC: Bureau of Justice Statistics, 2015), http://www.bjs.gov /content/pub/pdf/cpus14.pdf.

192. Bureau of Justice Statistics, "U.S. Correctional Population Declined By Less Than 1 Percent for the Second Consecutive Year," December 19, 2014, http://www.bjs .gov/content/pub/press/cpus13pr.cfm; see also, Pew Charitable Trust, *One in 100: Behind Bars in America 2008* (Washington, DC: Pew Charitable Trusts, 2008), http:// www.pewtrusts.org/en/research-and -analysis/reports/2008/02/28/one-in -100-behind-bars-in-america-2008.

193. William Spelman, "Specifying the Relationship Between Crime and Prisons," *Journal of Quantitative Criminology* 24 (2008): 149–178.

194. Steven Levitt, "Why Do Increased Arrest Rates Appear to Reduce Crime: Deterrence, Incapacitation, or Measurement Error?" *Economic Inquiry* 36 (1998): 353–372; see also Thomas Marvell and Carlisle Moody, "The Impact of Prison Growth on Homicide," *Homicide Studies* 1 (1997): 205–233.

195. Benjamin Meade, Benjamin Steiner, Matthew Makarios, and Lawrence Travis, "Estimating a Dose–Response Relationship Between Time Served in Prison and Recidivism," *Journal of Research in Crime and Delinquency* November 50 (2013): 525–550.

196. John Wallerstedt, *Returning to Prison, Bureau of Justice Statistics Special Report* (Washington, DC: U.S. Department of Justice, 1984).

197. Michael Ostermann and Joel Caplan, "How Much Do the Crimes Committed by Released Inmates Cost?" *Crime and Delinquency*, first published online November 5, 2013.

198. James Marquart, Victoria Brewer, Janet Mullings, and Ben Crouch, "The Implications of Crime Control Policy on HIV/AIDS-Related Risk Among Women Prisoners," *Crime and Delinquency* 45 (1999): 82–98.

199. Jose Canela-Cacho, Alfred Blumstein, and Jacqueline Cohen, "Relationship Between the Offending Frequency of Imprisoned and Free Offenders," *Criminology* 35 (1997): 133–171.

200. American Civil Liberties Union, "At America's Expense: The Mass Incarceration of the Elderly," 2012, https://www.aclu.org/criminal-law-reform/report-americas-expense-mass-incarceration-elderly.

201. Office of the Inspector General, U.S. Department of Justice, "The Impact of an Aging Inmate Population on the Federal Bureau of Prisons," revised February 2016, https://oig.justice.gov/reports/2015/e1505.pdf.

202. James Lynch and William Sabol, "Prisoner Reentry in Perspective," Urban Institute, http://www.urban.org/research/publication/prisoner-reentry-perspective.

203. Cook and Ludwig, "The Economist's Guide to Crime Busting."

204. David Cole and Marc Mauer, "Reducing Crime by Reducing Incarceration: Longer Sentences Don't Mean Fewer Crimes," *Washington Times*, November 14, 2013, http://www.washingtontimes.com/news/2013/nov/14/cole-and-mauer-reducing-crime-by-reducing-incarcer/.

205. Daniel Nagin, "Deterrence in the Twenty-first Century: A Review of the Evidence," in *Crime and Justice: An Annual Review of Research*, ed. Michael Tonry (Chicago: University of Chicago Press, 2013).

206. Lawrence Sherman, "Police Crackdowns: Initial and Residual Deterrence," in *Crime and Justice: An Annual Review of Research*, Vol. 12, ed. Michael Tonry and Norval Morris (Chicago: University of Chicago Press 1990): pp. 1–48.

207. Anthony Braga, David Hureau, and Andrew Papachristos, "Deterring Gang-Involved Gun Violence: Measuring the Impact of Boston's Operation Ceasefire on Street Gang Behavior," *Journal of Quantitative Criminology* 30 (2014): 113–139.

208. Marc Mauer, testimony before the U.S. Congress, House Judiciary Committee, on "Three Strikes and You're Out," March 1, 1994.

209. James Stephan and Tracy Snell, *Capital Punishment, 1994* (Washington, DC: Bureau of Justice Statistics, 1996), p. 8.

210. Cass R. Sunstein and Adrian Vermeule, "Is Capital Punishment Morally Required? Acts, Omissions, and Life-Life Tradeoffs," *Stanford Law Review* 58 (2006) 703–750, at 749.

211. Andrew von Hirsch, *Doing Justice* (New York: Hill and Wang, 1976).

212. Ibid.

213. Richard Frase, "Punishment Purposes," *Stanford Law Review* 67 (2005): 67–85.

214. Ibid.

Students, staff, and faculty are evacuated from Umpqua Community College.

LEARNING OBJECTIVES

L01 Trace the development of trait theory

L02 Differentiate between the biochemical conditions that produce crime

L03 Clarify the neurophysiological conditions associated with crime

L04 Cite examples of the different research techniques used to link genetics to crime

L05 Explain the evolutionary view of crime

L06 Discuss the elements of the psychodynamic perspective

L07 Link behavioral theory to crime

L08 Articulate the cognitive processes related to crime

L09 Identify the elements of personality related to crime

L010 Comment upon the controversy over the association between intelligence and crime

5 TRAIT THEORIES

A neighbor said that 26-year-old Chris Harper-Mercer would "sit by himself in the dark in the balcony with this little light." Harper-Mercer was the man who opened fire at Umpqua Community College in Roseburg, Oregon, on October 1, 2015, killing nine people and wounding seven others; he shot himself after exchanging gunfire with responding officers. Harper-Mercer left behind a long, rambling letter that told of being depressed and angry; he had a low opinion of himself and obsessed about his place in the world, which he apparently did not think was very good. He had an online blog that referenced other multiple shooting incidents. In one post he discussed Vester Flanagan, the man who on August 26, 2015, killed reporter Alison Parker and photojournalist Adam Ward while they were reporting live on camera in Moneta, Virginia. About this horrific case, Harper-Mercer wrote, "I have noticed that so many people like [Flanagan] are alone and unknown, yet when they spill a little blood, the whole world knows who they are. A man who was known by no one, is now known by everyone. His face splashed across every screen, his name across the lips of every person on the planet, all in the course of one day. Seems like the more people you kill, the more you're in the limelight."[1]

enseless tragedies such as these help convince some criminologists that the root cause of crime may be linked to mental or physical abnormality. How could a young man such as Chris Harper-Mercer engage in mass murder unless he were suffering from some form of mental instability or collapse? And yet, while in the aftermath of the killings there seemed to be ample evidence that he was under severe psychological stress, no one had been able to foresee or predict his violent actions.

This vision is neither new nor unique. The image of a disturbed, mentally ill offender seems plausible because more than one generation of Americans has grown up on films and TV shows that portray violent criminals as mentally deranged and physically abnormal.[2] Beginning with Alfred Hitchcock's film *Psycho*, producers have made millions depicting the ghoulish acts of people who at first seem normal and even friendly but turn out to be demented and dangerous. Lurking out there are fanatical patients (*Saw I* through *Saw VI*, plus *Saw 3D*), crazed babysitters (*The Hand that Rocks the Cradle*), frenzied airline passengers (*Red Eye*, *Turbulence*), deranged roommates (*Single White Female*), cracked neighbors (*Disturbia, Last House on the Left*), psychotic tenants (*Pacific Heights*), demented secretaries (*The Temp*), unhinged police (*Maniac Cop*), mad cab drivers (*The Bone Collector*), irrational fans (*The Fan, Misery*), abnormal girlfriends (*Obsessed, Fatal Attraction*) and boyfriends (*Fear*), unstable husbands (*Enough, Sleeping with the Enemy*) and wives (*Black Widow*), loony fathers (*The Stepfather*), mothers (*Mama, Friday the 13th, Part 1*), and grandparents (*The Visit*), unbalanced crime victims (*I Know What You Did Last Summer*), maniacal children (*The Good Son, Children of the Corn*), manical hotel owners (*Psycho, Hostel* and *Hostel: Parts II and III*), lunatic high school friends (*Scream*) and college classmates (*Scream II*), possessed dolls (*Child's Play 1* through *3*) and their mates (*Bride of Chucky*), and nutsy teenaged admirers in person (*The Crush*). Sometimes they even try to kill each other (*Freddy vs. Jason*), and some are not even totally human but spirits out for revenge (*Unfriended, Insidious,* and *Insidious: Chapters 2 and 3*). No one can ever be safe when doctors, psychologists, and psychiatrists who should be treating these disturbed people turn out to be demonic murderers themselves (*The Human Centipede, Hannibal, Silence of the Lambs*). And of course, even if they are killed they may come back as zombies (*World War Z, Evil Dead, I Am Legend*). Is it any wonder that we respond to a particularly horrible crime by saying of the perpetrator, "That guy must be crazy" or "She is a monster"!

The view that criminals bear physical and/or mental traits that make them different and abnormal is not restricted to the moviegoing public. Since the nineteenth century, criminologists have suggested that biological and psychological traits have the power to influence behavior. People develop physical or mental traits at birth or soon after that affect their social functioning over the life course and influence their behavior choices. Because these mental and physical traits are rare and occur infrequently, only a few people in any social environment embark on criminal careers. As you may recall, only a small percentage of all offenders go on to become persistent repeaters; most people age out of crime. It makes logical sense that what sets these chronic offenders apart from the "average" criminal is an abnormal biochemical makeup, brain structure, genetic constitution, or some other personal trait.[3] The fact that each of us has a unique physical makeup and personality structure explains why, when faced with the same life situations, one person commits crime and becomes a chronic offender, whereas another attends school, church, and neighborhood functions and obeys the laws of society.

To understand this view of crime causation, we begin with a brief review of the development of trait theories.

Foundations of Trait Theory

 L01 Trace the development of trait theory

During the late nineteenth century, the scientific method was beginning to take hold in Europe. Rather than relying on pure thought and reason, scientists began to use careful observation and analysis of natural phenomena in their experiments. This movement inspired new discoveries in biology, astronomy, and chemistry. Charles Darwin's (1809–1882) discoveries on the evolution of man encouraged a nineteenth-century "cult of science." Darwin's discoveries encouraged other scholars to be certain that all human activity could be verified by scientific principles. If the scientific method could be applied to the study of the natural world, then why not use it to study human behavior?

Auguste Comte (1798–1857), considered the founder of sociology, applied scientific methods to the study of society. According to Comte, societies pass through stages that can be grouped on the basis of how people try to understand the world in which they live. People in primitive societies consider inanimate objects as having life (for example, the sun is a god); in later social stages, people embrace a rational, scientific view of the world. Comte called this final stage the positive stage, and those who followed his writings became known as positivists. As we understand it today, **positivism** has two main elements:

■ All true knowledge is acquired through direct observation and not through conjecture or belief. Statements that cannot be backed up by direct observation—for instance, "all babies are born innocent"—are invalid and worthless.

positivism The branch of social science that uses the scientific method of the natural sciences and suggests that human behavior is a product of social, biological, psychological, or economic forces.

Cesare Lombroso

INTERFOTO/Alamy Stock Photo

■ The scientific method must be used if research findings are to be considered valid. This involves such steps as identifying problems, collecting data, forming hypotheses, conducting experiments, and interpreting results (see Exhibit 5.1).

According to the positivist tradition, social processes are a product of the measurable interaction between relationships and events. Human behavior therefore is a function of a variety of forces. Some are social, such as the effect of wealth and class; others are political and historical, such as war and famine. Other forces are more personal and psychological, such as an individual's brain structure and his or her biological makeup or mental ability. Each of these forces influences and shapes human behavior. People are born neither "good" nor "bad," and are neither "saints" nor "sinners." They are a product of their social and psychological traits, influenced by their upbringing and environment.

BIOLOGICAL POSITIVISM

The earliest "scientific" studies applying the positivist model to criminology were conducted by physiognomists, such as J. K. Lavater (1741–1801), who studied the facial features of criminals to determine whether the shape of ears, nose, and eyes and the distance between them were associated with antisocial behavior. Phrenologists, such as Franz Joseph Gall (1758–1828) and Johann K. Spurzheim (1776–1832), studied the shape of the skull and bumps on the head to determine whether these physical attributes were linked to criminal behavior. Phrenologists believed that external cranial characteristics dictate which areas of the brain control physical activity. The brain, they suggested, has 30 different areas or faculties that control behavior. The size of a brain could be determined by inspecting the contours of the skull—the larger the organ, the more active it was. The relative size of brain organs could be increased or decreased through exercise and self-discipline.[4] Though phrenology techniques and methods are no longer practiced or taken seriously, these efforts were an early attempt to use a "scientific" method to study crime.

By the early nineteenth century, abnormality in the human mind was being linked to criminal behavior patterns.[5] Philippe Pinel (1745–1826), one of the founders of French psychiatry, claimed that some people behave abnormally even without being mentally ill. He coined the phrase *manie sans delire* to denote what today is referred to as a **psychopathic personality**. In 1812, an American, Benjamin Rush (1745–1813), described patients with an "innate preternatural moral depravity."[6] Another early criminological pioneer, English physician Henry Maudsley (1835–1918), believed that insanity and criminal behavior were strongly linked. He stated: "Crime is a sort of outlet in which their unsound tendencies are discharged; they would go mad if they were not criminals, and they do not go mad because they are criminals."[7] These early research efforts shifted attention to brain functioning and personality as the keys to criminal behavior. When Sigmund Freud's (1856–1939) work on the unconscious gained worldwide notoriety, the psychological basis of behavior was forever established.

CESARE LOMBROSO

In Italy, Cesare Lombroso (1835–1909), a physician who served much of his career in the Italian army, was studying the cadavers of executed criminals in an effort to scientifically determine whether law violators were physically different from people of conventional values and behavior.[8] Lombroso believed that serious offenders—those who engaged in repeated assault- or theft-related activities—were "born criminals" who had inherited a set of primitive physical traits that he referred to as **atavistic anomalies**. Physically, born criminals were throwbacks to more primitive savage people. Among the crime-producing traits Lombroso identified were enormous jaws and strong canine teeth common to carnivores and savages who devour raw flesh. These criminogenic traits can be acquired through *indirect heredity*, from a degenerate family whose members suffered

from such ills as insanity, syphilis, and alcoholism, or *direct heredity*—being the offspring of criminal parents.

Lombroso's version of criminal anthropology was brought to the United States via articles and textbooks that adopted his ideas. He attracted a circle of followers who expanded on his vision of **biological determinism** and helped stimulate interest in what is referred to as **criminal anthropology**.[9] Ironically, Lombroso's research was more popular in the United States than it was in Europe, and by the turn of the century, American social thinkers were discussing "the science of penology" and "the science of criminology."[10]

 To read an interesting analysis of Lombroso written in 1912 by Charles Ellwood, go to **http://scholarlycommons.law.northwestern.edu/jclc/vol2/iss5/6**.

What do you think of the concept of the "born criminal"? Is such a thing possible? Are some people "born to be bad" or are people "made to be bad"?

Lombroso's Contemporaries   Lombroso was not alone in his views on the biological basis of crime. A contemporary, Raffaele Garofalo (1852–1934), shared the belief that certain physical characteristics indicate a criminal nature: "a lower degree of sensibility to physical pain seems to be demonstrated by the readiness with which prisoners submit to the operation of tattooing."[11] Enrico Ferri (1856–1929) added a social dimension to Lombroso's work and argued that criminals should not be held personally or morally responsible for their actions because forces outside their control caused criminality.[12]

Advocates of the **inheritance school**, such as Henry Goddard, Richard Dugdale, and Arthur Estabrook, traced several generations of crime-prone families (referred to by pseudonyms such as the "Jukes" and the "Kallikaks"), finding evidence that criminal tendencies were based on genetics.[13] Their conclusion: traits deemed socially inferior could be passed down from generation to generation through inheritance. Modern scholars point out that these families lived in severe poverty so that social rather than biological factors may have been at the root of their problems.[14]

The body build or **somatotype** school, developed more than 50 years ago by William Sheldon, held that criminals manifest distinct physiques that make them susceptible to particular types of antisocial behavior. Three types of body builds were identified:

- *Mesomorphs* have well-developed muscles and an athletic appearance. They are active, aggressive, sometimes violent, and the most likely to become criminals.
- *Endomorphs* have heavy builds and are slow moving. They are known for lethargic behavior, rendering them unlikely to commit violent crime and more willing to engage in less strenuous criminal activities such as fencing stolen property.

psychopathic personality A personality characterized by a lack of warmth and feeling, inappropriate behavior responses, and an inability to learn from experience. Some psychologists view psychopathy as a result of childhood trauma; others see it as a result of biological abnormality.

atavistic anomalies According to Lombroso, the physical characteristics that distinguish born criminals from the general population and are throwbacks to animals or primitive people.

biological determinism A belief that criminogenic traits can be acquired through indirect heredity from a degenerate family whose members suffered from such ills as insanity, syphilis, and alcoholism, or through direct heredity—being related to a family of criminals.

criminal anthropology Early efforts to discover a biological basis of crime through measurement of physical and mental processes.

inheritance school Advocates of this view trace the activities of several generations of families believed to have an especially large number of criminal members.

somatotype A system developed for categorizing people on the basis of their body build.

- *Ectomorphs* are tall, thin, and less social and more intellectual than the other types. These types are the least likely to commit crime.[15]

Sheldon recognized that pure types are rare and that most people have elements of all three types. He identified a Dionysian temperament, a person who has an excess of mesomorphy with a deficiency in ectomorphic restraint, thereby rendering them impulsive and into self-gratification, a condition that would produce crime.

THE LEGACY OF BIOLOGICAL CRIMINOLOGY

The work of Lombroso and his contemporaries is regarded today as a historical curiosity, not scientific fact. Strict biological determinism is no longer taken seriously (later in his career even Lombroso recognized that not all criminals were biological throwbacks). Early biological determinism has been discredited because it is methodologically flawed; most studies did not use control groups from the general population to compare results, a violation of the scientific method. Many of the traits assumed to be inherited are not really genetically determined but could be caused by deprivation in surroundings and diet. Even if most criminals shared some biological traits, they might be products not of heredity but of some environmental condition, such as poor nutrition or health care. Unusual appearance, and not behavior, may have prompted people to be labeled and punished by the justice system.

Because of these deficiencies the validity of a purely biological/psychological explanation of criminality became questionable and is no longer considered valid. Today, criminologists believe that environmental conditions interact with human traits and conditions to influence behavior. Hence, the term **biosocial theory** has been coined to reflect the assumed link between physical and mental traits, the social environment, and behavior.[16]

SOCIOBIOLOGY

What seems no longer tenable at this juncture is any theory of human behavior which ignores biology and relies exclusively on socio-cultural learning. . . . Most social scientists have been wrong in their dogmatic rejection and blissful ignorance of the biological parameters of our behavior.[17]

At midcentury, sociology dominated the study of crime and scholarship and any suggestion that antisocial behavior may have an individual-level cause was treated with enmity.[18] Some criminologists label this position as **biophobia**, the view that no serious consideration should be given to biological factors when attempting to understand human nature.[19]

Then in the early 1970s, spurred by the publication of *Sociobiology*, by biologist Edmund O. Wilson, the biological basis for crime once again emerged into the limelight.[20] **Sociobiology** differs from earlier theories of behavior in that it stresses that biological and genetic conditions affect how social behaviors are learned and perceived. These perceptions, in turn, are linked to existing environmental structures.

Sociobiologists view the gene as the ultimate unit of life that controls all human destiny. Although they believe environment and experience also have an impact on behavior, their main premise is that most actions are controlled by a person's "biological machine." Most important, people are controlled by the innate need to have their genetic material survive and dominate others. Consequently, they do everything in their power to ensure their own survival and that of others who share their gene pool (relatives, fellow citizens, and so forth). Even when they come to the aid of others, which is called **reciprocal altruism**, people are motivated by the belief that their actions will be reciprocated and that their gene survival capability will be enhanced.

CONTEMPORARY TRAIT THEORIES

The study of sociobiology revived interest in finding a biological basis for crime and delinquency. If, as it suggests, biological (genetic) makeup controls human behavior, it follows that it should also be responsible for determining whether a person chooses law-violating or conventional behavior. This view of crime causation is referred to as **trait theory**.

Linking personal traits to crime is a significant departure for mainstream criminologists who for many years maintained that social factors, such as poverty and racism, were responsible for antisocial behavior. Today, that view is softening, and trait theory has entered the criminological mainstream. As criminologists John Paul Wright and Francis Cullen put it:

. . . the ideological dam preventing the development of biosocial perspectives is weakening and has sprung some leaks. The reality that humans are biological creatures who vary in biological traits is becoming too obvious to ignore.[21]

---

biosocial theory An approach to criminology that focuses on the interaction between biological and social factors as they relate to crime.

biophobia A view held by sociologists that no serious consideration should be given to biological factors when attempting to understand human nature.

sociobiology The scientific study of the determinants of social behavior, based on the view that such behavior is influenced by both the individual's genetic makeup and interactions with the environment.

reciprocal altruism According to sociobiology, acts that are outwardly designed to help others but that have at their core benefits to the self.

trait theory The view that criminality is a product of abnormal biological and/or psychological traits.

As a result of this newfound acceptance, more criminologists are conducting research on the individual traits related to crime, and their findings are being published in mainstream journals.

Unlike their forebears, contemporary trait theorists do not suggest that a single biological or psychological attribute adequately explains all criminality. Rather, each offender is considered physically and mentally unique; consequently, there must be different explanations for each person's behavior. Some may have inherited criminal tendencies; others may be suffering from neurological problems; still others may have blood chemistry disorders that heighten their antisocial activity. But no matter what that trait may be, possession of it makes the bearer at risk to antisocial behavior. What sometimes appears to be an effect of environment and socialization may actually be caused by genetically determined physical and/or mental traits.[22]

Individual Vulnerability versus Differential Susceptibility

Trait theorists today recognize that crime-producing interactions involve both personal traits (such as defective intelligence, impulsive personality, and abnormal brain chemistry) and environmental factors (such as family life, educational attainment, socioeconomic status, and neighborhood conditions). People living in a disadvantaged community may be especially at risk to crime, but that risk is significantly increased if they also bear a genetic makeup that makes them vulnerable to the crime-producing influences in their environment.[23]

There are actually two views on how this interaction unfolds. The **individual vulnerability model** supposes a direct link between traits and crime: some people develop physical or mental conditions at birth, or soon thereafter, that affect their social functioning no matter where they live or how they are raised.[24]

In contrast, the **differential susceptibility model** suggests that there is an indirect association between traits and crime: some people possess physical or mental traits that make them vulnerable to adverse environmental influences.[25] While a positive environment provides benefits, unfortunately those people whose genetic makeup makes them predisposed to violence manifest more aggression when their surroundings become troubled. Someone like Chris Harper-Mercer may have benefited from a supportive, therapeutic environment, but a more adverse one triggered a violent response.[26]

Regardless of whether the connection between physical and psychological traits and crime is direct or indirect,

individual vulnerability model Assumes there is a direct link between traits and crime; some people are vulnerable to crime from birth.

differential susceptibility model The belief that there is an indirect association between traits and crime.

contemporary trait theories can be divided into two major subdivisions: one that stresses psychological functioning and another that stresses biological (biosocial) makeup. Although there is often overlap between these views (i.e., brain functioning may have a biological basis), each branch has its unique characteristics and will be discussed separately.

Biosocial Theory

Rather than viewing the criminal as a person whose behavior is controlled solely by conditions determined at birth, most biocriminologists believe that physical, environmental, and social conditions work in concert to produce human behavior; this integrated approach is commonly referred to as biosocial theory. The following subsections will examine some of the more important schools of thought within biosocial theory.[27] First, we look at the biochemical factors that are believed to affect behavior. Then the relationship of brain function and crime will be considered, followed by an analysis of genetics and crime. Finally, evolutionary views of crime causation are evaluated.

BIOCHEMICAL CONDITIONS AND CRIME

 L02 Differentiate between the biochemical conditions that produce crime

Some trait theorists believe biochemical conditions, including both those that are genetically predetermined and those acquired through diet and environment, control and influence antisocial behavior.[28] The influence of damaging chemical and biological contaminants may begin before birth if the mother's diet either lacks or has an excess of important nutrients (such as manganese) that may later cause developmental problems in her offspring.[29] In sum, exposure to harmful chemicals and poor diet *in utero*, at birth, and beyond may then affect people throughout their life course. Some of the more important biochemical factors that have been linked to criminality are set out in detail here.

Exposure to Smoking and Drinking Maternal alcohol abuse and/or smoking during gestation have long been linked to prenatal damage and subsequent antisocial behavior in adolescence.[30] Exposure to smoke has been associated with increased psychopathology in offspring, and that exposure to secondhand cigarette smoke during pregnancy predicts later conduct disorder.[31] Having a smoking parent had a greater effect on behavior than other influences, including prematurity, low birth weight, and poor parenting practices.

Research now shows that people who start drinking by the age of 14 are five times more likely to become alcoholics than people who hold off on drinking until the age of 21. It is possible that early exposure of the brain to alcohol may short-circuit the growth of brain cells, impairing the learning and memory processes that protect against addiction; adolescent drinking has a direct and harmful influence on behavior.[32]

Exposure to Chemicals and Minerals   Research shows that an over- or undersupply of certain chemicals and minerals—including sodium, mercury, potassium, calcium, amino acids, monoamines, and peptides—can lead to depression, mania, cognitive problems, memory loss, and abnormal sexual activity, all of which have proved to be correlates of crime.[33] Common food additives such as calcium propionate, which is used to preserve bread, have been linked to problem behaviors.[34] Even some commonly used medicines may have detrimental side effects: research links sildenafil, more commonly known as Viagra, with aggressive and violent behavior.[35]

Excessive intake of certain metals such as mercury, iron, and manganese may be linked to neurological dysfunctions such as intellectual impairment and attention deficit hyperactivity disorder (ADHD).[36] These neurological conditions are believed to be a precursor of delinquent and criminal behaviors.[37]

Diet and Crime   If biochemical makeup can influence behavior, then it stands to reason that food intake and diet are related to crime.[38] Those biocriminologists who believe in a diet–aggression association claim that in every segment of society there are violent, aggressive, and amoral people whose improper food, vitamin, and mineral intake may be responsible for their antisocial behavior.[39] If diet could be improved, they believe, the frequency of violent behavior would be reduced.[40]

In some instances, the absence in the diet of certain chemicals and minerals—including sodium, potassium, calcium, amino acids, magnesium, monoamines, and peptides—can lead to depression, mania, cognitive problems, memory loss, and abnormal sexual activity.[41] In contrast, research shows that excessive amounts of harmful substances such as caffeine, food dyes, and artificial flavors seem to provoke hostile, impulsive, and otherwise antisocial behaviors.[42] Ingredients that are routinely used in candy and soda have been linked to elevated hyperactivity scores, a condition that has been linked to antisocial behaviors.[43]

Diet can have a long-term influence on behavior. In a famous experiment, Adrian Raine and his colleagues charted the long-term effects of a two-year diet enrichment program for 3-year-olds and found that 20 years later the youngsters given a more nutritious diet still did better on personality tests, had greater levels of mental health, and had lower levels of self-reported crimes than the malnourished children who not been placed in the program.[44]

Sugar Intake   One area of diet that has received a great deal of attention is the association between high intake of both sugar and high fructose corn syrup and antisocial/aggressive behavior. Experiments have been conducted in which children's diets were altered so that sweet drinks were replaced with fruit juices, table sugar with honey, molasses substituted for sugar in cooking, and so on; results indicate that aggression levels are associated with sugar intake.[45] A British study of the long-term effects of childhood diet on adult violence found that kids age 10 who engaged in excessive consumption of confectionary (food items that are rich in sugar such as candy and soda) were the ones most likely to be convicted for violence in adulthood.[46] More recently, a study conducted in Boston with high school students found that adolescents who drank more than five cans of soft drinks per week were significantly more likely to carry weapons and to engage in violence with peers, family members, and intimate partners. [47]

Although these results are impressive, some questions remain about the actual interaction between sugar intake and violence, and not all research projects have found a significant sugar–violence effect. One recent study by Nathan DeWall and his associates found that some sugar intake may actually help *reduce* aggression.[48] They found that people who drank a glass of lemonade sweetened with sugar acted less aggressively a few minutes later than did people who consumed lemonade with a sugar substitute. The sugary drink helped provide the short-term energy needed to avoid lashing out at others. People who have trouble metabolizing or using glucose in their bodies show more evidence of aggression and less willingness to forgive others.

Glucose Metabolism/Hypoglycemia   In addition to the DeWall research, other efforts show that persistent abnormality in the way the brain metabolizes glucose (sugar) can be linked to antisocial behaviors such as substance abuse.[49] **Hypoglycemia** occurs when glucose in the blood falls below levels necessary for normal and efficient brain functioning. The brain is sensitive to the lack of blood sugar because it is the only organ that obtains its energy solely from the combustion of carbohydrates. Thus, when the brain is deprived of blood sugar, it has no alternate food supply to call upon, and brain metabolism slows down, impairing function. Symptoms of hypoglycemia include irritability, anxiety, depression, crying spells, headaches, and confusion.

Research studies have linked hypoglycemia to outbursts of antisocial behavior and violence.[50] Several studies have related assaults and fatal sexual offenses to hypoglycemic reactions.[51] Hypoglycemia has also been connected with a syndrome characterized by aggressive and assaultive behavior, glucose disturbance, and brain dysfunction. Some attempts have been made to measure hypoglycemia using subjects with a known history of criminal activity. Studies of jail and prison inmate populations have found a higher

hypoglycemia A condition that occurs when glucose (sugar) levels in the blood fall below the necessary level for normal and efficient brain functioning.

than normal level of hypoglycemia.[52] High levels of reactive hypoglycemia have been found in groups of habitually violent and impulsive offenders.[53]

Hormonal Influences Criminologist James Q. Wilson, in his book *The Moral Sense,* concludes that hormones, enzymes, and neurotransmitters may be the keys to understanding human behavior. According to Wilson, they help explain gender differences in the crime rate. Males, he writes, are biologically and naturally more aggressive than females, while women are naturally more nurturing due to the fact they are the ones who bear and raise children.[54] Hormone levels also help explain the aging-out process. Levels of testosterone, the principal male steroid hormone, decline during the life cycle and may explain why violence rates diminish over time.[55]

A number of biosocial theorists are now evaluating the association between criminal activities ranging from fraud to violent behavior episodes and hormone levels.[56] The most important findings suggest that abnormal levels of male sex hormones (**androgens**) do in fact produce aggressive behavior.[57] High androgen levels require people to seek excess stimulation and to be willing to tolerate pain in their quest for thrills. Androgens are linked to brain seizures that, under stressful conditions, can result in emotional volatility. Androgens affect the brain structure itself. They influence the left hemisphere of the **neocortex**, the part of the brain that controls sympathetic feelings toward others.[58] One area of interest has been the influence of **testosterone**, the most abundant androgen, which controls secondary sex characteristics, such as facial hair and voice timbre. Excessive levels of testosterone have been linked to violence and aggression.[59] Studies of prisoners show that testosterone levels are higher in men who commit violent crimes than in the general population. Hormone treatments that decrease testosterone levels have been administered to sex offenders to decrease their sexual potency.[60]

Lee Ellis and his associates found that self-reported violent criminality was positively correlated with masculine mannerisms, masculine body appearance, physical strength, strength of sex drive, low/deep voice, upper body strength, lower body strength, and amount of body hair.[61] Other androgen-related male traits include sensation seeking, impulsivity, dominance, and lesser verbal skills; all of these androgen-related male traits are related to antisocial behaviors.[62] There is a growing body of evidence suggesting that hormonal changes are also related to mood and behavior and, concomitantly, that adolescents experience more intense mood swings, anxiety, and restlessness than their elders.[63] An association between hormonal activity and antisocial behavior is suggested because rates of both factors peak in adolescence.[64]

Hormonal differences may be a key to understanding gender differences in the crime rate. Females may be biologically protected from deviant behavior in the same way they are immune from some diseases that strike males.[65] Girls who have high levels of testosterone or are exposed to testosterone *in utero* may become more aggressive in adolescence.[66] Conversely, boys who were prenatally exposed to steroids that decrease androgen levels display decreased aggressiveness in adolescence. Gender differences in the crime rate then may be explained by the relative difference in androgens between the two sexes. Nonetheless, abnormal hormone levels can also affect females and are correlated with higher violence levels.[67]

Hormonal changes may also be able to explain regional and temporal differences in the crime rate. It is possible they are due to the side effects of stress hormones such as adrenaline, which the body generates to cope with thermal heat stress. As heat rises, people get irritable, and the body produces excess hormones, which are directly related to aggression and antisocial behaviors.[68] Hence, crime rates are higher in the summer and in regions with warmer climates.

Premenstrual Syndrome Hormonal research has not been limited to male offenders. The suspicion has long existed that the onset of the menstrual cycle triggers excessive amounts of the female sex hormones, which affect antisocial, aggressive behavior. This condition is commonly referred to as **premenstrual syndrome**, or **PMS**.[69] The link between PMS and delinquency was first popularized more than 40 years ago by Katharina Dalton, whose studies of English women indicated that females are more likely to commit suicide and be aggressive and otherwise antisocial just before or during menstruation.[70] Based on her findings, lawyers began using PMS as a legal criminal defense that was accepted in courts in England and the United States.[71]

Dalton's research is often cited as evidence of the link between PMS and crime, but methodological problems make it impossible to accept her findings at face value. There is still significant debate over any link between PMS and aggression. Some doubters argue that the relationship is spurious; it is equally likely that the psychological and physical stress of aggression brings on menstruation and not vice versa.[72]

Diana Fishbein, a noted expert on biosocial theory, concludes that there is in fact an association between elevated levels of female aggression and menstruation. Research efforts, she argues, show (a) that a significant number of

androgens Male sex hormones.

neocortex A part of the human brain; the left side of the neocortex controls sympathetic feelings toward others.

testosterone The principal male steroid hormone. Testosterone levels decline during the life cycle and may explain why violence rates diminish over time.

premenstrual syndrome (PMS) The stereotype that several days prior to and during menstruation females are beset by irritability and poor judgment as a result of hormonal changes.

incarcerated females committed their crimes during the premenstrual phase and (b) that at least a small percentage of women appear vulnerable to cyclical hormonal changes, which makes them more prone to anxiety and hostility.[73] While the debate is ongoing, it is important to remember that the overwhelming majority of females who do suffer anxiety reactions prior to and during menstruation do not actually engage in violent criminal behavior; so any link between PMS and crime is tenuous at best.[74]

Allergies Allergies are defined as unusual or excessive reactions of the body to foreign substances.[75] For example, hay fever is an allergic reaction caused when pollen cells enter the body and are fought or neutralized by the body's natural defenses. The result of the battle is itching, red eyes, and active sinuses.

Cerebral allergies cause an excessive reaction in the brain, whereas **neuroallergies** affect the nervous system. Neuroallergies and cerebral allergies are believed to cause the allergic person to produce enzymes that attack wholesome foods as if they were dangerous to the body.[76] They may also cause swelling of the brain and produce sensitivity in the central nervous system, conditions linked to mental, emotional, and behavioral problems. Research indicates a connection between allergies and hyperemotionality, depression, aggressiveness, and violent behavior.[77]

Neuroallergy and cerebral allergy problems have also been linked to hyperactivity in children, a condition also linked to antisocial behavior. The foods most commonly involved in producing such allergies are cow's milk, wheat, corn, chocolate, nuts, peanut butter, citrus, and eggs; however, about 300 other foods have been identified as allergens. The potential seriousness of the problem has been raised by studies linking the average consumption of one suspected cerebral allergen, corn, to cross-national homicide rates.[78]

Environmental Contaminants In 2014, the city of Flint, Michigan, changed its water source from treated Detroit Water and Sewerage Department water to the Flint River. Because city officials failed to apply corrosion inhibitors to the pipes used to bring water to the city, lead from the aging pipes leached into the city's water supply. Up to 12,000 children in the city were then exposed to drinking water with high levels of lead, causing numerous long-term health problems.[79] Criminal charges have been filed against city officials and some have already entered guilty pleas.

While the Flint water crisis exposed the perils of lead contamination to the general public, the danger of exposure

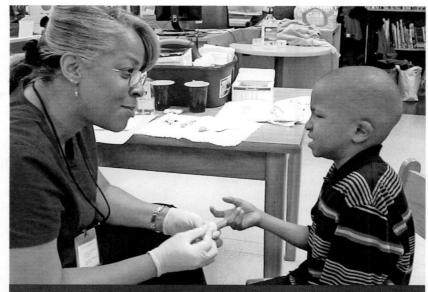

University of Michigan–Flint lecturer Veronica Robinson is shown drawing blood from 7-year-old Zyontae Looney during a lead-testing clinic in Flint, Michigan. Thousands of Flint parents have had their children tested at free clinics run by the Genesee County Health Department since residents became aware that their water was contaminated with lead after the city began drawing water from the Flint River to save money. The overworked health department has gotten help administering lead tests from nursing faculty and students from UM-Flint.

AP Images/Mike Householder

to heavy metals has been known for quite some time. The Centers for Disease Control and Prevention warns that exposure to dangerous substances in the environment, including lead, copper, cadmium, mercury, polybrominated diphenyl ethers (PBDEs), polychlorinated biphenyls (PCBs), polycyclic aromatic hydrocarbons (PAHs), and inorganic gases such as chlorine and nitrogen dioxide can cause severe illness or death. These environmental contaminants can be especially harmful to the brains of babies and small children because they may affect the developing nervous system; babies can be exposed to harmful chemicals even before they are born.[80]

Among the suspected contaminants that have been linked to developmental delays and emotional problems are chemicals used in the agricultural business in insecticides and pesticides. Another suspected cause with dysfunctional behavior is phthalates, industrial chemicals widely used as solvents and ingredients in plastics. Thousands of

cerebral allergies A physical condition that causes brain malfunction due to exposure to some environmental or biochemical irritant.

neuroallergies Allergies that affect the nervous system and cause the allergic person to produce enzymes that attack wholesome foods as if they were dangerous to the body. They may also cause swelling of the brain and produce sensitivity in the central nervous system—conditions that are linked to mental, emotional, and behavioral problems.

household items, from shampoos to flooring products, contain phthalates, and research shows that exposure is related to childhood misbehavior and improper functioning.[81] One such substance, chlorpyrifos, is now banned for residential use but is still allowed for agriculture and commercial enterprises. Virginia Rauh and her colleagues found that children exposed to large amounts of chlorpyrifos before birth maintain an increased risk for personal problems such as attention deficit hyperactivity disorder (highly exposed children were significantly more likely to score lower on measures of psychomotor and mental development).[82] These outcomes have been linked to antisocial behavior.

A number of recent research studies have suggested that lead ingestion is linked to aggressive behaviors.[83] This association is especially important because so many children suffer harmful levels of lead exposure. According to the Centers for Disease Control and Prevention, even low levels of lead in the blood have been shown to affect IQ, the ability to pay attention, and academic achievement. And effects of lead exposure cannot be corrected. Experts now use a reference level of 5 micrograms per deciliter (of blood) to identify children with blood lead levels that are much higher than most children's levels.[84] That means that about 2 million kids 18 and under have dangerously high lead levels according to CDC standards.

There is significant evidence of a lead–aggression linkage. Areas with the highest concentrations of lead also report the highest levels of homicide.[85] Examining changes in lead levels in the United States, Britain, Canada, France, Australia, Finland, Italy, West Germany, and New Zealand (lead levels changed when nations phased out lead-containing paint and gasoline), economist Rick Nevin found that long-term worldwide trends in crime levels correlate significantly with changes in environmental levels of lead. Nevin discovered that children exposed to higher levels of lead during the preschool developmental years engaged in higher rates of offending when they reached their late teens and early twenties. His conclusion: 65 to 90 percent or more of the substantial variation in violent crime in all of these countries was explained by lead. In the United States, juvenile arrest rates skyrocketed in the 1960s, an increase that tracked the increase in the use of leaded gas usage after World War II. As the use of leaded gas declined, so too did crime rates.[86]

Research also shows that even limited exposure to lead can have a deleterious influence on a child's development and subsequent behavior.[87] Delinquents are almost four times more likely to have high bone-lead levels than children in the general population.[88] A number of research studies have linked lead ingestion to antisocial behaviors.[89] Recent research shows that almost any elevated level of lead ingestion is related to lower IQ scores, a factor linked to aggressive behavior.[90] There is also evidence linking lead

exposure to mental illnesses, such as schizophrenia, which have been linked to antisocial behaviors.[91]

Research also shows that lead effects may actually begin in the womb due to the mother's dietary consumption of foods, such as seafood, that are high in lead content.[92] Improved prenatal care may help mothers avoid the danger of lead exposure and reduce long-term crime rates.

NEUROPHYSIOLOGICAL CONDITIONS AND CRIME

 L03 Clarify the neurophysiological conditions associated with crime

Some researchers focus their attention on **neurophysiology**, the study of brain activity.[93] Neurological and physical abnormalities are acquired as early as the fetal or prenatal stage or through birth delivery trauma, and they control behavior throughout the life span.[94]

Studies conducted in the United States and in other nations have indicated that the relationship between impairment in executive brain functions (such as abstract reasoning, problem-solving skills, and motor behavior skills) and aggressive behavior is significant.[95] Children who suffer from measurable neurological deficits at birth are believed to also suffer from a number of antisocial traits throughout their life course, ranging from habitual lying to antisocial violence.[96]

The association between neurological disorder and antisocial behaviors may take a number of different paths:

- *Direct association.* Neurological deficits may be a direct cause of antisocial behavior, including violent offending.[97] The presence of brain abnormality causes irrational and destructive behaviors. Clinical analysis of convicted murderers found that a significant number show evidence of brain abnormalities, including epilepsy, traumatic brain injury, childhood encephalitis, or meningitis causing brain damage, genetic disorders, and unspecified brain damage.[98]
- *Indirect association.* Being in possession of a neurological impairment leads to the development of personality traits that are linked to antisocial behaviors. For example, impulsivity and lack of self-control have been linked to antisocial behavior. There is now evidence that self-control may in fact be regulated and controlled by the prefrontal cortex of the brain.[99] Neurological impairment to the prefrontal cortex reduces levels of self-control, and this reduction in self-control leads to increased levels of aggression.
- *Interactive cause.* Neurological deficits may interact with another trait or social condition to produce antisocial behaviors. Take for instance the research conducted by Adrian Raine, which found that kids who had experienced birth complications indicative of neurological impairment and had also experienced maternal

neurophysiology The study of brain activity.

rejection as they matured were more likely to engage in criminal offending than those youth who did not experience these symptoms.[100] The combination of neurological dysfunction and maternal rejection had a more powerful influence on behavior than either of these conditions alone.

Measuring Neurological Impairment   There are numerous ways to measure neurological functioning, including memorization and visual awareness tests, short-term auditory memory tests, and verbal IQ tests. These tests have been found to distinguish criminal offenders from noncriminal control groups.[101]

Traditionally, the most important measure of neurophysiological functioning is the **electroencephalograph (EEG)**, which records the electrical impulses given off by the brain.[102] It represents a signal composed of various rhythms and transient electrical discharges, commonly called brain waves, which can be recorded by electrodes placed on the scalp. The frequency is given in cycles per second, measured in hertz (Hz), and usually ranges from 0.5 to 30 Hz. Studies using the EEG find that violent criminals have far higher levels of abnormal EEG recordings than nonviolent or one-time offenders. Although about 5 percent of the general population have abnormal EEG readings, about 50 to 60 percent of adolescents with known behavior disorders display abnormal recordings.[103] Behaviors highly correlated with abnormal EEG include poor impulse control, inadequate social adaptation, hostility, temper tantrums, and destructiveness.[104] Studies of adults have associated slow and bilateral brain waves with hostile, hypercritical, irritable, nonconforming, and impulsive behavior.[105]

Newer brain-scanning techniques using electronic imaging such as positron emission tomography (PET), brain electrical activity mapping (BEAM), single photon emission computed tomography (SPECT), and the superconducting quantum interference device (SQUID) have made it possible to assess which areas of the brain are directly linked to antisocial behavior.[106] Some research using PET shows that domestic violence offenders have lower metabolism in the right hypothalamus and decreased correlations between cortical and subcortical brain structures than a group of control subjects.[107] Daniel Amen and his colleagues employed SPECT to test a sample of people convicted of an impulsive murder. They found that these offenders suffered from a condition that reduced blood flow to a region of the brain involved with planning and self-control. Because this area of the brain is believed to control anger management, those who suffer reduced blood flow may be limited in their self-control, planning, and understanding of future consequences when challenged or forced to concentrate.[108]

It is possible that antisocial behavior is influenced by what is referred to as prefrontal dysfunction, a condition that occurs when demands on brain activity overload the prefrontal cortex and result in a lack of control over antisocial behaviors. Because the prefrontal lobes have not fully developed in adolescence, it is not surprising that this is the time that violent behavior peaks.[109]

Studies carried out in the United States and elsewhere have shown that both violent criminals and substance abusers have impairment in the prefrontal lobes, thalamus, medial temporal lobe, and superior parietal and left angular gyrus areas of the brain.[110] Such damage may be associated with a reduction in executive functioning (EF), a condition that refers to impairment of the cognitive processes that facilitate the planning and regulation of goal-oriented behavior (such as abstract reasoning, problem solving, and motor skills). Impairments in EF have been implicated in a range of developmental disorders, including attention deficit hyperactivity disorder (ADHD), conduct disorder (CD), autism, and Tourette syndrome. EF impairments also have been implicated in a range of neuropsychiatric and medical disorders, including schizophrenia, major depression, alcoholism, structural brain disease, diabetes mellitus, and normal aging.[111]

There is a suspected link between brain dysfunction and conduct disorder (CD), which is considered a precursor of long-term chronic offending. Children with CD lie, steal, bully other children, get into fights frequently, and break schools' and parents' rules; many are callous and lack empathy and/or guilt.[112] Adolescent boys with antisocial substance disorder (ASD) repeatedly engage in risky antisocial and drug-using behaviors. Research has linked this behavior with misfiring in particular areas of the brain and suppressed neural activity.[113]

Brain Development   Research psychiatrist Guido Frank finds that aggressive teen behavior may be linked to the amygdala, an area of the brain that processes information regarding threats and fear, and to a lessening of activity in the frontal lobe, a brain region linked to decision making and impulse control. Frank investigated why some teenagers are more prone than others to "reactive" aggression—that is, unpremeditated aggression in response to a trigger (for instance, an accidental bump from a passerby). He found that reactively aggressive adolescents—most commonly boys—frequently misinterpret their surroundings, feel threatened, and act inappropriately aggressive. They tend to strike back when being teased, blame others when getting into a fight, and overreact to accidents. Their behavior is emotionally "hot," defensive, and impulsive; teens with this behavior are at high risk for lifelong social, career, or legal problems.

Frank's research helps explain what goes on in the brains of some teenage boys who respond with inappropriate anger and aggression to perceived threats. It is possible that rather than having a social or environmental basis, such behavior

---

electroencephalograph (EEG)   A device that can record the electronic impulses given off by the brain, commonly called brain waves.

is associated with brain functioning and not environment, socialization, personality, or other social and psychological functions.[114]

Minimal Brain Dysfunction   Minimal brain dysfunction (MBD) is related to an abnormality in cerebral structure. It has been defined as an abruptly appearing, maladaptive behavior that interrupts an individual's lifestyle and life flow. In its most serious form, MBD has been linked to serious antisocial acts, an imbalance in the urge-control mechanisms of the brain, and chemical abnormality. Included in the category of minimal brain dysfunction are several abnormal behavior patterns: dyslexia, visual perception problems, hyperactivity, poor attention span, temper tantrums, and aggressiveness. One type of minimal brain dysfunction is manifested through episodic periods of explosive rage. This form of the disorder is considered an important cause of such behavior as spouse beating, child abuse, suicide, aggressiveness, and motiveless homicide. One perplexing feature of this syndrome is that people who are afflicted with it often maintain warm and pleasant personalities between episodes of violence. Some studies measuring the presence of MBD in offender populations have found that up to 60 percent exhibit brain dysfunction on psychological tests.[115] Criminals have been characterized as having a dysfunction of the dominant hemisphere of the brain.[116] Researchers using brain wave data have predicted with 95 percent accuracy the recidivism of violent criminals.[117] More sophisticated brain scanning techniques, such as PET, have also shown that brain abnormality is linked to violent crime.[118]

Learning Disabilities   One specific type of MBD that has generated considerable interest is learning disability (LD), a disorder in one or more of the basic psychological processes involved in understanding or using spoken or written languages. Learning-disabled children usually exhibit poor motor coordination (for example, problems with poor hand–eye coordination, trouble climbing stairs, clumsiness), have behavior problems (lack of emotional control, hostility, cannot stay on task), and have improper auditory and vocal responses (do not seem to hear, cannot differentiate

minimal brain dysfunction (MBD) An abruptly appearing, maladaptive behavior that interrupts an individual's lifestyle and life flow. In its most serious form, MBD has been linked to serious antisocial acts, an imbalance in the urge-control mechanisms of the brain, and chemical abnormality.

learning disability (LD) A disorder in one or more of the basic psychological processes involved in understanding or using spoken or written languages.

attention deficit hyperactivity disorder (ADHD) A psychological disorder in which a child shows developmentally inappropriate impulsivity, hyperactivity, and lack of attention.

sounds and noises).[119] There are some indications that children with LD are more likely to engage in aggressive behaviors than non-LD children.[120] Institutionalized youth in the United States and abroad are more likely to manifest learning disabilities than children in the general population.[121]

What is the association between learning disabilities and crime? There are two popular explanations:

- *Susceptibility rationale* argues that the link is caused by certain side effects of learning disabilities, such as impulsiveness, poor ability to learn from experience, and inability to take social cues.
- *School failure rationale* assumes that the frustration caused by the LD produces poor school performance leading to a negative self-image and acting-out behavior.

Some recent research conducted by Tomer Einat and Amela Einat in Israel might help settle this issue. They found that a far higher percentage of Israeli prison inmates (69.6 percent) were characterized as learning disabled, as opposed to an estimated 10 to 15 percent of the general Israeli population. Among the inmates, learning disabilities were correlated both with low level of education (dropping out of school at an early age) and early age of criminal onset. Their conclusion: people with learning disabilities who give up school at early stages due to their disabilities are more likely to initiate a criminal career at an early age, as compared to individuals—with or without learning disabilities—who do not leave school. Helping LD kids adjust to school may also help them avoid criminal careers.[122]

Attention Deficit Hyperactivity Disorder (ADHD)
Many parents have noticed that their children do not pay attention to them—they run around and do things in their own way. Sometimes this inattention is a function of age; in other instances, it is a symptom of attention deficit hyperactivity disorder (ADHD), in which a child shows a developmentally inappropriate lack of attention, impulsivity, and hyperactivity. The various symptoms of ADHD are described in Exhibit 5.2.

According to the latest data from the Centers for Disease Control and Prevention, as of 2011–2012 approximately 6.4 million U.S. children aged 4 to 17 (11 percent) were reported by parents to have a diagnosis of ADHD, a 42 percent increase since 2003. Nearly one-third of children with ADHD (approximately 2 million) received the diagnosis before age 6. Among children described by their parents as having severe ADHD, half of the cases were diagnosed by age 4.[123]

Children with ADHD have higher rates of retention in grade level, high school dropout, unintentional injuries, and emergency department visits.[124] ADHD has been associated with poor school performance, placement in special needs classes, bullying, stubbornness, and lack of response to discipline. Although the origin of ADHD is still unknown, suspected causes include neurological damage, prenatal stress, and even reactions to food additives and chemical allergies.

EXHIBIT 5.2

Symptoms of Attention Deficit Hyperactivity Disorder (ADHD)

LACK OF ATTENTION

- Frequently fails to finish projects
- Does not seem to pay attention
- Does not sustain interest in play activities
- Cannot sustain concentration on schoolwork or related tasks
- Is easily distracted

IMPULSIVITY

- Frequently acts without thinking
- Often "calls out" in class
- Does not want to wait his or her turn in lines or games
- Shifts from activity to activity
- Cannot organize tasks or work
- Requires constant supervision

HYPERACTIVITY

- Constantly runs around and climbs on things
- Shows excessive motor activity while asleep
- Cannot sit still; is constantly fidgeting
- Does not remain in his or her seat in class
- Is constantly on the go like a "motor"

SOURCE: Adapted from American Psychiatric Association, *Diagnostic and Statistical Manual of Mental Disorders*, 5th ed. (Washington, DC: American Psychiatric Press, 2013).

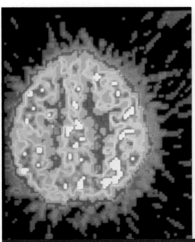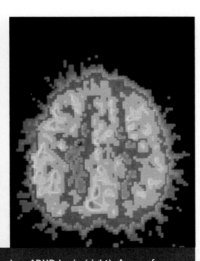

This scan compares a normal brain (left) and an ADHD brain (right). Areas of orange and white demonstrate a higher rate of metabolism, while areas of blue and green represent an abnormally low metabolic rate. Why is ADHD so prevalent in the United States today? Some experts believe that our immigrant forebears, risk takers who impulsively left their homelands for life in a new world, may have brought with them a genetic predisposition for ADHD.

Dr. Alan Zametkin/Clinical Brain Imaging, courtesy of Office of Scientific Information, NIMH

Some psychologists believe that the syndrome is essentially a chemical problem, specifically, an impairment in the chemical system that supports rapid and efficient communication in the brain's management system.[125] Among one-third of children with ADHD, the disorder persists into adulthood; among adults with ADHD, the prevalences of lesser educational and career attainment, co-occurring psychiatric disorders, and death by suicide are higher. The U.S. societal costs of childhood ADHD are estimated between $38 billion and $72 billion annually.[126]

There are also ties to family turmoil: parents of ADHD children are more likely to be divorced or separated, and ADHD children are much more likely to move to new locales than non-ADHD children.[127] It may be possible, then, that emotional turmoil either produces symptoms of ADHD or, if they already exist, causes them to intensify.

A series of research studies now links ADHD to the onset and sustenance of a criminal career. Children with ADHD are more likely than non-ADHD youths to use illicit drugs, alcohol, and cigarettes, be physically aggressive, and engage in sex offenses in adolescence. In addition to adolescent misbehavior, hyperactive or ADHD children are at greater risk for antisocial activity and drug use/abuse that persists into adulthood.[128] They are more likely to be arrested, to be charged with a felony, and to have multiple arrests.[129]

Among the many studies that have evaluated the ADHD–crime link, Jason Fletcher and Barbara Wolfe evaluated data on nearly 14,000 individuals participating in the National Longitudinal Study of Adolescent Health (also known as Add Health) and found that children with ADHD are at a heightened risk for criminality as adults.[130] Another study, by Patricia Westmoreland and her associates, assessed more than 300 randomly selected prison inmates. This study found that more than 20 percent could be diagnosed with ADHD. These inmates were more likely to report emotional and social problems and also had higher rates of mood, anxiety, psychotic, antisocial, and borderline personality disorders.[131]

There are two views on the association between ADHD and aggressive behavior. One view is that the association is direct and that hyperactivity leads to aggressive antisocial behaviors.[132] Others view the association as being more indirect: hyperactivity results in poor school achievement; school failure leads to substance abuse and depression, conditions that have long been associated with the onset of antisocial behaviors.[133]

How is ADHD treated? Today, the most typical treatment is doses of stimulants, such as Adderall and Ritalin, which ironically help control emotional and behavioral outbursts. However, treatment is not always effective. While some treated children with ADHD improve, many do not and continue to show a greater occurrence of externalizing (acting-out) behaviors and significant deficits in areas such as social skills, peer relations, and academic performance over the life course.[134]

Brain Chemistry   Chemical compounds called neurotransmitters influence or activate brain functions. Those studied in relation to aggression and other antisocial behaviors include dopamine, norepinephrine, serotonin, monoamine oxidase (MAO), and gamma-aminobutryic acid (GABA).[135]

Research efforts have linked low levels of MAO to high levels of violence and property crime, as well as defiance of punishment, impulsivity, hyperactivity, poor academic performance, sensation seeking and risk taking, and recreational drug use.[136] Abnormal levels of MAO may explain both individual and group differences in the crime rate. For example, females have higher levels of MAO than males, a condition that may explain gender differences in the crime rate.[137] The effect of MAO on crime persists throughout the life span: individuals with the low-activity form of monoamine oxidase-A who are exposed to violence in youth have a greater likelihood of engaging in physical aggression later in adulthood.[138]

What is the link between brain chemistry and crime? One view is that prenatal exposure of the brain to high levels of androgens can result in a brain structure that is less sensitive to environmental inputs and more prone to criminal behavior choices.[139] Because of this linkage, it is not uncommon for violence-prone people to be treated with antipsychotic drugs such as Haldol, Stelazine, Prolixin, and Risperdal, which help control levels of neurotransmitters; these are sometimes referred to as **chemical restraints** or **chemical straitjackets**.

AROUSAL THEORY

It has long been suspected that obtaining thrills is a crime motivator. Adolescents may engage in crimes such as shoplifting and vandalism simply because they offer the attraction of "getting away with it"; from this perspective, delinquency is a thrilling demonstration of personal competence.

According to **arousal theory**, for a variety of genetic and environmental reasons, some people's brains function differently in response to environmental stimuli. All of us seek to maintain a preferred or optimal level of arousal: too much stimulation leaves us anxious and stressed out; too little makes us feel bored and weary. There is, however, variation in the way people's brains process sensory input. Some nearly always feel comfortable with little stimulation, whereas others require a high degree of environmental input to feel comfortable. The latter are "sensation seekers," who seek out stimulating activities, which may include aggressive, violent behavior patterns.[140]

Evidence that some people may have lower levels of arousal comes from studies on resting heart rate levels conducted by Jill Portnoy, Adrian Raine, and associates, who found that antisocial children have lower resting heart rates than the general population.[141] In one recent study, Olivia Choy, Adrian Raine, and associates found that low heart rate may produce a need for stimulation that is associated with aggressive behavior patterns. It is also associated with impulsivity, which in turn is associated with lack of self-control and involvement in delinquent and criminal behaviors.[142]

Raine has also speculated that some people lack fear and are nonresponsive to the threat of punishment, a condition that allows them to feel relatively comfortable while engaging in antisocial encounters. People who have low arousal levels will seek out risky situations and become more involved with criminal behavior as an avenue toward thrill seeking. Because lack of fear and thrill-seeking behavior are characteristics of adult psychopaths, antisocial children might therefore develop into psychopaths as adults.[143]

The factors that determine a person's level of arousal are not fully determined, but suspected sources include:

- *Brain chemistry (and brain structure)*. Some people have brains with many more nerve cells with receptor sites for neurotransmitters than others.
- *Heart rate*. Another view is that people with low heart rates are more likely to commit crime because they seek stimulation to increase their feelings of arousal to normal levels.[144]
- *Autonomic nervous system*. Some biosocial theorists link arousal to the autonomic nervous system as measured by skin conductance response. People with abnormally

chemical restraints or chemical straitjackets Antipsychotic drugs such as Haldol, Stelazine, Prolixin, and Risperdal, which help control levels of neurotransmitters (such as serotonin/dopamine), that are used to treat violence-prone people.

arousal theory A view of crime suggesting that people who have a high arousal level seek powerful stimuli in their environment to maintain an optimal level of arousal. These stimuli are often associated with violence and aggression. Sociopaths may need greater than average stimulation to bring them up to comfortable levels of living; this need explains their criminal tendencies.

CONNECTIONS

Gottfredson and Hirschi's self-control theory of delinquency, which proposes that low self-control constitutes the most important causal factor in explaining antisocial behavior, will be discussed in Chapter 9.

ASK YOURSELF . . .

If low self-control causes crime, how can business fraud be explained? Is it possible that bankers and stockbrokers are really impulsive and not cold and calculating?

exaggerated skin conductivity may react with above average negative emotional intensity to stimulus that would have little effect on the average person. As a result, provocations that some people might merely shrug off are viewed as highly confrontational, inflammatory, insulting, and deserving of an aggressive reply.[145]

In sum, brain structure, chemistry, and development are believed to exert a strong influence on human behavior.

GENETICS AND CRIME

 LO4 Cite examples of the different research techniques used to link genetics to crime

Another biosocial theme is that the human traits associated with criminality have a genetic basis.[146] There are actually two views of the genetics of crime. According to the direct view, (1) antisocial behavior is inherited, (2) the genetic makeup of parents is passed on to children, and (3) genetic abnormality is directly linked to a variety of antisocial behaviors.[147] Over the course of human history, the most aggressive violent people have gained reproductive advantages that ensure survival of their genetics and have created a population of aggressive young males. The genes that produce aggression are still present in the population and those who inherit them are responsible for violent crimes.[148]

According to the indirect view, genes are related to some personality or physical trait which in turn is linked to antisocial behavior.[149] Genetic makeup may shape friendship patterns and orient people toward deviant peer associations which cause them to become crime prone.[150] Adolescent attachment to parents may be controlled by their genetic makeup; attachment that is weak and attenuated has been linked to criminality.[151]

Testing Genetic Theory If criminal tendencies are inherited, then it stands to reason that the children of criminal parents should be more likely to become law violators than the offspring of conventional parents. A number of studies have found that parental criminality and deviance do, in fact, have a powerful influence on delinquent behavior.[152] One recent study of violent offending in Sweden used a variety of pairing comparisons, between spouses of siblings and half-siblings, and across consecutive spouses, and found evidence that the genetic basis for violence crime was moderate to strong.[153]

Some of the most important data on parental deviance have been gathered as part of a long-term study of English youth called the Cambridge Study in Delinquent Development (CSDD). This research followed a group of about 1,000 males from the time they were 8 years old until they reached adulthood. The males in the study were repeatedly interviewed and their school and police records evaluated. These cohort data indicate that a significant number of delinquent youths had criminal fathers.[154]

While 8 percent of the sons of noncriminal fathers eventually became chronic offenders, about 37 percent of youths with criminal fathers were multiple offenders.[155] Analysis of the data confirms that delinquent youths grow up to become the parents of antisocial children.[156] One specific form of aggressive behavior that seems to be inherited is school yard bullying: bullies have children who bully others, and these second-generation bullies grow up to become the fathers of children who are also bullies, in a never-ending cycle.[157]

The Cambridge findings are not unique. Data from the Rochester Youth Development Study (RYDS), a longitudinal analysis that has been monitoring the behavior of 1,000 upstate New York area youths since 1988, also find an intergenerational continuity in antisocial behavior.[158]

It is possible, of course, that the genetic effect of parental deviance may be exaggerated by mating practices. For example, if an antisocial male partners with an antisocial female and breeds antisocial children, it appears to be a genetic effect. But it is also possible that this "antisocial" family consists of people who have suffered labeling and stigma, isolating them from the mainstream and increasing their chances of criminality. While it may appear that they produce children who are genetically predisposed to crime, it is also possible that what appears to be a genetic effect is actually the product of social processes.[159]

Sibling Similarities It stands to reason that if the cause of crime is in part genetic, then the behavior of siblings should be similar because they share genetic material. Research does show that if one sibling engages in antisocial behavior, so do his/her brothers and sisters. The effect is greatest among same-sex siblings.[160] Sibling pairs who report warm, mutual relationships and share friends are the most likely to behave in a similar fashion; those who maintain a close relationship also have similar rates of crime and drug abuse.[161]

While the similarity of siblings' behavior seems striking, what appears to be a genetic effect may also be explained by other factors:

- Siblings who live in the same environment are influenced by similar social and economic factors.
- Deviant siblings may grow closer because of shared interests.
- Younger siblings who admire their older siblings may imitate the elders' behavior.
- The deviant sibling forces or threatens the brother or sister into committing criminal acts.
- Siblings living in a similar environment may develop similar types of friends; it is peer behavior that is the critical influence. The influence of peers may negate any observed interdependence of sibling behavior.[162]

Twin Behavior As mentioned above, because siblings are usually brought up in the same household and share common life experiences, any similarity in their antisocial behavior might be a function of environmental influences and experiences and not genetics at all. To guard against this, biosocial theorists have compared the behavior of same-sex twins and again found concordance in their behavior patterns.[163]

However, an even more rigorous test of genetic theory involves comparison of the behavior of identical monozygotic (MZ) twins with fraternal dizygotic (DZ) twins; while the former have an identical genetic makeup, the latter share only about 50 percent of their genetic combinations. Research has shown that MZ twins are significantly closer in their personal characteristics, such as intelligence, than are DZ twins.[164]

The earliest studies conducted on the behavior of twins detected a significant relationship between the criminal activities of MZ twins and a much lower association between those of DZ twins. A review of relevant studies conducted between 1929 and 1961 found that 60 percent of MZ twins shared criminal behavior patterns (if one twin was criminal, so was the other), whereas only 30 percent of DZ twin behavior was similarly related.[165] These findings may be viewed as powerful evidence that a genetic basis for criminality exists.

One famous study of twin behavior still under way is the Minnesota Twin Family Study. This research compares the behavior of MZ and DZ twin pairs who were raised together with others who were separated at birth and in some cases did not even know of each other's existence. The study shows some striking similarities in behavior and ability for twin pairs raised apart. An MZ twin reared away from a co-twin has about as good a chance of being similar to the co-twin in terms of personality, interests, and attitudes as one who has been reared with his or her co-twin. The conclusion: similarities between twins are due to genes, not the environment.[166]

Not all research efforts have found that MZ twin pairs are more closely related in their criminal behavior than DZ or ordinary sibling pairs, and some that have found an association note that it is at best "modest."[167] Even if the behavior similarities between MZ twins are greater than those between DZ twins, the association may be explained by environmental factors. MZ twins are more likely to look alike and to share physical traits than DZ twins, and they are more likely to be treated similarly. Similarities in their shared behavior patterns may therefore be a function of socialization and/or environment and not heredity.[168]

It is also possible that what appears to be a genetic effect picked up by the twin research is actually the effect of sibling influence on criminality, referred to as the **contagion effect**: genetic predispositions and early experiences make some people, including twins, susceptible to deviant behavior, which is transmitted by the presence of antisocial siblings in the household.[169]

The contagion effect may explain in part the higher concordance of deviant behaviors found in identical twins as compared to fraternal twins or mere siblings. The relationship between identical twins may be stronger and more enduring than other sibling pairs so that contagion and not genetics explains their behavioral similarities. According to Marshall Jones and Donald Jones, the contagion effect may also help explain why the behavior of twins is more similar in adulthood than in adolescence.[170] Youthful misbehavior is influenced by friends and peer group relationships. As adults, the influence of peers may wane as people marry and find employment. In contrast, twin influence is everlasting; if one twin is antisocial, it legitimizes and supports the criminal behavior in his or her co-twin. This effect may grow even stronger in adulthood because twin relations are more enduring than any other. What seems to be a genetic effect may actually be the result of sibling interaction with a brother or sister who engages in antisocial activity.

Adoption Studies   One way of avoiding the pitfalls of twin studies is to focus attention on the behavior of adoptees. It seems logical that if the behavior of adopted children is more closely aligned to that of their biological parents than to that of their adoptive parents, then the idea of a genetic basis for criminality would be supported. If, on the other hand, adoptees are more closely aligned to the behavior of their adoptive parents than their biological parents, an environmental basis for crime would seem more valid.

Several studies indicate that some relationship exists between biological parents' behavior and the behavior of their children, even when their contact has been nonexistent.[171] One analysis of Swedish adoptees also found that genetic factors are highly significant, accounting for 59 percent of the variation in their petty crime rates. Boys who had criminal parents were significantly more likely to violate the law. Environmental influences and economic status were significantly less important, explaining about 19 percent of the variance in crime. Nonetheless, having a positive environment, such as being adopted into a more affluent home, helped inhibit genetic predisposition.[172]

Evaluating Genetic Research   The genes–crime relationship is controversial because it implies that the propensity to commit crime is present at birth and cannot be altered. It raises moral dilemmas: if *in utero* genetic testing could detect a gene for violence, and a violence gene was found to be present, what could be done as a precautionary measure?

contagion effect Genetic predispositions and early experiences make some people, including twins, susceptible to deviant behavior, which is transmitted by the presence of antisocial siblings in the household.

Some critics suggest that available evidence provides little conclusive proof that crime is genetically predetermined. Detractors point to the inadequate research designs and weak methodologies of supporting research. The newer, better-designed research studies, critics charge, provide less support than earlier, less methodically sound studies.[173] Some critics, such as Callie Burt and Ronald Simons, believe the social environment plays a more critical role in shaping behavior than genes and heredity, especially during the critical periods of childhood and adolescence. The environment, they argue, shapes biological processes and enables people to function and survive in existing social conditions; human biological makeup helps people respond to the everyday situations and events they face in their social world. As environmental conditions change, so do the brain and nervous system. Adverse, dangerous, and negative environments sculpt or change an individual's brain functioning, causing them to respond to environmental events with aggression, violence, and coercion.[174] Thus, if antisocial behavior is shaped at the genetic level, it's because environmental factors influence biological functioning and not because criminal tendencies are inherited.

Burt and Simons call for an end to research using twins to study heritability because that type of research does not adequately control for environmental impact. While persuasive, their conclusions have challenged by criminologists who find fault with their assumptions. The counterargument is that a great deal of human behavior is shaped by inherited rather than environmentally influenced traits and that twin studies have merit.[175] Abandoning twin research may be premature.[176] Needless to say, the debate over the heritability of criminal tendencies remains an open issue among criminologists.

EVOLUTIONARY THEORY

 L05 Explain the evolutionary view of crime

Some criminologists believe the human traits that produce violence and aggression are produced through the long process of human evolution.[177] According to this evolutionary view, the competition for scarce resources has influenced and shaped the human species.[178] Over the course of human existence, people whose personal characteristics enable them to accumulate more than others are the most likely to breed and dominate the species. People have been shaped to engage in actions that promote their well-being and ensure the survival and reproduction of their genetic line. Males who are impulsive risk takers may be able to father more children because they are reckless in their social relationships and have sexual encounters with numerous partners. If, according to evolutionary theories, such behavior patterns are inherited, impulsive behavior becomes intergenerational, passed down from father to son. It is not surprising, then, that human history has been marked by war, violence, and aggression.

There are a number of individual theories of evolutionary criminology, three of which are discussed in detail below.

Rushton's Theory of Race and Evolution One of the most controversial versions of evolutionary theory was formulated by J. Philippe Rushton and first appeared in his 1995 book, *Race, Evolution and Behavior.*[179] According to Rushton, there is evidence that modern humans evolved in Africa about 200,000 years ago and then began to migrate outward to present-day Europe and Asia. He posits that the farther north elements of the populations migrated, the more they encountered harsher climates, which produce the need to gather and store food, gain shelter, make clothes, and raise children successfully during prolonged winters. As these populations evolved into present-day Europeans and Asians, their brain mass increased, and they developed slower rates of maturation and lower levels of sex hormones. This physical change produced reductions in sexual potency and aggression and increases in family stability and longevity. These evolutionary changes are responsible for present-day crime rate differences between the races.

Rushton's work was received harshly by critics, who condemned his definitions of race and crime and accused him of racial bias.[180] Among the many criticisms hurled at Rushton has been his singular focus on street crimes, such as theft, while giving short shrift to white-collar and organized crimes, which are predominantly committed by whites. Rushton ignores the fact that men are much more criminal than women even though there is little evidence of significant differences in intelligence or brain size between the genders.

R/K Selection Theory R/K selection theory holds that all organisms can be located along a continuum based upon their reproductive drives.[181] Those along the "R" end reproduce rapidly whenever they can and invest little in their offspring; those along the "K" end reproduce slowly and cautiously and take care in raising their offspring. Evolutionary theorists believe males today "lean" toward R-selection because they can reproduce faster without the need for investing in their offspring; females are K-selected because they have fewer offspring but give more care and devotion to them. K-oriented people are more cooperative and sensitive to others, whereas R-oriented people are more cunning and deceptive. Males, therefore, tend to partake in more criminal behavior. In general, people who commit violent crimes seem to exhibit R-selection traits, such as a premature birth and early and frequent sexual activity. They are more likely to have been neglected as children and to have a short life expectancy.

Cheater Theory Cheater theory suggests that a subpopulation of men has evolved with genes that incline them toward extremely low parental involvement. They are sexually aggressive and use their cunning to gain sexual conquests with as many females as possible. Because females would not willingly choose them as mates, they use stealth to gain sexual access, including such tactics as mimicking the behavior of more stable males. They use devious and illegal means to acquire resources they need for sexual domination. Their deceptive reproductive tactics spill over into other endeavors, where their talent for irresponsible, opportunistic behavior supports their antisocial activities. Deception in reproductive strategies, then, is linked to a deceitful lifestyle.

Psychologist Byron Roth notes that cheater-type males may be especially attractive to those younger, less intelligent women who begin having children at a very early age.[182] State-sponsored welfare, claims Roth, removes the need for potential mates to have the resources needed to be stable providers and family caregivers. With the state meeting their financial needs, these women are attracted to men who are physically attractive and flamboyant. Their fleeting courtship process produces children with low IQs, aggressive personalities, and little chance of proper socialization in father-absent families. Because the criminal justice system treats them leniently, argues Roth, sexually irresponsible men are free to prey on young girls. Over time, their offspring will supply an ever-expanding supply of cheaters who are both antisocial and sexually aggressive.

Violence and Evolution In their classic book *Homicide,* Martin Daly and Margo Wilson suggest that violent offenses are often driven by evolutionary and reproductive factors. High rates of spouse abuse in modern society may be a function of aggressive men seeking to control and possess mates. When females are murdered by their husbands, the motivating factor is typically fear of infidelity and the threat of attachment to a new partner. Infidelity challenges male dominance and future reproductive rights. It comes as no surprise that in some cultures, including our own, sexual infidelity discovered in progress by the aggrieved husband is viewed legally as a provocation that justifies retaliatory killing.[183] Men who feel most threatened over the potential of losing mates to rivals are the ones most likely to engage in sexual violence. Research shows that women in common-law marriages, especially those who are much younger than their husbands, are at greater risk than older married women. Abusive males may fear the potential loss of their younger mates, especially if they are not bound by a marriage contract, and may use force for purposes of control and possession.[184]

Armed robbery is another crime that may have evolutionary underpinnings. Though most robbers are caught and severely punished, it remains an alluring pursuit for men who want to both show their physical prowess and display resources with which to conquer rivals and attract mates. Violent episodes are far more common among men who are unemployed and unmarried—in other words, those who may want to demonstrate their allure to the opposite sex but who are without the benefit of position or wealth.[185]

Gender and Evolution Evolutionary concepts have been linked to gender-based differences in the crime rate. To ensure survival of the gene pool (and the species), it is beneficial for a male of any species to mate with as many suitable females as possible since each can bear his offspring. Rather than forming stable families and developing parenting skills, the most aggressive males have a strong sexual drive, a reduced ability to form strong emotional bonds, a lack of conscience, and aggressive and violent tendencies. These traits, which express themselves in instances of antisocial behavior throughout the life span, beginning in early childhood.[186] These antisocial men produce many offspring, who are prone to criminal behaviors.[187] In contrast, because of the long period of gestation, females require a secure home and a single, stable, nurturing partner to ensure their survival. Because of these differences in mating patterns, the most aggressive males mate most often and have the greatest number of offspring. Therefore, over the history of the human species, aggressive males have had the greatest impact on the gene pool. The descendants of these aggressive males now account for the disproportionate amount of male aggression and violence.[188]

EVALUATION OF THE BIOSOCIAL BRANCH OF TRAIT THEORY

Contemporary biosocial theorists distinguish their views with Lombrosian, deterministic biology. Rather than suggest that there are born criminals and noncriminals, they maintain that some people carry the potential to be violent or antisocial and that environmental conditions can sometimes trigger antisocial responses.[189] This would explain why some otherwise law-abiding citizens engage in a single, seemingly unexplainable antisocial act, and conversely, why some people with long criminal careers often engage in conventional behavior. It also explains why there are geographic and temporal patterns in the crime rate: people who are predisposed to crime may simply have more opportunities to commit illegal acts in the summer in Los Angeles and Atlanta than in the winter in Bedford, New Hampshire, and Minot, North Dakota, or perhaps their hormonal levels become activated as the temperature rises.

The biosocial view is that behavior is a product of interacting biological and environmental events.[190] Physical impairments may make some people "at risk" to crime, but it is when they are linked to social and environmental problems, such as family dysfunction, that they trigger criminal acts.[191] People who possess a biological trait that makes them at risk to crime can avoid involvement in antisocial behaviors if their environment does not contain stimuli that trigger aggression and violence.[192] Biological traits, social relationships, and routine opportunities all interact to predict criminal involvement. Concept Summary 5.1 summarizes the various biosocial theories of crime.

Psychological Trait Theories

The second branch of trait theories focuses on the psychological aspects of crime, including the associations among intelligence, personality, learning, and criminal behavior.

Psychological theories of crime have a long history. In *The English Convict*, Charles Goring (1870–1919) studied the mental characteristics of 3,000 English convicts.[193] He found little difference in the physical characteristics of criminals and noncriminals, but he uncovered a significant relationship between crime and a condition he referred to as **defective intelligence**, which involves such traits as feeblemindedness, epilepsy, insanity, and defective social instinct.[194] Goring believed criminal behavior was inherited and could, therefore, be controlled by regulating the reproduction of families who produced mentally defective children.

Gabriel Tarde (1843–1904) is the forerunner of modern-day learning theorists.[195] Tarde believed people learn from one another through a process of imitation. Tarde's ideas are similar to modern social learning theorists who believe that both interpersonal and observed behavior, such as a movie or television, can influence criminality.

Since the pioneering work of people like Tarde and Goring, psychologists, psychiatrists, and other mental health professionals have long played an active role in formulating criminological theory. In their quest to understand and treat all varieties of abnormal mental conditions, psychologists have encountered clients whose behavior falls within categories society has labeled as criminal, deviant, violent, and antisocial.

This section is organized along the lines of the predominant psychological views most closely associated with the causes of criminal behavior. Some psychologists view antisocial behavior from a **psychoanalytic** or **psychodynamic perspective**: their focus is on early childhood experience and its effect on personality. In contrast, **behaviorism** stresses social learning and behavior modeling as the keys to criminality. **Cognitive theory** analyzes human perception and how it affects behavior.

PSYCHODYNAMIC THEORY

 Discuss the elements of the psychodynamic perspective

Psychodynamic (or psychoanalytic) psychology was originated by Viennese psychiatrist Sigmund Freud (1856–1939) and has since remained a prominent segment of psychological theory.[196]

---

defective intelligence Traits such as feeblemindedness, epilepsy, insanity, and defective social instinct, which Goring believed had a significant relationship to criminal behavior.

psychoanalytic or psychodynamic perspective Branch of psychology holding that the human personality is controlled by unconscious mental processes developed early in childhood.

behaviorism The branch of psychology concerned with the study of observable behavior rather than unconscious motives. It focuses on the relationship between particular stimuli and people's responses to them.

cognitive theory The study of the perception of reality and of the mental processes required to understand the world in which we live.

For a collection of links to libraries, museums, and biographical materials related to Sigmund Freud and his works, go to **http://www.freudarchives .org/**.

Do you believe we are all guided by unconscious thoughts and feelings?

Freud believed that we all carry with us residue of the most significant emotional attachments of our childhood, which then guide future interpersonal relationships. Today, the term *psychodynamic* refers to a broad range of theories that focus on the influence of instinctive drives and forces and the importance of developmental processes in shaping personality. Contemporary psychodynamic theory places greater emphasis on conscious experience and its interaction with the unconscious, in addition to the role that social factors play in development. Nonetheless, it still focuses on the influence of early childhood experiences on the development of personality, motivation, and drives.

id The primitive part of people's mental makeup, present at birth, that represents unconscious biological drives for food, sex, and other life-sustaining necessities. The id seeks instant gratification without concern for the rights of others.

pleasure principle According to Freud, a theory in which id-dominated people are driven to increase their personal pleasure without regard to consequences.

ego The part of the personality, developed in early childhood, that helps control the id and keep people's actions within the boundaries of social convention.

reality principle According to Freud, the ability to learn about the consequences of one's actions through experience.

superego Incorporation within the personality of the moral standards and values of parents, community, and significant others.

conscience One of two parts of the superego; it distinguishes between what is right and wrong.

ego ideal Part of the superego; directs the individual into morally acceptable and responsible behaviors, which may not be pleasurable.

eros The instinct to preserve and create life, a basic human drive present at birth.

thanatos According to Freud, the instinctual drive toward aggression and violence.

oral stage In Freud's schema, the first year of life, when a child attains pleasure by sucking and biting.

anal stage In Freud's schema, the second and third years of life, when the focus of sexual attention is on the elimination of bodily wastes.

phallic stage In Freud's schema, the third year, when children focus their attention on their genitals.

Elements of Psychodynamic Theory   According to the classic version of the theory, the human personality contains a three-part structure. The **id** is the primitive part of an individual's mental makeup present at birth. It represents unconscious biological drives for sex, food, and other life-sustaining necessities. The id follows the **pleasure principle**: it requires instant gratification without concern for the rights of others.

The **ego** develops early in life, when a child begins to learn that his or her wishes cannot be instantly gratified. The ego is that part of the personality that compensates for the demands of the id by helping the individual guide his or her actions to remain within the boundaries of social convention. The ego is guided by the **reality principle**: it takes into account what is practical and conventional by societal standards.

The **superego** develops as a result of incorporating within the personality the moral standards and values of parents, community, and significant others. It is the moral aspect of an individual's personality; it passes judgments on behavior. The superego is divided into two parts: **conscience** and **ego ideal**. Conscience tells what is right and wrong. It forces the ego to control the id and directs the individual into morally acceptable and responsible behaviors, which may not be pleasurable. Exhibit 5.3 summarizes Freud's model of the personality structure.

Psychosexual Stages of Human Development   The most basic human drive present at birth is **eros**, the instinct to preserve and create life. The other is the death instinct (**thanatos**), which is expressed as aggression.

Eros is expressed sexually. Consequently, very early in their development, humans experience sexuality, which is expressed by seeking pleasure through various parts of the body. During the first year of life, a child attains pleasure by sucking and biting; Freud called this the **oral stage**. During the second and third years of life, the focus of sexual attention is on the elimination of bodily wastes—the **anal stage**. The **phallic stage** occurs during the third year,

---

EXHIBIT 5.3

Freud's Model of the Personality Structure

Personality Structure	Guiding Principle	Description
Id	Pleasure principle	Unconscious biological drives; requires instant gratification
Ego	Reality principle	Helps the personality refine the demands of the id; helps person adapt to conventions
Superego	The conscience	The moral aspect of the personality

SOURCE: © Cengage Learning

when children focus their attention on their genitals. Males begin to have sexual feelings for their mothers (the **Oedipus complex**) and girls for their fathers (the **Electra complex**). **Latency** begins at age 6. During this period, feelings of sexuality are repressed until the genital stage begins at puberty; this marks the beginning of adult sexuality.

If conflicts are encountered during any of the psychosexual stages of development, a person can become **fixated** at that point. This means, as an adult, the fixated person will exhibit behavior traits characteristic of those encountered during infantile sexual development. For example, an infant who does not receive enough oral gratification during the first year of life is likely as an adult to engage in such oral behavior as smoking, drinking, or drug abuse or to be clinging and dependent in personal relationships. Thus, according to Freud, the roots of adult behavioral problems can be traced to problems developed in the earliest years of life.

The Psychodynamics of Antisocial Behavior

Psychologists have long linked criminality to abnormal mental states produced by early childhood trauma. For example, Alfred Adler (1870–1937), the founder of individual psychology, coined the term **inferiority complex** to describe people who have feelings of inferiority and compensate for them with a drive for superiority. Controlling others may help reduce personal inadequacies. Erik Erikson (1902–1984) described the **identity crisis**—a period of serious personal questioning people undertake in an effort to determine their own values and sense of direction. Adolescents undergoing an identity crisis might exhibit out-of-control behavior and experiment with drugs and other forms of deviance.

The psychoanalyst whose work is most closely associated with criminality is August Aichorn.[197] After examining many delinquent youths, Aichorn concluded that societal stress, though damaging, could not alone result in a life of crime unless a predisposition existed that psychologically prepared youths for antisocial acts. This mental state, which he labeled **latent delinquency**, is found in youngsters whose personality requires them to act in these ways:

- Seek immediate gratification (to act impulsively)
- Consider satisfying their personal needs more important than relating to others
- Satisfy instinctive urges without considering right and wrong (that is, they lack guilt)

The psychodynamic model of the criminal offender depicts an aggressive, frustrated person dominated by events that occurred early in childhood. Perhaps because they may have suffered unhappy experiences in childhood or had families that could not provide proper love and care, criminals suffer from weak or damaged egos that make them unable to cope with conventional society. Weak egos are associated with immaturity, poor social skills, and excessive dependence on others. People with weak egos may be easily led into crime by antisocial peers and drug abuse.

Some offenders have underdeveloped superegos and consequently lack internalized representations of those behaviors that are punished in conventional society. They commit crimes because they have difficulty understanding the consequences of their actions.[198]

Offenders may suffer from a wide variety of mood and/or behavior **disorders**. They may be histrionic, depressed, antisocial, or narcissistic.[199] They may suffer from **conduct disorders**, which include long histories of antisocial behavior, or mood disorders characterized by disturbance in expressed emotions. Among the latter is **bipolar disorder**, in which moods alternate between periods of wild elation and deep depression.[200] Some offenders are driven by an unconscious desire to be punished for prior sins, either real or imaginary. As a result, they may violate the law to gain attention or to punish their parents.

According to this view, crime is a manifestation of feelings of oppression and people's inability to develop the proper psychological defenses and rationales to keep these feelings under control. Criminality enables troubled people to survive by producing positive psychic results: it helps them to feel free and independent, and it gives them the possibility of excitement and the chance to use their skills and imagination. Crime also provides them with the promise of positive gain; it allows them to blame others for their predicament (for example, the police), and it gives them a chance to rationalize their sense of failure ("If I hadn't gotten into trouble, I could have been a success").[201]

Oedipus complex A stage of development when males begin to have sexual feelings for their mothers.

Electra complex A stage of development when girls begin to have sexual feelings for their fathers.

latency A developmental stage that begins at age 6. During this period, feelings of sexuality are repressed until the genital stage begins at puberty; this marks the beginning of adult sexuality.

fixated An adult who exhibits behavior traits characteristic of those encountered during infantile sexual development.

inferiority complex People who have feelings of inferiority and compensate for them with a drive for superiority.

identity crisis A psychological state, identified by Erikson, in which youth face inner turmoil and uncertainty about life roles.

latent delinquency A psychological predisposition to commit antisocial acts because of an id-dominated personality that renders an individual incapable of controlling impulsive, pleasure-seeking drives.

disorders Any type of psychological problems (formerly labeled neuroses or psychoses), such as anxiety disorders, mood disorders, and conduct disorders.

conduct disorder (CD) A pattern of repetitive behavior in which the rights of others or social norms are violated.

bipolar disorder An emotional disturbance in which moods alternate between periods of wild elation and deep depression.

ATTACHMENT THEORY

Attachment theory, a view most closely associated with psychologist John Bowlby, is also connected to the psychodynamic tradition. Bowlby believed that the ability to form attachments—that is, emotionally bond to another person—has important lasting psychological implications that follow people across the life span. Attachments are formed soon after birth, when infants bond with their mothers. They will become frantic, crying and clinging, to prevent separation or to reestablish contact with a missing parent. Bowlby noted that this behavior is not restricted to humans and occurs in all mammals, indicating that separation anxiety may be instinctual or evolutionary. After all, attachment figures, especially the mother, provide support and care, and without attachment an infant would be helpless and could not survive. Bowlby also challenged Freud's view of the development of the ego and superego, claiming that at birth these were bound up in the relationship with one's mother.[202]

Bowlby's most important finding was that to grow up mentally healthy "the infant and young child should experience a warm, intimate, and continuous relationship with his mother (or permanent mother substitute) in which both find satisfaction and enjoyment."[203]

According to this view, failing to develop proper attachment may cause people to fall prey to a number of psychological disorders. Psychologists believe that children with attachment problems lack trust and respect for others. They often display many psychological symptoms, some of which resemble attention deficit hyperactivity disorder (ADHD). They may be impulsive and have difficulty concentrating, and consequently experience difficulty in school. As adults, they often have difficulty initiating and sustaining relationships with others and find it difficult to sustain romantic relationships. Criminologists have linked people having detachment problems with a variety of antisocial behaviors, including sexual assault and child abuse.[204] Boys disproportionately experience disrupted attachment, and these disruptions are causally related to disproportionate rates of male offending.[205] Those who are not attached to parents and get little parental support are at risk to engage in risky sexual behavior and sexual assaults as teens and young adults.[206] There is also evidence that disrupted parental attachment is related to the onset and persistence of substance abuse and misuse.[207]

MENTAL DISORDERS AND CRIME

According to the psychodynamic tradition, traumatic life events can bring about severe mental disorders that have been linked to the onset of crime and deviance. Mental

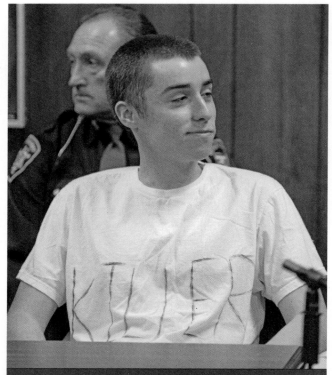

On March 19, 2013, in Chardon, Ohio, T. J. Lane smirks as he listens to the judge during sentencing. Lane was given three lifetime prison sentences without the possibility of parole for opening fire in a high school cafeteria in a rampage that left three students dead and three others wounded. Lane, 18, had pleaded guilty to shooting students at Chardon High School, east of Cleveland. He admitted to the shooting but said he didn't know why he killed the students. Before the case went to adult court, a juvenile court judge ruled that Lane was mentally competent to stand trial despite evidence he suffered from hallucinations, psychosis, and fantasies. Should someone like Lane be sent to prison or a mental health institution?

AP Images/News-Herald, Duncan Scott, Pool

disorders typically involve a psychological condition that disrupts thinking, feeling, and other important psychological processes. They may cause people to deviate from social expectations and impair their everyday functioning. Less severe forms are mood disorders—prolonged and intense emotional upheavals that shape and color a person's psychic life. A more severe mental disorder is referred to as psychosis and is characterized by derangement of personality and loss of contact with reality, thereby causing deterioration of normal social functioning. These are discussed more fully in the following pages.

Mood Disorders and Crime Psychologists recognize a variety of mental disorders that may be linked to antisocial behavior. Adolescents who are frequently uncooperative and hostile and who seem to be much more difficult than other children the same age may be suffering from a psychological condition known as disruptive behavior disorder

attachment theory The belief that the ability to form attachments—that is, emotionally bond to another person—has important lasting psychological implications that follow people across the life span.

(DBD), which can take on two distinct forms: oppositional defiant disorder (ODD) and conduct disorder (CD).[208]

Children suffering from ODD experience an ongoing pattern of uncooperative, defiant, and hostile behavior toward authority figures that seriously interferes with the youngsters' day-to-day functioning. Symptoms of ODD may include frequent loss of temper and constant arguing with adults; defying adults or refusing adult requests or rules; deliberately annoying others; blaming others for mistakes or misbehavior; being angry and resentful; being spiteful or vindictive; swearing or using obscene language; or having low self-esteem. The person with ODD is moody and easily frustrated and may abuse drugs as a form of self-medication.[209] ODD has been linked to a great many social problems, including delinquency and bullying.[210]

Conduct disorders are typically considered a more serious group of behavioral and emotional problems.[211] Children suffering from CD engage in repetitive and persistent patterns of behavior in which the rights of others or basic social rules are disrupted. These involve aggressive behavior, such as bullying or intimidating others, fighting, sexual assaults, and animal cruelty. Kids suffering from conduct disorder are also prone to vandalism, fire setting, lying, theft, and rule infractions such as truancy and running away. They are often viewed by other children, adults, and social agencies as severely antisocial.[212]

What causes CD? Numerous biosocial and psychological factors are suspected. There is evidence, for example, that interconnections between the frontal lobes and other brain regions may influence CD. There is also research showing that levels of serotonin can influence the onset of CD and that CD has been shown to aggregate in families, suggesting a genetic basis of the disorder.[213]

ODD and CD are not the only mood disorders associated with antisocial behavior. Some people find it impossible to cope with feelings of oppression or depression. Research shows that people who are clinically depressed are more likely to engage in a variety of illegal acts.[214] Some people suffer from **alexithymia**, a deficit in emotional cognition that prevents them from being aware of their feelings or being able to understand or talk about their thoughts and emotions; they seem robotic and emotionally dead.[215] Others may suffer from eating disorders and are likely to use fasting, vomiting, and drugs to lose weight or to keep from gaining weight.[216]

Psychosis and Crime   David Berkowitz (also known as "Son of Sam" or the "44-calibre killer"), a noted serial killer who went on a rampage from 1976 to 1977, claimed that his killing spree began when he received messages from a neighbor's dog. His symptoms made him appear to suffer from a severe form of mental illness referred to as **psychosis**, characterized by extreme impairment of a person's ability to think clearly, respond emotionally, communicate effectively, understand reality, and behave appropriately. People suffering from psychosis may hear nonexistent voices,

hallucinate, and make inappropriate behavioral responses. People with severe mental disorders exhibit illogical and incoherent thought processes and a lack of insight into their own behavior. They may see themselves as agents of the devil, avenging angels, or recipients of messages from animals and plants. Psychosis is brought about by a variety of mental disorders, including depression, manic depression, bipolar disorder, and **schizophrenia**.

There is evidence that law violators, especially those involved in violent crime, suffer from a disproportionate amount of severe mental health problems.[217] Recently, Richard Dorn and his associates examined the association between mental disorder and violence using a longitudinal sample of about 35,000 subjects. They found that when compared to the mentally sound, people suffering mental illness were significantly more likely to engage in subsequent violent episodes, especially if they abused drugs and alcohol.[218] The diagnosed mentally ill also appear in arrest and court statistics at a rate disproportionate to their presence in the population.[219] They may also be more prone to recidivism once released from prison.[220]

The association between mental health issues and crime crosses gender, age, and cultural lines.[221] Kids growing up in homes where parents suffer from mental illness are much more likely to be at risk for family instability, poverty, and other factors that are related to future delinquency and crime. So not only may mental illness be a cause of crime, but its effect may be intergenerational.[222] The Profiles in Crime feature looks at one of the most notorious crimes committed by a mentally ill young man.

To hear Adam Lanza's call-in to a radio show, go to **http://www.usatoday.com/story/news /nation/2014/01/16/adam-lanza-newtown -sandy-hook-radio-program/4505649/.**
Does he sound delusional or rational and calculating?

alexithymia A deficit in emotional cognition that prevents people from being aware of their feelings or being able to understand or talk about their thoughts and emotions; they seem robotic and emotionally dead.

psychosis A mental state in which the perception of reality is distorted. People experiencing psychosis hallucinate, have paranoid or delusional beliefs, change personality, exhibit disorganized thinking, and engage in unusual or bizarre behavior.

schizophrenia A type of psychosis often marked by bizarre behavior, hallucinations, loss of thought control, and inappropriate emotional responses. Schizophrenic types include catatonic, which characteristically involves impairment of motor activity; paranoid, which is characterized by delusions of persecution; and hebephrenic, which is characterized by immature behavior and giddiness.

Adam Lanza and the Newtown Massacre

On December 14, 2012, Adam Lanza shot his mother at her home in Newtown, Connecticut, and then took her car to nearby Sandy Hook Elementary School, where he shot and killed 20 young students, between the ages of 5 and 10, and six adult teachers and school employees. After firing 50 to 100 shots at the children and staff, Lanza fatally shot himself in the head as first responders began arriving on scene.

What could have driven this seemingly intelligent and articulate young man to commit one of the worst crimes in American history? Adam Peter Lanza was born in Exeter, New Hampshire, on April 22, 1992. His parents, Peter and Nancy Lanza, were both wealthy and successful. He had an older brother, Ryan Lanza, four years his senior. Then in 2008, when Adam was 16 years old, his parents divorced. Soon after, his classmates began to describe his behavior as "fidgety" and "deeply troubled"; he may have suffered from Asperger's syndrome. Adam began to lose his connection to reality and

developed severe mental illness. By 2010, his illness had become so severe he broke off relations with almost everyone in his life and secluded himself in his bedroom, where he spent hours playing violent video games and obsessing over mass murderers. The fact that his mother was a gun enthusiast did not help matters. Lanza's home was filled with weapons and ammunition to which he had easy access. Lanza also had a number of books and articles on other mass killings.

Adam joined the Columbine mass murder website, *Shocked Beyond Belief*, using the screen name "Smiggles," and began to express his paranoia and his belief that society was trying to manipulate him into following an immoral value system that led to both mental and physical sickness. On December 7, 2011, he posted a note showing his disdain for society and his interest in mass murder:

When civilization exists in a form where all forms of alienation (among

many other things) are rampant . . . new children will end up "not well" in all sorts of ways. You don't even have to touch a topic as cryptic as mass murder to see an indication of this: you can look at a single symptom as egregious as the proliferation of antidepressants.

In Adam's worldview, children were indoctrinated from a very young age to become part of a sick society. They were manipulated to live unhealthy lives and doomed to live in a joyless world where they would be used and abused. By killing them, he'd be doing them a favor, saving them from the hell he was enduring. Lanza's father said in his first public comments about the massacre that what his son did couldn't "get any more evil" and that he wished his son had never been born.

SOURCE: Matthew Lysiak, "Why Adam Lanza Did It," *Newsweek*, January 17, 2014, http://www.newsweek.com/why-adam-lanza-did-it-226565 (accessed May 2016).

The National Mental Health Association (NMHA) is the country's oldest and largest nonprofit organization addressing all aspects of mental health and mental illness. It is dedicated to improving the mental health of all individuals and achieving victory over mental illnesses. Learn more at **http://www.mentalhealthamerica.net/**.

Direct or Indirect Linkage? It is still uncertain whether the link between mental illness and crime is direct or indirect. While it's possible that crime is a direct result of the delusions and illogical thinking associated with mental illness, it is also possible that some intervening factor associated with mental illness is the primary cause of antisocial behaviors. Suspected associations include the following:

- Mentally ill people may be more likely than the mentally sound to lack financial resources. They are thus forced to reside in deteriorated high-crime neighborhoods, a social factor that may increase involvement with criminal behavior.[223] It is also possible that a lack of resources

may inhibit the mentally ill from obtaining the proper treatment, which, if made available, would result in reduced criminality.[224]
- The police may be more likely to arrest the mentally ill, which fosters the impression that they are crime prone.[225]
- Those suffering from mental illness may self-medicate by using illegal substances, a practice linked to criminal behavior.[226]
- People with severe mental illness are more at risk to violent victimization than the mentally healthy.[227] Violent victimization has been linked to increased crime rates. Ironically, efforts to deinstitutionalize the mentally ill and treat them in more humane community settings may expose them to higher rates of both victimization and criminality.[228]

BEHAVIORAL THEORY

 LO7 Link behavioral theory to crime

Psychological behavior theory maintains that human actions are developed through learning experiences. Rather

An Ethical Dilemma

Something Snapped

The American Psychiatric Association (APA) believes a person should not be held legally responsible for a crime if his or her behavior meets the following standard developed by legal expert Richard Bonnie:

> A person charged with a criminal offense should be found not guilty by reason of insanity if it is shown that as a result of mental disease or mental retardation he was unable to appreciate the wrongfulness of his conduct at the time of the offense.

> As used in this standard, the terms *mental disease* and *mental retardation* include only those severely abnormal mental conditions that grossly and demonstrably impair a person's perception or understanding of reality and that are not attributable primarily to the voluntary ingestion of alcohol or other psychoactive substances.

You are part of a research team with expertise on forensic criminology. Your team has been asked by the judge to investigate the case of Bill W., a young man who has murdered his father, and to make a written sentencing recommendation. You discover that Bill has a history of horrendous sexual and physical abuse at the hands of his father. When interviewed, Bill admits that "it is wrong to kill," but that something just "snapped" when he saw his dad with his arm around his younger brother, who also had cuts and bruises. Have one half of the research team write a brief recommending that Bill's behavior be excused because of his prior history of mistreatment. Have the other half write an opinion supporting a criminal conviction because he fails to meet the test of insanity according to the APA definition. Have each group make an oral presentation of their findings and have the team leader choose the most persuasive argument to present to the judge.

than focusing on unconscious personality traits or cognitive development patterns produced early in childhood, behavior theorists are concerned with the actual behaviors people engage in during the course of their daily lives. The major premise of behavior theory is that people alter their behavior according to the reactions it receives from others. Behavior is supported by rewards and extinguished by negative reactions or punishments. With respect to criminal activity, the behaviorist views crimes, especially violent acts, as learned responses to life situations that do not necessarily represent psychologically abnormal responses.

Social Learning Theory **Social learning** is the branch of behavior theory most relevant to criminology.[229] Social learning theorists, most notably Albert Bandura, argue that people are not actually born with the ability to act violently, but that they learn to be aggressive through their life experiences.

To read about the life and work of Albert Bandura, visit http://www.simplypsychology.org/bandura.html and http://faculty.frostburg.edu/mbradley/psyography/albertbandura.html.
Is your behavior altered when you observe people acting aggressively to achieve a goal and succeeding when others fail?

These experiences include personally observing others acting aggressively to achieve some goal or watching people being rewarded for violent acts on television or in movies. People learn to act aggressively when, as children, they model their behavior after the violent acts of adults. Later in life, these violent behavior patterns persist in social relationships. For example, the boy who sees his father repeatedly strike his mother with impunity is the one most likely to grow up to become a battering husband and parent.

Though social learning theorists agree that mental or physical traits may predispose a person toward violence, they believe that activating a person's violent tendencies is achieved by factors in the environment. The specific forms that aggressive behavior takes, the frequency with which it is expressed, the situations in which it is displayed, and the specific targets selected for attack are largely determined by social learning. However, people are self-aware and engage in purposeful learning. Their interpretations of behavior outcomes and situations influence the way they learn from experiences. One adolescent who spends a weekend in jail for drunk driving may find it the most awful experience of her life—one that teaches her to never drink and drive again. Another person, however, may find it an exciting experience about which he can brag to his friends.

social learning theory The view that human behavior is modeled through observation of human social interactions, either directly from observing those who are close and from intimate contact or indirectly through the media. Interactions that are rewarded are copied, while those that are punished are avoided.

Violent Media/Violent Crime?

`04`

Does the media influence behavior? Does violence depicted in TV shows, movies, games, music lyrics, and graphic novels cause aggressive behavior in viewers? This has become a hot topic because of the persistent theme of violence in these media. Critics have called for drastic measures, ranging from banning media violence to putting warning labels on video games.

If there is in fact a media–violence link, the problem is indeed alarming. Marketing research indicates that adolescents ages 11 to 14 view violent horror movies at a higher rate than any other age group. Children this age use older peers and siblings and apathetic parents to gain access to R-rated films. Most U.S. households now have either cable TV or smart TVs that can access the Internet and bring violent material into the home that is unavailable on broadcast networks.

There have been numerous anecdotal cases of violence linked to media. In one famous historical incident, John Hinckley shot President Ronald Reagan due to his obsession with actress Jodie Foster, which developed after he watched her play a prostitute in the violent film *Taxi Driver*. Hinckley viewed the film at least 15 times.

While not all experts believe that media violence is a direct *cause* of violent behavior (because if it were, there would be millions of daily incidents in which viewers imitated the aggression they watched on TV or in movies), many do agree that media violence *contributes* to aggression. Viewing media violence in both film and printed images has been related to both short- and long-term increases in aggressive attitudes, values, and behaviors. Teens who watch violent media are the ones most likely to engage in dating violence, especially if they do not hold strong antiviolence attitudes. There is also evidence of a significant association between watching and engaging in relational aggression (behavior intended to harm or manipulate relationships or the social standing of an individual who does not wish to be harmed). For example, kids who observe "mean girls" harassing someone on TV are more likely to engage in that behavior themselves.

Even relatively brief exposure to violent movie clips increased anxiety among late adolescents, indicating that media can create personality change. This change may account for the long-term effect of violent media: adolescents exposed to violent media are more likely to persist in aggressive behavior as adults. Children who watch more than an hour of TV each day show an increase in assaults, fights, robberies, and other acts of aggression later in life and into adulthood.

How Are the Media and Violence Connected?

There are several explanations for the effects of television and film violence on behavior:

- Media violence can provide aggressive "scripts" that children store in memory. Repeated exposure to these scripts can increase their retention and lead to changes in attitudes.

- Children learn from what they observe. In the same way they learn cognitive and social skills from their parents and friends, children learn to be violent from television.

- Television violence increases the arousal levels of viewers and makes them more prone to act aggressively. Studies measuring the galvanic skin response of subjects—a physical indication of arousal based on the amount of electricity conducted across the palm of the hand—show that viewing violent television shows led to increased arousal levels in young children.

- Watching television violence promotes such negative attitudes as suspiciousness and the expectation that the viewer will become involved in violence. Those who watch television frequently come to view aggression and violence as common and socially acceptable behavior.

- Television violence allows aggressive youths to justify their behavior. It is possible that, instead of causing violence, television helps violent youths rationalize their behavior as a socially acceptable and common activity.

Social Learning and Violence   Social learning theorists view violence as something learned through a process called **behavior modeling**. In modern society, aggressive acts are usually modeled after three principal sources:

- *Family interaction.* Studies of family life show that aggressive children have parents who use similar tactics when dealing with others. For example, the children of wife batterers are more likely to use aggressive tactics themselves than children in the general population, especially if the victims (their mothers) suffer psychological distress from the abuse.

- *Environmental experiences.* People who reside in areas in which violence is a daily occurrence are more likely to act violently than those who dwell in low-crime areas whose norms stress conventional behavior.

- *Mass media.* Films and television shows commonly depict violence graphically. Moreover, violence is often portrayed as an acceptable behavior, especially for heroes who never have to face legal consequences for their actions.

behavior modeling Process of learning behavior (notably aggression) by observing others. Aggressive models may be parents, criminals in the neighborhood, or characters on television or in video games and movies.

- Television violence may disinhibit aggressive behavior, which is normally controlled by other learning processes. Disinhibition takes place when adults are viewed as being rewarded for violence and when violence is seen as socially acceptable. This contradicts previous learning experiences in which violent behavior was viewed as wrong.

Debating the Media–Violence Link

While this research is quite persuasive, not all criminologists accept that watching TV and movies or playing violent video games actually leads to interpersonal violence. Just because kids who are exposed to violent media also engage in violent behaviors is not proof of a causal connection. It is also possible that kids who are violent later seek out violent media: What would we expect violent gang boys to watch on TV? *Harry the Bunny*? There is little evidence that areas that experience the highest levels of violent TV viewing also have rates of violent crime that are above the norm. Millions of children watch violence every night but do not become violent criminals. If violent TV shows did, indeed, cause interpersonal violence, then there should be few ecological and regional patterns in the crime rate, but there are many. Put another way, how can regional differences in the violence rate be explained considering the fact that people all across the nation watch the same TV shows and films? Nor can the media–violence link explain recent crime trends. Despite a rampant increase in violent TV shows, films, and video games, the violence rate among teens has been in a significant decline.

One reason for the ongoing debate may be that media violence may affect one subset of the population but have relatively little effect on others. Sociologist George Comstock has identified attributes that make some people especially prone to the effects of media violence:

- Predisposition for aggressive or antisocial behavior
- Rigid or indifferent parenting
- Unsatisfactory social relationships
- Low psychological well-being
- Having been diagnosed as suffering from disruptive behavior disorders (DBDs)

So if the impact of media on behavior is not in fact universal, it may have the greatest effect on those who are the most socially and psychologically vulnerable.

 CRITICAL THINKING

1. Should the government control the content of TV shows and limit the amount of weekly violence? How could the national news be shown if violence were omitted? What about boxing matches or hockey games?
2. How can we explain the fact that millions of kids watch violent TV shows and remain nonviolent?
3. If there is a TV–violence link, how can we explain the fact that violence rates may have been higher in the Old West than they are today?
4. Do you think violent gang kids stay home and watch TV shows?

SOURCES: Sarah Coyne, "Effects of Viewing Relational Aggression on Television on Aggressive Behavior in Adolescents: A Three-Year Longitudinal Study," *Developmental Psychology* 52 (2016): 284–295; Sarah Coyne, Mark Callister, Laura Stockdale, Holly Coutts, and Kevin Collier, "Just How Graphic Are Graphic Novels? An Examination of Aggression Portrayals in Manga and Associations with Aggressive Behavior in Adolescents," *Violence and Victims* 30 (2015): 208–224; Sukkyung You, Euikyung Kim, and Unkyung No, "Impact of Violent Video Games on the Social Behaviors of Adolescents: The Mediating Role of Emotional Competence," *School Psychology International* 36 (2015): 94–111; Morgan Tear and Mark Nielsen, "Video Games and Prosocial Behavior: A Study of the Effects of Non-Violent, Violent, and Ultra-Violent Gameplay," *Computers in Human Behavior* 41 (2014): 8; Seth Gitter, Patrick Ewell, Rosanna Guadagno, Tyler Stillman, and Roy Baumeister, "Virtually Justifiable Homicide: The Effects of Prosocial Contexts on the Link Between Violent Video Games, Aggression, and Prosocial and Hostile Cognition," *Aggressive Behavior* 39 (2013): 346; Ingrid Möller, Barbara Krahé, Robert Busching, and Christina Krause, "Efficacy of an Intervention to Reduce the Use of Media Violence and Aggression: An Experimental Evaluation with Adolescents in Germany," *Journal of Youth and Adolescence* 41 (2012): 105–120; Laura Friedlander, Jennifer Connolly, Debra Pepler, and Wendy Craig, "Extensiveness and Persistence of Aggressive Media Exposure as Longitudinal Risk Factors for Teen Dating Violence," *Psychology of Violence* 3 (2013): 310–322; Anjana Madan, Sylvie Mrug, and Rex Wright, "The Effects of Media Violence on Anxiety in Late Adolescence," *Journal of Youth and Adolescence* 43 (2014): 116–126; George Comstock, "A Sociological Perspective on Television Violence and Aggression," *American Behavioral Scientist* 51 (2008): 1184–1211; Craig Anderson and Brad J. Bushman, "The Effects of Media Violence on Society," *Science* 295 (2002): 2377–2379.

The Criminology in Action feature "Violent Media/Violent Crime" has more on the effects of the media and violent behavior.

Social learning theorists have tried to determine what triggers violent acts. One position is that a direct, pain-producing physical assault will usually trigger a violent response. Yet the relationship between painful attacks and aggressive responses has been found to be inconsistent. Whether people counterattack in the face of physical attack depends, in part, on their skill in fighting and their perception of the strength of their attackers. Verbal taunts and insults have also been linked to aggressive responses. People who are predisposed to aggression by their learning experiences are likely to view insults from others as a challenge to their social status and to react with violence. Still another violence-triggering mechanism is a perceived reduction in one's life conditions. Prime examples of this phenomenon are riots and demonstrations in poverty-stricken ghetto areas. Studies have shown that discontent also produces aggression in the more successful members of lower-class groups who have been led to believe they can succeed but then have been thwarted in their aspirations. While it is still uncertain how this relationship is constructed, it is apparently complex. No matter how deprived some individuals are, they will not resort to violence. It seems evident that people's perceptions of their relative deprivation have different effects on their aggressive responses.

In summary, social learning theorists have said that the following four factors may contribute to violent and/or aggressive behavior:

- *An event that heightens arousal.* Such as a person frustrating or provoking another through physical assault or verbal abuse.
- *Aggressive skills.* Learned aggressive responses picked up from observing others, either personally or through the media.
- *Expected outcomes.* The belief that aggression will somehow be rewarded. Rewards can come in the form of reducing tension or anger, gaining some financial reward, building self-esteem, or gaining the praise of others.
- *Consistency of behavior with values.* The belief, gained from observing others, that aggression is justified and appropriate, given the circumstances of the current situation.

COGNITIVE THEORY

L08 Articulate the cognitive processes related to crime

One area of psychology that has received increasing recognition in recent years is the cognitive school. Psychologists with a cognitive perspective focus on mental processes and how people perceive and mentally represent the world around them and solve problems. The pioneers of this school were Wilhelm Wundt (1832–1920), Edward Titchener (1867–1927), and William James (1842–1920). Today, there are several subdisciplines within the cognitive area. The **moral development** branch is concerned with the way people morally represent and reason about the world. **Humanistic psychology** stresses self-awareness and "getting in touch with feelings." The **information processing** branch focuses on the way people process, store, encode, retrieve, and manipulate information to make decisions and solve problems.

Moral and Intellectual Development Theory The moral and intellectual development branch of cognitive psychology is perhaps the most important for criminological theory. Jean Piaget (1896–1980), the founder of this approach, hypothesized that people's reasoning processes develop in an orderly fashion, beginning at birth and continuing into their maturity.[230] At first, children respond to the environment in a simple manner, seeking interesting objects and developing their reflexes. By the fourth and final stage, the formal operations stage, they have developed into mature adults who can use logic and abstract thought.

Lawrence Kohlberg first applied the concept of moral development to issues in criminology.[231] He found that people travel through stages of moral development during which their decisions and judgments on issues of right and wrong are made for different reasons. It is possible that serious offenders have a moral orientation that differs from that of law-abiding citizens. Kohlberg classified people according to the stage on this continuum at which their moral development ceased to grow. Kohlberg and his associates conducted studies in which criminals were found to be significantly lower in their moral judgment development than noncriminals of the same social background.[232] Since his pioneering efforts, researchers have continued to show that criminal offenders are more likely to be classified in the lowest levels of moral reasoning (Stages 1 and 2), whereas noncriminals have reached a higher stage of moral development (Stages 3 and 4).[233]

The decision not to commit crimes may be influenced by one's stage of moral development. People at the lowest levels report that they are deterred from crime because of their fear of sanctions. Those in the middle consider the reactions of family and friends. Those at the highest stages refrain from crime because they believe in duty to others and universal rights.[234]

Moral development theory suggests that people who obey the law simply to avoid punishment or have outlooks mainly characterized by self-interest are more likely to commit crimes than those who view the law as something that benefits all of society. Those at higher stages of moral reasoning tend to sympathize with the rights of others and are associated with conventional behaviors, such as honesty, generosity, and nonviolence. Subsequent research has found that a significant number of noncriminals display higher stages of moral reasoning than criminals and that engaging in criminal behavior leads to reduced levels of moral reasoning, which in turn produces more delinquency in a never-ending loop.[235]

moral development The way people morally represent and reason about the world.

humanistic psychology A branch of psychology that stresses self-awareness and "getting in touch with feelings."

information processing A branch of cognitive psychology that focuses on the way people process, store, encode, retrieve, and manipulate information to make decisions and solve problems.

CONNECTIONS

The deterrent effect of informal sanctions and feelings of shame discussed in Chapter 4 may hinge on the level of a person's moral development. The lower one's state of moral development, the less impact informal sanctions may have; increased moral development and informal sanctions may be better able to control crime.

ASK YOURSELF . . .

Can a person's state of moral development be altered by life events? Or, once formed, does it remain resistant to change?

Social Information Processing When cognitive theorists who study information processing try to explain antisocial behavior, they do so in terms of mental perception and how people use information to understand their environment. When people make decisions, they engage in a sequence of cognitive thought processes:

1. Encode information so that it can be interpreted.
2. Search for a proper response.
3. Decide on the most appropriate action.
4. Act on the decision.[236]

Not everyone processes information in the same way, and the differences in interpretation may explain the development of radically different visions of the world. According to this cognitive approach, people who use information properly, who are better conditioned to make reasoned judgments, and who can make quick and reasoned decisions when facing emotion-laden events are the ones best able to avoid antisocial behavior choices.[237] Crime-prone people may have cognitive deficits and use information incorrectly when they make decisions.[238] Law violators may lack the ability to perform cognitive functions in a normal and orderly fashion.[239] Some may be sensation seekers who are constantly looking for novel experiences, whereas others lack deliberation and rarely think through problems. Others maintain inappropriate attitudes and beliefs; they are thrill-seeking, manipulative, callous, deceptive, and hold rule-breaking attitudes.[240] Some may give up easily, whereas others act without thinking when they get upset.[241]

People with inadequate cognitive processing perceive the world as stacked against them; they believe they have little control over the negative events in their life.[242] Chronic offenders come to believe that crime is an appropriate means to satisfy their immediate personal needs, which take precedence over more distant social needs such as obedience to the law.[243] They have a distorted view of the world that shapes their thinking and colors their judgments. Because they have difficulty making the right decision while under stress, they pursue behaviors that they perceive as beneficial and satisfying, but that turn out to be harmful and detrimental.[244] They may take aggressive action because they wrongly believe that a situation demands forceful responses. Parents who believe that forceful physical discipline is necessary to control children are much more likely to actually engage in abusive behavior practices.[245] They find it difficult to understand or sympathize with other people's feelings and emotions, which leads them to blame their victims for their problems.[246] Thus, the sexual

offender believes his target either led him on or secretly wanted the forcible sex to occur: "She was asking for it."[247]

Shaping Perceptions To violence-prone kids, people seem more aggressive than they actually are and seem to intend them ill when there is no reason for alarm. According to information processing theory, as these children mature, they use fewer cues than most people to process information. Some use violence in a calculating fashion as a means of getting what they want; others react in an overly volatile fashion to the slightest provocation. Aggressors are more

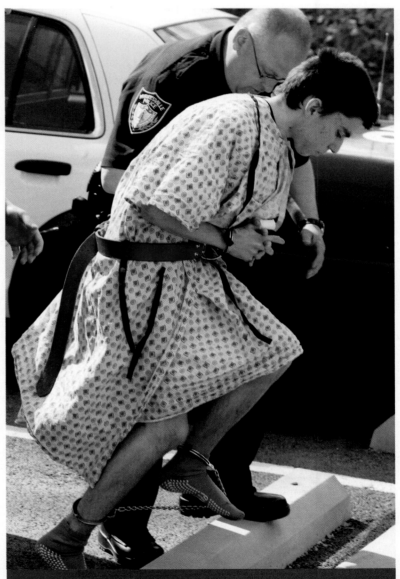

On April 9, 2014, Alex Hribal, 16, was arrested for stabbing and slashing 20 students and a security guard at Franklin Regional High School in Murrysville, Pennsylvania. Here he is shown being escorted by police to a district magistrate to be arraigned. Is it possible that Hribal's unexplained outburst was a function of a cognitive deficit that convinced him he had to retaliate against some imagined grievance? When told to drop his weapons after his rampage, he responded, "No, I am not dropping them; my work is not done. I have more people to kill."

AP Images/Keith Srakocic

likely to be vigilant, on edge, or suspicious. When they attack victims, they may believe they are defending themselves, even though they are misreading the situation.[248]

 To read more about information processing theory, go to http://www.education.com/reference/article/information-processing-theory/.

Do you ever wonder whether you are misinterpreting cues and behavior, such as thinking that someone is standoffish and arrogant when they really are just shy?

There is evidence that delinquent boys who engage in theft are more likely to exhibit cognitive deficits than nondelinquent youth. For example, they have a poor sense of time, leaving them incapable of dealing with or solving social problems in an effective manner.[249] Information processing theory has been used to explain the occurrence of date rape. Sexually violent males believe that when their dates say no to sexual advances the women are really "playing games" and actually want to be taken forcefully.[250]

Errors in cognition and information processing have been used to explain the behavior of child abusers. Distorted thinking patterns abusers express include the following:

- *Child as a sexual being.* Children are perceived as being able to and wanting to engage in sexual activity with adults.[251]
- *Nature of harm.* The offender perceives that sexual activity does not cause harm (and may in fact be beneficial) to the child.
- *Entitlement.* The child abuser perceives that he is superior and more important than others and hence is able to have sex with whomever and whenever he wants.
- *Dangerous world.* An offender perceives that others are abusive and rejecting, and he must fight to be safe.
- *Uncontrollable.* The world is perceived as uncontrollable, and circumstances are outside of his control.

Cause and Treatment of Cognitive Deficits Why do some individuals develop cognitive deficits that prevent them from conforming to social expectations and adjusting properly to society? One reason may be damage to the frontal lobe, the area of the brain that controls executive functions, attention, working memory, verbal skills, and intelligence. Such damage can occur prenatally as a result of maternal substance abuse, during birth trauma, or even later in development as a result of child abuse or injury.[252]

People whose cognitive processes are skewed or faulty may be relying on mental scripts learned in childhood that tell them how to interpret events, what to expect, how they should react, and what the outcome of the interaction should be. Hostile children may have learned improper scripts by observing how others react to events; their own

parents' aggressive and inappropriate behavior would have considerable impact. Some may have had early and prolonged exposure to violence (for example, child abuse), which increases their sensitivity to slights and maltreatment. Oversensitivity to rejection by their peers is a continuation of sensitivity to rejection by their parents.[253] Violent behavior responses learned in childhood become a stable behavior because the scripts that emphasize aggressive responses are repeatedly rehearsed as the child matures.[254] There is also evidence that adolescents who use violence as a coping technique with others are more likely to exhibit other social problems, such as drug and alcohol abuse.[255] Most likely there are not one but several compounding causes of impaired cognitive functioning, which encompass genetic, biological, psychological, and social influences.[256]

The various psychological theories of crime are set out in Concept Summary 5.2.

CONCEPT SUMMARY 5.2
Psychological Trait Theories

Psychodynamic
- The major premise of the theory is that the development of the unconscious personality early in childhood influences behavior for the rest of the person's life. Criminals have weak egos and damaged personalities.
- The strengths of the theory are that it explains the onset of crime and why crime and drug abuse cut across class lines.
- The research focuses of the theory are on mental disorders, personality development, and unconscious motivations and drives.

Behavioral
- The major premise of the theory is that people commit crime when they model their behavior after others they see being rewarded for similar acts. Behavior is reinforced by rewards and extinguished by punishment.
- The strengths of the theory are that it explains the role of significant others in the crime process; it shows how the media can influence crime and violence.
- The research focuses of the theory are the media and violence, as well as the effects of child abuse.

Cognitive
- The major premise of the theory is that individual reasoning processes influence behavior. Reasoning is influenced by the way people perceive their environment.
- The strengths of the theory are that it shows why criminal behavior patterns change over time as people mature and develop their reasoning powers. It may explain the aging-out process.
- The research focuses of the theory are perception and cognition.

Personality and Crime

L09 Identify the elements of personality related to crime

Personality can be defined as the reasonably stable patterns of behavior, including thoughts and emotions, that distinguish one person from another.[257] One's personality reflects a characteristic way of adapting to life's demands and problems. The way we behave is a function of how our personality enables us to interpret life events and make appropriate behavioral choices. Can the cause of crime be linked to personality?

The association between personality traits and crime has a long history. Sheldon Glueck and Eleanor Glueck identified a number of personality traits that they believe characterize antisocial youth:[258]

self-assertiveness	lack of concern for others
defiance	extroversion
feeling unappreciated	ambivalence
distrust of authority	impulsiveness
poor personal skills	narcissism
mental instability	suspicion
hostility	destructiveness
resentment	sadism

Psychologist Hans Eysenck linked personality to crime when he identified two traits that he associated with antisocial behavior: *extroversion-introversion* and *stability-instability*. Extreme introverts are overaroused and avoid sources of stimulation; in contrast, extreme extroverts are unaroused and seek sensation. Introverts are slow to learn and be conditioned; extroverts are impulsive individuals who lack the ability to examine their own motives and behaviors. Those who are unstable, a condition Eysenck calls "neuroticism," are anxious, tense, and emotionally unstable.[259] People who are both neurotic and extroverted lack self-insight and are impulsive and emotionally unstable; they are unlikely to have reasoned judgments of life events. While extrovert neurotics may act self-destructively (e.g., abusing drugs), more stable people will be able to reason that such behavior is ultimately

harmful and life threatening. Eysenck believes that personality is controlled by genetic factors and is heritable.

A large number of factors are believed to contribute to the development of a criminal personality.[260] Some are related to improper socialization, such as having a psychopathic parent, experiencing parental rejection and lack of love during childhood, and maternal cigarette smoking and receiving inconsistent discipline.[261] Others are psychological pathologies, including impulsivity, hostility, aggressiveness, and callousness.[262] These personality defects have been linked not only to aggressive antisocial behaviors such as assault and rape but also to white-collar and business crimes.[263]

According to this view, the personality is the key to understanding antisocial behavior. The more severe the disorder, the greater the likelihood that the individual will engage in serious and repeated antisocial acts.[264] Take for instance **sadistic personality disorder**, defined as a repeating pattern of cruel and demeaning behavior. People suffering from this type of extreme personality disturbance seem prone to engage in serious violent attacks, including homicides motivated by sexual sadism.[265]

THE ANTISOCIAL PERSONALITY

The Diagnostic and Statistical Manual of the American Psychiatric Association (APA) defines the antisocial personality as a pervasive pattern of disregard for, and violation of, the rights of others that begins in childhood or early adolescence and continues into adulthood. In addition, those suffering from this disease usually exhibit at least three of the following behaviors:

- Failure to conform to social norms with respect to lawful behaviors as indicated by repeatedly performing acts that are grounds for arrest
- Deceitfulness, as indicated by repeatedly lying, use of aliases, or conning others for personal profit or pleasure
- Impulsivity or failure to plan ahead
- Irritability and aggressiveness, as indicated by repeated physical fights or assaults
- Reckless disregard for safety of self or others
- Consistent irresponsibility, as indicated by repeated failure to sustain consistent work behavior or honor financial obligations
- Lack of remorse, as indicated by being indifferent to or rationalizing having hurt, mistreated, or stolen from another[266]

personality The reasonably stable patterns of behavior, including thoughts and emotions, that distinguish one person from another.

sadistic personality disorder A repeating pattern of cruel and demeaning behavior. People suffering from this type of extreme personality disturbance seem prone to engage in serious violent attacks, including homicides motivated by sexual sadism.

The terms **psychopath** and **sociopath** are still commonly used to describe people who have an antisocial personality. Though these terms are often used interchangeably, some psychologists distinguish between sociopaths and psychopaths, suggesting that the former are a product of a destructive upbringing marked by neglect and abuse, whereas the latter are a product of an inherited genetic defect or condition present at birth or soon after.[267]

From an early age, people suffering from antisocial behavior disorder experience home lives filled with frustration, bitterness, and quarreling. Antisocial youths exhibit low levels of guilt and anxiety and persistently violate the rights of others. Unlike most other offenders, high intelligence appears to enhance their destructive potential.[268] As a result of this instability and frustration, antisocial individuals develop personalities that are unreliable, unstable, demanding, and egocentric.

There are different types of psychopaths/sociopaths who fall along a continuum of critical behavior and personality traits, such as instability, inhibition, and attachment.[269] Most but not all are risk takers and sensation seekers who are constantly involved in a wide variety of antisocial behaviors. There are also differences in the need for stimulation. Some may become almost addicted to thrill seeking, resulting in repeated and dangerous risky behaviors. Others can be described as grandiose, egocentric, manipulative, forceful, and cold-hearted, with shallow emotions and the inability to feel remorse, empathy with others, or anxiety over their misdeeds. When they commit antisocial acts, they are less likely to feel shame or empathize with their victims. Considering these personality traits, it is not surprising that research studies show that antisocials tend to continue their criminal careers long after other offenders burn out or age out of crime.

After reviewing available data, forensic psychologist James Blair and his colleagues conclude that approximately 15 to 25 percent of U.S. prison inmates meet diagnostic criteria for psychopathy. Once they are released, former inmates who suffer from psychopathy are three times more likely to reoffend within a year of release than other prisoners, and four times more likely to reoffend violently.[270]

psychopath People who have an antisocial personality that is a product of a defect or aberration within themselves.

sociopath Personality disorder characterized by superficial charm and glibness, a lack of empathy for others, amoral conduct, and lack of shame, guilt, or remorse for antisocial behavior. The term may be used interchangeably with psychopath, but both terms have been replaced by antisocial behavior disorder.

Minnesota Multiphasic Personality Inventory (MMPI) A widely used psychological test that has subscales designed to measure many different personality traits, including psychopathic deviation (Pd scale), schizophrenia (Sc scale), and hypomania (Ma scale).

The Cause of Antisocial Personality Disorder There is still disagreement on the cause of antisocial personality disorder. Some explanations reflect sociopathy and focus on family experiences, such as the influence of an unstable parent, parental rejection, lack of love during childhood, and inconsistent discipline. Children who lack the opportunity to form an attachment to a mother figure in the first three years of life, who suffer sudden separation from the mother figure, or who see changes in the mother figure are most likely to develop psychopathic personalities. According to this view, the path runs from antisocial parenting to sociopathy to criminality.[271]

A second view is that antisocial personality disorder is passed down genetically and inherited.[272] Supporting evidence shows that psychopaths may suffer from lower than normal levels of arousal.[273] Research studies show that psychopaths have lower skin conductance levels and fewer spontaneous responses than normal subjects. There may be a link between psychopathy and autonomic nervous system (ANS) dysfunction. The ANS mediates physiological activities associated with emotions and is manifested in such measurements as heart rate, blood pressure, respiration, muscle tension, capillary size, and electrical activity of the skin (called galvanic skin resistance). Psychopaths may be less capable of regulating their activities than other people. While some people may become anxious and afraid when facing the prospect of committing a criminal act, psychopaths in the same circumstances feel no such fear. Their reduced anxiety levels result in behaviors that are more impulsive and inappropriate and in deviant behavior, apprehension, and incarceration.

Another view is that psychopathy is related to abnormal brain structures. Consequently, psychopaths may need greater than average stimulation to bring them up to comfortable levels (similar to arousal theory, discussed earlier). This may be linked to an impairment of the amygdala, that part of the brain that plays a crucial role in processing emotions. As James Blair and his colleagues suggest, amygdala dysfunction gives rise to impairments in aversive conditioning, instrumental learning, and the processing of fearful and sad expressions.[274]

This condition is discussed in the Criminology in Action feature "The Iceman: A True Sociopath?"

Research on Personality Since maintaining a deviant personality has been related to crime and delinquency, numerous attempts have been made to devise accurate measures of personality and determine whether they can predict antisocial behavior. One of the most widely used psychological tests is the **Minnesota Multiphasic Personality Inventory**, commonly called the **MMPI**. This test has subscales designed to measure many different personality traits, including psychopathic deviation (Pd scale), schizophrenia (Sc), and hypomania (Ma).[275] Research studies have detected an association between scores on the Pd scale and criminal involvement.[276] Another frequently administered

The Iceman: A True Sociopath?

04

Richard Kuklinski, known as the Iceman, fit the description of sociopath better than almost anyone on record. Kuklinski's early life was punctuated by savage abuse from his father, who beat his wife and children so badly that one son, Florian, died at his hands. Fearing for their lives, the family covered up the crime. Richard, an eighth-grade dropout, worked out his hatred of his father by killing his neighbors' pets. He soon progressed to people. His first victim, whom he killed when he was just 14, was a young boy who had bullied him at school. Kuklinski dumped his victim's body off a bridge in South Jersey after removing his teeth and chopping off his fingertips in an effort to prevent identification of the body. Kuklinski routinely made trips to New York City looking for victims to beat and kill.

At 6-foot-5, 300 pounds, Kuklinski soon became known to organized crime families in New Jersey looking for a cold-blooded enforcer. His career took off when he became one of the top enforcers for the Gambino family. He killed his victims with guns, ice picks, crossbows, and chainsaws. One innovative method: he attached a bomb to a remote-control toy car. Richard's favorite weapon was cyanide solution administered from a nasal-spray bottle in the victim's face. He earned his nickname by his practice of freezing corpses to disguise the time of death and confound authorities.

During his career, he killed somewhere between 100 and 200 people, but through the efforts of undercover agents, the Iceman was convicted of five murders and given consecutive life sentences. While in prison, he confessed to killing Peter Calabro, a New York City police detective, and got another 30 years tacked on to his life sentence.

Never shy or remorseful, Kuklinski gave many interviews and appeared in two HBO documentaries before he died in prison in 2006 at age 70.

Kuklinski's home life was not what you would expect from a mass killer. He married his wife, Barbara, in 1961, lived a suburban, relatively affluent lifestyle, and had three kids. His wife called them "the all-American family." And while he occasionally struck his wife, the Iceman would never harm a child, including his own.

Was Kuklinski a true sociopath? The evidence is mixed. His murderous behavior seems to have been a product of his disturbed, violent childhood. He exhibited a great deal of superficial charm and had above-average intelligence, positive traits that often mask a disturbed personality that continually involves sociopaths in deviant behaviors such as violence, risk taking, substance abuse, and impulsivity.

Another indicator: Kuklinski was a chronic offender, beginning in childhood and continuing until he was caught and imprisoned as an adult. As many as 80 percent of high-end chronic offenders

exhibit sociopathic behavior patterns. Though comprising about 4 percent of the total male population and less than 1 percent of the total female population, they are responsible for half of all serious felony offenses committed annually. Not all high-rate chronic offenders are sociopaths, but enough are to support a strong link between personality dysfunction and long-term criminal careers.

Despite this evidence, one factor remains puzzling: Kuklinski had a long-term marriage and was a loving father; sociopaths are believed to be incapable of forming enduring relationships with others.

CRITICAL THINKING

1. Should people diagnosed as sociopaths be separated from society and treated even if they have not yet committed a crime?
2. Should sociopathic murderers such as Richard Kuklinski be spared the death penalty because they lack the capacity to control their behavior?

SOURCES: Douglas Martin, "Richard Kuklinski, 70, a Killer of Many People and Many Ways, Dies," *New York Times*, March 9, 2006, http://www.nytimes.com/2006/03/09/nyregion/09kuklinski.html (accessed May 2016); Philip Carlo, *The Ice Man: Confessions of a Mafia Contract Killer* (New York: Macmillan, 2009).

---

personality test, the **California Personality Inventory (CPI)**, has also been used to distinguish deviants from nondeviant groups.[277] The **Multidimensional Personality Questionnaire (MPQ)** allows researchers to assess such personality traits as control, aggression, alienation, and well-being.[278] Evaluations using this scale indicate that adolescent offenders who are crime prone maintain "negative emotionality," a tendency to experience aversive affective states, such as anger, anxiety, and irritability. They also are predisposed to weak personal constraints, and they have difficulty

California Personality Inventory (CPI) A frequently administered personality test used to distinguish deviant groups from nondeviant groups.

Multidimensional Personality Questionnaire (MPQ) A test that allows researchers to assess such personality traits as control, aggression, alienation, and well-being. Evaluations using this scale indicate that adolescent offenders who are crime prone maintain negative emotionality, a tendency to experience aversive affective states such as anger, anxiety, and irritability.

controlling impulsive behavior urges. Because they are both impulsive and aggressive, crime-prone people are quick to take action against perceived threats.

Evidence that personality traits predict crime and violence is important because it suggests that the root cause of crime can be found in the forces that influence human development at an early stage of life. If these results are valid, rather than focus on job creation and neighborhood improvement, crime control efforts might be better focused on helping families raise children who are reasoned and reflective and enjoy a safe environment.

INTELLIGENCE AND CRIME

 LO10 Comment upon the controversy over the association between intelligence and crime

Intelligence refers to a person's ability to reason, think abstractly, understand complex ideas, learn from experience, and discover solutions to complex problems. It was long believed that people who maintain a below-average intelligence quotient (IQ) were at risk to criminality. According to the **nature theory**, intelligence is largely determined genetically, ancestry determines IQ, and low intelligence, as demonstrated by low IQ, is linked to criminal behavior. When the newly developed IQ tests were administered to inmates of prisons and juvenile training schools in the first decades of the twentieth century, the nature position gained support because a very large proportion of the inmates scored low on the tests. During his studies in 1920, Henry Goddard found that many institutionalized persons were what he considered "feebleminded"; he concluded that at least half of all juvenile delinquents were mental defectives.[279] In 1926, William Healy and Augusta Bronner tested groups of delinquent boys in Chicago and Boston and found that 37 percent were subnormal in intelligence. They concluded that delinquents were five to ten times more likely to be mentally deficient than normal boys.[280] These and other early studies were embraced as proof that low IQ scores identified potentially delinquent children and that a correlation existed between innate low intelligence and deviant behavior. IQ tests were believed to measure the inborn genetic makeup of individuals, and many criminologists accepted the idea that individuals with substandard IQs were predisposed toward delinquency and adult criminality.

Nurture Theory The rise of culturally sensitive explanations of human behavior in the 1930s led to the nurture school of intelligence. **Nurture theory** states that intelligence must be viewed as partly biological but primarily sociological. Because intelligence is not inherited, low-IQ parents do not necessarily produce low-IQ children.[281] Nurture theorists discredited the notion that people commit crimes because they have low IQs. Instead, they postulated that environmental stimulation from parents, relatives, social contacts, schools, peer groups, and innumerable others create a child's IQ level and that low IQs result from an environment that also encourages delinquent and criminal behavior. Thus, if low IQ scores are recorded among criminals, these scores may reflect criminals' cultural background, not their mental ability.[282]

Debating Intelligence Affects In the 1970s, Travis Hirschi and Michael Hindelang resurrected the IQ–crime debate.[283] Their examination of then-existing research data led them to the conclusion that IQ is a more important factor than race and socioeconomic class for predicting criminal involvement.[284] They proposed that low IQ increases the likelihood of criminal behavior through its effect on school performance. Kids with low IQs do poorly in school; school failure and academic incompetence are highly related to delinquency and later to adult criminality. Because of their prominence in the field, Hirschi and Hindelang's inferences were taken quite seriously.[285] Richard Herrnstein and Charles Murray came down firmly for an IQ–crime link in their controversial book *The Bell Curve*.[286]

On an individual level, there is evidence linking low IQ scores with violent crimes, including murder.[287] There is also evidence of a macro-level association between IQ and crime.[288] Macro-level state and county data show that IQ and crime rates are associated: states and counties whose residents have higher IQs experience lower crime rates than those with less intelligent citizens.[289] On an international level, some research claims that nations whose population scores higher on IQ tests have lower crime rates than those with lower scoring populations.[290]

IQ Controversy While some studies cited previously found an IQ–crime association, others suggest that IQ level has negligible influence on criminal behavior.[291] An evaluation of existing knowledge on intelligence conducted by the American Psychological Association concluded that the strength of an IQ–crime link was "very low."[292] Those who question the IQ–crime link suggest that any association may be based on spurious data and inadequate research methodologies:

- IQ tests are biased and reflect middle-class values. As a result, socially disadvantaged people do poorly on IQ tests, and members of that group are also the ones most likely to commit crime. The low IQ–crime association is

intelligence A person's ability to reason, think abstractly, understand complex ideas, learn from experience, and discover solutions to complex problems.

nature theory The view that intelligence is largely determined genetically and that low intelligence is linked to criminal behavior.

nurture theory The view that intelligence is not inherited but is largely a product of environment. Low IQ scores do not cause crime but may result from the same environmental factors.

spurious: people who suffer disadvantages such as poverty and limited educational resources do poorly on IQ tests and also commit crime.

- The measurement of intelligence is often varied and haphazard, and results may depend on the particular method used. The correlation between intelligence and antisocial behavior using IQ tests as a measure of aptitude is slight; it is stronger if attendance in special programs or special schools is used as an indicator of intellectual ability.[293]
- People with low IQs are stigmatized and negatively labeled by middle-class decision makers such as police officers, teachers, and guidance counselors. It is not a low IQ that causes criminal behavior but the reaction to negative labels: alienation, stigma, and resentment.
- Research using official record data may be flawed. It's possible that criminals with high IQs are better able to avoid detection and punishment than low-IQ people. Research using data from arrestees may omit the more intelligent members of the criminal subclass. And even if they are caught, high-IQ offenders are less likely to be convicted and punished. Because their favorable treatment helps higher-IQ offenders avoid the pains of criminal punishment, it lessens their chances of recidivism.
- Maintaining a low IQ may influence some criminal patterns, such as arson and sex crimes, but not others, further clouding the waters.[294]
- The association between IQ and crime is curvilinear: people with very high or very low IQs commit less crime than those who fall in the middle.[295]
- It is difficult to explain many patterns in the crime rate if low IQ is a significant cause of crime. Why do crime rates vary by region, time of year, and even weather patterns? Why does aging out occur? IQs do not increase with age, so why should crime rates fall?

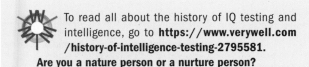

To read all about the history of IQ testing and intelligence, go to **https://www.verywell.com/history-of-intelligence-testing-2795581**. **Are you a nature person or a nurture person?**

Public Policy Implications of Trait Theory

For most of the twentieth century, biological and psychological views of criminality have influenced crime control and prevention policy. The result has been front-end or **primary prevention programs** that seek to treat personal problems before they manifest themselves as crime. To this end, thousands of family therapy organizations, substance abuse clinics, and mental health associations operate throughout the United States. Teachers, employers, relatives, welfare agencies, and others make referrals to these facilities. These services are based on the premise that if a person's problems can be treated before they become overwhelming, some future crimes will be prevented. **Secondary prevention programs** provide treatment such as psychological counseling to youths and adults who are at risk for law violation. **Tertiary prevention programs** may be a requirement of a probation order, part of a diversionary sentence, or aftercare at the end of a prison sentence.

Biologically oriented therapy is also being used in the criminal justice system. Programs have altered diets, changed lighting, compensated for learning disabilities, treated allergies, and so on.[296] More controversial has been the use of mood-altering chemicals, such as lithium, pemoline, imipramine, phenytoin, and benzodiazepines, to control behavior.

Numerous psychologically based treatment methods range from individual counseling to behavior modification. For example, treatment based on how people process information takes into account that people are more likely to respond aggressively to provocation if thoughts intensify the insult or otherwise stir feelings of anger. Cognitive therapists attempt to teach explosive people to control aggressive impulses by viewing social provocations as problems demanding a solution rather than retaliation. Therapeutic interventions designed to make people better problem solvers may involve measures that enhance:

- Coping and problem-solving skills
- Relationships with peers, parents, and other adults
- Conflict resolution and communication skills, and methods for resisting peer pressure related to drug use and violence
- Consequential thinking and decision-making abilities
- Prosocial behaviors, including cooperation with others, self-responsibility, respecting others, and public-speaking efficacy
- Empathy[297]

While it is often difficult to treat people with severe mental and personality disorders, there is evidence that positive outcomes can be achieved with the right combination of treatment modalities.[298] The findings of a recent study on biological and psychological–based crime prevention efforts is discussed in the Policy and Practice in Criminology feature.

primary prevention programs Treatment programs that seek to correct or remedy personal problems before they manifest themselves as crime.

secondary prevention programs Treatment programs aimed at helping offenders after they have been identified.

tertiary prevention programs Crime control and prevention programs that may be a requirement of a probation order, part of a diversionary sentence, or aftercare at the end of a prison sentence.

POLICY AND PRACTICE IN CRIMINOLOGY

Trait Theory and Crime Prevention

Recently, criminologists Michael Rocque, Brandon Welsh, and Adrian Raine reviewed treatment programs that consider biological and psychological traits and conditions in their approach. They believe that this approach might work because effective crime prevention strategies start from the premise that responding to crime after it happens is a missed opportunity; treatment and prevention must take place before a crime occurs. Crime prevention, according to their view, can be crafted in the same manner that doctors avert public health problems. Rather than identifying and treating a problem after it occurs, they use their knowledge of risk factors to provide guidance to those at risk in order to avoid illness before it occurs. Treatment based on psychological and biological traits identify at-risk people and then design plans to prevent future bouts of antisocial behaviors.

One approach has been parenting programs that are aimed at treating neuropsychological or cognitive deficits along with a host of other risk factors, such as impulsivity. One technique is to teach mothers to avoid the hazards of smoking or ingesting narcotics during pregnancy, in an attempt to help reduce neuropsychological impairment of the infant. Some programs take place in a school setting. Enriched preschool programs are designed to provide economically disadvantaged children with stimulus that helps them develop cognitively as well as provide them with enriching experiences that their

parents are unlikely to provide at home. The main goal here is to develop improved cognitive skills, enhance school readiness, and encourage social and emotional development.

Other programs are aimed at the prevention of serious mental illnesses or disorders. There is strong evidence that a variety of illnesses, ranging from psychosis to anxiety disorders, can be successfully treated before their effects have an overtly negative impact. This suggests that programs designed to reduce mental illness, such as a schizotypal personality, can work and help prevent crime. Rocque and his colleagues suggest that considering the demonstrated link among cognitive deficits, brain functioning, and crime, it is perhaps not surprising that nutrition can help prevent antisocial behavior. Family/parenting programs focus on nutrition and healthy development, relying on evidence that nutritional supplements may have a large impact on behavior through cognitive functioning. Finally, a very relevant crime prevention strategy is developmental. Recognizing the interaction between the person and the environment, this approach tends to focus on identifying risk factors for children or families and seeks to improve environmental conditions in order to facilitate healthy development of the child. Some programs focus on helping at-risk kids very early in life in order to foster healthy brain development. There is evidence that early prevention programs can improve cognitive functioning in a

cumulative fashion. In cases where risk factors are heritable or genetic, programs can prevent crime through identifying environmental triggers that may increase criminal behavior. In the future, it is reasonable to assume, more programs or strategies concentrating on biological risk factors will emerge.

Research suggests that the earlier the intervention, the better. It is possible that treatment will begin during pregnancy and continue through the first two years of life, as technology can now measure growth and maturation of cognitive functions during this period. Research has found that trauma during this period can be especially impactful, affecting brain development into adulthood. Thus, early intervention is of paramount importance in addressing the psychological and biological causes of crime.

 CRITICAL THINKING

Which approach to treatment do you believe could be most effective in curbing antisocial behaviors? Should the focus be on helping at the individual level or dealing with social problems such as unemployment and family functioning?

SOURCE: Michael Rocque, Brandon C. Welsh, and Adrian Raine, "Biosocial Criminology and Modern Crime Prevention," *Journal of Criminal Justice* 40 (2012): 306–312.

SUMMARY

 L01 **Trace the development of trait theory**

The view that criminals have physical or mental traits that make them different began with the Italian physician and criminologist Cesare Lombroso. Biological theory had many supporters in the early twentieth century who linked criminality to such traits as body build and the structure of the skull.

There were also early efforts to link criminality to mental illness, intelligence, and maladaptive personality. This work fell out of favor as social theories of crime were developed. In the early 1970s, spurred by the publication of *Sociobiology: The New Synthesis*, by Edmund O. Wilson, biological explanations of crime once again emerged. Trait theorists today recognize that crime-producing interactions involve both personal traits and environmental factors. If only a few offenders become persistent repeaters, what sets them apart from the rest of the criminal population may be some crime-producing trait.

L02 Differentiate between the biochemical conditions that produce crime

Biochemical conditions are believed to influence antisocial behavior. Biocriminologists maintain that an improper diet can cause chemical and mineral imbalance and lead to cognitive and learning deficits and problems, and these factors in turn are associated with antisocial behaviors. Abnormal levels of male sex hormones (androgens) can produce aggressive behavior. Excessive amounts of testosterone, the principal male hormone, has been linked to aggressive behaviors. Exposure to lead and other environmental contaminants has been linked to emotional and behavioral disorders.

L03 Clarify the neurophysiological conditions associated with crime

Inherited or acquired neurological abnormalities are believed to control behavior throughout the life span. Brain damage that is acquired prenatal, during birth, or soon after may lead to learning disabilities and other problems that are linked to antisocial behaviors.

L04 Cite examples of the different research techniques used to link genetics to crime

Another biosocial theme is that the human traits associated with criminality have a genetic basis. According to this view, (1) antisocial behavior is inherited, (2) the genetic makeup of parents is passed on to children, and (3) genetic abnormality is linked to a variety of antisocial behaviors. To test this view, criminologists have compared the behavior of siblings, adoptees, and identical twins.

L05 Explain the evolutionary view of crime

Human traits that produce violence and aggression have been advanced by the long process of human evolution. According to evolutionary theory, males who are aggressive and violent produce the most children, and these traits have dominated human society. Crime and violence are the products of millions of years of human breeding.

L06 Discuss the elements of the psychodynamic perspective

The id is the primitive part of people's mental makeup, the ego is shaped by learning and experience, and the superego reflects the morals and values of parents and significant others. Criminals are id-driven people who suffer from weak or damaged egos. Crime is a manifestation of feelings of oppression and the inability to develop the proper psychological defenses and rationales to keep these feelings under control.

L07 Link behavioral theory to crime

People are not born with the ability to act violently; rather, they learn to be aggressive through their life experiences. These experiences include personally observing others acting aggressively to achieve some goal or observing people being rewarded for violent acts. Kids who watch violent media may learn that violence is rewarded and that violence can be used as a solution to problems encountered in everyday life.

L08 Articulate the cognitive processes related to crime

Crime-prone people may have cognitive deficits and use information incorrectly when they make decisions. They view crime as an appropriate means to satisfy their immediate personal needs, which take precedence over more distant social needs such as obedience to the law. People with cognitive deficits may misread behavioral cues and misinterpret what others are doing. They see a harmless gesture as a provocation and react accordingly.

L09 Identify the elements of personality related to crime

Sociopathic, psychopathic, or antisocial people cannot empathize with others and are short-sighted and hedonistic. These traits make them prone to problems ranging from psychopathology to drug abuse, sexual promiscuity, and violence. Factors related to personality problems include improper socialization, having a psychopathic parent, experiencing parental rejection and lack of love during childhood, and receiving inconsistent discipline.

L010 Comment upon the controversy over the association between intelligence and crime

Proponents of nature theory argue that intelligence is largely determined genetically, that ancestry determines IQ, and that low intelligence is linked to criminal behavior. Proponents of nurture theory argue that intelligence is not inherited and that low-IQ parents do not necessarily produce low-IQ children. The IQ–criminality debate is unlikely to be settled soon. Measurement is beset by many methodological problems.

CRITICAL THINKING QUESTIONS

1. What should be done with the young children of violence-prone criminals if in fact research could show that the tendency to commit crime is inherited?

2. After considering the existing research on the subject, would you recommend that young children be forbidden from eating foods with a heavy sugar content?

3. Knowing what you do about trends and patterns in crime, how would you counteract the assertion that people who commit crime are physically or mentally abnormal? For example, how would you explain the fact that crime is more likely to occur in western and urban areas than in eastern or rural areas?

4. Aside from becoming a serial killer, what other career paths are open to psychopaths?

5. Research shows that kids who watch a lot of TV in adolescence are more likely to behave aggressively in adulthood. This has led some to conclude that TV watching is responsible for adult violence. Can this relationship be explained in another way?

KEY TERMS

positivism (140)
psychopathic personality (142)
atavistic anomalies (142)
biological determinism (142)
criminal anthropology (142)
inheritance school (142)
somatotype (142)
biosocial theory (143)
biophobia (143)
sociobiology (143)
reciprocal altruism (143)
trait theory (143)
individual vulnerability model (144)
differential susceptibility model (144)
hypoglycemia (145)
androgens (146)
neocortex (146)
testosterone (146)
premenstrual syndrome (PMS) (146)
cerebral allergies (147)
neuroallergies (147)

neurophysiology (148)
electroencephalograph (EEG) (149)
minimal brain dysfunction (MBD) (150)
learning disability (LD) (150)
attention deficit hyperactivity disorder (ADHD) (150)
chemical restraints or chemical straitjackets (152)
arousal theory (152)
contagion effect (154)
defective intelligence (157)
psychoanalytic or psychodynamic perspective (157)
behaviorism (157)
cognitive theory (157)
id (158)
pleasure principle (158)
ego (158)
reality principle (158)
superego (158)
conscience (158)

ego ideal (158)
eros (158)
thanatos (158)
oral stage (158)
anal stage (158)
phallic stage (158)
Oedipus complex (159)
Electra complex (159)
latency (159)
fixated (159)
inferiority complex (159)
identity crisis (159)
latent delinquency (159)
disorders (159)
conduct disorder (CD) (159)
bipolar disorder (159)
attachment theory (160)
alexithymia (161)
psychosis (161)
schizophrenia (161)
social learning (163)
behavior modeling (164)
moral development (166)
humanistic psychology (166)
information processing (166)

personality (169)
sadistic personality disorder (169)
psychopath (170)
sociopath (170)
Minnesota Multiphasic Personality Inventory (MMPI) (170)
California Personality Inventory (CPI) (171)
Multidimensional Personality Questionnaire (MPQ) (171)
intelligence (172)
nature theory (172)
nurture theory (172)
primary prevention programs (173)
secondary prevention programs (173)
tertiary prevention programs (173)

NOTES

All URLs accessed in 2016.

1. Jack Healy and Ian Lovett, "Oregon Killer Described as Man of Few Words, Except on Topic of Guns," *New York Times*, October 2, 2015, http://www.nytimes.com/2015/10/03/us/chris-harper-mercer-umpqua-community-college-shooting.html; CBS News, "What We Know About Oregon Shooter Chris Harper Mercer," http://www.cbsnews.com/news/umpqua-community-college-shooting-chris-harper-mercer/.

2. Scott Parrott and Caroline Parrott, "Law & Disorder: The Portrayal of Mental Illness in U.S. Crime Dramas," *Journal of Broadcasting and Electronic Media* (2015): 640–657.

3. Israel Nachshon, "Neurological Bases of Crime, Psychopathy, and Aggression," in *Crime in Biological, Social and Moral Contexts*, ed. Lee Ellis and Harry Hoffman (New York: Praeger, 1990), p. 199.

4. Nicole Rafter, "The Murderous Dutch Giddler: Criminology, History and the Problem of Phrenology," *Theoretical Criminology* 9 (2005): 65–97.

5. Nicole Rafter, "The Unrepentant Horse-Slasher: Moral Insanity and the Origins of Criminological Thought," *Criminology* 42 (2004): 979–1008.

6. Described in David Lykken, "Psychopathy, Sociopathy, and Crime," *Society* 34 (1996): 29–38.

7. See Peter Scott, "Henry Maudsley," in *Pioneers in Criminology*, ed. Hermann

Concern about the ecological distribution of crime, the effect of social change, and the interactive nature of crime itself has made sociology the foundation of modern criminology. This chapter reviews sociological theories that emphasize the relationship between social status and criminal behavior. In Chapter 7, the focus shifts to sociological social psychology theories that emphasize socialization and its influence on crime and deviance; Chapter 8 covers theories based on the concept of social conflict.

ASK YOURSELF . . .

Have you ever felt that your behavior was influenced by the environment in which you were raised? I grew up in the Bronx and it certainly had an effect on me!

Socioeconomic Structure and Crime

L02 Clarify the association between social structure and crime

People in the United States live in a **stratified society**. Social strata are created by the unequal distribution of wealth, power, and prestige. **Social classes** are segments of the population whose members have a relatively similar portion of desirable things and who share attitudes, values, norms, and an identifiable lifestyle.

In U.S. society, it is common to identify people as belonging to the upper, middle, or lower socioeconomic class, although a broad range of economic variations exist within each group. The upper-upper class is reserved for a small number of exceptionally well-to-do families who control enormous financial and social resources; income inequality has become a national social and political concern. The top 1 percent of households have an annual income of about $396,000 and/or about $1.5 million in liquid assets. The top 1/10th of the 1 percent have an income of almost $2 million a year; the top 1/100th of the top 1 percent have an annual income of at least $10 million.[17] The 16,000 wealthiest families in the United States have $6 trillion in total assets.[18] The 80 richest people on the planet have the same amount of wealth as the poorest 3.5 billion people combined.[19]

In contrast, there are now about 46 million Americans living in poverty, defined as a family of four earning about $24,000 per year, who have scant, if any, resources, and suffer socially and economically as a result; this number has been increasing during the past decade.[20] Those living below the poverty line are often forced to live in inadequate housing, have poor health care, and suffer from disrupted family lives, underemployment, and despair. They are more prone to depression, less likely to have achievement motivation, and are unable to put off immediate gratification for future gain; kids living in poverty areas may drop out before graduation because the rewards for educational achievement are in the distant future.

Clearly the wealth gap creates two Americas, one that can afford the finest luxuries the world can offer and the other just scraping by, often with government assistance to supplement meager earnings. The Criminology in Action feature "*Labor's Love Lost*" shows how social and income inequality impact human lives.

For an analysis of wealth and power in the United States, go to **http://www2.ucsc.edu /whorulesamerica/power/wealth.html.**
Do you believe that the unequal distribution of wealth is a growing social problem and the government should do something to redistribute wealth?

THE UNDERCLASS

Fifty years ago, sociologist Oscar Lewis coined the term the **underclass** to describe the crushing lifestyle experienced by those living in the American "**culture of poverty**," which is passed from one generation to the next.[21] Apathy, cynicism, helplessness, and mistrust of social institutions such as schools, government agencies, and the police mark the culture of poverty. Lewis's work was the first of a group that described the plight of **at-risk** children and adults. In 1970, Swedish economist Gunnar Myrdal described a worldwide underclass that was cut off from society, its members lacking the education and skills needed to be effectively in demand in modern society.[22]

stratified society A social structure that places people along a status-based hierarchy. In the United States, status is based primarily on wealth, power, and prestige.

social class Segment of the population whose members are at a relatively similar economic level and who share attitudes, values, norms, and an identifiable lifestyle.

underclass The lowest social stratum in any country, whose members lack the education and skills needed to function successfully in modern society.

culture of poverty The view that people in the lower class of society form a separate culture with its own values and norms that are in conflict with conventional society; the culture is self-maintaining and ongoing.

at-risk Children and adults who lack the education and skills needed to be effectively in demand in modern society.

04

Labor's Love Lost

In his recent book, *Labor's Love Lost*, Andrew Cherlin provides an explanation of the toll income and educational inequality takes on society. Cherlin points out that 50 years ago high-school graduates were able to enter the workforce and have plentiful opportunities in industrial occupations that at that time sustained the middle-class ideal of a male-breadwinner family. Such jobs have all but vanished due to automation and globalization, and in their place are low-paid jobs with few fringe benefits. Ever-growing numbers of young adults now face insecure economic prospects. Consequently, less-educated young adults, both men and women, are increasingly forgoing marriage and are having children within unstable cohabiting relationships. This has created a large marriage gap between the marginally educated and more affluent, college-educated peers, exacerbating the income gap in American society. These social and economic shifts have contributed to the collapse of this once stable lower-middle social class.

Cherlin points out that the marriage gap today seems similar to what occurred during the late-nineteenth century, when society was divided between families of great wealth and the working poor. Sadly, the prosperity of working-class families in the mid-twentieth century, when both income inequality and the marriage gap were low, was unique in the history of the American family. The changing economy, the end of high-paid factory jobs, and their replacement with low-paid service jobs have had such a significant impact that traditional working-class family patterns have largely disappeared.

The primary problem of the end of the working-class family is not that the traditional male-breadwinner family has declined, but that it has not been replaced with any other stable model. As a result of the breakdown, there are serious consequences for children of low-income families, many of whom underperform in school, thereby reducing their future employment prospects and perpetuating an intergenerational cycle of economic disadvantage. American children experience the highest rates of family turnover in the developed world. Large numbers live with single parents or with parents in cohabitating unions of short duration and high breakup rates. As a result, American children experience parents, parents' partners, and stepparents moving in and out of their households far more than in other developed countries. The percentage of children who aren't living with two biological parents has increased sharply among the moderately educated. It is now common for high-school-educated women to have at least one child outside of marriage. Cherlin finds that these problems are more pronounced in the African American community where men did not fully share in the wage gains of the post–World War II period. As a result, marriage rates among African Americans did not rise as high as whites during the 1950s and 1960s, and now they have fallen further.

Can This Cycle Be Broken?

Cherlin argues that rather than stress college as the answer for all, vocational opportunities for working-class children must be enhanced through programs stressing apprenticeships and internships as paths to steady employment for high school graduates. Wage subsidies and other income enhancements may also help break the cycle.

CRITICAL THINKING

Should the government create social programs to change the course of human lives? Is this the government's job? Do you think such social engineering can be successful?

SOURCE: Andrew Cherlin, *Labor's Love Lost* (New York: Russell Sage Foundation, 2014).

Economic disparity will continually haunt members of the underclass and their children over the course of their life span. Desperate life circumstances prevent them from developing the skills, habits, and lifestyles that lead first to educational success and later to success in the workplace.[23] Their ability to maintain social ties in the neighborhood become weak and attenuated, destabilizing community cohesiveness and interfering with mechanisms of informal social control such as the school, church, and family.[24] The poor are constantly bombarded by media advertisements linking material possessions (driving the right car, wearing the right clothes, taking the right vacations) to self-worth. Though they are members of a society that extols material success above any other, they are unable to satisfactorily compete for such success with members of the upper classes. As a result, they may turn to illegal solutions to their economic plight: they may deal drugs for profit, join gangs, boost cars and sell them to "chop shops," or commit armed robbery. They may become so depressed that they take alcohol and drugs as a form of self-tranquilization.

To read more about Oscar Lewis and the culture of poverty go to **http://www.encyclopedia.com/topic/Oscar_Lewis.aspx**.

Can people break out of poverty if they really try? Or are the odds against them too great?

CHILD POVERTY

About 15 million youths under 18 in the United States—nearly 22 percent of all youth—live in families with incomes below the poverty line. Another 22 percent escape poverty but live in families considered "poor."[25] Many kids living in poverty have working parents, but low wages and unstable employment leave their families struggling to make ends meet.[26] Being a child in a low-income or poor family does not happen by chance and is a function of parental education and employment, race/ethnicity, and other factors associated with economic insecurity.

Economic disadvantage and poverty can be especially devastating to younger children.[27] Children who grow up in low-income homes are less likely to achieve in school and less likely to complete their schooling than children with more affluent parents.[28] Poor kids are also more likely to suffer from health problems and to receive inadequate health care. Not only are they poor, but the number of homeless children in the United States has surged in recent years to an all-time high, amounting to one child in every 30. The National Center on Family Homelessness calculates that nearly 2.5 million American children were homeless at some point in the past year.[29]

A young girl walks by an abandoned building and lot in Camden, New Jersey. Crime rates are higher in deteriorated, disorganized neighborhoods, and minority group members are all too often forced to live in these high-risk communities.

Shannon Stapleton/Reuters

Kids Count, a project of the Annie E. Casey Foundation, is a national and state-by-state effort to track the relative status of children in the United States. Visit them at http://www.aecf.org/work/kids-count/.
What are some of the most significant social problems facing America's youth?

MINORITY GROUP POVERTY

The burdens of underclass life are often felt most acutely by minority group members. The median family income of Hispanics and African Americans is two-thirds that of whites, and the percentage of racial and ethnic minorities living in poverty is double that of European Americans.[30] As Figure 6.1 shows, the African American household median income is about $35,000 compared to $54,000 for non-Hispanic white households and almost $75,000 for Asian households. About 28 percent of African Americans are living at the poverty level, compared to 11 percent of non-Hispanic whites. The unemployment rate for blacks is twice that for non-Hispanic whites (about 10 percent versus about 5 percent), a finding consistent for both men and women.[31] There are also race-based differences in high school completion; white and Asian rates are higher than those of Hispanics and African Americans.[32]

These economic and social disparities haunt members of the minority underclass and their children despite efforts to erase race-based inequality.[33] Though most minority group members value education and other middle-class norms, their desperate life circumstances, such as high unemployment and nontraditional family structures, prevent them from developing the skills and habits that lead first to educational success and later to success in the workplace; these deficits have been linked to crime and drug abuse.[34]

Race-based social and economic disparity can take a terrific toll. Whereas many urban European Americans use their economic, social, and political advantages—that is, white privilege—to live in sheltered gated communities patrolled by security guards and police, most minorities do not have access to similar protections and opportunities (though the value of gating is still being debated: some research says yes for burglary, no for robbery).[35] In contrast, a significant proportion of minority group members are relegated to living in segregated inner-city areas, where they are hit hard by race-based disparity such as income inequality and institutional racism.[36] As Ruth Peterson and Lauren Krivo point out in

More than Just Race

William Julius Wilson, one of the nation's most prominent sociologists, has produced an impressive body of work that details racial problems and racial politics in American society. He has described the plight of the lowest levels of the underclass, which he labels the truly disadvantaged. These socially isolated people live in areas in which the basic institutions of society—family, school, housing—have long since declined. Their weakening triggers similar breakdowns in the strengths of inner-city areas, including the loss of community cohesion and the ability of people living in the area to control the flow of drugs and criminal activity. In more affluent areas, neighbors might complain to parents that their children are acting out. In distressed areas, this element of informal social control may be absent because parents are under stress or all too often

absent. These effects magnify the isolation of the underclass from mainstream society and promote a ghetto culture and behavior.

Because the truly disadvantaged rarely come into contact with the actual source of their oppression, they direct their anger and aggression at those with whom they are in close and intimate contact, such as neighbors, businesspeople, and landlords. Members of this group, plagued by under- or unemployment, begin to lose self-confidence, a feeling supported by the plight of kin and friendship groups who also experience extreme economic marginality. Self-doubt is a neighborhood norm, overwhelming those forced to live in areas of concentrated poverty.

In an important book, *When Work Disappears*, Wilson assesses the effect of joblessness and underemployment on residents in poor neighborhoods on Chicago's

south side. He argues that for the first time since the nineteenth century, most adults in inner-city ghetto neighborhoods are not working during a typical week. He finds that inner-city life is only marginally affected by changes in the nation's economy and unaffected by technological development. Poverty in these inner-city areas is eternal and unchanging and, if anything, worsening as residents are further shut out of the economic mainstream. Growth in the manufacturing sector fueled upward mobility and provided the foundation of today's African American middle class. Those opportunities no longer exist as manufacturing plants have moved to inaccessible rural and overseas locations where the cost of doing business is lower. With manufacturing opportunities all but obsolete in the United States, service and retail establishments, which depended on blue-collar spending, have similarly disappeared,

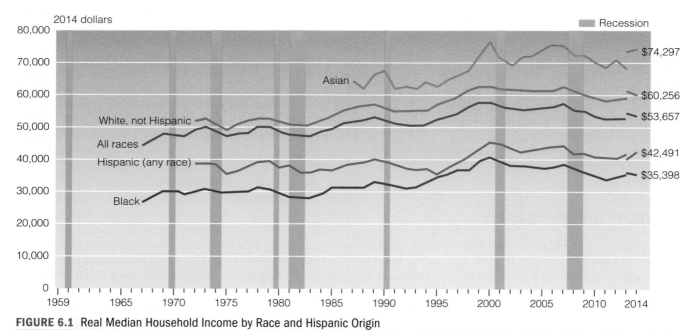

FIGURE 6.1 Real Median Household Income by Race and Hispanic Origin

SOURCE: Carmen DeNavas-Walt and Bernadette Proctor, *Income and Poverty in the United States: 2014, Current Population Reports,* U.S. Department of Commerce, September 2015, https://www.census.gov/content/dam/Census/library/publications/2015/demo/p60-252.pdf (accessed May 2016).

leaving behind an economy based on welfare and government supports. In less than 20 years, formerly active African American communities have become crime-infested inner-city neighborhoods.

Beyond sustaining inner-city poverty, the absence of employment opportunities has torn at the social fabric of the nation's inner-city neighborhoods. Work helps socialize young people into the wider society, instilling in them such desirable values as hard work, caring, and respect for others. When work becomes scarce, the discipline and structure it provides are absent. Community-wide underemployment destroys social cohesion, increasing the presence of neighborhood social problems ranging from drug use to educational failure. Schools in these areas are unable to teach basic skills and because desirable employment is lacking, there are few adults to serve as role models. In contrast to more affluent suburban households where daily life is organized around job and career demands, children in inner-city areas are not socialized in the workings of the mainstream economy.

Wilson finds that racism is becoming more subtle and harder to detect. Whites believe that blacks are responsible for their inferior economic status because of their cultural traits. Because even affluent whites fear corporate downsizing, they are unwilling to vote for governmental assistance to the poor because it means more taxes and lower corporate profits, a condition that threatens their jobs. Whites are continuing to be suburban dwellers, further isolating poor minorities in central cities and making their problems distant and unimportant. Wilson continues to believe that the changing marketplace, with its reliance on sophisticated computer technologies, is continually decreasing demand for low-skilled workers, which impacts African Americans more negatively than other better educated and affluent groups.

In his most recent work, *More than Just Race: Being Black and Poor in the Inner City*, Wilson shows that a law-and-order political philosophy and fear of racial conflict have led to high incarceration rates among African American males. While black women can get jobs in service industries, employers are less likely to hire black men, especially those with a criminal record. As a result, there has been a decline in the ability of black men to be providers and further stress on the stability of the African American family. Here we can see how structure and culture intertwine to produce stress in the African American community. In an era of high unemployment, the picture Wilson paints is not encouraging.

 CRITICAL THINKING

1. Is it unrealistic to assume that a government-sponsored public works program can provide needed jobs in this era of budget cutbacks?
2. What are some of the hidden costs of unemployment in a community setting?
3. How would a biocriminologist explain Wilson's findings?

SOURCES: William Julius Wilson, *More than Just Race: Being Black and Poor in the Inner City* (New York: Norton, 2009); William Julius Wilson and Richard Taub, *There Goes the Neighborhood: Racial, Ethnic, and Class Tensions in Four Chicago Neighborhoods and Their Meaning for America* (New York: Knopf, 2006); William Julius Wilson, *The Truly Disadvantaged* (Chicago: University of Chicago Press, 1987); *When Work Disappears: The World of the Urban Poor* (New York: Alfred Knopf, 1996); *The Bridge over the Racial Divide: Rising Inequality and Coalition Politics* (Wildavsky Forum Series, 2) (Berkeley: University of California Press, 1999).

their groundbreaking book *Divergent Social Worlds*, among urban dwellers more than two-thirds of all whites, half of all African Americans, and one-third of Hispanics live in segregated local neighborhoods. While fewer than 10 percent of white neighborhoods can be considered poverty stricken, 75 percent of black, Latino, and other minority communities can be considered poverty areas.[37]

There is also the perception in the minority community that the justice system is biased and racist. Minority citizens often believe that the police are overzealous in their duties when dealing with minorities, stopping them for no reason, searching them, and arresting them when they would treat whites informally, a practice that has spurred the creation of the Black Lives Matter movement. And if they do commit crime, minority youth are more likely to be officially processed to the juvenile court than white youths, helping them develop an official record at an early age, an outcome that may increase their chances of incarceration as adults.[38] In the United States today, about 1 in 30 men between the ages of 20 and 34 is behind bars, for black males in that age group the figure is 1 in 9. One in 100 African American women in their mid- to late-30s are incarcerated compared to 1 in 355 European American women.[39] In some neighborhoods a significant portion—up to half—of all minority males are under criminal justice system control.[40]

Interracial differences in the crime rate could be significantly reduced by improving levels of education, lowering levels of poverty, ending racial segregation in housing and neighborhood makeup, and reducing the extent of male unemployment among minority populations.[41] The issue of minority poverty is explored further in the Race, Culture, Gender, and Criminology feature "More than Just Race," which discusses the works of William Julius Wilson, one of the nation's leading experts on race and culture.

 The World Wealth Report provides information on global income trends. See more at **https://www.capgemini.com/resources/video/world-wealth-report-2015**.

The number of wealthy, high net worth individuals is growing around the world. Is that a good sign or troubling trend?

Social Structure Theories

 L03 Give examples of the elements of social disorganization theory

The problems caused by poverty and income inequality are not lost on criminologists. They recognize that the various sources of crime data show that crime rates are highest in neighborhoods characterized by poverty and social disorder. Although members of the middle and upper classes sometimes engage in crime, these are generally nonviolent acts, such as embezzlement and fraud, which present little danger to the general public. In contrast, lower-class crime is often the violent, destructive product of youth gangs and marginally and underemployed young adults. The real crime problem is essentially a lower-class phenomenon. Recognizing this phenomenon, criminologists have formulated **social structure theories**, which as a group suggest that social and economic forces operating in disorganized lower-class areas are the key determinant of criminal behavior patterns. Social forces begin to affect people while they are relatively young and continue to influence them throughout the life course.

> **social structure theory** The view that disadvantaged economic class position is a primary cause of crime.
>
> **social disorganization theory** Branch of social structure theory that focuses on the breakdown of institutions such as the family, school, and employment in inner-city neighborhoods.

Though not all youthful offenders become adult criminals, those who are exposed to the incivility present in deteriorated inner-city neighborhoods are the ones most likely to persist in their criminal careers.[42]

Social structure theorists challenge those who suggest that crime is an expression of some personal trait or individual choice. They argue that people living in equivalent social environments tend to behave in a similar, predictable fashion. If the environment did not influence human behavior, then crime rates would be distributed equally across the social structure, which they are not.[43] Because crime rates are higher in poor urban centers than in middle-class suburbs, social forces must be operating in these blighted inner-city areas that influence or control behavior.[44]

There are three independent yet overlapping branches within the social structure perspective—social disorganization, strain theory, and cultural deviance theory (outlined in Figure 6.2):

- **Social disorganization theory** focuses on the conditions within the urban environment that affect crime rates. A disorganized area is one in which institutions of social control—such as the family, commercial establishments, and schools—have broken down and can no longer carry out their expected or stated functions. Indicators of social disorganization include high unemployment, school dropout rates, deteriorated housing, low-income levels, and large numbers of single-parent households. Residents in these areas experience conflict and despair, and, as a result, antisocial behavior flourishes.

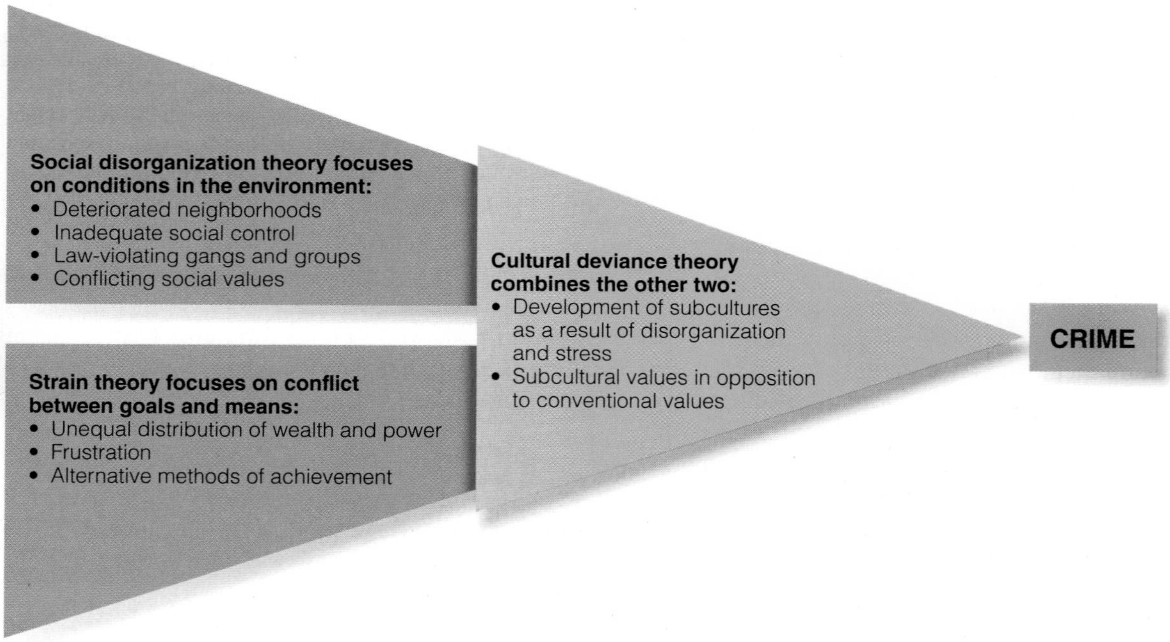

Social disorganization theory focuses on conditions in the environment:
- Deteriorated neighborhoods
- Inadequate social control
- Law-violating gangs and groups
- Conflicting social values

Strain theory focuses on conflict between goals and means:
- Unequal distribution of wealth and power
- Frustration
- Alternative methods of achievement

Cultural deviance theory combines the other two:
- Development of subcultures as a result of disorganization and stress
- Subcultural values in opposition to conventional values

CRIME

FIGURE 6.2 The Three Branches of Social Structure Theory

SOURCE: © Cengage Learning

- **Strain theory** holds that crime is a function of the conflict between the goals people have and the means they can use to obtain them legally. Because members of the lower class are unable to achieve success through conventional means, they feel anger, frustration, and resentment, referred to as **strain**. They can either live out their days as socially responsible, if unrewarded, citizens, or they can choose an alternative means of achieving success, that includes criminal acts such as theft, violence, or drug trafficking.
- **Cultural deviance theory**, the third variation of structural theory, combines elements of both strain and social disorganization: In lower-class neighborhoods a unique subculture develops that maintains a unique set of values and beliefs that are in conflict with conventional social norms. Rather than being deviant or unusual, criminal behavior is a natural expression of conformity to lower-class subcultural values that are handed down from one generation to the next.

In Baltimore, Angelo, a homeless man, displays a pin that holds his jaw together, which he said he received after being beaten and robbed while sleeping in a vacant row house, seen behind him. A census of Baltimore's homeless population counted more than 4,000 homeless people. Some choose to find shelter in the city's estimated 16,000 vacant or abandoned buildings. According to social structure theory, crime rates are highest in these disorganized neighborhoods, where social control is weak and attenuated.

AP Images/Patrick Semansky, Semansky

Although each of these views is distinct and independent, at its core each holds the view that socially isolated people, living in disorganized neighborhoods, are the ones most likely to experience crime-producing social forces: a person's place in the social structure controls their behavior. Each branch of social structure theory will now be discussed in some detail.

SOCIAL DISORGANIZATION THEORY

Social disorganization theory links crime rates to neighborhood ecological characteristics. Communities where the fabric of social life has become frayed and torn are unable to provide essential services to their residents, such as education, health care, and proper housing. Residents in these crime-ridden neighborhoods want to flee the area at the earliest opportunity. Because they want out, they become uninterested in community matters. As a result, these neighborhoods are destabilized. There is constant population turnover; people are not interested in investing in these communities. Soon streets are littered and untidy, housing becomes deteriorated, and the neighborhood is rezoned for mixed use (i.e., residential and commercial property exist side by side).

Because the area is undergoing stress, the normal sources of *social control* common to most neighborhoods—the family, school, neighbors, business owners, church, law enforcement, and social service agencies—become ineffective, weak, and disorganized. Personal relationships are strained because neighbors are constantly relocating to better areas. Resident turnover further weakens communication and blocks the establishment of common goals. The result: any attempt at community-level problem solving ends in frustration.[45] As social institutions become frayed

strain theory Branch of social structure theory that sees crime as a function of the conflict between people's goals and the means available to obtain them.

strain The emotional turmoil and conflict caused when people believe they cannot achieve their desires and goals through legitimate means. Members of the lower class might feel strain because they are denied access to adequate educational opportunities and social support.

cultural deviance theory Branch of social structure theory that sees strain and social disorganization together resulting in a unique lower-class culture that conflicts with conventional social norms.

or absent, law-violating youth groups and gangs form and are free to recruit neighborhood youth. Both boys and girls who feel detached and alienated from their social world are at risk to become gang members.[46] Gangs form their own subculture with unique names, slang, signs, and graffiti.

The problems encountered in this type of disorganized area take the form of a contagious disease, destroying the inner workings that enable neighborhoods to survive; the community becomes "hollowed out."[47] Crime and violence are like a "slow epidemic," spreading to surrounding areas and infecting them with inner-city problems.[48]

The elements of social disorganization theory are shown in Figure 6.3.

Poverty
• Development of isolated lower-class areas
• Lack of conventional social opportunities
• Racial and ethnic discrimination

Social disorganization
• Breakdown of social institutions and organizations such as school and family
• Lack of informal and formal social control

Breakdown of traditional values
• Development of law-violating gangs and groups
• Deviant values replace conventional values and norms

Criminal areas
• Neighborhood becomes crime prone
• Stable pockets of crime develop
• Lack of external support and investment

Cultural transmission
Adults pass norms (focal concerns) to younger generation, creating stable lower-class culture

Criminal careers
Most youths age out of delinquency, marry, and raise families, but some remain in life of crime

FIGURE 6.3 Social Disorganization Theory

SOURCE: © Cengage Learning

transitional neighborhoods Areas undergoing a shift in population and structure, usually from middle-class residential to lower-class mixed use.

 LO4 Explain the views of Shaw and McKay

Foundations of Social Disorganization Theory Social disorganization theory was first popularized by the work of two Chicago sociologists, Clifford R. Shaw and Henry D. McKay, who linked life in disorganized, transitional urban areas to neighborhood crime rates. Shaw and McKay began their pioneering work on crime in Chicago during the early 1920s while working as researchers for a state-supported social service agency.[49] They were heavily influenced by Chicago School sociologists Ernest Burgess and Robert Park, who had pioneered the ecological analysis of urban life.

Shaw and McKay began their analysis during a period when Chicago was experiencing a rapid population expansion, fueled by a dramatic influx of foreign-born immigrants and, later, migrating southern families. Congregating in the central city, the newcomers occupied the oldest housing areas and therefore faced numerous health and environmental hazards.

Sections of the city started to physically deteriorate, prompting the city's wealthy, established citizens to become concerned about the moral fabric of Chicago society. There was concern among the moneyed classes that immigrants from Europe and the rural South were crime prone and morally dissolute. Local citizens groups called "child savers" were formed, whose stated purpose was protecting the children of poor families from succumbing to the moral decadence of their parents.[50]

Transitional Neighborhoods While it was then popular to view crime as the property of inferior racial and ethnic groups, Shaw and McKay instead focused on the context of the changing urban environment and ecological development of the city. They saw that Chicago had developed into distinct neighborhoods (natural areas), some affluent and others wracked by extreme poverty. These poverty-ridden, **transitional neighborhoods** suffered high rates of population turnover; those who remained were incapable of defending the neighborhood against criminal groups.

The relatively low rents attracted newly arrived immigrants from Europe and the South. Children were torn between assimilating into a new culture and/or abiding by the traditional values of their parents. Informal social control mechanisms that had restrained behavior in the "old country" or rural areas were disrupted, exposing neighborhood youth to the lure of criminal gangs and groups.

In transitional areas, successive changes in the population composition, disintegration of traditional cultures, diffusion of divergent cultural standards, and gradual industrialization of the area resulted in dissolution of neighborhood culture and organization. The continuity of conventional neighborhood traditions and institutions was broken, leaving children feeling displaced and without a strong or definitive set of values. The culture of urban areas was the spawning grounds of young criminals.

Concentric Zones   Shaw and McKay identified the areas in Chicago that had excessive crime rates. Using a model of analysis pioneered by Ernest Burgess, they noted that distinct ecological areas had developed in the city, comprising a series of five concentric circles, or zones, and that there were stable and significant differences in interzone crime rates (Figure 6.4). The areas of heaviest concentration of crime appeared to be the transitional inner-city zones, where large numbers of foreign-born citizens had recently settled.[51] The zones farthest from the city's center had correspondingly lower crime rates.

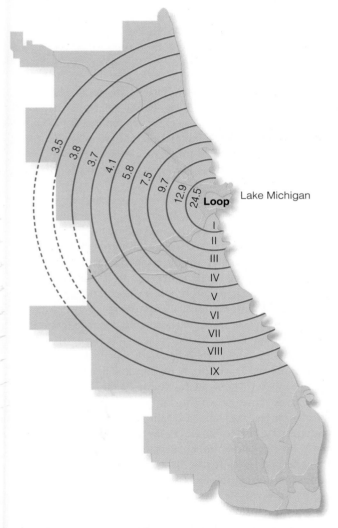

FIGURE 6.4 Shaw and McKay's Concentric Zones Map of Chicago

NOTE: Arabic numerals represent the rate of male delinquency.
SOURCE: Clifford R. Shaw et al., *Delinquency Areas* (Chicago: University of Chicago Press, 1929), p. 99.

Analysis of these data indicated a surprisingly stable pattern of criminal activity in the various ecological zones over a 65-year period. Shaw and McKay concluded that, in the transitional neighborhoods, multiple cultures and diverse values, both conventional and deviant, coexist. Children growing up in the street culture often find that adults who have adopted a deviant lifestyle are the most financially successful people in the neighborhood: the gambler, the pimp, or the drug dealer. Required to choose between conventional and deviant lifestyles, many inner-city kids see the value in opting for the latter. They join with other like-minded youths and form law-violating gangs and cliques. The development of teenage law-violating groups is an essential element of youthful misbehavior in lower-class areas. The values that inner-city youths adopt are often in conflict with existing middle-class norms, which demand strict obedience to the legal code. Consequently, a value conflict occurs that sets the delinquent youth and his peer group even further apart from conventional society. The result is a more solid embrace of deviant goals and behavior. To justify their choice of goals, these youths seek support by recruiting new members and passing on the delinquent tradition.

Shaw and McKay's statistical analysis confirmed their theoretical suspicions. Even though crime rates changed, they found that the highest rates were always in Zones I and II (central city and a transitional area). The areas with the highest crime rates retained high rates even when their ethnic composition changed (in the areas Shaw and McKay examined, from German and Irish to Italian and Polish).[52]

The Legacy of Shaw and McKay   Social disorganization concepts articulated by Shaw and McKay have remained a prominent fixture of criminological scholarship and thinking for more than 75 years. While cultural and social conditions have changed and American society today is much more heterogeneous and mobile than during Shaw and McKay's time, the most important elements of their findings still hold up:[53]

- Crime rates are sensitive to the destructive social forces operating in lower-class urban neighborhoods.
- Environmental factors, rather than individual differences, are the root cause of crime.
- Crime is a constant fixture in distressed areas regardless of racial or ethnic makeup.
- Neighborhood disorganization weakens formal and informal social control, the primary cause of criminal behavior.
- Community values, norms, and cohesiveness affect individual behavior choices.

Shaw and McKay's formulation of social disorganization provides a valuable contribution to our understanding of the causes of criminal behavior. By introducing a new variable—the ecology of the city—to the study of crime, these pioneering criminologists paved the way for a focus on the social influences of criminal and delinquent behavior.

THE SOCIAL ECOLOGY SCHOOL

 L05 Differentiate between the various elements of ecological theory

More than 30 years ago, a group of criminologists began to reexamine ecological conditions that support criminality.[54] Contemporary social ecologists developed a "purer" form of structural theory that emphasizes the association of community deterioration and economic decline to criminality, but places less emphasis on the value and norm conflict that lay at the core of Shaw and McKay's vision.

Social ecologists have focused their attention on the association between crime rates and community deterioration: disorder, poverty, alienation, disassociation, and fear of crime.[55] They find that neighborhoods with a high percentage of deserted houses and apartments experience high crime rates; abandoned buildings serve as a "magnet for crime."[56] Areas in which houses are in poor repair, boarded up, and burned out, and whose owners are best described as "slumlords," are also the location of the highest violence rates and gun crime.[57] These are neighborhoods in which retail establishments often go bankrupt, are abandoned, and deteriorate physically.[58]

According to this more contemporary view, living in these deteriorated, crime-ridden neighborhoods exerts a powerful influence over behavior that is strong enough to neutralize the positive effects of a supportive family and close social ties. If individual or family status influences criminality and violence, it is because of the nature of the communities in which disadvantaged persons and families reside and not the strength of family relationships themselves.[59]

Broken Windows One of the sparks that renewed interest in a structural view of crime was the publication of a highly regarded and widely read article written by James Q. Wilson and George Kelling, "Broken Windows."[60] These prominent scholars argued that serious crime is the result of neighborhood disorder that creates fear in the minds of residents and reduces the community's ability to exert social control. Once good citizens become convinced that the area in which they reside is unsafe, they withdraw physically and/or emotionally from the neighborhood, weakening the social controls that previously kept criminals in check. Once this process begins, it creates a feedback loop: disorder causes crime; crime causes further disorder.

As neighborhood disorder takes hold, the physical structure of the neighborhood begins a slow decline. Vacant buildings abound, vehicles are abandoned on the street, and garbage is not collected. When someone breaks a window or litters in a yard, there is no attempt to repair the damage.

There is also incivility and social disorder, which is typified by aggressive youths congregating on street corners and/or homeless people aggressively panhandling for money. Community deterioration, exhibited by unrepaired broken windows, serves as a magnet for crime because it sends a message: deviant and disorderly behavior will be tolerated. People interested in engaging in larceny, prostitution, and drug dealing know this is a safe place to ply their trade; those wishing to procure illicit and illegal substances and guns know where to purchase them safely. While different, these two types of disorder are both thought to increase fear among citizens with an resulting escalation in the neighborhood crime rate.

The popularity of the broken windows model helped focus attention on the association between neighborhood conditions and crime and also provided a game plan for reducing crime at the neighborhood level: if broken windows could somehow be fixed, then community crime rates would decline.[61]

Poverty Concentration William Julius Wilson describes how working- and middle-class families flee inner-city poverty areas, resulting in a poverty **concentration effect** in which the most disadvantaged population is consolidated in the most disorganized urban neighborhoods; population density interacts with lack of opportunity to produce high crime rates.

Poverty concentration has been associated with income and wealth disparities, nonexistent employment opportunities, inferior housing patterns, and unequal access to health care.[62] Urban areas marked by concentrated poverty become isolated and insulated from the social mainstream and more prone to criminal activity, violence, and homicide.[63] Young men growing up in neighborhoods characterized by poverty concentration are the most likely to engage in risk taking and delinquency, especially those who perceive few opportunities for legitimate success.[64]

How does neighborhood poverty concentration produce high crime rates? Middle-class families flee an area when they perceive that it is in economic decline.[65] As the middle classes move out to the suburbs, they take with them their financial and institutional resources and support, undermining the community's level of informal social control.[66] People left behind are socially isolated and have even a tougher time managing urban decay and conflict and/or controlling youth gangs and groups; after all, the most successful people in the community have left for "greener pastures."[67] Businesses are disinclined to locate in poverty areas; banks become reluctant to lend money for new housing or businesses.[68] The resulting deterioration in social capital in high-poverty areas reduces community social control, opening the door forever to expanding community crime rates.[69]

concentration effect Working- and middle-class families flee inner-city poverty areas, resulting in the most disadvantaged population being consolidated in the most disorganized urban neighborhoods.

Chronic Unemployment The association between unemployment and crime is still unsettled. Aggregate crime rates and aggregate unemployment rates seem weakly related: crime rates sometimes rise during periods of economic prosperity and fall during periods of economic decline.[70] Yet, as Shaw and McKay claimed, neighborhoods that experience chronic unemployment also encounter social disorganization and crime.[71] How can these divergent trends be explained?

One possibility is that even though short-term national economic trends may have little effect on crime, chronic unemployment and resulting poverty may have a more significant impact on conditions at the community or neighborhood level. Even in times of economic prosperity, some neighborhoods maintain stubbornly high unemployment rates.[72]

How does job loss lead to crime? Unemployment destabilizes households, and unstable families are the ones most likely to produce children who put a premium on violence and aggression as a means of dealing with limited opportunity. Conflict may also occur when people of the same age cohort compete for relatively scant resources.[73]

Limited employment opportunities also reduce the stabilizing influence of parents and other adults, who may have once been able to counteract the allure of youth gangs. Sociologist Elijah Anderson's analysis of Philadelphia neighborhood life found that "old heads" (i.e., respected neighborhood residents) who at one time played an important role in socializing youth have been displaced by younger street hustlers and drug dealers. While the old heads complain that these newcomers may not have earned or worked for their fortune in the "old-fashioned way," the old heads also admire and envy these kids whose gold chains and luxury cars advertise their wealth amid poverty.[74] The old heads may admire the fruits of crime, but they disdain the violent manner in which they were acquired.

Community Fear People feel safe in neighborhoods that are orderly and in repair.[75] In contrast, those living in neighborhoods that suffer social and physical **incivilities**—rowdy youth, trash and litter, graffiti, abandoned storefronts, burned-out buildings, littered lots, strangers, drunks, vagabonds, loiterers, prostitutes, noise, congestion, angry words, dirt, and stench—are much more likely to be fearful. Put another way, disorder breeds fear.[76]

In neighborhoods where people help one another, residents are less likely to fear crime and be afraid of becoming a crime victim.[77] When people feel distant from one another, disconnected from others in the community, they are more likely to view their environment as a dangerous place.[78] Not surprisingly, people living in areas with especially high crime rates are the ones most likely to experience fear.[79]

People who live in public housing projects, who may be approached by someone selling drugs, who come into daily contact with civil disorder, are not surprisingly the ones most likely to experience fear.[80] They may fear that their

children will also be approached and will be seduced into the drug life.[81] Residents who have already been victimized, or know someone else who has, are more fearful of the future than those who have escaped crime.

The presence of such incivilities, especially when accompanied by relatively high crime rates, helps convince residents that their neighborhood is dangerous; becoming a crime victim seems inevitable.[82] Eventually, they become emotionally numb, and as their exposure to crime increases, they experience indifference to the suffering of others.[83]

Fear can become contagious. People tell others when they have been victimized, spreading the word that the neighborhood is getting dangerous and that the chances of future victimization are high.[84] They dread leaving their homes at night and withdraw from community life.

When people live in areas where the death rates are high and life expectancies are short, they may alter their behavior out of fear. They may feel, "Why plan for the future when there is a significant likelihood that I may never see it?" In such areas, young boys and girls may psychologically assimilate by taking risks and discounting the future. Teenage birthrates soar and so do violence rates.[85] For these children, the inevitability of death skews their perspective of how they live their lives.

When fear grips a neighborhood, business conditions begin to deteriorate, population mobility increases, and a "criminal element" begins to drift into the area.[86] In essence, the existence of fear incites more crime, increasing the chances of victimization, producing even more fear, in a never-ending loop.[87] Fear is often associated with other community-level factors:

- *Race and fear.* Fear of crime is also bound up in anxiety over racial and ethnic conflicts. Residents experience the most fear in areas undergoing rapid and unexpected

Incivilities Rude and uncivil behavior; behavior that indicates little caring for the feelings of others.

racial and age-composition changes, especially when they are out of proportion to the rest of the city.[88] Minority group members often experience greater levels of fear than European Americans, especially when they believe they have fewer resources to address ongoing social problems.[89]

- *Gangs and fear.* Gangs flourish in deteriorated neighborhoods with high levels of poverty, lack of investment, high unemployment rates, and population turnover.[90] Unlike any other crime, however, gang activity is frequently undertaken out in the open, on the public ways, and in full view of the rest of the community.[91] Brazen criminal activity undermines community solidarity because it signals that the police can't do anything to curb gang activity. The fact that gangs are willing to openly engage in drug sales and other types of criminal activity shows their confidence to control or intimidate. The police and the community alike become hopeless about their ability to restore community stability, producing greater levels of community fear.

- *Mistrust and fear.* People who report living in neighborhoods with high levels of crime and civil disorder become suspicious and mistrusting.[92] They develop a sense of powerlessness, which amplifies the effect of neighborhood disorder and increases levels of mistrust. Some residents become so suspicious of authority that they develop a **siege mentality**: they believe there are forces in the outside world that set out to destroy the neighborhood. Elijah Anderson found that residents in the African American neighborhoods he studied believed in the existence of a secret plan to eradicate the population by such strategies as permanent unemployment, police brutality, imprisonment, drug distribution, and AIDS.[93] White officials and political leaders were believed to have hatched this conspiracy, and it was demonstrated by the lax law enforcement efforts in poor areas. Residents felt that police cared little about black-on-black crime because it helped reduce the population. Rumors abounded that federal government agencies, such as the CIA, controlled the drug trade and used profits to fund illegal overseas operations. This siege mentality results in mistrust of critical social institutions, including business, government, and schools. Government officials seem arrogant and haughty. Residents become self-conscious, worried about garnering any respect, and are particularly attuned to anyone who disrespects them. Considering this feeling of mistrust, when police ignore crime in poor areas or, conversely, when they are violent and corrupt, anger flares, and people take to the streets and react in violent ways.[94]

siege mentality Residents who become so suspicious of authority that they consider the outside world to be the enemy out to destroy the neighborhood.

Community Change In our postmodern society, the urban areas undergoing rapid structural changes in racial and economic composition also seem to experience the greatest change in crime rates. In contrast, stable neighborhoods, even those with a high rate of poverty, experience relatively low crime rates and have the strength to restrict substance abuse and criminal activity.[95]

Recent studies recognize that change, not stability, is the hallmark of inner-city areas. A neighborhood's residents, wealth, density, and purpose are constantly evolving. Even disorganized neighborhoods acquire new identifying features. Some may become multiracial, while others become racially homogeneous. Some areas become stable and family oriented, while in others, mobile, never-married people predominate.[96]

As areas decline, some residents flee to safer, more stable localities. Those who cannot leave because they cannot afford to live in more affluent communities face an increased risk of victimization. Some of course adapt and create new friendship networks which may cross ethnic and racial lines. While multicultural networks should be a good thing, they often exist in neighborhoods that have limited forces of social control.[97]

Those who can move to more affluent neighborhoods find that their lifestyles and life chances improve immediately and continue to do so over their life span.[98] Take for instance the Gautreaux Assisted Housing Program, a major initiative ordered by the courts in 1976 to provide a metropolitan-wide remedy for racial discrimination in Chicago's public housing program. The program helped inner-city families relocate to more affluent white suburbs. Research on the effects of the Gautreaux program shows that most families who moved to Chicago's suburbs were still living in those suburbs 10 and even 20 years later. Despite some race-based problems, children's attitudes toward school improved and their grades did not drop. Moreover, as children in these Gautreaux families grew up and left home, they moved to neighborhoods that were far safer and more affluent than the inner-city neighborhoods their families had left behind.[99]

High population turnover can have a devastating effect on community culture because it thwarts communication and information flow.[100] In response to this turnover, a culture may develop that dictates standards of dress, language, and behavior to neighborhood youth that are in opposition to those of conventional society. All these factors are likely to produce increased crime rates.

The Cycles of Community Change During periods of population turnover, communities may undergo changes that undermine their infrastructure. Urban areas seem to have life cycles, which begin with building residential dwellings and are followed by a period of decline, with marked decreases in socioeconomic status and increases in population density. Later stages in this life cycle include changing racial or ethnic makeup, population thinning, and finally, a renewal stage in which obsolete housing is replaced and upgraded (**gentrification**). Areas undergoing such change seem to experience an increase in their crime rates.[101]

As communities go through cycles, neighborhood deterioration precedes increasing rates of crime and delinquency.[102] Neighborhoods most at risk for high crime rate increases contain large numbers of single-parent families and unrelated people living together. They go from having owner-occupied to renter-occupied units, and have an economic base that has lost semiskilled and unskilled jobs (indicating a growing residue of discouraged workers who are no longer seeking employment).[103] These ecological disruptions strain existing social control mechanisms and inhibit their ability to control crime and delinquency.

COLLECTIVE EFFICACY

 LO6 Discuss the association between collective efficacy and crime

Cohesive communities, whether urban or rural, with high levels of social control and social integration, where people know one another and develop interpersonal ties, may also develop **collective efficacy**: mutual trust, a willingness to intervene in the supervision of children, and the maintenance of public order.[104] It is the cohesion among neighborhood residents combined with shared expectations for informal social control of public space that promotes collective efficacy.[105] Residents in these areas are able to enjoy a better life because the fruits of cohesiveness can be better education, health care, and housing opportunities.[106]

In contrast, in socially disorganized neighborhoods, where the population is transient and interpersonal relationships remain superficial and nonsupportive, efforts at social control are weak and attenuated.[107] In these unstable neighborhoods, residents find that the social support they need to live a conventional life is absent or lacking. The resulting lack of social cohesion produces an atmosphere where

antisocial behavior becomes normative.[108] As the number of people who have a stake in the community (i.e., they are homeowners) increases, crime rates drop.[109] These more cohesive neighborhoods report less disorder than less-unified communities.[110]

When community social control efforts are weak and attenuated, crime rates increase, further diminishing neighborhood cohesiveness.[111] There are actually three forms of collective efficacy: informal, institutional, and public social control.

Informal Social Control Some elements of collective efficacy operate on the primary or private level and involve peers, families, and relatives. These sources exert informal control by either awarding or withholding approval, respect, trust, and admiration. Informal control mechanisms include direct criticism, ridicule, ostracism, desertion, or physical punishment.[112] Crime rates and the chances of victimization are lower in communities where residents trust one another and are ready to lend help and assistance when needed.[113]

Because they already have a propensity to commit crime without informal social controls, some people will be unable to avoid entanglements in antisocial behaviors.[114] The most important wielder of informal social control is the family, which may keep at-risk kids in check through such mechanisms as corporal punishment, withholding privileges, or ridiculing lazy or disrespectful behavior. The importance of the family to apply informal social control takes on greater importance in neighborhoods with few social ties among adults and limited collective efficacy. In these areas, parents cannot call upon neighborhood resources to take up the burden of controlling children and face the challenge of providing adequate supervision.[115]

The family is not the only force of informal social control. In some neighborhoods, residents create informal social networks and groups, some organized around the theme of community preservation. Some are committed to preserving their immediate environment by confronting destabilizing forces such as teen gangs.[116] By helping neighbors become more resilient and self-confident, adults in these areas provide the external support systems that enable youth to desist from crime. Residents teach one another that they have moral and social obligations to their fellow citizens; children learn to be sensitive to the rights of others and to respect differences.

gentrification A residential renewal stage in which obsolete housing is replaced and upgraded; areas undergoing such change seem to experience an increase in their crime rates.

collective efficacy Social control exerted by cohesive communities, based on mutual trust, including intervention in the supervision of children and maintenance of public order.

In some areas, neighborhood associations and self-help groups form.[117] The threat of skyrocketing violence rates may draw people together to help each other out. While criminologists believe that crime rates are lower in cohesive neighborhoods, it is also possible that an escalating crime rate may bring people closer together to fight a common problem.[118] Some neighbors may get involved in informal social control through surveillance practices—for example, by keeping an eye out for intruders when their neighbors go out of town. Informal surveillance has been found to reduce the levels of some crimes such as street robberies; however, if robbery rates remain high, surveillance may be terminated because people become fearful for their safety.[119]

Institutional Social Control   Social institutions such as schools and churches cannot work effectively in a climate of alienation and mistrust. Unsupervised peer groups and gangs, which flourish in disorganized areas, disrupt the influence of those neighborhood control agents that do exist.[120]

People who reside in these neighborhoods find that involvement with conventional social institutions, such as schools and afternoon programs, is often attenuated or blocked.[121] Children are at risk for recruitment into gangs and law-violating groups when there is a lack of effective public services. Gangs become an attractive alternative when adolescents have little to do after school and must rely on out-of-home care rather than more structured school-based programs.[122] As a result, crime may flourish and neighborhood fear increases, conditions that decrease a community's cohesion and thwart the ability of its institutions to exert social control over its residents.[123]

To combat these influences, communities that have collective efficacy attempt to utilize their local institutions to control crime. Sources of institutional social control include businesses, stores, schools, churches, and social service and volunteer organizations. When these institutions are effective, crime rates decline.[124]

Some institutions, such as neighborhood youth organizations and recreation centers for teens, have been found to lower crime rates because they exert a positive effect on both the individual level (e.g., they improve participants' self-control) and institutional level (e.g., they encourage informal social control).[125] In contrast, the presence of disruptive institutions, such as taverns and bars, destabilize neighborhoods and increase the rate of violent crimes.[126]

Public Social Control   Stable neighborhoods are also able to arrange for external sources of social control. If they can draw on outside help and secure external resources—a process referred to as public social control—they are better able to reduce the effects of disorganization and maintain lower levels of crime and victimization.[127] Community organizations in low-income areas that are able to develop ties with the larger community experience a decrease in crime.[128]

Racial differences in crime and violence rates may be explained in part by the ability of citizens in affluent, predominantly white neighborhoods to use their economic resources, and the political power they bring, to their own advantage. They demand and receive a level of protection in their communities that is not enjoyed in less affluent minority communities.[129]

The level of policing, one of the primary sources of public social control, may vary from neighborhood to neighborhood.[130] The police presence is typically greatest when community organizations and local leaders have sufficient political clout to get funding for additional law enforcement personnel. An effective police presence, cracking down on hot spots and strictly enforcing the law at a neighborhood level, sends a message that the area will not tolerate deviant behavior.[131] Because they can respond vigorously to crime, the police prevent criminal groups from gaining a toehold in the neighborhood.[132] Criminals and drug dealers avoid such areas and relocate to easier and more appealing targets.[133] In contrast, crime rates are highest in areas where police are mistrusted because they engage in misconduct, such as use of excessive force, or because they are seemingly indifferent to neighborhood problems.[134]

In more disorganized areas, the absence of political powerbrokers limits access to external funding and protection.[135] Without outside funding, a neighborhood may lack the ability to get back on its feet.[136] In these areas, there are fewer police, and those that do patrol the area are less motivated and their resources are stretched tighter. These communities cannot mount an effective social control effort because as neighborhood disadvantage increases, the level of informal social control decreases.[137]

The government can also reduce crime by providing economic and social supports through publicly funded welfare programs. Though welfare is often criticized by conservative politicians as being a government handout, there is evidence of a significant association between the amount of welfare money people receive and lowered crime rates.[138] Government assistance may help people improve their social status by providing them with the financial resources to clothe, feed, and educate their children while at the same time reducing stress, frustration, and anger. Using government subsidies to reduce crime is controversial and not all research has found that it actually works as advertised.[139]

People living in disorganized areas may also be able to draw on resources from their neighbors in more affluent surrounding communities, helping to keep crime rates down.[140] This phenomenon may explain, in part, why violence rates are high in poor African American neighborhoods cut off from outside areas for support.[141]

The Effect of Collective Efficacy   In areas that maintain collective efficacy, children are less likely to become involved with deviant peers and engage in problem behaviors.[142] In these more stable areas, kids are able to use their wits to avoid violent confrontations and to feel safe in their own neighborhood, a concept referred to as **street efficacy**.[143] This association is important because adolescents living in communities with high levels of efficacy are less likely to resort to violence themselves or to associate with delinquent peers.[144]

In contrast, adolescents who live in neighborhoods with concentrated disadvantage and low collective efficacy begin to lose confidence in their ability to avoid violence. They perceive, and rightly so, that the community cannot provide the level of social control needed to neutralize or make up for what individuals lack in personal self-control.[145] The lack of community controls may convince them to take matters into their own hands—for example, joining a gang or carrying a weapon for self-protection. Thus community cohesion is an effect: cohesive neighborhoods help control crime; the more crime, the lower levels of community cohesion.[146]

Collective efficacy has other benefits. When residents are satisfied that their neighborhoods are good places to live, they feel a sense of obligation to maintain order themselves and are more willing to work hard to encourage informal social control. In areas where social institutions and processes—such as police protection—are working adequately, residents are willing to intervene personally to help control unruly children and uncivil adults.[147]

Concept Summary 6.1 sets out the features of social disorganization theory.

 To read a famous *Atlantic* magazine article titled "Broken Windows," which discusses the concept of community deterioration and crime, go to **http://www.theatlantic.com/magazine/archive/1982/03/broken-windows/304465/.**

Strain Theories

 L07 Articulate what is meant by the concepts of strain and anomie

As a group, strain theorists believe that most people share similar values and goals. They want to earn money, have a nice home, drive a great car, and wear stylish clothes. They also want to care for their families and educate their children. Unfortunately, the ability to achieve these personal goals is stratified by socioeconomic class. While the affluent may live out the American Dream, the poor are shut out from achieving their goals. Because they can't always get what they want, they begin to feel frustrated and angry, a condition that is referred to as strain.

Strain is related to criminal motivation. People who feel economically and socially humiliated may perceive the right to humiliate others in return.[148] Psychologists warn that under these circumstances those who consider themselves "losers" begin to fear and envy "winners" who are doing very well at their expense. If they fail to use risky, aggressive tactics, they are surely going to lose out in social competition and have little chance of future success.[149] These generalized feelings of **relative deprivation** are precursors to high crime rates.[150]

> **street efficacy** A concept in which more cohesive communities with high levels of social control and social integration foster the ability for kids to use their wits to avoid violent confrontations and to feel safe in their own neighborhood. Adolescents with high levels of street efficacy are less likely to resort to violence themselves or to associate with delinquent peers.
>
> **relative deprivation** The condition that exists when people of wealth and poverty live in close proximity to one another. Some criminologists attribute crime rate differentials to relative deprivation.

CONCEPT SUMMARY 6.1
Social Disorganization Theories

Theory	Major Premise	Strengths	Research Focus
Shaw and McKay's concentric zones theory	Crime is a product of transitional neighborhoods that manifest social disorganization and value conflict.	Identifies why crime rates are highest in slum areas. Points out the factors that produce crime. Suggests programs to help reduce crime.	Poverty; disorganization; gangs; neighborhood change; community context of crime.
Social ecology theory	The conflicts and problems of urban social life and communities, including fear, unemployment, deterioration, and siege mentality, influence crime rates.	Accounts for urban crime rates and trends. Identifies community-level factors that produce high crime rates.	Social control; fear; collective efficacy; unemployment.

According to the strain view, sharp divisions between the rich and poor create an atmosphere of envy and mistrust that may lead to violence and aggression.[151] People who feel deprived because of their race or economic class standing eventually develop a sense of injustice and discontent. The less fortunate begin to distrust the society that has nurtured social inequality and obstructed their chances of progressing by legitimate means. The constant frustration that results from these feelings of inadequacy produces pent-up aggression and hostility and, eventually, leads to violence and crime. The effect of inequality may be greatest when the impoverished population believes they are becoming less able to compete in a society where the balance of economic and social power is shifting further toward the already affluent. Under these conditions, the likelihood that the poor will choose illegitimate life-enhancing activities increases.[152] The basic components of strain theory are set out in Figure 6.5.

THE CONCEPT OF ANOMIE

The roots of strain theories can be traced to Émile Durkheim's notion of **anomie** (from the Greek *a nomos*, "without norms"). According to Durkheim, an anomic society is one in which rules of behavior (i.e., values, customs, and norms) have broken down or become inoperative during periods of rapid social change or social crisis such as war or famine. Anomie is most likely to occur in societies that are moving from a preindustrial society, which is held together by traditions, shared values, and unquestioned beliefs (i.e., **mechanical solidarity**) to a postindustrial social system, which is highly developed and dependent upon the division of labor. In this modern society, people are connected by their interdependent needs for one another's services and production (i.e., **organic solidarity**). The shift in traditions and values creates social turmoil. Established norms begin to erode and lose meaning. If a division occurs between what the population expects and what the economic and productive forces of society can realistically deliver, a crisis situation develops that can manifest itself in normlessness or anomie.

anomie According to Durkheim, an anomic society is one in which rules of behavior (i.e., values, customs, and norms) have broken down or become inoperative during periods of rapid social change or social crisis.

mechanical solidarity A characteristic of a preindustrial society that is held together by traditions, shared values, and unquestioned beliefs.

organic solidarity Postindustrial social systems, which are highly developed and dependent upon the division of labor; people are connected by their interdependent needs for one another's services and production.

Poverty
- Relative deprivation
- Feelings of inadequacy
- Siege mentality

Maintenance of conventional rules and norms
Despite adversity, people remain loyal to conventional values and rules of dominant middle-class culture.

Strain
People who desire conventional success but lack means and opportunity will experience strain and frustration.

Formation of gangs and groups
People form law-violating groups to seek alternative means of achieving success.

Crime and delinquency
People engage in antisocial acts to achieve success and relieve their feelings of strain.

Criminal careers
Feelings of strain may endure, sustaining criminal careers.

FIGURE 6.5 The Basic Components of Strain Theory

SOURCE: © Cengage Learning

Anomie undermines society's social control function. Every society works to limit people's goals and desires. If a society becomes anomic, it can no longer establish and maintain control over its population's wants and desires. Because people find it difficult to control their appetites, their demands become unlimited. Under these circumstances, obedience to legal codes may be strained, and alternative behavior choices, such as crimes, may be inevitable.

Contemporary strain theories come in two distinct formulations:

- *Structural strain*. Using a sociological lens, structural strain suggests that economic and social sources of strain shape collective human behavior.
- *Individual strain*. Using a psychological reference, individual strain theories suggest that individual life experiences cause some people to suffer pain and misery, feelings that are then translated into antisocial behaviors.

Following, three popular strain theories are discussed in some detail. Two, anomie theory and American Dream theory, are structural, while the third, general strain theory, relies more on a social psychological framework.

MERTON'S THEORY OF ANOMIE

LO8 Compare and contrast between the different elements in Merton's theory of anomie

Durkheim's ideas were applied to criminology by sociologist Robert Merton in his **theory of anomie**.[153] Merton used a modified version of the concept of anomie to fit social, economic, and cultural conditions found in modern U.S. society.[154] He found that two elements of culture interact to produce potentially anomic conditions: culturally defined goals and socially approved means for obtaining them. Contemporary society stresses the goals of acquiring wealth, success, and power. Socially permissible means include hard work, education, and thrift.

In the United States, Merton argued, legitimate means to acquire wealth are stratified across class and status lines. Those with little formal education and few economic resources soon find that they are denied the ability to legally acquire wealth—the preeminent success symbol. When socially mandated goals are uniform throughout society and access to legitimate means is bound by class and status, the resulting strain produces anomie among those who are locked out of the legitimate opportunity structure. Consequently, they may develop criminal or delinquent solutions to the problem of attaining goals.

Social Adaptations Merton argued that each person has his or her own concept of the goals of society and the means at his or her disposal for their attainment. Here is a brief description of each of these modes of adaptation to the association of goals and means:

- *Conformity.* Conformity occurs when individuals embrace conventional social goals and also have the means of attainment at their disposal. The conformist desires wealth and success and can obtain them through education and a high-paying job. In a balanced, stable society, this is the most common social adaptation. If a majority of its people did not practice conformity, the society would cease to exist.
- *Innovation.* Innovation occurs when an individual accepts the goals of society but rejects or is incapable of attaining them through legitimate means. Many people desire material goods and luxuries but lack the financial ability to attain them. The resulting conflict forces them to adopt innovative solutions to their dilemma: they steal, sell drugs, or extort money. Of the five adaptations, innovation is most closely associated with criminal behavior.

If successful, innovation can have serious, long-term social consequences. Criminal success helps convince otherwise law-abiding people that innovative means work better and faster than conventional ones. The prosperous drug dealer's expensive car and flashy clothes give out the message that crime pays. Merton claims, "The process thus enlarges the extent of anomie within the system, so that others, who did not respond in the form of deviant behavior to the relatively slight anomie which they first obtained, come to do so as anomie is spread and is intensified."[155] This explains why crime is initiated and sustained in certain low-income ecological areas.

- *Ritualism.* Ritualists have gained the tools to accumulate wealth—for example, they are educated and informed—but reject established cultural goals of contemporary society. These are people who enjoy the routine of work without having the ambition to climb to the top of their profession; they are not risk takers. Some may enjoy being midlevel government bureaucrats. Some are the professors who want to get tenure but do not strive to become chairperson of the department. Some ritualists gain pleasure from practicing traditional ceremonies regardless of whether they have a real purpose or goal. The rules and customs in religious orders, clubs, and college fraternities are appealing to ritualists. Ritualists should have the lowest level of criminal behavior because they have abandoned the success goal, which is at the root of criminal activity.
- *Retreatism.* Retreatists reject both the goals and the means of society. Merton suggests that people who adjust in this fashion are "in the society but not of it." Included in this category are "psychotics, psychoneurotics, chronic autists, pariahs, outcasts, vagrants, vagabonds, tramps, chronic drunkards, and drug addicts." Because such people are morally or otherwise incapable of using both legitimate and illegitimate means, they attempt to escape their lack of success by withdrawing, either mentally or physically.
- *Rebellion.* Rebellion involves substituting an alternative set of goals and means for conventional ones. Revolutionaries who wish to promote radical change in the existing social structure and who call for alternative lifestyles, goals, and beliefs are engaging in rebellion. Rebellion may be a reaction against a corrupt and hated government or an effort to create alternate opportunities and lifestyles within the existing system.

theory of anomie A modified version of the concept of anomie developed by Merton to fit social, economic, and cultural conditions found in modern U.S. society. He found that two elements of culture interact to produce potentially anomic conditions: culturally defined goals and socially approved means for obtaining them.

Strain can produce resistance or rebellion to the existing political and social order. On March 30, 2016, Mica Grimm of Black Lives Matter Minneapolis speaks to a group of protestors outside the Hennepin County Courthouse after the county attorney announced there would be no charges brought against police officers involved in the death of a young black man, Jamar Clark.

Evaluation of Anomie Theory According to anomie theory, social inequality leads to perceptions of anomie. To resolve the goals–means conflict and relieve their sense of strain, some people innovate by stealing or extorting money, others retreat into drugs and alcohol, others rebel by joining revolutionary groups, and still others get involved in ritualistic behavior by joining a religious cult.

Merton's view of anomie has been one of the most enduring and influential sociological theories of criminality. By linking deviant behavior to the success goals that control social behavior, anomie theory attempts to pinpoint the cause of the conflict that produces personal frustration and consequent criminality. By acknowledging that society unfairly distributes the legitimate means to achieving success, anomie theory helps explain the existence of high-crime areas and the apparent predominance of delinquent and criminal behavior among the lower class. By suggesting that social conditions, not individual personalities, produce crime, Merton greatly influenced the direction taken

to reduce and control criminality during the latter half of the twentieth century.

A number of questions are left unanswered by anomie theory.[156] Merton does not explain why people choose to commit certain types of crime. For example, why does one anomic person become a mugger and another deal drugs? Anomie may be used to explain differences in crime rates, but it cannot explain why most young criminals desist from crime as adults. Does this mean that perceptions of anomie dwindle with age? Is anomie short-lived?

Critics have also suggested that people pursue a number of different goals, including educational, athletic, and social success. Juveniles may be more interested in immediate goals, such as having an active social life or being a good athlete, than in long-term "ideal" achievements, such as monetary success. Achieving these goals is not a matter of social class alone; other factors, including athletic ability, intelligence, personality, and family life, can either hinder or assist goal attainment.[157] Anomie theory also assumes that all people share the same goals and values, which is false.[158]

Some contemporary theories are grounded on Merton's visionary concepts. Some of these are macro-level theories that hold that the success goal integrated within American society influences the nature and extent of the aggregate crime rate. There are also individual micro-level versions of the theory, which focus on how an individual is affected by feelings of alienation and strain.

INSTITUTIONAL ANOMIE THEORY (IAT)

An important addition to the strain literature is the book *Crime and the American Dream*, by Steven Messner and Richard Rosenfeld.[159] Their macro-level version of anomie theory views antisocial behavior as a function of cultural and institutional influences in U.S. society, a model they refer to as **institutional anomie theory (IAT)**. Messner and Rosenfeld agree with Merton's view that the success goal is pervasive in American culture. They refer to this as the *American Dream*, a term they employ as both a goal and a process. As a goal, the **American Dream** involves accumulating material goods and wealth via open individual competition. As a process, it involves both being socialized to pursue material success and believing that prosperity is an achievable goal

institutional anomie theory (IAT) The view that anomie pervades U.S. culture because the drive for material wealth dominates and undermines social and community values.

American Dream The goal of accumulating material goods and wealth through individual competition; the process of being socialized to pursue material success and to believe it is achievable.

in American culture. In the United States, the capitalist system encourages innovation in pursuit of monetary rewards. Businesspeople such as Mitt Romney, Bill Gates, Jeff Bezos, Warren Buffett, Mark Zuckerberg, and Donald Trump are admired as pundits, authorities, and leaders; they are often considered as possible (or actual, in the case of Romney and Trump) presidential candidates.

According to Messner and Rosenfeld, the relatively high U.S. crime rates can be explained by the interrelationship between culture and institutions. The dominance of the American Dream mythology ensures that many people will develop wishes and desires for material goods that cannot be satisfied by legitimate means. People are willing to do anything to get ahead, from cheating on tests to get higher grades to engaging in corporate fraud and tax evasion.[160] Those who cannot succeed become willing to risk everything, including a prison sentence. At the institutional level, the dominance of economic concerns weakens the informal social control exerted by the family, church, and school. These institutions have lost their ability to regulate behavior and have instead become a conduit for promoting material success. Parents push their kids to succeed at any cost; schools encourage kids to get into the best colleges; religious institutions promote their wealth and power.[161] Crime rates may rise even in a healthy economy because national prosperity heightens the attractiveness of monetary rewards, encouraging people to gain financial success by any means possible, including illegal ones. Meanwhile, the importance of social institutions as a means of exerting social control is reduced. In this "culture of competition," self-interest prevails and generates amorality, acceptance of inequality, and disdain for the less fortunate.[162]

Anomic conditions occur because the desire to succeed at any cost drives people apart, weakens the collective sense of community, fosters ambition, and restricts desires to achieve anything that is not material wealth. Achieving a "good name" and respect is not sufficient. Capitalist culture "exerts pressures toward crime by encouraging an anomic cultural environment, an environment in which people are encouraged to adopt an 'anything goes' mentality in the pursuit of personal goals . . . the anomic pressures inherent in the American Dream are nourished and sustained by an institutional balance of power dominated by the economy."[163]

What is distinct about American society, according to Messner and Rosenfeld, and what most likely determines the exceedingly high national crime rate, is that anomic conditions have been allowed to "develop to such an extraordinary degree."[164] There do not seem to be any alternatives that would serve the same purpose or strive for the same goal.

Impact of Anomie Why does anomie pervade American culture? According to Messner and Rosenfeld, it is because capitalist culture promotes intense pressures for economic success. Prosocial, noneconomic institutions that might otherwise control the exaggerated emphasis on financial success, such as religious or charitable institutions, have been rendered powerless or obsolete. As a result, the value structure of society is dominated by economic realities that weaken institutional social control. In other words, people are so interested in making money that their behavior cannot be controlled by the needs of family or the restraints of morality.

There are three reasons social institutions have been undermined. First, noneconomic functions and roles have been devalued. Performance in other institutional settings—the family, school, or community—is assigned a lower priority than the goal of financial success. Few students go to college to study the classics; most want to major in a field with good job prospects. Second, when conflicts emerge, noneconomic roles become subordinate to and must accommodate economic roles. The schedules, routines, and demands of the workplace take priority over those of the home, the school, the community, and other aspects of social life. A parent given the opportunity for a promotion thinks nothing of uprooting his family and moving them to another part of the country. And third, economic language, standards, and norms penetrate into noneconomic realms. Economic terms become part of the common vernacular. People want to get to the "bottom line"; spouses view themselves as "partners" who "manage" the household. Retired people say they want to "downsize" their household; we "outsource" home repairs instead of doing them ourselves. Corporate leaders run for public office promising to "run the country like a business." People join social clubs to make connections and "network," not to make close friends.

Testing the IAT A number of research efforts have found support for the principles set out in the IAT. On a macro level, research shows that there is an association between national homicide rates and cultural stress on individual achievement and the fetishism of money.[165] On an individual or micro level, commitment to economic success is positively related to criminality. The more people say that making money is what's important to them, the more likely they are to get involved in criminal pursuits.[166]

While there is general support for the IAT, a number of issues remain, such as developing an understanding of gender differences in the crime rate.[167] Assuming women desire money, success, and the American Dream as much as men, why is their crime rate lower? There is also evidence that the American Dream mythology had a greater effect on whites than African Americans. Cernkovich reasons that whites may have greater expectations of material success than African Americans, whose aspirations have been tempered by a long history of racial and economic deprivation. When whites experience strain, they are more apt to react with anger and antisocial behavior.[168]

The Messner-Rosenfeld version of anomie strain may be a blueprint for crime-reduction strategies: if citizens are provided with an economic safety net, they may be able to resist the influence of economic deprivation and commit less crime. Nations that provide such resources—welfare, pension benefits, health care—have significantly lower crime rates.[169] In contrast, crime and violence rates are highest in nations that experience high levels of income inequality.[170]

RELATIVE DEPRIVATION THEORY

There is ample evidence that neighborhood-level income inequality is a significant predictor of neighborhood crime rates.[171] Sharp divisions between the rich and the poor create an atmosphere of envy and mistrust. Criminal motivation is fueled both by perceived humiliation and by the perceived right to humiliate a victim in return.[172] Psychologists warn that under these circumstances young males will begin to fear and envy "winners" who are doing very well at their expense. If they fail to use risky aggressive tactics, they are surely going to lose out in social competition and have little chance of future success.[173] These generalized feelings of relative deprivation are precursors to high crime rates.[174]

The concept of relative deprivation was proposed by sociologists Judith Blau and Peter Blau, who combined concepts from anomie theory with those derived from social disorganization models.[175] According to the Blaus' view, lower-class people may feel both deprived and embittered when they compare their life circumstances to those of the more affluent. People who feel deprived because of their race or economic class eventually develop a sense of injustice and discontent. The less fortunate begin to distrust the society that has nurtured social inequality and reduced their chances of progressing by legitimate means. The constant frustration that results from these feelings of inadequacy produces pent-up aggression and hostility, eventually leading to violence and crime. The effect of inequality may be greatest when the impoverished believe that they are becoming less able to compete in a society whose balance of economic and social power is shifting further toward the already affluent. Under these conditions, the relatively poor are increasingly likely to choose illegitimate life-enhancing activities.[176] Research studies using national data sets do show a strong positive association between income inequality and violent crime, a finding that supports the relative deprivation concept.[177]

Relative deprivation is felt most acutely by African American youths because they consistently suffer racial discrimination and economic deprivation that inflict on them a lower status than that of other urban residents.[178] Wage inequality may motivate young African American males to enter the drug trade, an enterprise that increases the likelihood that they will become involved in violent crimes.[179]

In sum, according to the relative deprivation concept, people who perceive themselves as economically deprived relative to people they know, as well as to society in general, may begin to form negative self-feelings and hostility, which motivate them to engage in deviant and criminal behaviors.[180]

GENERAL STRAIN THEORY (GST)

Sociologist Robert Agnew's **general strain theory (GST)** helps identify the social-psychological, individual-level influences that produce strain. Whereas structural, macro-level strain theories explain how interclass socioeconomic differences produce strain and anomie in the lower class, Agnew sees strain as an individual phenomenon. People of any class can feel stress and strain and are then more likely to commit crimes. Agnew therefore offers a more general explanation of criminal activity: it can occur among all elements of society if they experience stress-producing events.[181] If members of the lower class commit more crime, it's because strain is a product of a lower-class lifestyle. Kids growing up poor in a gang-infested community are bound to experience more strain than their wealthier peers being raised in affluent suburban neighborhoods. According to Agnew, the greater the intensity and frequency of strain experiences, the greater their impact and the more likely they are to cause criminality. Each type of strain will increase the likelihood of experiencing such negative emotions as disappointment, depression, fear, and, most important, anger. Anger increases perceptions of being wronged and produces a desire for revenge, energizes individuals to take action, and lowers inhibitions. Violence and aggression seem justified if you have been wronged and are righteously angry.

Because it produces these emotions, strain can be considered a predisposing factor for criminality when it is chronic and repetitive and creates a hostile, suspicious, and aggressive attitude. Individual strain episodes may serve as a situational event or trigger that produces crime, such as when a particularly stressful event ignites a violent reaction. Strain may predispose people toward antisocial behaviors rather than cause them to commit a specific act to relieve strain. So the person who feels strain because of financial need may be as likely to beat up a rival as he is to rob a liquor store.[182]

L09 Clarify what Agnew means by the concept of negative affective states

Causes of Strain   Agnew suggests that criminality is the direct result of **negative affective states**—the anger, frustration, and adverse emotions that emerge in the wake of negative and destructive social relationships. He finds that negative affective states are produced by a variety of sources of strain (Figure 6.6).

general strain theory (GST) According to Agnew, the view that multiple sources of strain interact with an individual's emotional traits and responses to produce criminality.

negative affective states According to Agnew, anger, depression, disappointment, fear, and other adverse emotions that derive from strain.

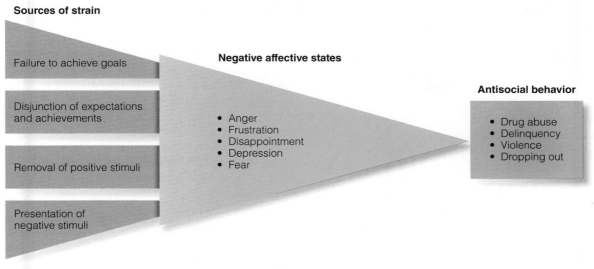

Sources of strain

Failure to achieve goals

Disjunction of expectations and achievements

Removal of positive stimuli

Presentation of negative stimuli

Negative affective states

- Anger
- Frustration
- Disappointment
- Depression
- Fear

Antisocial behavior

- Drug abuse
- Delinquency
- Violence
- Dropping out

FIGURE 6.6 Elements of General Strain Theory (GST)

SOURCE: © Cengage Learning

- *Failure to achieve positively valued goals.* This category of strain, similar to what Merton speaks of in his theory of anomie, is a result of the disjunction between aspirations and expectations. This type of strain occurs when people aspire for wealth and fame, but, lacking financial and educational resources, assume that such goals are impossible to achieve. These people, racked by despair, who feel few opportunities for success, are at risk for crime.[183]
- *The failure to achieve is relative.* Some very successful people may consider themselves failures. When people compare themselves to peers who seem to be doing a lot better financially or socially (such as making more money or getting better grades), even those doing relatively well feel strain. For example, when a high school senior is accepted at a good college but not a "prestige school" like some of her friends, she will feel strain. Perhaps she is not being treated fairly because the "playing field" is tilted against her; "other kids have connections," she may say. Perceiving inequity may result in adverse reactions, ranging from running away from its source to lowering the benefits of others through physical attacks or vandalizing their property. Strain then can also be produced when there is a disjunction between expectations and achievements.
- *Removal of positively valued stimuli.* Strain may occur because of the actual or anticipated removal or loss of a positively valued stimulus from the individual. Divorce, romantic breakup, the loss of a friend who moves away, and the death of a loved one can all produce strain.[184] The loss of positive stimuli may lead to criminality when a person tries to prevent the loss, retrieve what has been lost, obtain substitutes, or seek revenge against those responsible for the loss.[185]
- *The effect of removal of positive stimuli may be class bound.* Middle-class people may be less able to cope with the removal of positive stimuli. When you are expected to

succeed because of your class position, failure may be harder to swallow; those who have limited opportunities and lower expectations may be able to take failure in stride.[186]

- *Presentation of negative stimuli.* Strain is also produced by the application of negative or noxious stimuli. Included within this category are painful social interactions such as child abuse and neglect.[187] Stressful life events ranging from unemployment to crime victimization can produce strain that may develop into angry emotionality and subsequent antisocial behaviors.[188] Nor is the effect of negative stimuli a one-shot deal: victims forced to continually interact with the source of negative stimuli (the school yard bully, the abusive parent, the demanding boss) may find that the cumulative effects of strain are overwhelming; negative affective states experienced in childhood can follow a person to the grave.[189]

SOURCES OF STRAIN

There are a variety of sources of strain. Sometimes it can be a particular individual who is causing problems, such as a peer group rival. When individuals identify a target to blame for their problems, they are more likely to respond with retaliatory action (for example, "Joe stole my wife away by lying about me, so I beat him up!"). Sometimes the source of strain is difficult to pinpoint (for example, "I feel depressed because of the way the world is going"); this type of ambiguous strain is unlikely to produce an aggressive response.

Social Sources of Strain People may begin to feel strain because of their membership in a peer or social group. The relationship may be reciprocal. People who report feelings of stress and anger are more likely to interact with others who are similarly stressed out.[190] Peer group membership has its benefits, such as friendship, companionship, and support, but such groups also force members into behavior patterns (such as using drugs) that can be the source of unwelcome stress. Feelings of strain and being overwhelmed may become magnified as individuals attempt to comply with peer group demands. People may, for example, get involved in an unwanted shoplifting spree to pay for drugs, creating even more stress in their lives.[191] Experiments show that people who perceive strain because they are being treated unfairly report (1) high levels of situational anger that lead to (2) higher levels of theft from an employer.[192] People who live in strain-producing social conditions are more likely to cope with their negative emotions through crime.[193]

Adolescent Sources of Strain   Crime peaks during late adolescence because this is a period of social stress caused by the weakening of parental supervision and the development of relationships with a diverse peer group. Because many families are unstable, kids going through the trauma of family breakup and frequent changes in family structure find themselves feeling a high degree of strain. Some may react by becoming involved in precocious sexuality or by turning to substance abuse to mask the strain.[194] Adolescence is also a period during which hormone levels peak, and the behavior moderating aspects of the brain have not fully developed—two factors that make adolescents susceptible to environmental sources of strain.[195]

As they mature, children's expectations increase; some find that they are unable to meet academic and social demands. Adolescents are very concerned about their standing with peers. Those deficient in these areas may find they are social outcasts, another source of strain. While positive peer influence may help adolescents cope with stress, those who turn for help and guidance from peers who themselves are involved in criminality place themselves at risk for crime.[196]

Community Sources of Strain   The GST generally focuses on individual-level sources of strain, yet there are distinct ecological variations in the crime rate. Some regions, cities, and neighborhoods are more crime prone than others. Can ecological differences produce "negative affective states" in large segments of the population, which account for these differences? Agnew suggests that there are, in fact, community-level factors, such as blocked opportunities and lack of social support, that produce feelings of strain. According to Agnew, communities contribute to strain in several ways:

- They influence the goals people pursue and the ability people have to meet these goals.
- They influence feelings of relative deprivation and exposure to aversive stimuli, including family conflict, incivility, and economic deprivation.
- They influence the likelihood that angry, strain-filled individuals will interact with one another.

Consequently, not only does GST predict deviance on an individual level, but it can also account for community-level differences in the crime rate.

COPING WITH STRAIN

Not all people who experience strain fall into a life of crime and eventually resort to criminality. Some are able to marshal their emotional, mental, and behavioral resources to cope with the anger and frustration produced by strain. Personal temperament, high self-esteem, and a strong self-image underpin the ability to cope.[197] In contrast, people who are impulsive and lack attachments to others are less able to cope than those who are bonded to others and maintain higher levels of self-control.[198] Those high in negative emotionality and low in constraint will be more likely to react to strain with antisocial behaviors.[199] In contrast, those people who can call on family, friends, and social institutions for help and support are better able to cope with strain.[200]

Some defenses are cognitive; individuals may be able to rationalize frustrating circumstances. Not getting the career they desire is "just not that important"; they may be poor, but the "next guy is worse off"; and if things didn't work out, then they "got what they deserved." Others seek behavioral solutions: they run away from adverse conditions or seek revenge against those who caused the strain. Others will try to regain emotional equilibrium with techniques ranging from physical exercise to drug abuse. Some may change their daily routine in order to avoid the negative influences that are causing emotional duress.[201]

Strain and Criminal Careers   While some people can effectively cope with strain, others cannot and may turn to antisocial acts to help them relieve the pressures produced by negative affective states. Although it may be socially disapproved, criminality can provide relief and satisfaction for someone living an otherwise stress-filled life. Who is most likely to use crime to cope with strain? GST recognizes that certain people have traits that may make them particularly sensitive to strain.[202] These include an explosive temperament, being overly sensitive or emotional, low tolerance for adversity, and poor problem-solving skills.[203]

Agnew created the concept of storylines to help explain how people deal with the stressors of everyday life. This concept is discussed in the Criminology in Action feature, "Storylines."

CONNECTIONS

Explaining continuity and change in offending rates over the life course has become an important goal of criminologists. Analysis of latent trait and life course theories in Chapter 9 provides some recent thinking on this topic.

ASK YOURSELF . . .

Crime rates decline with age. Does that mean feelings of strain also fall off as we grow older?

04

Storylines

Criminologist Robert Agnew has identified a concept—storylines—to help explain why people commit crimes. He finds that when criminals are asked why they offend, they typically tell a story explaining why they engaged in crime. These stories describe the stressful events and conditions leading up to the crime and how they dealt with the pressure and strain. Very often it is some unusual or unplanned event that led them to feel strain and resort to criminal actions to solve their problems: they were insulted by a rival and sought revenge; they lost money gambling and, needing to pay off their debt, had to commit a burglary; some guy was hitting on their girl so they were forced to give them a beatdown. A storyline is a temporally limited, interrelated set of events and conditions that increases the likelihood that individuals will engage in a crime or a series of related crimes.

Storylines begin with a particular event; that is, "something happens" that is upsetting. This event affects the characteristics of the individual, leads to increased feelings of strain, and alters their associations and interactions. The feeling was temporary; they may claim "that's not really like me." They turn into a new person—jealous, angry, desperate, violent—that is out of character. The storyline ends when some event restores the individual's normal level of functioning, ending the temporary drama in their lives.

What are some typical stories that are told?

- *A Desperate Need for Money.* Offenders often report that they engage in crime during those periods when something has happened that creates a temporary but desperate need for money, and the individual believes that there are no good legitimate options for obtaining such money. Usually cited for this turn of events are unexpected expenses, poor budgeting between paydays, temporary employment problems, the temporary loss of other sources of financial support, demands that debts be repaid, gambling losses, drug binges, or the pressure to pay legal fines or fees. So this storyline might go: "I knew the Knicks were going to beat the Celtics, so I borrowed $500 for a bet, and then they lost on a lucky shot. I had to pay the loan back so I stole my brother-in-law's TV and sold it on the street."

- *An Unresolved Dispute.* This storyline begins when someone does or says something that the individual does not like, or challenges and/or threatens a core identity value or status. The individual experiences one or more negative emotions, such as anger and humiliation, and then finds someone to blame for this negative treatment. This type of storyline often has a romantic twist: "I thought someone was hitting on my girl because she was acting very strange. I thought she was trying to hook up with someone and I was really upset. Then I saw this guy with her. I was afraid she was going to be unfaithful, so I hit him in the face with a pipe."

- *A Brief but Close Involvement with a Criminal Other(s).* Individuals often develop close associations with criminal others over long periods of time, but sometimes the associations are more fleeting—lasting only hours, days, or weeks. This storyline can have a number of elements. The individual gets involved with another individual or group who entices them into committing a crime they would never have committed on their own. Success in a crime might lead to invitations for other crimes. Using this storyline, a person might say, "I was in a bar drinking when these guys I met told me that I could get some great weed for only $100 an ounce. I usually don't do things like that, but the price seemed so good I couldn't pass it up."

- *A Brief, Tempting Opportunity for Crime.* Individuals may develop or encounter tempting opportunities for crime that last from several hours to weeks. Being tempted means that the cost of crime is perceived as being low while the benefits are high and that this advantaged circumstance will persist for some time. This storyline might be, "I know this guy who is working as a security guard in an electronics store. He will sell me video games for $10 each that I know I can peddle on the street for $30. He can get me 50 games next week. Why pass up an easy $1,000? And besides, I can't get in trouble because I didn't really take the stuff myself."

Of course, individuals may experience more than one storyline at a time, each one contributing to or influencing another: a kid runs away from home, creating a desperate need for money; this gets him into disputes with other kids on the street, putting him in temporary contact with antisocial peers, and creates tempting opportunities for crime.

Agnew believes that storylines are the key to understanding the immediate cause of crime. The ebb and flow of storylines, partly a function of luck and chance, help explain why some people commit crime, then stop, only to start again. They also help us understand the context of crime, why it occurs in some situations and not others. A person may commit a violent act when he or she is in the midst of a domestic crisis, but resolve the same situation peacefully at another point in his or her life.

CRITICAL THINKING

1. What storylines do college students use when they cheat on tests? Smoke pot? Get drunk at a frat party? Are they similar to Agnew's vision?
2. If people use storylines to get involved in crime, are there ones that prevent or inhibit illegal activities?

SOURCE: Robert Agnew, "Storylines as a Neglected Cause of Crime," *Journal of Research in Crime and Delinquency* 43 (2006): 119–147.

Theory	Major Premise	Strengths	Research Focus
Anomie theory	People who adopt the goals of society but lack the means to attain them seek alternatives, such as crime.	Points out how competition for success creates conflict and crime. Suggests that social conditions and not personality can account for crime. Explains high lower-class crime rates.	Frustration; anomie; effects of failure to achieve goals.
Institutional anomie theory	The desire to accumulate wealth and material goods pervades all aspects of American life.	Explains why crime rates are so high in American culture.	Frustration; effects of materialism.
General strain theory	Strain has a variety of sources. Strain causes crime in the absence of adequate coping mechanisms.	Identifies the complexities of strain in modern society. Expands on anomie theory. Shows the influence of social events on behavior over the life course. Explains middle-class crimes.	Strain; inequality; negative affective states; influence of negative and positive stimuli.

EVALUATING GST

Agnew's work is important because it both clarifies the concept of strain and directs future research agendas. The model has been shown to predict crime and deviance within a number of subject, racial, gender, and age groups and in different cultures and nations.[204] It also addresses the dynamic nature of criminal behavior: levels of strain vary over the life course and so do crime rates. As levels of strain increase, so does involvement in antisocial activities; as strain levels decrease, so do individual crime rates.[205] Feelings of strain then appear to play a key role in offending continuity and change.[206]

One of the biggest question marks about GST is its ability to adequately explain gender differences in the crime rate. Females experience as much or more strain, frustration, and anger as males, but their crime rate is much lower. Is it possible that there are gender differences either (a) in the relationship between strain and criminality or (b) in the ability to cope with the effects of strain? Not all sources of strain produce the anger envisioned by Agnew.[207] Although females may experience more strain, males may be more deeply affected by interpersonal stress.[208]

There is evidence that stress influences both males and females equally; however, the degree to which it leads to criminal behavior is much higher among males than females.[209] When presented with similar types of strain,

males and females respond with a different constellation of negative emotions. Females may be socialized to internalize stress, blaming themselves for their problems; males may take the same type of strain and relieve it by striking out at others and deflecting criticism with aggression.[210] Consequently, males may resort to criminality in the face of stressors of any magnitude, but only extreme levels of strain produce violent reactions from women.[211] Males may also seek out their peers when they are faced with strain, whereas females are less inclined to confide in others. Male bonding with peers may actually increase their involvement with deviant behavior, a risk that is avoided by females. More effort is certainly needed to understand the cross-gender impact of strain.[212]

These issues aside, general strain theory has proven to be an enduring vision of the cause of criminality. Researchers have continued to show that people who perceive strain are the ones most likely to engage in delinquent activity.[213] Concept Summary 6.2 sets out the features of strain theories.

Cultural Deviance Theories

 Differentiate between the different forms of cultural deviance theory

The third branch of social structure theory combines the effects of social disorganization and strain to explain how people living in deteriorated neighborhoods react to social isolation and economic deprivation. Because their lifestyle is draining, frustrating, and dispiriting, members of the lower class create an independent **subculture** with its own set of

subcultures Groups that are loosely part of the dominant culture but maintain a unique set of values, beliefs, and traditions.

rules and values. Middle-class culture stresses hard work, delayed gratification, formal education, and being cautious; the lower-class subculture stresses excitement, toughness, risk taking, fearlessness, immediate gratification, and "street smarts." The lower-class subculture is an attractive alternative because the urban poor find that it is impossible to meet the behavioral demands of middle-class society.

Unfortunately, subcultural norms often clash with conventional values. People who have close personal ties to the neighborhood, especially when they are to deviant networks such as gangs and criminal groups, may find that community norms interfere with their personal desire for neighborhood improvement. So when the police are trying to solve a gang-related killing, neighbors may find that their loyalty to the gang boy and his family outweighs their desire to create a more stable crime-free community by giving information to the police.

Cultural deviance theory maintains that gang activity is a function of lack of opportunity that leads to an alternative lifestyle, often with tragic results. Here, a fight breaks out near mourners lining up before the funeral of Hadiya Pendleton, who was fatally shot on January 29, 2013, in what police say was a case of mistaken identity in a gang turf war. Pendleton, 15 and a sophomore at Martin Luther King Jr. College Prep, was shot as she and her friends shielded themselves from rain under a canopy in a Chicago park. She had performed with her school band eight days earlier at President Barack Obama's inauguration.

John Gress/Reuters/Landov

CONDUCT NORMS

The concept that the lower class develops a unique culture in response to strain can be traced to Thorsten Sellin's classic 1938 work, *Culture Conflict and Crime*, a theoretical attempt to link cultural adaptation to criminality.[214] Sellin's main premise is that criminal law is an expression of the rules of the dominant culture. The content of the law, therefore, may create a clash between conventional, middle-class rules and splinter groups, such as ethnic and racial minorities who are excluded from the social mainstream. These groups maintain their own set of **conduct norms**—rules governing the day-to-day living conditions within these subcultures.[215] Conduct norms can be found in almost any culture and are not the property of any particular group, culture, or political structure.

Complicating matters is the fact that most of us belong to several social groups. In a complex society, the number of groups people belong to—family, peer, occupational, and religious—is quite large. "A conflict of norms is said to exist when more or less divergent rules of conduct govern the specific life situation in which a person may find himself."[216] According to Sellin, **culture conflict** occurs when the rules expressed in the criminal law clash with the demands of group conduct norms. To make his point, Sellin cited the case of a Sicilian father in New Jersey who killed the 16-year-old boy who seduced his daughter and then expressed surprise at being arrested. He claimed that he had "merely defended his family honor in a traditional way."[217]

FOCAL CONCERNS

In his classic 1958 paper, "Lower Class Culture as a Generating Milieu of Gang Delinquency," Walter Miller identified the unique value system that defines lower-class culture.[218] Conformance to these **focal concerns** dominates life among

conduct norms Behaviors expected of social group members. If group norms conflict with those of the general culture, members of the group may find themselves described as outcasts or criminals.

culture conflict According to Sellin, a condition brought about when the rules and norms of an individual's subcultural affiliation conflict with the role demands of conventional society.

focal concerns According to Miller, the value orientations of lower-class cultures; features include the needs for excitement, trouble, smartness, and personal autonomy.

the lower class. According to Miller, clinging to lower-class focal concerns promotes illegal or violent behavior. Toughness may mean displaying fighting prowess; street smarts may lead to drug deals; excitement may result in drinking, gambling, or drug abuse. Focal concerns do not necessarily represent a rebellion against middle-class values; rather, these values have evolved specifically to fit conditions in lower-class areas. The major lower-class focal concerns are set out in Exhibit 6.1.[219]

It is this adherence to the prevailing cultural demands of lower-class society that causes urban crime. Research, in fact, shows that members of the lower class value toughness and want to show they are courageous in the face of provocation.[220] A reputation for toughness helps them acquire social power while at the same time insulating them from becoming victims. Violence is also seen as a means to acquire the accouterments of wealth (nice clothes, flashy cars, or access to clubs), control or humiliate another person, defy authority, settle drug-related "business" disputes, attain retribution, satisfy the need for thrills or risk taking, and respond to challenges to one's manhood.[221]

To some criminologists, the influence of lower-class focal concerns and culture seems as relevant today as when first identified by Miller more than 50 years ago. The Race, Culture, Gender, and Criminology feature "The Code of the Streets" discusses a more recent version of the concept of cultural deviance.

THEORY OF DELINQUENT SUBCULTURES

Albert Cohen first articulated the theory of delinquent subcultures in his classic 1955 book *Delinquent Boys*.[222] Cohen's central position was that delinquent behavior of lower-class youths is actually a protest against the norms and values of middle-class U.S. culture. Because social conditions make them incapable of achieving success legitimately, lower-class youths experience a form of culture conflict that Cohen labels **status frustration**.[223] As a result, many of them join together in gangs and engage in behavior that is "nonutilitarian, malicious, and negativistic."[224]

Cohen viewed the delinquent gang as a separate subculture, possessing a value system directly opposed to that of the larger society. He describes the subculture as one that "takes its norms from the larger culture, but turns them upside down. The delinquent's conduct is right by the standards of his subculture precisely because it is wrong by the norms of the larger culture."[225]

According to Cohen, the development of the delinquent subculture is a consequence of socialization practices found in the ghetto or inner-city environment. These children lack

status frustration A form of culture conflict experienced by lower-class youths because social conditions prevent them from achieving success as defined by the larger society.

EXHIBIT 6.1

Miller's Lower-Class Focal Concerns

TROUBLE

In lower-class communities, people are evaluated by their actual or potential involvement in making trouble. Getting into trouble includes such behavior as fighting, drinking, and sexual misconduct. Dealing with trouble can confer prestige—for example, when a man establishes a reputation for being able to handle himself well in a fight. Not being able to handle trouble, and having to pay the consequences, can make a person look foolish and incompetent.

TOUGHNESS

Lower-class males want local recognition of their physical and spiritual toughness. They refuse to be sentimental or soft and instead value physical strength, fighting ability, and athletic skill. Those who cannot meet these standards risk getting a reputation for being weak, inept, and effeminate.

SMARTNESS

Members of the lower-class culture want to maintain an image of being streetwise and savvy, using their street smarts, and having the ability to outfox and out-con the opponent. Though formal education is not admired, knowing essential survival techniques, such as gambling, conning, and outsmarting the law, is a requirement.

EXCITEMENT

Members of the lower class search for fun and excitement to enliven an otherwise drab existence. The search for excitement may lead to gambling, fighting, getting drunk, and sexual adventures. In between, the lower-class citizen may simply "hang out" and "be cool."

FATE

Lower-class citizens believe their lives are in the hands of strong spiritual forces that guide their destinies. Getting lucky, finding good fortune, and hitting the jackpot are all slum dwellers' daily dreams.

AUTONOMY

Being independent of authority figures, such as the police, teachers, and parents, is required. Losing control is an unacceptable weakness, incompatible with toughness.

SOURCE: Walter Miller, "Lower Class Culture as a Generating Milieu of Gang Delinquency," *Journal of Social Issues* 14 (1958): 5–19.

the basic skills necessary to achieve social and economic success in the demanding U.S. society. They also lack the proper education and therefore do not have the skills upon which to build a knowledge or socialization foundation. He suggests that lower-class parents are incapable of teaching children the necessary techniques for entering the dominant

The Code of the Streets

A widely cited view of the interrelationship of culture and behavior is Elijah Anderson's concept of the "code of the streets." He sees that life circumstances are tough for the "ghetto poor"—lack of jobs that pay a living wage, stigma of race, fallout from rampant drug use and drug trafficking, and alienation and lack of hope for the future. Living in such an environment places young people at special risk of crime and deviant behavior.

There are two cultural forces running through the neighborhood that shape their reactions. *Decent values* are taught by families committed to middle-class values and representing mainstream goals and standards of behavior. Though they may be better off financially than some of their street-oriented neighbors, they are generally "working poor." They value hard work and self-reliance and are willing to sacrifice for their families; they harbor hopes for a better future for their children. Most go to church and take a strong interest in education. Some see their difficult situation as a test from God and derive great support from their faith and from the church community.

In opposition, *street values* are born in the despair of inner-city life and are in opposition to those of mainstream society. The street culture has developed what Anderson calls a code of the streets, a set of informal rules setting down both proper attitudes and ways to respond if challenged. If the rules are violated, there are penalties and sometimes violent retribution.

At the heart of the code is the issue of respect—loosely defined as being "treated right." The code demands that disrespect be punished or hard-won respect will be lost. With the right amount of respect, a person can avoid being bothered in public. If he is bothered, not only may he be in physical danger, but he has been disgraced or "dissed" (disrespected). Some forms of dissing, such as maintaining eye contact for too long, may seem pretty mild. But to street kids who live by the code, these actions become serious indications of the other person's intentions and a warning of imminent physical confrontation.

These two orientations—decent and street—socially organize the community.

Their coexistence means that kids who are brought up in decent homes must be able to successfully navigate the demands of the street culture. Even in decent families, parents recognize that the code must be obeyed or at the very least negotiated; it cannot simply be ignored.

The Respect Game

Young men in poor inner-city neighborhoods build their self-image on the foundation of respect. Having "juice" (as respect is sometimes called on the street) means that they can take care of themselves even if it means resorting to violence. For street youth, losing respect on the street can be damaging and dangerous. Once they have demonstrated that they can be insulted, beaten up, or stolen from, they become an easy target. Kids from decent families may be able to keep their self-respect by getting good grades or a scholarship. Street kids do not have that luxury. With nothing to fall back on, they cannot walk away from an insult. They must retaliate with violence.

One method of preventing attacks is to go on the offensive. Aggressive, violence-prone people are not seen as easy prey. Robbers do not get robbed, and street fighters are not the favorite targets of bullies. A youth who communicates an image of not being afraid to die and not being afraid to kill has given himself a sense of power on the street.

Testing the Theory

A number of researchers have found that the code of the streets does in fact exist and that Anderson's observations are in fact valid. Jeffrey Fagan found that the street code's rules for getting and maintaining respect through aggressive behavior forced many "decent" youths to situationally adopt a tough demeanor and behave violently in order to survive an otherwise hostile and dangerous environment. Eric Stewart and Ronald Simons found that adolescents living in urban neighborhoods are often forced to accept the street code even if it violates their own personal values and attitudes. Failure to do so threatens their life and well-being. In another recent study, Kristy Matsuda and

her associates found that kids who join a gang also increase their street code–related attitudes and emotions. Those whose loyalty to the code of the streets is the greatest also experience the greatest frequency of violent offending.

Gender and social differences have also been found to exist. Males seem more likely to accept the code than females, though many girls also embrace the code. Boys who report experiencing racial discrimination maintain stronger street code beliefs that last into adulthood. Adolescents with strong family ties are more likely to embrace decent values, while those whose family is less influential are more likely to hold street code beliefs. In sum, the weight of the evidence supports the validity of Anderson's groundbreaking research.

CRITICAL THINKING

1. Does the code of the street, as described by Anderson, apply in the neighborhood in which you were raised? That is, is it universal?
2. Is there a form of "respect game" being played out on college campuses? If so, what is the substitute for violence?

SOURCES: Elijah Anderson, *Code of the Street: Decency, Violence, and the Moral Life of the Inner City* (New York: Norton, 2000); Richard Moule, Jr., Callie Burt, Eric Stewart, and Ronald Simons, "Developmental Trajectories of Individuals' Code of the Street Beliefs Through Emerging Adulthood," *Journal of Research in Crime and Delinquency* 52 (2015) 342–372; Jeffrey Nowacki, "Sugar, Spice, and Street Codes: The Influences of Gender and Family Attachment on Street Code Adoption," *Deviant Behavior* 33 (2012): 831–844; Eric Stewart and Ronald Simons, "Race, Code of the Street, and Violent Delinquency: A Multilevel Investigation of Neighborhood Street Culture and Individual Norms of Violence," *Criminology* 482 (2010): 569–606; Eric Stewart and Ronald Simons, "Structure and Culture in African American Adolescent Violence: A Partial Test of the 'Code of the Street' Thesis," *Justice Quarterly* 23 (2006): 1–33; Jeffrey Fagan, "Adolescent Violence: A View from the Street," NIJ Research Preview (Washington, DC: National Institute of Justice, 1998); Kristy Matsuda, Chris Melde, Terrance Taylor, Adrienne Freng, and Finn-Aage Esbensen, "Gang Membership and Adherence to the 'Code of the Street,'" *Justice Quarterly* 30 (2013): 440–468.

middle-class culture. The consequences of this deprivation include developmental handicaps, poor speech and communication skills, and inability to delay gratification.

Middle-Class Measuring Rods   One significant handicap that lower-class children face is the inability to positively impress authority figures, such as teachers, employers, or supervisors. Cohen calls the standards set by these authority figures **middle-class measuring rods**. The conflict and frustration lower-class youths experience when they fail to meet these standards is a primary cause of delinquency. For example, the fact that a lower-class student is deemed by those in power to be substandard or below the average of what is expected can have an important impact on his or her future life chances. A school record may be reviewed by juvenile court authorities and by the military. Because a military record can influence whether or not someone is qualified for certain jobs, it is quite influential.[226] Negative evaluations become part of a permanent file that follows an individual for the rest of his or her life. When he or she wants to improve, evidence of prior failures is used to discourage advancement.

The Formation of Deviant Subcultures   Cohen believes lower-class boys who suffer rejection by middle-class decision makers usually elect to join one of three existing subcultures: the corner boy, the college boy, or the delinquent boy. The **corner boy** role is the most common response to middle-class rejection. The corner boy is not a chronic delinquent, but may be a truant who engages in petty or status offenses, such as precocious sex and recreational drug abuse. His main loyalty is to his peer group, on which he depends for support, motivation, and interest. His values,

therefore, are those of the group with which he is in close personal contact. The corner boy, well aware of his failure to achieve the standards of the American Dream, retreats into the comforting world of his lower-class peers and eventually becomes a stable member of his neighborhood, holding a menial job, marrying, and remaining in the community.

The **college boy** embraces the cultural and social values of the middle class. Rather than scorning middle-class measuring rods, he actively strives to be successful by those standards. Cohen views this type of youth as one who is embarking on an almost hopeless path since he is ill-equipped academically, socially, and linguistically to achieve the rewards of middle-class life.

The **delinquent boy** adopts a set of norms and principles in direct opposition to middle-class values. He engages in short-run hedonism, living for today and letting "tomorrow take care of itself."[227] Delinquent boys strive for group autonomy. They resist efforts by family, school, or other sources of authority to control their behavior. They may join a gang because it is perceived as autonomous, independent, and the focus of "attraction, loyalty, and solidarity."[228] Frustrated by their inability to succeed, these boys resort to a process Cohen calls **reaction formation**. Symptoms of reaction formation include overly intense responses that seem disproportionate to the stimuli that trigger them. For the delinquent boy, this takes the form of irrational, malicious, and unaccountable hostility to the enemy, which in this case are "the norms of respectable middle-class society."[229] Reaction formation causes delinquent boys to overreact to any perceived threat or slight. They sneer at the college boy's attempts at assimilation and scorn the corner boy's passivity. The delinquent boy is willing to take risks, violate the law, and flout middle-class conventions.

Cohen's work helps explain the factors that promote and sustain a delinquent subculture. By introducing the concepts of status frustration and middle-class measuring rods, Cohen makes it clear that social forces and not individual traits promote and sustain a delinquent career. By introducing the corner boy, college boy, delinquent boy triad, he helps explain why many lower-class youth fail to become chronic offenders: there is more than one social path open to indigent youth.[230] His work is a skillful integration of strain and social disorganization theories and has become an enduring element of the criminological literature.

THEORY OF DIFFERENTIAL OPPORTUNITY

In their classic work *Delinquency and Opportunity*, written more than 50 years ago, Richard Cloward and Lloyd Ohlin combined strain and social disorganization principles into a portrayal of a gang-sustaining criminal subculture.[231] Cloward and Ohlin agreed with Cohen and found that independent delinquent subcultures exist within society. They consider a delinquent subculture to be one in which certain forms of delinquent activity are essential requirements for performing the dominant roles supported by the subculture.[232]

---

middle-class measuring rods According to Cohen, the standards by which teachers and other representatives of state authority evaluate lower-class youths. Because they cannot live up to middle-class standards, lower-class youths are bound for failure, which gives rise to frustration and anger at conventional society.

corner boy According to Cohen, a role in the lower-class culture in which young men remain in their birth neighborhood, acquire families and menial jobs, and adjust to the demands of their environment.

college boy A disadvantaged youth who embraces the cultural and social values of the middle class and actively strives to be successful by those standards. This type of youth is embarking on an almost hopeless path because he is ill-equipped academically, socially, and linguistically to achieve the rewards of middle-class life.

delinquent boy A youth who adopts a set of norms and principles in direct opposition to middle-class values, engaging in short-run hedonism, living for today and letting tomorrow take care of itself.

reaction formation According to Cohen, rejecting goals and standards that seem impossible to achieve. Because a boy cannot hope to get into college, for example, he considers higher education a waste of time.

The lack of opportunity creates the social condition in which gangs thrive. Violence then becomes routine. On April 6, 2015, Frank Reyos (right) sits with his defense team during his sentencing in Salt Lake City. Reyos, convicted in the shooting death of a teenage boy, was sentenced to life in prison without parole. Reyos killed 16-year-old Kenyatta Winston with a single bullet to the back of the head in 2012 as retribution after Winston left him behind during a gunfight with gang members the day before.

AP Images/Al Hartmann

Youth gangs are an important part of the delinquent subculture. Although not all illegal acts are committed by gang youth, they are the source of the most serious, sustained, and costly criminal behaviors. Delinquent gangs spring up in disorganized areas where youths lack the opportunity to gain success through conventional means. True to strain theory principles, Cloward and Ohlin portray inner-city kids as individuals who want to conform to middle-class values but lack the means to do so.[233]

Differential Opportunities   The centerpiece of the Cloward and Ohlin theory is the concept of **differential opportunity**, which states that people in all strata of society share the same success goals but that those in the lower class have limited means of achieving them. People who perceive themselves as failures within conventional society will seek alternative or innovative ways to gain success. People who conclude that there is little hope for advancement by legitimate means may join with like-minded peers to form a gang. Gang members provide the emotional support to handle the shame, fear, or guilt they may develop while engaging in illegal acts. Delinquent subcultures then reward these acts that conventional society would punish. The youth who is considered a failure at school and is only qualified for a menial job at a minimum wage can earn thousands of

dollars plus the respect of his or her peers by joining a gang and engaging in drug deals or armed robberies.

Cloward and Ohlin recognize that the opportunity for both successful conventional and criminal careers is limited. In stable areas, adolescents may be recruited by professional criminals, drug traffickers, or organized crime groups. Unstable areas, however, cannot support flourishing criminal opportunities. In these socially disorganized neighborhoods, adult role models are absent, and young criminals have few opportunities to join established gangs or to learn the fine points of professional crime. Cloward and Ohlin's most important finding, then, is that all opportunities for success, both illegal and conventional, are closed for the most truly disadvantaged youth.

Because of differential opportunity, kids are likely to join one of three types of gangs:

- *Criminal gangs.* Criminal gangs exist in stable lower-class areas in which close connections among adolescent, young adult, and adult offenders create an environment for successful criminal enterprise.[234] Youths are recruited into established criminal gangs that provide a training ground for a successful criminal career. Gang membership provides a learning experience in which the knowledge and skills needed for success in crime are acquired. During this "apprenticeship stage," older, more experienced members of the criminal subculture hold youthful "trainees" on tight reins, limiting activities that might jeopardize the gang's profits (for example, engaging in nonfunctional, irrational violence). Over time, new recruits learn the techniques and attitudes of the criminal world and how to "cooperate successfully with others in criminal enterprises."[235] To become a fully accepted member of the criminal gang, novices must prove themselves reliable and dependable in their contacts with their criminal associates.

- *Conflict gangs.* Conflict gangs develop in communities unable to provide either legitimate or illegitimate opportunities. These highly disorganized areas are marked by transient residents and physical deterioration. Crime in this area is "individualistic, unorganized, petty, poorly paid, and unprotected."[236] There are no successful adult criminal role models from whom youths can learn criminal skills. When such severe limitations on both criminal and conventional opportunity intensify frustrations of the young, violence is used as a means of gaining status. The image of the conflict gang member is the swaggering, tough adolescent who fights with weapons to win respect from rivals and engages in unpredictable and destructive assaults on people and property. Conflict

differential opportunity The view that lower-class youths, whose legitimate opportunities are limited, join gangs and pursue criminal careers as alternative means to achieve universal success goals.

gang members must be ready to fight to protect their own and their gang's integrity and honor. By doing so, they acquire a "rep," which provides them with a means for gaining admiration from their peers and consequently helps them develop their own self-image. Conflict gangs, according to Cloward and Ohlin, "represent a way of securing access to the scarce resources for adolescent pleasure and opportunity in underprivileged areas."[237]

■ *Retreatist gangs.* Retreatists are double failures, unable to gain success through legitimate means and unwilling to do so through illegal ones. Some retreatists have tried crime or violence but are too clumsy, weak, or scared to be accepted in criminal or violent gangs. They then retreat into a role on the fringe of society. Members of the retreatist subculture constantly search for ways of getting high—alcohol, pot, heroin, unusual sexual experiences, music. They are always "cool," detached from relationships with the conventional world. To feed their habit, retreatists develop a "hustle"—pimping, conning, selling drugs, and committing petty crimes. Personal status in the retreatist subculture is derived from peer approval.

EVALUATING SOCIAL STRUCTURE THEORIES

The social structure approach has significantly influenced both criminological theory and crime-prevention strategies. Its core concepts seem to be valid in view of the relatively high crime and delinquency rates and gang activity occurring in the deteriorated inner-city areas of the nation's largest cities.[238] The public's image of the disorganized inner city includes roaming bands of violent teenage gangs, drug users, prostitutes, muggers, and similar frightening examples of criminality. All of these are present today in inner-city areas.

Critics of the approach charge that we cannot be sure that it is lower-class culture itself that promotes crime and not some other force operating in society. They deny that residence in urban areas alone is sufficient to cause people to violate the law.[239] It is possible, they counter, that lower-class crime rates may be an artifact of bias in the criminal justice system. Numerous studies indicate that police use extensive discretion when arresting people and that social status is one factor that influences their decisions.[240] It is possible that adolescents in middle-class neighborhoods commit criminal acts that never show up in official statistics, whereas people in lower-class areas face a far greater chance of arrest and court adjudication.[241] In addition, police are more aggressive in lower-class areas and residents are more likely to be arrested and prosecuted for acts that would be treated informally (for example, a warning) in middle-class suburbs. After all, police and prosecutors are members of the middle and upper classes themselves, so it's not surprising that they exhibit class and racial bias.[242]

Even if the higher crime rates recorded in lower-class areas are valid, it is still true that most members of the lower class are not criminals. The discovery of the chronic offender indicates that a significant majority of people living in lower-class environments are not criminals and that a relatively small proportion of the population commits most crimes. If social forces alone could be used to explain crime, how can we account for the vast number of urban poor who remain honest and law abiding? Given these circumstances, law violators must be motivated by some individual mental, physical, or social process or trait.[243]

It is also questionable whether a distinct lower-class culture actually exists. Several researchers have found that gang members and other delinquent youths seem to value

CONCEPT SUMMARY 6.3
Cultural Deviance Theories

Theory	Major Premise	Strengths	Research Focus
Miller's focal concern theory	Citizens who obey the street rules of lower-class life (focal concerns) find themselves in conflict with the dominant culture.	Identifies the core values of lower-class culture and shows their association to crime.	Cultural norms; focal concerns.
Cohen's theory of delinquent gangs	Status frustration of lower-class boys, created by their failure to achieve middle-class success, causes them to join gangs.	Shows how the conditions of lower-class life produce crime. Explains violence and destructive acts. Identifies conflict of lower class with middle class.	Gangs; culture conflict; middle-class measuring rods; reaction formation.
Cloward and Ohlin's theory of opportunity	Blockage of conventional opportunities causes lower-class youths to join criminal, conflict, or retreatist gangs.	Shows that even illegal opportunities are structured in society. Indicates why people become involved in a particular type of criminal activity. Presents a way of preventing crime.	Gangs; cultural norms; culture conflict; effects of blocked opportunity.

middle-class concepts, such as sharing, earning money, and respecting the law, as highly as middle-class youths. Criminologists contend that lower-class youths also value education as highly as middle-class students do.[244] Public opinion polls can also be used as evidence that a majority of lower-class citizens maintain middle-class values. National surveys find that people in the lowest income brackets want tougher drug laws, more police protection, and greater control over criminal offenders.[245] These opinions seem similar to conventional middle-class values rather than representative of an independent, deviant subculture. While this evidence contradicts some of the central ideas of social structure theory, the discovery of stable patterns of lower-class crime, the high crime rates found in disorganized inner-city areas, and the rise of teenage gangs and groups support a close association between crime rates and social class position.

Concept Summary 6.3 sets out the features of cultural deviance theories.

Public Policy Implications of Social Structure Theory

Social structure theory has had a significant influence on public policy. If the cause of criminality is viewed as a schism between lower-class individuals and conventional goals, norms, and rules, it seems logical that alternatives to criminal behavior can be provided by giving inner-city dwellers opportunities to share in the rewards of conventional society. One approach is to give indigent people direct financial aid through welfare programs that assist needy families. Although welfare has been curtailed through the Federal Welfare Reform Act of 1996, research shows that crime rates decrease when families receive supplemental income through public assistance payments.[246]

There are also efforts to reduce crime by improving the community structure in high-crime inner-city areas. Crime-prevention efforts based on social structure precepts can be traced back to the Chicago Area Project, supervised by Clifford R. Shaw. This program attempted to organize existing community structures to develop social stability in otherwise disorganized lower-class neighborhoods. The project sponsored recreation programs for children in the neighborhoods, including summer camping. It campaigned for community improvements in such areas as education, sanitation, traffic safety, physical conservation, and law enforcement. Project members also worked with police and court agencies to supervise and treat gang youth and adult offenders. In a 25-year assessment of the project, Solomon Kobrin found that it was successful in demonstrating the feasibility of creating youth welfare organizations in high-delinquency areas.[247] Kobrin also discovered that the project made a distinct contribution to ending the isolation of urban males from the mainstream of society.

Washington Post/Getty Images

While gentrification can produce dramatic positive change in neighborhood dynamics, it may also cause community-wide strain. Signs of transition can be seen in the Park View neighborhood in Washington, D.C. As the neighborhood shows clear signs of gentrification, crime and violence have spiked in the area.

Social structure concepts, especially Cloward and Ohlin's views, were a critical ingredient in the Kennedy and Johnson administrations' War on Poverty, begun in the early 1960s. Some of the War on Poverty programs—Head Start, Neighborhood Legal Services, and the Community Action Program—have continued to help people to this day.

More recently, a government-funded program, Weed and Seed, involved a two-pronged approach: law enforcement agencies and prosecutors cooperated in "weeding out" violent criminals and drug abusers, and public agencies and community-based private organizations collaborated to "seed" much-needed human services, including prevention, intervention, treatment, and neighborhood restoration programs. However, funding for this program ended in 2012.

Another contemporary approach is the Communities That Care (CTC) model, a national program that emphasizes the reduction of risk factors and the enhancement of protective factors against crime and delinquency. One example of the CTC approach is Project COPE, which serves the Lynn, Massachusetts, area. Established in 2004, COPE works collaboratively with multiple local agencies, including Girls Incorporated of Lynn, the city's health department, police department, public schools, and other agencies whose goals include reducing risk factors for youth and promoting healthy family and neighborhood development. The coalition includes a large and active youth subcommittee. Originally focused on substance abuse prevention in youth, the coalition expanded its initiatives to include the prevention of fatal and nonfatal opiate overdoses, teen suicide, teen pregnancy, bullying and violence, and obesity. Project COPE cares for individuals of all ages. As an advocate for individuals needing specialized services, COPE assumes the responsibility for leadership in developing new and creative programs and addressing the needs of the many populations it serves.[248] In 2014, COPE merged with Bridgewell, a larger service organization that provides residential services, day habilitation, behavioral health services, employment training, transitional homeless services, affordable housing, and substance abuse and addiction services.

COMMUNITY POLICING

The criminal justice system has also been shaped by social structure theory. Corresponding to the broken windows concept of community disorder, police programs have been designed to reduce social disorder by concentrating on lifestyle crimes such as panhandling, loitering, and vandalism. Broken windows policing, more commonly called community policing, holds that police administrators would be well advised to deploy their forces where they can encourage public confidence, strengthen feelings of safety, and elicit cooperation from citizens. Community preservation, public safety, and order maintenance—not crime fighting—become the primary focus of patrol. Put another way, just as physicians and dentists practice preventive medicine and dentistry, police should help maintain an intact community structure rather than simply fighting crime.

Community-oriented policing (COP) also emphasizes sharing power with local groups and individuals. A key element of the community-oriented policing philosophy is that citizens must actively participate with police to fight crime. Such participation is essential because the community climate is influenced by the informal social control created by a concerned citizenry coupled with effective policing.[249] Participation might involve providing information in area-wide crime investigations or helping police reach out to troubled youths. To achieve the goals

THINKING LIKE A CRIMINOLOGIST

An Ethical Dilemma

Reducing Poverty, Crime, and Drug Abuse in an Urban Neighborhood

You have just been appointed as a presidential adviser on urban problems. The president informs you that she wants to initiate a demonstration project in a major city aimed at showing that the government can do something to reduce poverty, crime, and drug abuse. The area she has chosen for development is a large inner-city neighborhood with more than a hundred thousand residents. The neighborhood suffers from disorganized community structure, poverty, and hopelessness. Predatory delinquent gangs run free and terrorize local merchants and citizens. The school system has failed to provide opportunities and education experiences sufficient to dampen enthusiasm for gang recruitment. Stores, homes, and public buildings are deteriorated and decayed. Commercial enterprise has fled the area, and civil servants are reluctant to enter the neighborhood. There is an uneasy truce among the various ethnic and racial groups that populate the area. Residents feel that little can be done to bring the neighborhood back to life.

You are faced with suggesting an urban redevelopment program that can revitalize the area and eventually bring down the crime rate. You can bring any element of the public and private sector to bear on this rather overwhelming problem—including the military! You can also ask private industry to help in the struggle, promising them tax breaks for their participation. But before you even begin to create the program you have to ask yourself these basic questions:

Does living and growing up in such an area contribute to high crime and delinquency rates? Is poverty a cause of crime or merely an excuse used to rationalize crime and drug use? Do deviant places create deviant people, or vice versa? After all, when middle-class yuppies move into a poor area and gentrify it, crime rates eventually go down and property values go up. Is it ethical to ask the government to help revitalize communities? Why should my tax money go to increasing the real estate values in another neighborhood owned by another person? Is that fair and just? Answer these questions in a memo to the president.

of COP, some police agencies have tried to decentralize.[250] According to this view, problem solving is best done at the neighborhood level where issues originate, not at a far-off central headquarters. Because each neighborhood has its own particular needs, police decision making must be flexible and adaptive. Neighborhoods undergoing change in racial composition may experience high levels of racially motivated violence and require special police initiatives to reduce tensions.[251]

Does it work? New York City's emphasis on broken windows policing was credited with producing significant declines in that city's crime rate. In one of the most rigorous tests of broken windows theory, researchers identified 34 crime-ridden areas in Lowell, Massachusetts, half of which received broken windows policing, the other half regular patrol. Results revealed substantial reductions in crime, disorder, and calls for service in the treatment areas but not in the control areas.[252]

SUMMARY

L01 Trace the history of sociological criminology

The application of sociological concepts to criminology can be traced to the works of pioneering sociologists L. A. J. (Adolphe) Quetelet, who used data and statistics in performing research on criminal activity, and (David) Émile Durkheim, who defined crime as a normal and necessary social event. These perspectives have been extremely influential on modern criminology. The primacy of sociological positivism as the intellectual basis of criminology was secured by research begun by the sociology department at the University of Chicago, which pioneered research on the social ecology of the city. Regardless of their race, religion, or ethnicity, the everyday behavior of people was controlled by the social and ecological climate in which they dwelled. According to the Chicago School views, criminal behavior is not then a function of personal traits or choice but is linked to environmental conditions that fail to provide residents with proper human relations and development.

L02 Clarify the association between social structure and crime

According to social structure theory, the root cause of crime can be traced directly to the socioeconomic disadvantages that have become embedded in American society. People in the United States live in a stratified society; social strata are created by the unequal distribution of wealth, power, and prestige. The crushing lifestyle of lower-class areas produces a culture of poverty that is passed from one generation to the next and is stained by apathy, cynicism, helplessness, and mistrust of social institutions. Lower-class people are driven to desperate measures, such as crime and substance abuse, to cope with their economic plight. Aggravating this dynamic is the constant media bombardment linking material possessions to self-worth.

L03 Give examples of the elements of social disorganization theory

Crime occurs in disorganized areas where institutions of social control, such as the family, commercial establishments, and schools, have broken down and can no longer perform their expected or stated functions. Indicators of social disorganization include high unemployment and school dropout rates, deteriorated housing, low income levels, and large numbers of single-parent households. Residents in these areas experience conflict and despair, and, as a result, antisocial behavior flourishes.

L04 Explain the views of Shaw and McKay

Shaw and McKay explained crime and delinquency within the context of the changing urban environment and ecological development of the city. Poverty-ridden transitional neighborhoods suffered high rates of population turnover and were incapable of inducing residents to remain and defend the neighborhoods against criminal groups. The values that slum youths adopt often conflict with existing middle-class norms, which demand strict obedience to the legal code. Consequently, a value conflict further separates the delinquent youth and his or her peer group from conventional society; the result is a more solid embrace of deviant goals and behavior.

L05 Differentiate between the various elements of ecological theory

Crime rates and the need for police services are associated with community deterioration: disorder, poverty, alienation, disassociation, and fear of crime. In larger cities, neighborhoods with a high percentage of deserted houses and apartments experience high crime rates. In disorganized neighborhoods that suffer social and physical incivilities that cause fear, as fear increases, quality of life deteriorates. People who live in neighborhoods that experience high levels of crime and civil disorder become suspicious and mistrusting and may develop a "siege mentality." As areas decline, residents flee to safer, more stable localities. Transitional neighborhoods have very high crime rates.

L06 Discuss the association between collective efficacy and crime

Cohesive communities develop collective efficacy: mutual trust, a willingness to intervene in the supervision of children, and the maintenance of public order. Some elements of collective efficacy operate on the primary, or private, level and involve peers, families, and relatives. Communities that have collective efficacy attempt to use their local institutions to control crime. Stable neighborhoods are also able to arrange for external sources of social control, such as more police on patrol, that further reduce crime rates.

L07 Articulate what is meant by the concepts of strain and anomie

Anomie is a condition that occurs because while social and economic goals are common to people in all economic strata, the ability to obtain these goals is class dependent. Most people in the United States desire wealth, material possessions, power, prestige, and other life comforts. Anomie occurs among members of the lower class who are unable to achieve these symbols of success through conventional means. Consequently, they feel anger, frustration, and resentment, referred to collectively as strain.

L08 Compare and contrast between the different elements in Merton's theory of anomie

Merton argues that in the United States legitimate means to acquire wealth are stratified across class and status lines. Some people have inadequate means of attaining success; others who have the means reject societal goals. To resolve the goals–means conflict and relieve their sense of strain, some people innovate by stealing or extorting money; others retreat into drugs and alcohol; some rebel by joining revolutionary groups; and still others get involved in ritualistic behavior by joining a religious cult.

L09 Clarify what Agnew means by the concept of negative affective states

Agnew suggests that criminality is the direct result of negative affective states—the anger, frustration, and adverse emotions that emerge in the wake of destructive social relationships. He finds that negative affective states are produced by a variety of sources of strain, including the failure to achieve success, application of negative stimuli, and removal of positive stimuli.

L010 Differentiate between the different forms of cultural deviance theory

Cultural deviance theory combines elements of both strain and social disorganization theories. A unique lower-class culture has developed in disorganized neighborhoods. These independent subcultures maintain unique values and beliefs that conflict with conventional social norms. Criminal behavior is an expression of conformity to lower-class subcultural values and traditions, not a rebellion from conventional society. Subcultural values are handed down from one generation to the next.

CRITICAL THINKING QUESTIONS

1. Is there a "transition" area in your town or city? Does the crime rate remain constant in this neighborhood regardless of the racial, ethnic, or cultural composition of its residents?
2. Do you believe a distinct lower-class culture exists? Do you know anyone who has the focal concerns Miller talks about? Did you experience elements of these focal concerns while you were in high school? Do forms of communication such as the Internet reduce cultural differences and create a more homogenous society, or are subcultures resistant to such influences?
3. Do you agree with Agnew that there is more than one cause of strain? If so, are there other sources of strain that he did not consider?
4. How would a structural theorist explain the presence of middle-class crime?
5. How would biosocial theories explain the high levels of violent crime in lower-class areas?

KEY TERMS

socially disorganized (190)
stratified society (191)
social classes (191)
underclass (191)
culture of poverty (191)
at-risk (191)
social structure theory (196)
social disorganization theory (196)
strain theory (197)
strain (197)

cultural deviance theory (197)
transitional neighborhoods (198)
concentration effect (200)
incivilities (201)
siege mentality (202)
gentrification (203)
collective efficacy (203)
street efficacy (205)
relative deprivation (205)
anomie (206)

mechanical solidarity (206)
organic solidarity (206)
theory of anomie (207)
institutional anomie theory (IAT) (208)
American Dream (208)
general strain theory (GST) (210)
negative affective states (210)
subcultures (214)
conduct norms (215)

culture conflict (215)
focal concerns (215)
status frustration (216)
middle-class measuring rods (218)
corner boy (218)
college boy (218)
delinquent boy (218)
reaction formation (218)
differential opportunity (219)

NOTES

All URLs accessed in 2016.

1. U.S. Attorney's Office, Northern District of Georgia, "MS-13 Members Sentenced for a Murder and Shooting," February 13, 2015, http://www.justice.gov/usao-ndga /pr/ms-13-members-sentenced-murder -and-shooting.

2. Alexandra Limon, "Spike in Homicides Linked to MS-13," Fox News, January 7, 2016, http://www.fox5dc.com/news/local -news/70663508-story.

3. Arian Campo-Flores, "The Most Dangerous Gang in the United States," *Newsweek*, March 28, 2006; Ricardo Pollack, "Gang Life Tempts Salvador Teens," BBC News, http://news.bbc.co.uk/2/hi/americas /4201183.stm.

4. FBI, "The MS-13 Threat, A National Assessment," January 14, 2008, http:// www.fbi.gov/page2/jan08/ms13_011408 .html.

5. Arlen Egley, Jr., James Howell, and Meena Harris, *Highlights of the 2012 National Youth Gang Survey* (Washington, DC: Office of Juvenile Justice and Delinquency Prevention, 2014), http://www.ojjdp.gov /pubs/248025.pdf.

6. Steven Messner and Richard Rosenfeld, *Crime and the American Dream* (Belmont, CA: Wadsworth, 1994), p. 11.

7. Gregory M. Zimmerman, "Impulsivity, Offending, and the Neighborhood: Investigating the Person–Context Nexus," *Journal of Quantitative Criminology*, published online June 3, 2010.

8. See, generally, Robert Nisbet, *The Sociology of Émile Durkheim* (New York: Oxford University Press, 1974).

9. L. A. J. Quetelet, *A Treatise on Man and the Development of His Faculties* (Gainesville, FL: Scholars' Facsimiles and Reprints, 1969), pp. 82–96.

10. Ibid., p. 85.

11. Émile Durkheim, *Rules of the Sociological Method*, reprint ed., trans. W. D. Halls (New York: Free Press, 1982).

12. Émile Durkheim, *The Division of Labor in Society*, reprint ed. (New York: Free Press, 1997).

13. Robert E. Park, "The City: Suggestions for the Investigation of Human Behavior in the City Environment," *American Journal of Sociology* 20 (1915): 579–583.

14. Harvey Zorbaugh, *The Gold Coast and the Slum* (Chicago: University of Chicago Press, 1929); Frederick Thrasher, *The Gang* (Chicago: University of Chicago Press, 1927); Louis Wirth, *The Ghetto* (Chicago: University of Chicago Press, 1928).

15. Robert Park, Ernest Burgess, and Roderic McKenzie, *The City* (Chicago: University of Chicago Press, 1925).

16. Ibid.

17. National Tax Foundation, "Who Pays Income Tax?" http://www.ntu.org /foundation/page/who-pays-income-taxes; Richard Fry and Rakesh Kochha, "America's Wealth Gap Between Middle-Income and Upper-Income Families Is Widest on Record," December 17, 2014, Pew Research Center, http://www.pewresearch.org/fact -tank/2014/12/17/wealth-gap-upper -middle-income/.

18. Drew DeSilver, "High-Income Americans Pay Most Income Taxes, But Enough to Be 'Fair'?" March 24, 2015, http://www .pewresearch.org/fact-tank/2015/03/24 /high-income-americans-pay-most-income -taxes-but-enough-to-be-fair/; Phil DeMuth, "Are You Rich Enough? The Terrible Tragedy of Income Inequality Among the 1%," *Forbes Magazine*, November 25, 2013, http://www.forbes.com/sites/phildemuth /2013/11/25/are-you-rich-enough-the -terrible-tragedy-of-income-inequality -among-the-1/.

19. Faith Karimi, "Wealthiest 1% Will Soon Own More than the Rest of Us Combined, Oxfam Says," CNN, January 19, 2015, http://www.cnn.com/2015/01/19/world /wealth-inequality/.

20. U.S. Census Bureau, "Poverty," http://www .census.gov/hhes/www/poverty/about /overview/.

21. Oscar Lewis, "The Culture of Poverty," *Scientific American* 215 (1966): 19–25.

22. Gunnar Myrdal, *The Challenge of World Poverty* (New York: Vintage Books, 1970).

23. James Ainsworth-Darnell and Douglas Downey, "Assessing the Oppositional Culture Explanation for Racial/Ethnic Differences in School Performances," *American Sociological Review* 63 (1998): 536–553.

24. Barbara Warner, "The Role of Attenuated Culture in Social Disorganization Theory," *Criminology* 41 (2003): 73–97.

25. National Center for Children in Poverty (NCCP), *Child Poverty, 2015*, http://www .nccp.org/topics/childpoverty.html.

26. Ibid.

27. Jeanne Brooks-Gunn and Greg J. Duncan, "The Effects of Poverty on Children," *Future of Children* 7 (1997): 34–39.

28. Greg Duncan, W. Jean Yeung, Jeanne Brooks-Gunn, and Judith Smith, "How Much Does Childhood Poverty Affect the Life Chances of Children?" *American Sociological Review* 63 (1998): 406–423.

29. National Center on Family Homelessness, "America's Youngest Outcasts," http://new .homelesschildrenamerica.org/mediadocs /275.pdf.

30. U.S. Department of Census Data, "Poverty Main," http://www.census.gov/hhes/www /poverty/.

31. U.S. Department of Health and Human Services, "Profile: Black/African Americans," http://www.minorityhealth.hhs.gov/omh /browse.aspx?lvl=3&lvlid=61.

32. National Center for Education Statistics, *The Condition of Education 2014* (NCES 2014-083), Status Dropout Rates, http://www.nces.ed.gov/fastfacts/display .asp?id=16.

33. Deirdre Bloome, "Racial Inequality Trends and the Intergenerational Persistence of Income and Family Structure," *American Sociological Review* 79 (2014): 1196–1225.

34. James Ainsworth-Darnell and Douglas Downey, "Assessing the Oppositional Culture Explanation for Racial/Ethnic Differences in School Performances," *American Sociological Review* 63 (1998): 536–553.

35. Bruce Jacobs and Lynn Addington, "Gating and Residential Robbery," *Prevention and Community Safety* 18 (2016): 19–37; Lynn Addington and Callie Marie Rennison, "Keeping the Barbarians Outside the Gate? Comparing Burglary Victimization in Gated and Non-Gated Communities," *Justice Quarterly* 32 (2015): 168–192; Maria Velez, Lauren Krivo, and Ruth Peterson, "Structural Inequality and Homicide: An Assessment of the Black-White Gap in Killings," *Criminology* 41 (2003): 645–672.

36. Karen Parker and Matthew Pruitt, "Poverty, Poverty Concentration, and Homicide," *Social Science Quarterly* 81 (2000): 555–582.

37. Ruth Peterson and Lauren Krivo, *Divergent Social Worlds: Neighborhood Crime and the Racial-Spatial Divide*, reprint ed. (New York: Russell Sage, 2012).

38. Michael Leiber and Joseph Johnson, "Being Young and Black: What Are Their Effects on Juvenile Justice Decision Making?" *Crime and Delinquency* 54 (2008): 560–581.

39. Pew Foundation, *One in 100: Behind Bars in America 2008*, http://www.pewtrusts.org/en /topics/state-policy.

40. John Hagan, Carla Shedd, and Monique Payne, "Race, Ethnicity, and Youth Perceptions of Criminal Injustice," *American Sociological Review* 70 (2005): 381–407.

41. John Hipp, "Spreading the Wealth: The Effect of the Distribution of Income and Race/Ethnicity Across Households and Neighborhoods on City Crime Trajectories," *Criminology* 49 (2011): 631–665; Julie A. Phillips, "White, Black, and Latino Homicide Rates: Why the Difference?" *Social Problems* 49 (2002): 349–374.

42. Justin Patchin, Beth Huebner, John McCluskey, Sean Varano, and Timothy Bynum, "Exposure to Community Violence and Childhood Delinquency," *Crime and Delinquency* 52 (2006): 307–332.

43. David Brownfield, "Social Class and Violent Behavior," *Criminology* 24 (1986): 421–438.

44. Charles Tittle and Robert Meier, "Specifying the SES/Delinquency Relationship," *Criminology* 28 (1990): 271–295, at 293.

45. Ruth Kornhauser, *Social Sources of Delinquency* (Chicago: University of Chicago Press, 1978), p. 75.

46. Kerryn E. Bell, "Gender and Gangs: A Quantitative Comparison," *Crime and Delinquency* 55 (2009): 363–387.

47. Jonathan Crane, "The Epidemic Theory of Ghettos and Neighborhood Effects on Dropping Out and Teenage Childbearing," *American Journal of Sociology* 96 (1991): 1226–1259; Rodrick Wallace, "Expanding Coupled Shock Fronts of Urban Decay and Criminal Behavior: How U.S. Cities Are Becoming 'Hollowed Out,'" *Journal of Quantitative Criminology* 7 (1991): 333–355.

48. Jeffrey Fagan and Garth Davies, "The Natural History of Neighborhood Violence," *Journal of Contemporary Criminal Justice* 20 (2004): 127–147.

49. Clifford R. Shaw and Henry D. McKay, *Juvenile Delinquency and Urban Areas*, rev. ed. (Chicago: University of Chicago Press, 1972).

50. Anthony Platt, *The Child Savers: The Invention of Delinquency* (Chicago: University of Chicago Press, 1968).

51. Shaw and McKay, *Juvenile Delinquency and Urban Areas*, p. 52.

52. Ibid., p. 171.

53. Claire Valier, "Foreigners, Crime and Changing Mobilities," *British Journal of Criminology* 43 (2003): 1–21.

54. For a general review, see James Byrne and Robert Sampson, eds., *The Social Ecology of Crime* (New York: Springer Verlag, 1985).

55. See, generally, Robert J. Bursik, "Social Disorganization and Theories of Crime and Delinquency," *Criminology* 26 (1988): 519–552.

56. William Spelman, "Abandoned Buildings: Magnets for Crime?" *Journal of Criminal Justice* 21 (1993): 481–493.

57. Keith Harries and Andrea Powell, "Juvenile Gun Crime and Social Stress: Baltimore, 1980–1990," *Urban Geography* 15 (1994): 45–63.

58. Ellen Kurtz, Barbara Koons, and Ralph Taylor, "Land Use, Physical Deterioration, Resident-Based Control, and Calls for Service on Urban Streetblocks," *Justice Quarterly* 15 (1998): 121–149.

59. Stacy De Coster, Karen Heimer, and Stacy Wittrock, "Neighborhood Disadvantage, Social Capital, Street Context, and Youth Violence," *Sociological Quarterly* (2006): 723–753.

60. George Kelling and James Q. Wilson, "Broken Windows: The Police and Neighborhood Safety," *Atlantic Monthly* 249 (1982): 29–38.

61. Adam Boessen and John Hipp, "Close-Ups and the Scale of Ecology: Land Uses and the Geography of Social Context and Crime," *Criminology* 53 (2015): 399–426.

62. Gregory Squires and Charis Kubrin, "Privileged Places: Race, Uneven Development and the Geography of Opportunity in Urban America," *Urban Studies* 42 (2005): 47–68; Matthew Lee, Michael Maume, and Graham Ousey, "Social Isolation and Lethal Violence Across the Metro/Nonmetro Divide: The Effects of Socioeconomic Disadvantage and Poverty Concentration on Homicide," *Rural Sociology* 68 (2003): 107–131.

63. Lee, Maume, and Ousey, "Social Isolation and Lethal Violence Across the Metro/Nonmetro Divide"; Charis E. Kubrin, "Structural Covariates of Homicide Rates: Does Type of Homicide Matter?" *Journal of Research in Crime and Delinquency* 40 (2003): 139–170; Darrell Steffensmeier and Dana Haynie, "Gender, Structural Disadvantage, and Urban Crime: Do Macrosocial Variables Also Explain Female Offending Rates?" *Criminology* 38 (2000): 403–438.

64. Corina Graif, "Delinquency and Gender Moderation in the Moving to Opportunity Intervention: The Role of Extended Neighborhoods," *Criminology* 53 (2015): 366–398.

65. Kyle Crowder and Scott South, "Spatial Dynamics of White Flight: The Effects of Local and Extralocal Racial Conditions on Neighborhood Out-Migration," *American Sociological Review* 73 (2008): 792–812.

66. Paul Jargowsky and Yoonhwan Park, "Cause or Consequence? Suburbanization and Crime in U.S. Metropolitan Areas," *Crime and Delinquency* 55 (2009): 28–50.

67. Edward S. Shihadeh, "Race, Class, and Crime: Reconsidering the Spatial Effects of Social Isolation on Rates of Urban Offending," *Deviant Behavior* 30 (2009): 349–378.

68. Jeffrey Morenoff, Robert Sampson, and Stephen Raudenbush, "Neighborhood Inequality, Collective Efficacy, and the Spatial Dynamics of Urban Violence," *Criminology* 39 (2001): 517–560.

69. Jargowsky and Park, "Cause or Consequence?"

70. Steven Messner, Lawrence Raffalovich, and Richard McMillan, "Economic Deprivation and Changes in Homicide Arrest Rates for White and Black Youths, 1967–1998: A National Time Series Analysis," *Criminology* 39 (2001): 591–614.

71. Steven Messner and Kenneth Tardiff, "Economic Inequality and Levels of Homicide: An Analysis of Urban Neighborhoods," *Criminology* 24 (1986): 297–317.

72. Adam Dobrin, Daniel Lee, and Jamie Price, "Neighborhood Structure Differences Between Homicide Victims and Nonvictims," *Journal of Criminal Justice* 33 (2005): 137–143; G. David Curry and Irving Spergel, "Gang Homicide, Delinquency, and Community," *Criminology* 26 (1988): 381–407; Darrell Steffensmeier and Dana Haynie, "Gender, Structural Disadvantage, and Urban Crime: Do Macrosocial Variables Also Explain Female Offending Rates?" *Criminology* 38 (2000): 403–438; Richard McGahey, "Economic Conditions, Organization, and Urban Crime," in *Communities and Crime*, ed. Albert Reiss and Michael Tonry (Chicago: University of Chicago Press, 1986), pp. 231–270.

73. Scott Menard and Delbert Elliott, "Self-Reported Offending, Maturational Reform, and the Easterlin Hypothesis," *Journal of Quantitative Criminology* 6 (1990): 237–268.

74. Elijah Anderson, *Streetwise: Race, Class, and Change in an Urban Community* (Chicago: University of Chicago Press, 1990), pp. 243–244.

75. Joseph Schafer, Beth Huebner, and Timothy Bynum, "Fear of Crime and Criminal Victimization: Gender-Based Contrasts," *Journal of Criminal Justice* 34 (2006): 285–301.

76. Xu Yili, Mora Fiedler, and Karl Flaming, "Discovering the Impact of Community Policing," *The Journal of Research in Crime and Delinquency* 42 (2005): 147–186.

77. Marc Swatt, Sean Varano, Craig Uchida, and Shellie Solomon, "Fear of Crime, Incivilities, and Collective Efficacy in Four Miami Neighborhoods," *Journal of Criminal Justice* 41 (2013): 1–11; Matthew Lee and Terri Earnest, "Perceived Community Cohesion and Perceived Risk of Victimization: A Cross-National Analysis," *Justice Quarterly* 20 (2003): 131–158.

78. John Hipp, "Micro-Structure in Micro-Neighborhoods: A New Social Distance Measure, and Its Effect on Individual and Aggregated Perceptions of Crime and Disorder," *Social Networks* 32 (2010): 148–159.

79. Michael Hanslmaier, "Crime, Fear and Subjective Well-Being: How Victimization and Street Crime Affect Fear and Life Satisfaction," *European Journal of Criminology* 10 (2013): 515–533.

80. Wendy Kilewer, "The Role of Neighborhood Collective Efficacy and Fear of Crime in Socialization of Coping with Violence in Low-Income Communities," *Journal of Community Psychology* 41 (2013): 920–930; Danielle Wallace, "A Test of the Routine Activities and Neighborhood Attachment Explanations for Bias in Disorder Perceptions," *Crime and Delinquency*, first published online December 7, 2011; Michele Roccato, Silvia Russo, and Alessio Vieno, "Perceived Community Disorder

Moderates the Relation Between Victimization and Fear of Crime," *Journal of Community Psychology* 39 (2011): 884–888.

81. C. L. Storr, C. Y. Chen, and J. C. Anthony, "'Unequal Opportunity': Neighborhood Disadvantage and the Chance to Buy Illegal Drugs," *Journal of Epidemiology and Community Health* 58 (2004): 231–238.

82. Pamela Wilcox Rountree and Kenneth Land, "Burglary Victimization, Perceptions of Crime Risk, and Routine Activities: A Multilevel Analysis Across Seattle Neighborhoods and Census Tracts," *Journal of Research in Crime and Delinquency* 33 (1996): 147–180.

83. Tim Phillips and Philip Smith, "Emotional and Behavioural Responses to Everyday Incivility," *Journal of Sociology* 40 (2004): 378–399.

84. Wesley Skogan, "Fear of Crime and Neighborhood Change," in *Communities and Crime*, ed. Albert Reiss and Michael Tonry (Chicago: University of Chicago Press, 1986), pp. 191–232.

85. Margo Wilson and Martin Daly, "Life Expectancy, Economic Inequality, Homicide, and Reproductive Timing in Chicago Neighbourhoods," *British Journal of Medicine* 314 (1997): 1271–1274.

86. Skogan, "Fear of Crime and Neighborhood Change."

87. Ibid.

88. Ralph Taylor and Jeanette Covington, "Community Structural Change and Fear of Crime," *Social Problems* 40 (1993): 374–392; Ted Chiricos, Michael Hogan, and Marc Gertz, "Racial Composition of Neighborhood and Fear of Crime," *Criminology* 35 (1997): 107–131.

89. Jodi Lane and James Meeker, "Social Disorganization Perceptions, Fear of Gang Crime, and Behavioral Precautions Among Whites, Latinos, and Vietnamese," *Journal of Criminal Justice* 32 (2004): 49–62.

90. Curry and Spergel, "Gang Homicide, Delinquency, and Community."

91. Lawrence Rosenthal, "Gang Loitering and Race," *Journal of Criminal Law and Criminology* 91 (2000): 99–160.

92. Catherine E. Ross, John Mirowsky, and Shana Pribesh, "Powerlessness and the Amplification of Threat: Neighborhood Disadvantage, Disorder, and Mistrust," *American Sociological Review* 66 (2001): 568–580.

93. Anderson, *Streetwise: Race, Class, and Change in an Urban Community*, p. 245.

94. William Terrill and Michael Reisig, "Neighborhood Context and Police Use of Force," *Journal of Research in Crime and Delinquency* 40 (2003): 291–321.

95. Bridget Freisthler, Elizabeth Lascala, Paul Gruenewald, and Andrew Treno, "An Examination of Drug Activity: Effects of Neighborhood Social Organization on the Development of Drug Distribution Systems," *Substance Use and Misuse* 40 (2005): 671–686.

96. Finn-Aage Esbensen and David Huizinga, "Community Structure and Drug Use: From a Social Disorganization Perspective," *Justice Quarterly* 7 (1990): 691–709.

97. Barbara Warner, Kristin Swartz, and Shila René Hawk, "Racially Homophilous Social Ties and Informal Social Control," *Criminology* 53 (2015): 204–230.

98. Micere Keels, Greg Duncan, Stefanie Deluca, Ruby Mendenhall, and James Rosenbaum, "Fifteen Years Later: Can Residential Mobility Programs Provide a Long-Term Escape from Neighborhood Segregation, Crime, and Poverty?" *Demography* 42 (2005): 51–72.

99. Greg J. Duncan, "New Lessons from the Gautreaux and Moving to Opportunity Residential Mobility Programs," University of California, Irvine, http://merage.uci.edu/ResearchAndCenters/CRE/Resources/Documents/Duncan.pdf.

100. Wesley Skogan, *Disorder and Decline: Crime and the Spiral of Decay in American Neighborhoods* (New York: Free Press, 1990), pp. 15–35.

101. Yan Lee, "Gentrification and Crime: Identification Using the 1994 Northridge Earthquake in Los Angeles," *Journal of Urban Affairs* 32 (2010): 549–577.

102. Leo Scheurman and Solomon Kobrin, "Community Careers in Crime," in *Communities and Crime*, ed. Albert Reiss and Michael Tonry (Chicago: University of Chicago Press, 1986), pp. 67–100.

103. Ibid.

104. Jeffrey Michael Cancino, "The Utility of Social Capital and Collective Efficacy: Social Control Policy in Nonmetropolitan Settings," *Criminal Justice Policy Review* 16 (2005): 287–318; Chris Gibson, Jihong Zhao, Nicholas Lovrich, and Michael Gaffney, "Social Integration, Individual Perceptions of Collective Efficacy, and Fear of Crime in Three Cities," *Justice Quarterly* 19 (2002): 537–564.

105. Robert J. Sampson and Stephen W. Raudenbush, *Disorder in Urban Neighborhoods: Does It Lead to Crime?* (Washington, DC: National Institute of Justice, 2001).

106. Andrea Altschuler, Carol Somkin, and Nancy Adler, "Local Services and Amenities, Neighborhood Social Capital, and Health," *Social Science and Medicine* 59 (2004): 1219–1230.

107. Kelly Socia and Janet Stamatel, "Neighborhood Characteristics and the Social Control of Registered Sex Offenders," *Crime and Delinquency* 58 (2012): 565–587.

108. Todd A. Armstrong, Charles M. Katz, and Stephen M. Schnebly, "The Relationship Between Citizen Perceptions of Collective Efficacy and Neighborhood Violent Crime," *Crime and Delinquency* 61 (2015): 121–142.

109. M. R. Lindblad, K. R. Manturuk, and R. G. Quercia, "Sense of Community and Informal Social Control Among Lower Income Households: The Role of Homeownership and Collective Efficacy in Reducing Subjective Neighborhood Crime and Disorder," *American Journal of Community Psychology* 51 (2013): 123–139.

110. Rebecca Wickes, John Hipp, Renee Zahnow, and Lorraine Mazerolle, "'Seeing' Minorities and Perceptions of Disorder: Explicating the Mediating and Moderating Mechanisms of Social Cohesion," *Criminology* 51 (2013): 519–560.

111. Robert Sampson, Jeffrey Morenoff, and Felton Earls, "Beyond Social Capital: Spatial Dynamics of Collective Efficacy for Children," *American Sociological Review* 64 (1999): 633–660.

112. Donald Black, "Social Control as a Dependent Variable," in *Toward a General Theory of Social Control*, ed. D. Black (Orlando: Academic Press, 1990).

113. Justin Medina, "Neighborhood Firearm Victimization Rates and Social Capital Over Time," *Violence and Victims* 30 (2015): 81–96.

114. Shayne Jones and Donald R. Lynam, "In the Eye of the Impulsive Beholder: The Interaction Between Impulsivity and Perceived Informal Social Control on Offending," *Criminal Justice and Behavior* 36 (2009): 307–321.

115. Jennifer Beyers, John Bates, Gregory Pettit, and Kenneth Dodge, "Neighborhood Structure, Parenting Processes, and the Development of Youths' Externalizing Behaviors: A Multilevel Analysis," *American Journal of Community Psychology* 31 (2003): 35–53.

116. Ralph Taylor, "Social Order and Disorder of Street Blocks and Neighborhoods: Ecology, Microecology, and the Systemic Model of Social Disorganization," *Journal of Research in Crime and Delinquency* 34 (1997): 113–155.

117. April Pattavina, James Byrne, and Luis Garcia, "An Examination of Citizen Involvement in Crime Prevention in High-Risk versus Low- to Moderate-Risk Neighborhoods," *Crime and Delinquency* 52 (2006): 203–231.

118. Steven Messner, Eric Baumer, and Richard Rosenfeld, "Dimensions of Social Capital and Rates of Criminal Homicide," *American Sociological Review* 69 (2004): 882–905.

119. Paul Bellair, "Informal Surveillance and Street Crime: A Complex Relationship," *Criminology* 38 (2000): 137–170.

120. Skogan, *Disorder and Decline*.

121. Robert Sampson and W. Byron Groves, "Community Structure and Crime: Testing Social Disorganization Theory," *American Journal of Sociology* 94 (1989): 774–802;

Denise Gottfredson, Richard McNeill, and Gary Gottfredson, "Social Area Influences on Delinquency: A Multilevel Analysis," *Journal of Research in Crime and Delinquency* 28 (1991): 197–206.

122. Jodi Eileen Morris, Rebekah Levine Coley, and Daphne Hernandez, "Out-of-School Care and Problem Behavior Trajectories Among Low-Income Adolescents: Individual, Family, and Neighborhood," *Child Development* 75 (2004): 948–965.

123. Ruth Triplett, Randy Gainey, and Ivan Sun, "Institutional Strength, Social Control, and Neighborhood Crime Rates," *Theoretical Criminology* 7 (2003): 439–467; Fred Markowitz, Paul Bellair, Allen Liska, and Jianhong Liu, "Extending Social Disorganization Theory: Modeling the Relationships Between Cohesion, Disorder, and Fear," *Criminology* 39 (2001): 293–320.

124. George Capowich, "The Conditioning Effects of Neighborhood Ecology on Burglary Victimization," *Criminal Justice and Behavior* 30 (2003): 39–62.

125. Gregory Zimmerman, Brandon Welsh, and Chad Posick, "Investigating the Role of Neighborhood Youth Organizations in Preventing Adolescent Violent Offending: Evidence from Chicago," *Journal of Quantitative Criminology* 31 (2015): 565–593.

126. Ruth Peterson, Lauren Krivo, and Mark Harris, "Disadvantage and Neighborhood Violent Crime: Do Local Institutions Matter?" *Journal of Research in Crime and Delinquency* 37 (2000): 31–63.

127. Maria Velez, "The Role of Public Social Control in Urban Neighborhoods: A Multi-Level Analysis of Victimization Risk," *Criminology* 39 (2001): 837–864.

128. Lee Ann Slocum, Andres Rengifo, Tiffany Choi, and Christopher Herrmann, "The Elusive Relationship Between Community Organizations and Crime: An Assessment Across Disadvantaged Areas of the South Bronx," *Criminology* 51 (2013): 167–216.

129. Velez, Krivo, and Peterson, "Structural Inequality and Homicide."

130. Tammy Rinehart Kochel, "Robustness of Collective Efficacy on Crime in a Developing Nation: Association with Crime Reduction Compared to Police Services," *Journal of Crime and Justice* 36 (2013): 334–352.

131. David Weisburd, Michael Davis, and Charlotte Gill, "Increasing Collective Efficacy and Social Capital at Crime Hot Spots: New Crime Control Tools for Police," *Policing: A Journal of Policy and Practice* 9 (2015): 265–327.

132. David Klinger, "Negotiating Order in Patrol Work: An Ecological Theory of Police Response to Deviance," *Criminology* 35 (1997): 277–306.

133. Rodney Stark, "Deviant Places: A Theory of the Ecology of Crime," *Criminology* 25 (1987): 893–911.

134. Robert Kane, "Compromised Police Legitimacy as a Predictor of Violent Crime in Structurally Disadvantaged Communities," *Criminology* 43 (2005): 469–498.

135. Robert Sampson, "Neighborhood and Community," *New Economy* 11 (2004): 106–113.

136. Robert Bursik and Harold Grasmick, "Economic Deprivation and Neighborhood Crime Rates, 1960–1980," *Law and Society Review* 27 (1993): 263–278.

137. Delbert Elliott, William Julius Wilson, David Huizinga, Robert Sampson, Amanda Elliott, and Bruce Rankin, "The Effects of Neighborhood Disadvantage on Adolescent Development," *Journal of Research in Crime and Delinquency* 33 (1996): 389–426.

138. James DeFronzo, "Welfare and Homicide," *Journal of Research in Crime and Delinquency* 34 (1997): 395–406.

139. John Worrall, "Reconsidering the Relationship Between Welfare Spending and Serious Crime: A Panel Data Analysis with Implications for Social Support Theory," *Justice Quarterly* 22 (2005): 364–391.

140. Sampson, Morenoff, and Earls, "Beyond Social Capital."

141. Thomas McNulty, "Assessing the Race–Violence Relationship at the Macro Level: The Assumption of Racial Invariance and the Problem of Restricted Distribution," *Criminology* 39 (2001): 467–490.

142. Suzanna Fay-Ramirez, "The Comparative Context of Collective Efficacy: Understanding Neighbourhood Disorganisation and Willingness to Intervene in Seattle and Brisbane," *Australian and New Zealand Journal of Criminology* 48 (2015): 513–542; Keri Burchfield and Eric Silver, "Collective Efficacy and Crime in Los Angeles Neighborhoods: Implications for the Latino Paradox," *Sociological Inquiry* 83 (2013): 154–176.

143. Patrick Sharkey, "Navigating Dangerous Streets: The Sources and Consequences of Street Efficacy," *American Sociological Review* 71 (2006): 826–846.

144. Sampson, Morenoff, and Earls, "Beyond Social Capital."

145. Per-Olof H. Wikström and Kyle Treiber, "The Role of Self-Control in Crime Causation," *European Journal of Criminology* 4 (2007): 237–264.

146. John R. Hipp and Wouter Steenbeek, "Types of Crime and Types of Mechanisms: What Are the Consequences for Neighborhoods Over Time?" *Crime and Delinquency*, first published online September 9, 2015.

147. Eric Silver and Lisa Miller, "Sources of Informal Social Control in Chicago Neighborhoods," *Criminology* 42 (2004): 551–585.

148. John Braithwaite, "Poverty Power, White-Collar Crime, and the Paradoxes of Criminological Theory," *Australian and New Zealand Journal of Criminology* 24 (1991): 40–58.

149. Wilson and Daly, "Life Expectancy, Economic Inequality, Homicide, and Reproductive Timing in Chicago Neighbourhoods."

150. Judith Blau and Peter Blau, "The Cost of Inequality: Metropolitan Structure and Violent Crime," *American Sociological Review* 147 (1982): 114–129.

151. P. M. Krueger, S. A. Huie, R. G. Rogers, and R. A. Hummer, "Neighborhoods and Homicide Mortality: An Analysis of Race/Ethnic Differences," *Journal of Epidemiology and Community Health* 58 (2004): 223–230.

152. Gary LaFree and Kriss Drass, "The Effect of Changes in Intraracial Income Inequality and Educational Attainment on Changes in Arrest Rates for African Americans and Whites, 1957 to 1990," *American Sociological Review* 61 (1996): 614–634; Ralph B. Taylor and Jeanette Covington, "Neighborhood Changes in Ecology and Violence," *Criminology* 26 (1988): 553–590; Richard Block, "Community Environment and Violent Crime," *Criminology* 17 (1979): 46–57; Robert Sampson, "Structural Sources of Variation in Race-Age-Specific Rates of Offending Across Major U.S. Cities," *Criminology* 23 (1985): 647–673; Richard Rosenfeld, "Urban Crime Rates: Effects of Inequality, Welfare Dependency, Region and Race," in *The Social Ecology of Crime*, ed. James Byrne and Robert Sampson (New York: Springer Verlag, 1985), pp. 116–130.

153. Robert Merton, *Social Theory and Social Structure*, enlarged ed. (New York: Free Press, 1968).

154. For an analysis, see Richard Hilbert, "Durkheim and Merton on Anomie: An Unexplored Contrast in Its Derivatives," *Social Problems* 36 (1989): 242–256.

155. Ibid., p. 243.

156. Albert Cohen, "The Sociology of the Deviant Act: Anomie Theory and Beyond," *American Sociological Review* 30 (1965): 5–14.

157. Robert Agnew, "The Contribution of Social Psychological Strain Theory to the Explanation of Crime and Delinquency," in *Advances in Criminological Theory*, Vol. 6, *The Legacy of Anomie*, ed. Freda Adler and William Laufer (New Brunswick, NJ: Transaction Press, 1995), pp. 111–122.

158. These criticisms are articulated in Messner and Rosenfeld, *Crime and the American Dream*, p. 60.

159. Ibid.

160. Lisa Mufti, "Advancing Institutional Anomie Theory," *International Journal of Offender Therapy and Comparative Criminology* 50 (2006): 630–653.

161. Jon Gunnar Bernburg, "Anomie, Social Change, and Crime: A Theoretical Examination of Institutional-Anomie Theory," *British Journal of Criminology* 42 (2002): 729–743.

162. John Hagan, Gerd Hefler, Gabriele Classen, Klaus Boehnke, and Hans Merkens, "Subterranean Sources of Subcultural Delinquency Beyond the American Dream," *Criminology* 36 (1998): 309–340.

163. Ibid., p. 61.

164. Steven Messner and Richard Rosenfeld, "An Institutional-Anomie Theory of the Social Distribution of Crime," paper presented at the annual meeting of the American Society of Criminology, Phoenix, November 1993.

165. Lorine Hughes, Lonnie Schaible, and Benjamin Gibbs, "Economic Dominance, the 'American Dream,' and Homicide: A Cross-National Test of Institutional Anomie Theory," *Sociological Inquiry* 85 (2015): 100–128.

166. Brian Stults and Christi Falco, "Unbalanced Institutional Commitments and Delinquent Behavior: An Individual-Level Assessment of Institutional Anomie Theory," *Youth Violence and Juvenile Justice* 12 (2014): 77–100.

167. Steven Messner and Samantha Applin, "Her American Dream: Bringing Gender into Institutional-Anomie Theory," *Feminist Criminology* 10 (2015): 36–59.

168. Stephen Cernkovich, Peggy Giordano, and Jennifer Rudolph, "Race, Crime, and the American Dream," *Journal of Research in Crime and Delinquency* 37 (2000): 131–170.

169. Jukka Savolainen, "Inequality, Welfare State and Homicide: Further Support for the Institutional Anomie Theory," *Criminology* 38 (2000): 1021–1042.

170. Kate Pickett, Jessica Mokherjee, and Richard Wilkinson, "Adolescent Birth Rates, Total Homicides, and Income Inequality in Rich Countries," *American Journal of Public Health* 95 (2005): 1181–1183.

171. Morenoff, Sampson, and Raudenbush, "Neighborhood Inequality, Collective Efficacy, and the Spatial Dynamics of Urban Violence."

172. John Braithwaite, "Poverty, Power, White-Collar Crime and the Paradoxes of Criminological Theory," *Australian and New Zealand Journal of Criminology* 24 (1991): 40–58.

173. Wilson and Daly, "Life Expectancy, Economic Inequality, Homicide, and Reproductive Timing in Chicago Neighbourhoods."

174. Judith Blau and Peter Blau, "The Cost of Inequality: Metropolitan Structure and Violent Crime," *American Sociological Review* 147 (1982): 114–129.

175. Ibid.

176. Tomislav Kovandzic, Lynne Vieraitis, and Mark Yeisley, "The Structural Covariates of Urban Homicide: Reassessing the Impact of Income Inequality and Poverty in the Post-Reagan Era," *Criminology* 36 (1998): 569–600.

177. Aki Roberts and Dale Willits, "Income Inequality and Homicide in the United States: Consistency Across Different Income Inequality Measures and Disaggregated Homicide Types," *Homicide Studies* 19 (2015): 28–57.

178. Scott South and Steven Messner, "Structural Determinants of Intergroup Association," *American Journal of Sociology* 91 (1986): 1409–1430; Steven Messner and Scott South, "Economic Deprivation, Opportunity Structure, and Robbery Victimization," *Social Forces* 64 (1986): 975–991.

179. Richard Fowles and Mary Merva, "Wage Inequality and Criminal Activity: An Extreme Bounds Analysis for the United States 1975–1990," *Criminology* 34 (1996): 163–182.

180. Beverly Stiles, Xiaoru Liu, and Howard Kaplan, "Relative Deprivation and Deviant Adaptations: The Mediating Effects of Negative Self Feelings," *Journal of Research in Crime and Delinquency* 37 (2000): 64–90.

181. Robert Agnew, "Foundation for a General Strain Theory of Crime and Delinquency," *Criminology* 30 (1992): 47–87.

182. Stacy De Coster and Lisa Kort-Butler, "How General Is General Strain Theory?" *Journal of Research in Crime and Delinquency* 43 (2006): 297–325.

183. Stephen Baron, "Street Youth, Strain Theory, and Crime," *Journal of Criminal Justice* 34 (2006): 209–223.

184. Matthew Larson and Gary Sweeten, "Breaking Up Is Hard to Do: Romantic Dissolution, Offending, and Substance Use During the Transition to Adulthood," *Criminology* 50 (2012): 605–636.

185. Cesar Rebellon, "Reconsidering the Broken Homes/Delinquency Relationship and Exploring Its Mediating Mechanism(s)," *Criminology* 40 (2002): 103–135.

186. G. Roger Jarjoura, "The Conditional Effect of Social Class on the Dropout–Delinquency Relationship," *Journal of Research in Crime and Delinquency* 33 (1996): 232–255.

187. Stephen Watts and Thomas McNulty, "Childhood Abuse and Criminal Behavior: Testing a General Strain Theory Model," *Journal of Interpersonal Violence.* 28 (2013): 3023–3040.

188. Robert Agnew, "Experienced, Vicarious, and Anticipated Strain: An Exploratory Study on Physical Victimization and Delinquency," *Justice Quarterly* 19 (2002): 603–633; Carter Hay and Michelle Evans, "Violent Victimization and Involvement in Delinquency: Examining Predictions from General Strain Theory," *Journal of Criminal Justice* 34 (2006): 261–274.

189. Susan Sharp, Mitchell Peck, and Jennifer Hartsfield, "Childhood Adversity and Substance Use of Women Prisoners: A General Strain Theory Approach," *Journal of Criminal Justice* 40 (2012): 202–211.

190. Paul Mazerolle, Velmer Burton, Francis Cullen, T. David Evans, and Gary Payne, "Strain, Anger, and Delinquent Adaptations Specifying General Strain Theory," *Journal of Criminal Justice* 28 (2000): 89–101; Paul Mazerolle and Alex Piquero, "Violent Responses to Strain: An Examination of Conditioning Influences," *Violence and Victimization* 12 (1997): 323–345.

191. George E. Capowich, Paul Mazerolle, and Alex Piquero, "General Strain Theory, Situational Anger, and Social Networks: An Assessment of Conditioning Influences," *Journal of Criminal Justice* 29 (2001): 445–461.

192. Cesar Rebellon, Nicole Leeper Piquero, Alex Piquero, and Sherod Thaxton, "Do Frustrated Economic Expectations and Objective Economic Inequity Promote Crime? A Randomized Experiment Testing Agnew's General Strain Theory," *European Journal of Criminology* 6 (2009): 47–71.

193. Joanne Kaufman, Cesar Rebellon, Sherod Thaxton, and Robert Agnew, "A General Strain Theory of Racial Differences in Criminal Offending," *Australian and New Zealand Journal of Criminology* 41 (2008): 421–437.

194. Lawrence Wu, "Effects of Family Instability, Income, and Income Instability on the Risk of Premarital Birth," *American Sociological Review* 61 (1996): 386–406.

195. Anthony Walsh, "Behavior Genetics and Anomie/Strain Theory," *Criminology* 38 (2000): 1075–1108.

196. John Hoffman, "A Life-Course Perspective on Stress, Delinquency, and Young Adult Crime," *American Journal of Criminal Justice* 35 (2010): 105–120.

197. Ravinder Barn and Jo-Pei Tan, "Foster Youth and Crime: Employing General Strain Theory to Promote Understanding," *Journal of Criminal Justice* 40 (2012): 212–220.

198. Hay and Evans, "Violent Victimization and Involvement in Delinquency: Examining Predictions from General Strain Theory."

199. Robert Agnew, Timothy Brezina, John Paul Wright, and Francis T. Cullen, "Strain, Personality Traits, and Delinquency: Extending General Strain Theory," *Criminology* 40 (2002): 43–71.

200. Wan-Ning Bao, Ain Haas, and Yijun Pi, "Life Strain, Coping, and Delinquency in the People's Republic of China," *International Journal of Offender Therapy and Comparative Criminology* 51 (2007): 9–24.

201. Fawn T. Ngo and Raymond Paternoster, "Toward an Understanding of the Emotional and Behavioral Reactions to Stalking: A Partial Test of General Strain

Theory," *Crime and Delinquency*, first published online November 7, 2013.

202. Robert Agnew, "When Criminal Coping Is Likely: An Extension of General Strain Theory," *Deviant Behavior* 34 (2013): 653–670.

203. Agnew, Brezina, Wright, and Cullen, "Strain, Personality Traits, and Delinquency"; Robert Agnew, "Stability and Change in Crime over the Life Course: A Strain Theory Explanation," in *Advances in Criminological Theory*, Vol. 7, *Developmental Theories of Crime and Delinquency*, ed. Terence Thornberry (New Brunswick, NJ: Transaction Books, 1995), pp. 113–137.

204. Ekaterina Botchkovar and Lisa Broidy, "Accumulated Strain, Negative Emotions, and Crime: A Test of General Strain Theory in Russia," *Crime and Delinquency* 59 (2013): 837–860; Michael Ostrowsky and Steven Messner, "Explaining Crime for a Young Adult Population: An Application of General Strain Theory," *Journal of Criminal Justice* 33 (2005): 463–476.

205. Jacob Bucher, Michelle Manasse, and Jeffrey Milton, "Soliciting Strain: Examining Both Sides of Street Prostitution Through General Strain Theory," *Journal of Crime and Justice* 38 (2015): 435–453.

206. Lee Ann Slocum, Sally Simpson, and Douglas Smith, "Strained Lives and Crime: Examining Intra-Individual Variation in Strain and Offending in a Sample of Incarcerated Women," *Criminology* 43 (2005): 1067–1110.

207. Lisa Broidy, "A Test of General Strain Theory," *Criminology* 39 (2001): 9–36.

208. Robert Agnew and Timothy Brezina, "Relational Problems with Peers, Gender and Delinquency," *Youth and Society* 29 (1997): 84–111.

209. John Hoffmann and S. Susan Su, "The Conditional Effects of Stress on Delinquency and Drug Use: A Strain Theory in Assessment of Sex Differences," *Journal of Research in Crime and Delinquency* 34 (1997): 46–78.

210. Lisa Broidy and Robert Agnew, "Gender and Crime: A General Strain Theory Perspective," *Journal of Research in Crime and Delinquency* 34 (1997): 275–306.

211. Robbin Ogle, Daniel Maier-Katkin, and Thomas Bernard, "A Theory of Homicidal Behavior Among Women," *Criminology* 33 (1995): 173–193.

212. Nicole Leeper Piquero and Miriam Sealock, "Gender and General Strain Theory: A Preliminary Test of Broidy and Agnew's Gender/GST Hypothesis," *Justice Quarterly* 21 (2004): 125–158.

213. Teresa LaGrange and Robert Silverman, "Investigating the Interdependence of Strain and Self-Control," *Canadian Journal of Criminology and Criminal Justice* 45 (2003): 431–464.

214. Thorsten Sellin, *Culture Conflict and Crime*, Bulletin No. 41 (New York: Social Science Research Council, 1938).

215. Ibid., p. 22.

216. Ibid., p. 29.

217. Ibid., p. 68.

218. Walter Miller, "Lower Class Culture as a Generating Milieu of Gang Delinquency," *Journal of Social Issues* 14 (1958): 5–19.

219. Ibid., pp. 14–17.

220. Fred Markowitz and Richard Felson, "Social-Demographic Attitudes and Violence," *Criminology* 36 (1998): 117–138.

221. Jeffrey Fagan, *Adolescent Violence: A View from the Street*, NIJ Research Preview (Washington, DC: National Institute of Justice, 1998).

222. Albert Cohen, *Delinquent Boys* (New York: Free Press, 1955).

223. Ibid., p. 25.

224. Ibid., p. 28.

225. Ibid.

226. Clarence Schrag, *Crime and Justice American Style* (Washington, DC: U.S. Government Printing Office, 1971), p. 74.

227. Cohen, *Delinquent Boys*, p. 30.

228. Ibid., p. 31.

229. Ibid., p. 133.

230. J. Johnstone, "Social Class, Social Areas, and Delinquency," *Sociology and Social Research* 63 (1978): 49–72; Joseph Harry, "Social Class and Delinquency: One More Time," *Sociological Quarterly* 15 (1974): 294–301.

231. Richard Cloward and Lloyd Ohlin, *Delinquency and Opportunity* (New York: Free Press, 1960).

232. Ibid., p. 7.

233. Ibid., p. 85.

234. Ibid., p. 171.

235. Ibid., p. 23.

236. Ibid., p. 73.

237. Ibid., p. 24.

238. Finn-Aage Esbensen and David Huizinga, "Gangs, Drugs and Delinquency in a Survey of Urban Youth," *Criminology* 31 (1993): 565–587.

239. For a general criticism, see Kornhauser, *Social Sources of Delinquency*.

240. Robert Sampson, "Effects of Socioeconomic Context of Official Reaction to Juvenile Delinquency," *American Sociological Review* 51 (1986): 876–885.

241. Jeffrey Fagan, Ellen Slaughter, and Eliot Hartstone, "Blind Justice? The Impact of Race on the Juvenile Justice Process," *Crime and Delinquency* 33 (1987): 224–258; Merry Morash, "Establishment of a Juvenile Police Record," *Criminology* 22 (1984): 97–113.

242. Charles Tittle, "Social Class and Criminal Behavior: A Critique of the Theoretical Foundations," *Social Forces* 62 (1983): 334–358.

243. James Q. Wilson and Richard Herrnstein, *Crime and Human Nature* (New York: Simon & Schuster, 1985).

244. Kenneth Polk and F. Lynn Richmond, "Those Who Fail," in *Schools and Delinquency*, ed. Kenneth Polk and Walter Schafer (Englewood Cliffs, NJ: Prentice Hall, 1974), p. 67.

245. Kathleen Maguire and Ann Pastore, *Sourcebook of Criminal Justice Statistics, 1996* (Washington, DC: U.S. Government Printing Office, 1996), pp. 150–166.

246. James DeFronzo, "Welfare and Burglary," *Crime and Delinquency* 42 (1996): 223–230.

247. Solomon Kobrin, "The Chicago Area Project—25-Year Assessment," *Annals of the American Academy of Political and Social Science* 322 (1959): 20–29.

248. Project COPE, http://www.bridgewell.org/projectcope/.

249. Brian Renauer, "Reducing Fear of Crime," *Police Quarterly* 10 (2007): 41–62.

250. Susan Sadd and Randolph Grinc, *Implementation Challenges in Community Policing* (Washington, DC: National Institute of Justice, 1996).

251. Donald Green, Dara Strolovitch, and Janelle Wong, "Defended Neighborhoods: Integration and Racially Motivated Crime," *American Journal of Sociology* 104 (1998): 372–403.

252. Anthony A. Braga and Brenda J. Bond, "Policing Crime and Disorder Hot Spots: A Randomized Controlled Trial," *Criminology* 46 (2008): 577–606.

Ethan Couch

AP Images/LM Otero

LEARNING OBJECTIVES

LO1 Analyze the associations among socialization, social process, and crime

LO2 Assess the effect of families and education on crime

LO3 Comment on the link between peers and delinquency

LO4 Explain how personal beliefs impact on criminality

LO5 Compare and contrast among social learning, control, and reaction theories

LO6 Comment upon the different forms social learning theory has taken

LO7 Set out the principles of Hirschi's social bond theory

LO8 Summarize the basic elements of social reaction or labeling theory

LO9 Review the research that underpins the labeling approach

LO10 Review the efforts to link social process theory to crime prevention efforts

7 SOCIAL PROCESS THEORIES: SOCIALIZATION AND SOCIETY

O n June 15, 2013, Ethan Couch, a 16-year-old Texas boy, killed four people while driving drunk. It seems that Couch and seven friends had been drinking for hours before the crash, and some of them were caught on a surveillance video stealing two cases of beer from a nearby Walmart. At around 11:45 P.M., the intoxicated teens were in a Ford F350 pickup going 70 mph (30 over the speed limit) when Couch swerved off the road and into a stalled SUV on the roadside. The SUV owner and three good Samaritans who were trying to help her get the car going were thrown 60 yards. They were killed on impact; the kids driving with Couch were severely injured. Couch was three times over the legal alcohol limit when he slammed into the victims.

In a decision that received national attention, Couch was sentenced to probation even though prosecutors had sought a maximum sentence of 20 years. One reason for the light sentence was that during his trial a defense psychologist testified that Couch suffered from "affluenza"—in other words, on the night of the crash he did not understand the consequences of his actions because of his privileged upbringing. His parents had taught him that wealth buys privilege and he could do anything he wanted without consequences because they were wealthy. If that were true, the state helped fuel those feelings further. Couch was supposed to go to a rehab clinic that would have cost his family approximately $500,000 annually. Instead, he was sent to a state facility which required the family to pay only $1,100 per month for a $750 per day facility, leaving taxpayers to pay the remaining bill for his therapy. The facility offers a 90-day treatment program that includes horseback riding, mixed martial arts, massage, cookery classes, a swimming pool, basketball, and six acres of land.[1]

But that was not the end of the saga of Ethan Couch. On December 2, 2015, a video surfaced showing Couch at a party where alcohol was being served, a clear violation of his probation agreement. The next day Couch was contacted by his probation officer and told to report for a drug test. Instead of complying, his mother withdrew $30,000 from her bank account and the two fled to Mexico. A directive to apprehend Couch for probation violation was issued, and on December 28, Ethan Couch and Tonya Couch were taken into custody in the Mexican resort city of Puerto Vallarta. Tonya was deported and jailed in Texas on a charge of hindering the apprehension of a felon.[2] On April 16, 2016, Ethan was sentenced to two years in prison—four consecutive sentences of 180 days for the four people he killed in 2013. His mother was indicted on charges of hindering apprehension for helping her son flee to Mexico and for money laundering for allegedly using $30,000 to finance the trip.[3]

he Couch case sadly illustrates the belief that the way we are brought up or socialized can have long-term influence over behavior. If we are to believe the defense, Couch was brought up to believe that his wealth shielded him from responsibility for his actions, freeing him to engage in deviant and criminal behaviors. And the state reinforced these values by granting him a lenient sentence and subsidizing his rehabilitation costs. Who could blame him if he walked away believing that his parents were correct? According to the victims' families, he showed no remorse for killing four innocent people.

Here we can see how social processes influence both the definition of what is to be considered a crime and who is to be considered a criminal. How people are socialized and how they are perceived by others are critical determinants of a person's status and behavior. And as the Couch case illustrates, agents of the justice system who hold legal power are often swayed by a person's life story. In most instances, the suspect's background includes growing up in a home with poor or absent drug-abusing parents or being sexually assaulted as a child. Such hardships often mitigate guilt and can result in a reduced sentence. In this instance, being raised in affluence was considered a determining factor in a young man's behavior choices.

In this chapter, we will review those theories that associate socialization and criminal behaviors. We begin with an analysis of the elements of socialization.

Socialization and Crime

L01 Analyze the associations among socialization, social process, and crime

The Couch case shows how socialization and social processes can influence both crime and criminality. Crime and criminality are social constructs: people are not born criminals, they are made that way; bad acts become crime when they are defined as such through a social process.

This notion of crime and criminality became popular during the 1930s and 1940s: a group of sociologists began to link social-psychological interactions to criminological behavior. **Sociological social psychology** (also known as psychological sociology) is the study of human interactions and

---

sociological social psychology The study of human interactions and relationships, emphasizing such issues as group dynamics and socialization.

socialization The interactions people have with various organizations, institutions, and processes of society.

social process or socialization theory The view that criminality is a function of people's interactions with various organizations, institutions, and processes in society.

---

relationships that emphasizes such issues as group dynamics and socialization.

According to this school of thought, an individual's relationship to important social processes, such as education, family life, and peer relations, is the key to understanding human behavior. Poverty and social disorganization alone are not sufficient to cause criminal activity because, after all, the great majority of people living in the most deteriorated areas do not become criminal offenders. More than 46 million Americans live below the poverty line. Even if we were to assume that all criminals come from the lower class—which they do not—it is evident that the great majority of the most indigent Americans do not commit criminal acts even though they may have a great economic incentive. Relatively few adolescents living in the most deteriorated areas become persistent offenders. Thirty million American kids are considered poor or living in poverty yet there are "only" 850,000 gang members; clearly even the most indigent young people do not turn to ganging. And for those who do, most desist when they reach their adulthood despite the continuing pressure of poverty and social decay.

Some other social forces, then, must be at work to explain why the majority of at-risk individuals do not become persistent criminal offenders and to explain why some who have no economic or social reason to commit crime do so anyway. According to social process theorists, that missing ingredient is **socialization**—the interactions people have with various organizations, institutions, and processes of society. Most people are influenced by their family relationships, peer group associations, educational experiences, and interactions with authority figures, including teachers, employers, and agents of the justice system. If these relationships are positive and supportive, people are able to function effectively within society; if these relationships are dysfunctional and destructive, conventional success may be impossible, and criminal solutions may become a feasible alternative. Taken together, this view of crime is referred to as **social process or socialization theory**.[4] Criminologists have long studied the critical elements of socialization to determine how they contribute to a burgeoning criminal career. Prominent among these elements are the family, the peer group, and the school.

FAMILY RELATIONS

L02 Assess the effect of families and education on crime

For some time, family relationships have been considered a major determinant of criminal behavior.[5] In fact, there is abundant evidence that parenting factors, such as the ability to communicate and to provide proper discipline, may play a critical role in determining whether people misbehave as children and even later as adults.

Youths who grow up in households characterized by conflict and tension, and where there is a lack of familial love and support, are susceptible to the crime-promoting forces in the environment.[6] Adolescents who live in this type of environment develop poor emotional well-being, externalizing problems, and antisocial behavior.[7]

Even those children living in so-called high-crime areas will be better able to resist the temptations of the streets if they receive fair discipline, care, and support from parents who provide them with strong, positive role models. Even gang boys will be better able to reduce their criminal activity if they receive parental monitoring; those left alone to engage in unstructured and unsupervised socializing, partying, and drinking with peers significantly increased their likelihood of delinquent and criminal involvement.[8]

Family Stress While the family can help neutralize the lure of the streets, living in a disadvantaged neighborhood places terrific strain on family functioning, especially in single-parent families that experience social isolation from relatives, friends, and neighbors. Children who are raised within such distressed families are at risk for delinquency.[9] Ongoing studies by sociologist Rand Conger and his associates find economic stress appears to have a harmful effect on parents and children.[10] According to his family stress model of economic hardship, such factors as low income and income loss increase parents' sadness, pessimism about the future, anger, despair, and withdrawal from other family members. Economic stress has this impact on parents' social-emotional functioning through the daily pressures it creates for them, such as being unable to pay bills or acquire basic necessities such as adequate food, housing, clothing, and medical care. Disrupted parenting, in turn, increases children's risk of suffering developmental problems, such as depressed mood, substance abuse, and engaging in delinquent behaviors. These economic stress processes also decrease children's ability to function in a competent manner in school and with peers.

The Effects of Divorce The relationship between family structure and crime is critical when the high rates of divorce and single parents are considered. Today more than 35 percent of children live in single-family homes.[11] Family disruption or change can have a long-lasting impact on children. Research conducted in both the United States and abroad shows that children raised in homes with one or both parents absent may be prone to antisocial behavior.[12] It is not surprising that the number of single-parent households in the population is significantly related to arrest rates.[13]

Why is the effect of divorce or separation so devastating? Even if single mothers (or fathers) can make up for the loss of a second parent, it is difficult to do so and the chances of failure increase. Single parents may find it difficult to provide adequate supervision, exposing kids to the negative effects of antisocial peers.[14] Single moms and dads are more likely to work outside the home, leaving kids alone after school, thereby reducing hours of parental supervision. Of course, most kids growing up in single-parent homes do not become delinquents or criminals, and most go on to live highly productive lives.[15] The strain created by family breakup can take a lifelong toll on children's emotional lives and make them vulnerable to the crime-producing forces in the environment.[16]

The association between crime and divorce may be due to economic factors. Because their incomes may decrease substantially in the aftermath of marital breakup, some divorced parents are forced to move to residences in deteriorated neighborhoods that may place children at risk of crime and drug abuse. In poor neighborhoods, single parents cannot call upon neighborhood resources to take up the burden of controlling children, and, as a result, a greater burden is placed on families to provide adequate supervision.[17] Some groups (i.e., Hispanics, Asians) have been raised in cultures where divorce is rare and parents have less experience in developing child-rearing practices that buffer the effects of family breakup on adolescent problem behavior.[18]

When a parent remarries, it does not seem to mitigate the effects of divorce on youth. Children living with a stepparent exhibit as many problems as youth in single-parent families and considerably more problems than those who are living with both original parents.[19]

Family Deviance A number of studies have found that parental deviance has a powerful influence on children's future behavior. When parents drink, take drugs, and commit crimes, the effects can be both devastating and long term. If they get arrested and wind up in prison, the effects of parental misbehavior are enhanced.[20]

The effect is intergenerational: the children of deviant parents produce delinquent children themselves.[21] Some of the most important data on the influence of parental deviance were gathered by British criminologist David Farrington, whose longitudinal research data were gathered in the long-term Cambridge Study in Delinquent Development (CSDD):

- A significant number of delinquent youths have criminal fathers. About 8 percent of the sons of noncriminal fathers became chronic offenders, compared to 37 percent of youths with criminal fathers.[22]
- School yard bullying may be both inter- and intragenerational. Bullies have children who bully others, and these "second-generation bullies" grow up to become the parents of children who are also bullies.[23] Thus, one family may have a grandfather, father, and son who are or were school yard bullies.[24]
- Kids whose parents go to prison are much more likely to be at risk for delinquency than children of nonincarcerated parents.[25]

Things only get worse when deviant parents wind up in the arms of the law. Children of incarcerated parents are more likely to act out and engage in expressive crimes of violence.[26] Perhaps having a parent in prison produces strain

Parents who support their children and use effective parenting skills help neutralize socially constructed crime-producing pulls and pushes. Here, students, teachers, staff, and parents participate in family fitness night at the International Community School (ICS) in Decatur, Georgia. A public charter school for grades K–5, ICS has about 400 students from 30 nations speaking 25 languages. ICS was designed to bring together refugee, immigrant, and local children in an academically challenging and nurturing environment. The surrounding community is noted for its ethnic diversity.

forces in society.[29] Effective parenting can help neutralize the effect of both individual (e.g., emotional problems) and social (e.g., delinquent peers) forces that promote delinquent behaviors.[30] Even kids who are at risk for delinquency because of personality problems or neurological syndromes, such as ADHD, have a much better prognosis if they receive effective, supportive parenting.[31]

Research shows that antisocial behavior will be reduced if parents provide the type of structure that integrates children into families, while giving them the ability to assert their individuality and regulate their own behavior—a phenomenon referred to as **parental efficacy**.[32] In some cultures, emotional support from the mother is critical, whereas in others the father's support remains the key factor.[33]

Numerous studies have uncovered links between the quality of family life and delinquency. Children who feel inhibited with their parents and refuse to discuss important issues with them are more likely to engage in deviant activities. Kids who report having troubled home lives also exhibit lower levels of self-esteem and are more prone to antisocial behaviors.[34] One reason for poor communication is parents who rely on authoritarian disciplinary practices, holding a "my way or the highway" orientation. Telling kids that "as long as you live in my house you will obey my rules" does little to improve communication and may instead produce kids who are rebellious and crime prone.[35]

and anger; these kids are more likely to manifest "internalizing" problems (like depression) and more "externalizing" problems (like aggression and delinquency). In the long term, children of incarcerated parents have more physical health problems (migraines, asthma, and high cholesterol), school problems (absenteeism and dropping out), and adult life problems (lower incomes, homelessness, and feelings of powerlessness).[27]

Of course, not all parents who have problems with the law produce children who will grow up to be similarly law violating. One key is the age at which child rearing takes place: the younger the parent, the greater the risk of intergenerational criminality.[28]

Parental Efficacy While poor parenting and parental deviance may increase exposure to criminality, children raised by parents who have excellent parenting skills, who are supportive and can effectively control their children in a noncoercive fashion, are more insulated from crime-producing

parental efficacy Parenting that is supportive, effective, and non-coercive.

CONNECTIONS

While it is possible that those who delay having children may have reached a higher level of maturity and are better able to care for their offspring, it's also possible that older parents have more self-control than those who have children earlier in the life course. High levels of self-control may be genetically transmitted to their offspring. For more on the association between self-control and crime, see Chapter 9's discussion of the General Theory of Crime.

ASK YOURSELF . . .

What other factors may link older parents with better adjusted children? Higher incomes? More stable, long-lasting marriages?

Child Maltreatment There is also a suspected link between crime and child abuse, neglect, and sexual abuse.[36] Numerous studies conducted in the United States and abroad show that there is a significant association between child maltreatment and serious self-reported and official delinquency, even when taking into account gender, race, and class.[37] The more often a child is physically disciplined and the harsher the discipline, the more likely they will engage in antisocial behaviors.[38] Children, both males and females, black and white, who experience abuse, neglect, or sexual abuse are believed to be more crime prone and suffer from other social problems such as depression, suicide attempts, substance abuse, and self-injurious behaviors.[39] Nor does the abuse have to be direct: children who observe the physical abuse of a sibling are more likely to externalize misbehavior themselves.[40]

The effects of abuse are felt well beyond childhood. Kids who were abused are less likely to graduate from high school, hold a job, and be happily married; they are more likely to have juvenile and adult arrests.[41] Thus, the seeds of adult dysfunction are planted early in childhood.[42]

The Chicken or the Egg? Which comes first, bad parents or bad kids? Does poor parenting cause delinquency or do delinquents undermine their parents' supervisory abilities? According to David Huh and his colleagues, bad kids create bad parents. They found little evidence that poor parenting is a direct cause of children's misbehavior problems but instead discovered that a child's problem behaviors undermine parenting effectiveness. *Increases* in adolescent behavior problems, such as substance abuse, result in a *decrease* in parental control and support.[43] While not everyone agrees with that turn of events, others support Huh's view that parental control weakens *after* kids get involved in delinquency and not before.[44] Parents actually tend to stick by their kids, even when their children are chronic troublemakers; parents do not give up easily on their troubled teens.[45]

EDUCATIONAL EXPERIENCE

The educational process and adolescent achievement in school have been linked to criminality. Children who do poorly in school, fail at their coursework, do not have a strong bond to the educational experience, lack educational motivation, and feel alienated are the most likely to engage in criminal acts.[46] Children who fail in school commit more serious and violent offenses and persist in their offending into adulthood.[47]

Schools contribute to criminality when they label problem youths and set them apart from conventional society. One way in which schools perpetuate this stigmatization is the "track system," which identifies some students as college bound and others as special needs.[48]

Dropping Out Another significant educational problem is that many students leave high school without gaining a diploma. Each year, approximately 1.2 million students fail to graduate from high school.

When surveyed, most dropouts say they left either because they did not like school or because they wanted to get a job. Kids who grow up fast, who are involved in drug abuse or other risky behaviors, may drop out of school in order to pursue an adult lifestyle.[49] Other risk factors include low academic achievement, poor problem-solving ability, low self-esteem, dissatisfaction with school, and being too old for their grade level.[50] Some dropouts could not get along with teachers and had been expelled or were under suspension. Almost half of all female dropouts left school because they were pregnant or had already given birth.

The research on the effect of dropping out is a mixed bag. Some research findings indicate that school dropouts face a significant chance of entering a criminal career, but other efforts using sophisticated methodological tools have failed to find a dropout effect.[51] If there *is* a "dropout effect," it is because those who leave school early already have a long history of poor school performance and antisocial behaviors.[52] In other words, poor school performance predicts both dropping out and antisocial activity. Even if dropping out is not directly related to crime, it reduces earnings and dampens future life achievements.

PEER RELATIONS AND CRIME

 L03 Comment on the link between peers and delinquency

Criminologists have long recognized that the peer group has a powerful effect on human conduct and can have a dramatic influence on decision making and behavior choices.[53] Peers guide each other and help each other learn to share and cooperate, to cope with aggressive impulses, and to discuss feelings they would not dare bring up at home. Youths can compare their own experiences with peers and learn that others have similar concerns and problems.[54] It is not surprising, then, that peer influence on criminal behavior appears to be a universal norm.[55] Kids who hang out with delinquent friends, who spend time socializing with them without parental supervision, and who admire and want to emulate them are the ones most likely to increase involvement in antisocial behaviors.[56]

The more antisocial the peer group, the more likely its members will engage in delinquency; nondelinquent friends will help moderate delinquency.[57] One study found that kids involved in delinquency are five times more likely than nonoffenders to associate with delinquent peers.[58] Peer relations may be more important than parental nurturance in the development of long-term behavior.[59] Even children born into high-risk families—such as those with single teen mothers—can avoid delinquency if their friends refrain from drug use and criminality.[60]

Peer effects follow people over the life course, through adolescence into adulthood. Prolonged attachment and exposure to deviant friends eventually shapes the content and character of illegal involvement: those who have violent friends eventually become violent themselves; those whose friends abuse substances will eventually specialize in substance abuse.[61] This relationship continues into college: having a roommate who is a binge drinker is highly correlated with personal binge drinking.[62]

While there is general agreement that the association between peers and criminality exists, there is some debate over the path of the relationship:

- Delinquent friends cause law-abiding youth to get in trouble. Kids who fall in with a bad crowd are at risk for delinquency.[63] For teenage girls, a "bad crowd" usually means teenage boys![64]

- Antisocial youths seek out and join up with like-minded friends; deviant peers sustain and amplify delinquent careers.[65] Those who choose aggressive or violent friends are more likely to begin engaging in antisocial behavior themselves and suffer psychological deficits.[66]

- As children move through their life course, antisocial friends help youths maintain delinquent careers and obstruct the aging-out process.[67] In stable friendships, the more accepted popular partner exerts greater influence over the less accepted partner. If the more popular friend continually engages in delinquency and alcohol use, the less popular "follower" will also.[68]

- Troubled kids choose delinquent peers out of necessity rather than desire. The social baggage they cart around prevents them from developing associations with conventional peers. Because they are impulsive, they may join cliques whose members are dangerous and get them into trouble.[69]

- The most at-risk kids may choose older peers, perhaps because they believe these older, tougher friends can provide some level of protection; their choices may backfire when their more mature companions enmesh them in a deviant subculture.[70] Older peers do not cause straight kids to go bad, but they amplify the likelihood of a troubled kid getting further involved in antisocial behaviors.[71] The fear of punishment is diminished among kids who hang with delinquent friends, and loyalty to delinquent peers may outweigh the fear of punishment.[72]

- Members of friendship groups created in disorganized neighborhoods are all exposed to destructive, crime-producing social forces. What appears to be a peer effect on crime is in reality an ecological one.[73]

While the direction of the peer–delinquency association is still being studied, the fact remains that people who get involved with delinquent peers are more likely to engage in delinquent behavior themselves and more likely to engage in the same types of acts as their friends.

RELIGION AND BELIEF

 L04 Explain how personal beliefs impact on criminality

Logic would dictate that people who hold high moral values and beliefs, who have learned to distinguish right from wrong, and who regularly attend religious services should also eschew crime and other antisocial behaviors.[74] Religion binds people together and forces them to confront the consequences of their behavior. Having high moral beliefs may enhance the deterrent effect of punishment by convincing even motivated offenders not to risk apprehension and punishment.[75] Committing crimes would violate the principles of all organized religions.

More than 40 years ago in a now classic study, Travis Hirschi and Rodney Stark found that, contrary to expectations, the association between religious attendance and belief and delinquent behavior patterns is negligible and insignificant.[76] Since the publication of their milestone study, there have been numerous research efforts to review the influence of religion on misbehavior, and a majority have reached an opposite conclusion: maintaining religious beliefs and attending religious services significantly helps reduce crime.[77] Richard Petts used data from a national survey and found that adolescents residing within two-parent families are less likely to become delinquent and that supportive parenting practices reduce the likelihood of their becoming delinquent even further. However, whether they reside in single-parent or two-parent families, kids who are involved in religion are less likely to engage in delinquency. Religion enhances the effect of parental affection in two-parent homes and also helps kids living in single-parent homes resist the influence of deviant peers. Petts found that religious participation helps reduce deviant behavior involvement throughout the life course, from adolescence until marriage.[78]

SOCIALIZATION AND CRIME

 L05 Compare and contrast among social learning, control, and reaction theories

To many criminologists these elements of social process, social interaction, and socialization are the chief determinants of criminal behavior. While a person's place in the social structure may contribute to crime, environment alone is not enough to explain criminality. People living in even the most deteriorated urban areas can successfully resist inducements to crime if they have a positive self-image, learn moral values, and have the support of their parents, peers, teachers, and neighbors. The girl with a positive self-image who is chosen for a college scholarship has the warm, loving support of her parents and is viewed by friends and neighbors as someone who is "going places." She is less likely to adopt a criminal way of life than another adolescent who is abused at home, lives with criminal parents, and whose bond to her

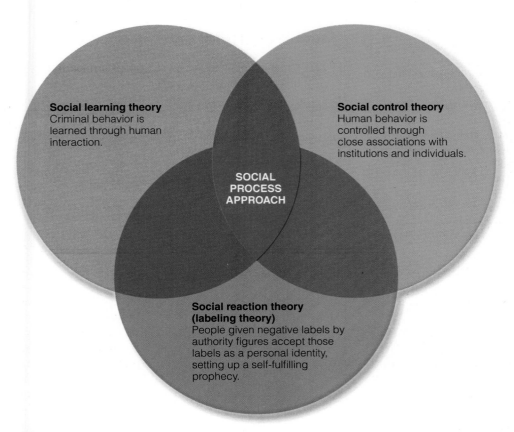

FIGURE 7.1 The Social Processes that Control Human Behavior

SOURCE: © Cengage Learning

school and peer group is shattered because she is labeled a troublemaker.[79] The boy who has learned criminal behavior from his parents and siblings and then joins a neighborhood gang is much more likely to become an adult criminal than his next-door neighbor who idolizes his hard-working, deeply religious parents. It is socialization, not the social structure, that determines life chances. The more social problems encountered during the socialization process, the greater the likelihood that youths will encounter difficulties and obstacles as they mature, such as being unemployed or becoming a teenage mother.

Theorists who believe that an individual's socialization determines the likelihood of criminality adopt the social process approach to human behavior. The social process approach has several independent branches (Figure 7.1):

- **Social learning theory** suggests that people learn the techniques and attitudes of crime from close and intimate relationships with criminal peers; crime is a learned behavior.
- **Social control theory** maintains that everyone has the potential to become a criminal, but that most people are controlled by their bonds to society. Crime occurs when the forces that bind people to society are weakened or broken.

- **Social reaction theory (labeling theory)** says people become criminals when significant members of society label them as such, and they accept those labels as a personal identity.

Put another way, social learning theory assumes people are born good and learn to be bad; social control theory assumes people are born bad and must be controlled in order to be good; social reaction theory assumes that, whether good or bad, people are controlled by the reactions of others. Each of these independent branches will be discussed separately.

social learning theory The view that human behavior is modeled through observation of human social interactions, either directly from observing those who are close and from intimate contact, or indirectly through the media. Interactions that are rewarded are copied, while those that are punished are avoided.

social control theory The view that people commit crime when the forces that bind them to society are weakened or broken.

social reaction theory (labeling theory) The view that people become criminals when significant members of society label them as such and they accept those labels as a personal identity.

To learn about the Institute for Child and Family Health, whose goal is to stimulate and coordinate the cross-disciplinary work required to make progress on the most difficult child and family policy issues facing the United States, go to **http://www.icfhinc.org/**.

Make a list of all the social process factors that you believe influence a child's future behavior. Can positive socialization overcome the social forces present in disorganized neighborhoods?

FAMOUS CRIMINOLOGISTS

Social Process Theory

ORIGIN Mid-twentieth century

FOUNDERS Edwin Sutherland, Ronald Akers, Travis Hirschi, Gresham Sykes, David Matza, Edwin Lemert, Howard Becker

MOST IMPORTANT WORKS Sutherland, *Principles of Criminology* (1939); Hirschi, *Causes of Delinquency* (1969); Becker, *The Outsiders* (1963)

CORE IDEAS How people are socialized is the key to understanding human behavior. People are a product of their upbringing. Those who are influenced by deviant others may become deviant themselves. Labeling and stigma lock people into criminal careers.

MODERN OUTGROWTHS Differential reinforcement theory, control theory, social reaction theory

Howard Becker

differential association theory According to Sutherland, the principle that criminal acts are related to a person's exposure to an excess amount of antisocial attitudes and values.

Social Learning Theory

 L06 Comment upon the different forms social learning theory has taken

Social learning theorists believe crime is a product of learning the norms, values, and behaviors associated with criminal activity. Social learning can involve the actual techniques of crime—how to hot-wire a car or illegally download videos—as well as the psychological aspects of criminality—how to deal with the guilt or shame associated with illegal activities. This section briefly reviews the three most prominent forms of social learning theory: differential association theory, differential reinforcement theory, and neutralization theory.

DIFFERENTIAL ASSOCIATION THEORY

One of the most prominent social learning theories is Edwin H. Sutherland's **differential association theory**. Often considered the preeminent U.S. criminologist, Sutherland first put forth his theory in his 1939 text, *Principles of Criminology*.[80] The final version of the theory appeared in 1947. When Sutherland died in 1950, Donald Cressey, his long-time associate, continued his work. Cressey was so successful in explaining and popularizing his mentor's efforts that differential association remains one of the most enduring explanations of criminal behavior.

Sutherland's research on white-collar crime, professional theft, and intelligence led him to dispute the notion that crime was a function of the inadequacy of people in the lower classes.[81] To Sutherland, criminality stemmed neither from individual traits nor from socioeconomic position; instead, he believed it to be a function of a learning process that could affect any individual in any culture. Acquiring a behavior is a social learning process, not a political or legal process. Skills and motives conducive to crime are learned as a result of contacts with procrime values, attitudes, and definitions and other patterns of criminal behavior.

Principles of Differential Association The basic principles of differential association are explained as follows:[82]

- *Criminal behavior is learned.* This statement differentiates Sutherland's theory from prior attempts to classify criminal behavior as an inherent characteristic of criminals. By suggesting that delinquent and criminal behavior is learned, Sutherland implied that it can be classified in the same manner as any other learned behavior, such as writing, painting, or reading.
- *Learning is a by-product of interaction.* Criminal behavior is learned as a by-product of interacting with others. Sutherland believed individuals do not start violating the law simply by living in a criminogenic environment or by manifesting personal characteristics, such as low IQ or family problems, associated with criminality. People—family, friends, peers—have the

greatest influence on their deviant behavior and attitude development. Relationships with these influential individuals color and control the way people interpret everyday events. For example, research shows that children who grow up in homes where parents abuse alcohol are more likely to view drinking as being socially and physically beneficial.[83] The intimacy of these associations far outweighs the importance of any other form of communication, such as movies or television. Even on those rare occasions when violent motion pictures seem to provoke mass criminal episodes, these outbreaks can be more readily explained as a reaction to peer group pressure than as a reaction to the films themselves.

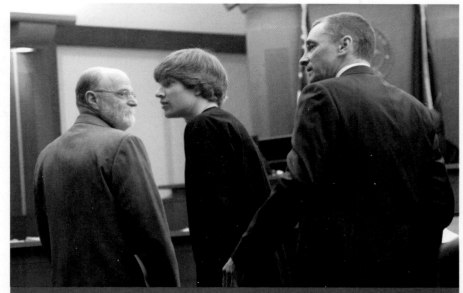

James Wesley Robinson (right) and his son Zachary Robinson wait for their initial court appearance in Salt Lake City Third District Court, March 13, 2014. Robinson, 50, was charged with operation of a clandestine laboratory, possession of a controlled substance with intent to distribute, and possession or use of a controlled substance. His two sons, Alexander, 21, and Zachary, 18, were charged with similar violations. They were accused of manufacturing the marijuana by-product called "Dab" or "Shatter," a concentrated, caramel-like substance produced from raw pot.

- *Criminal techniques are learned.* Learning criminal behavior involves acquiring the techniques of committing the crime, which are sometimes very complicated and sometimes very simple. This requires learning the specific direction of motives, drives, rationalizations, and attitudes. Some kids may meet and associate with criminal "mentors" who teach them how to be successful criminals and gain the greatest benefits from their criminal activities.[84] They learn the proper way to pick a lock, shoplift, and obtain and use narcotics. In addition, novice criminals learn to use the proper terminology for their acts and then acquire "proper" reactions to law violations. For example, getting high on marijuana and learning the proper way to smoke a joint are behavior patterns usually acquired from more experienced companions. Moreover, criminals must learn how to react properly to their illegal acts, such as when to defend them, rationalize them, or show remorse for them.

- *Perceptions of the legal code influence motives and drives.* The specific direction of motives and drives is learned from perceptions of various aspects of the legal code as being favorable or unfavorable. The reaction to social rules and laws is not uniform across society, and people constantly come into contact with others who maintain different views on the utility of obeying the legal code. Some people they admire may openly disdain or flout the law or ignore its substance. People experience what Sutherland calls *culture conflict* when they are exposed to different and opposing attitudes toward what is right and wrong, moral and immoral. The conflict of social attitudes and cultural norms is the basis for the concept of differential association.

- *Differential associations may vary in frequency, duration, priority, and intensity.* Whether a person learns to obey the law or to disregard it is influenced by the quality of social interactions. Those of lasting *duration* have greater influence than those that are brief. Similarly, *frequent* contacts have greater effect than rare and haphazard contacts. Sutherland did not specify what he meant by *priority*, but Cressey and others have interpreted the term to mean the age of children when they first encounter definitions of criminality. Contacts made early in life probably have a greater and more far-reaching influence than those developed later on. Finally, *intensity* is generally interpreted to mean the importance and prestige attributed to the individual or groups from whom the definitions are learned. For example, the influence of a father, mother, or trusted friend far outweighs the effect of more socially distant figures.

- *The process of learning criminal behavior by association with criminal and anticriminal patterns involves all of the mechanisms involved in any other learning process.* This suggests that learning criminal behavior patterns is similar to learning nearly all other patterns and is not a matter of mere imitation.

- *Criminal behavior is an expression of general needs and values, but it is not excused by those general needs and values because noncriminal behavior is also an expression of those same needs and values.* This principle suggests that the motives for criminal behavior cannot logically be the same as those for conventional behavior. Sutherland rules out such motives as desire to accumulate money or social status, personal frustration, or low self-concept as causes of crime because they are just as likely to produce noncriminal behavior, such as getting a better education or working harder on a job. It is only the learning of deviant norms through contact with an excess of definitions favorable toward criminality that produces illegal behavior.

A person becomes a criminal when he or she perceives more favorable than unfavorable consequences to violating the law. According to Sutherland's theory, individuals become law violators when they are in contact with people, groups, or events that produce an excess of definitions favorable toward criminality and are isolated from counteracting forces. A definition favorable toward criminality occurs, for example, when a person is exposed to friends sneaking into a theater to avoid paying for a ticket or talking about the virtues of getting high on drugs. A definition unfavorable toward crime occurs when friends or parents demonstrate their disapproval of crime. Neutral behavior, such as reading a book, is neither positive nor negative with respect to law violation. Neutral behavior, such as helping parents around the house, is important; when a child is occupied with activities, it prevents him or her from being in contact with those involved in criminal behaviors.[85]

In sum, differential association theory holds that people learn criminal attitudes and behavior while in their adolescence from close and trusted friends and/or relatives. A criminal career develops if learned antisocial values and behaviors are not at least matched or exceeded by conventional attitudes and behaviors. Criminal behavior, then, is learned in a process that is similar to learning any other human behavior.

Testing Differential Association Theory Numerous research efforts have supported the core principles of differential association. These generally show a correlation between (a) having deviant parents and friends, (b) holding deviant attitudes, and (c) committing deviant acts. Taken as a whole, the research shows that the relationship between crime and measures of differential association are quite strong.[86] Among the most important findings are:

- Crime appears to be intergenerational. Kids whose parents are deviant and criminal are more likely to become criminals themselves and eventually to produce criminal children. This supports the contention that children learn from deviant parents.[87]
- The more deviant an adolescent's social network and network of affiliations, including parents, peers, and romantic partners, the more likely that adolescent is to engage in antisocial behavior.[88] This finding supports the hypothesis that children learn criminal attitudes from exposure to deviant others, rather than crime being a function of inherited criminal traits.[89]

- People who report having attitudes that support deviant behavior are also likely to engage in deviant behavior.[90] As people mature, having delinquent friends who support criminal attitudes and behavior is strongly related to developing criminal careers.[91]
- Association with deviant peers has been found to sustain the deviant attitudes.[92]
- The influence of deviant friends is highly supportive of delinquency, regardless of race and/or class.[93] One reason is that within peer groups, high-status leaders will influence and legitimize deviant behavior. If an admired friend drinks and smokes, it makes it a lot easier for a follower to engage in those behaviors and to believe they are appropriate.[94]
- Romantic partners who engage in antisocial activities may influence their partner's behavior, which suggests that partners learn from one another.[95] Adolescents with deviant romantic partners are more delinquent than those youths with more prosocial partners, regardless of friends' and parents' behavior.[96]
- Kids who associate and presumably learn from deviant peers are more likely to get involved in delinquency.[97] Deviant peers keep kids in criminal careers.[98]
- People who engage in antisocial activities also perceive and believe that their best friends and close associates engage in antisocial activities as well. [99]
- Differential association is multicultural. Scales measuring differential association have been significantly correlated with criminal behaviors among samples taken in other nations and cultures.[100]

Differential association also seems especially relevant in trying to explain the onset of substance abuse and a career in the drug trade. This requires learning proper techniques and attitudes from an experienced user or dealer.[101] In his interview study of low-level drug dealers, Kenneth Tunnell found that many novices were tutored by a more experienced criminal dealer who helped them make connections with buyers and sellers. One told him:

> I had a friend of mine who was an older guy, and he introduced me to selling marijuana to make a few dollars. I started selling a little and made a few dollars. For a young guy to be making a hundred dollars or so, it was a lot of money. So I got kind of tied up in that aspect of selling drugs.[102]

Tunnell found that making connections is an important part of the dealer's world. Adolescent drug users are likely to have intimate relationships with a peer friendship network that supports their substance abuse and teaches them how to deal within the drug world.[103]

Differential association may also be used to explain the gender difference in the crime rate. Males are more likely to socialize with deviant peers than females and, when they do, are more deeply influenced by peer relations.[104] Females are shielded by their unique moral sense, which makes caring about people and avoiding social harm a top priority. Males, in contrast, have a more cavalier attitude toward others and are more interested in their own self-interests. They are therefore more susceptible to the influence of deviant peers.[105]

Analysis of Differential Association Theory There have been a number of important critiques of the theory. According to the *cultural deviance critique*, differential association is invalid because it suggests that criminals are people "properly" socialized into a deviant subculture; that is, they are taught criminal norms by significant others. Supporters counter that differential association also recognizes that individuals can embrace criminality because they have been improperly socialized into the normative culture.[106]

Differential association theory also fails to explain why one youth who is exposed to delinquent definitions eventually succumbs to them, while another, living under the same conditions, is able to avoid criminal entanglements. It also fails to account for the origin of delinquent definitions: How did the first "teacher" learn delinquent attitudes and definitions in order to pass them on? Who taught the teacher?

Differential association theory assumes that youths learn about crime and then commit criminal acts, but it is also possible that experienced delinquents and criminals seek out like-minded peers after they engage in antisocial acts and that the internalization of deviant attitudes follows, rather than precedes, criminality ("birds of a feather flock together").[107] Research on gang boys shows that they are involved in high rates of criminality before they join gangs, indicating that the group experience facilitates their antisocial behavior rather than playing a role in its creation.[108]

Despite these criticisms, differential association theory maintains an important place in the study of criminal behavior. For one thing, it provides a consistent explanation of all types of delinquent and criminal behavior. Unlike social structure theories, it is not limited to the explanation of a single facet of antisocial activity, such as lower-class gang activity. The theory can also account for the extensive delinquent behavior found even in middle- and upper-class areas, where youths may be exposed to a variety of pro-delinquent definitions from such sources as overly opportunistic parents and friends. The theory appears flexible and able to explain current trends in crime and is not bound by those that existed when the theory was first created. For example, Sameer Hinduja and Jason Ingram found that adolescents who pirate music off the Internet are influenced by both personal friends and also online friends they meet on social media. Internet music piracy is not a crime that Sutherland had in mind when he first proposed the theory more than 70 years ago.[109]

DIFFERENTIAL REINFORCEMENT THEORY

Differential reinforcement theory is another attempt to explain crime as a type of learned behavior. First proposed

 Edwin H. Sutherland served as the 29th president of the American Sociological Society. His presidential address, "White-Collar Criminality," was delivered at the organization's annual meeting in Philadelphia in December 1939. Read this groundbreaking address and paper at **http://www.asanet.org/about /presidents/Edwin_Sutherland.cfm.**
  According to Sutherland, all crimes are learned, even white-collar offenses. Do you agree?

CONNECTIONS

Psychological learning theories were first discussed in Chapter 5. These trait theories maintain that human actions are developed through learning experiences. Behavior is supported by rewards and extinguished by negative reactions or punishments. In contrast, sociological learning theory holds that behavior is constantly being shaped by life experiences.

ASK YOURSELF . . .

Do you believe that someone can actually learn to be a deviant or criminal from others, or is that merely an excuse, that a "good kid" can learn to be bad?

by Ronald Akers in collaboration with Robert Burgess in 1966, it is a version of the social learning view that employs both differential association concepts along with elements of psychological learning theory.

According to Akers, the same process is involved in learning both deviant and conventional behavior. People learn to be neither "all deviant" nor "all conforming," but rather strike a balance between the two opposing poles of behavior. This balance is usually stable, but it can undergo revision over time.[110]

A number of learning processes shape behavior. **Direct conditioning**, also called **differential reinforcement**, occurs when behavior is reinforced by being either rewarded or punished

differential reinforcement theory An attempt to explain crime as a type of learned behavior. First proposed by Akers in collaboration with Burgess in 1966, it is a version of the social learning view that employs differential association concepts as well as elements of psychological learning theory.

direct conditioning Behavior is reinforced by being either rewarded or punished while interacting with others; also called differential reinforcement.

differential reinforcement Behavior is reinforced by being either rewarded or punished while interacting with others; also called direct conditioning.

while interacting with others. When behavior is punished, this is referred to as **negative reinforcement**. This type of reinforcement can be distributed either by using negative stimuli (punishment) or by loss of a positive reward. Whether deviant or criminal behavior has been initiated or persists depends on the degree to which it has been rewarded or punished and the rewards or punishments attached to its alternatives.

According to Akers, people learn to evaluate their own behavior through their interactions with significant others and groups in their lives. These groups control sources and patterns of reinforcement, define behavior as right or wrong, and provide behaviors that can be modeled through observational learning. The more individuals learn to define their behavior as good or at least as justified, rather than as undesirable, the more likely they are to engage in it. Adolescents who join a drug-abusing peer group whose members value drugs and alcohol, encourage their use, and provide opportunities to observe people abusing substances will be encouraged, through this social learning experience, to use drugs themselves.

Akers's theory posits that the principal influence on behavior comes from "those groups that control individuals' major sources of reinforcement and punishment and expose them to behavioral models and normative definitions."[111] The important groups are the ones with which a person is in differential association—peer and friendship groups, schools, churches, and similar institutions. Within the context of these critical groups, according to Akers, "deviant behavior can be expected to the extent that it has been differentially reinforced over alternative behavior . . . and is defined as desirable or justified."[112] Once people are indoctrinated into crime, their behavior can be reinforced by being exposed to deviant behavior models—associating with deviant peers—without being subject to negative reinforcements for their antisocial acts. The deviant behavior, originally executed by imitating someone else's behavior, is sustained by social support. For example, kids who engage in computer crime and computer hacking may find their behavior reinforced by peers who are playing the same game.[113]

It is possible that differential reinforcements help establish criminal careers and are a key factor in explaining persistent criminality.

Testing Differential Reinforcement The principles of differential reinforcement have been subject to empirical

review by Akers and other criminologists.[114] In an important test of his theory, Akers and his associates surveyed 3,065 male and female adolescents on drug- and alcohol-related activities and their perception of variables related to social learning and differential reinforcement. Items in the scale included the respondents' perceptions of esteemed peers' attitudes toward drug and alcohol abuse, the number of people they admired who actually used controlled substances, and whether people they admired would reward or punish them for substance abuse. Akers found a strong association between drug and alcohol abuse and social learning variables: those who believed they would be rewarded for deviance by those they respect were the ones most likely to engage in deviant behavior.[115] Aker's efforts have been supported by research showing that kids whose deviant behavior (such as smoking pot) is reinforced by significant others (such as parents or peers) are more likely to accelerate their rates of deviance.[116]

Akers also found that the learning–deviant behavior link is not static. The learning experience continues within a deviant group as behavior is both influenced by and exerts influence over group processes. For example, adolescents may learn to smoke because their friends are smoking and, therefore, approve of this behavior. Over time, smoking influences friendships and peer group memberships as smokers seek out one another for companionship and support.[117]

Differential reinforcement theory is an important perspective that endeavors to determine the cause of criminal activity. It considers how the content of socialization conditions crime. Because not all socialization is positive, it accounts for the fact that negative social reinforcements and experiences can produce criminal results. This concurs with research that demonstrates that parental deviance is related to adolescent antisocial behavior.[118] Parents may reinforce their children's deviant behavior by supplying negative social reinforcements. Akers's work also fits well with rational choice theory because they both suggest that people learn the techniques and attitudes necessary to commit crime. Criminal knowledge is gained through experience. After considering the outcome of their past experiences, potential offenders decide which criminal acts will be profitable and which are dangerous and should be avoided.[119] Integrating these perspectives, people make rational choices about crime because they have learned to balance risks against the potential for criminal gain.

NEUTRALIZATION THEORY

Neutralization theory is identified with the writings of David Matza and his associate Gresham Sykes.[120] They view the process of becoming a criminal as a learning experience in which potential delinquents and criminals master techniques that enable them to counterbalance or neutralize conventional values and drift back and forth between

negative reinforcement Using either negative stimuli (punishment) or loss of reward (negative punishment) to curtail unwanted behaviors.

neutralization theory Neutralization theory holds that offenders adhere to conventional values while "drifting" into periods of illegal behavior. In order to drift, people must first overcome (neutralize) legal and moral values.

illegitimate and conventional behavior. One reason this is possible is the subterranean value structure of American society. **Subterranean values** are morally tinged influences that have become entrenched in the culture but are publicly condemned. They exist side by side with conventional values and while condemned in public may be admired or practiced in private. Examples include viewing pornographic films, drinking alcohol to excess, and gambling on sporting events. In American culture, it is common to hold both subterranean and conventional values; few people are "all good" or "all bad."

Matza argues that even the most committed criminals and delinquents are not involved in criminality all the time; they also attend schools, family functions, and religious services. Their behavior can be conceived as falling along a continuum between total freedom and total restraint. This process, which he calls **drift**, refers to the movement from one extreme of behavior to another, resulting in behavior that is sometimes unconventional, free, or deviant and at other times constrained and sober.[121] Learning techniques of neutralization enables a person to temporarily "drift away" from conventional behavior and get involved in more subterranean values and behaviors, including crime and drug abuse.[122]

Sykes and Matza base their theoretical model on these observations:[123]

- *Criminals sometimes voice a sense of guilt over their illegal acts.* If a stable criminal value system existed in opposition to generally held values and rules, it would be unlikely that criminals would exhibit any remorse for their acts, other than regret at being apprehended.
- *Offenders frequently respect and admire honest, law-abiding people.* Really honest people are often revered, and if for some reason such people are accused of misbehavior, the criminal is quick to defend their integrity. Those admired may include sports figures, priests and other clergy, parents, teachers, and neighbors.
- *Criminals draw a line between those whom they can victimize and those whom they cannot.* Members of similar ethnic groups, churches, or neighborhoods are often off limits. This practice implies that criminals are aware of the wrongfulness of their acts.
- *Criminals are not immune to the demands of conformity.* Most criminals frequently participate in many of the same social functions as law-abiding people—for example, in school, church, and family activities.

Because of these factors, Sykes and Matza conclude that criminality is the result of the neutralization of accepted social values through the learning of a standard set of techniques that allow people to counteract the moral dilemmas posed by illegal behavior.[124]

Techniques of Neutralization Sykes and Matza suggest that people develop a distinct set of justifications for their law-violating behavior (Figure 7.2). These neutralization techniques enable them to temporarily drift away from the rules of the normative society and participate in subterranean behaviors. These techniques of neutralization include the following patterns:

- *Deny responsibility.* Young offenders sometimes claim their unlawful acts were simply not their fault. Criminal acts resulted from forces beyond their control or were accidents.
- *Deny injury.* By denying the wrongfulness of an act, criminals are able to neutralize illegal behavior. For example, stealing is viewed as borrowing; vandalism is considered mischief that has gotten out of hand. Delinquents may find that their parents and friends support their denial of injury. In fact, they may claim that the behavior was merely a prank, helping affirm the offender's perception that crime can be socially acceptable. Since no one was "really hurt" the act was not "really a crime."
- *Deny the victim.* Criminals sometimes neutralize wrongdoing by maintaining that the victim of crime "had it coming." Vandalism may be directed against a disliked teacher or neighbor; homosexuals may be beaten up by a gang because their behavior is considered offensive. Denying the victim may also take the form of ignoring the rights of an absent or unknown victim—for example, stealing from the unseen owner of a department store. It becomes morally acceptable for the criminal to commit such crimes as vandalism when the victims, because of their absence, cannot be sympathized with or respected.
- *Condemn condemners.* An offender views the world as a corrupt place with a dog-eat-dog code. Because police and judges are on the take, teachers show favoritism, and parents take out their frustrations on their kids, it is ironic and unfair for these authorities to condemn his or her misconduct. By shifting the blame to others, criminals are able to repress the feeling that their own acts are wrong.
- *Appeal to higher loyalties.* Novice criminals often argue that they are caught in the dilemma of being loyal to their own peer group while at the same time attempting to abide by the rules of the larger society. The needs of the group take precedence over the rules of society because the demands of the former are immediate and localized.

In sum, the theory of neutralization presupposes a condition that allows people to neutralize unconventional norms and values by using such slogans as "I didn't mean to do it," "I didn't really hurt anybody," "They had it coming to

subterranean values Morally tinged influences that have become entrenched in the culture but are publicly condemned. They exist side by side with conventional values and while condemned in public may be admired or practiced in private.

drift According to Matza, the view that youths move in and out of delinquency and that their lifestyles can embrace both conventional and deviant values.

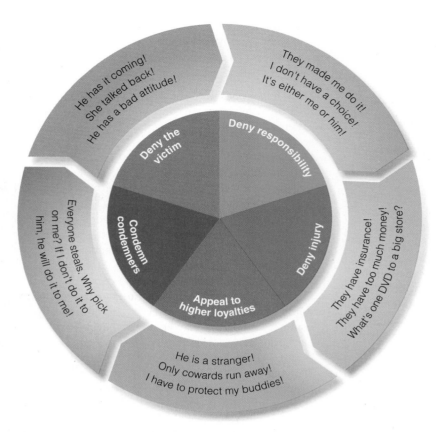

FIGURE 7.2 Techniques of Neutralization

SOURCE: © Cengage Learning

them," "Everybody's picking on me," and "I didn't do it for myself." These excuses allow people to drift into criminal modes of behavior.

Testing Neutralization Theory Attempts have been made to verify the assumptions of neutralization theory empirically, but the results have been inconclusive.[125] One area of research has been directed at determining whether there really is a need for law violators to neutralize moral constraints. The thinking behind this research is this: if criminals hold values *in opposition* to accepted social norms, then there is really no need to neutralize. So far, the evidence is mixed. Some studies show that law violators approve of criminal behavior, such as theft and violence, and still others find evidence that even though they may be active participants themselves, criminals voice disapproval of illegal behavior.[126] Some studies indicate that law violators approve of social values such as honesty and fairness; others come to the opposite conclusion.[127]

In addition to youthful delinquent behaviors, the adoption of neutralization techniques has also been used to explain the onset of white-collar crime.[128] Businessmen may find it easier to cut corners by claiming that "the government exaggerates dangers to the consumer" (denial of injury) or the "markets are generally safe so the corporate

producers should not have to take blame for the few injuries that occur" (denial of responsibility) or "the bottom line is all that matters" (appeal to higher loyalty). The need to get ahead in the corporate world may help them neutralize the moral constraints that their parents may have taught them in adolescence, such as play fair, don't cheat, take responsibility.

The theory of neutralization, then, is a major contribution to the literature of crime and delinquency. It can account for the aging-out process: youths can forgo criminal behavior as adults because they never really rejected the morality of normative society. It helps explain the behavior of the occasional or nonchronic delinquent, who is able to successfully age out of crime. Because teens are not committed to criminality, as they mature they simply drift back into conventional behavior patterns. While they are young, justifications and excuses neutralize guilt and enable individuals to continue to feel good about themselves.[129] In contrast, people who remain criminals as adults, such as white-collar criminals, may be using newly learned techniques to neutralize the wrongfulness of their actions and avoid guilt (see the Criminology in Action feature). One study found psychotherapists accused of sexually exploiting their clients blame the victim for "seducing them"; some claim there was little injury caused by the sexual encounter; others seek scapegoats to blame for their actions.[130]

White-Collar Neutralization

04

Do white-collar criminals use neutralization techniques before engaging in business crimes? To find out, Paul M. Klenowski interviewed 40 inmates in federal custody who had been convicted of white-collar crimes.

Klenowski found that, like common-law criminals, white-collar offenders routinely used neutralizations before committing law violations. The most commonly used technique for all offenders was the appeal to higher loyalties. Those using this technique believed they committed their crimes for the betterment of others, namely family and friends. One inmate, incarcerated for his wrongdoings in the investment industry, told Klenowski:

> My parents never really supported me. So, I guess when I was committing my acts, I believed that maybe I was doing some of this for my family. I wanted to have the time and the financial security to be around my family to make sure I would be there for my children, so I guess family also subconsciously played into why I did what I did.

The denial of injury technique was the second most frequently offered account by participants. Some explained that "nobody is getting hurt," "it's only money," or "I am only borrowing it." One respondent incarcerated for bribery said, "I wasn't stealing from anybody. I didn't take that money. It wasn't for me." Some claimed that they did not intend to cause any real harm and if given more time they would have paid their victims back in full.

It was not uncommon for the offenders to redirect the focus of their own actions toward those whom they felt unfairly condemned or judged their actions. Those who used this technique typically pointed out hypocrisy within the government that allowed them to carry out their illicit activities. Some said the laws are too strict and almost force people to be criminals if they are going to make any money. One asked, "Why should we follow regulations that the government itself does not follow?"

Another common white-collar neutralization technique was to put blame for crime onto the victims: victims were deserving of victimization. The offenders were actually the real victims, and the people they were stealing from "had it coming" for the way they had treated others. Greedy corporations and banks should not be considered victims because of their prior actions of preying on individuals. Some felt it was okay to cheat on their taxes because the government did things they disagreed with, such as legalize abortion. Why give tax money to an organization that will only spend it on disagreeable activities?

Many participants claimed that they should not be held responsible for the commission of their crimes because their actions were the result of social conditions or bad advice from others whom they trusted. They blamed the business culture or their colleagues for their decision to engage in their trust-violating behavior.

Those using the defense of necessity claimed to be in a desperate situation and that their crimes were born out of need and not greed. They had no choice. One told how she was desperate for money, her husband was ill and had filed bankruptcy, and she committed crime only to protect her family's ability to stay in their home.

Offenders using the defense of necessity technique often coupled it with the fulfilling of the caregiver role (i.e., appeal to higher loyalties). They claimed that the necessity of their crimes was heightened because of their desire to protect or shield their family from harm.

Some of the neutralizations used seemed unique to white-collar crime. They claimed that what they did was common business practice and that their crimes were justifiable because others in their respective industries were committing the same types of behaviors with impunity. They had to commit crime to keep up with the competition. Others simply felt that they worked so hard they were entitled to a greater share of profit than they were actually getting. One engaged in theft because the boss denied her a raise that she felt entitled to; she compensated herself through larceny. When participants were asked what had allowed them to psychologically cross that moral and legal boundary to commit their individual acts, all of those using this technique indicated that their legitimate efforts were not meeting their financial expectations. Thus, they were entitled to the extra benefits that they obtained.

Where did they learn to use these techniques? Most of the research sample said that they learned from coworkers or colleagues both the knowledge of how to and the language necessary to pacify the feelings of guilt prior to the commission of their crimes. Thus, neutralizations can be learned through interaction with others, especially coworkers and colleagues in the field.

CRITICAL THINKING

Do you believe that people learn and assimilate neutralization techniques prior to committing crime or are they actually rationalizations formulated after the act to explain away their illegal acts? In other words, are neutralizations a cause or an effect of crime?

SOURCE: Paul Klenowski, "'Learning the Good with the Bad': Are Occupational White-Collar Offenders Taught How to Neutralize Their Crimes?" *Criminal Justice Review* 37 (2012) 461–477.

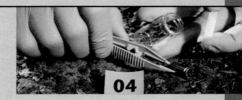

CRIMINOLOGY IN ACTION

When Being Good Is Bad

04

In their neutralization theory, Sykes and Matza claim that neutralizations provide offenders with a means of preserving a noncriminal self-concept even as they engage in crime and deviance. Sykes and Matza's vision assumes that most criminals believe in conventional norms and values and must use neutralizations in order to shield themselves from the shame attached to criminal activity. Recent research by criminologist Volkan Topalli finds that Sykes and Matza may have ignored the influential street culture that exists in highly disadvantaged neighborhoods. Using data gleaned from 191 in-depth interviews with active criminals in St. Louis, Missouri, Topalli finds that street criminals living in disorganized, gang-ridden neighborhoods "disrespect authority, lionize honor and violence, and place individual needs above those of all others." Rather than having to neutralize conventional values in order to engage in deviant ones, these offenders do not experience guilt that requires neutralizations; they are "guilt free." There is no need for them to "drift" into criminality, Topalli finds, because their allegiance to nonconventional values and lack of guilt perpetually leave them in a state of openness to crime.

Rather than being contrite or ashamed, the offenders Topalli interviewed took great pride in their criminal activities and abilities. Bacca, a street robber who attacked a long-time neighbor without provocation, exemplified such sentiments:

> Actually I felt proud of myself just for robbing him, just for doing what I did I felt proud of myself. I didn't feel like I did anything wrong, I didn't feel like I lost a friend 'cause the friends I do have . . . are lost, they're dead. I feel like I don't have anything to lose. I wanted to do just what I wanted to do.

Topalli refers to streetwise offenders such as Bacca as "hardcores," who experience no guilt for their actions and

operate with little or no regard for the law. They have little contact with agents of formal social control or conventional norms because their crimes are not directed toward conventional society— they rob drug dealers. Most hardcores maintain no permanent home, staying in various residences as their whim dictates. Their lifestyles are almost entirely dominated by the street ethics of violence, self-sufficiency, and opportunism. Obsessed with a constant need for cash, drugs, and alcohol in order to "keep the party going" on the one hand, and limited by self-defeating and reckless spending habits on the other, they often engage in violent crime to bankroll their street life activities. They do not have to neutralize conventional values, because they have none.

Rather than neutralizing conventional values, hardcore criminals often have to neutralize deviant values: they are expected to be "bad" and have to explain good behavior. Even if they themselves are the victims of crime, they can never help police or even talk to them, a practice defined as snitching and universally despised and discouraged. Smokedog, a carjacker and drug dealer, described the anticipated guilt of colluding with the police in this way: "You know I ain't never told on nobody and I ain't never gonna tell on nobody 'cause I would feel funny in the world if I told on somebody. You know, I would feel funny, I would have regrets about what I did."

Street criminals are also expected to seek vengeance if they are the target of theft or violence. If they don't, their self-image is damaged, and they look weak and ineffective. If they decide against vengeance, they must neutralize their decision by convincing themselves that they are being merciful, respecting direct appeals by their target's family and friends. T-dog, a young drug dealer and car thief, told Topalli how he neutral-

ized the decision not to seek revenge by allowing his uncle to "calm him down." The older man, a robber and drug dealer himself, intervened before T-dog could leave his house armed with two 9mm automatics: "That's basically what he told me, 'Calm down.' He took both my guns and gave me a little .22 to carry when I'm out to put me back on my feet. Gave me an ounce of crack and a pound of weed. That's what made me let it go." In other cases, offenders claimed the target was just not worth the effort, reserving their vengeance for those who were worthy opponents.

Do these findings indicate that neutralization theory is invalid? Topalli concludes that the strength of the theory is its emphasis on cognitive processes that occur prior to offending. He suggests that neutralization theory's current emphasis on a conventional cultural value orientation must be expanded to accommodate the values of the street culture.

 CRITICAL THINKING

1. Are there deviant norms and values that you have to neutralize in order to engage in conventional behaviors? What neutralizations have you come up with in order to save face when your friends wanted to engage in some forms of deviance but you decided not to take the risk?

2. Do you agree with Topalli that kids in disorganized neighborhoods shun conventional values? Or do you agree with Sykes and Matza that everyone shares conventional norms and values?

SOURCE: Volkan Topalli, "When Being Good Is Bad: An Expansion of Neutralization Theory," *Criminology* 43 (2005): 797–836.

ARE LEARNING THEORIES VALID?

Learning theories make a significant contribution to our understanding of the onset of criminal behavior. Nonetheless, the general learning model has been subject to some criticism. One complaint is that learning theorists fail to account for the origin of criminal definitions. How did the first "teacher" learn criminal techniques and definitions? Who came up with the original neutralization technique? And, as the Criminology in Action feature "When Being Good Is Bad" suggests, hardcore offenders feel little need to neutralize moral restraints—they may not have any!

Learning theories also imply that people systematically learn techniques that enable them to be active and successful criminals, but they fail to adequately explain spontaneous and wanton acts of violence and damage and other expressive crimes that appear to have little utility or purpose. Principles of differential association can easily explain shoplifting, but is it possible that a random shooting is caused by excessive deviant definitions? It is estimated that about 70 percent of all arrestees were under the influence of drugs and alcohol when they committed their crime. Do "crack heads" pause to neutralize their moral inhibitions before mugging a victim? Do drug-involved kids stop to consider what they have "learned" about moral values?[131]

Little evidence exists substantiating that people learn the techniques that enable them to become criminals before they actually commit criminal acts. It is equally plausible that people who are already deviant seek out others with similar lifestyles. Early onset of deviant behavior is now considered a key determinant of criminal careers. It is difficult to see how extremely young adolescents had the opportunity to learn criminal behavior and attitudes within a peer group setting.

Despite these criticisms, learning theories maintain an important place in the study of delinquent and criminal behavior. Unlike social structure theories, these theories are not limited to the explanation of a single facet of antisocial activity—for example, lower-class gang activity; they may be used to explain criminality across all class structures. Even corporate executives may be exposed to a variety of procriminal definitions and learn to neutralize moral constraints.

Social Control Theory

Social control theories maintain that all people have the potential to violate the law and that modern society presents many opportunities for illegal activity. Criminal activities, such as drug abuse and car theft, are often exciting pastimes that hold the promise of immediate reward and gratification.

Considering the attractions of crime, the question control theorists pose is: why do people obey the rules of society? A choice theorist would respond that it is the fear of punishment; structural theorists would say that obedience is a function of having access to legitimate opportunities; learning theorists would explain that obedience is acquired through contact with law-abiding parents and peers. In contrast, social control theorists argue that people obey the law because behavior and passions are being controlled by internal and external forces. Because they have been properly socialized, most people have developed a strong moral sense, which renders them incapable of hurting others and violating social norms. They develop a **commitment to conformity**, which requires that they obey the rules of society.[132] Properly socialized people believe that getting caught at criminal activity will hurt a dearly loved parent or jeopardize their chance at a college scholarship, or perhaps they feel that their job will be forfeited if they get in trouble with the law. In other words, people's behavior, including criminal activity, is controlled by their attachment and commitment to conventional institutions, individuals, and processes. On the other hand, those who have not been properly socialized, who lack a commitment to others or themselves, are free to violate the law and engage in deviant behavior. Those who are "uncommitted" are not deterred by the threat of legal punishments because they have little to lose.[133]

SELF-CONCEPT AND CRIME

Early versions of control theory speculated that control was a product of social interactions. Maladaptive social relations produced weak self-concept and poor self-esteem, rendering kids at risk to crime. In contrast, youths who felt good about themselves and maintained a positive attitude were able to resist the temptations of the streets. As early as 1951, sociologist Albert Reiss described how delinquents had weak egos.[134] Scott Briar and Irving Piliavin noted that youths who believe criminal activity will damage their self-image and their relationships with others will be most likely to conform to social rules; they have a commitment to conformity. In contrast, those less concerned about their social standing are free to violate the law.[135] In his **containment theory**, pioneering control theorist Walter Reckless argued that a strong self-image insulates a youth from the pressures and pulls of criminogenic influences in the environment.[136] In a series of studies conducted within the school setting, Reckless and his colleagues found that nondelinquent youths are able to maintain a positive self-image in the face of environmental pressures toward delinquency.[137]

It is Travis Hirschi's vision of social control, articulated in his highly influential 1969 book *Causes of Delinquency*, that remains the dominant version of the theory.[138]

---

commitment to conformity A strong personal investment in conventional institutions, individuals, and processes that prevents people from engaging in behavior that might jeopardize their reputation and achievements.

containment theory The idea that a strong self-image insulates a youth from the pressures and pulls of criminogenic influences in the environment.

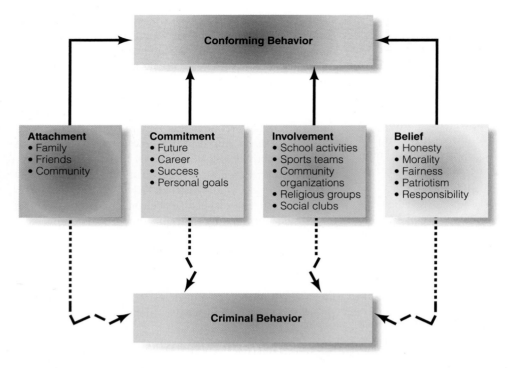

FIGURE 7.3 Elements of the Social Bond

SOURCE: © Cengage Learning

HIRSCHI'S SOCIAL BOND THEORY

 Set out the principles of Hirschi's social bond theory

In his insightful work, Hirschi links the onset of criminality to the weakening of the ties that bind people to society. He assumes that all individuals are potential law violators, but they are kept under control because they fear that illegal behavior will damage their relationships with friends, parents, neighbors, teachers, and employers. Without these social ties or bonds, and in the absence of sensitivity to and interest in others, a person is free to commit criminal acts. Hirschi does not view society as containing competing subcultures with unique value systems. Most people are aware of the prevailing moral and legal codes. He suggests, however, that in all elements of society people vary in how they respond to conventional social rules and values. Among all ethnic, religious, racial, and social groups, people whose bond to society is weak may fall prey to criminogenic behavior patterns.

Elements of the Social Bond Hirschi argues that the **social bond** a person maintains with society is divided into four main elements: attachment, commitment, involvement, and belief (Figure 7.3).

- *Attachment.* Attachment refers to a person's sensitivity to and interest in others.[139] Without a sense of attachment, psychologists believe, a person becomes a psychopath and loses the ability to relate coherently to the world. The acceptance of social norms and the development of a social conscience depend on attachment to and caring for other human beings.

   When people are attached to others they learn the kinds of behavior that are required to maintain these relationships and what behavior others expect in return. Through this process of attachment, people develop a shared understanding of social behaviors and boundaries that prevent self-focus and self-interest. A person who is able to form strong attachments feels

Though his work has achieved a prominent place in criminological literature, Hirschi, along with Michael Gottfredson, has restructured his concept of control by integrating biosocial, psychological, and rational choice theory ideas into a "General Theory of Crime." This theory of self-control is discussed more fully in Chapter 9.

ASK YOURSELF . . .

Have you experienced a lack of self-control that led to involvement with deviant behavior?

social bond Ties a person has to the institutions and processes of society. According to Hirschi, elements of the social bond include attachment, commitment, involvement, and belief.

250 **PART TWO** Theories of Crime Causation

like part of the social group, internalizing norms and values that produce conventional behavior choices—that is, they would not do anything to jeopardize the relationships they have formed. In contrast, a person who does not form strong attachments to others will be less likely to internalize or recognize the importance of these social boundaries and more likely to engage in risky behaviors—why not get drunk and stay out all night if I don't care about my parents and they don't care about me?

Hirschi views parents, peers, and schools as the important social institutions with which a person should maintain ties. Attachment to parents is the most important. Even if a family is shattered by divorce or separation, a child must retain a strong attachment to one or both parents in order to avoid involvement with antisocial behaviors.[140]

- *Commitment.* Commitment involves the time, energy, and effort expended in conventional lines of action, such as getting an education and saving money for the future. Commitment represents a person's willingness to accept and observe social norms. People who are unattached to others are probably less likely to be devoted to conventional social behaviors.

  If people build a strong commitment to conventional society, they will be less likely to engage in acts that will jeopardize their hard-won position. Conversely, the lack of commitment to conventional values may foreshadow a condition in which risk-taking behavior, such as crime, becomes a reasonable behavior alternative. The association may be reciprocal. Kids who drink and engage in deviant behavior are more likely to fail in school; kids who fail in school are more likely to later drink and engage in deviant behavior.[141]

- *Involvement.* Heavy involvement in conventional activities leaves little time for illegal behavior. When people become involved in school, recreation, and family, Hirschi believes, it insulates them from the potential lure of criminal behavior, whereas idleness enhances it.

- *Belief.* People who live in the same social setting often share common moral beliefs; they may adhere to such values as sharing, sensitivity to the rights of others, and admiration for the legal code. If these beliefs are absent or weakened, individuals are more likely to participate in antisocial or illegal acts.

Hirschi further suggests that the interrelationship of social bond elements controls subsequent behavior. People who feel kinship with and sensitivity to parents and friends should be more likely to adopt and work toward legitimate goals or gain skills that help them avoid antisocial or dangerous behaviors. Girls, for example, who have higher levels of bonding to parents and develop good social skills in adolescence are less likely to experience dating violence as young adults. The reason: a close bond to parents reduces early adolescent alcohol use, a factor that shields girls from victimization.[142]

Testing Social Bond Theory   One of Hirschi's most significant contributions was his attempt to test the principal hypotheses of social bond theory. He administered a detailed self-report survey to a sample of more than 4,000 junior and senior high school students in Contra Costa County, California.[143] In a detailed analysis of the data, Hirschi found considerable evidence to support the control theory model. Among Hirschi's more important findings are the following:

- Youths who were strongly attached to their parents were less likely to commit criminal acts.
- Commitment to conventional values, such as striving to get a good education and refusing to drink alcohol and "cruise around," was indicative of conventional behavior.

People who are committed to approved and conventional social norms and values are also more likely to succeed. Here, Dania Darwish speaks with her mother following Hunter College graduation ceremonies held at Madison Square Garden on May 27, 2015. Dania, a first-generation Syrian American, has been accepted into a master's degree program at three schools in England: Oxford, University of London, and the London School of Economics. She plans to pursue a career in law or diplomacy.

Robert Nickelsberg/Getty Images

- Youths involved in conventional activity, such as homework, were less likely to engage in criminal behavior.
- Youths involved in unconventional behavior, such as smoking and drinking, were more delinquency prone.
- Youths who maintained weak and distant relationships with people tended toward delinquency.
- Those who shunned unconventional acts were attached to their peers.
- Delinquents and nondelinquents shared similar beliefs about society.

Supporting Research   Hirschi's data lent important support to the validity of control theory. Even when the statistical significance of his findings was less than he expected, the direction of his research data was notably consistent. Only in very rare instances did his findings contradict the theory's most critical assumptions.

Hirschi's version of social control theory has been corroborated by numerous research studies, in the United States and abroad, showing that delinquent youth often feel detached from society.[144] Their relationships within the family, peer group, and school often appear strained, indicative of a weakened social bond and lack of attachment to significant others.[145] In contrast, strong positive attachments help control delinquency.[146]

- *Attachment.* Research indicates that, as Hirschi predicts, kids who are attached to their families, friends, and school are less likely to get involved in a deviant peer group and consequently less likely to engage in criminal activities.[147] In contrast, family detachment—including intrafamily conflict, abuse of children, and lack of affection, supervision, and family pride—are predictive of delinquent conduct.[148] Attachment to education is equally important. Youths who are detached from the educational experience are at risk of criminality; those who are committed to school are less likely to engage in delinquent acts.[149] Detachment and alienation from school may be even more predictive of delinquency than school failure and/or educational underachievement.[150]
- *Belief.* There is support for Hirschi's view that holding positive beliefs is inversely related to criminality. Children who are involved in religious activities and hold conventional religious beliefs are less likely to become involved in substance abuse.[151] Kids who live in areas marked by strong religious values and who hold strong religious beliefs themselves are less likely to engage in delinquent activities than adolescents who do not hold such beliefs or who live in less devout communities.[152]
- *Commitment.* As predicted by Hirschi, kids who are committed to future success and achievement are less likely to become involved in delinquent behaviors than those who lack such commitment.[153]
- *Involvement.* Research shows that youths who are involved in conventional leisure activities, such as supervised social activities and noncompetitive sports, are less likely

THINKING LIKE A CRIMINOLOGIST

An Ethical Dilemma

Bound for College/Bound for Trouble

The principal of the local high school, a big fan of control theory (she used to be in your class), asks for your opinion on a new policy she intends to propose to the school board. She wants to increase students' bond to education and the school experience by creating three tracks of students: one college bound, the other average, and the third for kids who need remedial help. The college bound would take advanced math and science, the average track would be reserved for those who plan to forgo college, and the remedial track would offer less-challenging course work and be designed to get the students through high school. She argues that the college-bound students will be recognized for their achievements and rewarded for their efforts, a process that will solidify their bond to the educational experience, all the while insulating them from more disruptive teens.

The principal wants you to comment on her plan. Write a memo outlining the pros and cons of the three-track plan. What is the major downside of placing kids in tracks? Will it help create or weaken bonds to education? Is it ethical to label kids educationally deficient at a young age? Might that create a self-fulfilling prophecy and encourage them to drop out?

to engage in delinquency than those who are involved in unconventional leisure activities and unsupervised, peer-oriented social pursuits.[154] Students who engage in a significant amount of prosocial extracurricular activities are more likely to experience high academic achievement and prosocial behaviors extending into young adulthood.[155]

Cross-national surveys have also supported the general findings of Hirschi's control theory.[156] For example, one study of Canadian youth found that perception of parental attachment was the strongest predictor of delinquent or law-abiding behavior. Teens who are attached to their parents may develop the social skills that equip them both to maintain harmonious social ties and to escape life stresses such as school failure.[157]

Opposing Views   A great deal of scholarly research has been conducted to corroborate social control theory by replicating Hirschi's original survey techniques.[158] There has been significant empirical support for Hirschi's work, but there are also those who question some or all of its elements. Here are some elements that have come under criticism and need further study:

- *Friendship.* One significant criticism concerns Hirschi's contention that delinquents are detached loners whose bond to their family and friends has been broken. Some critics have questioned whether delinquents (a) do have strained relations with family and peers and (b) may be influenced by close relationships with deviant peers and family members. A number of research efforts do show that delinquents maintain relationships with deviant peers and are influenced by members of their deviant peer group.[159] Delinquents, however, may not be "lone wolves" whose only personal relationships are exploitive; their friendship patterns seem quite close to those of conventional youth.[160] In fact, some types of offenders, such as drug abusers, may maintain even more intimate relations with their peers than nonabusers.[161] Hirschi would counter that what appears to be a close friendship is really a relationship of convenience and that "birds of a feather flock together" only when it suits their criminal activities. His view is supported by research conducted by criminologists Lisa Stolzenberg and Stewart D'Alessio, who found that most juvenile offenses are committed by individuals acting alone and that group offending, when it does occur, is incidental and of little importance to explaining the onset of delinquency.[162]

- *Not all elements of the bond are equal.* Hirschi makes little distinction between the importance of each element of the social bond, yet research evidence suggests that there may be differences. Some adolescents who report high levels of "involvement," which Hirschi suggests should reduce delinquency, are involved in criminal behavior. As kids get involved in behaviors outside the home, it is possible that parental control weakens, and youths have greater opportunity to commit crime.[163] When asked, children report that concepts such as "involvement" and "belief" have relatively little influence over behavior patterns."[164]

- *Deviant involvement.* Adolescents who report high levels of involvement, which Hirschi suggests should reduce delinquency, actually report high levels of criminal behavior. Typically, these are kids who are involved in activities outside the home without parental supervision.[165] Kids who spend a lot of time hanging out with their friends, unsupervised by parents and/or other authority figures, and who own cars that give them the mobility to get into even more trouble are the ones most likely to get involved in antisocial acts such as drinking and taking drugs.[166] This is especially true of dating relationships: kids who date, especially if they have multiple partners, are the ones who are likely to get into trouble and engage in delinquent acts.[167] It is possible that although involvement is important, it depends on the behavior in which a person is involved!

- *Deviant peers and parents.* Hirschi's conclusion that any form of social attachment is beneficial, even to deviant peers and parents, has also been disputed. Rather than deter delinquency attachment to deviant peers, it may support and nurture antisocial behavior. In a now classic study, criminologist Michael Hindelang found that attachment to delinquent peers escalated rather than

restricted criminality.[168] In a similar fashion, a number of research efforts have found that youths attached to drug-abusing parents are more likely to become drug users themselves.[169] Attachment to deviant family members, peers, and associates may help motivate youths to commit crime and facilitate their antisocial acts.[170]

- *Restricted in scope.* There is some question as to whether the theory can explain all modes of criminality (as Hirschi maintains) or is restricted to particular groups or forms of criminality. Control variables seem better able to explain minor delinquency (such as alcohol and marijuana abuse) than more serious criminal acts and associations (such as the association between child abuse and violence).[171] Research efforts have found control variables are more predictive of female than male behavior.[172] Perhaps girls are more deeply influenced by the quality of their bond to society.

- *Crime and social bonds.* It is possible that Hirschi miscalculated the direction of the relationship between criminality and a weakened social bond.[173] Social bond theory projects that a weakened bond leads to delinquency, but it is possible that the chain of events may flow in the opposite direction: kids who break the law find that their bond to parents, schools, and society eventually becomes weak and attenuated.[174]

Despite these criticisms, the weight of existing empirical evidence supports control theory, and it has emerged as one of the preeminent theories in criminology. For many criminologists, it is perhaps the most important way of understanding the onset of youthful misbehavior.

Social Reaction Theory

 L08 Summarize the basic elements of social reaction or labeling theory

Social reaction theory, commonly called labeling theory (the two terms are used interchangeably here), explains how the creation of criminal careers rests on social interactions and encounters. Its roots are found in the **symbolic interaction theory** of sociologists Charles Horton Cooley and George Herbert Mead, and later, Herbert Blumer.[175] Symbolic interaction theory holds that people communicate via symbols—gestures, signs, words, or images—that stand for or represent something else. A gold band on your ring finger conveys many meanings: married, stable, sexually off limits, conventional.

People interpret symbolic gestures from others and incorporate them in their self-image. When a teacher puts an A

symbolic interaction theory The sociological view that people communicate through symbols. People interpret symbolic communication and incorporate it within their personality. A person's view of reality, then, depends on his or her interpretation of symbolic gestures.

on your paper, it tells you that you are an excellent student, and the symbol pumps up your self-image. Symbols are used by others to let people know how well they are doing and whether they are liked or appreciated. Wearing a Rolex and driving a Mercedes is a symbolic way of letting people know that you are quite successful. Designer clothes carry a distinctive name or logo to make sure an observer knows the wearer is affluent and stylish—for example, a polo player symbol on a shirt or a double-C on a handbag. How people view reality then depends on the content of the messages and situations they encounter, the subjective interpretation of these interactions, and how they shape future behavior.

These symbolic messages and their interpretation also determine how people view themselves—that is, develop a self-image. More than 100 years ago, Charles Horton Cooley presented his idea of the "looking-glass self": an individual's view of self is formed by interpreting how others in society view him or her. People shape their self-concepts based on their understanding of how they are perceived by others.[176] If we believe others see us as smart, attractive, and appealing, this appraisal will form the basis of our own self-image; if we believe, through thought or action, that people view us as unappealing, foolish, or dangerous, these negative traits will shape our selves.

DEFINING CRIME AND DEVIANCE

Using an interactionist perspective, labeling theorists see crime as a social construct. A crime exists only when an act is labeled a crime; a criminal is someone so labeled. Even murder and rape are social constructs: When someone takes another person's life, it could be labeled as self-defense or cold-blooded murder, depending on how people interpret the act. The difference between a forcible rape and a consensual sexual encounter rests on how members of a jury interpret the events that took place and whom they believe. The difference between an excusable act and a criminal one is often subject to change and modification.

Because crime is a social construct, as the social world and its values change over time so too does the concept of what is crime and who is a criminal. At one time there was no national standard on when people were allowed to purchase and possess alcohol. In 1984, Congress passed the National Minimum Drinking Age Act, which required states to set the legal age for purchase and public possession of alcohol to 21 by October 1986 or lose 10 percent of their federal highway funds; the law was later upheld by the Supreme Court.[177]

Other criminal definitions have changed to reflect social realities. As you may recall (Chapter 2), the FBI recently changed its definition of rape from "the carnal knowledge of a female forcibly and against her will" to the current one of "penetration, no matter how slight, of the vagina or anus with any body part or object, or oral penetration by a sex organ of another person, without the consent of the victim."

The effect of social reaction on the definition of crime has been recognized by the founders of social reaction theory. In a defining statement, sociologist Kai Erickson argues, "Deviance is not a property inherent in certain forms of behavior, it is a property conferred upon those forms by the audience which directly or indirectly witnesses them."[178] Crime and deviance, therefore, are defined by the social audience's reaction to people and their behavior and the subsequent effects of that reaction; they are not defined by the moral content of the illegal act itself.[179]

In another famous statement, Howard Becker sums up the importance of the audience's reaction:

> Social groups create deviance by making rules whose infractions constitute deviance, and by applying those rules to particular people and labeling them as outsiders. From this point of view, deviance is not a quality of the act a person commits, but rather a consequence of the application by others of rules and sanctions to an "offender." The deviant is one to whom the label has successfully been applied; deviant behavior is behavior that people so label.[180]

Becker refers to people who create rules as *moral entrepreneurs*. An example of moral entrepreneurs today might be members of an ultra-orthodox religious group who continue to fight against same-sex marriage despite the fact that it was legalized by the Supreme Court in 2015.[181] In the aftermath of the decision, conservative religious leaders mounted a campaign for legislation that would prevent the federal government from penalizing federal employees, contractors, or religiously affiliated organizations that oppose gay marriage.[182] One group of conservative pastors released a declaration saying they wouldn't "capitulate on marriage." "We will not allow the government to coerce or infringe upon the rights of institutions to live by the sacred belief that only men and women can enter into marriage."[183]

Interaction and Interpretation   Social reaction theory rests on the concepts of *interaction* and *interpretation*.[184] Throughout their lives, people are given a variety of symbolic labels and ways to interact with others. These labels represent behavior and attitude characteristics; labels help define not just one trait but the whole person. People labeled insane are also assumed to be dangerous, dishonest, unstable, violent, strange, and otherwise unsound. Valued labels, including smart, honest, and hard working, suggest overall competence. These labels can improve self-image and social standing. Research shows that people who are labeled with one positive trait, such as being physically attractive, are assumed to maintain other traits, such as being intelligent and competent.[185] In contrast, negative labels—including troublemaker, mentally ill, and stupid—help stigmatize the recipients of these labels and reduce their self-image. Those who have accepted these labels are more prone to engage in deviant behaviors than those whose self-image has not been so tarnished.[186] Though a label may be a function of rumor, innuendo, or unfounded suspicion, its adverse impact can be immense.

Stigma can harm and diminish both the public and private self. Some groups bear public stigma, and being labeled as part of a stigmatized group "robs people of social opportunities."[187] Public stigma occurs when there is prejudice about a group that stigmatizes members (i.e., sex workers, mental patients) and helps exclude them from social opportunities, including housing and work. In contrast, self-stigma occurs when negative social attitudes are internalized, subsequently harming a person's self-esteem and inducing shame.

The long-term effects of stigma were observed in a recent study conducted by David Ramey.[188] He found that students who are punished for behavioral problems by being suspended or expelled from school—as opposed to receiving mental health treatment and medication—are more likely to be involved in the criminal justice system later in life. Black and Hispanic students are more likely to receive punishment rather than medical treatment. Kids who are labeled troublemakers are more likely to be suspended. If they miss school, they have lower grade point averages and perform worse on standardized aptitude tests. In contrast, those viewed as being in need of therapy and/or medication during childhood are more likely to be involved in the mental health system as adults.

LABELING EFFECTS AND CONSEQUENCES

Depending on the visibility of the label and the manner and severity with which it is applied, a person will have an increasing commitment to a deviant career. They may be watched and become the leading suspect when a similar crime occurs. Labeled people may find themselves turning to others similarly stigmatized for support and companionship. Isolated from conventional society, they may identify themselves as members of an outcast group and become locked into a deviant career.

Negative labeling can be quite damaging to a person's well-being. Kids who perceive that they have been negatively labeled by significant others are at risk of adopting a deviant self-concept. They may seek out deviant friends and join deviant groups and gangs.[189] If their deviant activities land them in court, the official label increases the risk of their later dropping out of high school. Rather than deterring crime, court intervention increases the likelihood of future criminality.[190] The effects of this stigma become permanent, locking people out of jobs and conventional careers.[191]

Labeling, however, is rarely a one-way street; what some people are quick to reject, others are quite willing to defend. When they learn that their child has been in trouble at school or in the community, some parents are willing to join in and condemn their kid as a "troublemaker," thereby helping to add to the label's impact and further damage their child's self-image; this process is referred to as **reflected appraisals**.[192] In contrast, when parents are supportive, the effect of negative labels bestowed by others can be neutralized, helping to ward off the damaging effects of labeling.[193]

Labeling and Deviance Depending on the visibility of the label and the manner and severity with which it is applied, a person will have an increasing commitment to a deviant career. They may be watched and become the leading suspect when a similar crime occurs. Labeled people may find themselves turning to others similarly stigmatized for support and companionship. Isolated from conventional society, they may identify themselves as members of an outcast group and become locked into a deviant career. If during the self-stigma process a devalued status is conferred by an authority figure such as a police officer or judge, the negative label may cause permanent harm. A negative label given by agents of the justice system—delinquent, criminal—may affect treatment at home, at work, at school, and in other social situations. Children may find that their parents consider them a bad influence on younger brothers and sisters. School officials may limit them to classes reserved for students with behavioral problems.

Labels conferred early in life can have lifelong consequences. Getting arrested during adolescence is associated with future offending; rather than deterring crime, formal labels increase its occurrence.[194] Official labels also increase financial hardship during young adulthood, which, in turn, decreases the odds of entering into a stable and sustaining marriage. Because marriage is viewed as a barrier to a criminal career, this means that even minimally invasive contact with the criminal justice system during adolescence has long-lasting consequences for success as an adult.[195]

Joining Deviant Cliques When people are labeled as deviant, they may join up with similarly outcast delinquent peers who facilitate their behavior.[196] Eventually, antisocial behavior becomes habitual and automatic.[197] The desire to join deviant cliques and groups may stem from a self-rejecting attitude ("at times, I think I am no good at all"), which eventually results in a weakened commitment to conventional values and behaviors. In turn, these people may acquire motives to deviate from social norms. Facilitating this attitude and value transformation is the bond social outcasts form with similarly labeled peers in the form of a deviant subculture.[198]

Membership in a deviant subculture often involves conforming to group norms that conflict with those of conventional society. Deviant behaviors that defy conventional values can serve a number of different purposes. Some acts are designed to show contempt for the source of the negative labels. Other acts are planned to distance the transgressor

---

stigma An enduring label that taints a person's identity and changes him or her in the eyes of others.

reflected appraisals When parents are alienated from their children, their negative labeling reduces their children's self-image and increases delinquency.

Michael Appleton/*New York Times*/Redux Pictures

New York mayoral candidate Anthony Weiner and his wife, Huma Abedin, a top aide to Hillary Rodham Clinton, during a news conference at the Gay Men's Health Crisis offices in New York. The revelation that Weiner had been involved in sexting damaged his identity and destroyed his political career.

forced his new employers to let him go after only a few months. The firm's head, Michael Kempner, stated about Weiner, "He understands that his presence here has created noise and distraction that just isn't helpful."[201]

A damaged identity provokes some people into repeating their antisocial behaviors, creating new labels and amplifying old ones.[202] Once their identity has been damaged, the target may reassess their own self-image: "If everyone says I am a deviant, it must be true."[203] Although labels may not have caused them to initiate antisocial behaviors, once applied, they increase the likelihood of persistent offending.

from further contact with the source of criticism (for example, an adolescent runs away from critical parents).[199]

Damaged Identity People who are given deviant labels and become notorious public figures suffer damaged identities. Their bad behavior can even be captured by cell phone cameras and show up on the Internet almost instantly. People engaging in sexual impropriety find their image online, their career in tatters. Take the case of Anthony Weiner, the former U.S. representative who served New York's 9th congressional district from January 1999 until June 2011 and was a rising political star until his "sexting" forced his resignation. Damaged identities are hard to shake. They follow you around and limit conventional opportunities, such as educational attainment and employment.[200] Weiner tried a political comeback, running for New York City mayor in 2013, but his past was too hard to overcome and his bid failed badly.

In July 2015, Weiner was hired by MWW Group, a PR firm in New York City, as a part-time consultant to serve on the company's board of advisers. But his notoriety

Retrospective Reading After someone is labeled because of some unusual or inexplicable act, people begin to reconstruct the culprit's identity so that the act and the label become understandable (e.g., "we always knew there was something wrong with that boy"). It is not unusual for the media to lead the way and interview boyhood friends of an assassin or serial killer. On news programs we can hear them report that the suspect was withdrawn, suspicious, and negativistic as a youth, expressing violent thoughts and ideation, a loner, troubled, and so on. Yet, until now no one was suspicious and nothing was done. This is referred to as **retrospective reading**, a process in which the past of the labeled person is reviewed and reevaluated to fit his or her current status. By conducting a retrospective reading, we can now understand what prompted his current behavior; therefore, the label must be accurate.[204]

Dramatization of Evil Labels become the basis of personal identity. As the negative feedback of law enforcement agencies, parents, friends, teachers, and other figures amplifies the force of the original label, stigmatized offenders may begin to reevaluate their own identities. If they are not really evil or bad, they may ask themselves, why is everyone making such a fuss? Frank Tannenbaum, a social reaction theory pioneer, referred to this process as the **dramatization of evil**. With respect to the consequences of labeling delinquent behavior, Tannenbaum stated:

> The process of making the criminal, therefore, is a process of tagging, defining, identifying, making conscious and self-conscious; it becomes a way of stimulating, suggesting and evoking the very traits that are complained of. If the theory of relation of response to stimulus has any meaning, the entire process of dealing with the young

retrospective reading The reassessment of a person's past to fit a current generalized label.

dramatization of evil As the negative feedback of law enforcement agencies, parents, friends, teachers, and other figures amplifies the force of the original label, stigmatized offenders may begin to reevaluate their own identities. The person becomes the thing he is described as being.

delinquent is mischievous insofar as it identifies him to himself or to the environment as a delinquent person. The person becomes the thing he is described as being.[205]

PRIMARY AND SECONDARY DEVIANCE

One of the best-known views of the labeling process is Edwin Lemert's concept of primary deviance and secondary deviance.[206] According to Lemert, **primary deviance** involves norm violations or crimes that have very little influence on the actor and can be quickly forgotten. For example, a college student takes a "five-finger discount" at the campus bookstore. He successfully steals a textbook, uses it to get an A in a course, goes on to graduate, is admitted into law school, and later becomes a famous judge. Because his shoplifting goes unnoticed, it is a relatively unimportant event that has little bearing on his future life.

In contrast, **secondary deviance** occurs when a deviant event comes to the attention of significant others or social control agents who apply a negative label. The newly labeled offender then reorganizes his or her behavior and personality around the consequences of the deviant act. The shoplifting student is caught by a security guard and expelled from college. With his law school dreams dashed and his future cloudy, his options are limited; people who know him say he "lacks character," and he begins to share their opinion. He eventually becomes a drug dealer and winds up in prison (Figure 7.4).

Secondary deviance involves resocialization into a deviant role. The labeled person is transformed into one who, according to Lemert, "employs his behavior or a role based upon it as a means of defense, attack, or adjustment to the overt and covert problems created by the consequent social reaction to him."[207] Secondary deviance produces a deviance amplification effect. Offenders feel isolated from the mainstream of society and become firmly locked within their deviant role. They may seek out others similarly labeled to form deviant subcultures or groups. Ever more firmly enmeshed in their deviant role, they are locked into an escalating cycle of deviance, apprehension, more powerful labels, and identity transformation. Lemert's concept of secondary deviance expresses the core of social reaction theory: deviance is a process in which one's identity is transformed. Efforts to control the offenders, whether by treatment or punishment, simply help lock them in their deviant role.

RESEARCH ON SOCIAL REACTION THEORY

L09 Review the research that underpins the labeling approach

Research on social reaction theory can be classified into two distinct categories. The first focuses on the characteristics of offenders who are chosen for labels. The theory maintains that these offenders should be relatively powerless people who are unable to defend themselves against the negative labeling. The second type of research attempts to discover the effects of being labeled. Labeling theorists predict that people who are negatively labeled should view themselves as deviant and commit increasing amounts of criminal behavior.

WHO GETS LABELED? DIFFERENTIAL ENFORCEMENT

An important principle of social reaction theory is that the law is differentially applied, benefiting those who hold economic and social power and penalizing the powerless. From the police officer's decision on whom to arrest to the prosecutor's decisions on whom to charge and for how many and what kind of charges, to the court's decision on release or bail, to the grand jury's decision on indictment, to the judge's decision on the length of the sentence, discretion works to the detriment of minorities, including African Americans, Hispanics, Asian Americans, and Native Americans.[208]

The term *racial profiling* has been used to signify that police suspicion is often directed at minority group males. Minorities and the poor are more likely to be prosecuted for criminal offenses and to receive harsher punishments when convicted.[209] Judges may sympathize with white defendants and help them avoid criminal labels, especially if they seem to come from "good families," whereas minority defendants are not afforded that luxury.[210]

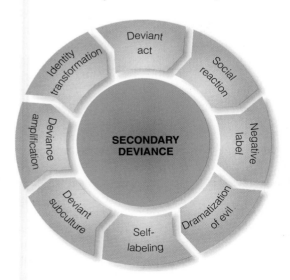

FIGURE 7.4 The Process of Creating Secondary Deviance

SOURCE: © Cengage Learning

primary deviance According to Lemert, deviant acts that do not help redefine the self-image and public image of the offender.

secondary deviance According to Lemert, accepting deviant labels as a personal identity. Acts become secondary when they form a basis for self-concept, as when a drug experimenter becomes an addict.

Nowhere is this dynamic more visible than in the so-called "war on drugs." African American drug offenders have a significantly higher likelihood of suffering drug arrests, which grow substantially with age. Before age 17, whites and blacks have similar likelihoods of drug arrest. In early adulthood, race disparities in drug arrest increase significantly: by age 22, African Americans have an 83 percent greater odds of a drug arrest than whites, and at age 27 this disparity is 235 percent. These differences exist while controlling for differences in both the nature and extent of drug offending.[211] Clearly, this evidence supports the labeling theory assertion that personal characteristics and social interactions are more important variables in developing criminal identities than merely violating the law.

Labeling Effects   Considerable evidence indicates social sanctions lead to self-labeling and deviance amplification.[212] Children negatively labeled by their parents routinely suffer a variety of problems, including antisocial behavior and school failure.[213] This process has been observed in the United States and abroad, indicating that the labeling process is universal, especially in nations in which a brush with the law brings personal dishonor, such as China and Japan.[214]

Empirical evidence supports the view that labeling plays a significant role in persistent offending.[215] Although labels may not cause adolescents to initiate criminal behaviors, those who do are significantly more likely to continue offending if they believe their parents and peers view them in a negative light; they now have a "damaged identity."[216] Maintaining a damaged identity after official labeling may, along with other negative social reactions from society, produce a *cumulative disadvantage*, which provokes some adolescents into repeating their antisocial behaviors.[217]

There is also evidence that people who are involved with official labeling agencies such as the police are the ones most likely to engage in future deviant and criminal behaviors, especially if they are the most vulnerable, at-risk adolescents.[218] Using data collected from middle-school students in seven cities to examine the deviance amplification process, Stephanie Ann Wiley and her associates compared youth with no police contact, those who were stopped by police, and those who were arrested; the latter group reported higher levels of future delinquency.[219] Those with weak social bonds and delinquent peers are the ones most likely to be affected by the negative consequences of police contact. Arrest may amplify a person's cumulative disadvantage and trigger exclusionary processes that limit conventional opportunities, such as educational attainment and employment.[220]

IS LABELING THEORY VALID?

Labeling theory has been the subject of academic debate in criminological circles. Those who criticize it point to its inability to specify the conditions that must exist before an act or individual is labeled deviant—that is, why some people are labeled and others remain "secret deviants."[221] There

are also questions about whether stigma produces crime. Labeling often comes after, rather than before, chronic offending.[222] Getting labeled by the justice system and having an enduring criminal record may have little effect on people who have been burdened with social and emotional problems since birth.[223]

While these criticisms are telling, there has been significant research showing that, as the theory predicts, people who suffer official labels are prone to a delinquent and criminal way of life. Recent research by Emily Restivo and Mark Lanier found that official labeling may lead to an increased delinquent self-identity, decreased prosocial expectations, and an increased association with delinquent peers, which then lead to an increased likelihood of engaging in subsequent delinquency. Restivo and Lanier conclude that the labeling process creates a new damaged identity for the individual that places them in the company of other damaged people. The result is they are expected to fail and their association with delinquent peers helps make sure that happens.[224]

In a now classic work, criminologists Raymond Paternoster and Leeann Iovanni identified features of the labeling perspective that are important contributions to the study of criminality:[225]

- The labeling perspective identifies the role played by social control agents in the process of crime causation. Criminal behavior cannot be fully understood if the agencies and individuals empowered to control and treat it are neglected.
- Labeling theory recognizes that criminality is not a disease or pathological behavior. It focuses attention on the social interactions and reactions that shape individuals and their behavior.
- Labeling theory distinguishes between criminal acts (primary deviance) and criminal careers (secondary deviance) and shows that these concepts must be interpreted and treated differently.

Labeling theory is also important because of its focus on interaction as well as the situations surrounding the crime. Rather than viewing the criminal as a robot-like creature whose actions are predetermined, it recognizes that crime is often the result of complex interactions and processes. The decision to commit crime involves actions of a variety of people, including peers, the victim, the police, and other key characters. Labels may expedite crime because they guide the actions of all parties involved in these criminal interactions. Actions deemed innocent when performed by one person are considered provocative when someone who has been labeled as deviant engages in them. Similarly, labeled people may be quick to judge, take offense, or misinterpret behavior of others because of past experience.

Labeling theory is also supported by research showing that convicted criminals who are placed in treatment programs aimed at reconfiguring their self-image may be able to develop revamped identities and desist from crime. Some go through "redemption rituals" in which they cast off their damaged identities and develop new ones. As a result, they develop an improved self-concept, which reflects the positive reinforcement they receive while in treatment.[226]

Evaluating Social Process Theories

The branches of social process theory—social learning, social control, and social reaction—are compatible because they suggest that criminal behavior is part of the socialization process. When interactions with critically important social institutions and processes—family, schools, justice system, peer groups, employers, and neighbors—are troubled and disturbed, people may turn to criminal solutions for their problems.

Though there is some disagreement about the relative importance of those influences and the form they take, there seems to be little question that social interactions shape the behavior, beliefs, values, and self-image of the offender. People who have learned deviant social values, find themselves detached from conventional social relationships, or are the subject of stigma and labels from significant others will be the most likely to fall prey to criminal behavior.

These negative influences can affect people in all walks of life, beginning in their youth and continuing through their majority. The major strength of the social process view is the vast body of empirical data showing that delinquents and criminals are people who grew up in dysfunctional families, who had troubled childhoods, and who failed at school, at work, and in marriage. Prison data show that these characteristics are typical of inmates.

Although persuasive, these theories do not always account for the patterns and fluctuations in the crime rate. If social process theories are valid, for example, people in the West and South must be socialized differently from those in the Midwest and New England because these latter regions have much lower crime rates. How can the fact that crime rates are lower in October than in July be explained if crime is a function of learning or control? How can social processes explain why criminals escalate their activity or why they desist from crime as they age? Once a social bond is broken, how can it be "reattached"? Once crime is "learned," how can it be "unlearned"?

Concept Summary 7.1 sets out the premises, strengths, and research focus of social process theories.

CONCEPT SUMMARY 7.1
Social Process Theories

THEORY	MAJOR PREMISE	STRENGTHS	RESEARCH FOCUS
Social Learning Theories			
Differential association theory	People learn to commit crime from exposure to antisocial definitions.	Explains onset of criminality. Explains the presence of crime in all elements of social structure. Explains why some people in high-crime areas refrain from criminality. Can apply to adults and juveniles.	Measuring definitions toward crime; influence of deviant peers and parents.
Differential reinforcement theory	Criminal behavior depends on the person's experiences with rewards for conventional behaviors and punishment for deviant ones. Being rewarded for deviance leads to crime.	Adds psychological learning theory principles to differential association. Links sociological and psychological principles.	The cause of criminal activity; how the content of socialization conditions crime.
Neutralization theory	Youths learn ways of neutralizing moral restraints and periodically drift in and out of criminal behavior patterns.	Explains why many delinquents do not become adult criminals. Explains why youthful law violators can participate in conventional behavior.	Identifying the neutralizations people use to commit crime without jeopardizing their cherished beliefs and values.
Social Control Theory			
Hirschi's control theory	A person's bond to society prevents him or her from violating social rules. If the bond weakens, the person is free to commit crime.	Explains the onset of crime; can apply to both middle- and lower-class crime. Explains its theoretical constructs adequately so they can be measured. Has been empirically tested.	Measuring the association between commitment, attachment, involvement, belief, and crime.
Social Reaction Theory			
Labeling theory	People enter into law-violating careers when they are labeled for their acts and organize their personalities around the labels.	Explains the role of society in creating deviance. Explains why some juvenile offenders do not become adult criminals. Develops concepts of criminal careers.	Determining whether self-concept is related to crime. Showing how the differential application of labels produces crime; measuring the effect of stigma.

Second Chance for Ex-Offenders Act

I am writing this letter . . . out of desperation and to tell you a little about the struggles of reentering society as a convicted felon. I have worked hard to turn my life around. I have remained clean for nearly eight years, I am succeeding in college, and I continue to share my story in schools, treatment facilities, and correctional institutions, yet I have nothing to show for it. . . . I have had numerous interviews and sent out more than 200 résumés for jobs for which I am more than qualified. I have had denial after denial because of my felony. I do understand that you are not responsible for the choices that have brought me to this point. Furthermore, I recognize that if I was not abiding by the law, if I was not clean, and if I was not focusing my efforts toward a successful future, I would have no claim to make.

So writes Jay, a man convicted of involuntary vehicular manslaughter and sentenced to 38 months in state prison nine years before. He is not alone: a criminal label can haunt people for the rest of their life, well beyond their offending years and despite the fact that they have stayed "clean" for quite some time.

Many people with records suffer stigma that prevents them from getting jobs. A recent study shows that nearly one-third of American adults have been arrested by age 23. This record will keep many people from obtaining employment, even if they have paid their dues, are qualified for the job, and are unlikely to reoffend.

Criminal records run the gamut from one-time arrests where charges are dropped to lengthy, serious, and violent criminal histories. Many people who have been arrested—and, therefore, technically have a criminal record that shows up on a background check—were never convicted of a crime. This is true not only among those charged with minor crimes but also for many individuals arrested for serious offenses.

The impact of having a criminal record is most often felt among African Americans, who may already experience racial discrimination in the labor market and are more likely than whites to have a criminal record. Research shows that a criminal record reduces the likelihood of a job callback or offer by approximately 50 percent. This criminal record "penalty" is substantially greater for African Americans than for white applicants. Hispanics suffer similar penalties in the employment market.

In addition to these significant and often overlapping challenges, an extra set of punishments, or "collateral consequences," is imposed on individuals as a direct result of their criminal convictions. These legal restrictions create barriers to jobs, housing, benefits, and voting. More than 80 percent of the statutes that place restrictions on people convicted of crime operate as denial of employment opportunities. Although some of these consequences serve important public safety purposes, others may be antiquated and create unnecessary barriers to legitimate work opportunities. A commonly cited example is that in some states formerly incarcerated people who were trained as barbers cannot hold those jobs after release because state laws prohibit felons from practicing the trade, presumably because their access to sharp objects makes them a threat to the public. Regardless of the legal restrictions, the majority of employers indicate they would "probably" or "definitely" not be willing to hire an applicant with a criminal record. There is frequent use of blanket "no-hire" policies among major corporations. Employers do not want to hire individuals who might commit future crimes and who may be a risk to their employees' and customers' safety. The assumption, of course, is that a prior record signals higher odds that the individual will commit more crimes in the future.

States are taking steps to help the situation by passing laws allowing people to erase (expunge) or seal low-level offenses after a number of years have gone by without reoffending; some states have passed laws to limit the liability of employers that hire people with criminal records.

There are also efforts afoot to reduce the stigma of a stay in prison. New York Congressman Charles Rangel proposed the Second Chance for Ex-Offenders Act of 2011, a bill that would expunge the record of any felon who (a) hadn't been convicted of a violent crime, (b) served a full sentence and completed all court-ordered requirements, (c) had been free of alcohol or drug dependency for at least a year, (d) received a high school diploma or its equivalent, and (e) completed a year of community service. So far the bill has not gotten much support in Congress, but it may eventually gain traction and serve as a means of helping former inmates avoid stigma and successfully reintegrate back into society.

CRITICAL THINKING

1. Should records be expunged within a certain time frame if a person does not reoffend? Or should knowledge of a prior criminal record be available since an employer or neighbor has a right to know about the background of people they are considering hiring?

2. Does the stigma of a criminal label serve a deterrent purpose? Are people less willing to commit a criminal act because they know that the record will follow them around forever? Would people be more willing to break the law if they knew their record would eventually be expunged?

SOURCES: H.R. 2065 (112th): Second Chance for Ex-Offenders Act of 2011, https://www.govtrack.us/congress/bills/112/hr2065; Amy Solomon, "In Search of a Job: Criminal Records as Barriers to Employment," *NIJ Journal* 270 (2012), http://www.nij.gov/journals/270/pages/criminal-records.aspx (URLs accessed May 2016).

Public Policy Implications of Social Process Theory

LO10 Review the efforts to link social process theory to crime prevention efforts

Social process theories have had a major influence on policy making since the 1950s. Learning theories have greatly influenced the way criminal offenders are dealt with and treated. The effect of these theories has mainly been felt by young offenders, who are viewed as being more salvageable than "hardened" criminals. If people become criminal by learning definitions and attitudes toward criminality, advocates of the social learning approach argue that they can "unlearn" them by being exposed to definitions toward conventional behavior. It is common today for residential and nonresidential programs to offer treatment programs that teach offenders about the harmfulness of drugs, how to forgo delinquent behavior, and how to stay in school. If learning did not affect behavior, such exercises would be futile.

Control theories have also influenced criminal justice and other public policy. Programs have been developed to increase people's commitment to conventional lines of action. Some work at creating and strengthening bonds early in life before the onset of criminality. The educational system has been the scene of numerous programs designed to improve basic skills and create an atmosphere in which youths will develop a bond to their schools. The most famous of these efforts is the Head Start program. Today, Head Start is administered by the Head Start Bureau, the Administration on Children, Youth, and Families (ACFY), the Administration for Children and Families (ACF), and the Department of Health and Human Services (DHHS). It receives annual funding of more than $8.5 billion, enrolls close to 1 million children, and provides support to more than 1,600 individual programs.[227]

Control theories have focused on the family and have played a key role in putting into operation programs designed to strengthen the bond between parent and child. Others attempt to repair bonds that have been broken and frayed. Examples of this approach are the career, work furlough, and educational opportunity programs being developed in the nation's prisons. These programs are designed to help inmates maintain a stake in society so they will be less willing to resort to criminal activity on their release.

Labeling theorists caution against too much intervention. Rather than ask social agencies to attempt to rehabilitate people having problems with the law, they argue, "less is better." Put another way, the more institutions try to "help" people, the more these people will be stigmatized and labeled. For example, a special education program designed to help problem readers may cause them to label themselves and others as slow or stupid. Similarly, a mental health rehabilitation program created with the best intentions may cause clients to be labeled as crazy or dangerous.

Diversion programs are designed to remove both juvenile and adult offenders from the normal channels of the criminal justice process by placing them in programs designed for rehabilitation. A college student whose drunken driving causes injury to a pedestrian may, before a trial occurs, be placed for six months in an alcohol treatment program. If he successfully completes the program, charges against him will be dismissed; he avoids the stigma of a criminal label.

Another label-avoiding innovation that has gained popularity is restitution. Rather than face the stigma of a formal trial, an offender is asked to either pay back the victim of the crime for any loss incurred or do some useful work in the community in lieu of receiving a court-ordered sentence.

There are efforts to reduce labeling and stigma if someone has been charged, convicted, and even sent to prison. Some important ones are discussed in the Policy and Practice in Criminology feature.

Despite their good intentions, stigma-reducing programs have not met with great success. Critics charge that they substitute one kind of stigma for another—for instance, attending a mental health program in place of a criminal trial. In addition, diversion and restitution programs usually screen out violent offenders and repeat offenders. Finally, there is little hard evidence that the recidivism rate of people placed in alternative programs is less than that of people sent to traditional programs.

> **diversion programs** Programs of rehabilitation that remove offenders from the normal channels of the criminal justice system, thus avoiding the stigma of a criminal label.

SUMMARY

LO1 Analyze the associations among socialization, social process, and crime

Social process theories view criminality as a function of people's interaction with various organizations, institutions, and processes in society. People in all walks of life have the potential to become criminals if they maintain destructive social relationships. Improper socialization is a key component of crime. Social learning theory stresses that people learn how to commit crimes and suggests that people learn criminal behaviors much as they learn conventional behavior. Social control theory analyzes the failure of society to control criminal tendencies. Social reaction (labeling) theory maintains that negative labels produce criminal careers.

L02 Assess the effect of families and education on crime

Kids growing up in troubled families are crime prone. Parental efficacy reduces crime. Divorce can strain families. School failure is linked to delinquency. Dropping out may influence later criminality. School violence and conflict are also problems.

L03 Comment on the link between peers and delinquency

Delinquent peers sustain individual offending patterns. Delinquent friends may help kids neutralize the fear of punishment. The greater the exposure to delinquent peers, the greater the likelihood of criminal behavior.

L04 Explain how personal beliefs impact on criminality

People with high moral standards can resist crime. Church attendance is related to low crime rates: the more people attend religious services, the less likely they will engage in antisocial behaviors.

L05 Compare and contrast among social learning, control, and reaction theories

According to social learning theory, people learn the techniques and attitudes to support crime from close and intimate relationships with criminal peers; crime is a learned behavior. Social control theory maintains that people are controlled by their bonds to society. Crime occurs when the forces that bind people to society are weakened or broken. At its core, social reaction theory (labeling theory) holds that a criminal career is sustained by social labels and stigma; when significant members of society label them as deviants and criminals, people accept those labels as a personal identity.

L06 Comment upon the different forms social learning theory has taken

Differential association theory was formulated by Edwin Sutherland. It holds that criminality is a result of a person's perceiving an excess of definitions in favor of crime. Gresham Sykes and David Matza created the theory of neutralization, which stresses that youths learn mental techniques that enable them to overcome societal values and drift into delinquency. Ronald Akers has posed a behavioral version of social learning called differential reinforcement theory.

L07 Set out the principles of Hirschi's social bond theory

Control theory maintains that all people have the potential to become criminals, but their bonds to conventional society prevent them from violating the law. This view suggests that a person's self-concept aids his or her commitment to conventional action. Travis Hirschi's social bond theory describes the social bond as containing elements of attachment, commitment, involvement, and belief. Weakened bonds allow youths to behave antisocially.

L08 Summarize the basic elements of social reaction or labeling theory

Social reaction or labeling theory holds that criminality is promoted by becoming negatively labeled by significant others. Such labels as "criminal," "ex-con," and "junkie" isolate people from society and lock them into lives of crime. Crime and criminality are social constructs. One person may be labeled deviant, while another finds their behavior excused. Criminality is in the eye of the beholder.

L09 Review the research that underpins the labeling approach

Labels create expectations that the labeled person will act in a certain way; labeled people are always watched and suspected. Eventually these people begin to accept their labels as personal identities, locking them further into lives of crime and deviance. People begin to view themselves as others do: troublemaker, drug addict, criminal. Edwin Lemert suggests that people who accept labels are involved in secondary deviance while primary deviants are able to maintain an undamaged identity.

L010 Review the efforts to link social process theory to crime prevention efforts

Social process theories have greatly influenced social policy. They have been applied in treatment orientations as well as community action policies. Some programs teach kids conventional attitudes and behaviors. Others are designed to improve the social bond they have with parents and teachers. Another approach is to reduce the stigma of a criminal conviction by creating alternative treatments and expunging the records of criminal offenders.

CRITICAL THINKING QUESTIONS

1. Do negative labels cause crime? Or do people who commit crime become negatively labeled? That is, are labels a cause of crime or a result?

2. Once weakened, can a person's bonds to society become reattached? What social processes might help reattachment?

3. Can you devise a test of Sutherland's differential association theory? How would you go about measuring an excess of definitions favorable toward criminality?

4. Can you think of ways you may have supported your peers' or siblings' antisocial behavior by helping them learn criminal techniques or attitudes?

5. Do you recall neutralizing any guilt you might have felt for committing a criminal or illegal act? Did your neutralizations come before or after you committed the act in question?

KEY TERMS

sociological social psychology (234)
socialization (234)
social process or socialization theory (234)
parental efficacy (236)
social learning theory (239)
social control theory (239)

social reaction theory (labeling theory) (239)
differential association theory (240)
differential reinforcement theory (243)
direct conditioning (243)
differential reinforcement (243)

negative reinforcement (244)
neutralization theory (244)
subterranean values (245)
drift (245)
commitment to conformity (249)
containment theory (249)
social bond (250)

symbolic interaction theory (253)
stigma (255)
reflected appraisals (255)
retrospective reading (256)
dramatization of evil (256)
primary deviance (257)
secondary deviance (257)
diversion programs (261)

NOTES

All URLs accessed in 2016.

1. Hunter Stuart, "Ethan Couch, 'Affluenza' Teen, Facing 5 Lawsuits," *Huffington Post*, December 12, 2013, http://www.huffingtonpost.com/2013/12/18/ethan-couch-affluenza-lawsuits-car-crash-texas_n_4461585.html; Ramit Plushnick-Masti, "'Affluenza' Isn't a Recognized Diagnosis, Experts Say After 'Brat' Spared from Jail in Drunk Driving Case," *National Post*, December 12, 2013, http://news.nationalpost.com/2013/12/12/affluenza-defence-used-to-protect-teen-driver-who-killed-four-was-never-meant-to-be-used-in-court-expert-says/.

2. USA Today, "'Affluenza' Teen Ethan Couch Transferred to Adult Jail," http://www.usatoday.com/story/news/nation-now/2016/02/06/affluenza-teen-ethan-couch-jail-time-adult/79920884/.

3. Fox4 News, Fort Worth, "Affluenza Teen Ethan Couch Gets 2 Years in Jail," http://www.fox4news.com/news/121811068-story.

4. Charles Tittle and Robert Meier, "Specifying the SES/Delinquency Relationship," *Criminology* 28 (1990): 271–299, at 274.

5. Sheldon Glueck and Eleanor Glueck, *Unraveling Juvenile Delinquency* (Cambridge, MA: Harvard University Press, 1950); Ashley Weeks, "Predicting Juvenile Delinquency," *American Sociological Review* 8 (1943): 40–46.

6. Diana Formoso, Nancy Gonzales, and Leona Aiken, "Family Conflict and Children's Internalizing and Externalizing Behavior: Protective Factors," *American Journal of Community Psychology* 28 (2000): 175–199.

7. Ming Cui and Rand D. Conger, "Parenting Behavior as Mediator and Moderator of the Association Between Marital Problems and Adolescent Maladjustment," *Journal of Research on Adolescence* 18 (2008): 261–284; James Unnever, Francis Cullen, and Robert Agnew, "Why Is 'Bad' Parenting Criminogenic? Implications from Rival Theories," *Youth Violence and Juvenile Justice* 4 (2006): 3–33.

8. Lorine Hughes and James Short, "Partying, Cruising, and Hanging in the Streets: Gangs, Routine Activities, and Delinquency and Violence in Chicago, 1959–1962," *Journal of Quantitative Criminology* 30 (2014): 415–451.

9. Roslyn Caldwell, Jenna Silverman, Noelle Lefforge, and Clayton Silver, "Adjudicated Mexican-American Adolescents: The Effects of Familial Emotional Support on Self-Esteem, Emotional Well-Being, and Delinquency," *American Journal of Family Therapy* 32 (2004): 55–69.

10. Monica J. Martin, Rand D. Conger, Thomas J. Schofield, Shannon J. Dogan, Keith F. Widaman, M. Brent Donnellan, and Tricia K. Neppl, "Evaluation of the Interactionist Model of Socioeconomic Status and Problem Behavior: A Developmental

Cascade Across Generations," Center for Poverty Research at University of California, Davis, http://poverty.ucdavis.edu/research-paper/evaluation-interactionist-model-socioeconomic-status-and-problem-behavior; Rand Conger and Katherine Conger, "Understanding the Processes Through Which Economic Hardship Influences Families and Children," in *Handbook of Families and Poverty*, ed. D. Russell Crane and Tim B. Heaton (Thousand Oaks, CA: Sage Publications, 2008), pp. 64–81.

11. Annie E. Casey Foundation, Kids Count, 2014, http://datacenter.kidscount.org/.

12. Andre Sourander, Henrik Elonheimo, Solja Niemelä, Art-Matti Nuutila, Hans Helenius, Lauri Sillanmäki, Jorma Piha, Tuulk Tamminen, Kirsti Kumpulkinen, Irma Moilanen, and Frederik Almovist, "Childhood Predictors of Male Criminality: A Prospective Population-Based Follow-Up Study from Age 8 to Late Adolescence," *Journal of the American Academy of Child and Adolescent Psychiatry* 45 (2006): 578–586.

13. Jukka Savolainen, "Relative Cohort Size and Age-Specific Arrest Rates: A Conditional Interpretation of the Easterlin Effect," *Criminology* 38 (2000): 117–136.

14. Cesar Rebellon, "Reconsidering the Broken Homes/Delinquency Relationship and Exploring Its Mediating Factors," *Criminology* 40 (2002): 103–136.

15. Joongyeup Lee, Hyunseok Jang, and Leana A. Bouffard, "Maternal Employment and

Juvenile Delinquency: A Longitudinal Study of Korean Adolescents," *Crime and Delinquency*, first published online December 7, 2011; Thomas Vander Ven and Francis Cullen, "The Impact of Maternal Employment on Serious Youth Crime: Does the Quality of Working Conditions Matter?" *Crime and Delinquency* 50 (2004): 272–292; Thomas Vander Ven, Francis Cullen, Mark Carrozza, and John Paul Wright, "Home Alone: The Impact of Maternal Employment on Delinquency," *Social Problems* 48 (2001): 236–257.

16. Judith Rich Harris, *The Nurture Assumption: Why Children Turn Out the Way They Do* (New York: Free Press, 1998).

17. Jennifer Beyers, John Bates, Gregory Pettit, and Kenneth Dodge, "Neighborhood Structure, Parenting Processes, and the Development of Youths' Externalizing Behaviors: A Multilevel Analysis," *American Journal of Community Psychology* 31 (2003): 35–53.

18. En-Ling Pan and Michael Farrell, "Ethnic Differences in the Effects of Intergenerational Relations on Adolescent Problem Behavior in U.S. Single-Mother Families," *Journal of Family Issues* 27 (2006): 1137–1158.

19. Paul Amato and Bruce Keith, "Parental Divorce and the Well-Being of Children: A Meta-Analysis," *Psychological Bulletin* 110 (1991): 26–46.

20. Michael Roettger and Raymond Swisher, "Associations of Fathers' History of Incarceration with Sons' Delinquency and Arrest Among Black, White, and Hispanic Males in the United States," *Criminology* 49 (2011): 1109–1148; Marieke van de Rakt, Joseph Murray, and Paul Nieuwbeerta, "The Long-Term Effects of Paternal Imprisonment on Criminal Trajectories of Children," *Journal of Research in Crime and Delinquency* 49 (2012): 81–108.

21. Daniel Shaw, "Advancing Our Understanding of Intergenerational Continuity in Antisocial Behavior," *Journal of Abnormal Child Psychology* 31 (2003): 193–199.

22. Donald J. West and David P. Farrington, eds., "Who Becomes Delinquent?" in *The Delinquent Way of Life* (London: Heinemann, 1977); Donald J. West, *Delinquency: Its Roots, Careers, and Prospects* (Cambridge, MA: Harvard University Press, 1982).

23. David Farrington, "Understanding and Preventing Bullying," in *Crime and Justice*, Vol. 17, ed. Michael Tonry (Chicago: University of Chicago Press, 1993), pp. 381–457.

24. Carolyn Smith and David Farrington, "Continuities in Antisocial Behavior and Parenting Across Three Generations," *Journal of Child Psychology and Psychiatry* 45 (2004): 230–247.

25. Joseph Murray and David Farrington, "Parental Imprisonment: Effects on Boys' Antisocial Behaviour and Delinquency Through the Life-Course," *Journal of Child Psychology and Psychiatry* 46 (2005): 1269–1278.

26. Lauren Porter and Ryan King, "Absent Fathers or Absent Variables? A New Look at Paternal Incarceration and Delinquency," *Journal of Research in Crime and Delinquency* 52 (2015): 414–443.

27. Christopher Uggen and Suzy McElrath, "Parental Incarceration: What We Know and Where We Need to Go," *Journal of Criminal Law and Criminology* 104 (2014): 596–604.

28. Alan Lizotte, Matthew Phillips, Marvin Krohn, Terence Thornberry, and Shawn Bushway, "Like Parent, Like Child? The Role of Delayed Childrearing in Breaking the Link Between Parent's Offending and Their Children's Antisocial Behavior," *Justice Quarterly* 32 (2015): 410.

29. John Paul Wright and Francis Cullen, "Parental Efficacy and Delinquent Behavior: Do Control and Support Matter?" *Criminology* 39 (2001): 677–706.

30. Christopher Sullivan, "Early Adolescent Delinquency: Assessing the Role of Childhood Problems, Family Environment, and Peer Pressure," *Youth Violence and Juvenile Justice* 4 (2006): 291–313.

31. Andrea Chronis, Heather Jones, Benjamin Lahey, Paul Rathouz, William Pelham, Jr., Stephanie Hall Williams, Barbara Baumann, and Heidi Kipp, "Maternal Depression and Early Positive Parenting Predict Future Conduct Problems in Young Children with Attention-Deficit/Hyperactivity Disorder," *Developmental Psychology* 43 (2007): 70–82.

32. Carter Hay, "Parenting, Self-Control, and Delinquency: A Test of Self-Control Theory," *Criminology* 39 (2001): 707–736.

33. Sonia Cota-Robles and Wendy Gamble, "Parent-Adolescent Processes and Reduced Risk for Delinquency: The Effect of Gender for Mexican American Adolescents," *Youth and Society* 37 (2006): 375–392.

34. Robert Vermeiren, Jef Bogaerts, Vladislav Ruchkin, Dirk Deboutte, and Mary Schwab-Stone, "Subtypes of Self-Esteem and Self-Concept in Adolescent Violent and Property Offenders," *Journal of Child Psychology and Psychiatry* 45 (2004): 405–411.

35. Jacinta Bronte-Tinkew, Kristin Moore, and Jennifer Carrano, "The Father-Child Relationship, Parenting Styles, and Adolescent Risk Behaviors in Intact Families," *Journal of Family Issues* 27 (2006): 850–881.

36. Jennifer Lansford, Laura Wager, John Bates, Gregory Pettit, and Kenneth Dodge, "Forms of Spanking and Children's Externalizing Behaviors," *Family Relations* 6 (2012): 224–236.

37. Carolyn Smith and Terence Thornberry, "The Relationship Between Childhood Maltreatment and Adolescent Involvement in Delinquency," *Criminology* 33 (1995): 451–479.

38. Lansford, Wager, Bates, Pettit, and Dodge, "Forms of Spanking and Children's Externalizing Behaviors."

39. Kristi Holsinger and Alexander Holsinger, "Differential Pathways to Violence and Self-Injurious Behavior: African American and White Girls in the Juvenile Justice System," *Journal of Research in Crime and Delinquency* 42 (2005): 211–242; Eric Slade and Lawrence Wissow, "Spanking in Early Childhood and Later Behavior Problems: A Prospective Study of Infants and Young Toddlers," *Pediatrics* 113 (2004): 1321–1330; Fred Rogosch and Dante Cicchetti, "Child Maltreatment and Emergent Personality Organization: Perspectives from the Five-Factor Model," *Journal of Abnormal Child Psychology* 32 (2004): 123–145.

40. Lynette Renner, "Single Types of Family Violence Victimization and Externalizing Behaviors Among Children and Adolescents," *Journal of Family Violence* 27 (2012): 177–186.

41. Maureen A. Allwood and Cathy Spatz Widom, "Child Abuse and Neglect, Developmental Role Attainment, and Adult Arrests," *Journal of Research in Crime and Delinquency* 50 (2013): 551–578.

42. Todd Herrenkohl, Rick Kosterman, David Hawkins, and Alex Mason, "Effects of Growth in Family Conflict in Adolescence on Adult Depressive Symptoms: Mediating and Moderating Effects of Stress and School Bonding," *Journal of Adolescent Health* 44 (2009): 146–152.

43. David Huh, Jennifer Tristan, Emily Wade, and Eric Stice, "Does Problem Behavior Elicit Poor Parenting? A Prospective Study of Adolescent Girls," *Journal of Adolescent Research* 21 (2006): 185–204.

44. Martha Gault-Sherman, "It's a Two-Way Street: The Bidirectional Relationship Between Parenting and Delinquency," *Journal of Youth and Adolescence* 41 (2012): 121–145.

45. Sonja Siennick, "Tough Love? Crime and Parental Assistance in Young Adulthood," *Criminology* 49 (2011): 163–196.

46. Daniel Seddig, "Crime-Inhibiting, Interactional and Co-Developmental Patterns of School Bonds and the Acceptance of Legal Norms," *Crime and Delinquency*, first published online April 1, 2015.

47. Eugene Maguin and Rolf Loeber, "Academic Performance and Delinquency," in *Crime and Justice: A Review of Research*, Vol. 20, ed. Michael Tonry (Chicago: University of Chicago Press, 1996), pp. 145–264.

48. Jeannie Oakes, *Keeping Track, How Schools Structure Inequality* (New Haven, CT: Yale University Press, 1985).

49. Joseph Gasper, *Drug Use and Delinquency: Causes of Dropping Out of High School?* (El Paso, TX: LFB Scholarly Publishing, 2012).

50. Spencer Rathus, *Voyages in Childhood* (Belmont, CA: Wadsworth, 2004).

51. Gary Sweeten, Shawn D. Bushway, and Raymond Paternoster, "Does Dropping Out of School Mean Dropping into Delinquency?" *Criminology* 47 (2009): 47–91; G. Roger Jarjoura, "Does Dropping Out of School Enhance Delinquent Involvement? Results from a Large-Scale National Probability Sample," *Criminology* 31 (1993): 149–172; Terence Thornberry, Melanie Moore, and R. L. Christenson, "The Effect of Dropping Out of High School on Subsequent Criminal Behavior," *Criminology* 23 (1985): 3–18.

52. Sweeten, Bushway, and Paternoster, "Does Dropping Out of School Mean Dropping into Delinquency?"

53. Irving Janis, *Groupthink: Psychological Studies of Policy Decisions and Fiascoes* (Boston: Houghton Mifflin, 1982).

54. Ibid., p. 463.

55. Olena Antonaccio, Charles Tittle, Ekaterina Botchkovar, and Maria Kranidioti, "The Correlates of Crime and Deviance: Additional Evidence," *Journal of Research in Crime and Delinquency*, first published online April 28, 2010, http://jrc.sagepub.com/content/47/3/297.

56. Jean Marie McGloin, "Delinquency Balance and Time Use: A Research Note," *Journal of Research in Crime and Delinquency* 49 (2012): 109–121.

57. Callie H. Burt and Carter Rees, "Behavioral Heterogeneity in Adolescent Friendship Networks," *Justice Quarterly*, first published online January 3, 2014.

58. Paul Friday, Xin Ren, Elmar Weitekamp, Hans-Jürgen Kerner, and Terrance Taylor, "A Chinese Birth Cohort: Theoretical Implications," *Journal of Research in Crime and Delinquency* 42 (2005): 123–146.

59. Harris, *The Nurture Assumption*.

60. J. C. Barnes and Robert Morris, "Young Mothers, Delinquent Children: Assessing Mediating Factors Among American Youth," *Youth Violence and Juvenile Justice* 10 (2012): 172–189.

61. Kyle Thomas, "Delinquent Peer Influence on Offending Versatility: Can Peers Promote Specialized Delinquency?" *Criminology* 5 (2015): 280–308.

62. Guang Guo, Yi Li, Hongyu Wang, Tianji Cai, and Greg J. Duncan, "Peer Influence, Genetic Propensity, and Binge Drinking: A Natural Experiment and a Replication," *American Journal of Sociology* 121 (2015): 914–954.

63. Kate Keenan, Rolf Loeber, Quanwu Zhang, Magda Stouthamer-Loeber, and Welmoet van Kammen, "The Influence of Deviant Peers on the Development of Boys' Disruptive and Delinquent Behavior: A Temporal Analysis," *Development and Psychopathology* 7 (1995): 715–726.

64. Brett Johnson Solomon, "Other-Sex Friendship Involvement Among Delinquent Adolescent Females," *Youth Violence and Juvenile Justice* 4 (2006): 75–96.

65. Terence Thornberry and Marvin Krohn, "Peers, Drug Use, and Delinquency," in *Handbook of Antisocial Behavior*, ed. David Stoff, James Breiling, and Jack Maser (New York: Wiley, 1997), pp. 218–233; Thomas Dishion, Deborah Capaldi, Kathleen Spracklen, and Fuzhong Li, "Peer Ecology of Male Adolescent Drug Use," *Development and Psychopathology* 7 (1995): 803–824.

66. Sylvie Mrug, Betsy Hoza, and William Bukowski, "Choosing or Being Chosen by Aggressive-Disruptive Peers: Do They Contribute to Children's Externalizing and Internalizing Problems?" *Journal of Abnormal Child Psychology* 32 (2004): 53–66.

67. Mark Warr, "Age, Peers, and Delinquency," *Criminology* 31 (1993): 17–40.

68. Brett Laursen, Christopher Hafen, Margaret Kerr, and Hakin Stattin, "Friend Influence over Adolescent Problem Behaviors as a Function of Relative Peer Acceptance: To Be Liked Is to Be Emulated," *Journal of Abnormal Psychology* 121 (2012): 88–94.

69. Stephen W. Baron, "Self-Control, Social Consequences, and Criminal Behavior: Street Youth and the General Theory of Crime," *Journal of Research in Crime and Delinquency* 40 (2003): 403–425.

70. David Harding, "Violence, Older Peers, and the Socialization of Adolescent Boys in Disadvantaged Neighborhoods," *American Sociological Review* 74 (2009): 445–464.

71. Daneen Deptula and Robert Cohen, "Aggressive, Rejected, and Delinquent Children and Adolescents: A Comparison of Their Friendships," *Aggression and Violent Behavior* 9 (2004): 75–104.

72. Shelley Keith Matthews and Robert Agnew, "Extending Deterrence Theory: Do Delinquent Peers Condition the Relationship Between Perceptions of Getting Caught and Offending?" *Journal of Research in Crime and Delinquency* 45 (2008): 91–118.

73. Jacob Young, Cesar Rebellon, J. C. Barnes, and Frank Weerman, "Unpacking the Black Box of Peer Similarity in Deviance: Understanding the Mechanisms Linking Personal Behavior, Peer Behavior, and Perceptions," *Criminology* 52 (2014): 60–86.

74. T. David Evans, Francis Cullen, R. Gregory Dunaway, and Velmer Burton, Jr., "Religion and Crime Reexamined: The Impact of Religion, Secular Controls, and Social Ecology on Adult Criminality," *Criminology* 33 (1995): 195–224.

75. Alex R. Piquero, Jeffrey A. Bouffard, Nicole Leeper Piquero, and Jessica M. Craig, "Does Morality Condition the Deterrent Effect of Perceived Certainty Among Incarcerated Felons?" *Crime and Delinquency*, first published online October 20, 2013.

76. Travis Hirschi and Rodney Stark, "Hellfire and Delinquency," *Social Problems* 17 (1969): 202–213.

77. Colin Baier and Bradley Wright, "If You Love Me, Keep My Commandments: A Meta-Analysis of the Effect of Religion on Crime," *Journal of Research in Crime and Delinquency* 38 (2001): 3–21; Byron Johnson, Sung Joon Jang, David Larson, and Spencer De Li, "Does Adolescent Religious Commitment Matter? A Reexamination of the Effects of Religiosity on Delinquency," *Journal of Research in Crime and Delinquency* 38 (2001): 22–44; Sung Joon Jang and Byron Johnson, "Neighborhood Disorder, Individual Religiosity, and Adolescent Use of Illicit Drugs: A Test of Multilevel Hypothesis," *Criminology* 39 (2001): 109–144.

78. Richard Petts, "Family and Religious Characteristics' Influence on Delinquency Trajectories from Adolescence to Young Adulthood," *American Sociological Review* 74 (2009): 465–483.

79. Walter Miller, *Violence by Youth Gangs and Youth Groups as a Crime Problem in Major American Cities* (Washington, DC: U.S. Government Printing Office, 1975).

80. Edwin H. Sutherland, *Principles of Criminology* (Philadelphia: Lippincott, 1939).

81. See, for example, Edwin Sutherland, "White-Collar Criminality," *American Sociological Review* 5 (1940): 2–10.

82. See Edwin Sutherland and Donald Cressey, *Criminology*, 8th ed. (Philadelphia: Lippincott, 1970), pp. 77–79.

83. Sandra Brown, Vicki Creamer, and Barbara Stetson, "Adolescent Alcohol Expectancies in Relation to Personal and Parental Drinking Patterns," *Journal of Abnormal Psychology* 96 (1987): 117–121.

84. Carlo Morselli, Pierre Tremblay, and Bill McCarthy, "Mentors and Criminal Achievement," *Criminology* 44 (2006): 17–43.

85. Ibid.

86. Travis C. Pratt, Francis T. Cullen, Christine S. Sellers, L. Thomas Winfree, Jr., Tamara D. Madensen, Leah E. Daigle, Noelle E. Fearn, and Jacinta M. Gau, "The Empirical Status of Social Learning Theory: A Meta-Analysis" *Informaworld*, November 2009, http://www.tandfonline.com/doi/abs/10.1080/07418820903379610.

87. Daniel Shaw, "Advancing Our Understanding of Intergenerational Continuity in Antisocial Behavior," *Journal of Abnormal Child Psychology* 31 (2003): 193–199.

88. Robert Lonardo, Peggy Giordano, Monica Longmore, and Wendy Manning, "Parents, Friends, and Romantic Partners: Enmeshment in Deviant Networks and Adolescent Delinquency Involvement," *Journal of Youth and Adolescence* 38 (2009): 367–383.

89. Terence P. Thornberry, "The Apple Doesn't Fall Far from the Tree (Or Does It?): Intergenerational Patterns of Antisocial Behavior—The American Society of Criminology 2008 Sutherland Address," *Criminology* 47 (2009): 297–325; Terence Thornberry, Adrienne Freeman-Gallant, Alan Lizotte, Marvin Krohn, and Carolyn Smith, "Linked Lives: The Intergenerational Transmission of Antisocial Behavior," *Journal of Abnormal Child Psychology* 31 (2003): 171–184.

90. Paul Vowell and Jieming Chen, "Predicting Academic Misconduct: A Comparative Test of Four Sociological Explanations," *Sociological Inquiry* 74 (2004): 226–249.

91. Glenn Walters, "Proactive Criminal Thinking and the Transmission of Differential Association: A Cross-Lagged Multi-Wave Path Analysis," *Criminal Justice and Behavior* 42 (2015): 1128–1144.

92. Andy Hochstetler, Heith Copes, and Matt DeLisi, "Differential Association in Group and Solo Offending," *Journal of Criminal Justice* 30 (2002): 559–566.

93. Wesley Church II, Tracy Wharton, and Julie Taylor, "An Examination of Differential Association and Social Control Theory: Family Systems and Delinquency," *Youth Violence and Juvenile Justice* 7 (2009): 3–15.

94. Wesley Younts, "Status, Endorsement and the Legitimacy of Deviance," *Social Forces* 87 (2008): 561–590.

95. Dana Haynie, Peggy Giordano, Wendy Manning, and Monica Longmore, "Adolescent Romantic Relationships and Delinquency Involvement," *Criminology* 43 (2005): 177–210.

96. Lonardo, Giordano, Longmore, and Manning, "Parents, Friends, and Romantic Partners."

97. Joel Hektner, Gerald August, and George Realmuto, "Effects of Pairing Aggressive and Nonaggressive Children in Strategic Peer Affiliation," *Journal of Abnormal Child Psychology* 31 (2003): 399–412; Matthew Ploeger, "Youth Employment and Delinquency: Reconsidering a Problematic Relationship," *Criminology* 35 (1997): 659–675; William Skinner and Anne Fream, "A Social Learning Theory Analysis of Computer Crime Among College Students," *Journal of Research in Crime and Delinquency* 34 (1997): 495–518; Denise Kandel and Mark Davies, "Friendship Networks, Intimacy, and Illicit Drug Use in Young Adulthood: A Comparison of Two Competing Theories," *Criminology* 29 (1991): 441–467.

98. Warr, "Age, Peers, and Delinquency."

99. Ryan Meldrum and Jamie Flexon, "Is Peer Delinquency in the Eye of the Beholder?: Assessing Alternative Operationalizations of Perceptual Peer Delinquency," *Criminal Justice and Behavior: An International Journal* 42 (2015): 938–951.

100. Clayton Hartjen and S. Priyadarsini, "Gender, Peers, and Delinquency," *Youth and Society* 34 (2003): 387–414.

101. Denise Kandel and Mark Davies, "Friendship Networks, Intimacy, and Illicit Drug Use in Young Adulthood: A Comparison of Two Competing Theories," *Criminology* 29 (1991): 441–467.

102. Kenneth Tunnell, "Inside the Drug Trade: Trafficking from the Dealer's Perspective," *Qualitative Sociology* 16 (1993): 361–381, at 367.

103. Marvin Krohn and Terence Thornberry, "Network Theory: A Model for Understanding Drug Abuse Among African-American and Hispanic Youth," published online July 3, 2009.

104. Daniel Mears, Matthew Ploeger, and Mark Warr, "Explaining the Gender Gap in Delinquency: Peer Influence and Moral Evaluations of Behavior," *Journal of Research in Crime and Delinquency* 35 (1998): 251–266.

105. Ibid.

106. Ronald Akers, "Is Differential Association/Social Learning Cultural Deviance Theory?" *Criminology* 34 (1996): 229–247; for an opposing view, see Travis Hirschi, "Theory Without Ideas: Reply to Akers," *Criminology* 34 (1996): 249–256.

107. Robert Burgess and Ronald Akers, "A Differential Association–Reinforcement Theory of Criminal Behavior," *Social Problems* 14 (1966): 128–147.

108. Mons Bendixen, Inger Endresen, and Dan Olweus, "Joining and Leaving Gangs: Selection and Facilitation Effects on Self-Reported Antisocial Behaviour in Early Adolescence," *European Journal of Criminology* 3 (2006): 85–114.

109. Sameer Hinduja and Jason Ingram, "Social Learning Theory and Music Piracy: The Differential Role of Online and Offline Peer Influences," *Criminal Justice Studies: A Critical Journal of Crime, Law and Society* 22 (2009): 405–420.

110. Ronald Akers, *Deviant Behavior: A Social Learning Approach*, 2nd ed. (Belmont, CA: Wadsworth, 1977).

111. Ronald Akers, Marvin Krohn, Lonn Lanza-Kaduce, and Marcia Radosevich, "Social Learning and Deviant Behavior: A Specific Test of a General Theory," *American Sociological Review* 44 (1979): 638.

112. Ibid.

113. Robert G. Morris and Ashley G. Blackburn, "Cracking the Code: An Empirical Exploration of Social Learning Theory and Computer Crime," *Journal of Crime and Justice* 32 (2009): 1–34.

114. Marvin Krohn, William Skinner, James Massey, and Ronald Akers, "Social Learning Theory and Adolescent Cigarette Smoking: A Longitudinal Study," *Social Problems* 32 (1985): 455–471.

115. L. Thomas Winfree, Christine Sellers, and Dennis L. Clason, "Social Learning and Adolescent Deviance Abstention: Toward Understanding the Reasons for Initiating, Quitting, and Avoiding Drugs," *Journal of Quantitative Criminology* 9 (1993): 101–125.

116. Jonathan Brauer, "Testing Social Learning Theory Using Reinforcement's Residue: A Multilevel Analysis of Self-Reported Theft and Marijuana Use in the National Youth Survey," *Criminology* 47 (2009): 929–970.

117. Ronald Akers and Gang Lee, "A Longitudinal Test of Social Learning Theory: Adolescent Smoking," *Journal of Drug Issues* 26 (1996): 317–343.

118. Gary Jensen and David Brownfield, "Parents and Drugs," *Criminology* 21 (1983): 543–554.

119. Ronald Akers, "Rational Choice, Deterrence and Social Learning Theory in Criminology: The Path Not Taken," *Journal of Criminal Law and Criminology* 81 (1990): 653–676.

120. Gresham Sykes and David Matza, "Techniques of Neutralization: A Theory of Delinquency," *American Sociological Review* 22 (1957): 664–670; David Matza, *Delinquency and Drift* (New York: Wiley, 1964).

121. Matza, *Delinquency and Drift*, p. 51.

122. Sykes and Matza, "Techniques of Neutralization," pp. 664–670; see also David Matza, "Subterranean Traditions of Youths," *Annals of the American Academy of Political and Social Science* 378 (1961): 116.

123. Sykes and Matza, "Techniques of Neutralization," pp. 664–670.

124. Ibid.

125. Ian Shields and George Whitehall, "Neutralization and Delinquency Among Teenagers," *Criminal Justice and Behavior* 21 (1994): 223–235; Robert A. Ball, "An Empirical Exploration of Neutralization Theory," *Criminologica* 4 (1966): 22–32. See also M. William Minor, "The Neutralization of Criminal Offense," *Criminology* 18 (1980): 103–120; Robert Gordon, James Short, Desmond Cartwright, and Fred Strodtbeck, "Values and Gang Delinquency: A Study of Street

Corner Groups," *American Journal of Sociology* 69 (1963): 109–128.

126. Robert Agnew, "The Techniques of Neutralization and Violence," *Criminology* 32 (1994): 555–580; Michael Hindelang, "The Commitment of Delinquents to Their Misdeeds: Do Delinquents Drift?" *Social Problems* 17 (1970): 500–509; Robert Regoli and Eric Poole, "The Commitment of Delinquents to Their Misdeeds: A Reexamination," *Journal of Criminal Justice* 6 (1978): 261–269.

127. Larry Siegel, Spencer Rathus, and Carol Ruppert, "Values and Delinquent Youth: An Empirical Reexamination of Theories of Delinquency," *British Journal of Criminology* 13 (1973): 237–244.

128. Nicole Leeper Piquero, Stephen Tibbetts, and Michael Blankenship, "Examining the Role of Differential Association and Techniques of Neutralization in Explaining Corporate Crime," *Deviant Behavior* 26 (2005): 159–188.

129. John Hamlin, "Misplaced Role of Rational Choice in Neutralization Theory," *Criminology* 26 (1988): 425–438.

130. Mark Pogrebin, Eric Poole, and Amos Martinez, "Accounts of Professional Misdeeds: The Sexual Exploitation of Clients by Psychotherapists," *Deviant Behavior* 13 (1992): 229–252.

131. Eric Wish, *Drug Use Forecasting 1990* (Washington, DC: National Institute of Justice, 1991).

132. Scott Briar and Irving Piliavin, "Delinquency: Situational Inducements and Commitment to Conformity," *Social Problems* 13 (1965–1966): 35–45.

133. Lawrence Sherman and Douglas Smith, with Janell Schmidt and Dennis Rogan, "Crime, Punishment, and Stake in Conformity: Legal and Informal Control of Domestic Violence," *American Sociological Review* 57 (1992): 680–690.

134. Albert Reiss, "Delinquency as the Failure of Personal and Social Controls," *American Sociological Review* 16 (1951): 196–207.

135. Briar and Piliavin, "Delinquency: Situational Inducements and Commitment to Conformity."

136. Walter Reckless, *The Crime Problem* (New York: Appleton-Century-Crofts, 1967), pp. 469–483.

137. Among the many research reports by Reckless and his colleagues are Walter Reckless, Simon Dinitz, and Ellen Murray, "The Good Boy in a High Delinquency Area," *Journal of Criminal Law, Criminology, and Police Science* 48 (1957): 12–26; Frank Scarpitti, Ellen Murray, Simon Dinitz, and Walter Reckless, "The Good Boy in a High Delinquency Area: Four Years Later," *American Sociological Review* 23 (1960): 555–558; Walter Reckless, Simon Dinitz, and Ellen Murray, "Self-Concept as an Insulator Against Delinquency," *American Sociological Review* 21 (1956): 744–746; Walter Reckless and Simon Dinitz, "Pioneering with Self-Concept as a Vulnerability Factor in Delinquency," *Journal of Criminal Law, Criminology, and Police Science* 58 (1967): 515–523; Walter Reckless, Simon Dinitz, and Barbara Kay, "The Self-Component in Potential Delinquency and Potential Non-Delinquency," *American Sociological Review* 22 (1957): 566–570.

138. Travis Hirschi, *Causes of Delinquency* (Berkeley: University of California Press, 1969).

139. Ibid., p. 231.

140. Tiffiney Barfield-Cottledge, "The Triangulation Effects of Family Structure and Attachment on Adolescent Substance Use," *Crime and Delinquency* 61 (2015): 297–320.

141. Robert Crosnoe, "The Connection Between Academic Failure and Adolescent Drinking in Secondary School," *Sociology of Education* 79 (2006): 44–60.

142. Carl Maas, Charles Fleming, Todd Herrenkohl, and Richard Catalano, "Childhood Predictors of Teen Dating Violence Victimization," *Violence and Victims* 25 (2010): 131–149.

143. Hirschi, *Causes of Delinquency*, pp. 66–74.

144. Øzden Øzbay and Yusuf Ziya Øzcan, "A Test of Hirschi's Social Bonding Theory," *International Journal of Offender Therapy and Comparative Criminology* 50 (2006): 711–726; Michael Wiatrowski, David Griswold, and Mary K. Roberts, "Social Control Theory and Delinquency," *American Sociological Review* 46 (1981): 525–541.

145. Patricia van Voorhis, Francis Cullen, Richard Mathers, and Connie Chenoweth Garner, "The Impact of Family Structure and Quality on Delinquency: A Comparative Assessment of Structural and Functional Factors," *Criminology* 26 (1988): 235–261.

146. Bobbi Jo Anderson, Malcolm Holmes, and Erik Ostresh, "Male and Female Delinquents' Attachments and Effects of Attachments on Severity of Self-Reported Delinquency," *Criminal Justice and Behavior* 26 (1999): 435–452.

147. Abigail A. Fagan, M. Lee Van Horn, J. David Hawkins, and Thomas Jaki, "Differential Effects of Parental Controls on Adolescent Substance Use: For Whom Is the Family Most Important?" *Journal of Quantitative Criminology* 29 (2013): 347–368; Helen Garnier and Judith Stein, "An 18-Year Model of Family and Peer Effects on Adolescent Drug Use and Delinquency," *Journal of Youth and Adolescence* 31 (2002): 45–56.

148. Van Voorhis, Cullen, Mathers, and Garner, "The Impact of Family Structure and Quality on Delinquency."

149. Allison Ann Payne, "A Multilevel Analysis of the Relationships Among Communal School Organization, Student Bonding, and Delinquency," *Journal of Research in Crime and Delinquency* 45 (2008): 429–455.

150. Norman White and Rolf Loeber, "Bullying and Special Education as Predictors of Serious Delinquency," *Journal of Research in Crime and Delinquency* 45 (2008): 380–397.

151. John Cochran and Ronald Akers, "An Exploration of the Variable Effects of Religiosity on Adolescent Marijuana and Alcohol Use," *Journal of Research in Crime and Delinquency* 26 (1989): 198–225.

152. Mark Regnerus and Glen Elder, "Religion and Vulnerability Among Low-Risk Adolescents," *Social Science Research* 32 (2003): 633–658; Mark Regnerus, "Moral Communities and Adolescent Delinquency: Religious Contexts and Community Social Control," *Sociological Quarterly* 44 (2003): 523–554.

153. Michael Cretacci, "Religion and Social Control: An Application of a Modified Social Bond of Violence," *Criminal Justice Review* 28 (2003): 254–277.

154. Robert Agnew and David Peterson, "Leisure and Delinquency," *Social Problems* 36 (1989): 332–348.

155. Lisa Kort-Butler and David Martin, "The Influence of High School Activity Portfolios on Risky Behaviors in Emerging Adulthood," *Justice Quarterly* 32 (2015): 381; Jonathan Zaff, Kristin Moore, Angela Romano Papillo, and Stephanie Williams, "Implications of Extracurricular Activity Participation During Adolescence on Positive Outcomes," *Journal of Adolescent Research* 18 (2003): 599–631.

156. Marianne Junger and Ineke Haen Marshall, "The Interethnic Generalizability of Social Control Theory: An Empirical Test," *Journal of Research in Crime and Delinquency* 34 (1997): 79–112; Josine Junger-Tas, "An Empirical Test of Social Control Theory," *Journal of Quantitative Criminology* 8 (1992): 18–29.

157. Teresa LaGrange and Robert Silverman, "Perceived Strain and Delinquency Motivation: An Empirical Evaluation of General Strain Theory," paper presented at the annual meeting of the American Society of Criminology, Boston, November 1995.

158. Kimberly Kempf, "The Empirical Status of Hirschi's Control Theory," in *Advances in Criminological Theory*, ed. Bill Laufer and Freda Adler (New Brunswick, NJ: Transaction Books, 1992).

159. Vander Ven, Cullen, Carrozza, and Wright, "Home Alone: The Impact of Maternal Employment on Delinquency," 253.

160. Peggy Giordano, Stephen Cernkovich, and M. D. Pugh, "Friendships and Delinquency," *American Journal of Sociology* 91 (1986): 1170–1202.

161. Denise Kandel and Mark Davies, "Friendship Networks, Intimacy, and Illicit Drug Use in Young Adulthood: A Comparison of Two Competing Theories," *Criminology* 29 (1991): 441–467.

162. Lisa Stolzenberg and Stewart D'Alessio, "Co-Offending and the Age–Crime Curve," *Journal of Research in Crime and Delinquency* 45 (2008): 65–86.

163. Velmer Burton, Francis Cullen, T. David Evans, R. Gregory Dunaway, Sesha Kethineni, and Gary Payne, "The Impact of Parental Controls on Delinquency," *Journal of Criminal Justice* 23 (1995): 111–126.

164. Kimberly Kempf Leonard and Scott Decker, "The Theory of Social Control: Does It Apply to the Very Young?" *Journal of Criminal Justice* 22 (1994): 89–105.

165. Burton, Cullen, Evans, Dunaway, "The Impact of Parental Controls on Delinquency."

166. Amy Anderson and Lorine Hughes, "Exposure to Situations Conducive to Delinquent Behavior: The Effects of Time Use, Income, and Transportation," *Journal of Research in Crime and Delinquency* 46 (2009): 5–34.

167. Patrick Seffrin, Peggy Giordano, Wendy Manning, and Monica Longmore, "The Influence of Dating Relationships on Friendship Networks, Identity Development, and Delinquency," *Justice Quarterly* 26 (2009): 238–267.

168. Michael Hindelang, "Causes of Delinquency: A Partial Replication and Extension," *Social Problems* 21 (1973): 471–487.

169. Gary Jensen and David Brownfield, "Parents and Drugs," *Criminology* 21 (1983): 543–554; see also M. Wiatrowski, D. Griswold, and M. Roberts, "Social Control Theory and Delinquency," *American Sociological Review* 46 (1981): 525–541.

170. Leslie Samuelson, Timothy Hartnagel, and Harvey Krahn, "Crime and Social Control Among High School Dropouts," *Journal of Crime and Justice* 18 (1990): 129–161.

171. Cesar Rebellon and Karen van Gundy, "Can Control Theory Explain the Link Between Parental Physical Abuse and Delinquency? A Longitudinal Analysis," *Journal of Research in Crime and Delinquency* 42 (2005): 247–274; Marvin Krohn and James Massey, "Social Control and Delinquent Behavior: An Examination of the Elements of the Social Bond," *Sociological Quarterly* 21 (1980): 529–543.

172. Jill Leslie Rosenbaum and James Lasley, "School, Community Context, and Delinquency: Rethinking the Gender Gap," *Justice Quarterly* 7 (1990): 493–513.

173. Robert Agnew, "Social Control Theory and Delinquency: A Longitudinal Test," *Criminology* 23 (1985): 47–61.

174. Alan E. Liska and M. D. Reed, "Ties to Conventional Institutions and Delinquency: Estimating Reciprocal Effects," *American Sociological Review* 50 (1985): 547–560.

175. George Herbert Mead, *Mind, Self and Society* (Chicago: University of Chicago Press, 1934); George Herbert Mead, *The Philosophy of the Act* (Chicago: University of Chicago Press, 1938); Charles Horton Cooley, *Human Nature and the Social Order* (New York: Schocken, 1964, first published 1902); Herbert Blumer, *Symbolic Interactionism: Perspective and Method* (Englewood Cliffs, NJ: Prentice Hall, 1969).

176. Cooley, *Human Nature and the Social Order*.

177. *South Dakota v. Dole*, 483 U.S. 203 (1987); The National Minimum Drinking Age Act of 1984 (23 U.S.C. § 158).

178. Kai Erickson, "Notes on the Sociology of Deviance," *Social Problems* 9 (1962): 397–414.

179. Edwin Schur, *Labeling Deviant Behavior* (New York: Harper & Row, 1972), p. 21.

180. Howard Becker, *Outsiders, Studies in the Sociology of Deviance* (New York: Macmillan, 1963), p. 9.

181. *Obergefell v. Hodges* 576 U.S. ___ (2015).

182. Tamara Audi and Jacob Gershman, "Religious Groups Vow to Fight Gay Marriage Despite Supreme Court," *Wall Street Journal*, June 26, 2015, http://www.wsj.com/articles/religious-groups-vow-to-fight-same-sex-marriage-despite-supreme-court-1435329751.

183. Ibid.

184. Bruce Link, Elmer Streuning, Francis Cullen, Patrick Shrout, and Bruce Dohrenwend, "A Modified Labeling Theory Approach to Mental Disorders: An Empirical Assessment," *American Sociological Review* 54 (1989): 400–423.

185. Linda Jackson, John Hunter, and Carole Hodge, "Physical Attractiveness and Intellectual Competence: A Meta-Analytic Review," *Social Psychology Quarterly* 58 (1995): 108–122.

186. Mike Adams, Craig Robertson, Phyllis Gray-Ray, and Melvin Ray, "Labeling and Delinquency," *Adolescence* 38 (2003): 171–186.

187. Patrick Corrigan, "How Stigma Interferes with Mental Health Care," *American Psychologist* 59 (2004): 614–625, at 614.

188. David Ramey, "The Influence of Early School Punishment and Therapy/Medication on Social Control Experiences During Young Adulthood," *Criminology*, first published online 2016.

189. Jón Gunnar Bernburg, Marvin Krohn, and Craig Rivera, "Official Labeling, Criminal Embeddedness, and Subsequent Delinquency: A Longitudinal Test of Labeling Theory," *Journal of Research in Crime and Delinquency* 43 (2006): 67–88.

190. Lee Michael Johnson, Ronald Simons, and Rand Conger, "Criminal Justice System Involvement and Continuity of Youth Crime," *Youth and Society* 36 (2004): 3–29.

191. Melvin Ray and William Downs, "An Empirical Test of Labeling Theory Using Longitudinal Data," *Journal of Research in Crime and Delinquency* 23 (1986): 169–194.

192. Ross Matsueda, "Reflected Appraisals: Parental Labeling, and Delinquency: Specifying a Symbolic Interactionist Theory," *American Journal of Sociology* 97 (1992): 1577–1611.

193. Dylan Jackson and Carter Hay, "The Conditional Impact of Official Labeling on Subsequent Delinquency: Considering the Attenuating Role of Family Attachment," *Journal of Research in Crime and Delinquency* 50 (2013): 300–322.

194. Daniel Ryan Kavish, Christopher Mullins, and Danielle Soto, "Interactionist Labeling: Formal and Informal Labeling's Effects on Juvenile Delinquency," *Crime and Delinquency*, first published online July 15, 2014.

195. Nicole Schmidt, Giza Lopes, Marvin Krohn, and Alan Lizotte, "Getting Caught and Getting Hitched: An Assessment of the Relationship Between Police Intervention, Life Chances, and Romantic Unions," *Justice Quarterly* 32 (2015): 976–1005.

196. Bernburg, Krohn, and Rivera, "Official Labeling, Criminal Embeddedness, and Subsequent Delinquency."

197. Heimer and Matsueda, "Role-Taking, Role-Commitment, and Delinquency."

198. See, for example, Howard Kaplan and Hiroshi Fukurai, "Negative Social Sanctions, Self-Rejection, and Drug Use," *Youth and Society* 23 (1992): 275–298; Howard Kaplan and Robert Johnson, "Negative Social Sanctions and Juvenile Delinquency: Effects of Labeling in a Model of Deviant Behavior," *Social Science Quarterly* 72 (1991): 98–122; Howard Kaplan, Robert Johnson, and Carol Bailey, "Deviant Peers and Deviant Behavior: Further Elaboration of a Model," *Social Psychology Quarterly* 30 (1987): 277–284.

199. Howard Kaplan, *Toward a General Theory of Deviance: Contributions from Perspectives on Deviance and Criminality* (College Station: Texas A&M University, n.d.).

200. Jón Gunnar Bernburg and Marvin Krohn, "Labeling, Life Chances, and Adult Crime: The Direct and Indirect Effects of Official Intervention in Adolescence on Crime in Early Adulthood," *Criminology* 41 (2003): 1287–1319.

201. Emily Smith, "Anthony Weiner Out of His Job at Powerhouse PR Firm," *Page Six*, September 16, 2015, http://pagesix.com/2015/09/16/anthony-weiner-out-of-his-job-at-powerhouse-p-r-firm/.

202. Robert Sampson and John Laub, "A Life-Course Theory of Cumulative Disadvantage and the Stability of Delinquency," in

Developmental Theories of Crime and Delinquency, ed. Terence Thornberry (New Brunswick, NJ: Transaction Press, 1997), pp. 133–161.

203. Suzanne Ageton and Delbert Elliott, *The Effect of Legal Processing on Self-Concept* (Boulder, CO: Institute of Behavioral Science, 1973).

204. John Lofland, *Deviance and Identity* (Englewood Cliffs, NJ: Prentice Hall, 1969).

205. Frank Tannenbaum, *Crime and the Community* (New York: Columbia University Press, 1938), pp. 19–20.

206. Edwin Lemert, *Social Pathology* (New York: McGraw-Hill, 1951).

207. Ibid., p. 75.

208. Bruce Western, *Punishment and Inequality in America* (New York: Russell Sage Foundation, 2006); Sara Steen, Rodney Engen, and Randy Gainey, "Images of Danger and Culpability: Racial Stereotyping, Case Processing, and Criminal Sentencing," *Criminology* 43 (2005): 435–468; Stephanie Bontrager, William Bales, and Ted Chiricos, "Race, Ethnicity, Threat and the Labeling of Convicted Felons," *Criminology* 43 (2005): 589–622.

209. Marjorie Zatz, "Race, Ethnicity and Determinate Sentencing," *Criminology* 22 (1984): 147–171.

210. Christina DeJong and Kenneth Jackson, "Putting Race into Context: Race, Juvenile Justice Processing, and Urbanization," *Justice Quarterly* 15 (1998): 487–504.

211. Ojmarrh Mitchell and Michael S. Caudy, "Examining Racial Disparities in Drug Arrests," *Justice Quarterly* 32 (2015): 288–313.

212. Howard Kaplan and Robert Johnson, "Negative Social Sanctions and Juvenile Delinquency: Effects of Labeling in a Model of Deviant Behavior," *Social Science Quarterly* 72 (1991): 98–122.

213. Ruth Triplett, "The Conflict Perspective, Symbolic Interactionism, and the Status Characteristics Hypothesis," *Justice Quarterly* 10 (1993): 540–558.

214. Lening Zhang, "Official Offense Status and Self-Esteem Among Chinese Youths," *Journal of Criminal Justice* 31 (2003): 99–105.

215. Charles Tittle, "Two Empirical Regularities (Maybe) in Search of an Explanation: Commentary on the Age/Crime Debate," *Criminology* 26 (1988): 75–85.

216. Sampson and Laub, "A Life-Course Theory of Cumulative Disadvantage and the Stability of Delinquency"; Douglas Smith and Robert Brame, "On the Initiation and Continuation of Delinquency," *Criminology* 4 (1994): 607–630.

217. Sampson and Laub, "A Life-Course Theory of Cumulative Disadvantage and the Stability of Delinquency."

218. Robert Morris and Alex Piquero, "For Whom Do Sanctions Deter and Label?" *Justice Quarterly* 30 (2013): 837–868.

219. Stephanie Ann Wiley, Lee Ann Slocum, and Finn-Aage Esbensen, "The Unintended Consequences of Being Stopped or Arrested: An Exploration of the Labeling Mechanisms Through Which Police Contact Leads to Subsequent Delinquency," *Criminology* 51 (2013): 927–966.

220. Bernburg and Krohn, "Labeling, Life Chances, and Adult Crime."

221. Jack Gibbs, "Conceptions of Deviant Behavior: The Old and the New," *Pacific Sociological Review* 9 (1966): 11–13.

222. Charles Tittle, "Labeling and Crime: An Empirical Evaluation," in *The Labeling of Deviance: Evaluating a Perspective*, ed. Walter Gove (New York: Wiley, 1975), pp. 157–179.

223. Megan Kurlychek, Robert Brame, and Shawn Bushway, "Enduring Risk? Old Criminal Records and Predictions of Future Criminal Involvement," *Crime and Delinquency* 53 (2007): 64–83.

224. Emily Restivo and Mark Lanier, "Measuring the Contextual Effects and Mitigating Factors of Labeling Theory," *Justice Quarterly* 32 (2015): 116–141.

225. Raymond Paternoster and Leeann Iovanni, "The Labeling Perspective and Delinquency: An Elaboration of the Theory and an Assessment of the Evidence," *Justice Quarterly* 6 (1989): 358–394.

226. Shadd Maruna, Thomas Lebel, Nick Mitchell, and Michelle Maples, "Pygmalion in the Reintegration Process: Desistance from Crime Through the Looking Glass," *Psychology, Crime, and Law* 10 (2004): 271–281.

227. National Head Start Association, http://www.nhsa.org/; Office of Head Start, http://www.acf.hhs.gov/programs/ohs.

Brendan Smialowski/Getty Images

LEARNING OBJECTIVES

L01 Define the concept of social conflict and how it shapes behavior

L02 Trace the history of critical theory and its roots in Marxist thought

L03 List the core ideas of critical criminology

L04 Define the concept of globalization and analyze its association with crime

L05 Comment on the concept of state-organized crime

L06 Compare and contrast structural and instrumental theory

L07 Analyze critical criminology and discuss criticisms of the theory

L08 Assess the concept of left realism

L09 Articulate the central themes of critical feminism and gendered criminology

L010 Explain peacemaking criminology and restorative justice

8 SOCIAL CONFLICT, CRITICAL CRIMINOLOGY, AND RESTORATIVE JUSTICE

To some, the 2016 presidential primary campaign revealed the conflict that has overrun traditional political and social institutions. On one side, billionaire candidate Donald Trump claimed that America was losing ground and was being brought to heel by outsiders who were undermining the nation. He focused his attention on religious and ethnic minorities, calling for a ban on Muslims entering the United States and promising to build a wall along the Mexican border to keep out illegal immigrants. He said: "We are not talking about isolation, we're talking about security. We're not talking about religion, we're talking about security. Our country is out of control." "Tens of thousands of people" were entering America with "cell phones with ISIS flags on them . . . I don't think so." He said he would triple the number of federal agents to enforce immigration laws, end birthright citizenship, and deport more than 11 million illegal immigrants if he was elected president. "They have to go," Trump said. "What they're doing, they're having a baby. And then all of a sudden, nobody knows . . . the baby's here." Trump said he would get Mexico to construct the border wall. If Mexico refused, a Trump administration would penalize the U.S. ally with measures such as increasing fees on border crossings and visas, imposing tariffs, and cutting foreign aid.[1]

Among those opposing Trump was Democrat Bernie Sanders, the senator from Vermont. Rather than blame Mexicans and Muslims for the nation's woes, he targeted the wealthy, claiming that the rich get richer and the poor get poorer because of government policies that benefit the very wealthy at the expense of the vast majority of Americans.[2] He was furious because, according to his calculations, the super-rich and the largest corporations and banks in America don't pay their fair share of taxes. As a result, there is not enough funding for programs that will alleviate systemic inequalities. He called the justice system "broken" and claimed it perpetuated inequality, particularly among people of color, breeding crime and poverty instead of community and economic opportunity. Sanders promised to break up the big banks, create jobs by rebuilding infrastructure, and move toward public funding of elections—and provide free tuition at public universities, all paid for by a tax on Wall Street speculation.

The campaigns of both Trump and Sanders hoped to capitalize on the anger and conflict that pervade American society. One side directed their fury at the "outsider"—immigrants and religious minorities—hoping to capture Tea Party members, while the other raged against the "insider," the wealthy and successful, reflecting the beliefs of the Occupy Wall Street movement. But both camps tapped into the fact that contemporary society can be characterized as contentious and fractious.

271

The political conflict that dominated the 2016 primary season is nothing new or unusual. We live in a world rife with political, social, and economic conflict in nearly every corner of the globe. Conflict comes in many forms, occurs at many levels of society, and involves a whole slew of adversaries: workers and bosses, the United States and its overseas enemies, religious zealots and apostates, citizens and police. It occurs within cities, in neighborhoods, and even within the family.

Conflict can be destructive when it leads to war, violence, and death. It can be functional when it results in positive social change, though sometimes it's hard to discern when change is positive. The uprisings referred to as the Arab Spring that occurred in the Middle East between 2010 and 2014 brought political and social change to Egypt, Libya, and Tunisia, but at the same time produced a civil war in Syria that has killed at least 250,000 people and displaced millions, causing a major refugee crisis in Europe.[3]

Conflict promotes crime by creating a social atmosphere in which the law is a mechanism for controlling dissatisfied,

critical criminologists Researchers who view crime as a function of the capitalist mode of production and not the social conflict that might occur in any society regardless of its economic system.

critical criminology The view that capitalism produces haves and have-nots, each engaging in a particular branch of criminality. The mode of production shapes social life. Because economic competitiveness is the essence of capitalism, conflict increases and eventually destabilizes social institutions and the individuals within them.

have-not members of society while the wealthy maintain their power. This is why crimes that are the province of the wealthy, such as illegal corporate activities, are sanctioned much more leniently than those, such as burglary, that are considered lower-class activities.

Criminologists who view crime as a function of social conflict and economic rivalry have in the past been known by a number of titles, such as conflict, Marxist, left, or radical criminologists, but today most commonly they are referred to as **critical criminologists** and their field of study as **critical criminology**.

L01 Define the concept of social conflict and how it shapes behavior

As their title hints, critical criminologists view themselves as social critics who dig beneath the surface of society to uncover its inequities. They reject the notion that law is designed to maintain a tranquil, fair society and that criminals are malevolent people who wish to trample the rights of others. They believe that the law is an instrument of power, wielded by those who control society in order to maintain their wealth, social position, and class advantage. The ability to control the law has resulted in the accumulation of wealth in the hands of a relatively few creating income inequality that threatens to undermine the economy. They consider acts of racism, sexism, imperialism, unsafe working conditions, inadequate child care, substandard housing, pollution of the environment, and war-making as a tool of foreign policy to be "true crimes." The crimes of the helpless—burglary, robbery, and assault—are often an expression of rage over unjust social and economic conditions rather than selfish acts of greedy people.[4]

Contemporary critical criminologists try to explain crime within economic and social contexts and to express the connections among social class, crime, and social control.[5] They are concerned with issues such as these:

- The role government plays in creating a crime-producing environment
- The relationship between personal or group power and the shaping of criminal law
- The prevalence of bias in justice system operations
- The relationship between a capitalist, free-enterprise economy and crime rates

Libyans attend a celebration marking the "Friday of Victory" in Tripoli on October 28, 2011, a week after former strongman Muammar Gaddafi was captured and killed. Rather than ending the violence, Gaddafi's death was followed by civil war and death across the country. The ongoing crisis in Libya resulted in tens of thousands of casualties and the collapse of its oil-based economy.

Mahmud Turkia/Getty Images

Critical criminologists often take the broader view, opposing what they consider to be "real crimes"—racism, sexism, and genocide—rather than focusing on street crimes such as burglary, robbery, and rape.[6] They want to publicize the fact that while conservative, right-wing politicians propose spending cuts for social programs, they are all for military expansion, presumably to control people in third-world countries so that American corporations can flourish abroad. Other elements of the conservative agenda include the buildup of the prison system and passage of draconian criminal laws that threaten civil rights and liberties, such as the death penalty and three-strikes laws. Critical criminologists believe they are responsible both for informing the public about the dangers of these developments and promoting social change through their teaching and research.[7]

This chapter reviews the historical development of critical criminology. It covers its principal ideas and then looks at policies that have been embraced by critical thinkers, which focus on peace and restoration rather than punishment and exclusion. Figure 8.1 illustrates the various independent branches of social conflict theory.

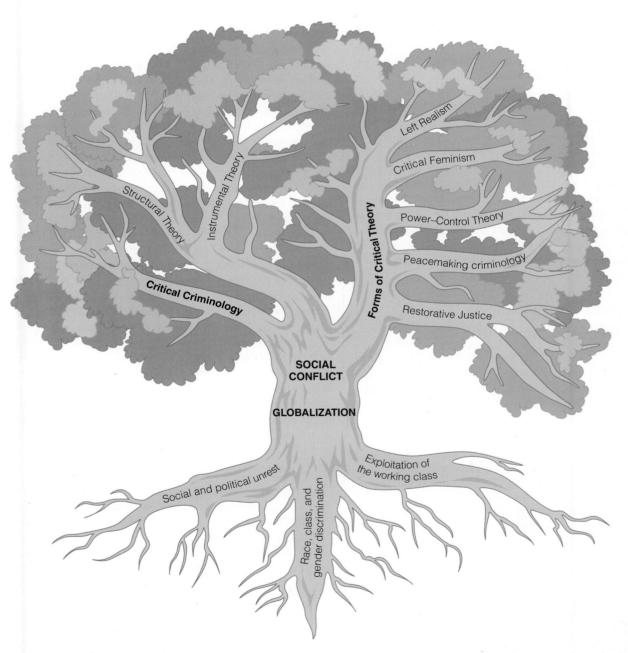

FIGURE 8.1 The Branches of Social Conflict Theory

SOURCE: © Cengage Learning

The Historical Development of Critical Criminology

L02 Trace the history of critical theory and its roots in Marxist thought

The roots of critical criminology can be traced to the social philosopher Karl Marx (1818–1883), who identified the economic structures in society that control all human relations. Marx's view of society was shaped by the economic trends and structures of that period. He lived in an era of unrestrained capitalist expansion.[8] The tools of the Industrial Revolution had become regular features of society by 1850. Mechanized factories, the use of coal to drive steam engines, and modern transportation all inspired economic development. Production had shifted from cottage industries to large factories. Industrialists could hire workers on their own terms; as a result, conditions in factories were atrocious. Factory owners and the government enforcement agents in their pay ruthlessly suppressed trade unions that promised workers salvation from these atrocities.

Marx's early career as a journalist was interrupted by government suppression of the newspaper where he worked because of the paper's liberal editorial policy. He then moved to Paris, where he met Friedrich Engels (1820–1895), who would become his friend and economic patron. By 1847, Marx and Engels had joined with a group of primarily German socialist revolutionaries known as the Communist League.

PRODUCTIVE FORCES AND PRODUCTIVE RELATIONS

In 1848, Marx issued his famous **Communist Manifesto** in which he described the oppressive labor conditions prevalent during the rise of industrial capitalism. The exploitation of the working class, he believed, would eventually lead to class conflict and the end of the capitalist system.

Communist Manifesto In this document, Marx focused his attention on the economic conditions perpetuated by the capitalist system. He stated that its development had turned workers into a dehumanized mass who lived an existence that was at the mercy of their capitalist employers.

productive forces Technology, energy sources, and material resources.

productive relations The relationships that exist among the people producing goods and services.

capitalist bourgeoisie The owners of the means of production.

proletariat A term used by Marx to refer to the working class members of society who produce goods and services but who do not own the means of production.

lumpen proletariat The fringe members at the bottom of society who produce nothing and live, parasitically, off the work of others.

Marx focused his attention on the economic conditions perpetuated by the capitalist system. He stated that its development had turned workers into a dehumanized mass who lived an existence that was at the mercy of their capitalist employers. He wrote of the injustice of young children being sent to work in mines and factories from dawn to dusk. He focused on the people who were being beaten down by a system that demanded obedience and cooperation and offered little in return. These oppressive conditions led Marx to conclude that the character of every civilization is determined by its mode of production—the way its people develop and produce material goods (materialism).

Marx identified the economic structures in society that control all human relations. Production has two components: **productive forces**, which include such things as technology, energy sources, and material resources, and **productive relations**, which are the relationships that exist among the people producing goods and services. The most important relationship in industrial culture is between the owners of the means of production, the **capitalist bourgeoisie**, and the people who do the actual labor, the **proletariat**.

Throughout history, society has been organized this way: master–slave, lord–serf, and now capitalist–proletariat. According to Marx, capitalist society is subject to the development of a rigid class structure with the capitalist bourgeoisie at the top, followed by the working proletariat, who actually produce goods and services, and at the bottom, the fringe, nonproductive members who produce nothing and live, parasitically, off the work of others—the **lumpen proletariat**.

In Marxist theory, the term *class* does not refer to an attribute or characteristic of a person or a group; rather, it denotes position in relation to others. Thus, it is not necessary to have a particular amount of wealth or prestige to be a member of the capitalist class; it is more important to have the power to exploit others economically, legally, and socially. The political and economic philosophy of the dominant class influences all aspects of life. Consciously or unconsciously, artists, writers, and teachers bend their work to the whims of the capitalist system. Thus, the economic system controls all facets of human life. Consequently, people's lives revolve around the means of production.

As Marx said:

> In all forms of society, there is one specific kind of production which predominates over the rest, whose relations thus assign rank and influence to the others. It is a general illumination which bathes all the other colours and modifies their particularity. It is a particular ether which determines the specific gravity of every being which has materialized within it.[9]

Marx believed societies and their structures were not stable and, therefore, could change through slow evolution or sudden violence. If social conflicts are not resolved, they tend to destabilize society, leading to social change.

The ebb and flow of the capitalist business cycle creates social conflicts that contain the seeds of its own destruction.

Marx predicted that from its ashes would grow a socialist state in which the workers themselves would own the means of production. In his analysis, Marx used the **dialectic method**, based on the analysis developed by the philosopher Georg Hegel (1770–1831). Hegel argued that for every idea, or **thesis**, there exists an opposing argument, or **antithesis**. Since neither position can ever be truly accepted, the result is a merger of the two ideas, a **synthesis**. Marx adapted this analytic method for his study of class struggle. History, argued Marx, is replete with examples of two opposing forces whose conflict promotes social change. When conditions are bad enough, the oppressed will rise up to fight the owners and eventually replace them. Thus, in the end, the capitalist system will destroy itself.

A MARXIST VISION OF CRIME

Marx did not write a great deal on the subject of crime, but he mentioned it in a variety of passages scattered throughout his writing. He viewed crime as the product of law enforcement policies akin to a labeling process theory.[10] He also saw a connection between criminality and the inequities found in the capitalist system. He reasoned: "There must be something rotten in the very core of a social system which increases in wealth without diminishing its misery, and increases in crime even more rapidly than in numbers."[11]

His collaborator, Friedrich Engels, however, did spend some time on the subject in his work *The Condition of the Working Class in England in 1844*.[12] Engels portrayed crime as a function of social demoralization—a collapse of people's humanity reflecting a decline in society. Workers, demoralized by capitalist society, are caught up in a process that leads to crime and violence. According to Engels, workers are social outcasts, ignored by the structure of capitalist society and treated as brutes.[13] Left to their own devices, working people commit crime because their choice is a slow death of starvation or a speedy one at the hands of the law. The brutality of the capitalist system, he believed, turns workers into animal-like creatures without a will of their own.

The writings of Karl Marx greatly influenced the development of the view of crime that rested on the concept of social conflict. Even though Marx himself did not write much on the topic of crime, his views on the relationship between the concept of crime and social conflict were first applied to criminology by three distinguished scholars: Willem Bonger, Ralf Dahrendorf, and George Vold. In some instances, their works share the Marxist view that industrial society is wracked by conflict between the proletariat and the bourgeoisie; in other instances, their writings diverge from Marxist dogma. The writing of each of these pioneers is briefly described in Exhibit 8.1.

---

dialectic method For every idea, or thesis, there exists an opposing argument, or antithesis. Because neither position can ever be truly accepted, the result is a merger of the two ideas, a synthesis. Marx adapted this analytic method for his study of class struggle.

thesis In the philosophy of Hegel, an original idea or thought.

antithesis An opposing argument.

synthesis A merger of two opposing ideas.

Marxist/Conflict Theory

ORIGIN About 1848

FOUNDERS Karl Marx, Willem Bonger, Ralf Dahrendorf, George Vold

MOST IMPORTANT WORKS Friedrich Engels, *The Condition of the Working Class in England in 1844* (1845); Marx and Engels, *The Communist Manifesto* (1848); Bonger, *Criminality and Economic Conditions* (1916); George Rusche and Otto Kircheimer, *Punishment and Social Structure* (1939); Dahrendorf, *Class and Class Conflict in Industrial Society* (1959); Vold, *Theoretical Criminology* (1958)

CORE IDEAS Crime is a function of class struggle. The capitalist system's emphasis on competition and wealth produces an economic and social environment in which crime is inevitable.

MODERN OUTGROWTHS Critical theory, conflict theory, radical theory, radical feminist theory, left realism, peacemaking, power–control theory, postmodern theory, reintegrative shaming, restorative justice

Ralf Dahrendorf

Roland Magunia/afp/ddp/Getty Images

Willem Bonger, Ralf Dahrendorf, and George Vold on Crime

WILLEM BONGER

Bonger believed that society is divided into have and have-not groups, not on the basis of people's innate ability, but because of the system of production that is in force. In every society that is divided into a ruling class and an inferior class, penal law serves the will of the ruling class. Even though criminal laws may appear to protect members of both classes, hardly any act is punished that does not injure the interests of the dominant ruling class. Crimes, then, are considered to be antisocial acts because they are harmful to those who have the power at their command to control society. Under capitalism, the legal system discriminates against the poor by defending the actions of the wealthy. Because the proletariat are deprived of the materials that are monopolized by the bourgeoisie, they are more likely to violate the law.

RALF DAHRENDORF

Dahrendorf argued that modern society is organized into what he called imperatively coordinated associations. These associations comprise two groups: those who possess authority and use it for social domination and those who lack authority and are dominated. Society is a plurality of competing interest groups. He proposed a unified conflict theory of human behavior, which can be summarized as follows:

- Every society is at every point subject to processes of change; social change is everywhere.
- Every society displays at every point dissent and conflict; social conflict is everywhere.
- Every element in a society renders a contribution to its disintegration and change.
- Every society is based on the coercion of some of its members by others.

GEORGE VOLD

Vold argued that laws are created by politically oriented groups, who seek the government's assistance to help them defend their rights and protect their interests. If a group can marshal enough support, a law will be created to hamper and curb the interests of some opposition group. Every stage of the process—from passing the law to prosecuting the case to developing relationships between inmate and guard, parole agent and parolee—is marked by conflict. Criminal acts are a consequence of direct contact between forces struggling to control society.

SOURCE: Willem Bonger, *Criminality and Economic Conditions*, abridged ed. (Bloomington: Indiana University Press, 1969, first published 1916); Ralf Dahrendorf, *Class and Class Conflict in Industrial Society* (Palo Alto, CA: Stanford University Press, 1959); George Vold, *Theoretical Criminology* (New York: Oxford University Press, 1958).

 To read about Marx and his vision, visit **http:// plato.stanford.edu/entries/marx/**. Marx is always associated with the Russian revolution, but he actually never traveled there, being born in Germany and living in France and England.

Could a Marxist-style society have benefits if it could be created without the baggage of Russian-style communism— that is, ruthless dictators and thought control?

Creating a Critical Criminology

The social ferment of the 1960s gave birth to critical criminology. In 1968, a group of British sociologists formed the National Deviancy Conference (NDC). With about 300 members, this organization sponsored several national symposia and dialogues. Members came from all walks of life, but at its core the NDC was a group of academics who were critical of the positivist criminology being taught in British and American universities. More specifically, they rejected the conservative stance of criminologists and their close financial relationship with government funding agencies.

The NDC called attention to ways in which social control might actually cause deviance rather than just respond to antisocial behavior. Many conference members became concerned about the political nature of social control.

In 1973, critical theory was given a powerful academic boost when British scholars Ian Taylor, Paul Walton, and Jock Young published *The New Criminology*.[14] This brilliant, thorough, and well-constructed critique of existing concepts in criminology called for the development of new methods of criminological analysis and critique. *The New Criminology* became the standard resource for scholars critical of both the field of criminology and the existing legal process. Since its publication there has been a tradition for critical criminologists to turn their attention to the field itself, questioning the role criminology plays in supporting the status quo and aiding in the oppression of the poor and powerless.[15]

U.S. scholars were also influenced during the late 1960s and early 1970s by the widespread unrest and social change that shook the world. The war in Vietnam, prison struggles, and the civil rights and feminist movements produced a climate in which criticism of the ruling class seemed a natural by-product. Mainstream, positivist criminology was criticized as being overtly conservative, pro-government, and antihuman. Critical criminologists scoffed when their fellow scholars used statistical analysis of computerized data to describe criminal and delinquent behavior. Several influential scholars embraced the idea that the social conflict produced by the unequal distribution of power and wealth was at the root cause of crime. William Chambliss and Robert Seidman wrote the well-respected treatise *Law, Order and Power*, which documented how the justice system protects the rich and powerful.[16] Chambliss and Seidman's work showed how control of the political and economic system affects the way criminal justice is administered and that the definitions of crime used in contemporary society favor those who control the justice system.

In another influential work, *The Social Reality of Crime*, Richard Quinney also proclaimed that in contemporary society criminal law represents the interests of those who hold power.[17] Where there is conflict between social groups—the wealthy and the poor—those who hold power will create laws that benefit themselves and keep rivals in check. Law is not an abstract body of rules that represents an absolute moral code; rather, law is an integral part of society, a force that represents a way of life and a method of doing things. Crime is a function of power relations and an inevitable result of social conflict. Criminals are not simply social misfits but people who have come up short in the struggle for success and are seeking alternative means of achieving wealth, status, or even survival.

As a group, these social thinkers began to show how in our postindustrial, capitalist society the economic system invariably produces haves and have-nots.[18] The mode of production shapes social life. Because economic competitiveness is the essence of capitalism, conflict increases and eventually destabilizes both social institutions and social groups.[19]

CONTEMPORARY CRITICAL CRIMINOLOGY

 L03 List the core ideas of critical criminology

From these early roots, a robust critical criminology was formed. At first, these alternative forms of criminology were considered Marxist and radical. They have morphed into a critical criminology that is antiestablishment and questioning of the socioeconomic structures that produce crime and criminality.[20]

Today, critical criminologists devote their attention to a number of important themes and concepts. One is the use and misuse of power, or the ability of persons and groups to determine and control the behavior of others and to shape public opinion to meet their personal interests. Because those in power shape the content of the law, it comes as no surprise that their behavior is often exempt from legal sanctions. Those who deserve the most severe sanctions (wealthy white-collar criminals whose crimes cost society millions of dollars) usually receive lenient punishments, while those whose relatively minor crimes are committed out of economic necessity (petty thieves and drug dealers) receive stricter penalties, especially if they are minority group members who lack social and economic power.[21] And once they have done their time, they face a bleak future in a jobless economy in

CONNECTIONS

The USA Patriot Act, discussed in Chapter 11, made it easier for the government to monitor and prosecute terrorists. While some welcome its provisions that make it easier for the government to control people considered dangerous, critical thinkers fear the loss of individual freedom at the expense of state power.

ASK YOURSELF . . .

Are you willing to give up elements of your privacy and individual liberty, such as having government agents monitor your emails, if it would help reduce the threat of terrorist attacks?

which the poor, minority group members and those with a criminal record are typically un- or under-employed.[22]

Critical criminologists are also deeply concerned about the current state of the American political system and the creation of what they consider to be an American empire abroad. The wars in Iraq and Afghanistan are viewed as elements of a global policy designed to control the world through the application of military power, tax cuts for the wealthy, and less money for social programs. Critical criminologists believe they are responsible for informing the public about the dangers of these developments.[23]

How Critical Criminologists Define Crime

According to critical theorists, crime is a political concept designed to protect the power and position of the upper classes at the expense of the poor. Some, but not all, would include in a list of "real" crimes such acts as violations of human rights due to racism, sexism, and imperialism and other violations of human dignity and physical needs and necessities. Take for instance what Alette Smeulers and Roelof Haveman call supranational crimes: war crimes, crimes against humanity, genocide, and other human rights violations. Smeulers and Haveman believe that these types of crimes should merit more attention by criminologists, and therefore they call for a separate specialization, **supranational criminology**.[24]

The nature of a society controls the direction of its criminality; criminals are not social misfits but products of the society and its economic system.[25] Criminals are not a group of outsiders who can be controlled by increased law enforcement. Criminality, instead, is a function of social and

supranational criminology The study of war crimes, crimes against humanity, and the supranational penal system in which such crimes are prosecuted and tried.

economic organization. To control crime and reduce criminality, societies must remove the social conditions that promote crime.[26]

In our advanced technological society, those with economic and political power control the definition of crime and the manner in which the criminal justice system enforces the law.[27] Consequently, the only crimes available to the poor are the severely sanctioned "street crimes": rape, murder, theft, and mugging. Members of the middle class cheat on their taxes and engage in petty corporate crime (employee theft), acts that generate social disapproval but are rarely punished severely. The wealthy routinely are involved in corporate acts that should be described as crimes but escape sanctions. Regulatory laws control illegal business activities, but these are rarely enforced, and violations are lightly punished. One reason is that an essential feature of capitalism is the need to expand business and create new markets. This goal often conflicts with laws designed to protect the environment and creates clashes with those who seek their enforcement. The need for expansion usually triumphs over the need to protect society. Corporate spokespeople and their political allies brand environmentalists as "tree huggers" who stand in the way of jobs and prosperity.[28]

The rich are insulated from street crimes because they live in areas far removed from crime. Those in power use the fear of crime as a tool to maintain their control over society. The poor are controlled through incarceration, and the middle class is diverted from caring about the crimes of the powerful by their fear of the crimes of the powerless.[29] Ironically, they may have more to lose from the economic crimes committed by the rich than from the street crimes of the poor. Stock market swindles and savings and loan scams cost the public billions of dollars but are typically settled with fines and probationary sentences.

Because private ownership of property is the true measure of success in American society (as opposed to, say, being a worthy person), the state becomes an ally of the wealthy in protecting their property interests. As a result, theft-related crimes are often punished more severely than are acts of violence because although the former may be interclass, the latter are typically intraclass.

How Critical Criminologists View the Cause of Crime

Critical thinkers believe that the key crime-producing element of modern corporate capitalism is the effort to create **surplus value**—the profits produced by the laboring classes

surplus value The Marxist view that the laboring classes produce wealth that far exceeds their wages and goes to the capitalist class as profits.

marginalization Displacement of workers, pushing them outside the economic and social mainstream.

that are accrued by business owners. Once accumulated, surplus value can be either reinvested or used to enrich the owners. To increase the rate of surplus value, workers can be made to toil harder for less pay, be made more efficient, or be replaced by machines or technology. Therefore, economic growth does not benefit all elements of the population, and in the long run it may produce the same effect as a depression or recession.

As the rate of surplus value increases, more people are displaced from productive relationships and the size of the marginal population swells. As corporations downsize to increase profits, high-paying labor and managerial jobs are lost to computer-driven machinery. Displaced workers are forced into service jobs at minimum wage. Many become temporary employees without benefits or a secure position.

As more people are thrust outside the economic mainstream, a condition referred to as **marginalization**, a larger portion of the population is forced to live in areas conducive to crime. Once people are marginalized, commitment to the system declines, creating another crime-producing force: a weakened bond to society.

The government may be quick to respond during periods of economic decline because those in power assume that poverty breeds crime and social disorder. When unemployment is increasing, public officials assume the worst and devote greater attention to the criminal justice system, perhaps building new prisons to prepare for the coming "crime wave."[30] Empirical research confirms that economic downturns are indeed linked to both crime rate increases and government activities such as passing anticrime legislation.[31] As the level of surplus value increases, so too do police expenditures, most likely because of the perceived or real need for the state to control those on the economic margin.[32]

 The theory of surplus value can be quite complex. To read more about it, go to **http://www .internationalviewpoint.org/spip.php?article287. How do the Internet and web commerce influence the concept of surplus value?**

FAILING SOCIAL INSTITUTIONS

Critical thinkers often focus on contemporary social institutions to show how they operate as instruments of class and racial oppression. Critical scholars find that class bias and racial oppression exist from the cradle to the grave. There are significant race-based achievement differences in education, ranging from scores on standardized tests to dropout and high school completion rates. There are high schools, mostly in poverty-stricken inner-city neighborhoods, where the high school completion rate is 40 percent or less; these are referred to as **dropout factories**. There are more than 1,700 of these failing schools in the United States. Although they represent only a small fraction of all public high schools in America, they account for about half of all high school dropouts each year.[33]

One reason for these persistent problems may be linked to differences in discipline meted out in poor and wealthy districts. Research shows that African American children receive more disciplinary infractions than children from other racial categories, despite the fact that their behavior is quite similar. Having a higher percentage of black students in a school translates into a greater use of disciplinary tactics, a factor that may explain why minority students fare less well and are more likely to disengage from school at a younger age than whites.[34] Critical thinkers might suggest that these class- and race-based burdens make crime inevitable.

GLOBALIZATION

 Define the concept of globalization and analyze its association with crime

Globalization, which usually refers to the process of creating transnational markets and political and legal systems, has shifted the focus of critical inquiry to a world perspective. Globalization began when large companies decided to establish themselves in foreign markets by adapting their products or services to the local culture. The process took off with the fall of the Soviet Union, which opened new European markets. The development of China into an industrial superpower encouraged foreign investors to take advantage of China's huge supply of workers. Capitalists hailed China's entry into the World Trade Organization in 2001 as a significant economic event. However, critical thinkers point out that the economic boom has significant costs. While the average manufacturing wage in China has risen quite a bit, it remains at about $1.75 per hour, less than a tenth of what a worker in the United States earns; many thousands of workers are killed at work each year and millions more disabled.[35]

As the Internet and communication revolution unfolded, companies were able to establish instant communications with their far-flung corporate empires, a technological breakthrough that further aided trade and foreign investments. A series of transnational corporate mergers and takeovers (such as when Ford bought Swedish car maker Volvo in 1999 and then in 2010 sold Volvo to the Chinese car company Geely) produced ever-larger transnational corporations. In some instances the mergers were designed to avoid paying taxes in the United States. In 2015, Pfizer and the Irish pharmaceutical Allergan announced a $160 billion merger that created the world's largest drug maker. Though the company is still called Pfizer, with headquarters in New York City, the deal was structured so that Allergan is technically the buyer. The reason is that corporate taxes in Ireland are significantly lower than those in the

United States; Pfizer is subject to a tax rate of more than 25 percent, while Allergan enjoys a 4.8 percent tax rate. As a result, tax proceeds from this giant company will go to Ireland even though most of its business is in the United States.[36]

Some experts believe globalization can improve the standard of living in third-world nations by providing jobs and training, but critical theorists question the altruism of multinational corporations. Their motives are exploiting natural resources, avoiding regulation, and taking advantage of desperate workers. When these giant corporations set up a factory in a developing nation, it is not to help the local population but to get around environmental laws and take advantage of needy workers who may be forced to labor in substandard conditions. In some instances, transnational companies take advantage of national unrest and calamity in order to engage in profiteering.[37] While millions have died in African civil unrest, mining operations go on unabated. Conflict diamonds are those sold in order to fund armed conflict and civil war and profits are in the billions. Conflict diamonds mined in Côte d'Ivoire and Liberia are also being smuggled into neighboring countries and exported as part of the legitimate diamond trade.[38]

Globalization has replaced imperialism and colonization as a new form of economic domination and oppression and now presents, according to critical thinkers, a threat to the world economy:

- Growing global dominance and the reach of the free-market capitalist system, which disproportionately benefits wealthy and powerful organizations and individuals
- Increasing vulnerability of indigenous people with a traditional way of life to the forces of globalized capitalism
- Growing influence and impact of international financial institutions (such as the World Bank) and the related relative decline of power of local or state-based institutions
- Nondemocratic operation of international financial institutions[39]

Globalization may have a profound influence on class relations. Workers in the United States may be replaced in high-paying manufacturing jobs not by machines but by foreign workers. Instant communication via the Internet and global communications, a development that Marx could not have foreseen, has sped the effect immeasurably. Globalization will have a profound effect both on the economy and eventually on crime rates.

Globalization and Crime   Globalization may be responsible for unrest in financial systems and in so doing has created a fertile ground for contemporary enterprise crimes.[40]

---

dropout factories High schools in which the completion rate is consistently 40 percent or less.

globalization The process of creating transnational markets, politics, and legal systems in an effort to form and sustain a global economy.

With money and power to spare, criminal enterprise groups can recruit new members, bribe government officials, and even fund private armies. International organized crime has globalized its activities for the same reasons legitimate multinational corporations have expanded around the world: new markets bring new sources of profits. As international crime expert Louise Shelley puts it:

> Just as multinational corporations establish branches around the world to take advantage of attractive labor or raw material markets, so do illicit businesses. Furthermore, international businesses, both legitimate and illicit, also establish facilities worldwide for production, marketing, and distribution needs. Illicit enterprises are able to expand geographically to take advantage of these new economic circumstances thanks to the communications and international transportation revolution.[41]

state-organized crime Acts defined by law as criminal and committed by state officials, either elected or appointed, in pursuit of their jobs as government representatives.

Because of globalization, crime has no national boundaries. Here, Canadian nationals James Clayton Riach (right) and Ali Memar Mortazavi Shirazi wait for their inquest proceeding at the Department of Justice in Manila, Philippines. The Anti-Organized and Transnational Crime Division of the National Bureau of Investigation (NBI) arrested Riach and Shirazi for trafficking illegal drugs from Mexico. The suspects have alleged links to a Mexican cartel and were undercutting Chinese traffickers dominating the local market, which could trigger a drug war, according to the NBI. During the arrest, agents seized at least three suitcases full of cocaine, methamphetamines, and MDMA.

AP Images/Bullit Marquez

CONNECTIONS

Transnational organized crime will be discussed in greater detail in Chapter 13. There seems to be little question that organized crime cartels have been rejuvenated by globalization. While traditional groups are in decline, new ones are constantly emerging.

ASK YOURSELF . . .

What organized crimes are aided by globalization? How does the anonymity of the Internet encourage transnational crimes?

Shelley argues that two elements of globalization encourage criminality: one technological, the other cultural. Technological advances such as efficient and widespread commercial airline traffic, improvements in telecommunications (ranging from global cell phone connectivity to the Internet), and the growth of international trade have all aided the growth in illicit transnational activities. These changes have facilitated the cross-border movement of goods and people, conditions exploited by criminals who now use Internet chat rooms to plan their activities. On a cultural level, globalization brings with it an ideology of free markets and free trade. The cultural shift means less intervention and regulation, conditions exploited by crime groups to cross unpatrolled borders and to expand their activities to new regions of the world. Transnational crime groups freely exploit this new freedom to travel to regions where they cannot be extradited, base their operations in countries with ineffective or corrupt law enforcement, and launder their money in countries with bank secrecy or few effective controls. Globalization has allowed both individual offenders and criminal gangs to gain tremendous operational benefits while reducing risks of apprehension and punishment.

STATE-ORGANIZED CRIME

L05 Comment on the concept of state-organized crime

While mainstream criminologists focus on the crimes of the poor and powerless, critical criminologists focus their attention on the law violations of the powerful. One area of concern is referred to as **state-organized crime**—acts defined by law as criminal and committed by state officials, elected or appointed, in pursuit of their jobs as government representatives. Their actions, or in some cases failure to act, amount to a violation of the criminal law they are bound by oath or duty to uphold.

Among the most controversial claims made by critical criminologists are those linking the United States to state-organized crime and violence. Those who study state-organized crime argue that these antisocial behaviors arise from efforts to either maintain governmental power or to uphold the race, class, and gender advantages of those who support the government. In industrial society, the state will do everything to protect the property rights of the wealthy while opposing the real interests of the poor. They might even go to war to support the capitalist classes who need the wealth and resources of other nations. The desire for natural resources such as rubber, oil, and metals was one of the primary reasons for Japan's invasion of China and other Eastern nations that sparked their entry into World War II. Sixty years later, the United States was accused by many media commentators and political pundits of invading Iraq in order to secure its oil for American use.[42]

Why do states and their representatives get caught up in illegal enterprises such as money laundering and human trafficking? There are a variety of reasons ranging from gaining revenue to controlling more territory.[43] Some of the categories of state-organized crime are discussed here.[44]

Illegal Domestic Surveillance   In 2013, Edward Snowden set off an international firestorm when he released documents showing that the National Security Agency (NSA) had programs that gave it access to a vast quantity of emails, chat logs, and other data directly from Internet companies, including Google, Facebook, and Apple. Snowden revealed that the NSA was collecting millions of email and instant messaging contact lists, searching email content, and tracking and mapping the location of cell phones.[45]

Before fleeing to Russia, Edward Snowden's illegal copying and dissemination of NSA documents showed that the U.S. government was engaging in a wide range of domestic and foreign surveillance activities. Among other things, without a warrant the agency was collecting and analyzing the content of communications of foreigners talking to persons inside the United States. The NSA was collecting data and information off of fiber optic cables used by the communications industry. Was this a crime? The government was quick to point out that the programs were designed to combat terrorism and protect U.S. citizens. While the NSA programs disturbed many people in the United States and abroad, the programs would only be considered criminal if government agents listen in on telephone conversations or intercept emails without proper approval in order to stifle dissent and monitor political opponents.

The dangers of illegal surveillance by government agencies have become magnified because technology now allows snoopers wide latitude to intercept messages and to enter computers through the Internet without being detected. In addition, closed-circuit TV cameras are now routinely used by metropolitan police agencies. Britain employs an estimated 6 million CCTV cameras, one for every 11 citizens; many cities in the United States, including Washington, New York, Chicago, and Los Angeles, have installed significant numbers of police-operated cameras trained on public spaces. Globally, there are now almost 250 million security cameras in operation.[46] This capability worries civil libertarians as well as critical criminologists.[47]

Human Rights Violations   Some governments, such as Iran, routinely deny their citizens basic civil rights, holding them without trial and using "disappearances" and summary executions to rid themselves of political dissidents. The Chinese government has been criticized for taking a heavy hand with the Muslim Uighur minority. The Beijing government claims that its crackdown is necessary to fight separatism and terrorism, but its tactic is to impose discriminatory policies against Uighurs, including prohibitions on wearing beards and veils, restrictions on fasting, and overt discrimination with respect to religious education.[48] Another example: the United Arab Emirates (UAE) government has been accused of serious human rights problems. The government detains, and in some cases forcibly disappears, individuals who criticize the authorities, and its security forces have used torture against detainees. Most troubling has been allegations that imported foreign workers are used as slave labor. The workers obtain the visas needed to work in the UAE by paying hefty fees to "labor-supply agencies"; many workers sell their homes or land or borrow money at high rates of interest to pay the agencies' fees. Upon arrival in the UAE, the indebted workers—many of whom are illiterate—are required to sign contracts with the construction companies on much worse terms than they had been promised back home, ensuring that their debts can never be paid off. In the worst cases, they are subjected to what may be considered forced labor or virtual slavery.[49] Female domestic workers are excluded from regulations that apply to workers in other sectors.

Another state-organized crime involves the operation of the correctional systems in nations that are notorious for depriving detainees of basic necessities and routinely using hard labor and torture to punish political dissidents. The CIA has made use of their brutal regimes to soften up terror suspects for interrogation and sent suspected terror suspects to secret prisons abroad, without trial or indictment. There they can be subject to harsh interrogation tactics forbidden in the United States.[50]

State-Corporate Crime   This type of state-organized crime is committed by individuals who abuse their state authority or who fail to exercise it when working with people and organizations in the private sector. For example, a state environmental agency may fail to enforce laws, resulting in the

Are Wrongful Convictions a State Crime?

04

Before 1990, most lawyers and judges thought that wrongful convictions were extremely rare. The use of DNA profiling to exonerate factually innocent prisoners made it clear that wrongful convictions regularly occur. In mid-2016, the National Registry of Exonerations listed about 1,800 exonerations of innocent prisoners occurring since 1989. Although this is a tiny percentage of all felony convictions, experts believe that about 10,000 wrongful felony convictions occur every year, or about 1 percent of all convictions.

In 1992, attorneys Barry Scheck (who gained notoriety by serving on O. J. Simpson's defense team) and Peter Neufeld formed the Innocence Project in collaboration with the Cardozo Law School in New York. The Innocence Project's mission is to exonerate wrongfully convicted persons through DNA testing.

The Innocence Project receives in excess of 200 letters per month from convicted individuals who claim their innocence. Yet the organization has only a handful of attorneys and can take on around 160 cases at a time. To date, more than 240 innocent persons have been freed through DNA testing in the United States. The Innocence Project provided direct representation or critical assistance in most of these cases.

The reasons uncovered for miscarriages of justice have included mistaken eyewitness identification, faulty forensic science, false confessions, perjury by jailhouse snitches and others, police and prosecutorial misconduct, and ineffective assistance of counsel. Jon Gould and John Firman found that the accused's age matters the most: younger defendants

are the ones most likely to be falsely convicted. Why is that? First, younger defendants are not as sophisticated as more mature and experienced defendants and are unable to be as helpful to their attorneys in preparing a defense. Second, younger defendants are less likely to be employed. Older defendants often clock into work at a particular time, providing corroborating evidence that they could not have been at the crime scene—"Look here, I was at work"—hence, fewer false convictions.

Another important factor is having any prior criminal record. Being known to the police or having your photo in a mug shot book means that you are more likely—even if you are innocent—to be erroneously identified and thereafter wrongly convicted.

Does this amount to state crime? A number of criminologists think so. Greg Stratton finds that most false convictions are a function of errors of omission or commission or purposeful obstruction by investigators. Saundra Westervelt and Kimberly Cook interviewed exonerees and found that they faced a myriad of social problems even after they were found innocent of the crimes of which they were accused. Police, prosecutors, and judges have engaged in activities that fall short of criminal behavior but nonetheless result in convictions of innocent people, including carelessness, sloppiness, short-cutting, cynicism, routine processing, stereotyping, and/or the presumption of guilt. Westervelt and Cook charge that police create inducements to falsely confess, feed information to witnesses, conduct misleading lineups and photo arrays, lose and contaminate evidence, ignore

conflicting evidence or alternative leads due to tunnel vision, and mishandle informants. Prosecutors fail to provide complete files to the defense, lose evidence, mishandle witnesses, use inflammatory and misleading evidence at trial, and intentionally exempt people of color from juries. Westervelt and Cook find that many aspects of false convictions coincide with the concept of state crime:

- Victims are powerless.
- Victimizers generally fail to recognize and understand the nature, extent, and harmfulness of institutional policies.
- Victimizers have a sense of entitlement.
- Illegal state policies and practices are manifestations of the attempt to achieve organizational, bureaucratic, or institutional goals.

 CRITICAL THINKING

Do you agree with this analysis? Are wrongful convictions really a state crime or merely sloppy police work or lazy prosecution? Is there really intent to commit a state crime here?

SOURCES: Jon Gould and John Firman, "Wrongful Convictions: The Latest Scientific Research and Implications for Law Enforcement," presentation at a National Institute of Justice Seminar, March 25, 2013, http://www.nij.gov/multimedia/presenter/presenter-gould-firman/pages/presenter-gould-firman-transcript.aspx (accessed May 2016); Greg Stratton, "Wrongfully Convicting the Innocent: A State Crime?" *Critical Criminology* 23 (2015): 21–37; Saundra D. Westervelt and Kimberly J. Cook, "Framing Innocents: The Wrongly Convicted as Victims of State Harm," *Crime Law and Social Change* 53 (2010): 259–275.

pollution of public waterways or airways. This oversight can cause significant damage. When Michael Lynch and Kimberly Barrett examined deaths and diseases associated with pollution from coal-fired power plants (CFPPs), they found that the small-particle pollution these plants produce causes more deaths in the United States each year than homicide.[51]

State-corporate crime is particularly alarming considering that regulatory law aimed at controlling private

corporations is being scaled back while globalization has made corporations worldwide entities both in production and in advancing the consumption of their products.[52]

State Violence Sometimes nations engage in violence to maintain their power over dissident groups. Army or police officers form death squads—armed vigilante groups that kill suspected political opponents or other undesirables.

Russian State-Organized Crime

Russia has not hesitated to send troops to neighboring countries that threaten its hegemony, a practice that amounts to state-organized crime. Russian troops have intimidated and attacked local populations when they desire independence. Its two wars against breakaway province Chechnya went on from the mid-1990s until 2009, when with massive firepower they crushed the separatist rebel groups; hundreds of thousands died during the conflict. Enraged by terrorist attacks by Chechen fighters who attacked targets in the homeland, the Russians created death squads made up of elite Russian special forces commandos who would stop at nothing to find, torture, and kill enemy combatants. Intelligence was often extracted by breaking limbs with a hammer, administering electric shocks, and forcing men to perform sexual acts on each other. The bodies were either buried in unmarked pits or pulverized. The scenes would occasionally be filmed and circulated among enemy combatants as a form of psychological warfare.

In February and March of 2014, the independent nation of Ukraine was in turmoil after days and nights of clashes between antigovernment protesters and police that ended with a vote in parliament to oust President Viktor Yanukovych, a close ally and supporter of Russia and its leader Vladimir Putin. The cause of the rioting was the government's rejection of an accord with the European Union in favor of stronger ties with Russia. With a population of 45 million people, a majority of Ukrainians sought ties with the West, something that was considered unacceptable to the Russian premier. On February 20, 2014, the streets became a battlefield. At least 77 people were killed and hundreds wounded in clashes between protesters and police, including many shot by uniformed snipers. Russia then sent in troops with the pretext that it was necessary to protect Russian citizens. Most were sent to Ukraine's autonomous republic of Crimea where Russia's Black Sea fleet is based at Sevastopol. Pro-Russian forces gradually took control of the Crimean peninsula. Soon the Crimean parliament and the city council of Sevastopol adopted a resolution to show their intention of joining the Russian Federation. A vote was held and 96 percent of those who voted in Crimea supported joining Russia.

On March 17, 2014, the Crimean parliament officially declared its independence from Ukraine and requested to join the Russian Federation; a day later, President Putin declared Crimea a part of Russia.

 CRITICAL THINKING

Is it the responsibility of the United States to intervene when a nation such as Russia commits state-organized crimes?

SOURCES: Andrew Osborn, "Russia Uses Death Squads and Torture in Chechnya, Says Amnesty," *The Independent*, June 24, 2004, http://www.independent .co.uk/news/world/europe/russia-uses-death-squads -and-torture-in-chechnya-says-amnesty-733296. html; BBC News, "Why Is Ukraine in Turmoil?" February 22, 2014, http://www.bbc.com/news/world -europe-25182823; Human Rights Watch, "Chechnya: Research Shows Widespread and Systematic Use of Torture," https://www.hrw.org/news/2006/11/12 /chechnya-research-shows-widespread-and -systematic-use-torture; Emad El-Din Shahin, "Brutality, Torture, Rape: Egypt's Crisis Will Continue Until Military Rule Is Dismantled," *The Guardian*, March 5, 2014, http://www.theguardian.com/commentisfree/2014 /mar/06/brutality-torture-rape-egypt-military-rule. (URLs accessed May 2016.)

These groups commit assassinations and kidnappings using extremely violent methods to intimidate the population and deter political activity against the government. Manoel Mattos, human rights activist and vice president of the Workers' Party (Partido dos Trabalhadores) in the state of Pernambuco, Brazil, was shot in his own home by intruders. Mattos had received repeated death threats as a result of his work denouncing killings and abuses by death squads across northeast Brazil. Despite the threats, federal police had recently withdrawn the protection he was receiving, allegedly because they felt it was no longer necessary.[53]

While the use of death squads is common in third-world countries, police violence and use of deadly force are not uncommon in Western industrialized nations. In some nations, almost all political detainees are subjected to torture, including electric shocks, burnings, and severe beating with boots, sticks, plastic bottles filled with water or sand, and heavy rubber-coated cables. The rest are subject to psychological pressure, such as threats or imitation of sexual abuse or execution, as well as threats to harm their relatives.

Critical criminologists go as far to link state-organized crime to attacks on other nations, and they do not exempt the United States from blame. In his book *Mass Deception*, criminologist Scott Bonn argues that the George W. Bush administration manufactured public support for war with Iraq by falsely claiming that (a) its leader, Saddam Hussein, was involved in the terrorist attacks of 9/11, (b) Iraq possessed weapons of mass destruction, and (c) Iraq represented a grave and growing threat to U.S. security. Bonn explains that the war was a function of a "moral panic" engineered by the Bush administration with the support of the U.S. news media.[54] Bonn believes that the war in Iraq amounts to state-organized crime.

The United States is not alone in getting involved in large-scale conflicts. The Profiles in Crime feature discusses two famous incidents of state-organized crime involving state violence. And read the Criminology in Action feature "Are Wrongful Convictions a State Crime?"

Instrumental vs. Structural Theory

 LO6 Compare and contrast structural and instrumental theory

Not all critical thinkers share a similar view of society and its control by the means of production. **Instrumental theorists** view criminal law and the criminal justice system solely as instruments for controlling the poor, have-not members of society. They view the state as the tool of capitalists. In contrast, **structural theorists** believe that the law is not the exclusive domain of the rich; rather, it is used to maintain the long-term interests of the capitalist system and to control members of any class who threaten its existence.

INSTRUMENTAL THEORY

According to the instrumental view, the law and the justice system serve the powerful and rich and enable them to impose their morality and standards of behavior on the entire society. Those who wield economic power are able to extend their self-serving definition of illegal or criminal behavior to encompass those who might threaten the status quo or interfere with their quest for ever-increasing profits.[55] The concentration of economic assets in the nation's largest industrial firms translates into the political power needed to control tax laws to limit the firms' tax liabilities.[56] Some have the economic clout to hire top attorneys to defend them against antitrust actions, making them almost immune to regulation.

The poor, according to this branch of critical theory, may or may not commit more crimes than the rich, but they certainly are arrested and punished more often. Under the capitalist system, the poor are driven to crime because a natural frustration exists in a society in which affluence is well publicized but unattainable. When class conflict becomes unbearable, frustration can spill out in riots and urban unrest. Because of class conflict, a deep-rooted hostility is generated among members of the lower class toward a social order they are not allowed to shape and whose benefits are unobtainable.[57]

Instrumental theorists consider it essential to **demystify** law and justice—that is, to unmask its true purpose. Criminological theories that focus on family structure, intelligence, peer relations, and school performance keep the lower classes servile by showing why they are more criminal, less intelligent, and more prone to school failure and family problems than the middle class. Demystification involves identifying the destructive intent of capitalist inspired and funded criminology. Instrumental theory's goal for criminology is to show how capitalist law preserves ruling-class power.[58]

STRUCTURAL THEORY

Structural theorists disagree with the view that the relationship between law and capitalism is unidirectional, always working for the rich and against the poor.[59] If law and justice were purely instruments of the wealthy, why would laws controlling corporate crimes, such as price fixing, false advertising, and illegal restraint of trade, have been created and enforced?

To a structuralist, the law is designed to keep the system operating efficiently, and anyone, worker or owner, who rocks the boat is targeted for sanction. For example, antitrust legislation is designed to prevent any single capitalist from dominating the system. If the free enterprise system is to function, no single person can become too powerful at the expense of the economic system as a whole. Structuralists would regard the efforts of the U.S. government to break up Microsoft as an example of a conservative government using its clout to keep the system on an even keel. The long prison sentences given to corporate executives who engage in insider trading are a warning to capitalists that they must play by the rules.

Research on Critical Criminology

Among the most important research carried out by critical criminologists are studies aimed at determining whether the criminal justice system operates as an instrument of class oppression or as a fair, even-handed social control agency.

Critical researchers have found disturbing evidence that at every stage of justice, criminal members of powerless, disenfranchised groups are treated less favorably than the wealthy and powerful.[60] Those convicted of crime tend to receive stricter sentences if their personal characteristics (single, young, urban, male) show them to be members of the "dangerous classes."[61] Research has found that jurisdictions with significant levels of economic disparity are also the most likely to have large numbers of people killed by police officers. Police may act more forcefully in areas where class conflict creates the perception that extreme forms of social control are needed to maintain order.[62]

---

instrumental theory The view that criminal law and the criminal justice system are capitalist instruments for controlling the lower class.

structural theory The view that criminal law and the criminal justice system are means of defending and preserving the capitalist system.

demystify To unmask the true purpose of law, justice, or other social institutions.

CONNECTIONS

The enforcement of laws against illegal business activities such as price fixing, restraint of trade, environmental crimes, and false advertising is discussed in Chapter 13. Although some people are sent to prison for these white-collar offenses, many offenders are still punished with a fine or economic sanction.

ASK YOURSELF . . .

Should white-collar criminals be sent to prison or merely pay large fines? After all, they are not too dangerous.

RACE AND JUSTICE

Critical research also shows that racial bias is present in the justice system, beginning with police contact and continuing through arrest, prosecution, and sentencing. As the numbers of racial and ethnic minorities in the population increase, so too do calls for harsher punishments. As you may recall (Chapter 2), the *racial threat hypothesis* states that as the number of minority group members in the community increases, law enforcement agents become more punitive.[63] There are cries for more "law and order" even when crime rates are declining. As a result, charges of racial profiling have become common. Police are more likely to use racial profiling to stop black motorists as they travel farther into the boundaries of predominantly white neighbor-

Racine County (Wisconsin) Sheriff's Deputy Ed Drewitz tickets a motorist stopped for speeding on I-94 near Racine. The officer's laser speed-measuring device clocked the motorist at 80 mph. Drewitz said he cannot tell a driver's gender or racial characteristics or the car's license plate as he clocks speeders, sometimes at a distance of 1,600 feet. Despite his disclaimer, racial profiling remains a hot button issue in the United States. Do you think that such practices exist? Or has awareness of racial inequality changed the way officers use their discretion to stop, search, investigate, and arrest?

AP Images/Mark Hertzberg

hoods: black motorists driving in an all-white neighborhood set up a red flag because they are "out of place."[64] All too often these unwarranted stops lead to equally unfair arrests.[65] Police brutality complaints are highest in minority neighborhoods, especially those that experience relative deprivation (African American residents earn significantly less money than the European American majority).[66]

African American defendants are more likely to be prosecuted under habitual offender statutes if they commit crimes where there is a greater likelihood of a white victim—for example, larceny and burglary—than if they commit violent crimes that are largely intraracial; where there is a perceived "racial threat," punishment is enhanced.[67] After conviction, criminal courts also are more likely to dole out harsh punishments to members of powerless, disenfranchised groups.[68] Unemployed racial minorities may be perceived as "social dynamite" who present a real threat to society and must be controlled and incapacitated.[69] States with a substantial minority population have a much higher imprisonment rate than those with predominantly white populations.[70] Critical analysis also shows that despite legal controls the use of the death penalty seems to be skewed against racial minorities.[71]

Taken in sum, critical criminologists claim that these and other studies underpin the foundations of their view: social institutions are designed to favor the rich and powerful and to oppress those who lack economic power and social standing.

Critique of Critical Criminology

 L07 Analyze critical criminology and discuss criticisms of the theory

Critical criminology has been sharply criticized by some members of the criminological mainstream, who charge that its contribution has been "hot air, heat, but no real light."[72] In turn, critical thinkers have accused mainstream criminologists of being culprits in developing state control over individual lives and selling out their ideals for the chance to receive government funding.

Mainstream criminologists have also attacked the substance of critical thought. Some argue that critical theory simply rehashes the old tradition of helping the underdog, in which the poor steal from the rich to survive.[73] In reality, most theft is for luxury, not survival. While the wealthy do commit their share of illegal acts, these are nonviolent and leave no permanent injuries.[74] People do not live in fear of corrupt businessmen and stock traders; they fear muggers and rapists.

Other critics suggest that critical theorists unfairly neglect the capitalist system's efforts to regulate itself—for example, by instituting antitrust regulations and putting violators in jail. Similarly, they ignore efforts to institute social reforms aimed at helping the poor.[75] There seems to be no logic in condemning a system that helps the poor and empowers them to take on corporate interests in a court of law. Even inherently conservative institutions such as police departments have made attempts at self-regulation when they become aware of class- and race-based inequality, such as the use of racial profiling in making traffic stops.[76]

Some argue that critical thinkers refuse to address the problems and conflicts that exist in socialist countries, such as the gulags and purges of the Soviet Union under Stalin. Similarly, they fail to explain why some highly capitalist countries, such as Japan, have extremely low crime rates. Critical criminologists are too quick to blame capitalism for every human vice without adequate explanation or regard for other social and environmental factors.[77] In so doing, they ignore objective reality and refuse to acknowledge that members of the lower classes tend to victimize one another. They ignore the plight of the lower classes, who must live in crime-ridden neighborhoods, while condemning the capitalist system from the security of the "ivory tower."

Alternative Views of Critical Theory

Critical criminologists are exploring avenues of inquiry that fall outside the traditional models of conflict and critical theories. The following sections discuss in detail some of these alternative views of the conflict approach to crime.

LEFT REALISM

 Assess the concept of left realism

Some critical scholars are now addressing the need for the left wing to respond to the increasing power of right-wing conservatives. They are troubled by the emergence of a strict "law and order" philosophy, which has as its centerpiece a policy of punishing juveniles severely in adult court. At the same time, they find the focus of most left-wing scholarship—the abuse of power by the ruling elite—too narrow. It is wrong, they argue, to ignore inner-city gang crime and violence, which often target indigent people.[78] The approach of **left realism** is most often connected to the writings of British scholars John Lea and Jock Young. In their well-respected 1984 work *What Is to Be Done About Law and Order?*, they reject the utopian views of idealists who portray street criminals as revolutionaries.[79] They take the more "realistic" approach that street criminals prey on the poor and disenfranchised, thus making the poor doubly abused, first by the capitalist system and then by members of their own class.

left realism An approach that views crime as a function of relative deprivation under capitalism and that favors pragmatic, community-based crime prevention and control.

preemptive deterrence Efforts to prevent crime through community organization and youth involvement.

Lea and Young's view of crime causation borrows from conventional sociological theory and closely resembles the relative deprivation approach, which posits that experiencing poverty in the midst of plenty creates discontent and breeds crime. As they put it, "The equation is simple: relative deprivation equals discontent; discontent plus lack of political solution equals crime."[80]

In *Crime in Context: A Critical Criminology of Market Societies*, Ian Taylor recognizes that anyone who expects an instant socialist revolution to take place is simply engaging in wishful thinking.[81] He uses data from both Europe and North America to show that the world is currently in the midst of multiple crises that are shaping all human interaction, including criminality. These crises include lack of job creation, social inequality, social fear, political incompetence and failure, gender conflict, and family and parenting issues. These crises have led to a society in which the government seems incapable of creating positive social change: people have become more fearful and isolated from one another and some are excluded from the mainstream because of racism and discrimination; manufacturing jobs have been exported overseas to nations that pay extremely low wages; and fiscal constraints inhibit the possibility of reform. These problems often fall squarely on the shoulders of young black men, who suffer from exclusion and poverty and who now feel the economic burden created by the erosion of manufacturing jobs due to the globalization of the economy. In response, they engage in a form of hypermasculinity, which helps increase their crime rates.[82]

Crime Protection   Left realists argue that crime victims in all classes need and deserve protection; crime control reflects community needs. They do not view police and the courts as inherently evil tools of capitalism whose tough tactics alienate the lower classes. In fact, they recognize that these institutions offer life-saving public services. The left realists wish, however, that police would reduce their use of force and increase their sensitivity to the public.[83] They want the police to be more responsive to community needs, end racial profiling, and improve efforts at self-regulation and enforcement through citizen review boards and other control mechanisms.

Preemptive deterrence is an approach in which community organization efforts eliminate or reduce crime before police involvement becomes necessary. The reasoning behind this approach is that if the number of marginalized youths (those who feel they are not part of society and have nothing to lose by committing crime) could be reduced, then delinquency rates would decline.[84]

Although implementing a socialist economy might help eliminate the crime problem, left realists recognize that something must be done to control crime under the existing capitalist system. To develop crime control policies, left realists not only welcome critical ideas but also build on the work of strain theorists, social ecologists, and other mainstream views. Community-based efforts seem to hold the greatest promise of crime control.

Left Realism and Terrorism

04

Left realists typically have focused their attention on street crime and how it affects its targets: lower-class citizens are forced to live in dangerous neighborhoods and communities. Left realist Jennifer Gibbs uses a different lens and applies the basic concepts to explain the motivation for terrorist activity.

Gibbs finds four key elements of left realism that should, if valid, underpin terrorist involvement:

- People are recruited into terrorist organizations because of relative deprivation.
- Terrorist organizations are subcultures that provide peer support.
- Victims/targets are selected based on opportunity/routine activities.
- "Get tough" policies that create a police state may backfire.

Gibbs finds evidence to support the first proposition: terrorists are drawn not from extremely poor populations but from those who realize they have fallen behind other groups. Absolute deprivation (e.g., the inability to provide basic necessities) is not the cause of terrorism; relative deprivation (e.g., being less well off than one's peers) seems to carry more weight, an association predicted by left realism. Feelings of deprivation are exacerbated by new technology. Advancements like the Internet make communication easier and people can see how much better off oth-

ers are, increasing the perception of relative deprivation.

Second, left realist theory argues that men who experience stress as a result of relative deprivation and do not have socially appropriate coping mechanisms turn to similarly situated peers who provide support; they often form subcultures. Likewise, terrorist group members seek peer support with like-minded people, forming subcultures supportive of these values or ideology. In today's postmodern world, technology has created the opportunity for virtual peer groups and subcultures. Peer support does not necessarily need to be face to face within groups but can exist in blogs and chat rooms. Those adhering to a particular ideology may find peer support in written communications such as listservs, magazines, and other media.

Gibbs finds weaker support for the role of opportunity in terrorist activities because they tend to be planned rather than spontaneous events. However, there is some evidence that opportunity plays a role in choosing victims: targeting businesses and citizens is easier than targeting government entities or military installations or personnel. Other reasons may include having the "biggest bang for the buck" by targeting businesses—symbolic of capitalism—or civilians, whose deaths generate widespread attention.

The final proposition of left realist theory addressed by Gibbs is that "get

tough" policies will not reduce crime. She notes that left realism focuses on individualized or community-focused responses to crime. Get-tough policies alienate people and legitimate terrorist organizations. The "war" on terror legitimized groups like al-Qaeda, attracting more terrorism instead of decreasing it. Also, the military response to terrorism is not a deterrent. Military "solutions," in particular, lead to retaliation, generating a cycle of violence because they tend to be reactive rather than proactive. They provide short-term solutions that fail to address the underlying causes that lead to terrorism in the first place. Instead, left realism theory directs policy toward minimal official response and maximizing informal social control. With terrorism, attempting to address the underlying grievances may be helpful.

CRITICAL THINKING

Do you agree that the way to fight terror is to address the underlying grievances? Sounds good, but is it truly possible in a world with shifting conflicts and myriad points of view? Can we ever satisfy a terrorist? And would we even if we knew how?

SOURCE: Jennifer Gibbs, "Looking at Terrorism Through Left Realist Lenses," *Crime, Law and Social Change* 54 (2010): 171–185.

Left Realism and Incarceration   Left realists also decry the use of mass incarceration as a crime control device, fearing that it has racial overtones. In *The New Jim Crow: Mass Incarceration in the Age of Colorblindness* (2010), legal scholar Michelle Alexander notes that the number of people in prison has skyrocketed in the past 30 years; there are now more African Americans behind bars than there were slaves at the time of the Civil War. This system of mass incarceration now works as a tightly networked system of laws, policies, customs, and institutions that operate collectively to ensure racial subordination.[85] In a sense, the Jim Crow laws, which worked to segregate minorities and prevented

them from voting, have been replaced by the War on Drugs, which has placed millions behind bars and restricted their civil rights upon release; existing laws prevent convicted felons from gaining employment, education, and housing, as well as obtaining loans, and voting.

Surprisingly, this left realist perspective may be gaining traction even in the nation's most conservative states (including Texas), which have begun to reduce their prison expenditures while funding treatment, reentry, and alternative to incarceration programs. In part this policy shift corresponds to a change in public opinion: as crime rates have declined and state budgets are in crisis, the public demands low-cost alternatives to the "lock 'em up" policies that have been predominant for the past few decades. It's possible that a more realistic vision of punishment may be on the horizon.[86]

In the Criminology in Action feature "Left Realism and Terrorism," a left realist focuses on the onset of terrorist activity.

Left realism has been criticized by critical thinkers as legitimizing the existing power structure: by supporting existing definitions of law and justice, it suggests that the "deviant" and not the capitalist system causes society's problems. Critics question whether left realists advocate the very institutions that "currently imprison us and our patterns of thought and action."[87] In rebuttal, left realists say that it is unrealistic to speak of a socialist state lacking a police force or a system of laws and justice. They believe the criminal code does, in fact, represent public opinion.

CRITICAL FEMINIST THEORY: GENDERED CRIMINOLOGY

LO9 Articulate the central themes of critical feminism and gendered criminology

Like so many theories in criminology, most of the efforts of critical theorists have been devoted to explaining male criminality.[88] To remedy this theoretical lapse, a number of feminist writers have attempted to explain the cause of crime, gender differences in crime rates, and the exploitation of female victims from a critical perspective.

Critical feminism views gender inequality as stemming from the unequal power of men and women in a capitalist society, which leads to the exploitation of women by fathers and husbands. Under this system, women are considered a commodity worth possessing, like land or money.[89] Some of the most important issues focused upon by critical feminist criminologists include the unique role of women in policing and corrections, fields that have traditionally been dominated by men. Another important area of study is the role of masculinity in creating the gender gap in serious crime. There is also concern with the role of media in "demonizing" girls and women of color.[90]

Queer Criminology As part of their interest in gender roles and crime, critical scholars are also focusing attention on the treatment of the lesbian, gay, bisexual, transgender, and queer (LGBTQ) population by society in general and the justice system in particular. Among the issues being studied is how damaging stereotypes and representations of people as sexual deviants developed.[91] They claim that mainstream criminologists have either ignored LGBTQ people or portrayed them in a negative light. Areas of interest include defining deviance, crimes against LGBTQ people, and gaining equality before the law.[92]

Gender Differences in Society The origin of gender differences can be traced to the development of private property and male domination of the laws of inheritance, which led to male control over property and power.[93] A patriarchal system developed in which men's work was valued and women's work was devalued. As capitalism prevailed, the division of labor by gender made women responsible for the unpaid maintenance and reproduction of the current and future labor force, which was derisively called "domestic work." Although this unpaid work done by women is crucial and profitable for capitalists, who reap these free benefits, such labor is exploitative and oppressive for women.[94] Even when women gained the right to work for pay, they were exploited as cheap labor. The dual exploitation of women within the household and in the labor market means that women produce far greater surplus value for capitalists than men.

Patriarchy, or male supremacy, has been and continues to be supported by capitalists. This system sustains female oppression at home and in the workplace.[95] Although the number of traditional patriarchal families is in steep decline, in those that still exist, a wife's economic dependence ties men more securely to wage-earning jobs, further serving the interests of capitalists by undermining potential rebellion against the system.

Patriarchy and Crime Critical feminists link criminal behavior patterns to the gender conflict created by the economic and social struggles common in postindustrial societies. In *Capitalism, Patriarchy, and Crime*, James Messerschmidt argues that capitalist society is marked by both patriarchy and class conflict. Capitalists control the labor of workers, and men control women both economically and biologically.[96] This "double marginality" explains why females in a capitalist society commit fewer crimes than males. Because they are isolated in the family, they have fewer opportunities to engage in elite deviance (white-collar and economic crimes). Although powerful females as well as males will commit white-collar crimes, the female crime rate is restricted because of the patriarchal nature of the capitalist system.[97] Women are also denied access to male-dominated street crimes.

Because capitalism renders lower-class women powerless, they are forced to commit less serious, nonviolent, self-destructive crimes, such as abusing drugs. Recent efforts of the capitalist classes to undermine the social support of the poor has hit women particularly hard. The end of welfare, concentration on welfare fraud, and cutbacks to social services have all directly and uniquely affected women.[98]

critical feminism An area of scholarship whose focus is on the effects of gender inequality and the unequal power of men and women in a capitalist society.

patriarchy A society in which men dominate public, social, economic, and political affairs.

Powerlessness also increases the likelihood that women will become targets of violent acts.[99] When lower-class males are shut out of the economic opportunity structure, they try to build their self-image through acts of machismo; such acts may involve violent abuse of women. This type of reaction accounts for a significant percentage of female victims who are attacked by a spouse or intimate partner. It is not surprising to find that incarcerated female offenders report higher rates of mental health problems than incarcerated men and that there is a strong association between suffering intimate partner violence, mental health issues, and involvement with the justice system.[100]

According to this view, female victimization should decline as women's place in society is elevated, and they are able to obtain more power at home, in the workplace, and in government. Recent research by Lynne Vieraitis, Sarah Britto, and Robert Morris found that, as predicted, as gender equality increases, female homicide victimization declines. While some scholars have predicted a "backlash effect"—angry males victimizing women who are invading their turf—that has not really occurred.[101]

In *Masculinities and Crime*, Messerschmidt expands on these themes.[102] He suggests that in every culture males try to emulate "ideal" masculine behaviors. In Western culture, this means being authoritative, in charge, combative, and controlling. Failure to adopt these roles leaves men feeling effeminate and unmanly. Their struggle to dominate women in order to prove their manliness is called "doing gender." Crime is a vehicle for men to "do gender" because it separates them from the weak and allows them to demonstrate physical bravery. Violence directed toward women is an especially economical way to demonstrate manhood. Would a weak, effeminate male ever attack a woman?

Feminist writers have supported this view by maintaining that in contemporary society men achieve masculinity at the expense of women. In the best-case scenario, men must convince others that in no way are they feminine or have female qualities. For example, they are sloppy and don't cook or do housework because these are "female" activities. More ominously, men may work at excluding, hurting, denigrating, exploiting, or otherwise abusing women. Even in all-male groups, men often prove their manhood by treating the weakest member of the group as "woman-like" and abusing him accordingly. Men need to defend themselves at all costs from being contaminated with femininity, and these efforts begin in children's playgroups and continue into adulthood and marriage.[103]

Exploitation and Criminality   Critical feminists also focus on the social forces that shape women's lives and experiences to explain female criminality.[104] They attempt to show how the sexual victimization of girls is a function of male socialization because so many young males learn to be aggressive and to exploit women. Males seek out same-sex peer groups for social support; these groups encourage members to exploit and sexually abuse women. On college campuses, peers encourage sexual violence against women who are considered "teasers," "bar pickups," or "loose women." These derogatory labels allow the males to justify their actions; a code of secrecy then protects the aggressors from retribution.[105]

This attitude has produced numerous incidents of sexual assault against young women, in which gender-centered humiliation, such as taking nude photos and videos of unsuspecting victims and posting them online, plays a major role. College fraternities have become notorious for this type of behavior, prompting closings or suspensions at major schools such as Penn State.[106] This attitude also helps explain the sexual assault culture that dominates the club scene in which men feel free to victimize women because that is just what men do. According to Philip Kavanaugh, various types of unwanted sexual contact become expected in bars, clubs, and lounges because sexually aggressive or coercive behavior is considered a normal part of gendered interactions in public places devoted to urban nightlife.[107]

Being Victimized   Critical feminists also show how sexual and other victimization of girls is a function of male socialization because so many young males learn to be aggressive and to exploit women. Males seek out same-sex peer groups for social support; these groups encourage members to exploit and sexually abuse women. On college campuses, peers encourage sexual violence against women who are considered "sluts." Such derogatory labels allow the males to justify their actions. Slut-shaming—the practice of embarrassing, humiliating, or attacking a woman for being sexual or acting on sexual feelings—has now become common on college campuses.

According to the critical feminist view, when female victims run away and abuse substances, they may be reacting to abuse they have suffered at home or at school.[108] Those who are on the street, who are homeless, are more likely to have experienced significant social problems, including childhood molestation, adult sexual assault, and arrests for prostitution and to have been in treatment for substance misuse.[109]

Empirical research seems to support this view. In nations where the status of women is generally high, sexual violence rates are significantly lower than in nations where women do not enjoy similar educational and occupational opportunities.[110] Women's victimization rates decline as they are empowered socially, economically, and legally.[111]

Gender and the Justice System   When the exploited girl finds herself in the arms of the justice system, her problems may just be beginning. Boys who get in trouble may be considered "overzealous" youth or kids who just went too far. Girls who get in trouble are seen as a threat to acceptable images of femininity; their behavior is considered even more unusual and dangerous than male delinquency.[112]

Critical feminists such as Meda Chesney-Lind have found gender differences not only in criminality but also in the way girls and women are treated in both the juvenile and criminal justice system.[113] While it is true males are sanctioned more heavily than females, and they are overrepresented in the correctional system, it is also true that they commit more serious violent crimes.

These outcomes may be misleading. As Chesney-Lind has repeatedly found, women and girls receive more punitive treatment than men and boys, especially in cases involving sexual matters or offenses. Nor is this a recent phenomenon. Throughout history females have been more likely to be punished for their immoral behavior than for their criminal activities. Chesney-Lind's now classic research first identified the fact that police are more likely to arrest female adolescents for sexual activity while ignoring similar behaviors when engaged in by males. Girls are more likely than boys to be picked up by police for status offenses such as being truant, runaways, or disobedient, and are more likely to be kept in detention for such offenses.[114]

The sexual stigmatization of girls is not a thing of the past. Critical feminists note that girls are still disadvantaged if their behavior is viewed as morally incorrect by government officials or if they are considered beyond parental control.[115] Girls may still be subject to harsh punishments if they are considered dangerously immoral or fail to measure up to stereotypes of proper female behavior.[116] Research by Tia Stevens and her associates found that over the past decades, regardless of racial/ethnic group, young girls who are involved in behavior considered inappropriate for females are more likely to be formally charged and involved in the juvenile justice system. Tolerance for misbehavior significantly decreases when girls violate gender norms.[117] Lisa Pasko's research confirms that the focus of the juvenile justice system continues to be on girls' sexual behavior. While girls are not directly arrested and adjudicated for sexual immorality, they are still told to take responsibility for their "bad choices." In the contemporary era, the correctional focus remains on the control and micromanagement of girls' bodies and sexuality.[118]

The justice system also seems biased against people who identify as lesbian, gay, bisexual, transgender, or queer (LGBTQ), who are disproportionately incarcerated. Though they make up approximately 6 percent of the youth population, it is now estimated that LGBTQ youth comprise 13 to 15 percent of youth involved in the juvenile justice system.[119]

As they mature, women may become more adept at navigating the justice system and use their street smarts and savvy to control their experience. When Corey S. Shdaimah and Chrysanthi Leon interviewed prostitute women who were placed within justice system programs they found that rather than acting passively, the women demonstrated skills and moral reasoning that included the ability to make choices, work the systems that dominate their lives, and assert power and control. Rather than being passive, they were creative, resilient, and rational in their efforts to deal with the life circumstances in which they were placed.[120]

POWER–CONTROL THEORY

John Hagan and his associates have created a critical feminist model that uses gender differences to explain the onset of criminality.[121] Hagan's view is that crime and delinquency rates are a function of two factors: class position (power) and family functions (control).[122] The link between these two variables is that, within the family, parents reproduce the power relationships they hold in the workplace; a position of dominance at work is equated with control in the household. As a result, parents' work experiences and class position influence the criminality of children.[123]

In **paternalistic families**, fathers assume the traditional role of breadwinners, while mothers tend to have menial jobs or remain at home to supervise domestic matters. Within the paternalistic home, mothers are expected to control the behavior of their daughters while granting greater freedom to sons. In such a home, the parent–daughter relationship can be viewed as a preparation for the "cult of domesticity," which makes girls' involvement in delinquency unlikely, whereas boys are freer to deviate because they are not subject to maternal control. Girls growing up in patriarchal families are socialized to fear legal sanctions more than are males; consequently, boys in these families exhibit more delinquent behavior than their sisters. The result is that boys not only engage in more antisocial behaviors but have greater access to legitimate adult behaviors, such as working at part-time jobs or possessing their own transportation. In contrast, without these legitimate behavioral outlets, girls who are unhappy or dissatisfied with their status are forced to seek out risky **role exit behaviors**, including such desperate measures as running away or contemplating suicide.

In **egalitarian families**—those in which the husband and wife share similar positions of power at home and in the workplace—daughters gain a kind of freedom that reflects reduced parental control. These families produce daughters whose law-violating behavior mirrors their brothers'. In an egalitarian family, girls may have greater opportunity to engage in legitimate adult status behaviors and less need to enact deviant role exits.[124]

Ironically, Hagan believes that these relationships also occur in female-headed households with absent fathers. Hagan and his associates found that when fathers and mothers hold equally valued managerial positions, the similarity between the rates of their daughters' and sons' delinquency is greatest. By implication, middle-class girls are the most likely to violate the law because they are less closely

paternalistic families Traditional family model in which fathers assume the role of breadwinners, while mothers tend to have menial jobs or remain at home to supervise domestic matters.

role exit behaviors In order to escape from a stifling life in male-dominated families, girls may try to break away by running away or even attempting suicide.

egalitarian families Families in which spouses share similar positions of power at home and in the workplace.

controlled than their lower-class counterparts. In homes in which both parents hold positions of power, girls are more likely to have the same expectations of career success as their brothers. Consequently, siblings of both sexes will be socialized to take risks and engage in other behavior related to delinquency.

Evaluating Power–Control Theory This **power–control theory** has received a great deal of attention in the criminological community because it encourages a new approach to the study of criminality, one that includes gender differences, class position, and family structure. Empirical analysis of its premises has generally been supportive. Brenda Sims Blackwell's research supports a key element of power–control theory: females in paternalistic households have learned to fear legal sanctions more than have their brothers.[125]

Not all research is as supportive.[126] Some critics have questioned its core assumption that power and control variables can explain crime. More specifically, critics fail to replicate the finding that upper-class girls are more likely to deviate than their lower-class peers or that class and power interact to produce delinquency.[127] Some researchers have found few gender-based supervision and behavior differences in worker-, manager-, or owner-dominated households.[128] Research indicates that single-mother families may be different from two-parent egalitarian families, though Hagan's theory equates the two.[129] Some suggest that the theory may be more valid with white populations and only gets mixed support when used in cross-cultural settings.[130]

It is possible that the concept of family employed by Hagan may have to be reconsidered. Power–control theorists should consider the multitude of power and control relationships that are emerging in postmodern society: blended families, families where mothers hold managerial positions and fathers are blue-collar workers, and so forth.[131]

Finally, power and control may interact with other personal traits, such as personality and self-control, to shape behavior.[132] Further research is needed to determine whether power–control can have an independent influence on behavior and can explain gender differences in the crime rate.

PEACEMAKING CRIMINOLOGY

L010 Explain peacemaking criminology and restorative justice

To members of the **peacemaking** movement, the main purpose of criminology is to promote a peaceful, just society. Rather than standing on empirical analysis of data, peacemaking draws its inspiration from religious and philosophical teachings ranging from Quakerism to Zen.[133] For example, rather than seeing socioeconomic status as a "variable" that is correlated with crime, as do mainstream criminologists, peacemakers view poverty as a source of suffering—almost a crime in and of itself. Poverty enervates people, makes them suffer, and becomes a master status that

subjects them to lives filled with suffering. From a peacemaking perspective, a key avenue for preventing crime is, in the short run, diminishing the suffering poverty causes and, in the long run, embracing social policies that reduce the prevalence of economic suffering in contemporary society.[134]

Peacemakers view the efforts of the state to punish and control as crime-encouraging rather than crime-discouraging. These views were first articulated in a series of books with an anarchist theme written by criminologists Larry Tifft and Dennis Sullivan in 1980.[135] Tifft argues, "The violent punishing acts of the state and its controlling professions are of the same genre as the violent acts of individuals. In each instance these acts reflect an attempt to monopolize human interaction."[136]

Sullivan stresses the futility of correcting and punishing criminals in the context of our conflict-ridden society: "The reality we must grasp is that we live in a culture of severed relationships, where every available institution provides a form of banishment but no place or means for people to become connected, to be responsible to and for each other."[137] Sullivan suggests that mutual aid rather than coercive punishment is the key to a harmonious society. In *Restorative Justice*, Sullivan and Tifft reaffirm their belief that society must seek humanitarian forms of justice without resorting to brutal punishments:

> By allowing feelings of vengeance or retribution to narrow our focus on the harmful event and the person responsible for it—as others might focus solely on a sin committed and the "sinner"—we tell ourselves we are taking steps to free ourselves from the effects of the harm or the sin in question. But, in fact, we are putting ourselves in a servile position with respect to life, human growth, and the further enjoyment of relationships with others.[138]

Today, advocates of the peacemaking movement try to find humanist solutions to crime and other social problems.[139] Rather than punishment and prison, they advocate such policies as mediation and conflict resolution.[140] They reject the vocabulary that social problems should be met with a "War on . . ." approach, such as the War on Drugs. Instead, peaceful and collaborative solutions can be found for social problems ranging from narcotics addiction to climate change.[141]

Concept Summary 8.1 summarizes the various emerging forms of critical criminology.

power–control theory The view that gender differences in crime are a function of economic power (class position, one-earner versus two-earner families) and parental control (paternalistic versus egalitarian families).

peacemaking An approach that considers punitive crime control strategies to be counterproductive and favors the use of humanistic conflict resolution to prevent and control crime.

THEORY	MAJOR PREMISE	STRENGTHS	RESEARCH FOCUS
Left realism	Crime is a function of relative deprivation; criminals prey on the poor.	Represents a compromise between conflict and traditional criminology	Deterrence; protection
Critical feminist theory	The capitalist system creates patriarchy, which oppresses women.	Explains gender bias, violence against women, and repression	Gender inequality; oppression; patriarchy
Power–control theory	Girls are controlled more closely than boys in traditional male-dominated households. There is gender equity in contemporary egalitarian homes.	Explains gender differences in the crime rate as a function of class and gender conflict	Power and control; gender differences; domesticity
Peacemaking criminology	Peace and humanism can reduce crime; conflict resolution strategies can work.	Offers a new approach to crime control through mediation	Punishment; nonviolence; mediational

Critical Theory and Public Policy

At the core of all the varying branches of social conflict theory is the fact that conflict causes crime. If conflict and competition in society could somehow be reduced, it is possible that crime rates would fall. Some critical theorists believe this goal can only be accomplished by thoroughly reordering society so that capitalism is destroyed and a socialist state is created. Others call for a more "practical" application of conflict principles. Nowhere has this been more successful than in applying peacemaking principles in the criminal justice system.

Rather than punish law violators harshly and make them outcasts of society, peacemakers look for ways to bring them back to the community. This peacemaking movement has adopted nonviolent methods and applied them to what is known as **restorative justice**. Springing both from academia and justice system personnel, the restorative approach relies on nonpunitive strategies for crime prevention and control.[142] The next sections discuss the foundation and principles of restorative justice.

THE CONCEPT OF RESTORATIVE JUSTICE

The term *restorative justice* is often hard to define because it encompasses a variety of programs and practices. According to a leading restorative justice scholar, Howard Zehr, restorative justice requires that society address victims' harms and needs, hold offenders accountable to put right those harms,

restorative justice Using humanistic, nonpunitive strategies to right wrongs and restore social harmony.

THINKING LIKE A CRIMINOLOGIST

An Ethical Dilemma

Is It a Bribe?

A student wants to discuss a personal matter. It seems that a few weeks ago she was at a party when she was sexually assaulted by a fellow student. The attack was quite traumatic, and she suffered both physical and emotional injury. The police were called and the boy charged with rape. Now that a few weeks have passed, she has been contacted by a local program that bills itself as a restorative treatment program. It seems that her attacker is now a client and wants to engage in some form of reconciliation. At an arranged meeting, he professes his regret for the attack and wishes to make amends. He and the program director have worked out a schedule in which the victim will be compensated for her pain and suffering in the amount of $5,000 in exchange for her agreeing to a recommendation to the prosecutor that the case be treated informally rather than going to trial. She doesn't know what to do: she needs the money, having missed work after the attack, but at the same time is concerned that people will think she has accepted a bribe to withdraw the charges.

Write a paper describing the advice you would give to the student in this situation. How would you suggest that she respond to the program director? Do you consider the payment a bribe or restitution for an evil deed? Can restorative justice be used in a crime such as rape?

and involve victims, offenders, and communities in the process of healing. Zehr maintains that the core value of the restoration process can be translated into respect for all, even those who are different from us, even those who seem to be our enemies. At its core, Zehr argues, restorative justice is a set of principles, a philosophy, an alternate set of guiding questions that provide an alternative framework for thinking about wrongdoing.[143] Restorative justice would reject concepts such as "punishment," "deterrence," and "incarceration" and embrace "apology," "rehabilitation," "reparation," "healing," "restoration," and "reintegration."

Restorative justice has grown out of a belief that the traditional justice system has done little to involve the community in the process of dealing with crime and wrongdoing. What has developed is a system of coercive punishments, administered by bureaucrats, that are inherently harmful to offenders and reduce the likelihood offenders will ever become productive members of society. This system relies on punishment, stigma, and disgrace. In his controversial book *The Executed God: The Way of the Cross in Lockdown America*, theology professor Mark Lewis Taylor discusses the similarities between this contemporary, coercive justice system and that which existed in imperial Rome when Jesus and many of his followers were executed because they were an inspiration to the poor and slave populations. They represented a threat to the ruling Roman power structure. So, too, is our modern justice system designed to keep the downtrodden in their place. Taylor suggests that there should be a movement to reduce such coercive elements of justice as police brutality and the death penalty before our "lockdown society" becomes the model used around the globe.[144]

Advocates of restorative justice argue that rather than today's lockdown mentality, what is needed is a justice policy that repairs the harm caused by crime and that includes all parties who have suffered from that harm: the victim, the community, and the offender. They have made an ongoing effort to reduce the conflict created by the criminal justice system when it hands out harsh punishments to offenders, many of whom are powerless social outcasts. Based on the principle of reducing social harm, restorative justice advocates argue that the old methods of punishment are a failure: after all, upwards of two-thirds of all prison inmates recidivate soon after their release. And tragically, not all inmates are released. Some are given life sentences for relatively minor crimes under three-strikes laws, which mandate such a sentence for a third conviction; some are given sentences of life with no parole, which are in essence death sentences.[145]

REINTEGRATIVE SHAMING

One of the key foundations of the restoration movement is contained in John Braithwaite's influential book *Crime, Shame, and Reintegration*.[146] Braithwaite's vision rests on the concept of **shame**: the feeling we get when we don't meet the standards we have set for ourselves or that significant others have set for us. Shame can lead people to believe that they are defective, that there is something wrong with them. Braithwaite notes that countries such as Japan in which conviction for crimes brings an inordinate amount of shame have extremely low crime rates. In Japan, criminal prosecution proceeds only when the normal process of public apology, compensation, and the victim's forgiveness breaks down.

Shame is a powerful tool of informal social control. Citizens in cultures in which crime is not shameful, such as the United States, do not internalize an abhorrence for crime because when they are punished, they view themselves as mere victims of the justice system. Their punishment comes at the hands of neutral strangers, such as police and judges, who are being paid to act. In contrast, shaming relies on the victim's participation.[147]

Braithwaite divides the concept of shame into two distinct types. The most common form of shaming typically involves stigmatization, an ongoing process of degradation in which the offender is branded as an evil person and cast out of society. Shaming can occur at a school disciplinary hearing or a criminal court trial. Bestowing stigma and degradation may have a general deterrent effect: it makes people afraid of social rejection and public humiliation. As a specific deterrent, stigma is doomed to failure; people who suffer humiliation at the hands of the justice system "reject their rejectors" by joining a deviant subculture of like-minded people who collectively resist social control. Despite these dangers, there has been an ongoing effort to brand offenders and make their shame both public and permanent. For example, all fifty states have passed sex offender registry and notification laws that make public the names of those convicted of sex offenses and warn neighbors of their presence in the community.[148]

But the fear of shame can backfire or be neutralized. When shame is managed well, people acknowledge they made mistakes and suffered disappointments, and try to work out what can be done to make things right; this is referred to as shame management. However, in some cases, to avoid the pain of shaming, people engage in improper shame management, a psychological process in which they deny shame by shifting the blame of their actions to their target or to others.[149] They may get angry and take out their frustrations on those whom they can dominate. Improper shame management of this sort has been linked to antisocial acts ranging from school yard bullying to tax evasion.[150]

Massive levels of improper shame management may occur on a societal scale during periods of social upheaval. Because of this, some nations that previously have had low crime rates may experience a surge of antisocial behavior during periods of war and revolution. Rape, an act

shame The feeling we get when we don't meet the standards we have set for ourselves or that significant others have set for us.

which may have been unthinkable to most men, suddenly becomes commonplace because of the emergence of narcissistic pride, feeling dominant and arrogant, and developing a sense of superiority over others, in this case the enemy. This sense of hubris fosters aggressive actions and allows combatants to rape women whom they perceive as belonging to an enemy group.[151]

Braithwaite argues that crime control can be better achieved through a policy of **reintegrative shaming**. Here disapproval is extended to the offenders' evil deeds, while at the same time they are cast as respected people who can be reaccepted by society. A critical element of reintegrative shaming occurs when the offenders begin to understand and recognize their wrongdoing and shame themselves. To be reintegrative, shaming must be brief and controlled and then followed by ceremonies of forgiveness, apology, and repentance.

To prevent crime, Braithwaite charges, society must encourage reintegrative shaming. For example, the women's movement can reduce domestic violence by mounting a crusade to shame spouse abusers. Similarly, parents who use reintegrative shaming techniques in their childrearing practices may improve parent–child relationships and ultimately reduce the delinquent involvement of their children.[152] Because informal social controls may have a greater impact than legal or formal ones, it may not be surprising that the fear of personal shame can have a greater deterrent effect than the fear of legal sanctions. It may also be applied to produce specific deterrence. Offenders can meet with victims so that the offenders can experience shame. Family members and peers can be present to help the offender reintegrate. Such efforts can humanize a system of justice that today relies on repression rather than forgiveness as the basis of specific deterrence.

reintegrative shaming A method of correction that encourages offenders to confront their misdeeds, experience shame because of the harm they caused, and then be reincluded in society.

THE PROCESS OF RESTORATION

The restoration process begins by redefining crime in terms of a conflict among the offender, the victim, and affected constituencies (families, schools, workplaces, and so forth). Therefore, it is vitally important that the resolution take place within the context in which the conflict originally occurred rather than being transferred to a specialized institution that has no social connection to the community or group from which the conflict originated. In other words, most conflicts are better settled in the community than in a court.

By maintaining "ownership" or jurisdiction over the conflict, the community is able to express its shared outrage about the offense. Shared community outrage is directly communicated to the offender. The victim is also given a chance to voice his or her story, and the offender can directly communicate his or her need for social reintegration and treatment. All restoration programs involve an understanding among all the parties involved in a criminal act: the victim, offender, and community. Although processes differ in structure and style, they generally include these elements:

- The offender is asked to recognize that he or she caused injury to personal and social relations along with a determination and acceptance of responsibility (ideally accompanied by a statement of remorse). Only then can the offender be restored as a productive member of the community.
- Restoration involves turning the justice system into a "healing" process rather than being a distributor of retribution and revenge.
- Reconciliation is a big part of the restorative approach. Most people involved in offender–victim relationships actually know one

High school student Cameron Wallace, 17, and his father, Johnny Wallace, attend a restorative justice class at the Augustus F. Hawkins High School in Los Angeles. In the Los Angeles Unified School District, the suspension rate has dropped from 8 percent in 2008 to 1.5 percent. The reason: a district-wide push to stop punishing children by removing them from class for minor disruptions, costing them important time in the classroom and potentially affecting lifelong academic achievement. In Los Angeles, restorative justice is one of the most important alternatives to suspension.

AP Images/Damian Dovarganes

another or were related in some way before the criminal incident took place. Instead of treating one of the involved parties as a victim deserving of sympathy and the other as a criminal deserving of punishment, it is more productive to address the issues that produced conflict between these people.[153]

■ The effectiveness of justice ultimately depends on the stake a person has in the community (or a particular social group). If a person does not value his or her membership in the group, the person will be unlikely to accept responsibility, show remorse, or repair the injuries caused by his or her actions. In contrast, people who have a stake in the community and its principal institutions, such as work, home, and school, find that their involvement enhances their personal and familial well-being.[154]

■ The offender must make a commitment to both material (monetary) restitution and symbolic reparation (an apology). A determination must also be made of community support and assistance for both victim and offender.

The intended result of the process is to repair injuries suffered by the victim and the community while ensuring reintegration of the offender.

Restoration Programs Negotiation, mediation, consensus building, and peacemaking have been part of the dispute resolution process in European and Asian communities for centuries.[155] Native American and First Nations (native Canadian) people have long used the type of community participation in the adjudication process (for example, sentencing circles, sentencing panels, elders panels) that restorative justice advocates are now embracing.[156]

In some Native American communities, people accused of breaking the law meet with community members, victims (if any), village elders, and agents of the justice system in a **sentencing circle**. Each member of the circle expresses his or her feelings about the act that was committed and raises questions or concerns. The accused can express regret about his or her actions and a desire to change the harmful behavior. People may suggest ways the offender can make things up to the community and those he or she harmed. A treatment program, such as Alcoholics Anonymous, can be suggested, if appropriate.

Restorative justice is now being embraced on many levels within our society and the justice system:

■ *Community.* Communities that isolate people and have few mechanisms for interpersonal interaction encourage and sustain crime. Those that implement forms of community dialogue to identify problems and plan tactics for their elimination, guided by restorative justice practices and principles, may create a climate in which violent crime is less likely to occur.[157]

■ *Schools.* Some schools have embraced restorative justice practices to deal with students who are involved in drug and alcohol abuse without having to resort to more punitive measures such as expulsion. Schools in Minnesota, Colorado, and elsewhere are now trying to involve students in "relational rehabilitation" programs that strive to improve individuals' relationships with key figures in the community who may have been harmed by their actions.[158]

■ *Police.* Restorative justice has also been implemented by police when crime is first encountered. The new community policing models are an attempt to bring restorative concepts into law enforcement. Restorative justice relies on the fact that criminal justice policymakers need to listen and respond to the needs of those who are to be affected by their actions, and community policing relies on policies established with input and exchanges between officers and citizens.[159]

■ *Courts.* Restorative programs in the courts typically involve diverting the formal court process. These programs encourage meeting and reconciling the conflicts between offenders and victims via victim advocacy, mediation programs, and sentencing circles, in which crime victims and their families are brought together with offenders and their families in an effort to formulate a sanction that addresses the needs of each party. Victims are given a chance to voice their stories, and offenders can help compensate them financially or provide some service (for example, fixing damaged property).[160] The goal is to enable offenders to appreciate the damage they have caused, to make amends, and to be reintegrated back into society.

Restoration programs are being used in court systems around the world. One example is the justice system in Australia, which makes use of a conferencing process to divert offenders from the justice system.[161] This offers offenders the opportunity to attend a conference to discuss and resolve their offense instead of being charged and appearing in court. (Those who deny guilt are not offered conferencing.) The conference, normally lasting one to two hours, is attended by the victims and their supporters, the defendant and his or her supporters, and other concerned parties. The conference coordinator focuses the discussion on condemning the act without condemning the character of the actor. Offenders are asked to tell their side of the story, what happened, how they have felt about the crime, and what they think should be done. The victims and others are asked to describe the physical, financial, and emotional consequences of the crime. This discussion may lead the offenders, their families, and their friends to experience the shame of the act, prompting an apology to the victim. A plan of action is developed and signed by key participants. The plan may include the offender paying compensation

---

sentencing circle A peacemaking technique in which offenders, victims, and other community members are brought together in an effort to formulate a sanction that addresses the needs of all.

The Center for Restorative Justice (CRJ)

There are numerous restorative justice initiatives now in operation around the United States and overseas. One prominent example is the Center for Restorative Justice (CRJ) in Vermont, a nonprofit community justice agency that for more than 30 years has provided a variety of restorative justice programming and services helping both young people and adults. Originally incorporated in 1982 as the Bennington County Court Diversion Program, the agency now known as CRJ provides programming that begins with prevention and intervention work in the schools through reentry work helping people returning to the community from incarceration. The services discussed following provide an example of the various forms that restorative justice now take in the community.

Pre-Charge and KAOS Programs

These programs are designed to provide early intervention and support to prevent young people from entering the juvenile justice system. Students identified as having broken school rules or who have committed chargeable offenses on school grounds may be offered this program as an alternative to school punitive sanctions. Using restorative justice principles, the Pre-Charge Program at Mount Anthony Union High School and the Kids Are Our Strength (KAOS) Program at Mount Anthony Union Middle School help first-time offenders make amends to those affected by their actions as well as the school community.

Truancy Project

The program is designed to work with students whose chronic truancy issues have not responded to school interventions. The Truancy Project is offered as a final option to the student and his or her parents as a way to address and correct the truancy problems before the case is filed with family court. Through identifying barriers, case management, community resources, and integrating contract conditions, students are supported to successfully attend school on a daily basis.

Court Diversion

Court diversion is a community-based alternative to the formal court process and gives the offender a chance to make amends to the victim and community. Restorative justice panels hold offenders accountable to victims and the community. Court diversion is a confidential and voluntary program that results in the offender's record being sealed upon successful completion of the program.

Youth Substance Abuse Safety Program (YSASP)

The focus of YSASP is to help young people (ages 16–20) who have been civilly cited for underage drinking or possession of marijuana get proper screening, education, and treatment for identified substance abuse problems. Once a young person successfully completes the program their civil ticket is voided. This is a voluntary program; individuals who choose not to participate in the program face a $300 fine from the State of Vermont, 90-day driver's license suspension with a $71 reinstatement fee, dramatically increased insurance rates, and civil conviction on their driving record.

Civil DLS Diversion Program

This diversion program is designed to help people regain their driver's license while they pay off their fines and fees. Participants work with a case manager to develop a contract and payment plan that is presented to the Vermont Judicial Bureau for review and approval. Some people may be eligible for a reduction in their debt, and some may provide community service and/or participate in an educational program in

---

to the victim, doing work for the victim or the community, or similar solutions. It is the responsibility of the conference participants to determine the outcomes that are most appropriate for these particular victims and these particular offenders. All eight states and territories in Australia have used the conference model at one time or another. Research indicates the conferencing approach is well received by young offenders, who believe the outcomes are fair, but it remains to be seen whether it can reduce future crime rates.[162]

Reconciliation   Restoration has also been used as a national policy to heal internal rifts. For example, after 50 years of oppressive white rule in South Africa, the race-dividing apartheid policy was abolished in the early 1990s, and in 1994 Nelson Mandela, leader of the African National Congress (ANC), was elected president.[163] Some black leaders wanted revenge for the political murders carried out during the apartheid era, but Mandela established the Truth and Reconciliation Commission. Rather than seeking vengeance for the crimes, this government agency investigated the atrocities with the mandate of granting amnesty to those individuals who confessed their roles in the violence and could prove that their actions served some political motive rather than being based on personal factors such as greed or jealousy.

Supporters of the commission believed that this approach would help heal the nation's wounds and prevent years of racial and ethnic strife. Mandela, who had been unjustly jailed for 27 years by the regime, had reason to desire vengeance. Yet he wanted to move the country forward after the truth of what happened in the past had been established. Though many South Africans, including

exchange for a reduction in fines and fees owed. Upon successful completion of their contract, an individual's prior suspensions are removed from their record.

Juvenile Restorative Programs

The Juvenile Restorative Probation Program (JRPP) provides restorative justice panels and restitution case management to youth on probation. Restorative justice panels hold youth accountable to victims and their community. Case managers provide follow-up services to ensure that restorative conditions of probation are completed. In addition, the program provides young offenders with an opportunity to increase their skills and participate in a variety of community activities.

The Juvenile Direct Court Referral Program is offered to youth as an alternative sentence set by the Family Court judge. Youth may be adjudicated in Family Court, but not placed on probation. The youth participate in a restorative justice panel, learn new skills, and repair harm caused to their victims.

Community Support and Supervision (Street Checker Program)

This program provides progressive levels of community support and supervision for at-risk youth or for youth who are on probation. Community case managers provide home-based support such as curfew checks and ensuring youth's activities are consistent with probation conditions. This program offers youth opportunities to build their skills and successfully reintegrate into their own communities.

Life Skills Development

CRJ offers a wide array of skill-building opportunities. Groups vary throughout the year and cover topics such as anger management, conflict resolution, impact on victims, self-esteem, peer pressure, and substance abuse. Individualized life skills instruction is available year-round.

Adult Restorative Programs

The Reparative Probation Program is offered to adults through the criminal court as a condition of their probation. Restorative justice panels run by trained volunteers provide an offender the opportunity to take responsibility for his or her actions and repair the harm caused to victims and communities. Offenders who participate in this program must accept responsibility for their role in the crime that was committed.

The Direct Referral Reparative Program is offered to offenders convicted in criminal court but not placed on probation. Participants meet with a restorative justice panel to discuss the impact of their crime and develop a contract that helps make amends to their victim and community. Only those offenders who take responsibility for their crime qualify for the program.

The Suspended Fine Program provides an alternative sentencing option with a fine reduction upon successful program completion.

Community Reentry Program

The Reentry Program provides intensive case management services to help individuals who are returning to the community from incarceration. Providing support to individuals who are struggling to reintegrate into the community is the key to their success. Area case managers' focuses include housing, employment, prosocial leisure activities, transportation, connection to community resources, and mentoring.

Circle of Support and Accountability (COSA)

A team of trained community volunteers helps individuals returning to the community from incarceration meet the challenges of everyday living and learn ways to become productive, contributing members of the community. In addition to supporting the individual to successfully reintegrate into the community, volunteers help guide the offender to make amends to those impacted by his or her past behavior.

 CRITICAL THINKING

What do you think about restorative justice? Is it better to help people reintegrate into the community than to cast them out and stigmatize them as "criminals" and "convicts"? Or is the restorative justice movement simply wishful thinking?

SOURCE: Information provided by the Center for Restorative Justice, Bennington, Vermont, 2015, http://www.bcrj.org/programs/ (accessed May 2016).

---

some ANC members, believed that the commission was too lenient, Mandela's attempts at reconciliation prevailed. The commission was a model of restoration over revenge.

In sum, restoration can be or has been used at the following stages of justice:

- As a form of final warning to young offenders
- As a tool for school officials
- As a method of handling complaints to police
- As a diversion from prosecution
- As a presentencing, postconviction add-on to the sentencing process
- As a supplement to a community sentence (probation)
- As a preparation for release from long-term imprisonment[164]

The Policy and Practice in Criminology feature reviews a successful restorative justice agency.

THE CHALLENGE OF RESTORATIVE JUSTICE

Restorative justice holds great promise, but there are also some concerns:

- Is it a political movement or a treatment process? Restorative justice is viewed as an extremely liberal alternative, and its advocates often warn of the uneven exercise of state power. Some view it as a social movement rather than a method of rehabilitation.[165] Can it survive in a culture that is becoming increasingly conservative and focused on security rather than personal freedom?
- Restorative justice programs must be wary of the cultural and social differences that can be found throughout our heterogeneous society. What may be considered "restorative" in one subculture may be considered insulting and damaging in another.[166]

- There is still no single definition of what constitutes restorative justice.[167] Consequently, many diverse programs that call themselves restorative-oriented pursue objectives that seem remote from the restorative ideal.
- Restorative justice programs face the difficult task of balancing the needs of offenders with those of their victims. If programs focus solely on victims' needs, they may risk ignoring the offenders' needs and increase the likelihood of reoffending. Declan Roache, a lecturer in law at the London School of Economics, makes the argument that the seductive promise of restorative justice may blind admirers to the benefits of traditional methods and prevent them from understanding or appreciating some of the pitfalls of restoration. There is danger, he warns, in a process that is essentially informal, without lawyers, and with little or no oversight on the outcome. The restoration process gives participants unchecked power without the benefit of procedural safeguards.[168]
- Benefits may only work in the short term while ignoring long-term treatment needs. Sharon Levrant and her colleagues suggest that restorative justice programs that feature short-term interactions with victims fail to help offenders learn prosocial ways of behaving. Restorative justice advocates may falsely assume that relatively brief interludes of public shaming will change deeply rooted criminal predispositions.[169]

These are a few of the obstacles that restorative justice programs must overcome to be successful and productive. Yet because the method holds so much promise, criminologists are conducting numerous demonstration projects to find the most effective means of returning the ownership of justice to the people and the community.[170]

SUMMARY

L01 Define the concept of social conflict and how it shapes behavior

Social conflict theorists view crime as a function of the conflict that exists in society. Conflict theorists suggest that crime in any society is caused by class conflict. Laws are created by those in power to protect their own rights and serve their own interests.

L02 Trace the history of critical theory and its roots in Marxist thought

Marx's view of society was shaped by the economic trends and structures of that period. He lived in an era of unrestrained capitalist expansion. During this period owners ruthlessly suppressed workers. The economic system was biased against the poor and designed to protect the wealthy. A view developed that social and political oppression produce crime. Crime would disappear if equality rather than discrimination was the norm.

L03 List the core ideas of critical criminology

Critical criminology views the competitive nature of the capitalist system as a major cause of crime. The poor commit crimes because of their frustration, anger, and need. The wealthy engage in illegal acts because they are used to competition and because they must do so to maintain their positions in society. Critical scholars have attempted to show that the law is designed to protect the wealthy and powerful and to control the poor, "have-not" members of society.

L04 Define the concept of globalization and analyze its association with crime

Globalization is a product of the cyber age that allows mega corporations to operate around the world with instant communication and rapid travel. It also allows criminal groups to operate on a global scale and to pick up new recruits from oppressed workers who are being exploited by international capitalists.

L05 Comment on the concept of state-organized crime

State-organized crimes involve a violation of citizen trust. They are acts defined by law as criminal and committed by state officials in pursuit of their jobs as government representatives. Some state-organized crimes are committed by individuals who abuse their state authority, or fail to exercise it, when working with people and organizations in the private sector. State-corporate crime involves the deviant activities by which the privileged classes strive to maintain or increase their power.

L06 Compare and contrast structural and instrumental theory

Critical theorists subscribe to either instrumental theory or structural theory. Instrumental theorists hold that those in authority wield their power to control society and keep the lower classes in check. Structural theorists believe that the justice system is designed to maintain the status quo and is used to punish the wealthy, as well as members of the lower classes, when they break the rules governing capitalism.

L07 Analyze critical criminology and discuss criticisms of the theory

Critical criminology has been criticized by traditional criminologists. Some critics suggest that critical criminologists make fundamental errors in their concepts of ownership and class interest. Other critics suggest that critical theorists unfairly neglect the capitalist system's efforts to regulate itself—for example, by instituting antitrust regulations and putting white-collar criminals behind bars. Others question whether socialist and communist nations are any more crime free than capitalist countries.

LO8 **Assess the concept of left realism**

Left realism sees crime as a function of relative deprivation under capitalism and views the justice system as necessary to protect the lower classes until a socialist society can be developed, which will end crime.

LO9 **Articulate the central themes of critical feminism and gendered criminology**

Critical feminist writers draw attention to the influence of patriarchal society on crime. They assess how capitalism has created gender conflict and the exploitation of women. They also look at how the concept of masculinity is related to crime, especially the victimization of women. According to power–control theory, gender differences in the crime rate can be explained by the structure of the family in a capitalist society.

LO10 **Explain peacemaking criminology and restorative justice**

Peacemaking criminology brings a call for humanism to criminology. The restorative justice model holds that reconciliation rather than retribution should be applied to prevent and control crime. Restoration programs are now being used around the United States in schools, justice agencies, and community forums. They employ mediation, sentencing circles, and other techniques.

KEY TERMS

critical criminologists (272)
critical criminology (272)
Communist Manifesto (274)
productive forces (274)
productive relations (274)
capitalist bourgeoisie (274)
proletariat (274)
lumpen proletariat (274)
dialectic method (275)

thesis (275)
antithesis (275)
synthesis (275)
supranational criminology (277)
surplus value (278)
marginalization (278)
dropout factories (279)
globalization (279)

state-organized crime (280)
instrumental theory (284)
structural theory (284)
demystify (284)
left realism (286)
preemptive deterrence (286)
critical feminism (288)
patriarchy (288)
paternalistic families (290)

role exit behaviors (290)
egalitarian families (290)
power–control theory (291)
peacemaking (291)
restorative justice (292)
shame (293)
reintegrative shaming (294)
sentencing circle (295)

CRITICAL THINKING QUESTIONS

1. How would a conservative reply to a call for more restorative justice? How would a restorative justice advocate respond to a conservative call for more prisons?

2. Considering recent changes in American culture, how would a power–control theorist explain recent drops in the U.S. crime rate? Can it be linked to changes in the structure of the American family?

3. Is conflict inevitable in all cultures? If not, what can be done to reduce the level of conflict in our own society?

4. If Marx were alive today, what would he think about the prosperity enjoyed by the working class in industrial societies? Might he alter his vision of the capitalist system?

5. Has religious conflict replaced class conflict as the most important issue facing modern society? Can anything be done to heal the rifts between people of different faiths?

NOTES

All URLs accessed in 2016.
1. Donald Trump, "Immigration Reform that Will Make America Great Again," 2016, https://www.donaldjtrump.com /positions/immigration-reform; Russell Berman, "Donald Trump's Call to Ban Muslim Immigrants," *Atlantic*, December 7, 2015, http://www.theatlantic.com /politics/archive/2015/12/donald -trumps-call-to-ban-muslim-immigrants /419298/.

2. Margaret Talbot, "The Populist Prophet," *New Yorker*, October 12, 2015, http://www .newyorker.com/magazine/2015/10/12/the -populist-prophet.

3. United Nations, "Alarmed by Continuing Syria Crisis, Security Council Affirms Its Support for Special Envoy's Approach in Moving Political Solution Forward," August 17, 2015, http://www.un.org/press /en/2015/sc12008.doc.htm; Emad El-Din Shahin, "Brutality, Torture, Rape: Egypt's Crisis Will Continue Until Military Rule Is Dismantled," *Guardian*, March 5, 2014, http://www.theguardian.com/commentisfree /2014/mar/06/brutality-torture-rape-egypt -military-rule.

4. Michael Lynch and W. Byron Groves, *A Primer in Radical Criminology*, 2nd ed. (Albany, NY: Harrow & Heston, 1989), pp. 32–33.

5. Michael Lynch, "Rediscovering Criminology: Lessons from the Marxist Tradition," in

Marxist Sociology: Surveys of Contemporary Theory and Research, ed. Donald McQuarie and Patrick McGuire (New York: General Hall, 1994).

6. Andrew Woolford, "Making Genocide Unthinkable: Three Guidelines for a Critical Criminology of Genocide," *Critical Criminology* 14 (2006): 87–106.

7. Tony Platt and Cecilia O'Leary, "Patriot Acts," *Social Justice* 30 (2003): 5–21.

8. See, generally, Karl Marx and Friedrich Engels, *Capital: A Critique of Political Economy*, trans. E. Aveling (Chicago: Charles Kern, 1906); Karl Marx, *Selected Writings in Sociology and Social Philosophy*, trans. P. B. Bottomore (New York: McGraw-Hill, 1956). For a general discussion of Marxist thought, see Lynch and Groves, *A Primer in Radical Criminology*, pp. 6–26.

9. Karl Marx, *Grundrisse: Introduction to the Critique of Political Economy*, trans. Martin Nicolaus (New York: Vintage, 1973), pp. 106–107.

10. Lynch, "Rediscovering Criminology."

11. Karl Marx, "Population, Crime and Pauperism," in *Karl Marx and Friedrich Engels, Ireland and the Irish Question* (Moscow: Progress, 1859, reprinted 1971), p. 92.

12. Friedrich Engels, *The Condition of the Working Class in England in 1844* (London: Allen & Unwin, 1950).

13. Lynch, "Rediscovering Criminology," p. 5.

14. Ian Taylor, Paul Walton, and Jock Young, *The New Criminology: For a Social Theory of Deviance* (London: Routledge & Kegan Paul, 1973).

15. Biko Agozino, "Imperialism, Crime and Criminology: Towards the Decolonisation of Criminology," *Crime, Law, and Social Change* 41 (2004): 343–358.

16. William Chambliss and Robert Seidman, *Law, Order and Power* (Reading, MA: Addison-Wesley, 1971), p. 503.

17. Richard Quinney, *The Social Reality of Crime* (Boston: Little, Brown, 1970).

18. This section borrows heavily from Richard Sparks, "A Critique of Marxist Criminology," in *Crime and Justice*, Vol. 2, ed. Norval Morris and Michael Tonry (Chicago: University of Chicago Press, 1980), pp. 159–208.

19. Barbara Sims, "Crime, Punishment, and the American Dream: Toward a Marxist Integration," *Journal of Research in Crime and Delinquency* 34 (1997): 5–24.

20. Gregg Barak, "Revisionist History, Visionary Criminology, and Needs-Based Justice," *Contemporary Justice Review* 6 (2003): 217–225.

21. John Braithwaite, "Retributivism, Punishment, and Privilege," in *Punishment and Privilege*, ed. W. Byron Groves and Graeme Newman (Albany, NY: Harrow & Heston, 1986), pp. 55–66.

22. Michael Hallett, "Reentry to What? Theorizing Prisoner Reentry in the Jobless Future," *Critical Criminology* 20 (2012): 213–228.

23. Tony Platt and Cecilia O'Leary, "Patriot Acts," *Social Justice* 30 (2003): 5–21.

24. Alette Smeulers and Roelof Haveman, eds., *Supranational Criminology: Towards a Criminology of International Crimes* (Belgium: Intersentia, 2008).

25. Ibid., p. 4.

26. Lynch and Groves, *A Primer in Radical Criminology*, p. 7.

27. Jeffery Reiman, *The Rich Get Richer and the Poor Get Prison* (New York: Wiley, 1984), pp. 43–44.

28. Rob White, "Environmental Harm and the Political Economy of Consumption," *Social Justice* 29 (2002): 82–102.

29. Sims, "Crime, Punishment, and the American Dream."

30. Steven Box, *Recession, Crime, and Unemployment* (London: Macmillan, 1987).

31. David Barlow, Melissa Hickman-Barlow, and W. Wesley Johnson, "The Political Economy of Criminal Justice Policy: A Time-Series Analysis of Economic Conditions, Crime, and Federal Criminal Justice Legislation, 1948–1987," *Justice Quarterly* 13 (1996): 223–241.

32. Mahesh Nalla, Michael Lynch, and Michael Leiber, "Determinants of Police Growth in Phoenix, 1950–1988," *Justice Quarterly* 14 (1997): 144–163.

33. America's Promise Alliance, "Building a Grad Nation: Progress and Challenge in Ending the High School Dropout Epidemic," November 30, 2010, http://www.americaspromise.org/Our-Work/Grad-Nation/Building-a-Grad-Nation.aspx.

34. Michael Rocques and Raymond Paternoster, "Understanding the Antecedents of the 'School-to-Jail' Link: The Relationship Between Race and School Discipline," *Journal of Criminal Law and Criminology* 101 (2011): 633–665.

35. Bureau of Labor Statistics, Manufacturing in China, 2012, http://www.bls.gov/ilc/china.htm#data_tables.

36. Jim Puzzanghera and Samantha Masunaga, "Pfizer and Allergan's $160-billion Pharmaceutical Merger Puts New Twist on Tax-Avoiding Inversion," *Los Angeles Times*, November 23, 2015, http://www.latimes.com/business/la-fi-pfizer-allergan-merger-20151123-story.html.

37. Dawn L. Rothe, Jeffrey Ian Ross, Christopher W. Mullins, David Friedrichs, Raymond Michalowski, Gregg Barak, David Kauzlarich, and Ronald C. Kramer, "That Was Then, This Is Now, What About Tomorrow? Future Directions in State Crime Studies," *Critical Criminology* 17 (2009): 3–13.

38. Amnesty International, "Conflict Diamonds: Did Someone Die for that Diamond?" http://www.amnestyusa.org/our-work/issues/business-and-human-rights/oil-gas-and-mining-industries/conflict-diamonds.

39. David Friedrichs and Jessica Friedrichs, "The World Bank and Crimes of Globalization: A Case Study," *Social Justice* 29 (2002): 13–36.

40. Ibid.

41. Louise Shelley, "The Globalization of Crime and Terrorism," State Department's Bureau of International Information Programs (IIP), 2006, http://iipdigital.usembassy.gov/st/english/publication/2008/06/20080608103639xjyrrep4.218692e-02.html.

42. Greg Palast, "Secret US Plan for Iraqi Oil, BBC News," March 17, 2005, http://news.bbc.co.uk/1/hi/programmes/newsnight/4354269.stm.

43. Jonathan H. C. Kelman, "States Can Play, Too: Constructing a Typology of State Participation in Illicit Flows," *Crime, Law and Social Change* 64 (2015): 37–55.

44. Jeffrey Ian Ross, *The Dynamics of Political Crime* (Thousand Oaks, CA: Sage, 2003).

45. Charlie Savage and Mark Mazzetti, "Cryptic Overtures and a Clandestine Meeting Gave Birth to a Blockbuster Story," *New York Times*, June 10, 2013, http://www.nytimes.com/2013/06/11/us/how-edward-j-snowden-orchestrated-a-blockbuster-story.html.

46. Philip Ingram, "How Many CCTV Cameras Are There Globally?" *Security News Desk*, June 11, 2015, http://www.securitynewsdesk.com/how-many-cctv-cameras-are-there-globally/.

47. American Civil Liberties Union, "What's Wrong with Public Video Surveillance? The Four Problems with Public Video Surveillance," http://www.aclu.org/technology-and-liberty/whats-wrong-public-video-surveillance.

48. Human Rights Watch, World Report 2015, https://www.hrw.org/sites/default/files/wr2015_web.pdf.

49. Human Rights Watch, United Arab Emirates, https://www.hrw.org/middle-east/n-africa/united-arab-emirates.

50. MSNBC News, "Bush Acknowledges Secret CIA Prisons," September 6, 2006, http://www.msnbc.msn.com/id/14689359/; American Civil Liberties Union, "FBI Inquiry Details Abuses Reported by Agents at Guantanamo," January 3, 2007, http://www.aclu.org/safefree/torture/27816prs20070103.html.

51. Michael Lynch and Kimberly Barrett, "Death Matters: Victimization by Particle Matter from Coal Fired Power Plants in the US, a Green Criminological View," *Critical Criminology* 23 (2015): 219–234.

52. Ross, *The Dynamics of Political Crime*.

53. Amnesty International, "Brazil: One More Human Rights Defender Lost to the Scourge of 'Death-Squads,'" January 26, 2009, https://www.amnesty.org/en/press-releases/2009/01/brazil-one-more-human-rights

-defender-lost-scourge-death-squads
-20090126/.

54. Scott A. Bonn, *Mass Deception: Moral Panic and the U.S. War on Iraq* (Piscataway, NJ: Rutgers University Press, 2010).

55. Gresham Sykes, "The Rise of Critical Criminology," *Journal of Criminal Law and Criminology* 65 (1974): 211–229.

56. David Jacobs, "Corporate Economic Power and the State: A Longitudinal Assessment of Two Explanations," *American Journal of Sociology* 93 (1988): 852–881.

57. Richard Quinney, "Crime Control in Capitalist Society," in *Critical Criminology*, ed. Ian Taylor, Paul Walton, and Jock Young (London: Routledge & Kegan Paul, 1975), p. 199.

58. Ibid.

59. John Hagan, *Structural Criminology* (New Brunswick, NJ: Rutgers University Press, 1989), pp. 110–119.

60. Darrell Steffensmeier and Stephen Demuth, "Ethnicity and Judges' Sentencing Decisions: Hispanic-Black-White Comparisons," *Criminology* 39 (2001): 145–178; Alan Lizotte, "Extra-Legal Factors in Chicago's Criminal Courts: Testing the Conflict Model of Criminal Justice," *Social Problems* 25 (1978): 564–580.

61. Terance Miethe and Charles Moore, "Racial Differences in Criminal Processing: The Consequences of Model Selection on Conclusions About Differential Treatment," *Sociological Quarterly* 27 (1987): 217–237.

62. David Jacobs and David Britt, "Inequality and Police Use of Deadly Force: An Empirical Assessment of a Conflict Hypothesis," *Social Problems* 26 (1979): 403–412.

63. Graham Ousey and James Unnever, "Racial-Ethnic Threat, Out-Group Intolerance, and Support for Punishing Criminals: A Cross-National Study," *Criminology* 50 (2012): 565–603.

64. Albert Meehan and Michael Ponder, "Race and Place: The Ecology of Racial Profiling African American Motorists," *Justice Quarterly* 29 (2002): 399–431.

65. Tammy Rinehart Kochel, David Wilson, and Stephen Mastrofski, "Effect of Suspect Race on Officers' Arrest Decisions," *Criminology* 49 (2011): 473–512.

66. Malcolm Homes, "Minority Threat and Police Brutality: Determinants of Civil Rights Criminal Complaints in Municipalities," *Criminology* 38 (2000): 343–368.

67. Charles Crawford, Ted Chiricos, and Gary Kleck, "Race, Racial Threat, and Sentencing of Habitual Offenders," *Criminology* 36 (1998): 481–511.

68. Steffensmeier and Demuth, "Ethnicity and Judges' Sentencing Decisions"; Alan Lizotte, "Extra-Legal Factors in Chicago's Criminal Courts: Testing the Conflict Model of Criminal Justice," *Social Problems* 25 (1978): 564–580.

69. Tracy Nobiling, Cassia Spohn, and Miriam DeLone, "A Tale of Two Counties: Unemployment and Sentence Severity," *Justice Quarterly* 15 (1998): 459–485.

70. David Greenberg and Valerie West, "State Prison Populations and Their Growth, 1971–1991," *Criminology* 39 (2001): 615–654.

71. Michael Lenza, David Keys, and Teresa Guess, "The Prevailing Injustices in the Application of the Missouri Death Penalty (1978 to 1996)," *Social Justice* 32 (2005): 151–166.

72. Jack Gibbs, "An Incorrigible Positivist," *Criminologist* 12 (1987): 2–3.

73. Jackson Toby, "The New Criminology Is the Old Sentimentality," *Criminology* 16 (1979): 513–526.

74. Richard Sparks, "A Critique of Marxist Criminology," in *Crime and Justice*, Vol. 2, ed. Norval Morris and Michael Tonry (Chicago: University of Chicago Press, 1980), pp. 159–208.

75. Carl Klockars, "The Contemporary Crises of Marxist Criminology," in *Radical Criminology: The Coming Crisis*, ed. J. Inciardi (Beverly Hills, CA: Sage, 1980), pp. 92–123.

76. Matthew Petrocelli, Alex Piquero, and Michael Smith, "Conflict Theory and Racial Profiling: An Empirical Analysis of Police Traffic Stop Data," *Journal of Criminal Justice* 31 (2003): 1–10.

77. Ibid.

78. Anthony Platt, "Criminology in the 1980s: Progressive Alternatives to 'Law and Order,'" *Crime and Social Justice* 21–22 (1985): 191–199.

79. John Lea and Jock Young, *What Is to Be Done About Law and Order?* (Harmondsworth, England: Penguin, 1984).

80. Ibid., p. 88.

81. Ian Taylor, *Crime in Context: A Critical Criminology of Market Societies* (Boulder, CO: Westview Press, 1999).

82. Ibid., pp. 30–31.

83. Richard Kinsey, John Lea, and Jock Young, *Losing the Fight Against Crime* (London: Blackwell, 1986).

84. Martin Schwartz and Walter DeKeseredy, *Contemporary Criminology* (Belmont, CA: Wadsworth, 1993), p. 249.

85. Michelle Alexander, *The New Jim Crow: Mass Incarceration in the Age of Colorblindness* (New York: New Press, 2010), p. 2.

86. Michael Jacobson and Lynn Chancer, "From Left Realism to Mass Incarceration: The Need for Pragmatic Vision in Criminal Justice Policy," *Crime, Law and Social Change* 55 (2011): 187–196.

87. Martin D. Schwartz and Walter S. DeKeseredy, "Left Realist Criminology: Strengths, Weaknesses and the Feminist Critique," *Crime, Law, and Social Change* 15 (1991): 51–72.

88. For a general review of this issue, see Kathleen Daly and Meda Chesney-Lind, "Feminism and Criminology," *Justice Quarterly* 5 (1988): 497–538; Douglas Smith and Raymond Paternoster, "The Gender Gap in Theories of Deviance: Issues and Evidence," *Journal of Research in Crime and Delinquency* 24 (1987): 140–172; and Pat Carlen, "Women, Crime, Feminism, and Realism," *Social Justice* 17 (1990): 106–123.

89. Herman Schwendinger and Julia Schwendinger, *Rape and Inequality* (Newbury Park, CA: Sage, 1983).

90. Meda Chesney-Lind and Merry Morash, "Transformative Feminist Criminology: A Critical Re-thinking of a Discipline," *Critical Criminology* 21 (2013): 287–304.

91. Jordan Blair Woods, "Queer Contestations and the Future of a Critical 'Queer' Criminology," *Critical Criminology* 22 (2014): 5–19.

92. Matthew Ball, "What's Queer About Queer Criminology?" in *Handbook of LGBT Communities, Crime, and Justice*, ed. Dana Peterson and Vanessa Panfil (New York: Springer Science + Business Media, 2014), pp. 531–555.

93. Daly and Chesney-Lind, "Feminism and Criminology."

94. Janet Saltzman Chafetz, "Feminist Theory and Sociology: Underutilized Contributions for Mainstream Theory," *Annual Review of Sociology* 23 (1997): 97–121.

95. Ibid.

96. James Messerschmidt, *Capitalism, Patriarchy, and Crime* (Totowa, NJ: Rowman & Littlefield, 1986); for a critique of this work, see Herman Schwendinger and Julia Schwendinger, "The World According to James Messerschmidt," *Social Justice* 15 (1988): 123–145.

97. Kathleen Daly, "Gender and Varieties of White-Collar Crime," *Criminology* 27 (1989): 769–793.

98. Gillian Balfour, "Re-imagining a Feminist Criminology," *Canadian Journal of Criminology and Criminal Justice* 48 (2006): 735–752.

99. Jane Roberts Chapman, "Violence Against Women as a Violation of Human Rights," *Social Justice* 17 (1990): 54–71.

100. Shannon Lynch, April Fritch, and Nicole Heath, "Looking Beneath the Surface: The Nature of Incarcerated Women's Experiences of Interpersonal Violence, Treatment Needs, and Mental Health," *Feminist Criminology* 7 (2012): 381–400.

101. Lynne Vieraitis, Sarah Britto, and Robert Morris, "Assessing the Impact of Changes in Gender Equality on Female Homicide Victimization: 1980–2000," *Crime and Delinquency* 61 (2015): 428–453.

102. James Messerschmidt, *Masculinities and Crime: Critique and Reconceptualization of Theory* (Lanham, MD: Rowman & Littlefield, 1993).

103. Angela P. Harris, "Gender, Violence, Race, and Criminal Justice," *Stanford Law Review* 52 (2000): 777–810.

104. Suzie Dod Thomas and Nancy Stein, "Criminality, Imprisonment, and Women's Rights in the 1990s," *Social Justice* 17 (1990): 1–5.

105. Walter DeKeseredy and Martin Schwartz, "Male Peer Support and Woman Abuse: An Expansion of DeKeseredy's Model," *Sociological Spectrum* 13 (1993): 393–413.

106. Fox News, "Penn State Frat Suspended for Year over Nude Facebook Pics," March 17, 2015, http://www.foxnews.com/us/2015/03/17/penn-state-frat-suspended-for-year-over-nude-facebook-pics/.

107. Philip Kavanaugh, "The Continuum of Sexual Violence: Women's Accounts of Victimization in Urban Nightlife," *Feminist Criminology* 8 (2013): 20–39.

108. Daly and Chesney-Lind, "Feminism and Criminology." See also Drew Humphries and Susan Caringella-MacDonald, "Murdered Mothers, Missing Wives: Reconsidering Female Victimization," *Social Justice* 17 (1990): 71–78.

109. Kia Asberg and Kimberly Renk, "Safer in Jail? A Comparison of Victimization History and Psychological Adjustment Between Previously Homeless and Non-homeless Incarcerated Women," *Feminist Criminology* 10 (2015): 165–187.

110. Carrie Yodanis, "Gender Inequality, Violence Against Women, and Fear," *Journal of Interpersonal Violence* 19 (2004): 655–675.

111. Victoria Titterington, "A Retrospective Investigation of Gender Inequality and Female Homicide Victimization," *Sociological Spectrum* 26 (2006): 205–236.

112. Kjersti Ericsson and Nina Jon, "Gendered Social Control: 'A Virtuous Girl' and 'a Proper Boy,'" *Journal of Scandinavian Studies in Criminology and Crime Prevention* 9 (2006): 126–141.

113. Meda Chesney-Lind and Vickie Paramore, "Are Girls Getting More Violent? Exploring Juvenile Robbery Trends," *Journal of Contemporary Criminal Justice* 17 (2001): 142–166; Joanne Belknap, Kristi Holsinger, and Melissa Dunn, "Understanding Incarcerated Girls," *Prison Journal* 77 (1997): 381–404.

114. Thomas J. Gamble, Sherrie Sonnenberg, John Haltigan, and Amy Cuzzola-Kern, "Detention Screening: Prospects for Population-Management and the Examination of Disproportionality by Race, Age, and Gender," *Criminal Justice Policy Review* 13 (2002): 380–395; Kimberly Kempf-Leonard and Lisa Sample, "Disparity Based on Sex: Is Gender-Specific Treatment Warranted?" *Justice Quarterly* 17 (2000): 89–128.

115. Holly Hartwig and Jane Myers, "A Different Approach: Applying a Wellness Paradigm to Adolescent Female Delinquents and Offenders," *Journal of Mental Health Counseling* 25 (2003): 57–75; Meda Chesney-Lind and Randall Shelden, *Girls, Delinquency, and Juvenile Justice* (Belmont, CA: West/Wadsworth, 1998).

116. Hartwig and Myers, "A Different Approach: Applying a Wellness Paradigm to Adolescent Female Delinquents and Offenders."

117. Tia Stevens, Merry Morash, and Meda Chesney-Lind, "Are Girls Getting Tougher, or Are We Tougher on Girls? Probability of Arrest and Juvenile Court Oversight in 1980 and 2000," *Justice Quarterly* 28 (2011): 719–744.

118. Lisa Pasko, "Damaged Daughters: The History of Girls' Sexuality and the Juvenile Justice System," *Journal of Criminal Law and Criminology* 100 (2010): 1099–1130.

119. Kristi Holsinger and Jessica P. Hodge, "The Experiences of Lesbian, Gay, Bisexual, and Transgender Girls in Juvenile Justice Systems," *Feminist Criminology*, first published online February 2014.

120. Corey S. Shdaimah and Chrysanthi Leon, "First and Foremost They're Survivors: Selective Manipulation, Resilience, and Assertion Among Prostitute Women," *Feminist Criminology* 1–22, first published online 2014.

121. Hagan, *Structural Criminology.*

122. John Hagan, A. R. Gillis, and John Simpson, "The Class Structure and Delinquency: Toward a Power-Control Theory of Common Delinquent Behavior," *American Journal of Sociology* 90 (1985): 1151–1178; John Hagan, John Simpson, and A. R. Gillis, "Class in the Household: A Power-Control Theory of Gender and Delinquency," *American Journal of Sociology* 92 (1987): 788–816.

123. John Hagan, Bill McCarthy, and Holly Foster, "A Gendered Theory of Delinquency and Despair in the Life Course," *Acta Sociologica* 45 (2002): 37–47.

124. Brenda Sims Blackwell, Christine Sellers, and Sheila Schlaupitz, "A Power-Control Theory of Vulnerability to Crime and Adolescent Role Exits—Revisited," *Canadian Review of Sociology and Anthropology* 39 (2002): 199–219.

125. Brenda Sims Blackwell, "Perceived Sanction Threats, Gender, and Crime: A Test and Elaboration of Power-Control Theory," *Criminology* 38 (2000): 439–488.

126. Christopher Uggen, "Class, Gender, and Arrest: An Intergenerational Analysis of Workplace Power and Control," *Criminology* 38 (2001): 835–862.

127. Gary Jensen and Kevin Thompson, "What's Class Got to Do with It? A Further Examination of Power-Control Theory," *American Journal of Sociology* 95 (1990): 1009–1023. For some critical research, see Simon Singer and Murray Levine, "Power-Control Theory, Gender and Delinquency: A Partial Replication with Additional Evidence on the Effects of Peers," *Criminology* 26 (1988): 627–648.

128. Kevin Thompson, "Gender and Adolescent Drinking Problems: The Effects of Occupational Structure," *Social Problems* 36 (1989): 30–38.

129. Kristin Mack and Michael Leiber, "Race, Gender, Single-Mother Households, and Delinquency: A Further Test of Power-Control Theory," *Youth and Society* 37 (2005): 115–144.

130. David Eitle, Fallon Niedrist, and Tamela McNulty Eitle, "Gender, Race, and Delinquent Behavior: An Extension of Power-Control Theory to American Indian Adolescents," *Deviant Behavior* 35 (2014): 1023–1042; Helmut Hirtenlehner, Brenda Sims Blackwell, Heinz Leitgoeb, and Johann Bacher, "Explaining the Gender Gap in Juvenile Shoplifting: A Power-Control Theoretical Analysis," *Deviant Behavior* 35 (2014): 41–65.

131. See, generally, Uggen, "Class, Gender, and Arrest."

132. Brenda Sims Blackwell and Alex Piquero, "On the Relationships Between Gender, Power Control, Self-Control, and Crime," *Journal of Criminal Justice* 33 (2005): 1–17.

133. Liz Walz, "One Blood," *Contemporary Justice Review* 6 (2003): 25–36.

134. John F. Wozniak, "Poverty and Peacemaking Criminology: Beyond Mainstream Criminology," *Critical Criminology* 16 (2008): 209–223.

135. See, for example, Dennis Sullivan and Larry Tifft, *Restorative Justice: Healing the Foundations of Our Everyday Lives* (Monsey, NY: Willow Tree Press, 2005); Dennis Sullivan, *The Mask of Love: Corrections in America, Toward a Mutual Aid Alternative* (Port Washington, NY: Kennikat Press, 1980).

136. Larry Tifft, "Foreword," in Sullivan, *The Mask of Love*, p. 6.

137. Sullivan, *The Mask of Love*, p. 141.

138. Sullivan and Tifft, *Restorative Justice.*

139. Richard Quinney, "The Way of Peace: On Crime, Suffering, and Service," in *Criminology as Peacemaking*, ed. Harold Pepinsky and Richard Quinney (Bloomington: Indiana University Press, 1991), pp. 8–9.

140. For a review of Quinney's ideas, see Kevin B. Anderson, "Richard Quinney's Journey: The Marxist Dimension," *Crime and Delinquency* 48 (2002): 232–242.

141. Bill McClanahan and Avi Brisman, "Climate Change and Peacemaking Criminology: Ecophilosophy, Peace and Security in the 'War on Climate Change,'" *Critical Criminology* 23 (2015): 417–443.

142. Kathleen Daly and Russ Immarigeon, "The Past, Present and Future of Restorative Justice: Some Critical Reflections," *Contemporary Justice Review* 1 (1998): 21–45.

143. Howard Zehr, *The Little Book of Restorative Justice* (Intercourse, PA: Good Books, 2002), pp. 1–10.

144. Mark Lewis Taylor, *The Executed God: The Way of the Cross in Lockdown America* (Minneapolis: Fortress Press, 2001).

145. Alfred Villaume, "'Life Without Parole' and 'Virtual Life Sentences': Death Sentences by Any Other Name," *Contemporary Justice Review* 8 (2005): 265–277.

146. John Braithwaite, *Crime, Shame, and Reintegration* (Melbourne, Australia: Cambridge University Press, 1989).

147. Ibid., p. 81.

148. Anthony Petrosino and Carolyn Petrosino, "The Public Safety Potential of Megan's Law in Massachusetts: An Assessment from a Sample of Criminal Sexual Psychopaths," *Crime and Delinquency* 45 (1999): 140–158.

149. Eliza Ahmed, Nathan Harris, John Braithwaite, and Valerie Braithwaite, *Shame Management Through Reintegration* (Cambridge, England: Cambridge University Press, 2001).

150. Eliza Ahmed, "'What, Me Ashamed?' Shame Management and School Bullying," *Journal of Research in Crime and Delinquency* 41 (2004): 269–294.

151. John Braithwaite, "Rape, Shame and Pride," *Journal of Scandinavian Studies in Criminology and Crime Prevention* 7 (2006): 2–16.

152. Carter Hay, "An Exploratory Test of Braithwaite's Reintegrative Shaming Theory," *Journal of Research in Crime and Delinquency* 38 (2001): 132–153.

153. Gene Stephens, "The Future of Policing: From a War Model to a Peace Model," in *The Past, Present and Future of American Criminal Justice*, ed. Brendan Maguire and Polly Radosh (Dix Hills, NY: General Hall, 1996), pp. 77–93.

154. Rick Shifley, "The Organization of Work as a Factor in Social Well-Being," *Contemporary Justice Review* 6 (2003): 105–126.

155. Kay Pranis, "Peacemaking Circles: Restorative Justice in Practice Allows Victims and Offenders to Begin Repairing the Harm," *Corrections Today* 59 (1997): 74–78.

156. Carol LaPrairie, "The 'New' Justice: Some Implications for Aboriginal Communities," *Canadian Journal of Criminology* 40 (1998): 61–79.

157. Diane Schaefer, "A Disembodied Community Collaborates in a Homicide: Can Empathy Transform a Failing Justice System?" *Contemporary Justice Review* 6 (2003): 133–143.

158. David R. Karp and Beau Breslin, "Restorative Justice in School Communities," *Youth and Society* 33 (2001): 249–272.

159. Paul Jesilow and Deborah Parsons, "Community Policing as Peacemaking," *Policing and Society* 10 (2000): 163–183.

160. Gordon Bazemore and Curt Taylor Griffiths, "Conferences, Circles, Boards, and Mediations: The 'New Wave' of Community Justice Decision Making," *Federal Probation* 61 (1997): 25–37.

161. Heather Strang, "Restorative Justice Programs in Australia," http://www .criminologyresearchcouncil.gov.au/reports /strang/report.pdf.

162. Hennessey Hayes, Tara Renae McGee, Helen Punter, and Michael John Cerruto, "Agreements in Restorative Justice Conferences: Exploring the Implications of Agreements for Post-conference Offending Behaviour," *British Journal of Criminology* 54 (2014): 109–127.

163. John W. De Gruchy, *Reconciliation: Restoring Justice* (Minneapolis: Fortress, 2002).

164. Lawrence W Sherman and Heather Strang, *Restorative Justice: The Evidence* (London: Smith Institute, 2007).

165. John Braithwaite, "Setting Standards for Restorative Justice," *British Journal of Criminology* 42 (2002): 563–577.

166. David Altschuler, "Community Justice Initiatives: Issues and Challenges in the U.S. Context," *Federal Probation* 65 (2001): 28–33.

167. Lois Presser and Patricia van Voorhis, "Values and Evaluation: Assessing Processes and Outcomes of Restorative Justice Programs," *Crime and Delinquency* 48 (2002): 162–189.

168. Declan Roche, *Accountability in Restorative Justice* (Clarendon Studies in Criminology) (London: Oxford University Press, 2004).

169. Sharon Levrant, Francis Cullen, Betsy Fulton, and John Wozniak, "Reconsidering Restorative Justice: The Corruption of Benevolence Revisited?" *Crime and Delinquency* 45 (1999): 3–28.

170. Edward Gumz, "American Social Work, Corrections and Restorative Justice: An Appraisal," *International Journal of Offender Therapy and Comparative Criminology* 48 (2004): 449–460.

Dr. William Petit Jr.

Cloe Poisson/*Hartford Courant*/MCT/Getty Images

Steven Hayes

Joshua Komisarjevsky

LEARNING OBJECTIVES

LO1 Discuss the history of developmental theory

LO2 Compare and contrast life course, latent trait, and trajectory theories

LO3 Enumerate the principles of the life course theory

LO4 Give examples of problem behaviors that cluster together

LO5 Explain why age of onset is an important factor in crime

LO6 Outline the basic principles of Sampson and Laub's age-graded theory

LO7 Interpret the terms *propensity* and *latent trait*

LO8 Comment upon Wilson and Herrnstein's views on crime and human nature

LO9 Understand the basic principles of the General Theory of Crime

LO10 Recognize that there are a variety of criminal trajectories

9 DEVELOPMENTAL THEORIES: LIFE COURSE, LATENT TRAIT, AND TRAJECTORY

ew crimes are as horrific as the murder of Jennifer, Michaela, and Hayley Petit during a home invasion in the leafy suburb of Cheshire, Connecticut. The crime began on July 23, 2007, when career criminals Steven Hayes and Joshua Komisarjevsky spotted the Petits at a grocery store, followed them home, burst into the house, beat and tied up Dr. William Petit Jr., raped and assaulted his wife, Jennifer Hawke-Petit, and their 11-year-old daughter Michaela, and tied up and terrorized 17-year-old Hayley. They forced Hawke-Petit to go to a local bank to withdraw funds when they considered the household haul insufficient. She was able to inform a bank employee who then called local police. William Petit managed to free himself, escape, and call to a neighbor for help. While police surrounded the home, Hayes and Komisarjevsky strangled Hawke-Petit before setting the house on fire with the two girls tied to their beds. The crime was so gruesome that some jurors had to be treated for PTSD.

During the trial, defense lawyers presented evidence in an effort to spare Hayes and Komisarjevsky the death penalty. Komisarjevsky was portrayed as a damaged person who was sexually abused as a child, suffered mood disorders and head injuries, abused drugs, and cut himself with glass, knives, and razors. His evangelical Christian adoptive parents denied him proper care, relying instead on religion.

Dr. Eric Goldsmith, a psychiatrist who interviewed Hayes for about 37 hours on eight occasions, noted that Hayes had a troubled and abusive upbringing, was sexually abused by a teenage babysitter when he was 10 or 11, and had developed a sexual fetish that caused him to associate an object—a woman's old sneaker—with sexual arousal; he said Hayes sought out women who shared his fetish. Hayes claimed that he had killed 17 women in the Northeast and also committed date rapes.

Despite defense efforts, Hayes and Komisarjevsky were convicted of the murders and sentenced to death.[1] Connecticut Governor M. Jodi Rell issued a statement soon after the verdict was released: "The crimes that were committed on that brutal July night were so far out of the range of normal understanding that now, more than three years later, we still find it difficult to accept that they happened in one of our communities." Komisarjevsky's family also issued a statement: "From the very beginning, we have spoken out about the horror of the crime and taken the position that whatever verdict the jury reached was the right verdict. With today's jury decision, our view is the same. The crime was monstrous and beyond comprehension. There are no excuses." When Connecticut ended capital punishment in 2015, the sentence was automatically amended to life in prison.

305

career criminals such as Hayes and Komisarjevsky defy what is commonly known about criminal behavior. They do not age out of crime as do most youthful offenders but persist into their adulthood. Nor do they get involved in a single crime and then forgo illegal activity; they have a long history of antisocial behavior, continually planning and getting involved in criminal acts of greater seriousness until they are captured and imprisoned. Criminologists have struggled to understand the factors that explain the onset and continuation of a criminal career. Rather than look at a single factor, such as poverty or low intelligence, and suggest that people who maintain this trait are predisposed to crime, those who engage in **developmental criminology** attempt to provide a more global vision of a criminal career encompassing its onset, continuation, and termination. This chapter reviews the most important issues in developmental criminology, and discusses major concepts and theories in some detail.

Foundations of Developmental Theory

L01 Discuss the history of developmental theory

During the twentieth century, some criminologists began to integrate sociological, psychological, and economic elements into more complex developmental views of crime causation. Hans Eysenck published *Crime and Personality* in 1964 and proclaimed that antisocial behavior was linked to psychological conditions that were a product of heredity.[2] His controversial theory integrated social, biological, and psychological factors, a vision that upset the sociologists who controlled the field at that time.[3]

However, it is Sheldon (1896–1980) and Eleanor (1898–1972) Glueck who are today considered founders of the developmental branch of criminological theory. While at Harvard University in the 1930s, they conducted research on the careers of known criminals to determine the factors that predicted persistent offending, making extensive use of interviews and records in their elaborate comparisons of criminals and noncriminals.

The Gluecks' research focused on early onset of delinquency as a harbinger of a criminal career: "[T]he deeper the roots of childhood maladjustment, the smaller the chance of adult adjustment."[4] They also noted the stability of offending careers: children who are antisocial early in life are the most likely to continue their offending careers into adulthood.

In a series of longitudinal research studies, the Gluecks followed the careers of known delinquents to determine the characteristics that predicted persistent offending.[5] The Gluecks identified a number of personal and social factors related to persistent offending, the most important of which was family relations. This factor was considered in terms of quality of discipline and emotional ties with parents. The adolescent raised in a large, single-parent family of limited economic means and educational achievement was the most vulnerable to delinquency. Not restricting their analysis to social variables, the Gluecks measured such biological and psychological traits as body type, intelligence, and personality, and found that physical and mental factors also played a role in determining behavior. Children with low intelligence, who had a background of mental disease and who had a powerful ("mesomorph") physique, were the most likely to become persistent offenders.

Integrating biological, social, and psychological elements, the Gluecks' research suggested that the initiation and continuity of a criminal career was a developmental process influenced by both internal and external situations, conditions, and circumstances. While impressive, their research was heavily criticized by sociologists such as Edwin Sutherland, who wanted to keep criminology within the field of sociology and feared or disparaged efforts to integrate biological or psychological concepts into the field.[6]

All but forgotten, the Gluecks were rediscovered when two highly thought of criminologists, Robert Sampson and John Laub, found their original data and used modern statistical techniques to reanalyze their carefully drawn empirical measurements. Laub and Sampson's findings, published in a series of books and articles, fueled the popularity of what is now referred to as developmental criminology.[7]

CRIMINAL CAREER RESEARCH

The Philadelphia cohort research by Marvin Wolfgang and his associates was another milestone prompting interest in

developmental criminology A view of criminal behavior that places emphasis on the changes people go through over the life course. It presents a criminal career as a dynamic process involving onset, continuity, persistence, acceleration, and eventual desistance from criminal behavior, controlled by individual level traits and conditions.

CONNECTIONS

Social process theories lay the foundation for assuming that peer, family, educational, and other interactions, which vary over the life course, influence behaviors. See the first few sections of Chapter 7 for a review of these issues. As you may recall from Chapter 2, a great deal of research has been conducted on the relationship of age and crime and the activities of chronic offenders. This scholarship has prompted interest in the life cycle of crime.

ASK YOURSELF . . .

Are you less "deviant" now than when you were younger? If so, why? If not, why not?

Multifactor/Integrated Theory

ORIGIN About 1930

FOUNDERS Sheldon and Eleanor Glueck; Hans Eysenck

MOST IMPORTANT WORKS Sheldon and Eleanor Glueck: *Five Hundred Delinquent Women* (1934); *Later Criminal Careers* (1937); *Criminal Careers in Retrospect* (1943); *Juvenile Delinquents Grown Up* (1940); *Unraveling Juvenile Delinquency* (1950); Hans Eysenck: *Crime and Personality*

CORE IDEAS Crime is a function of environmental, socialization, physical, and psychological factors. Each makes an independent contribution to shaping and directing behavior patterns. Deficits in these areas of human development increase the risk of crime. People at risk for crime can resist antisocial behaviors if these traits and conditions can be strengthened.

MODERN OUTGROWTHS Developmental theory, life course theory, propensity/latent trait theory, trajectory theory

Hans Eysenck

Daily Mail/Rex/Alamy Stock Photo

explaining criminal career development.[8] As you may recall (Chapter 2), Wolfgang found that while many offenders commit a single criminal act and desist from crime, a small group of chronic offenders engage in frequent and repeated criminal activity and continue to do so across their life span. Wolfgang's research focused attention on criminal careers rather than criminal acts. Rather than asking why one person offends and another remains law abiding, developmental criminologists focus their attention on the factors that prompt one person to engage in persistent criminal activity leading to a criminal career.

A 1990 review paper by Rolf Loeber and Marc LeBlanc was another important event that generated interest in developmental theory. In this landmark work, Loeber and LeBlanc proposed that criminologists should devote time and effort to understanding some basic questions about the evolution of criminal careers: Why do people begin committing antisocial acts? Why do some stop while others continue? Why do some escalate the severity of their criminality (that is, go from shoplifting to drug dealing to armed robbery) while others deescalate and commit less serious crimes as they mature? If some terminate their criminal activity, what, if anything, causes them to begin again? Why do some criminals specialize in certain types of crime, whereas others are generalists engaging in a variety of antisocial behavior? According to Loeber and LeBlanc's developmental view, criminologists must pay attention to how a criminal career unfolds, how it begins, why it is sustained, and how it comes to an end.[9]

LIFE COURSE, LATENT TRAITS, AND TRAJECTORIES

 LO2 Compare and contrast life course, latent trait, and trajectory theories

These scholarly advances created enormous excitement among criminologists and focused their attention on criminal career research. As research on criminal careers has evolved, three distinct viewpoints have taken shape: life course view, latent trait view, and trajectory view. **Life course theories** see criminality as a dynamic process, influenced by a multitude of individual characteristics, traits, and social experiences. As people travel through the life course, they are constantly bombarded by changing perceptions and experiences, and as a result their behavior will change directions, sometimes for the better and sometimes for the worse (Figure 9.1). In contrast, **latent trait theories** hold that human development is controlled by a stable propensity or "master trait," present at birth or soon after. As people mature from childhood to adolescence to adulthood, this

> **life course theories** Theoretical views studying changes in criminal offending patterns over a person's entire life.
>
> **latent trait theories** Theoretical views that criminal behavior is controlled by a master trait, present at birth or soon after, that remains stable and unchanging throughout a person's lifetime.

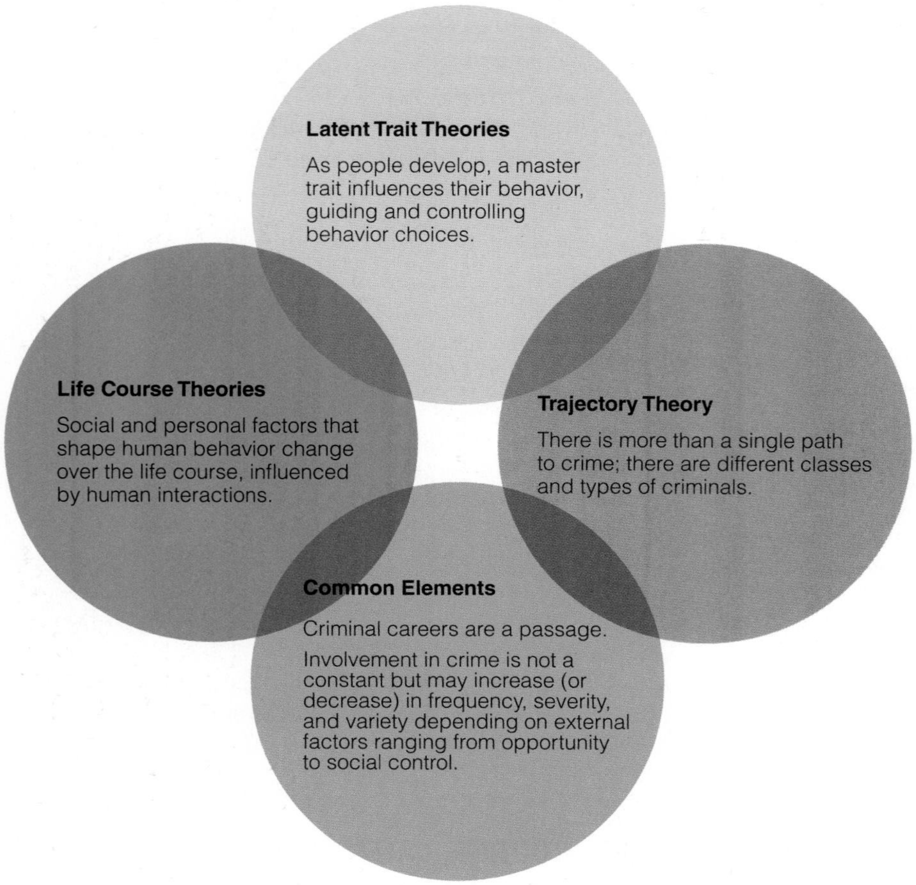

FIGURE 9.1 Developmental Theories

SOURCE: © Cengage Learning

Within the figure:

Latent Trait Theories

As people develop, a master trait influences their behavior, guiding and controlling behavior choices.

Life Course Theories

Social and personal factors that shape human behavior change over the life course, influenced by human interactions.

Trajectory Theory

There is more than a single path to crime; there are different classes and types of criminals.

Common Elements

Criminal careers are a passage.

Involvement in crime is not a constant but may increase (or decrease) in frequency, severity, and variety depending on external factors ranging from opportunity to social control.

---

trait is always there, directing their behavior and shaping life events. Because this master trait is enduring and unchanging, the ebb and flow of criminal behavior are directed by the impact of external forces such as interpersonal interactions and criminal opportunity.

A third view, **trajectory theory**, suggests there are multiple trajectories in a criminal career. According to this approach, there are numerous subgroups within a population that follow distinctively different criminal career trajectories. Some people may begin involvement in antisocial activities in childhood and adolescence and demonstrate a precocious propensity for crime, while others begin later and are influenced by a different set of life circumstances. This view suggests that there are different types and classes of offenders and each must be studied independently.[10]

Each of these positions is discussed in detail in the following sections.

trajectory theory A view of criminal career formation that holds there are multiple paths to crime.

population heterogeneity The view that the propensity of an individual to participate in antisocial behavior is a relatively stable trait, unchanging over their life course.

POPULATION HETEROGENEITY VS. STATE DEPENDENCE

Are people truly different, or are we more or less all the same but shaped by our different experiences? This question is the core issue separating the various branches of developmental theory.

The concept of **population heterogeneity** assumes that the propensity of an individual to participate in antisocial and/or criminal behaviors is a relatively stable trait, unchanging over their life course. Within a given population people differ in their behavior choices: some are hotheaded, violent, and inclined to commit crime, while others remain reasoning, unruffled, and presumably law abiding. According to this view, individual differences remain stable and are not affected by the consequences of participation in crime or any other changing life circumstances.[11] Because people affect their environment and not vice versa, the best predictor of future behavior is past behavior: people who are criminally active in their childhood should remain so in their adulthood, no matter what happens to them in the meantime. Propensity theorists embrace this concept because it suggests that the cause of misbehavior remains the same as people traverse the life course.

In contrast, the concept of **state dependence** suggests that people change and develop as they mature; life events have a significant influence on future behavior. Life course and trajectory theorists embrace this concept because it can explain continuity and desistance from crime: while positive experiences can help the troubled person adjust and conform, damaging encounters and events have the potential to increase future criminal involvement. Even kids who are at risk for crime can avoid a criminal way of life if they encounter people who help, nurture, and support them in their adolescence and adulthood. If past antisocial behavior influences future offending, it's not because they have a similar cause, but because offending disrupts prosocial bonds and informal mechanisms of social controls.[12]

Life Course Fundamentals

L03 Enumerate the principles of the life course theory

According to the life course view, even as toddlers people begin relationships and behaviors that will determine their adult life course. At first they must learn to conform to social rules and function effectively in society. Later they are expected to begin to think about careers, leave their parental homes, find permanent relationships, and eventually marry and begin their own families.[13] These transitions are expected to take place in order—beginning with finishing school, then entering the workforce, getting married, and having children.

Some individuals, however, are incapable of maturing in a reasonable and timely fashion because of family, environmental, or personal problems.[14] In some cases, transitions can occur too early—an adolescent girl who engages in precocious sex gets pregnant and is forced to drop out of high school. In other cases, transitions may occur too late—a teenage male falls in with the wrong crowd, goes to prison, and finds it difficult to break into the job market upon release; he puts off getting married because of his diminished economic circumstances. Sometimes interruption of one transition can harm another. A teenager who has family problems may find that her educational and career development is upset or that she suffers from psychological impairments.[15]

Kids who get in trouble early may find it difficult to shake the criminal way of life as they mature. Those who join gangs are more likely to get involved in antisocial behavior after they leave the gang than before they joined; gang membership creates long-term disruptions.[16] One reason is that joining a gang can lead to educational underachievement, a factor routinely associated with career criminality. Youths who join gangs are 30 percent less likely to graduate from high school and 58 percent less likely to earn a four-year degree than youths of similar background who do not become gang members.[17]

DISRUPTION PROMOTES CRIMINALITY

Because the shift from one stage of life to another can be a bumpy ride, the propensity to commit crimes is neither stable nor constant: it is a developmental process. A positive life experience may help some criminals desist from crime, whereas a negative one may cause them to resume their activities. Criminal careers are said to be developmental because people are constantly being influenced by the behavior of those around them, and they, in turn, influence others' behavior. A youth's antisocial behavior may turn his more conventional friends against him; their rejection solidifies and escalates his antisocial behavior.[18]

Disruptions in life's major transitions can be destructive and ultimately can promote criminality. Those who are already at risk because of socioeconomic problems or family dysfunction are the most susceptible to these awkward transitions. Criminality, according to this view, cannot be attributed to a single cause nor does it represent a single underlying tendency.[19] People are influenced by different factors as they mature. Consequently, a factor that may have an important influence at one stage of life (such as delinquent peers) may have little influence later on.[20]

These negative life events can become cumulative: as people acquire more personal deficits, the chance of acquiring additional ones increases.[21] The cumulative impact of these disruptions sustains criminality from childhood into adulthood.[22]

CHANGING LIFE INFLUENCES

Life course theories also recognize that as people mature, the factors that influence their behavior change.[23] As people make important life transitions—from child to adolescent, from adolescent to adult, from unwed to married—the nature of social interactions changes.[24]

At first, family relations may be most influential; it comes as no shock to life course theorists when research shows that criminality runs in families and that having criminal relatives is a significant predictor of future misbehaviors.[25] In later adolescence, school and peer relations predominate; in adulthood, vocational achievement and marital relations may be the most critical influences. Some antisocial children who are in trouble throughout their adolescence may manage to find stable work and maintain intact marriages as adults; these life events help them desist from crime. In contrast, less fortunate adolescents who develop arrest records and get involved with the wrong crowd may find themselves limited to menial jobs and at risk for criminal careers. However, even the ability to change wilts with age as people become embedded in a criminal lifestyle. What may help a

state dependence The propensity to commit crime profoundly and permanently disrupts normal socialization. Early rule breaking strengthens criminal motivation and increases the probability of future rule breaking.

person resist a life of crime while they are still in their teens (e.g., school achievement and positive family relations) may have little impact once they reach their 20s.[26]

Life Course Concepts

A view of crime has emerged that incorporates personal change and growth. The factors that produce crime and delinquency at one point in the life cycle may not be relevant at another; as people mature, the social, physical, and environmental influences on their behavior are transformed. People may show a propensity to offend early in their lives, but the nature and frequency of their activities are often affected by forces beyond their control, which elevate and sustain their criminal activity.[27]

The next sections review some of the more important concepts associated with the developmental perspective and discuss some prominent life course theories.

PROBLEM BEHAVIOR SYNDROME

LO4 Give examples of problem behaviors that cluster together

Most criminological theories portray crime as the outcome of social problems. Learning theorists view a troubled home life and deviant friends as precursors of criminality; structural theorists maintain that acquiring deviant cultural values leads to criminality. In contrast, the developmental view is that criminality may best be understood as one of many social problems faced by at-risk youth, a view called **problem behavior syndrome (PBS)**. According to this view, crime is one among a group of interrelated antisocial behaviors that cluster together. PBS has been linked to individual-level personality problems (such as impulsiveness, rebelliousness, and low ego), family problems (such as intra-family conflict and parental mental disorder), substance abuse, poor health, and educational failure.[28] People who suffer from one of these conditions typically exhibit many symptoms of the rest.[29] All varieties of criminal behavior, including violence, theft, and drug offenses, may be part of a generalized PBS, indicating that all forms of antisocial behavior have similar developmental patterns (Exhibit 9.1).[30]

Many examples support the existence of PBS:[31]

- Adolescents with a history of gang involvement are more likely to have been expelled from school, be binge drinkers, test positive for marijuana, have been in three or more fights in the past six months, have promiscuous partners, and test positive for sexually transmitted diseases.[32]

problem behavior syndrome (PBS) A cluster of antisocial behaviors that may include family dysfunction, substance abuse, smoking, precocious sexuality and early pregnancy, educational underachievement, suicide attempts, sensation seeking, and unemployment, as well as crime.

- Kids who gamble and take risks at an early age also take drugs and commit crimes.[33]
- People who exhibit one of these conditions typically exhibit many of the others.[34]

Considering the types of problems that cluster together, it is not surprising that people who have a long and varied criminal career are more likely to die early and to have greater than average mortality rates.[35] Criminal conduct has been found to increase the chances of premature death due to both natural and unnatural causes, including deaths from accidents, homicide, and suicide. The more crime a person commits, the more likely he or she is to suffer premature death.[36] Kids with limited intelligence and mental health problems may use drugs to feel more relaxed.[37] These connections cut across racial, gender, and socioeconomic lines.[38]

In sum, problem behavior syndrome portrays crime as a type of social problem rather than the product of other social problems.[39] People involved in crime may fall prey to other social problems, ranging from poverty to premature death.[40]

OFFENSE SPECIALIZATION/GENERALIZATION

Some offenders are specialists, limiting their criminal activities to a cluster of crime such as theft offenses, including burglary and larceny, or violent offenses such as assault and rape.[41] Others are generalists who engage in a variety of criminal activities such as drug abuse, burglary, and/or rape, depending on the opportunity to commit crime and the likelihood of success.[42] There is an ongoing debate over generalization/specialization: some criminologists believe that most criminals are generalists, while others have found evidence that more serious offenders tend to specialize in a narrower range of antisocial activities.[43] The answer may lie in between these two positions; there is evidence for specialization, but it is neither overwhelming nor universal.[44] Some offenders may specialize in the short term but engage in a wider variety of offenses when presented with opportunities to commit crime.[45]

EARLY ONSET

L05 Explain why age of onset is an important factor in crime

Children who will later become the most serious offenders begin their deviant careers at a very early (preschool) age, and the earlier the onset of criminality, the more frequent, varied, and sustained the criminal career.[46] If children are aggressive and antisocial during their public school years, they are much more likely to be troublesome and exhibit aggressive behavior in adulthood.[47]

These early-onset criminals seem to be more involved in aggressive acts ranging from cruelty to animals to peer-directed violence.[48] In contrast, late starters are more likely to be involved in nonviolent crimes such as theft.[49] The peak frequency of physical aggression occurs during early childhood and generally declines thereafter.[50]

Why is early onset so important? Starting early in delinquent behavior creates a downward spiral in a young person's life.[51] Thereafter tension may begin to develop with parents and other family members, emotional bonds to conventional peers become weakened and frayed, and opportunities to pursue conventional activities like sports dry up and wither away. Replacing them are closer involvement with more deviant peers and involvement in a delinquent way of life.[52] As they emerge into adulthood, persisters report less emotional support, lower job satisfaction, distant peer relationships, and more psychiatric problems than those who desist.[53]

The Cause of Early Onset What causes some kids to begin offending at an early age? Among the suspected root causes are poor parental discipline and monitoring, inadequate emotional support, distant peer relationships, and psychological issues and problems.[54] These influences may follow kids into their adulthood, helping them shift from one form of deviant lifestyle to another.[55] The psychic scars of childhood are hard to erase.[56]

Children who are improperly socialized by unskilled parents are the most likely to rebel by wandering the streets with deviant peers.[57] Parental influences may be replaced: in middle childhood, social rejection by conventional peers and academic failure sustain antisocial behavior; in later adolescence, commitment to a deviant peer group creates a training ground for crime. While the youngest and most serious offenders may persist in their criminal activity into late adolescence and even adulthood, others are able to age out of crime or desist.

PERSISTENCE AND DESISTANCE

The best predictor of future criminality is past criminality. Children who are repeatedly in trouble during early adolescence will generally still be antisocial in their middle teens; those who display conduct problems in youth are the ones most likely to commit crime as adults.[58] As adults, people involved in the most serious crimes continue to misbehave even when they are behind bars.[59]

Criminal persistence appears to be state dependent: criminal activity is sustained because law violators and rule breakers seem to lack the social survival skills necessary to find work or to develop the interpersonal relationships they need to allow them to desist. As a result, antisocial behavior may be *contagious*: people at risk for criminality infect those around them, thereby creating an ever-widening circle of peers and acquaintances who support deviant behavior.[60]

Considering that persistence is the norm, why then are some offenders able to desist? The answer is complex. Using data gathered by the Cambridge Study in Delinquent Development, a longitudinal study of 411 London boys born in 1953, David Farrington found that life experiences shape the direction and flow of behavior choices and that factors that predict crime at one point in the life course may not be the ones that foretell criminality.[61] As they mature, former delinquents are able to desist if they enter adult worlds of work and marriage and relocate to a more hospitable environment. Not that this transition is easy: even if they can leave a life of crime they still face overwhelming social problems. Farrington found that desisters tended to live in unkempt homes and have large debts and low-paying jobs. They were also more likely to remain single, live alone, and experience social isolation. So while these people may avoid a life of crime, they cannot avoid correlate social problems.

Peggy Giordano and her associates found that desistance involves cognitive transformation.[62] In their study of intimate partner violence, Giordano found that offenders must go through a constant learning process in order to discontinue their criminal activity. It is not merely changing life events, such as getting into trouble with the law, that promotes desistance. A wide range of social experiences encourages change: those who learn from experience are the ones most able to change. While transition events such as marriage may contribute to desistance, they are not enough; cognitive change is also needed.

Gender and Desistance As they mature, both males and females who have early experiences with antisocial behavior are the ones most likely to persist throughout their life course. Like boys, early-onset girls continue to experience difficulties—increased drug and alcohol use, poor school adjustment, mental health problems, poor sexual health, psychiatric problems, higher rates of mortality, criminal behavior, insufficient parenting skills, relationship dysfunction, lower performance in academic and occupational environments, involvement with social service assistance, and adjustment problems—as they enter young adulthood and beyond.[63]

There are also some distinct gender differences. For males, the path runs from early onset in childhood to later problems at work and involvement with substance abuse. For females, the path seems somewhat different: early antisocial behavior leads to relationship problems, depression, a tendency to commit suicide, and poor health in adulthood.[64] Males seem to be more deeply influenced by an early history of childhood aggression: males who exhibited chronic physical aggression during the elementary school years exhibit the risk of continued physical violence and delinquency during adolescence. There is less evidence of a linkage between childhood physical aggression and adult aggression among females.[65]

Theories of the Criminal Life Course

A number of systematic theories have been formulated that account for onset, continuance, and desistance from crime. As a group they integrate societal level variables such as measures of social control, social learning, and structural models. It is not uncommon for life course theories to interconnect *personal factors* such as personality and intelligence, *social factors* such as income and neighborhood, *socialization factors* such as marriage and military service, *cognitive factors* such as information processing and attention/perception, and *situational factors* such as criminal opportunity, effective guardianship, and apprehension risk into complex multifactor explanations of human behavior. In this sense they are **integrated theories** because they incorporate social, personal, and developmental factors into complex explanations of human behavior. They do not focus on the relatively simple question—why do people commit crime?—but on more complex issues: why do some offenders persist in criminal careers while others desist from or alter their criminal activity as they mature?[66] Why do some people continually escalate their criminal involvement, whereas others slow down and turn their lives around? Are all criminals similar in their offending patterns, or are there different types of offenders and paths to offending? Life course theorists want to know not only why people enter a criminal way of life, but why, once they do, they are able to alter the trajectory of their criminal involvement. One of the more important life course theories, Sampson and Laub's **age-graded theory**, is set out in some detail. Exhibit 9.2 outlines the principles of some other important life course theories.

integrated theories Models of crime causation that weave social and individual variables into a complex explanatory chain.

age-graded theory A developmental theory that posits that (a) individual traits and childhood experiences are important to understand the onset of delinquent and criminal behavior; (b) experiences in young adulthood and beyond can redirect criminal trajectories or paths; (c) serious problems in adolescence undermine life chances; (d) positive life experiences and relationships can help a person knife off from a criminal career path; (e) positive life experiences such as gaining employment, getting married, or joining the military create informal social control mechanisms that limit criminal behavior opportunities; (f) former criminals may choose to desist from crime because they find more conventional paths more beneficial and rewarding.

EXHIBIT 9.2

Principal Life Course Theories

NAME Social Development Model (SDM)

PRINCIPAL THEORISTS J. David Hawkins, Richard Catalano

MAJOR PREMISE Community-level risk factors make some people susceptible to antisocial behaviors. Preexisting risk factors are either reinforced or neutralized by socialization. To control the risk of antisocial behavior, a child must maintain prosocial bonds. Over the life course, involvement in prosocial or antisocial behavior determines the quality of attachments. Commitment and attachment to conventional institutions, activities, and beliefs insulate youths from the criminogenic influences in their environment. The prosocial path inhibits deviance by strengthening bonds to prosocial others and activities. Without the proper level of bonding, adolescents can succumb to the influence of deviant others.

NAME Interactional Theory

PRINCIPAL THEORISTS Terence Thornberry and Marvin Krohn, Alan Lizotte, Margaret Farnworth

MAJOR PREMISE The onset of crime can be traced to a deterioration of the social bond during adolescence, marked by weakened attachment to parents, commitment to school, and belief in conventional values. The cause of crime and delinquency is bidirectional: weak bonds lead kids to develop friendships with deviant peers and get involved in delinquency. Frequent delinquency involvement further weakens bonds and makes it difficult to reestablish conventional ones. Delinquency-promoting factors tend to reinforce one another and sustain a chronic criminal career. Kids who go through stressful life events such as a family financial crisis are more likely to later get involved in antisocial behaviors and vice versa. Criminality is a developmental process that takes on different meaning and form as a person matures. During early adolescence, attachment to the family is critical; by mid-adolescence, the influence of the family is replaced by friends, school, and youth culture; by adulthood, a person's behavioral choices are shaped by his or her place in conventional society and his or her own nuclear family. Although crime is influenced by these social forces, it also influences these processes and associations. Therefore, crime and social processes are interactional.

SOURCES: Terence Thornberry, "Toward an Interactional Theory of Delinquency," *Criminology* 25 (1987): 863–891; Richard Catalano and J. David Hawkins, "The Social Development Model: A Theory of Antisocial Behavior," in *Delinquency and Crime: Current Theories*, ed. J. David Hawkins (New York: Cambridge University Press, 1996), pp. 149–197.

SAMPSON AND LAUB: AGE-GRADED THEORY

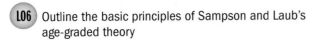 **L06** Outline the basic principles of Sampson and Laub's age-graded theory

Most theories focus on why people get involved in crime. In an important 1993 work, *Crime in the Making*, Robert Sampson and John Laub instead focus on whether there are trails back to conformity. In formulating their *Age-Graded Theory of Informal Social Control* (Figure 9.2), Laub and Sampson relied on the data originally collected by the Gluecks more than 50 years before. Using modern statistical analysis, Laub and Sampson used these data to formulate a life course/developmental view of crime.[67] Some of the principles of age-graded theory are listed here:

- Individual traits and childhood experiences are important to understand the onset of delinquent and criminal behavior. But these alone cannot explain the continuity of crime into adulthood.
- Experiences in young adulthood and beyond can redirect criminal transitions. In some cases people can be turned in a positive direction, while in others negative life experiences can be harmful and injurious.
- Repeat negative experiences create a condition called cumulative disadvantage. Serious problems in adolescence undermine life chances and reduce employability and social relations. People who increase their cumulative disadvantage risk continue offending.

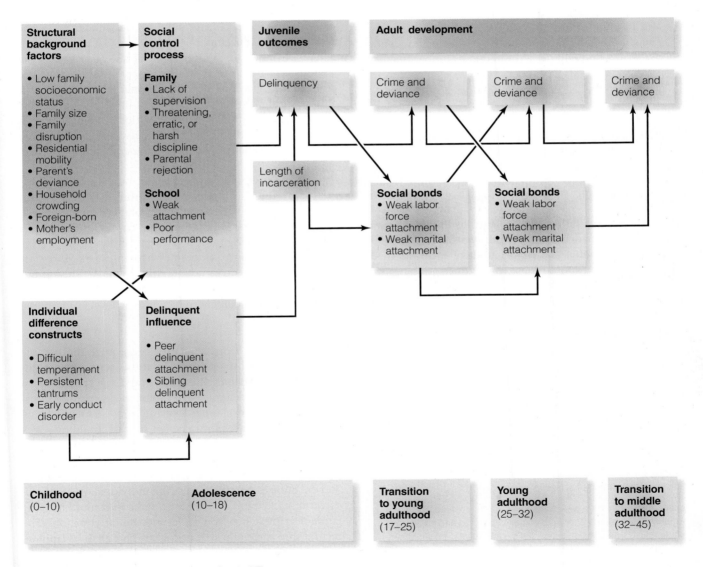

FIGURE 9.2 Sampson and Laub's Age-Graded Theory

SOURCE: Reprinted by permission of the publisher from Robert Sampson and John Laub, *Crime in the Making: Pathways and Turning Points Through Life* (Cambridge, MA: Harvard University Press, Copyright © 1993 by the President and Fellows of Harvard College), pp. 244–245. All rights reserved.

- Positive life experiences and relationships can help a person become reattached to society and allow him or her to knife off from a criminal career path.
- Positive life experiences such as gaining employment, getting married, or joining the military create informal social control mechanisms that limit criminal behavior opportunities. These elements of informal social control are called *turning points in crime*.
- Two critical elements of informal social control/turning points are marriage and career. Adolescents who are at risk for crime can live conventional lives if they can find good jobs, achieve successful military careers, or enter into a successful marriage. Turning points may be serendipitous and unexpected: success may hinge on a lucky break; someone takes a chance on them; they win the lottery.
- Another vital feature that helps people desist from crime is "human agency" or the purposeful execution of choice and free will. Former delinquents may choose to go straight and develop a new sense of self and an identity. They can choose to desist from crime and become family men and hard workers.[68] Human agency seems to play a role both in choosing to commit crime and the decision to desist.
- While some people persist in crime simply because they find it lucrative or perhaps because it serves as an outlet for their frustrations, others choose not to participate because as human beings they find other, more conventional paths more beneficial and rewarding. Human choice cannot be left out of the equation.

Trajectories, Transitions, and Turning Points   One of Laub and Sampson's most important contributions is identifying the life events that enable adult offenders to desist from crime. According to them, trajectories are long-term patterns in life, while transitions are "short-term events embedded in trajectories."[69] Both transitions and trajectories can have a positive or negative connotation. A positive transition, for example, might include graduating from college and getting a good job; a negative trajectory might be joining a gang.

A major concept in the Sampson and Laub theory is that criminal careers are a dynamic process in which an important life event can (a) produce a transition in the life course and (b) change the direction of a person's life course trajectory;

they refer to these as **turning points**. Two critical turning points are marriage and career. Adolescents who are at risk for crime can live conventional lives if they can find good jobs or achieve successful careers. Even those who have been in trouble with the law may turn from crime if employers are willing to give them a chance despite their records.

Cumulative Disadvantage   According to age-graded theory, some people experience repeated and varied social problems that weigh down their life chances. Nor do their social problems simply go away as they mature; they linger and vex people throughout their lives. Miscues accumulated in childhood hurt people further down the life path—for example, kids who get arrested are less likely to find jobs as adults.[70] People who acquire this **cumulative disadvantage** are more likely to commit criminal acts and become crime victims themselves.[71] When faced with personal crisis, they lack the social supports that can help them reject deviant solutions to their problems and instead maintain a conventional behavior trajectory.

Acquiring disadvantage begins at an early age. People who get in trouble early in life, especially those who are arrested and given an official criminal label, may find it difficult to shake the criminal way of life as they mature.[72] Racial disparity in the criminal justice system helps put minority group members at a disadvantage, increasing the likelihood that they will become embedded in criminal careers.[73]

Adolescents whose parents have a criminal record, were convicted of crime, and suffered incarceration are more likely to become law violators themselves.[74] Parental incarceration erases social capital and escalates cumulative disadvantage: it reduces family income, gives kids the opportunity to gain antisocial peers, and subjects them to negative labels and stigma.[75] That is not their only problem: people who accumulate disadvantages are also more likely to become the target of criminal victimization.[76]

Social Capital   Social scientists recognize that people build **social capital**—positive relations with individuals and institutions that are life sustaining. Laub and Sampson view the development of social capital as essential for desistance. In the same manner that building financial capital improves the chances for personal success, building social capital supports conventional behavior and inhibits deviant behavior. A successful marriage creates social capital when it improves a person's stature, creates feelings of self-worth, and encourages people to trust the individual. A successful career inhibits crime by creating a stake in conformity; why commit crime when you are doing well at your job? The relationship is reciprocal. If people are chosen to be employees, they return the favor by doing the best job possible; if they are chosen as spouses, they blossom into devoted partners. In contrast, people who fail to accumulate social capital are more prone to commit criminal acts.[77]

turning points   According to Laub and Sampson, the life events that alter the development of a criminal career.

cumulative disadvantage   A condition in which repeated negative experiences in adolescence undermine life chances and reduce employability and social relations. People who increase their cumulative disadvantage risk continued offending.

social capital   Positive relations with individuals and institutions that are life sustaining.

The fact that social capital influences the trajectory of a criminal career underscores the life course view that events that occur in later adolescence and adulthood do in fact influence behavior choices. Life events that occur in adulthood can help either terminate or sustain deviant careers.

Testing Age-Graded Theory   There have been a number of research efforts that support the basic assumptions of age-graded theory:

- Empirical research now shows that, as predicted by Sampson and Laub, people change over the life course and that the factors that predict crime in adolescence, such as a weak bond to parents, may have less of an impact on adult crime when other factors, such as marriage and family, take on greater importance.[78]
- Criminality appears to be dynamic and is affected both by the erosion of informal social control and by interaction with antisocial influences. Accumulating deviant peers helps sustain criminality: the more deviant friends one accumulates over time, the more likely one is to maintain a criminal career.[79]
- As levels of cumulative disadvantage increase, crime-resisting elements of social life are impaired. Adolescents who are convicted of crime at an early age are more likely to develop antisocial attitudes later in life. They later develop low educational achievement, declining occupational status, and unstable employment records.[80] People who get involved with the justice system as adolescents may find that their career paths are blocked well into adulthood.[81] The relationship is reciprocal: men who are unemployed or underemployed report higher criminal participation rates than employed men.[82]
- Criminal career trajectories can be reversed if life conditions improve and they gain social capital.[83] First, communities that have social capital opportunities such as group recreation centers and job prospects have lower rates of crime and victimization than areas that lack the ability to improve life chances.[84] Second, kids whose life circumstances improve because their parents escape poverty and move to these more attractive environments find that they can knife off from criminal trajectories.[85] Relocating may place them in better educational environments where they can have a positive high school experience, facilitated by occupationally oriented course work, small class size, and positive peer climates; having a positive school experience has been shown to be one of the most important factors that helps people knife off from crime.[86]
- Gaining social capital helps with behavior reversal.[87] As predicted by Laub and Sampson, those who enter the military, serve overseas, and receive veterans' benefits enhance their occupational status (social capital) while reducing criminal involvement.[88] Similarly, people who

are fortunate enough to obtain high-quality jobs are likely to reduce their criminal activities even if they had a prior history of offending.[89]

THE MARRIAGE FACTOR

Age-graded theory places a lot of emphasis on the stability brought about by romantic relationships. People headed toward a life of crime can knife off that path if they meet the right mate, fall in love, and get married.[90] On an individual level, falling in love and getting married reduces criminal activity. On a social level, communities with high marriage rates have correspondingly low crime rates.[91] And it is marriage and not merely cohabiting that has a crime suppression effect.[92]

The marriage benefit is intergenerational: children who grow up in two-parent families are more likely to later have happy marriages themselves than children who are the product of divorced or never-married parents. If people with marital problems are more crime prone, their children will also suffer a greater long-term risk of marital failure and antisocial activity.[93]

Sometimes it is tough to get married and stay married when life circumstances are chaotic, especially when people are in trouble with the law. When people get involved in crime they are more likely to experience financial hardship, a condition that decreases the odds of entering into a stable marriage.[94] For those people who can form a stable relationship despite having prior police contact, the effects can be dramatic.[95]

Why Does Marriage Work?   What prompts some people to engage in loving relationships, while others are doomed to fall in and out of love without finding lasting happiness? Sociologist Rand Conger and his colleagues have discovered that the seeds of marital success are planted early in childhood: kids who grow up with warm, nurturing parents are the ones most likely to have positive romantic relationships and later intact marriages. Well-nurtured kids develop into warm and supportive romantic partners who have relationships that are likely to endure.[96] It is the quality of parenting, not the observation of adult romantic relations, that socializes a young person to engage in behaviors likely to promote successful and lasting romantic unions as an adult.

Why does domestic bliss help people desist from crime? Marriage both transforms people and reduces their opportunity to commit crimes. It helps cut off a person's past, provides new relationships, creates new levels of supervision, and helps the former offender develop structured routines focused on family life. Happy marriages are life sustaining, and marital quality can even improve over time (as people work less and have fewer parental responsibilities). Spending time in marital and family activities also reduces exposure to deviant peers, which in turn reduces

Katja Heinemann/Do! Thing.org/Redux

Can a warm and loving relationship help people turn their lives around and knife off from crime? Griffin Kinard, shown here with girlfriend Melissa Castillo, is a poet and writer. Born in Brooklyn, Griffin spent his childhood and teenage years in a series of New York state institutions—larger residence programs for at-risk youths such as Children's Village in Dobbs Ferry and Green Chimneys in Brewster. After aging out of the system he found himself back in New York City, finishing high school while living in a Salvation Army group home. A seven-month stint in jail was followed by his 21st birthday and a new commitment to writing. Since then he served as a senior writer at *Represent* magazine, a bimonthly publication for and by youth in foster care by the nonprofit organization Youth Communication. While working on the magazine, Griffin stayed at his older sister's home in Harlem most nights, with occasional stints in drop-in shelters when the siblings argued. Melissa is in recovery with a history of institutionalization in group homes and psychiatric programs. Does a relationship like the one Griffin and Melissa entered into help people go straight? Or are people on the verge of going straight capable of forming a committed relationship?

What Happens When It Ends? Romantic break-ups, pre- and post-marriage, are a precursor to increased delinquent and criminal activity.[100] Even unstable marriages appear to reduce conviction frequency, at least while they last.[101] However, instability can be damaging, and things don't always work out as planned. Many relationships end in a breakup: an estimated 40 to 50 percent of first marriages, 67 percent of second marriages, and 74 percent of third marriages end in divorce. And while a happy marriage can reduce crime, separation and divorce seem to have an opposite effect. Both men and women have a greater likelihood of arrest when divorced (or legally separated) compared with when they were married.[102]

Recently, Bianca Bersani and Elaine Eggleston Doherty evaluated the divorce effect with a sample of 3,000 people.[103] They found that the detrimental effects of divorce are long lasting and not related to the immediate turmoil that ended the marriage. The length of marriage had a big effect on its aftermath: the detrimental effects of divorce seem to be most pronounced for longer marriages, prompting an immediate increase in offending. In contrast, offending rates are statistically similar when married and when divorced among those people involved in short marriages, especially if they dissolve prior to the first anniversary. However, among the short-marriage group, offending rates are significantly higher when married compared with when single. It's possible, Bersani and Doherty speculate, that "bad marriages," those that are doomed to quickly fail, are criminogenic and may increase rather than decrease antisocial behaviors—or conversely, the most antisocial people enter quickly into doomed marriages. In either event, not all marriages are the same, but those who can find the right mate and stick with them for the duration are also the people most likely to live happier, crime-free lives.

AGE-GRADED THEORY VALIDITY

Despite the theory's popularity and importance, a number of issues remain to be fully analyzed. The most important is causal ordering: Are people who desist from crime able to

the opportunity to become involved in criminal activities.[97] As Mark Warr states:

> For many individuals, it seems, marriage marks a transition from heavy peer involvement to a preoccupation with one's spouse. That transition is likely to reduce interaction with former friends and accomplices and thereby reduce the opportunities as well as the motivation to engage in crime.[98]

Researchers Alex Piquero, John MacDonald, and Karen Parker tracked 524 men in their late teens and early 20s for seven years after they were paroled from the California Youth Authority during the 1970s and 1980s. They found that former offenders were far less likely to return to crime if they settled down into the routines of a solid marriage. People who get married are more likely to have nine-to-five jobs, come home for dinner, take care of children if they have them, watch television, go to bed, and repeat that cycle over and over again. Single people have a lot of free time to do what they want, especially if they are not employed. There's something about crossing the line of getting married that helps these men stay away from crime.[99]

find a suitable mate, get married, and find a good job? Or are people who find an appropriate mate and a good job then able to desist from crime? Does desistance precede the accumulation of social capital or does the accumulation of social capital produce desistance? Laub and Sampson believe the latter, but there is also evidence that people who desist from crime undergo a cognitive change, and only after they quit a criminal way of life are they able to acquire mates, jobs, and other benefits that support their life change.[104] People who are aging out of crime, who want to end their criminal way of life, are only then ready to get married and settle down, and not vice versa.[105] Further research is needed on the time order of this important association.

Probably the most important issue surrounding age-graded theory that must be addressed is whether the relationships that underpin age-graded theory are still valid today. Laub and Sampson's theory relies heavily on the Glueck data collected more than 50 years ago. The Glueck sample lived in a world that was quite different from contemporary society: they did not watch violent video games or TV shows; they used alcohol but were not part of a drug culture; marriage was the norm and the divorce rate was much lower; globalization and wide-scale job loss were not issues. It is possible that getting involved in the drug culture has a much more damaging effect today than when the Gluecks collected their data.[106] Similarly, joining the military may have a significantly different meaning and produce different effects today than it did for the men in the Glueck sample.[107] An important research task, then, is to determine whether the theory's basic premises are still valid considering these structural changes in society.

To answer some of these questions, Laub and Sampson contacted the surviving members of the Glueck cohort. Some of their findings are discussed in the Criminology in Action feature "Shared Beginnings, Divergent Lives."

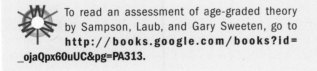
To read an assessment of age-graded theory by Sampson, Laub, and Gary Sweeten, go to **http://books.google.com/books?id=_ojaQpx6OuUC&pg=PA313.**

Social Schematic Theory (SST)

Age-graded theory is not the only life course view; there have been a number of other attempts to chart the course of a criminal career. In what they call a life-course learning approach, social schematic theory (SST), criminologists Ronald Simons and Callie Burt propose that social factors—especially persistent, reoccurring, or memorable ones—blunt humans' innate tendencies toward sympathy, fairness, and cooperation.[108] While they assume that most people are naturally benevolent and altruistic, they ponder how it is that some become unkind and egoistic, willing to hurt others and take their property. The answer is that most offenders do not believe that their illegal acts are evil or immoral because they have learned that their acts are actually justified, sensible, and normative considering the situation in which their crime occurs. Crime then is a result of an individual learning to define situations as requiring or justifying aggression, coercion, or cheating.

Why does this cognitive transformation occur? Simons and Burt highlight the role of learning: the lessons communicated by "the persistent and recurring interactions that comprise an individual's everyday existence."[109] These lessons are stored as **social schemas**, cognitive frameworks that help people quickly process and sort through information; they are the key theoretical mechanisms that account for the development of criminal behavior patterns.

The SST relies on how people develop these cognitive shortcuts to organize and interpret information. In some instances schemas can exclude pertinent information and instead focus only on things that confirm preexisting beliefs and ideas. If a member of some group commits a notorious crime, we think "those people are all criminals," forgetting that the vast majority in any grouping are law-abiding citizens. If someone is hassled by a police officer, the experience can shape the way they view all police officers and cause them to alter their behavior accordingly (i.e., avoid contact with cops, refuse to cooperate, call them names, and so on). Schemas can contribute to stereotypes and make it difficult to retain new information that does not conform to our established ideas about the world.

Simons and Burt argue that seemingly unrelated family, peer, and community conditions—harsh parenting, racial discrimination, and community disadvantage—lead to crime because the lessons communicated by these events are actually similar to one another and promote social schemas involving (a) a hostile view of people and relationships, (b) a preference for immediate rewards, and (c) a cynical view of conventional norms. Because these negative schemas are interconnected they combine to form a **criminogenic knowledge structure (CKS)**. When someone with a CKS forged by negative life events encounters a stressful situation, their past experiences compel them to respond with criminal and antisocial behavior. Prior negative life experiences allow them to legitimize their behavior: "people abused me, so it's okay to abuse other people." CKS exists on a continuum; those at the low end possess benign views of relationships, see the wisdom of following conventional norms, and recognize the value of delaying gratification.

social schemas Cognitive frameworks that help people quickly process and sort through information.

criminogenic knowledge structure (CKS) The view that negative life events are connected and produce a hostile view of people and relationships, preference for immediate rewards, and a cynical view of conventional norms.

CRIMINOLOGY IN ACTION

Shared Beginnings, Divergent Lives

04

Why are some delinquents destined to become persistent criminals as adults? John Laub and Robert Sampson have conducted a follow-up to their reanalysis of Sheldon and Eleanor Glueck's study that matched 500 delinquent boys with 500 nondelinquents. The individuals in the original sample were reinterviewed by the Gluecks at ages 25 and 32. Sampson and Laub located and interviewed the survivors of the delinquent sample, the oldest 70 years old and the youngest 62.

Persistence and Desistance

Laub and Sampson find that delinquency and other forms of antisocial conduct in childhood are strongly related to adult delinquency and drug and alcohol abuse. Former delinquents also suffer consequences in other areas of social life, such as school, work, and family life. For example, delinquents are far less likely to finish high school than are nondelinquents and subsequently are more likely to be unemployed, receive welfare, and experience separation or divorce as adults.

In their latest research, Laub and Sampson address one of the key questions

posed by life course theories: is it possible for former delinquents to turn their lives around as adults? They find that most antisocial children do not remain antisocial as adults. For example, of men in the study cohort who survived to age 50, 24 percent had no arrests for delinquent acts of violence and property after age 17 (6 percent had no arrests for total delinquency); 48 percent had no arrests for predatory delinquency after age 25 (19 percent for total delinquency); 60 percent had no arrests for predatory delinquency after age 31 (33 percent for total delinquency); and 79 percent had no arrests for predatory delinquency after age 40 (57 percent for total delinquency). They conclude that desistance from delinquency is the norm and that most, if not all, serious delinquents desist from delinquency.

Why Do Delinquents Desist?

Laub and Sampson's earlier research indicated that building social capital through marriage and jobs was a key component of desistance from delinquency. However, in this new round of research, Laub and Sampson were able to find out more about long-term desistance by interviewing 52 men as they

approached age 70. The follow-up showed a dramatic drop in criminal activity as the men aged. Between the ages of 17 and 24, 84 percent of the subjects had committed violent crimes; in their 30s and 40s, that number dropped to 14 percent; it fell to just 3 percent as the men reached their 60s and 70s. Property crimes and alcohol- and drug-related crimes also showed significant decreases. They found that men who desisted from crime were rooted in structural routines and had strong social ties to family and community. Drawing on the men's own words, they found that one important element for "going straight" is the "knifing off" of individuals from their immediate environment and offering the men a new script for the future. Joining the military can provide this knifing-off effect, as does marriage or changing one's residence. One former delinquent (age 69) told them:

> I'd say the turning point was, number one, the Army. You get into an outfit, you had a sense of belonging, you made your friends. I think I became a pretty good judge of character. In the Army, you met some good ones, you met some foul balls. Then I met the wife. I'd say probably that would be the turning

---

Those at the high end of the CKS have a learned view of the world that is more harsh, unpredictable, and unforgiving, and thus are more likely to define situations as requiring or justifying crime.[110]

While developed at an early age, the CKS can improve when people experience positive life events, such as having a healthy romantic relationship, or worsen when experiencing some negative life event, such as racial discrimination. Negative social schemas combined with situational events that set them off produce antisocial behavior. Actions, including crime, result from the combination of individual characteristics and situational cues. Moreover, individuals are not randomly placed in various contexts, they actively seek out settings consistent with their aims and preferences. Consequently, any preexisting thought patterns will be reinforced by surrounding influences in a never-ending loop. Individuals who are frequently exposed to harsh, unpredictable, and unfair social

environments internalize messages that the world is a hostile, unpredictable place, delayed rewards rarely materialize, and social rules and punishments do not apply to everyone equally.

Although it is still being tested, early results have given strong support for the SST.[111] In one recent study, Burt and Simons found that racial discrimination has a profound effect on young black women and that learning to deal with racial bias helps mitigate its effect.[112]

Propensity/Latent Trait Theories

L07 Interpret the terms *propensity* and *latent trait*

In a critical 1990 article, David Rowe, D. Wayne Osgood, and W. Alan Nicewander proposed the concept of latent traits to explain the flow of crime over the life cycle.

point. Got married, then naturally, kids come. So now you got to get a better job, you got to make more money. And that's how I got to the Navy Yard and tried to improve myself.

Former delinquents who went straight were able to put structure into their lives. Structure often led the men to disassociate from delinquent peers, reducing the opportunity to get into trouble. Getting married, for example, may limit the number of nights men can "hang with the guys." As one wife of a former delinquent said, "It is not how many beers you have, it's who you drink with." Even multiple offenders who did time in prison were able to desist with the help of a stabilizing marriage.

Former delinquents who can turn their life around, who have acquired a degree of maturity by taking on family and work responsibilities, and who have forged new commitments are the ones most likely to make a fresh start and find new direction and meaning in life. It seems that men who desisted changed their identity as well, and this, in turn, affected their outlook and sense of maturity and responsibility. The ability to change did not reflect delinquency "specialty": violent offenders followed the same path as property offenders.

While many former delinquents desisted from delinquency, they still faced the risk of an early and untimely death. Thirteen percent of the delinquent as compared to only 6 percent of the nondelinquent subjects died of unnatural deaths such as violence, cirrhosis of the liver caused by alcoholism, poor self-care, suicide, and so on. By age 65, 29 percent (N=139) of the delinquent and 21 percent (N=95) of the nondelinquent subjects had died from natural causes. Frequent delinquent involvement in adolescence and alcohol abuse were the strongest predictors of an early and unnatural death. So while many troubled youth are able to reform, their early excesses may haunt them across their life span.

Policy Implications

Laub and Sampson find that youth problems—delinquency, substance abuse, violence, dropping out, teen pregnancy—often share common risk characteristics. Intervention strategies, therefore, should consider a broad array of antisocial, criminal, and deviant behaviors and not limit the focus to just one subgroup or delinquency type. Because criminality and other social problems are linked, early prevention efforts that reduce delinquency will probably also reduce alcohol abuse, drunk driving, drug abuse, sexual promiscuity, and family violence. The best way to achieve these goals is through four significant life-changing events: marriage, joining the military, getting a job, and changing one's environment or neighborhood. What appears to be important about these processes is that they all involve, to varying degrees, the following items: a knifing off of the past from the present, new situations that provide both supervision and monitoring as well as new opportunities of social support and growth, and new situations that provide the opportunity for transforming identity. Prevention of delinquency must be a policy at all times and at all stages of life.

CRITICAL THINKING

1. Do you believe that the factors that influenced the men in the original Glueck sample are still relevant for change? For example, considering the high current divorce rate, is marriage still a stabilizing force?

2. Recent reports show that male U.S. veterans are twice as likely to die by suicide than people with no military service, and are more likely to kill themselves with a gun than others who commit suicide. Considering this recent finding, do you agree with Laub and Sampson that military service might be beneficial and help troubled kids turn their lives around?

SOURCES: John Laub and Robert Sampson, *Shared Beginnings, Divergent Lives: Delinquent Boys to Age 70* (Cambridge, MA: Harvard University Press, 2003); John Laub and Robert Sampson, "Understanding Desistance from Delinquency," in *Delinquency and Justice: An Annual Review of Research*, Vol. 28, ed. Michael Tonry (Chicago: University of Chicago Press, 2001), pp. 1–71; John Laub and George Vaillant, "Delinquency and Mortality: A 50-Year Follow-Up Study of 1,000 Delinquent and Non-delinquent Boys," *American Journal of Psychiatry* 157 (2000): 96–102.

Their model assumes that a number of people in the population have a personal attribute or characteristic that controls their inclination or **propensity** to commit crimes.[113] This disposition, or **latent trait**, may be either present at birth or established early in life, and it can remain stable over time. Suspected latent traits include defective intelligence, damaged or impulsive personality, genetic abnormalities, the physical-chemical functioning of the brain, and environmental influences on brain function such as drugs, chemicals, and injuries.[114] Some of these master traits are inflexible, stable, and unchanging throughout a person's lifetime; others can be altered, influenced, or changed by experiences and interactions (Exhibit 9.3).

Regardless of gender or environment, those who possess one or more of these latent traits may be at risk to crime and in danger of becoming career criminals; those who lack the propensity to commit crime have a much lower risk.[115]

Because the propensity to commit crime is stable over the life course, people who are antisocial during adolescence are the most likely to develop criminal careers. The positive association between past and future criminality detected in the cohort studies of career criminals reflects the presence of this underlying stable criminal propensity. That is, if an impulsive personality contributes to delinquency in childhood, it should also cause the same people to offend as adults because personality traits remain stable over the life span.

propensity An inclination or tendency to behave in a particular way.

latent trait A stable feature, characteristic, property, or condition, present at birth or soon after, that makes some people crime prone over the life course.

EXHIBIT 9.3

Two Types of Latent Traits

CONSTANT LATENT TRAIT	EVOLVING LATENT TRAIT
Inflexible	Flexible
Unchanging	Varying
Influenced by psychological and biological traits and conditions	Influenced by human interaction, personal relationships, contact, and associations

SOURCE: © Cengage Learning

HOW CAN THE AGING-OUT PROCESS BE EXPLAINED?

Because latent traits are stable, people who are antisocial during adolescence are the most likely to persist in crime. The positive association between past and future criminality detected in the cohort studies of career criminals reflects the presence of this underlying stable criminal propensity. That is, if an impulsive personality contributes to delinquency in childhood, it should also cause the same people to offend as adults because personality traits remain stable over the life span. According to the concept of state dependence, kids who have the propensity to commit crime will find that this latent trait profoundly and permanently disrupts normal socialization. Disruptions in socialization thereafter increase the risk of prolonged antisocial behavior. In this view, early rule breaking increases the probability of future rule breaking because it weakens inhibitions to crime and strengthens criminal motivation. In other words, once kids get a taste of antisocial behavior, they like it and want to continue down a deviant path.[116]

How then can a latent trait theorist explain the well-known fact that people do commit less crime as they mature? It's possible that declining criminal activity may not be a valid indicator of real behavioral change. Why does this illusion exist? Whereas the propensity to commit crime is stable, the opportunity to commit crime fluctuates over time. People may appear to age out of crime as they mature and develop simply because there are fewer opportunities to commit crimes and greater inducements to remain straight. They may marry, have children, and obtain jobs. The former delinquents' newfound adult responsibilities leave them little time to hang with their friends, abuse substances, and get into scrapes with the law. So while their propensity to commit crime remains stable, their opportunity to commit crime has changed.

General Theory of Crime (GTC) According to Gottfredson and Hirschi, a developmental theory that modifies social control theory by integrating concepts from biosocial, psychological, routine activities, and rational choice theories.

To understand this concept of stable criminal propensity better, assume that intelligence as measured by IQ tests is a stable latent trait associated with crime. Intelligence remains stable and unchanging over the life course, but crime rates decline with age. How can latent trait theory explain this phenomenon? Teenagers have more opportunity to commit crime than adults, so at every level of intelligence, adolescent crime rates will be higher. As they mature, however, teens with both high and low IQs will commit less crime because their adult responsibilities provide them with fewer criminal opportunities. They may get married and raise a family, get a job, and buy a home. And like most people, as they age they lose strength and vigor, qualities necessary to commit crime. Though their IQ remains stable and their propensity to commit crime is unchanged, their living environment and physical condition have undergone radical change. Even if they wanted to engage in criminal activities, the former delinquents may lack the opportunity and energy to do so.

CRIME AND HUMAN NATURE

 Comment upon Wilson and Herrnstein's views on crime and human nature

Latent trait theorists were encouraged when two prominent social scientists, James Q. Wilson and Richard Herrnstein, published *Crime and Human Nature* in 1985 and suggested that personal traits—such as genetic makeup, intelligence, and body build—may outweigh the importance of social variables as predictors of criminal activity.[117]

According to Wilson and Herrnstein, all human behavior, including criminality, is determined by its perceived consequences. A criminal incident occurs when an individual chooses criminal over conventional behavior (referred to as *noncrime*) after weighing the potential gains and losses of each: "The larger the ratio of net rewards of crime to the net rewards of noncrime, the greater the tendency to commit the crime."[118]

Wilson and Herrnstein's model assumes that both biological and psychological traits influence the crime–noncrime choice. They see a close link between a person's decision to choose crime and such biosocial factors as low intelligence, mesomorphic body type, genetic influences (parental criminality), and possessing an autonomic nervous system that responds too quickly to stimuli. Psychological traits, such as an impulsive or extroverted personality or generalized hostility, also determine the potential to commit crime.

In their focus on the association between these constitutional and psychological factors and crime, Wilson and Herrnstein seem to be suggesting the existence of an elusive latent trait that predisposes people to commit crime.[119] Their vision helped inspire other criminologists to identify the elusive latent trait that causes criminal behavior. The most prominent latent trait theory is Gottfredson and Hirschi's **General Theory of Crime (GTC)**. Exhibit 9.4 discusses some other important contributions to the latent trait model.

NAME Integrated Cognitive Antisocial Potential (ICAP) Theory

PRINCIPAL THEORIST David Farrington

LATENT TRAIT Antisocial potential

MAJOR PREMISE People maintain a range of *antisocial potential (AP)*, the potential to commit antisocial acts. AP can be viewed as both a long- and short-term phenomenon. Those with high levels of long-term AP are at risk for offending over the life course; those with low AP levels live more conventional lives. Though AP levels are fairly consistent over time, they peak in the teenage years because of the effects of maturational factors—such as increase in peer influence and decrease in family influence—that directly affect crime rates. Long-term AP can be reduced by life-changing events such as marriage. There is also short-term AP when immediate life events may increase a personal antisocial potential so that, in the immediate moment, people may advance their location on the AP continuum. For example, a person with a relatively low long-term AP may suffer a temporary amplification if he is bored, angry, drunk, or frustrated. According to the ICAP theory, the commission of offenses and other types of antisocial acts depends on the interaction between the individual (with his immediate level of AP) and the social environment (especially criminal opportunities and victims).

NAME Differential Coercion Theory

PRINCIPAL THEORIST Mark Colvin

LATENT TRAIT Perceptions of coercion

MAJOR PREMISE Perceptions of coercion begin early in life when children experience punitive forms of discipline—both physical attacks and psychological coercion, including negative commands, critical remarks, teasing, humiliation, whining, yelling, and threats. Through these destructive family interchanges, coercion becomes ingrained and guides reactions to adverse situations that arise in both family and nonfamily settings.

There are two sources of coercion: interpersonal and impersonal. Interpersonal coercion is direct, involving the use or threat of force and intimidation from parents, peers, and significant others. Impersonal coercion involves pressures beyond individual control, such as economic and social pressure caused by unemployment, poverty, or competition among businesses or other groups. High levels of coercion produce criminality, especially when the episodes of coercive behavior are inconsistent and random, because this teaches people that they cannot control their lives. Chronic offenders grew up in homes where parents used erratic control and applied it in an inconsistent fashion.

NAME Control Balance Theory

PRINCIPAL THEORIST Charles Tittle

LATENT TRAIT Control/balance

MAJOR PREMISE The concept of control has two distinct elements: the amount of control one is subject to by others and the amount of control one can exercise over others. Conformity results when these two elements are in balance; control imbalances produce deviant and criminal behaviors.

Those people who sense a deficit of control turn to three types of behavior to restore balance:

- *Predation* involves direct forms of physical violence, such as robbery, sexual assault, or other forms of assault.
- *Defiance* challenges control mechanisms but stops short of physical harm: for example, vandalism, curfew violations, and unconventional sex.
- *Submission* involves passive obedience to the demands of others, such as submitting to physical or sexual abuse without response.

An excess of control can result in crimes of (a) *exploitation*, which involves using others to commit crimes, such as contract killers or drug runners, (b) *plunder*, which involves using power without regard for others, such as committing a hate crime or polluting the environment, or (c) *decadence*, which involves spur of the moment, irrational acts such as child molesting.

SOURCES: David P. Farrington, "Developmental and Life-Course Criminology: Key Theoretical and Empirical Issues," Sutherland Award address presented at the annual meeting of the American Society of Criminology, Chicago, November 2002, revised March 2003; Charles Tittle, *Control Balance: Toward a General Theory of Deviance* (Boulder, CO: Westview Press, 1995); Mark Colvin, *Crime and Coercion: An Integrated Theory of Chronic Criminality* (New York: Palgrave Press, 2000).

GENERAL THEORY OF CRIME

 Understand the basic principles of the General Theory of Crime

In their important work *A General Theory of Crime*, Michael Gottfredson and Travis Hirschi link the propensity to commit crime to two latent traits: an impulsive personality and a lack of self-control.[120]

Gottfredson and Hirschi attribute the tendency to commit crimes to a person's level of **self-control**. People with limited self-control tend to be impulsive; they are insensitive to other people's feelings, physical (rather than mental), risk takers, shortsighted, and nonverbal.[121] They have a here-and-now orientation and refuse to work for distant goals; they lack diligence, tenacity, and persistence. People lacking self-control tend to be adventuresome, active, and self-centered. As they mature, they often have unstable marriages, jobs, and friendships.[122] They are less likely to feel shame if they engage in deviant acts and are more likely to find them pleasurable.[123] They are also more likely to engage in

> **self-control** A strong moral sense that renders a person incapable of hurting others or violating social norms.

Bloomberg/Getty Images

Are white-collar criminals impulsive? Here, on August 11, 2015, Vitaly Korchevsky is escorted in handcuffs from his home by agents from the Federal Bureau of Investigation in Glen Mills, Pennsylvania. Korchevsky, 50, was one of several men arrested in the biggest case of insider trading linked to the fast-growing threat of global cybercrime. The alleged scheme stretched from the affluent suburbs of Philadelphia, where Korchevsky ran the small investment firm NTS Capital Fund, to the darkest realms of the Internet. The scheme involved paying hackers to steal yet-to-be published financial news releases and then using them in illegal trading that generated an alleged $30 million in profits. This allowed the schemers to trade ahead of about 800 corporate news releases, hours or even days before the releases went public. The traders used foreign shell companies to share the profits. Are these criminals impulsive and lacking in self-control or cold and calculating?

agility, speed, and power, than conventional acts, which demand long-term study and cognitive and verbal skills. As Gottfredson and Hirschi put it, they derive satisfaction from "money without work, sex without courtship, revenge without court delays."[125] Many of these individuals who have a propensity for committing crime also engage in other risky, impulsive behaviors such as smoking, drinking, gambling, and illicit sexuality.[126] Although these acts are not illegal, they too provide immediate, short-term gratification.

What Causes Impulsivity?
Gottfredson and Hirschi trace the root cause of poor self-control to inadequate childrearing practices that begin soon after birth and can influence neural development. Parents who refuse or are unable to monitor a child's behavior, to recognize deviant behavior when it occurs, and to punish that behavior will produce children who lack self-control. Children who are not attached to their parents, who are poorly supervised, and whose parents are criminal or deviant themselves are the most likely to develop poor self-control.[127] Even in disadvantaged communities, children whose parents provide adequate and supportive discipline are the ones most likely to develop self-control.[128]

The association between poor parenting and children's antisocial behavior may be both reciprocal and intergenerational. Kids who have low self-control may strain parental attachments and the ability of parents to control children. Parents who themselves have low self-control are the ones

dangerous behaviors such as drinking, smoking, and reckless driving; all of these behaviors are associated with criminality (see Exhibit 9.5 for a list of factors that indicate low self-control).[124]

Because those with low self-control enjoy risky, exciting, or thrilling behaviors with immediate gratification, they are more likely to enjoy criminal acts, which require stealth,

---

EXHIBIT 9.5

The Elements of Impulsivity: Signs that a Person Has Low Self-Control

- Insensitive
- Physical
- Shortsighted
- Nonverbal
- Here-and-now orientation
- Unstable social relations
- Enjoys deviant behaviors
- Risk taker
- Refuses to work for distant goals

- Lacks diligence
- Lacks tenacity
- Adventuresome
- Self-centered
- Shameless
- Imprudent
- Lacks cognitive and verbal skills
- Enjoys danger and excitement

SOURCE: © Cengage Learning

CONNECTIONS

In his original version of control theory, discussed in Chapter 7, Hirschi focused on the social controls that attach people to conventional society and insulate them from criminality. In this newer work, he concentrates on self-control as a stabilizing force. The two views are connected, however, because both social control (or social bonds) and self-control are acquired through early experiences with effective parenting.

ASK YOURSELF . . .

Can you imagine a criminal offender who exhibits both social control and self-control? What would they be like and what crimes would they commit?

most likely to use damaging and inappropriate supervision and punishment mechanisms. Impulsive kids grow up to become poor parents who themselves use improper discipline, producing yet another generation of impulsive kids who lack self-control.[129]

Learning or Biology? There may also be a genetic/biosocial component to the development of impulsivity. Children of impulsive parents are the ones most likely to exhibit a lack of self-control.[130] Research shows that antisocial behavior runs in families and that having criminal relatives is a significant predictor of future misbehaviors.[131] While these studies are not definitive, they raise the possibility that the intergenerational transfer of impulsivity has a biological basis.

Measures of neuropsychological deficits, birth complications, and low birth weight have all been found to have significant direct or indirect effects on levels of self-control.[132] Recent research shows that children who suffer anoxia (oxygen starvation) during the birthing process are the ones most likely to lack self-control later in life, which suggests that impulsivity may have a biological basis.[133] When Kevin Beaver and his associates examined impulsive personality and self-control in twin pairs, they discovered evidence that these traits may be inherited rather than developed. That might help explain the stability of these latent traits over the life course.[134]

Another biological basis for impulsivity may be low resting heart rate. People with low heart rates may seek out dangerous and arousing behaviors, such as criminality, to compensate for their biological condition; they become thrill seekers who engage in dangerous behaviors simply because it gives them the jolt they need to they feel good, that is, normal.[135]

Crime Rate Variations If individual differences are stable over the life course, why do crime rates vary? Why do people commit less crime as they age? Why are some regions more crime prone than others? Why are some groups more crime prone than others? Does that mean there are between-group differences in self-control? If male crime rates are higher than female rates, does that mean men are more impulsive and lacking in self-control? How does the GTC address these issues?

Gottfredson and Hirschi remind us that criminal propensity and criminal acts are separate concepts (Figure 9.3). On the one hand, criminal acts, such as robberies or burglaries, are illegal events or deeds that offenders engage in when they perceive them to be advantageous. Burglaries are typically committed by young males looking for cash, liquor, and entertainment; the crime provides "easy, short-term gratification."[136] Crime is rational and predictable: people commit crime when it promises rewards with minimal threat of pain; the threat of punishment can deter crime. If targets are well guarded, crime rates diminish. Only the truly irrational offender would dare to strike under those circumstances.

On the other hand, while criminal offenders are people predisposed to commit crimes, they are not robots who commit crime without restraint; their days are also filled with conventional behaviors, such as going to school, parties, concerts, and church. But given the same set of criminal opportunities, such as having a lot of free time for mischief and living in a neighborhood with unguarded homes containing valuable merchandise, crime-prone people have a much higher probability of violating the law than do noncriminals. The propensity to commit crimes remains stable throughout a person's life. Change in the frequency of criminal activity is purely a function of change in criminal opportunity.

If we accept this provision of the GTC, then both criminal propensity and criminal opportunity must be considered to explain criminal participation. So if males and females are equally impulsive but their crime rates vary, the explanation is that males have more opportunity to commit crime. Young teenage girls may be more closely monitored by their parents and therefore lack the freedom to offend. Girls are also socialized to have more self-control than boys: although females get angry as often as males, many have been taught

Criminal Offender

Impulsive personality
- Physical
- Insensitive
- Risk taking
- Short-sighted
- Nonverbal

Low self-control
- Poor parenting
- Deviant parents
- Lack of supervision
- Active
- Self-centered

Weakening of social bonds
- Attachment
- Commitment
- Involvement
- Belief

Criminal Opportunity
- Presence of gangs
- Lack of supervision
- Lack of guardianship
- Suitable targets

+

Criminal/Deviant Act
- Delinquency
- Smoking
- Drinking
- Underage sex
- Crime

=

FIGURE 9.3 Gottfredson and Hirschi's General Theory of Crime

SOURCE: © Cengage Learning

to blame themselves for such feelings. Females are socialized to fear that anger will harm relationships; males are encouraged to react with "moral outrage," blaming others for their discomfort.[137]

Opportunity can also be used to explain ecological variation in the crime rate. How does the GTC explain the fact that crime rates are higher in the summer than the winter? The number of impulsive people lacking in self-control is no higher in August than it is in December. Gottfredson and Hirschi would argue that seasonal differences are explained by opportunity: during the summer kids are out of school and have more opportunity to commit crime. Similarly, if crime rates are higher in Los Angeles than Minneapolis, it is because either there are more criminal opportunities in this western city, or because the fast-paced life of L.A. attracts more impulsive people than the laid-back Midwest.

To read an article by Bruce J. Arneklev, Lori Elis, and Sandra Medlicott that tests the General Theory of Crime, go to **http://www.westerncriminology .org/documents/WCR/v07n3/arneklev.pdf.**

Self-Control and Crime   Gottfredson and Hirschi claim that the principles of **self-control theory** can explain all varieties of criminal behavior and all the social and behavioral correlates of crime. That is, such widely disparate crimes as burglary, robbery, embezzlement, drug dealing, murder, rape, and insider trading all stem from a deficiency of self-control. Likewise, gender, racial, and ecological differences in crime rates can be explained by discrepancies in self-control.

Unlike other theoretical models that explain only narrow segments of criminal behavior (i.e., teenage gang formation), Gottfredson and Hirschi's self-control theory

CONNECTIONS

As you may recall, in Chapter 3 the association between risky lifestyle and victimization was set out in detail. People who are impulsive and lack self-control are also the ones most likely to have a risky lifestyle.

ASK YOURSELF . . .

Does this mean the causes of both crime and victimization are actually the same?

self-control theory According to Gottfredson and Hirschi, the view that the cause of delinquent behavior is an impulsive personality. Kids who are impulsive may find that their bond to society is weak.

applies to all crimes and deviant acts, ranging from murder to suicide.[138] White-collar crime rates remain low, they claim, because people who lack self-control rarely attain the positions necessary to commit those crimes. However, the relatively few white-collar criminals lack self-control to the same degree and in the same manner as criminals such as rapists and burglars.

Empirical Support for GTC   Since the publication of *A General Theory of Crime*, numerous researchers have attempted to test the validity of Gottfredson and Hirschi's theoretical views.[139] The general consensus of this research is that people with low self-control and poor impulse control are the most likely to engage in serious crime.[140]

One approach has been to identify indicators of impulsiveness and self-control to determine whether these factors correlate with measures of criminal activity. As a group they suggest that the lower a person's self-control, the more likely they are to engage in antisocial behaviors.[141] Kids with low self-control are the ones most likely to fall in with a bad crowd, and once they do so their impulsivity makes them vulnerable to antisocial peer influence.[142] It is not surprising that career criminals have been shown to have significantly lower levels of self-control than non-offenders, and that the lower the level of a person's self-control, the greater his or her chance of becoming a career criminal.[143] Some studies have found self-control to be the strongest predictor of career criminality, exceeding the impact of age, race, ethnicity, gender, socioeconomic status, mental illness, attention deficit hyperactivity disorder diagnosis, and trauma experience.[144]

Analyzing the General Theory of Crime   By integrating the concepts of socialization and criminality, Gottfredson and Hirschi help explain why some people who lack self-control can escape criminality, and, conversely, why some people who have self-control might not escape. People who are at risk because they have impulsive personalities may forgo criminal careers because there are no criminal opportunities that satisfy their impulsive needs; instead, they may find other outlets for their impulsive personalities. In contrast, if the opportunity is strong enough, even people with relatively strong self-control may be tempted to violate the law; the incentives to commit crime may overwhelm self-control.

Integrating criminal propensity and criminal opportunity can explain why some children enter into chronic offending while others living in similar environments are able to resist criminal activity. It can also help us understand why the corporate executive with a spotless record gets caught up in business fraud. Even a successful executive may find self-control inadequate if the potential for illegal gain is large. The driven executive, accustomed to both academic and financial success, may find that the fear of failure can neutralize his or her self-control. During tough economic times, the impulsive manager who fears dismissal may be tempted to circumvent the law to improve the bottom line.[145]

Questions Remaining About the GTC Although the General Theory of Crime seems persuasive, several questions and criticisms remain unanswered. One of the most important issues is the assumption that criminal propensity does not change. Research shows that changing life circumstances, such as starting and leaving school, becoming a member of an antisocial peer group, abusing substances and then getting straight, and starting or ending personal relationships all influence the frequency of offending.[146]

There is also the question of whether the theory is tautological or involves circular reasoning: How do we know when people are impulsive? When they commit crimes! Are all criminals impulsive? Of course, or else they would not have broken the law![147] Gottfredson and Hirschi counter by saying that impulsivity is not itself a propensity to commit crime but a condition that inhibits people from appreciating the long-term consequences of their behavior. Consequently, if given the opportunity, they are more likely to indulge in criminal acts than their non-impulsive counterparts.[148] According to Gottfredson and Hirschi, impulsivity and criminality are neither identical nor equivalent. Some impulsive people may channel their reckless energies into noncriminal activity, such as trading on the commodities markets or real estate speculation, and make a legitimate fortune for their efforts. Others, more impulsive, may bend the rules for their own benefit.

In addition to these basic issues, numerous studies have attempted to explain or address environmental and individual level differences in the crime rate and determine whether the GTC can explain why they occur:

- *People change and so does their level of self-control.* The General Theory of Crime assumes that criminal propensity does not change; opportunities change. This is a critical issue because it assumes that the human personality is stable from childhood into adulthood. However, social scientists recognize that behavior-shaping factors that are dominant in early adolescence, such as peer groups, may fade in adulthood and be replaced by others, such as the nuclear family.[149] Personality also undergoes change and so does its impact on antisocial behavior.[150]

A scene from *In the Blood* (2014): from left, Danny Trejo, Amaury Nolasco, Gina Carano. A child drug addict and criminal, Danny Trejo was in and out of jail for 11 years. While serving time in San Quentin, he won the lightweight and welterweight boxing titles. Imprisoned for armed robbery and drug offenses, he successfully completed a 12-step rehabilitation program that changed his life. While speaking at a Cocaine Anonymous meeting in 1985, Trejo met a young man who later called him for support. Trejo went to meet him at what turned out to be the set of the film *Runaway Train* (1985). Trejo was immediately offered a role as a convict extra, probably because of his tough, tattooed appearance. Also on the set was a screenwriter who did time with Trejo in San Quentin. Remembering Trejo's boxing skills, the screenwriter offered him $350 per day to train the actors for a boxing match. Director Andrei Konchalovsky saw Trejo training Eric Roberts and immediately offered him a featured role as Roberts's opponent in the film. Now in his 70s, Trejo has appeared in more than 300 films and TV shows, including *From Dusk Till Dawn: The Series*, where he plays the Regulator.

Francisco Roman/Anchor Bay Films/courtesy Everett Collection

It is not surprising that research efforts show that the stability in self-control predicted by Gottfredson and Hirschi may be an illusion: some research efforts find stability in social control over the life course, while others find significant change and fluctuations.[151] As people mature, the focus of their lives likewise changes and they may be better able to control their impulsive behavior.[152] As Callie Burt and her associates recently found, adolescence is a period of dramatic biological, behavioral, and social changes; a young person's physical and neurological makeup is undergoing remodeling and restructuring. Environmental influences operate in concert with neurobiological changes to create a period of heightened change. During this period levels of impulsivity also change, a result that is not predicted by the GTC.[153]

- *Environmental patterns are not adequately explained.* The GTC fails to address ecological patterns in the crime rate. If crime rates are higher in Los Angeles than in Albany, New York, can it be assumed that residents of Los Angeles are more impulsive than residents of Albany? There is little evidence of regional differences in impulsivity or self-control. Gottfredson and Hirschi might counter that crime rate differences may reflect criminal opportunity:

one area may have more effective law enforcement, more draconian laws, and higher levels of guardianship. If crime rates are lower in Albany it is because there are fewer opportunities to commit crime.

Environments may interact with personality to shape behaviors, a condition not foreseen by the GTC.[154] Some research indicates that social factors do in fact mediate the influence of self-control on crime and that such factors as community solidarity, morality and general levels of self-control moderate the effects of individual-level low self-control.[155] Take what criminologist Gregory Zimmerman found when he examined how environment and personality interact. In high-crime neighborhoods, being impulsive and lacking self-control are not associated with criminal behavior. In contrast, in low-crime, safer areas, impulsive kids are the ones most likely to commit criminal acts. How can this environmental effect be explained? In disadvantaged neighborhoods, where crime is omnipresent, maintaining low self-control means relatively little. In contrast, in safer, low-crime areas, most kids conform and it's only the most impulsive ones, the few bad apples, who risk engaging in criminal acts. In stable neighborhoods, where legitimate opportunity abounds, only the most reckless kids are foolish enough to commit crime.[156] In sum, environment may influence criminal decision making, an observation that contradicts the GTC.

- *Racial and gender differences in the crime rate are not adequately explained.* Impulsivity may not be able to explain all the gender and racial variations in the crime rate; it has different cross-group effects.[157] Although distinct gender differences in the crime rate exist, there is little evidence that males are more impulsive than females (although females and males differ in many other personality traits).[158] Some research efforts have found gender differences in the association between self-control and crime; the theory predicts no such difference should occur.[159]

Looking at this relationship from another perspective, males who persist in crime exhibit characteristics that are different from female persisters. Women seem to be influenced by their place of residence, childhood and recent abuses, living with a criminal partner, selling drugs, stress, depression, fearfulness, their romantic relationships, their children, and whether they have suicidal thoughts. In contrast, men are more likely to persist because of their criminal peer associations, carrying weapons, alcohol abuse, and aggressive feelings. Impulsivity alone may not be able to explain why males and females persist or desist.[160]

Similarly, Gottfredson and Hirschi explain racial differences in the crime rate as a failure of childrearing practices in the African American community.[161] In so doing, they overlook issues of institutional racism, poverty, and relative deprivation, which have been shown to have a significant impact on crime rate differentials.

African Americans are more influenced by their perception of police bias than others, a fact overlooked by Hirschi and Gottfredson.[162]

- *Socialization differences.* A number of research efforts show that the quality of peer relations either enhances or controls criminal behavior and that these influences vary over time.[163] As children mature, peer influence continues to grow. Research shows that kids who lack self-control also have trouble maintaining relationships with law-abiding peers. They may either choose or be forced to seek out friends who are similarly limited in their ability to maintain self-control.[164] Similarly, as they mature they may seek out romantic relationships with law-violating boyfriends or girlfriends, and these entanglements enhance the likelihood that they will get further involved in crime (girls seem more deeply influenced by their delinquent boyfriends than boys by their delinquent girlfriends).[165] This finding contradicts the GTC, which suggests the influence of friends should be stable and unchanging and that a relationship established later in life (making deviant friends) should not influence criminal propensity. Gottfredson and Hirschi might counter that it should come as no surprise that impulsive kids, lacking in self-control, seek out peers with similar personality characteristics.

Gottfredson and Hirschi propose that children either develop self-control by the end of early childhood or fail to develop it at all. Research shows, however, that some kids who are predisposed toward delinquency may find their life circumstances improved and their involvement with antisocial behavior diminished if they are exposed to positive and effective parenting that appears later in life.[166] Parenting can influence self-control in later adolescence and kids who receive improved parenting may improve their self-control much later in the life course than predicted by the GTC.[167]

- *Personality differences.* Not all people have similar personalities and not all criminals are impulsive.[168] The personality is too complex to suggest that only a single element can account for antisocial behavior. There is too much variety in personality traits, ranging from psychopathy to decision-making style to say that a single element is responsible for all crimes.[169] It is also possible that other elements of the personality—including but not limited to temperament, risk-seeking, and self-centeredness—are more potent predictors of antisocial behavior than impulsivity.[170]

While Gottfredson and Hirschi assume that criminals are impatient or "present-oriented," there is also evidence that some choose to commit crime for future rewards. When Steven Levitt and Sudhir Alladi Venkatesh interviewed gang boys, they found that many young gang boys are willing to wait years to "rise through the ranks" before becoming gang leaders and earning high wages. Their stay in the gang is fueled by the promises of future compensation, a fact that contradicts Gottfredson and Hirschi's vision of an impulsive criminal who lives for today without worrying about tomorrow.[171]

Despite these unresolved issues, the GTC remains one of the most important and influential criminological theories. By integrating concepts of criminal choice, criminal opportunity, socialization, and personality, Gottfredson and Hirschi have created a plausible roadmap to understand and explain the onset and continuity of crime.

Trajectory Theory

L010 Recognize that there are a variety of criminal trajectories

Trajectory theory is a third developmental approach that combines elements of propensity and life course theory. The basic premise is that there is more than one path to crime and more than one class of offender; there are different *trajectories* in a criminal career. Because all people are different, no single model of criminality can hope to describe every person's journey through life. Some people are social and have a large peer group, while others are loners who make decisions on their own.[172]

People offend at a different pace, commit different kinds of crimes, and are influenced by different external forces.[173] Those who begin offending at an early age may engage in more age-appropriate crimes as they mature: the violent adolescent school yard bully may mature into an abusive husband in adulthood, but he remains violent over the life course.[174]

Factors that predict offending in males may have little influence on females; there are significant gender differences in offending careers.[175] Criminal trajectories may also vary according to offending specialty: people who commit violent crimes maintain a unique set of personality traits and problem behaviors that separate them from nonviolent property and drug offenders.[176] There are also differences in the onset of criminal careers: some people begin at an early age and later become adult offenders, while others begin their violent careers in adulthood, having escaped and/or avoided crime as juveniles.[177]

One reason that all these different trajectories exist may be that some of the specific causes of crime such as mental disease and personality disorders progress differently, affecting some people in early adolescence while affecting others later in life.[178] As external influences shift and change so too do offending trajectories. For example, as parents change their parenting style, their children alter their antisocial behavior involvement.[179] In sum, people offend at a different pace, commit different kinds of crimes, and are influenced by different external forces.[180]

Because propensity theories disregard social influences during the life span, and life course theories maintain that social events seem to affect all people equally, they both miss the fact that there are different classes and types of offenders.

Consequently, criminologists have sought to identify different paths or trajectories to crime.[181] Some important concepts contained within this model will be discussed in some detail.

EARLY, LATE, AND NONSTARTERS

Not all persistent offenders begin at an early age. Some are precocious, beginning their criminal careers early and persisting into adulthood.[182]

Others stay out of trouble in early adolescence and do not violate the law until later in early adulthood. Some offenders may peak their criminal activity during adolescence, whereas others persist into adulthood. Some people maximize their offending rates at a relatively early age and then reduce their antisocial activity; others persist into their 20s. Some are high-rate offenders, whereas others offend at relatively low rates.[183] Some may suffer from mental disease, for example, psychosis, that onsets later in adolescence and results in nonstarters suddenly beginning an offending career.[184]

CHRONIC OFFENDING

There may even be different classes of chronic offenders. As you may recall, when Wolfgang first identified the concept of chronicity he did not distinguish within that grouping. Now research shows that chronic offenders can be divided into subgroupings: some are very high-rate offenders, whereas other chronics offend relatively infrequently but are persistent in their criminal activities, never really stopping.[185] Alex Piquero and his associates examined data from the Cambridge Study in Delinquent Development (CSDD), a longitudinal survey of 411 South London males, most born in 1953, and found that the group could be further subdivided into five classes based on their offending histories:

- Non-offenders (62 percent)
- Low-adolescence peak offenders (19 percent)
- Very low-rate chronic offenders (11 percent)
- High-adolescence peak offenders (5 percent)
- High-rate chronic offenders (3 percent)

Following them over time until they reached their 40s, Piquero found that boys in each of these offending trajectories faced a different degree of social and personal problems, such as poor housing, a troubled romantic life, mental illness, and drug involvement. Not surprisingly, those youth classified as high-rate chronic offenders were more likely to experience life failure than kids placed in the other groups. The research shows that people who fall into different offender trajectories have different outcomes reaching into midlife.[186] Each of these categories of offenders presents unique problems, and each presents serious social and economic cost differentials over the life course. Piquero, along with Wesley Jennings and David Farrington, found that the cost to society presented by each high-rate chronic offender can be up to 10 times greater than the cost of those in the other offending categories.[187]

In sum, propensity theories maintain that most persistent offenders are early starters, beginning their delinquent careers in their adolescence and persisting into adulthood. In contrast, trajectory theory holds that people begin their offending careers at different points of their lives and follow different offending trajectories. Those who engage in repeated and sustained involvement with the law in early adolescence are the ones most likely to continue to violate the law late into their adulthood.[188]

Abstainers and Late Bloomers There is also a group of abstainers or non-offenders. Despite the fact that most of their peers engage in a wide variety of antisocial activities, these people never break the law; their conventional behavior makes them deviant because offending is the norm!

Why do some people refrain from antisocial activity of any sort? Who are these folks who never ever shoplifted, smoked pot, got drunk, or had a fight? According to social psychologist Terrie Moffitt, abstainers are social introverts as teens, whose unpopularity shielded them from group pressure to commit delinquent acts.[189] Other experts disagree, suggesting that conformity may be related more to close parental monitoring and involvement with prosocial peer groups than it is to being unpopular. Kids who do not learn delinquent behaviors from role models are the ones most likely to be abstainers.[190] Still another explanation may be biological: abstainers maintain a genetic code that insulates them from criminality-producing factors in the environment.[191] Not surprisingly, abstainers are more likely than other youth to become successful, well-adjusted adults.[192]

There are also late bloomers who abstain during childhood and early adolescence and then decide to commit crime relatively late in the life cycle.[193] Even though their criminal careers are delayed they may still get involved in serious adult offending.[194] Because late bloomers combine psychopathology with risk-taking behavior and poor social skills, their behavior becomes increasingly violent over time.[195]

First Offenders The reason why some offenders start early, others late, and some not at all may be linked to psychological problems and disturbance. Mental disease and personality disorders progress differently, affecting some people in early adolescence and others later in life.[196] Research shows that offending trajectories do in fact differ among people with mental disorders, creating different classes of offenders. There are early starters (ES) who begin to engage in antisocial behavior at a young age before the onset of the psychiatric disorder, most likely because they maintain other psychological issues such as an antisocial

personality. There are also late starters (LS) who begin to engage in antisocial behavior after the onset of the psychiatric disorder. Their criminal and deviant behavior is attributed to symptoms of the disorder. The final category, called first offenders (FO), are men in their late thirties with a schizophrenia disorder who suddenly commit a violent offense. Though they are late starters, they differ from those people in the LS grouping because while the latter start a criminal career with a variety of less serious offenses, the FO men suddenly commit a very serious (often fatal) offense without prior identified psychological abnormality.[197]

PATHWAYS TO CRIME

Trajectory theory recognizes that criminals may travel more than a single road. Some may specialize in violence and extortion; some may be involved in theft and fraud; others may engage in a variety of criminal acts.[198] Each type of specialist may be unique: kids who commit violent crimes may be different from nonviolent property and drug offenders.[199]

There may also be distinct career paths. Some start out as violent kids whose violent behavior declines with age and who eventually desist. Another group are *escalators* whose severity of violence increases over time. Escalators are more likely to live in racially mixed communities, experience racism, and have less parental involvement than people who avoid or decrease their violent behaviors.[200]

Pathways may also be created by the effect of early childhood risk factors. Kids who experience risk factors (difficult infant temperament, low cognitive ability, weak parental closeness, and disadvantaged family background) very early in their lives, by age 3, seem to travel down a variety of paths: a normative, prosocial pathway; a pathway marked by oppositional behavior and fighting; a pathway marked by impulsivity and inattention; and a few who engage a wide range of antisocial tendencies. Children who enter on an antisocial pathway early in their lives are more likely to engage in preteen delinquency and substance use by 11 years of age.[201]

But not all enter the path to crime at an early age. Another group—referred to late-onset escalators—begin their violent careers relatively late in their adolescence after suffering a variety of psychological and social disturbances earlier in childhood, including high levels of social anxiety.[202]

Some of the most important research on delinquent paths or trajectories has been conducted by Rolf Loeber and his associates. Using data from a longitudinal study of Pittsburgh youth, Loeber has identified three distinct paths to a criminal career (Figure 9.4):[203]

- The **authority conflict pathway** begins at an early age with stubborn behavior. This leads to defiance (doing things one's own way, disobedience) and then to authority avoidance (staying out late, truancy, running away).
- The **covert pathway** begins with minor, underhanded behavior (lying, shoplifting) that leads to property damage (setting nuisance fires, damaging property). This behavior

authority conflict pathway The path to a criminal career that begins with early stubborn behavior and defiance of parents.

covert pathway A path to a criminal career that begins with minor underhanded behavior and progresses to fire starting and theft.

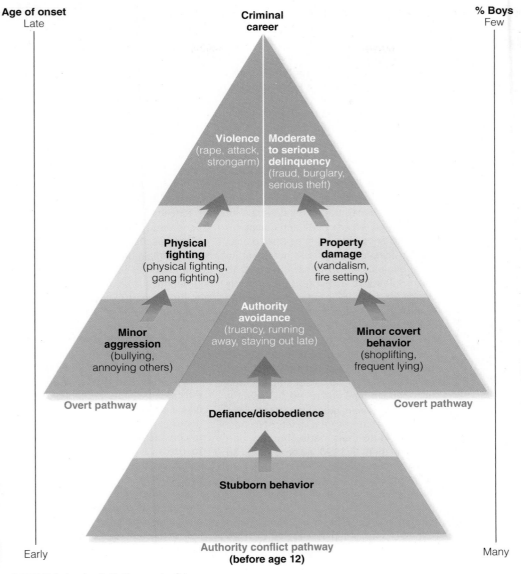

Age of onset
Late

Criminal career

% Boys
Few

Violence (rape, attack, strongarm)

Moderate to serious delinquency (fraud, burglary, serious theft)

Physical fighting (physical fighting, gang fighting)

Property damage (vandalism, fire setting)

Authority avoidance (truancy, running away, staying out late)

Minor aggression (bullying, annoying others)

Minor covert behavior (shoplifting, frequent lying)

Overt pathway

Covert pathway

Defiance/disobedience

Stubborn behavior

Early

Authority conflict pathway (before age 12)

Many

FIGURE 9.4 Loeber's Pathways to Crime

eventually escalates to more serious forms of criminality, ranging from joyriding, pocket picking, larceny, and fencing to passing bad checks, using stolen credit cards, stealing cars, dealing drugs, and breaking and entering.

- The **overt pathway** escalates to aggressive acts beginning with aggression (annoying others, bullying), leading to physical (and gang) fighting, and then to violence (attacking someone, forced theft).

The Loeber research indicates that each of these paths may lead to a sustained deviant career. Some people enter two and even three paths simultaneously: they are stubborn, lie to teachers and parents, are bullies, and commit petty thefts. Those taking more than one path are the most likely to become persistent offenders as they mature.

Although some persistent offenders may specialize in one type of behavior, others engage in varied criminal acts and antisocial behaviors as they mature. As adolescents, they cheat on tests, bully kids in the school yard, take drugs, commit burglary, steal a car, and then shoplift from a store. Later as adults, some specialize in a particular criminal activity such as drug trafficking, while others are involved in an assortment of deviant acts—selling drugs, committing robberies, and getting involved in break-ins—when the situation arises and the opportunities are present.[204] There may be a multitude of criminal career subgroupings (for example, prostitutes, drug dealers), each with its own distinctive career path.

> **overt pathway** Pathway to a criminal career that begins with minor aggression, leads to physical fighting, and eventually escalates to violent crime.

An Ethical Dilemma

The Xbox Killers

In the hot summer months of 2004, Troy Victorino and friends Robert Cannon, Jerome Hunter, and Michael Salas were illegally squatting in a Deltona, Florida, home and using it as a "party house." The owners, who were spending the summer in Maine, asked their granddaughter, Erin Belanger, to check up on the property. When she saw what was going on she called the police in order to get the squatters removed from the premises. Victorino (who was in jail on an unrelated matter at the time his friends were evicted) left behind an Xbox game system and some clothes, and Belanger took possession of these items. Once he was released from jail on bond, Victorino, feeling disrespected because the police had been called and his stuff confiscated, threatened Belanger and slashed the tires on her car. He warned her that unless she returned the items, he was going to come back and beat her with a baseball bat while she was sleeping. It was not an idle threat. On August 6, 2004, in what is now known either as the *Xbox murders* or the *Deltona massacre*, Victorino, Cannon, Hunter, and Salas armed themselves with aluminum bats, put on all-black clothing, covered their faces with scarves, kicked in the front door, and attacked Belanger and her roommates as they slept. All six

victims, including Erin Belanger, were beaten and stabbed beyond recognition. All six died.

The perpetrators of the deadly attack left a trail of clues that resulted in their quick arrest and indictment on murder charges. It was a pretty sad bunch; they all seemed to have lived troubled lives. Michael Salas was abused even before his birth by his mother, who used drugs during her pregnancy, traded food stamps for cocaine, and left her three sons alone for long periods during the winter. Child protective services found cigarette burns on the boys' bodies. Salas's father died of AIDS when Salas was 9. Hunter is a clinically depressed, mentally ill man whose parents were both committed to mental hospitals at the time of the massacre. As early as age 3, Hunter conversed with his identical twin brother Jeremy, who died from pneumonia at 6 months old. But it was Victorino, a 6-foot-6, 300-pound career criminal, who most outraged the public. He had spent 8 of the last 11 years before the killings serving prison sentences for a variety of crimes, including auto theft, battery, arson, burglary, and theft. In 1996, he beat a man so severely that doctors needed 15 titanium plates to rebuild the victim's face. Not surprisingly, Victorino also had a long history of physical and sexual abuse that began at the time he was 2 years old. He suffered from neurological impairment that resulted in poor impulse control and the inability to manage his violent temper.

The Xbox killers followed a classic developmental path: early abuse and problems in childhood leading to a long and sustained criminal career. These killers did not age out of crime but persisted and escalated their criminal involvement until it culminated in unspeakable tragedy.

Despite their personal problems, on August 2, 2006, Victorino and Hunter were sentenced to death by lethal injection, and Cannon and Salas to life in prison without the possibility of parole. Victorino and Hunter remain on death row at the Florida State Prison in Starke because the average length of incarceration of a Florida inmate prior to execution is more than 12 years.

Recently the governor has been asked to review the sentence in light of the troubled histories of Victorino and Hunter. Would it be ethical to execute someone who has had a horrendous upbringing? Anti–death penalty groups have asked him to consider commuting the sentences to life in prison considering their childhood traumas. He has asked for your opinion on the matter. Write a memo stating whether you believe that developmental factors should mitigate their culpability in the case. Would it be fair to execute someone who commits a similar crime but had a relatively problem-free childhood?

ADOLESCENT-LIMITED OFFENDERS VS. LIFE COURSE PERSISTERS

According to psychologist Terrie Moffitt, most young offenders follow one of two paths. **Adolescent-limited offenders** may be considered "typical teenagers" who get into minor scrapes and engage in what might be considered rebellious

adolescent-limited offender Offender who follows the most common criminal trajectory, in which antisocial behavior peaks in adolescence and then diminishes.

life course persister One of the small group of offenders whose criminal career continues well into adulthood.

teenage behavior with their friends.[205] As they reach their mid-teens, adolescent-limited delinquents begin to mimic the antisocial behavior of more troubled teens, only to reduce the frequency of their offending as they mature to around age 18.[206] So while it may be cool for some kids to swagger around and get into trouble during their teenage years, they are ready to settle down and assume more conventional roles as they enter young adulthood.

The second path is the one taken by a small group of **life course persisters** who begin their offending career at a very early age and continue to offend well into adulthood.[207] Moffitt finds that the seeds of life course persistence are planted early in life and may combine the effects of abnormal traits, such as neurological deficits, with severe family dysfunction. Life course persisters also manifest more abnormal personal traits such as low verbal ability, impaired reasoning skills, limited learning ability, and weak spatial and memory functions than do adolescent-limited offenders.[208] Individual traits rather than environment seem to have the greatest influence on life course persistence.[209]

Many life course persisters display elements of problem behavior syndrome, including mental health problems, lower than average verbal ability, psychiatric pathologies, limited school achievement, ADHD, impaired spatial and memory functions, and health issues.[210] It is not surprising, then, that life course persisters display social and personal dysfunctions.

Supporting research shows that the persistence patterns predicted by Moffitt are valid and accurate.[211] There may also be a genetic basis to life course persistence; some recent research links it to neurological deficiencies.[212] Life course persisters may be aggressive as part of a strategy to increase their reproductive options, a view that jibes with the sociobiology view discussed in Chapter 5.[213]

Evaluating Developmental Theories

Although the differences among the views presented in this chapter may seem irreconcilable, they in fact share some common ground. They indicate that a criminal career must be understood as a passage along which people travel, that it has a beginning and an end, and that events and life circumstances influence the journey. The factors that affect a criminal career may include structural factors, such as income and status; socialization factors, such as family and peer relations; biological factors, such as size and strength; psychological factors, including intelligence and personality; and opportunity factors, such as free time, inadequate police protection, and a supply of easily stolen merchandise.

Life course theories emphasize the influence of changing interpersonal and structural factors (that is, people change along with the world they live in). Latent trait theories place more emphasis on the fact that behavior is linked less to personal change and more to changes in the surrounding world. Trajectory theory finds that there are different classes of offenders who may change at different points of their criminal career.

These perspectives differ in their view of human development. Do people constantly change, as life course theories suggest, or are they stable, constant, and changeless, as the latent trait view indicates? Are the factors that produce criminality different at each stage of life, as the life course view suggests, or does a master trait—such as control balance, self-control, or coercion—steer the course of human behavior? Is there a single path to crime or are there different paths and different trajectories?

It is also possible that these positions are not mutually exclusive, and each may make a notable contribution to understanding the onset and continuity of a criminal career. In other words, stable individual characteristics—latent traits—may interact with or modify the effects of life course–varying social factors to increase their effect and shape the direction of criminal careers.[214] Is it possible that people take different paths to crime because they have different levels of criminal propensity? Needless to say, measuring these effects is quite complex and relies on sophisticated research techniques. One research effort by Bradley Entner Wright and his associates found evidence supporting both latent trait and life course theories.[215] Their research, conducted with subjects in New Zealand, indicates that low self-control in childhood predicts disrupted social bonds and criminal offending later in life, a finding that supports latent trait theory. They also found that maintaining positive social bonds helps reduce criminality and that maintaining prosocial bonds could even counteract the effect of low self-control. Latent traits are an important influence on crime, but their findings indicate that social relationships that form later in life appear to influence criminal behavior "above and beyond" individuals' preexisting characteristics.[216] This finding may reflect the fact that there are different classes of criminals: a less serious group who are influenced by life events, and a more chronic group whose latent traits insulate them from any positive prosocial relationships; this finding supports trajectory theory concepts.[217]

Concept Summary 9.1 sets out the most important life course, latent trait, and trajectory theories.

Public Policy Implications of Developmental Theory

There have been a number of policy initiatives based on premises of developmental theory. These typically feature multisystemic treatment efforts designed to provide at-risk kids with personal, social, educational, and family services. For example, one program found that an intervention that promotes academic success, social competence, and educational enhancement during the elementary grades can reduce risky sexual practices and their accompanying health consequences in early adulthood.[218]

Other programs are now employing multidimensional strategies and are aimed at targeting children in preschool through the early elementary grades in order to alter the direction of their life course. Many of the most successful programs focus on strengthening children's social-emotional competence and positive coping skills and suppressing the development of antisocial, aggressive behavior.[219] Research evaluations indicate that the most promising multicomponent crime and substance abuse prevention programs for youths, especially those at high risk, are aimed at improving their developmental skills. They may include a school component, an after-school component, and a parent-involvement component.[220] Take for instance the Boys and Girls Clubs and School Collaborations' Substance Abuse Prevention Program, which includes a school component

THEORY	MAJOR PREMISE	STRENGTHS	RESEARCH FOCUS
LIFE COURSE THEORIES	As people go through the life course, social and personal traits undergo change and influence behavior.	Explains why some at-risk children desist from crime.	Identify critical moments in a person's life course that produce crime.
Interactional Theory	Criminals go through lifestyle changes during their offending career. Crime influences lifestyle, and changing lifestyle influences crime.	Combines sociological and psychological theories.	Identify crime-producing interpersonal interactions and their reciprocal effects.
General Theory of Crime and Delinquency (GTCD)	Five critical life domains shape criminal behavior and are shaped by criminal behavior.	Shows that crime and other aspects of social life are interactive and developmental.	Measure the relationship between life domains and crime.
Age-Graded Theory	As people mature, the factors that influence their propensity to commit crime change. In childhood, family factors are critical; in adulthood, marital and job factors are key.	Shows how crime is a developmental process that shifts in direction over the life course.	Identify critical points in the life course that produce crime. Analyze the association between social capital and crime.
LATENT TRAIT THEORIES	A master trait controls human development.	Explains the continuity of crime and chronic offending.	Identify master trait that produces crime.
Integrated Cognitive Antisocial Potential (ICAP) Theory	People with antisocial potential (AP) are at risk to commit antisocial acts. AP can be viewed as both a long- and short-term phenomenon.	Identifies different types of criminal propensities and shows how they may influence behavior in both the short and long term.	Identify the components of long- and short-term AP.
General Theory of Crime	Crime and criminality are separate concepts. People choose to commit crime when they lack self-control. People lacking self-control will seize criminal opportunities.	Integrates choice and social control concepts. Identifies the difference between crime and criminality.	Measure associations among impulsivity, low self-control, and criminal behaviors.
Differential Coercion Theory	Individuals exposed to coercive environments develop social-psychological deficits that enhance their probability of engaging in criminal behavior.	Explains why a feeling of coercion is a master trait that determines behavior.	Measuring the sources of coercion.
Control Balance Theory	A person's "control ratio" influences his or her behavior.	Explains how the ability to control one's environment is a master trait.	Measuring control balance and imbalance.
TRAJECTORY THEORY	There is more than one pathway to crime.	Explains the existence of different types and classes of criminals.	Measuring different criminal paths.
Life Course Persistent/ Adolescent Limited	People begin their criminal activities at different points in their lives.	Explains why most adolescent misbehavior is limited to youthful misadventures.	Measuring the starting and stopping points of criminal activity.

called SMART (Skills Mastery and Resistance Training) Teachers, an after-school component called SMART Kids, and a parent-involvement component called SMART Parents. Each component is designed to reduce specific risk factors in the children's school, family, community, and personal environments.[221]

Another successful program, Fast Track, is designed to prevent serious antisocial behavior and related adolescent problems in high-risk children entering first grade.

The intervention is guided by a developmental approach that suggests that antisocial behavior is the product of the interaction of multiple social and psychological influences:

- Residence in low-income, high-crime communities places stressors and influences on children and families that increase their risk levels. In these areas, families characterized by marital conflict and instability make consistent and effective parenting difficult to achieve, particularly with children who are impulsive and of difficult temperament.

- Children of high-risk families usually enter the education process poorly prepared for its social, emotional, and cognitive demands. Their parents often are unprepared to relate effectively with school staff, and a poor home–school bond often aggravates the child's adjustment problems. They may be grouped with other children who are similarly unprepared. This peer group may be negatively influenced by disruptive classroom contexts and punitive teachers.
- Over time, aggressive and disruptive children are rejected by families and peers and tend to receive less support from teachers. All of these processes increase the risk of antisocial behaviors, in a process that begins in elementary school and lasts throughout adolescence. During this period, peer influences, academic difficulties, and dysfunctional personal identity development can contribute to serious conduct problems and related risky behaviors.

Compared with children in the control group, children in the intervention group displayed significantly less aggressive behavior at home, in the classroom, and on the playground. By the end of the third grade, 37 percent of the intervention group had become free of conduct problems, in contrast with 27 percent of the control group. By the end of elementary school, 33 percent of the intervention group had a developmental trajectory of decreasing conduct problems, as compared with 27 percent of the control group.

Programs based on developmental theories are aimed at young kids before they enter a path that leads to crime. Here, children in New York attend the Boys & Girls Clubs of America's launch of the Great Futures campaign to call attention to the critical role of out-of-school time for kids. BGCA took over Times Square to "redefine the opportunity equation" and garner support for after-school and summer programs that empower youth toward success.

AP Images/John Minchillo

Furthermore, placement in special education by the end of elementary school was about one-fourth lower in the intervention group than in the control group.

Group differences continued through adolescence. Court records indicate that by eighth grade, 38 percent of the intervention group boys had been arrested, in contrast with 42 percent of the control group. Finally, psychiatric interviews after ninth grade indicate that the Fast Track intervention has reduced serious conduct disorder by over a third, from 27 percent to 17 percent. These effects generalized across gender and ethnic groups and across the wide range of child and family characteristics measured by Fast Track.

SUMMARY

L01 Discuss the history of developmental theory

The foundation of this theory is Sheldon and Eleanor Glueck's integration of biological, psychological, and social factors. Later the Glueck data was rediscovered by criminologists Robert Sampson and John Laub. The Philadelphia cohort research by Marvin Wolfgang and his associates investigated criminal career development. Rolf Loeber and Marc LeBlanc proposed that criminologists should devote time and effort to understanding basic questions about the evolution of criminal careers.

L02 Compare and contrast life course, latent trait, and trajectory theory

Life course theorists view criminality as a dynamic process influenced by a multitude of individual characteristics, traits, and social experiences. Life course theories look at such issues as the onset of crime, the escalation of offenses, the persistence of crime, and desistance from crime. Latent trait theorists believe that human development is controlled by a "master trait" that guides human development and gives some people an increased propensity to commit crime. Trajectory theory holds that there are multiple pathways to crime.

LO3 Enumerate the principles of the life course theory

At an early age, people begin relationships and behaviors that will determine their adult life course. Some individuals are incapable of maturing in a reasonable and timely fashion. A positive life experience may help some criminals desist from crime for a while, but a negative experience may cause them to resume their criminal activities. As people mature, the factors that influence their behavior change. The social, physical, and environmental influences on their behavior are transformed.

LO4 Give examples of problem behaviors that cluster together

Crime is one of a group of interrelated antisocial behaviors that cluster together. Problem behaviors typically involve family dysfunction, sexual and physical abuse, substance abuse, smoking, precocious sexuality and early pregnancy, educational underachievement, suicide attempts, sensation seeking, and unemployment. People who suffer from one of these conditions typically exhibit many symptoms of the rest.

LO5 Explain why age of onset is an important factor in crime

Early onset of antisocial behavior predicts later and more serious criminality. Adolescent offenders whose criminal behavior persists into adulthood are likely to have begun their deviant careers at a very early (preschool) age. Early-onset kids tend to have poor parental discipline and monitoring, inadequate emotional support, distant peer relationships, and psychological issues and problems.

LO6 Outline the basic principles of Sampson and Laub's age-graded theory

Sampson and Laub find that the maintenance of a criminal career can be affected by events that occur later in life. They recognize the role of social capital and its influence on the trajectory of a criminal career. When faced with personal crisis, offenders lack the social supports that can help them reject criminal solutions. Sampson and Laub view criminal careers as a dynamic process in which important life events can change the direction of a person's life course trajectory; these key events are called turning points.

LO7 Interpret the terms *propensity* and *latent trait*

A propensity or latent trait is a personal attribute or characteristic that controls the inclination to commit crimes. It is a stable feature, characteristic, property, or condition, present at birth or soon after, that makes some people crime prone over the life course. Suspected latent traits include defective intelligence, damaged or impulsive personality, genetic abnormalities, the physical-chemical functioning of the brain, and environmental influences on brain function, such as drugs, chemicals, and injuries.

LO8 Comment upon Wilson and Herrnstein's views on crime and human nature

According to Wilson and Herrnstein, all human behavior, including criminality, is determined by its perceived consequences. A criminal incident occurs when an individual chooses criminal over conventional behavior. Wilson and Herrnstein assume that both biological and psychological traits influence the choice between crime and noncrime. Wilson and Herrnstein suggest the existence of an elusive latent trait that predisposes people to committing crime.

LO9 Understand the basic principles of the General Theory of Crime

Gottfredson and Hirschi link the propensity to commit crime to an impulsive personality and a lack of self-control. People with limited self-control tend to be impulsive; they are insensitive to other people's feelings, predisposed toward physical (rather than mental) activities and solutions, and are risk takers, shortsighted, and nonverbal. Because those with low self-control enjoy risky, exciting, or thrilling behaviors with immediate gratification, they are more likely to enjoy criminal acts. Gottfredson and Hirschi trace the root cause of poor self-control to inadequate child-rearing practices.

LO10 Recognize that there are a variety of criminal trajectories

There are different pathways to crime and different types of criminals. Some career criminals may specialize in violence and extortion; some may be involved in theft and fraud; some may engage in a variety of criminal acts. Some offenders begin their careers early in life, whereas others are late bloomers who begin committing crime at about the time when most people desist.

KEY TERMS

developmental criminology (306)
life course theories (307)
latent trait theories (307)
trajectory theory (308)
population heterogeneity (308)
state dependence (309)

problem behavior syndrome (PBS) (310)
integrated theories (312)
age-graded theory (312)
turning points (314)
cumulative disadvantage (314)
social capital (314)
social schemas (317)

criminogenic knowledge structure (CKS) (317)
propensity (319)
latent trait (319)
General Theory of Crime (GTC) (320)
self-control (321)
self-control theory (324)

authority conflict pathway (328)
covert pathway (328)
overt pathway (329)
adolescent-limited offenders (330)
life course persister (330)

CRITICAL THINKING QUESTIONS

1. Do you consider yourself to have social capital? If so, what form does it take?
2. Someone you know gets a perfect score on the SAT. What personal, family, and social characteristics do you think this individual has? Another person becomes a serial killer. Without knowing this person, describe their personal, family, and social characteristics. If bad behavior is explained by multiple problems, is good behavior explained by multiple strengths?
3. Do you believe it is a latent trait that makes a person crime prone, or is crime a function of environment and socialization?
4. Do you agree with Loeber's multiple pathways model? Do you know people who have traveled down those paths?
5. Do people really change, or do they stay the same but appear to be different because their life circumstances have changed?

NOTES

All URLs accessed in 2016.

1. David Gardner. "'Things Got Out of Control': Chilling Confession of Connecticut Massacre 'Killer,'" *Daily Mail*, September 23, 2010; Alaine Griffin, "Judge Sentences Komisarjevsky to Death," Courant.com, January 27, 2012, http://www.courant.com/community/cheshire/cheshire-home-invasion/hc-komisarjevsky-sentenced-0128-20120127,0,1199254.story.
2. Hans Eysenck, *Crime and Personality* (London: Methuen, 1964).
3. Nicole Hahn Rafter, "H. J. Eysenck in Fagin's Kitchen: The Return to Biological Theory in 20th-Century Criminology," *History of the Human Sciences* 19 (2006): 37–56.
4. Sheldon Glueck and Eleanor Glueck, *Unraveling Juvenile Delinquency* (Cambridge: Harvard University Press, 1950), p. 48.
5. See, generally, Sheldon Glueck and Eleanor Glueck, *500 Criminal Careers* (New York: Knopf, 1930); Glueck and Glueck, *One Thousand Juvenile Delinquents* (Cambridge, MA: Harvard University Press, 1934); Glueck and Glueck, *Predicting Delinquency and Crime* (Cambridge, MA: Harvard University Press, 1967), pp. 82–83; Glueck and Glueck, *Unraveling Juvenile Delinquency* (Cambridge, MA: Harvard University Press, 1950).
6. John Laub and Robert Sampson, "The Sutherland-Glueck Debate: On the Sociology of Criminological Knowledge," *American Journal of Sociology* 96 (1991): 1402–1440.
7. See, generally, Laub and Sampson, "The Sutherland–Glueck Debate"; John Laub and Robert Sampson, "Unraveling Families and Delinquency: A Reanalysis of the Gluecks' Data," *Criminology* 26 (1988): 355–380.
8. Marvin E. Wolfgang, Robert M. Figlio, and Thorsten Sellin, *Delinquency in a Birth Cohort* (Chicago: University of Chicago Press, 1972).
9. Rolf Loeber and Marc LeBlanc, "Toward a Developmental Criminology," in *Crime and Justice*, Vol. 12, ed. Norval Morris and Michael Tonry (Chicago: University of Chicago Press, 1990), pp. 375–473; Loeber and LeBlanc, "Developmental Criminology Updated," in *Crime and Justice*, Vol. 23, ed. Michael Tonry (Chicago: University of Chicago Press, 1998), pp. 115–198.
10. Alex Piquero, "Taking Stock of Developmental Trajectories of Criminal Activity over the Life Course," in *The Long View of Crime: A Synthesis of Longitudinal Research*, ed. Akiva Liberman (New York: Springer, 2008), pp. 23–78.
11. Shawn Bushway, Robert Brame, and Raymond Paternoster, "Assessing Stability and Change in Criminal Offending: A Comparison of Random Effects, Semiparametric, and Fixed Effects Modeling Strategies," *Journal of Quantitative Criminology* 15 (1999) 23–61.
12. Sarah Bacon, Raymond Paternoster, and Robert Brame, "Understanding the Relationship Between Onset Age and Subsequent Offending During Adolescence," *Journal of Youth and Adolescence* 38 (2009): 301–311.
13. Marvin Krohn, Alan Lizotte, and Cynthia Perez, "The Interrelationship Between Substance Use and Precocious Transitions to Adult Sexuality," *Journal of Health and Social Behavior* 38 (1997): 87–103, at 88.
14. Jennifer M. Beyers and Rolf Loeber, "Untangling Developmental Relations Between Depressed Mood and Delinquency in Male Adolescents," *Journal of Abnormal Child Psychology* 31 (2003): 247–266.
15. Stephanie Milan and Ellen Pinderhughes, "Family Instability and Child Maladjustment Trajectories During Elementary School," *Journal of Abnormal Child Psychology* 34 (2006): 43–56.
16. Chris Melde and Finn-Aage Esbensen, "The Relative Impact of Gang Status Transitions: Identifying the Mechanisms of Change in Delinquency," *Journal of Research in Crime and Delinquency*, first published October 30, 2013.
17. David Pyrooz, "From Colors and Guns to Caps and Gowns? The Effects of Gang Membership on Educational Attainment," *Journal of Research in Crime and Delinquency* 51 (2014): 56–87.
18. Bradley Entner Wright, Avshalom Caspi, Terrie Moffitt, and Phil Silva, "The Effects of Social Ties on Crime Vary by Criminal Propensity: A Life-Course Model of Interdependence," *Criminology* 39 (2001): 321–352.
19. Joan McCord, "Family Relationships, Juvenile Delinquency, and Adult Criminality," *Criminology* 29 (1991): 397–417.
20. Paul Mazerolle, "Delinquent Definitions and Participation Age: Assessing the Invariance Hypothesis," *Studies on Crime and Crime Prevention* 6 (1997): 151–168.
21. Peggy Giordano, Stephen Cernkovich, and Jennifer Rudolph, "Gender, Delinquency, and Desistance: Toward a Theory of Cognitive Transformation?" *American Journal of Sociology* 107 (2002): 990–1064.
22. John Hagan and Holly Foster, "S/He's a Rebel: Toward a Sequential Stress Theory of Delinquency and Gendered Pathways to Disadvantage in Emerging Adulthood," *Social Forces* 82 (2003): 53–86.
23. G. R. Patterson, Barbara DeBaryshe, and Elizabeth Ramsey, "A Developmental Perspective on Antisocial Behavior," *American Psychologist* 44 (1989): 329–335.
24. Robert Sampson and John Laub, "Crime and Deviance in the Life Course," *American Review of Sociology* 18 (1992): 63–84.
25. David Farrington, Darrick Jolliffe, Rolf Loeber, Magda Stouthamer-Loeber, and Larry Kalb, "The Concentration of Offenders in Families, and Family Criminality in the Prediction of Boys' Delinquency," *Journal of Adolescence* 24 (2001): 579–596.
26. Shawn D. Bushway, Marvin D. Krohn, Alan J. Lizotte, Matthew D. Phillips, and Nicole M. Schmidt, "Are Risky Youth Less Protectable as They Age? The Dynamics of Protection During Adolescence and Young Adulthood," *Justice Quarterly* 30 (2013): 84–116.
27. Raymond Paternoster, Charles Dean, Alex Piquero, Paul Mazerolle, and Robert Brame,

"Generality, Continuity, and Change in Offending," *Journal of Quantitative Criminology* 13 (1997): 231–266.

28. John Stogner, Chris Gibson, and J. Mitchell Miller, "Examining the Reciprocal Nature of the Health-Violence Relationship: Results from a Nationally Representative Sample," *Justice Quarterly* 31 (2014): 473–499.

29. Richard Miech, Avshalom Caspi, Terrie Moffitt, Bradley Entner Wright, and Phil Silva, "Low Socioeconomic Status and Mental Disorders: A Longitudinal Study of Selection and Causation During Young Adulthood," *American Journal of Sociology* 104 (1999): 1096–1131.

30. Deborah Capaldi and Gerald Patterson, "Can Violent Offenders Be Distinguished from Frequent Offenders? Prediction from Childhood to Adolescence," *Journal of Research in Crime and Delinquency* 33 (1996): 206–231.

31. For an analysis of more than 30 studies, see Mark Lipsey and James Derzon, "Predictors of Violent or Serious Delinquency in Adolescence and Early Adulthood: A Synthesis of Longitudinal Research," in *Serious and Violent Juvenile Offenders: Risk Factors and Successful Interventions*, ed. Rolf Loeber and David Farrington (Thousand Oaks, CA: Sage, 1998).

32. Gina Wingood, Ralph DiClemente, Rick Crosby, Kathy Harrington, Susan Davies, and Edward Hook III, "Gang Involvement and the Health of African American Female Adolescents," *Pediatrics* 110 (2002): 57.

33. David Husted, Nathan Shapira, and Martin Lazoritz, "Adolescent Gambling, Substance Use, and Other Delinquent Behavior," *Psychiatric Times* 20 (2003): 52–55.

34. Krohn, Lizotte, and Perez, "The Interrelationship Between Substance Use and Precocious Transitions to Adult Sexuality," p. 88; Richard Jessor, "Risk Behavior in Adolescence," *Journal of Adolescent Health* 12 (1991): 597–605.

35. Alex Piquero, David Farrington, Jonathan Shepherd, and Katherine Auty, "Offending and Early Death in the Cambridge Study in Delinquent Development," *Justice Quarterly* 31 (2014): 445–472.

36. Paul Nieuwbeerta and Alex Piquero, "Mortality Rates and Causes of Death of Convicted Dutch Criminals 25 Years Later," *Journal of Research in Crime and Criminality* 45 (2008): 256–286.

37. David Fergusson, L. John Horwood, and Elizabeth Ridder, "Show Me the Child at Seven II: Childhood Intelligence and Later Outcomes in Adolescence and Young Adulthood," *Journal of Child Psychology and Psychiatry and Allied Disciplines* 46 (2005): 850–859.

38. Krysia Mossakowski, "Dissecting the Influence of Race, Ethnicity, and Socioeconomic Status on Mental Health in Young Adulthood," *Research on Aging* 30 (2008): 649–671.

39. Fergusson, Horwood, and Ridder, "Show Me the Child at Seven II."

40. Mossakowski, "Dissecting the Influence of Race, Ethnicity, and Socioeconomic Status on Mental Health in Young Adulthood."

41. Jacqueline Schneider, "The Link Between Shoplifting and Burglary: The Booster Burglar," *British Journal of Criminology* 45 (2005): 395–401.

42. Glenn Deane, Richard Felson, and David Armstrong, "An Examination of Offense Specialization Using Marginal Logit Models," *Criminology* 43 (2005): 955–988.

43. Christopher Sullivan, Jean Marie McGloin, Travis Pratt, and Alex Piquero, "Rethinking the 'Norm' of Offender Generality: Investigating Specialization in the Short-Term," *Criminology* 44 (2006): 199–233.

44. Christopher J. Sullivan, Jean Marie McGloin, James V. Ray, and Michael S. Caudy, "Detecting Specialization in Offending: Comparing Analytic Approaches," *Journal of Quantitative Criminology* 25 (2009): 419–441.

45. Jean Marie McGloin, Christopher J. Sullivan, and Alex R. Piquero, "Aggregating to Versatility? Transitions Among Offender Types in the Short Term," *British Journal of Criminology* 49 (2009): 243–264.

46. David Nurco, Timothy Kinlock, and Mitchell Balter, "The Severity of Preaddiction Criminal Behavior Among Urban, Male Narcotic Addicts and Two Nonaddicted Control Groups," *Journal of Research in Crime and Delinquency* 30 (1993): 293–316.

47. Hanno Petras, Nicholas Alongo, Sharon Lambert, Sandra Barrueco, Cindy Schaeffer, Howard Chilcoat, and Sheppard Kellam, "The Utility of Elementary School TOCA-R Scores in Identifying Later Criminal Court Violence Among Adolescent Females," *Journal of the American Academy of Child and Adolescent Psychiatry* 44 (2005): 790–797; Hanno Petras, Howard Chilcoat, Philip Leaf, Nicholas Ialongo, and Sheppard Kellam, "Utility of TOCA-R Scores During the Elementary School Years in Identifying Later Violence Among Adolescent Males," *Journal of the American Academy of Child and Adolescent Psychiatry* 43 (2004): 88–96.

48. W. Alex Mason, Rick Kosterman, J. David Hawkins, Todd Herrenkohl, Liliana Lengua, and Elizabeth McCauley, "Predicting Depression, Social Phobia, and Violence in Early Adulthood from Childhood Behavior Problems," *Journal of the American Academy of Child and Adolescent Psychiatry* 43 (2004): 307–315; Rolf Loeber and David Farrington, "Young Children Who Commit Crime: Epidemiology, Developmental Origins, Risk Factors, Early Interventions, and Policy Implications," *Development and Psychopathology* 12 (2000): 737–762; Patrick Lussier, Jean Proulx, and Marc LeBlanc, "Criminal Propensity, Deviant Sexual Interests and Criminal Activity of Sexual Aggressors Against Women: A Comparison of Explanatory Models," *Criminology* 43 (2005): 249–281.

49. Dawn Jeglum Bartusch, Donald Lynam, Terrie Moffitt, and Phil Silva, "Is Age Important? Testing a General versus a Developmental Theory of Antisocial Behavior," *Criminology* 35 (1997): 13–48.

50. Daniel Nagin and Richard Tremblay, "What Has Been Learned from Group-Based Trajectory Modeling? Examples from Physical Aggression and Other Problem Behaviors," *Annals of the American Academy of Political and Social Science* 602 (2005): 82–117.

51. Mason, Kosterman, Hawkins, Herrenkohl, Lengua, and McCauley, "Predicting Depression, Social Phobia, and Violence in Early Adulthood from Childhood Behavior Problems"; Ronald Prinz and Suzanne Kerns, "Early Substance Use by Juvenile Offenders," *Child Psychiatry and Human Development* 33 (2003): 263–268.

52. Bacon, Paternoster, and Brame, "Understanding the Relationship Between Onset Age and Subsequent Offending During Adolescence."

53. Glenn Clingempeel and Scott Henggeler, "Aggressive Juvenile Offenders Transitioning into Emerging Adulthood: Factors Discriminating Persistors and Desistors," *American Journal of Orthopsychiatry* 73 (2003): 310–323.

54. Mary Campa, Catherine Bradshaw, John Eckenrode, and David Zielinski, "Patterns of Problem Behavior in Relation to Thriving and Precocious Behavior in Late Adolescence," *Journal of Youth and Adolescence* 37 (2008): 627–640; Mason, Kosterman, Hawkins, Herrenkohl, Lengua, and McCauley, "Predicting Depression, Social Phobia, and Violence in Early Adulthood from Childhood Behavior Problems"; Loeber and Farrington, "Young Children Who Commit Crime"; Lussier, Proulx, and LeBlanc, "Criminal Propensity, Deviant Sexual Interests and Criminal Activity of Sexual Aggressors Against Women"; Clingempeel and Henggeler, "Aggressive Juvenile Offenders Transitioning into Emerging Adulthood: Factors Discriminating Persistors and Desistors."

55. Kristin Carbone-Lopez and Jody Miller, "Precocious Role Entry as a Mediating Factor in Women's Methamphetamine Use: Implications for Life-Course and Pathways Research," *Criminology* 50 (2012): 187–220.

56. David Gadd and Stephen Farrall, "Criminal Careers, Desistance and Subjectivity: Interpreting Men's Narratives of Change," *Theoretical Criminology* 8 (2004): 123–156.

57. G. R. Patterson, L. Crosby, and S. Vuchinich, "Predicting Risk for Early Police Arrest," *Journal of Quantitative Criminology* 8 (1992): 335–355.

10 INTERPERSONAL VIOLENCE

The leaders of a Dominican street gang in Lawrence, Massachusetts, known as the Joloperros (loosely translated as "the stick-up guys") thought they had the perfect illegal enterprise: kidnap drug dealers, bookmakers, and money launderers, steal their cash and drugs, and then hold them for ransom. After all, it seemed unlikely that the victims and their families, involved in criminal enterprise themselves, would report the abductions and get involved with police.

The gang members were organized, armed, and violent. They targeted anyone they thought would be able to pay large sums of money to be released. They used GPS devices to track individuals, conducted surveillance to learn targets' routes and movements, and also tried to identify dealers' stash houses. They did not target street-level dealers but rather suppliers who were selling multiple kilos of heroin and cocaine on a monthly basis. When the actual abductions took place, the crew would grab the victim, duct tape his hands, and put a cover over his head. Some were made to wear masks to hide their identity (the actual mask used by the gang is shown in the opening photo). Victims were taken to safe houses, and large ransoms were demanded from their families. If they did not cooperate immediately, the victims were tortured, sometimes with hot irons.

When the Joloperros' activities became known, the North Shore Gang Task Force—made up of the FBI, Massachusetts State Police, Lawrence Police Department, Massachusetts Department of Corrections, and federal Drug Enforcement Administration started to build a case against the crew. The investigation was hampered by the fact that victims and their families refused to cooperate, but eventually the case was broken when gang members held a gun to a victim, kidnapped him from a street in the Jamaica Plain neighborhood in Boston, and demanded a $100,000 ransom for the victim's release; they held the victim in Lawrence for five days. Law enforcement agents were alerted, the victim was rescued unharmed, and members of the crew were identified by fingerprint and DNA evidence.

After trial, the leader, Edgar Acevedo, 34, was sentenced to 16 years in prison and two years of supervised release; 20 other members were indicted. Before imposing sentence, Judge Nathaniel Gorton termed Acevedo's crime "heinous" and remarked:

> You deserve to be severely punished here because you played an integral role in a sophisticated, well-planned kidnapping that involved the use of violence, firearms, and an abduction for at least several days and the demand for and pursuit of a ransom after death threats. This kind of an egregious crime is rightly dealt with harshly in the sentencing guidelines, particularly to deter the commission of such crimes. And because you were part of the conspiracy to carry out this potentially deadly kidnapping, you are deserving of the long sentence you are about to receive. This sentence is intended not only to deter you from ever committing such a crime again but also to deter anyone else, whether engaged in drug trafficking or otherwise, from committing such dastardly crimes.[1]

The Joloperros case illustrates the toll violent crime takes on society in the United States. It can divide a community, damage reputations, and cause lifelong harm. It tells people that no matter where they go, they may encounter violent acts—at a movie theater, a public park, or walking down the street. No one is safe, not even drug dealers and hard-core criminals. Violence can be committed by gang boys and drug dealers but also husbands and wives, boyfriends and girlfriends. Some violent acts, such as the kidnappings and torture committed by the Joloperros are considered **instrumental violence**—acts designed to improve the financial or social position of the criminal. Others are termed **expressive violence**—acts that vent rage, anger, or frustration—such as a random shooting of a stranger. Media accounts of interpersonal violence cause people to live in fear, staying home at night and avoiding dangerous neighborhoods. It can also bring disorder to whole communities, disrupting services and driving down real estate values, further destabilizing areas already reeling from the shock of violent crimes.[2]

This chapter explores the concept of violence in some depth. First, it reviews the suggested causes of violent crime. Then it focuses on specific types of interpersonal violence—rape, homicide, assault, robbery, and newly recognized types of interpersonal violence such as stalking and workplace violence. Finally, it briefly examines political violence and terrorism.

The Causes of Violence

L01 Differentiate among the various causes of violent crime

What sets off a violent person? Criminologists have a variety of views on this subject. Some believe that violence is a function of human traits and makeup. Others point to improper socialization and upbringing. Violent behavior may be culturally determined and relate to dysfunctional social values. The various sources of violence are set out in Figure 10.1.

PSYCHOLOGICAL/BIOLOGICAL ABNORMALITY

On March 13, 1996, an ex-Scout leader named Thomas Hamilton took four automatic handguns into the primary school of the peaceful Scottish town of Dunblane and

instrumental violence Violence used in an attempt to improve the financial or social position of the criminal.

expressive violence Violence that is designed not for profit or gain but to vent rage, anger, or frustration.

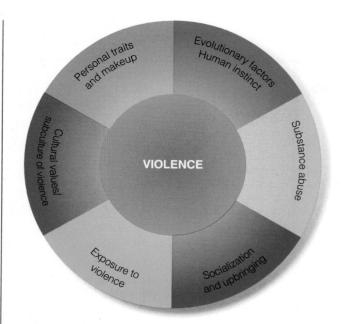

FIGURE 10.1 Sources of Violence

SOURCE: © Cengage Learning

slaughtered 16 kindergarten children and their teacher before taking his own life. This horrific crime shocked the British Isles into implementing strict controls on all guns.[3] Many of those in the school who were spared, such as tennis star Andy Murray, bear lifelong psychic scars from the tragedy.[4] Bizarre outbursts such as Hamilton's support a link between violence and some sort of mental or biological abnormality.

People who are involved in violent episodes may be suffering from severe mental abnormalities.[5] Psychologist Dorothy Otnow Lewis suggested that kids who kill may be suffering from multiple symptoms of psychological abnormality: neurological impairment (e.g., abnormal EEGs, multiple psychomotor impairments, and severe seizures), low intelligence, and psychotic symptoms such as paranoia, illogical thinking, and hallucinations.[6] In her now classic book *Guilty by Reason of Insanity*, Lewis found that death row inmates have a history of mental impairment and intellectual dysfunction.[7]

Lewis's research is not unique. Abnormal personality structures, including such traits as depression, impulsivity, aggression, dishonesty, pathological lying, lack of remorse, borderline personality syndrome, and psychopathology, have all been associated with various forms of violence, ranging from serial murder to elder abuse.[8] It comes as no surprise to psychologists that many murderers kill themselves shortly after committing their crime.[9]

There is also evidence that personality disturbance is linked to some physical trait or characteristic. Neuroscientists claim to have found differences in both the limbic system and the prefrontal cortex of the brain that separates aggressive, violent people from the more level-headed and reasonable. According to this view, if some defect or injury impairs communication between the limbic system and the frontal cortex, a person might not be entirely able to moderate his or her emotional reactions.[10] This view supports Lewis's findings: People convicted of murder have in fact been shown to suffer signs of neurological impairment (abnormal EEGs, psychomotor impairments, severe seizures), low intelligence as measured on standard IQ tests, psychotic close relatives, mental impairment and intellectual dysfunction, animal cruelty, and psychotic symptoms.[11]

If there is a connection between psychological instability and violence, does the availability of mental health treatment help reduce violence rates? A significant relationship has been found between mental health treatment opportunities and global crime rate trends. It is possible that a significant drop in the violence rate may be due to expanded mental health treatment.[12]

Shooting suspect James Holmes appears in court in Centennial, Colorado. Holmes killed 12 people and wounded dozens more at an Aurora, Colorado, movie theater in 2012. His lawyers claimed he was "in the throes of a psychotic episode" at the time. Does the frequency of mass killings by psychologically impaired criminals seem to be increasing? Or is this trend merely a function of the availability of high-powered weapons that make their violent outbursts ever more lethal?

AP Images/Andy Cross

HUMAN INSTINCT

Some anthropologists trace the roots of violence back to our prehistory, when our ancestors lived in social groups and fought for dominance. The earliest humans would not hesitate to retaliate violently against aggressors, and it was common for family, tribe, or clan members to protect one another if they were attacked.[13] According to Harvard psychologist Steven Pinker, the remains of earliest humans indicate that a significant number were the victims of violence rather than dying from natural causes. The violence declined during the period of human evolution when our hunter-gatherer ancestors began to settle into agricultural civilizations, which Pinker calls the pacification process.[14] About 15 percent of all tribe members died violently, compared to about 3 percent of the citizens of the earliest organized states or empires, when rulers created and sustained men at arms to protect the population from harm.

The fact that our ancient ancestors were so violent seems to suggest that violence is instinctual and part of the human condition. Sigmund Freud believed that human behavior is shaped by two instinctual drives: *eros*, the life instinct, which drives people toward self-fulfillment and enjoyment, and *thanatos*, the death instinct, which produces self-destruction. Thanatos can be expressed externally (e.g., violence and sadism) or internally (e.g., suicide, alcoholism, or other self-destructive habits).[15]

In his celebrated book *On Aggression*, anthropologist Konrad Lorenz argued that aggressive energy is produced by inbred instincts that are independent of environmental forces.[16] In the animal kingdom, aggression usually serves a productive purpose—for example, it leads members of grazing species such as zebras and antelopes to spread out over available territory to ensure an ample food supply and the survival of the fittest. Lorenz found that humans possess some of the same aggressive instincts as animals. But within lower species, aggression is rarely fatal; when a conflict occurs, the winner is determined through a test of skill or endurance. This inhibition against killing members of their own species protects animals from self-extinction. Humans, lacking this inhibition against fatal violence, are capable of killing their own kind in war or as a result of interpersonal conflicts such as those arising over finding suitable mates.[17] Lorenz feared that as technology develops and more lethal weapons are produced, the extinction of the human species becomes a significant possibility. As the Criminology in

Violence and Human Nature

04

In his important work *Violence: A Micro-sociological Theory*, sociologist Randall Collins proposes a theory of violence that seems diametrically opposed to Lorenz: humans are inherently passive, and violence is a function of social interaction. Collins argues that most humans shrink from violence and even those who are verbally aggressive are fearful and tense during violent encounters. Humans typically resort to violence only when they have overwhelming superiority over their opponents in terms of arms and numbers. While the thought of violence makes most people weak and scared, a supportive audience helps it become more palatable. Whether it's gang boys acting in a group or terrorists being supported by their leaders, violence is more of a group process than an individual choice.

Collins finds that the myth that humans enjoy bloodshed is perpetuated by media depictions of violence. Take for instance the barroom brawl shown in numerous films. A fight breaks out in a bar and soon everyone joins in, joyously punching one another and breaking up the premises. If the crowd doesn't join in, they generally will make a space for the individuals to fight, cheering and shouting encouragement from the sidelines. Fights are drawn out with two evenly matched opponents punching each other for long periods of combat. While normative in the movies, Collins points out that these events never

actually happen in real life. When a fight does break out, most patrons typically back away as far as possible and watch from a safe distance. Rather than shouting encouragement, onlookers tend to withdraw vocally as well as physically. And rather than drawn-out brawls, fights are over quickly, typically with a single punch.

If violence is against human nature and not normative, what enables some people to become violent? The core of Collins's micro-sociological theory is the concept of "confrontational tension." When antagonistic interactions occur, the prospective combatants begin to feel tension and fear, emotions that will typically dampen their martial spirit; these emotions form a roadblock to violence. In order to engage in violence, people must find a pathway around this roadblock, leading them into a "tunnel of violence." There are several pathways into this tunnel, one being "forward panic." In these situations, confrontational tension builds up and is suddenly and violently released, allowing people to engage in inexplicable atrocities. "A forward panic," Collins states, "is a zone in time where the emotional impulses are overwhelming, above all because they are shared by everyone: by one's supporters and fellow attackers, and in a reciprocal way, by the passive victims." Forward panics may occur when police confront an aggressive suspect and a beating occurs, or when sports fans riot when their team wins

(or loses). Other pathways that open to relieve confrontational tension are to attack a weak victim or to be encouraged by an audience to do violence. These pathways can be interactive: a bully is encouraged by a crowd to beat up a weaker student. So, though most brawlers are willing to quit without a clear-cut victory as soon as a few punches are launched, a fight can get out of hand when there is a group brawl and people are encouraging violent confrontations. Prior organization, group identity, and support, Collins finds, are what enable individuals to overcome their own pervasive fear of violence and confrontation; if it were not well organized, wide-participation group fighting would not be possible.

 CRITICAL THINKING

1. What is your immediate reaction when violence breaks out: flee or fight? Do you agree with Collins that most of us are not violent by nature and will only resort to aggressive behavior under the most extreme circumstances?
2. How do we explain the behavior of people drawn to terrorist groups if violence is neither instinctual nor normative?

SOURCE: Randall Collins, *Violence: A Micro-sociological Theory* (Princeton, NJ: Princeton University Press, 2008).

Action feature "Violence and Human Nature" suggests, not all criminologists are convinced that Lorenz's views on violence are correct.

 To learn more about Konrad Lorenz, who won the Nobel Prize in Medicine in 1973, go to **https://www.nobelprize.org/nobel_prizes/medicine/laureates/1973/lorenz-bio.html**.

Do you think humans are aggressive by nature? If not, why have we been so violent since the beginning of time? Why are we constantly involved in war and conquest?

SUBSTANCE ABUSE

Substance abuse has been associated with violence on both the individual and social levels: substance abusers have higher rates of violence than non-abusers; neighborhoods with high levels of substance abuse have higher violence rates when compared to areas with low use rates.[18] A direct association has been found between community levels of crack cocaine and heroin use and the incidence of street robberies.[19] High-use areas may also face social disorganization, poverty, and unemployment, factors that further escalate violence rates.[20]

The link between substance abuse and violence appears in three different formats:[21]

- *Psychopharmacological relationship.* Violence may be the direct consequence of ingesting mood-altering substances.[22] High doses of drugs such as PCP and amphetamines and the binge drinking of alcohol produce violent, aggressive behavior and are associated with violent crime rates.[23] Heavy drinking reduces cognitive ability, information processing skills, and the ability to process and react to verbal and nonverbal behavior. As a result, miscommunication becomes more likely and the capacity for rational dialogue is compromised.[24] It is not surprising that males involved in sexual assaults often claim that they were drinking and misunderstood their victims' intentions.[25] Drinking becomes particularly dangerous when abusers have access to firearms; guns and alcohol do not mix well.[26] When Eric Sevigny and Andrea Allen used survey data collected from incarcerated inmates they found that while, surprisingly, most drug market participants do not routinely use firearms to commit crimes, those who were under the influence at the time they committed the crime were also the ones most likely to be carrying. They speculate that drug use induces a reactive or brazen temperament among drug market participants that increases the likelihood of gun possession.[27]
- *Economic compulsive behavior.* Drug users resort to violence to obtain the financial resources to support their habit. Studies conducted in the United States and Europe show that addicts commit hundreds of crimes each year.[28]
- *Systemic link.* Violence escalates when drug-dealing gangs flex their muscle to dominate territory and drive out rivals. Those involved in the sale of illicit drugs in urban street markets face an elevated risk for serious victimization. Despite their fierce image, drug dealers are not immune to violence from robbers who realize they carry a lot of cash and cannot call the police when they are victimized. Only those dealers who are very active in the drug market and willing to use violence to protect their turf are immune from violent victimization; there are actually less aggressive dealers who are fair game for armed robbers.[29]

SOCIALIZATION AND UPBRINGING

Another view is that improper socialization and upbringing are responsible for the onset of violent acts. Absent or deviant parents, inconsistent discipline, physical abuse, and lack of supervision have all been linked to persistent violent offending.[30]

Although infants demonstrate individual temperaments, who they become may have a lot to do with how they are treated during their early years. Some children are harder to soothe than others; in some cases, difficult infant temperament has been associated with later aggression and behavioral problems.[31] Parents who fail to set adequate limits or

to use proper, consistent discipline reinforce a child's coercive behavior.[32] The effects of inadequate parenting and early rejection may affect violent behavior throughout life.[33]

Abuse and Violence   There are also indications that children who are subject to even minimal amounts of physical punishment may be more likely one day to use violence themselves.[34] Sociologist Murray Straus reviewed the concept of discipline in a series of surveys and found a powerful relationship between exposure to physical punishment and later aggression.[35] We now know that the more often a child is physically disciplined and the harsher the punishment, the more likely he or she will later engage in antisocial behaviors.[36] When kids experience physical punishment they feel angry and unjustly treated and are more willing to defy their parents and engage in antisocial behavior.[37] Abuse has long-term effects: physical abuse leads to childhood antisocial behavior and later to adult criminality; emotional abuse is directly related to adult antisocial behavior. The more intense and longer lasting the abuse, the more likely the later occurrence of adult criminality.[38]

In a series of research studies, criminologist Cathy Spatz Widom identified a **cycle of violence**, in which physical abuse by parents or caregivers is a direct cause of subsequent violent behavior among youth.[39] Kids who were abused are then likely to grow up to be abusers themselves, creating a never-ending cycle of abuse and violence. They are significantly more likely to be arrested for violent crime sometime during their life course.

The abuse–violence link can take different forms. Some violent offenders have long histories of abuse and neglect and this condition is a direct conduit to their personal involvement in violence. Others develop posttraumatic stress disorder (PTSD) in the aftermath of their abuse; their subsequent violence can be linked to the emotional upheaval brought on by their history of personal traumas. Whatever its form, the abuse–violence association is quite significant.[40]

Since Widom's pioneering efforts, there has been a significant amount of research supporting the cycle of violence concept, showing that people who suffer abuse in childhood and adolescence are more likely to get involved in violent behavior as teens and adults.[41] Not surprisingly, abused kids also experience involvement with the juvenile justice system.[42] People who have been abused are 59 percent more likely to be arrested as a juvenile, 28 percent more likely to be arrested as an adult, and 30 percent more likely to commit violent crime as the non-abused. As many as two-thirds of the people in treatment for drug abuse reported being abused or neglected as children.[43]

cycle of violence A hypothesis that suggests that a childhood history of physical abuse predisposes survivors to becoming violent themselves in later years.

There are also distinct class and gender patterns in the abuse–crime association. Lower-class children are more likely to be mistreated than those in the upper and middle classes; abused boys are at greater risk to commit crime than are girls. Children suffering sexual abuse have a greater chance of getting involved in crime and substance abuse than those who are physically abused.[44]

Ironically, while lower-class youth suffer abuse more than their upper- and middle-class peers, it seems to have less effect. One reason: abuse and violence may be more common in lower-class neighborhoods, more culturally accepted, and therefore may have less of an effect on its targets, who view themselves and their upbringing as normative.[45]

Of course, not all abused children become violent criminals. Many do not, and many violent youths come from what appear to be model homes.[46] Widom herself finds that the majority of both abused and non-abused kids do not engage in antisocial behavior, so more research is needed to clarify this very important association.

 LO2 Articulate the stages in Athens's violentization process

The Violentization Process Lonnie Athens, a well-known criminologist who links violence to early experiences with child abuse, has coined the phrase **violentization process** to describe how abused kids are turned into aggressive adults.[47] The stages of this process are described in Exhibit 10.1. Athens recognizes that abuse alone is not a sufficient condition to cause someone to become a dangerous violent criminal. One must complete the full cycle of the violentization process—brutalization, belligerence, violent performances, and virulency—to become socialized into violence. Many brutalized children do not go on to become violent criminals, and some later reject the fact that they were abused as youths and redefine their early years as normative.

EXPOSURE TO VIOLENCE

People who are constantly exposed to violence in the environment may adopt violent methods themselves.[48] Children living in areas marked by extreme violence may eventually become desensitized to the persistent brutality.[49]

In disadvantaged neighborhoods people of all ages are exposed to violence on a routine basis.[50] Much of the difference in violent crime rates between whites and racial minorities can be explained by the fact that the latter are often

violentization process According to Lonnie Athens, the process by which abused children are turned into aggressive adults. This process takes violent youths full circle from being the victims of aggression to being its initiators; they are now the same person they grew up despising, ready to begin the process with their own children.

forced to live in poverty areas, which increases their risk of exposure to violence.[51] Areas where people have little confidence in the police and are therefore reluctant to call for help—a condition common in the minority community—may also experience higher levels of violent behavior.[52]

In a famous study, social scientist Felton Earls conducted interviews with youths ages 9 to 15 in Chicago neighborhoods and found that large numbers of these children have been victims of or witnesses to violence.[53] Between 30 and 40 percent of the children who reported exposure to violence also displayed significant violent behavior themselves. Other research efforts support Earls's conclusions: even a single exposure to firearm violence doubles the chance that a young person will later engage in violent behavior.[54]

Children living in these conditions become **crusted over**: they do not let people inside nor do they express their feelings. They exploit others and in turn are exploited by those older and stronger; as a result, they develop a sense of hopelessness. They find that parents and teachers focus on their failures and problems, not their achievements. Consequently, they are vulnerable to the lure of delinquent gangs and groups.[55]

CULTURAL VALUES: SUBCULTURE OF VIOLENCE

Violence may be the product of cultural beliefs, values, and behaviors that develop in poor and disorganized neighborhoods.[56] In a classic work, criminologists Marvin Wolfgang and Franco Ferracuti formulated the famous concept that some areas contain an independent **subculture of violence**.[57]

The subculture of violence's norms are separate from society's central, dominant value system. In this subculture, a potent theme of violence influences lifestyles, the socialization process, and interpersonal relationships. Even though the subculture's members share some of the dominant culture's values, they expect that violence will be used to solve social conflicts and dilemmas. In some cultural subgroups, then, violence has become legitimized by custom and norms. It is considered appropriate behavior within culturally defined conflict situations in which an individual who has been offended by a negative outcome in a dispute seeks reparations through violent means—a concept referred to as **disputatiousness**.[58]

There is evidence that a subculture of violence may be found in areas that experience concentrated poverty and social disorganization.[59] Though most people abhor violence, income inequality and racial disparity may help instill a sense of hopelessness that nourishes pro-violence norms and values.[60] In these areas people are more likely to carry weapons and use them in assaults and robberies. Victims are aware of these tactics and are less likely to fight back forcibly when attacked.[61] However, when pressed to the limit, even passive victims may eventually fight back. When Charis Kubrin and Ronald Weitzer studied homicide

in St. Louis, Missouri, they discovered that a certain type of killing referred to as *cultural retaliatory homicide* is common in neighborhoods that suffer economic disadvantage. In these areas, residents resolve interpersonal conflicts informally—without calling the police—even if it means killing their opponent; neighbors understand and support their violent methods.[62] Because police and other agencies of formal social control are viewed as weak and devalued, understaffed and/or corrupt, people are willing to take matters into their own hands and violence rates increase accordingly.[63]

The Gang Subculture Empirical evidence shows that violence rates are highest in urban areas where subcultural values support teenage gangs whose members typically embrace the use of violence.[64] Gang boys are more likely to own guns and other weapons than non–gang members. They are also more likely to have peers who are gun owners and are more likely to carry guns outside the home.[65]

While many boys are predisposed toward violence before joining a gang, research shows that once in gangs their violent behavior quickly escalates; after they leave, it significantly declines.[66] Andrew Papachristos finds that members do not kill because they are poor, young, or live in a socially disadvantaged neighborhood, but rather because they live in a culture that maintains norms conducive to violent retaliation.[67] When a gang boy kills a rival, murders spread through a process of social contagion as gangs are forced to respond in order to maintain their social status and honor through a display of solidarity. The culture that houses gangs associates honor with hypermasculinity and the use of violence to protect reputation. Because formal social control (i.e., the police) is absent in gang areas, violence is condoned or promoted as an acceptable form of social control. The need to conform to cultural values and to protect the gang's rep is more important than individual thoughts and feelings. While some may link gang violence to "turf wars," disputes that lead to murder are less about a parcel of land than about a gang's status and perceived dominance.

CULTURAL VALUES: NATIONAL VALUES

Some nations—including Colombia, Brazil, Sri Lanka, Angola, Uganda, and the Philippines—have relatively high

crusted over Children who have been victims of or witnesses to violence and do not let people inside, nor do they express their feelings. They exploit others and in turn are exploited by those older and stronger; as a result, they develop a sense of hopelessness.

subculture of violence Norms and customs that, in contrast to society's dominant value system, legitimize and expect the use of violence to resolve social conflicts.

disputatiousness Behavior within culturally defined conflict situations in which an individual who has been offended by a negative outcome in a dispute seeks reparations through violent means.

violence rates, while others, such as Japan, are relatively nonviolent. There are two possible explanations for this discrepancy. One is that nations with high violence rates embrace value structures that support violence, while those that have a strong communitarian spirit and an emphasis on forgiveness and restorative justice have low violence rates.[68]

The other view is that nations with high violence rates also have negative structural factors such as a high level of poverty, income inequality, illiteracy, and alcohol consumption, and it is these components, rather than a regional culture of violence, that produce high crime rates.[69]

Does the United States Maintain Values that Promote Violence? In a recent front page story, a group of *New York Times* reporters gathered and analyzed data on the 358 shootings in 2015 that resulted in four or more casualties.[70] These incidents—nearly one per day—left 462 people dead and 1,330 injured. Few made the national headlines. Most followed some minor local conflict or interaction that occurred in an outdoor location: at a neighborhood barbecue, family reunion, music festival, basketball tournament, movie theater, housing project courtyard, teen party, or public park. Roughly half involved crime or gang activity, while others stemmed from interpersonal conflicts that spun out of control; domestic disputes often led to mass violence. The typical victim was a male between 18 and 30, but more than 1 in 10 were 17 or younger.

Most of the shootings occurred in economically downtrodden neighborhoods. Of the zip codes where four or more people were shot during a single encounter in 2015, 86 percent are poorer than the nation as a whole. There was also a racial element to these shootings. While domestic violence incidents and mass shootings tended to involve white shooters, nearly three-fourths of victims and suspected assailants were black; African Americans die from gun attacks at 6 to 10 times the rate of whites.

Why does the United States suffer a mass shooting almost every day? Is this a function of our own culture and national values? According to historian David Courtwright, relatively high violence rates in the United States can be traced to a frontier culture that was characterized by racism and preoccupation with personal honor.[71] Westerners drank heavily and frequented saloons and gambling halls, where petty arguments could become lethal because most patrons carried guns and knives. Violent acts often went unpunished because law enforcement agencies were unable or unwilling to take action. The population of the frontier was mostly young bachelors who were sensitive about honor, morally indifferent, heavily armed, and unchecked by adequate law enforcement. Many died from disease, but others succumbed to drink and violence. Smoking, gambling, and heavy drinking became a cultural imperative, and those who were disinclined to indulge were considered social outcasts. Courtwright claims that over time gender ratios equalized as more men brought families to the frontier and children of both sexes were born. Many men died, returned home, or drifted elsewhere. By the mid-twentieth century, America's overall male surplus was disappearing, and a balanced population helped bring down the crime rate, but remnants of the frontier mentality still exist in contemporary American society.

Rape

 L03 Discuss the history of rape and the different types of rape and rapists

Rape (from the Latin *rapere*, to take by force) is defined in common law as "the carnal knowledge of a female forcibly and against her will."[72] It is one of the most loathed, misunderstood, and frightening crimes. Under traditional common-law definitions, rape involves nonconsensual sexual intercourse that a male performs against a female he is neither married to nor cohabitating with.[73] There are of course other forms of sexual assault, including male on male, female on female, and female on male sexual assaults, but these are not considered within the traditional definition of rape.[74] However, recognizing changing contemporary standards, almost every state and the federal government (as in the Uniform Crime Reports) have now revised their rape statutes, making them gender neutral and including other forms of sexual assault beyond nonconsensual sexual intercourse.[75] In addition, states now recognize that rape can occur among married couples and people who previously have been sexually intimate.[76] And of course, regardless of what form it takes, rape has long-term effects on the victim's emotional and physical well-being.[77]

HISTORY OF RAPE

Rape has been a recognized crime throughout history. It has been the subject of art, literature, film, and theater. Paintings such as *The Rape of the Sabine Women* by Nicolas Poussin, novels such as *Clarissa* by Samuel Richardson, poems such as *The Rape of Lucrece* by William Shakespeare, and films such as *The Girl with the Dragon Tattoo* and *The General's Daughter* have sexual violence as a central theme.

In early civilization rape was common. Men staked a claim of ownership on women by forcibly abducting and raping them. This practice led to males' solidification of power and their historical domination of women.[78] Under Babylonian and Hebraic law, the rape of a virgin was a crime punishable by death. However, if the victim was married, then both she and her attacker were considered equally to blame, and unless her husband intervened, both were put to death.

During the Middle Ages, it was common for ambitious men to abduct and rape wealthy women in an effort to force them into marriage. The practice of "heiress stealing" illustrates how feudal law gave little thought or protection to women and equated them with property.[79] Only in the late fifteenth century, after a monetary economy developed, was forcible sex outlawed. Thereafter, the violation of a virgin caused an economic hardship on her family, who expected a significant dowry for her hand in marriage. However, the law only applied to the wealthy; peasant women and married women were not considered rape victims until well into the sixteenth century. The Christian condemnation of sex during this period was also a denunciation of women as evil, having lust in their hearts, and redeemable only by motherhood. A woman who was raped was almost automatically suspected of contributing to her attack.

RAPE AND WAR

The link between the military and rape is inescapable. Throughout recorded history, rape has been associated with armies and warfare. Soldiers of conquering armies have considered sexual possession of their enemies' women one of the spoils of war. Among the ancient Greeks, rape was socially acceptable within the rules of warfare. During the Crusades, even knights and pilgrims, ostensibly bound by vows of chivalry and Christian piety, took time to rape as they marched toward Constantinople.

The belief that women are part of the spoils of war has continued. During World War II, the Japanese army forced as many as 200,000 Korean women into frontline brothels, where they were repeatedly raped. In a 1998 Japanese ruling, the surviving Korean women were awarded the equivalent of $2,300 each in compensation.[80] Russian soldiers routinely raped German women as they marched to Berlin in 1945. By the end of World War II millions had been raped, including least 1.4 million women in East Prussia, Pomerania, and Silesia alone.[81]

The use of rape as a weapon of war did not end with World War II. The systematic rape of Bosnian and Kosovar women by Serbian army officers during the civil war in the former Yugoslavia horrified the world in the 1990s. These crimes seemed particularly atrocious because they appeared to be part of an official policy of genocide: rape was deliberately used to impregnate Bosnian women with Serbian children.

On March 9, 1998, Dragoljub Kunarac, 37, a former Bosnian Serb paramilitary commander, admitted before an international tribunal in the Netherlands that he had raped Muslim women during the Bosnian war in 1992. His confession made him the first person to plead guilty to rape as a war crime.[82] Human rights groups have estimated that more than 30,000 women and young girls were sexually abused in the Balkan fighting.

Though shocking, the war crimes discovered in Bosnia have not deterred conquering armies from using rape as a weapon. In 2004, pro-government militias in the Darfur region of Sudan were accused of using rape and other forms of sexual violence "as a weapon of war" to humiliate black African women and girls as well as the rebels fighting the Sudanese government in Khartoum.[83] In April 2014, the Nigerian terror group Boko Haram kidnapped 276 high school girls with the intent of selling them into sexual slavery, an act that prompted worldwide outrage; fewer than 60 girls have been found or rescued.[84] Members of the terror group ISIL were given a free hand to rape captured Yazidi women after being told that this would turn these followers of a unique religion that blends elements of Islam, Judaism, and Christianity into Muslims.[85]

In a provocative article, Eileen Zurbriggen proposes that rape is prevalent during war because military socialization emphasizes elements of hypermasculinity that produce both conditions: status and achievement; toughness and aggression; restricted emotionality; and power, dominance, and control. She argues that society's need for effective soldiers is the root cause of traditional masculine socialization and that this socialization ensures that rape will be prevalent.[86]

INCIDENCE OF RAPE

According to the most recent UCR data, about 84,000 rapes or attempted rapes are now being reported to U.S. police each year, a rate of about 30 per 100,000 inhabitants.[87] According to the NCVS, about 285,000 people are the victims of rape and sexual assault each year.[88]

Like other violent crimes, the rape rate had been in a decade-long decline, but preliminary 2015 data indicate that the number of rapes increased by about 1 percent over the prior year using the traditional definition and 9.6 percent if the new definition (penetration, no matter how slight, of the vagina or anus with any body part or object, or oral penetration by a sex organ of another person, without the consent of the victim) is employed. Whether this increase in the incidence of rape is the beginning of a long-term trend remains to be seen.

While the overwhelming percentage of rape victims are female, hundreds of men report being sexually assaulted each year. One significant difference: while women most often are attacked by strangers, almost every male rape involves a friend or acquaintance. Male sexual victimization is most common among a small strata of men that includes gay and bisexual men, veterans, inmates, and men seeking mental and physical health services.[89]

Population density influences the rape rate. Metropolitan areas today have rape rates significantly higher than rural areas; nonetheless, urban areas have experienced a much greater drop in rape reports than rural areas. The police make arrests in about 40 percent of all reported rape offenses. Of the offenders arrested, typically about half are under 25 years of age, and about two-thirds are white. The racial and age pattern of rape arrests has been fairly consistent for some time. Finally, rape is a warm-weather crime—most incidents occur during July and August, with the lowest rates occurring during December, January, and February.

Underreporting Rape   Rape is a traditionally underreported crime, and some criminologists estimate that as many as 10 percent of all adult women may have been raped during their lifetime.[90] In one important study, Dean Kilpatrick and his research team surveyed more than 5,000 women across the nation and found that 18 percent of women in the United States have been raped; this amounts to more than 25 million women. Only 16 percent of all rapes were reported to law enforcement authorities, helping to explain the discrepancy between NCVS findings and UCR data.[91]

Why is rape, one of the most serious violent crimes, also one of the most underreported? Many victims fail to report rapes because they are embarrassed, believe nothing can be done, or blame themselves. Some victims of sexual assaults may even question whether they have really been raped; research indicates that when the assault involves an acquaintance, such as a boyfriend, and the victim had been drinking or taking drugs, they are unlikely to label their situations as being a "real" rape. Similarly, if the assault involved oral or digital sex it is less likely to be labeled a "real" rape.[92] Women are more likely to report rape when it is committed by a stranger who uses a weapon or causes physical injury, or when the rape occurred in a public place—or if at home, was the result of "home blitz" (in which an attacker broke in or entered without permission).[93] Therefore it is likely that many acquaintance rapes and date rapes go unreported.

There may be many more rape victims than the official data allow.[94] But even if victims fail to acknowledge that their attack was "real" and refuse to report it to the police, the experience can have a long-lasting psychological effect.[95]

TYPES OF RAPE AND RAPISTS

Some rapes are planned, others are spontaneous; some focus on a particular victim, whereas others occur almost as an afterthought during the commission of another crime, such as a burglary. Some rapists commit a single crime, whereas others are multiple offenders; some attack alone, and others engage in group or gang rapes.[96] Some use force to attack their target, others prey upon those who are incapacitated by drugs and alcohol.[97] Because there is no single type of rape or rapist, criminologists have attempted to define and categorize the vast variety of rape situations.

Criminologists now recognize that there are numerous motivations for rape and as a result various types of rapists. There are many different typologies of rape and one of the best known is the classic work of psychologist A. Nicholas Groth, an expert on classifying and treating sex offenders. According to Groth, every rape encounter contains at least one of these three elements: anger, power, and sadism.[98]

gang rape Forcible sex involving multiple attackers.

serial rape Multiple rapes committed by one person over time.

EXHIBIT 10.2

Varieties of Forcible Rape

- *Anger rape.* This rape occurs when sexuality becomes a means of expressing and discharging pent-up anger and rage. The rapist uses far more brutality than would have been necessary if his real objective had been simply to have sex with his victim. His aim is to hurt his victim as much as possible; the sexual aspect of rape may be an afterthought.
- *Power rape.* This type of rape involves an attacker who does not want to harm his victim as much as he wants to possess her sexually. His goal is sexual conquest, and he uses only the amount of force necessary to achieve his objective. The power rapist wants to be in control, to be able to dominate women and have them at his mercy.
- *Sadistic rape.* This type of rape involves both sexuality and aggression. The sadistic rapist is caught up in ritual—he may torment his victim, bind her, or torture her. Victims are usually related, in the rapist's view, to a personal characteristic that he wants to harm or destroy.

SOURCE: A. Nicholas Groth and Jean Birnbaum, *Men Who Rape* (New York: Plenum Press, 1979).

Consequently, rapists can be classified according to one of the three dimensions described in Exhibit 10.2. In treating rape offenders, Groth found that about 55 percent were of the power type; about 40 percent, the anger type; and about 5 percent, the sadistic type.[99]

Gang Rape   Research studies estimate that as many as 25 percent or more of rapes involve multiple offenders.[100] There is generally little difference in the demographic characteristics of single- or multiple-victim rapes. However, women who are attacked by multiple offenders are subject to more violence, such as beatings and the use of weapons, and the rapes are more likely to be completed than individual rapes. **Gang rape** victims are more likely to resist and face injury than those attacked by single offenders. They are more likely to call police, to seek therapy, and to contemplate suicide. Gang rapes then, as might be expected, are more severe in violence and outcome.

Serial Rape   Some rapists are one-time offenders, but others engage in multiple or **serial rapes**. Some serial rapists constantly increase their use of force; others do not. Increasers (about 25 percent of serial rapists) tend to be white males who attack multiple victims who are typically older than the norm. During these attacks, the rapist uses excessive profanity and takes more time than during typical rapes. Increasers have a limited criminal history for other crimes, a fact suggesting that their behavior is focused almost solely on sexual violence.[101]

Some serial rapists commit "blitz rapes," in which they attack their victims without warning, whereas others try to "capture" their victims by striking up a conversation or offering them a ride. Others use personal or professional relationships to gain access to their targets.[102]

Acquaintance Rape   **Acquaintance rape** involves someone known to the victim, including family members and friends. Included within acquaintance rapes are the subcategories of **date rape**, which involves a sexual attack during a courting relationship; **statutory rape**, in which the victim is underage; and **marital rape**, which is forcible sex between people who are legally married to each other.[103] It is difficult to estimate the ratio between rapes involving strangers and those in which victim and assailant are in some way acquainted because women may be more reluctant to report acts involving acquaintances. By some estimates, about 50 percent of rapes involve acquaintances, a number that is not surprising considering the prevalence of negative attitudes toward women and attitudes that support sexual coercion among some groups of young men.[104]

Stranger rapes are typically more violent than acquaintance rapes; attackers are more likely to carry a weapon, threaten the victim, and harm her physically. Stranger rapes may also be less likely to be prosecuted than acquaintance rapes because victims may be more reluctant to recount their ordeal at trial if the attack involved a stranger than if their attacker was someone they knew or had been involved with in an earlier relationship.[105]

Date Rape   Date rape was first identified as a significant social problem in the 1980s when Mary Koss conducted surveys finding that a significant number of college-age women had been sexually assaulted by a dating partner; about 27 percent of the respondents were the victim of rape or attempted rape. However, only about a quarter of the women considered what had happened to them "real" rape; the majority either blamed themselves or denied they had really been raped.[106] The Koss research helped identify a social problem that all too long had remained below the radar.

There is no single form of date rape. Some occur on first dates, others after a relationship has been developing, and still others occur after the couple has been involved for some time. In long-term or close relationships, the male partner may feel he has invested so much time and money in his partner that he is owed sexual relations or that sexual intimacy is an expression that the involvement is progressing. He may make comparisons to other couples who have dated as long and are sexually active.[107] Some use a variety of strategies to coerce sex, including getting their dates drunk, threatening them with termination of the relationship, threatening to disclose negative information, making them feel guilty, or uttering false promises (i.e., "we'll get engaged") to obtain sex.[108]

The actual incidence of date rape may be even higher than surveys indicate because many victims blame themselves and do not recognize the incident as a rape, saying, for example, "I should have fought back harder" or "I shouldn't have gotten drunk."[109] Victims tend to have histories of excessive drinking and prior sexuality, conditions which may convince them that their intemperate and/or immoderate behavior contributed to their own victimization.[110] Some victims do not report rapes because they do not view their experience as a real rape, which, they believe, involves a strange man "jumping out of the bushes." Other victims are embarrassed and frightened. Many will tell their friends about their rape but refuse to let authorities know what happened. Reporting is most common in the most serious cases, such as when a weapon is used; it is less common when drugs and alcohol are involved.[111]

Rape on Campus   In 2016, Brock Turner, a Stanford University student and champion swimmer, was convicted on charges of intent to commit rape of an intoxicated/unconscious person, penetration of an intoxicated person, and penetration of an unconscious person. For his attack on a 23-year-old female student behind a dumpster, Turner was sentenced to only six months behind bars. The controversial sentence received national attention when two letters hit the Internet. The first was from the victim, who described her ordeal, the pain and suffering she endured, and how it changed her life. She wrote of her humiliating examination in a local hospital and said, "After a few hours of this, they let me shower. I stood there examining my body beneath the stream of water and decided, I don't want my body anymore. I was terrified of it, I didn't know what had been in it, if it had been contaminated, who had touched it. I wanted to take off my body like a jacket and leave it at the hospital with everything else."

The other letter was from Turner's father, who dismissed his son's crime as "20 minutes of action" and made it sound like he considered his son the real victim. Adding fuel to the fire, Santa Clara County Superior Court Judge Aaron Persky said that Turner's age and lack of criminal history made him feel that imposing a six-month jail sentence with probation was appropriate; Turner also has to register as a sex offender. "A prison sentence would have a severe impact on him," Persky wrote. "I think he will not be a danger to others."[112] Incensed at what they considered to be a very lenient punishment, more than 1 million people signed a

---

acquaintance rape Forcible sex in which offender and victim are acquainted with each other.

date rape Forcible sex during a courting relationship.

statutory rape Sexual relations between an underage individual and an adult; though not coerced, an underage partner is considered incapable of giving informed consent.

marital rape Forcible sex between people who are legally married to each other.

petition calling for the judge's ouster. The case acquired so much national attention that Vice President Joe Biden felt compelled to write a public letter in support of the victim.

Brock Turner's victim is not alone. A great deal of date and acquaintance rape is committed on college campuses. One recent survey of college women found that 15 to 30 percent of all college women are victims of rape or attempted rape; 27 percent of the sample had experienced unwanted sexual contact ranging from kissing and petting to sexual intercourse.[113] But some women, especially those in marginalized populations such as lesbian and transgendered, may even be more vulnerable than the norm. For instance, recent research found that within a sample of female undergraduate students who are hearing impaired, more than two-thirds (69 percent) experienced at least one assault and more than half (56 percent) experienced multiple assaults.[114]

Despite their prevalence, many rapes on college campuses go unreported; relatively few victims (less than 20 percent) report the incident to police. A recent survey by the Bureau of Justice Statistics found that rape and sexual assault victimizations were more likely to go unreported to police among victims who were college students (80 percent) than nonstudents (67 percent); in both groups far less than half of the incidents were reported.[115]

One reason for underreporting may be that many campus police officers are not sensitive to rape victims and believe in "rape myths" that the victim is somehow responsible for the assault or that they made it up to conceal consensual sex.[116] Campus police are less likely to believe victims who admitted drinking before the attack or who knew their attacker. In contrast, campus police officers who attend training on victim sensitivity, the trauma of victimization, the identification of drug-facilitated sexual assaults, and the role of alcohol and/or intoxication in sexual assault were significantly less likely to accept rape myths than those who had not received such training.[117]

Another reason for the limited reporting of campus rapes is that many incidents, many of which occur in fraternity houses and dorms, involve the victim's voluntary involvement in drinking or substance abuse before the assault occurred, and therefore victims hold themselves somewhat responsible for the attack; they may not believe the incident was a "real" rape because they were at fault. Misplaced guilt may also explain why so many college women suffer PTSD and other disorders soon after they were attacked. And when they do report rape and file a lawsuit against the frat house or university, the defense is to blame the victim: if she had not been drinking and taking risks, the attack would never have occurred.

Yet another reason for the lack of reporting may be that colleges and universities are notorious for trying to sweep sexual assault incidents under the rug to protect their image of a safe environment for young women—this despite the protections of Title IX of the Education Amendments of 1972, a federal civil rights law that prohibits discrimination on the basis of sex in any education program or activity that receives federal funding.[118] Under Title IX, discrimination on the basis of sex can include sexual harassment, rape, and sexual assault. A college or university that receives federal funds may be held legally responsible when it knows about and ignores sexual harassment or assault in its programs or activities. The school can be held responsible whether the harassment is committed by a faculty member, staff, or a student.[119] Despite this injunction, critics claim that schools either fail to prosecute miscreants or treat them with a slap on the wrist—making them send a letter of apology or perform a community service. Even these sanctions may not be enforced.

The Profiles in Crime feature discusses a notorious case of rape on campus.

Marital Rape   In 1978, Greta Rideout filed rape charges against her husband, John. This Oregon case grabbed headlines because it was the first in which a husband was prosecuted for raping his wife while sharing a residence with her. John was acquitted, and the couple briefly reconciled; later, continued violent episodes culminated in divorce and a jail term for John.[120]

Traditionally, a legally married husband could not be charged with raping his wife; this was referred to as the **marital exemption**. The origin of this legal doctrine can be traced to the sixteenth-century pronouncement by Matthew Hale, England's chief justice, who wrote:

> But the husband cannot be guilty of rape committed by himself upon his lawful wife, for by their mutual matrimonial consent and contract the wife hath given up herself in this kind unto the husband which she cannot retract.[121]

Research indicates that many women are raped each year by their husbands as part of an overall pattern of spousal abuse, and they deserve the protection of the law. Many spousal rapes are accompanied by brutal, sadistic beatings and have little to do with normal sexual interests.[122] Not surprisingly, the marital exemption has undergone significant revision. In 1980, only three states had laws against marital rape; today every state recognizes marital rape as a crime.[123] Piercing the marital exemption is not unique to U.S. courts; more than 100 nations have abolished the marital exemption.[124] However, although marital rape is now recognized, most states do not give wives the same legal protection as they would unmarried couples, and when courts do recognize marital rape, the perpetrators are sanctioned less harshly than are those accused of nonmarital sexual assaults.[125] For example, in 30 states, a husband is exempt from charges of rape when he does not have to

---

marital exemption The practice of prohibiting the prosecution of husbands for the rape of their wives.

Rape on a Prep School Campus

In 2015, in a case that made national news, 19-year-old Owen Labrie was tried for raping a fellow student at the exclusive St. Paul's School in Concord, New Hampshire. Labrie, who was 18 at the time the attack took place, used email to convince the 15-year-old freshman to meet him as part of the "senior salute" ritual in which graduating seniors seduce younger students. She claimed that she had intended merely to kiss or make out with Labrie, but then as things got out of hand said no to his sexual advances and resisted him as best she could. In the end her resistance was futile; he forced himself on her and engaged in three unwanted sex acts.

Labrie, a popular scholarship student and athlete who was accepted at Harvard, testified that the young woman consented to his advances and that sexual intercourse had not actually taken place. They had exchanged pleasant emails after the assault, evidence of her consent.

The jury found Labrie not guilty of the most serious charge of forcible rape but convicted him of several lesser charges, including endangering the welfare of a child and using a computer and the Internet to "seduce, solicit, lure, or entice a child" in order to commit a sexual assault. He was also found guilty of three counts of misdemeanor sexual assault. Why was he found not guilty of the most serious charge even though the jury believed he did have sex with the young woman, who was still a minor? The reason is that under New Hampshire law, an individual can be found guilty of aggravated felonious sexual assault only if the victim clearly indicates that she doesn't "freely consent," or before she has "an adequate chance to flee and/or resist." The jury obviously concluded that Labrie did have sex with the girl, but there was no real proof that she resisted. Also, under New Hampshire law, if a person has penetrative consensual sex with a minor between the ages of 13 and 16 but is within four years of that age, they are guilty of *misdemeanor* sexual assault. If the age difference is more than four years, they are guilty of *felony* sexual assault. Since Labrie was 18 and the young woman 15, he could only be convicted of a misdemeanor.

The judge suspended his sentence on the Internet charge and sentenced him to a year in a county jail. Out on bail while his attorneys seek a new trial, Labrie lives at his mother's home with a 5 P.M. curfew, monitored by GPS. He served time in jail when he violated his bail conditions but was once again released. He is registered as a sex offender, a status that will follow him for the rest of his life. Meanwhile, the victim's parents have filed suit against St. Paul's School, alleging that the school turned a blind eye to a "warped culture of sexual misconduct" by "fostering, permitting, and condoning a tradition of ritualized statutory rape."

 CRITICAL THINKING

The St. Paul's case illustrates some of the problems associated with bringing rape cases to trial. The young woman testified under oath that she did not consent to sex, but the jury did not believe her story. Despite all we know about sexual assault, the victim is still on trial in rape cases. The unanswered questions are: What would she gain by lying? What could possibly motivate someone to bring false charges in this case?

SOURCES: Jess Bidgood, "Owen Labrie of St. Paul's School Not Guilty of Main Rape Charge," *New York Times*, August 28, 2015, http://www.nytimes.com/2015/08/29/us/st-pauls-school-rape-trial-owen-labrie.html; Andy Rosen and Peter Schworm, "Labrie Acquitted of Felony Rape in St. Paul's School Trial," *Boston Globe*, August 28, 2015; Jennifer Levitz, "Parents Sue St. Paul's School After 'Senior Salute' Sexual-Assault Case," *Wall Street Journal*, June 1, 2016, http://www.wsj.com/articles/parents-sue-st-pauls-school-after-senior-salute-sexual-assault-case-1464830358.

---

use force; because of the marital contract, a wife's consent is assumed unless she overtly refuses her husband's advances. The existence of some spousal exemptions in the majority of states indicates that rape in marriage is still treated as a lesser crime than other forms of rape.[126]

Statutory Rape   The term *statutory rape* refers to sexual relations between an underage minor and an adult. Although the sex is not forced or coerced, the law says that young people are incapable of giving informed consent, so the act is legally considered nonconsensual. Typically a state's law will define an age of consent above which there can be no criminal prosecution for sexual relations. Although each state is different, most evaluate the age differences between the parties to determine whether an offense has taken place.

The purpose of such "Romeo and Juliet provisions" is to prevent a sexual act that occurred between individuals with a few years' age difference from being considered a criminal offense. The age range allowed is typically between two and four years. In some states, it can only apply if the younger of the individuals has reached a certain age, such as 15. The state may also require the older of the individuals to be under a certain age, such as 21.

Romeo and Juliet provisions typically do not protect an older individual accused of abusing a relationship that involves the imposition of authority over a younger person—for example, between a teacher and his student or a coach and an athlete on his team. Individuals accused of sexual acts that involve violence or threat of violence typically do not fall under these laws.

In some states, defendants can claim they mistakenly assumed their victims were above the age of consent, whereas in others, "mistake-of-age" defenses are ignored. An American Bar Association (ABA) survey found that prosecution is often difficult in statutory rape cases because the young victims are reluctant to testify. Often parents have given their blessing to the relationships, and juries are reluctant to convict men involved in consensual sex even with young teenage girls.[127]

Rape by Deception   Rape by deception occurs when the rapist uses fraud or trickery to convince the victim to engage in sex or impersonates someone with whom the victim has been intimate.[128] In one Massachusetts case, a man was convicted of rape after he allegedly impersonated his brother in order to have sex with his brother's girlfriend in the middle of the night. The conviction was overturned because Massachusetts law does not recognize that sex without force can be considered rape. However, a number of other states recognize rape by deception. In Tennessee, rape is defined to include "sexual penetration . . . accomplished by fraud." In Idaho, sex with a woman is defined as rape when because of his "artifice, pretense, or concealment" the victim believes him to be someone other than who he is.[129]

THE CAUSES OF RAPE

What factors predispose some men to commit rape? Criminologists' responses to this question are almost as varied as the crime itself. However, most explanations can be grouped into a few consistent categories.

Evolutionary, Biological Factors   One explanation is that rape may be instinctual, developed over the ages as a means of perpetuating the species. In more primitive times, forcible sexual contact may have helped spread genes and maximize offspring. Some believe that these prehistoric drives remain: males still have a natural sexual drive that encourages them to have intimate relations with as many women as possible.[130] The evolutionary view is that the sexual urge corresponds to the unconscious need to preserve the species by spreading one's genes as widely as possible. Men who are sexually aggressive will have a reproductive edge over their more passive peers.[131]

From the evolutionary perspective, it makes sense that women at the peak of their fertility would be preferential targets, and rape studies have documented that younger women are most often victimized by rapists.[132] However, in contemporary society sexual violence is subject to both social condemnation and legal punishment so that any

linkage between rape and evolutionary drives seems rather dubious.[133]

Male Socialization   Some researchers argue that rape is a function of modern male socialization. Some men have been socialized to be aggressive with women and believe that the use of violence or force is legitimate if their sexual advances are rebuffed—that is, "women like to play hard to get and expect to be forced to have sex." Those men who have been socialized to believe that "no means yes" are more likely to be sexually aggressive.[134] The use of sexual violence is aggravated if pro-force socialization is reinforced by peer group members who share similar values.[135]

Diana Russell, a leading expert on sexual violence, suggests that rape is actually not a deviant act but one that conforms to the qualities regarded as masculine in U.S. society.[136] Russell maintains that from an early age boys are taught to be aggressive, forceful, tough, and dominating. Men are taught to dominate at the same time that they are led to believe that women want to be dominated. Russell describes the **virility mystique**—the belief that males must separate their sexual feelings from needs for love, respect, and affection. She believes men are socialized to be the aggressors and expect to be sexually active with many women; consequently, male virginity and sexual inexperience are shameful. Similarly, sexually aggressive women frighten some men and cause them to doubt their own masculinity. Sexual insecurity may lead some men to commit rape to bolster their self-image and masculine identity.[137]

A rape culture is not unique to the United States. India has experienced a number of globally publicized rapes. Jyoti Singh, a 23-year-old medical intern, was attacked as she and a friend took a bus home after seeing a movie. Five men raped and beat Singh as the bus driver drove them around. Singh later died from the horrific injuries she sustained during the attack. When one of the rapists, Mukesh Singh, was interviewed in prison, he claimed, "A decent girl won't roam around at 9 o'clock at night. A girl is far more responsible for rape than a boy. Housework and housekeeping is for girls, not roaming in discos and bars at night doing wrong things, wearing wrong clothes."[138]

Feminists suggest that as the nation moves toward gender equality there may be an immediate increase in rape rates because of increased threats to male virility and dominance. However, in the long term, gender equality will reduce rape rates because there will be an improved social climate toward women.[139]

Psychological Abnormality   Another view is that rapists suffer from some type of personality disorder or mental illness. Research shows that a significant percentage of incarcerated rapists exhibit psychotic tendencies, and many others have hostile, sadistic feelings toward women.[140] A high proportion of serial rapists and repeat sexual offenders exhibit psychopathic personality structures.[141] There is

virility mystique   The belief that males must separate their sexual feelings from needs for love, respect, and affection.

evidence linking rape proclivity with **narcissistic personality disorder**, a pattern of traits and behaviors that indicate infatuation and fixation with one's self to the exclusion of all others and the egotistic and ruthless pursuit of one's gratification, dominance, and ambition.[142]

Social Learning This perspective submits that men learn to commit rapes much as they learn any other behavior. For example, sexual aggression may be learned through interaction with peers who articulate attitudes supportive of sexual violence.[143] Nicholas Groth found that 40 percent of the rapists he studied were sexually victimized as adolescents.[144] A growing body of literature links personal sexual trauma with the desire to inflict sexual trauma on others.[145] Watching violent or pornographic films featuring women who are beaten, raped, or tortured has been linked to sexually aggressive behavior in men.[146]

Gender Conflict View According to the gender conflict view, as women make progress toward social, political, and economic equality, men fear them as a threat to their long-held dominance.[147] Men react through efforts of formal and informal controls over women. One informal method of social control is to dominate women sexually through the commission of rape. The male-dominated criminal justice system may exert less effort in handling rape cases in an effort to maintain male superiority. Research by Richard Johnson does in fact show that regions with higher levels of progress toward gender equality actually experience higher rates of rape and lower rates of rape case clearances.[148]

Sexual Motivation Most criminologists believe rape is a violent act that is not sexually motivated. Yet it might be premature to dismiss the sexual motive from all rapes.[149] NCVS data reveal that rape victims tend to be young and that rapists prefer younger, presumably more attractive, victims. Richard Felson and his associates found this effect when they studied the risk of sexual and physical assault in prisons and jails.[150] Felson found that male inmates of all ages tend to sexually assault young men and that the young are sexually assaulted because of their sexual attractiveness rather than because of their vulnerability.

Older rapists tend to harm their victims more than younger rapists. This pattern indicates that older criminals may rape for motives of power and control, whereas younger offenders may be seeking sexual gratification and may therefore be less likely to harm their victims.

RAPE AND THE LAW

 Assess the legal issues in rape prosecution

On March 13, 2006, after a performance by two strippers at a private residence, three members of Duke University's men's lacrosse team were accused of raping one of the women who had been hired to entertain the team. Media outlets had a field day with a case involving a young African American victim and her alleged attackers, who were wealthy and white. However, evidence soon emerged that the charges were false, the players falsely accused and wrongfully vilified.[151]

The Duke case is not the only false accusation that made national headlines. In 2014, a *Rolling Stone* article claimed that a University of Virginia student identified only as "Jackie" was gang raped at a frat house. The article made headlines when it described a culture of binge-drinking and casual sex tolerated by a university administration that ignored protocol when students filed sexual assault complaints. A thorough investigation turned up no evidence of a sexual assault or any wrongdoing by the school, suggesting the entire incident was a made-up story.[152]

The Duke and UVA rape accusations are especially troubling because they support the notion that a great many rape accusations are false, making it more difficult to prosecute and gain conviction in those that are valid. Unlike other crime victims, women may find that their claim of sexual assault is greeted with some skepticism by police and court personnel.[153] They will soon discover that they have to prove they did not engage in consensual sex and then develop remorse afterward. Their background and sexual history may impact on whether charges are filed. Police officers may be hesitant to make arrests and testify in court when the alleged assaults do not yield obvious signs of violence or struggle (presumably showing the victim strenuously resisted the attack). Research shows that people are more likely to "blame the victim" in a case of sexual assault than they are in other common-law crimes such as armed robbery. Victim blaming is exacerbated if a prior relationship existed or if the victim did not fight back because she was intoxicated, a factor that may have influenced the judge's lenient sentencing in the Stanford rape case cited earlier.[154] Victim blaming is also common when a woman agrees to a limited sexual encounter but her attacker takes it much farther without her consent; this is what occurred in the St. Paul School rape case.

Proving Rape Because of these attitudes, proving guilt in a rape case is extremely challenging for prosecutors. Although the law does not recognize it, jurors are sometimes swayed by the insinuation that the rape was victim precipitated; thus the blame is shifted from rapist to victim. To get a conviction, prosecutors must establish that the act was forced and violent and that no question of voluntary compliance exists. They may be reluctant to prosecute cases where they have questions about the victim's moral

narcissistic personality disorder A condition marked by a persistent pattern of self-importance, need for admiration, lack of empathy, and preoccupation with fantasies of unlimited success, power, brilliance, beauty, or ideal love.

character or if they believe that the victim's demeanor and attitude (i.e., they were dressed provocatively) will turn off the jury and undermine the chance of conviction.[155] Prosecutors may be more willing to bring charges in interracial rape cases because they know that juries are more likely to believe victims and convict defendants in cases involving interracial rape than in intraracial rapes.[156]

There is also the fear that a frightened and traumatized victim may identify the wrong man, which happened in the case of Dennis Maher, a Massachusetts man freed after spending more than 19 years in prison for rapes he did not commit. Though three victims provided eyewitness identification at trial, DNA testing proved that Maher could not have been the rapist.[157]

Consent   Rape represents a major legal challenge to the criminal justice system for a number of reasons.[158] One issue involves the concept of **consent**. It is essential to prove that the attack was forced and that the victim did not give voluntary consent to her attacker. In a sense, the burden of proof is on the victim to show that her character is beyond question and that she in no way encouraged, enticed, or misled the accused rapist. On the other hand, some states, such as California and Illinois, now recognize that once given consent can be withdrawn if a woman changes her mind about sex even after relations have begun. Once she says stop, the act must end or else a rape has occurred.

Proving victim dissent is not a requirement in any other violent crime: robbery victims do not have to prove they did not entice their attackers by flaunting expensive jewelry, yet the defense counsel in a rape case can create reasonable doubt about the woman's credibility. A common defense tactic is to introduce suspicion in the minds of the jury that the woman may have consented to the sexual act and later regretted her decision. Research shows that even when a defendant is found guilty in a sexual assault case, punishment is significantly reduced if the victim's personal characteristics are viewed as being negative (e.g., transient, hitchhiker, gold digger, or substance abuser).[159] Proving the victim has a good character is not a requirement in any other crime.

Conversely, it is difficult for a prosecuting attorney to establish that a woman's character is so impeccable that the absence of consent is a certainty. Such distinctions are important in rape cases because male jurors may be sympathetic to the accused if the victim is portrayed as unchaste. Referring to the woman as "sexually liberated" or "promiscuous" may be enough to result in exoneration of the accused, even if violence and brutality were used in the attack.[160] When Cassia Spohn and David Holleran studied prosecutors' decisions in rape cases, they found that perception of the victim's character was still a critical factor in their decision to file charges. In cases involving acquaintance rape, prosecutors were reluctant to file charges when the victim's character was questioned—for example, when police reports described the victim as sexually active or engaged in a sexually oriented occupation such as stripper. In cases involving strangers, prosecutors were more likely to take action if a gun or knife was used. Spohn and Holleran state that prosecutors are still influenced by perceptions of what constitutes "real rape" and who are "real victims."[161]

Reform   Because of the difficulty rape victims have in obtaining justice, there has been an ongoing effort to create sensitivity to sexual assault victims. Police receive training in the proper methods of investigating rape allegations and are now just as likely to investigate acquaintance rapes as they are **aggravated rapes** involving multiple offenders, weapons, and victim injuries.

Efforts for rape law reform include changing the language of statutes, dropping the condition of victim resistance, and changing the requirement of use of force to include the threat of force or injury.[162] A number of states and the federal government have replaced rape laws with the more gender-neutral term *crimes of sexual assault*.[163] Sexual assault laws outlaw any type of forcible sex, including homosexual rape.[164]

Most states and the federal government have developed **shield laws**, which protect women from being questioned about their sexual history unless it directly bears on the case. In some instances these laws are quite restrictive, whereas in others they grant the trial judge considerable discretion to admit prior sexual conduct in evidence if it is deemed relevant for the defense. In an important 1991 case, *Michigan v. Lucas*, the U.S. Supreme Court upheld the

consent In prosecuting rape cases, it is essential to prove that the attack was forced and that the victim did not give voluntary consent to her attacker. In a sense, the burden of proof is on the victim to show that her character is beyond question and that she in no way encouraged, enticed, or misled the accused rapist. Proving victim dissent is not a requirement in any other violent crime.

aggravated rape Rape involving multiple offenders, weapons, and victim injuries.

shield laws Laws designed to protect rape victims by prohibiting the defense attorney from inquiring about their previous sexual relationships.

CONNECTIONS

As you may recall, Chapter 2 covered the new definition of rape used by the FBI in collecting UCR data. The changing definition better reflects how the crime is now defined in state legal codes.

ASK YOURSELF . . .

Do you agree with the FBI that all methods of sexual penetration should be considered rape?

validity of shield laws and ruled that excluding evidence of a prior sexual relationship between the parties did not violate the defendant's right to a fair trial.[165]

In addition to requiring evidence that consent was not given, the common-law definition of rape required corroboration that the crime of rape actually took place. This involved the need for independent evidence from police officers, physicians, and witnesses that the accused was actually the person who committed the crime, that sexual penetration took place, and that force was present and consent absent. This requirement shielded rapists from prosecution in cases where the victim delayed reporting the crime or in which physical evidence had been compromised or lost. Corroboration is no longer required except under extraordinary circumstances, such as when the victim is too young to understand the crime, has had a previous sexual relationship with the defendant, or gives a version of events that is improbable and self-contradictory.[166]

The federal government may have given rape victims another source of redress when it passed the Violence Against Women Act in 1994. This statute allows rape victims to sue in federal court on the grounds that sexual violence violates their civil rights; the provisions of the act have so far been upheld by appellate courts.[167]

International Trends Rape reform is not unique to the United States and has become an international movement.[168] A number of nations have made rape a gender-neutral crime. For example, South Africa removed gender from its rape law in 1988, dropping the restriction that perpetrators be male and victims female. The Caribbean nation of Antigua and Barbuda dropped their marital-exclusion clause in 1995, thereafter criminalizing nonconsensual sex between a husband and wife. The kinds of persons and acts subject to and protected by rape laws have expanded dramatically. In Zimbabwe, Article 8 of the 2001 Sexual Offences Act punishes any kind of illegal sexual assault with the same kind of penalties provided by law for rape. With this reform, Zimbabwe greatly increased the range of nonconsensual sexual activities that fall under the umbrella of rape. There has also been an international effort to unify rape laws so that they apply equally to men and women of all classes and statuses. Take rape law in the South American nation of Paraguay. Until 1989, Article 315 of that nation's penal code (*Código Penal*) set harsher penalties for the rape of a married woman (four to eight years in prison) than the rape of an unmarried woman (three to six years), even if the latter were "an honest woman of good name." Why the distinction? It was assumed that the rapist could make things right by marrying his victim if she was an unmarried woman! Today, few codes still include such differential treatments.

 To read a report on a victim-oriented approach to dealing with statutory rape, visit **http://ojp .gov/ovc/publications/infores/statutoryrape /trainguide/victimoriented.pdf.**

If it were up to you, would a 17-year-old boy be prosecuted for having sexual relations with his 15-year-old girlfriend? If not, what about a 21-year-old? Or 25-year-old?

Murder and Homicide

Murder is defined in common law as "the unlawful killing of a human being with malice aforethought."[169] It is the most serious of all common-law crimes and the only one that can still be punished by death. Western society's abhorrence of murderers is illustrated by the fact that there is no statute of limitations in murder cases. Whereas state laws limit prosecution of other crimes to a fixed period, usually 7 to 10 years,

> **murder** The unlawful killing of a human being (homicide) with malicious intent.

A billboard showing that the suspect known as the "Grim Sleeper" had been arrested stands near a freeway in Compton, California. The Grim Sleeper is the nickname for convicted serial killer Lonnie David Franklin Jr., who is believed to have killed at least 10 people in Los Angeles. Franklin was nicknamed the Grim Sleeper because he appeared to have taken a 14-year break from his crimes, from 1988 to 2002. He was convicted and sentenced to death in 2016.

AP Images/Nick Ut

accused killers can be brought to justice at any time after their crimes were committed:

- In 2012, 72-year-old Jack McCullough was found guilty of killing Maria Ridulph in 1957 when he was 17 years old; 55 years had gone by before the murder was solved.[170]
- In 2013, Conrado Juarez was arrested in New York City 22 years after killing four-year-old Anjelica Castillo, known as "Baby Hope," whose abused and decomposed body was found in an ice chest by the side of a New York roadway in 1991.[171]
- In 2015, Michael R. Jones, 62, of Champaign, Illinois, was arrested and charged with two counts of murder and one count of aggravated criminal sexual assault in the 1985 death of Kristina Wesselman.[172]

To legally prove that a murder has taken place, most state jurisdictions require prosecutors to show that the accused maliciously intended to kill the victim. "Express or actual malice" is the state of mind assumed to exist when someone kills another person in the absence of any apparent provocation. "Implied or constructive malice" is considered to exist when a death results from negligent or unthinking behavior. In these cases, even though the perpetrator did not wish to kill the victim, the killing resulted from an inherently dangerous act and therefore is considered murder. An unusual example of this concept is the attempted-murder conviction of Ignacio Perea, an AIDS-infected Miami man who kidnapped and raped an 11-year-old boy. Perea was sentenced to up to 25 years in prison when the jury agreed with the prosecutor's contention that the AIDS virus is a deadly weapon.[173]

DEGREES OF MURDER

 LO5 Compare and contrast the different degrees of murder

There are different levels or degrees of homicide.[174] **First-degree murder** is an intentional killing that is deliberate and premeditated. **Premeditation** means that the killing was considered beforehand and suggests that it was motivated by more than a simple desire to engage in an act of violence; the murder was planned after careful thought rather than being carried out on impulse. Planning need not be long term and may be an almost instantaneous decision to take another's life. Also, a killing accompanying a felony, such as robbery or rape, usually constitutes first-degree murder (**felony murder**). In some states, statutes have defined murder in the first to include crimes involving multiple deaths, the killing of a child, an agent of the justice system, such as police officer or prison guard, or murder for hire.

Second-degree murder requires the killer to have malice aforethought but not premeditation or **deliberation**. There are three situations that are typically defined as second-degree murder:

- A killing done impulsively without premeditation but with malice aforethought. This occurs when two people get into a heated argument and one pulls out a knife and stabs the victim. The killer did not have an original intent to kill or plan to kill, but he did intend to kill once the argument started or else why did he pull out and use his knife?
- A killing that results from an act intended to cause serious bodily harm. During a fight, someone grabs a baseball bat and hits her opponent, resulting in death. Even though she merely intended to seriously injure and not kill her opponent, her actions caused death.
- A person can also be held criminally liable for the death of another even if she or he did not intend to injure another person but exhibited *deliberate indifference* to the danger her or his actions might cause. The deliberate indifference standard is met when a person knows of, and yet disregards or ignores, an excessive risk to another's health or safety.

One of the most famous cases illustrating deliberate indifference murder occurred on January 26, 2001, when Diane Whipple, a San Francisco woman, died after two large dogs attacked her in the hallway of her apartment building. One of the dogs' owners/keepers, Robert Noel, was found guilty of manslaughter, and his wife, Marjorie Knoller, was convicted on charges of second-degree murder because they knew that the dogs were highly dangerous but did little or nothing to control the animals' behavior. Their deliberate indifference put their neighbor at risk, with tragic consequences. After a long series of appeals, on June 1, 2007, the California Supreme Court ruled that a dog owner who knows the animal is a potential killer and exposes other people to that danger may be guilty of murder even though he or she did not intend that particular victim to be injured or killed. In a unanimous decision, the appellate court ruled that Knoller could be convicted of murder because she acted with "conscious disregard of the danger to human life." On September 22, 2008, the court sentenced Marjorie Knoller to serve 15 years to life for the death of Diane Whipple.[175]

first-degree murder Unlawful killing that is both willful and premeditated, committed after planning or "lying in wait" for the victim.

premeditation Consideration of a homicide before it occurs.

felony murder A homicide in the context of another felony, such as robbery or rape; legally defined as first-degree murder.

second-degree murder A homicide with malice but not premeditation or deliberation, as when a desire to inflict serious bodily harm and a wanton disregard for life result in the victim's death.

deliberation Planning a homicide after careful thought, however brief, rather than acting on sudden impulse.

Homicide without malice is called **manslaughter**. **Voluntary manslaughter**, also called **nonnegligent manslaughter**, refers to a killing, typically without a weapon, committed in the heat of passion or during a sudden quarrel that provoked violence. Death resulting from a misdemeanor is considered voluntary manslaughter: Two people get into an argument and exchange blows. One falls, hits his head, and dies. The punch is technically a battery, a misdemeanor, and the resulting death would be considered manslaughter.

Involuntary manslaughter or **negligent manslaughter** refers to a killing that occurs when a person's acts are negligent and without regard for the harm they may cause others. Many involuntary manslaughter cases involve motor vehicle deaths—for example, when a drunk driver kills a pedestrian. While the motorist did not intend to kill anyone, they knew or should have known that drinking and driving was both an illegal act and one that could cause death. Involuntary manslaughter can also be a result of otherwise legal behavior that is performed in a negligent manner: a person leaves a heavy object on her tenth floor windowsill, it falls and strikes a pedestrian, killing them instantly. A reasonable person should know that an object left by an open window could fall out and strike someone below.

"Born and Alive"   One issue that has received national attention is whether a murder victim can be a fetus that has not yet been delivered; this is referred to as **feticide**. Today at least 38 states have some form of fetal homicide laws and more than two-thirds of the states have passed some form of legislation that criminalizes the killing of a fetus as murder even if it is not "born and alive."[176] In some states, there exists legislation creating a separate class of crime that increases criminal penalties when a person causes injury to a woman they know is pregnant, and the injury results in miscarriage or stillbirth. At the federal level, the Unborn Victims of Violence Act of 2004 makes it a separate crime to harm a fetus during an assault on the mother. If the attack causes death or bodily injury to a child who is *in utero* at the time the conduct takes place, the penalty is the same as that for conduct had the injury or death occurred to the unborn child's mother.

Some states have prosecuted women for endangering or killing their unborn fetuses by their drug or alcohol abuse. Some of these convictions have been overturned because the law applies only to a "human being who has been born and is alive."[177] However, in *Whitner v. State of South Carolina*, the Supreme Court of South Carolina ruled that a woman could be held liable for actions during pregnancy that could affect her viable fetus.[178] In holding that a fetus is a "viable person," the court opened the door for a potential homicide prosecution if a mother's action resulted in fetal death. As for third-party actions, only 12 states still follow the common-law "born alive" rule: Colorado, Connecticut, Delaware, Hawaii, Montana, New Hampshire, New Jersey, New Mexico, North Carolina, Oregon, Vermont, and Wyoming.

There is still a great deal of state-to-state variation in feticide laws. Some make it a separate crime to kill a fetus or commit an act of violence against a pregnant woman. Others have a viability requirement: feticide can only occur if the unborn child could at the time potentially live outside the mother's body.[179]

THE NATURE AND EXTENT OF MURDER

It is possible to track U.S. murder rate trends from 1900 to the present with the aid of coroners' reports and UCR data. The murder rate peaked in 1933, a time of high unemployment and lawlessness, and then fell until 1958. Then the homicide rate began to skyrocket, doubling from the mid-1960s to a peak in 1991 when almost 25,000 people were killed in a single year, a rate of about 10 per 100,000 people. The murder rate has since been in a decline. In 2014, there were about 14,000 murders, a rate of about 4.5 per 100,000 population. Preliminary 2015 data show that the decline in the murder rate may be over: murders increased more than 6 percent in the first half of 2015.

What else do official crime statistics tell us about murder today? Murder tends to be an urban crime. More than half of homicides occur in cities with a population of 100,000 or more; almost one-quarter of homicides occur in cities with a population of more than 1 million. Why is homicide an urban phenomenon? Large cities experience the greatest rates of structural disadvantage—poverty, joblessness, racial heterogeneity, residential mobility, family disruption, and income inequality—that are linked to high murder rates.[180] Not surprisingly, large cities are much more commonly the site of drug-related killings and gang-related murders, and relatively less likely to be the location of family-related homicides, including murders of intimates.

Murder victims and offenders tend to be males: about 80 percent of homicide victims and nearly 90 percent of offenders are male. Males are more likely to kill others of similar social standing in more public contexts; women kill family members and intimate partners in private locations.[181]

Murder, like rape, tends to be an intraracial crime: about 90 percent of victims are slain by members of their own race. About half of all murder victims are African Americans. Approximately one-third of murder victims and almost half the offenders are under the age of 25.

manslaughter A homicide without malice.

voluntary or nonnegligent manslaughter A homicide committed in the heat of passion or during a sudden quarrel; although intent may be present, malice is not; also called voluntary manslaughter.

involuntary or negligent manslaughter A homicide that occurs as a result of acts that are negligent and without regard for the harm they may cause others, such as driving under the influence of alcohol or drugs.

feticide Endangering or killing an unborn fetus.

Some murders involve babies, a crime referred to as **infanticide**; killing one's own child is called **filicide**; and others involve senior citizens, referred to as **eldercide**.[182] The UCR indicates that about 350 juveniles are murdered each year. The younger the child, the greater the risk. At the opposite end of the age spectrum, less than 5 percent of all homicides involve people age 65 or older. Males age 65 or older are more likely than females of the same age to be homicide victims. Although most of the offenders who committed eldercide were age 50 or younger, elderly females were more likely than elderly males to be killed by an elderly offender.[183]

Murderers typically have a long involvement in crime; few people begin a criminal career by killing someone. Research shows that people arrested for homicide are significantly more likely to have been in trouble with the law prior to their arrest than people arrested for other crimes.[184] David Farrington and his associates found that among the risk predictors for homicide, prior criminal offenses up to age 14 was the most important; 95 percent of offenders had records of violence at the time they committed murder.[185]

A murderer's choice of weapon is related to their association with the victim. Those who knew or who had an intimate relationship with the victim are more likely to use a weapon found at the scene—a knife or blunt instrument—and attack their target in the head or face; stranger homicides are more likely to use a gun.[186]

Unlike other crimes, more than two-thirds of all murders are cleared by arrest or other means. Why are murders so solvable? Police devote more time and resources to identifying murderers, most victims and killers were acquainted, and there is a significant chance of forensic evidence being left at the scene.

MURDEROUS RELATIONS

Most murders are expressive—that is, motivated by rage or anger—and they typically involve friends, relatives, and acquaintances. What other forms do murderous relations take?

Acquaintance Murders   Most murders occur among people who are acquainted. Although on the surface the killing might seem senseless, it is often the result of a long-simmering dispute motivated by revenge, dispute resolution, jealousy, drug deals, racial bias, or threats to identity or status.[187] For example, a prior act of violence motivated by profit or greed, such as when a buyer robs his dealer during a drug transaction, may generate revenge killing.

Intimate Partner Murder   Many murders involve husbands and wives, boyfriends and girlfriends, and others involved in romantic relationships. In some jurisdictions, upward of 40 percent of all murders involve an intimate partner.[188]

Intimate partner murder is a gendered phenomenon. When women commit homicide, the most likely victim is an intimate partner; about 40 percent of all female homicide incidents involve killing a male partner. Less than 10 percent of all murders committed by men involve a female partner. Men who kill romantic partners typically have a long history of violence, while for women killing their partner may be their first violent offense.[189] This may be the reason that there is a "chivalry effect" in domestic violence murders. In death penalty states such as California the death-sentence rate for single-victim domestic violence murders is significantly lower than the overall death-sentence rate for other kinds of killings. Not surprisingly, when women in these states are found guilty of capital murder, they are far less likely than men to be sentenced to death.[190]

Research also shows most females who kill their mates do so after suffering repeated violent attacks.[191] Women who kill or seriously assault intimate partners are often battered women unable to flee a troubled relationship.[192] Perhaps the number of males killed by their partners has declined because alternatives to abusive relationships, such as shelters for battered women, are becoming more prevalent around the United States. Regions that provide greater social support for battered women and that have passed legislation to protect abuse victims also have lower rates of female-perpetrated homicide.[193] This escape valve may help them avoid retaliation through lethal violence.

Sexually Based Murders   Some people kill their mates because they find themselves involved in a love triangle.[194]

CONNECTIONS

It is possible that men who perceive loss of face aim their aggression at rivals who are competing with them for a suitable partner. Biosocial theory (Chapter 5) suggests that this behavior is motivated by the male's instinctual need to replenish the species and protect his place in the gene pool. Killing a rival would help a spouse maintain control over a potential mother for his children.

ASK YOURSELF . . .

Is it really possible that murder is truly instinctual and based on the need to maintain the species? If that were true, what patterns in murder would you expect to see?

---

infanticide The murder of a newborn or very young baby.

filicide The murder of one's own child.

eldercide The murder of a senior citizen.

Interestingly, women who kill out of jealousy aim their aggression at their partners; in contrast, men are more likely to kill their rivals (their mates' suitors). Love triangles tend to become lethal when the offenders believe they have been misled. Lethal violence is more common when (1) the rival initiated the affair, (2) the killer knew the spouse was already in a steady relationship outside the marriage, and (3) the killer was repeatedly lied to or betrayed.[195]

Research indicates that sexually related homicide can take a variety of different forms:[196]

- Domestic disputes involving husbands and wives, men and women, boyfriends and girlfriends, same-sex couples, and even on occasion siblings. Sometimes these events are triggered by a partner's unwanted or unexpected pregnancy: homicidal injury is a leading cause of death among pregnant and postpartum women in the United States.[197]
- Love triangles involving former husbands and/or wives and jilted lovers.
- Rape and/or sodomy–oriented assault in which a person intends to commit a rape or sexual assault but uses excessive force to overcome resistance, resulting in the victim's death.
- "Lust murders" that are motivated by obsessive sexual fantasies.
- Vengeance for sexual violence. In these cases, someone exacts vengeance on a sexual violence perpetrator, either on his or her own behalf or on the behalf of a sexual violence victim.
- Self-defense during sexual violence. In these incidents, sexual violence was taking place and the victim defended herself or himself resulting in the death of the sexual violence perpetrator; or another person intervened to defend the sexual violence victim and this resulted in the death of the sexual violence perpetrator.

Sexual homicide is typically part of a long history of antisocial acts that included a variety of violent crimes in addition to murder; physical abuse and parental conflict are often present.[198]

These killers displayed behavioral problems, were poor achievers, and experienced social isolation. In adulthood, they became isolated single men who abuse substances and have criminal records.[199]

The Race, Culture, Gender, and Criminology feature discusses one type of sexually based murder: a woman killed by relatives for damaging the family's honor.

 Assess stranger and acquaintance homicide

Stranger Murders   About 20 percent of all murders involve strangers. Stranger homicides occur most often as felony murders during rapes, robberies, and burglaries, where the perpetrator applied too much force in completing the crime. Others are random acts of urban violence that fuel public fear: a homeowner tells a motorist to move his car because it is blocking the driveway, an argument ensues, and the owner gets a pistol and kills the motorist. Stranger homicides can also result from random gang violence—for example, when a bystander is killed inadvertently in a drive-by shooting. They can also stem from a hate crime (see later in this chapter) directed at a victim merely because of their race, class, gender, and so on. The killing of homeless people by adolescent groups and gangs has also become all too common.[200]

How do these murderous interactions develop between two people who may have had little prior conflict? In a classic study, David Luckenbill examined murder transactions to determine whether particular patterns of behavior are common between the killer and the victim.[201] He found that many homicides follow a sequential pattern. First, the victim makes what the offender considers an offensive move. The offender typically retaliates verbally or physically. An agreement to end things violently is forged with the victim's provocative response. The battle ensues, leaving the victim dead or dying. The offender's escape is shaped by his or her relationship to the victim or by the reaction of the audience, if any.

School Murders   Sadly, violence in schools has become commonplace. There have been a number of mass killings such as the April 20, 1999, shootings at Columbine High School in Colorado, which resulted in the deaths of 15 people, and the Newtown, Connecticut, massacre on December 14, 2012, in which Adam Lanza killed 20 children and 6 staff members.

On average, about 25 students are killed each year at school, or on the way to or returning from regular sessions at school, or while the victim was attending or traveling to or from an official school-sponsored event.[202]

Research shows that most shooting incidents occur around the start of the school day, the lunch period, or the end of the school day.[203] In most of the shootings (55 percent), a note, threat, or other action indicating risk for violence occurred before the event. Shooters were also likely to have expressed some form of suicidal behavior and to have been bullied by their peers.[204] School massacres tend to be committed by both males and females, the former most likely to use a firearm, the latter a knife or some other instrument.[205]

MULTIPLE MURDERS

 Analyze the differences among serial killing, mass murder, and spree killing

For 17 years, a killer terrorized Wichita, Kansas. Known as the BTK Killer (for Bind, Torture, Kill), he sent taunting letters and packages to the police and the media with details of the 10 murders he committed between 1979 and 1991, when he suddenly went underground and disappeared from view. In 2004, he renewed his communications with a local

Honor Killing

I n 2014, a 19-year-old Pakistani woman named Saba Qaiser fell in love and ran off to marry her boyfriend against her family's wishes. Hours after the wedding, her father and uncle got her into their car and took her to a spot along a riverbank to murder her for her defiance. After beating her, Saba's uncle held her so that her father could shoot her in the head. The two men then packed her bloody body into a sack and threw it into the river to sink, not realizing that Saba was unconscious but alive. The river water revived her and she managed to claw her way out of the sack and find help.

After her father and uncle were arrested, Saba's father said, "She took away our honor . . . If you put one drop of piss in a gallon of milk, the whole thing gets destroyed. That's what she has done. . . . So I said, 'No, I will kill you myself.'"

Saba was pressured by other relatives to formally forgive her father and uncle, and she reluctantly complied; the father and uncle were released from prison. "After this incident, everyone says I am more respected," her father later boasted. "I can proudly say that for generations to come none of my descendants will ever think of doing what Saba did." He promised not to try again to kill Saba. Her story was made into an Oscar-winning 2015 documentary, *A Girl in the River: The Price of Forgiveness*, by filmmaker Sharmeen Obaid-Chinoy.

Saba's story is sadly not unique: more than 1,000 people are the victims of honor killings in Pakistan each year. In 2014, a young newlywed couple, Sajjad Ahmed, 26, and Muawia Bibi, 18, were killed by the bride's family in northeastern Pakistan because they did not approve of the marriage. The bride's father and uncles lured the couple back to the village of Satrah in the Punjab province, where the pair were tied up and decapitated. The family members turned themselves in to the police, maintaining that their brutal attack was a matter of honor.

Honor killing and honor crime involve violence against women and girls, including such acts as beating, battering, or killing, by a family member or relative. The attacks are provoked by the belief or perception that an individual's or family's honor has been threatened because of the actual or perceived sexual misconduct of the female. The United Nations now estimates that 5,000 of these honor killings occur each year, and they are increasing rapidly in areas such as Palestinian territories, where the number of honor killings has more than doubled in the past few years. They are most common in traditional societies in the Middle East, Southwest Asia, India, China, and Latin America but are now being exported to Europe and North America. In 2008, Egyptian-born Texas resident Yaser Abdel Said took his two teenage daughters for a ride in his taxi cab, under the guise of taking them out to eat, then allegedly shot both girls to death. The reason: dating boys against his will.

The killings often seem illogical to an outsider. Even when a woman is raped she may be accused of being the sexual aggressor who must be punished. Honor killing/crime is based on the shame that a loss of control of the woman or girl brings to the family and to the male heads of the family. Most of the victims are women killed by husbands or brothers. "Illicit relations" is most often cited as a motive, and demanding to marry a partner of their choice is another motivating factor.

According to criminologist Linda Williams, men consider honor killings culturally necessary because any suspicion that a girl or woman is unchaste is enough to raise questions about the family's honor. Strict control of women and girls within the home and outside the home is justified. Women are restricted in their activities in the community, religion, and politics. These institutions, in turn, support the control of females. Williams believes that honor killing is designed for maintaining male dominance. Submissiveness may be seen as a sign of sexual purity, and a woman's or girl's attempts to assert her rights is a violation of the family's honor that needs to be redressed. Rules of honor and threats against females who violate such rules reinforce the control of women and have a powerful impact on their lives. Honor killings/crimes serve to keep women and girls from "stepping out of line." The manner in which such behaviors silence women and kill their spirit has led some to label honor killings/crimes more broadly as "femicide."

 CRITICAL THINKING

While the idea of honor killings may seem primitive, are there elements of American culture and life that you consider harmful to women yet are still tolerated? What can be done to change them?

SOURCES: Nicholas Kristof, "Her Father Shot Her in the Head, as an 'Honor Killing'" *New York Times*, January 30, 2016, http://www.nytimes.com/2016/01/31/opinion/sunday/her-father-shot-her-in-the-head-as-an-honor-killing.html; Shelby Lin Erdman, "Pakistani Newlyweds Decapitated by Bride's Family in Honor Killing," CNN, June 29, 2014, http://www.cnn.com/2014/06/28/world/asia/pakistan-honor-murders/; Anne-Marie O'Connor, "Honor Killings Rise in Palestinian Territories, Sparking Backlash," *Washington Post*, March 3, 2014, http://www.washingtonpost.com/world/middle_east/honor-killings-rise-in-palestinian-territories-sparking-backlash/2014/03/02/1392d144-940c-11e3-9e13-770265cf4962_story.html; Julia Dahl, "'Honor Killing' Under Growing Scrutiny in the U.S.," CBS News, April 5, 2012, http://www.cbsnews.com/news/honor-killing-under-growing-scrutiny-in-the-us/; Linda M. Williams, "Honor Killings," in *Encyclopedia of Interpersonal Violence*, ed. Claire M. Renzetti and Jeffrey I. Edelson (Thousand Oaks, CA: Sage Publications, 2007). (URLs accessed June 2016.)

news station. His last communication contained a computer disk, which was traced to 59-year-old Dennis Rader after FBI analysis of deleted data on the disk. Rader later confessed to the 10 murders in an effort to escape the death penalty.

Multiple murderers, such as Dennis Rader, are people who have killed more than one victim. Based on the patterns of their murders, multiple killers are classified into three basic categories—serial killers, mass murderers, and spree killers. Each type of these multiple killers is discussed below.

SERIAL MURDER

Criminologists consider a **serial killer**, such as Dennis Rader, to be a person who kills three or more persons in three or more separate events. In between the murders, the serial killer reverts to his normal lifestyle. Rader worked as a supervisor of the Compliance Department at Park City, Kansas, which put him in charge of animal control, housing problems, zoning, general permit enforcement, and a variety of nuisance cases. A married father of two, he served as a county commissioner, a Cub Scout leader, and a member of Christ Lutheran Church where he had been elected president of the Congregation Council. Rader's biography and personal life give few clues to his murderous path, which is perhaps why it took more than three decades to track him down.[206]

There is a great deal of fascination with serial killers, and they are frequent subjects for films like *Silence of the Lambs* and TV shows like *Criminal Minds*. They are sometimes portrayed as heroes, as anyone who watched *Dexter* soon found out. They inspire a great many myths and legends (see Exhibit 10.3).

Types of Serial Killers There are different types of serial killers. Some wander the countryside killing at random; others hide themselves in a single locale and lure victims to their death.[207] Theodore Bundy, convicted killer of three young women and suspected killer of many others, roamed the country in the 1970s, killing as he went. John Wayne Gacy, during the same period, killed more than 30 boys and young men without leaving Chicago.

Some serial killers are sadists who gain satisfaction from torturing and killing.[208] Sadists wish to gain complete control over their victims through humiliation, shame, enslavement, and terror. Dr. Michael Swango, who is suspected of killing between 35 and 60 patients, wrote in his diary of the pleasure he obtained from murder. He wrote of the "sweet, husky, close smell of indoor homicide" and how murders were "the only way I have of reminding myself that I'm still alive."[209]

While Swango obtained pleasure from killing, other health care workers who have committed serial murder rationalize their behavior by thinking they are helping patients end their suffering when they put them to death.

Harold Frederick Shipman, Britain's most notorious serial killer, was a general practitioner convicted of 15 murders, most involving elderly patients. After he committed suicide in 2004, further investigation found that he actually killed 218 patients and perhaps even more.[210]

Another type, the psychopathic killer, is motivated by a character disorder that causes an inability to experience shame, guilt, sorrow, or other normal human emotions; these murderers are concerned solely with their own needs and passions.

Serial murder experts James Alan Fox and Jack Levin have developed the following typology of serial killer motivations:

- *Thrill killers* strive for either sexual sadism or dominance. This is the most common form of serial murderer.
- *Mission killers* want to reform the world or have a vision that drives them to kill.
- *Expedience killers* are out for profit or want to protect themselves from a perceived threat.[211]

Female Serial Killers Female serial killers have been around for quite some time. Locusta, a poisoner, was active in Rome during the first century CE. Slave trader Martha Patricia "Patty" Cannon, the first known female serial killer in the United States, was active between 1802 and 1829 in Delaware. Cannon confessed to more than 24 murders of runaway slaves and free blacks. Sensational accounts of her crimes dubbed her Lucretia P. Cannon to associate her with Lucrezia Borgia.[212]

An estimated 17 percent of serial killers are women. They are typically white, educated, have been married, and held a caregiving role (e.g., mother, health care worker); about 40 percent experience some form of mental illness. Why do they kill? Usually for financial gain: they tend to poison family members or friends in order to collect an inheritance or insurance policy. They target people who have little chance of fighting back, children, elderly, or the infirm.[213]

There are striking differences between male and female serial killers.[214] Males are much more likely than females to use extreme violence and torture, beating, bludgeoning, and strangling their victims. In contrast, females are more likely to poison or smother their victims.[215] Men choose victims whom they can render helpless, and women choose victims who are already helpless.[216]

There are also gender-based differences in personality and behavior characteristics. Female killers, somewhat older than their male counterparts, abuse both alcohol and drugs; males are not likely to be substance abusers. Women were diagnosed as having histrionic, manic-depressive, borderline, dissociative, and antisocial personality disorders; men

serial killer The killing of a large number of people over time by an offender who seeks to escape detection.

EXHIBIT 10.3

The Myth and Reality of Serial Killers

MYTH #1: ALL SERIAL KILLERS ARE MEN

Reality: This is simply not true, but it is understandable why the public would hold this erroneous belief. As late as 1998, a highly regarded former FBI profiler said, "There are no female serial killers." The news and entertainment media also perpetuate the stereotypes that all serial offenders are male and that women do not engage in horrible acts of violence. In fact, approximately 17 percent of all serial homicides in the United States are committed by women; in contrast, only 10 percent of total murders in the United States are committed by women. Therefore, relative to men, women represent a larger percentage of serial murders than all other homicide cases in the United States.

MYTH #2: ALL SERIAL KILLERS ARE CAUCASIAN

Reality: Contrary to popular mythology, not all serial killers are white. Serial killers span all racial and ethnic groups in the United States. The racial diversity of serial killers generally mirrors that of the overall U.S. population. There are well-documented cases of African American, Hispanic, and Asian American serial killers. African Americans comprise the largest racial minority group among serial killers, representing approximately 20 percent of the total. Significantly, however, only white (and normally, male) serial killers such as Ted Bundy become popular culture icons.

MYTH #3: ALL SERIAL KILLERS ARE ISOLATED AND DYSFUNCTIONAL LONERS

Reality: Real-life serial killers are not the isolated monsters of fiction. The majority of serial killers are not reclusive, social misfits who live alone. Frequently, they do not appear to be strange or stand out from the public in any meaningful way. Many serial killers are able to hide out in plain sight for extended periods of time. Those who successfully blend in are typically employed, have families and homes, and outwardly appear to be nonthreatening, normal members of society. In fact, many are highly functioning and appear to be completely normal.

MYTH #4: ALL SERIAL MURDERERS TRAVEL WIDELY AND KILL INTERSTATE

Reality: The roaming, homicidal maniac such as Freddy Krueger in the cult film *A Nightmare on Elm Street* is another stereotype that is rarely found in real life. Serial killers typically have a comfort zone—that is, an area that they are intimately familiar with and where they like to stalk and kill their prey. The comfort zone of a serial killer is often defined by an anchor point such as a place of residence or employment. Crime statistics reveal that serial killers are most likely to commit their first murder very close to their place of residence due to the comfort and familiarity it offers them.

MYTH #5: ALL SERIAL KILLERS ARE EITHER MENTALLY ILL OR EVIL GENIUSES

Reality: The images presented in the news and entertainment media suggest that serial killers either have a debilitating mental illness such as psychosis or they are brilliant but demented geniuses like Dr. Hannibal Lecter. Neither of these two stereotypes is quite accurate. In fact, very few serial killers suffer from any mental illness. Serial killers such as John Wayne Gacy and Dennis Rader may be psychopaths, but they were entirely aware of the illegality of murder while in the process of killing their victims. Their understanding of right and wrong does nothing to impede their crimes, however, because psychopaths have an overwhelming desire and compulsion to kill that causes them to ignore the criminal law with impunity.

There is a popular culture stereotype that serial killers are cunning, criminal geniuses. The reality is that most serial killers who have had their IQ tested score between borderline and above average intelligence. This is very consistent with the general population. Contrary to mythology, it is not high intelligence that makes serial killers successful. Instead, it is obsession, meticulous planning, and a cold-blooded, often psychopathic personality that enable serial killers to operate over long periods of time without detection.

MYTH #6: ALL SERIAL KILLERS MUST KEEP ON KILLING

Reality: Another common myth is that once serial killers start killing, they cannot stop. Although this claim may seem reasonable, it is inaccurate. There are serial killers who stop murdering altogether before ever being caught.

MYTH #7: ALL SERIAL KILLERS WANT TO GET CAUGHT

Reality: It is popularly believed that serial killers secretly want to get caught. For the vast majority of them, however, this is simply not true. They love the act of killing. Serial killers take satisfaction in their success, particularly at the beginning of their killing careers. The skills and confidence gained through their experience make serial killers very difficult to apprehend. As they continue to operate and avoid capture, serial killers become increasingly emboldened and empowered.

MYTH #8: ALL SERIAL KILLER VICTIMS ARE FEMALE

Reality: According to the stereotypical imagery presented in Hollywood films and best-selling novels, male serial killers prey exclusively on female victims. This is not true. Just as not all serial killers are male, not all serial-killer victims are female, although females do represent the majority of victims. The presence of a sexual motive often leads a male serial killer to prey on women, but in reality about 30 percent of victims are men.

SOURCE: Scott Bonn, *Why We Love Serial Killers: The Curious Appeal of the World's Most Savage Murderers* (New York: Skyhorse Press, 2014).

were more often diagnosed as having antisocial personalities. Aileen Wuornos, executed for killing seven men, was diagnosed with a severe psychopathic personality, which probably arose from her horrific childhood marred by beatings, alcoholism, rape, incest, and prostitution.[217] Because they use stealth and cunning rather than overt brutality, and are older and more mature, women are more likely to remain at large longer before arousing suspicion than males.

The misconception that women cannot be serial murderers may also help them avoid capture.[218]

Why Do Serial Killers Kill? The cause of serial murder eludes criminologists. Such disparate factors as mental illness, sexual frustration, neurological damage, child abuse and neglect, smothering relationships with mothers (David Berkowitz, the notorious Son of Sam, slept in his parents' bed until he was 10), and childhood anxiety are suspected. Most experts view serial killers as sociopaths who from early childhood demonstrate bizarre behavior, such as torturing animals. Some are sadists who enjoy the sexual thrill of murdering and who are both pathological and destructive narcissists.[219]

This behavior extends to the pleasure they reap from killing, their ability to ignore or enjoy their victims' suffering, and their propensity for basking in the media limelight when apprehended for their crimes. Killing provides a way to fill their emotional hunger and reduce their anxiety levels.[220] Wayne Henley, Jr., who along with Dean Corill killed 27 boys in Houston, offered to help prosecutors find the bodies of additional victims so he could break Chicago killer John Wayne Gacy's record of 33 murders.[221]

According to experts Fox and Levin, serial killers enjoy the thrill, the sexual gratification, and the dominance they achieve over the lives of their victims. The serial killer rarely uses a gun because this method is too quick and would deprive him of his greatest pleasure, exulting in his victim's suffering. Fox and Levin dispute the notion that serial killers have some form of biological or psychological problems, such as genetic anomalies or schizophrenia. Even the most sadistic serial murderers are not mentally ill or driven by delusions or hallucinations. Instead, they typically exhibit a sociopathic personality that deprives them of pangs of conscience or guilt to guide their behavior. Serial killers are not insane, they claim, but "more cruel than crazy."[222]

Controlling Serial Killers Serial killers come from diverse backgrounds. To date, law enforcement officials have been at a loss to control random killers who leave few clues, constantly move, and have little connection to their victims. Catching serial killers is often a matter of luck. To help local law enforcement officials, the FBI has developed a profiling system to identify potential suspects. Because serial killers often use the same patterns in each attack, they leave a signature that might help in their capture.[223]

In addition, the Justice Department's Violent Criminal Apprehension Program (VICAP), a computerized information service, gathers information and matches offense characteristics on violent crimes around the country.[224] This program links crimes to determine if they are the product of a single culprit.

MASS MURDERS

In contrast to serial killings, **mass murder** involves the killing of four or more victims by one or more assailants within a single event.[225] Some of the most notorious of these mass killings include:

- Charles Whitman killed 14 people and wounded 30 others from atop the 307-foot tower on the University of Texas campus in August 1966.
- James Huberty killed 21 people in a McDonald's restaurant in San Ysidro, California, in July 1984.
- George Hennard killed 22 people in a Killeen, Texas, cafeteria in October 1991.
- Seung-Hui Cho killed 32 people and wounded 25 at Virginia Tech in April 2007.
- James Holmes killed 12 people and wounded 70 others in a movie theater in Aurora, Colorado, in July 2012.
- Adam Lanza killed 20 children and 6 adult staff members at the Sandy Hook Elementary School in Newtown, Connecticut, in December 2012.
- Aaron Alexis killed 12 people and wounded 4 others at the Washington Navy Yard in Washington, D.C., in September 2013.
- Syed Rizwan Farook and Tashfeen Malik killed 14 people and wounded 22 others at the Inland Regional Center in San Bernardino, California, in December 2015.
- Omar Mateen killed 49 people and wounded more than 50 others at the Pulse nightclub in Orlando, Florida, in June 2016.

In some instances police and law enforcement agents are present as the crime unfolds; these are known as **active shooter incidents**.

A recent survey by the FBI of active shooting incidents between 2000 and 2013 found an average of 11 active shooting incidents occurred annually, including 6 incidents in the first seven years studied, and an average of 16 in the last seven years. As the data show, active shooting incidents have now become routine. About 70 percent of the incidents occurred in either a commerce/business or educational environment. Shootings occurred in 40 of 50 states and the District of Columbia. In all, active shooting incidents produced 1,043 casualties: 486 victims killed and 557 wounded. All but two incidents involved a single shooter. In at least nine incidents, the shooter first shot and killed one or more family members in a residence before moving to a more public location to continue shooting. In 64 incidents (40 percent), the shooters committed suicide; 54 shooters did so at the scene of the crime.[226] Why is it so common

mass murder The killing of a large number of people in a single incident by an offender who typically does not seek concealment or escape.

active shooter incident A term used by law enforcement to describe a situation in which a mass shooting is in progress when police and law enforcement agents arrive at the scene.

Mass Shooters: Why Do Some Live and Why Do Some Die?

04

A recent study by Adam Lankford compared mass murderers who took their own life with those who survived their attacks. Lankford found that while only 4 percent of murderers commit murder-suicide and fewer than 3 percent of terrorist attacks are suicidal in nature, about 38 percent of mass shooters commit suicide by their own hand. Others commit "suicide by cop," pointing a weapon at police until they are shot and killed themselves. In all, 48 percent of mass shooters died as a result of their attacks, a consequence that suggests that mass shooters are quite different than other perpetrators of murder or terrorism.

Lankford found that there are significant differences between mass shooters who die as a result of their attacks and those who survive their attacks. Mass shooters who died had unique behavior patterns: they armed themselves with more weapons, killed more victims, and often struck at different locations—public places, open commercial establishments—than those who survived their attacks.

There are also psychological factors that distinguish the suicidal killer from those who want to live. Suicidal killers tend to engage in profound self-loathing, whereby they feel guilty and ashamed about their inadequacies and weaknesses, including their uncontrolled anger and violent tendencies. It is possible that those who commit suicide are not only consumed by hopelessness and guilt but also by a vengeful desire to punish themselves. Those who feel the most rage and the greatest desire to punish others—and who therefore kill more victims—may also feel the most self-loathing about their own murderous desires, and thus be the most likely to punish themselves by taking their own lives in one way or another.

Mass killers' murderous outbursts may also be propelled by powerful perceptions of personal victimization, social injustice, and general hopelessness, which helps explain why they are more likely to end up dead. They may be acting in response to perceived failures in social control; they feel like they can no longer count on the system to protect them, so they take matters into their own hands. Mass murder is their violent exercise of direct control—an attempt to right past wrongs. Many attackers claim to have been fighting (and killing) to correct previous injustices and revenge their unanswered calls for help. Mass shooters who attack random victims at open commercial sites may be lashing out against perceived failures of social control—another sign that they feel hopeless about their ability to have a healthy future anywhere in society.

There are also those mass shooters who target specific individuals at the factories, offices, and warehouses where they work. Because working men have embraced masculine ideals, they may prefer to go out in a blaze of glory, killing themselves or shooting it out with cops, rather than showing they are weak or effeminate by surrendering to law enforcement.

CRITICAL THINKING

According to Lankford's research, the behavioral and psychological differences between offenders who lived and those who died as a result of their attacks may reflect fundamental differences in their motives and intent. Considering this knowledge, is there anything that can be done to prevent mass murders from taking place?

SOURCE: Adam Lankford, "Mass Shooters in the USA, 1966–2010: Differences Between Attackers Who Live and Die," *Justice Quarterly* 32 (2015): 360–379.

for mass shooters to take their own life? The Criminology in Action feature "Mass Shooters: Why Do Some Live and Why Do Some Die?" addresses this issue in some detail.

While these highly publicized incidents make it appear that mass murder is a product of contemporary society, more than 900 mass killings took place between 1900 and 1999. Mass killings were nearly as common during the 1920s and 1930s as they are today. More of the earlier incidents involved familicide (killing one's family), and killers were more likely to be older and more suicidal than they are today. The most significant difference between contemporary mass murders and those in the past: more killers use guns today and more incidents involve drug trafficking.[227]

Why Mass Murder? What group of personality traits and social conditions produce mass murder? Some of these killers were suffering from obvious mental distress and their violent outburst might be considered a product of mental disease. The shotgun Aaron Alexis used had etched into the barrel the words "End to the torment!" "Not what yall say!" "Better off this way!" and "My ELF weapon!" ELF referred to his delusional belief that he was being controlled or influenced by extremely low frequency electromagnetic waves. On his computer, law enforcement agents found the statement that "Ultra low frequency attack is what I've been subject to for the last 3 months, and to be perfectly honest that is what has driven me to this."[228]

James Alan Fox and Jack Levin have identified at least four other types of mass murderers:

- *Revenge killers* seek to get even with individuals or society at large. Their typical target is an estranged wife and "her" children or an employer and "his" employees.
- *Love killers* are motivated by a warped sense of devotion. They are often despondent people who commit suicide and take others, such as a wife and children, with them.
- *Profit killers* are usually trying to cover up a crime, eliminate witnesses, and carry out a criminal conspiracy.
- *Terrorist killers* are trying to send a message. Gang killings tell rivals to watch out; cult killers may actually leave a message behind to warn society about impending doom.[229]

SPREE KILLERS

Michael McLendon, 28, killed 10 people in rural Alabama before taking his own life. He had a target list that detectives found in his home. After killing seven members of his family, he drove around the county and killed three more people at random.[230] Spree killers like McLendon engage in a rampage of violence taking place over a period of days or weeks. Unlike mass murderers, their killing is not confined to a single outburst, and unlike serial killers, they don't have a "cooling off" period between murders or return to their "normal" identities in between killings.

The most notorious spree killing to date occurred in October 2002, in the Washington, D.C., area.[231] John Lee Malvo, 17, a Jamaican citizen, and his traveling companion John Allen Muhammad, 41, an army veteran with an expert's rating in marksmanship, went on a rampage that left more than 10 people dead.

Some spree killers target a specific group or class. Joseph Paul Franklin targeted mixed-race couples, African Americans, and Jews, committing more than 20 murders in 12 states in an effort to instigate a race war (Franklin also shot and paralyzed *Hustler* publisher Larry Flynt because he published pictures of interracial sex). Franklin was executed on November 20, 2013.[232] Others, like the D.C. snipers Malvo and Muhammed, kill randomly and do not seek out a specific class of victim; their targets included young and old, African Americans and whites, men and women.[233]

Assault and Battery

Although many people mistakenly believe the term *assault and battery* refers to a single act, they are actually two separate crimes. *Battery* requires offensive touching, such as slapping, hitting, or punching a victim. *Assault* requires no actual touching but involves either attempted battery or intentionally frightening the victim by word or deed. Although common law originally intended these twin crimes to be misdemeanors, most jurisdictions now upgrade them to felonies either when a weapon is used or when they occur during the commission of a felony (for example, when a person is assaulted during a robbery). In the UCR, the FBI defines serious assault, or aggravated assault, as "an unlawful attack by one person upon another for the purpose of inflicting severe or aggravated bodily injury"; this definition is similar to the one used in most state jurisdictions.[234]

Under common law, battery required bodily injury, such as broken limbs or wounds. However, under modern law, battery occurs if the victim suffers a temporarily painful blow, even if no injury results. Battery can also involve offensive touching, such as if a man kisses a woman against her will or puts his hands on her body.

NATURE AND EXTENT OF ASSAULT

The pattern of criminal assault is similar to that of homicide; one could say that the only difference between the two is that the victim survives.[235] Assaults may be common in our society simply because of common life stresses. Motorists who assault each other have become such a familiar occurrence that the term **road rage** has been coined. There have even been frequent incidents of violent assault among frustrated passengers who lose control while traveling.

Every citizen is bound by the law of assault, even police officers. Excessive use of force can result in criminal charges being filed even if it occurs while police officers are arresting a dangerous felony suspect. Only the minimum amount of force needed to subdue the suspect is allowed by law, and if police use more aggressive tactics than required, they may find themselves the target of criminal charges and civil lawsuits that can run into the millions of dollars.[236]

The FBI records about 740,000 assaults each year, a rate of about 230 per 100,000 inhabitants. Like other violent crimes, the number of assaults has been in decline, down about 20 percent in the past decade. Preliminary 2014 data indicate that that trend may be over; assaults increased about 2 percent in the first 6 months of 2014.

The NCVS also indicates that the number of assault victimizations has been in steep decline, dropping more than 50 percent during the past decade; even weapon-related assaults have dropped sharply. However, unlike the UCR data, the NCVS found that more than 1 million serious assaults occur each year and that the number of assaults actually rose slightly (1 percent) between 2013 and 2014.[237]

People arrested for assault and those identified by victims are usually young, male (about 80 percent), and white, although the number of African Americans arrested for assault (about one-third of the total) is disproportionate to their representation in the population. Assault victims tend to be male, but females also face a significant danger. Assault rates are highest in urban areas, during summer, and in southern and western regions. The most common

road rage A term used to describe motorists who assault each other.

weapons used in assaults are blunt instruments and hands and feet. The NCVS indicates that only about half of all serious assaults are reported to the police.

ASSAULT IN THE HOME

Violent attacks in the home are one of the most frightening types of assault. Criminologists recognize that intrafamily violence is an enduring social problem in the United States and abroad.

The UN's World Health Organization (WHO) found that around the world, women often face the greatest risk for violence in their own homes and in familiar settings. Almost half the women who die due to homicide are killed by their current or former husbands or boyfriends; in some countries about 70 percent of all female deaths are domestic homicides. It is possible that nearly one in four women will experience violence by an intimate partner in their lifetime, and most of these are subjected to multiple acts of violence over extended periods of time. In addition to physical abuse, a third to over half of these cases are accompanied by sexual violence; in some countries, up to one-third of adolescent girls report forced sexual initiation. The WHO report found that the percentage of women assaulted by a spouse or intimate partner varied considerably around the world: less than 3 percent in the United States, Canada, and Australia, up to 38 percent of the married women in the Republic of Korea, and 52 percent of Palestinian women on the West Bank and Gaza Strip. In many places, assaults and even murders occur because men believe that their partners have been defiled sexually, either through rape or sex outside of marriage. In some societies, the only way to cleanse the family honor is by killing the offending female. In Alexandria, Egypt, for example, 47 percent of the women who were killed by a relative were murdered after they had been raped.

Child Abuse   One area of intrafamily violence that has received a great deal of media attention is **child abuse**.

Child abuse can take many forms, including abandonment and neglect. Here, Lake Stevens, Washington, police detective Jerad Wachtveitl searches a home of a man and woman accused of abandoning their three young children without food or heat. It wasn't known how long the children had been unattended when police removed them from the filthy home.

AP Images/Mark Mulligan

child abuse Any physical, emotional, or sexual trauma to a child for which no reasonable explanation, such as an accident, can be found. Child abuse can also be a function of neglecting to give proper care and attention to a young child.

neglect Not providing a child with the care and shelter to which he or she is entitled.

This term describes any physical or emotional trauma to a child for which no reasonable explanation, such as an accident or ordinary disciplinary practices, can be found.[238] Child abuse can result from actual physical beatings administered to a child by hands, feet, weapons, belts, sticks, burning, and so on. Another form of abuse results from **neglect**—not providing a child with the care and shelter to which he or she is entitled.

The U.S. Department of Health and Human Services (HHS) has been monitoring the extent of child maltreatment through its annual survey of child protective services (CPS).[239] The most recent survey found that state and local CPS received an estimated 3.4 million referrals of children being abused or neglected each year. Of these, CPS estimate that 678,000 children (9 per 1,000) were actual and confirmed victims of maltreatment. Of the child victims, 78 percent were victims of neglect, 18 percent of physical abuse, 9 percent of sexual abuse, and 11 percent were victims of other types of maltreatment, including emotional and threatened abuse, parent's drug/alcohol abuse, or lack of supervision. The most serious cases of abuse result in death, and the last available data indicate that about 1,600 children die from maltreatment each year (2.2 per 100,000). If anything, the CPS data underestimate the true occurrence of abuse because so many cases go unreported and many victims are too young to seek help.

Though these figures are staggering, the number and rate of abuse have actually been in decline. Fifteen years ago more than 1 million children were identified as victims of abuse or neglect nationwide, and the rate of victimization of children was approximately 15 per 1,000 children. While these results are encouraging, trends in reported child maltreatment may be more reflective of the effect budgetary cutbacks have on CPS's ability to monitor, record, and investigate reports of abuse than an actual decline in child abuse rates.

L08 Point out the root causes of child abuse

Causes of Child Abuse   The great majority of child abuse cases involve parents. Why do parents physically assault their children? Such maltreatment is a highly complex problem with neither a single cause nor a readily available solution. It cuts across ethnic, religious, and socioeconomic lines. Abusive parents cannot be categorized by sex, age, or educational level; they come from all walks of life.[240]

A number of factors have been commonly linked to abuse and neglect:

- *Family violence* seems to be perpetuated from one generation to another within families. The behavior of abusive parents can often be traced to negative experiences in their own childhood—physical abuse, lack of love, emotional neglect, incest, and so on.
- *Blended families*, which include children living with an unrelated adult such as a stepparent or another unrelated co-resident, have also been linked to abuse. Children who live with a mother's boyfriend are at much greater risk for abuse than children living with two genetic parents. Some stepparents do not have strong emotional ties to their nongenetic children, nor do they reap emotional benefits from the parent–child relationship.[241]
- *Parents* may also become abusive if they are isolated from friends, neighbors, or relatives who can help in times of crisis. Potentially abusive parents are often alienated from society; they have carried the concept of the shrinking nuclear family to its most extreme form and are cut off from ties of kinship and contact with other people in the neighborhood.[242]

Sexual Abuse   Another aspect of the abuse syndrome is **sexual abuse**—the exploitation of children through rape, incest, and molestation by parents or other adults. It is difficult to estimate the incidence of sexual abuse, but a number of attempts have been made to gauge the extent of the problem. The most recent national survey indicates that about 61,000 cases of sexual abuse were reported. However, these reported cases may vastly undercount the true nature of the problem. In a classic study, Diana Russell's survey of women in the San Francisco area found that 38 percent had experienced intra- or extrafamilial sexual abuse by the time they reached age 18.[243]

Although sexual abuse is still prevalent, the number of reported cases has been in a significant decline, being reduced from about 78,000 reported cases in 2003.[244]

This trend must be interpreted with caution. While it is possible that the actual number of cases is truly in decline because of the effectiveness of prevention programs, increased prosecution, and public awareness campaigns, declines might be the result of more cases being overlooked because of (a) increased evidentiary requirements to substantiate cases, (b) increased caseworker caution due to new legal rights for caregivers, and (c) increasing limitations on the types of cases that agencies accept for investigation.[245]

Sexual abuse is of particular concern because children who have been abused experience a long list of symptoms, including fear, posttraumatic stress disorder, behavior problems, sexualized behavior, and poor self-esteem.[246] Women who were abused as children are also at greater risk to be reabused as adults than those who avoided childhood victimization.[247] The amount of force used during the abuse, its duration, and its frequency are all related to the extent of the long-term effects and the length of time needed for recovery.

Regardless of its cause, child abuse can have devastating long-term effects, ranging from depression to loss of self-esteem.[248] Not surprisingly, a history of childhood sexual and physical abuse among persons with severe mental illness is disproportionately high.[249]

Parental Abuse   Parents are sometimes the target of abuse from their own children. Research conducted by Arina Ulman and Murray Straus found:

- The younger the child, the higher the rate of child-to-parent violence (CPV).
- At all ages, more children were violent to mothers than to fathers.
- Both boys and girls hit mothers more often than fathers.
- At all ages, slightly more boys than girls hit parents.

Ulman and Straus found that child-to-parent violence was associated with some other form of violence by parents, which could either be husband-to-wife, wife-to-husband, corporal punishment of children, or physical abuse. They suggest that if the use of physical punishment could be eliminated or curtailed, then child-to-parent violence would similarly decline.[250]

Spousal Abuse   Spousal abuse has occurred throughout recorded history. Roman men had the legal right to beat their wives for minor acts such as attending public games without permission, drinking wine, or, walking outdoors with their faces uncovered.[251] More serious transgressions, such as adultery, were punishable by death. During the later stages of the Roman Empire, the practice of wife beating

sexual abuse Exploitation of a child through rape, incest, or molestation by a parent or other adult.

abated, and by the fourth century, excessive violence on the part of husband or wife was grounds for divorce.[252] During the early Middle Ages, there was a separation of love and marriage.[253] The ideal woman was protected, cherished, and loved from afar. In contrast, the wife, with whom marriage had been arranged by family ties, was guarded jealously and could be punished severely for violating her duties. A husband was expected to beat his wife for "misbehaviors" and might himself be punished by neighbors if he failed to do so.[254]

Through the later Middle Ages and into modern times (from 1400 to 1900), there was little community objection to a man using force against his wife as long as the assault did not exceed certain limits, usually construed as death or disfigurement. By the mid-nineteenth century, severe wife beating fell into disfavor, and accused wife beaters were subject to public ridicule. Nonetheless, limited chastisement was still the rule. By the close of the nineteenth century, England and the United States outlawed wife beating. Yet the long history of husbands' domination over their wives made physical coercion hard to control. Until recent times, the subordinate position of women in the family was believed to give husbands the legal and moral obligation to manage their wives' behavior. Even after World War II, English courts found physical assault a reasonable punishment for a wife who had disobeyed her husband.[255] These ideas form the foundation of men's traditional physical control of women and have led to severe cases of spousal assault.

The Nature and Extent of Spousal Abuse It is difficult to estimate how widespread spousal abuse is today; however, some statistics indicate the extent of the problem. In their classic study of family violence, Richard Gelles and Murray Straus found that 16 percent of surveyed families had experienced husband–wife assaults.[256] In police departments around the country, 60 to 70 percent of evening calls involve domestic disputes.

Males are also the target of abuse. One recent study of 12,000 male abuse victims serving in the U.S. Army found that abused men were at greater risk for early army discharge and hospitalization than were nonvictims—particularly hospitalizations for depression, alcohol dependence, and mental health problems.[257]

Some of the personal attributes and characteristics of spouse abusers and abusive situations are listed in Exhibit 10.4.

DATING VIOLENCE

Date rape is not the only form of violence aimed at a boyfriend or girlfriend.[258] A significant portion of all teens have been the target of dating violence, and it is estimated that one high school girl in five may suffer sexual or physical abuse from a boyfriend. Dating violence has been linked to substance abuse, unsafe sex, and eating disorders.[259]

EXHIBIT 10.4

Factors that Predict Spousal Abuse

- *Presence of alcohol.* Excessive alcohol use may turn otherwise docile husbands into wife abusers.
- *Access to weapons.* A perpetrator's access to a gun and previous threats with a weapon may lead to abuse.
- *Stepchild in the home.* Having a stepchild living in the home may provoke abuse because the stepparent may have a more limited bond to the child.
- *Estrangement.* This may occur especially in the case of a controlling partner and subsequent involvement with another partner.
- *Hostility toward dependency.* Some husbands who appear docile and passive may resent their dependence on their wives and react with rage and violence; this reaction has been linked to sexual inadequacy.
- *Excessive brooding.* Obsession with a wife's behavior, however trivial, can result in violent assaults.
- *Social learning.* Some males believe society approves of spouse or mate abuse and use these beliefs to justify their violent behavior. Peer support helps shape their attitudes and behaviors.
- *Socioeconomic factors.* Men who fail as providers and are under economic stress may take their frustrations out on their wives.
- *Flashes of anger.* Research shows that a significant amount of family violence results from a sudden burst of anger after a verbal dispute.
- *Military service.* Spousal abuse among men who have served in the military service is extremely high. Those serving in the military are more likely to assault their wives than civilian husbands. The reasons for this phenomenon may be the violence promoted by military training and the close proximity in which military families live to one another.
- *Having been battered children.* Husbands who assault their wives were generally battered as children.
- *Unpredictability.* Batterers are unpredictable, unable to be influenced by their wives, and impossible to prevent from battering once an argument has begun.

SOURCES: Christine Sellers, John Cochran, and Kathryn Branch, "Social Learning Theory and Partner Violence: A Research Note," *Deviant Behavior* 26 (2005) 379–395; Jacquelyn Campbell, Daniel Webster, Jane Koziol-McLain, Carolyn Block, Doris Campbell, Mary Ann Curry, Faye Gary, Nancy Glass, Judith McFarlane, Carolyn Sachs, Phyllis Sharps, Yvonne Ulrich, Susan Wilt, Jennifer Manganello, Xiao Xu, Janet Schollenberger, Victoria Frye, and Kathryn Laughon, "Risk Factors for Femicide in Abusive Relationships: Results from a Multisite Case Control Study," *American Journal of Public Health* 93 (2003): 1089–1097.

Physical dating violence can involve a wide spectrum of activities—scratching, slapping, pushing, slamming or holding someone against a wall, biting, choking, burning, beating someone up, and assault with a weapon—ranging from moderate to severe. There is also emotional and psychological abuse, including insulting, criticizing, threatening, humiliating, or berating. An emerging form of emotional abuse is referred to as **relational aggression** in which a partner tries to damage a person's relationship with friends by spreading smears and false rumors or by revealing information or images intended to be private.

 Read more about teen dating violence at the Centers for Disease Control and Prevention (CDC) webpage: http://www.cdc.gov /violenceprevention/intimatepartnerviolence/teen _dating_violence.html.
Is there something we can do to prevent dating violence? What would you suggest?

Robbery

 LO9 Understand the crime of robbery and discuss why it is a rational crime

The common-law definition of robbery (and the one used by the FBI) is "the taking or attempting to take anything of value from the care, custody or control of a person or persons by force or threat of force or violence and/or by putting the victim in fear."[260] A robbery is considered a violent crime because it involves the use of force to obtain money or goods. Robbery is punished severely because the victim's life is put in jeopardy. In fact, the severity of punishment is based on the amount of force used during the crime, not the value of the items taken.

The FBI records about 325,000 robberies each year, a rate of about 102 per 100,000 population. As with most other violent crimes, there has been a significant reduction in the robbery rate during the past decade; the robbery rate is down almost 40 percent.

The ecological pattern for robbery is similar to that of other violent crimes, with one significant exception: northeastern states have the highest robbery rates by far. Whereas most crime rates are higher in the summer, robberies seem to peak during the winter months. One reason may be that the cold weather allows for greater disguise; another reason is that robbers may be attracted to the large amounts of cash people and merchants carry during the Christmas shopping season.[261] Robbers may also be more active in winter because days are shorter, affording them greater concealment in the dark.

TYPES OF ROBBERS/TYPES OF ROBBERIES

Attempts have been made to classify and explain the nature and dynamics of robbery. One approach is to characterize robberies by type (Exhibit 10.5), and another is to characterize types of robbers based on their specialties (Exhibit 10.6).

As these typologies indicate, the typical armed robber is unlikely to be a professional who carefully studies targets while planning a crime. People walking along the street,

---

convenience stores, and gas stations are much more likely robbery targets than banks or other highly secure environments. Robbers, therefore, seem to be diverted by modest defensive measures, such as having more than one clerk in a store or locating stores in strip malls; they are more likely to try an isolated store.[262]

THE CALCULATING ROBBER

While many robbers are amateurs, robbery remains a crime of rationality and planning. Some robbers target fellow

relational aggression Psychological and emotional abuse that involves the spreading of smears, rumors, and private information in order to harm a person's partner.

EXHIBIT 10.6

Types of Robbers

- *Professional robbers.* These robbers have a long-term commitment to crime as a source of livelihood. This type of robber plans and organizes crimes prior to committing them and seeks money to support a hedonistic lifestyle. Some professionals are exclusively robbers, whereas others engage in additional types of crimes. Professionals are committed to robbing because it is direct, fast, and profitable. They hold no other steady job and plan three or four "big scores" a year to support themselves. Planning and skill are the trademarks of the professional robber, who usually operates in groups with assigned roles. Professionals usually steal large amounts from commercial establishments. After a score, they may stop for a few weeks until "things cool off."

- *Opportunist robbers.* These robbers steal to obtain small amounts of money when an accessible target presents itself. They are not committed to robbery but will steal from cab drivers, drunks, the elderly, and other vulnerable persons if they need some extra spending money. Opportunists are usually teens and gang members who do not plan their crimes. Although they operate within the milieu of the juvenile gang, they are seldom organized and spend little time discussing weapon use, getaway plans, or other strategies.

- *Addict robbers.* These people steal to support their drug habits. They have a low commitment to robbery because of its danger but a high commitment to theft because it supplies needed funds. The addict is less likely to plan crime or use weapons than the professional robber but is more cautious than the opportunist. Addicts choose targets that present minimal risk; however, when desperate for funds, they are sometimes careless in selecting the victim and executing the crime. They rarely think in terms of the big score; they just want enough money to get their next fix.

- *Alcoholic robbers.* These people steal for reasons related to their excessive consumption of alcohol. Alcoholic robbers steal (a) when, in a disoriented state, they attempt to get some money to buy liquor or (b) when their condition makes them unemployable and they need funds. Alcoholic robbers have no real commitment to robbery as a way of life. They plan their crimes randomly and give little thought to their victim, circumstance, or escape. For that reason, they are the most likely to be caught.

SOURCES: Katie Willis, *Armed Robbery: Who Commits It and Why?* (Canberra: Australian Institute of Criminology, 2006); John Conklin, *Robbery and the Criminal Justice System* (New York: Lippincott, 1972), pp. 1–80.

criminals—for example, drug dealers.[263] Although these fellow criminals may be dangerous, robbers recognize that people with "dirty hands" are unlikely to call police and get entangled with the law. Ripping off a dealer kills three birds with one stone, providing both money and drugs at the same time, while targeting victims who are quite unlikely to call the police.[264]

When Bruce Jacobs interviewed armed robbers, he found that some specialize in targeting drug dealers because they believe that even though their work is hazardous, the rewards outweigh the risks: drug dealers are plentiful, visible, and accessible, and they carry plenty of cash. Their merchandise is valuable, is easily transported, and can be used by the robber or sold to another. Drug dealers are not particularly popular, so they cannot rely on bystanders to come to their aid. Of course, drug dealers may be able to "take care of business" themselves, but surprisingly, Jacobs found that many choose not to carry a pistol.[265] Drug dealers may be tough and bad, the robbers claim, but *they* are tougher and badder.

In their important book *Armed Robbers in Action: Stickups and Street Culture,* Scott Decker and Richard Wright interviewed active robbers in St. Louis, Missouri, and found that robbers are rational decision makers who look for easy prey. One ideal target is the married man who is looking for illicit sexual adventures and hires a prostitute, only to be robbed by her and her pimp. The robbers know that this victim will not be inclined to call the police and bring himself to their attention.

Because they realize that the risk of detection and punishment is the same whether the victim is carrying a load of cash or is penniless, experienced robbers use discretion in selecting targets. People whose clothing, jewelry, and demeanor mark them as carrying substantial amounts of cash make suitable targets; people who look like they can fight back are avoided. Some robbers station themselves at cash machines to spot targets who are flashing stacks of money.[266]

Wright and Decker are not the only researchers who found that most robbers seek out vulnerable victims. According to research by criminologist Jody Miller, female armed robbers are likely to choose female targets, reasoning that they will be more vulnerable and offer less resistance.[267] When robbing males, women "set them up" to catch them off guard; some feign sexual interest or prostitution to gain the upper hand.[268]

Wright and Decker found that most armed robberies are motivated by a pressing need for cash. Many robbers careen from one financial crisis to the next, prompted by their endless quest for stimulation and thrills. Interviewees described how they partied, gambled, drank, and abused substances until they were broke. Their partying not only provided excitement but also helped generate a street reputation as someone who can "make things happen." Robbers had a "here and now" mentality and required a constant supply of cash to fuel their appetites.

Marcus Felson describes robbers as foragers, predators who search for victims, preferably close to their homes, where numerous "nutritious" victims are abundant, where the robbers know the territory so that their prey cannot easily escape, and where their victims may be less vigilant because they are on their home turf.[269] Robbers, then, select targets that are *vulnerable, accessible,* and *profitable.* If a victim looks tough—"street credible"—the robber may choose to use violence at the outset rather than wait for the victim to resist. During the robbery itself, victims who fight back are the ones most likely to be attacked and injured. Victim passivity may be the best way to avoid injury during a robbery.[270]

Carjacking We can see this element of rationality and planning in the strategies of one type of robber: carjackers, who attack occupied vehicles for the purpose of theft. Carjacking is not a random event committed by amateurs but is carefully planned and carried out by experienced criminals. To be successful, carjackers must develop both perceptual (choosing the vehicle) and procedural (commandeering the vehicle) skills.[271] Carjackers must learn when their efforts are having a desired effect—scaring the victim. Developing these perceptual skills lets carjackers know exactly how effective their efforts are and helps them instantly adjust the application of those skills. They must constantly process information and make split-second decisions to react properly to a rapidly changing environment, not a task for amateurs.

When Heith Copes, Andy Hochstetler, and Michael Cherbonneau interviewed a sample of carjackers, they were told that, to get the upper hand, robbers avoid the likelihood of victims fighting back by devoting attention to selecting "proper victims" who are the least likely to resist.[272] Ironically, some steer clear of women drivers, fearing that their victims will panic and start to yell for help or act erratically, making them difficult to control.

Once a victim has been chosen, carjackers carefully form a line of attack designed to shock the victim into compliance. Some use a blitz method, attacking so rapidly that the target does not have time to respond. Others manipulate their appearance, posing as a street vendor, in order to approach potential victims without causing alarm. Some wait for an opportune moment, lurking in parking lots and approaching inattentive victims as they enter their cars, demanding that they surrender their keys. The research uncovered the fact that carjackers used and reused scripts when committing their crimes. Sticking to their scripts enabled carjackers to reduce danger and to use their skills and experience to prevent detection. Sticking to the script also prolongs a criminal career. It builds confidence and helps the carjacker act quickly and decisively, analyzing the situation and figuring out what must be done. No matter what the strategy, carjackers seem rational and calculating.

ACQUAINTANCE ROBBERY

As Exhibit 10.6 suggests, one type of robber may focus on people they know, a phenomenon referred to as acquaintance robbery. This seems puzzling because victims can easily identify their attackers and report them to the police. However, despite this threat, acquaintance robbery may be attractive for a number of rational reasons:[273]

- Victims may be reluctant to report these crimes because they do not want to get involved with the police. They may be involved in crime themselves (drug dealers, for example), or they may fear retaliation if they report the crime. Some victims may be reluctant to gain the label of "rat" or "fink" if they go to the police.
- Some robberies are motivated by street justice. The robber has a grievance against the victim and settles the dispute by stealing the victim's property. In this instance, robbery may be considered a substitute for an assault: the robber wants retribution and revenge rather than remuneration.[274]
- Because the robber knows the victim personally, the robber has inside information that there will be a "good take." Offenders may target people they know to be carrying a large amount of cash or who just purchased expensive jewelry.
- A person in desperate need of immediate cash may target people in close proximity simply because they are convenient targets.

When Richard Felson and his associates studied acquaintance robbery, they found that victims were more likely to be injured in acquaintance robberies than in stranger robberies, indicating that revenge rather than reward was the primary motive.[275] Similarly, robberies of family members were more likely to have a bigger payoff than stranger robberies, an indication that the offender was aware that the target had a large amount of cash on hand.

Emerging Forms of Interpersonal Violence

L010 Describe emerging forms of violence such as stalking, hate crimes, and workplace violence

Assault, rape, robbery, and murder are traditional forms of interpersonal violence. As more data become available, criminologists have recognized relatively new subcategories within these crime types, such as serial murder and date rape. Additional new categories of interpersonal violence are now receiving attention in criminological literature; the next sections describe three of these forms of violent crime.

acquaintance robbery Robbers who focus their thefts on people they know.

HATE CRIMES

Hate crimes usually involve convenient, vulnerable targets who are unlikely to fight back: vagrants, homeless people, religious minorities, LGBTQ people, and the mentally and physically challenged.

The factors that precipitate hate crimes are listed in Exhibit 10.7.

The Roots of Hate   Why do people commit bias crimes? In their book *Hate Crimes*, Jack McDevitt and Jack Levin identify three motivations for hate crimes: **thrill-seeking hate crimes**, **reactive (defensive) hate crimes**, and **mission hate crimes**:

- *Thrill-seeking hate crimes.* In the same way some kids like to get together to shoot hoops, hatemongers join forces to have fun by bashing minorities or destroying property. Inflicting pain on others gives them a sadistic thrill.
- *Reactive (defensive) hate crimes.* Perpetrators of these crimes rationalize their behavior as a defensive stand taken against outsiders whom they believe threaten their community or way of life. A gang of teens that attacks a new family in the neighborhood because they are the "wrong" race is committing a reactive hate crime.
- *Mission hate crimes.* Some disturbed individuals see it as their duty to rid the world of evil. Those on a "mission," such as skinheads, the Ku Klux Klan (KKK), and white supremacist groups, may seek to eliminate people who threaten their religious beliefs because they are members

Images of Deah Barakat, 23, a University of North Carolina student, and his wife, Yusor Abu-Salha, 21, are projected as friends speak to thousands who gathered for a vigil and memorial. The two were killed along with Yusor's sister, Razan Abu-Salha, 19, on February 11, 2015. Craig Hicks, 46, of Chapel Hill was charged with three counts of first-degree murder. Was this a hate crime or the outcome of a dispute over a parking space? Postings on Facebook suggest the former. Hicks wrote, "I don't deny you your right to believe whatever you'd like; but I have the right to point out it's ignorant and dangerous for as long as your baseless superstitions keep killing people."

Justin Cook/Redux

of a different faith or threaten "racial purity" because they are of a different race.[276]

More recent research by McDevitt and Levin with Susan Bennett used data from the Community Disorders Unit (CDU) of the Boston Police Department to uncover a new category of hate crime: **retaliatory hate crimes**. These offenses are committed in response to a hate crime, whether real or perceived; whether the original incident

---

hate crimes Acts of violence or intimidation designed to terrorize or frighten people considered undesirable because of their race, religion, ethnic origin, or sexual orientation.

thrill-seeking hate crimes Acts by hatemongers who join forces to have fun by bashing minorities or destroying property; inflicting pain on others gives them a sadistic thrill.

reactive (defensive) hate crimes Perpetrators believe they are taking a defensive stand against outsiders whom they believe threaten their community or way of life.

mission hate crimes Violent crimes committed by disturbed individuals who see it as their duty to rid the world of evil.

retaliatory hate crimes A hate crime motivated by revenge for another hate crime, either real or imaginary, which may spark further retaliation.

EXHIBIT 10.7

Factors that Precipitate Hate Crimes

- Poor or uncertain economic conditions
- Racial stereotypes in films and on television
- Hate-filled discourse on talk shows or in political advertisements
- The use of racial code language such as "welfare mothers" and "inner-city thugs"
- An individual's personal experiences with members of particular minority groups
- Scapegoating—blaming a minority group for the misfortunes of society as a whole

SOURCE: "A Policymaker's Guide to Hate Crimes," *Bureau of Justice Assistance Monograph* (Washington, DC: Bureau of Justice Assistance, 1997).

actually occurred is irrelevant. Their more recent research indicates that most hate crimes can be classified as thrill motivated (66 percent) followed by defensive (25 percent) and retaliatory (8 percent). Few cases were mission-oriented offenders.[277]

In his book *The Violence of Hate*, Levin notes that in addition to the traditional hatemongers, hate crimes can be committed by "dabblers"—people who are not committed to hate but drift in and out of active bigotry. They may be young people who get drunk on Saturday night and assault a gay couple or attack an African American man who happens by; they then go back to work or school on Monday. Some are thrill seekers, while others may be reacting to the presence of members of a disliked group in their neighborhood. Levin also notes that some people are "sympathizers": they may not attack African Americans but think nothing of telling jokes with racial themes or agreeing with people who despise gays. Finally, there are "spectators," who may not actively participate in bigotry but who do nothing to stop its course. They may even vote for politicians who are openly bigoted because they agree with their tax policies or some other positions, neglecting to process the fact that their vote empowers prejudice and leads to hate.[278]

Nature and Extent of Hate Crime

According to the FBI, about 6,000 hate crime incidents are reported to police each year.[279] And like other violent crimes, the number has been in decline since they peaked at about 8,000 in 2005. However, according to data collected by the NCVS, this number significantly undercounts the actual incidence of hate crimes. The latest data indicate that an estimated 293,800 nonfatal violent and property hate crime victimizations occurred in the United States. While there has been no significant change in the number of reported hate crimes, motivations have shifted significantly during the past decade. Today, about half of hate crimes were motivated by ethnicity bias (i.e., the victim's ancestral, cultural, social, or national affiliation), up from 22 percent in 2004. The percentage of hate crimes motivated by religious bias nearly tripled from 10 percent in 2004 to 28 percent, and the percentage of hate crimes motivated by gender bias more than doubled, from 12 percent to 26 percent during the same period. About 90 percent of all hate crimes are violent victimizations, and about 27 percent of hate crimes were classified as serious violent crimes—rape or sexual assault, robbery and aggravated assault—while the majority of hate crimes (63 percent) were simple assaults. In all, hate crimes accounted for 1.2 percent of total victimizations, 4.2 percent of violent victimizations, and 0.2 percent of property victimizations.[280]

In crimes where victims could actually identify the culprits, most victims reported that they were acquainted with their attackers or that their attackers were actually friends, coworkers, neighbors, or relatives. Younger victims were more likely to be victimized by people known to them. Hate crimes can occur in many settings, but most are perpetrated in public settings.

To learn more about the FBI's hate crime data collections and to access information on hate crimes, go to **http://www.fbi.gov/about-us /investigate/civilrights/hate_crimes.**
Do hate crimes support rational choice theory?

Controlling Hate Crimes

Today almost every state jurisdiction has enacted some form of legislation designed to combat hate crimes: 45 states have enacted laws against bias-motivated violence and intimidation; 27 states have statutes that specifically mandate the collection of hate crime data.[281]

Some critics argue that it is unfair to punish criminals motivated by hate any more severely than those who commit similar crimes whose motivation is revenge, greed, or anger. There is also the danger that what appears to be a hate crime, because the target is a minority group member, may actually be motivated by some other factor such as vengeance or monetary gain. In November 2004, Aaron McKinney (who is serving a life sentence for killing Matthew Shepard) told *ABC News* correspondent Elizabeth Vargas that he was high on methamphetamine when he killed Shepard, and that his intent was robbery and not hate. His partner, Russell Henderson, claimed that the killing was simply a robbery gone bad: "It was not because me and Aaron had anything against gays."[282]

However, in his important book *Punishing Hate: Bias Crimes Under American Law*, Frederick Lawrence argues that criminals motivated by bias deserve to be punished more severely than those who commit identical crimes for other motives.[283] He suggests that a society dedicated to the equality of all its people must treat bias crimes differently from other crimes and in so doing enhance the punishment of these crimes.[284]

Some criminals choose their victims randomly; others select specific victims, as in crimes of revenge. Bias crimes are different. They are crimes in which (a) distinct identifying characteristics of the victim are critical to the perpetrator's choice of victim, and (b) the individual identity of the victim is irrelevant.[285] Lawrence views a bias crime as one that would not have been committed but for the victim's membership in a particular group.[286] Bias crimes should be punished more severely because the harm caused will exceed that caused by crimes with other motivations:[287]

- Bias crimes are more likely to be violent and involve serious physical injury to the victim.
- Bias crimes will have significant emotional and psychological impact on the victim; they result in a "heightened sense of vulnerability," which causes depression, anxiety, and feelings of helplessness.
- Bias crimes harm not only the victim but also the "target community."

- Bias crimes violate the shared value of equality among citizens and racial and religious harmony in a heterogeneous society.

Recent research by McDevitt and his associates that made use of bias crime records collected by the Boston police supports Lawrence's position. McDevitt found that the victims of bias crime experience more severe post-crime psychological trauma, for a longer period of time, than do victims of similar crimes that are not motivated by hate or bias. Hate crime victims are more likely to suffer intrusive thoughts, feelings of danger, nervousness, and depression at a higher level than other crime victims.[288] Considering the damage caused by bias crimes, it seems appropriate that they be punished more severely than typical common-law crimes.

Legal Controls Should symbolic acts of hate such as drawing a swastika or burning a cross be banned or are they protected by the free speech clause of the First Amendment? The U.S. Supreme Court helped answer this question in the case of *Virginia v. Black* (2003) when it upheld a Virginia statute that makes it a felony "for any person . . . with the intent of intimidating any person or group . . . to burn . . . a cross on the property of another, a highway or other public place," and specifies that "[a]ny such burning . . . shall be prima facie evidence of an intent to intimidate a person or group." The Court ruled that cross burning was intertwined with the Ku Klux Klan and its reign of terror throughout the South. The Court has long held that statements in which the speaker intends to communicate intent to commit an act of unlawful violence to a particular individual or group of individuals is not protected free speech and can be criminalized; the speaker need not actually intend to carry out the threat.[289]

WORKPLACE VIOLENCE

In a shocking case of workplace violence, two WDBJ (Roanoke, Virginia) television journalists, Alison Parker and Adam Ward, were killed on air while doing a live newsfeed.

workplace violence Irate employees or former employees attack coworkers or sabotage machinery and production lines; now considered the third leading cause of occupational injury or death.

Here, on August 26, 2015, in Moneta, Virginia, police investigators look at the body of WDBJ cameraman Adam Ward after he and reporter Alison Parker were fatally shot during an on-air interview. Authorities identified the suspect as Vester Lee Flanagan II, who appeared on WDBJ as Bryce Williams. The motive: Flanagan was fired from the station for what he considered to be unfair racist reasons and blamed Ward and Parker for his dismissal. After a five-hour manhunt, Flanagan shot himself during a car chase with police officers and died later at a local hospital.

AP Images/Steve Helber

The two were gunned down by a former coworker named Vester Flanagan (professional name Bryce Williams), who had a grudge against the station and its employees.[290] The shooter later took his own life rather than surrender to police.

Workplace violence is now considered one of the leading causes of occupational injury or death.[291] It consists of such acts as overt violence causing physical harm, nonfatal assaults with or without weapons, and lethal violence. It may also involve disruptive, aggressive, hostile, or emotionally abusive conduct that interrupts the flow of the workplace and causes employees concern for their personal safety, such as bullying, stalking, and threatening.[292]

Workplace violence can take a number of different forms:

- Violent acts by criminals who have no other connection with the workplace but enter to commit robbery or another crime
- Violence directed at employees by customers, clients, patients, students, inmates, or any others for whom an organization provides services
- Violence against coworkers, supervisors, or managers by a present or former employee
- Violence committed in the workplace by someone who doesn't work there but has a personal relationship with an employee—an abusive spouse or domestic partner[293]

Who engages in workplace violence? The typical offender is a middle-aged white male who faces termination in a worsening economy. The fear of economic ruin is especially strong in agencies such as the U.S. Postal Service, where long-term employees fear job loss because of automation and reorganization. In contrast, younger workers usually kill while committing a robbery or another felony.

Creating Workplace Violence   Experts believe that workplace violence is not spontaneous—individuals do not "snap" and suddenly become violent. Instead, the path to violence is taken in small steps, consisting of such behaviors of concern as brooding and odd writings or drawings, which keep building in intensity.[294]

A number of factors precipitate workplace violence. One suspected cause is a management style that appears cold and insensitive to workers. As corporations cut their staffs because of some economic downturn or workers are summarily replaced with cost-effective technology, long-term employees may become irate and irrational; their unexpected layoff can lead to violent reactions. The effect is most pronounced when managers are unsympathetic and nonsupportive; their callous attitude may help trigger workplace violence.

Not all workplace violence is triggered by management-induced injustice. In some incidents coworkers have been killed because they refused romantic relationships with the assailants or reported them for sexual harassment. Others have been killed because they got a job the assailant coveted.

Irate clients and customers have also killed because of poor service or perceived slights. While hospital employees are taught to handle agitated patients, sometimes people whose demands have not been met may turn on these caregivers: health care and social services workers have the highest rate of nonfatal assault injuries. Nurses are three times more likely to experience workplace violence than any other professional group.[295] In one Los Angeles incident, a former patient shot and critically wounded three doctors because his demands for painkillers had gone unheeded.[296] There are a variety of responses to workplace provocations. Some people take out their anger and aggression by attacking their supervisors in an effort to punish the company that dismissed them; this is a form of murder by proxy.[297] Disgruntled employees may also attack family members or friends, misdirecting the rage and frustration caused by their work situation. Others are content with sabotaging company equipment; computer databases are particularly vulnerable to tampering. The aggrieved party may do nothing to rectify the situation; this inaction is referred to as **sufferance**. Over time, the unresolved conflict may be compounded by other events that cause an eventual eruption.

The Extent of Workplace Violence   While a handful of high-profile mass shootings at a workplace have led to increased public awareness of the problem, nonfatal workplace violence is actually a much more common phenomenon. According to the Bureau of Justice Statistics, more than 572,000 nonfatal violent crimes—rape, robbery, or assault—occur annually against persons age 16 or older while they were at work or on duty. The number of incidents has declined by almost 75 percent since 1993.[298] About 750 workplace violence incidents involved homicides; 40 percent of workplace homicide offenders were robbers and 32 percent were committed by some other non-workplace assailant. Work associates—current and former co-workers, customers, and clients—accounted for about 21 percent of workplace homicide offenders. Spouses, relatives, and other personal acquaintances accounted for about 8 percent of offenders.

It is estimated that these events cost the American workforce approximately $36 billion per year, including lost work time, employee medical benefits, legal expenses, replacing lost employees and retraining new ones, decreased productivity, higher insurance premiums, raised security costs, bad publicity, lost business, and expensive litigation.[299]

Can Workplace Violence Be Controlled?   One approach is to use third parties to mediate disputes. The restorative justice movement (discussed in Chapter 8) advocates the use of mediation to resolve interpersonal disputes. Restorative justice techniques may work particularly well in the workplace, where disputants know one another and tensions may have been simmering over a long period. This may help control the rising tide of workplace violence. Another idea is a human resources approach, with aggressive job retraining and continued medical coverage after layoffs; it is also important to use objective, fair hearings to thwart unfair or biased terminations. Perhaps rigorous screening tests can help identify violence-prone workers so they can be given anger management training. Most importantly, employers may want to establish policies restricting weapons in the workplace: recent research shows that workplaces where guns were specifically permitted are five to seven times more likely to be the site of a worker homicide than those where all weapons were prohibited.[300]

STALKING

Frank Mendoza began a romantic relationship with a woman in Jacksonville, Florida. When he became emotionally and psychologically abusive toward the victim she broke it off and moved to Connecticut, telling him that

---

sufferance The aggrieved party does nothing to rectify a conflict situation; over time, the unresolved conflict may be compounded by other events that cause an eventual eruption.

she was moving to Rhode Island for a work-related training program. When Mendoza found out about the ruse, he began to stalk his victim. For almost 10 years he made harassing and threatening phone calls to her, her friends, and her work colleagues. He then traveled to Connecticut and placed bottles containing hydrochloric acid in her car, set to explode. When the victim noticed the bombs she ran from the car before the acid bottles blew up. In 2014, Mendoza was sentenced to 10 years in prison for what is now a recognized form of long-term and repeat victimization: **stalking**.[301] Stalking is generally defined as a course of conduct directed at a specific person that involves repeated physical or visual proximity, nonconsensual communication, or verbal, written, or implied threats sufficient to cause fear in a reasonable person.[302]

All 50 states and the federal government now have stalking statutes that cover a wide range of behavior, ranging from physical attacks such as those Mendoza planned to using surveillance technology such as GPS-equipped cell phones or involving third parties such as family and friends in the stalking scheme.

There are significant differences in how the states legally define stalking.[303] Some require that the defendant's behavior cause the victim actual fear, which typically requires the victim to show how his or her behavior changed due to the stalking; others only require that the behavior would cause a reasonable person to feel fear. There are also state-level differences in the amount of fear required before an act can be considered stalking, ranging from mere emotional distress to feelings of being terrorized, intimidated, or threatened; some require that the victim fear serious bodily injury or death. Many states require that the offender pose a credible threat.

Fourteen states classify stalking as a felony upon first offense. Thirty-five states classify it as a felony only if there is a second offense and/or when the crime involves aggravating factors such as use of a weapon or violation of a court order.

How big a problem is stalking? National studies indicate that stalking is now a routine behavior. The Centers for Disease Control and Prevention found that 16 percent of women and 5 percent of men had been stalked during their lifetime and "felt very fearful or believed that they or someone close to them would be harmed or killed as a result of the perpetrator's behavior."[304]

While this research is disturbing, it may actually undercount the problem. The most recent national data indicate that stalkers victimize more than 3 million people each year; while males can be victims, females are nearly three times

as likely to be stalked.[305] For example, one study of college-age women found that 13 percent reported being stalked. Considering that there are more than 6.5 million women attending college in the United States, about 700,000 women are being stalked each year on college campuses alone.[306]

Most victims know their stalker in some way; in about 30 percent of cases, the stalker is a current or former intimate partner. Former partners have leverage over their victim; they can use the information they have about their former partner's friends and family members—where they work, shop, and go for entertainment—to terrorize victims.[307]

Women are most likely to be stalked by an intimate partner—a current spouse, a former spouse, someone they lived with, or even a date. In contrast, men typically are stalked by a stranger or an acquaintance. The typical female victim is stalked because her assailant wants to control her, scare her, or keep her in a relationship.

While national data indicate that women are much more likely to be stalked than men, this may be misleading. Recent research by Jennifer Owens shows that females are much more likely to report being afraid of their stalkers, a criterion to define an act as stalking under the law. When women and men were similarly subjected to serious stalking behaviors, females were far more likely than males to meet the fear criterion, helping to explain gender differences in the stalking rate.[308]

Why Stalkers Stalk   Victims of both genders find that there is a clear relationship between stalking and other emotionally controlling and physically abusive behavior. Some psychologists believe that most stalkers are persons with mental illness who create social and public problems due to their violent behavior.[309]

Stalkers behave in ways that induce fear, but they do not always make overt threats against their victims. Many follow or spy upon their victims, some threaten to kill pets, and others vandalize property. Criminologist Mary Brewster found that stalkers who make verbal threats are the ones most likely to later attack their victims.[310] However, it is not uncommon for stalking to end in violence.

Though stalking is a serious problem, research indicates that many cases are dropped by the courts even though the stalkers often have extensive criminal histories and are frequently the subject of protective orders. A lenient response may be misplaced considering that there is evidence that stalkers repeat their criminal activity within a short time of the lodging of a stalking charge with police authorities.[311] Victims experience its social and psychological consequences long afterward. About one-third seek psychological treatment, and about one-fifth lose time from work; some never return to work.

Why does stalking stop? Most often because the victim moved away or the police got involved or, in some cases, when the stalker met another love interest.

stalking A pattern of behavior directed at a specific person that includes repeated physical or visual proximity, unwanted communications, and/or threats sufficient to cause fear in a reasonable person.

LO1 Differentiate among the various causes of violent crime

Violence has become an all-too-common aspect of modern life. Among the various explanations of sources of violent crime are exposure to violence, personal traits and makeup, evolutionary factors and human instincts, cultural values and a subculture of violence, substance abuse, and socialization and upbringing.

LO2 Articulate the stages in Athens's violentization process

According to Lonnie Athens, violence is the product of a full cycle of the violentization process—brutalization, belligerence, violent performances, and virulency—to become socialized into violence. Many brutalized children do not go on to become violent criminals, and some later reject the fact that they were abused as youths and redefine their early years as normative. Only those who are brutalized become violent themselves.

LO3 Discuss the history of rape and the different types of rape and rapists

Rape, defined in common law as "the carnal knowledge of a female forcibly and against her will," has been known throughout history, but the view of rape has evolved. Rape has been an instrument of war for thousands of years. There are different types of rapists, including those motivated by anger, power, and sadism. There are numerous forms of rape, including statutory, acquaintance, and date rape.

LO4 Assess the legal issues in rape prosecution

Rape is an extremely difficult charge to prove in court. The victim's lack of consent must be proven; therefore, it almost seems that the victim is on trial. Rape shield laws have been developed to protect victims from having their personal life placed on trial.

LO5 Compare and contrast the different degrees of murder

Murder is defined as killing a human being with malice aforethought. There are different degrees of murder, and punishments vary accordingly. First-degree murder involves malice and premeditation. Second-degree murder requires malice aforethought but not premeditation or deliberation. Voluntary manslaughter refers to a killing, typically without a weapon, committed in the heat of passion or during a sudden quarrel that provoked violence. Although intent may be present, malice is not. Involuntary or negligent manslaughter refers to a killing that occurs when a person's acts are negligent and without regard for the harm they may cause others.

LO6 Assess stranger and acquaintance homicide

One important characteristic of murder is that the victim and criminal often know each other. Murder can be a family affair, the result of a love triangle or relationship gone wrong. Some murders are sexually based. There are also stranger killings that occur during robberies and other crimes. Some occur in schools when shooters kill random students. Stranger murder often involves an interpersonal transaction in which a hostile action by the victim precipitates a murderous relationship. In some instances, it is the victim who initiates the murderous transaction, such as a barroom brawl, and is killed in the aftermath.

LO7 Analyze the differences among serial killing, mass murder, and spree killing

Murder can involve a single victim or be a serial killing, mass murder, or spree killing, which involve multiple victims. The difference between a spree killer and a serial killer is that the latter retains his or her identity and kills secretly. The spree killer abandons his or her normal identity and continues killing until he or she is identified and captured.

LO8 Point out the root causes of child abuse

A number of factors have been commonly linked to abuse and neglect. Family violence seems to be perpetuated from one generation to another within families. The behavior of abusive parents can often be traced to negative experiences in their own childhood. Blended families, which include children living with an unrelated adult such as a stepparent or another unrelated co-resident, have also been linked to abuse. Parents may also become abusive if they are isolated from friends, neighbors, or relatives who can help in times of crisis.

LO9 Understand the crime of robbery and discuss why it is a rational crime

The definition of robbery is "the taking or attempting to take anything of value from the care, custody or control of a person or persons by force or threat of force or violence and/or by putting the victim in fear." A robbery is considered a violent crime because it involves the use of force to obtain money or goods. Robbery is punished severely because the victim's life is put in jeopardy. In fact, the severity of punishment is based on the amount of force used during the crime, not the value of the items taken. Robbery that involves people who know each other is acquaintance robbery. Robbers carefully analyze targets and avoid those who seem dangerous. Robbers therefore appear rational in their choice of crime.

LO10 Describe emerging forms of violence such as stalking, hate crimes, and workplace violence

Hate crimes usually involve convenient, vulnerable targets who are incapable of fighting back. People become the target of hate crimes because of their religion, ethnicity, or race, or because they engage in behavior that is considered unacceptable to their attacker, such as being gay. Workplace violence is now considered one of the leading causes of occupational injury or death. It has become commonplace to read of irate employees or former employees attacking coworkers or sabotaging machinery and production lines. Stalking is a course of conduct directed at a specific person that involves repeated physical or visual proximity, nonconsensual communication, or verbal, written, or implied threats sufficient to cause fear in a reasonable person.

CRITICAL THINKING QUESTIONS

1. Should different types of rape receive different legal sanctions? For example, should someone who rapes a stranger be punished more severely than someone who is convicted of marital rape or date rape? If your answer is yes, do you also think that someone who kills a stranger should be more severely punished than someone who kills his wife or girlfriend?

2. Is there a subculture of violence in your home city or town? If so, how would you describe its environment and values?

3. There have been significant changes in rape laws regarding issues such as corroboration and shield laws. What other measures would you take to protect the victims of rape when they are forced to testify in court? Should the names of rape victims be published in the press? Do they deserve more protection than those accused of rape?

4. Should hate crimes be punished more severely than crimes motivated by greed, anger, or revenge? Why should crimes be distinguished by the motivations of the perpetrator? Is hate a more heinous motivation than revenge?

5. Do you believe that murder is an interactive event? If so, does that amount to "blaming the victim"? If there is a murder transaction, should we not consider rape, domestic assault, and so forth as "transactions"?

KEY TERMS

instrumental violence (346)
expressive violence (346)
cycle of violence (349)
violentization process (350)
crusted over (351)
subculture of violence (351)
disputatiousness (351)
gang rape (354)
serial rape (354)
acquaintance rape (355)
date rape (355)
statutory rape (355)
marital rape (355)
marital exemption (356)

virility mystique (358)
narcissistic personality
 disorder (359)
consent (360)
aggravated rape (360)
shield laws (360)
murder (361)
first-degree murder (362)
premeditation (362)
felony murder (362)
second-degree murder
 (362)
deliberation (362)
manslaughter (363)

voluntary or nonnegligent
 manslaughter (363)
involuntary or negligent
 manslaughter (363)
feticide (363)
infanticide (364)
filicide (364)
eldercide (364)
serial killer (367)
mass murder (369)
active shooter incident (369)
road rage (371)
child abuse (372)
neglect (372)

sexual abuse (373)
relational aggression (375)
acquaintance robbery (377)
hate crimes (378)
thrill-seeking hate crimes
 (378)
reactive (defensive) hate
 crimes (378)
mission hate crimes (378)
retaliatory hate crimes
 (378)
workplace violence (380)
sufferance (381)
stalking (382)

NOTES

All URLs accessed in 2016.
1. U.S. Attorney's Office, District of Massachusetts, "Member of Lawrence Kidnapping Crew Sentenced to 16 Years in Prison," March 17, 2015, https://www.fbi.gov/boston/press-releases/2015/member-of-lawrence-kidnapping-crew-sentenced-to-16-years-in-prison; FBI, "Violent Gangs: Kidnapping Crew Targeted Criminal Community," April 10, 2015, https://www.fbi.gov/news/stories/2015/april/violent-gangs-kidnapping-crew-targeted-criminal-community/violent-gangs-kidnapping-crew-targeted-criminal-community.

2. George Tita, Tricia Petras, and Robert Greenbaum, "Crime and Residential Choice: A Neighborhood Level Analysis of the Impact of Crime on Housing Prices," *Journal of Quantitative Criminology* 22 (2006): 299–317.

3. Stryker McGuire, "The Dunblane Effect," *Newsweek*, October 28, 1996, p. 46.

4. Benedict Moore-Bridger, "Andy Murray Breaks His Silence on Dunblane School Massacre," *London Evening Standard*, June 24, 2013, http://www.standard.co.uk/news/london/andy-murray-breaks-his-silence-on-dunblane-school-massacre-8671255.html.

5. Rokeya Farrooque, Ronnie Stout, and Frederick Ernst, "Heterosexual Intimate Partner Homicide: Review of Ten Years of Clinical Experience," *Journal of Forensic Sciences* 50 (2005): 648–651; Miltos Livaditis, Gkaro Esagian, Christos Kakoulidis, Maria Samakouri, and Nikos Tzavaras, "Matricide by Person with Bipolar

Disorder and Dependent Overcompliant Personality," *Journal of Forensic Sciences* 50 (2005): 658–661.

6. Dorothy Otnow Lewis, Ernest Moy, Lori Jackson, Robert Aaronson, Nicholas Restifo, Susan Serra, and Alexander Simos, "Biopsychosocial Characteristics of Children Who Later Murder," *American Journal of Psychiatry* 142 (1985): 1161–1167.

7. Dorothy Otnow Lewis, *Guilty by Reason of Insanity* (New York: Fawcett Columbine, 1998).

8. Travis Labrum and Phyllis Solomon, "Physical Elder Abuse Perpetrated by Relatives with Serious Mental Illness: A Preliminary Conceptual Social-Ecological Model," *Aggression and Violent Behavior* 25 (2015): 293–303; Marissa Harrison, Erin Murphy, Lavinia Ho, Thomas Bowers, and Claire Flaherty, "Female Serial Killers in the United States: Means, Motives, and Makings," *Journal of Forensic Psychiatry and Psychology* 26 (2015): 383–406; Richard Rogers, Randall Salekin, Kenneth Sewell, and Keith Cruise, "Prototypical Analysis of Antisocial Personality Disorder," *Criminal Justice and Behavior* 27 (2000): 234–255.

9. Katherine van Wormer and Chuk Odiah, "The Psychology of Suicide-Murder and the Death Penalty," *Journal of Criminal Justice* 27 (1999): 361–370.

10. Daniel Strueber, Monika Lueck, and Gerhard Roth, "The Violent Brain," *Scientific American Mind* 17 (2006): 20–27.

11. David P. Farrington, Rolf Loeber, and Mark T. Berg, "Young Men Who Kill: A Prospective Longitudinal Examination from Childhood," *Homicide Studies* 16 (2012): 99–128; Christopher Hensley and Suzanne Tallichet, "Childhood and Adolescent Animal Cruelty Methods and Their Possible Link to Adult Violent Crimes," *Journal of Interpersonal Violence* 24 (2009): 147–158.

12. Dave Marcotte and Sara Markowitz, "A Cure for Crime? Psycho-Pharmaceuticals and Crime Trends," *Journal of Policy Analysis and Management* 30 (2011): 29–56.

13. Christopher Boehm, "Retaliatory Violence in Human Prehistory," *British Journal of Criminology* 51 (2011): 518–534.

14. Steven Pinker, *The Better Angels of Our Nature: Why Violence Has Declined* (New York: Viking, 2011).

15. Sigmund Freud, *Beyond the Pleasure Principle* (London: Inter-Psychoanalytic Press, 1922).

16. Konrad Lorenz, *On Aggression* (New York: Harcourt Brace Jovanovich, 1966).

17. Nigel Barber, "Why Is Violent Crime So Common in the Americas?" *Aggressive Behavior* 32 (2006): 442–450.

18. William Alex Pridemore and Tony Grubesic, "Alcohol Outlets and Community Levels of Interpersonal Violence: Spatial Density, Outlet Type, and Seriousness of Assault," *Journal of Research in Crime*, first published May 17, 2011; Chris Allen, "The Links Between Heroin, Crack Cocaine, and Crime: Where Does Street Crime Fit In?" *British Journal of Criminology* 45 (2005): 355–372; Arnie Nielsen, Ramiro Martinez, and Matthew Lee, "Alcohol, Ethnicity, and Violence: The Role of Alcohol Availability for Latino and Black Aggravated Assaults and Robberies," *Sociological Quarterly* 46 (2005): 479–502.

19. Allen, "The Links Between Heroin, Crack Cocaine, and Crime."

20. Steven Messner, Glenn Deane, Luc Anselin, and Benjamin Pearson-Nelson, "Locating the Vanguard in Rising and Falling Homicide Rates Across Cities," *Criminology* 43 (2005): 661–696.

21. Paul Goldstein, Henry Brownstein, and Patrick Ryan, "Drug-Related Homicide in New York: 1984–1988," *Crime and Delinquency* 38 (1992): 459–476.

22. Lena Lundholm, Thomas Frisell, Paul Lichtenstein, and Niklas Långström, "Anabolic Androgenic Steroids and Violent Offending: Confounding by Polysubstance Abuse Among 10,365 General Population Men," *Addiction* 110 (2015): 100–108.

23. Robert Brewer and Monica Swahn, "Binge Drinking and Violence," *JAMA: Journal of the American Medical Association* 294 (2005): 16–20.

24. Tomika Stevens, Kenneth Ruggiero, Dean Kilpatrick, Heidi Resnick, and Benjamin Saunders, "Variables Differentiating Singly and Multiply Victimized Youth: Results from the National Survey of Adolescents and Implications for Secondary Prevention," *Child Maltreatment* 10 (2005): 211–223; James Collins and Pamela Messerschmidt, "Epidemiology of Alcohol-Related Violence," *Alcohol Health and Research World* 17 (1993): 93–100.

25. Antonia Abbey, Tina Zawacki, Philip Buck, Monique Clinton, and Pam McAuslan, "Sexual Assault and Alcohol Consumption: What Do We Know About Their Relationship and What Types of Research Are Still Needed?" *Aggression and Violent Behavior* 9 (2004): 271–303.

26. Scott Phillips, Jacqueline Matusko, and Elizabeth Tomasovic, "Reconsidering the Relationship Between Alcohol and Lethal Violence," *Journal of Interpersonal Violence* 22 (2007): 66–84.

27. Eric Sevigny and Andrea Allen, "Gun Carrying Among Drug Market Participants: Evidence from Incarcerated Drug Offenders," *Journal of Quantitative Criminology* 31 (2015): 435–458.

28. Martin Grann and Seena Fazel, "Substance Misuse and Violent Crime: Swedish Population Study," *British Medical Journal* 328 (2004): 1233–1234; Susanne Rogne Gjeruldsen, Bjørn Myrvang, and Stein Opjordsmoen, "Criminality in Drug Addicts: A Follow-Up Study over 25 Years," *European Addiction Research* 10 (2004): 49–56.

29. Bruce Jacobs, *Robbing Drug Dealers: Violence beyond the Law* (New York: Aldine de Gruyter. 2000).

30. Todd Herrenkhol, Bu Huang, Emiko Tajima, and Stephen Whitney, "Examining the Link Between Child Abuse and Youth Violence," *Journal of Interpersonal Violence* 18 (2003): 1189–1208; Pamela Lattimore, Christy Visher, and Richard Linster, "Predicting Rearrest for Violence Among Serious Youthful Offenders," *Journal of Research in Crime and Delinquency* 32 (1995): 54–83.

31. Rolf Loeber and Dale Hay, "Key Issues in the Development of Aggression and Violence from Childhood to Early Adulthood," *Annual Review of Psychology* 48 (1997): 371–410.

32. Deborah Capaldi and Gerald Patterson, "Can Violent Offenders Be Distinguished from Frequent Offenders: Prediction from Childhood to Adolescence," *Journal of Research in Crime and Delinquency* 33 (1996): 206–231.

33. Adrian Raine, Patricia Brennan, and Sarnoff Mednick, "Interaction Between Birth Complications and Early Maternal Rejection in Predisposing Individuals to Adult Violence: Specificity to Serious, Early-Onset Violence," *American Journal of Psychiatry* 154 (1997): 1265–1271.

34. Eric Slade and Lawrence Wissow, "Spanking in Early Childhood and Later Behavior Problems: A Prospective Study of Infants and Young Toddlers," *Pediatrics* 113 (2004): 1321–1330.

35. Murray Straus, "Discipline and Deviance: Physical Punishment of Children and Violence and Other Crime in Adulthood," *Social Problems* 38 (1991): 101–123.

36. Jennifer Lansford, Laura Wager, John Bates, Gregory Pettit, and Kenneth Dodge, "Forms of Spanking and Children's Externalizing Behaviors," *Family Relations* 6 (2012): 224–236.

37. Ronald Simons, Chyi-In Wu, Kuei-Hsiu Lin, Leslie Gordon, and Rand Conger, "A Cross-Cultural Examination of the Link Between Corporal Punishment and Adolescent Antisocial Behavior," *Criminology* 38 (2000): 47–79.

38. Hyunzee Jung, Todd Herrenkohl, Jungeun Lee, Bart Klika, and Martie Skinner, "Effects of Physical and Emotional Child Abuse and Its Chronicity on Crime into Adulthood," *Violence and Victims* 30 (2015): 1004–1018.

39. Cathy Spatz Widom, "The Cycle of Violence," *Science* 244 (1989): 160–166; "Understanding Child Maltreatment and Juvenile Delinquency: The Research," Welfare League of America, 2010, http://66.227.70.18/programs/juvenilejustice/ucmjd03.pdf.

40. Cathy Spatz Widom, "Varieties of Violent Behavior," *Criminology* 52 (2014): 313–344.

41. See, for example, Egbert Zavala, "Testing the Link Between Child Maltreatment and Family Violence Among Police Officers," *Crime and Delinquency*, first published online November 22, 2010; Cesar Rebellon and Karen Van Gundy, "Can Control Theory Explain the Link Between Parental Physical Abuse and Delinquency? A Longitudinal Analysis," *Journal of Research in Crime and Delinquency* 42 (2005): 247–274.

42. Wan-Yi Chen, Jennifer Propp, Ellen deLara, and Kenneth Corvo, "Child Neglect and Its Association with Subsequent Juvenile Drug and Alcohol Offense," *Child and Adolescent Social Work Journal* 28 (2011): 273–290.

43. Childhelp, National Child Abuse Statistics, https://www.childhelp.org/child-abuse-statistics/.

44. Janet Currie and Erdal Tekin, "Does Child Abuse Cause Crime?" National Bureau of Economic Research, April 2006, http://www.nber.org/papers/w12171.

45. Emily M. Wright and Abigail A. Fagan, "The Cycle of Violence in Context: Exploring the Moderating Roles of Neighborhood Disadvantage and Cultural Norms," *Criminology* 51 (2013): 217–249.

46. Ibid.

47. Lonnie Athens, *The Creation of Dangerous Violent Criminals* (Urbana: University of Illinois Press, 1992), pp. 27–80.

48. David Kirk and Margaret Hardy, "The Acute and Enduring Consequences of Exposure to Violence on Youth Mental Health and Aggression," *Justice Quarterly*, first published online November 9, 2012.

49. Eric Stewart, Ronald Simons, and Rand Conger, "Assessing Neighborhood and Social Psychological Influences on Childhood Violence in an African-American Sample," *Criminology* 40 (2002): 801–830.

50. Gregory M. Zimmerman, "Do Age Effects on Youth Secondary Exposure to Violence Vary Across Social Context?" *Justice Quarterly* 32 (2015): 193–222.

51. Darrell Steffensmeier, Ben Feldmeyer, Casey T. Harris, and Jeffery T. Ulmer, "Reassessing Trends in Black Violent Crime, 1980–2008: Sorting Out the 'Hispanic Effect' in Uniform Crime Reports Arrests, National Crime Victimization Survey Offender Estimates, and U.S. Prisoner Counts," *Criminology* 49 (2011): 197–251.

52. Barbara Warner, "Robberies with Guns: Neighborhood Factors and the Nature of Crime," *Journal of Criminal Justice* 35 (2007): 39–50.

53. Felton Earls, *Linking Community Factors and Individual Development* (Washington, DC: National Institute of Justice, 1998).

54. Jeffrey B. Bingenheimer, Robert T. Brennan, and Felton J. Earls, "Firearm Violence Exposure and Serious Violent Behavior," *Science* 308 (2005): 1323–1326;

"Witnessing Gun Violence Significantly Increases Likelihood that a Child Will Also Commit Violent Crime; Violence May Be Viewed as Infectious Disease," *AScribe Health News Service*, May 26, 2005.

55. Michael Greene, "Chronic Exposure to Violence and Poverty: Interventions that Work for Youth," *Crime and Delinquency* 39 (1993): 106–124.

56. Robert Baller, Luc Anselin, Steven Messner, Glenn Deane, and Darnell Hawkins, "Structural Covariates of U.S. County Homicide Rates Incorporating Spatial Effects," *Criminology* 39 (2001): 561–590.

57. Marvin Wolfgang and Franco Ferracuti, *The Subculture of Violence* (London: Tavistock, 1967).

58. David Luckenbill and Daniel Doyle, "Structural Position and Violence: Developing a Cultural Explanation," *Criminology* 27 (1989): 419–436.

59. Robert Sampson and William Julius Wilson, "Toward a Theory of Race, Crime, and Urban Inequality," in *Crime and Inequality*, ed. John Hagan and Ruth Peterson (Stanford, CA: Stanford University Press, 1995), p. 51.

60. Liqun Cao, Anthony Adams, and Vickie Jensen, "A Test of the Black Subculture of Violence Thesis," *Criminology* 35 (1997): 367–379.

61. Eric Baumer, Julie Horney, Richard Felson, and Janet Lauritsen, "Neighborhood Disadvantage and the Nature of Violence," *Criminology* 41 (2003): 39–71.

62. Charis Kubrin and Ronald Weitzer, "Retaliatory Homicide: Concentrated Disadvantage and Neighborhood Culture," *Social Problems* 50 (2003): 157–180.

63. Robert J. Kane, "Compromised Police Legitimacy as a Predictor of Violent Crime in Structurally Disadvantaged Communities," *Criminology* 43 (2005): 469–499.

64. Steven Messner, "Regional and Racial Effects on the Urban Homicide Rate: The Subculture of Violence Revisited," *American Journal of Sociology* 88 (1983): 997–1007; Steven Messner and Kenneth Tardiff, "Economic Inequality and Levels of Homicide: An Analysis of Urban Neighborhoods," *Criminology* 24 (1986): 297–317.

65. Beth Bjerregaard and Alan Lizotte, "Gun Ownership and Gang Membership," *Journal of Criminal Law and Criminology* 86 (1995): 37–58.

66. Rachel Gordon, Benjamin Lahey, Eriko Kawai, Rolf Loeber, Magda Stouthamer-Loeber, and David Farrington, "Antisocial Behavior and Youth Gang Membership," *Criminology* 42 (2004): 55–88.

67. Andrew Papachristos, "Murder by Structure: Dominance Relations and the Social Structure of Gang Homicide," *American Journal of Sociology* 115 (2009): 74–128.

68. Lonnie Schaible and Lorine Hughes, "Crime, Shame, Reintegration, and

Cross-national Homicide: A Partial Test of Reintegrative Shaming Theory," *Sociological Quarterly* 52 (2011): 104–131.

69. Marc Ouimet, "A World of Homicides: The Effect of Economic Development, Income Inequality, and Excess Infant Mortality on the Homicide Rate for 165 Countries in 2010," *Homicide Studies* 16 (2012): 238–258; Don Chon, "Contributing Factors for High Homicide Rate in Latin America: A Critical Test of Neapolitan's Regional Subculture of Violence Thesis," *Journal of Family Violence* 26 (2011): 299–307.

70. Sharon LaFraniere, Daniela Porat, and Agustin Armendariz, "Untold Damage: America's Overlooked Gun Violence," *New York Times*, May 22, 2016, http://www.nytimes.com/2016/05/23/us/americas-overlooked-gun-violence.html.

71. David Courtwright, "Violence in America," *American Heritage* 47 (1996): 36–52, at 36; David Courtwright, *Violent Land: Single Men and Social Disorder from the Frontier to the Inner City* (Cambridge, MA: Harvard University Press, 1996).

72. William Green, *Rape* (Lexington, MA: Lexington Books, 1988), p. 5.

73. Susan Randall and Vicki McNickle Rose, "Forcible Rape," in *Major Forms of Crime*, ed. Robert Meyer (Beverly Hills: Sage, 1984), p. 47.

74. Barbara Krah, Renate Scheinberger-Olwig, and Steffen Bieneck, "Men's Reports of Nonconsensual Sexual Interactions with Women: Prevalence and Impact," *Archives of Sexual Behavior* 32 (2003): 165–176.

75. Siegmund Fred Fuchs, "Male Sexual Assault: Issues of Arousal and Consent," *Cleveland State Law Review* 51 (2004): 93–108.

76. Raquel Kennedy Bergen and Paul Bukovec, "Men and Intimate Partner Rape: Characteristics of Men Who Sexually Abuse Their Partner," *Journal of Interpersonal Violence* 21 (2006): 1375–1384.

77. Heidi Zinzow, Heidi Resnick, Ananda Amstadter, Jenna McCauley, Kenneth Ruggiero, and Dean Kilpatrick, "Drug- or Alcohol-Facilitated, Incapacitated, and Forcible Rape in Relationship to Mental Health Among a National Sample of Women," *Journal of Interpersonal Violence* 25 (2010): 2217–2236.

78. Susan Brownmiller, *Against Our Will: Men, Women, and Rape* (New York: Simon & Schuster, 1975).

79. Green, *Rape*, p. 6.

80. Yuri Kageyama, "Court Orders Japan to Pay Sex Slaves," *Boston Globe*, April 28, 1998, p. A2.

81. Anthony Beever, *Berlin: The Downfall 1945* (New York: Viking Press, 2002).

82. Marlise Simons, "Bosnian Serb Pleads Guilty to Rape Charge Before War Crimes Tribunal," *New York Times*, March 10, 1998, p. 8.

83. Marc Lacey, "Amnesty Says Sudan Militias Use Rape as Weapon," *New York Times*, July 19, 2004, p. A9.

84. CNN, "Boko Haram Kidnapping of Nigerian Schoolgirls, a Year Later," April 14, 2015, http://www.cnn.com /2015/04/14/africa/nigeria-kidnapping -anniversary/.

85. Atika Shubert and Bharati Naik, "ISIS Soldiers Told to Rape Women 'to Make Them Muslim,'" CNN, October 8, 2015, http://www.cnn.com/2015/10/08/middleeast /isis-rape-theology-soldiers-rape-women-to -make-them-muslim/.

86. Eileen Zurbriggen, "Rape, War, and the Socialization of Masculinity: Why Our Refusal to Give Up War Ensures that Rape Cannot Be Eradicated," *Psychology of Women Quarterly* 34 (2010): 538–549.

87. FBI, *Crime in the United States, 2014*. Crime data in this chapter come from this source and from preliminary 2015 data, https:// www.fbi.gov/about-us/cjis/ucr/crime-in-the -u.s/2014/crime-in-the-u.s.-2014/offenses -known-to-law-enforcement/rape/.

88. Jennifer L. Truman and Lynn Langton, *Criminal Victimization, 2014* (Washington, DC: Bureau of Justice Statistics, 2015), http:// www.bjs.gov/content/pub/pdf/cv14.pdf.

89. Samantha Lundrigan and Katrin Mueller-Johnson, "Male Stranger Rape: A Behavioral Model of Victim-Offender Interactions," *Criminal Justice and Behavior* 40 (2013): 763–783.

90. Sarah Cook, Christine Gidycz, Mary Koss, and Megan Murphy, "Emerging Issues in the Measurement of Rape Victimization," *Violence Against Women* 17 (2011): 201–218; Bonnie S. Fisher, "The Effects of Survey Question Wording on Rape Estimates: Evidence from a Quasi-Experimental Design," *Violence Against Women* 15 (2009): 133–147.

91. Dean G. Kilpatrick, Heidi S. Resnick, Kenneth J. Ruggiero, Lauren M. Conoscenti, and Jenna McCauley, "Drug-Facilitated, Incapacitated, and Forcible Rape: A National Study," U.S. Department of Justice, 2007, http://www.ncjrs.gov /pdffiles1/nij/grants/219181.pdf.

92. Carol Vanzile-Tamsen, Maria Testa, and Jennifer Livingston, "The Impact of Sexual Assault History and Relationship Context on Appraisal of and Responses to Acquaintance Sexual Assault Risk," *Journal of Interpersonal Violence* 20 (2005): 813–822; Arnold Kahn, Jennifer Jackson, Christine Kully, Kelly Badger, and Jessica Halvorsen, "Calling It Rape: Differences in Experiences of Women Who Do or Do Not Label Their Sexual Assault as Rape," *Psychology of Women Quarterly* 27 (2003): 233–242.

93. Jody Clay-Warner and Jennifer McMahon-Howard, "Rape Reporting: 'Classic Rape' and the Behavior of Law," *Violence and Victims* 24 (2009): 723–743.

94. For an analysis of the validity of rape data, see Bonnie S. Fisher, "The Effects of Survey Question Wording on Rape Estimates: Evidence from a Quasi-Experimental Design," *Violence Against Women* 15 (2009): 133–147.

95. Heather Littleton and Craig Henderson, "If She Is Not a Victim, Does That Mean She Was Not Traumatized? Evaluation of Predictors of PTSD Symptomatology Among College Rape Victims," *Violence Against Women* 15 (2009): 148–167.

96. Mark Warr, "Rape, Burglary, and Opportunity," *Journal of Quantitative Criminology* 4 (1988): 275–288.

97. Maria Testa, Jennifer Livingston, and Carol Vanzile-Tamsen, "The Role of Victim and Perpetrator Intoxication on Sexual Assault Outcomes," *Journal of Studies on Alcohol* 65 (2004): 320–329.

98. A. Nicholas Groth and Jean Birnbaum, *Men Who Rape* (New York: Plenum Press, 1979).

99. For another typology, see Raymond Knight, "Validation of a Typology of Rapists," in *Sex Offender Research and Treatment: State-of-the-Art in North America and Europe*, ed. W. L. Marshall and J. Frenken (Beverly Hills: Sage, 1997), pp. 58–75.

100. Sarah Ullman, "A Comparison of Gang and Individual Rape Incidents," *Violence and Victimization* 14 (1999): 123–134.

101. Janet Warren, Roland Reboussin, Robert Hazlewood, Natalie Gibbs, Susan Trumbetta, and Andrea Cummings, "Crime Scene Analysis and the Escalation of Violence in Serial Rape," *Forensic Science International* (1998): 56–62.

102. James LeBeau, "Patterns of Stranger and Serial Rape Offending Factors Distinguishing Apprehended and At-Large Offenders," *Journal of Criminal Law and Delinquency* 78 (1987): 309–326.

103. Bonnie Fisher, Francis Cullen, and Leah Daigle, "The Discovery of Acquaintance Rape," *Journal of Interpersonal Violence* 20 (2005): 493–500.

104. Leah Adams-Curtis and Gordon Forbes, "College Women's Experiences of Sexual Coercion," *Trauma, Violence and Abuse* 5 (2004): 91–122.

105. Cassia Spohn, Dawn Beichner, and Erika Davis-Frenzel, "Prosecutorial Justifications for Sexual Assault Case Rejection: Guarding the 'Gateway to Justice,'" *Social Problems* 48 (2001): 206–235.

106. Mary Koss, "Hidden Rape: Sexual Aggression and Victimization in a National Sample of Students in Higher Education," in *Rape and Sexual Assault*, Vol. 2, ed. Ann Wolbert Burgess (New York: Garland Publishing, 1988), p. 824.

107. R. Lance Shotland, "A Model of the Causes of Date Rape in Developing and Close Relationships," in *Close Relationships*, ed. C. Hendrick (Newbury Park, CA: Sage, 1989), pp. 247–270.

108. Kimberly Tyler, Danny Hoyt, and Les Whitbeck, "Coercive Sexual Strategies," *Violence and Victims* 13 (1998): 47–63.

109. Julie A. Allison and Lawrence S. Wrightsman, *Rape: The Misunderstood Crime* (Newbury Park, CA: Sage Publications, 1993), p. 64.

110. Amy Buddie and Maria Testa, "Rates and Predictors of Sexual Aggression Among Students and Nonstudents," *Journal of Interpersonal Violence* 20 (2005): 713–725.

111. Bonnie Fisher, Leah Daigle, Francis Cullen, and Michael Turner, "Reporting Sexual Victimization to the Police and Others: Results from a National-Level Study of College Women," *Criminal Justice and Behavior* 30 (2003): 6–39.

112. Ashley Fantz, "Outrage over 6-Month sentence for Brock Turner in Stanford Rape Case," CNN, June 7, 2016, http://www.cnn .com/2016/06/06/us/sexual-assault-brock -turner-stanford/.

113. David Cantor, Bonnie Fisher, Susan Chibnall, Reanne Townsend, Hyunshik Lee, Carol Bruce, and Gail Thomas, *Report on the AAU Campus Climate Survey on Sexual Assault and Sexual Misconduct* (Rockville, MD: Westat, 2015).

114. Rebecca Elliott Smith and Lawrence Pick, "Sexual Assault Experienced by Deaf Female Undergraduates: Prevalence and Characteristics," *Violence and Victims* 30 (2015): 948–959.

115. Lynn Langton, *Rape and Sexual Assault Among College-Age Females, 1995–2013* (Washington, DC: Bureau of Justice Statistics, 2014), http://www.bjs.gov /content/pub/pdf/rsavcaf9513.pdf.

116. Molly Smith, Nicole Wilkes, and Leana Bouffard, "Rape Myth Adherence Among Campus Law Enforcement Officers," *Criminal Justice and Behavior*, first published September 4, 2015.

117. Ibid.

118. United States Department of Justice, "Overview of Title IX of the Education Amendments of 1972, 20 U.S.C. A§ 1681 Et. Seq," http://www.justice.gov/crt /overview-title-ix-education-amendments -1972-20-usc-1681-et-seq.

119. American Civil Liberties Union, "Know Your Rights: Title IX and Sexual Assault," https://www.aclu.org/know-your-rights /title-ix-and-sexual-assault.

120. Allison and Wrightsman, *Rape: The Misunderstood Crime*, pp. 85–87.

121. Cited in Diana Russell, "Wife Rape," in *Acquaintance Rape: The Hidden Crime*, ed. A. Parrot and L. Bechofer (New York: Wiley, 1991), pp. 129–139, at 129.

122. David Finkelhor and K. Yllo, *License to Rape: Sexual Abuse of Wives* (New York: Holt, Rinehart & Winston, 1985).

123. Allison and Wrightsman, *Rape: The Misunderstood Crime*, p. 89.

124. Raquel Kennedy Bergen, with contributions from Elizabeth Barnhill, "Marital Rape: New Research and Directions," National Online Resource Center for Violence Against Women, http://vawnet.org/assoc_files _vawnet/ar_maritalraperevised.pdf; Associated Press, "British Court Rejects Precedent, Finds a Man Guilty of Raping Wife," *Boston Globe*, March 15, 1991, p. 68.

125. Jill Elaine Hasday, "Contest and Consent: A Legal History of Marital Rape," *California Law Review* 88 (2000): 1373–1433.

126. Bergen and Barnhill, "Marital Rape: New Research and Directions."

127. Sharon Elstein and Roy Davis, *Sexual Relationships Between Adult Males and Young Teen Girls: Exploring the Legal and Social Responses* (Chicago: American Bar Association, 1997).

128. Jed Rubenfeld, "The Riddle of Rape-by-Deception and the Myth of Sexual Autonomy," *Yale Law Journal* 122 (2013): 1372–1443.

129. Tenn. Codeann. § 39-i3-5O3(a)(4) (2010); Idaho Codeann. § 18-6101(8) (Supp. 2011).

130. Donald Symons, *The Evolution of Human Sexuality* (Oxford: Oxford University Press, 1979).

131. Lee Ellis and Anthony Walsh, "Gene-Based Evolutionary Theories in Criminology," *Criminology* 35 (1997): 229–276.

132. Lawrence Miller "Rape: Sex Crime, Act of Violence, or Naturalistic Adaptation?" *Aggression and Violent Behavior* 19 (2014): 67–81.

133. Ibid.

134. Suzanne Osman, "Predicting Men's Rape Perceptions Based on the Belief that 'No' Really Means 'Yes,'" *Journal of Applied Social Psychology* 33 (2003): 683–692.

135. Martin Schwartz, Walter DeKeseredy, David Tait, and Shahid Alvi, "Male Peer Support and a Feminist Routine Activities Theory: Understanding Sexual Assault on the College Campus," *Justice Quarterly* 18 (2001): 623–650.

136. Diana Russell, *The Politics of Rape* (New York: Stein and Day, 1975).

137. Diana Russell and Rebecca M. Bolen, *The Epidemic of Rape and Child Sexual Abuse in the United States* (Thousand Oaks, CA: Sage, 2000).

138. Lynn Elber, "Student's Horrific, Fatal Rape Inspires 'India's Daughter,'" *Washington Post*, November 13, 2015, https://www .washingtonpost.com/entertainment/tv /students-horrific-fatal-rape-inspires-indias -daughter/2015/11/13/812e9cbe-8a74 -11e5-bd91-d385b244482f_story.html.

139. Rachel Bridges Whaley, "The Paradoxical Relationship Between Gender Inequality and Rape: Toward a Refined Theory," *Gender and Society* 15 (2001): 531–555.

140. Paul Gebhard, John Gagnon, Wardell Pomeroy, and Cornelia Christenson, *Sex Offenders: An Analysis of Types* (New York:

Harper & Row, 1965), pp. 198–205; Richard Rada, ed., *Clinical Aspects of the Rapist* (New York: Grune & Stratton, 1978), pp. 122–130.

141. Stephen Porter, David Fairweather, Jeff Drugge, Huues Herve, Angela Birt, and Douglas Boer, "Profiles of Psychopathy in Incarcerated Sexual Offenders," *Criminal Justice and Behavior* 27 (2000): 216–233.

142. Brad Bushman, Angelica Bonacci, Mirjam van Dijk, and Roy Baumeister, "Narcissism, Sexual Refusal, and Aggression: Testing a Narcissistic Reactance Model of Sexual Coercion," *Journal of Personality and Social Psychology* 84 (2003): 1027–1040.

143. Schwartz, DeKeseredy, Tait, and Alvi, "Male Peer Support and a Feminist Routine Activities Theory."

144. Groth and Birnbaum, *Men Who Rape*, p. 101.

145. See, generally, Edward Donnerstein, Daniel Linz, and Steven Penrod, *The Question of Pornography* (New York: Free Press, 1987); Diana Russell, *Sexual Exploitation* (Beverly Hills: Sage, 1985), pp. 115–116.

146. Neil Malamuth and John Briere, "Sexual Violence in the Media: Indirect Effects on Aggression Against Women," *Journal of Social Issues* 42 (1986): 75–92.

147. Richard Johnson, "Rape and Gender Conflict in a Patriarchal State," *Crime and Delinquency* 60 (2014): 1110–1128.

148. Ibid.

149. Richard Felson and Marvin Krohn, "Motives for Rape," *Journal of Research in Crime and Delinquency* 27 (1990): 222–242.

150. Richard Felson, Patrick Cundiff, and Noah Painter-Davis, "Age and Sexual Assault in Correctional Facilities: A Blocked Opportunity Approach," *Criminology* 50 (2012): 887–911.

151. "Duke Lacrosse 'Rape' Accuser Changes Story Again, Says Seligmann Didn't Touch Her," Associated Press, January 12, 2007, http://www.foxnews.com/story/2007/01/12 /duke-lacrosse-rape-accuser-changes-story -again-says-seligmann-didnt-touch-her .html; Sal Ruibal, "Rape Allegations Cast Pall at Duke," *USA Today*, March 29, 2006, http:// usatoday30.usatoday.com/sports/college /lacrosse/2006-03-29-duke-fallout_x.htm.

152. Juliet Linderman, "Victim Advocates Worry About Discredited UVa Rape Account," Associated Press, March 24, 2015, koin .com/ap/police-report-on-virginia-gang -rape-not-the-final-word/.

153. Laura Monroe, Linda Kinney, Mark Weist, Denise Spriggs Dafeamekpor, Joyce Dantzler, and Matthew Reynolds, "The Experience of Sexual Assault: Findings from a Statewide Victim Needs Assessment," *Journal of Interpersonal Violence* 20 (2005): 767–776.

154. Steffen Bieneck and Barbara Krahe, "Blaming the Victim and Exonerating the Perpetrator in Cases of Rape and Robbery: Is There a Double Standard?" *Journal of Interpersonal Violence* 26 (2011): 1785–1797.

155. Mark Whatley, "The Effect of Participant Sex, Victim Dress, and Traditional Attitudes on Causal Judgments for Marital Rape Victims," *Journal of Family Violence* 20 (2005): 191–200; Spohn, Beichner, and Davis-Frenzel, "Prosecutorial Justifications for Sexual Assault Case Rejection."

156. Patricia Landwehr, Robert Bothwell, Matthew Jeanmard, Luis Luque, Roy Brown III, and Marie-Anne Breaux, "Racism in Rape Trials," *Journal of Social Psychology* 142 (2002): 667–670.

157. "Man Wrongly Convicted of Rape Released 19 Years Later," *Forensic Examiner* (May–June 2003): 44.

158. Gerald Robin, "Forcible Rape: Institutionalized Sexism in the Criminal Justice System," *Crime and Delinquency* 23 (1977): 136–153.

159. Rodney Kingsworth, Randall MacIntosh, and Jennifer Wentworth, "Sexual Assault: The Role of Prior Relationship and Victim Characteristics in Case Processing," *Justice Quarterly* 16 (1999): 276–302.

160. Associated Press, "Jury Stirs Furor by Citing Dress in Rape Acquittal," *Boston Globe*, October 6, 1989, p. 12.

161. Cassia Spohn and David Holleran, "Prosecuting Sexual Assault: A Comparison of Charging Decisions in Sexual Assault Cases Involving Strangers, Acquaintances, and Intimate Partners," *Justice Quarterly* 18 (2001): 651–688.

162. Susan Estrich, *Real Rape* (Cambridge, MA: Harvard University Press, 1987), pp. 58–59.

163. See, for example, Mich. Comp. Laws Ann. 750.5200-(1); Florida Statutes Annotated, Sec. 794.011; see, generally, Gary LaFree, "Official Reactions to Rape," *American Sociological Review* 45 (1980): 842–854.

164. Martin Schwartz and Todd Clear, "Toward a New Law on Rape," *Crime and Delinquency* 26 (1980): 129–151.

165. *Michigan v. Lucas* 90-149 (1991); Comment, "The Rape Shield Paradox: Complainant Protection Amidst Oscillating Trends of State Judicial Interpretation," *Journal of Criminal Law and Criminology* 78 (1987): 644–698.

166. Andrew Karmen, *Crime Victims* (Pacific Grove, CA: Brooks/Cole, 1990), p. 252.

167. "Court Upholds Civil Rights Portion of Violence Against Women Act," *Criminal Justice Newsletter* 28 (1997): 3.

168. This section relies on David John Frank, Tara Hardinge, and Kassia Wosick-Correa, "The Global Dimensions of Rape-Law Reform: A Cross-National Study of Policy Outcomes," *American Sociological Review* 74 (2009): 272–290.

169. Donald Lunde, *Murder and Madness* (San Francisco: San Francisco Book Company, 1977), p. 3.

170. Clifford Ward, "Former Neighbor Found Guilty of Killing Girl, 7, in 1957," *Chicago Tribune*, September 14, 2012, http://www .chicagotribune.com/news/local/breaking

/chi-mccullough-guilty-of-killing-girl-7-in
-1957-20120914,0,2995426.story.

171. "'Baby Hope' Case: Cousin Confesses to Sexually Assaulting, Killing Toddler Anjelica Castillo More than Two Decades Ago," *New York Daily News*, October 13, 2013, http://www.nydailynews.com/news /crime/relative-arrested-baby-hope-case -article-1.1483690.

172. Genevieve Bookwalter, "30-Year-Old Glen Ellyn Murder Case Had Twists, Turns—and Now an Arrest," *Chicago Tribune*, September 21, 2015, http://www .chicagotribune.com/suburbs/glen-ellyn /news/ct-dupage-cold-case-kristy-wesselman -20150920-story.html.

173. Lisa Baertlein, "HIV Ruled Deadly Weapon in Rape Case," *Boston Globe*, March 2, 1994, p. 3.

174. The legal principles here come from Wayne LaFave and Austin Scott, *Criminal Law* (St. Paul: West, 1986; updated 1993). The definitions and discussion of legal principles used in this chapter lean heavily on this work.

175. Bob Egelko, "State's Top Court OKs Dog Maul Murder Charge, Judge Ordered to Reconsider Owner's Original Conviction," *San Francisco Chronicle*, June 1, 2007, http://www.sfgate.com/bayarea/article /SAN-FRANCISCO-State-s-top-court-OKs -dog-maul-2557910.php; Evelyn Nieves, "Woman Gets 4-Year Term in Fatal Dog Attack," *New York Times*, July 16, 2002, p.1.

176. The National Conference of State Legislatures, "Fetal Homicide Laws," April 2012, http://www.ncsl.org/issues-research /health/fetal-homicide-state-laws.aspx.

177. Pauline Arrillaga, "Jurors Give Drunk Driver 16 Years in Fetus's Death," *Manchester Union Leader*, October 22, 1996, p. B20.

178. *Whitner v. State of South Carolina*, Supreme Court of South Carolina, Opinion Number 24468, July 15, 1996.

179. The National Conference of State Legislatures, "Fetal Homicide Laws."

180. Dana Haynie and David Armstrong, "Race and Gender-Disaggregated Homicide Offending Rates: Differences and Similarities by Victim-Offender Relations Across Cities," *Homicide Studies* 10 (2006): 3–32.

181. Terance Miethe and Wendy Regoeczi with Kriss Drass, *Rethinking Homicide: Exploring the Structure and Process Underlying Deadly Situations* (Cambridge, MA: Cambridge University Press, 2004).

182. Todd Shackelford, Viviana Weekes-Shackelford, and Shanna Beasley, "An Exploratory Analysis of the Contexts and Circumstances of Filicide-Suicide in Chicago, 1965–1994," *Aggressive Behavior* 31 (2005): 399–406.

183. Ibid.

184. Philip Cook, Jens Ludwig, and Anthony Braga, "Criminal Records of Homicide Offenders," *JAMA: Journal of the American Medical Association* 294 (2005): 598–601.

185. Farrington, Loeber, and Berg, "Young Men Who Kill."

186. William Parkin, Joshua Freilich, and Steven Chermak, "Ideological Victimization: Homicides Perpetrated by Far-Right Extremists," *Homicide Studies* 19 (2015): 211–236.

187. Scott Decker, "Deviant Homicide: A New Look at the Role of Motives and Victim–Offender Relationships," *Journal of Research in Crime and Delinquency* 33 (1996): 427–449.

188. Victoria Frye, Vanessa Hosein, Eve Waltermaurer, Shannon Blaney, and Susan Wilt, "Femicide in New York City: 1990 to 1999," *Homicide Studies* 9 (2005): 204–228.

189. Carol E. Jordan, James Clark, Adam Pritchard, and Richard Charnigo, "Lethal and Other Serious Assaults: Disentangling Gender and Context," *Crime and Delinquency* 58 (2012): 425–455.

190. Steven Shatz and Naomi Shatz, "Chivalry Is Not Dead: Murder, Gender, and the Death Penalty," *Berkeley Journal of Gender, Law and Justice* 27 (2012): 64–112.

191. Linda Saltzman and James Mercy, "Assaults Between Intimates: The Range of Relationships Involved," in *Homicide: The Victim/Offender Connection*, ed. Anna Victoria Wilson (Cincinnati: Anderson Publishing, 1993), pp. 65–74.

192. Jordan, Clark, Pritchard, and Charnigo, "Lethal and Other Serious Assaults."

193. Angela Browne and Kirk Williams, "Exploring the Effect of Resource Availability and the Likelihood of Female-Perpetrated Homicides," *Law and Society Review* 23 (1989): 75–94.

194. Richard Felson, "Anger, Aggression, and Violence in Love Triangles," *Violence and Victimization* 12 (1997): 345–363.

195. Ibid., p. 361.

196. Sharon Smith, Kathleen Basile, and Debra Karch, "Sexual Homicide and Sexual Violence–Associated Homicide: Findings from the National Violent Death Reporting System," *Homicide Studies* 15 (2011): 132–153; Vernon J. Geberth, "The Classification of Sex-Related Homicides," http://www.practicalhomicide.com/Research /sexrelatedhomicides.htm.

197. Peter Lin and James Gill, "Homicides of Pregnant Women," *American Journal of Forensic Medicine and Pathology* 32 (2011): 161–163.

198. Paul Greenall and Michelle Wright, "Exploring the Criminal Histories of Stranger Sexual Killers," *Journal of Forensic Psychiatry and Psychology* 26 (2015): 242–259.

199. Paul V. Greenall and Clare Richardson, "Adult Male-on-Female Stranger Sexual Homicide: A Descriptive (Baseline) Study from Great Britain," *Homicide Studies* 19 (2015): 237–25.

200. Jeff Gruenewald, "A Comparative Examination of Homicides Perpetrated by Far-Right Extremists," *Homicide Studies* 15 (2011): 177–203.

201. David Luckenbill, "Criminal Homicide as a Situational Transaction," *Social Problems* 25 (1977): 176–186.

202. National Center for Education Statistics, "Violent Deaths at School and Away from School," https://nces.ed.gov/programs /crimeindicators/mobile/characteristic_3 .aspx.

203. Mark Anderson, Joanne Kaufman, Thomas Simon, Lisa Barrios, Len Paulozzi, George Ryan, Rodney Hammond, William Modzeleski, Thomas Feucht, Lloyd Potter, and the School-Associated Violent Deaths Study Group, "School-Associated Violent Deaths in the United States, 1994–1999," *Journal of the American Medical Association* 286 (2001): 2695–2702.

204. Bryan Vossekuil, Marisa Reddy, Robert Fein, Randy Borum, and William Modzeleski, *Safe School Initiative, An Interim Report on the Prevention of Targeted Violence in Schools* (Washington, DC: United States Secret Service, 2000).

205. Laura Agnich, "A Comparative Analysis of Attempted and Completed School-Based Mass Murder Attacks," *American Journal of Criminal Justice* 40 (2015): 1–22.

206. "BTK Killer Blames 'Demon' for Murders," *USA Today*, July 7, 2005, http://www .usatoday.com/news/nation/2005-07-07 -btk-killings_x.htm.

207. Alasdair Goodwill and Laurence Alison, "Sequential Angulation, Spatial Dispersion and Consistency of Distance Attack Patterns from Home in Serial Murder, Rape and Burglary," *Journal of Psychology, Crime and Law* 11 (2005): 161–176.

208. Ronald Holmes and Stephen Holmes, *Murder in America* (Thousand Oaks, CA: Sage, 1994): pp. 13–14.

209. "Ex-N.Y. Doctor Pleads Guilty in 3 Deaths," *Los Angeles Times*, September 07, 2000, http://articles.latimes.com/2000/sep/07 /news/mn-16969.

210. Aneez Esmail, "Physician as Serial Killer—The Shipman Case," *New England Journal of Medicine* 352 (2005): 1483–1844.

211. James Alan Fox and Jack Levin, *Overkill: Mass Murder and Serial Killing Exposed* (New York: Plenum, 1994); James Alan Fox, Jack Levin, and Kenna Quinet, *The Will to Kill: Making Sense of Senseless Murder*, 2nd ed. (Boston: Allyn & Bacon, 2004).

212. Amanda L. Farrell, Robert D. Keppelm, and Victoria B. Titterington, "Lethal Ladies: Revisiting What We Know About Female Serial Murderers," *Homicide Studies* 15 (2011): 228–252.

213. Harrison, Murphy, Ho, Bowers, and Flaherty, "Female Serial Killers in the United States."

214. Belea Keeney and Kathleen Heide, "Gender Differences in Serial Murderers:

A Preliminary Analysis," *Journal of Interpersonal Violence* 9 (1994): 37–56.

215. Farrell, Keppel, and Titterington, "Lethal Ladies."

216. Ibid.

217. Wade Myers, Erik Gooch, and Reid Meloy, "The Role of Psychopathy and Sexuality in a Female Serial Killer" *Journal of Forensic Sciences* 50 (2005): 652–658.

218. Farrell, Keppel, and Titterington, "Lethal Ladies," p. 245.

219. Zelda Knight, "Some Thoughts on the Psychological Roots of the Behavior of Serial Killers as Narcissists: An Object Relations Perspective," *Social Behavior and Personality: An International Journal* 34 (2006): 1189–1206.

220. Terry Whitman and Donald Akutagawa, "Riddles in Serial Murder: A Synthesis," *Aggression and Violent Behavior* 9 (2004): 693–703.

221. Holmes and Holmes, *Murder in America*, p. 106.

222. Ibid., p. 17; James Alan Fox and Jack Levin, *Overkill: Mass Murder and Serial Killing Exposed* (New York: Plenum, 1994).

223. Gabrielle Salfati and Alicia Bateman, "Serial Homicide: An Investigation of Behavioural Consistency," *Journal of Investigative Psychology and Offender Profiling* 2 (2005): 121–144.

224. Jennifer Browdy, "VI-CAP System to Be Operational This Summer," *Law Enforcement News*, May 21, 1984, p. 1.

225. James Alan Fox and Jack Levin, "Multiple Homicide: Patterns of Serial and Mass Murder," in *Crime and Justice: An Annual Edition*, Vol. 23, ed. Michael Tonry (Chicago: University of Chicago Press, 1998), pp. 407–455; Fox and Levin, *Overkill: Mass Murder and Serial Killing Exposed*; Fox, Levin, and Quinet, *The Will to Kill*; James Allan Fox and Jack Levin, "A Psycho-Social Analysis of Mass Murder," in *Serial and Mass Murder: Theory, Policy, and Research*, ed. Thomas O'Reilly-Fleming and Steven Egger (Toronto: University of Toronto Press, 1993).

226. FBI, "A Study of Active Shooter Incidents in the United States Between 2000 and 2013," https://www.fbi.gov/news/stories/2014 /september/fbi-releases-study-on-active -shooter-incidents/pdfs/a-study-of-active -shooter-incidents-in-the-u.s.-between -2000-and-2013.

227. Grant Duwe, "The Patterns and Prevalence of Mass Murder in Twentieth-Century America," *Justice Quarterly* 21 (2004): 729–761.

228. Federal Bureau of Investigation, "Law Enforcement Shares Findings of the Investigation into the Washington Navy Yard Shootings," September 25, 2013, http://www.fbi.gov/washingtondc/press -releases/2013/law-enforcement-shares -findings-of-the-investigation-into-the -washington-navy-yard-shootings.

229. James Alan Fox and Jack Levin, "Mass Murder: An Analysis of Extreme Violence,"

Journal of Applied Psychoanalytic Studies 5 (2003): 47–64.

230. Fox News, "Gunman in Alabama Massacre Had Hit List," March 11, 2009, http://www .foxnews.com/story/0,2933,508507,00.html.

231. Elissa Gootman, "The Hunt for a Sniper: The Victim; 10th Victim Is Recalled as Motivator on Mission," *New York Times*, October 14, 2002, p. A15; Sarah Kershaw, "The Hunt for a Sniper: The Investigation; Endless Frustration but Little Evidence in Search for Sniper," *New York Times*, October 14, 2002, p. A1.

232. Murderpedia, "Joseph Paul Franklin," http://murderpedia.org/male.F/f/franklin -joseph.htm.

233. Francis X. Clines with Christopher Drew, "Prosecutors to Discuss Charges as Rifle Is Tied to Sniper Killings," *New York Times*, October 25, 2002, p. A1.

234. Federal Bureau of Investigation, *Crime in the United States, 2005*.

235. Keith Harries, "Homicide and Assault: A Comparative Analysis of Attributes in Dallas Neighborhoods, 1981–1985," *Professional Geographer* 41 (1989): 29–38.

236. Kevin Flynn, "Record Payouts in Settlements of Lawsuits Against the New York City Police Are Set for Year," *New York Times*, October 1, 1999, p. 12.

237. Jennifer Truman and Lynn Langton, "Criminal Victimization, 2014," Bureau of Justice Statistics, http://www.bjs.gov /content/pub/pdf/cv14.pdf.

238. See, generally, Ruth S. Kempe and C. Henry Kempe, *Child Abuse* (Cambridge, MA: Harvard University Press, 1978).

239. Data in this and the following sections come from Department of Health and Human Services, "Child Maltreatment: Facts at a Glance," 2014, http://www.cdc.gov /violenceprevention/pdf/childmaltreatment -facts-at-a-glance.pdf; Centers for Disease Control and Prevention, "Child Abuse and Neglect Prevention, http://www.cdc.gov /violenceprevention/childmaltreatment /index.html.

240. G. D. Wolfner and R. J. Gelles, "A Profile of Violence Toward Children," *Child Abuse and Neglect* 17 (1993): 197–212.

241. Martin Daly and Margo Wilson, "Violence Against Step Children," *Current Directions in Psychological Science* 5 (1996): 77–81.

242. Ruth Inglis, *Sins of the Fathers: A Study of the Physical and Emotional Abuse of Children* (New York: St. Martin's, 1978), p. 53.

243. Diana Russell, "The Incidence and Prevalence of Intrafamilial and Extrafamilial Sexual Abuse of Female Children," *Child Abuse and Neglect* 7 (1983): 133–146; see also David Finkelhor, *Sexually Victimized Children* (New York: Free Press, 1979), p. 88.

244. Lisa Jones and David Finkelhor, *The Decline in Child Sexual Abuse Cases* (Washington, DC: Office of Juvenile Justice and Delinquency Prevention, 2001); Emily M.

Douglas and David Finkelhor, "Child Sexual Abuse Fact Sheet," May 2005, Crimes Against Children Research Center, http://www.unh.edu/ccrc/factsheet/pdf /childhoodSexualAbuseFactSheet.pdf.

245. Lisa Jones, David Finkelhor, and Kathy Kopie, "Why Is Sexual Abuse Declining? A Survey of State Child Protection Administrators," *Child Abuse and Neglect* 25 (2001): 1139–1141.

246. Eva Jonzon and Frank Lindblad, "Adult Female Victims of Child Sexual Abuse," *Journal of Interpersonal Violence* 20 (2005): 651–666.

247. Jane Siegel and Linda Williams, "Risk Factors for Sexual Victimization of Women," *Violence Against Women* 9 (2003): 902–930.

248. April Chiung-Tao Shen, "Self-Esteem of Young Adults Experiencing Interparental Violence and Child Physical Maltreatment: Parental and Peer Relationships as Mediators," *Journal of Interpersonal Violence* 24 (2009): 770–794.

249. Christina Meade, Trace Kershaw, Nathan Hansen, and Kathleen Sikkema, "Long-Term Correlates of Childhood Abuse Among Adults with Severe Mental Illness: Adult Victimization, Substance Abuse, and HIV Sexual Risk Behavior," *AIDS and Behavior* 13 (2009): 207–216.

250. Arina Ulman and Murray Straus, "Violence by Children Against Mothers in Relation to Violence Between Parents and Corporal Punishment by Parents," *Journal of Comparative Family Studies* 34 (2003): 41–63.

251. R. Emerson Dobash and Russell Dobash, *Violence Against Wives* (New York: Free Press, 1979).

252. Julia O'Faolain and Laura Martines, eds., *Not in God's Image: Women in History* (Glasgow: Fontana/Collins, 1974).

253. Laurence Stone, "The Rise of the Nuclear Family in Modern England: The Patriarchal Stage," in *The Family in History*, ed. Charles Rosenberg (Philadelphia: University of Pennsylvania Press, 1975), p. 53.

254. Dobash and Dobash, *Violence Against Wives*, p. 46.

255. John Braithwaite, "Inequality and Republican Criminology," paper presented at the annual meeting of the American Society of Criminology, San Francisco, November 1991, p. 20.

256. Richard Gelles and Murray Straus, "Violence in the American Family," *Journal of Social Issues* 35 (1979): 15–39.

257. Nicole Bell, "Health and Occupational Consequences of Spouse Abuse Victimization Among Male U.S. Army Soldiers," *Journal of Interpersonal Violence* 24 (2009): 751–769.

258. This section leans heavily on Priscilla Offenhauer and Alice Buchalter, *Teen Dating Violence: A Literature Review and Annotated*

Bibliography, April 2011, https://www.ncjrs .gov/pdffiles1/nij/grants/235368.pdf.

259. Jay G. Silverman, Anita Raj, Lorelei A. Mucci, and Jeanne E. Hathaway, "Dating Violence Against Adolescent Girls and Associated Substance Abuse, Unhealthy Weight Control, Sexual Risk Behavior, Pregnancy and Suicidality," *JAMA* 286 (2001): 572–579.

260. FBI, *Crime in the United States*, 2012.

261. Peter Van Koppen and Robert Jansen, "The Time to Rob: Variations in Time of Number of Commercial Robberies," *Journal of Research in Crime and Delinquency* 36 (1999): 7–29.

262. James Calder and John Bauer, "Convenience Store Robberies: Security Measures and Store Robbery Incidents," *Journal of Criminal Justice* 20 (1992): 553–566.

263. Elizabeth Ehrhardt Mustaine and Richard Tewksbury, "Predicting Risks of Larceny Theft Victimization: A Routine Activity Analysis Using Refined Lifestyle Measures," *Criminology* 36 (1998): 829–858.

264. Volkan Topalli, Richard Wright, and Robert Fornango, "Drug Dealers, Robbery and Retaliation: Vulnerability, Deterrence and the Contagion of Violence," *British Journal of Criminology* 42 (2002): 337–351.

265. Bruce A. Jacobs, *Robbing Drug Dealers: Violence Beyond the Law* (Hawthorne, NY: Aldine de Gruyter, 2000).

266. Richard Wright and Scott Decker, *Armed Robbers in Action: Stickups and Street Culture* (Boston: Northeastern University Press, 1997).

267. Jody Miller, "Up It Up: Gender and the Accomplishment of Street Robbery," *Criminology* 36 (1998): 37–67.

268. Ibid., pp. 54–55.

269. Marcus Felson, *Crime and Nature* (Thousand Oaks, CA: Sage, 2006).

270. Marie Rosenkrantz Lindegaard, Wim Bernasco, and Scott Jacques, "Consequences of Expected and Observed Victim Resistance for Offender Violence During Robbery Events," *Journal of Research in Crime and Delinquency* 52 (2015): 32–61.

271. Volkan Topalli, Scott Jacques, and Richard Wright, "It Takes Skills to Take a Car: Perceptual and Procedural Expertise in Carjacking," *Aggression and Violent Behavior* (2014): 19–25.

272. Heith Copes, Andy Hochstetler, and Michael Cherbonneau, "Getting the Upper Hand: Scripts for Managing Victim Resistance in Carjackings," *Journal of Research in Crime and Delinquency*, published online May 3, 2011.

273. Richard Felson, Eric Baumer, and Steven Messner, "Acquaintance Robbery," *Journal of Research in Crime and Delinquency* 37 (2000): 284–305.

274. Ibid., p. 287.

275. Ibid.

276. Jack Levin and Jack McDevitt, *Hate Crimes: The Rising Tide of Bigotry and Bloodshed* (New York: Plenum Press, 1993).

277. Jack McDevitt, Jack Levin, and Susan Bennett, "Hate Crime Offenders: An Expanded Typology," *Journal of Social Issues* 58 (2002): 303–318.

278. Jack Levin, *The Violence of Hate: Confronting Racism, Anti-Semitism, and Other Forms of Bigotry* (Boston: Allyn & Bacon, 2002), pp. 29–56.

279. FBI, *Hate Crime Statistics, 2014* (Washington, DC: FBI, 2015), https://www .fbi.gov/about-us/cjis/ucr/hate-crime/2014 /topic-pages/incidentsandoffenses_final.

280. Bureau of Justice Statistics, "U.S. Residents Experienced About 293,800 Hate Crime Victimizations in 2012—Unchanged from 2004," http://www.bjs.gov/content/pub /press/hcv0412stpr.cfm.

281. National Gay and Lesbian Task Force, "Hate Crime Laws Map," http://www.thetaskforce .org/hate-crimes-laws-map/.

282. Felicia Lee, "Gays Angry Over TV Report on a Murder," *New York Times*, November 26, 2004, p. A3.

283. Frederick M. Lawrence, *Punishing Hate: Bias Crimes Under American Law* (Cambridge, MA: Harvard University Press, 1999).

284. Ibid., p. 3.

285. Ibid., p. 9.

286. Ibid., p. 11.

287. Ibid., pp. 39–42.

288. Jack McDevitt, Jennifer Balboni, Luis Garcia, and Joann Gu, "Consequences for Victims: A Comparison of Bias- and Non-Bias-Motivated Assaults," *American Behavioral Scientist* 45 (2001): 697–714.

289. *Virginia v. Black et al.* No. 01-1107. 2003.

290. Eliott McLaughlin and Catherine Shoichet, "Police: Bryce Williams Fatally Shoots Self After Killing Journalists on Air," CNN, August 27, 2015, http://www.cnn.com /2015/08/26/us/virginia-shooting-wdbj/.

291. James Alan Fox and Jack Levin, "Firing Back: The Growing Threat of Workplace Homicide," *Annals* 536 (1994): 16–30.

292. Stephen Romano, Micòl E. Levi-Minzi, Eugene A. Rugala, and Vincent Van Hasselt, "Workplace Violence Prevention: Readiness and Response," *FBI Law Enforcement Bulletin*, January 2011, https://leb.fbi.gov/2011 /january/workplace-violence-prevention -readiness-and-response.

293. FBI, *Workplace Violence: Issues in Response* (Quantico, VA: National Center for the Analysis of Violent Crime, 2001), http:// www.fbi.gov/stats-services/publications /workplace-violence.

294. Romano, Levi-Minzi, Rugala, and Van Hasselt, "Workplace Violence Prevention: Readiness and Response."

295. Janet R. Cooper, "Response to 'Workplace Violence in Health Care: Recognized but Not Regulated,' by Kathleen M. McPhaul and Jane A. Lipscomb (September 30, 2004)," *Online Journal of Issues in Nursing* 10 (2005): 53–55.

296. Associated Press, "Gunman Wounds 3 Doctors in L.A. Hospital," *Cleveland Plain Dealer*, February 9, 1993, p. 1B.

297. Fox and Levin, "Firing Back," p. 5.

298. Erika Harrell, "Workplace Violence, 1993–2009," Bureau of Justice Statistics, March 29, 2011, http://www.bjs.gov /content/pub/pdf/wv09.pdf.

299. Romano, Levi-Minzi, Rugala, and Van Hasselt, "Workplace Violence Prevention: Readiness and Response."

300. Dana Loomis, Stephen Marshall, and Myduc Ta, "Employer Policies Toward Guns and the Risk of Homicide in the Workplace," *American Journal of Public Health* 95 (2005): 830–832.

301. The following sections rely heavily on Patricia Tjaden, *The Crime of Stalking: How Big Is the Problem?* (Washington, DC: National Institute of Justice, 1997); see also Robert M. Emerson, Kerry O. Ferris, and Carol Brooks Gardner, "On Being Stalked," *Social Problems* 45 (1998): 289–298.

302. Patrick Kinkade, Ronald Burns, and Angel Ilarraza Fuentes, "Criminalizing Attractions: Perceptions of Stalking and the Stalker," *Crime and Delinquency* 51 (2005): 3–25.

303. This section relies on "Analyzing Stalking Laws," National Center for Victims of Crime, 2016, https://www.victimsofcrime .org/docs/src/analyzing-stalking-statute.pdf.

304. Michael Black, Kathleen Basile, Matthew Breiding, Sharon Smith, Mikel Walters, Melissa Merrick, Jieru Chen, and Mark Stevens, *The National Intimate Partner and Sexual Violence Survey (NISVS): 2010 Summary Report* (Atlanta: National Center for Injury Prevention and Control, Centers for Disease Control and Prevention, 2011).

305. Michelle Garcia, "Voices from the Field: Stalking," *NIJ Journal* 266 (2010) http://www .nij.gov/journals/266/pages/stalking.aspx.

306. Bonnie Fisher, Francis Cullen, and Michael Turner, "Being Pursued: Stalking Victimization in a National Study of College Women," *Criminology and Public Policy* 1 (2002): 257–309.

307. Garcia, "Voices from the Field: Stalking."

308. Jennifer Gatewood Owens, "A Gender-Biased Definition: Unintended Impacts of the Fear Requirement in Stalking Victimization," *Crime and Delinquency*, first published November 18, 2015.

309. Reid Meloy, "Stalking: The State of the Science," *Criminal Behaviour and Mental Health* 17 (2007): 1–7.

310. Mary Brewster, "Stalking by Former Intimates: Verbal Threats and Other Predictors of Physical Violence," *Violence and Victims* 15 (2000): 41–51.

311. Carol Jordan, T. K. Logan, and Robert Walker, "Stalking: An Examination of the Criminal Justice Response," *Journal of Interpersonal Violence* 18 (2003): 148–165.

Liang sen Xinhua/eyevine/Redux

Orlando Police/*New York Times*/Redux

Omar Marteen

LEARNING OBJECTIVES

L01 Define the term *political crime*

L02 Assess the cause of political crime

L03 Compare and contrast the terms *espionage* and *treason*

L04 List the components of state political crime

L05 Debate the use and misuse of torture

L06 Distinguish among terrorists, insurgents, guerillas, and revolutionaries

L07 Enumerate the various forms of terrorism

L08 Explain what motivates the terrorist to commit violent acts

L09 Give examples of the efforts being made to centralize intelligence gathering

L010 Rate the efforts by the FBI and DHS to fight terrorism

11 POLITICAL CRIME AND TERRORISM

On June 12, 2016, Omar Mateen, age 29, an American-born man of Afghan descent, gunned down 49 people at Pulse, a gay nightclub in Orlando. It was the deadliest mass shooting in the United States and the nation's worst terror attack since 9/11.

Mateen, who was living in Fort Pierce, Florida, at the time of the shooting, had worked since 2007 as a security officer for one of the world's largest private security companies. Twice investigated by the FBI over the past several years for terrorism-related associations, Mateen wasn't arrested and both cases were closed for lack of evidence. His background in security and lack of arrest by the FBI allowed him to legally purchase guns and ammunition.

During the attack, Mateen called 911 to pledge allegiance to Abu Bakr al-Baghdadi, leader of ISIL (the Islamic State of Iraq and the Levant, also known as ISIS). According to the FBI, he also mentioned his admiration for the Boston Marathon bombers and for Moner Abu-Salha, the son of a Palestinian father and American mother, who on May 24, 2014, at the age of 22, drove a truck packed with explosives into a government outpost in Syria, detonating the charge. Evidence emerged that Mateen had visited Pulse a number of times and also scouted Disney World as another possible target.

As the attack began, an Orlando police officer was on duty outside the club and moved to confront the gunman. The officer drew the gunman outside, where they exchanged fire; the officer was outgunned and called for backup. The shooter re-entered the club and started firing again with his assault rifle, killing 20 people. After a hostage standoff that lasted three hours, and fearing for the lives of people trapped inside the club, police crashed into the building with an armored vehicle and stun grenades and killed Mateen, but not before he was able to kill another 29 victims. Many others were seriously wounded.

In the aftermath of the attack, a message posted in Arabic on a dark-web site associated with the ISIL news agency Amaq said, "The armed attack that targeted a gay night club in the city of Orlando in the American state of Florida and that bore more than a 100 killed and wounded was carried out by an Islamic state fighter." Despite such pronouncements, there was little evidence that Mateen had been directed by ISIL to attack the club. Rather, he appeared to be a disturbed person whose obsessions led him to ISIL's jihad against the West.[1]

olitical crime, which can range from the non-violent, such as election fraud, to the extremely violent, such as Omar Mateen's murderous rampage, has become an important area of criminological inquiry. Today, many criminologists who previously paid scant attention to the interaction between political motivation and crime have now made it the focus of intense study.

In this chapter, we will briefly discuss the concept of political crime and some of the forms it takes. We will then go into its most extreme form, terrorism, which now occupies the center stage of both world opinion and government policy. It is important for students of criminology to develop a basic understanding of terrorism's definition, history, and structure, and review the steps being taken to limit or eliminate its occurrence.

Political Crime

LO1 Define the term *political crime*

The term **political crime** is used to signify illegal acts that are designed to undermine an existing government and threaten its survival.[2] However, unlike other crimes, it is often difficult to decide who is the criminal and who is the victim. Take the series of uprisings that began in 2011 and are known as the "Arab Spring." Some targeted people widely viewed as dictators, such as the popular revolt in February 2011 that toppled the regime of long-term Egyptian dictator Hosni Mubarak. Similar protests broke out in Tunisia and Yemen and Libya, where the regime of dictator Muammar Gaddafi was ousted. These revolts were not viewed as terrorist acts but popular political upheavals against hated and evil dictators. The world did not recoil when Gaddafi was apprehended and killed brutally on camera.

When an act becomes a political crime and when an actor is considered a political criminal are often extremely subjective. In highly repressive nations, any form of unsanctioned political activity, including writing a newspaper article critical of the regime, may be considered a political crime, punishable by a prison term or even death. In contrast, people whom some label as terrorists and insurrectionists are viewed by others as freedom fighters and revolutionaries. What would have happened to George Washington and

political crime Illegal acts that are designed to undermine an existing government and threaten its survival. Political crimes can include both violent and nonviolent acts and range in seriousness from dissent, treason, and espionage to violent acts such as terrorism or assassination.

al-Qaeda (Arabic for "the base") An international fundamentalist Islamist organization comprising independent and collaborative cells, whose goal is reducing Western influence upon Islamic affairs. Also spelled al-Qa'ida.

 Edward Snowden's brush with espionage is but one of many forms of political crime—a term used to signify illegal acts that undermine an existing government and threaten its survival. To read more about Snowden, go to **http://www.cnn.com/2013/06/10 /politics/edward-snowden-profile/**.
Do you believe Snowden was actually motivated by his conviction that government spying was an evil that had to be stopped?

Benjamin Franklin had the British won the Revolutionary War? Would they have been hanged for their political crimes or considered heroes and freedom fighters? Another well-known figure involved in political rebellion, Edward Snowden, is discussed in the Profiles in Crime feature.

The moral ambivalence of political crimes can be viewed in the ongoing civil war in Syria. In 2011, troops loyal to the ruling party cracked down hard when protests erupted against the government of Bashar al-Assad. The world watched in horror and dismay as state security forces killed hundreds of protesters and arbitrarily arrested thousands, many of whom, including children, were beaten and tortured. The conflict evolved into a full-blown civil war in which hundreds of thousands of combatants and noncombatants have been killed, many by chemical weapons used by government forces.[3]

At first, world leaders denounced the violence: Turkish Prime Minister (now President) Recep Tayyip Erdoğan called the crackdown a "barbarity" that is "inhumane" and "cannot be digested."[4] However, as in many political conflicts, things soon became murky. Syrian government officials blamed the violence on "terrorist groups" and "armed gangs." One rebel group, the Al-Nusra Front (ANF), is associated with **al-Qaeda** and the Syrian Islamic Front, whose aim is overthrowing the Syrian government and establishing an Islamic state. The fighting soon took on sectarian overtones, and Shia and Sunni factions emerged. According to the government, the rebels were really jihadists looking to establish a base in Syria; according to the opposition, the rebels were freedom fighters looking to oust an evil dictator and establish democracy. In the midst of the turmoil, the Islamic State of Iraq and the Levant, more commonly known as ISIL or ISIS, emerged and carved out a caliphate spanning part of Syria and Iraq. In response to horrific terror acts, first the United States and then Russia began a bombing campaign against ISIL as the three-way civil war dragged on.

 To read a series of *New York Times* articles on the Syrian conflict, go to **http://www.nytimes .com/topic/destination/syria**.
Is joining a terror group such as ISIL similar to joining a gang such as MS-13 or the Crips? If not, why?

Edward Snowden

Edward Snowden, born in North Carolina in 1983, worked for Booz Allen Hamilton, a provider of management and technology consulting services to the U.S. government. In May 2013, Snowden began collecting top-secret documents regarding National Security Agency (NSA) domestic surveillance practices and leaking them to the press. Why did he engage in what some people consider treason? He was disturbed that the NSA was engaged in spying on millions of American citizens, a practice he considered an illegal invasion of privacy. When the documents appeared in the press, Snowden was charged with two counts of violating the Espionage Act of 1917 and theft of U.S. government or foreign government property. He fled to Russia in order to avoid prosecution, where he has been given asylum and remains to this day.

In a series of interviews given in Hong Kong and Russia, Snowden told the press, "I'm willing to sacrifice [my former life] because I can't in good conscience allow the U.S. government to destroy privacy, Internet freedom, and basic liberties for people around the world with this massive surveillance machine they're secretly building." He saw himself as a truth teller, informing the press that the American people have a right to know about government abuses that were being kept hidden. "The secret continuance of these programs represents a far greater danger than their disclosure. . . . So long as there's broad support amongst a people, it can be argued there's a level of legitimacy even to the most invasive and morally wrong program, as it was an informed and willing decision. . . . However, programs that are implemented in secret, out of public oversight, lack that legitimacy, and that's a problem. It also represents a dangerous normalization of 'governing in the dark,' where decisions with enormous public impact occur without any public input." Is Snowden a patriot who exposed illegal government practices or a political criminal who engaged in treasonous activity that endangered national security?

 CRITICAL THINKING

Whether Snowden is a political criminal is still a matter of some debate. What would you do if you came into possession of documents suggesting that the government was spying on political opponents? Reveal them to the press or keep them hidden from public view?

SOURCES: Charlie Savage and Mark Mazzetti, "Cryptic Overtures and a Clandestine Meeting Gave Birth to a Blockbuster Story," *New York Times*, June 10, 2013, http://www.nytimes.com/2013/06/11/us/how-edward-j-snowden-orchestrated-a-blockbuster-story.html; James Risen, "Snowden Says He Took No Secret Files to Russia," *New York Times*, January 20, 2014, http://www.nytimes.com/2013/10/18/world/snowden-says-he-took-no-secret-files-to-russia.html; Gordon Hunt, "Edward Snowden: I've Applied for Asylum in 21 Countries," *Silicon Republic*, June 5, 2015, https://www.siliconrepublic.com/enterprise/2015/06/05/edward-snowden-ive-applied-for-asylum-in-21-countries. (URLs accessed June 2016.)

THE NATURE OF POLITICAL CRIMES

The political criminal and political crimes may stem from religious or ideological sources. Because their motivations shift between selfish personal needs and selfless, noble, or altruistic desires, political crimes often occupy a gray area between conventional and outlawed behavior. It is easy to condemn interpersonal violent crimes such as rape or murder because their goals are typically selfish and self-centered (e.g., revenge or profit). In contrast, political criminals may be motivated by principle, faith, or conviction. While it is true that some political crime involves profit (such as selling state secrets for money), most political criminals, including Edward Snowden, do not consider themselves antisocial but instead patriotic and altruistic. They are willing to sacrifice themselves for what they consider to be the greater good. While some concoct elaborate schemes to hide or mask their actions, others are quite brazen, hoping to provoke the government to overreact in their zeal to crack down on dissent. Because state authorities may engage in a range of retaliatory actions that result in human rights violations, even those who support the government may begin to question its activities: maybe the government is corrupt and authoritarian? On the other hand, if the government does nothing, it appears weak and corrupt and unable to protect citizens.

Even those political criminals who profit personally from their misdeeds, such as someone who spies for an enemy nation for financial payoffs, may believe that their acts are motivated by a higher calling than common theft. "My ultimate goal is to weaken or overthrow a corrupt government," they reason, "so selling secrets to the enemy is justified." Political criminals may believe that their acts are criminalized only because the group holding power fears them and wants to curtail their behavior. And while the general public has little objection to laws that control extreme behaviors such as plotting a bloody revolution, they may have questions when a law criminalizes ordinary political dissent or bans political meetings in order to control suspected political criminals.

THE GOALS OF POLITICAL CRIMINALS

One survivor of a bombing attack in Iraq told reporters, "There may be a state, there may be a government. But what can that state do? What can they do with all the terrorists?

Are they supposed to set up a checkpoint in every house?" In their attack, the bombers succeeded in their efforts to create an atmosphere of intimidation and fear designed to oust the government.[5] Unsettling the populace and reducing faith in the government may be one goal of political criminals; some of the others include:

- *Intimidation.* Some political criminals want to intimidate or threaten an opponent who does not share their political orientation or views.
- *Revolution.* Some political criminals plot to overthrow the existing government and replace it with one that holds views they find more acceptable.
- *Profit.* Another goal of political crime is profit: selling state secrets for personal enrichment or trafficking in stolen arms and munitions.
- *Conviction.* Some political criminals are motivated by altruism; they truly believe their crimes will benefit society and are willing to violate the law and risk punishment in order to achieve what they see as social improvement.
- *Pseudo-conviction.* These political criminals conceal conventional criminal motivations behind a mask of conviction and altruism. They may form a revolutionary movement out of a hidden desire to engage in violence rather than their stated goal of reforming society. The pseudo-convictional criminal is particularly dangerous because they convince followers to join them in their crimes without fully revealing their true motivations.[6]

BECOMING A POLITICAL CRIMINAL

L02 Assess the cause of political crime

Why does someone become a political criminal? There is no set pattern or reason; motivations vary widely. Some use political crime as a stepping stone to public office, while others use it as a method to focus their frustrations. Others hope they can gain respect from their friends and family. Although the motivations for political crime are complex and varied, there does appear to be some regularity in the way ideas are formed. Political crime expert Randy Borum finds that this pattern takes the form of a series of cognitive stages:

- Stage 1: *"It's not right."* An unhappy, dissatisfied individual identifies some type of undesirable event or condition. It could be economic (e.g., poverty, unemployment, poor living conditions), social (e.g., government-imposed restrictions on individual freedoms, lack of order, or morality), or personal ("I am being cheated because of discrimination against my religious beliefs."). While the conditions may vary, those involved perceive the experience as "things are not as they should be."
- Stage 2: *"It's not fair."* The prospective political criminal concludes that the undesirable condition is a product of "injustice"—that is, it does not apply to everyone equally. A worker may believe that because of racial or religious bias someone with less skill is making more money and getting more benefits. Feeling deprived facilitates emotions of resentment and injustice.
- Stage 3: *"It's your fault."* Someone or some group must be held accountable for the extremist's displeasure. It always helps to identify a potential target—for example, an angry employee is convinced that minorities get all the good jobs while he is underpaid and suffering financially. He becomes receptive to propaganda put out by extremist groups looking to attract recruits and decides to join.
- Stage 4: *"You're evil."* Because good people would not intentionally hurt others, targeted groups are appropriate choices for revenge and/or violence. The disaffected worker concludes that since his country has let him down he is justified in joining a terrorist group or even taking matters in his own hands. Aggression becomes justifiable when aimed against bad people, particularly those who intentionally cause harm to others. By casting the target as evil, they are dehumanized and appropriate targets for aggression.[7]

This chain of events described by Borum can be seen in the events that led up to Dylann Roof's attack on the Emanuel African Methodist Episcopal Church, which left nine people dead. In his online manifesto, Roof stated:

The event that truly awakened me was the Trayvon Martin case. I kept hearing and seeing his name, and eventually I decided to look him up. I read the Wikipedia article and right away I was unable to understand what the big deal was. It was obvious that Zimmerman was in the right. But more importantly this prompted me to type in the words "black on White crime" into Google, and I have never been the same since that day. The first website I came to was the Council of Conservative Citizens. There were pages upon pages of these brutal black on White murders. I was in disbelief. At this moment I realized that something was very wrong. How could the news be blowing up the Trayvon Martin case while hundreds of these black on White murders got ignored?[8]

Here we can see how Roof thought in terms of "it's not right, it's not fair, it's your fault, and you're evil" as justifications for what amounts to a terror attack. His beliefs made him receptive to propaganda put out by radical groups.

CONNECTIONS

Borum's typology seems similar to the techniques of neutralization discussed in Chapter 7.

ASK YOURSELF . . .

Is it possible that terrorists must neutralize feelings of guilt and shame before planting their bombs? Or do their religious and political beliefs negate any need for a psychological process to reduce personal responsibility for violence?

Types of Political Crimes

Considering this cognitive thought that produces political crime and terrorism, what are the specific crimes and what form do they take?

ELECTION FRAUD

In 2012, officials in the small town of Cudahy, California, took part in a widespread corruption scheme that included accepting cash bribes, abusing drugs at city hall, and throwing out absentee ballots that favored election challengers. After a lengthy investigation, former head of code enforcement Angel Perales admitted to tampering with mail-in ballots in city elections. Perales and other city officials opened absentee ballots to see for whom the vote went. Ballots cast in favor of the incumbent candidates were resealed and returned to the mail to be counted. Ballots for non-incumbent candidates were discarded. Mayor David Silva was sentenced to one year in federal prison; Perales was sentenced to five years' probation.[9]

Some political criminals want to shape elections to meet their personal needs (even elections for student council president). In some instances their goal is altruistic: the election of candidates who reflect their personal political views. In others, their actions are motivated by profit: they are paid by a candidate to rig the election. And in some cases, such as David Silva and Angel Perales, they simply want to get elected!

Whatever the motive, **election fraud** is illegal interference with the political process. Acts of fraud tend to involve affecting vote counts to bring about a desired election outcome, whether by increasing the vote share of the favored candidate, depressing the vote share of the rival candidates, or both.

Election fraud has been a feature of political life since Roman times. In addition to discarding absentee ballots, it includes a variety of behaviors designed to give a candidate or his/her party an unfair advantage:

- *Intimidation.* Voters can be scared away from the polls through threats or intimidation. Having armed guards posted at polling places may convince people it is dangerous to vote. Lists of registered voters can be obtained and people subjected to threatening calls before the election.
- *Disruption.* Bomb threats can be called into voting places in areas that are known to heavily favor the opposing party, with the goal of suppressing the vote. There can be outright sabotage of polling places, ballots, ballot boxes, and voting machines.
- *Misinformation.* Flyers are sent out to voters registered with the opposition party containing misleading information such as the wrong election date or saying that rules have been changed about who is eligible to vote.
- *Registration fraud.* Political operatives may try to shape the outcome of an election by busing in ineligible voters from other districts. Because many jurisdictions require minimal identification and proof of citizenship, political criminals find it easy to get around residency requirements. They may provide conspirators with "change of address" forms to allow them to vote in a particular election, when in fact no actual change of address has occurred.
- *Vote buying.* Securing votes by payment or other rewards or the selling of one's vote is an age-old problem that still exists. One popular method is to buy absentee ballots from people who are in need of cash. The fraudulent voter can then ensure that the vote goes their way, an outcome that cannot be guaranteed if the conspirator casts a secret ballot at a polling place.

Most states have created laws to control and punish vote fraud. The federal government has a number of statutes designed to control and/or restrict fraud, including 18 U.S.C. § 594, which provides:

> Whoever intimidates, threatens, coerces, or attempts to intimidate, threaten, or coerce, any other person for the purpose of interfering with the right of such other person to vote or to vote as he may choose, or of causing such other person to vote for, or not to vote for, any candidate for the office of President, Vice President, Presidential elector, Member of the Senate, Member of the House of Representatives, Delegate from the District of Columbia, or Resident Commissioner, at any election held solely or in part for the purpose of electing such candidate, shall be fined under this title or imprisoned not more than one year, or both.

Another provision that applies to voting is 18 U.S.C. § 245(b)(1)(A):

> Whoever, whether or not acting under color of law, by force or threat of force willfully injures, intimidates or interferes with, or attempts to injure, intimidate or interfere with (1) any person because he is or has been, or in order to intimidate such person or any other person or any class of persons from (A) voting or qualifying to vote, qualifying or campaigning as a candidate for elective office, or qualifying or acting as a poll watcher, or any legally authorized election official, in any primary, special, or general election. . . .

This provision is in the Civil Rights section of Title 18, the federal criminal code, and it protects the right of all citizens to vote and campaign for office.

---

election fraud Illegal interference with the process of an election. Acts of fraud tend to involve affecting vote counts to bring about a desired election outcome, whether by increasing the vote share of the favored candidate, depressing the vote share of the rival candidates, or both. Varieties of election fraud include intimidation, disruption of polling places, distribution of misinformation such as the wrong election date, registration fraud, and vote buying.

How Common Is Voter Fraud? According to NYU Law School's Brennan Center for Justice, while claims of voter fraud are common, actual cases in the United States are relatively rare. There have only been a handful of substantiated cases of individual ineligible voters attempting to defraud the election system. One reason is that fraud by individual voters is an ineffective way to attempt to win an election. Each act of voter fraud in connection with a federal election risks five years in prison and a $10,000 fine, in addition to any state penalties, and yields at most one vote. When properly investigated, most fraud turns out to be a matter of mistake rather than intentional fraud (e.g., a person attempting to vote under a false name can be traced back to a typo).[10] Not all groups are convinced election fraud is a rare occurrence and many government officials consider it rampant.[11]

In response, most states have passed laws requiring voter IDs in order to cut down on fraud. As of February 2016, 33 states enforced voter identification requirements; 19 states required voters to present photo identification; 14 accepted other forms of identification. Most common IDs are a driver's license, a state-issued identification card, or a military identification card.

ABUSE OF OFFICE/PUBLIC CORRUPTION

In 2015, Senator Robert Menendez became the 12th senator to be indicted while in office. Menendez, the top Democrat on the Senate Foreign Relations Committee, was indicted on corruption charges alleging that he used his office to help Salomon Melgen, a Florida ophthalmologist and political donor, who was accused of overbilling Medicare.[12] Menendez is believed to have received personal favors from Melgen including plane tickets to vacation resorts; he denied all charges. He is by far not the only well-known politician accused of using their office for personal enrichment:

- In 2015, Sheldon Silver, a powerful member of the New York State legislature, was convicted on seven counts of honest services fraud, extortion, and money laundering stemming from schemes by which he obtained nearly $4 million in exchange for using his position to help benefit a cancer researcher and two real estate developers.
- In 2013, former Congressman Jesse L. Jackson Jr. was sentenced to 30 months in prison for conspiring to defraud his reelection campaigns by converting $750,000 in campaign funds to pay for personal items and expenses, including high-end appliances and electronics.[13]
- Former Illinois Governor Rod Blagojevich is serving a 14-year sentence in federal prison following conviction for corruption and the soliciting of bribes for political appointments, including an attempt to sell the U.S. Senate seat formerly occupied by Barack Obama.
- In 2013, Detroit Mayor Kwame Kilpatrick was sentenced to a 28-year prison term for his role in a wide-ranging racketeering conspiracy that included extortion, bribery, and fraud. Kilpatrick extorted money from people doing business with the city, rigged bids, and took bribes. He illegally appropriated funds from nonprofit civic organizations.[14]

Public corruption involves a breach of public trust and/or abuse of position by government officials and their private sector accomplices. Whether elected, appointed, or hired, they are committing a crime if while in office they demand, solicit, accept, or agree to receive anything of value in return for being manipulated in the performance of their official duties. They and their relatives and friends may be the recipients of illegal funds paid for by businesspeople willing to bribe to gain public contracts and other government actions. The victims of public corruption are the general public, who pay for corruption through inflated costs and sometimes higher taxes.

TREASON

 L03 Compare and contrast the terms *espionage* and *treason*

John Walker Lindh, the so-called American Taliban, was captured during the American invasion of Afghanistan. Lindh, who had spent

Former New York State assembly speaker Sheldon Silver is surrounded by media and police as he exits federal court on May 3, 2016, in New York City. Silver was sentenced to 12 years in prison for abuse of office and corruption schemes that federal officials said captured $5 million over a span of two decades.

Eduardo Munoz Alvarez/Getty Images

his early years in an affluent northern California community, converted to Islam and through a convoluted path wound up first in an al-Qaeda training camp and then fighting with the Taliban on the front lines in Afghanistan. He was captured on November 25, 2001, by Afghan Northern Alliance forces, and questioned by CIA agents. Later that day, there was a violent uprising in the prison in which he was being held and during the attack a CIA agent was killed. Walker escaped only to be recaptured seven days later. At his trial, he apologized for fighting alongside the Taliban, saying, "Had I realized then what I know now . . . I never would have joined them." The 21-year-old said Osama bin Laden was against Islam and that he "never understood jihad to mean anti-American or terrorism." (See Exhibit 11.1.) "I understand why so many Americans were angry when I was first discovered

---

EXHIBIT 11.1

What Is Jihad?

When John Walker Lindh used the word *jihad*, he made reference to a term that has become all too familiar in contemporary society. Often assumed to mean "holy war," the term is more complex than that simple meaning. According to terror expert Andrew Silke, the term derives from the Arabic for "struggle," and within Islam there are two forms of jihad: the Greater Jihad and the Lesser Jihad. The Greater Jihad refers to a Muslim's personal struggle to live a good and charitable life and adhere to God's commands. In this sense, jihad is a strictly personal and nonviolent phenomenon. The Lesser Jihad refers to violent struggle on behalf of Islam. Jihadists are "those who struggle" and refers to individuals who have volunteered to fight in the Lesser Jihad. The term is used by members of groups such as al-Qaeda to describe themselves and their goals. Jihadists sometimes call themselves *mujahideen*, meaning "holy warriors," and the term is commonly used to refer to Muslims engaged in the Lesser Jihad.

SOURCE: Andrew Silke, "Holy Warriors: Exploring the Psychological Processes of Jihadi Radicalization," *European Journal of Criminology* 5 (2008) 99–123.

---

in Afghanistan. I realize many still are, but I hope in time that feeling will change." After a plea agreement, John Walker Lindh was sentenced to 20 years in prison.[15] He is expected to be released in 2019.

Lindh's behavior amounts to what is commonly called **treason**, an act of disloyalty to one's nation or state. While the crime of treason is well known and the word *traitor* is a generic term, there have actually been fewer than 40 prosecutions for treason in the entire history of the United States and most have resulted in acquittal. In fact, though his behavior might be considered treasonous, Lindh was not actually charged or convicted of treason but was charged with serving in the Taliban army and carrying weapons.

Because treason is considered such a heinous crime, and to deter would-be traitors, many nations apply or have applied the death penalty to those convicted of attempting to overthrow the existing government. Treason was considered particularly loathsome under English common law, and until the nineteenth century it was punishable by being "drawn and quartered," a method of execution that involved hanging the offender, removing their intestines while still living, and finally cutting the offender into four pieces for public display. William Wallace, the Scottish patriot made famous in the film *Braveheart*, was so displayed after his execution.

Acts can be considered treasonous in order to stifle political dissent. In eighteenth-century England, it was considered treasonous to merely criticize the king or his behavior, and not surprisingly, the American colonists feared giving their own central government that much power. Therefore treason *is the only crime mentioned in the United States Constitution*, which defines treason as levying war against the United States or "in adhering to their Enemies, giving them Aid and Comfort," and requires the testimony of two witnesses or a confession in open court for conviction. The purpose of this was to limit the government's ability to bring charges of treason against opponents and to make it more difficult to prosecute those who are so charged.[16]

Today, the United States Criminal Code codifies treason as "whoever, owing allegiance to the United States, levies war against them or adheres to their enemies, giving them aid and comfort within the United States or elsewhere, is guilty of treason and shall suffer death, or shall be imprisoned not less than five years and fined under this title but not less than $10,000; and shall be incapable of holding any office under the United States."[17] Helping or cooperating with the enemy in a time of war (as Lindh did) would be considered treason; so too would be creating or recruiting a military force to help a foreign nation overthrow the government.

treason An act of disloyalty to one's nation or state.

Some of the most famous cases of treason in U.S. history include:

- In 1807 former Vice President Aaron Burr, a man best known for killing Secretary of the Treasury Alexander Hamilton in 1804 in a duel over a matter of honor, was accused of hatching a plot to separate the western states from the union. When that plot went awry, he conspired to seize Mexico and set up a puppet government with himself as king! Arrested on charges of treason, he was acquitted when the federal court, headed by John Marshall, ruled that to be guilty of treason an overt act must be committed; planning is not enough.[18]
- On the evening of October 16, 1859, John Brown, a staunch abolitionist, and a group of his supporters captured prominent citizens and seized the federal armory and arsenal at Harper's Ferry (West Virginia). Brown had hopes of creating a popular slave rebellion. He was convicted of treason against the Commonwealth of Virginia in 1859 and executed for attempting to organize armed resistance to slavery.[19]
- After World War II, two women, Iva Ikuko Toguri D'Aquino, a Japanese American born in Los Angeles and known as Tokyo Rose, and Mildred Elizabeth Gillars, born in Portland, Maine, and known as Axis Sally, served prison terms for broadcasting for the Axis powers in an effort to demoralize American troops.[20]

Espionage involves spying by governments to obtain political and military information from a rival nation. Master spy Andrei Bezrukov was born in Siberia. He and his cover wife, Yelena Vavilova, were recruited in the 1980s by the KGB and trained to pose as model Western citizens named Donald Heathfield and Tracy Foley. After living in Europe and Canada, the couple moved to Massachusetts, where Bezrukov earned a master's degree from Harvard and owned a consulting company, all the while being the head of a Russian spy network. The pair were arrested in the United States in 2010 and later exchanged for U.S. citizens being held in Russia for espionage activities. Their two sons claim that they had no idea their parents were Russian agents; they had always thought they were Canadian.

Kommersant Photo/Getty Images

ESPIONAGE

Americans have become very familiar with a once obscure website called WikiLeaks, an international organization that publishes classified and secret documents submitted by unnamed and anonymous sources. Launched in 2006 and run by Julian Assange, an Australian who emigrated to Sweden, WikiLeaks has supporters around the globe. A few years ago, the site began to post videos and documents that had been illegally appropriated from U.S. diplomatic and military computers by unknown hackers. One video showed a 2007 incident in which Iraqi civilians and journalists were killed by U.S. forces. The site also leaked more than 76,000 classified war documents from Afghanistan, including U.S. State Department cables. In the aftermath of the leaks, Army Specialist Bradley Manning, 22, was arrested after an informant told federal authorities that he had overheard him bragging about giving WikiLeaks a video of a helicopter assault in Iraq plus more than 260,000 classified U.S. diplomatic cables taken from government computers. Both the U.S. and foreign governments were embarrassed when the confidential cables hit the Net.[21] Wanted on a series of charges stemming from an alleged sexual assault in Sweden and threatened with extradition to the United States to face charges of espionage, Assange was granted asylum by the government of Ecuador and is currently residing in their London embassy. Bradley Manning (now Chelsea Elizabeth Manning) was convicted under the Espionage Act and sentenced to up to 35 years in prison.

There are many people who believe that Chelsea Manning is a hero, not a traitor. According to her supporters' website, she revealed information that showed us "the true human cost of our wars in Iraq and Afghanistan, and changed journalism forever," for revealing the video that exposed the killing of unarmed civilians and two Reuters journalists by a U.S. Apache helicopter crew in Iraq and the release of U.S. diplomatic cables that revealed the role that corporate interests and spying play in international diplomacy. Among the awards she received:

- Person of the Year 2012, *The Guardian*
- 2013 Peace Prize, U.S. Peace Memorial Foundation
- Peacemaker of the Year 2013, Peace and Justice Center of Sonoma County
- Hero of Peace Award 2013, Eisenhower Chapter of Veterans for Peace[22]

Espionage (more commonly called spying) is the practice of obtaining information about a government, organization, or society that is considered secret or confidential without the permission of the holder of the information. Espionage involves obtaining the information illegally by covertly entering the area where the information is stored, secretly photographing forbidden areas, or subverting through threat or payoff people who know the information and will divulge it through subterfuge.[23]

Espionage is typically associated with spying on potential or actual enemies by a foreign agent who is working for his or her nation's intelligence service. With the end of the Cold War, the threat of espionage seemed reduced until 2010 when a major Russian spy group was unraveled and 10 people arrested. These were sleeper agents who had spent decades fitting seamlessly in their new environment. Neighbors were shocked to find out that "Richard Murphy" and "Cynthia Murphy" were actually spies named Vladimir Guryev and Lydia Guryev, while "Michael Zottoli" and "Patricia Mills" were in reality agents of the Russian Federation. The case was settled when the Russians were exchanged for four American spies being held in Russian prisons.

Not all spies are foreign nationals. There are numerous cases of homegrown spies who are motivated by misguided altruism or belief. Perhaps the most famous international case involved a group of five upper-crust students recruited during the Cold War at prestigious Cambridge University in England by Russia's foreign intelligence service, the KGB. The five were motivated by the belief that capitalism was corrupt and that the Soviet Union offered a better model for society. After graduation, they secured sensitive government posts that gave them access to valuable intelligence they then passed on to the Soviet Union. Two of the conspirators, Guy Burgess and Donald Maclean, were exposed in 1951 and defected to the Soviet Union before they could be captured; Kim Philby, who had worked as a high-level intelligence agent, defected to Russia in 1963 but not before passing on information that cost hundreds of lives. The last two members of the ring, Anthony Blunt and John Cairncross, went undetected for many years.[24]

While some spies, like the Cambridge Five, are motivated by ideology, others, like CIA operative Harold Nicholson and FBI agent Robert Hanssen, were looking for profit. Nicholson was convicted in 1997 of selling U.S. intelligence to Russia for $180,000 and was sentenced to 23.5 years imprisonment; Nicholson was the highest ranking CIA official ever convicted for spying for a foreign country. Robert Hanssen was a counterintelligence agent for the FBI assigned to detect and identify Russian spies. A former Chicago police officer, Hanssen's assignment required him to have access to sensitive top-secret information. He volunteered to become a paid spy for the KGB during the Cold War and over a period of 15 years received at least $1.4 million in cash and diamonds. He was arrested on February 18, 2001, after leaving a package of classified documents for his Russian handlers under a footbridge in a park outside Washington, D.C. On July 6, 2001, he pleaded guilty to 15 counts of espionage and was sentenced to 15 life terms without the possibility of parole. During his years as a double agent, Hanssen not only provided more than 6,000 pages of documents to the Soviet Union but also caused the death of two U.S. double agents whose identities were uncovered with the aid of his secret documents. The Hanssen case was the subject of the 2007 film *Breach*, which starred Chris Cooper as the corrupt agent.[25]

One of the most infamous of these cases, that of CIA double agent Aldrich Ames, is set out in the Profiles in Crime feature.

Industrial Espionage   In 2014, five Chinese men were indicted for stealing thousands of sensitive internal communications from U.S. companies, including Alcoa, United States Steel Corporation, and Westinghouse.[26] The concept of espionage has been extended to spying involving corporations, referred to as **industrial espionage**. This involves such unethical or illegal activities as bribing employees to reveal trade secrets such as computer codes or product formulas. The traditional methods of industrial espionage include recruiting agents and inserting them into the target company or breaking into an office to take equipment and information. It can also involve surveillance and spying on commercial organizations to determine the direction of their new product line or even what bid they intend to make on a government contract. Such knowledge can provide vast profits when it allows a competitor to save large sums on product development or to win an undeserved contract by underbidding.[27]

A report from the National Counterintelligence Center lists biotechnology, aerospace, telecommunications, computer software, transportation, advanced materials, energy research, defense, and semiconductor companies as the top targets for foreign economic espionage.[28] The FBI has seen a 53 percent increase in economic espionage cases aimed at U.S. companies, leading to the loss of hundreds of billions of dollars. The vast majority of the perpetrators originate from China and have ties to that nation's government. Large corporations successfully targeted in the past include DuPont, Lockheed Martin, and Valspar. In a survey conducted by the FBI, half of the 165 private companies surveyed claimed to be victims of economic espionage or theft of trade secrets.[29] Espionage is often carried out with "insider threats," or employees who are familiar with the inner workings of a particular technology being recruited by foreign agents in exchange for large amounts of cash.

> **espionage** The practice of obtaining information about a government, organization, or society that is considered secret or confidential without the permission of the holder of the information. Commonly called spying.
>
> **industrial espionage** Activities designed to gain illegal competitive advantage over a business rival, such as bribing employees to reveal trade secrets and product formulas.

Aldrich Hazen Ames

Aldrich Hazen Ames was arrested by the FBI in Arlington, Virginia, on espionage charges on February 24, 1994. At the time of his arrest, Ames was a 31-year veteran of the Central Intelligence Agency (CIA) who had been spying for the Russians since 1985. Arrested with him was his wife, Rosario Ames, who had aided and abetted his espionage activities.

Ames was a CIA case officer who spoke Russian and specialized in the Russian intelligence services, including the KGB, the USSR's foreign intelligence service. His initial overseas assignment was in Ankara, Turkey, where he targeted Russian intelligence officers for recruitment. Later, he worked in New York City and Mexico City. On April 16, 1985, while assigned to the CIA's Soviet/East European Division at CIA Headquarters in Langley, Virginia, he secretly volunteered to KGB officers at the USSR embassy in Washington, D.C. Shortly thereafter, the KGB paid him $50,000. During the summer of 1985, Ames met several times with a Russian diplomat to whom he passed classified information about CIA and FBI human sources, as well as technical operations targeting the Soviet Union. In December 1985, Ames met with a Moscow-based KGB officer in Bogota, Colombia. In July 1986, Ames was transferred to Rome.

In Rome, Ames continued his meetings with the KGB, including a Russian diplomat assigned to Rome and a Moscow-based KGB officer. At the conclusion of his assignment in Rome, Ames received instructions from the KGB regarding clandestine contacts in the Washington, D.C., area, where he would next be assigned. In the four years after he volunteered, the KGB paid Ames $1.88 million.

Upon his return to Washington in 1989, Ames continued to pass classified documents to the KGB, using "dead drops" or prearranged hiding places where he would leave the documents to be picked up later by KGB officers from the USSR embassy in Washington. In return, the KGB left money and instructions for Ames, usually in other dead drops.

In the meantime, the CIA and FBI learned that Russian officials who had been recruited by them were being arrested and executed. These human sources had provided critical intelligence information about the USSR, which was used by U.S. policy makers in determining U.S. foreign policy. Following analytical reviews and receipt of information about Ames's unexplained wealth, the FBI opened an investigation in May 1993.

FBI special agents and investigative specialists conducted intensive physical and electronic surveillance of Ames during a 10-month investigation. Searches of Ames's residence revealed documents and other information linking Ames to the Russian foreign intelligence service. On October 13, 1993, investigative specialists observed a chalk mark Ames made on a mailbox confirming to the Russians his intention to meet them in Bogota, Colombia. On November 1, special agents observed him and, separately, his Russian handler in Bogota. When Ames planned foreign travel, including a trip to Moscow, as part of his official duties, a plan to arrest him was approved.

Following guilty pleas by both Ames and his wife on April 28, 1994, Ames was sentenced to incarceration for life without the possibility of parole. Rosario Ames was sentenced on October 20, 1994, to 63 months in prison. Ames also forfeited his assets to the United States, and $547,000 was turned over to the Justice Department's Victims Assistance Fund. Ames is serving his sentence in the federal prison system. Rosario Ames completed her sentence and was released.

 CRITICAL THINKING

How can you explain the criminal motivation of someone like Aldrich Ames? Which theory of crime causation would best explain his treasonous behavior?

SOURCE: FBI, "Famous Cases and Criminals: Aldrich Hazen Ames," http://www.fbi.gov/about-us/history/famous-cases/aldrich-hazen-ames/ (accessed June 2016).

Industrial espionage by foreign agents' efforts have eroded the U.S. military advantage by enabling foreign militaries to acquire sophisticated capabilities that might otherwise have taken years to develop. Such efforts also undercut the U.S. economy by making it possible for foreign firms to gain a competitive economic edge over U.S. companies.

A number of factors have combined to facilitate private-sector technology theft. Globalization, while generating major gains for the U.S. economy, has given foreigners unprecedented access to U.S. firms and to sensitive technologies. There has also been a proliferation of devices that have made it easy for private-sector experts to illegally retrieve, store, and transfer massive amounts of information, including trade secrets and proprietary data; such devices are increasingly common in the workplace.

In addition to private citizens conducting espionage, foreign government organizations also mount their own operations, including:

- Targeting U.S. firms for technology that would strengthen their foreign defense capabilities
- Posting personnel at U.S. military bases to collect classified information to bolster military modernization efforts
- Employing commercial firms in the United States in a covert effort to target and acquire U.S. technology
- Recruiting students, professors, scientists, and researchers to engage in technology collection
- Making direct requests for classified, sensitive, or export-controlled information via personal contacts, telephone, email, fax, and other forms of communication

- Forming ventures with U.S. firms in the hope of placing collectors in proximity to sensitive technologies or else establishing foreign research

Foreign companies seek entrée into U.S. firms and other targeted institutions by pursuing business relationships that provide access to sensitive or classified information, technologies, or projects:

- *Conferences, conventions, and trade shows.* These public venues offer opportunities for foreign adversaries to gain access to U.S. information and experts in dual-use and sensitive technologies.
- *Official foreign visitors and exploitation of joint research.* Foreign government organizations, including intelligence services, use official visits to U.S. government and cleared defense contractor facilities, as well as joint research projects between foreign and U.S. entities, to target and collect information.
- *Foreign targeting of U.S. visitors overseas.* Whether traveling for business or personal reasons, U.S. travelers overseas—businesspeople, U.S. government employees, and contractors—are routinely targeted by foreign collectors, especially if they are assessed as having access to some sensitive information. Some U.S. allies engage in this practice, as do less friendly powers such as Russia and China. Targeting takes many forms: exploitation of electronic media and devices, surreptitious entry into hotel rooms, aggressive surveillance, and attempts to set up sexual or romantic entanglements.
- *Open source information.* Foreign collectors are aware that much U.S. economic and technological information is available in professional journals, social networking and other public websites, and the media.[30]

Legal Controls   Until 1996, there was no federal statute that explicitly penalized industrial espionage. Recognizing the increasingly important role that intellectual property plays in the well-being of the American economy, Congress enacted the Economic Espionage Act (EEA) of 1996, which criminalizes the theft of trade secrets. The EEA actually contains two separate provisions, one that penalizes foreign agents from stealing American trade secrets and one directed at domestic spying.

Convictions of foreign agents under the Economic Espionage Act have been relatively rare. It was not until 2006 that the first conviction occurred, when two Chinese Nationals, Fei Ye and Ming Zhong, pleaded guilty to stealing secret information from Sun Microsystems and Transmeta Corporation.[31]

STATE POLITICAL CRIME

 L04 List the components of state political crime

While some political crimes are committed by people who oppose the state, others are perpetrated by state authorities against the people they are supposed to serve; this is referred to as **state political crime**. Critical criminologists argue that rather than being committed by disaffected people, a great deal of political crime arises from the efforts of the state to either maintain governmental power or to uphold the race, class, and gender advantages of those who support the government. In industrial society, the state will do everything to protect the property rights of the wealthy while opposing the real interests of the poor. They might even go to war to support the capitalist classes who need the wealth and resources of other nations. The desire for natural resources such as rubber, oil, and metals was one of the primary reasons for Japan's invasion of China and other Eastern nations that sparked their entry into World War II.

USING TORTURE

 L05 Debate the use and misuse of torture

On February 23, 2007, Osama Hassan Mustafa Nasr, an Egyptian cleric, made worldwide headlines when he claimed that he had been kidnapped in Italy by American CIA agents and sent to Egypt for interrogation as part of the CIA's "extraordinary rendition." Nasr claimed, "I was subjected to the worst kind of torture in Egyptian prisons. I have scars of torture all over my body." Italy indicted 26 Americans and five Italian agents accused of seizing him and sending him to Egypt without trial or due process.[32]

Of all state political crimes, the use of **torture** to gain information from suspected political criminals is perhaps the most notorious.

Can the torture of a suspected terrorist determined to destroy the government and harm innocent civilians ever be permissible or is it always an example of state-sponsored political crime? While most people loathe the thought of torturing anyone, some experts argue that torture can sometimes be justified in what they call the **ticking bomb scenario**. Suppose the government found out that a captured terrorist knew the whereabouts of a dangerous explosive device that was set to go off and kill thousands of innocent people. Would it be permissible to engage in the use of torture on this single suspect if it would save the population of a city?

state political crime Political crime that arises from the efforts of the state to either maintain governmental power or to uphold the race, class, and gender advantages of those who support the government. It is possible to divide state political crimes into five varieties: (1) political corruption, (2) illegal domestic surveillance, (3) human rights violations, (4) state violence such as torture, illegal imprisonment, police violence and use of deadly force, and (5) state corporate crime committed by individuals who abuse their state authority or who fail to exercise it when working with people and organizations in the private sector.

torture An act that causes severe pain or suffering, whether physical or mental, that is intentionally inflicted on a person for such purposes as obtaining a confession, punishing them for a crime they may have committed, or intimidating or coercing them into a desired action.

ticking bomb scenario A scenario that some experts argue in which torture can perhaps be justified if the government discovers that a captured terrorist knows the whereabouts of a dangerous explosive device that is set to go off and kill thousands of innocent people.

The ticking bomb scenario has appeal. Famed social commentator and legal scholar Alan Dershowitz argues that the "vast majority" of Americans would expect law enforcement agents to use any means necessary to obtain information needed to prevent a terror attack. To protect against abuse, Dershowitz proposes the creation of a "torture warrant" that can only be issued by a judge in cases where (a) there is an absolute need to obtain immediate information in order to save lives and (b) there is probable cause that the suspect has such information and is unwilling to reveal it to law enforcement agents. The suspect would be given immunity from prosecution based on information elicited by the torture; it would be used only to save lives. The warrant would limit the torture to nonlethal means, such as sterile needles being inserted beneath the nails to cause excruciating pain without endangering life.[33]

Not everyone agrees with Dershowitz.[34] Opponents of torture believe that even imminent danger does not justify state violence. There is a danger that such state-sponsored violence would become calculated and premeditated; torturers would have to be trained, ready, and in place for the ticking bomb argument to work. We couldn't be running around looking for torturers when a bomb is set to go off, could we? Because torturers would be part of the government bureaucracy, there is no way to ensure that they would only use their skills in certain morally justifiable cases.[35] What happens if a superior officer tells them to torture someone, but they believe the order is unjustified? Should they follow orders or risk a court martial for being disobedient? Furthermore, there is very little empirical evidence suggesting that torture provides any real benefits and much more that suggests it can create serious problems. It can damage civil rights and democratic institutions and cause the general public to have sympathy for the victims of torture no matter their evil intent.[36]

The Waterboarding Controversy   During the 2016 presidential primaries, Republican candidate Donald Trump repeatedly defended enhanced interrogation techniques when dealing with terror detainees, saying torture works. "Of course waterboarding is bad, but it's not like chopping off heads," Trump said at an event in South Carolina.[37] Is Trump correct? Can a bright line be drawn between what is considered torture and what constitutes firm but legal interrogation methods?[38]

Waterboarding involves immobilizing a person on his or her back, with the head inclined downward, and pouring water over the face and into the breathing passages. It produces an immediate gag reflex and an experience akin to drowning; the subject believes his or her death is imminent.

The use of waterboarding is controversial because there seems to be no agreement on whether it is torture or a relatively harmless instrument of interrogation. While official U.S. government policy and government doctrine is vehemently opposed to torture, it has condoned harsh interrogation techniques that combine physical and psychological

An Ethical Dilemma

Torture or Not?

As a criminologist, your specialty is terrorism, so it comes as no surprise that the director of the CIA asks you to draw up a protocol setting out the rules for the use of torture with suspected terrorists. The reason for his request is that a series of new articles has exposed the agency's practice of sending suspected terrorists to friendly nations that are less squeamish about using torture. Shocking photo evidence of torture from detention facilities at the Guantanamo base in Cuba support these charges. Legal scholars have argued that these tactics violate both international treaties and domestic statutes prohibiting torture. Some maintain that the U.S. Constitution limits the authority of an executive agency like the CIA to act against foreigners abroad and also limits physical coercion by the government under the Fifth Amendment due process and self-incrimination clauses and the Eighth Amendment prohibition against cruel and unusual punishment. Legally, it is impermissible for United States authorities to engage in indefinite detention or torture regardless of the end, the place, or the victim.

 Write a memo to the CIA director outlining the protocol you recommend for the use of torture with suspected terrorists. In your document, address when torture should be used, whom it should be used on, and what tortures you recommend using. Of course, if you believe the use of torture is always unethical, you could let the director know why you have reached this conclusion.

tactics, including head slapping, waterboarding, and exposure to extreme cold. Waterboarding was also an issue during the 2008 presidential campaign, when Republican nominee Senator John McCain, a former prisoner of war who experienced torture firsthand in a North Vietnamese prison camp, told the press, "All I can say is that it was used in the Spanish Inquisition, it was used in Pol Pot's genocide in Cambodia, and there are reports that it is being used against Buddhist monks today. They should know what it is. It is not a complicated procedure. It is torture."[39]

Terrorism

LO6 Distinguish among terrorists, insurgents, guerillas, and revolutionaries

On November 13, 2015, in a series of terrorist attacks in Paris, suicide bombings and mass shootings were aimed at a stadium, cafés, restaurants, and the Le Bataclan theater, where an American rock group was playing. The attacks took the lives of

EXHIBIT 11.2

Definitions of Terrorism

LEAGUE OF NATIONS CONVENTION (1937)

All criminal acts directed against a State and intended or calculated to create a state of terror in the minds of particular persons or a group of persons or the general public.

UNITED NATIONS RESOLUTION LANGUAGE (1999)

1. *Strongly condemns* all acts, methods and practices of terrorism as criminal and unjustifiable, wherever and by whomsoever committed;

2. *Reiterates* that criminal acts intended or calculated to provoke a state of terror in the general public, a group of persons or particular persons for political purposes are in any circumstance unjustifiable, whatever the considerations of a political, philosophical, ideological, racial, ethnic, religious or other nature that may be invoked to justify them. (GA Res. 51/210, "Measures to Eliminate International Terrorism.")

SHORT LEGAL DEFINITION PROPOSED BY A. P. SCHMID TO UNITED NATIONS CRIME BRANCH (1992)

Act of Terrorism = Peacetime Equivalent of War Crime

ACADEMIC CONSENSUS DEFINITION USED BY THE UNITED NATIONS

Terrorism is an anxiety-inspiring method of repeated violent action, employed by (semi-) clandestine individual, group or state actors, for idiosyncratic, criminal or political reasons, whereby—in contrast to assassination—the direct targets of violence are not the main targets. The immediate human victims of violence are generally chosen randomly (targets of opportunity) or selectively (representative or symbolic targets) from a target population, and serve as message generators. Threat- and violence-based communication processes between terrorist (organization), (imperiled) victims, and main targets are used to manipulate the main target (audience[s]), turning it into a target of terror, a target of demands, or a target of attention, depending on whether intimidation, coercion, or propaganda is primarily sought.

UNITED STATES DEPARTMENT OF STATE

The term "terrorism" means premeditated, politically motivated violence perpetrated against noncombatant targets by subnational groups or clandestine agents, usually intended to influence an audience.

The term "international terrorism" means terrorism involving citizens or the territory of more than one country.

The term "terrorist group" means any group practicing, or that has significant subgroups that practice, international terrorism.

SOURCES: *Patterns of Global Terrorism* (Washington: U.S. Department of State) http://www.state.gov/j/ct/rls/pgtrpt/; National Institute of Justice, *Terrorism*, http://www.nij.gov/topics/crime/terrorism/; Alex Schmid, *Routledge Handbook of Terrorism Research* (London: Routledge, 2013).

---

130 people and injured 368. Seven of the attackers were killed while a number were able to flee. The attack was a follow-up to the January 2015 attacks on the offices of the satirical newspaper *Charlie Hebdo* and a Jewish supermarket in Paris, which killed 17 people and wounded 22, including civilians and police officers.[40] ISIL claimed responsibility for all of these attacks.

The Paris attacks hammered home the fact that the political crime that many people are most concerned with is terrorism. What could possibly motivate people to commit such horrific acts of random violence? While scholars and experts debated the cause, ISIL had begun warning Western nations a year earlier that its fighters kill enemies of Islam wherever they could be found. The attackers were not seeking a homeland or to topple a government, they merely wanted bloody retribution for perceived wrongs. Because terrorism is so important and salient, the remainder of this chapter focuses on the history, nature, and extent of terrorism and the methods being employed for its control.

Despite its long history, it is often difficult to precisely define terrorism (from the Latin *terrere*, which means to frighten) and to separate terrorist acts from interpersonal crimes of violence. If a group robs a bank to obtain funds for its revolutionary struggles, should the act be treated as terrorism or as a common bank robbery? In this instance, defining a crime as terrorism depends on the kind of legal response the act evokes from those in power. To be considered **terrorism**, which is a political crime, an act must carry with it the intent to disrupt and change the government and must not be merely a common-law crime committed for greed or egotism.

Because of its complexity, an all-encompassing definition of terrorism is difficult to formulate, although most experts agree that it generally involves the illegal use of force against innocent people to achieve a political objective. According to the U.S. State Department, the term *terrorism* means premeditated, politically motivated violence perpetrated against noncombatant targets by subnational groups or clandestine agents, usually intended to influence an audience. The term *international terrorism* means terrorism involving citizens or the territory of more than one country. A terrorist group is any group practicing, or that has significant subgroups that practice, international terrorism.[41] Exhibit 11.2 sets out a number of definitions of terrorism drafted or used by prominent governmental agencies or organizations.

terrorism The illegal use of force against innocent people to achieve a political objective.

Terrorism usually involves a type of political crime that emphasizes violence as a mechanism to promote change. Whereas some political criminals sell secrets, spy, and the like, terrorists systematically murder and destroy or threaten such violence to terrorize individuals, groups, communities, or governments into conceding to the terrorists' political demands.[42] Because terrorists lack large armies and formidable weapons, their use of subterfuge, secrecy, and hit-and-run tactics is designed to give them a psychological advantage and the power to neutralize the physical superiority of their opponents.

However, it may be erroneous to assume that all terrorists have political goals. Some may try to bring about what they consider to be social reform—for example, by attacking women wearing fur coats or sabotaging property during a labor dispute. Terrorism must also be distinguished from conventional warfare because it requires secrecy and clandestine operations to exert social control over large populations.[43] So terrorist activities may be aimed at promoting an ideology other than political change.

TERRORIST AND GUERILLA

The word *terrorist* is often used interchangeably with the word *guerilla*, but the terms are quite different. **Guerilla** comes from the Spanish term meaning "little war," which developed out of the Spanish rebellion against French troops after Napoleon's 1808 invasion of the Iberian Peninsula.[44] Terrorists have an urban focus. Operating in small bands, called cells or cadres, they target the property or persons of their enemy, such as members of the ruling class. However, terrorists may not have political ambitions, and their actions may be aimed at stifling or intimidating other groups who oppose their political, social, or economic views. Terrorists who kill abortion providers in order to promote their "pro-life" agenda are not aiming for regime change. Guerillas, on the other hand, are armed military bands, typically located in rural areas, that attack military, police, and government officials in an effort to destabilize the existing government. Their organizations can grow quite large and eventually take the form of a conventional military force. Some guerilla bands infiltrate urban areas (urban guerillas). For the most part, guerillas are a type of insurgent band.

TERRORIST AND INSURGENT

An insurgency is a political movement that may use terror tactics to achieve their goals. **Insurgents** wish to confront the existing government for control of all or a portion of its territory, or force political concessions in sharing political power by competing with the opposition government for popular support.[45] What makes the insurgent unique is that they have the luxury of receiving aid from neighboring sympathizers, allowing them to base their insurgency outside the target nation, thereby protecting them from their enemies. Taliban members took shelter in Pakistan when the U.S. military drove them out of Afghanistan. Insurgencies may attract recruits who do not actually live in the disputed area but are sympathetic to the cause. In 2014, insurgents from **ISIL** surged into Iraq from Syria, routed the Iraqi army, and occupied major cities such as Mosul. ISIL is a violent Sunni extremist group that has the goal of creating a caliphate, based on a very conservative Islamic religious code, that

guerilla The term means "little war" and developed out of the Spanish rebellion against French troops after Napoleon's 1808 invasion of the Iberian Peninsula. Today the term is often used interchangeably with the term *terrorist*.

insurgent The typical goal of an insurgency is to confront the existing government for control of all or a portion of its territory, or force political concessions in sharing political power. While terrorists may operate in small bands with a narrow focus, insurgents represent a popular movement and may also seek external support from other nations to bring pressure on the government.

Islamic State of Iraq and the Levant (ISIL) A jihadist militant group that follows an Islamic fundamentalist version of Sunni Islam. Their objective is to create an independent caliphate in lands seized from Syria and Iraq. Also known as ISIS and Daesh.

ISIS has emerged as the foremost terrorist group in the world. It is known for broadcasting its brutal tactics on the Internet and in the media. In August 2014, US journalist James Wright Foley was beheaded on camera by ISIS fighter Mohammed Emwazi aka "Jihadi John." On November 12, 2015, Emwazi was killed in a targeted drone strike in Syria.

AP Images/REX

	TERRORIST	GUERILLA	INSURGENT	REVOLUTIONARY
Description	Groups who engage in premeditated, politically motivated violence perpetrated against noncombatant targets.	Armed groups operating in rural areas who attack the military, the police, and other government officials.	Groups who engage in armed uprising or revolt against an established civil or political authority.	Engages in civil war against sovereign power that holds control of the land.
Examples	Al-Qaeda, Hamas	Mao's People's Liberation Army, Ho Chi Minh's Viet Cong	Iraqi insurgent groups	American Revolution, French Revolution, Russian Revolution
Goals	Personal, criminal, or political gain or change.	Replace or overthrow existing government.	Win over population by showing government's incompetence. Force government into political concessions and/or power sharing.	Gain independence or oust existing government or monarchy.
Methods	Small, clandestine cells who use systematic violence for purpose of intimidation.	Use unconventional warfare and mobile tactics. May grow large and use tactics similar to conventional military force.	May use violent (bombings and kidnappings) or nonviolent means (food distribution centers and creating schools).	Can use violent armed conflict or nonviolent methods such as Gandhi used in India.

spans Sunni-dominated sections of Iraq and Syria. ISIL is made up of Islamic fighters from around the world, highly trained and motivated. They were able to launch their insurgency after organizing outside of Iraq and then filtering through the porous border with Syria where they had played a major role in the ongoing civil war.[46]

Insurgents tend to live isolated and stressful lives and enjoy varying levels of public support.[47] Although insurgents may engage in violence, they also may use nonviolent methods or political tactics. They may set up food distribution centers and schools in areas in which they gain control in order to provide the population with needed services while contrasting their benevolent rule with the government's incompetence and corruption.

TERRORIST AND REVOLUTIONARY

A revolution (from the Latin *revolutio*, "a revolving," and *revolvere*, "turn, roll back") is generally seen as a civil war fought between nationalists and a sovereign power that holds control of the land, or between the existing government and local groups over issues of ideology and power. Historically, the American Revolution may be considered an example of a struggle between nationalistic groups and an imperialistic overseas government. Classic examples of ideological rebellions are the French Revolution, which pitted the middle class and urban poor against the aristocracy, and the Russian Revolution of 1917, during which the Tsarist government was toppled by the Bolsheviks. More recent ideological revolutions have occurred in China, Cuba, Nicaragua, and Chile, to name but a few.

While some revolutions (such as the American, French, and Russian) rely on armed force, terror activities, and violence, others can be nonviolent, depending on large urban protests and threats. Such was the case when the Shah Mohammad Reza Pahlavi was toppled in Iran in the 1979 revolution that transformed Iran into an Islamic republic under the rule of Ayatollah Ruhollah Khomeini. Similar events unfolded in Egypt in early 2011 in the effort to topple the government of Hosni Mubarak that had been in power for 30 years.

Concept Summary 11.1 describes the components of various types of radical political groups.

A Brief History of Terrorism

Acts of terrorism have been known throughout history. The assassination of Julius Caesar on March 15, 44 BCE is considered an act of terrorism. Terrorism became widespread at the end of the Middle Ages, when political leaders were frequently subject to assassination by their enemies.

RELIGIOUS ROOTS

The first organized terrorist activities were committed by members of minority religious groups who engaged in violence to (a) gain the right to practice their own form of religion, (b) establish the supremacy of their own religion over others, or (c) meet the requirements of the bloodthirsty gods they worshipped.[48]

In some instances, a conquered people used force and violence to maintain their right to worship in their own faith. **Zealots**, Hebrew warrior groups, were active during the Roman occupation of Palestine during the first century CE. A subgroup of the Zealots, the Sciari (literally translated as "daggermen"), were so named for the long curved knives they favored as a weapon to assassinate Romans or their sympathizers. The Zealots carried out their attacks in broad daylight, typically with witnesses around, in order to send a message that the Roman authorities and those Jews who collaborated with them would not be safe. Ironically, this tactic is still being used by contemporary terrorists. The Zealots and Sciari led the revolt in 66 CE against Roman occupation of the Holy Land, during which they occupied the fortress of Masada. Here they held out for more than seven months before engaging in mass suicide rather than surrender to the Roman legions. The revolt ended badly and the Romans destroyed the Jewish temple and sent the population into exile.

Some religious terrorists want to promote the supremacy of their own sect over a rival group. The (Shi'ite) Muslim Order of the Assassins (*assassin* literally means "hashish-eater," a reference to the commonly held belief that gang members engaged in acts of ritual intoxication and smoked hashish just prior to undertaking their missions) was active in Persia, Syria, and Palestine from 1090 to 1272, killing a great number of their enemies, mainly Sunnis whom they considered apostates, but also Christians who were then the rulers of the kingdom of Jerusalem.[49] The Assassins also were prone to stabbing their victims in an effort to spread their vision of Islam, and carried out missions in public places on holy days in order to publicize their cause. Successful assassinations guaranteed them a place in heaven.

Another form of religious terror is inspired by the requirements of belief. Some religious beliefs have focused on violence, the gods demanding the death of nonbelievers. In India, members of the Thugee cult (from which the modern term *thug* was derived) were devoted to Kali, the goddess of death and destruction. The thugs believed each murder prevented Kali's arrival for 1,000 years, thus sparing the nation. The thugs traveled in gangs of up to 100 with each member having a defined role—some lured unwary travelers, while others strangled the chosen victim. The gang used secret argot and jargon, which only they could understand, and signs so that members could recognize each other even in the most remote parts of India. Cult members may have killed hundreds of thousands of victims over a 300-year span. They would attach themselves to travelers and when the opportunity arose, strangle them with a noose around their necks, steal their money, and bury their bodies. The killings were highly ritualistic and involved religious rites and prayers. By the mid-nineteenth century the British made it a policy to end Thugee activities, hanged nearly 4,000, and all but eradicated the cult. Thugees represented the last serious religion-inspired terrorist threat until the emergence of Islamic terrorism in the 1980s.

POLITICAL ROOTS

When rulers had absolute power, terrorist acts were viewed as one of the only means of gaining political rights. At times European states encouraged terrorist acts against their enemies. In the sixteenth century, Queen Elizabeth I empowered her naval leaders, including famed captains John Hawkins and Francis Drake, to attack the Spanish fleet and take prizes. These privateers would have been considered pirates had they not operated with government approval. American privateers attacked the British during the Revolutionary War and the War of 1812 and were considered heroes for their actions against the English navy.

The term *terrorist* first became popular during the French Revolution. Use of the word *terrorism* began in 1793 in reference to the **Reign of Terror** initiated by the revolutionary government during which agents of the Committee of Public Safety and the National Convention were referred to as terrorists. In response, royalists and opponents of the Revolution employed terrorist tactics in resistance to the Revolutionists. The widespread use of the guillotine is an infamous reminder of the revolutionary violence; urban mobs demanded blood, and many government officials and aristocrats were beheaded in gruesome public spectacles. From the fall of the Bastille on July 14, 1789, until July 1794, thousands suspected of counterrevolutionary activity were killed on the guillotine. Here again, the relative nature of political crime is documented: most victims of the French Reign of Terror were revolutionaries who had been denounced by rival factions, whereas thousands of the hated nobility lived in relative tranquility. The end of the terror was signaled by the death of its prime mover, Maximilien Robespierre, on July 28, 1794, as the result of a successful plot to end his rule. He was executed on the same guillotine to which he had sent almost 20,000 people.

In the hundred years following the French Revolution, terrorism continued to be a political tool around the world. Terrorist acts became the preferred method of political action for national groups in the early years of the twentieth century. In Eastern Europe, the Internal Macedonian Revolutionary Organization campaigned against the Turkish government, which controlled its homeland (Macedonia became part of the former Yugoslavia). Similarly, the protest of the Union of Death Society, or Black Hand, against the Austro-Hungarian Empire's control of Serbia led to the group's assassination of Archduke Franz Ferdinand, which started World War I. Russia was the scene of left-wing

zealot The original Zealots were Hebrew warrior groups active during the Roman occupation of Palestine during the first century BCE. Today the term commonly refers to a fanatical or over-idealistic follower of a political or religious cause.

Reign of Terror The origin of the term *terrorism*, the French Revolution's Reign of Terror began in 1793 and was initiated by the revolutionary government during which agents of the Committee of Public Safety and the National Convention were referred to as terrorists.

revolutionary activity, which killed the Tsar in 1917 and gave birth to the Marxist state.

After the war ended, the Treaty of Versailles restructured Europe and broke up the Austro-Hungarian Empire. The result was a hodgepodge of new nations controlled by majority ethnic groups. Self-determination was limited to European nations and ethnic groups and denied to others, especially the colonial possessions of the major European powers, creating bitterness and setting the stage for the long conflicts of the anticolonial period. The Irish Republican Army, established around 1916, steadily battled British forces from 1919 to 1923, culminating in the Republic of Ireland gaining independence.

Between the World Wars, right-wing terrorism existed in Germany, Spain, and Italy. One source of tension, according to author Michael Kellogg, was the virulently anti-Communist exiles who fled Russia after the 1917 Revolution (called White Russians) and took up residence in Germany and other Western nations. According to Kellogg, between 1920 and 1923, Adolf Hitler was deeply influenced by the Aufbau (Reconstruction), the émigrés' organization. Members of the Aufbau allied with the Nazis to overthrow the legitimate German government and thwart German communists from seizing power. The White Russians' deep-seated anti-Semitism may have inspired Hitler to go public with his campaign to kill the European Jews, prompting both the Holocaust and the invasion of Russia, which spelled the eventual doom of Hitler and National Socialism.[50]

During World War II, resistance to the occupying German troops was common throughout Europe. The Germans considered the resistors to be terrorists, but the rest of the world considers them heroes. Meanwhile, in Palestine, Jewish terrorist groups—the Haganah, Irgun, and Stern Gang, whose leaders included Menachem Begin, who later became Israel's prime minister—waged war against the British to force them to allow Jewish survivors of the Holocaust to settle in their traditional homeland. Today, of course, many of these alleged terrorists are considered freedom fighters who laid down their lives for a just cause.

After the war, Arab nationalists felt that they had been betrayed. Believing they were promised postwar independence, they were doubly disappointed—first when the French and British were given authority over their lands, and then especially when the British allowed Zionist immigration into Palestine in keeping with a promise contained in the Balfour Declaration.

Since the end of World War II, terrorism has accelerated its development into a major component of contemporary conflict. Primarily in use immediately after the war as a subordinate element of anticolonial insurgencies, it expanded beyond that role. In the service of various ideologies and aspirations, terrorism sometimes supplanted other forms of conflict completely. It became a far-reaching weapon capable of effects no less global than the intercontinental bomber or missile. It has also proven to be a significant tool of diplomacy and international power for states inclined to use it.

Contemporary Forms of Terrorism

 L07 Enumerate the various forms of terrorism

Today the term *terrorism* encompasses many different behaviors and goals. Some of the more common forms are briefly described here.

REVOLUTIONARY TERRORISTS

Revolutionary terrorists use violence to frighten those in power and their supporters in order to replace the existing government with a regime that holds acceptable political or religious views. Terrorist actions such as kidnapping, assassination, and bombing are designed to draw repressive responses from governments trying to defend themselves. These responses help revolutionaries to expose, through the skilled use of media coverage, the government's inhumane nature. The original reason for the government's harsh response may be lost as the effect of counterterrorist activities is felt by uninvolved people.

Jemaah Islamiyah, an Indonesian terrorist organization aligned with al-Qaeda, is believed to be intent on driving away foreign tourists and ruining the nation's economy so they can usurp the government and set up a pan-Islamic nation in Indonesia and neighboring Malaysia.

POLITICAL TERRORISTS

Political terrorism is directed at people or groups who oppose the terrorists' political ideology or whom the terrorists define as "outsiders" who must be destroyed. Political terrorists may not want to replace the existing government but to shape it so that it accepts the terrorists' views.

Right-Wing Political Groups Domestic terrorists in the United States can be found across the political spectrum. On the right, they tend to be heavily armed groups organized around such themes as white supremacy, anti-abortion, militant tax resistance, and religious revisionism. Identified groups have included, at one time or another, the Aryan Republican Army, the Aryan Nation, the Posse Comitatus, and the Ku Klux Klan. These groups want to shape U.S. government policy over a range of matters, including ending abortion rights, extending the right to bear arms, and eliminating federal taxation. According to federal officials they are often organized into paramilitary groups that follow a military-style rank hierarchy.[51] They tend to stockpile illegal weapons and ammunition, trying illegally to get their hands on fully automatic firearms or attempting to convert weapons to fully automatic. They also try to buy or manufacture improvised explosive devices and typically engage in wilderness, survival, or other paramilitary training.

Many militia extremists view themselves as protecting the U.S. Constitution, other U.S. laws, or their own individual liberties. They believe that the Constitution grants citizens the power to take back the federal government by force or violence if they feel it's necessary. They oppose gun control efforts and fear the widespread disarming of Americans by the federal government. Militia extremists often subscribe to various conspiracy theories regarding government. One of their primary theories is that the United Nations—which they refer to as the New World Order, or NWO—has the right to use its military forces anywhere in the world. The extremists often train and prepare for what they foresee as an inevitable invasion of the U.S. by United Nations forces. Many militia extremists also wrongly believe that the federal government will relocate citizens to camps controlled by the Federal Emergency Management Agency (FEMA) or force them to undergo vaccinations. Although unlikely to topple the government, these individualistic acts of terror are difficult to predict or control. On April 19, 1995, in the most deadly right-wing attack, 168 people were killed during the Oklahoma City bombing, the most severe example of political terrorism in the United States so far.

Some right-wing militants target specific groups. Anti-abortion activists have demonstrated at clinics, attacked patients, bombed offices, and killed doctors who perform abortions. On October 23, 1998, Dr. Barnett Slepian was shot by a sniper and killed in his Buffalo, New York, home; he was one of a growing number of abortion providers believed to be the victims of terrorists who ironically claim to be "pro-life."

A favorite target is law enforcement officers. Between 1990 and 2013 far-right extremists killed 50 federal, state, and local law enforcement officers in the line of duty in 33 separate incidents. More than two-thirds were killed during ideologically motivated attacks; the remaining officers were killed in non-ideological confrontations (e.g., while arresting an individual during a bank robbery). In addition, corrections officers, private security guards, and a judge have been killed during ideologically motivated attacks.[52]

Left-Wing Political Groups   During the turmoil of the 1960s, a number of left-wing political groups emerged to challenge the existing power structure. Some, such as the Black Panther Party—founded in 1966 in Oakland, California, by Bobby Seale and Huey Newton—demanded the right to control community schools, police, and public assistance programs. While many of their activities were productive, such as sponsoring breakfast programs and medical clinics in poor neighborhoods, they also began to openly carry rifles and shotguns while patrolling areas where the Oakland police were rumored to be harassing the community's black citizens. The Panthers' confrontational style led to clashes with police, shootings, and arrests. Because its leaders were faced with criminal charges of varying degrees, the Black Panthers steadily eroded.

Another influential 1960s group, the Students for a Democratic Society (SDS) was founded in Chicago in 1962 and was active on college campuses throughout the sixties protesting the United States' involvement in Vietnam.

Though the SDS was nonviolent, a splinter group known as the Weather Underground (or Weathermen) utilized terror tactics to achieve their goals. They were involved in a number of bombings at corporation headquarters and federal institutions, though they typically sent out warnings to evacuate the buildings. The group lost influence when on March 6, 1970, a bomb accidentally exploded in one of their safe houses in New York City. The detonations were so powerful that they collapsed the three-story house, killing three members. The Weathermen disbanded in 1977.

The most recent left-leaning domestic terror groups are committed to the protection of the environment. Of these groups, the Earth Liberation Front (ELF) is perhaps the best known. Founded in 1992 in Brighton, England, by members of the Earth First! environmental movement, ELF has been active since 1994 throughout the world, including the United States. Operating in secret, ELF cells have conducted a series of actions intent on damaging individuals or corporations that they consider a threat to the environment. On October 19, 1998, ELF members claimed responsibility for fires that were set atop Vail Mountain, a luxurious ski resort in Colorado, claiming that the action was designed to stop the resort from expanding into animal habitats (especially that of the mountain lynx); the fires caused an estimated $12 million in damages.

 Read more about the Earth Liberation Front by visiting their website at **http://earth-liberation -front.com/**.
Do you think environmental activists should really be considered terrorists?

Another group, the Animal Liberation Front (ALF), focuses their efforts on protecting animals from being used as food, in clothing, or as experimental subjects. Their philosophy is that animals are entitled to the moral right to possess their own lives and control their own bodies, while rejecting the view that animals are merely capital goods or property intended for the benefit of humans and can be bought, sold, or killed by humans.[53] In 2015, ALF members were responsible for "liberating" 5,740 mink from farms in Idaho, Iowa, Pennsylvania, Wisconsin, and Minnesota and also vandalizing property and destroying breeding records in an attempt to disrupt the fur breeding economy.[54]

Despite a few such incidents, left-wing terror groups have all but ceased operations.

NATIONALIST TERRORISM

Nationalist terrorism promotes the interests of a minority ethnic or religious group that believes it has been persecuted under majority rule and wishes to carve out its own independent homeland.

In the Middle East, terrorist activities have been linked to the Palestinians' desire to wrest their former homeland from Israel. At first, the Palestinian Liberation Organization (PLO), led by Yasser Arafat, directed terrorist activities against Israel. Now the group Hamas is perpetuating the conflict with Israel and is behind a spate of suicide bombings and terrorist attacks designed to elicit a sharp response from Israel and set back any chance for peace in the region. Hundreds on both sides of the conflict have been killed during terrorist attacks and reprisals. In Lebanon, Hezbollah (from the Arabic, meaning "party of God") is a Lebanese Shi'ite Islamist organization founded in 1982 in response to the presence of Israeli forces in southern Lebanon. At inception, its goals were to both drive Israeli troops out of Lebanon and to form a Shi'ite Islamic republic in Lebanon. Taking its inspiration from Iran, Hezbollah members follow a distinct version of Shia ideology developed in Iran and have also received arms and financial support from Iran. Hezbollah is anti-West and anti-Israel and has engaged in a series of terrorist actions including kidnappings, car bombings, and airline hijackings.[55] Recently, Hezbollah has shifted its focus and has become increasingly embroiled in the Syrian civil war, fighting for the Assad regime. Ironically, this shift has alienated some of its Lebanese constituents and prompted deadly reprisals in Beirut from partisans of the predominantly Sunni Muslim Syrian rebels. The U.S. government and its European allies consider Hezbollah a global terrorist threat and a menace to Middle East stability.

The Middle East is not the only source of nationalistic terrorism. The Chinese government has been trying to suppress separatist groups fighting for an independent state in the northwestern province of Xinjiang. The rebels are drawn from the region's Uyghur people, most of whom practice Sufi Islam, speak a Turkic language, and wish to set up a Muslim state called Eastern Turkistan. During the past decade, the Uyghur separatists have organized demonstrations, bombings, and political assassinations.[56] Russia fought a series of protracted wars with Chechen nationalists intent on creating a free Chechen homeland before the uprising was finally crushed in 2009.

Today, the most well-known group seeking to carve out a homeland is ISIL, described in some detail in the Criminology in Action feature "The Islamic State of Iraq and the Levant (ISIL)."

RETRIBUTIVE TERRORISM

In September 2012, U.S. Ambassador to Libya J. Christopher Stevens and three other Americans were killed in an attack on the U.S. consulate in Benghazi. At first it was suspected that the deaths were the result of rioting prompted by an American-produced film that insulted the prophet Muhammad. Later it appeared that the attack was planned because the attackers used military-grade weapons, including RPGs (rocket-propelled grenades), and knew details of the consulate and a safe house where U.S. personnel fled after the attack began. Some authorities believe the attack was coordinated by elements of the former Gaddafi

government while others claim that the raid was planned by a Libyan-based terrorist group with links to al-Qaeda.[57]

Some terrorist groups are not nationalist, political, or revolutionary organizations. They do not wish to set up their own homeland or topple a government but are motivated by anger against the existing social and political regime whose policies they find offensive.[58] One prime example is the Boko Haram group operating in Nigeria. It made international news when the group abducted 276 schoolgirls attending a Western school, saying it would treat them as slaves and marry them off—a reference to an ancient Islamic belief that women captured in conflict are part of the "war booty."[59] Its followers take to heart a phrase from the Quran that says: "Anyone who is not governed by what Allah has revealed is among the transgressors." Therefore, the group promotes a version of Islam that makes it *haram*, or forbidden, for Muslims to take part in any political or social activity associated with Western society, including voting in elections, wearing shirts and trousers, or receiving a secular education.

In Somalia, the al-Shabaab terror group has shifting goals and priorities. They do not hesitate to attack real or imagined opponents in other nations. In 2013, they attacked the Westgate Mall in Nairobi, Kenya, which resulted in hundreds of casualties and more than 60 deaths; on April 2, 2015, al-Shabaab gunmen attacked the Garissa University campus in Kenya, killing 148 students before being rooted out by security forces. In the aftermath of the attack, al-Shabaab spokespersons pledged a "long, gruesome war" in retaliation for Kenya's security forces joining with other nations of the African Union to fight al-Shabaab.[60] The group has also been linked to criminal activity. They require a share of the payment of ransoms given to Somali pirates who launch cross-ocean raids from the al-Shabaab–controlled territory; piracy would be impossible without cooperation from al-Shabaab. The group is also heavily involved in smuggling, slapping taxes on illegal charcoal exports to the Gulf, arms shipments from Yemen, and electronic goods destined for the region.[61]

Retributive terrorists such as Al-Shabaab and Boko Haram have a number of characteristics that are unique and separate them from guerrillas, revolutionaries, and other terrorists:[62] Victims are usually selected for their maximum propaganda value, usually ensuring a high degree of media coverage. The message is that the target population had better comply with their demands because the terrorists are desperate enough to "do anything." Sometimes this may backfire if the attack results in the death of innocents, especially children, along with the symbolic targets.

retributive terrorists Terror groups who refrain from tying specific acts to direct demands for change. They want to instead redirect the balance between what they believe is good and evil. They see their revolution as existing on a spiritual plane; their mission is to exact retribution against sinners.

The Islamic State of Iraq and the Levant (ISIL)

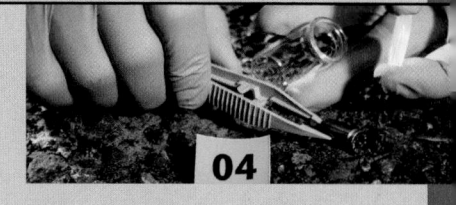

04

The Islamic State of Iraq and the Levant (ISIL), also known as the Islamic State of Iraq and Syria (ISIS), startled the world in the summer of 2014 when it took control of cities in Syria and Iraq defended by large contingents of enemy soldiers, who threw down their weapons and abandoned their posts. Those who actually fought were captured and killed in extremely brutal ways, through burning or decapitation. These militant insurgents then carried out mass executions, captured major cities, and created havoc in their ongoing struggle to topple the governments of Syria and Iraq. Their immediate goal is to combine those nations—or at least the Sunni-controlled parts—into a caliphate operating under strict Sharia law. The group's ultimate goal is to take over much of the Middle East, including Israel, southern Turkey, Jordan, and Lebanon, and remove all Western influence. Nonbelievers and opponents are killed in public executions. When Iraqi and Syrian forces tried to recapture lost territory, they only made headway under cover of U.S. and other allies' air strikes. Despite this show of force, ISIL still holds sway over significant territory.

Where did this deadly group come from? How did it get its start? ISIL origins can be traced back to 2002, when Abu Musab al-Zarqawi founded a jihadist organization called Tawhid wal-Jihad in the north of Iraq. Affiliated with al-Qaeda, Tawhid wal-Jihad focused its attention on elements of the Islamic world rather than the West. When the United States invaded Iraq, Zarqawi's organization morphed into al-Qaeda in Iraq (AQI), and began to recruit locally as a jihadist organization, while at the same time allowing al-Qaeda to gain a foothold in Iraq.

Al-Qaeda in Iraq was involved in internal conflicts until Zarqawi was killed in an airstrike in 2006 and the group joined with other hard-core Islamist groups to create the Islamic State of Iraq (ISI), whose goal was creating an ultra-religious caliphate, governed by Islamic law, to whom all Muslims owed allegiance. Drone attacks by the U.S. helped degrade ISI until Abu Bakr al-Baghdadi took over in 2010. This change in leadership, coupled with the withdrawal of U.S. forces from Iraq and the start of the Syrian civil war, helped revive the group's prospects. ISI, now renamed ISIL, gained significant amounts of territory in both Syria and Iraq, including the Syrian city of Raqqa. The major Iraqi cities of Tikrit and Fallujah fell in 2014, followed by Mosul, Iraq's second-largest city.

In 2014, more than 16,000 foreign terrorist fighters from more than 90 countries traveled to Syria to join ISIL. One reason for this successful recruiting is that ISIL has shown a particular capability in the use of media and online products to address a wide spectrum of audiences: local Sunni Arab populations, potential recruits, and governments of coalition members and other populations around the world, including English-speaking audiences. ISIL is now proficient in using the most popular social media platforms—YouTube, Facebook, and Twitter—to disseminate its propaganda, which include brutal images such as hostage beheadings and boasts of slave markets of girls and women.

ISIL also began to foster relationships with potential affiliates beyond Iraq and Syria. Ansar al-Shari'a in Darnah pledged allegiance to ISIL; Ansar Bayt al-Maqdis, operating primarily out of Egypt's Sinai Peninsula, officially declared allegiance to ISIL; Boko Haram in Nigeria have also allied themselves with ISIL.

In 2015, ISIL began to be the target of attacks by Kurdish forces, mainly the Peshmerga in Iraq. In March 2015, Iraqi military forces retook Tikrit. Other Muslim nations, including Jordan and Turkey, have either heavily criticized or actually attacked ISIL.

In addition to its terrorist activities, ISIL is a governing body that imposes a very strict version of Islamic law in the territory it holds. It guarantees protection in exchange for the payment of a tax and the acceptance of second-class citizenship for minorities, including Shia Muslims. ISIL has engaged in massacres, beheadings, burnings, and executions of foreign journalists and humanitarian aid workers who have fallen into their hands. Ironically, this brutality has helped them draw recruits from the Western world who applaud their ruthlessness and want to be part of an Islamic caliphate that will not abide any element of Western culture. Western leaders fear that some of the recruits will return to their homes after being trained in jihad, creating tremendous danger for their home nations since they can blend in and have families and friends for support.

 **CRITICAL THINKING**

Considering the refugee crisis caused by people desperately trying to flee violence, should Western states intervene militarily every time a group such as ISIL or the Taliban forms in the Middle East? Are there other solutions than military intervention?

SOURCES: U.S. Department of State, *Country Reports on Terrorism*, 2014, http://www.state.gov/j/ct/rls/crt/2014/index.htm; Peter Welby, "What Is ISIS?" Tony Blair Faith Foundation, November 16, 2015, http://tonyblairfaithfoundation.org/religion-geopolitics/commentaries/backgrounder/what-isis; BBC News, "What Is 'Islamic State'?" December 2, 2015, http://www.bbc.com/news/world-middle-east-29052144; Tim Arango, Kareem Fahim, and Ben Hubbard, "Rebels' Fast Strike in Iraq Was Years in the Making," *New York Times*, June 14, 2014, http://www.nytimes.com/2014/06/15/world/middleeast/rebels-fast-strike-in-iraq-was-years-in-the-making.html; Andrew Silke, "Holy Warriors: Exploring the Psychological Processes of Jihadi Radicalization," *European Journal of Criminology* 5 (2008): 99–123; Farouk Chothia, "Who Are Nigeria's Boko Haram Islamists?" BBC News Africa, May 4, 2015, http://www.bbc.com/news/world-africa-13809501. (URLs accessed June 2016.)

Unconventional military tactics are used, especially secrecy and surprise, as well as targeting civilians, including women and children. Because the goal is to inflict maximum horror, it makes sense to choose targets that contain the largest number of victims from all walks of life. The message: everyone is a target; no one is safe.

Al-Qaeda is the paradigm of the new retributive terrorist organization. Rather than fighting for a homeland, its message is a call to take up a cause: there is a war of civilizations in which "Jews and Crusaders" want to destroy Islam and must therefore be defeated. Armed jihad is the individual obligation of every Muslim; terrorism and violence are appropriate methods for defeating even the strongest powers. The end product would be a unified Muslim world, the caliphate, ruled under Muslim law free of Western influence.

These themes are preached in schools, on the Internet, and disseminated in books, CDs, and pamphlets. Videos are distributed in which al-Qaeda's leaders expound on political topics, going as far as calling Western leaders liars and drunkards. As a result of this media strategy, al-Qaeda's messages have penetrated deeply into Muslim communities around the world, finding a sympathetic response among many Muslims who have a sense of helplessness both in the Arab world and in the Western Muslim diaspora. Al-Qaeda appears to have had an impact by offering a sense of empowerment to young men who feel lost in their adopted cultures.[63]

STATE-SPONSORED TERRORISM

State-sponsored terrorism occurs when a repressive government regime forces its citizens into obedience, oppresses minorities, and stifles political dissent. Death squads and the use of government troops to destroy political opposition parties are often associated with political terrorism. Much of what we know about state-sponsored terrorism comes from the efforts of human rights groups such as London-based Amnesty International, whose research shows that tens of thousands of people continue to become victims of security operations that result in disappearances and executions. Political prisoners are now being tortured in about 100 countries, people have disappeared or are being held in secret detention in about 20 countries, and government-sponsored death squads have been operating in more than 35 countries. Countries known for encouraging violent control of dissidents include Brazil, Colombia, Guatemala, Honduras, Peru, Iraq, and Sudan.

State-sponsored terrorism became a world issue when South and Central American dictatorships in the 1970s and 1980s unleashed state violence against political dissidents through forced disappearance, political imprisonment, torture, blacklisting, and massive exile. The region-wide state repression in this period emerged in response to the rise of the 1960s radical movements, which demanded public reforms and programs to help the lower classes in urban areas and agricultural workers in the countryside. Local authoritarian governments, which used repression to take control of radical political groups, were given financial support by the economic elites who dominated Latin American politics and were fearful of a socialist revolution.[64]

As might be expected, governments claim that repressive measures are needed to control terror and revolutionary groups that routinely use violence. Thus the use of terror is sometimes a way of defending the nation against violence, a conundrum that supports the idea that a state is both protective and destructive.[65]

It is sometimes difficult to assess blame for state terror—is it a few rogue government agents who act on their own authority or the government itself? The issue of responsibility for improper acts hit home during the Abu Ghraib scandal in Iraq. Photos beamed around the world embarrassed the United States when they showed military personnel victimizing suspected insurgents. The government's response was to prosecute and imprison the perpetrators. However, some critics, such as criminologist Mark Hamm, suggest that these images constitute the photographic record of a state-sponsored crime.[66] He argues that rather than being the work of a few rogue officers, the sophisticated interrogation practices at Abu Ghraib were designed and executed by the CIA and that the torturing of detainees at Abu Ghraib followed directly from decisions made by top government officials to get tough with prisoner interrogations. So while we condemn state-sponsored violence, it is not easy to identify who is truly responsible.

LONE-ACTOR TERRORISTS

On April 15, 2013, brothers Dzhokhar and Tamerlan Tsarnaev set off bombs at the finish line of the Boston Marathon, killing three people, and maiming and injuring at least 260 more. The two had conspired for many months to use improvised explosive devices (IEDs) to harm and kill people in the crowds of spectators who were cheering the runners on toward the marathon finish line. The IEDs were constructed from pressure cookers, explosive powder, shrapnel, adhesives, and other items and were designed to shred skin, shatter bone, and cause extreme pain and suffering, as well as death. After the explosions, the Tsarnaevs, armed with five IEDs, a Ruger P95 semi-automatic handgun, ammunition, a machete, and a hunting knife, drove to the MIT campus, where they shot police officer Sean Collier in an attempt to steal his service weapon.

Who were these killers? Tamerlan Tsarnaev was born in the Kalmyk Autonomous Soviet Socialist Republic, North Caucasus; Dzhokhar was born in Kyrgyzstan. Because their

state-sponsored terrorism Terrorism that occurs when a repressive government regime forces its citizens into obedience, oppresses minorities, and stifles political dissent.

father was a Chechen, they identified themselves as being of Chechen descent. Though the family prospered in the United States and Dzhokhar attended a state university, the brothers clung to radical Islamic views and blamed the U.S. government for conducting a war against Islam in Iraq and Afghanistan. They viewed the Boston bombing victims as "collateral damage" in their war against the West. Their actions were disavowed by Islamic, Chechen, and other groups, all of whom quickly distanced themselves from the Tsarnaev brothers.[67]

The marathon bombing and the Orlando mass shooting carried out by Omar Mateen (discussed in the opening vignette) are examples of a lone-actor terrorist attack. Sometimes called a lone-wolf terrorist (LWT), these individuals use violence or the threat of violence to achieve some political or social goal. While they may admire a particular terrorist group, they do not receive orders, direction, support, or aid from any such group.

Thorough evaluation of this phenomenon by Mark Hamm and Ramon Spaaj found evidence that most LWTs are unemployed, single white males with a criminal record.[68] Compared to members of terrorist groups, lone wolves are older, less educated, and more prone to mental illness. They are more likely to be unmoored from society, deprived of what they perceive as the lifestyle to which they are entitled; this encourages them to form grievances against the government they hold responsible for unemployment, discrimination, and injustices. One reason for this relatively high level of alienation is that more than half of the lone wolves embrace right-wing or anti-government ideologies. Nationalistic movements—such as American white supremacy movements—have tended to produce terrorists from the lower classes, while religious terrorists like al-Qaeda come from all classes.

LWTs are in sympathy with extremist groups, but they are neither guided by nor answer to some collective entity. However, most are enabled through either direct means in the form of people who unwittingly assist in planning attacks, or indirectly by people who provide inspiration for terrorism. They are often helped or encouraged by an enabler, someone who either unknowingly performs tasks that make an attack possible, or someone who indirectly encourages terrorism by example.

While lone wolves physically isolate from society, at the same time they communicate with outsiders through spoken statements, threats, letters, manifestos, and videotaped proclamations. They are prone to proclaim that an attack is imminent; broadcasting intent may occur in the weeks, days, and even hours before an attack.

The Criminology in Action feature takes a closer look at lone-actor terrorism.

How Are Terror Groups Organized?

Terror groups tend to be networked or hierarchical. Newer terrorist organizations tend to be formed as **networks**, loosely organized groups located in different parts of a city, state, or country (or worldwide) that share a common theme or purpose, but have a diverse leadership and command structure and are only in intermittent communication with one another. While there may be a variety of antigovernment groups operating in the United States, there is little evidence that they share a single command structure or organizational fabric. These groups have few resources and little experience, so it is critical that they operate under cover and with as little public exposure as possible.

When needed, networked groups can pull factions together for larger-scale operations, such as an attack on a military headquarters, or conversely, they can readily splinter off into smaller groups to avoid detection when a counterterrorism operation is under way. The advent of the Internet has significantly improved communications among networked terror groups.

As terror organizations evolve and expand, they may eventually develop a hierarchical organization with a commander at the top, captains, local area leaders, and so on. Ideological and religious groups tend to gravitate toward this model since a common creed/dogma controls their operations and a singular leader may be needed to define and disseminate group principles and maintain discipline. In a hierarchical model, the leader has the power to increase or decrease levels of violence for political purposes (i.e., they may order their followers to initiate a bombing campaign to influence an election). Schools may be off limits so that the population is not antagonized, or schools may become a target to show that the government cannot protect their children.

Regardless of what organizational structure is used, most groups subdivide their affiliates into **terror cells** for both organizational and security purposes. To enhance security, each cell may be functionally independent so that each member has little knowledge of other cells, their members, locations, and so on. However, individual cell members provide emotional support to one another and maintain loyalty and dedication. Because only the cell leader knows how to

networks When referring to terrorist organizations, networks are loosely organized groups located in different parts of the city, state, or country (or world) that share a common theme or purpose, but have a diverse leadership and command structure and are only in intermittent communication with one another.

terror cells Divisions of terrorist group affiliates, each of which may be functionally independent so that each member has little knowledge of other cells, their members, locations, and so on. The number of cells and their composition depend on the size of the terrorist group. Local or national groups will have fewer cells than international terrorist groups that may operate in several countries, such as the al-Qaeda group.

Lone-Actor Terrorists

04

In addition to the Orlando massacre and the Boston Marathon bombing, there have been a number of mass casualty incidents involving lone-actor terrorists who plan and carry out an attack without assistance from others. On November 5, 2009, U.S. Major Nidal Malik Hasan attacked fellow soldiers at Fort Hood, leaving 12 dead and 31 wounded. On July 22, 2011, Anders Breivik killed 77 civilians in and around Oslo, Norway. Clark McCauley and Sophia Moskalenko conducted research in order to answer the basic question: Why would any individual take this kind of risk and choose to sacrifice themselves for a cause?

They found that lone actors may see themselves as representing some larger group or cause and may have had some experience in a group, organization, or social movement related to this cause. However, it was difficult for them to stay or be part of a group because they tend to suffer from some form of psychological disturbance, are socially isolated, and tend to be loners with few friends.

Many have a military background and have recently suffered some form of serious personal disruption that triggered a violent attack, such as divorce or the death of a partner. Major Hasan had experience with weapons and no close relationships. He had turned to the Quran after the death of his parents and was about to be transferred to Afghanistan. He saw himself discriminated against as a Muslim and viewed the war on terrorism as a war on Islam, thereby developing both personal and political grievances.

Taken together, these results provide a portrait of the typical lone actor as grievance-fueled individual, likely to have weapons experience, who suffers from depression or other mental disorders, and experiences temporary or chronic social isolation. McCauley and Moskalenko call this the *disconnected-disordered profile*.

However, not all lone-actor terrorists fit the disconnected-disordered profile: there are some who are neither loners nor suffer mental disorder, but who nonetheless undertake lone-actor terrorist violence. They may be motivated by some emotionally charged event that sets them off on a destructive path: the political becomes personal. They are radicalized by feelings of moral obligation to right a perceived wrong: a man bombs abortion clinics after a family member loses a child at birth; a woman burns down a factory farm after witnessing the suffering of animals. The Tsarnaev brothers were motivated by their sensitivity to what they perceived as the oppression of Muslims by the West. A note that Dzhokhar Tsarnaev wrote while hiding from authorities on a dry-docked boat said in part: "God has a plan for each person. Mine was to hide in this boat and shed some light on our actions. . . . Stop killing our innocent people and we will stop."

What sets this type of lone terrorist apart is their unusual capacity to care about the suffering of others. Those who fit this *caring-compelled profile* have social relations and are not mentally ill. But they care too much and find that there is a dark side to caring greatly about others. Individuals can kill for love, including love of strangers seen as victimized.

In sum, McCauley and Moskalenko believe that lone-actor terrorists fit one of these two profiles: disconnected-disordered or caring-compelled. They suspect that the caring-compelled profile is less common than the disconnected-disordered profile—not least because self-sacrifice for others is less common than self-interest—but this hypothesis remains to be tested.

CRITICAL THINKING

Sometimes after a terror attack we hear that the suspect was on the government's watch list. Should something more be done to monitor these potential mass killers?

SOURCES: Clark McCauley and Sophia Moskalenko, "Two Possible Profiles of Lone-Actor Terrorists," National Consortium for the Study of Terrorism and Responses to Terrorism (START), 2013, http://www.start.umd .edu/publication/two-possible-profiles-lone-actor -terrorists; Jeff Gruenewald, Steven Chermak, and Joshua Freilich, "Distinguishing 'Loner' Attacks from Other Domestic Extremist Violence," *Criminology and Public Policy* 12 (2013): 65–91; *Boston Globe*, "Text from Dzhokhar Tsarnaev's Note Written in Watertown Boat," May 22, 2014, http://www.bostonglobe.com /metro/2014/05/22/text-from-dzhokhar-tsarnaev -note-left-watertown-boat/KnRleqqr95rJQbAbfnj5EP /story.html. (URLs accessed June 2016.)

communicate with other cells and/or a central command, capture of one cell does not then compromise other group members.

Terror cell formations may be based on location, employment, or family membership. Some are formed on the basis of function: some are fighters, others political organizers. The number of cells and their composition depend on the size of the terrorist group: local or national groups will have fewer cells than international terrorist groups that may operate in several countries, such as the al-Qaeda group.

The various forms that terror groups take are summarized in Concept Summary 11.2.

What Motivates the Terrorist?

L08 Explain what motivates the terrorist to commit violent acts

In the aftermath of the September 11, 2001, destruction of the World Trade Center in New York City, many Americans asked themselves the same simple question: Why? What could motivate someone like Osama bin Laden to order the deaths of thousands of innocent people? How could someone who had never been to the United States or suffered personally at its hands develop such lethal hatred? Some experts believed the attacks had a political basis, claiming

CONCEPT SUMMARY 11.2
The Variety of Terror Groups

Revolutionary terrorists	Use violence to frighten those in power and their supporters in order to replace the existing government with a regime that holds acceptable political or religious views.
Political terrorists	Political terrorism is directed at people or groups who oppose the terrorists' political ideology or whom the terrorists define as "outsiders" who must be destroyed.
Eco-terrorists	Political terror groups involved in violent actions to protect the environment.
Nationalist terrorists	Groups whose actions promote the interests of a minority ethnic or religious group that has been persecuted under majority rule and/or wishes to carve out its own independent homeland.
Retributive terrorists	Groups that use violence as a method of influence, persuasion, or intimidation in order to achieve a particular aim or objective.
State-sponsored terrorism	Carried out by a repressive government regime in order to force its citizens into obedience, oppress minorities, and stifle political dissent.
Lone-actor terrorists	Individuals who carry out terror acts without involvement or participation in an organized group.

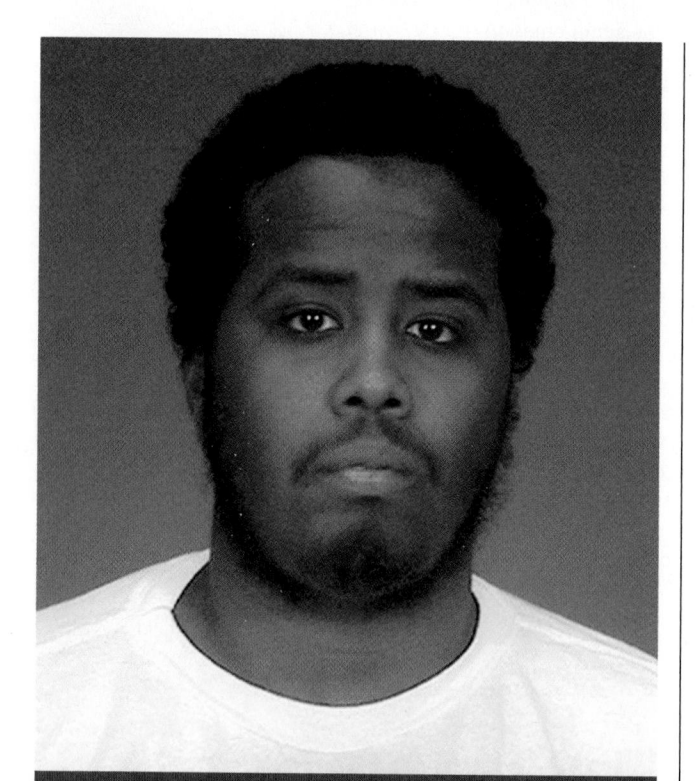

Six young Minnesota men of Somali descent, including Mohamed Abdihamid Farah (shown here) and his younger brother, Adnan Abdihamid Farah, are facing trial for allegedly plotting to join ISIL. What could possibly motivate someone like Farah to leave the United States and return as a terrorist? William Braniff, executive director of the National Consortium for the Study of Terrorism and Responses to Terrorism (START), believes that an intimate relationship—like that of family members—is often the key that will lead someone with extremist views to action. It's hard to conspire with others over the phone or in emails or meetings without getting caught; it is much easier to make plans with a sibling at home.

AP Images/Uncredited

that bin Laden's anger was fueled by the U.S.'s Middle East policies. Others saw a religious motivation and claimed that bin Laden was a radical Muslim at war with the liberal religions of the West. Another view was that bin Laden's rage was fueled by deep-rooted psychological problems.

Who was this man who caused so much death and destruction before his own death at the hands of SEAL Team Six? And what motivated him to choose a terrorist path? He came from a wealthy family founded by his father, Mohammed bin Laden, whose industrial empire continued to expand even after his death until it employed more than 40,000 people. So poverty and alienation were certainly not motives.

Bin Laden was a devout Muslim, and his terrorist activity may have been motivated by religious beliefs and anger over the presence of Western influences in the Middle East. In a 1995 interview with a French journalist, bin Laden explained why he chose to join the *mujahideen* fight against the Russians at that time:

> To counter these atheist Russians, the Saudis chose me as their representative in Afghanistan. . . . I did not fight against the communist threat while forgetting the peril from the West. For us, the idea was not to get involved more than necessary in the fight against the Russians, which was the business of the Americans, but rather to show our solidarity with our Islamist brothers. I discovered that it was not enough to fight in Afghanistan, but that we had to fight on all fronts against communist or Western oppression. The urgent thing was communism, but the next target was America. . . . This is an open war up to the end, until victory.[69]

It is also possible that bin Laden's motivation was psychological, and his efforts an unconscious attempt to gain his father's approval. "My father was very keen that one of his sons should fight against the enemies of Islam. So I am the one son who is acting according to the wishes of his father." Perhaps this need for acceptance explains bin Laden's religious zeal, which was in excess of anyone else's in his large extended family.

Whether his motivations were psychological, political, or religious—or a combination of all three—is still uncertain. It is likely that we will never truly understand bin Laden's motivations to attack the West.[70]

Before terrorism can be effectively fought, controlled, and eradicated, it is important to understand something about the kind of people who become terrorists, what motivates their behavior, and how their ideas are formed. Unfortunately, this is not an easy task. Terrorism researchers have generally concluded that there is no single personality trait or behavior pattern that distinguishes the majority of terrorists or sets them apart so they can be easily identified and apprehended. Some seem truly disturbed, whereas many others have not suffered long-term mental illness or displayed sociopathic traits and/or tendencies; if that were so, bizarre or violent behavior in their early childhood would be a giveaway.[71] As such, there have been a number of competing visions of why terrorists engage in criminal activities such as bombings, shootings, and kidnappings to achieve a political end. Four views stand out.

PSYCHOLOGICAL VIEW

One of the most controversial views of terrorists is that some if not all suffer from psychological deficits, and that the typical terrorist can be described as an emotionally disturbed individual who acts out his or her psychoses within the confines of violent groups. According to this view, terrorist violence is not so much a political instrument as an end in itself; it is the result of compulsion or psychopathology. Terrorists do what they do because of garden variety emotional problems, including but not limited to self-destructive urges and disturbed emotions combined with problems with authority.[72] As terrorism expert Jerrold M. Post puts it, "Political terrorists are driven to commit acts of violence as a consequence of psychological forces, and . . . their special psychology is constructed to rationalize acts they are psychologically compelled to commit."[73]

Some terror experts say that the majority of research on terrorists indicates that most are not psychologically abnormal.[74] Even suicide bombers, a group that should show signs of psychological abnormality, exhibit few signs of the mental problems such as depression that are typically found in people who choose to take their own life. Rather than acting disturbed and disoriented, those terrorists willing to die for their cause display a heightened sense of purpose, group allegiance, and task focus.[75] After carefully reviewing existing evidence on the psychological state of terrorists, mental health expert Randy Borum concludes:

- Mental illness is not a critical factor in explaining terrorist behavior. Also, most terrorists are not psychopaths.

- There is no "terrorist personality," nor is there any accurate profile—psychological or otherwise—of the terrorist.
- Histories of childhood abuse and trauma and themes of perceived injustice and humiliation often are prominent in terrorist biographies, but do not really help to explain terrorism.[76]

ALIENATION VIEW

Another explanation for terrorist activity is that a lack of opportunity creates a sense of alienation that motivates men and women to embrace terrorism.[77] Regions such as South Asia breed terrorists because they house an incendiary mix of strong ethnic identities and diverse religious communities, many of which are concentrated within exclusionary ghettos. Young men and women residing in these areas are motivated to join terror groups when they feel left out of the social and economic mainstream because of their religious or ethnic status.[78] According to this view, terror recruits suffer alienation from friends, family, and society.[79] Many have been raised to hate the groups who are in power and believe that they have been victimized by state authorities whom they view as oppressors.

Terrorism has also become an alternative for people whose religious beliefs alienate them from our postmodern, technological, global society in which foreign influences routinely clash with age-old traditions. They may believe that modern forms of communication, entertainment, and social interaction have brought foreign influences that are corrupting and disrespectful to their traditional way of life. Some may join terror groups whose goal is to eliminate these corrupting external influences—for example, the name of the terrorist group Boko Haram can be translated as "Western education is sin." Alienation can become so powerful that the terrorist may even believe that a suicide mission will help cleanse them of the corruption of the modern world while at the same time scaring off outsiders.

While at first glance terrorists seem alienated from modern society, when Marc Sageman studied members of extremist Islamist groups he found that most tend to be well educated; about 60 percent had some form of higher education. More than 75 percent came from upper- or middle-class backgrounds. When they joined a terror organization, the majority had professional occupations such as doctor or engineer, or semiskilled employment, such as a civil servant; fewer than 25 percent were unemployed or working in unskilled jobs. Surprisingly, Sageman found that almost three-quarters were married and that most had children.[80] These findings suggest that terrorists are not suffering from the social problems usually associated with alienation: poverty, lack of education, and ignorance.

Family Conflict View   Terrorists report that they are products of dysfunctional families in which the father was absent or, even if present, was a distant and cold figure.[81] Because of this family estrangement, the budding terrorist may have been swayed to join a group or cult by a charismatic leader who serves as an alternative father figure. Some find it in religious schools run by strong leaders who demand strict loyalty from their followers while indoctrinating them in political causes.[82] In this sense, terror groups, similar to what happens in urban street gangs, provide a substitute family–like environment, which can nurture a heretofore emotionally underprivileged youth.

Political View   When people are left out of the political process, having their votes restricted or even losing the right to vote, they may be inclined to join terror groups.[83] Analyzing cross-national data, Laura Dugan and Gary LaFree, of the National Consortium for the Study of Terrorism and Responses to Terrorism, found that most of the risk for political violence lies in those nations that are nearly democracies, which experience three times as many terror attacks as full democracies. Ironically, the most autocratic countries, governed by dictators and without free elections, generally had the lowest average number of attacks. In contrast, **failed states**—those where governments have lost physical control of their own territory, are unable to provide reasonable public services, and cannot interact properly with other states—have extremely high rates of terrorist activity. Dugan and LaFree also found evidence that terrorist attacks against failed states were much more lethal than attacks against other nations. Their finding suggests that nations that provide access to the political process for people holding a wide range of diverse viewpoints create a culture that helps reduce the frustration that could lead to terrorist violence. Those states that cannot maintain order or provide services to its citizens are fertile grounds for terrorists. And while iron-handed dictators may keep terrorism under control in the short term, their long-term prospects are sketchy at best, as recent events in Egypt, Libya, and Syria have shown.[84]

SOCIALIZATION/FRIENDSHIP VIEW

Many jihadist recruits were living in foreign countries when they got involved with terrorist organizations. Feeling homesick, they sought out people with similar backgrounds, whom they would often find at mosques. If they appeared to be motivated by religious fervor, it was because they were seeking friends in a foreign land. They moved in together in order to share the rent and also to eat together under strict Muslim dietary laws. The group solidified their beliefs and created a sense of solidarity with like-minded people. If one became committed to terror, others may follow rather than let him down.

failed state A nation whose government has lost control of its own territory, is unable to provide public services and protection, and lacks the ability to interact with other states as a full member of the international community.

IDEOLOGICAL VIEW

Another view is that terrorists hold extreme ideological beliefs that prompt their behavior. They may have developed heightened perceptions of oppressive conditions, believing they are being victimized by some group or government for their beliefs or way of life. Once they conclude that the government will not help people with their beliefs, they decide to resort to violence to encourage change.

Facilitating the use of violence is the ability to divide people based on religious, ethnic, racial, or other cultural criteria into two categories: those with common interests and beliefs who are avenged through terrorist activities ("us") and those against whom the terrorist activities are to be directed ("them"). Those associated with "us" are viewed as moral, right, good, and strong. Those associated with "them" are seen as immoral, wrong, bad, and weak.[85] Once this division is made, the terrorist can act with impunity to further their ideological beliefs because those harmed have beliefs that make them less than human.

Religious Fanaticism   Some terrorists, like the Tsarnaev brothers, are motivated by extreme religious beliefs, which often coincide with their ideological views. But how can they justify using violence if they are truly religious, since most of the world's religions eschew violence? Islamic terrorists believe that their commitment to God justifies their extreme actions. They regard the actions of people they trust as a testimony to the righteousness of their acts. They trust significant others, and rely on their wisdom, experience, and testimony and accept their expressions of faith. To the terrorist, someone like Osama bin Laden has demonstrated the strength of his faith by living in poverty and giving up a more luxurious and leisurely life in the name of God. When he calls them to jihad, they are likely to follow, even if it means killing those who deny their faith or beliefs. Perceived miracles, such as the defeat of a superpower through faith alone (e.g., the Soviet/Afghan war or the fight against the United States in Iraq), also increase confidence in the righteousness of the cause. Some have mystical experiences during prayers or dreams that demonstrate the existence of God and reinforce faith. In a videotape in the fall of 2001, Osama bin Laden said that he had banned the reporting of dreams of airplanes flying into buildings prior to September 11 for fear of revealing the plot.[86]

EXPLAINING STATE-SPONSORED TERRORISM

How can state-sponsored terrorism be explained? After all, these violent acts are not directed at a foreign government or overseas adversaries but against natives of one's own country. In her book *Reigns of Terror*, Patricia Marchak finds that people willing to kill or maim their fellow countrymen are likely to be highly susceptible to unquestioning submission to authority. They are conformists who want to be part of the central group and who are quite willing to be part of a state regime. They are vulnerable to ideology that dehumanizes their targets and can utilize propaganda to distance themselves psychologically from those they are terrorizing.[87] So the Nazis had little trouble recruiting people to carry out horrific acts during the Holocaust because many Germans wanted to be part of the popular social/political movement and were easily indoctrinated by the Nazi propaganda that branded Jews as subhuman. Stalin was able to carry out his reign of terror in Russia because his victims were viewed as state enemies who were trying to undermine the Communist regime. How can these tendencies be neutralized? Marchak sees little benefit to international intervention that results in after-the-fact punishment of the perpetrators, a course of action that was attempted in the former Yugoslavia after death squads had performed "ethnic cleansing" of undesirables. Instead she argues for a prevention strategy that involves international aid and economic development by industrialized nations to those in the Third World that are on the verge of becoming collapsed states, the construction of social welfare systems, and the acceptance of international legal norms and standards of human rights.[88]

Terrorists are now operating all over the world. Here, security forces evacuate a man from an area surrounding the Radisson Blu Hotel in Bamako, Mali, on November 20, 2015. Two gunmen went on a shooting rampage at the luxury hotel, seizing 170 guests and staff in a hostage-taking that left at least 20 people dead.

HABIBOU KOUYATE/Getty Images

Extent of the Terrorism Threat

Does the pressure being put on ISIL, al-Qaeda, the Taliban, and other terror groups through drone attacks and commando raids mean that the end of the global terrorism threat is at hand? Not likely. Terror cells have now dispersed around the world, helping to offset this loss in leadership. When one leader is killed, a new and even more violent one may take command. Take for instance the death of Hakimullah Mehsud, the leader of the Pakistani Taliban, who died in a drone strike on November 1, 2013.[89] Upon the death of Mehsud, hardline commander Mullah Fazlullah was elected the new leader of the Pakistani Taliban and soon promised a wave of terror attacks in revenge for the death of his predecessor. Fazlullah refuses to consider peace talks, opposes educating females, was blamed for ordering the beheading of 17 Pakistani soldiers in a check-post attack in June 2012 and planting a bomb that killed a Pakistani major general—hardly an improvement over the brutal Mehsud.

The most recent data from the National Consortium for the Study of Terrorism and Responses to Terrorism (START) support the fact that the terrorist danger has not diminished—quite the opposite in fact: 80 Americans were killed in terrorist attacks from 2004 to 2013, including perpetrators and excluding deaths in Afghanistan and Iraq. Of those 80 Americans killed, 36 were killed in attacks that occurred in the United States. More broadly, 3,066 Americans have been killed in terrorist attacks from September 11, 2001, through December 31, 2014, including perpetrators and excluding deaths in Afghanistan and Iraq. The majority of these deaths (2,902) occurred during the attacks on September 11, 2001.[90]

Globally, the number of recent attacks and deaths is staggering. In 2014, more than 16,800 terrorist attacks took place worldwide, causing more than 43,500 deaths and more than 40,900 injuries. More than 11,800 people were taken hostage in terrorist attacks in 2014.[91] Worldwide patterns of terrorism in 2014 were heavily influenced by conflicts in key locations. Although terrorist attacks took place in 99 countries, nearly half of all attacks (47 percent) took place in Iraq, Pakistan, and Afghanistan. Likewise, more than half (60 percent) of all fatalities took place in Iraq, Nigeria, and Afghanistan.

Who were the most active groups? They included the Taliban in Afghanistan, Boko Haram in Nigeria, al-Qaeda in the Arabian Peninsula, Tehrik-i-Taliban Pakistan, al-Qaeda in Iraq, and al-Shabaab in Somalia. While many of these organizations have been active for many years, if not decades, two new organizations emerged in 2014 and immediately became highly active. The Donetsk People's Republic and the Luhansk People's Republic, both active in Ukraine, carried out bombings, armed assaults, kidnappings, and facility/infrastructure attacks. The Donetsk People's Republic was attributed responsibility for more than 1,000 total fatalities, including the deaths of nearly 300 passengers killed by a surface-to-air missile launched at a Malaysia Airlines commercial flight.[92]

Response to Terrorism

LO9 Give examples of the efforts being made to centralize intelligence gathering

After the 9/11 attacks, agencies of the criminal justice system began to focus their attention on combating the threat of terror. Even local police agencies created anti-terror programs designed to protect their communities from the threat of attack. How should the nation best prepare itself to thwart potential attacks? The National Commission on Terrorist Attacks Upon the United States (also known as the 9/11 Commission), an independent, bipartisan commission, was created in late 2002 and given the mission of preparing an in-depth report of the events leading up to the 9/11 attacks. Part of their goal was to create a comprehensive plan to ensure that no further attacks of that magnitude take place.

To monitor the more than 500 million people who annually cross into and out of America, the commission recommended that a single agency should be created to screen border crossings. They also recommended creation of an investigative agency to monitor all aliens in the United States and to gather intelligence on the way terrorists travel across borders. The commission suggested that people who want passports be tagged with biometric measures to make them easily identifiable.

In response to the commission report, a **Director of National Intelligence (DNI)** was created and charged with coordinating data from the nation's primary intelligence-gathering agencies. The DNI serves as the principal intelligence adviser to the president and the statutory intelligence adviser to the National Security Council. On February 17, 2005, President George W. Bush named U.S. Ambassador to Iraq John Negroponte to be the first person to hold the post; he was confirmed on April 21, 2005; the current director is James R. Clapper, a former air force general and director of the Defense Intelligence Agency.

Among the agencies reporting to the DNI are the National Counterterrorism Center (NCTC), which is staffed by terrorism experts from the CIA, FBI, and the Pentagon; the Privacy and Civil Liberties Board; and the National Counterproliferation Center. The NCTC serves as the primary organization in the U.S. government for analyzing and integrating all intelligence possessed or acquired by the government pertaining to terrorism and counterterrorism, excepting purely domestic counterterrorism information.

While the 9/11 Commission report outlines what has already been done, what has not been done, and what needs to be done, agencies of the justice system are now responding to the challenge.

CONFRONTING TERRORISM WITH LAW ENFORCEMENT

Ending the threat of terror is not easy. One reason is the very nature of American society. Because we live in a free and open nation, it is extremely difficult to seal the borders and prevent the entry of terrorist groups. In his book *Nuclear Terrorism*, Graham Allison, an expert on nuclear weapons and national security, describes the almost superhuman effort it would take to seal the nation's borders from nuclear attack considering the thousands of trucks, rail cars, and ships that deliver goods every day. The potential for terrorists to obtain bombs is significant: there are more than 100 nuclear research reactors now in operation around the world, and many are contained in countries hostile to the United States, such as Iran and North Korea. Even if terrorists lack the knowledge to build their own bomb, they may be able to purchase an intact device on the black market. Russia alone has thousands of nuclear warheads and material for many thousands of additional weapons; all of these are vulnerable to theft. Terrorists may also be able to buy the knowledge to construct bombs. In one well-known incident, Pakistan's leading nuclear scientist, A. Q. Khan, sold comprehensive "nuclear starter kits" that included advanced centrifuge components, blueprints for nuclear warheads, and uranium samples in quantities sufficient to make a small bomb, and even provided personal consulting services to assist in nuclear development.[93]

Recognizing this problem, law enforcement agencies around the country began to realign their resources to combat future terrorist attacks. In response to 9/11, law enforcement agencies undertook a number of steps: increasing the number of personnel engaged in emergency response planning; updating response plans for chemical, biological, or radiological attacks; and reallocating internal resources or increasing departmental spending to focus on terrorism preparedness.[94] Actions continue to be taken on the federal, state, and local levels.

LO10 Rate the efforts by the FBI and DHS to fight terrorism

Federal Law Enforcement One of the most significant changes has been a realignment of the Federal Bureau of Investigation (FBI), the federal government's main law enforcement agency. The FBI announced a reformulation of its priorities, making protecting the United States

---

Director of National Intelligence (DNI) Government official charged with coordinating data from the nation's primary intelligence-gathering agencies.

from terrorist attack its number one commitment. It is charged with coordinating intelligence collection with the Border Patrol, Secret Service, and the CIA. The FBI must also work with and share intelligence with the National Counterterrorism Center (NCTC). Another initiative has been the creation of Joint Terrorism Task Forces (JTTFs), which are located in 104 cities nationwide. The JTTFs include approximately 4,000 members nationwide, hailing from over 500 state and local agencies and 55 federal agencies (the Department of Homeland Security, the U.S. military, Immigration and Customs Enforcement, and the Transportation Security Administration, to name a few). JTTFs enable a shared intelligence base across many agencies, among other benefits.[95]

Department of Homeland Security (DHS)

Soon after the 2001 attacks, President George W. Bush proposed the creation of a new cabinet-level agency called the **Department of Homeland Security (DHS)**, which is engaged in:

- Preventing terrorist attacks within the United States
- Reducing America's vulnerability to terrorism
- Minimizing the damage and recovering from attacks that do occur

Rather than start from the ground up, the DHS combined a number of existing agencies into a superagency. Among its components are:

- *Border and transportation security.* The Department of Homeland Security is responsible for securing our nation's borders and transportation systems, which include 350 ports of entry. The department manages who and what enters the country, and works to prevent the entry of terrorists and the instruments of terrorism while simultaneously ensuring the speedy flow of legitimate traffic. The DHS also is in charge of securing territorial waters, including ports and waterways.
- *Emergency preparedness and response.* The department ensures the preparedness of emergency response professionals, provides the federal government's response, and aids America's recovery from terrorist attacks and natural disasters. The department is responsible for reducing the loss of life

and property and protecting institutions from all types of hazards through an emergency management program of preparedness, mitigation, response, and recovery.

- *Chemical, biological, radiological, and nuclear countermeasures.* The department leads the federal government's efforts in preparing for and responding to the full range of terrorist threats involving weapons of mass destruction. To do this, the department sets national policy and establishes guidelines for state and local governments. It directs exercises and drills for federal, state, and local chemical, biological, radiological, and nuclear (CBRN) response teams and plans. The department is assigned to prevent the importation of nuclear weapons and material.
- *Information analysis and infrastructure protection.* The department analyzes information from multiple available sources, including the CIA and FBI, in order to assess the dangers facing the nation. It also analyzes law enforcement and intelligence information.[96]

Department of Homeland Security (DHS) An agency of the federal government charged with preventing terrorist attacks within the United States, reducing America's vulnerability to terrorism, and minimizing the damage and aiding recovery from attacks that do occur.

An agent at work at the National Cybersecurity and Communications Integration Center, an arm of the Homeland Security Department, in Arlington, Virginia. In 2013, an executive order was issued requiring increased information sharing about cyberthreats between the government and private companies that oversee the country's critical infrastructure.

The DHS has numerous and varied duties. It is responsible for port security and transportation systems and manages airport security with its Transportation Security Administration (TSA). It has its own intelligence section, and it covers every special event in the United States, including political conventions.

State and County Law Enforcement In the wake of the 9/11 attacks, a number of states have beefed up their intelligence-gathering capabilities and aimed them directly at homeland security. Arizona maintains the Arizona Counter Terrorism Information Center (ACTIC), a statewide intelligence system designed to combat terrorism.[97] It consists of two divisions. One is unclassified and draws together personnel from various public safety agencies. The other operates in a secretive manner and is made up of personnel from the FBI's Joint Terrorism Task Force. Its Fusion Center is responsible for sharing information about situations that might affect jurisdictions in the state and combs through diverse informational sources to provide early warning of incidents at the local, regional, and state levels.[98] ACTIC also has an outreach program known as the Community Liaison Program (CLP). Community partners, including religious groups, businesses, and community crime watches, provide intelligence information to ACTIC personnel as the need arises.

Some counties are now engaging in anti-terror and homeland security activities. The Harris County, Texas, Office of Homeland Security and Emergency Management (OHSEM) is responsible for an emergency management plan that prepares for public recovery in the event of natural disasters or human-caused catastrophes or attacks. It works in conjunction with state, federal, and local authorities, including the city of Houston and other municipalities in the surrounding Harris County area when required. If needed, OHSEM activates an Emergency Operations Center to facilitate coordination of all support agencies to provide continuity of services to the public. OHSEM is responsible for advisement, notification, and assembly of services that are in the best interest of the citizens of Harris County. It prepares and distributes information and procedures governing the same.[99]

Local Law Enforcement Federal and state law enforcement agencies are not alone in responding to the threat of terrorism. And, of course, nowhere is the threat of terrorism being taken more seriously than in New York City, one of the main targets of the 9/11 attacks, which has established a Counterterrorism Bureau.[100] After the 9/11 attacks, the NYPD augmented its anti-terrorism forces from 17 to 125 and assigned them to the operational control of the Counterterrorism Bureau. Teams within the bureau have been trained to examine potential targets in the city and attempt to insulate them from possible attack.

Viewed as prime targets are the city's bridges, the Empire State Building, Rockefeller Center, and the United Nations. Bureau detectives are assigned overseas to work with the police in several foreign cities, including cities in Canada and Israel. Detectives have been assigned as liaisons with the FBI and with INTERPOL, in Lyon, France. The city recruits detectives with language skills from Pashtun and Urdu to Arabic, Fujianese, and other dialects. The New York City Police Intelligence Division has been revamped, and agents are examining foreign newspapers and monitoring Internet sites. The department has set up several backup command centers in different parts of the city in case a terror attack puts headquarters out of operation. Backup senior command teams have been created so that if people at the highest levels of the department are killed, individuals will already have been tapped to step into their jobs. The Lower Manhattan Security Initiative (LMSI) is a networked surveillance project designed to detect threats and perform preoperational terrorist surveillance south of Canal Street in lower Manhattan.

The department is also drawing on the expertise of other institutions around the city. Medical specialists have been enlisted to monitor daily developments in the city's hospitals to detect any suspicious outbreaks of illness that might reflect a biological attack. And the police are conducting joint drills with the New York Fire Department to avoid the problems in communication and coordination that marked the emergency response on September 11. In January 2015, the NYPD announced it was expanding the counterterrorism unit by creating a Strategic Response Group, whose officers will receive training on counterterrorism and be equipped with heavy protective gear, including long rifles and machine guns.[101]

COMBATING TERRORISM WITH THE COURTS

In April 2009, the U.S. attorney for the Southern District of New York brought federal charges against Haji Juma Khan, an Afghan who allegedly provided the Taliban with funding through his lucrative (and illegal) opium, morphine, and heroin trafficking organization, dubbed the "Khan Organization."[102] In the same month, Wesam al-Delaema pleaded guilty to conspiring to kill U.S. personnel in Iraq.[103] These are but two of the many terrorism-related cases that have been tried in the nation's court system. Prosecutions began to spike right after 9/11 and continue to grow today; there have been more than 800 prosecutions of suspected terrorists in the United States in the last decade.[104]

In addition to the trial courts, the Supreme Court has been involved in terror issues ever since Congress authorized President Bush to use "all necessary and appropriate force" against those responsible for the attacks in New York and Washington, D.C. Yaser Hamdi, an American citizen who had left the United States in his youth, was captured in Afghanistan and detained by military forces at Guantanamo Bay, Cuba, for supposedly aiding the Taliban. He was later moved to a military prison in Norfolk, Virginia, where he filed a writ of *habeas corpus*, arguing that, as a U.S. citizen, he was entitled to challenge the constitutionality of his confinement in federal court. In *Hamdi v. Rumsfeld* (2004), the Supreme Court agreed with his argument, holding in a 6–3 decision that the due process clause of the Fifth Amendment requires that U.S. citizens be given the opportunity to challenge their confinement in this way.[105] The Court also decided in *Rasul v. Bush* (2004) that the federal courts have jurisdiction to hear *habeas corpus* petitions from foreign nationals captured outside the United States.[106]

One year later, the Supreme Court heard a case involving Salim Hamdan, a Yemeni and former driver for Osama bin Laden. He was captured by Afghan warlords and turned over to U.S. forces in 2001. He was then transferred in 2002 to Guantanamo Bay and, in 2003, was slated to be tried for various conspiracy offenses before a military tribunal. He filed a *habeas corpus* petition in the U.S. District Court for the Western District of Washington, claiming that he could not legally be tried by a military tribunal. In a 5–3 decision, the Supreme Court agreed.[107] It held that the military commission at issue violated the Uniform Code of Military Justice and the four Geneva Conventions signed in 1949. Charges against him were subsequently dropped, but Hamdan was later deemed an "unlawful enemy combatant," tried once again before a military tribunal, and convicted. He was sentenced to five-and-a-half years in prison, given credit for time served, and sent back to Yemen. He was not named a combatant before going into his first trial, which is partly why the first military tribunal was illegal.

Shortly after Hamdan's case was decided, Congress passed the Military Commissions Act of 2006, which stripped the federal courts of jurisdiction to hear *habeas corpus* petitions from detainees who have been designated as "enemy combatants." In a 5–4 decision, the Supreme Court held that prisoners (even foreign nationals held at Guantanamo Bay) had the right to *habeas corpus* under the U.S. Constitution and that their arguments could be heard in the federal courts.[108] In effect, the Court held that the Military Commissions Act of 2006 was an unconstitutional suspension of the right to *habeas corpus*. In October 2009, President Obama signed into law the Military Commissions Act of 2009, which attempted to improve on—and address some of the deficiencies of—the earlier legislation. The law does not permit a U.S. citizen to be tried by a military commission.[109]

As a result of these cases, detainees, enemy combatants, terror suspects, and the like enjoy greater protection now than they did in the past. Indeed, all but a few of them enjoy the same rights as anyone else, whether or not they are U.S. citizens.

CONFRONTING TERRORISM WITH THE LAW

Soon after the September 11 terrorist attacks, the U.S. government enacted several laws focused on preventing further acts of violence against the United States and creating greater flexibility in the fight to control terror activity. Most importantly, Congress passed the **USA Patriot Act (USAPA)** on October 26, 2001.

The USA Patriot Act   USAPA expanded all four traditional tools of surveillance—wiretaps, search warrants, pen/trap orders (installing devices that record phone calls), and subpoenas. The Foreign Intelligence Surveillance Act (FISA), allowed domestic operations by intelligence agencies. USAPA gave greater power to the FBI to check and monitor phone, Internet, and computer records without first needing to demonstrate that they were being used by a suspect or target of a court order.

The government was given permission to serve a single wiretap, or pen/trap order, on any person regardless of whether that person or entity is named in a court order. Prior to the Patriot Act, telephone companies could be ordered to install pen/trap devices on their networks that would monitor calls coming to a surveillance target and to whom the surveillance target made calls; the USAPA extended this monitoring to the Internet. Law enforcement agencies were able to obtain the email addresses and websites visited by a target, and emails of the people with whom they communicated. It was possible to require that an Internet service provider install a device that records email and other electronic communications on its servers, looking for communications initiated or received by the target of an investigation. Under USAPA, the government did not need to show a court that the information or communication is relevant to a criminal investigation, nor does it have to report where it served the order or what information it received.

The act also allowed enforcement agencies to monitor cable operators and obtain access to their records and systems. Before the act, a cable company had to give prior notice to the customer, even if that person was a target of an investigation. Information could be obtained on people with whom the cable subscriber communicated, the content of the person's communications, and the person's subscription

USA Patriot Act (USAPA) Legislation giving U.S. law enforcement agencies a freer hand to investigate and apprehend suspected terrorists.

records; prior notice was still required if law enforcement agencies wanted to learn what television programming a subscriber purchases.

The act also expanded the definition of terrorism and enabled the government to monitor more closely those people suspected of "harboring" and giving "material support" to terrorists (Sections 803, 805). It increased the authority of the U.S. attorney general to detain and deport noncitizens with little or no judicial review. The attorney general may certify that he has "reasonable grounds to believe" that a noncitizen endangers national security and is therefore eligible for deportation. The attorney general and secretary of state were also given the authority to designate domestic groups as terrorist organizations and deport any noncitizen who is a member.

USA Freedom Act   When the Patriot Act ended in 2015, it was replaced by the USA Freedom Act.[110] The main change was to Section 215, the section that most bothered civil libertarians. Under Section 215 of the Patriot Act, the National Security Agency routinely collected metadata from some of the biggest cellular companies—not the contents of conversations, but the phone numbers, dates, times, and duration of the calls. If someone inside the United States called a number linked to major terrorist organizations (such as al-Qaeda), an NSA alert system would note that fact. The NSA could then ask the U.S. Foreign Intelligence Surveillance Court (the federal court authorized under the Foreign Intelligence Surveillance Act of 1978 [FISA] to oversee requests for surveillance warrants against foreign spies inside the United States) for permission to search the database for a list of all the other numbers that the American phone had called, as well as all the numbers that those numbers had called, going back as far as five years. If this search revealed a suspicious pattern, the NSA could then turn the materials over to the FBI, which could seek a warrant to listen to conversations.

Under the new reform law, the NSA would no longer possess the database, so it would seek a FISA court order to get it from the telecom companies—and the FISA court would now include a privacy advocate who could argue against relinquishing the data. If the court sided with the NSA, what happened next would be exactly the same as before the new law passed.

COMBATING TERRORISM WITH POLITICS

In the long run, it may simply be impossible to defeat terror groups and end terrorism using military, law enforcement, or legal solutions. Using force may play into terrorists' hands and convince them that they are freedom fighters valiantly struggling against a better-armed and more ruthless foe. No matter how many terrorists are killed and/or captured, military/deterrence-based solutions may be doomed. Aggressive reprisals will cause terrorist ideology to spread and gain greater acceptance in the underdeveloped world. The resulting anger and alienation will produce more terrorists than can be killed off through violent responses. In contrast, if the terrorist ideology is countered and discredited, the appeal of terror groups such as al-Qaeda and ISIL will wither and die.

One approach suggested by policy experts is to undermine support for terrorist groups by being benevolent nation-builders, giving aid to the nations that house terror groups.[111] This is the approach the United States took after World War II to rebuild Germany and Japan (the Marshall Plan) all the while gaining support for its Cold War struggle against the Soviet Union. According to the Rand Corporation, a nonprofit research group, the following steps are required to defeat jihadist groups such as al-Qaeda:

- Attack the ideological underpinnings of global jihadism
- Sever ideological and other links between terrorist groups
- Strengthen the capabilities of front-line states to counter local jihadist threats

This approach may work because al-Qaeda's goal of toppling "apostate" regimes in Saudi Arabia, Egypt, and Pakistan and creating an ultraorthodox pan-Islamic government spanning the world does not sit well with large groups of Muslims; their monolithic vision has no room for other Muslim sects such as Shi'ites and Sunni moderates. Therefore, political and social appeals may help fracture local support for al-Qaeda. In addition, the United States should seek to deny sanctuaries to terrorist groups and strengthen the capabilities of foreign governments to deal with terrorist threats, but in an advisory capacity by providing intelligence. In his book *Unconquerable Nation*, Brian Michael Jenkins, a noted expert on the topic, identifies the strategic principles he believes are the key to combating terror in contemporary society. These beliefs are summarized in Exhibit 11.3.

To access the websites of two leading government agencies that are involved in anti-terror activity and information gathering, go to:
- The Office of the Director of National Intelligence, **http://www.dni.gov/**
- The National Counterterrorism Center (NCTC), **http://www.nctc.gov/**

   Do you believe the threat of terror in the United States has diminished because of governmental efforts? Or is it impossible to stop lone-wolf terrorists who act on their own?

EXHIBIT 11.3

Countering Terror

- *Destroy the jihadist enterprise.* Jihadists have proven to be flexible and resistant and capable of continued action despite sustained military actions. They remain the primary threat to U.S. national security and will continue to be so for the foreseeable future. Therefore, they must be outright destroyed or at the least have their ability to operate damaged.

- *Conserve resources for a long war.* These include blood, treasure, the will of the American people, and the support of needed allies. This means picking future fights carefully, making security measures both effective and efficient, maintaining domestic support, avoiding extreme measures that alienate the people, and cultivating rather than bullying other countries.

- *Wage more-effective political warfare.* Political solutions must be pragmatic. We must be ready to compromise. Amnesty should be offered to terrorists who have become disillusioned. Local leaders should be accommodated and deals cut to co-opt enemies.

- *Break the cycle of jihadism.* Jihadism is a cycle beginning with recruitment and ending with death, arrest, or detention. Combating terror must involve neutralizing terror groups' ability to radicalize and indoctrinate potential recruits before the cycle begins and then, at the end of the cycle, deal effectively with terror suspects once they have been captured and detained.

- *Impede recruitment.* Recruitment sites must be identified and made dangerous and therefore unusable. Alternatives to terror must be offered. Former, now disillusioned terrorists can be used to denounce terror and counteract its appeal with potential recruits.

- *Encourage defections and facilitate exits.* Potential defectors must be identified and encouraged to quit through the promise of amnesty, cash, job training, and homes.

- *Persuade detainees to renounce terrorism.* Rehabilitation of known terror suspects may be more important than prosecution and imprisonment.

- *Maintain international cooperation.* International cooperation is a prerequisite to success, a precious commodity not to be squandered by bullying, unreciprocated demands, indifference to local realities, or actions that repel even America's closest friends.

- *Reserve the right to retaliate—a muscular deterrent.* Terror groups and their sponsors should know that any attack using weapons of mass destruction will be met with all-out warfare against any group or government known to be or even suspected of being responsible.

SOURCE: Brian Michael Jenkins, *Unconquerable Nation: Knowing Our Enemy, Strengthening Ourselves* (Santa Monica, CA: Rand Corporation, 2006).

SUMMARY

L01 Define the term *political crime*

Political crime is used to signify illegal acts that are designed to undermine an existing government and threaten its survival. Political crimes can include both violent and nonviolent acts and range in seriousness from dissent, treason, and espionage to violent acts such as terrorism or assassination.

L02 Assess the cause of political crime

The political criminal and political crimes may stem from religious or ideological sources. They often occupy a gray area between conventional and outlawed behavior. While common criminals may be motivated by greed, vengeance, or jealousy, political criminals have a somewhat different agenda from common criminals. There is no set pattern or reason why someone becomes a political criminal. Some use political crime as a stepping stone to public office while others use it as a method to focus their frustrations.

L03 Compare and contrast the terms *espionage* and *treason*

Helping or cooperating with the enemy in a time of war would be considered treason. Espionage is the practice of obtaining information about a government, organization, or a society that is considered secret or confidential without the permission of the holder of the information. Industrial espionage involves unethical or illegal activities such as bribing employees to reveal trade secrets such as computer codes or product formulas.

L04 List the components of state political crime

While some political crimes are committed by people who oppose the state, others are perpetrated by state authorities against the people they are supposed to serve. State political crime has five components: political corruption, illegal domestic surveillance, human rights violations, state violence, and state-corporate crime.

L05 Debate the use and misuse of torture

The use of torture to gain information from suspected political criminals is highly controversial. The use of waterboarding has become a national issue because there seems to be no agreement on whether it is torture or a relatively harmless instrument of interrogation.

L06 Distinguish among terrorists, insurgents, guerillas, and revolutionaries

Terrorism is generally defined as the illegal use of force against innocent people to achieve a political objective.

The term *guerilla* refers to antigovernment forces located in rural areas that attack the military, the police, and government officials. The typical goal of an insurgency is to confront the existing government for control of all or a portion of its territory, or force political concessions in sharing political power. A revolution is generally seen as a civil war fought between nationalists and a sovereign power that holds control of the land, or between the existing government and local groups over issues of ideology and power.

L07 **Enumerate the various forms of terrorism**

Revolutionary terrorists use violence to frighten those in power and their supporters in order to replace the existing government with a regime that holds acceptable political or religious views. Political terrorism is directed at people or groups who oppose the terrorists' political ideology or whom the terrorists define as "outsiders" who must be destroyed. Nationalist terrorism promotes the interests of a minority ethnic or religious group that believes it has been persecuted under majority rule and wishes to carve out its own independent homeland. Retributive terrorists want to impose their social and religious code on others. State-sponsored terrorism occurs when a repressive government regime forces its citizens into obedience, oppresses minorities, and stifles political dissent. Sometimes terrorist groups become involved in common-law crimes such as drug dealing and kidnapping, even selling nuclear materials.

L08 **Explain what motivates the terrorist to commit violent acts**

While not all terrorists suffer from psychological deficits, enough do so that the typical terrorist can be described as an emotionally disturbed individual who acts out his or her psychoses within the confines of violent groups. Another view is that because they are out of the political and social mainstream, young men and women are motivated to join terror groups because they suffer alienation and lack the tools to compete in a post-technological society. Yet another view is that terrorists hold extreme religious and/or ideological beliefs that prompt their behavior.

L09 **Give examples of the efforts being made to centralize intelligence gathering**

The Director of National Intelligence (DNI) is charged with coordinating data from the nation's primary intelligence-gathering agencies. The National Counterterrorism Center (NCTC) serves as the primary organization in the U.S. government for analyzing and integrating all intelligence possessed or acquired by the government pertaining to terrorism and counterterrorism, excepting purely domestic counterterrorism information.

L010 **Rate the efforts by the FBI and DHS to fight terrorism**

The FBI announced a reformulation of its priorities, making protecting the United States from terrorist attack its number one commitment. It is now charged with coordinating intelligence collection with the Border Patrol, Secret Service, and the CIA. The Department of Homeland Security (DHS) is the federal agency responsible for preventing terrorist attacks within the United States, reducing America's vulnerability to terrorism, and minimizing the damage and recovering from attacks that do occur.

CRITICAL THINKING QUESTIONS

1. Would you be willing to give up some of your civil rights in order to aid the war on terror?
2. Should terror suspects arrested in a foreign land be given the same rights and privileges as an American citizen accused of crime?
3. What elements of American culture might encourage terrorist activity in the United States?
4. In light of the 9/11 attacks, should acts of terrorism be treated differently from other common-law violent crimes?

Should terrorists be executed for their acts even if no one is killed during their attack?
5. Can the use of torture ever be justified? Is the "ticking bomb" scenario valid?
6. A spy gives plans for a new weapon to the enemy. They build the weapon and use it to kill American soldiers. Is the spy guilty of murder?

KEY TERMS

political crime (394)
al-Qaeda (394)
election fraud (397)
treason (399)
espionage (401)
industrial espionage (401)
state political crime (403)

torture (403)
ticking bomb scenario (403)
terrorism (405)
guerilla (406)
insurgent (406)
Islamic State of Iraq and the Levant (ISIL) (406)

zealot (408)
Reign of Terror (408)
retributive terrorists (411)
state-sponsored terrorism (413)
networks (414)
terror cells (414)

failed states (418)
Director of National Intelligence (DNI) (420)
Department of Homeland Security (DHS) (421)
USA Patriot Act (USAPA) (423)

All URLs accessed in 2016.

1. Camila Domonoske, "Reports: Gunman Had Visited Nightclub Before, Used Gay Dating Apps," National Public Radio, June 14, 2016, http://www.npr.org/sections /thetwo-way/2016/06/14/481986819 /reports-gunman-had-visited-nightclub-before -used-gay-dating-apps; Michael Edison Hayden, "Gunman's Wife Says She Tried to Talk Him Out of Attack, Officials Say," ABC News, June 14, 2016, http://abcnews.go .com/US/gunmans-wife-talk-attack-officials /story?id=39841580.

2. Jeffrey Ian Ross, *The Dynamics of Political Crime* (Thousand Oaks, CA: Sage, 2003).

3. Micah Zenko, "Counting the Dead in Syria," *The Atlantic*, September 15, 2015, http:// www.theatlantic.com/international/archive /2015/09/syria-civil-war-civilian-deaths /405496/.

4. Human Rights Watch, "UN: Reject Syria's Human Rights Council Candidacy, Country Under Investigation by Rights Body Not Fit to Join," May 6, 2011, http://www.hrw.org /en/news/2011/05/06/un-reject-syria-s -human-rights-council-candidacy.

5. Stephen Farrell and Anthony Shadid, "Dozens Killed in Wave of Attacks Across Iraq," *New York Times*, August 25, 2010, http://www.nytimes.com/2010/08/26 /world/middleeast/26iraq.html.

6. Stephen Schafer, *The Political Criminal, The Problem of Morality and Crime* (New York: Free Press, 1974), pp. 154–157.

7. Randy Borum, "Understanding the Terrorist Mind-Set," *FBI Law Enforcement Bulletin* 72 (2003): 7–10.

8. Brendan O'Connor, "Here Is What Appears to Be Dylann Roof's Racist Manifesto," *Gawker*, June 20, 2015, http://gawker.com /here-is-what-appears-to-be-dylann-roofs -racist-manifest-1712767241.

9. Olsen Ebright, Melissa Pamer, and Jason Kandel, "Election Fraud Alleged in Cudahy; 2 Accept Plea Deal," http://www .nbclosangeles.com/news/local/Cudahy -Officials-Corruption-Bribery-Ballots -Voting-162259065.html.

10. Justin Levitt, *The Truth About Voter Fraud* (New York: Brennan Center for Justice, 2007), https://www.brennancenter.org/sites /default/files/legacy/The%20Truth%20 About%20Voter%20Fraud.pdf.

11. Michael Gilbert, "The Problem of Voter Fraud," *Columbia Law Review* 115 (2015): 739–775.

12. Evan Perez and Shimon Prokupecz, "Sen. Bob Menendez: 'I Am Not Going Anywhere,'" CNN, March 9, 2015, http:// www.cnn.com/2015/03/06/politics/robert -menendez-criminal-corruption-charges -planned/.

13. Internal Revenue Service, "Examples of Public Corruption Investigations—Fiscal Year 2013."

14. U.S. Attorney's Office, Eastern District of Michigan, "Former Detroit Mayor Kwame Kilpatrick, Contractor Bobby Ferguson, and Bernard Kilpatrick Sentenced on Racketeering, Extortion, Bribery, Fraud, and Tax Charges," press release, October 17, 2013, http://www.fbi.gov/detroit/press -releases/2013/former-detroit-mayor-kwame -kilpatrick-contractor-bobby-ferguson -and-bernard-kilpatrick-sentenced-on -racketeering-extortion-bribery-fraud-and -tax-charges.

15. BBC news, "Profile of John Walker Lindh," January 24, 2002, http://news.bbc.co.uk/2 /hi/americas/1779455.stm.

16. John Ziff and Austin Sarat, *Espionage and Treason* (New York: Chelsea House, 1999).

17. United States Criminal Code at 18 U.S.C. § 2381.

18. University of Missouri–Kansas City School of Law, Douglas Linder, "The Treason Trial of Aaron Burr," http://www.law.umkc.edu /faculty/projects/ftrials/burr/burraccount .html.

19. Civil War Trust, "John Brown's Harpers Ferry Raid," http://www.civilwar.org /150th-anniversary/john-browns-harpers -ferry.html.

20. HistoryNet, "Tokyo Rose: They Called Her a Traitor," http://www.historynet.com /tokyo-rose-they-called-her-a-traitor.htm.

21. John F. Burns and Ravi Somaiya, "WikiLeaks Founder on the Run, Trailed by Notoriety," *New York Times*, October 23, 2010, http:// www.nytimes.com/2010/10/24/world /24assange.html.

22. Free Chelsea Manning website, https://www .chelseamanning.org/learn-more/bradley -manning.

23. David Owen, *Hidden Secrets: The Complete History of Espionage and the Technology Used to Support It* (Ontario, Canada: Firefly Books, 2002).

24. BBC News, "Key Cases in Soviet-UK Espionage," January 23, 2006, http://news .bbc.co.uk/2/hi/europe/4639130.stm.

25. CNN, "Accused FBI Spy Hanssen Pleads Not Guilty," May 31, 2001, http://edition .cnn.com/2001/LAW/05/31/hanssen .arraignment.02/; Lawrence Schiller, *Into the Mirror: The Life of Master Spy Robert P. Hanssen* (Darby, PA: Diane Publications, 2004).

26. Tim Culpan, "China's Clock-Punching Hackers Show Spying as Routine Job," *Bloomberg News*, May 27, 2014, http://www .bloomberg.com/news/2014-05-27/china -s-clock-punching-hackers-show-spying -as-routine-job.html.

27. Hedieh Nasheri, *Economic Espionage and Industrial Spying* (Cambridge, England: Cambridge University Press, 2004).

28. Office of the National Counterintelligence Executive, "Annual Report to Congress on Foreign Economic Collection and Industrial Espionage, 2005," http://www.fas.org/irp /ops/ci/docs/2005.pdf.

29. Wesley Bruer, "FBI Sees Chinese Involvement Amid Sharp Rise in Economic Espionage Cases," CNN, July 24, 2015, http://www.cnn .com/2015/07/24/politics/fbi-economic -espionage/.

30. Office of the National Counterintelligence Executive, "Foreign Spies Stealing US Economic Secrets in Cyberspace," 2011, https://www.ncsc.gov/publications/reports /fecie_all/Foreign_Economic_Collection _2011.pdf.

31. Department of Justice news release, "Two Men Plead Guilty to Stealing Trade Secrets from Silicon Valley Companies to Benefit China," December 14, 2006, https://www.justice.gov/archive/criminal /cybercrime/press-releases/2006/yePlea .htm.

32. Nadia Abou El-Magd, "Accuser in Case vs. CIA Agents Tells of Torture: Muslim Cleric Says Egyptians Used Electricity," *Boston Globe*, February 23, 2007, A3.

33. Alan M. Dershowitz, *Shouting Fire: Civil Liberties in a Turbulent Age* (New York: Little, Brown, 2002); Dershowitz, "Want to Torture? Get a Warrant," *San Francisco Chronicle*, January 22, 2002.

34. Human Rights Watch, "The Twisted Logic of Torture," January 2005, http://hrw.org /wr2k5/darfurandabughraib/6.htm.

35. Jessica Wolfendale, "Training Torturers: A Critique of the 'Ticking Bomb' Argument," *Social Theory and Practice* 31 (2006): 269–287; Elizabeth Sepper, "The Ties that Bind: How the Constitution Limits the CIA's Actions in the War on Terror," *New York University Law Review* 81 (2006): 1805–1843.

36. Vittorio Bufacchi and Jean Maria Arrigo, "Torture, Terrorism and the State: A Refutation of the Ticking-Bomb Argument," *Journal of Applied Philosophy* 23 (2006): 355–373.

37. Jim Acosta, Jim Sciutto and Julia Manchester, "Donald Trump: Torture Works," CNN, February 17, 2016, http://www.cnn.com/2016/02/17/politics /donald-trump-torture-works/.

38. Scott Shane, David Johnston, and James Risen, "Secret U.S. Endorsement of Severe Interrogations" *New York Times*, October 4, 2007, http://www.nytimes .com/2007/10/04/washington /04interrogate.html.

39. Michael Cooper and Marc Santora, "McCain Rebukes Giuliani on Waterboarding Remark," *New York Times*, October 26, 2007, http://www.nytimes.com/2007/10/26/us/politics/26giuliani.html.

40. BBC News, "Paris Attacks: What Happened on the Night," http://www.bbc.com/news/world-europe-34818994.

41. Title 22 of the United States Code section 2656f (d) (1999).

42. Paul Wilkinson, *Terrorism and the Liberal State* (New York: Wiley, 1977), p. 49.

43. Jack Gibbs, "Conceptualization of Terrorism," *American Sociological Review* 54 (1989): 329–340, at 330.

44. Robert Friedlander, *Terrorism* (Dobbs Ferry, NY: Oceana Publishers, 1979), p. 14.

45. "Differences Between Terrorism and Insurgency," http://www.terrorism-research.com/insurgency/.

46. Tim Arango, Kareem Fahim, and Ben Hubbard, "Rebels' Fast Strike in Iraq Was Years in the Making," *New York Times*, June 15, 2014, http://www.nytimes.com/2014/06/15/world/middleeast/rebels-fast-strike-in-iraq-was-years-in-the-making.html.

47. Andrew Silke, "Holy Warriors: Exploring the Psychological Processes of Jihadi Radicalization," *European Journal of Criminology* 5 (2008): 99–123.

48. Walter Laqueur, *The New Terrorism: Fanaticism and the Arms of Mass Destruction* (New York: Oxford, 1999).

49. This section relies heavily on Friedlander, *Terrorism*, pp. 8–20.

50. Michael Kellogg. *The Russian Roots of Nazism: White Russians and the Making of National Socialism, 1917–1945* (New York: Cambridge University Press, 2005).

51. FBI, "Domestic Terrorism: Focus on Militia Extremism," September 22, 2011, https://www.fbi.gov/news/stories/2011/september/militia_092211.

52. National Consortium for the Study of Terrorism and Responses to Terrorism (START), "Far-Right Violence in the United States: 1990–2013," https://www.start.umd.edu/pubs/START_ECDB_FarRightViolence_FactSheet_June2014.pdf.

53. Fiona Proffitt, "Costs of Animal Rights Terror," *Science* 304 (2004): 1731–1739.

54. "Animal Activists Face 'Domestic Terrorism' Charge in Freeing 5,740 Mink," *The Guardian*, July 25, 2015, http://www.theguardian.com/us-news/2015/jul/25/animal-activists-minks-domestic-terrorism-charges.

55. Council on Foreign Relations, "Hezbollah," http://www.cfr.org/lebanon/hezbollah-k-hizbollah-hizbullah/p9155.

56. Chung Chien-Peng, "China's War on Terror," *Foreign Affairs* 81 (2002): 8–13.

57. CNN, "Benghazi Consulate Attack Fast Facts," http://www.cnn.com/2013/09/10/world/benghazi-consulate-attack-fast-facts/.

58. Angel Rabasa, Peter Chalk, Kim Cragin, Sara A. Daly, Heather S. Gregg, Theodore W. Karasik, Kevin A. O'Brien, and William Rosenau, *Beyond al-Qaeda Part 1, The Global Jihadist Movement*, xviii, and *Part 2, The Outer Rings of the Terrorist Universe* (Santa Monica, CA: Rand Corporation, 2006).

59. Farouk Chothia, "Who Are Nigeria's Boko Haram Islamists?" BBC News, May 20, 2014, http://www.bbc.com/news/world-africa-13809501.

60. Josh Levs and Holly Yan, "147 Dead, Islamist Gunmen Killed After Attack at Kenya College," CNN, April 2, 2015, http://www.cnn.com/2015/04/02/africa/kenya-university-attack/.

61. Richard Lough, "Piracy Ransom Cash Ends Up with Somali Militants," Reuters, July 6, 2011, http://www.reuters.com/article/2011/07/06/somalia-piracy-idUSLDE7650U320110706.

62. Lawrence Miller, "The Terrorist Mind: A Psychological and Political Analysis, Part I," *International Journal of Offender Therapy and Comparative Criminology* 50 (2006): 121–138.

63. Ibid.

64. Gabriela Fried, "Piecing Memories Together After State Terror and Policies of Oblivion in Uruguay: The Female Political Prisoner's Testimonial Project (1997–2004)," *Social Identities* 12 (2006): 543–562.

65. Martin Miller, "Ordinary Terrorism in Historical Perspective." *Journal for the Study of Radicalism* 2 (2008): 125–154.

66. Mark Hamm, "'High Crimes and Misdemeanors': George W. Bush and the Sins of Abu Ghraib," *Crime, Media, Culture: An International Journal* 3 (2007): 259–284.

67. U.S. Department of Justice, "Federal Grand Jury Returns 30-Count Indictment Related to Boston Marathon Explosions and Murder of MIT Police Officer Sean Collier," June 27, 2013, http://www.fbi.gov/boston/press-releases/2013/federal-grand-jury-returns-30-count-indictment-related-to-boston-marathon-explosions-and-murder-of-mit-police-officer-sean-collier.

68. Mark Hamm and Ramon Spaaj, "Lone Wolf Terrorism in America: Using Knowledge of Radicalization Pathways to Forge Prevention Strategies, Final Report to the U.S. Department of Justice," 2015.

69. *Frontline*, "Osama bin Laden v. the U.S.: Edicts and Statements," http://www.pbs.org/wgbh/pages/frontline/shows/binladen/who/edicts.html.

70. Michael Scott Doran, "Somebody Else's Civil War," *Foreign Affairs* 81 (2002): 22–25; Peter L. Bergen, *Holy War, Inc.: Inside The Secret World of Osama bin Laden* (New York, Free Press, 2001), pp. 41–50; Yonah Alexander and Michael S. Swetnam, *Usama bin Laden's al-Qaida: Profile of a Terrorist Network* (New York: Transnational Publishers, 2001); Michael Kranish and Anthony Shadid,

"Bin Laden Zeal for Stature Used Psychology, Religion," *Boston Globe*, November 19, 2001, p. 3; *Frontline*, "Osama bin Laden v. the U.S.: Edicts and Statements."

71. Stephen J. Morgan, *The Mind of a Terrorist Fundamentalist: The Psychology of Terror Cults* (Awe-Struck E-Books, 2001); Martha Crenshaw, "The Psychology of Terrorism: An Agenda for the 21st Century," *Political Psychology* 21 (2000): 405–420.

72. Andrew Silke, "Courage in Dark Places: Reflections on Terrorist Psychology," *Social Research* 71 (2004): 177–198.

73. Jerrold Post, "When Hatred Is Bred in the Bone: Psycho-cultural Foundations of Contemporary Terrorism," *Political Psychology* 25 (2005): 615–637.

74. Charles Ruby, "Are Terrorists Mentally Deranged?" *Analyses of Social Issues and Public Policy* 2 (2002): 15–26.

75. David Lester, Bijou Yang, and Mark Lindsay, "Suicide Bombers: Are Psychological Profiles Possible?" *Studies in Conflict and Terrorism* 27 (2004): 283–295.

76. Randy Borum, *Psychology of Terrorism* (Tampa: University of South Florida, 2004), http://www.ncjrs.gov/pdffiles1/nij/grants/208552.pdf.

77. Ethan Bueno de Mesquita, "The Quality of Terror," *American Journal of Political Science* 49 (2005): 515–530.

78. Saroj Kumar Rath, *Social Research Reports* 21 (2012): 23–36.

79. Arie Kruglanski and Shira Fishman, "Terrorism: Between 'Syndrome' and 'Tool,'" *Current Directions in Psychological Science* 15 (2006): 45–48.

80. Marc Sageman, *Understanding Terror Networks* (Philadelphia: University of Pennsylvania Press, 2004), Ch. 4.

81. This section leans heavily on Anthony Stahelski, "Terrorists Are Made, Not Born: Creating Terrorists Using Social Psychological Conditioning," *Journal of Homeland Security* (March 2004).

82. Sageman, *Understanding Terror Networks*, Ch. 4.

83. Seth Schwartz, Curtis Dunkel, and Alan Waterman, "Terrorism: An Identity Theory Perspective," *Studies in Conflict and Terrorism* 32 (2009): 537–559.

84. Gary LaFree and Laura Dugan, *Global Trends in Terrorism, 1970–2011* (New York: Paradigm Publishers, 2014).

85. Schwartz, Dunkel, and Waterman, "Terrorism: An Identity Theory Perspective."

86. Sageman, *Understanding Terror Networks*.

87. Patricia Marchak, *Reigns of Terror* (Montreal: McGill-Queen's University Press, 2003).

88. Ibid., pp. 153–155.

89. Ibid.

90. National Consortium for the Study of Terrorism and Responses to Terrorism (START), "American Deaths in Terrorist Attacks," https://www.start.umd.edu/pubs

/START_AmericanTerrorismDeaths _FactSheet_Oct2015.pdf.

91. National Consortium for the Study of Terrorism and Responses to Terrorism (START), "Despite Fewer Attacks in Western World, Global Terrorism Increasing," December 19, 2013, http://www.start.umd .edu//news/despite-fewer-attacks-western -world-global-terrorism-increasing.

92. William Braniff, "Discussion Point: The State of Al-Qaida, Its Affiliates and Associated Groups," House Armed Services Committee Oral Testimony, February 4, 2014, http://www.start.umd.edu/news /discussion-point-state-al-qaida-its -affiliates-and-associated-groups.

93. Graham Allison, *Nuclear Terrorism: The Ultimate Preventable Catastrophe* (New York: Times Books, 2004).

94. Rand Corporation, "How Prepared Are State and Local Law Enforcement for Terrorism?" http://www.rand.org/pubs /research_briefs/RB9093.html.

95. FBI, "Protecting America from Terrorist Attack: Our Joint Terrorism Task Forces," http://www.fbi.gov/about-us/investigate /terrorism/terrorism_jttfs.

96. Homeland Security, "Information Sharing," http://www.dhs.gov/topic/information -sharing. The section on homeland security relies heavily on "The Department of Homeland Security," http://www.whitehouse .gov/infocus/homeland/.

97. Arizona Department of Public Safety, *Arizona Fusion Center*, http://www.azdps.gov/about /Task_Forces/Fusion/. Also see http://www .azactic.gov/.

98. http://www.azactic.gov/About/Operation/.

99. Harris County Homeland Security and Emergency Management, http://www .hcoem.org.

100. NYPD, "Counterterrorism Units," http://www .nyc.gov/html/nypd/html/administration /counterterrorism_units.shtml.

101. Pervaiz Shallwani, "New York City Police Department to Create New Counterterrorism Unit," *Wall Street Journal*, January 29, 2015, http://www.wsj.com/articles/new-york -city-police-department-to-create-new -counterterrorism-unit-1422570131.

102. U.S. Attorney for the Southern District of New York Press Release No. 09-103, "Afghan Drug Kingpin Charged with Terrorist Financing for Funding Taliban Insurgency," April 21, 2009.

103. Del Quentin Wilbur, "U.S. Judge Sentences Dutch Man to 25 Years for Crimes in Iraq," *Washington Post*, April 17, 2009, A7.

104. Center on Law and Security, New York School of Law, *Terrorist Trial Report Card*.

105. *Hamdi v. Rumsfeld*, 542 U.S. 507 (2004).

106. *Rasul v. Bush*, 542 U.S. 466 (2004).

107. *Hamdan v. Rumsfeld*, 548 U.S. 557 (2006).

108. *Boumediene v. Bush*, 553 U.S. 723 (2008).

109. Section 948c of the Military Commissions Act of 2009.

110. USA Freedom Act (H.R. 2048, Pub.L. 114–23).

111. Rabasa et al., *Beyond al-Qaeda Part 1*.

MIXA Co. Ltd./Getty Images

LEARNING OBJECTIVES

L01 Discuss the history of theft offenses

L02 Compare and contrast professional and amateur thieves

L03 Comment on the activities of a professional fence

L04 Differentiate between petty and grand larceny

L05 Compare professional and amateur shoplifters

L06 Explain the concept of embezzlement

L07 Describe the elements of sexual burglary

L08 Compare the activities of male and female burglars

L09 Know what it takes to be a "good burglar"

L010 Discuss why people commit arson for profit

12 PROPERTY CRIME

Between 2010 and 2013, the 13 members of the infamous Pharmacy Burglars ring were responsible for more than 125 burglaries and attempted burglaries of pharmacies in New York City's boroughs of Manhattan, the Bronx, Queens, and Brooklyn. They used both high tech and brute strength to break into drugstores and take cash and prescription drugs. The thieves entered their targets through ceilings, walls, barred windows, and doors; nothing could stop them for long. In some instances, they used their muscles, crowbars, axes, and other tools to penetrate exterior walls. If a pharmacy was adjacent to a commercial establishment such as a laundry or hardware store, the gang would smash through the shared wall.

The Pharmacy Burglars always wore dark hooded sweatshirts, masks, and gloves, and employed countersurveillance techniques to avoid apprehension. They frequently circumvented or disabled burglar alarms and cameras. They communicated by cell phone with lookouts who monitored police scanners, allowing the gang to escape with the stolen goods and cash before law enforcement was able to catch them in the act. Their getaway cars were luxury vehicles—Mercedes-Benzes, a Bentley—purchased from the proceeds of their narcotics sales.

The Pharmacy Burglars' downfall came when a joint task force of federal, state, and local agencies received information provided by a former gang member who was turned into a cooperating witness. After their arrest and indictment, DNA evidence was used to link gang members to three of the pharmacy burglaries, and cell phone data linked various combinations of the defendants to more than 50 of the burglaries. In addition, investigators obtained numerous photographs showing gang members holding large amounts of cash, wearing expensive jewelry, and driving high-end automobiles.[1]

While the Pharmacy Burglars' crimes went on for years and netted them millions, they are by no means unique. NCVS data tell us that about 15 million theft-related property offenses occur each year. Since 1993, the rate of property crime declined from 351 to 118 victimizations per 1,000 households.[2]

As a group, theft offenses involve the intentional and unauthorized taking, keeping, or using of another's property. Theft can be accomplished through stealth, deceit, or fraud, but the intent is to misappropriate someone else's property for the thief's personal benefit. The range and scope of U.S. criminal activity motivated by the desire for financial gain are tremendous. Self-report studies show that property crime is widespread among the young in every social class. National surveys of criminal behavior indicate that millions of personal and household thefts occur annually. Though average citizens may be puzzled and enraged by violent crimes, believing them to be both senseless and cruel, they often view economic crimes with a great deal more ambivalence. Society generally disapproves of crimes involving theft and corruption, but the public seems quite tolerant of the "gentleman bandit," even to the point of admiring such figures. They pop up as characters in popular myths and legends—such as the famed English outlaw Robin Hood—and in films such as *Ocean's Eleven* (2001) *Ocean's Twelve* (2004), and *Ocean's Thirteen* (2007) in which a suave George Clooney and roguish Brad Pitt lead a band of thieves who loot hundreds of millions of dollars from casinos, galleries, and so on. (See also *The Italian Job* with Mark Wahlberg or *Focus* with Will Smith or Jesse Eisenberg in *Now You See Me* and *Now You See Me: The Second Act* for more films featuring gentlemen bandits.)

How can such ambivalence toward thievery be explained? For one thing, if self-report surveys are accurate, national tolerance toward economic criminals may be prompted by the fact that almost every U.S. citizen has at some time been involved in economic crime. Even those among us who would never consider ourselves lawbreakers may have at one time engaged in petty theft as a teen, stolen a textbook from a college bookstore, cheated on our income tax, or pilfered from our place of employment. Consequently, it may be difficult for society to condemn economic criminals without feeling hypocritical.

People may also be somewhat more tolerant of **economic crimes** because they never seem to seriously hurt anyone—banks are insured, large businesses pass along losses to consumers, stolen cars can be easily replaced and in most cases are insured. The true pain of economic crime often goes unappreciated. Convicted offenders, especially businesspeople who commit white-collar crimes involving millions of dollars, often are punished rather lightly.

This chapter is the first of two that review the nature and extent of economic crime in the United States. It is divided into two principal sections. The first deals with the concept of professional crime and focuses on different types of professional criminals, including the **fence**, a buyer and seller of stolen merchandise. The chapter then turns to a discussion of common-law theft-related offenses such as larceny, burglary, and arson. In Chapter 13, attention will be given to crimes that involve organizations devoted to criminal enterprise—white-collar, green-collar, and organized crime.

A Brief History of Theft

L01 Discuss the history of theft offenses

Theft is not a phenomenon unique to modern times; the illegal taking of the personal property of another has been known throughout recorded history. The Crusades of the eleventh century inspired peasants and downtrodden noblemen to leave the shelter of their estates to prey on passing pilgrims.[3] Crusaders felt it within their rights to appropriate the possessions of any infidels—Greeks, Jews, or Muslims—they happened to encounter during their travels.

By the thirteenth century, returning pilgrims, not content to live as serfs on feudal estates, gathered in the forests of England and the Continent to poach game that was the rightful property of their lord or king and, when possible, to steal from passing strangers. By the fourteenth century, many such highwaymen and poachers were full-time livestock thieves, stealing great numbers of cattle and sheep.[4] The fifteenth and sixteenth centuries brought hostilities between England and France in what has come to be known as the Hundred Years' War. Foreign mercenary troops fighting for both sides roamed the countryside; loot and pillage were viewed as a rightful part of their pay. As cities developed and a permanent class of property-less urban poor was established,[5] theft became more professional. By the eighteenth century, three separate groups of property criminals were active: skilled thieves, smugglers, and poachers.

- **Skilled thieves** typically worked in the larger cities, such as London and Paris. This group included pickpockets, forgers, and counterfeiters, who operated freely. They congregated in **flash houses**—public meeting places, often taverns, that served as headquarters for gangs.

---

economic crime An act in violation of the criminal law that is designed to bring financial gain to the offender.

fence A buyer and seller of stolen merchandise.

skilled thieves Thieves who typically work in the larger cities, such as London and Paris. This group includes pickpockets, forgers, and counterfeiters who operate freely.

flash houses Public meeting places in England, often taverns, that served as headquarters for gangs.

Here, deals were made, crimes were plotted, and the sale of stolen goods was negotiated.[6]

- **Smugglers** were the second group of thieves. They moved freely in sparsely populated areas and transported goods, such as spirits, gems, gold, and spices, without bothering to pay tax or duty.
- **Poachers**, the third type of thief, typically lived in the country and supplemented their diet and income with game that belonged to a landlord.

Professional thieves in the larger cities banded together into gangs to protect themselves, increase the scope of their activities, and help dispose of stolen goods. Jack Wild, perhaps London's most famous thief, perfected the process of buying and selling stolen goods and gave himself the title of Thief-Taker General of Great Britain and Ireland. Before he was hanged, Wild controlled numerous gangs and dealt harshly with any thief who violated his strict code of conduct.[7] During this period, individual theft-related crimes began to be defined by the common law. The most important of these categories are still used today.

To read more about Jack Wild and his times, go to the website of the Old Bailey Court in England: **http://www.oldbaileyonline.org/.** **Who would be the contemporary equivalent of Jack Wild? How about Whitey Bulger? Read about him here: http://www.biography.com/people/whitey-bulger--328770.**

THEFT IN THE NINETEENTH CENTURY: TRAIN ROBBERY AND SAFECRACKING

In the nineteenth century, two new forms of theft appeared. Train robbery hit the nation hard when, in 1866, $700,000 (the equivalent of more than $9 million in today's currency) was taken from an Adams Express car on the New York, New Haven, and Hartford Railroad; it was the first train robbery on record. Also in 1866, the Reno brothers stole $13,000 in their first train holdup. The four brothers and their gang went on to rob a number of banks and trains in southern Indiana and Illinois before being tracked down by the Pinkerton Detective Agency in 1868 (three of the four brothers were lynched by a gang of vigilantes who attacked the jail where they were being held before trial).[8]

To read about the colorful history of the Pinkerton detectives, go to their website: **http://www.pinkerton.com/history/.** **Would you consider the early Pinkerton detectives bounty hunters?**

Train robbery flourished toward the end of the nineteenth century because professional robbers considered trains easy pickings.[9] Law enforcement was decentralized, and robbers could escape over the border to a neighboring state to avoid detection. Security arrangements were minimal, and robbers could stop, board, and loot trains with little fear of capture. As the threat to trains increased, improvements were initiated in an effort to deter would-be robbers:

- Plainclothes officers were placed on trains and rode unobtrusively among the passengers.
- Baggage cars were equipped with ramps and stalls containing fleet horses that could be used to immediately pursue bandits.
- Cars were made with finer precision and strength to make them impregnable.
- Forensic science made it easier to identify robbers, and improved communication made it easier to capture them.

Federal involvement in train protection extended the ability of law enforcement beyond the county or state in which the robbery occurred. As a result of these innovations, the number of train robberies decreased from 29 in 1900 to 7 in 1905; by 1920, train robbers had all but disappeared.[10]

Safecracking Secured boxes and safes have existed for centuries, but it wasn't until early in the twentieth century that use of cast iron became widespread and was used to create solid metal boxes. Safecracking also underwent a dramatic change due to technological changes in the design of safes. In the early 1900s, safes were made of manganese steel because it was resistant to drilling and was fireproof. With the invention and distribution of acetylene torches in the latter part of the nineteenth century, safes constructed of manganese became vulnerable and encouraged safecrackers to commit bold crimes. Safe manufacturers fought back by constructing safes with alternating sheets of copper and steel. The copper diffused heat and made the safe resistant to being torched. In response, safecrackers shifted their approach to attacking safes' locks and locking mechanisms. They developed mechanical devices that either dismantled or destroyed locks. Some burglars developed methods of peeling the laminated layers of the safe apart.

After World War II, safecrackers began using carbide and then diamond drill bits, which tore through metal. Safe manufacturers responded by lining safes with new

smugglers Thieves who move freely in sparsely populated areas and transport goods, such as spirits, gems, gold, and spices, without bothering to pay tax or duty.

poachers Early English thieves who typically lived in the country and supplemented their diet and income with game that belonged to a landlord.

metals designed to chip or break drill bits. They also developed sophisticated security systems featuring light beams, which would trip an alarm if the beam was interrupted by an intruder. When thieves learned how to neutralize these alarms, motion detectors and ultrasonic systems were implemented, which fill the space with sound waves and set off alarms when they are disturbed. Though these systems can be defeated, it requires expensive electronic gear, which most criminals can neither afford nor operate. As a result, the number of safecrackers has declined, and the crime of safecracking is relatively rare.[11]

Contemporary Theft

L02 Compare and contrast professional and amateur thieves

Theft is still a popular criminal pastime, and millions of property and theft-related crimes occur each year. Most are committed by **occasional criminals** who do not define themselves by a criminal role or view themselves as committed career criminals; other theft-offenders are in fact skilled **professional criminals**. The following sections review these two orientations toward property crime.

OCCASIONAL THIEVES

Occasional offenders are not professional criminals; they do not make theft their occupation. Many are school-age youths who are unlikely to enter into a criminal career and whose behavior has been described as drifting between conventional and criminal. Added to the pool of amateur thieves are adults who may occasionally violate the criminal law—shoplifters, pilferers, petty thieves—but whose main source of income comes from conventional means and whose self-identity is not criminal. Added together, their behaviors form the bulk of theft crimes.

When amateurs decide to steal, their decision is spontaneous and based on **situational inducements**, short-term influences on a person's behavior that increase risk taking.[12] They include psychological factors, such as an immediate and unsolvable financial problem, and social factors, such as peer pressure to commit a spontaneous criminal act— taking a car for a drunken joyride or breaking into a store or home.

---

occasional criminals Offenders who do not define themselves by a criminal role or view themselves as committed career criminals.

professional criminals Offenders who make a significant portion of their income from crime.

situational inducement Short-term influence on a person's behavior, such as financial problems or peer pressure, that increases risk taking.

While members of every layer of the economy may at some time experience a situational inducement, the opportunity to solve economic crisis through criminal activity is structured by class. While the poor are forced to engage in low-profit, high-risk crimes, members of the upper class have the opportunity to engage in the more lucrative business-related crimes of price fixing, bribery, and embezzlement.

Unlike professionals, occasional thieves do not receive informal peer group support for their crimes. In fact, they will deny any connection to a criminal lifestyle and instead view their transgressions as being "out of character." They may see their crimes as being motivated by necessity. When apprehended, they say they were only "borrowing" the car the police caught them with; they were going to pay for the merchandise they stole from the store, they just "forgot" to go through the checkout line. Because of their lack of commitment to a criminal lifestyle, occasional offenders may be the most likely to respond to the general deterrent effect of the law.

PROFESSIONAL THIEVES

In contrast to occasional thieves, professional criminals make a significant portion of their income from crime. Professionals do not delude themselves with the belief that their acts are impulsive, one-time efforts, nor do they employ elaborate rationalizations to excuse the harmfulness of their action ("shoplifting doesn't really hurt anyone"). Consequently, professionals pursue their craft with vigor, attempting to learn from older, experienced criminals the techniques that will earn them the most money with the least risk. Though their numbers are relatively few, professionals engage in crimes that produce the greater losses to society and perhaps cause the more significant social harm.

Professional theft traditionally refers to nonviolent forms of criminal behavior that are undertaken with a high degree of skill for monetary gain and that exploit interests tending to maximize financial opportunities and minimize the possibilities of apprehension. The most typical forms include pickpocketing, burglary, shoplifting, forgery and counterfeiting, extortion, sneak theft, and confidence swindling.[13]

Relatively little is known about the career patterns of professional thieves and criminals. From the literature on crime and delinquency, three patterns emerge:

- Youth come under the influence of older, experienced criminals who teach them the trade.
- Juvenile gang members continue their illegal activities at a time when most of their peers have dropped out to marry, raise families, and take conventional jobs.
- Youth sent to prison for minor offenses learn the techniques of crime from more experienced thieves.

In a classic work, *Box Man: A Professional Thief's Journey*, Harry King, a professional thief, relates this story to criminologist William Chambliss about his entry into crime after being placed in a shelter-care home by his recently divorced mother:

> It was while I was at this parental school that I learned that some of the kids had been committed there by the court for stealing bikes. They taught me how to steal and where to steal them and where to sell them. Incidentally, some of the "nicer people" were the ones who bought bikes from the kids. They would dismantle the bike and use the parts: the wheels, chains, handlebars, and so forth.[14]

Here we can see how would-be criminals may be encouraged in their illegal activities by so-called honest people who are willing to buy stolen merchandise and gain from criminal enterprise.

There is some debate in the criminological literature over who may be defined as a professional criminal. In his classic works, Edwin Sutherland used the term to refer only to thieves who do not use force or physical violence in their crimes and who live solely by their wits and skill.[15] It is more common today for criminologists to use the term to refer to any criminal who identifies with a criminal subculture, who makes the bulk of his or her living from crime, and who possesses a degree of skill in his or her chosen trade.[16] Thus, one can become a professional safecracker, burglar, car thief, or fence. Some criminologists would not consider drug addicts who steal to support their habit as professionals; they lack skill and therefore are amateur opportunists rather than professional technicians. However, some professional criminals take drugs without losing their lofty status in the criminal hierarchy.

Becoming a Professional Thief   What we know about the lives of professional criminals has come to us through their journals, diaries, autobiographies, and the first-person accounts they have given to criminologists. The best-known account of professional theft is the life of Chic Conwell, in Edwin Sutherland's classic book *The Professional Thief*.[17] Conwell and Sutherland's concept of professional theft has two critical dimensions.

First, professional thieves engage in limited types of crime, which are described in Exhibit 12.1.[18] Professionals depend solely on their wit and skill. Thieves who use force or commit crimes that require little expertise are not considered worthy of the title "professional." Their areas of activity include "heavy rackets," such as bank robbery, car theft, burglary, and safecracking. You can see that Conwell and Sutherland's criteria for professionalism are weighted heavily toward con games and trickery and give little attention to common street crimes.

You can read selections from *The Professional Thief* on Google Books: http://books.google.com/books/about/The_professional_thief.html?id=G9nBxdMR4IAC.

Do books and stories like this glamorize crime and make it seem daring and appealing?

EXHIBIT 12.1

Sutherland's Typology of Professional Thieves

- Pickpocket (cannon)
- Thief in rackets related to confidence games
- Forger
- Extortionist from those engaging in illegal acts (shakedown artist)
- Confidence game artist (con artist)
- Thief who steals from hotel rooms (hotel prowl)
- Jewel thief who substitutes fake gems for real ones (pennyweighter)
- Shoplifter (booster)
- Sneak thief from stores, banks, and offices (heel)

SOURCE: Chic Conwell, *The Professional Thief*, ed. Edwin Sutherland (Chicago: University of Chicago Press, 1937).

The second requirement of professional theft is the exclusive use of wits, "front" (a believable demeanor), and talking ability. Manual dexterity and physical force are of little importance. Professional thieves must acquire status in their profession. Status is based on their technical skill, financial standing, connections, power, dress, manners, and wide knowledge base. In their world, "thief" is a title worn with pride. Conwell and Sutherland also argue that professional thieves share common feelings, sentiments, and behaviors. Of these, none is more important than the code of honor of the underworld; even under the threat of the most severe punishment, a professional thief must never inform (squeal) on his or her fellows. Sutherland and Conwell view professional theft as an occupation with much the same internal organization as that characterizing such legitimate professions as advertising, teaching, or police work. They conclude:

> A person can be a professional thief only if he is recognized and received as such by other professional thieves. Professional theft is a group way of life. One can get into the group and remain in it only by the consent of those previously in the group. Recognition as a professional thief by other professional thieves is the absolutely necessary, universal, and definitive characteristic of the professional thief.[19]

The following sections describe two types of professional thieves: fences and cargo thieves.

THE FENCE

L03   Comment on the activities of a professional fence

Some experts have argued that Sutherland's view of the professional thief may be outdated because modern thieves often work alone, are not part of a criminal subculture, and were not tutored early in their careers by other criminals.[20] However, some important research efforts show that the principles set down by Sutherland still have value for understanding the behavior of one contemporary criminal type—the fence, who earns his or her living solely by buying and reselling stolen merchandise. The fence's critical role in criminal transactions has been recognized since the eighteenth century.[21] They act as middlemen who purchase stolen merchandise—ranging from diamonds to auto hubcaps—and resell them to merchants who market them to legitimate customers.[22]

Much of what we know about fences comes from relatively few in-depth studies of the lives and activities of these specialized professional criminals. Carl Klockars examined the life and times of one successful fence who used the alias Vincent Swaggi. Through 400 hours of listening to and observing Swaggi, Klockars found that this highly professional criminal had developed techniques that made him almost immune to prosecution. During the course of a long and profitable career in crime, Swaggi spent only four months in prison. He stayed in business, in part, because of his sophisticated knowledge of the law of stolen property. To convict someone of receiving stolen goods, the prosecution must prove that the accused was in possession of the goods and knew that they had been stolen. Swaggi had the skills to make sure that these elements could never be proved. Also helping Swaggi stay out of the law's grasp were the close working associations he maintained with society's upper classes, including influential members of the justice system. Swaggi helped them purchase stolen items at below-cost, bargain prices. He also helped authorities recover stolen goods and therefore remained in their good graces. Klockars's work strongly suggests that fences customarily cheat their thief-clients and at the same time cooperate with the law.

Sam Goodman, a fence interviewed by sociologist Darrell Steffensmeier, lived in a world similar to Vincent Swaggi's. He also purchased stolen goods from a wide variety of thieves and suppliers, including burglars, drug addicts, shoplifters, dockworkers, and truck drivers. According to Goodman, to be successful, a fence must meet the following conditions:

- *Upfront cash.* All deals are cash transactions, so an adequate supply of ready cash must always be on hand.
- *Knowledge of dealing—learning the ropes.* The fence must be schooled in the knowledge of the trade, including developing a "larceny sense"; learning to "buy right" at acceptable prices; being able to "cover one's back" and not get caught; finding out how to make the right contacts; and knowing how to "wheel and deal" and how to create opportunities for profit.
- *Connections with suppliers of stolen goods.* The successful fence must be able to engage in long-term relationships with suppliers of high-value stolen goods who are relatively free of police interference. The warehouse worker

who pilfers is a better supplier than the narcotics addict, who is more likely to be apprehended and talk to the police.
- *Connections with buyers.* The successful fence must have continuing access to buyers of stolen merchandise who are inaccessible to the common thief. They must make contacts with local pawnshops and other distributors of secondhand goods and be able to move their material without drawing attention from the authorities.[23] Some sell stolen cigarettes to local convenience stores, while others restock pharmacies with goods taken by shoplifters from the same store. Ecommerce sites such as eBay are an alternative way of moving merchandise.
- *Complicity with law enforcers.* The fence must work out a relationship with law enforcement officials who invariably find out about the fence's operations. Steffensmeier found that to stay in business the fence must either bribe officials with good deals on merchandise and cash payments or act as an informer who helps police recover particularly important merchandise and arrest thieves.

Sam had a strong commitment to crime throughout the course of his life. The height of his personal commitment to crime was during the middle phase of his career when he was a "big, wide-open" fence. Nonetheless, his favorable attitudes toward crime and other criminals endured into the later "moonlighting" phase of his career when he was less involved in crime. At that point, he also developed more positive attitudes toward legitimate people and associations (such as his employees and legitimate antique dealers). Furthermore, the moonlighting phase of his career saw some changes in Sam's self-definition, as reflected in this assessment in the final weeks of his life:

I never cared how the cops saw me but I wanted the public to see me in a different light. Not as a guy who did time, not as a burglar, not even as a fence, but as a businessman. As a good Joe. In that way I knew what I done was wrong. . . . If they saw me as a crook, that I could handle. But not a [expletive] bum. I wanted the people to respect me as me. As a businessman taking care of business in my shop.

Deviants, even persistent criminals, are seldom deviant in all or even most aspects of their lives. Sam comfortably rubbed shoulders with thieves, gamblers, and quasi-legitimate businessmen but also courted respectability and pledged allegiance to some major normative standards. Sam was unapologetic about his criminal career. While he realized that his behavior may have violated the law, he took pride in the way he conducted himself and did business, as these deathbed comments illustrate:

I do not feel sad about my life. I did what I thought I had to do at the time. But I would not wish my life on somebody else. I made that very goddamn plain to your students—a life in crime can be a bitch. . . . I done wrong, pulled some very rank shit. But helped a whole lot of people, too. If somebody needed something, came into my shop, I more or less gave it away. Anyone that worked for me, I dealt with fairly. Got paid a good dollar and helped them out in little ways.[24]

Fences handle a tremendous variety of products, including televisions, cigarettes, stereo equipment, watches, autos, and cameras.[25] In dealing their merchandise, they operate through many legitimate fronts, including art dealers, antique stores, furniture and appliance retailers, remodeling companies, salvage companies, trucking companies, and jewelry stores.

In the Internet age, some fences have begun to sell their merchandise online on a variety of merchandising websites. Recent surveys estimate that one-third of auction and blog sites' listings for "new in box" or "new with tags" items are actually goods that were stolen through organized retail theft. E-fencers like to sell, at a discount, small items in bulk—razor blades, makeup, skincare products, baby formula, over-the-counter medications, and tooth-whitening strips—as well as more expensive items—digital cameras, electric shavers, and disposable cell phones—that can bring bigger online profits.[26]

When deciding what to pay the thief for goods, the fence uses a complex pricing policy: professional thieves who steal high-priced items are usually given the highest amounts—about 30 to 50 percent of the wholesale price. An item valued at $5,000 may be bought for $1,500. However, the amateur thief or drug addict who is not in a good bargaining position may receive only 10 cents on the dollar.

Fencing seems to contain many of the elements of professional theft as described by Sutherland: fences live by their wits, never engage in violence, depend on their skill in negotiating, maintain community standing based on connections and power, and share the sentiments and behaviors of their fellows. The only divergence between Sutherland's thief and the fence is the code of honor; it seems likely that the fence is much more willing to cooperate with authorities than most other professional criminals.

The Occasional Fence Professional fences have attracted the attention of criminologists, but like other forms of theft, fencing is not dominated solely by professional criminals. A significant portion of all fencing is performed by amateur or occasional criminals. Novice burglars, such as juveniles and drug addicts, often find it so difficult to establish relationships with professional fences that they turn instead to nonprofessionals to unload the stolen goods.[27]

One type of occasional fence is the part-timer who, unlike professional fences, has other sources of income. Part-timers are often "legitimate" businesspeople who integrate the stolen merchandise into their regular stock. A rental store manager who buys stolen merchandise and rents it along with his legitimate merchandise is a part-time fence. An added benefit of the illegitimate part of his work is the profit he makes on these stolen items, which is not reported for tax purposes.

Some merchants become actively involved in theft either by specifying the merchandise they want the burglars to steal or by "fingering" victims. Some businesspeople sell merchandise and then describe the customers' homes and vacation plans to known burglars so they can steal it back!

- *Associational fences* are amateur fences who barter stolen goods for services. These amateurs typically have legitimate professional dealings with known criminals such as bail bond agents, police officers, and attorneys. A lawyer may demand an expensive watch from a client in exchange for legal services. Bartering for stolen merchandise avoids taxes and becomes a transaction in the underground economy.
- *Neighborhood hustlers* buy and sell stolen property as one of the many ways they make a living. They keep some of the booty for themselves and sell the rest in the neighborhood. These dealmakers are familiar figures to neighborhood burglars looking to get some quick cash by selling them stolen merchandise.
- *Amateur receivers* can be complete strangers approached in a public place by someone offering a great deal on valuable commodities. It is unlikely that anyone buying a $2,000 home theater system for $500 cash would not suspect that it may have been stolen. Some amateur receivers make a habit of buying suspect merchandise at reasonable prices from a "trusted friend," establishing an ongoing relationship. This practice encourages crime because the criminals know that there will always be someone to buy their merchandise. In addition to the professional fence, the nonprofessional fence may account for a great deal of criminal receiving. Both professional and amateur thieves have a niche in the crime universe.

PROFESSIONAL CARGO THIEVES

Some professionals work in highly organized groups, targeting specific items and employing "specialists" who bring a different set of criminal skills to the table. Take for example professional cargo thieves, whose bases of operations are truck yards, hubs for commercial freight carriers, airports, and port cities. These thieves prey upon the huge fleet of cargo ships, planes, and trucks that bring in a daily array of valuable cargoes. While other thieves target cash and jewels, these professionals make off with frozen shrimp, clothing, and electronic goods. Their criminal activities cost the public billions of dollars each year. Cargo thieves use sophisticated operations with well-organized hierarchies of leadership. They employ specialists who carry out a variety of tasks, including thieves and brokers or fences who help unload the stolen goods on the black market. "Lumpers" physically move the goods and work with drivers in transporting the stolen merchandise from the docks.

Gangs usually employ a specialist who is an expert at foiling the antitheft locks on truck trailers. Cargo thieves heist whole truckloads of merchandise—the average freight on a trailer can be valued at up to $3 million.[28]

Criminologists and legal scholars recognize that common theft offenses fall into several categories linked together because they involve the intentional misappropriation of property for personal gain. In fencing, goods are bought from another who is in illegal possession of those goods. In the case of embezzlement, burglary, and larceny, the property is taken through stealth. In other kinds of theft, such as bad checks, fraud, and false pretenses, goods are obtained through deception. Some of the major categories of common theft offenses are discussed in the next sections in some detail.

Larceny/Theft

It was called the "body snatchers case." New York City detectives uncovered a scheme being run by a former Manhattan dentist named Michael Mastromarino, who had lost his practice and money because of a substance abuse addiction.

Fraud, a wrongful or criminal deception intended to result in illegal financial or personal gain, is a type of larceny. Celia Mitchell, a self-professed psychic, was convicted of grand larceny after a client who had spent $159,205 for her services filed a criminal complaint. At her hearing, Mitchell admitted she had no fortunetelling skills. "It was just going by what they would give you. It's all a scam."

Needing capital to maintain his lifestyle, he and three other men set up a body harvesting scheme, looting bones and tissue from more than a thousand corpses sent to a Brooklyn funeral home. The men then sold the body parts to legitimate companies that supplied hospitals around the United States. They forged death certificates to hide the fact that the donors were too old or sick to be used for medical purposes or when relatives refused to donate their loved ones' body parts. Hundreds of people in states as far away as Florida, Nebraska, and Texas received tissue and bone carved from looted corpses. The tissue was used in such procedures as joint and heart-valve replacements, back surgery, dental implants, and skin grafts; a single harvested body yielded $7,000 in parts. Some patients suffered severe infection, septic shock, and even paralysis due to having received an implant made from infected cadaver tissue from Mastromarino's company. After his arrest, Mastromarino was charged with, among other crimes, grand larceny vis-à-vis his body snatching.[29] He died in prison from bone cancer in 2013.

The body snatcher's case illustrates the wide variety of schemes that make up the crime of larceny: taking the possessions of another; in this case, the possessions were bodily organs and the victims were dead! Larceny/theft was one of the earliest common-law crimes created by English judges to define acts in which one person took for his or her own use the property of another.[30] According to common law, larceny was defined as "the trespassory taking and carrying away of the personal property of another with intent to steal."[31] Most state jurisdictions have incorporated the common-law crime of larceny in their legal codes. Today, definitions of larceny often include such familiar acts as shoplifting, passing bad checks, and other theft offenses that do not involve using force or threats on the victim (robbery) or forcibly breaking into a person's home or place of work (burglary).

When it was originally construed, larceny involved taking property that was in the possession of the rightful owners. For example, it would have been considered larceny for someone to go secretly into a farmer's field and steal a cow. Thus, the original common-law definition required a "trespass in the taking"; this meant that for an act to be considered larceny, goods must have been taken from the physical possession of the rightful owner. In creating this definition of larceny, English judges were more concerned with people disturbing the peace than they were with thefts. If someone tried to steal property from another's possession, they reasoned that the act could eventually lead to a physical confrontation and possibly the death of one party or the other, thereby disturbing the peace. Consequently, the original definition of larceny did not include crimes in which the thief had come into possession of the stolen property by trickery or deceit. It was therefore not considered larceny if someone entrusted with another person's property decided to keep it for themselves.

The growth of manufacturing and the development of the free enterprise system required greater protection for private property. The pursuit of commercial enterprise often required that one person's legal property be entrusted to a second party; therefore larceny evolved to include the theft of goods that had come into the thief's possession through legitimate means.

To get around the element of "trespass in the taking," English judges created the concept of **constructive possession**. This legal fiction applied to situations in which persons voluntarily and temporarily gave up custody of their property but still believed the property was legally theirs. If a person gave a jeweler her watch for repair, she would still believe she owned the watch even though she had handed it over to the jeweler. Similarly, when a person misplaces his wallet and someone else finds it and keeps it—although identification of the owner can be plainly seen—the concept of constructive possession makes the person who has kept the wallet guilty of larceny.

LARCENY TODAY

LO4 Differentiate between petty and grand larceny

Most U.S. state criminal codes separate larceny into **petit (petty) larceny** and **grand larceny**. The former involves small amounts of money or property and is punished as a misdemeanor. Grand larceny, involving merchandise of greater value, is a felony punished by a sentence in the state prison. Each state sets its own boundary between grand larceny and petty larceny. For example, in the Virginia Criminal Code the main distinction between petit and grand larceny is the value of the item taken: larceny of an item with a value of $200 or more is considered grand larceny, while taking something with a value of less than $200 is considered petit larceny. In Virginia, how the larceny is committed may affect its definition. For example, while grand larceny generally requires theft of property valued at more than $200, if the money or property is taken directly *from a person*, then anything over $5 is considered grand larceny; taking money or property with a value of less than $5 from a person is petit larceny. Taking a firearm from a home or car is automatically considered grand larceny.[32]

How larceny is categorized can have a significant influence on the level of punishment. Looking at Virginia again as an example, grand larceny is a felony with a specific punishment of not less than one year in prison but not more than 20, or at the discretion of a jury (or judge) trying the case, it can also be punished with a jail sentence of not more than 12 months and/or a fine not to exceed $2,500. In contrast, petit larceny is a class 1 misdemeanor punishable by up to 12 months in jail and/or a fine of up to $2,500.[33] In New York State, the cutoff is $1,000; there are different classes of grand larceny, the most serious being theft over $1,000,000.[34]

Larceny/theft is probably the most common criminal offense. According to the FBI, slightly less than 6 million larcenies are reported to the police annually, a rate of about 1,800 per 100,000 population.[35] The larceny rates have declined by about 20 percent during the past decade. The average value of property taken during larceny/thefts is now about $1,000 per offense. When the average value is applied to the estimated number of larceny/thefts, the loss to victims nationally is about $5.5 billion. Thefts of motor vehicle parts, accessories, and contents make up the largest portion of reported larcenies, almost 25 percent.

There are many different varieties of larceny. Most involve small items of little value. Many of these go unreported, however, especially if the victims were business owners who do not want to take the time to get involved with police. They simply write off the losses as part of doing business. Hotel owners estimate that guests filch millions a year in towels, bathrobes, ashtrays, bedspreads, showerheads, flatware, and even television sets and wall paintings.[36]

SHOPLIFTING

When it comes to shoplifting, Sameh Khaled Danhach knew how to run a serious and sophisticated operation.[37] Danhach employed teams who targeted major U.S. retail stores and pharmacies, walking out with stolen products of all kinds, from medicine and baby formula to beauty supplies. Team members received a small percentage of the actual value of the stolen property, always in cash so there'd be no paper trail. The shoplifting team then shipped the merchandise back to Danhach's warehouse using phony accounts with bogus business names, email addresses, and credit cards. Once the stolen merchandise was in Danhach's possession, he would have his people remove antitheft devices and store stickers, and then he would ship the goods to various wholesalers, who in some cases sold them right back to the companies from which they had been stolen. Danhach's scheme involved an estimated $10 million worth of products that were swiped *every year* from 2008 to 2012. To make matters worse, many of the goods—compromised by being stored and shipped under improper conditions and some sold past their expiration dates—eventually were resold to unsuspecting consumers.[38]

Though the Danhach gang's shoplifting scheme was unusual because of its scope and magnitude, **shoplifting**—the taking of goods from retail stores—is one of the most common form of larceny/theft. Usually shoplifters try to

---

constructive possession In the crime of larceny, willingly giving up temporary physical possession of property but retaining legal ownership.

petit (petty) larceny Theft of a small amount of money or property, punished as a misdemeanor.

grand larceny Theft of money or property of substantial value, punished as a felony.

shoplifting The taking of goods from retail stores.

snatch items—jewelry, clothes, or small electronics—when store personnel are otherwise occupied, hiding the goods on their person.

The "five-finger discount" is not a recent phenomenon and there are cases as early as the seventeenth century. Shoplifting became a common criminal act when London and Paris became mercantile centers in the nineteenth century. Consumers flocked to department stores such as Harrods and Le Bon Marché where they were left to shop on their own without a clerk keeping watch. Goods that were displayed to encourage buying inadvertently encouraged theft.[39] In a famous historical incident, in August 1799, Mrs. Jane Leigh-Perrot, the aunt of author Jane Austen, was arrested for theft, accused of stealing a length of lace from a local store. Though she insisted that it was a mistake, Leigh-Perrot was held in confinement for eight months in the home of the local jailer until her trial, where she was found not guilty. At the time the alleged shoplifting took place, theft of any item worth five shillings or more was punishable by hanging or, as was more likely in her case, deportation to Australia for 14 years.[40]

Extent of Shoplifting   Of the 6 million larcenies recorded each year by the UCR, about 20 percent or 1.2 million are shoplifting incidents; about 250,000 shoplifting arrests occur on an annual basis. Of course, not every shoplifting incident is reported to police nor is every shoplifter caught by store security staff arrested. Most are handled informally, their name kept on file; many are told never to return to the store. Hayes International, a loss prevention/shrinkage control consulting business, does an annual survey of major retailers around the United States. The 25 major retailers (with about 23,000 stores and over $700 billion in retail sales) they surveyed reported apprehending 1,192,194 shoplifters in 2014, up 7 percent from 2013. Over $159 million was recovered from apprehended shoplifters, an increase of 7.5 percent from 2013. An additional $82 million was recovered from shoplifters where no apprehension was made, up 15 percent from the prior year.[41] Hayes estimates that shoplifting results in a total of retail losses of approximately $44 billion annually, accounting for 30 to 40 percent of total retail shrink/losses.

Retail security measures add to the already high cost of this crime, all of which is passed on to the consumer. Some studies estimate that about one in every nine shoppers steals from department stores. Moreover, the increasingly popular discount stores, such as Costco, Walmart, and Target, have a minimum of sales help and depend on highly visible merchandise displays to attract purchasers, all of which makes them particularly vulnerable to shoplifters.

snitches Amateur shoplifters who do not self-identify as thieves but who systematically steal merchandise for personal use.

L05 Compare professional and amateur shoplifters

Shoplifters: Amateurs and Professionals   In a now classic study, Mary Owen Cameron found that the majority of shoplifters are amateur pilferers, called **snitches** in thieves' argot.[42] Snitches are usually respectable people who do not conceive of themselves as thieves but are systematic shoplifters who steal merchandise for their own use. Some snitches are simply overcome by an uncontrollable urge to snatch something that attracts them, while others arrive at the store intending to steal. Some adolescents become shoplifters because they have been coerced by older kids into becoming "proxy shoplifters," forced to steal goods with the understanding that if caught their youth will protect them from prosecution.[43]

When caught, they may try to rationalize or neutralize their behavior. When Paul Cromwell and Quint Thurman interviewed 137 apprehended shoplifters, they found widespread use of techniques of neutralizations—statements such as "I don't know what comes over me. It's like, you know, it's somebody else doing it, not me" (denial of responsibility) or "I like to get nice stuff for my kids, you know. I know it's not O.K., you know what I mean? But I want my kids to dress nice and stuff" (appeal to higher loyalties).[44]

If they are not professionals and want to deny their culpability, why do they steal? Some are impulsive sensation seekers who are driven to shoplift by their psychological need to live on the edge.[45] Others are motivated by rational choice and the desire to get something for nothing. Still another motivation for shoplifting seems to be psychological distress; some amateur shoplifters are looking for a release from anxiety and depression.[46] Another type of snitch needs to get quick cash to feed a drug habit. Research shows that products that serve a role in illicit drug use are actually the ones most often stolen from retail stores.[47] Both male and female drug users report that shoplifting is a form of work which helps support their habits, preferable and less dangerous than robbery for men and sex work for women.[48]

Regardless of their motives, snitches are likely to reform if caught because they are not part of a criminal subculture and do not think of themselves as criminals. Cameron reasoned that they are deterred by an initial contact with the law. Getting arrested has a traumatic effect on them, and they will not risk a second offense.

Professional Shoplifters   Professional shoplifters can walk into a department store, fill up a cart with expensive medicines, smart phones, tablets, and other high-cost items, and use deceptive techniques to slip past security guards. Hitting several stores in a day and the same store once a month, a professional thief can make between $100,000 and $200,000 a year.

Pros wear or carry devices and implements that help them avoid detection while shoplifting. They place a large open shopping bag obtained from another store, name prominently displayed, on the floor by their feet and casually drop in merchandise. They use a **booster box**, a device with a false bottom that can be opened and closed by the operator. The boxes are lined with metal or some other substance to prevent security tags from setting off alarms. The box is placed over merchandise, the bottom opened and then closed, capturing the goods.

A professional female shoplifter will stroll into a store with a baby carriage accompanied by a friend wearing maternity clothes. Carriages are useful because no one wants to disturb a sleeping baby wrapped in blankets, which of course can also be used to hide stolen merchandise. And who would suspect a visibly pregnant woman, even though the expandable outfit is perfect for stuffing in high-priced merchandise and walking casually out the door?

Pros will later sell the merchandise in their own discount stores, at flea markets, or through online auctions. Some sell to fences who repackage—or "scrub"—the goods and pawn them off on retailers at prices that undercut legitimate distributors. Ironically, some stolen merchandise can actually make its way back onto the shelves of the chain store from which it was stolen.[49] In her pioneering study, Mary Owen Cameron found that about 10 percent of all shoplifters were professionals, called boosters, or heels. Professional shoplifters steal with the intention of reselling stolen merchandise to pawnshops or fences, usually at half the original price.

Controlling Shoplifting

One major problem associated with combating shoplifting is that many customers who observe pilferage are reluctant to report it to security agents. Store employees themselves are often loathe to get involved in apprehending a shoplifter. It is also likely that a store owner's decision to prosecute shoplifters will be based on the value of the goods stolen, the nature of the goods stolen, and the manner in which the theft was realized. Shoplifters who planned their crime by using a concealed apparatus, such as a bag pinned to the inside of their clothing, are more apt to be prosecuted than those who impulsively put merchandise into their pockets.[50] The concealment indicates that the crime was premeditated and not a spur of the moment loss of control.

To encourage the arrest of shoplifters, a number of states have passed *merchant privilege laws* designed to protect retailers and their employers from litigation stemming from improper or false arrests of suspected shoplifters. These laws protect but do not immunize merchants from lawsuits. They typically require that arrests be made on reasonable grounds or probable cause, detention be of short duration, and store employees or security guards conduct themselves in a reasonable fashion.

Prevention Strategies

Retail stores initiate a number of strategies designed to reduce or eliminate shoplifting. **Target removal strategies** involve putting dummy or disabled goods on display while the real merchandise is kept under lock and key. Audio equipment with missing parts is displayed, and only after items are purchased are the necessary components installed. Some stores sell from a catalogue while keeping merchandise in stockrooms.

Target hardening strategies involve locking goods in place or having them monitored by electronic systems. Clothing stores may use racks designed to prevent large quantities of garments from being slipped off easily. Store owners may rely on electronic article surveillance (EAS) systems, featuring tags with small electronic sensors that trip sound and light alarms if not removed by employees before the item leaves the store. Security systems now feature source tagging, a process by which manufacturers embed the tag in the packaging or in the product itself. Thieves are hard-pressed to remove or defeat such tags, and retailers save on the time and labor needed to attach the tags at their stores.[51] Situational measures place the most valuable goods in the least vulnerable places, use warning signs to deter potential thieves, and use closed-circuit cameras.

Another approach to shoplifting prevention is to create specialized programs that use methods such as doing community service, paying monetary restitution, writing essays, watching anti-shoplifting videos, writing apology letters, and being placed in individual and/or family counseling. Evaluations indicate that such programs can be successful in reducing recidivism of young shoplifters.[52]

Overzealous Enforcement These methods may control shoplifting, but stores must be wary of becoming overzealous in their enforcement policies. Those falsely accused have won significant judgments in civil actions.[53] In one case, a woman accused of shoplifting at a JCPenney store in Media, Pennsylvania, was awarded $250,000, charging them with false confinement and malicious prosecution after she was mistakenly taken for a shoplifter.[54] In 2013, a Portland, Oregon, woman won a $67,000 judgment from Walgreens after an assistant store manager's accusations that the woman shoplifted makeup prompted a police investigation.[55]

Stores may be liable if security guards use excessive force when subduing a suspected shoplifter. There is also the danger of profiling based on gender, age, or racial and ethnic background, resulting in customers being targeted, detained, and searched for inappropriate reasons.[56] And of

booster box Device with a false bottom that can be opened and closed by a professional shoplifter, lined with metal or some other substance to prevent security tags from setting off alarms, placed over merchandise.

target removal strategies Displaying dummy or disabled goods as a means of preventing shoplifting.

target hardening strategies Making one's home or business crime proof through the use of locks, bars, alarms, and other devices.

course, searching and detaining customers based on stereotyping is legally indefensible: in one case, eight African American plaintiffs sued the Dillard's department store chain, claiming that employees and security workers questioned them while they were shopping in the stores and accused them of stealing merchandise, solely based on their race. In a separate case, Dillard's was ordered to pay a $1.2 million verdict to an African American woman who was detained on suspicion of shoplifting in a store in Overland Park, Kansas.[57]

BAD CHECKS

Another form of larceny is cashing bad bank checks, knowingly and intentionally drawn on a nonexistent or underfunded bank account, to obtain money or property. In general, for a person to be guilty of passing a bad check, the bank the check is drawn on must refuse payment, and the check casher must fail to make the check good within 10 days after finding out the check was not honored.

More than 60 years ago, Edwin Lemert conducted the best-known study of check forgers.[58] The majority of check forgers—**naive check forgers**—are amateurs who do not believe their actions will hurt anyone. Most naive check forgers come from middle-class backgrounds and have little identification with a criminal subculture. They cash bad checks because of a financial crisis that demands an immediate resolution—perhaps they have lost money at the horse track and have some pressing bills to pay. Lemert refers to this condition as **closure**. Naive check forgers are often socially isolated people who have been unsuccessful in their personal relationships. They are risk prone when faced with a situation that is unusually stressful for them. The willingness of stores and other commercial establishments to cash checks with a minimum of fuss to promote business encourages the check forger to risk committing a criminal act.

Not all check forgers are amateurs. Lemert found that a few professionals—whom he calls **systematic forgers**—make a substantial living by passing bad checks. However, professionals constitute a relatively small segment of the total population of check forgers. It is difficult to estimate the number of such forgeries committed each year or the

---

---

amounts involved. Stores and banks may choose not to press charges because the effort to collect the money due them is often not worth their while. It is also difficult to separate the true check forger from the neglectful shopper.

Some of the different techniques used in check fraud schemes, which may cost retail establishment upward of $1 billion per year, are set out in Exhibit 12.2.

CREDIT CARD THEFT

In 2013, ten individuals, including Babar Qureshi, Ijaz Butt, and Khawaja Ikram, were indicted in one of the largest credit card fraud schemes in the nation's history. The charges involved a plot to fabricate more than 7,000 false identities to obtain tens of thousands of credit cards and steal more than $200 million. The conspiracy involved a three-step process. First, the defendants made up a false identity by

---

naive check forgers Amateurs who cash bad checks because of some financial crisis but have little identification with a criminal subculture.

closure A term used by Lemert to describe a condition in which people from a middle-class background who have little identification with a criminal subculture cash bad checks because of a financial crisis that demands an immediate resolution.

systematic forgers Professionals who make a living by passing bad checks.

---

creating fraudulent identification documents and a fraudulent credit profile with the major credit bureaus. Then they
pumped up the credit of the false identity by providing false
information about that identity's creditworthiness to those
credit bureaus. Finally, they borrowed or spent as much as
they could, based on the phony credit history, but did not
repay the debts. The scope of the criminal fraud enterprise
required the conspirators to construct an elaborate network
of false identities. Across the country, the conspirators maintained more than 1,800 "drop addresses," including houses,
apartments, and post office boxes, which they used as the
mailing addresses for the false identities.[59]

This criminal conspiracy is by no means unique nor
is the elaborate planning and technical knowhow needed
to bring it off that unusual. Another similar scam, involving conspirators in Estonia, Ukraine, China, and Belarus,
stole 40 million credit and debit card numbers from companies such as Marshall's, T.J.Maxx, BJ's Wholesale Club,
OfficeMax, and Barnes and Noble by hacking into their
computer systems and installing "sniffer" programs designed
to capture credit card numbers, passwords, and account
information as they moved through the retailers' card processing networks. The thieves then concealed the data in
encrypted computer servers they controlled in the United
States and eastern Europe. Some of the credit and debit card
numbers were "cashed out" by encoding the numbers on
the magnetic strips of blank cards and using these cards to
withdraw tens of thousands of dollars at a time from automatic teller machines (ATMs). A card stolen in Amsterdam
could be used to make bogus online purchases in Prague
within hours.[60]

The use of stolen credit cards is a major problem in U.S.
society. It has been estimated that fraud has been responsible for a billion-dollar loss in the credit card industry. Most
credit card abuse is the work of amateurs who acquire stolen cards through theft or mugging and then use them for
two or three days. However, professional credit card rings
such as those described previously are getting into the act.
They collect or buy from employees the names and credit
card numbers of customers in retail establishments; then
they buy plain plastic cards and have the customers' numbers embossed on them. They create fictitious wholesale
companies and apply for and receive authorization to accept
credit cards from the customers. They then use the phony
cards to charge nonexistent purchases on the accounts of
the people whose names and card numbers they collected.
One approach is to first obtain the victim's address and card
number from a confederate (e.g., a store employee where
the victim shops). They may then call the victim, claiming
to be from the credit card company, and informing them
that their account has been flagged because of suspicious
activity. After offering credentials such as a bogus badge ID
number, the thief tells them that someone has used the card
to purchase a $1,500 television from a local store. When
the consumer denies making the purchase, the scammer
explains that he is starting a fraud investigation, gives the

CONNECTIONS

Similar credit card frauds are conducted over the Internet.
These will be discussed in Chapter 15.

ASK YOURSELF . . .

While some people refuse to give card information online or
on the phone, is that actually more risky than handing a waiter
your card in a restaurant?

consumer a "confirmation" number, and asks them for
the three-digit security number on the back of the card. The
security code allows the thief to make purchases over the
Internet or from local merchants.[61]

To combat losses from credit card theft, Congress passed
a law in 1971 limiting a person's liability to $50 per sto-
len card. Some states, such as California, have passed specific statutes making it a misdemeanor to obtain property
or services by means of cards that have been stolen, forged,
canceled, or revoked, or whose use is for any reason unauthorized.[62]

The most recent attempt to use technology to combat
credit card fraud is called EMV, for Europay, MasterCard,
and Visa. Cards are embedded with a microchip containing data that had previously been stored in the card's magnetic strip. The chip works with point-of-sale readers that
process payment transactions in a secure manner using
encryption. The chip is aimed at reducing fraud because
it contains a cryptographic key that authenticates the card
and generates a one-time code with each transaction. This
means thieves are prevented from using stolen account
numbers and embossing them onto the magnetic strip of
a random card or programming them onto the chip of a
random chip card.[63] It remains to be seen whether microchip technology can reduce credit card fraud or whether
high-tech thieves will discover ways to defeat the new
systems.

AUTO THEFT

Motor vehicle theft is another common larceny offense.
Because of its frequency and seriousness, it is treated as a
separate category in the Uniform Crime Report (UCR).
The FBI now records slightly less than 700,000 yearly auto
thefts, accounting for a total loss of $4.5 billion. Like other
crimes, there has been a significant reduction in motor vehicle theft rates over the past decade, and the number of car
thefts has declined more than 40 percent. UCR projections
on auto theft are similar to the projections of the National
Crime Victim Survey (NCVS), probably because almost
every state requires owners to insure their vehicles, and auto
theft is one of the most highly reported of all major crimes
(75 percent of all auto thefts are reported to police).

Carjacking is a particularly scary crime. A surveillance video shows carjacker Ryan Stone, 29, forcing a woman from her car, which he then stole and drove off on March 12, 2014, in Lone Tree, Colorado. Suspected of stealing an SUV with a 4-year-old boy inside, carjacking two other vehicles, and seriously injuring a state trooper, Stone was arrested after police tracked him, and at times chased him, around the Denver area during morning rush hour.

To read more about car theft, go to the National Insurance Crime Bureau (NICB) website at **https://www.nicb.org/.**

Has your car ever been stolen? If not, what do you do to prevent that from happening?

Which cars are stolen most often? According to the National Insurance Crime Bureau (NICB), the 10 most stolen vehicles in the United States in a single year (2014) include the following:

1.	Honda Accord	(53,995)
2.	Honda Civic	(45,001)
3.	Chevrolet Pickup (full size)	(27,809)
4.	Ford Pickup (full size)	(26,494)
5.	Toyota Camry	(14,420)
6.	Dodge Pickup (full size)	(11,347)
7.	Dodge Caravan	(10,911)
8.	Jeep Cherokee/Grand Cherokee	(9,272)
9.	Toyota Corolla	(9,010)
10.	Nissan Altima	(8,892)

Why these models? Many cars are stolen and then stripped for parts. Thieves target vehicles that can bring them the greatest return in the used-part market. The NICB found that older Honda Accords and Civics were by far the most stolen models.[64]

Amateur Auto Thieves

Amateur thieves steal cars for a number of reasons that involve some form of temporary personal use.[65] Among the reasons why an amateur would steal a car include:

- *Joyriding.* Many car thefts are motivated by teenagers' desire to acquire the power, prestige, sexual potency, and recognition associated with an automobile. Joyriders steal cars not for profit or gain but to experience, even briefly, the benefits associated with owning an automobile.
- *Short-term transportation.* Auto theft for short-term transportation is similar to joyriding. It involves the theft of a car simply to go from one place to another. In more serious cases, the thief may drive to another city or state and then steal another car to continue the journey.
- *Long-term transportation.* Thieves who steal cars for long-term transportation intend to keep the cars for their personal use. Usually older than joyriders and from a lower-class background, these auto thieves may repaint and otherwise disguise cars to avoid detection.
- *Profit.* Auto theft for profit is motivated by the hope of monetary gain. Some amateurs hope to sell the entire car, but most are auto strippers who steal batteries, tires, and wheel covers to sell or to reequip their own cars.
- *Commission of another crime.* A few auto thieves steal cars to use in other crimes, such as robberies and thefts. This type of auto thief desires both mobility and anonymity.

Professional Car Thieves At one time, most auto theft was the work of amateurs, and most cars were taken by relatively affluent, middle-class teenagers looking for excitement.[66] There appears to be a change in this pattern: fewer cars are being taken today, and fewer stolen cars are being recovered. Part of the reason is that there has been an increase in highly organized professionals who resell expensive cars after altering their identification numbers and falsifying their registration papers. Exporting stolen vehicles has become a global problem, and the emergence of capitalism in eastern Europe has increased the demand for U.S.-made cars.

Many cars are now stolen in order to be sold to chop shops for spare parts. Among the most attractive targets are these parts:

- *Global positioning system.* It now costs approximately $950 to replace one on a Mercedes. The whole unit for a Honda Odyssey can cost up to $1,200, navigation included.
- *Air conditioning.* Today, the air-conditioning compressor for a Toyota Camry costs up to $1,000. One for a Ford goes between $500 and $1,000.
- *Air bags.* These lifesavers do well in the auto-part seller's market. Air bags go for about $200.
- *Exhaust.* The exhaust system carries emissions from the engine to the atmosphere. An overall exhaust system—including catalytic converter in some vehicles—can range up to $2,800 for a BMW M1.[67]

Car Cloning   One form of professional auto theft is called "cloning." After stealing a luxury car from a mall or parking lot, car thieves later visit a large car dealership in another state and look for a car that's the exact make and model (and even the same color) of the stolen one. The thieves jot down the vehicle identification number (VIN) stamped on the top of the dashboard and drive off. The manufacturer-installed VIN plate on the stolen car is removed and replaced with a homemade counterfeit, similar to the original, only this one bears the VIN of the legitimate vehicle. Phony ownership and registration documents complete the cloning. At that point, the stolen vehicle can be easily registered with a motor vehicle agency in another state and sold to an unwary buyer. In one Tampa, Florida, case, more than 1,000 cloned cars were sold to buyers in 20 states and several countries, with estimated losses of more than $25 million to consumers, auto insurers, and other victims.[68]

Carjacking   You may have read the awful account of a young attorney, Justin Friedland, shot to death in 2013 by carjackers as he and his wife were Christmas shopping at the Mall at Short Hills in Millburn, New Jersey. Friedland, 30, was killed by two men after they approached him and his wife in the parking deck and tried to enter his car with his wife was in the front seat. Friedland's wife managed to escape the vehicle unharmed, but he was killed.[69] This type of auto theft is so common that it has its own name, **carjacking**. Carjacking is legally considered a type of robbery because it involves force to steal.[70]

Both victims and offenders in carjackings tend to be young men. Urban residents are more likely to experience carjacking than suburban or rural residents. About half of all carjackings are typically committed by gangs or groups. These crimes are most likely to occur in the evening, in the central city, in an open area, or in a parking garage. This pattern may reflect the fact that carjacking seems to be a crime of opportunity; it is the culmination of the carjacker's personal needs and desires coinciding with the immediate opportunity for gain.[71]

Weapons, most often guns, are used in about three-quarters of all carjacking victimizations.[72] Despite the presence of weapons, victims resist the offender in two-thirds of carjackings, and, not surprisingly, about one-third of victims of completed carjackings and about 20 percent of victims of attempted carjackings are injured. Serious injuries, such as gunshot or knife wounds, broken bones, or internal injuries, occur in about 10 percent of carjackings. More minor injuries, such as bruises and chipped teeth, occurred in about 15 percent of cases.

Combating Auto Theft   Auto theft is a significant target of situational crime prevention efforts. One approach to theft deterrence has been to increase the risks of apprehension. Hotlines offer rewards for information leading to the arrest of car thieves. Another approach has been to place fluorescent decals on windows that indicate that the car is never used between 1 A.M. and 5 A.M.; if police spot a car with the decal being operated during this period, they know it is stolen.[73]

Highly sophisticated tracking and security systems may also be deterring car thieves from stealing newer model cars. OnStar, a car safety device, provides a navigation system that can be used to track and disable stolen vehicles from afar through tracking and remote ignition blocking.[74] The LoJack system involves installing a hidden tracking device in cars that gives off a signal, enabling the police to pinpoint its location.[75] LoJack therefore has the advantage of tracking cars in some places GPS systems are ineffective. LoJack units are tied to a car's vehicle identification number, so when a car is reported stolen and the VIN is entered into the state police crime computer, it automatically triggers the LoJack unit in the vehicle.

Because car thieves cannot tell that LoJack has been installed, it does not reduce the likelihood that a protected car will be stolen. However, cars installed with LoJack have a much higher recovery rate. There may also be a general deterrent effect: areas with high rates of LoJack use experience significant reductions in their auto theft rates. Ironically, LoJack owners actually accrue a smaller than anticipated reward for their foresight than the general public because they have to pay for installation and maintenance of the device. Those without it actually gain more because they benefit from a lower auto theft rate in their community without paying any additional cost.

Other prevention efforts involve making it more difficult to steal cars. Take the VINshield program. Every vehicle has its own unique vehicle identification number (VIN) located on the dashboard, where it's viewable through the car's windshield and where it can be covered up by thieves. The VINshield program enables owners to etch the VIN number on all the car's windows, making it difficult and expensive to sell the car off for parts.[76]

Publicity campaigns have been directed at encouraging people to lock their cars. Parking lots have been equipped with theft-deterring closed-circuit TV cameras and barriers.

carjacking Theft of a car by force or threat of force.

Jason Martinez, a U.S. Marshals assistant program manager with the Asset Forfeiture Division, shows one of more than 500 bottles of counterfeit and unsellable wine being prepped for destruction at the Texas Disposal Systems recycling and compost facility in Austin. The wine was seized from Rudy Kurniawan, who was convicted of fraud in federal court for producing and selling millions of dollars' worth of counterfeit wine. A raid on his home turned up thousands of empty bottles, corks, fake labels, sealing wax, and other evidence of a wine-counterfeiting operation.

In 1757, the English Parliament defined false pretenses to cover an area of law left untouched by larceny statutes. The first false pretenses law punished people who "knowingly and designedly by false pretense or pretenses, [obtained] from any person or persons, money, goods, wares or merchandise with intent to cheat or defraud any person or persons of the same."[79]

False pretense differs from traditional larceny because the victims willingly give their possessions to the offender, and the crime does not, as does larceny, involve a "trespass in the taking." An example of false pretenses would be an unscrupulous merchant selling someone a chair by claiming it was an antique, but knowing all the while that it was a cheap copy. Another example would be a phony healer selling a victim a bottle of colored sugar water as an elixir that would cure a disease.

Swindlers have little shame when defrauding people out of their money; they often target the elderly, sick, and infirm. In the aftermath of Hurricane Katrina, in 2005, swindlers used the tragedy to solicit relief funds from charitable and well-meaning people and then converted the money for their own usage.[80] About 140,000 people are arrested for fraud schemes each year, though that is probably only the tip of the iceberg.[81]

Manufacturers have installed more sophisticated steering column locking devices and other security systems that make theft more difficult.

The most effective methods appear to be devices that immobilize a vehicle by cutting off the electrical power needed to start the engine when a theft is detected. However, car thieves with modest resources—just a few hundred dollars in off-the-shelf equipment—and some computer knowledge can crack the codes of millions of car keys and compromise these security systems.[77]

FALSE PRETENSES/FRAUD

The crime of **false pretenses**, or fraud, involves misrepresenting a fact in a way that causes a victim to willingly give his or her property to the wrongdoer, who then keeps it.[78]

false pretenses (fraud) Misrepresenting a fact in a way that causes a deceived victim to give money or property to the offender.

mark The target of a con man or woman.

confidence (con) game A swindle, usually involving a get-rich-quick scheme, often with illegal overtones, so that the victim will be afraid or embarrassed to call the police.

pigeon drop A con game in which a package or wallet containing money is "found" by a con man or woman, and the victims are bilked out of money they are asked to put up as collateral.

CONFIDENCE GAMES

Some fraudulent schemes involve getting a **mark** (target) interested in some get-rich-quick scheme, which may have illegal overtones; this is known as a **confidence (con) game**. The criminal's hope is that when victims lose their money, they will be either too embarrassed or too afraid to call the police. There are hundreds of varieties of con games, but the most common is called the **pigeon drop**.[82] Here, a package or shopping bag containing money is "found" by a con man or woman. A passing victim is stopped and asked for advice about what to do since there is no identification. Another "stranger," who is part of the con, approaches and enters the discussion. The three decide to split the money, but first, to make sure everything is legal, one of the swindlers goes off to consult a lawyer. Upon returning, he or she says that the lawyer claims the money can be split up; first, however, each party must prove he or she is financially stable or has the means to reimburse the original owner, should one show up. The victim then is asked to give some good-faith money for the lawyer to hold. Later, when the victim goes to the lawyer's office to pick up a share of the loot, he or she finds the address bogus and the money gone.

Other cons include:

- A self-proclaimed "contractor" offers an unusually low price for an expensive job such as driveway repair and then uses old motor oil rather than asphalt to make the "repairs." The first rain brings disaster. Some cons offer a free home inspection that turns up several expensive repairs. They then offer a cheap rate to fix the problem, but of course the repairs are actually bogus.
- A business office receives a mailing that looks like an invoice with a self-addressed envelope that makes it look like it comes from the phone company (walking fingers on a yellow background). It appears to be a contract for an ad in the Yellow Pages. On the back, in small print, will be written, "By returning this confirmation, you're signing a contract to be an advertiser in the upcoming, and all subsequent, issues." If the invoice is returned, the business soon finds that it has agreed to a long-term contract to advertise in some private publication that is not widely distributed.
- Con artists read the obituary column and then send a surviving spouse bills supposedly owed by the person deceased. Or they deliver an item, such as a Bible, that they say the deceased relative ordered just before he died.
- A con artist, posing as a bank employee, stops a customer as he or she is about to enter the bank. The con man claims to be an investigator who is trying to catch a dishonest teller. He asks the customer to withdraw cash to see if he or she gets the right amount. After the cash is withdrawn, the con man asks that it be turned over to him so he can check the serial numbers and promises to return the cash in a few minutes, gives the customer a receipt, and escapes through a back exit.
- An old musician carrying his violin enters a restaurant and orders an expensive meal. When asked to pay he claims that he left his wallet at home. He begs the owner to be allowed to retrieve his money and leaves his violin as collateral. While he's gone, another man presents himself to the owner as a rare instrument dealer—he has a personal business card. He wants to have a look at the violin he saw in passing, and as soon as it's produced, he claims it is a valuable antique, perhaps a Stradivarius worth hundreds of thousands of dollars! He asks the owner to give the old violinist his business card as soon as he returns. The old violinist returns and the business owner offers him $1,000 for his violin. While the old man seems clueless, he asks for more and they settle on a price of $5,000. He walks out with the money, and when the owner calls the number on the card, ready to resell, he finds out it's a false number. The old man and the "dealer" meet up later, split the cash, and buy another $50 violin. Hence the expression "fiddling around."

Third-Party Fraud   In some instances of false pretenses, the "victim" is a third party, such as an insurance company forced to pay for false claims or the people who have to pay higher claims because of the swindle. Cheating on an entrance exam may be considered third-party fraud because the victims are people who took the test honestly and received lower grades. One example of an innovative third-party cheating scheme was instituted by a man named Po Chieng Ma, who conspired to sell answers to the Graduate Management Administration Test (GMAT), the Graduate Record Examinations (GRE), and the Test of English as a Foreign Language (TOEFL) to an estimated 788 customers, each of whom had paid him between $2,000 and $9,000. In the scheme, people were paid to take the multiple-choice tests in Manhattan and then call California, where the same tests were to be given, with the answers. The answers were passed on to Ma, who, taking advantage of the three-hour time difference, carved the answers in code on the sides of pencils, which were then given to his customers. Ma pleaded guilty to conspiracy and obstruction of justice and received a four-year prison term for his efforts. In this case, there were many victims, including the testing service, universities, and the students who lost places in school because those who inflated their scores through the scheme were admitted instead.[83]

Auto Accident Fraud   Another common scheme involves fake auto accidents, including the ones described below:

- *The "swoop and squat."* A driver is stuck in heavy traffic on a busy highway. A confederate cuts off the driver in front, forcing him or her to slam on the brakes, resulting in a rear-end collision. After the "accident," everyone in the damaged car files bogus injury claims with the driver's insurance company. They may even go to crooked physical therapists, chiropractors, lawyers, or auto repair technicians to further exaggerate their claims.
- *The drive down.* A driver is attempting to merge into a traffic lane. Suddenly, another driver waves her forward, indicating he will allow her to merge. Instead of letting her in, he slams into the car, causing an accident. When the police arrive, the "injured" driver denies ever motioning, claims serious injury, and files an insurance claim with the victim's company.
- *The sideswipe.* As a driver rounds a corner at a busy intersection with multiple turn lanes, the driver drifts slightly into the next lane. The car in that lane, waiting for such an opportunity, steps on the gas and sideswipes the driver, producing an accident.
- *The t-bone.* A driver is crossing an intersection when a car coming from a side street accelerates and hits the car. When the police arrive, the driver and several planted "witnesses" claim that the driver ran a red light or stop sign.[84]

How common are such fraudulent schemes? Staged accidents cost the insurance industry about $20 billion a year. Some experts estimate that about one-third of auto insurance claims are either fraudulent or contain some form of misinformation.[85]

EMBEZZLEMENT

L06 Explain the concept of embezzlement

A decade ago, Reverend Willard Leonard Jones had the idea to build a community center not far from his church in a disadvantaged West Tulsa neighborhood called South Haven. The center would bring health care, a food and clothing bank, and other resources to the community. As the executive director of the Greater Cornerstone Community Development Project, Jones solicited donations from foundations, corporations, churches, and individuals—and raised about $7 million to help the community. Despite his promises, Jones used approximately $933,000 of community center money for his personal benefit—to pay his mortgage, buy luxury items like a Rolex watch, and to live a lavish lifestyle that included gambling and expensive hotel accommodations. After an investigation turned up the missing funds, Jones admitted that from 2007 to 2013 he embezzled the church's money and also failed to report nearly $400,000 to the IRS. He was sentenced to 37 months in prison for his crimes.[86]

Embezzlement occurs when someone who is trusted with property fraudulently converts it—that is, keeps it for his or her own use or the use of others. It can be distinguished from fraud on the basis of when the criminal intent was formed. Most U.S. courts require that a serious breach of trust must have occurred before a person can be convicted of embezzlement. The mere act of moving property without the owner's consent, or damaging it or using it, is not considered embezzlement. However, using it up, selling it, pledging it, giving it away, or holding it against the owner's will is considered to be embezzlement.

Embezzlement is not a recent crime phenomenon. It was mentioned in early Greek culture when, in his writings, Aristotle alluded to theft by road commissioners and other government officials.[87] It was first codified in law by the English Parliament during the sixteenth century to fill a gap in the larceny law.[88] Until then, to be guilty of theft, a person had to take goods from the physical possession of another (trespass in the taking). However, as explained earlier, this definition did not cover instances in which one person trusted another and willfully gave that person temporary custody of his or her property. Store clerks, bank tellers, brokers, and merchants gain lawful possession but not legal ownership of other people's money.

Although it is impossible to know how many embezzlement incidents occur annually, the 16,000 people arrested for embezzlement in 2014 is probably an extremely small percentage of all embezzlers.

Want to avoid credit card theft? The Federal Trade Commission has some important tips: **http://www.consumer.ftc.gov/articles/0216 -protecting-against-credit-card-fraud.**

Do you think that limiting personal liability on credit cards discourages people from taking special care to protect their cards?

Burglary

In common law, the crime of burglary is defined as "the breaking and entering of a dwelling house of another in the nighttime with the intent to commit a felony within."[89] Burglary is considered a much more serious crime than larceny/theft because it often involves entering another's home, a situation in which the threat of harm to occupants is great. Even though the home may be unoccupied at the time of the burglary, the potential for harm to the occupants is so significant that most state jurisdictions punish burglary as a felony.

The legal definition of burglary has undergone considerable change since its common-law origins. When first created by English judges during the late Middle Ages, laws against burglary were designed to protect people whose homes might be set upon by wandering criminals. Including the phrase "breaking and entering" in the definition protected people from unwarranted intrusions; if an invited guest stole something, it would not be considered a burglary. Similarly, the requirement that the crime be committed at nighttime was added because evening was considered the time when honest people might fall prey to criminals.[90]

In more recent times, state jurisdictions have changed the legal requirements of burglary, and most have discarded the necessity of a nighttime forced entry into a dwelling house. Nor does a burglary have to involve theft; the purpose of the crime could be to attack the occupant or damage their property. The Criminology in Action feature "Sexual Burglary" describes some burglaries that are not motivated by financial needs.

It is common for penal codes to recognize different degrees of burglary. Such issues as being armed, whether force was used, and whether the structure was a home or business can affect the level of crime seriousness and consequently the punishment attached to the crime. Typically, the more serious and severely punished burglaries involve a

---

embezzlement A type of larceny that involves taking the possessions of another (fraudulent conversion) that have been placed in the thief's lawful possession for safekeeping, such as a bank teller misappropriating deposits or a stockbroker making off with a customer's account.

Sexual Burglary

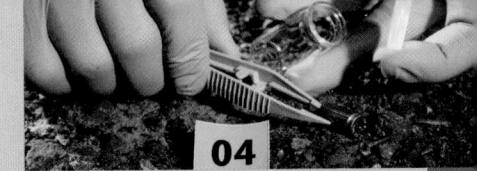

04

Some burglaries have a sexual motivation, while others involve sexual attacks that, though unplanned, occur when the burglar finds the residence unexpectedly occupied. To investigate this type of burglary, Amélie Pedneault, Danielle Harris, and Raymond Knight used a sample of 224 specific incidents of burglary that had evident sexual components. Sexual components were identified through offending behaviors, considering the nature of the property stolen (e.g., underwear) or the nature of the offender's actions (e.g., voyeurism, rape). The 224 burglaries were committed by 104 offenders sent to the Massachusetts Treatment Center for Sexually Dangerous Persons. The analysis showed that burglaries with a sexual component can be divided into three types.

Fetishistic Noncontact Burglaries

These burglaries typically occur in unoccupied houses and involve fetishistic behavior but no theft, violence, or weapon. This type of sexual burglary is motivated to fulfill a sexual fantasy but involves neither victim contact nor material gain. The covert type involves voyeurism (e.g., breaking and entering to see a woman getting undressed or showering). In contrast, the overt fetishistic burglary is motivated by sexual fantasies and typically involves breaking and entering into homes to steal objects with a sexually arousing value for the burglar (e.g., female underwear or accessories such as handbags or shoes);

neither type involves sexual contact with a victim.

Example: The offender was peeping through a house window at night. He illegally entered the house by forcing the lock and watched the female occupant undress and go to sleep. He then proceeded to steal a suitcase that he filled with the occupant's underwear before leaving.

Versatile Contact Burglaries

These burglaries are characterized by rapes occurring in homes and involving theft, violence, and weapons. An example of this type of burglary is an offender who, while burglarizing a residence he thought was unoccupied, finds a woman at home alone. The characteristics that render a residence at risk for burglary are the same characteristics as those that render the female occupant at greater risk for rape; isolation, easy access, and time were all considerations of the perpetrators of burglaries and rapes in residences.

Example: The offender entered the female victim's apartment by breaking a rear window at 1 A.M. while the victim was sleeping. The offender awoke the victim by leaning on her and threatened her with a knife. The victim struggled with the offender, which resulted in a deep laceration to her hand. The offender pushed the victim to the floor where he vaginally raped her while repeatedly threatening and hitting her. When he was done, the offender ransacked the apartment and left with money, jewelry, and electronic goods.

Sexually Oriented Contact Burglaries

In this type of sexually oriented burglary, the criminal rapes the victim at home, but these incidents rarely involve theft, violence, or weapons. This "home intruder rapist" uses breaking and entering primarily to gain access to his rape victim. These rapists appeared to be less concerned with the victim and more focused on the residence in their selection. More than half of serial rapists use breaking and entering to access their victim, without giving thought to material gain. These burglaries appear to have been perpetrated with the unique goal of gaining access to a sexual victim (with violence and theft being infrequent).

Example: At 2:30 A.M., the offender illegally entered an apartment occupied by a female and her child. The offender awoke the female occupant and vaginally raped her, forcing her compliance by threatening to harm her child. When he was done, the offender left without stealing anything.

CRITICAL THINKING

Does the fact that burglars seek out specific targets for specific needs indicate that burglary is a rational crime, rather than a spontaneous event committed by occasional criminals?

SOURCE: Amélie Pedneault, Danielle Harris, and Raymond A. Knight, "Toward a Typology of Sexual Burglary: Latent Class Findings," *Journal of Criminal Justice* 40 (2012): 278–284.

---

forced entry by an armed burglar into a home; the least serious an unforced entry into a nonresidential structure by an unarmed offender. Several gradations of the offense may be found between these extremes.

L07 Describe the elements of sexual burglary

THE NATURE AND EXTENT OF BURGLARY

According to the UCR, about 1.7 million burglaries occur annually; the NCVS reports that about 3 million residential burglaries are either attempted or completed annually. Both the UCR and NCVS estimate that burglaries have declined by about 20 percent during the past decade.

Most burglaries occur during daylight hours in residential structures (about two-thirds). The homes most likely to be burglarized are occupied by relatively poor Hispanic and African American families. Rural owner-occupied and single-family residences have lower burglary rates than urban, renter-occupied, and multiple-family dwellings. Households in the northeast are less likely to experience burglary than households in other regions of the country.

Gender Differences in Burglary

Does gender play a role in shaping burglary careers? Are there differences in the way professional male and female burglars approach their craft? Do gender roles influence the burglar lifestyle? To find out, Christopher Mullins and Richard Wright used interviews with 18 active female burglars and 36 males, matched approximately for age. Their findings indicate that significant gender-based differences exist in the way males and females begin and end their offending careers and how they carry out their criminal tasks.

There are similarities in the way most offenders, male or female, were initiated into residential burglary. Burglars of both genders became involved via interaction in intimate groups, such as older friends, family members, or street associates. One told how they got started in burglary:

> [M]e and my brother, we wanted, you know, he came and got me and say he know where a house at to break into. And, uhm, we go there and uh, we just do it . . . me and my brother, he and some more friends.

But there was one key difference between the male and female offenders: the men typically became involved in burglary with male peers; women more often were introduced to crime by their boyfriends. Males are more likely to bring their male peers and family members into their offending networks and resist working with women except their girlfriend or female relative. And when they do include women, they put them in a subservient role, such as a lookout.

Why do they get involved in a burglary career in the first place? Both males and females generally said they got involved in break-ins to finance a party lifestyle centered on drug use and to buy designer clothing and flashy jewelry. There were some differences: males reportedly wanted money to pursue sexual conquests; female burglars were far more likely to say that they needed money to buy necessities for their children.

When asked what they were looking for in a prospective residential burglary target, the male and female offenders expressed similar preferences; both wanted to find a dwelling that was (a) unoccupied and (b) contained something of value. Both the men and the women wanted to know something about the people who lived in the residence, be familiar with their day-to-day routine, and have an idea of the target's valuables. Male offenders used their legitimate jobs as home remodelers, cable television installers, or gardeners to scout potential burglary targets. Female burglars who lacked legitimate entry had to rely on information generated by the men in their immediate criminal social network. Some used sexual attraction to gain the victim's confidence and gather information.

Mullins and Wright also found that men preferred to commit residential burglaries by themselves, while women most often worked with others. Males seemed unwilling to trust accomplices and were also unwilling to share the proceeds. Females, on the other hand, reported that they lacked the knowledge or skills needed to break into a dwelling on their own and were therefore more willing to work with a team.

Finally, when asked what it would take to make them stop committing crime, both male and female offenders claimed that a good job that paid well and involved little or no disciplined subordination to authority would be required to get them to give up their careers in crime. Men also claimed they would probably give up burglary once they settled down and started a family. Because they were dependent on male help, female burglars needed to sever their relationships with criminally involved males in order to reduce their offending. Female burglars were also more sensitive than the males to shaming and ostracism at the hands of their relatives and might quit under family pressure.

Mullins and Wright found that residential burglary is a significantly gender-stratified offense; the processes of initiation, commission, and potential desistance are heavily structured by gender. Women have to negotiate the male-dominated world of burglary to accomplish their crimes. Gender, they found, plays a significant role in shaping opportunity (such as initiation) and the events leading up to residential burglaries (for example, information gathering), while playing a lesser but still important role in molding actual offense commission.

CRITICAL THINKING

1. Do the gender differences in burglary reflect the gender differences found in other segments of society?
2. Do you think gender discrimination helps reduce the female crime rate? If gender equality were achieved, would differences in the crime rate narrow?

SOURCE: Christopher Mullins and Richard Wright, "Gender, Social Networks, and Residential Burglary," *Criminology* 41 (2003): 813–839.

The UCR tells us that most people arrested for burglary are adults (80 percent), white (67 percent), and male (80 percent). While most burglars are male, about 25,000 women are arrested for burglary annually. What motivates female burglars, and how do they differ from males? These are the topics of the Race, Culture, Gender, and Criminology feature.

RESIDENTIAL BURGLARIES

About 75 percent of all burglaries involve entering a home or residence. Some residential burglars are crude thieves who will smash a window and enter a home or structure with minimal preparation; others plan out a strategy. In urban areas and their immediate suburbs, experienced burglars learn to avoid areas of the city in which most residents are renters and not homeowners, reasoning that renters are less likely to be suitable targets than are more affluent homeowners.[91]

Experienced residential burglars also learn that if they want to operate in daylight they have to be careful of their target choice. If they want to break into a home in an upscale neighborhood during the day, they'd better choose one that is set back from the street, providing better cover for their forced entry.

They may want to assess security measures. While at first they may believe they can defeat any alarm system, if they continue to fail they may either give up on burglary or move to a less well-guarded location.[92]

Social factors may also condition residential burglary planning. When unemployment rates increase, home guardianship does also because unemployed people are home during the workday protecting their possessions.[93]

Homeowners in affluent neighborhoods have higher employment levels, so daylight burglaries are a safer and more lucrative bet in wealthier communities. After dark, the patterns seem to change—burglars who operate at night may shift their targets to apartments and townhouses closer to home even though the risk of someone being home is greater.[94]

In a classic work, Frank Hoheimer, an experienced professional burglar, described how he learned the "craft of burglary" from a fellow inmate, Oklahoma Smith, when the two were serving time in the Illinois State Penitentiary. Among Smith's recommendations are these:

> Never wear deodorant or shaving lotion; the strange scent might wake someone up. The more people there are in a house, the safer you are. If someone hears you moving around, they will think it's someone else . . . If they call, answer in a muffled sleepy voice . . . Never be afraid of dogs, they can sense fear. Most dogs are friendly, snap your finger, they come right to you.[95]

Despite his elaborate preparations, Hoheimer spent many years in confinement.

Repeat Burglary   Residential burglars often attack the same target more than once. The reasons burglars like to return to the scene of the crime include the following:

- It takes less effort to burgle a home or apartment known to be a suitable target than an unknown or unsuitable one.
- The burglar is already aware of the target's layout.

An Ethical Dilemma

Rational Choice

You are a criminology professor at a local college. You are approached by the police chief, who is quite concerned about high burglary rates in some areas of the city. She is a former student of yours and well aware of recent developments in criminological theory. The chief is a strong advocate of rational choice theory and has already instituted a number of programs based on a deterrence/situational crime prevention model of control. The existing police initiatives include these programs:

- The police offer target-hardening measures to repeat victims. They install high-tech security equipment in homes so the homes can be monitored on a 24-hour basis. The police plan an advertising campaign to alert would-be offenders that they are on watch at prior target residences.
- A new police initiative identifies repeat burglars in the area and provides intervention designed to supply them with legitimate economic opportunities to reduce their criminal motivation.
- A new school-based program designed to reduce criminal motivation seeks to raise young people's awareness of the dangers of burglary and how it can result in a long prison sentence.
- The police have developed a series of environmental improvements in the target area with a view to minimizing burglary opportunities. These include improved visibility, better access control, and lighting in areas that have relatively high burglary rates. They have also instituted high-visibility police patrols in these areas to deter criminals from committing crimes there.
- A burglary control model house, fitted with low-cost methods of security such as strengthened door/window frames, bolts, locks, and so on, has been built and will be advertised to encourage residents to help themselves avoid burglary.

The chief has asked you to look over these initiatives and write a memo discussing their effectiveness. She wants you to develop a policy plan discussing whether you think there are any possible ethical pitfalls with these initiatives. If you do find problems, she wants you to suggest other policy initiatives that might prove effective in reducing the opportunity to commit burglary and deter potential burglars.

- The ease of entry of the target has probably not changed, and escape routes are known.
- The lack of protective measures and the absence of nosy and intrusive neighbors that made the first burglary a success have probably not changed.

- Goods have been observed that could not be taken out the first time.[96]
- Burgled items are often considered indispensable (e.g., televisions) and therefore are quickly replaced; burglars return to steal these newer replacement goods.[97]

COMMERCIAL BURGLARY

Some burglars prefer to victimize commercial property rather than private homes where occupants may be home, carry weapons, and under new "stand your ground" laws might be willing to shoot to protect their property. In states where "stand your ground" laws have been passed, some burglars seem willing to switch their targets from residential to commercial properties, while others may be deterred from committing future burglaries.[98]

Of all business establishments, retail stores are burglars' favorite targets. They display merchandise so that burglars know exactly what to look for, where it can be found, and—because the prices are displayed—how much they can hope to gain in resale to a fence. Burglars can legitimately enter a retail store during business hours and gain knowledge about what the store contains and where it is stored; they can also check for security alarms and devices. Commercial burglars perceive retail establishments as quick sources of merchandise that can be easily sold.

Other commercial establishments such as service centers, warehouses, and factories are less attractive targets because it is more difficult to gain legitimate access to plan the theft. The burglar must use a great deal of guile to scope out these places, perhaps posing as a delivery person. In addition, the merchandise is more likely to be used, and it may be more difficult to fence at a premium price.

If burglars choose to attack factories, warehouses, or service centers, the most vulnerable properties are those located far from major thoroughfares and away from pedestrian traffic. Establishments located within three blocks of heavily traveled thoroughfares have been found to be less vulnerable to burglary than those located farther away; commercial establishments in wealthier communities have a higher probability of burglary.[99]

Though alarms have been found to be an effective deterrent to burglary, they are less effective in isolated areas because it takes police longer to respond than on more heavily patrolled thoroughfares, and an alarm is less likely to be heard by a pedestrian who would be able to call for help. Even in the most remote areas, however, burglars are wary of alarms and try to choose targets without elaborate or effective security systems. One study found that the probability of burglary of non-alarmed properties is 4.57 times higher than that of similar properties with alarms.[100]

CAREERS IN BURGLARY

When Debbie Baskin and Ira Sommers evaluated the impact of forensic evidence on criminal case outcomes, they found that despite great technological strides in the collection of forensic evidence only about 12 percent of more than 1,000 burglaries they studied resulted in arrest and 3 percent resulted in a conviction.[101] One reason why burglars are rarely caught and punished is because they learn from experience and become good at their trade. Some make burglary their career and continually develop new and specialized skills to aid their profession. They learn to spot targets that contain valuables worth stealing and those that are most likely to prove to be a dry hole. Burglars avoid student-occupied apartments realizing their occupants have little worth stealing and target those whose residents are more affluent.[102]

Whether they operate alone or in groups, experienced burglars like to choose targets in neighborhoods they know so they can make their way home undetected if things go awry.[103] They avoid difficult and well-guarded targets with security gates.[104] While most prefer to burglarize in their own neighborhood where escape routes are well known, some are willing to travel farther to commit crimes when there are good roadways and getting around is easy.[105] And while security guards may deter some burglars, alarms and other devices designed to protect homes may actually have an opposite effect on a savvy burglar: why have an alarm unless there was something worth taking inside?[106]

There have been a number of important studies of the "burglary career" and these are described next.

L09 Know what it takes to be a "good burglar"

The Good Burglar In a now classic study, Neal Shover reviewed the careers of professional burglars and uncovered the existence of a particularly successful type, which he labels the "**good burglar**."[107] Professional burglars use this title to characterize colleagues who have distinguished themselves as burglars. Characteristics of the good burglar include:

CONNECTIONS

Chapter 1 mentioned "stand your ground" laws as an example of the evolution of the criminal law.

ASK YOURSELF . . .

Is the shift from residential to commercial burglary in "stand your ground" states a good example of the displacement effect discussed in Chapter 4?

---

good burglar Professional burglars use this title to characterize colleagues who have distinguished themselves as burglars. Characteristics of the good burglar include technical competence, maintenance of personal integrity, specialization in burglary, financial success, and the ability to avoid prison sentences.

- Technical competence
- Maintenance of personal integrity
- Specialization in burglary
- Financial success
- The ability to avoid prison sentences

Shover found that to receive recognition as good burglars novices must develop four key requirements of the trade. First, they must learn the many skills needed to commit lucrative burglaries. This process may include learning how to gain entry into homes and apartment houses; how to select targets with high potential payoffs; how to choose items with a high resale value; how to open safes properly, without damaging their contents; and how to use the proper equipment, including cutting torches, electric saws, explosives, and metal bars.

Second, the good burglar must be able to team up to form a criminal gang. Choosing trustworthy companions is essential if the obstacles to completing a successful job—police, alarms, and secure safes—are to be overcome.

Third, the good burglar must have inside information. Without knowledge of what awaits them inside, burglars can spend a tremendous amount of time and effort on empty safes and jewelry boxes.

Finally, the good burglar must cultivate fences or buyers for stolen wares. Once the burglar gains access to people who buy and sell stolen goods, he or she must also learn how to successfully sell these goods for a reasonable profit. Evidence of these skills was discovered in a study of more than 200 career burglars in Australia. Burglars reported that they had developed a number of relatively safe methods for disposing of their loot. Some traded stolen goods directly for drugs; others used fences, legitimate businesses, pawnbrokers, and secondhand dealers as trading partners. Surprisingly, many sold their illegal gains to family or friends. Burglars report that disposing of stolen goods was actually low risk and more efficient than expected. One reason was that in many cases fences and shady businesspeople put in a request for particular items, and the ready-made market allowed the stolen merchandise to be disposed of quickly, often in less than one hour. Though the typical markdown was 67 to 75 percent of the price of the goods, most reported that they could still earn a good living, averaging $2,000 per week. Those who benefited most from these transactions were the receivers of stolen property, who make considerable profits and are unlikely to be caught.[108]

According to Shover, a person becomes a good burglar by learning the techniques of the trade from older, more experienced burglars. During this process, the older burglar teaches the novice how to handle such requirements as dealing with defense attorneys, bail bond agents, and other agents of the justice system. Apprentices must be known to have the appropriate character before they are taken under the wing of the old pro. Usually, the opportunity to learn burglary comes as a reward for being a highly respected juvenile gang member, from knowing someone in the neighborhood who has made a living at burglary, or, more often,

CONNECTIONS

Shover finds that the process of becoming a professional burglar is similar to the process described in Sutherland's theory of differential association. You can read more about this theory in Chapter 7.

ASK YOURSELF . . .

What other criminal "occupations" involve professionalism?

from having built a reputation for being solid while serving time in prison. Consequently, the opportunity to become a good burglar is not open to everyone.

Burglars on the Job In an important book titled *Burglars on the Job*, Richard Wright and Scott Decker describe the working conditions of active professional burglars.[109] Most are motivated by the need for cash in order to get high; they want to enjoy the good life, "keeping the party going" without having to work. As Exhibit 12.3 shows, they approach their "job" in a rational workmanlike fashion, but their lives are controlled by their culture and environment. Unskilled and uneducated, urban burglars make the choices they do

EXHIBIT 12.3

Burglars on the Job

According to active burglars:

- Most avoid occupied residences, considering them high-risk targets.
- Most are not deterred by alarms and elaborate locks; in fact, these devices tell them there is something inside worth stealing.
- Once entering a residence, anxiety turns to calm as they first turn to the master bedroom for money and drugs. They also search kitchens, believing that some people keep money in a mayonnaise jar.
- Most work in groups, one serving as a lookout while another ransacks the place.
- Some dispose of goods through a professional fence; others try to pawn the goods. Some exchange goods for drugs, some sell them to friends and relatives, and a few keep the stolen items for themselves, especially guns and jewelry.
- Many approach a target masquerading as workmen, such as carpenters or house painters.
- Some stake out residences to learn occupants' routines.
- Tipsters help them select attractive targets.
- Drug dealers are favored targets because they tend to have a lot of cash and drugs, and victims are not going to call the police.
- Targets are often acquaintances.

SOURCE: Richard Wright and Scott Decker, *Burglars on the Job: Streetlife and Residential Break-Ins* (Boston: Northeastern University Press, 1994).

because there are few conventional opportunities for success. This rationality and cool decision making may help explain why most burglaries go unsolved. Most burglars do not like to travel far from their residence, choosing close-by neighborhoods with single-family homes.[110] However, experienced burglars are more willing to travel to find rich targets. They have access to transportation that enables them to select a wider variety of targets than younger, more inexperienced thieves.[111] They also seem to be sensitive to police anticrime efforts: when police are active and forceful, burglary rates decline. Experienced burglars may locate to safer areas or bide their time and wait for the police to reduce their anticrime initiatives as crime rates decline.[112]

The Burglary "Career Ladder" Paul Cromwell, James Olson, and D'Aunn Wester Avary interviewed 30 active burglars in Texas and found that burglars go through stages of career development. They begin as young *novices* who learn the trade from older, more experienced burglars, frequently siblings or relatives. Novices will continue to get this tutoring as long as they can develop their own markets (fences) for stolen goods. After their education is over, novices enter the *journeyman* stage, characterized by forays in search of lucrative targets and careful planning. At this point, they develop reputations as experienced, reliable criminals. Finally, they become *professional* burglars when they have developed advanced skills and organizational abilities that give them the highest esteem among their peers.

The Texas burglars also displayed evidence of rational decision making. Most seemed to carefully evaluate potential costs and benefits before deciding to commit crime. There is evidence that burglars follow this pattern in their choice of burglary sites. Burglars show a preference for corner houses because they are easily observed and offer the maximum number of escape routes.[113] They look for houses that show evidence of long-term care and wealth. Though people may erect fences and other barriers to deter burglars, these devices may actually attract crime because they are viewed as protecting something worth stealing.[114] Cromwell, Olson, and Avary also found that many burglars had serious drug habits and that their criminal activity was, in part, aimed at supporting their substance abuse.

Arson

Arson is the willful and malicious burning of a home, public building, vehicle, or commercial building. According to the UCR, almost 43,000 arsons are now being recorded each year. More than 45 percent of all arson offenses involved structures (e.g., residential, storage, public, etc.). Mobile property was involved in 23 percent of arsons, and other types of property (such as crops, timber, fences, etc.) accounted for 31 percent of reported arsons. The average dollar loss per arson was $16,055. However, it is likely that this undercounts the number of annual arsons since not all police departments gather data on the crime.

Los Angeles firefighters battle a fire on December 8, 2014, at the Da Vinci apartment complex under construction in Los Angeles. At a preliminary hearing on May 11, 2016, Dawud Abdulwali was ordered to stand trial for arson over the fire that incinerated the building and caused $100 million in damage.

Arson has been a common occurrence in America and was even tried as a weapon during the Civil War. In 1864, a small group of Confederate agents attempted to set New York City ablaze by using a liquid called "solidified Greek fire"; the plot failed because they improperly used the chemical.[115]

There are several motives for arson. Adult arsonists may be motivated by severe emotional turmoil. Some psychologists view fire starting as a function of a disturbed personality. They consider arson to be a symptom of illness, not merely a crime.[116] It is alleged that arsonists often experience sexual pleasure from starting fires and then observing their destructive effects. Although some arsonists may be aroused sexually by their activities, there is little evidence that most arsonists are psychosexually motivated.[117] It is equally likely that fires are started by angry people looking for revenge against property owners or by teenagers out to vandalize property. These findings support the claim that arson should be viewed as a mental health problem, not a criminal act and that it should be treated with counseling and other therapeutic measures rather than severe punishments.[118]

THE JUVENILE FIRE STARTER

Juveniles, the most prolific fire starters, may get involved in arson for a variety of reasons as they mature. Juvenile fire setting has long been associated with psychological abnormality, including depression conduct problems, such as disobedience, aggressiveness, anger, hostility, and resentment over parental rejection.[119] According to research by sociologist Wayne Wooden, juvenile arsonists can be classified in one of four categories:

- *The "playing with matches" fire setter.* This is the youngest fire starter, usually between the ages of 4 and 9, who sets fires because parents are careless with matches and lighters. Proper instruction on fire safety can help prevent fires set by these young children.

- *The "crying for help" fire setter.* This type of fire setter is a 7- to 13-year-old who is suffering emotional turmoil. The source of the stress could be family conflict, divorce, death, or abuse. These youngsters have difficulty expressing their feelings of sorrow, rage, or anger and turn to fire as a means of relieving stress or getting back at their antagonists.
- *The "delinquent" fire setter.* Some youths set fire to school property or surrounding areas to retaliate for some slight experienced at school. These kids may break into the school to vandalize property with friends and later set a fire to cover up their activities.
- *The "severely disturbed" fire setter.* This youngster is obsessed with fires and often dreams about them in "vibrant colors." This is the most disturbed type of juvenile fire setter and the one most likely to set numerous fires with the potential for death and damage.[120]

During the past decade, hundreds of jurisdictions across the nation have established programs to address the growing problem of juvenile fire setting. Housed primarily within the fire service, these programs are designed to identify, evaluate, and treat juvenile fire setters to prevent the recurrence of fire-setting behaviors. For example, in Broward County, Florida, the Juvenile Firesetter Prevention and Intervention Program provides specialized fire safety education for children ages 2 to 17. It targets at-risk adolescents who have displayed an interest in or a history of starting fires. By offering fire safety education, instruction, and community outreach presentations, the program helps reduce incidents of injury, property loss, and death.[121]

Another approach involves training programs that help practitioners develop a comprehensive strategy to combat the misuse of fire and incendiary devices by juveniles. They typically cover issues such as identification, intake, screening, disposition, and follow-up, all used to reduce youthful fire setting.[122]

To learn more about the Broward County program, go to **http://www.sheriff.org/about_bso/dfres /operations/jfp.cfm.**
Can this really help or are kids who start fires too psychologically damaged to be treated?

PROFESSIONAL ARSON

L010 Discuss why people commit arson for profit

Other arsons are set by professional arsonists who engage in **arson for profit**. People looking to collect insurance money, but who are afraid or unable to set the fire themselves, hire professional arsonists. These professionals have acquired the skills to set fires and make the cause seem accidental (for example, like an electrical short). Another form is **arson fraud**, which involves a business owner burning his or her property, or hiring someone to do it, to escape financial problems.[123] Over the years, investigators have found that businesspeople are willing to become involved in arson to collect fire insurance or for various other reasons, including but not limited to these:

- Obtaining money during a period of financial crisis
- Getting rid of outdated or slow-moving inventory
- Destroying outmoded machines and technology
- Paying off legal and illegal debt
- Relocating or remodeling a business; for example, when a theme restaurant has not been accepted by customers
- Taking advantage of government funds available for redevelopment
- Applying for government building money, pocketing it without making repairs, and then claiming that fire destroyed the "rehabilitated" building
- Planning bankruptcies to eliminate debts, after the merchandise supposedly destroyed was secretly sold before the fire
- Eliminating business competition by burning out rivals
- Employing extortion schemes that demand that victims pay up or the rest of their holdings will be burned
- Solving labor–management problems; arson may be committed by a disgruntled employee
- Concealing another crime, such as embezzlement

arson for profit People looking to collect insurance money, but who are afraid or unable to set the fire themselves, hire professional arsonists. These professionals have acquired the skills to set fires and make the cause seem accidental.

arson fraud A business owner burns his or her property, or hires someone to do it, to escape financial problems.

SUMMARY

L01 **Discuss the history of theft offenses**

Common theft offenses include larceny, fraud, and embezzlement. These are common-law crimes, originally defined by English judges. Skilled thieves included pickpockets, forgers, and counterfeiters, who operated freely. Smugglers transported goods, such as spirits, gems, gold, and spices, without paying tax or duty. Poachers supplemented their diet and income with game that belonged to a landlord.

LO2 **Compare and contrast professional and amateur thieves**

Economic crimes are designed to reap financial rewards for the offender. Opportunistic amateurs commit the majority of economic crimes. Economic crime has also attracted professional criminals. Professionals earn most of their income from crime, view themselves as criminals, and possess skills that aid them in their law-breaking behavior. An example of the professional criminal is the fence who buys and sells stolen merchandise.

LO3 **Comment on the activities of a professional fence**

Fences buy stolen goods and sell them at a profit. Some specialize in jewelry, auto parts, or electronic products, while others are generalists. They may act as middlemen and resell the stolen items to local merchants who market them to legitimate customers, or sell the items themselves in pawn shops or on the Internet. The key to becoming a successful fence is to develop relationships with people on both sides of the law: the criminals who steal, the merchants who sell, and members of the justice system with whom they come into contact.

LO4 **Differentiate between petty and grand larceny**

Larceny, the most common theft crime, involves taking the legal possessions of another. Petty larceny is typically theft of amounts under a particular amount, ranging from $5 to $1,000 (depending on state law); grand larceny is theft over that amount. Grand larceny is a felony, petty larceny a misdemeanor.

LO5 **Compare professional and amateur shoplifters**

Some shoplifters are amateurs who steal on the spur of the moment. These snitches are otherwise respectable persons who do not view themselves as thieves but take goods for their own use. Called boosters or heels, professional shoplifters steal with the intention of reselling stolen merchandise to pawnshops or fences, usually at half the original price. Boosters know how to hit stores without being detected, use devices to help them steal, and have partners who can unload merchandise after it is stolen.

LO6 **Explain the concept of embezzlement**

Embezzlement occurs when a person in a position of trust uses that position to convert or steal property or money from another without their consent. Embezzlement is premeditated, systematic, not spontaneous, and involves schemes that involve small amounts taken over a long period of time.

LO7 **Describe the elements of sexual burglary**

Fetishistic noncontact burglaries typically occur in unoccupied houses and involve fetishistic behavior but no theft, violence, or weapon. This type of sexual burglary is motivated to fulfill a sexual fantasy but involves neither victim contact nor material gain. Versatile contact burglaries are characterized by rapes occurring in the home and involving theft, violence, and weapons. In sexually oriented contact burglaries, the criminal raped the victim at home, but these incidents rarely involved theft, violence, or weapons.

LO8 **Compare the activities of male and female burglars**

Both male and female burglars engage in other forms of theft, such as shoplifting and assault. Males are more likely to steal cars to supplement their income. Female burglars are much more likely to work with a partner, whereas males are more likely to go it alone. Males begin their offending careers at an earlier age than females and are more likely to be repeat and recurrent offenders.

LO9 **Know what it takes to be a "good burglar"**

Because burglary involves planning and risk, it attracts professional thieves. The most competent have technical skill and personal integrity, specialize in burglary, are financially successful, and avoid prison sentences. Professional burglars size up the value of a particular crime and balance it against the perceived risks. Many have undergone training in the company of older, more experienced burglars.

LO10 **Discuss why people commit arson for profit**

Arson is the willful, malicious burning of a home, public building, vehicle, or commercial building. Most arsonists are teenage vandals. Professional arsonists specialize in burning commercial buildings for profit. The owners of commercial buildings may resort to arson to get rid of outdated inventory, to qualify for government redevelopment funds, to collect insurance money, to claim the loss of merchandise already sold, or to eliminate business competition (by burning a building owned by a competitor).

CRITICAL THINKING QUESTIONS

1. Differentiate between an occasional and a professional criminal. Which one would be more likely to resort to violence? Which one would be more easily deterred?
2. What crime occurs when a person who owns an antique store sells a client an "original Tiffany lamp" that the seller knows is a fake? Would it still be a crime if the person selling the lamp was not aware that it was a fake? As an antique dealer, should the seller have a duty to determine the authenticity of the products he or she sells?

3. What are the characteristics of good burglars? Can you compare their career path to any other professionals, such as doctors or lawyers? Which theory of criminal behavior best predicts the development of the good burglar?

4. You have been the victim of repeat burglaries. What could you do to reduce the chances of future victimization? (Hint: Buying a gun is not an option!)

KEY TERMS

economic crime (432)
fence (432)
skilled thieves (432)
flash houses (432)
smugglers (433)
poachers (433)
occasional criminals (434)
professional criminals (434)

situational inducement (434)
constructive possession (439)
petit (petty) larceny (439)
grand larceny (439)
shoplifting (439)
snitches (440)
booster box (441)

target removal strategies (441)
target hardening strategies (441)
naive check forgers (442)
closure (442)
systematic forgers (442)
carjacking (445)
false pretenses (fraud) (446)

mark (446)
confidence game (446)
pigeon drop (446)
embezzlement (448)
good burglar (452)
arson for profit (455)
arson fraud (455)

NOTES

All URLs accessed in 2016.

1. U.S. Attorney's Office, Southern District of New York, October 30, 2013, press release, "Thirteen Members of Pharmacy Burglary Ring Charged with Stealing and Distributing Millions of Dollars' Worth of Prescription-Controlled Substances and Hundreds of Thousands of Dollars in Cash," https://www.justice.gov/usao-sdny /pr/thirteen-members-pharmacy-burglary -ring-charged-stealing-and-distributing -millions.

2. Jennifer Truman and Lynn Langton, *Criminal Victimization, 2014* (Washington, DC: Bureau of Justice Statistics, 2015), http:// www.bjs.gov/content/pub/pdf/cv14.pdf.

3. Andrew McCall, *The Medieval Underworld* (London: Hamish Hamilton, 1979), p. 86.

4. Ibid., p. 104.

5. J. J. Tobias, *Crime and Police in England, 1700–1900* (London: Gill and Macmillan, 1979).

6. Ibid., p. 9.

7. Marilyn Walsh, *The Fence* (Westport, CT: Greenwood Press, 1977), pp. 18–25.

8. Don DeNevi, *Western Train Robberies* (Millbrae, CA: Celestial Arts, 1976); Harry Sinclair Drago, *Road Agents and Train Robbers: Half a Century of Western Banditry* (New York: Dodd, Mead, 1973).

9. Neal Shover, *Great Pretenders, Pursuits, and Careers of Persistent Thieves* (Boulder, CO: Westview Press, 1996).

10. Ibid., pp. 50–51.

11. Ibid.

12. John Hepburn, "Occasional Criminals," in *Major Forms of Crime*, ed. Robert Meier (Beverly Hills, CA: Sage, 1984), pp. 73–94.

13. James Inciardi, "Professional Crime," in *Major Forms of Crime*, p. 223.

14. Harry King and William Chambliss, *Box Man: A Professional Thief's Journey* (New York: Harper & Row, 1972), p. 24.

15. Edwin Sutherland, "White-Collar Criminality," *American Sociological Review* 5 (1940): 2–10.

16. Gilbert Geis, "Avocational Crime," in *Handbook of Criminology*, ed. D. Glazer (Chicago: Rand McNally, 1974), p. 284.

17. Chic Conwell, *The Professional Thief*, ed. Edwin Sutherland (Chicago: University of Chicago Press, 1937).

18. Ibid., pp. 197–198.

19. Ibid., p. 212.

20. See, for example, Edwin Lemert, "The Behavior of the Systematic Check Forger," *Social Problems* 6 (1958): 141–148.

21. Cited in Walsh, *The Fence*, p. 1.

22. Carl Klockars, *The Professional Fence* (New York: Free Press, 1976); Darrell Steffensmeier, *The Fence: In the Shadow of Two Worlds* (Totowa, NJ: Rowman and Littlefield, 1986); Walsh, *The Fence*, pp. 25–28.

23. Simon Fass and Janice Francis, "Where Have All the Hot Goods Gone? The Role of Pawnshops," *Journal of Research in Crime and Delinquency* 41 (2004): 156–179.

24. Darrell Steffensmeier and Jeffery Ulmer, *Confessions of a Dying Thief: Understanding Criminal Careers and Illegal Enterprise* (Piscataway, NJ: Transaction-Aldine, 2005), p. 375.

25. Walsh, *The Fence*, p. 34.

26. National Retail Federation, "Organized Retail Crime Survey," 2014, https://nrf.com /sites/default/files/NRF%202014%20ORC %20report%20REV2.pdf.

27. Paul Cromwell, James Olson, and D'Aunn Avary, "Who Buys Stolen Property? A New Look at Criminal Receiving," *Journal of Crime and Justice* 16 (1993): 75–95.

28. FBI, "Cargo Theft's High Cost: Thieves Stealing Billions Annually," July 26, 2006, http://www.fbi.gov/news/stories/2006/july /cargo_theft072106.

29. Michael Powell and David Segal, "In New York, a Grisly Traffic in Body Parts, Illegal Sales Worry Dead's Kin, Tissue Recipients," *Washington Post*, January 18, 2006, p. A03; William Sherman, "Clients Flee Biz Eyed in Ghoul Probe," *New York Daily News*, October 13, 2005.

30. This section depends heavily on a classic book, Wayne La Fave and Austin Scott, *Handbook on Criminal Law* (St. Paul, MN: West Publishing, 1972).

31. Ibid., p. 622.

32. Virginia Crime Codes, http://law.lis.virginia .gov/vacode/18.2-95/.

33. Ibid.

34. New York Penal Law, http://ypdcrime.com /penal.law/article155.htm.

35. Data in this chapter on crime rates and trends come from FBI, Uniform Crime Reports, *Crime in the United States, 2014*, https://www.fbi.gov/about-us/cjis/ucr/crime -in-the-u.s/2014/crime-in-the-u.s.-2014 /offenses-known-to-law-enforcement /property-crime/property-crime.

36. Margaret Loftus, "Gone: One TV," *U.S. News and World Report*, July 14, 1997, p. 61.

37. U.S. Attorney's Office, Southern District of Texas, "Foreign National Convicted in Multi-Million-Dollar, Multi-State Criminal Operation," March 04, 2013, http://www .fbi.gov/houston/press-releases/2013 /foreign-national-convicted-in-multi -million-dollar-multi-state-criminal -operation.

38. U.S. Attorney's Office, Southern District of Texas, "Foreign National Convicted in Multi-Million-Dollar, Multi-State Criminal Operation."

39. Rachel Shteir, *The Steal: A Cultural History of Shoplifting* (New York: Penguin Press, 2011).

40. Laura Boyle, "The Life and Crimes of Jane Leigh-Perrot," http://www.janeausten.co.uk/the-life-and-crimes-of-jane-leigh-perrot/.

41. Hayes International, "Annual Retail Theft Survey, 2014," http://hayesinternational.com/news/annual-retail-theft-survey/.

42. Mary Owen Cameron, *The Booster and the Snitch* (New York: Free Press, 1964).

43. Janne Kivivuori, "Crime by Proxy: Coercion and Altruism in Adolescent Shoplifting," *British Journal of Criminology* 47 (2007): 817–833.

44. Paul Cromwell and Quint Thurman, "The Devil Made Me Do It: Use of Neutralizations by Shoplifters," *Deviant Behavior* 24 (2003): 535–550.

45. Ellen Beate Hansen and Gunnar Breivik, "Sensation Seeking as a Predictor of Positive and Negative Risk Behavior Among Adolescents," *Personality and Individual Differences* 30 (2001): 627–640.

46. Yves Lamontagne, Richard Boyer, Celine Hetu, and Celine Lacerte-Lamontagne, "Anxiety, Significant Losses, Depression, and Irrational Beliefs in First-Offense Shoplifters," *Canadian Journal of Psychiatry* 45 (2000): 64–66.

47. Brian T. Smith and Ronald V. Clarke, "Shoplifting of Everyday Products that Serve Illicit Drug Uses," *Journal of Research in Crime and Delinquency* 52 (2015): 245–269.

48. Gail A. Caputo and Anna King, "Shoplifting by Male and Female Drug Users: Gender, Agency, and Work," *Criminal Justice Review* 40 (2015): 47–66.

49. Ibid.

50. Michael Hindelang, "Decisions of Shoplifting Victims to Invoke the Criminal Justice Process," *Social Problems* 21 (1974): 580–595.

51. Jill Jordan Sieder, "To Catch a Thief, Try This," *U.S. News and World Report*, September 23, 1996, p. 71.

52. Thomas Kelley, Daniel Kennedy, and Robert Homant, "Evaluation of an Individualized Treatment Program for Adolescent Shoplifters," *Adolescence* 38 (2003): 725–733.

53. Shaun Gabbidon and Patricia Patrick, "Characteristics and Outcomes of Shoplifting Cases in the U.S. Involving Allegations of False Arrest," *Security Journal* 18 (2005): 7–18.

54. *Rudity v. J.C. Penney Co.*, No. 02-4114 (Delaware Co., PA, Ct. C.P. 2003).

55. Helen Jung, "Walgreens Must Pay NE Portland Mother and Son in Case over Shoplifting Accusations, Jury Says," *The Oregonian*, November 20, 2013, http://www.oregonlive.com/portland/index.ssf/2013/11/walgreens_must_pay_ne_portland.html.

56. Dean Dabney, Laura Dugan, Volkan Topalli, and Richard Hollinger, "The Impact of Implicit Stereotyping on Offender Profiling: Unexpected Results from an Observational Study of Shoplifting," *Criminal Justice and Behavior* 33 (2006): 646–674.

57. Security Information Watch, "Lawsuit Claims Dillard's Used Racial Profiling to Fight Shoplifting," February 6, 2009, http://www.securityinfowatch.com/press_release/10593712/lawsuit-claims-dillards-used-racial-profiling-to-fight-shoplifting.

58. Edwin Lemert, "An Isolation and Closure Theory of Naive Check Forgery," *Journal of Criminal Law, Criminology and Police Science* 44 (1953): 297–298.

59. U. S. Attorney, District of New Jersey, "Ten Indicted in $200 Million International Credit Card Fraud Conspiracy," September 27, 2013, http://www.fbi.gov/newark/press-releases/2013/ten-indicted-in-200-million-international-credit-card-fraud-conspiracy.

60. CNN Money.com, "11 Charged in Theft of More than 40M Card Numbers," August 6, 2008, http://money.cnn.com/2008/08/05/news/companies/card_fraud/?postversion=2008080604.

61. Kimberly Palmer, "Beware the Latest Credit Card Scam," *U.S. News and World Report*, May 15, 2008, http://www.usnews.com/blogs/alpha-consumer/2008/05/15/beware-the-latest-credit-card-scam.html.

62. 15 U.S. Code § 1643, Liability of Holder of Credit, https://www.law.cornell.edu/uscode/text/15/1643.

63. Jim Zarroli, "U.S. Credit Cards Tackle Fraud with Embedded Chips, but No PINs," National Public Radio, January 5, 2015, http://www.npr.org/sections/alltechconsidered/2015/01/05/375164839/u-s-credit-cards-tackle-fraud-with-embedded-chips-but-no-pins.

64. National Insurance Crime Bureau, "NICB's *Hot Wheels*: America's 10 Most Stolen Vehicles," https://www.nicb.org/newsroom/news-releases/hot-wheels-report.

65. Charles McCaghy, Peggy Giordano, and Trudy Knicely Henson, "Auto Theft," *Criminology* 15 (1977): 367–381.

66. Donald Gibbons, *Society, Crime and Criminal Careers* (Englewood Cliffs, NJ: Prentice Hall, 1977), p. 310.

67. All prices here were obtained on eBay, March 2016.

68. CNN, FBI Breaks Up $25 Million 'Car Cloning' Ring," March 24, 2009, http://www.cnn.com/2009/CRIME/03/24/cloned.cars/.

69. Richard Cowen and Chris Harris, "Short Hills Mall Killing Latest Turn in Surge of Carjackings," NorthJersey.com, http://www.northjersey.com/news/short-hills-mall-killing-latest-turn-in-surge-of-carjackings-1.682194.

70. Patsy Klaus, *Carjacking, 1993–2002* (Washington, DC: Bureau of Justice Statistics, 2004).

71. Bruce Jacobs, Volkan Topalli, and Richard Wright, "Carjacking, Streetlife, and Offender Motivation," *British Journal of Criminology* 43 (2003): 673–688.

72. Klaus, *Carjacking, 1993–2002*.

73. Ronald Clarke and Patricia Harris, "Auto Theft and Its Prevention," in *Crime and Justice: An Annual Review*, ed. N. Morris and M. Tonry (Chicago: University of Chicago Press, 1992).

74. OnStar, https://www.onstar.com/.

75. LoJack, http://www.lojack.com/.

76. VINshield, http://www.vinshield.com/.

77. P. Weiss, "Outsmarting the Electronic Gatekeeper: Code Breakers Beat Security Scheme of Car Locks, Gas Pumps," *Science News* 167 (2005): 86.

78. La Fave and Scott, *Handbook on Criminal Law*, p. 655.

79. 30 Geo. III, C. 24 (1975).

80. Internet Crime Complaint Center, "Fraudulent Sites Capitalizing on Relief Efforts of Hurricane Katrina," http://www.ic3.gov/media/2005/050902.aspx.

81. FBI, *Crime in the United States, 2014*, Table 29, https://www.fbi.gov/about-us/cjis/ucr/crime-in-the-u.s/2014/crime-in-the-u.s.-2014/tables/table-29.

82. As described in Charles McCaghy, *Deviant Behavior* (New York: Macmillan, 1976), pp. 230–231.

83. Benjamin Weiser, "4-Year Sentence for Mastermind of Scheme to Cheat on Graduate School Tests," *New York Times*, October 3, 1998, p. 8.

84. FBI, "A Cautionary Tale: Staged Auto Accident Fraud: Don't Let It Happen to You," http://www.fbi.gov/news/stories/2005/february/staged_auto021805.

85. Auto Insurance Center, "Staged Car Accidents on the Rise," June 15, 2016, http://www.autoinsurancecenter.com/staged-car-accidents-on-the-rise.htm.

86. FBI, "Financial Fraud: Oklahoma Pastor Embezzled Nearly $1 Million from Community Center," May 15, 2015, https://www.fbi.gov/news/stories/financial-fraud.

87. Jerome Hall, *Theft, Law and Society* (Indianapolis: Bobbs-Merrill, 1952), p. 36.

88. La Fave and Scott, *Handbook on Criminal Law*, p. 644.

89. Ibid., p. 708.

90. E. Blackstone, *Commentaries on the Laws of England* (London: 1769), p. 224.

91. Elizabeth Groff and Nancy La Vigne, "Mapping an Opportunity Surface of Residential Burglary," *Journal of Research in Crime and Delinquency* 38 (2001): 257–278.

92. Graham Farrell, "Attempted Crime and the Crime Drop," *International Criminal Justice Review* 26 (2016): 1–30.

93. Stewart D'Alessio, David Eitle, and Lisa Stolzenberg, "Unemployment, Guardianship, and Weekday Residential Burglary," *Justice Quarterly* 29 (2012): 919–932.

94. Timothy Coupe and Laurence Blake, "Daylight and Darkness Targeting Strategies and the Risks of Being Seen at Residential Burglaries," *Criminology* 44 (2006): 431–464.

95. Frank Hoheimer, *The Home Invaders: Confessions of a Cat Burglar* (Chicago: Chicago Review, 1975).

96. Graham Farrell, Coretta Phillips, and Ken Pease, "Like Taking Candy: Why Does Repeat Victimization Occur?" *British Journal of Criminology* 35 (1995): 384–399, at 391.

97. Ronald Clarke, Elizabeth Perkins, and Donald Smith, Jr., "Explaining Repeat Residential Burglaries: An Analysis of Property Stolen," in *Repeat Victimization, Crime Prevention Studies*, Vol. 12, ed. Graham Farrell and Ken Pease (Monsey, NY: Criminal Justice Press, 2001), pp. 119–132.

98. Mitchell Chamlin and Andrea Krajewski, "Use of Force and Home Safety: An Impact Assessment of Oklahoma's Stand Your Ground Law," *Deviant Behavior* 37 (2016): 237–245; Ling Ren, Yan Zhang, and Jihong Solomon Zhao, "The Deterrent Effect of the Castle Doctrine Law on Burglary in Texas," *Crime and Delinquency* 61 (2015): 1127–1151.

99. Simon Hakim and Yochanan Shachmurove, "Spatial and Temporal Patterns of Commercial Burglaries," *American Journal of Economics and Sociology* 55 (1996): 443–457.

100. Ibid., pp. 443–456.

101. Deborah Baskin and Ira Sommers, "Solving Residential Burglaries in the United States: The Impact of Forensic Evidence on Case Outcomes," *International Journal of Police Science and Management* 13 (2011): 70–86.

102. Matthew Robinson, "Accessible Targets, but Not Advisable Ones: The Role of 'Accessibility' in Student Apartment Burglary," *Journal of Security Administration* 21 (1998): 28–44.

103. Wim Bernasco, "Co-Offending and the Choice of Target Areas in Burglary," *Journal of Investigative Psychology and Offender Profiling* 3 (2006): 139–155.

104. Lynn A. Addington and Callie Marie Rennison, "Keeping the Barbarians Outside the Gate? Comparing Burglary Victimization in Gated and Non-Gated Communities," *Justice Quarterly* 32 (2015): 168–192.

105. Christophe Vandeviver, Stijn Van Daele, and Tom Vander Beken, "What Makes Long Crime Trips Worth Undertaking? Balancing Costs and Benefits in Burglars' Journey to Crime," *British Journal of Criminology* 55 (2014): 399–420.

106. Nick Tilley, Rebecca Thompson, Graham Farrell, Louise Grove, and Andromachi Tseloni, "Do Burglar Alarms Increase Burglary Risk? A Counter-Intuitive Finding and Possible Explanations," *Crime Prevention and Community Safety* 17 (2015): 1–19.

107. See, generally, Neal Shover, "Structures and Careers in Burglary," *Journal of Criminal Law, Criminology and Police Science* 63 (1972): 540–549.

108. Richard Stevenson, Lubica Forsythe, and Don Weatherburn, "The Stolen Goods Market in New South Wales, Australia: An Analysis of Disposal Avenues and Tactics," *British Journal of Criminology* 41 (2001): 101–118.

109. Richard Wright and Scott Decker, *Burglars on the Job: Streetlife and Residential Break-Ins* (Boston: Northeastern University Press, 1994).

110. Wim Bernasco and Paul Nieuwbeerta, "How Do Residential Burglars Select Target Areas? A New Approach to the Analysis of Criminal Location Choice," *British Journal of Criminology* 45 (2005): 296–315.

111. Brent Snook, "Individual Differences in Distance Travelled by Serial Burglars," *Journal of Investigative Psychology and Offender Profiling* 1 (2004): 53–66.

112. John Worrall, "Does Targeting Minor Offenses Reduce Serious Crime? A Provisional, Affirmative Answer Based on an Analysis of County-Level Data," *Police Quarterly* 9 (2006): 47–72.

113. Paul Cromwell, James Olson, and D'Aunn Wester Avary, *Breaking and Entering: An Ethnographic Analysis of Burglary* (Newbury Park, CA: Sage, 1991), pp. 48–51.

114. See M. Taylor and C. Nee, "The Role of Cues in Simulated Residential Burglary: A Preliminary Investigation," *British Journal of Criminology* 28 (1988): 398–401; Julia MacDonald and Robert Gifford, "Territorial Cues and Defensible Space Theory: The Burglar's Point of View," *Journal of Environmental Psychology* 9 (1989): 193–205.

115. Jane Singer, *The Confederate Dirty War: Arson, Bombings, Assassination and Plots for Chemical and Germ Attacks on the Union* (Jefferson, NC, and London: McFarland & Company, 2005), p. 21.

116. Nancy Webb, George Sakheim, Luz Towns-Miranda, and Charles Wagner, "Collaborative Treatment of Juvenile Firestarters: Assessment and Outreach," *American Journal of Orthopsychiatry* 60 (1990): 305–310.

117. Vernon Quinsey, Terry Chaplin, and Douglas Unfold, "Arsonists and Sexual Arousal to Fire Setting: Correlations Unsupported," *Journal of Behavior Therapy and Experimental Psychiatry* 20 (1989): 203–209.

118. John Taylor, Ian Thorne, Alison Robertson, and Ginny Avery, "Evaluation of a Group Intervention for Convicted Arsonists with Mild and Borderline Intellectual Disabilities," *Criminal Behaviour and Mental Health* 12 (2002): 282–294.

119. Mark Dadds and Jennifer Fraser, "Fire Interest, Fire Setting and Psychopathology in Australian Children: A Normative Study," *Australian and New Zealand Journal of Psychiatry* 40 (2006): 581–586; Pekka Santtila, Helina Haikkanen, Laurence Alison, Laurence Whyte, and Carrie Whyte, "Juvenile Firesetters: Crime Scene Actions and Offender Characteristics," *Legal and Criminological Psychology* 8 (2003): 1–20.

120. Wayne Wooden, "Juvenile Firesetters in Cross-Cultural Perspective: How Should Society Respond?" in *Official Responses to Problem Juveniles: Some International Reflections*, ed. James Hackler (Onati, Spain: Onati Publications, 1991), pp. 339–348.

121. Broward County, Florida, Sheriff's Department, Juvenile Firesetter Prevention and Intervention Program, June 2016, http://www.sheriff.org/about_bso/dfres/operations/jfp.cfm.

122. See, for example, U.S. Fire Administration, Youth Firesetting Prevention and Intervention, June 2016, https://apps.usfa.fema.gov/nfacourses/catalog/details/10435.

123. Leigh Edward Somers, *Economic Crimes* (New York: Clark Boardman, 1984), pp. 158–168.

Woman: Brigitte Sporrer/Cultura/Getty Images; money: Nikolai Sorokin/Dreamstime.com

LEARNING OBJECTIVES

L01 Assess what is meant by the term *enterprise crime*

L02 Define white-collar crime

L03 Compare and contrast the various forms of white-collar crime

L04 Discuss efforts to control white-collar crime

L05 Be familiar with the concept of green crime

L06 List the components of green crime

L07 Trace the evolution of organized crime

L08 Be familiar with transnational organized crime

L09 Assess the efforts to control transnational organized crime

L010 Comment on the causes of enterprise crime

13 ENTERPRISE CRIME: WHITE-COLLAR, GREEN, AND TRANSNATIONAL ORGANIZED CRIME

Allison Layton owned a California company called Miracles Egg Donation. She claimed that she was in the business of helping infertile couples have children. Would-be parents paid Miracles tens of thousands of dollars—sometimes their life savings—for egg donation and surrogacy services that Layton promised to coordinate. But her business turned out to be a fraud, and she ended up stealing her victims' hopes and dreams as well as their money.

During a three-year period beginning in 2008, she defrauded couples, egg donors, and surrogate mothers while living a lavish lifestyle off the proceeds. Many of the victims were in a vulnerable place in their lives—working against their biological clocks and trying to afford this expensive and time-consuming procedure. The fees paid to Miracles by would-be parents—known in the surrogacy world as intended parents—were supposed to go into escrow accounts to be withdrawn for expenses related to surrogacy or egg donation. But Layton took the money and spent it on her own $60,000 wedding, a new vehicle for her husband, and high-end shopping sprees she flaunted on social media.

As a result, egg donors, surrogates, attorneys, and others often were not paid for the services they provided, and many intended parents—including some who lived overseas—failed to get the services they paid for in advance; some effectively missed the opportunity to have children.

Layton was running a Ponzi scheme. Early on, some people got the services they paid for, but then she began shuffling funds to cover some clients' services and not others. And when it all finally collapsed, nobody was getting anything. When confronted by clients, Layton lied about why payments had not been made and refunds not issued. She led victims to believe they might soon be paid, when, in fact, many were not. More than 40 victims lost in excess of $270,000.

Clients contacted law enforcement authorities and, in 2014, Layton was charged with wire fraud. In a plea agreement with federal prosecutors, she admitted to defrauding the victims; in September 2015, a judge sentenced the 38-year-old woman to 18 months in prison.[1]

Allison Layton's scheme may seem particularly cruel and harmful, but it is certainly not unusual. People like Layton who engage in **enterprise crimes** are involved in ongoing criminal conspiracies that are shady forms of business and commerce. These criminal acts either violate the laws regulating legitimate business or are intended to gain profit through illegitimate commercial enterprise.

In this chapter, we divide these crimes of illicit entrepreneurship into three distinct categories: white-collar crime, green crime, and (transnational) organized crime. White-collar crime involves illegal activities of people and institutions whose acknowledged purpose is illegal profit through legitimate business transactions. Green criminology is concerned with the study of environmental harm, environmental laws, and environmental regulation.[2] Organized crime involves illegal activities of people and organizations whose acknowledged purpose is profit through illegitimate business enterprise.

The Concept of Enterprise Crime

 L01 Assess what is meant by the term *enterprise crime*

Enterprise crimes are linked here because in each category offenders twist legal rules to enhance their personal economic position through ongoing illicit and illegal business practices. Because they are so connected, these three broad categories of crime often overlap:

- Corporate execs, in order to increase profits, may engage in environmental crimes.
- Green criminals may disguise their acts through elaborate corporate structures employing corrupt business practices.
- Organized criminals may buy legitimate businesses to launder money.

Business enterprise crimes taint and corrupt the free market system. They mix and match illegal and legal methods and legal and illegal products in all phases of commercial activity. They involve illegal business practices (embezzlement, price fixing, pollution, dumping, bribery, and so on) to merchandise what are normally legitimate commercial products (securities, medical care, disposing of computer equipment).[3] They can also involve using standard business methods and accounting to market illegal goods (drugs) and services (gambling, money laundering).

The public may not view enterprise crime as particularly dangerous. Nonetheless, hundreds of thousands of occupational deaths occur each year from illegal and unsafe working conditions; illegal pollution annually kills and injures more people than all street crimes combined.[4] So while business crimes typically involve stealth and fraud, they may also include violence and death.

White-Collar Crime

 L02 Define white-collar crime

While we sometimes think of enterprise crimes as a new phenomenon, they have been around for hundreds of years, ever since the Industrial Revolution began. The period between 1750 and 1850 witnessed the widespread and unprecedented emergence of financial offenses—such as fraud and embezzlement—frequently perpetrated by respectable middle-class offenders as the banking and commercial systems developed. Not surprisingly, scholars have long recognized that some unscrupulous businesspeople use their position of trust to fleece the public. In 1907, pioneering sociologist Edward Alsworth Ross recognized the phenomenon when he coined the phrase "the criminaloid" to describe the kind of person who hides behind his or her image as a pillar of the community and paragon of virtue to get personal gain through any means necessary.[5]

In the late 1930s, the distinguished criminologist Edwin Sutherland first used the phrase "white-collar crime" to describe the criminal activities of the rich and powerful. He defined white-collar crime as "a crime committed by a person of respectability and high social status in the course of his occupation."[6] As Sutherland saw it, white-collar crime involved conspiracies by members of the wealthy classes to use their position in commerce and industry for personal gain without regard to the law. Often these actions were handled by civil courts because injured parties were more concerned with recovering their losses than with seeing the offenders punished criminally. Consequently, Sutherland believed that the great majority of white-collar criminals did not become the subject of criminological study. Yet the cost of white-collar crime is probably several times greater than all the crimes customarily regarded as the crime problem. And, in contrast to street crimes, white-collar offenses breed distrust in economic and social institutions, lower public morale, and undermine faith in business and government.[7]

---

enterprise crimes Ongoing illegal activities by an individual or a group of individuals involved in commerce that either violate the laws regulating legitimate business or whose acknowledged purpose is profit through illegitimate commercial enterprise.

To read more about the history of white-collar crime and Edwin Sutherland, go to **http://www .heritage.org/research/reports/2004/10/the -sociological-origins-of-white-collar-crime.**

Is there a big difference between a corporate bigwig who scams millions and a low-level employee who pilfers some company supplies? Could their motives be the same?

Although Sutherland's work is considered a milestone in criminological history, his focus was on corporate criminality, including the crimes of the rich and powerful. Contemporary definitions of white-collar crime are typically much broader and include both middle-income Americans and corporate titans who use the marketplace for their criminal activity.[8] Included within recent views of white-collar crime are such acts as income tax evasion, credit card fraud, and bankruptcy fraud. Other white-collar criminals use their positions of trust in business or government to commit crimes. Their activities might include pilfering, soliciting bribes or kickbacks, and embezzlement. Some white-collar criminals set up business for the sole purpose of victimizing the general public. They engage in land swindles (i.e., representing a swamp as a choice building site), securities theft, medical fraud, and so on.

In addition to acting as individuals, some white-collar criminals become involved in criminal conspiracies designed to improve the market share or profitability of their corporations. This type of white-collar crime, which includes antitrust violations, price fixing, and false advertising, is known as **corporate crime**.

NATURE AND EXTENT OF WHITE-COLLAR CRIME

L03 Compare and contrast the various forms of white-collar crime

It is difficult to estimate the extent and influence of white-collar crime because these crimes are not tallied by either the UCR or NCVS. Some private and quasi-public organizations do conduct surveys on white-collar crime, which help determine the extent of the problem. The National White Collar Crime Center's most recent national survey of more than 2,500 adults taps into individual experiences with mortgage fraud, credit card fraud, identity theft, unnecessary home or auto repairs, price misrepresentation, and losses due to false stockbroker information, fraudulent business ventures, and Internet scams. The study gives a picture of how widespread white-collar crime is and how many citizens are affected by enterprise crimes:[9]

- Twenty-four percent of households and 17 percent of individuals reported experiencing at least one form of white-collar crime within the previous year.
- White-collar crimes happened at both household and individual levels, most often as a result of credit card fraud, price misrepresentation, and unnecessary repairs.
- More than half (55 percent) of the households surveyed reported at least one external recipient or agency (e.g., credit card company, business or person involved, law enforcement, consumer protection agency, personal attorney).
- Only about 12 percent of the crimes were reported to law enforcement or some other crime control agency.
- The general public views white-collar crimes seriously, considering them more damaging than traditional crimes.[10]

It is not surprising, then, that some estimates of the annual cost of white-collar crime are as high as $660 billion per year, losses that far outstrip the cost of any other type of crime.[11] Nor is it likely that the full extent of white-collar crime will ever be fully known because many victims (70 percent) are reluctant to report their crime to police, believing that nothing can be done and that getting further involved is pointless.[12]

Beyond the monetary cost, white-collar crime can cause significant economic, social, and personal damage. White-collar crime also destroys confidence, saps the integrity of commercial life, and has the potential for devastating destruction.

White-collar crime today represents a range of behaviors involving individuals acting alone and within the context of a business structure. The victims of white-collar crime can be the general public, the organization that employs

corporate crime White-collar crime involving a legal violation by a corporate entity, such as price fixing, restraint of trade, or hazardous waste dumping.

the offender, or a competing organization. There have been numerous attempts to create subcategories or typologies of white-collar criminality. The one used here contains seven elements, ranging from an individual using a business enterprise to swindle clients to large-scale corporate enterprises collectively engaging in illegitimate activity.[13]

WHITE-COLLAR SWINDLERS

Robert Allen Stanford was a financier who lived like a king on the tropical island of Antigua.[14] "Sir Robert" (as he liked to be called after being knighted by the Antiguan prime minister) ran a high-flying investment bank that offered investors high-yielding bank certificates of deposit. In 2008, at the height of his power, he was one of the richest men in the world, worth an estimated $2.2 billion. And he knew how to live the life: he spent $100 million on aircraft, including helicopters and private jets; another $12 million was spent lengthening his yacht by just six feet.[15]

Swindles are common in the digital age. On September 21, 2015, Trendon Shavers (right) exits Manhattan federal court after pleading guilty in the first U.S. criminal securities fraud case related to bitcoins, the digital currency. Authorities say Shavers defrauded investors after raising more than $4.5 million worth of bitcoins while operating "Bitcoin Savings and Trust" out of his home.

Darren Ornitz/REUTERS

Sir Robert's financial activities soon began to raise eyebrows among American authorities. His promises of lucrative returns on relatively safe certificates of deposit were often more than twice the going rate offered by mainstream banks. Stanford's investment opportunities sounded too good to be true, and unfortunately for investors, they were. Instead of the safe investments being promised, Stanford secretly used the money in very risky long-term real estate and private equity investments; $2 billion was actually lent to Stanford himself. Antiguan auditors did not examine the bank's portfolio or verify its assets because (according to witnesses) they had received bribes to cover up Stanford's scheme and misinform U.S. regulatory commissions. Stanford held these facts from investors, who were told that their money was totally safe thanks to monitoring by a team of more than 20 analysts and yearly audits by Antiguan bank regulators.

Before being seized by the government, Stanford's bank had misappropriated $8.5 billion in assets belonging to 30,000 clients in 131 countries. Stanford was convicted of

fraud in 2012 and is currently serving a 110-year prison sentence. He is eligible for release in 2105.

Swindlers such as Stanford and Allison Layton (from the opening vignette) use their position in the marketplace for illegal gains. As you may recall (Chapter 12), fraud is a common-law crime in which someone uses trickery and deceit to separate a mark from his money. A common-law swindle occurs when the con artist tells people she just inherited a Picasso from her deceased aunt and then sells it to an unsuspecting purchaser who later discovers it to be a forgery. In contrast, **white-collar swindles** such as the ones created by Stanford, involve a person using his or her institutional or business position to commit fraud and fleece victims over an extended period of time. It would be common-law fraud to sell a forged autograph of Peyton Manning or Tom Brady to someone you just met at a poker game. In contrast, someone who sets up an ongoing sports memorabilia business, advertises the sale of sports posters, photos, and other items allegedly signed by famous athletes, and then sells forgeries to unwitting customers is engaging in a white-collar swindle. Here, a criminal enterprise was created specifically to engage in illegal activity.

White-collar swindles take many forms, some of which are described in detail next.

Investment Swindles In 2015, a $40 million **Ponzi scheme** (see Exhibit 13.1) was uncovered by federal agents and the principals were sentenced to very long prison sentences. How did this scheme unfold? It seems that in 2007, Keith Franklin Simmons, a North Carolina businessman

white-collar swindle A crime in which people use an ongoing business enterprise to fraudulently expropriate money from unsuspecting victims.

Ponzi scheme An investment fraud that involves the payment of purported returns to existing investors from funds contributed by new investors.

What Is a Ponzi Scheme?

A Ponzi scheme is an investment fraud that involves the payment of purported returns to existing investors from funds contributed by new investors. Ponzi scheme organizers often solicit new investors by promising to invest funds in opportunities claimed to generate high returns with little or no risk. In many Ponzi schemes, the fraudsters focus on attracting new money to make promised payments to earlier-stage investors and to use for personal expenses, instead of engaging in any legitimate investment activity. With little or no legitimate earnings, the schemes require a consistent flow of money from new investors to continue. Ponzi schemes tend to collapse when it becomes difficult to recruit new investors or when a large number of investors ask to cash out.

Why are they called Ponzi schemes? The term comes from one Charles Ponzi, who duped thousands of New England residents into investing in a postage stamp speculation scheme back in the 1920s. At a time when the annual interest rate for bank accounts was 5 percent, Ponzi promised investors that he could provide a 50 percent return in just 90 days. Ponzi initially bought a small number of international mail coupons in support of his scheme, but quickly switched to using incoming funds to pay off earlier investors.

The most famous recent Ponzi scheme involved financier Bernard Madoff, whose Wall Street firm Bernard L. Madoff Investment Securities LLC handled the money of celebrities such as Kevin Bacon and Steven Spielberg. Madoff had not actually invested any of the money but instead deposited it in various banks and for a while paid dividends and interest while spending large sums on himself and his family. When investors wanted to cash in their stock, they found that all the money was gone. Losses amounted to about $18 billion, and Madoff was sentenced to life in prison.

SOURCE: "Ponzi Schemes," Securities and Exchange Commission, http://www.sec.gov/answers/ponzi.htm (accessed June 2016).

looking for a way to make easy money, formulated an investment scheme called Black Diamond, which he promoted as a legitimate hedge fund involved in foreign currency trading. Black Diamond, Simmons told investors, was highly safe, independently audited, and had steady rates of return. To help solicit investors from around the country, Simmons and his co-conspirators recruited "regional managers" to get investors involved, including friends, family, and acquaintances. These early investors were promised financial compensation for bringing new investors on board, so they in turn praised Black Diamond and its high rate of return to their friends, family, and acquaintances. Unfortunately, not a single dollar of investor funds was actually invested. While the fund claimed that investor accounts amounted to more than $120 million, in reality all of the accounts combined totaled less than $1 million. What happened to the money? As long as new money was coming in, Simmons and his partners were able to keep making some payments to their early investors while at the same time continuing to fund their lavish lifestyles, which included mansions, luxury vehicles, and expensive trips. Black Diamond began to collapse in on itself—there was not enough new money coming in to keep the old investors satisfied or to continue lining the pockets of the criminals running the fraud. So Simmons began a new Ponzi scheme and used the money from investors in the latest scheme to make some payments to the investors of the previous one while keeping the rest for himself and his partners in crime. Simmons received a 40-year prison sentence, one year for each million he stole![16]

To read more about Bernard Madoff, go to **http://topics.nytimes.com/top/reference /timestopics/people/m/bernard_l_madoff/. Should nondangerous people like Madoff be put in prison at the taxpayers' expense? Or should he be made to do community service after all his wealth has been confiscated?**

There have been numerous swindles in the financial world designed to fraudulently siphon off clients' money, some so great that they have threatened to collapse the world's financial markets (see Exhibit 13.2).

Telemarketing Swindles Telemarketing swindles occur when someone calls the victim, makes a false statement, and the misrepresentation causes the victim to give money to the caller. Some victims are told that they won a prize and personal information is required to receive the prize. In another example, the scammer calls the victim, claiming to be from an antivirus software company, and convinces the victim to allow the caller to access his or her computer in order to rid it of a fictional virus. Once the scammer has the victim's personal information, he can use it to access the victim's bank accounts. Here are some typical telemarketing swindle come-ons:

- You must act *now* or the offer won't be good.
- You've won a "free" gift, vacation, or prize—but you have to pay for "postage and handling" or other charges.
- You must send money, give a credit card or bank account number, or have a check picked up by courier. (You may hear this before you have had a chance to consider the offer carefully.)
- You don't need to check out the company with anyone.
- You don't need any written information about their company or their references.
- You can't afford to miss this "high-profit, no-risk" offer.[17]

Financial Swindles

- *The pyramid scheme.* Similar to Ponzi schemes, the money collected from newer victims of the fraud is paid to earlier victims to provide a veneer of legitimacy. In pyramid schemes, however, the victims themselves are induced to recruit further victims through the payment of recruitment commissions.

- *Prime bank investment swindle.* In these schemes, perpetrators claim to have access to a secret trading program endorsed by large financial institutions such as the Federal Reserve Bank, U.S. Treasury Department, World Bank, International Monetary Fund, and so on. Perpetrators often claim the unusually high rates of return and low risk are the result of a worldwide "secret" exchange open only to the world's largest financial institutions. Victims are often drawn into prime bank investment frauds because the criminals use sophisticated terms and legal-looking documents, and claim the investments are insured against loss.

- *Advance fee fraud.* This category of fraud encompasses a broad variety of schemes designed to induce their victims into remitting up-front payments in exchange for the promise of goods, services, and/or prizes. Victims are informed that in order to participate in a promising investment opportunity, they must first pay various taxes and/or fees.

- *Commodities swindle.* These schemes typically involve the deceptive or fraudulent sale of commodity investments. Victims are duped into providing funds for commodities transactions that either never occur or are inconsistent with the original sales pitches. Alternatively, commodities market participants may attempt to illegally manipulate the market for a commodity by such actions as fraudulently reporting price information or cornering the market to artificially increase the price of the targeted commodity.

- *Foreign currency exchange swindle.* These schemes are characterized by the use of false or deceptive sales practices, alleging high rates of return for minimal risk, to induce victims to invest in the foreign currency exchange market. The touted transactions either never occur, are inconsistent with the original sales pitches, or are executed for the sole purpose of generating excessive trading commissions in breach of fiduciary responsibilities to the victim client.

SOURCE: FBI, "Financial Crimes Report to the Public, Fiscal Years 2010–2011," http://www.fbi.gov/stats-services/publications/financial-crimes-report-2010-2011/financial-crimes-report-2010-2011#Financial (accessed June 2016).

Religious Swindles   Swindlers love to target the religious, taking advantage of their hope. Swindlers take in worshippers of all faiths: Jews, Muslims, Baptists, Lutherans, Catholics, Mormons, and Greek Orthodox have all fallen prey to religious swindles. How do religious swindlers operate? Some create fraudulent charitable organizations and convince devout people to contribute to their seemingly worthwhile cause while pocketing the contributions for themselves. Others create investment funds based on religious values, hoping to draw investors wary of secular investments. These scammers sometimes place scripture verses on their promotional literature to comfort hesitant investors. Others take advantage of people seeking religious pilgrimages. In 2015, Rashid Minhas was sentenced to more than nine years in prison for selling bogus travel packages to devout Muslims who wanted to travel to Saudi Arabia for the Hajj. He claimed he could obtain required Saudi Arabian entry visas, knowing full well he was not authorized to do so by the Saudi government. He sold travel deals to at least 50 customers and deposited approximately $525,000 into his own accounts.[18]

The Profiles in Crime feature "Aubrey Lee Price: Religious Swindler" looks at another swindle in some detail.

WHITE-COLLAR CHISELING

White-collar **chiseling** involves a business owner regularly cheating customers and clients, or an employee stealing from the organization they work for, by deception or deceit. When chiselers target an individual client, they may charge for something they never delivered or overbill them for services they did receive. Because the schemes are so subtle, the victim may not even realize they have been cheated. Hundreds of New York City cab drivers have lost their licenses overcharging customers by activating a switch that alters the meter, charging passengers out-of-town rates even though the ride has taken place within city limits.[19]

Auto repair shops have long been suspected of overcharging customers for bogus auto repairs that were not required or never performed.[20] When someone brings their car in for repair and are told the brakes are shot, how often do they examine them themselves? And auto repair clients seldom ask to see proof that new high-quality parts were used, making it easy for unscrupulous chiselers to substitute off-brands or used parts.

Chiseling the public can also involve schemes such as short weighting—intentionally tampering with the accuracy

chiseling   Crimes that involve using illegal means to cheat an organization, its consumers, or both on a regular basis.

Aubrey Lee Price: Religious Swindler

In 2014, Georgia native Aubrey Lee Price, formerly a devout Christian minister and trusted financial adviser, was sentenced to 30 years in prison for bank fraud, embezzlement, and other crimes,

How did this pillar of the community fall so far? Price got involved in the investment business to help fund his overseas missionary efforts. He worked for two well-known investment firms and later started his own company, PFG. Many of his clients were personal friends who knew him from church—he gave seminars on how to be a wise Christian investor. Others had been on mission trips with him. Eventually, he consolidated PFG to about 100 significant investors. Then unbeknownst to his clients, Price began gambling with their money, making risky investments and falsifying documents to hide the transactions. He had his clients invest in a local

bank and used it to fund his schemes. Price eventually gained access to more than $21 million in investor money and lost more than $16 million through risky investments—all the while telling his victims the money was being used to purchase securities. In the end, Price's deception resulted in the bank's failure and losses of more than $70 million.

When he knew he was in serious trouble, Price faked suicide on a boat in Key West, Florida. He fled first to Mexico and later back to Florida, where he grew and sold marijuana, dealt in cocaine, and sometimes worked as a bodyguard for prostitutes.

Price went from a preacher to a schemer who wiped out many of his clients' life savings and then faked his own death to avoid taking responsibility for what he had done. When a routine traffic stop in Georgia resulted in his

arrest on New Year's Eve in 2013—nearly 18 months after his disappearance—Price was tried and convicted.

 CRITICAL THINKING

Should swindlers who fleece religious people be punished more severely than those who scam the more secular? Is this a form of hate crime?

SOURCES: FBI, "The Fraudster Who Faked His Own Death: Inside the Aubrey Lee Price Case," December 18, 2014, http://www.fbi.gov/news /stories/2014/december/the-fraudster-who -faked-his-own-death-inside-the-aubrey-lee-price -case/; Arielle Kass and J. Scott Trubey, "'Dead' Banker Aubrey Lee Price Sentenced to 70 Years," *Atlanta Journal-Constitution*, October 27, 2014, http://www.ajc.com/news/business /dead-banker-aubrey-lee-price-scheduled-for -sentenc/nhsXH/. (URLs accessed June 2016.)

of scales used to weigh products in markets—or adding filler to what is being sold as unadulterated food products. A few years ago, whistleblowers let on that almost 70 percent of ground meat sold in supermarkets contained finely textured beef, better known as "**pink slime**," a substance made by gathering waste trimmings, simmering them at low heat so the fat separates easily from the muscle, and spinning the trimmings using a centrifuge to complete the separation. Next, the mixture is sent through pipes where it is sprayed with ammonia gas to kill bacteria—sounds appetizing.[21] While not illegal, a number of businesses (including McDonald's) stopped using pink slime after the story broke. Beef Products, Inc. (BPI), the South Dakota–based company that produced the stuff, was forced to close three of its four plants and laid off 700 employees. Within a year or two, BPI reopened one of its shuttered plants and the company has been gradually regaining business. The reason is the same one that made finely textured beef successful in the first place: it's cheap.[22]

Professional Chiseling   It is not uncommon for professionals to use their positions to chisel clients. Pharmacists have been known to alter prescriptions or substitute low-cost generic drugs for more expensive name brands.[23] In one of the most notorious cases in the nation's history,

Kansas City pharmacist Robert R. Courtney was charged with fraud when it was discovered that he had been selling diluted mixtures of the medications Taxol, Gemzar, Paraplatin, and Platinol, which are used to treat a variety of illnesses, including pancreatic and lung cancer, advanced ovarian and breast cancer, and AIDS-related Kaposi's sarcoma. In one instance, Courtney provided a doctor with only 450 milligrams of Gemzar for a prescription that called for 1,900 mg, a transaction that netted him a profit of $779.[24] After he pleaded guilty, Courtney told authorities that his drug dilution activities were not limited to the conduct he admitted to at the time of his guilty plea. His criminal activities had actually begun in 1992 or even earlier, affected the patients of 400 doctors, involved 98,000 prescriptions, and harmed approximately 4,200 patients.[25] There is no telling how many people died or suffered serious medical complications because of Courtney's criminal conduct.

pink slime A substance made by gathering waste trimmings, cooking them so the fat separates easily from the muscle, and using a centrifuge to complete the separation.

In May 2016, the Securities and Exchange Commission filed a complaint against pro golfer Phil Mickelson (shown here in the 2014 U.S. Open) related to insider trading. According to the SEC, in 2012 Billy Walters, a high-profile sports bettor, called Mickelson, who owed him money, and urged him to trade Dean Foods stock. The SEC says Mickelson did so the next day and made a profit of $931,000. The SEC says Walters received tips and business information about Dean Foods from former Dean Foods' director Thomas Davis between 2008 and 2012. The case was settled when Mickelson repaid $931,738.12 in trading profits and $105,291.69 in interest.

Securities Chiseling Mathew Martoma was an up-and-coming portfolio manager for the hedge fund company SAC Capital, taking millions of dollars each year in bonus money for his stock-picking prowess. But as it turns out, Martoma's success was based not on his investment savvy but on illegally obtained inside information. Martoma

insider trading Illegal buying of stock in a company based on information provided by someone who has a fiduciary interest in the company, such as an employee or an attorney or accountant retained by the firm. Federal laws and the rules of the Securities and Exchange Commission require that all profits from such trading be returned and provide for both fines and a prison sentence.

exploitation Forcing victims to pay for services to which they have a clear right.

arranged for dozens of "consultations" with doctors working for pharmaceutical firms in order to get inside information on how drug trials were going. He often engaged in subterfuge to disguise the nature of their communications (e.g., sending emails to schedule meetings or phone calls on bogus topics). Taking full advantage of his financial and personal relationships with them, Martoma and SAC Capital traded aggressively in the stocks, racking up hundreds of millions in profits for the company and himself.[26] Martoma was convicted of two counts of securities fraud, which carries a maximum 20-year term, and one count of conspiracy, which has a maximum 5-year term.[27]

It is against the law for securities to profit from inside business information, referred to as **insider trading**. The information can be used to buy and sell securities, giving the trader an unfair advantage over the general public. As originally conceived, insider trading made it illegal for corporate employees with direct knowledge of market-sensitive information to use that information for their own benefit—for example, by buying stock in a small company that is being taken over by their employer. In recent years, the definition of insider trading has been expanded by federal courts to include employees of financial institutions, such as law or banking firms, who use illegally obtained confidential information on pending corporate actions to purchase stock or give the information to a third party so that party can buy shares in the company. Courts have ruled that such actions are deceptive and violate security trading codes.[28]

Because there is no such thing as making too much money, a great deal of chiseling takes place on the commodities and stock markets, where individuals who are already rich engage in deceptive practices that are prohibited by federal law in order to become even richer.[29] Stockbrokers violate accepted practices when they engage in churning the client's account by repeated, excessive, and unnecessary buying and selling of stock.[30] Other broker fraud includes front running, in which brokers place personal orders ahead of a customer's large order to profit from the market effects of the trade, and bucketing, which is skimming customer trading profits by falsifying trade information.[31]

WHITE-COLLAR EXPLOITATION

White-collar **exploitation** occurs when an individual abuses their power or position in an organization to extort or coerce people into making payments to them for services to which they are already entitled. If the payments are not made, the services for which the victim is entitled to are withheld.

In most cases, exploitation occurs when the victim has a clear right to expect a service, and the offender threatens to withhold the service unless an additional payment or bribe is forthcoming. On the local and state levels, exploitation may occur when a government official who holds discretionary power—liquor license board members, food inspectors, fire inspectors—demand extortion money. People who want a license are told that unless they pay the board member he will turn down the request. A fire inspector demands payment for approving an addition to a business or demands that the owner of a restaurant pay him for an operating license to which they are by law entitled. Exploitation involves a threat: "If you don't pay me, I will cause you trouble."

Exploitation can also occur in private industry. Purchasing agents in large companies often demand a piece of the action for awarding contracts to suppliers and distributors. Managing agents in some of New York City's most luxurious buildings have been convicted on charges that they routinely extorted millions of dollars from maintenance contractors and building suppliers, steering repair and maintenance work to particular contractors in exchange for kickbacks.[32]

Exploitation is particularly troubling in the criminal justice system when police officers threaten victims with arrest if they do not make payments or when judges bully defendants, threatening conviction unless they are paid off. In one New York case, a police officer pretended to befriend a pizzeria owner who was being extorted by some hard-nosed criminals. When the owner asked for his help, the officer, Besnik Llakatura, actively discouraged him from going to the police and instead tried to persuade the victim that he had no choice but to make the demanded payments, warning the victim that he would by physically harmed if he did not pay. While Llakatura presented an outward façade of friendship, he was actually in cahoots with the extortionists and collected an equal share of the money the owner was forced to pay.[33]

WHITE-COLLAR INFLUENCE PEDDLING

In 2014, a scam was exposed in which corrupt state employees and their accomplices were selling California driver's licenses for cash. A man who owned a driving school let his students know that—for a price—he could guarantee them a license, even if they had already failed the driving test. Often they didn't even have to take the test, thanks to the man's connections at the Department of Motor Vehicles (DMV) office in El Cajon, California. Those willing to pay anywhere from $500 to $2,500 to corrupt DMV employees could get a license with no questions asked. The driving school catered mostly to Middle Eastern immigrants, and soon word of easy licenses in that community spread north to Los Angeles and beyond. People flew in from other states just to take a California driving test. A number of DMV employees who participated in the scam went to prison for up to 18 months.[34]

Sometimes individuals holding important institutional positions sell power, influence, and information to outsiders who have an interest in influencing the activities of the institution or buying information on what the institution may do in the future. In addition to DMV employees selling licenses to people who not deserve them, offenses within this category include government employees taking kickbacks from contractors in return for awarding them contracts they could not have won on merit, or outsiders bribing government officials, such as those in the Securities and Exchange Commission, who might sell information about future government activities. A police officer who sells information on future raids or takes a bribe in lieu of handing out a citation or making an arrest is engaging in influence peddling.

Though they are somewhat similar, **influence peddling** can be distinguished from exploitation. Exploiters force victims to pay for services to which they have a clear right; they are engaging in extortion. In contrast, influence peddlers take bribes to use their positions to grant favors and sell information to which their co-conspirators are not entitled. In sum, in crimes of exploitation, the victim is threatened and forced to pay, whereas the victim of influence peddling is the organization compromised by its employees for their own interests.

Influence Peddling in Government In 2015, Sheldon Silver, speaker of New York State's assembly and one of its most powerful politicians, was convicted of numerous charges of influence peddling. In one scheme, he secretly directed $500,000 in state money to Dr. Robert Taub's mesothelioma research at Columbia University. In return, the doctor gave Silver leads on his patients who were suffering from the deadly effects of asbestos exposure. Silver then directed those patients to the personal injury firm Weitz & Luxenberg, which paid Silver $3 million in referral fees. In the second scheme, Silver directed two major developers to use the law firm Goldberg & Iryami for litigation challenging city tax assessments. That firm secretly paid Silver $700,000 in referral fees.[35]

It has become all too common for elected and appointed government officials to be forced to resign or even to be jailed for accepting bribes to use their influence. The Silver case is by no means unique. On April 17, 2006, former Illinois Governor George Ryan was convicted of steering government contracts to people who were willing to give him kickbacks and bribes. The prosecution said Ryan and his family got fancy vacations, money, and other items worth at least $167,000, and in return offered special political favors and state business in the dozen years he served in the state's top roles.[36] Ryan's successor Governor Rod Blagojevich was forced to resign after he was overheard in federal wiretaps planning to sell president-elect Obama's open Senate seat to the highest bidder.[37] Blagojevich was subsequently impeached and removed from office on January 29, 2009. In March 2012, Blagojevich began serving a 14-year sentence in federal prison following conviction for corruption, including the soliciting of bribes; he will be eligible for parole in 2024.

---

influence peddling Using an institutional position to grant favors and sell information to which their co-conspirators are not entitled.

Influence Peddling in Criminal Justice Agents of the criminal justice system have also been accused of influence peddling. Police have routinely been accused and convicted of accepting bribes from individuals engaged in illegal activities. Some have been convicted on charges that they have provided protection and given warning of planned raids on brothels, gambling dens, and drug houses. Even customs inspectors have been convicted on charges that they were in the pay of drug cartels for looking the other way as large shipments of illegal substances were brought across the border.[38] In 1972, the Knapp Commission found that police corruption in New York City was pervasive and widespread, ranging from patrol officers accepting small gratuities from local businesspeople to senior officers receiving payoffs in the thousands of dollars from gamblers and narcotics violators.[39] Did the Knapp Commission end police dabbling in illicit activities? Hardly. In 2016, a Brooklyn cop named Eduardo Cornejo moonlighted as a pimp overseeing 11 prostitutes, sometimes heading straight from work at his NYPD precinct to his second occupation. He used his personal car to ferry the prostitutes to hot-sheets motels around the area—charging johns $100 for 15 minutes and $150 for 30 minutes.[40]

Police are not the only justice officials who have been caught in the web of bribery and influence peddling. Sadly, judges have been accused of taking bribes in order to influence their decision making. Louisiana judge Wayne G. Cresap was charged with accepting bribes in order to influence his bail decision making. Cresap released defendants on their own recognizance, without requiring cash bail, if their lawyers would later give him a payoff in return.[41] While Cresap's actions are troubling, they pale in comparison to what may be the most shocking case of judicial malfeasance on record. In 2009, two Pennsylvania judges, Mark Ciavarella and Michael Conahan, were indicted for accepting $2.6 million in bribes to place juvenile offenders in a privately run youth detention facility. Thousands of kids were put away for minor infractions so that the judges could earn millions in illegal payoffs while the owners of the private corrections facility received millions in state payments; both judges eventually pleaded guilty and received seven-year prison sentences.[42]

Influence Peddling in Business On August 13, 2010, the Apple manager in charge of selecting Asian suppliers, Paul Shin Devine, was arrested for disclosing confidential information to suppliers in exchange for payments. The information helped the suppliers gain an edge when bidding for Apple's business. Devine had the suppliers send payments to his wife's bank account to avoid attracting attention; unfortunately for him, he neglected to delete incriminating emails.[43]

Politicians and government officials are not the only ones accused of bribery; business has had its share of scandals. People who hold power in a business may force those wishing to work with the company to pay them some form of bribe or gratuity to gain a contract. In the building industry, a purchasing agent may demand a kickback from contractors hoping to gain a service contract. Sometimes influence peddling can benefit both parties. In the record industry, payola is the routine practice of paying radio stations or DJs to play songs. While the recording companies are forced to pay, they also benefit from having their recording artists receive air time they might not otherwise have gotten. Some large companies have been caught in payola scandals; Sony records paid $10 million to the State of New York to settle a claim that its promoters gave gifts to radio station managers to get songs played.[44]

Business-related bribery is not unique to the United States. In some foreign countries, soliciting bribes to do business is a common, even expected, practice. In some European countries, such as Italy and France, giving gifts to secure contracts is a routine practice.[45] It is common for foreign officials to solicit bribes to allow American firms to do business in their countries. In 2013, IBM settled a case and agreed to pay some $10 million over improper gifts to government officials in South Korea and China. That did not end IBM's ordeal: the Department of Justice continued to investigate allegations of illegal activity by a former IBM employee in Poland, as well as transactions in Argentina, Bangladesh, and Ukraine.[46] In response to these revelations, Congress passed the Foreign Corrupt Practices Act (FCPA), which makes it a criminal offense to bribe foreign officials or to make other questionable overseas payments. Violations of the FCPA draw strict penalties for both the defendant company and its officers.[47] Moreover, all fines imposed on corporate officers are paid by them, not absorbed by the company. If a domestic company violates the antibribery provisions of the FCPA, it can be fined up to $1 million. Company officers, employees, or stockholders who are convicted of bribery may have to serve a prison sentence of up to five years and pay a $10,000 fine.

WHITE-COLLAR EMBEZZLEMENT AND EMPLOYEE FRAUD

Another type of white-collar crime involves individuals' use of their positions to embezzle company funds or appropriate company property for themselves. Here the company or organization that employs the criminal, rather than an outsider, is the victim of white-collar crime.

Blue-Collar Pilferage Is nothing sacred? Three employees and a friend allegedly stole moon rocks from a NASA laboratory in Houston. FBI agents arrested them after they tried to sell the contraband to an undercover agent in Orlando, Florida. The would-be seller reportedly asked $2,000 per gram for the rocks initially but later bumped the price to $8,000 per gram.[48] While the theft of moon rocks does not happen very often, systematic theft of company property by employees, or pilferage, is common.[49]

Employee theft is most accurately explained by factors relevant to the work setting, such as job dissatisfaction and the workers' belief that they are being exploited by employers or supervisors; economic problems play a relatively small role in the decision to pilfer. So, although employers attribute employee fraud to economic conditions and declining personal values, workers themselves say they steal because of strain and conflict.

Management Fraud   Blue-collar workers are not the only employees who commit corporate theft. Management-level fraud is also quite common. Such acts include converting company assets for personal benefit; fraudulently receiving increases in compensation (such as raises or bonuses); fraudulently increasing personal holdings of company stock; retaining one's present position within the company by manipulating accounts; and concealing unacceptable performance from stockholders.[50]

Management fraud has involved some of the nation's largest companies and richest people. Multibillionaire L. Dennis Kozlowski was imprisoned in 2005 for taking excessive bonuses totaling $430 million, tax evasion, and stealing more than $100 million from his firm Tyco International; he was released on parole in 2014.[51] In an even greater scandal, chief financial officer (CFO) Andrew Fastow, chief executive officer (CEO) Jeffrey Skilling, and chairman and CEO Kenneth Lay of Enron, one of the nation's largest companies, were charged with conspiracy, securities fraud, wire fraud, bank fraud, and making false statements. The three fooled the public into believing that the company was doing great and would reach its profit targets, even though they knew it was losing billions of dollars. People who had invested heavily in Enron lost their life savings when the company collapsed. Fastow was sentenced to six years in prison for his role in the accounting scandal, and Skilling was sentenced to 24 years and four months in prison. CEO Kenneth Lay died of natural causes before he could be sentenced.[52] Why did they do it? Kenneth Lay alone received approximately $300 million from the sale of Enron stock options and restricted stock and made over $217 million in profit; he was also paid more than $19 million in salary and bonuses.

CLIENT FRAUD

Client fraud occurs when an organization that either (a) advances credit, (b) provides loans, (c) supports people financially, or (d) reimburses them for services provided to a third party is the target of criminal activity. Victims of client fraud might be an insurance company that pays out on false claims or repays health care providers that put in false claims for bogus charges. Included in this category are insurance fraud, bank fraud, credit card fraud, fraud related to welfare and Medicare programs, and tax evasion.

Health Care Fraud   In 2015, Paula Kluding, owner of Prairie View Hospice in Chandler, Oklahoma, was convicted on charges stemming from her submission of millions of dollars' worth of fraudulent claims to the Medicare program. From 2010 until July 2013, Kluding conspired with her general manager and two nurses to conceal the true medical conditions of hospice patients in her facility, and the quality and quantity of their care, in order to continue receiving payments from Medicare. She directed that medical documents be changed or written a certain way to make it appear as if nurses had visited patients or conducted assessments at the regular intervals required by Medicare—when, in fact, they hadn't. She also directed that nursing notes be falsified to make it appear that patients were in terrible health. Kluding used a substantial portion of the Medicare payments to fund her

Medicare fraud hurts many people. Dr. Farid Fata, a Detroit oncologist, prescribed chemotherapy drugs to many of his patients, telling them they had cancer when they were actually disease free. He also overtreated actual terminally ill cancer patients rather than letting them die peacefully. When he could profit from it, he also undertreated cancer patients. After an investigation, Fata was tried for Medicare fraud and sentenced to 45 years in prison, effectively a life sentence. He fraudulently diagnosed more than 550 patients while raking in more than $17 million from fraudulent billings. In this photo, Melinda Tolar holds a picture of her father, Stanton Richard Lamb, who died while being treated by Fata for cancer, even though he didn't have the disease.

lavish lifestyle—which included a 6,000-square-foot home on hundreds of acres of land.[53] Kluding was not only sent to prison but ordered to pay $2.5 million in restitution; she owes an additional $5.4 million to Medicare for overpayments.

Kluding's crimes are the mere tip of the iceberg. A single 2015 federal investigation of Medicare fraud resulted in the arrest of 240 individuals—including doctors, nurses, and other licensed professionals—for their participation in schemes involving approximately $712 million in false billings. The schemes included submitting claims to Medicare for treatments that were medically unnecessary and often not provided. In many of the cases, Medicare beneficiaries and other co-conspirators were allegedly paid cash kickbacks for supplying beneficiary information so providers could submit fraudulent bills to Medicare.[54]

One reason that thieves found Medicare an inviting target is because it operated under a system that paid providers first and investigated later. The so-called "pay and chase method" gave abusers 90 days' lag time to fleece the government out of millions before authorities were aware a crime had been committed.[55] In addition to individual physicians, some large health care providers and hospitals have been accused of routinely violating the law to obtain millions in illegal payments by overstating expenses to Medicare, filing false claims for reimbursement, billing for unnecessary procedures, and other practices.[56]

Crooked health care providers find it lucrative to engage in fraud in obtaining patients and administering their treatment and for patients to try to scam the system for their own benefit. The FBI estimates that health care fraud now costs the nation $80 billion per year.[57] There are numerous health care–related schemes, including:

- Billing for services that were never rendered by using genuine patient information to fabricate entire claims or by adding to claims with charges for procedures or services that did not take place.
- Billing for more expensive services or procedures than were actually provided or performed, commonly known as "upcoding." This practice requires "inflation" of the patient's diagnosis code to a more serious condition consistent with the false procedure code.
- Performing medically unnecessary services solely for the purpose of generating insurance payments. This scheme occurs most often in nerve-conduction and other diagnostic-testing schemes. Some Southern California clinics performed unnecessary, and sometimes harmful, surgeries on patients who had been recruited and paid to have these unnecessary surgeries performed.
- Misrepresenting noncovered treatments as medically necessary covered treatments for purposes of obtaining insurance payments. This scheme occurs in cosmetic-surgery in which noncovered cosmetic procedures such as nose jobs, tummy tucks, liposuction, or breast augmentations are billed to patients' insurers as deviated-septum repairs, hernia repairs, or lumpectomies.[58]

A central target of medical fraud is the federal Medicaid program. The Office of Inspector General of the U.S. Department of Health and Human Services estimates that 6 percent of all Medicaid payments (more than $12 billion) should not have been paid due to erroneous billing or payment, inadequate provider documentation of services to back up the claims, and/or outright fraud.[59] The government has attempted to tighten control over the industry in order to restrict the opportunity for physicians to commit fraud. Health care companies providing services to federal health care programs are also regulated by federal laws that prohibit kickbacks and self-referrals. The Health Insurance Portability and Accountability Act of 1996 (HIPAA) established health care fraud as an independent federal criminal offense, with the basic crime carrying a federal prison term of up to 10 years in addition to significant financial penalties.[60] HIPAA doubles the prison term to up to 20 years should a perpetrator's fraud result in injury to a patient; if the fraud results in a patient's death, the perpetrator can be sentenced to life in federal prison. It is a crime, punishable by up to five years in prison, to provide anything of value, money or otherwise, directly or indirectly, with the intent to induce a referral of a patient or a health care service. Liability attaches to both parties in the transaction—the entity or individual providing the kickbacks and the individual receiving payment of the referral. The law also prohibits physicians and other health care providers from referring beneficiaries in federal health care programs to clinics or other facilities in which the physician or health care provider has a financial interest. For example, it is illegal for a doctor to refer her patients to a blood-testing lab in which she has an ownership share. These practices—kickbacks and self-referrals—are prohibited under federal law because they would compromise a medical professional's independent judgment. Congress also mandated the establishment of a nationwide Coordinated Fraud and Abuse Control Program to coordinate federal, state, and local law enforcement efforts against health care fraud and to include "the coordination and sharing of data" with private health insurers.

Health care fraud is expected to continue to rise as people live longer and produce a greater demand for Medicare benefits. In the future, the utilization of long- and short-term care facilities such as skilled nursing, assisted living, and hospice services will expand substantially. Additionally, fraudulent billings and medically unnecessary services billed to health care insurers are prevalent throughout the country and are expected to grow in the future.

Bank Fraud Encompassing such diverse schemes as check kiting, check forgery, false statements on loan applications, sale of stolen checks, bank credit card fraud, unauthorized use of automatic teller machines (ATMs), auto title fraud, and illegal transactions with offshore banks, bank fraud can cost billions per year.[61] Among the schemes used to defraud banks are mortgage frauds in which a group of conspirators fraudulently obtain loans on overvalued or

EXHIBIT 13.3

Some Common Bank Fraud Schemes

- *Fraudulent property flipping*. Property is purchased, falsely appraised at a higher value, and then quickly sold at a higher value than the market. A home worth $200,000 may be appraised for $800,000 or higher and sold to a co-conspirator who gets a mortgage based on a phony appraisal. The new owner quickly defaults on the loan. This type of scheme typically involves one or more of the following: fraudulent appraisals, doctored loan documentation, and/or inflating buyer income. Kickbacks to buyers, investors, property/loan brokers, appraisers, or title company employees are common in this scheme.

- *Silent second*. The buyer of a property borrows the down payment from the seller through the issuance of a nondisclosed second mortgage. The primary lender believes the borrower has invested his own money in the down payment, when in fact it is borrowed. The second mortgage may not be recorded to further conceal its status from the primary lender.

- *Nominee loans/straw buyers*. The identity of the borrower is concealed through the use of a nominee who allows the borrower to use the nominee's name and credit history to apply for a loan.

- *Fictitious/stolen identity*. A fictitious/stolen identity may be used on the loan application. The applicant may be involved in an identity theft scheme: the applicant's name, personal identifying information, and credit history are used without the true person's knowledge.

- *Inflated appraisals*. A corrupt home appraiser acts in collusion with a borrower and provides a misleading appraisal report to the lender. The report inaccurately states an inflated property value.

- *Foreclosure schemes*. The perpetrator identifies homeowners who are at risk of defaulting on loans or whose houses are already in foreclosure. Perpetrators mislead the homeowners into believing that they can save their homes in exchange for a transfer of the deed and up-front fees. The perpetrator profits from these schemes by remortgaging the property or pocketing fees paid by the homeowner.

- *Equity skimming*. An investor may use a straw buyer, false income documents, and false credit reports to obtain a mortgage loan in the straw buyer's name. Subsequent to closing, the straw buyer signs the property over to the investor in a quit claim deed, which relinquishes all rights to the property and provides no guaranty to title. The investor does not make any mortgage payments and rents the property until foreclosure takes place several months later.

- *Air loans*. This is a nonexistent property loan where there is usually no collateral. An example of an air loan would be where a broker invents borrowers and properties, establishes accounts for payments, and maintains custodial accounts for escrows. They may set up an office with a bank of telephones, each one used as the employer, appraiser, credit agency, and so on, for verification purposes.

- *Hedge fund fraud*. Hedge funds (HFs) are private investment partnerships that routinely accept only high-wealth clients willing to invest at least hundreds of thousands of dollars. Historically, these high-wealth investors were deemed "financially sophisticated," and, as a result, HFs have been unregulated and are not required to register with any federal or state regulatory agency. More recently, many middle-class investors have been exposed to HFs through ancillary investments such as pensions and endowments. There are about 9,000 HFs currently operating, with over a trillion dollars in assets under management.

SOURCE: FBI, "Common Fraud Schemes," 2014, http://www.fbi.gov/scams-safety/fraud (accessed June 2016).

nonexistent property. Some of the more common schemes are set out in Exhibit 13.3.[62]

To be found guilty of bank fraud, one must knowingly execute or attempt to execute a scheme to fraudulently obtain money or property from a financial institution. A car dealer would commit bank fraud by securing loans on titles to cars it no longer owned. A real estate owner would be guilty of bank fraud if he or she obtained a false appraisal on a piece of property with the intention of obtaining a bank loan in excess of the property's real worth. Penalties for bank fraud include a maximum fine of $1 million and up to 30 years in prison.

Tax Evasion Another important aspect of client fraud is tax evasion. Here the victim is the government that is cheated by one of its clients, the errant taxpayer to whom it extended credit by allowing the taxpayer to delay paying taxes on money he or she had already earned. Tax fraud is a particularly challenging area for criminological study because so many U.S. citizens regularly underreport their income, and it is often difficult to separate honest error from deliberate tax evasion.

The basic law on tax evasion is contained in the U.S. Internal Revenue Code, section 7201, which states:

> Any person who willfully attempts in any manner to evade or defeat any tax imposed by this title or the payment thereof shall, in addition to other penalties provided by law, be guilty of a felony and, upon conviction thereof, shall be fined not more than $100,000 or imprisoned not more than five years, or both, together with the costs of prosecution.

To prove tax fraud, the government must find that the taxpayer either underreported his or her income or did not report taxable income. No minimum dollar amount is stated before fraud exists, but the government can take legal action when there is a "substantial underpayment of tax." A second element of tax fraud is "willfulness" on the part of the tax evader. In the major case on this issue, willfulness was defined as a "voluntary, intentional violation of a known legal duty and not the careless disregard for the truth."[63] Finally, to prove tax fraud, the government must show that the taxpayer has purposely attempted to evade or defeat a tax payment. If the offender is guilty of passive neglect, the offense is a misdemeanor. Passive neglect means simply not paying taxes, not reporting income, or not paying taxes when due. On the other hand, affirmative tax evasion, such as keeping double books, making false entries, destroying books or records, concealing assets, or covering up sources of income, constitutes a felony.

Although tax cheating is a serious crime, the great majority of major tax cheats (in some categories, four of five cheaters) are not prosecuted because the IRS lacks the money to enforce the law.[64]

CORPORATE CRIME

Yet another component of white-collar crime involves situations in which powerful institutions or their representatives willfully violate the laws that restrain these institutions from doing social harm or require them to do social good. This is also known as corporate or organizational crime.

Interest in corporate crime first emerged in the early 1900s, when a group of writers, known as muckrakers, targeted the monopolistic business practices of John D. Rockefeller and other corporate business leaders. In a 1907 article, sociologist Edward Alsworth Ross described the "criminaloid": a business leader who while enjoying immunity from the law victimized an unsuspecting public.[65] Edwin Sutherland focused theoretical attention on corporate crime when he began his research on the subject in the 1940s; corporate crime was probably what he had in mind when he coined the phrase "white-collar crime."[66]

Corporate crimes are socially injurious acts committed by people who control companies to further their business interests. The target of their crimes can be the general public, the environment, or even company workers. What makes these crimes unique is that the perpetrator is a legal fiction—a corporation—and not an individual. In reality, it is company employees or owners who commit corporate crimes and who ultimately benefit through career advancement or greater profits. For a corporation to be held criminally liable, the employee committing the crime must be acting within the scope of his employment and must have

Sherman Antitrust Act Law that subjects to criminal or civil sanctions any person "who shall make any contract or engage in any combination or conspiracy" in restraint of interstate commerce.

actual or apparent authority to engage in the particular act in question. Actual authority occurs when a corporation knowingly gives authority to an employee; apparent authority is satisfied if a third party, such as a customer, reasonably believes the agent has the authority to perform the act in question. Courts have ruled that actual authority may occur even when the illegal behavior is not condoned by the corporation but is nonetheless within the scope of the employee's authority.[67]

Some of the acts included within corporate crime are price fixing and illegal restraint of trade, false advertising, and the use of company practices that violate environmental protection statutes. The variety of crimes contained within this category is great, and they cause vast damage. The following subsections examine some of the most important offenses.

Illegal Restraint of Trade and Price Fixing In 2013, nine Japan-based companies pleaded guilty and were forced to pay a total of more than $740 million in criminal fines for their roles in conspiracies to fix the prices of more than 30 different products sold to U.S. car manufacturers, including Chrysler, Ford, and General Motors, as well as to the U.S. subsidiaries of Honda, Mazda, Mitsubishi, Nissan, Toyota, and Subaru. Executives in the companies attended meetings and communicated by telephone in the United States and Japan to set prices, to conspire to keep bids for merchandise higher than needed, and to control the supply of auto parts sold to the car manufacturers. They took measures to keep their conduct secret by using code names and meeting in remote locations. Afterward, they had further secret communications to monitor and enforce their illegal agreements.[68]

The executives at these auto part supply companies engaged in restraint of trade and price fixing. A restraint of trade involves a contract or conspiracy designed to stifle competition, create a monopoly, artificially maintain prices, or otherwise interfere with free market competition. The control of restraint of trade violations has its legal basis in the **Sherman Antitrust Act**, which subjects to criminal or civil sanctions any person "who shall make any contract or engage in any combination or conspiracy" in restraint of interstate commerce.[69] The Sherman Act carries maximum penalties of a $100 million criminal fine for corporations and a $1 million criminal fine and 10 years in prison for individuals. The maximum fine may be increased to twice the gain derived from the crime or twice the loss suffered by the victims of the crime, if either of those amounts is greater than the statutory maximum fine.[70] The act outlaws conspiracies between corporations designed to control the marketplace.

In most instances, the act lets the presiding court judge whether corporations have conspired to "unreasonably restrain competition." However, four types of market conditions are considered so inherently anticompetitive that federal courts, through the Sherman Antitrust Act, have defined them as illegal per se, without regard to the facts or circumstances of the case:

- *Division of markets.* Firms divide a region into territories, and each firm agrees not to compete in the others' territories.
- *Tying arrangement.* A corporation requires customers of one of its services to use other services it offers. For example, it would be an illegal restraint of trade if a railroad required that companies doing business with it or supplying it with materials ship all goods they produce on trains owned by the rail line.[71]
- *Group boycott.* An organization or company boycotts retail stores that do not comply with its rules or desires.
- *Price fixing.* A conspiracy to set and control the price of a necessary commodity is considered an absolute violation of the act.

Deceptive Pricing   Even the largest U.S. corporations commonly use deceptive pricing schemes when they respond to contract solicitations. Deceptive pricing occurs when contractors provide the government or other corporations with incomplete or misleading information on how much it will actually cost to fulfill the contracts on which they are bidding or use mischarges once the contracts are signed. For example, defense contractors have been prosecuted for charging the government for costs incurred on work they are doing for private firms or shifting the costs on fixed-price contracts to ones in which the government reimburses the contractor for all expenses ("cost-plus" contracts).

False Claims Advertising   Executives in even the largest corporations sometimes face stockholders' expectations of ever-increasing company profits that seem to demand that sales be increased at any cost. At times executives respond to this challenge by making claims about their products that cannot be justified by actual performance. However, the line between clever, aggressive sales techniques and fraudulent claims is fine. It is traditional to show a product in its best light, even if that involves resorting to fantasy. It is not fraudulent to show a delivery service vehicle taking off into outer space or to imply that taking one sip of beer will make people feel they have just jumped into a freezer. However, it is illegal to knowingly and purposely advertise a product as possessing qualities that the manufacturer realizes it does not have, such as the ability to cure the common cold, grow hair, or turn senior citizens into rock stars (though some rock stars are senior citizens these days).

In 2003, the U.S. Supreme Court, in the case of *Illinois Ex Rel. Madigan v. Telemarketing Associates*, helped define the line separating illegal claims from those that are artistic hyperbole protected by free speech.[72] Telemarketing Associates, a for-profit fundraising corporation, was retained by a charity to solicit donations to aid Vietnam veterans in the state of Illinois. Though donors were told that a significant portion of the money would go to the vets, the telemarketers actually retained 85 percent of all the money collected. The Illinois attorney general filed a complaint in state court, alleging that such representations were knowingly deceptive and materially false. The telemarketers said they were exercising their First Amendment free speech rights when they made their pitch for money.

The Supreme Court disagreed and found that states may charge fraud when fundraisers make false or misleading representations designed to deceive donors about how their donations will be used. The Court held that it is false and misleading for a solicitor to fool potential donors into believing that a substantial portion of their contributions would fund specific programs or services knowing full well that was not the case.

Worker Safety Violations   Some corporations have endangered the lives of their own workers by maintaining unsafe conditions in their plants and mines. It has been estimated that more than 20 million workers have been exposed to hazardous materials while on the job. Each year about 4 million workers are injured and 4,000 killed on the job. Some industries have been hit particularly hard by complaints and allegations. The control of workers' safety has been the province of the Occupational Safety and Health Administration (OSHA). OSHA sets industry standards for the proper use of such chemicals as benzene, arsenic, lead, and coke. Intentional violation of OSHA standards can result in criminal penalties.

The National Whistleblowers Center is a nonprofit educational advocacy organization that works for the enforcement of environmental laws, nuclear safety, civil rights, and government and industry accountability through the support and representation of employee whistleblowers. Learn more at **http://www .whistleblowers.org/**.

Should whistleblowers get a share of any penalties levied on white-collar criminals?

WHITE-COLLAR LAW ENFORCEMENT SYSTEMS

Who deals with these crimes and enforces the laws controlling violations of business enterprise law? The Commerce Clause of the U.S. Constitution gives the federal government the authority to regulate white-collar crime. Detection and enforcement are primarily in the hands of administrative departments and agencies, including the FBI, the Internal Revenue Service, the Secret Service, U.S. Customs, the Environmental Protection Agency, and the Securities and Exchange Commission.[73] The decision to pursue criminal rather than civil violations usually is based on the seriousness of the case and the perpetrator's intent, actions to conceal the violation, and prior record. Enforcement generally is reactive (generated by complaints) rather than proactive (involving ongoing investigations or the monitoring of activities). Investigations are carried out by the various federal agencies and the FBI. If criminal prosecution is called for, the case will be handled by attorneys from the criminal, tax, antitrust, and civil rights divisions of the Justice Department. If insufficient evidence is available to warrant a criminal prosecution, the case will be handled civilly or administratively by some other federal agency. The Federal Trade Commission can issue a cease-and-desist order in antitrust or merchandising fraud cases.

The number of state-funded technical assistance offices to help local prosecutors has increased significantly; more than 40 states offer such services. On the state and local levels, law enforcement officials have made progress in a number of areas, such as controlling consumer fraud. Local prosecutors pursue white-collar criminals more vigorously if they are part of a team effort involving a network of law enforcement agencies.[74] National surveys of local prosecutors find that many do not consider white-collar crimes particularly serious problems. They are more willing to prosecute cases if the offense causes substantial harm and if other agencies fail to act. Relatively few prosecutors participate in interagency task forces designed to investigate white-collar criminal activity.[75]

CONTROLLING WHITE-COLLAR CRIME

L04 Discuss efforts to control white-collar crime

In years past, it was rare for a corporate or white-collar criminal to receive a serious criminal penalty.[76] White-collar criminals are often considered nondangerous offenders because they usually are respectable older citizens who have families to support. These "pillars of the community" are not seen in the same light as a teenager who breaks into a drugstore to steal a few dollars. Their public humiliation at being caught is usually deemed punishment enough; a prison sentence seems unnecessarily cruel.

The main reason, according to legal expert Stuart Green, is that perception of white-collar crime is clouded by moral ambiguity. White-collar crimes are typically committed by society's success stories, by the rich and the powerful, and frequently have no visible victim at their root. Both the public and the justice system have had trouble distinguishing criminal fraud from mere lawful exaggeration, tax evasion from "tax avoidance," insider trading from "savvy investing," obstruction of justice from "zealous advocacy," bribery from "horse trading," and extortion from "hard bargaining."[77] Hence, white-collar criminals are treated more leniently than lower-class offenders.

The prevailing wisdom, then, is that many white-collar criminals avoid prosecution, and those who are prosecuted receive lenient punishment. What efforts have been made

to bring violators of the public trust to justice? White-collar criminal enforcement typically involves two strategies designed to control organizational deviance: compliance and deterrence.[78]

Compliance Strategies Compliance strategies aim for law conformity without the necessity of detecting, processing, or penalizing individual violators. At a minimum, they ask for cooperation and self-policing among the business community. Compliance systems attempt to create conformity by giving companies economic incentives to obey the law. They rely on administrative efforts to prevent unwanted conditions before they occur. Compliance systems depend on the threat of economic sanctions or civil penalties to control corporate violators.

One method of compliance is to set up administrative agencies to oversee business activity. The Securities and Exchange Commission regulates Wall Street activities, the Food and Drug Administration regulates drugs, cosmetics, medical devices, meats and other foods, and so on. The legislation creating these agencies usually spells out the penalties for violating regulatory standards.[79] It is easier and less costly to be in compliance, the theory goes, than to pay costly fines and risk criminal prosecution for repeat violations. Moreover, the federal government bars people and businesses from receiving government contracts if they have engaged in repeated business law violations.

Another compliance approach is to force corporate boards to police themselves and take more oversight responsibility. In the wake of the Enron and WorldCom cases, the federal government enacted the Sarbanes-Oxley (SOX) legislation in 2002 to combat fraud and abuse in publicly traded companies.[80] This law limits the services auditing firms can perform in order to make sure accounting firms do not fraudulently collude with corporate officers; it places greater responsibilities on boards to preserve an organization's integrity and reputation. It also penalizes any attempts to alter or falsify company records to delude shareholders:

> Sec. 802(a) Whoever knowingly alters, destroys, mutilates, conceals, covers up, falsifies, or makes a false entry in any record, document, or tangible object with the intent to impede, obstruct, or influence the investigation or proper administration of any matter within the jurisdiction of any department or agency of the United States or any case filed under title 11, or in relation to or contemplation of any such matter or case, shall be fined under this title, imprisoned not more than 20 years, or both.

In sum, compliance strategies attempt to create a marketplace incentive to obey the law. Compliance strategies avoid punishing, stigmatizing, and shaming businesspeople by focusing on the act, rather than the actor, in white-collar crime.[81]

Deterrence Strategies Some criminologists say that the punishment of white-collar crimes should include a retributive component similar to that used in common-law crimes. White-collar crimes, after all, are immoral activities that have harmed social values and deserve commensurate punishment.[82] Even the largest fines and penalties are no more than a slap on the wrist to multibillion-dollar companies. Corporations can get around economic sanctions by moving their rule-violating activities overseas, where legal controls over injurious corporate activities are lax or nonexistent.[83] They argue that the only way to limit white-collar crime is to deter potential offenders through fear of punishment.

Deterrence strategies involve detecting criminal violations, determining who is responsible, and penalizing the offenders to deter future violations.[84] Deterrence systems are oriented toward apprehending violators and punishing them rather than creating conditions that induce conformity to the law.

Deterrence strategies should work—and they have—because white-collar crime by its nature is a rational act whose perpetrators are extremely sensitive to the threat of criminal sanctions. Perceptions of detection and punishment for white-collar crimes appear to be powerful deterrents to future law violations. Although deterrence strategies may prove effective, federal agencies have traditionally been reluctant to throw corporate executives in jail. The government seeks criminal indictments in corporate violations only in "instances of outrageous conduct of undoubted illegality," such as price fixing.[85] The government has also been lenient with companies and individuals that cooperate voluntarily after an investigation has begun; leniency is not given as part of a confession or plea arrangement. Those who comply with the leniency policy are charged criminally for the activity reported.[86]

Despite years of neglect, there is growing evidence that white-collar crime deterrence strategies have become normative. This get-tough deterrence approach appears to be affecting all classes of white-collar criminals. Although many people believe affluent corporate executives usually avoid serious punishment, public displeasure with such highly publicized white-collar crimes may be producing a backlash that is resulting in more frequent use of prison sentences.[87] With the Enron scandal depriving so many people of their life savings, the general public has become educated as to the damage caused by white-collar criminals and may now consider white-collar crimes as more serious offenses than common-law theft offenses.[88]

 Since 1999, Florida's Department of Environmental Protection has fielded a multiagency Strike Force—led by the department's Division of Law Enforcement—to investigate pollutant discharges and the release of hazardous material statewide. Check it out at **http://www.dep.state.fl.us/**.
   Would you put polluters in prison or simply make them pay for the cleanup?

Green Crime

L05 Be familiar with the concept of green crime

The federal Environmental Protection Agency requires the proper handling and disposal of hazardous wastes. Before they are released into local sewers and wastewater treatment plants, EPA rules require that toxic chemicals be treated in order to protect rivers, lakes, and streams. In 2016, Southern Grease Company, based in Dickson, Tennessee, was ordered to pay a criminal fine of $280,000 and forfeit an additional $113,500 for felony violations arising from its illegal disposal of waste grease. Southern

SARAH RICE/The New York Times/Redux

The Flint, Michigan, water pollution case shocked the nation. Here, Flint resident Joyce Cruz uses bottled water to prepare dinner at home. The city's drinking water may have exposed tens of thousands of people to lead and other toxic chemicals, but few could see a way to pick up and move someplace safe.

DEFINING GREEN CRIME

There is no single vision to define the concept of green crimes. Three independent views exist:

- *Legalist.* According to the legalist perspective, environmental crimes are violations of existing criminal laws designed to protect people, the environment, or both. This definition would include crimes against workers such as occupational health and safety crimes, as well as laws designed to protect nature and the environment (e.g., Clean Air Act, Clean Water Act).
- *Environmental justice.* According to the environmental justice view, limiting environmental crimes to actual violations of the criminal law is too narrow. A great deal of environmental damage occurs in third-world nations desperate for funds and willing to give mining and oil companies a free hand to develop resources. These nations have meager regulatory laws and therefore allow businesses wide latitude in environmental contamination that would be forbidden in the United States. In addition, environmental justice advocates believe that corporations themselves have attempted to co-opt or manipulate environmental laws, thereby limiting their scope and reach. Executives fear that the environmental movement will force changes in their production practices and place limits on their growth and corporate power. Some try to co-opt green laws by public relations and advertising campaigns that suggest they are doing everything in their power to respect the environment, thereby reducing the need for government regulation. Criminologists must take a broader view of green crimes than the law allows.
- *Biocentric.* According to the biocentric approach, environmental harm is viewed as any human activity that disrupts a biosystem, destroying plant and animal life. This more radical approach would criminalize any intentional or negligent human activity or manipulation that impacts negatively on the earth's natural resources.[92] Environmental harm, according to this view, is much greater than what is defined by law as environmental crimes. As criminologist Rob White points out, this is because some of the most ecologically destructive activities, such as clear felling of old-growth forests, are quite legal. Environmental crimes are typically oriented toward protecting humans and their property and have a limited interest in the interests of animals and plants.[93] Environmental laws protect animal and fish processing plants that treat nature and wildlife simply and mainly as

Grease contracted with restaurants and other customers in Tennessee and Kentucky to collect and dispose of the customers' waste grease. Rather than hauling the grease to licensed waste treatment plants, Southern Grease discharged the toxic waste into grease interceptors that were connected to the municipal sewer systems. This illegal dumping of grease caused substantial damage to the sewer systems by clogging pipes and interrupting the operation of pump stations. In 2015 and 2016, company executives pleaded guilty to violating the Clean Water Act, conspiring to violate the Clean Water Act, and making false statements to EPA agents. They were sentenced to prison and also ordered to pay restitution to municipal authorities in Dickson and Clarksville.[89]

Green crime is a type of enterprise crime involving violation of laws protecting the environment. Illegal dumping schemes are just part of the green crime problem. Environmental activists have long called attention to a variety of ecological threats that they feel should be deemed criminal: green crimes involve a wide range of actions and outcomes that harm the environment and that stem from decisions about what is produced, where it is produced, and how it is produced.[90] Global warming, overdevelopment, population growth, and other changes will continue to bring these issues front and center.[91]

green crime Acts involving illegal environmental harm that violate environmental laws and regulations.

resources for human exploitation. Human beings are the cause of environmental harm and need to be controlled.

THE HARMS PERSPECTIVE

Green criminologists typically use what is known as the *harms perspective* when they conceptualize crime and deviance.[94] Accordingly, crime is a social construction that can and should be expanded to include all serious *social harms*, activities that cause any discomfort, present or future, to individuals. Harms may include physical, financial/economic, emotional or psychological, and cultural safety harm. Using the harms perspective, it would be appropriate to sanction toxic waste dumping or air pollution severely because they cause residual harm that will last many years, poisoning the environment and producing diseases such as cancer. However, in many instances this action is punished civilly, not criminally. For example, in 2013, AK Steel Corp. was fined a $1.65 million civil penalty to resolve alleged violations of air pollution laws that occurred at its now-closed coke plant in Ashland, Kentucky. In the Criminology in Action feature, one enterprise that may fit the harms test, chicken farming, is discussed in some detail.

 The American Humane Association is a champion of animal rights. Learn more at **http://www.americanhumane.org.**
Should people who kill animals be sent to prison? Before you answer, think about hunting, fishing, and bullfighting, not to mention chicken farming.

FORMS OF GREEN CRIME

 LO6 List the components of green crime

Green crime can take many different forms, ranging from deforestation and illegal logging to violations of worker safety. A few of the most damaging forms are set out next.

Illegal Logging   Illegal logging involves harvesting, processing, and transporting timber or wood products in violation of existing laws and treaties.[95] It is a universal phenomenon, occurring in major timber-producing countries, especially in the third world where enforcement is lax. Illegal logging operations rely on corruption and could not occur without some form of cooperation from government officials responsible for protecting forests, who may take bribes so that criminals can obtain logging permits, avoid detection, and export illegal timber. This results in the loss of crucial resources for developing countries, while damaging their economies, public trust, and institutional structures.[96]

Logging violations include taking trees in protected areas such as national parks, going over legally prescribed logging quotas, processing logs without acquiring licenses, and exporting logs without paying export duties. By sidestepping the law, loggers can reap greater profits than those generated through legal methods. The situation is serious because illegal logging can have severe environmental and social impact:

- Illegal logging exhausts forests, destroys wildlife, and damages its habitats. Illegal logging in central Africa is destroying the habitats and threatening the survival of populations of the great apes, including gorillas and chimpanzees.
- It causes ruinous damage to the forests, including deforestation and forest degradation worldwide. The destruction of forest cover can cause flash floods and landslides that have killed thousands of people. By reducing forest cover, illegal logging impairs the ability of land to absorb carbon emissions. This is especially troublesome because forests are vital to mitigating climate change because they absorb carbon dioxide from the atmosphere. Deforestation accounts for an estimated 17 percent of global carbon emissions, greater than from all the world's air, road, rail, and shipping traffic combined.[97]

Illegal logging costs billions each year in government revenue, impairing the ability of third-world nations to provide needed social services.

- It creates unsustainable economic devastation in the poorest countries. Vietnam, for example, has lost a third of its forest cover; in nearby Cambodia, illegal logging is at least 10 times the size of the legal harvest. These rates of extraction are clearly unsustainable, destroying valuable sources of employment and export revenues for the future.
- The substantial revenues from illegal logging fund national and regional conflict. In Cambodia, for several years Khmer Rouge insurgents were sustained primarily by revenue from logging areas under their control.[98]

According to INTERPOL, illegal logging accounts for 50 to 90 percent of all forestry activities in key producer tropical forests, such as those of the Amazon basin, central Africa, and Southeast Asia, and 15 to 30 percent of all wood traded globally. Illegal logging continues to occur in many formally protected forests, especially in tropical countries. And it's likely to continue since illegally harvested timber is highly lucrative and estimated to be worth between $30 billion and $100 billion annually.[99]

 INTERPOL is an international organization that enables police in 190 member countries to work together to fight international crime. They provide a range of policing expertise and capabilities, supporting three main crime programs: counterterrorism, cybercrime, and organized and emerging crime. Learn more at **http://www.interpol.int/en.**
In the era of globalization, should a true international police force be created to combat transnational crime and global criminal enterprise?

Is Chicken Farming Foul?

04

Green criminologists who favor the harms perspective believe that business enterprise that damages people and hurts animals should be a crime. One good example is the chicken farming industry, whose practices, though currently legal, are actually destructive and harmful.

Green criminologists point out that the modern poultry industry began about 50 years ago with the use of artificial incubators and food additives added to chicken feed. These additives stimulated unnatural and rapid growth and also staved off potential diseases that were spread due to the cramped confinement of the indoor farms. Some chemicals made chickens produce more eggs, while different mixtures were used to make chickens grow larger and faster. With the discovery of genetic and chemical manipulation, chickens became a moldable product used to embody what humans need for their own consumption.

The results of these modifications have created a bird that no longer resembles the natural chicken. From 1935 to 1995, the average weight of a broiler chicken increased by 65 percent. The time they took to grow to this size decreased by 60 percent, while their food was decreased by 57 percent. The chicken industry created a product that drove down costs by producing more meat in a shorter amount of time while spending far less on food.

The chicken industry has grown tremendously within the last 50 years. Today, America raises over 9 billion chickens, China 7 billion, and Europe about 6 billion. Some estimate about 50 billion chickens are raised around the world each year.

Of course, there is a price to pay. On average the modern chicken farm houses 30,000 to 40,000 birds. Of these chickens, up to 4 percent will die from sudden death syndrome, a cardiovascular disorder that can be compared to having a heart attack. This syndrome is most often associated with an abnormally fast growth rate. Five percent will develop excess fluid in their body cavities that is caused from growth rates, cold temperatures, and excessive salt in their feed; three out of four will be unable to walk. Other problems include bacterial infections in the bones, internal bleeding, respiratory disease, and weakened immune systems.

The process of preparing the chicken for consumption is also objectively cruel and harmful to the birds. Chickens are crated and typically travel hundreds of miles with no food or water. Often the chickens already have broken bones and injuries from the journey when they arrive at the processing plant. They are then strung up by their ankles and are moved through a water bath that is electrified in order to stun them. The chicken is then brought to a throat-slitter machine; this cuts the throat to drain blood from the carcass. It is common for the major arteries to be missed and for these cases they have "kill men" whose job it is to slaughter those chickens left alive; they also sometimes miss the arteries, causing severe pain. The birds are then dumped into a scald tank containing water heated to 140 degrees Fahrenheit, which loosens the chicken's feathers so they are easily removed without burning off the chicken skin; scald water may be a source of salmonella. When the birds are beheaded, a high-speed machine cuts the bodies vertically, often nicking the intestines and contaminating the body with feces. After inspection the chickens are dunked in a tank of cold water. In this tank the feces that released from the bowels are mixed with and sit in the water.

Beyond the inhumane treatment of chickens during the factory process, the process can have a devastating effect on the human consumer. It is clear that many birds are sent into the market covered in feces and bacteria. Between 39 and 75 percent of chickens in grocery stores are infected with E. coli, 8 percent contain salmonella, and 70 to 90 percent contain campylobacter, which causes diarrhea, nausea, and vomiting.

Despite these cruel and dangerous practices, chicken farming is legal. Green criminologists believe that the practices constitute a crime, and if changes cannot be made the practice should be abandoned entirely.

 CRITICAL THINKING

Is it realistic, considering how much chicken is produced and how critical it is for diets here and abroad, that chicken farming could be halted? Is this just the price that must be paid to feed 7 billion people around the world? Or would it be worth doubling or tripling the price of this food product to make it more humane?

SOURCES: Julie Stephens, "Capitalism and Green Crime: An Examination of Chicken Farming," University of South Florida, 2014; Jonathan Foer, *Eating Animals* (New York, NY: Little, Brown and Company, 2009); Humane Society of America, Cruel Confinement, 2014, http://www.humanesociety.org/issues/confinement_farm/ (accessed June 2016).

Illegal Wildlife Exports The smuggling of wildlife across national borders is a serious matter.[100] Exporters find a lucrative trade in the demand for such illicit wildlife commodities as tiger parts, caviar, elephant ivory, rhino horn, and exotic birds and reptiles. Wildlife contraband may include live pets, hunting trophies, fashion accessories, cultural artifacts, ingredients for traditional medicines, wild meat for human consumption (or bushmeat), and other products. Illegal profits can be immense.

In some instances, endangered species are killed and their hides and body parts are illegally exported abroad. Tigers are the target of a highly lucrative illegal trade spanning countries and continents. These big cats are killed for their fur, which is prized on the black market, and for their body parts for traditional medicines and other uses.[101] Elephants and rhinoceroses are prized by poachers for their tusks and horns. Since 2008, African and Asian rhinoceros populations have been experiencing unprecedented intensification of poaching. Two subspecies, the northern white rhinoceros and the western black rhinoceros, are being shot into extinction; the black rhino population, which was 70,000 in 1960, is now about 2,500.[102] Since 2010, record numbers of elephants, more than 30,000 per year, have been reported poached, and record amounts of contraband ivory have been seized by authorities. Why poach? Ivory is going for around $1,000 per pound on the black market. A pair of tusks measuring 92 inches along the outside curve and weighing over 100 pounds can fetch close to $100,000 on the black market.[103] Rhino horns go for about $45,000. While they can be safely harvested from farmed rhinos (rhino horns grow back after trimming), that has not stopped poachers from decimating the species.

In addition to species endangered by poaching, there are also numerous problems presented by illegal wildlife exporting. Poachers imperil endangered species and threaten them with extinction. By evading government controls, they create the potential for introducing pests and diseases into formerly unaffected areas.[104] They import non-native species that harm the receiving habitats. Florida's Everglades have been overrun with non-native species, such as pythons, that have escaped into the Everglades and now threaten native species. Illegal wildlife traders range from independent one-person operations that sell a single item to complex multi-ton, commercial-sized consignments shipped all over the world.

Adding all these sources together, the global trade in illegal wildlife is a growing phenomenon and is now estimated to be $10 billion annually. The United States is estimated to purchase nearly 20 percent of all illegal wildlife and wildlife products on the market, perhaps as much as $3 billion annually. The trade is so lucrative because exotic animals and animal parts are enormously expensive, providing an economic incentive that proves irresistible to smugglers in third-world nations.[105]

The U.S. Congress has passed numerous laws that regulate and restrict wildlife imports and exports, including the Endangered Species Act of 1973 and the Lacey Act, which protects both plants and wildlife by creating civil and criminal penalties for a wide array of violations. The original act was directed at preserving game and wild birds and prohibiting the introduction of non-native birds and animals into native ecosystems. The act has been amended and in 1981 was changed to include illegal trade in plants, fish, and wildlife both domestically and abroad. The maximum penalty was increased to $10,000 with possible imprisonment for one year. Additionally, the mental state required for a criminal violation was increased to "knowingly and willfully"; civil penalties were expanded to apply to negligent violations.[106]

These laws and others establish authorities and guidelines for wildlife trade inspection at ports of entry, and wildlife crime law enforcement and prosecution. There are international laws restricting the wildlife trade. The United Nations Convention on International Trade in Endangered Species of Wild Fauna and Flora (CITES) serves as the primary vehicle for regulating wildlife trade. Despite these controls, it has been argued that one way to effectively control the movements of creatures across regions is to allow commercial export of wildlife. However, where legalized trade is allowed, experience shows that this opens up opportunities for forging permits and other documentation, as well as for other types of enabling activity. Opening up a legal export trade in captive-bred birds would provide opportunities for laundering wild-caught birds and concealing rare species of similar appearance. In 1989, CITES prohibited international commercial trade in all elephant ivory. Following decades of a successful international ban on ivory trading, CITES approved the export of more than 150 metric tons of government-stockpiled ivory from Botswana, Namibia, Zambia, and South Africa. The move backfired: the flood of ivory revived demand in East Asia, and since then poaching has escalated dramatically. From 2003 to 2014, illegal elephant killings in central Africa have been occurring at unsustainable levels relative to natural population growth. This means that elephants are dying faster than they are able to reproduce. West Africa is also thought to be suffering from unsustainable levels of elephant poaching.[107]

Illegal Fishing Unlicensed and illegal fishing is another billion-dollar green crime. It can take many forms and involve highly different parties, ranging from huge factory ships operating on the high seas that catch thousands of tons of fish on each voyage, to smaller, locally operating ships that confine themselves to national waters. Illegal fishing occurs when these ships sign on to their home nation's rules but then choose to ignore their scope and boundary, or operate in a country's waters without permission or on the high seas without a flag. Because catches are not reported by the fishing vessels, their illegal fishing can have a detrimental effect on species, as government regulators have no idea how many fish are being caught. Stocks become depleted and species endangered; whole species of fish can be wiped out. Take for instance the global demand for shark fin soup, desired for its healing and medicinal value, which has led to a catastrophic decline in shark populations; some species have been reduced by 99 percent since the 1950s due to legal and illegal fishing. In 2013, animal rights groups in Thailand launched a campaign against the sale and consumption of shark fin soup, calling on businesses to ban the dish and advising people to refrain from eating the traditional Chinese delicacy.

In addition, illegal fishing techniques, including fishermen using the wrong sized nets or fishing in prohibited areas, can damage fragile marine ecosystems, threatening coral reefs, turtles, and seabirds. In underdeveloped nations, regulators may look the other way because the needs for short-term economic, social, or political gains are given more weight than long-term sustainability. As a result, species of whales, abalone, lobsters, and Patagonian toothfish (known in the United States as Chilean sea bass) have become endangered.[108]

Industrial fishing is mainly operated through joint ventures between the government and foreign companies from Japan and Spain. The main commercial species are lobster, crabs, gamba (deep-water shrimp), shrimp, crayfish, and squid. Lobster, shrimp, and gamba are the main exports with key markets in other African states, Hong Kong, Japan, Italy, Spain, Portugal, and the United Kingdom.

Illegal Dumping Some green criminals want to skirt local, state, and federal restrictions on dumping dangerous substances in the environment. Rather than pay expensive processing fees they may secretly dispose of hazardous wastes in illegal dump sites. Illegally dumped wastes can either be hazardous or nonhazardous materials that are discarded in an effort to avoid either disposal fees or the time and effort required for proper disposal. Materials dumped ranged from used motor oil to waste from construction sites.

One of the largest and fastest growing problems is the disposal of obsolete high-tech electronics, called e-waste, such as televisions, computers and computer monitors, notebooks and tablets, cell phones, and so on. In 2015, an estimated 42 million tons of e-waste was disposed of around the world.[109] While most e-waste in the United States is disposed of in landfills or is incinerated, the toxic material contained in electronic gear (such as lead) encourages illegal dumping in order to avoid recycling costs.[110] Consequently a considerable amount of e-waste is sent abroad to developing nations for recycling, often in violation of international laws restricting such commerce. All too often, the material overwhelms recycling plants and is instead dumped in local villages near people and water sources. Illegal dump sites have been documented in Nigeria, Ghana, China, the Philippines, Indonesia, Pakistan, and India, and they pose severe threats to both human health and the natural environment.

Illegal Polluting A great deal of attention is now paid to intentional or negligent environmental pollution caused by many large corporations. The numerous allegations in this area involve almost every aspect of U.S. business. Most environmental crime statutes contain overlapping civil, criminal, and administrative penalty provisions, which gives the government latitude in enforcement. Over time, Congress has elevated some violations from misdemeanors to felonies and has increased potential jail sentences and fines for those convicted.[111]

Criminal environmental pollution is defined as the intentional or negligent discharge of a toxic or contaminating substance into the biosystem that is known to have an adverse effect on the natural environment or life. It may involve the ground release of toxic chemicals such as kepone, vinyl chloride, mercury, PCBs, and asbestos. Illegal and/or controlled air pollutants include hydrochlorofluorocarbons

(HCFCs), aerosols, asbestos, carbon monoxide, chlorofluorocarbons (CFCs), criteria air pollutants, lead, mercury, methane, nitrogen oxides (NO_x), radon, refrigerants, and sulfur oxide (SO_2). Water pollution is defined as the dumping of a substance that degrades or alters the quality of the waters to an extent that is detrimental for use by humans or by an animal or a plant that is useful to humans. This includes the disposal into rivers, lakes, and streams of:

- Excess fertilizers, herbicides, and insecticides from agricultural lands and residential areas
- Oil, grease, and toxic chemicals from urban runoff and energy production
- Sediment from improperly managed construction sites, crop and forest lands, and eroding streambanks
- Salt from irrigation practices and acid drainage from abandoned mines
- Bacteria and nutrients from livestock, pet wastes, and faulty septic systems

The most serious of these incidents occurred in India in 1984, discussed in Exhibit 13.4.

CONTROLLING GREEN CRIME

The United States and most other nations have passed laws making it a crime to pollute or damage the environment. Among environmental laws in the U.S. are the following:

- *Clean Water Act (1972)*. Establishes and maintains goals and standards for U.S. water quality and purity. It was amended in 1987 to increase controls on toxic pollutants, and in 1990 to more effectively address the hazard of oil spills.

EXHIBIT 13.4

The Bhopal Incident

In December 1984, in Bhopal, India, thousands of people were affected by a leakage of methyl isocyanate gas and other chemicals from a Union Carbide pesticide plant. The government confirmed that 3,787 were killed outright soon after the leak, but as many as 8,000 may have died from medical complications caused by the chemical. Two years later, the Indian government claimed that almost 600,000 people may have been affected, 200,000 of them children. Many suffer from long-term and incurable respiratory complaints. Union Carbide claimed that the leak was sabotage and they should not be held responsible for what happened. But there had been previous complaints about safety violations, and there were other leaks that left workers injured or dead. Local authorities in Bhopal had warned the company on several occasions about the potential for accidents.

SOURCE: M. Arun Subramaniam and Ward Morehouse, *The Bhopal Tragedy: What Really Happened and What It Means for American Workers and Communities at Risk* (Washington, DC: Apex Press, 1986).

- *Emergency Planning and Community Right-to-Know Act (1986).* Requires companies to disclose information about toxic chemicals they release into the air and water and dispose of on land.
- *Endangered Species Act (1973).* Designed to protect and recover endangered and threatened species of fish, wildlife, and plants in the United States and beyond. The law works in part by protecting species' habitats.
- *Oil Pollution Act (1990).* Enacted in the aftermath of the *Exxon Valdez* oil spill in Alaska's Prince William Sound, this law streamlines federal response to oil spills by requiring oil storage facilities and vessels to prepare spill-response plans and provide for their rapid implementation. The law also increases polluters' liability for cleanup costs and damage to natural resources.

One of the most famous incidents of green crime and efforts by the government to punish offenders is covered in the Profiles in Crime feature *"Deepwater Horizon."*

Enforcing these federal laws is the Environmental Protection Agency, which was given full law enforcement authority in 1988. The EPA has successfully prosecuted significant violations across all major environmental statutes, including data fraud cases (for instance, private laboratories submitting false environmental data to state and federal environmental agencies); indiscriminate hazardous waste dumping that resulted in serious injuries and death; industry-wide ocean dumping by cruise ships; oil spills that caused significant damage to waterways, wetlands, and beaches; international smuggling of CFC refrigerants that damage the ozone layer and increase skin cancer risk; and illegal handling of hazardous substances such as pesticides and asbestos that exposed children, the poor, and other especially vulnerable groups to potentially serious illness.[112] Its Criminal Investigation Division (EPA CID) investigates allegations of criminal wrongdoing prohibited by various environmental statutes. Such investigations involve but are not limited to:

- The illegal disposal of hazardous waste
- The export of hazardous waste without the permission of the receiving country
- The illegal discharge of pollutants to a body of water of the United States
- The removal and disposal of regulated asbestos-containing materials in a manner inconsistent with the law and regulations
- The illegal importation of certain restricted or regulated chemicals into the United States
- Tampering with a drinking water supply
- Mail fraud
- Wire fraud
- Conspiracy and money laundering relating to environmental criminal activities

There are also local and state law enforcement efforts devoted to controlling green crimes and enforcing state environmental laws. The Environmental Crimes Strike Force in Los Angeles County is considered a model for the control of illegal dumping and pollution. Some of the more common environmental offenses investigated and prosecuted by the task force include:

- The illegal transportation, treatment, storage, or disposal of hazardous waste
- Oil spills
- Fraudulent certification of automobile smog tests[113]

Citizen Groups There have also been charges that efforts to control green crime are less than successful. One reason is that law enforcement efforts may be stratified by class and race: authorities seem to be less diligent when victims are poor or minority group members or the crimes take place in minority areas. When Michael Lynch and his associates studied petroleum refineries' law violations, they found that those polluting African American, Hispanic, and low-income communities receive smaller fines than refineries in white and affluent communities. They also found that violations of the Clean Air Act, the Clean Water Act, and/or the Resource Conservation and Recovery Act in minority areas received much smaller fines than the same types of violations occurring in white areas ($108,563 versus $341,590).[114]

Therefore, in addition to state and federal environmental agencies, citizen groups have also become active in environmental monitoring and combating green crime. One well-known organization, Group Against Smog and Pollution (GASP), was founded in 1969 by a group of 43 volunteers concerned about air quality issues in southwestern Pennsylvania. Since its founding, not only has GASP educated the public on questions of pollution, it has also used the courts to achieve its goal of a cleaner environment. GASP has cooperated in a number of cases with the EPA in bringing about enforcement of air quality standards. In each case the court action resulted in substantial fines and/or remedial actions being imposed on the defendant.[115]

Water quality is another concern of community groups. Citizen water-monitoring organizations have worked with environmental enforcement agencies across the United States. Community members help monitor water quality so they can help direct state action as well as identify sources of pollution that impact their communities. Citizen water-monitoring organizations engage in informal surveillance activities that are designed to identify environmental violations, and they can report those violations to authorities.

Have these groups been effective? Michael Lynch and Paul Stretesky found that while potentially effective, citizen-based groups may be skewed by the racial and ethnic makeup of the communities they serve.[116] Communities with fewer economic resources and those with higher concentrations of minority populations receive less official protection and hence a reduced level of environmental justice; these inequities also extend to informal organizations. Equipment to monitor pollution is expensive and not easily available in less well-off areas that actually need it the most.

Deepwater Horizon

On April 20, 2010, an explosion occurred on the *Deepwater Horizon* oil rig, killing 11 platform workers and injuring 17 others. The rig was built by Hyundai Heavy Industries of Korea, owned by the Transocean Drilling Corporation, and leased by BP (formerly British Petroleum) in order to drill a deepwater oil well in the Gulf of Mexico. The drilling was overseen by Halliburton.

Following the explosion, the *Deepwater Horizon* burned for 36 hours before sinking to the ocean floor 5,000 feet below, where oil was gushing from the now-uncapped well. At first, estimates of the oil spill were 5,000 barrels a day, but they quickly rose to 60,000. For more than three months, company officials frantically tried to stem the flow with a variety of failed schemes, while millions of barrels of escaping oil created a slick that covered thousands of square miles, devastating wildlife and causing one of the greatest natural disasters in U.S. history.

On June 1, 2010, the Obama administration announced that it had launched a criminal probe in order to "prosecute to the fullest extent of the law" any persons or companies that broke the law in the time leading up to the spill. Under federal environmental laws, a company may be charged with a misdemeanor for negligent conduct, or a felony if there is evidence that company personnel knowingly engaged in conduct risking injury. It would be a criminal act if, for example, employees of BP or its subcontractors, Transocean and Halliburton:

- Lied in the permit process for obtaining a drilling license
- Tried to cover up the severity of the spill
- Knowing of negligence in construction, chose to ignore the danger it imposed
- Engaged in or approved of unsafe, risky, or dangerous methods to remove the drill, knowing that such methods could injure those on board

To prove a felony, and potentially put BP executives in prison, the government had to show that company officials knew in advance that its actions would lead to the explosion and oil spill but chose to ignore the danger; a misdemeanor requires only mere negligence. But even a misdemeanor conviction would amp up the loss to the company because the Federal Alternative Fines Act allows the government to request monetary fines that are twice the loss associated with an offense. This provision can also have a devastating effect on employees because fines imposed on individuals under the act may *not* be paid by their employer.

On September 4, 2014, U.S. District Judge Carl Barbier ruled BP was guilty of gross negligence and willful misconduct. He apportioned 67 percent of the blame for the spill to BP, 30 percent to Transocean, and 3 percent to Halliburton. Judge Barbier found that BP had acted with "conscious disregard of known risks" and that "employees took risks that led to the largest environmental disaster in U.S. history." In the final tally, the company paid almost $54 billion in order to settle all claims: federal Clean Water Act fines, claims by states (Alabama, Florida, Louisiana, Mississippi, and Texas), and 400 local government entities. However, while a number of BP employees were indicted on criminal charges relating to their negligence in the spill and their efforts to cover up company involvement and responsibility, not one served jail time. On December 2, 2015, federal prosecutors moved—and a judge agreed—to drop manslaughter charges against two supervisors aboard the *Deepwater Horizon* when it exploded; they may face probation over Clean Water Act violations.

While some may argue that it is overly harsh to put company executives in prison for what is essentially an accident, civil penalties do not seem to deter companies such as BP. Before the Gulf of Mexico oil spill, BP had already paid hundreds of millions in civil penalties for similar if lesser disasters. One fine of $87 million was paid to the Occupational Safety and Health Administration—the largest fine in OSHA's history—for a Texas refinery explosion; an additional $50 million was paid to the Department of Justice for the same explosion. BP also paid $3 million to OSHA for 42 safety violations at an Ohio refinery and was fined $20 million by the Department of Justice for another spill that violated the Clean Water Act.

 CRITICAL THINKING

Should people responsible for environmental disasters such as *Deepwater Horizon* be held criminally responsible and eligible for a prison sentence? Or should they and the company they represent be held civilly responsible and forced to pay damages?

SOURCES: *The Guardian*, "Manslaughter Charges Dropped Against Two BP Employees in Deepwater Spill," December 2, 2015, http://www.theguardian.com/environment/2015/dec/03/manslaughter-charges-dropped-bp-employees-deepwater-horizon-oil-spill; Thomas Catan and Guy Chazan, "Spill Draws Criminal Probe," *Wall Street Journal*, June 2, 2010, http://online.wsj.com/article/SB10001424052748704875604575280983140254458.html; Tyson Slocum, "BP: The Worst Safety and Environmental Record of All Oil Companies Operating in the United States," *Monthly Review*, http://mrzine.monthlyreview.org/2010/slocum060510.html; Helene Cooper and Peter Baker, "U.S. Opens Criminal Inquiry into Oil Spill," *New York Times*, June 1, 2010, http://www.nytimes.com/2010/06/02/us/02spill.html; Alternative Fines Act, 18 U.S.C. § 3571(d); Terry Wade and Kristen Hays, "BP Reaches $18.7 Billion Settlement over Deadly 2010 Spill," Reuters, July 2, 2015, http://www.reuters.com/article/2015/07/02/us-bp-gulfmexico-settlement-idUSKCN0PC1BW20150702. (URLs accessed June 2016.)

CONNECTIONS

The Flint, Michigan, water crisis was covered in Chapter 5. The Flint case highlights the dangers of lead contamination and also shows how poor communities are most vulnerable to environmental hazards.

ASK YOURSELF . . .

Does the reality of environmental contamination explain the connection between poverty and crime?

Organized and Transnational Organized Crime

The third leg of enterprise crime, organized crime, involves ongoing criminal enterprise groups whose ultimate purpose is personal economic gain through illegitimate means. One component involves setting up a structured enterprise system to supply consumers with merchandise and services banned by criminal law but for which a ready market exists: prostitution, pornography, gambling, and narcotics.

A second component involves the use of illegitimate means to dominate and control legitimate enterprises. Organized crime groups enter, buy, or control legitimate industries such as construction and trash hauling. However, rather than play by the rules, they use violence and strong-arm tactics to remove rivals, collect money owed, and intimidate people into cooperation. Their ability to operate freely may be the result of their buying off corrupt officials and using graft, extortion, intimidation, and murder to maintain their operations.[117] The economic impact alone is staggering: it's estimated that global organized crime reaps illegal profits of around $1 trillion per year.[118]

Because of its secrecy, power, and fabulous wealth, a great mystique has grown up about organized crime. Its legendary leaders—Al Capone, Meyer Lansky, Lucky Luciano—have been the subjects of books and movies. The *Godfather* films popularized and humanized organized crime figures; the media often glamorizes them.[119] Watching the exploits of Tony Soprano and his family life became a national craze. This section briefly reviews the history of traditional organized crime, its decline, and the rise of its replacement: transnational organized crime groups.

ORIGINS OF ORGANIZED CRIME

 L07 Trace the evolution of organized crime

Organized crime itself is not a recent phenomenon and can be traced as far back as the 1600s when London was terrorized by organized gangs that called themselves Hectors, Bugles, Dead Boys, and other colorful names. In the seventeenth and eighteenth centuries, English gang members wore distinctive belts and pins marked with serpents, animals, stars, and the like. The first mention of youth gangs in America occurred in the late 1780s, when prison reformers noted the presence of gangs of young people hanging out on Philadelphia's street corners. By the 1820s, New York's Bowery and Five Points districts, Boston's North End and Fort Hill, and the outlying Southwark and Moyamensing sections of Philadelphia were the locales of youth gangs with colorful names like the Roach Guards, Chichesters, the Plug Uglies, and the Dead Rabbits.[120]

THE MAFIA

The Mafia originated in Sicily around 1860, and started as a criminal gang employed by wealthy landowners to function as agents of social and land control, keeping peasant workers in line. At the turn of the twentieth century, La Mano Nera (the Black Hand), an offshoot of Sicilian criminal groups, established themselves in northeastern urban centers. Gangsters demanded payments from local businessmen in return for "protection"; those who would not pay were beaten and

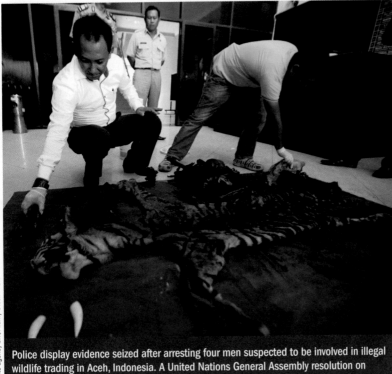

Police display evidence seized after arresting four men suspected to be involved in illegal wildlife trading in Aceh, Indonesia. A United Nations General Assembly resolution on "Tackling Illicit Trafficking in Wildlife" expresses concern that illicit trafficking in protected species of wild fauna and flora is an increasingly sophisticated form of transnational organized crime. The resolution declares that such trafficking poses a threat to health and safety, security, good governance, and the sustainable development of states.

epa european pressphoto agency b.v./Alamy Stock Photo

their shops vandalized. Eventually the Black Hand merged with gangs of Italian heritage to form larger urban-based gangs and groups.

A turning point in the development of organized gangs occurred on January 16, 1919, when the Eighteenth Amendment to the U.S. Constitution was ratified. The new amendment prohibited the sale, manufacture, and transportation of intoxicating liquors. Until then, gangs had remained relatively small and local, but now the national market for controlled substances opened the door to riches.

Charles "Lucky" Luciano, who had come to the United States during this era, is credited with helping to create a national syndicate, La Cosa Nostra, with rules and codes that all members were required to follow. When Luciano was deported back to Italy in 1946 for operating a prostitution ring, he became a liaison between the Sicilian Mafia and La Cosa Nostra.[121] What emerged was a national syndicate that was centrally coordinated and whose various component gangs worked cooperatively to settle disputes, dictate policy, and assign territory.[122] Despite these efforts at cooperation and control, numerous and bloody gang wars and individual vendettas were common.

Through the twentieth century, the power of the Mafia continued to grow. Meyer Lansky (1902–1983), a close associate of Luciano, was involved in a wide range of organized criminal activity from the 1920s to the 1970s. Lansky was especially active in gambling ventures, including the rise of Las Vegas, and led efforts by the mob to build casinos in Cuba before the communist revolution.

The Mafia remains active in the United States. The FBI estimates that the Mafia has approximately 25,000 members total, with 250,000 affiliates worldwide. The families control crime in distinct geographic areas. New York City, the most important organized crime area, contains five families—Gambino, Columbo (formerly Profaci), Lucchese, Bonanno, and Genovese—named after their founding "godfathers." In contrast, Chicago contains a single mob organization called the "outfit," which also influences racketeering in such cities as Milwaukee, Kansas City, and Phoenix. The families are believed to be ruled by a "commission" made up of the heads of the five New York families and bosses from Detroit, Buffalo, Chicago, and Philadelphia, which settles personal problems and jurisdictional conflicts and enforces rules that allow members to gain huge profits through the manufacture and sale of illegal goods and services.

The Mafia in Decline In recent years, the American Mafia has been in decline. One reason: high-profile criminal prosecutions using up-to-date IT methods for surveillance

and evidence collection. For example, Chicago mob boss Frank Calabrese Sr. was sentenced to life in prison in 2009 for his role in 18 gangland slayings dating back to 1970. His arrest—along with 13 others—meant that the Chicago mob does not have the power and influence it once had in the city. In another high-profile case, James "Whitey" Bulger was arrested and convicted of murder in 2013 after having been on the run for 16 years. Bulger, who once ran Boston's feared Winter Hill Gang, was wanted for his role in 19 murders.

The Mafia leadership is aging. A number of the reigning family heads are in their eighties and older. A younger generation of mob leaders has stepped in to take control of the families, and they seem to lack the skill and leadership of the older bosses. The code of silence that protected Mafia leaders is now broken regularly by younger members who turn informer rather than face prison terms. When Joe Calabrese was on trial, his own son testified against him in court. In addition, active government enforcement policies have halved what the estimated mob membership was 25 years ago, and a number of the highest-ranking leaders have been imprisoned.

Traditional organized crime has also been hurt by changing values in U.S. society. European American neighborhoods, which were the locus of Mafia power, have been shrinking as families move to the suburbs. Organized crime groups lost their urban-centered political and social bases of operation. In addition, success has hurt organized crime families: younger family members are better educated than their forebears and are equipped to seek their fortunes through legitimate enterprise. However, while their power may be eroding, traditional organized crime families are still in operation, as the Profiles in Crime feature "Mafia Looters" illustrates.

THE RISE OF TRANSNATIONAL ORGANIZED CRIME

L08 Be familiar with transnational organized crime

Transnational organized crime (TOC or transnational crime) is a form of organized crime operating across national borders. It involves groups or networks of individuals working in more than one state or even across cultures and nations, to plan and execute illegal business ventures. Cross-national gangs are often large criminal organizations, some with more than 20,000 members.

According to criminologist Jay Albanese, the distinction between these new organizations that operate across borders and the traditional Mafia whose activities were bounded by neighborhood territory is actually not that great. They overlap in terms of the crimes committed, the offenders involved, and how criminal opportunities are exploited for profit. They are, he concludes, manifestations of the same underlying conduct and the same pool of criminal offenders who exploit similar criminal opportunities.[123]

transnational organized crime A criminal enterprise that involves the planning and execution of the distribution of illicit materials or services by groups or networks of individuals working in more than one country.

Mafia Looters

A recent New Jersey case involving the Lucchese crime family—one of the families traditionally associated with La Cosa Nostra—is proof that traditional organized crime can still be a potent threat. In 2007, Lucchese family members Nicodemo "Nicky" Scarfo Jr., Salvatore Pelullo, and brothers William and John Maxwell orchestrated an illegal takeover of FirstPlus Financial Group (FPFG), a publicly held company in Texas. Once a billion-dollar financial organization that specialized in mortgages, FPFG had filed for bankruptcy during the housing downturn. The company was dormant but still had assets, thanks to the continued proceeds from all the mortgages it had financed.

Pelullo and Scarfo used threats and other tactics to intimidate and remove FPFG's management and board of directors. They were replaced with Mafia associates, including the Maxwell brothers—William was named special counsel to FPFG, while John became the company's CEO. Within several weeks of gaining control, Pelullo and Scarfo converted $7 million of company assets for their own use. Before they were arrested in 2011, more than $12 million of stockholders' assets was illegally funneled to the Lucchese gang members. In addition, between 2007 and 2008, Scarfo received $33,000 per month from FPFG as a "consultant"—at a time when he was on home detention in New Jersey for violating his parole from a previous conviction; Pelullo had a similar deal. With their ill-gotten gains, the mobsters purchased an airplane, a yacht, and expensive jewelry.

After a complex investigation by federal authorities, in 2015 Scarfo and Pelullo received 30-year sentences, while brothers William and John Maxwell received 20- and 10-year terms, respectively.

 CRITICAL THINKING

As traditional crime groups shrink in size they are being replaced by new groups of organized criminals. Does this mean that as long as people desire forbidden products, such as drugs and other contraband, criminals will emerge to provide a marketplace? In other words, is organized crime inevitable?

SOURCE: FBI, "La Cosa Nostra: Lengthy Prison Terms for Lucchese Crime Family Members," September 8, 2015, https://www.fbi.gov/news /stories/2015/september/la-cosa-nostra -members-sentenced/la-cosa-nostra-members -sentenced (accessed June 2016).

CHARACTERISTICS OF TRANSNATIONAL ORGANIZED CRIME

A precise description of the characteristics of transnational organized crime is difficult to formulate, but here are some of its general traits:

- Transnational organized crime is a conspiratorial activity, involving the coordination of numerous people in the planning and execution of illegal acts or in the pursuit of a legitimate objective by unlawful means (e.g., threatening a legitimate business to get a stake in it).
- An offense is transnational if:
  ○ It is committed in more than one state or nation.
  ○ It is committed in one state or nation but a substantial part of its preparation, planning, direction, or control takes place in another state or nation.
  ○ It is committed in one state or nation but involves an organized criminal group that engages in criminal activities in more than one state or nation.
  ○ It is committed in one state of nation but has substantial effects in another state of nation.[124]
- Transnational organized crime involves continuous commitment by primary members, although individuals with specialized skills may be brought in as needed.

- Transnational organized crime is usually structured along hierarchical lines—a chieftain supported by close advisers, lower subordinates, and so on.
- Transnational organized crime has economic gain as its primary goal, although power and status may also be motivating factors. Economic gain is achieved through global supply of illegal goods and services, including drugs, sex slaves, arms, and pornography.
- In addition to providing illegal material such as narcotics, contemporary global syndicates engage in business crimes such as laundering illegal money through legitimate businesses, land fraud, and computer crime.
- Transnational criminal syndicates employ predatory tactics, such as intimidation, violence, and corruption.
- Transnational organized crime groups are quick and effective in controlling and disciplining their members, associates, and victims, and will not hesitate to use lethal violence against those who flaunt organizational rules.
- Transnational crime depends heavily on the instruments of the IT age: the Internet, global communications, rapid global transportation systems, universal banking systems, and global credit card and payment systems.
- Transnational organized crime groups do not include terror organizations, though there may be overlap. Some terror groups are involved in criminality to fund their

Human Trafficking

I n the first movie in the popular *Taken* series, Bryan Mills, a former CIA agent played by Liam Neeson, must save his daughter Kim, who has been abducted while on a trip to Paris. Almost as soon as she arrives, Kim and a friend are kidnapped. As Bryan searches frantically for his beloved daughter, he uncovers an international scheme in which young women are taken, abused, forcibly addicted to drugs, and used as sex slaves. Luckily for Kim, Brian, who has a special set of skills, kills about 35 people and rescues her from her abductors. The film was so popular that the sequel *Taken 2* was released in 2012 and *Taken 3* in 2015. Can these dreadful scenarios be based on reality?

Unfortunately, they may be all too real. Every year, hundreds of thousands of women and children—primarily from Southeast Asia and eastern Europe—are lured by the promise of good jobs and then end up in the sex trade in industrialized countries. The data are notoriously unreliable, but estimates of the number of people trafficked internationally each year range between 600,000 and 1 million

men, women, and children from 124 different countries around the world, including the United States. Most victims are foreigners in the country where they have been abused and victimized, though most are from the region, often from neighboring countries (e.g., eastern European women trafficked to western Europe). Domestic trafficking is also widely practiced, and for one in three trafficking cases, the exploitation takes place in the victim's country of citizenship.

The majority of these victims are runaway or thrown-away youths who live on the streets and become victims of prostitution. These children generally come from homes where they have been abused or from families who have abandoned them. Often, they become involved in prostitution to support themselves financially or to get the things they feel they need or want (like drugs).

According to a report prepared by the United Nations, the most common form of human trafficking is sexual exploitation, and the victims are predominantly women and girls; about one-third of these victims are children. Others are taken for forced

labor, to be used as combat troops, or forced to beg on the streets.

Even though films such as *Taken* depict human traffickers as almost entirely men, many sex traffickers are women. On average, some 10 to 15 percent of convicted offenders are women. For trafficking in persons, however, even though males still make up the vast majority, the share of women offenders is nearly 30 percent. Many were in the sex trade themselves and were encouraged by their recruiter/trafficker to return home and recruit other women, often under the scrutiny of people working for the trafficker to make sure they don't try to escape.

Because it is a global enterprise, there is a great deal of cooperation in human trafficking. A single gang in eastern Europe may include Russians, Moldavians, Egyptians, and Syrians. Cooperation makes it possible to traffic sex slaves not only to neighboring countries but all around the globe. Victims from East Asia were detected in more than 20 countries in regions throughout the world, including Europe, the Americas, the Middle East, central Asia, and Africa.

political objectives, and some have morphed from politically motivated organizations to ones solely involved in for-profit criminal activity. Transnational criminal organizations may aid terror groups with transportation and communication.

ACTIVITIES OF TRANSNATIONAL ORGANIZED CRIME

What are the main activities of transnational organized crime? The traditional sources of income are derived from providing illicit materials, such as narcotics, and using force to enter into and maximize profits in legitimate businesses. Income is generated from such activities as narcotics distribution, extortion, gambling, pornography, and cargo theft rings. Other activities are discussed here.

Cultural Property Trafficking   Organized crime groups have become involved in trafficking in cultural property.

Antiques, artifacts, and relics stolen through illegal archaeological digs are sold to gangs who then smuggle the goods out of the country and sell them either through legitimate markets such as auctions and the Internet or in underground markets where collectors buy offered goods, no questions asked. Trafficking in cultural property is also becoming an important source for money laundering.

Piracy   Maritime piracy (a crime made famous in the 2013 film *Captain Phillips*, with Tom Hanks in the title role) is the specialty of Somali gangs. Pirates from this nation located on the Horn of Africa are now arming themselves with a higher grade of weaponry and basing themselves on "mother ships" from which they can send out smaller attack boats. This system allows them to hijack larger vessels over wider distances, hundreds of miles off the coast. Piracy is also linked to other forms of organized crime since it requires sophisticated intelligence collection networks and systematic corruption of local officials. Piracy is a key source of income

Contributing Factors

Human trafficking is facilitated by social problems and disorder, such as disruptions in the global economy, war, and social unrest. Economic crisis hits young girls especially hard. Female victims are often poor and aspire to a better life. They may be forced, coerced, deceived, and psychologically manipulated into industrial or agricultural work, marriage, domestic servitude, organ donation, or sexual exploitation. Some traffickers exploit victims' frustration with low salaries in their home countries, and others take advantage of a crisis in the victim's family that requires her to make money. The traffickers then promise the victim to take her abroad and find her a traditionally female service-sector job, such as waitress, salesperson, domestic worker, or au pair/babysitter.

Whereas victims often come from poorer countries, the market for labor and sex is found in wealthier countries or in countries that, though economically poor, cater to the needs of citizens from wealthy countries, of corporations, or of tourists.

Combating Human Trafficking

In recent years, the United States has made stopping the trafficking of women a top priority. In 2000, Congress passed the Trafficking Victims Protection Act (TVPA), which created the first comprehensive federal law to address trafficking, with a significant focus on the international dimension of the problem.

The law provides a three-pronged approach: *prevention* through public awareness programs overseas and a State Department–led monitoring and sanctions program; *protection* through a new visa and services for foreign national victims; and *prosecution* through new federal crimes that carry severe penalties.

As a result of the passing of the TVPA, the Office to Monitor and Combat Trafficking in Persons was established in October 2001. This enabling legislation led to the creation of a bureau within the State Department to specifically address human trafficking and exploitation on all levels and to take legal action against perpetrators. Along with the FBI, U.S. Immigration and Customs Enforcement (ICE) is one of the lead federal agencies charged with enforcing the TVPA. Human trafficking represents significant risks to homeland security. Would-be terrorists and criminals often can access the same routes and use the same methods as human traffickers. ICE's Human Smuggling and Trafficking Unit works to identify criminals and organizations involved in these illicit activities.

A number of local law enforcement agencies have also created special branches to combat trafficking. The Massachusetts Human Trafficking Task Force uses a two-pronged approach, addressing investigations focusing on international victims and those focusing on the commercial sexual exploitation of children. The New Jersey Human Trafficking Task Force attacks the problem by training law enforcement in the methods of identifying victims and signs of trafficking, coordinating statewide efforts in the identification and provision of services to victims of human trafficking, and increasing the successful interdiction and prosecution of trafficking of human persons.

 CRITICAL THINKING

1. If put in charge, what would you do to slow or end the international sex trade?
2. Should men who hire prostitutes be severely punished to deter them from getting involved in the exploitation of these vulnerable young women?

SOURCES: Michael Pittaro and Anthony Normore, "International Efforts by Police Leadership to Combat Human Trafficking," FBI Law Enforcement Bulletin, June 2016, https://leb.fbi.gov/2016/june/international-efforts-by-police-leadership-to-combat-human-trafficking; United States Department of State, *Trafficking in Persons Report, 2015*, https://www.state.gov/documents/organization/245365.pdf; United Nations Office on Drugs and Crime, *Global Reports on Trafficking in Persons, 2014*, http://www.unodc.org/documents/data-and-analysis/glotip/GLOTIP_2014_full_report.pdf; Amanda Walker-Rodriguez and Rodney Hill, "Human Sex Trafficking," FBI Law Enforcement Bulletin, 2011, http://leb.fbi.gov/2011/march/leb-march-2011. (URLs accessed June 2016.)

for many in the local communities, who receive funds from ransoms that their own governments fail to provide.

Human Trafficking Organized crime groups are quite active in human trafficking, the acquisition of people by improper means such as force, fraud, or deception, with the aim of exploiting them in such illegal activities as prostitution, sexual exploitation, forced labor, slavery, or similar practices. Every year, thousands of men, women, and children fall into the hands of traffickers in their own countries and abroad. Almost every country in the world is affected by trafficking, whether as a country of origin, transit, or destination for victims. For more on this global social problem, see the Policies and Practices in Criminology feature.

Migrant Smuggling Organized crime groups profit from smuggling migrants. Criminals are increasingly providing smuggling services to irregular migrants to evade national border controls, migration regulations, and visa requirements. Most irregular migrants resort to the assistance of profit-seeking smugglers because as border controls have improved in developed nations, migrants are deterred from attempting to illegally cross them themselves and are diverted into the hands of smugglers. Migrant smugglers are becoming more and more organized, establishing professional networks that transcend borders and regions. Nonetheless, thousands of people have lost their lives as a result of the indifferent or even deliberate actions of migrant smugglers.

Organ Trafficking The demand for organs has outstripped supply, creating an underground market for illicitly obtained organs. Desperate recipients and donors create an avenue ready for exploitation by international organ trafficking syndicates. Traffickers exploit the desperation of donors to improve the economic situation of themselves and their families, and they exploit the desperation of recipients who may have few other options to improve or prolong their lives.

Like other victims of trafficking in persons, those who fall prey to traffickers for the purpose of organ removal may be vulnerable by virtue of poverty. Traffickers may enlist the services of doctors, nurses, ambulance drivers, and health care professionals who are involved in legitimate activities when they are not participating in trafficking in persons for the purpose of organ removal.[125]

Because cross-national and transnational gangs are a product of the cyber age, members often use cyberspace to communicate and promote their illicit activities.[126] Gangs typically use cell phones (voice and text) to conduct drug transactions and prearrange meetings with customers. Prepaid cell phones are used when conducting drug trafficking operations. Social networking sites, encrypted email, Twitter, and instant messaging are commonly used by gang members to communicate with one another and with drug customers. Gang members use social media such as YouTube and Facebook as well as personal web pages to communicate and boast about their gang membership and related activities. Some use the Internet to intimidate rival gang members and maintain websites to recruit new members. Gang members flash gang signs and wear gang colors in videos and photos posted on the Web. Sometimes, rivals "spar" on Internet message boards or Facebook.[127] They rely on encrypted messenger services like WhatsApp, Telegram, and others to coordinate their activities and warn associates about police raids.[128]

TRANSNATIONAL GANGS

Traditional Eurocentric gangs are being replaced by transnational mega-gangs. Some, such as the Crips, Bloods, and MS-13, have expanded from local street gangs to national mega-gangs with thousands of members. The Sureños is an alliance of hundreds of individual Mexican American street gangs that originated in Southern California. Sureños gang members' main sources of income are retail-level distribution of cocaine, heroin, marijuana, and methamphetamine within prison systems and in the community as well as extortion of drug distributors on the streets. Some members have direct links to Mexican drug traffickers, brokering large drug transactions; they are also involved in other criminal activities such as assault, carjacking, home invasion, homicide, and robbery. While most members remain in Southern California cities, the gang has spread significantly and can be found throughout much of the United States.[129]

In addition to these home-grown gangs, international gangs based in Asia, eastern Europe, North, South, and Latin America use the Internet and IT devices to facilitate their operations across nations and continents. Emerging transnational crime syndicates are primarily located in nations whose governments are too weak to present effective opposition. If they believe that the government is poised to interfere with their illegal activities, they will carry out a terror campaign, killing police and other government officials

to achieve their goals. Easier international travel, expanded world trade, and financial transactions that cross national borders have enabled them to branch out of local and regional crime to target international victims and develop criminal networks within more prosperous countries and regions.[130]

Africa, a continent that has experienced fierce political turmoil, has also seen the rise of transnational gangs. African criminal enterprises in Nigeria, Ghana, and Liberia have developed quickly since the 1980s due to the globalization of the world's economies and the great advances in communications technology. Nigerian criminal enterprises, primarily engaged in drug trafficking and financial frauds, are the most significant of these groups and operate in more than 80 countries. They are infamous for their email-based financial frauds, which cost the United States alone an estimated $1 billion to $2 billion each year.

Some of the most prominent transnational gang clusters are described here in some detail.

Eastern European Gangs   Eastern European gangs trace their origins to countries spanning the Baltics, the Balkans, central/eastern Europe, Russia, the Caucasus, and central Asia. For example, Albanian organized crime activities in the United States include gambling, money laundering, drug trafficking, human smuggling, extortion, violent witness intimidation, robbery, attempted murder, and murder.[131]

Although ethnically based, they work with other ethnic groups when perpetrating crimes. Trading in illegal arms, narcotics, pornography, and prostitution, they operate a multibillion-dollar transnational crime cartel. Balkan organized crime groups have recently expanded into more sophisticated crimes, including real estate fraud. Take for instance Armenian Power (AP), an international organized crime group whose illegal activities allegedly range from bank fraud and identity theft to violent extortion and kidnapping. In one scheme, AP caused more than $2 million in losses when members secretly installed "skimming" devices in cash register credit card swipe machines at Southern California 99 Cents Only stores to steal customer account information and then used it to create counterfeit debit and credit cards to empty accounts. With 200 known members, AP got its start as a neighborhood gang in the 1980s, but has now morphed into a transnational crime group with close ties to other gangs, including the Mexican Mafia. AP's leadership also maintains ties to Armenia and Russia and deals directly with top organized crime figures in those countries, even to the point of using respected organized crime mediators—known as "thieves-in-law"—to settle disputes.[132] The government began to crack down on this group and eventually indicted 90 Armenian Power leaders, members, and associates, including the head man, Mher Darbinyan, aka "Hollywood Mike" and "Capone." Darbinyan was indicted for a bank fraud scheme that used middlemen and runners to deposit and cash hundreds of thousands of dollars in fraudulent checks drawn on the accounts of elderly bank customers and businesses. He also organized and operated a sophisticated debit card skimming scheme that involved the installation and use of skimmers to steal thousands of customers' debit card numbers and PIN codes. He was eventually sentenced to 32 years in prison; 87 other AP members have been convicted. The AP case shows how today's transnational crime groups rely more on sophisticated cybercrime conspiracies than they do on the brute force of yesterday's organized criminals.[133]

Organized groups prey upon women in the poorest areas of Europe—Romania, Ukraine, Bosnia—and sell them into virtual sexual slavery. Many of these women are transported as prostitutes around the world, some finding themselves in the United States.

Russian Transnational Crime Groups Since the collapse of the Soviet Union in 1991, criminal organizations in Russia and other former Soviet republics such as Ukraine have engaged in a variety of crimes: drugs and arms trafficking, stolen automobiles, trafficking in women and children, and money laundering.[134] No area of the world seems immune, especially not the United States. America is the land of opportunity for unloading criminal goods and laundering dirty money.

Russian organized crime is not primarily based on ethnic or family structures. It is based on economic necessity that was nurtured by the oppressive Soviet regime. A professional criminal class developed in Soviet prisons during the Stalinist period that began in 1924—the era of the gulag. These criminals adopted behaviors, rules, values, and sanctions that bound them together in what was called the thieves' world, led by the elite *vory v zakone*, criminals who lived according to the "thieves' law." This thieves' world, and particularly the *vory*, created and maintained the bonds and climate of trust necessary for carrying out organized crime. The following are some specific characteristics of Russian organized crime in the post-Soviet era:

- Russian criminals make extensive use of the state governmental apparatus to protect and promote their criminal activities. For example, most businesses in Russia—legal, quasi-legal, and illegal—must operate with the protection of a *krysha* (roof). The protection is often provided by police or security officials employed outside their "official" capacities for this purpose. In other cases, officials are "silent partners" in criminal enterprises that they, in turn, protect.
- As Communism collapsed, the privatization of industry resulted in the massive use of state funds for criminal gain. Valuable properties are purchased through insider deals for much less than their true value and then resold for lucrative profits.
- Criminals have been able to directly influence the state's domestic and foreign policy to promote the interests of organized crime, either by attaining public office themselves or by buying public officials.

Beyond these particular features, organized crime in Russia shares other characteristics that are common to organized crime elsewhere in the world:

- Systematic use of violence, including both the threat and use of force
- Hierarchical structure
- Limited or exclusive membership
- Specialization in types of crime and a division of labor
- Military-style discipline, with strict rules and regulations for the organization as a whole
- Possession of high-tech equipment, including military weapons
- Threats, blackmail, and violence used to penetrate business management and assume control of commercial enterprises or, in some instances, to found their own enterprises with money from their criminal activities

As a result of these activities, corruption and organized crime are globalized. Russian organized crime is active in Europe, Africa, Asia, and North and South America. Massive money laundering is now common, which allows Russian and foreign organized crime to flourish. In some cases, it is tied to terrorist funding.

The organized crime threat to Russia's national security is now becoming a global threat. Russian organized crime operates both on its own and in cooperation with foreign groups. The latter cooperation often comes in the form of joint money laundering ventures. Russian criminals have become involved in killings for hire in central and western Europe, Israel, Canada, and the United States.

In the United States, with the exception of extortion and money laundering, Russians have had little or no involvement in some of the more traditional types of organized crime, such as drug trafficking, gambling, and loan sharking. However, thousands of Russian immigrants are believed to be involved in criminal activity, primarily in Russian enclaves in New York City.[135] Russian criminal groups are extensively engaged in a broad array of frauds and scams, including health care fraud, insurance scams, stock frauds, antiquities swindles, forgery, and fuel tax evasion schemes. Russians are believed to be the main purveyors of credit card fraud in the United States. Legitimate businesses, such as the movie business and the textile industry, have become targets of criminals from the former Soviet Union, and they are often used for money laundering and extortion.

Italian Organized Crime Groups Italian criminal societies, aka the Mafia, are active in Italy and impact the world. There are several groups currently active in the United States: the Sicilian Mafia, the Camorra or Neapolitan Mafia, the 'Ndrangheta or Calabrian Mafia, and the Sacra Corona Unita (United Sacred Crown). These groups have approximately 25,000 members total, with 250,000 affiliates worldwide. There are more than 3,000 members and affiliates of the Italian Mafia in the U.S., scattered mostly throughout major cities in the Northeast, the Midwest, California, and the South. Their largest presence centers around New York, southern New Jersey, and Philadelphia. These groups are involved in drug trafficking and money laundering. They have been involved in heroin trafficking for decades, as well as illegal gambling, political corruption, extortion, kidnapping, fraud, counterfeiting, infiltration of legitimate businesses, murders, bombings, and weapons trafficking. Industry experts in Italy estimate that their worldwide criminal activity is worth more than $100 billion annually.[136]

Latin American and Mexican Drug Cartels Transnational crime cartels operate freely in South American nations such as Peru and Columbia. Caribbean nations such as Jamaica, the Dominican Republic, and Haiti are home to drug and gun smuggling gangs. The money from illicit trade strengthens and enlarges the gangs, enabling them to increase their involvement in intraregional and transnational dealing in order to gain more money. Furthermore, drug trafficking has contributed to a sharp increase in the availability and usage of firearms.[137]

However, while island groups flourish, it is the Mexican drug cartels that are now of greatest concern. These transnational gangs have become large-scale suppliers of narcotics, marijuana, and methamphetamines to the United States, and Mexico has become a drug-producing and transit country. In addition, an estimated 90 percent of cocaine entering the United States transits Mexico. Mexican drug gangs routinely use violence, and fighting for control of the border regions has affected U.S. citizens. More than 100 Americans are now being killed in Mexico each year, and Mexican drug cartel members have threatened to kill U.S. journalists covering drug violence in the border region.[138]

Although Mexican drug cartels, or drug trafficking organizations, have existed for quite some time, they have become more powerful since Colombia was able to crack down on the Cali and Medellín cartels in the 1990s. Mexican drug cartels now dominate the wholesale illicit drug market in the United States. As a result, Mexican cartels are the leading wholesale launderers of drug money from the United States. Mexican and Colombian trafficking organizations annually smuggle an estimated $25 billion in drug proceeds into Mexico for laundering.

There are numerous drug cartels operating in Mexico, the main ones being Gulf, Sinaloa, Knights Templar, and Juárez. Some are dominant in local regions, while the major gangs—Gulf, Sinaloa, Los Zetas—are present throughout all of Mexico. In recent years, new cartels have formed and others have become allies, in a constantly shifting landscape of drug activity.

Asian Transnational Crime Groups Asia-based transnational crime groups are also quite active in such areas as human trafficking, narcotics, and money laundering.[139] Chinese gangs are involved in importing heroin from the neighboring Golden Triangle area and distributing it throughout the country. They are also involved in gambling and prostitution, activities that had all but disappeared under Mao Zedong's Communist regime. The two leading organized crime problems in Cambodia are drug production/trafficking and human trafficking. Drug traffickers also use Cambodia as a transit country and traffic Cambodian women into Thailand for sex. In Taiwan, the number-one organized crime problem is *heijin*, the penetration of mobsters into the legitimate business sector and the political arena. Gangs are now heavily involved in the businesses of bid-rigging, waste disposal, construction, cable television networks, telecommunications, stock trading, and entertainment. Further, starting in the mid-1980s, many criminals have successfully run for public office in order to protect themselves from police crackdowns. Taiwan's gangs are involved in gambling, prostitution, loan sharking, debt collection, extortion, and gang violence; kidnapping for ransom is also a serious concern.

Among the best-known Asian crime groups are:

- *Yakuza.* Japanese criminal group. They are often involved in multinational criminal activities, including human trafficking, gambling, prostitution, and undermining licit businesses.
- *Fuk Ching.* Chinese organized criminal group in the United States. They have been involved in smuggling, street violence, and human trafficking.
- *Triads.* Underground criminal societies based in Hong Kong. They control secret markets and bus routes and are often involved in money laundering and drug trafficking.
- *Heijin.* Taiwanese gangsters who are often executives in large corporations. They are involved in white-collar crimes, such as illegal stock trading and bribery, and sometimes run for public office.
- *Jao Pho.* Organized crime group in Thailand. They are often involved in illegal political and business activity.
- *Red Wa.* Gangsters from Thailand. They are involved in manufacturing and trafficking methamphetamine.[140]

CONTROLLING TRANSNATIONAL CRIME

 L09 Assess the efforts to control transnational organized crime

Efforts to combat transnational organized crime are typically in the hands of federal agencies. One approach is to form international working groups to collect intelligence, share information, and plot unified strategies among member nations. The FBI belongs to several international working groups aimed at combating transnational gangs in various parts of the world. For example, to combat the influence and reach of Eurasian organized crime the FBI is involved in the following groups and activities:

- *Eurasian Organized Crime Working Group.* Established in 1994, it meets to discuss and jointly address the transnational aspects of Eurasian organized crime that impact member countries and the international community in general. The member countries are Canada, Great Britain, Germany, France, Italy, Japan, the United States, and Russia.

- *Central European Working Group*. This group is part of a project that brings together the FBI and central European law enforcement agencies to discuss cooperative investigative matters covering the broad spectrum of Eurasian organized crime. A principal concern is the growing presence of Russian and other Eurasian organized criminals in central Europe and the United States. The initiative works on practical interaction between the participating agencies to establish lines of communication and working relationships, to develop strategies and tactics to address transnational organized crime matters impacting the region, and to identify potential common targets.

- *Southeast European Cooperative Initiative*. This is an international organization intended to coordinate police and customs regional actions for preventing and combating transborder crime. It is headquartered in Bucharest, Romania, and has 12 fully participating member countries. The United States has been one of 14 countries with observer status since 1998. The initiative's center serves as a clearinghouse for information and intelligence sharing, allowing the quick exchange of information in a professional and trustworthy environment. The initiative also supports specialized task forces for countering transborder crime such as the trafficking of people, drugs, and cars; smuggling; financial crimes; terrorism; and other serious transborder crimes.

Anti–Organized Crime Laws Congress has passed a number of laws that have made it easier for agencies to bring transnational gangs to justice. One of the first measures aimed directly at organized crime was the Interstate and Foreign Travel or Transportation in Aid of Racketeering Enterprises Act (Travel Act).[141] The Travel Act prohibits travel in interstate commerce or use of interstate facilities with the intent to promote, manage, establish, carry on, or facilitate an unlawful activity; it also prohibits the actual or attempted engagement in these activities.

In 1970, Congress passed the Organized Crime Control Act. Title IX of the act, probably its most effective measure, is the **Racketeer Influenced and Corrupt Organization (RICO) Act**.[142] RICO did not create new categories of crimes but rather new categories of offenses in racketeering activity, which it defined as involvement in two or more acts prohibited by 24 existing federal and 8 state statutes. The offenses listed in RICO include state-defined crimes (such as murder, kidnapping, gambling, arson, robbery, bribery, extortion, and narcotics violations) and federally defined crimes (such as bribery, counterfeiting, transmission of gambling information, prostitution, and mail fraud). RICO is designed to limit patterns of organized criminal activity by prohibiting involvement in acts intended to do the following:

- Derive income from racketeering or the unlawful collection of debts and use or investment of such income
- Acquire through racketeering an interest in or control over any enterprise engaged in interstate or foreign commerce
- Conduct business through a pattern of racketeering
- Conspire to use racketeering as a means of making income, collecting loans, or conducting business

An individual convicted under RICO is subject to 20 years in prison and a $25,000 fine. Additionally, the accused must forfeit to the U.S. government any interest in a business in violation of RICO. These penalties are much more potent than simple conviction and imprisonment.

Why Is It So Difficult to Eradicate Transnational Gangs?

While international cooperation is now common and law enforcement agencies are willing to work together to fight transnational gangs, these criminal organizations are extremely hard to eradicate. The gangs are ready to use violence and well equipped to carry out threats. Take for instance Los Zetas, whose core members are former members of the Mexican military's elite Special Air Mobile Force Group (Grupo Aeromovil de Fuerzas Especiales, or GAFES). Military trained, Los Zetas are able to carry out complex operations and use sophisticated weaponry.[143] Los Zetas, who began as enforcers for the Gulf cartel's regional domination, are now their rivals and are considered the most powerful Mexican transnational gang. Their base is Nuevo Laredo, but the criminal organization's sphere of influence extends across Mexico and deep into Central America. Unlike most gangs, which obtain most of their income from narcotics, Los Zetas earns about half their income trafficking in arms, kidnapping, and competing for control of trafficking routes along the eastern half of the U.S.–Mexico border. The cartel is now considered Mexico's most brutal, and they are suspected of kidnapping and killing Central American migrants headed for the border as well as Mexican bus passengers who traveled through their territory.[144]

Even when a gang can be taken out, it is soon replaced as long as money can be made. Take the case of La Familia Michoacana cartel, which became an independent drug trafficking organization in Mexico and later allied itself with the Gulf cartel. Originated in the 1980s, La Familia was heavily armed and utilized violence to support its narcotics trafficking business, including murders, kidnappings, and assaults in the Michoacán state of Mexico. The killing of its founder

Racketeer Influenced and Corrupt Organizations (RICO) Act
Federal legislation that enables prosecutors to bring additional criminal or civil charges against people whose multiple criminal acts constitute a conspiracy. RICO features monetary penalties that allow the government to confiscate all profits derived from criminal activities. Originally intended to be used against organized criminals, RICO has also been used against white-collar criminals.

and leader Nazario Moreno González in 2011 spelled the end of La Familia. However, that did not spell the end of gang activity in the area. Two of his subordinates, Enrique Plancarte Solís and Servando Gómez Martínez, broke away and formed the Knights Templar gang (Caballeros Templarios). The Knights extort protection money from legitimate businesspeople in Michoacán and tax farmers' crops; they tell restaurant owners what to charge for food and then demand a kickback.

Adding to control problems is the fact that the drug trade is an important source of foreign revenue, and destroying the drug trade undermines the economies of third-world nations. Even if the government of one nation were willing to cooperate in vigorous drug suppression efforts, suppliers in other nations, eager to cash in on the sellers' market, would be encouraged to turn more acreage over to coca or poppy production. Today, almost every Caribbean country is involved with narcotrafficking, and illicit drug shipments in the region are worth more money than the top five legitimate exports combined. Drug gangs are able to corrupt the political structure and destabilize countries. Drug addiction and violent crime are now common in Jamaica, Puerto Rico, and even small islands like St. Kitts. The corruption of the police and other security forces has reached a crisis point, where an officer can earn the equivalent of half a year's salary by simply looking the other way on a drug deal.[145] There are also indications that the drug syndicates may be planting a higher yield variety of coca and improving refining techniques to replace crops lost to government crackdowns.

The United States has little influence in some key drug-producing areas such as Taliban-held Afghanistan and Myanmar (formerly Burma). War and terrorism also may make gang control strategies problematic. After the United States toppled Afghanistan's Taliban government, the remnants began to grow and sell poppy to support their insurgency; Afghanistan now supplies 90 percent of the world's opium.[146] And while the Colombian guerillas may not be interested in joining or colluding with crime cartels, they finance their war against the government by aiding drug traffickers and "taxing" crops and sales. Considering these problems, it is not surprising that transnational gangs continue to flourish.

The Causes of Enterprise Crime

LO10 Comment on the causes of enterprise crime

Why do people get involved in risky schemes to use their institutional positions to steal money? Why do people risk going to prison because they pollute the environment? Why do criminal gangs form? Can the same factors that predict other types of criminal offenses also apply to crimes of criminal enterprise? After all, unlike most common-law crimes, enterprise crimes are not committed by impoverished teenagers living in the inner city but by people who are often well-off, highly educated businesspeople. In order to commit an enterprise crime, someone must have already obtained a position of power and trust. This section describes some of the most prominent views of why people commit crimes of criminal enterprise.

RATIONAL CHOICE: GREED

When Kansas City pharmacist Robert Courtney was asked after his arrest why he substituted improper doses of drugs instead of what doctors had prescribed, he told investigators he cut the drugs' strength "out of greed."[147] Courtney is not alone. One view of enterprise crime is that greedy people

California Attorney General Kamala Harris addresses the Domestic Human Sex Trafficking symposium in Los Angeles on April 25, 2014, hoping to bring increased attention to the problem. Human trafficking, sexual servitude, and forced labor bring in more than $30 billion annually, making it the second most profitable criminal enterprise after illegal arms trafficking. The vast majority of those trafficked are women and children, from all milieus of society.

AP Images/Damian Dovarganes

CONNECTIONS

The rational choice view was first discussed in Chapter 4.

ASK YOURSELF . . .

Do you believe it's the most accurate way of explaining enterprise crime? Would the General Theory of Crime, discussed in Chapter 9, be a more appropriate and valid explanation? Think *Wolf of Wall Street*!

rationally choose to take shortcuts to acquire wealth, believing that the potential profits far outweigh future punishments. Most believe they will not get caught; they are far too clever to be detected by mere civil servants who work for government agencies.

Recently criminologists Neal Shover and Peter Grabosky introduced the concept of "lure" to help explain why some people choose the illegal yet alluring benefits of enterprise crime:[148] The lure of enterprise crime has diverse sources. When states create loopholes in the law that provide criminal opportunities, someone is bound to take advantage of the error. As the supply of lure expands, so too will the number of people willing to risk legal censure to acquire financial benefits. The lure of crime expands in the absence of capable control systems. When financial oversight was absent in the United States economic markets, the crash of 2008 became inevitable.

RATIONAL CHOICE: NEED

Greed is not the only motivation for enterprise crime; need also plays an important role. Some people turn to crime to fulfill an overwhelming financial or psychological need. Executives may tamper with company books because they feel the need to keep or improve their jobs, satisfy their egos, or support their children. Blue-collar workers may pilfer because they need to keep pace with inflation or buy a new car. People may join a transnational gang, despite the risks, because they can think of no other way to make a living. A lot of people convicted of white-collar crime typically work in lower-echelon positions, and their acts seem motivated more by economic survival than by greed and power.[149]

RATIONALIZATION/NEUTRALIZATION VIEW

Rationalizing guilt is a common trait of enterprise criminals.[150] What they did was not so bad; what some call crime is merely a "technicality"; the organized crime figure feels tremendous loyalty to his comrades. One offender convicted of price fixing denied the illegality of his actions: "We did not fix prices. I am telling you that all we did was recover costs."[151] Some white-collar criminals believe that everyone violates business laws, so it is not so bad if they do so themselves.

In his classic research on fraud, Donald Cressey found that the door to solving personal financial problems through criminal means is opened by the rationalizations people develop for white-collar crime: "Some of our most respectable citizens got their start in life by using other people's money temporarily." "In the real estate business, there is nothing wrong about using deposits before the deal is closed." "All people steal when they get in a tight spot."[152] Offenders use these and other rationalizations to resolve the conflict they experience over engaging in illegal behavior.

Organized crime figures rationalize their behavior by insisting they are only providing a service that people want, even if it's illegal. Some white-collar offenders feel free to engage in business crime because they can easily rationalize its effects. Some convince themselves that their actions are not really crimes because the acts involved do not resemble street crimes. A banker who uses his position of trust to lend his institution's assets to a company he secretly controls may see himself as a shrewd businessman, not as a criminal. A pharmacist who chisels customers on prescription drugs may rationalize her behavior by telling herself that it does not really hurt anyone. Further, some businesspeople feel justified in committing enterprise crimes because they believe government regulators do not really understand the business world or the problems of competing in the free enterprise system.[153] When asked, enterprise criminals often use techniques of neutralization to defuse guilt: (1) everyone else does it, (2) it's not my fault or responsibility, and (3) no one is hurt except insurance companies and they are wealthy.

CULTURAL VIEW

According to this view, some organizations promote criminal enterprise in the same way that lower-class culture encourages the development of juvenile gangs and street crime. According to the cultural view, some enterprises cause crime by placing excessive demands on employees while at the same time maintaining a business climate tolerant of employee deviance. New employees learn the attitudes and techniques needed to commit crime from their business peers. Under these circumstances, the attitudes of closest coworkers and the perceived attitudes of executives have a more powerful control over decision making than the attitudes of outsiders—closest friends and business professors—whose more moderate views might have tempered the decision to commit crime.[154]

Those holding the cultural view would point to the Enron scandal as a prime example of what happens when people work in organizations in which the cultural values stress profit over fair play, government scrutiny is limited and regulators are viewed as the enemy, and senior members encourage newcomers to believe that "greed is good." One method of controlling enterprise crime, then, is to redirect institutional culture and focus more on values and trust than profit and greed.[155]

SELF-CONTROL VIEW

In their General Theory of Crime, Travis Hirschi and Michael Gottfredson suggest that the motives that produce enterprise crimes—quick benefits with minimal effort—are the same as those that produce any other criminal behaviors.[156] Enterprise criminals have low self-control and are inclined to follow momentary impulses without considering the long-term costs of such behavior.[157] Even though bankers and stockbrokers are not a group known for being impulsive, those who commit enterprise crimes are the most impulsive of the bunch. Hirschi and Gottfredson collected data showing that the demographic distribution of white-collar crime is similar to other crimes. For example,

CONNECTIONS

The General Theory of Crime was covered in Chapter 9.

ASK YOURSELF . . .

Is it really possible, as Hirschi and Gottfredson claim, that corrupt bankers lack self-control? Is it possible that the crimes of inside traders and gang boys have a similar explanation?

gender, race, and age ratios are the same for crimes such as embezzlement and fraud as they are for street crimes such as burglary and robbery.

SUMMARY

L01 Assess what is meant by the term *enterprise crime*

Enterprise crime involves criminal acts that twist the legal rules of commercial enterprise for criminal purposes. They taint the free market system because they mix and match illegal and legal methods in all phases of commercial activity. They involve illegal business practices to merchandise what are normally legitimate commercial products. They can also involve the use of standard business methods and accounting to market illegal goods.

L02 Define white-collar crime

Edwin Sutherland first used the phrase "white-collar crime" to describe the criminal activities of the rich and powerful. He defined white-collar crime as "a crime committed by a person of respectability and high social status in the course of his occupation." Included within recent views of white-collar crime are such acts as income tax evasion, credit card fraud, and bankruptcy fraud. Other white-collar criminals use their positions of trust in business or government to commit crimes. Their activities might include pilfering, soliciting bribes or kickbacks, and embezzlement.

L03 Compare and contrast the various forms of white-collar crime

There are a variety of categories of white-collar crime. White-collar fraud involves using a business enterprise as a front to swindle people. Chiseling involves businesspeople and professionals who use their positions to cheat clients on a regular basis. Embezzlement and employee fraud occur when a person uses a position of trust to steal from an organization. White-collar exploitation occurs when an individual abuses his or her power or position in an organization to coerce people into making payments for services to which they are already entitled. If the payments are not made, the services are

withheld. In most cases, exploitation occurs when the victim has a clear right to expect a service, and the offender threatens to withhold the service unless an additional payment or bribe is forthcoming. In contrast, influence peddling occurs when individuals holding important institutional positions sell power, influence, and information to outsiders who have an interest in influencing the activities of the institution or buying information on what the institution may do in the future. Client fraud involves theft from an organization that advances credit, covers losses, or reimburses for services. Corporate, or organizational, crime involves various illegal business practices such as price fixing, restraint of trade, and false advertising.

L04 Discuss efforts to control white-collar crime

The government has used various law enforcement strategies to combat white-collar crime. Some involve deterrence, which uses punishment to frighten potential abusers. Others involve economic or compliance strategies, which create economic incentives to obey the law. Most offenders do not view themselves as criminals and therefore do not seem to be deterred by criminal statutes. Although thousands of white-collar criminals are prosecuted each year, their numbers are insignificant compared with the magnitude of the problem. Detection and enforcement are primarily in the hands of administrative departments and agencies, including the FBI, the Internal Revenue Service, the Secret Service, U.S. Customs, the Environmental Protection Agency, and the Securities and Exchange Commission. On the state and local levels, law enforcement officials have made progress in a number of areas, such as controlling consumer fraud. One approach is to ensure compliance with business rules and law by threatening economic sanction. Another is to deter white-collar crime by punishing individual offenders and putting them in prison as a deterrent to other would-be criminals.

LO5 Be familiar with the concept of green crime

Green crimes involve a wide range of actions and outcomes that harm the environment and that stem from decisions about what is produced, where it is produced, and how it is produced. There is more than one perspective on green crime: according to the legalist perspective, environmental crimes are violations of existing criminal laws designed to protect people, the environment, or both. According to the environmental justice (EJ) view, limiting environmental crimes to actual violations of the criminal law is too narrow and should be broader than the law allows. According to the biocentric approach, environmental harm is viewed as any human activity that disrupts a biosystem, destroying plant and animal life.

LO6 List the components of green crime

Green crime can take many different forms, ranging from deforestation and illegal logging to violations of worker safety. Elements of green crime include illegal dumping and pollution, illegal logging, illegal fishing, and the exportation of endangered species.

LO7 Trace the evolution of organized crime

Organized criminals used to be white ethnics—Jews, Italians, and Irish—but today African Americans, Latinos, and other groups have become involved in organized crime activities. The old-line "families" are now more likely to use their criminal wealth and power to buy into legitimate businesses. The most common view of organized crime today is an ethnically diverse group of competing gangs dedicated to extortion or to providing illegal goods and services. Efforts to control organized crime have been stepped up by the federal government, which has used antiracketeering statutes to arrest syndicate leaders.

LO8 Be familiar with transnational organized crime

Organized crime today is transnational. With the aid of the Internet and instant communications, groups are operating on a global scale to traffic drugs and people, to launder money, and to sell arms. Eastern European crime families are active abroad and in the United States. Russian organized crime has become a major problem for law enforcement agencies. Mexican and Latin American groups are quite active in the drug trade; Asian crime families are involved in smuggling and other illegal activities.

LO9 Assess the efforts to control transnational organized crime

Efforts to combat transnational organized crime are typically in the hands of federal agencies. One approach is to form international working groups to collect intelligence, share information, and plot unified strategies among member nations. The FBI belongs to several international working groups aimed at combating transnational gangs in various parts of the world. While international cooperation is now common and law enforcement agencies are willing to work together to fight transnational gangs, these criminal organizations are extremely hard to eradicate. The gangs are ready to use violence and well equipped to carry out threats.

LO10 Comment on the causes of enterprise crime

There are numerous explanations for enterprise crime. Some offenders are motivated by greed; others offend due to personal problems. They use rationalizations to allow their financial needs to be met without compromising their values. Culture theory suggests that some organizations actually encourage employees to cheat or cut corners. The self-control view is that enterprise criminals are like any other law violators: impulsive people who lack self-control.

CRITICAL THINKING QUESTIONS

1. How would you punish a corporate executive whose product killed people if the executive had no knowledge that the product was potentially lethal? What if the executive did know?

2. Is organized crime inevitable as long as people desire banned goods and services such as drugs, gambling, and prostitution?

3. Does the media glamorize organized crime? Does it paint an inaccurate picture of noble crime lords fighting to protect their families?

4. Apply traditional theories of criminal behavior to white-collar, green, and organized crime. Which one seems to best predict why someone would engage in these behaviors?

KEY TERMS

enterprise crimes (462)
corporate crime (463)
white-collar swindle (464)
Ponzi scheme (464)
chiseling (466)

pink slime (467)
insider trading (468)
exploitation (468)
influence peddling (469)
Sherman Antitrust Act (474)

green crime (478)
transnational organized crime (486)

Racketeer Influenced and Corrupt Organization Act (RICO) (493)

All URLs accessed in 2016.

1. U.S. Attorney's Office, Central District of California, "Owner of San Gabriel Valley Surrogacy Agency Sentenced to Federal Prison for Ripping Off Would-Be Parents Who Paid for Egg Donations," September 28, 2015, https://www.fbi.gov/losangeles/press -releases/2015/owner-of-san-gabriel-valley -surrogacy-agency-sentenced-to-federal -prison-for-ripping-off-would-be-parents -who-paid-for-egg-donations.

2. Rob White, "Researching Transnational Environmental Harm: Toward an Eco-Global Criminology," *International Journal of Comparative and Applied Criminal Justice* 33 (2009): 229–248.

3. Mark Haller, "Illegal Enterprise: A Theoretical and Historical Interpretation," *Criminology* 28 (1990): 207–235.

4. Nancy Frank and Michael Lynch, *Corporate Crime, Corporate Violence* (Albany, NY: Harrow & Heston, 1992), p. 7.

5. Edward Alsworth Ross, *Sin and Society: An Analysis of Latter-Day Iniquity* (Boston: Houghton Mifflin Company, 1907): 45–71.

6. Edwin Sutherland, *White-Collar Crime: The Uncut Version* (New Haven, CT: Yale University Press, 1983).

7. Edwin Sutherland, "White-Collar Criminality," *American Sociological Review* 5 (1940): 2–10.

8. David Weisburd and Kip Schlegel, "Returning to the Mainstream," in *White-Collar Crime Reconsidered*, ed. Kip Schlegel and David Weisburd (Boston: Northeastern University Press, 1992), pp. 352–365.

9. Rodney Huff, Christian Desilets, and John Kane, *2010 National Public Survey on White Collar Crime*, http://www.nw3c.org/docs /publications/2010-national-public-survey -on-white-collar-crime.pdf.

10. Ibid.

11. Ibid.

12. Natalie Taylor, "Under-Reporting of Crime Against Small Business: Attitudes Towards Police and Reporting Practices," *Policing and Society* 13 (2003): 79–90.

13. The typology used here leans closely on Mark Moore, "Notes Toward a National Strategy to Deal with White-Collar Crime," in *A National Strategy for Containing White-Collar Crime*, ed. Herbert Edelhertz and Charles Rogovin (Lexington, MA: Lexington Books, 1980), pp. 32–44.

14. Clifford Krauss, Phillip L. Zweig, and Julie Creswell, "Texas Firm Accused of $8 Billion Fraud," *New York Times*, February 18, 2009, http://www.nytimes.com/2009/02/18 /business/18stanford.html.

15. CNBC, "Allen Stanford: Descent from Billionaire to Inmate #35017-183," October 5, 2012, http://www.cnbc.com /id/49276842.

16. FBI, A Ponzi Scheme Collapses Financial Crime Ring Uncovered, Criminals Brought to Justice, 02/23/15, http://www.fbi.gov /news/stories/2015/february/a-ponzi -scheme-collapses/a-ponzi-scheme -collapses.

17. FBI, "Telemarketing Fraud," https://www .fbi.gov/scams-safety/fraud.

18. Jon Seidel, "Travel Agent Scammed People Trying to Get to Mecca, Gets 9 1/2 Years," *Chicago Sun-Times*, November 19, 2015, http://chicago.suntimes.com/news/travel -agent-scammed-people-trying-to-get-to -mecca-gets-9-12-years/.

19. Bao Ong, "Commission Seeks to Revoke Licenses of 633 Cabbies," *New York Times*, May 14, 2010, http://cityroom.blogs .nytimes.com/2010/05/14/633-cabbies -lose-their-licenses/.

20. Federal Trade Commission, "Auto Repair Basics," https://www.consumer.ftc.gov /articles/0211-auto-repair-basics.

21. Jim Avila, "70 Percent of Ground Beef at Supermarkets Contains 'Pink Slime,'" ABC News, March 7, 2012, http://abcnews.go .com/blogs/headlines/2012/03/70-percent -of-ground-beef-at-supermarkets-contains -pink-slime/.

22. Josh Sanborn, "The Surprising Reason 'Pink Slime' Meat Is Back," *Time*, August 24, 2014, http://time.com/3176714/pink -slime-meat-prices-bpi-beef/.

23. Richard Quinney, "Occupational Structure and Criminal Behavior: Prescription Violation of Retail Pharmacists," *Social Problems* 11 (1963): 179–185; see also John Braithwaite, *Corporate Crime in the Pharmaceutical Industry* (London: Routledge and Kegan Paul, 1984).

24. Pam Belluck, "Prosecutors Say Greed Drove Pharmacist to Dilute Drugs," *New York Times*, August 18, 2001, p. 3.

25. Federal Bureau of Investigation, Kansas City Division, press release, April 22, 2002.

26. FBI, "Historic Insider Trading Scheme: Stock Manager Busted," February 28, 2014, http://www.fbi.gov/news/stories/2014 /february/historic-insider-trading-scheme /historic-insider-trading-scheme.

27. Patricia Hurtado, "SAC's Martoma Faces Up to 20 Years at June 10 Sentencing," *Bloomberg News*, February 8, 2014, http:// www.bloomberg.com/news/2014-02-08 /sac-capital-s-martoma-faces-up-to -20-years-at-june-10-sentencing.html.

28. *Carpenter v. United States*, 484 U.S. 19 (1987); also see John Boland, "The SEC Trims the First Amendment," *Wall Street Journal*, December 4, 1986, p. 28.

29. Anish Vashista, David Johnson, and Muhtashem Choudhury, "Securities Fraud," *American Criminal Law Review* 42 (2005): 877–942.

30. James Armstrong et al., "Securities Fraud," *American Criminal Law Review* 33 (1995): 973–1016.

31. Scott McMurray, "Futures Pit Trader Goes to Trial," *Wall Street Journal*, May 8, 1990, p. C1; Scott McMurray, "Chicago Pits' Dazzling Growth Permitted a Free-for-All Mecca," *Wall Street Journal*, August 3, 1989, p. A4.

32. Charles V. Bagli, "Kickback Investigation Extends to Middle-Class Buildings in New York," *New York Times*, October 14, 1998, p. A19.

33. U.S. Attorney's Office, Eastern District of New York, "New York City Police Officer Pleads Guilty to Extortion and Firearms Charges," December 15, 2015, https://www .justice.gov/usao-edny/pr/new-york-city -police-officer-pleads-guilty-extortion-and -firearms-charges.

34. FBI, "A (Driver's) License to Steal: Corruption in a San Diego Motor Vehicle Office," February 25, 2014, http://www.fbi .gov/news/stories/2014/february/corruption -in-a-san-diego-motor-vehicle-office /corruption-in-a-san-diego-motor-vehicle -office.

35. Victoria Bekiempis and Stephen Rex Brown, "Sheldon Silver Guilty of All 7 Corruption Charges in Twin Kickback Schemes, Faces Up to 130 Years in Prison," *New York Daily News*, December 1, 2015, http://www .nydailynews.com/news/crime/sheldon -silver-guilty-7-corruption-charges-article -1.2450685.

36. Monica Davey and John O'Neil, "Ex-Governor of Illinois Is Convicted on All Charges," *New York Times*, April 18, 2006, p. 1.

37. MSNBC, "Feds: Governor Tried to 'Auction' Obama's Seat," December 9, 2008, http:// www.msnbc.msn.com/id/28139155/.

38. FBI, "Abuse of Trust: The Case of the Crooked Border Official," June 8, 2009, http://www.fbi.gov/news/stories/2009/june /border060809.

39. *The Knapp Commission Report on Police Corruption* (New York: George Braziller, 1973), pp. 1–3, 170–182.

40. 4 New York, NBC, "Ex-NYPD Cop Ran Prostitution Ring Across Tri-State," February 2, 2016, http://www.nbcnewyork .com/news/local/NYPD-Cop-Prostitution -Ring-Federal-Court-Eduardo-Cornejo -367410031.html.

41. FBI, New Orleans Division, "St. Bernard Parish Judge Wayne Cresap, Two Lawyers Charged in Bribery Scheme," July 1, 2009, http://www.fbi.gov/neworleans/press -releases/2009/no070109a.htm.

42. MSNBC, "Pa. Judges Accused of Jailing Kids for Cash: Judges Allegedly Took $2.6 Million in Payoffs to Put Juveniles in

Lockups," February 11, 2009, http://www.msnbc.msn.com/id/29142654/.

43. Henry Blodget, "Apple Manager Paul Shin Devine Busted in $1 Million Kickback Scheme," *Business Insider*, August 15, 2010, http://www.businessinsider.com/apple-manager-paul-shin-devine-busted-in-1-million-kickback-scheme-2010-8.

44. Disclosure of Payments to Individuals Connected with Broadcasts, United States Criminal Code, Title 47, Chapter 5, Subchapter V § 508.

45. Marshall Clinard and Peter Yeager, *Corporate Crime* (New York: Free Press, 1980), p. 67.

46. Alina Selyukh, "U.S. Judge Approves IBM's Foreign Bribery Case Settlement with SEC," Reuters, July 25, 2013, http://www.reuters.com/article/2013/07/25/us-ibm-sec-idUSBRE96O1FB20130725.

47. PL No. 95-213, 101-104, 91 Stat. 1494.

48. Adrian Cho, "Hey Buddy . . . Wanna Buy a Moon Rock?" *Science Now*, July 7, 2002, p. 1.

49. Charles McCaghy, *Deviant Behavior* (New York: Macmillan, 1976), p. 178.

50. J. Sorenson, H. Grove, and T. Sorenson, "Detecting Management Fraud: The Role of the Independent Auditor," in *White-Collar Crime, Theory and Research*, ed. G. Geis and E. Stotland (Beverly Hills: Sage, 1980), pp. 221–251.

51. Jason Knott, "Ex-Tyco CEO Dennis Kozlowski Released from Prison," January 17, 2014, http://www.cepro.com/article/ex_tyco_ceo_dennis_kozlowski_released_from_prison/.

52. Bethany McLean and Peter Elkind, *The Smartest Guys in the Room: The Amazing Rise and Scandalous Fall of Enron* (New York: Penguin, 2003); Kurt Eichenwald, "Ex-Andersen Partner Pleads Guilty in Record-Shredding," *New York Times*, April 12, 2002, p. C1; John A. Byrne, "At Enron, the Environment Was Ripe for Abuse," *BusinessWeek*, February 25, 2002, p. 12;. Peter Behr and Carrie Johnson, "Govt. Expands Charges Against Enron Execs," *Washington Post*, May 1, 2003, p. 1.

53. FBI, "Medicare Fraud: Hospice Owner Falsified Numerous Claims," August 20, 2015, https://www.fbi.gov/news/stories/2015/august/medicare-fraud/medicare-fraud.

54. FBI, "Health Care Fraud Takedown: 243 Arrested, Charged with $712 Million in False Medicare Billings," June 18, 2015, https://www.fbi.gov/news/stories/2015/june/health-care-fraud-takedown/health-care-fraud-takedown.

55. U.S. Department of Justice, "Three Miami Area Brothers and Physician's Assistant Charged in $110 Million Health Care Fraud Scheme," June 11, 2008, http://www.justice.gov/opa/pr/2008/June/08-crm-526.html.

56. U.S. Attorney's Office, Eastern District of Kentucky, "Saint Joseph London Hospital to Pay $16.5 Million to Settle False Claims Act Allegations of Unnecessary Heart Procedures," January 28, 2014, http://www.fbi.gov/louisville/press-releases/2014/saint-joseph-london-hospital-to-pay-16.5-million-to-settle-false-claims-act-allegations-of-unnecessary-heart-procedures.

57. FBI, "Rooting Out Health Care Fraud Is Central to the Well-Being of Both Our Citizens and the Overall Economy," 2014, http://www.fbi.gov/about-us/investigate/white_collar/health-care-fraud.

58. National Health Care Anti-Fraud Association, "The Challenge of Health Care Fraud," 2014, http://www.nhcaa.org/resources/health-care-anti-fraud-resources/the-challenge-of-health-care-fraud.aspx.

59. Ibid.

60. Health Insurance Portability and Accountability Act of 1996 (HIPAA), United States Code, Title 18, Section 1347.

61. 18 U.S.C. section 1344 (1994).

62. FBI, "Financial Crimes Report to the Public 2005," http://www.fbi.gov/stats-services/publications/fcs_report2005/fcs_2005.

63. *United States v. Bishop*, 412 U.S. 346 (1973).

64. David Cay Johnston, "Departing Chief Says I.R.S. Is Losing War on Tax Cheats," *New York Times*, November 5, 2002, p. 1.

65. Cited in Frank and Lynch, *Corporate Crime, Corporate Violence*, pp. 12–13.

66. Sutherland, "White-Collar Criminality," pp. 2–10.

67. Joseph S. Hall, "Corporate Criminal Liability," *American Criminal Law Review* 35 (1998): 549–560.

68. FBI, "Nine Automobile Parts Manufacturers and Two Executives Agree to Plead Guilty to Fixing Prices on Automobile Parts Sold to U.S. Car Manufacturers and Installed in U.S. Cars: Companies Agree to Pay Total of More than $740 Million in Criminal Fines," September 26, 2013, http://www.fbi.gov/news/pressrel/press-releases/nine-automobile-parts-manufacturers-and-two-executives-agree-to-plead-guilty-to-fixing-prices-on-automobile-parts-sold-to-u.s.-car-manufacturers-and-installed-in-u.s.-cars.

69. 15 U.S.C. section 1 (1994).

70. 15 U.S.C. § 1 - Trusts, Etc., in Restraint of Trade Illegal; Penalty, http://www.law.cornell.edu/uscode/text/15/1.

71. *Northern Pacific Railways v. United States*, 356 U.S. 1 (1958).

72. *Illinois Ex Rel. Madigan v. Telemarketing Associates, Inc., et al.* No. 01-1806 (2003).

73. This section relies heavily on Daniel Skoler, "White-Collar Crime and the Criminal Justice System: Problems and Challenges," in *A National Strategy for Containing White-Collar Crime*, ed. Edelhertz and Rogovin, (Lexington, MA: Lexington Books, 1980), pp. 57–76.

74. Michael Benson, Francis Cullen, and William Maakestad, "Local Prosecutors and Corporate Crime," *Crime and Delinquency* 36 (1990): 356–372.

75. Ibid., pp. 369–370.

76. David Simon and D. Stanley Eitzen, *Elite Deviance* (Boston: Allyn & Bacon, 1982), p. 28.

77. Stuart P. Green, *Lying, Cheating, and Stealing: A Moral Theory of White Collar Crime* (London: Oxford University Press, 2006).

78. This section relies heavily on Albert Reiss, Jr., "Selecting Strategies of Social Control over Organizational Life," in *Enforcing Regulation*, ed. Keith Hawkins and John M. Thomas (Boston: Kluwer Publications, 1984), pp. 25–37.

79. John Braithwaite, "The Limits of Economism in Controlling Harmful Corporate Conduct," *Law and Society Review* 16 (1981–1982): 481–504.

80. Sarbanes-Oxley Act, H.R. 3763-2 (2002).

81. Michael Benson, "Emotions and Adjudication: Status Degradation Among White-Collar Criminals," *Justice Quarterly* 7 (1990): 515–528; John Braithwaite, *Crime, Shame, and Reintegration* (Sydney: Cambridge University Press, 1989).

82. Kip Schlegel, "Desert, Retribution and Corporate Criminality," *Justice Quarterly* 5 (1988): 615–634.

83. Raymond Michalowski and Ronald Kramer, "The Space Between Laws: The Problem of Corporate Crime in a Transnational Context," *Social Problems* 34 (1987): 34–53.

84. Ibid.

85. Christopher M. Brown and Nikhil S. Singhvi, "Antitrust Violations," *American Criminal Law Review* 35 (1998): 467–501.

86. Howard Adler, "Current Trends in Criminal Antitrust Enforcement," *Business Crimes Bulletin* (April 1996): 1.

87. David Weisburd, Elin Waring, and Stanton Wheeler, "Class, Status, and the Punishment of White-Collar Criminals," *Law and Social Inquiry* 15 (1990): 223–243.

88. Sean Rosenmerkel, "Wrongfulness and Harmfulness as Components of Seriousness of White-Collar Offenses," *Journal of Contemporary Criminal Justice* 17 (2001): 308–328.

89. United States Attorney, Middle District of Tennessee, "Grease Hauling Company and Executives Sentenced for Clean Water Act Violations," February 19, 2016, https://www.epa.gov/sites/production/files/2016-02/documents/southern-grease-press-release.pdf.

90. Michael J. Lynch and Paul Stretesky, "Green Criminology in the United States," in *Issues in Green Criminology*, ed. Piers Beirne and Nigel South (Portland, OR: Willan, 2008), pp. 248–269, at p. 249.

91. Michael M. O'Hear, "Sentencing the Green-Collar Offender: Punishment, Culpability, and Environmental Crime," *Journal of Criminal Law and Criminology* 95 (2004): 133–276.

92. F. J. W. Herbig and S. J. Joubert, "Criminological Semantics: Conservation Criminology—Vision or Vagary?" *Acta Criminologica* 19 (2006): 88–103.

93. Rob White, "Researching Transnational Environmental Harm: Toward an Eco-Global Criminology," *International Journal of Comparative and Applied Criminal Justice* 33 (2009): 229–248.

94. Paddy Hillyard, Christina Pantazis, Dave Gordon, and Steve Tombs, *Beyond Criminology: Taking Harm Seriously* (London, Pluto Press, 2004).

95. Duncan Brack, "Illegal Logging," Chatham House, 2007, http://www.illegal-logging .info/uploads/1_Illegal_logging_bp_07_01 .pdf.

96. INTERPOL, Project Leaf, http://www .interpol.int/Crime-areas/Environmental -crime/Projects/Project-Leaf.

97. Ibid.

98. Brack, "Illegal Logging."

99. INTERPOL, Project Leaf.

100. Liana Sun Wyler and Pervaze A. Sheikh, *International Illegal Trade in Wildlife: Threats and U.S. Policy* (Washington, DC: Congressional Research Service, 2008), http://fpc.state.gov/documents/organization /110404.pdf.

101. INTERPOL, Project Predator, http://www .interpol.int/Crime-areas/Environmental -crime/Projects/Project-Predator.

102. INTERPOL, Project Wisdom, http://www .interpol.int/Crime-areas/Environmental -crime/Projects/Project-Wisdom.

103. Patterson Clark and Darryl Fears, "The Horn and Ivory Trade," *Washington Post*, August 10, 2014, https://www.washington post.com/apps/g/page/national/the-horn -and-ivory-trade/1163/.

104. White, "Researching Transnational Environmental Harm: Toward an Eco-Global Criminology."

105. Liana Sun Wyler and Pervaze A. Sheikh, *International Illegal Trade in Wildlife: Threats and U.S. Policy* (Washington, DC: Congressional Research Service, 2013), http://www.fas.org/sgp/crs/misc/RL34395 .pdf.

106. The Lacey Act, 16 U.S.C. §§ 3371-3378.

107. Poaching Facts, Elephant Poaching Statistics, http://www.poachingfacts.com /poaching-statistics/elephant-poaching -statistics/.

108. U. R. Sumaila, J. Alder, and H. Keith, "Global Scope and Economics of Illegal Fishing," *Marine Policy* 30 (2006) 696–703.

109. Adam Minter, "The Burning Truth Behind an E-Waste Dump in Africa," Smithsonian .com, January 13, 2016, http://www .smithsonianmag.com/science-nature /burning-truth-behind-e-waste-dump -africa-180957597/?no-ist.

110. Carole Gibbs, Edmund F. McGarrell, and Mark Axelrod, "Transnational White-collar Crime and Risk : Lessons from the Global Trade in Electronic Waste," *Criminology and Public Policy* 9 (2010): 543–560.

111. Andrew Oliveira, Christopher Schenck, Christopher Cole, and Nicole Janes, "Environmental Crimes (Annual Survey of White Collar Crime)," *American Criminal Law Review* 42 (2005): 347–380.

112. Environmental Protection Agency, Criminal Investigation Division, http://www3.epa.gov/.

113. Los Angeles County District Attorney's Office, Environmental Crimes, http://da .lacounty.gov/operations/environmental -crimes.

114. Michael Lynch, Paul Stretesky, and Ronald Burns, "Slippery Business," *Journal of Black Studies* 34 (2004): 421–440.

115. Group Against Smog and Pollution (GASP), http://gasp-pgh.org/.

116. Michael J. Lynch and Paul B. Stretesky, "The Distribution of Water-Monitoring Organizations Across States: Implications for Community Environmental Policing and Social Justice," *Policing: An International Journal of Police Strategies and Management* 36 (2013): 6–26.

117. FBI, "Organized Crime Overview," http:// www.fbi.gov/about-us/investigate /organizedcrime/overview.

118. Ibid.

119. Frederick Martens and Michele Cunningham-Niederer, "Media Magic, Mafia Mania," *Federal Probation* 49 (1985): 60–68.

120. Christopher Adamson, "Defensive Localism in White and Black: A Comparative History of European-American and African American Youth Gangs," *Ethnic and Racial Studies* 23 (2000): 272–298.

121. FBI, "Organized Crime Overview."

122. Donald Cressey, *Theft of the Nation* (New York: Harper & Row, 1969).

123. Jay Albanese, "Deciphering the Linkages Between Organized Crime and Transnational Crime," *Journal of International Affairs* 66 (2012): 1–16.

124. James O. Finckenauer and Ko-lin Chin, *Asian Transnational Organized Crime and Its Impact on the United States* (Washington, DC: National Institute of Justice, 2007), http://www.ncjrs.gov/pdffiles1/nij /214186.pdf.

125. United Nations Office on Drugs and Crime, "Emerging Crimes, 2014," https://www .unodc.org/unodc/en/organized-crime /emerging-crimes.html.

126. Information in this section comes from the National Gang Intelligence Center, *National Gang Report, 2015*, https://www.fbi.gov /stats-services/publications/national-gang -report-2015.pdf.

127. Ibid.

128. Council on Foreign Relations, "California's Gangs Go Digital and Global," June 22, 2016, http://blogs.cfr.org/cyber/2016 /06/22/californias-gangs-go-digital-and -global/.

129. National Gang Intelligence Center, *National Gang Report, 2015*.

130. FBI, "African Criminal Enterprises," http:// www.fbi.gov/about-us/investigate /organizedcrime/african/.

131. FBI, "Balkan Criminal Enterprises," http:// www.fbi.gov/about-us/investigate /organizedcrime/balkan/.

132. FBI, "Operation Power Outage: Armenian Organized Crime Group Targeted," March 3, 2011, http://www.fbi.gov/news/stories /2011/march/armenian_030311/.

133. FBI, "Armenian Power Leader Sentenced to 32 Years in Prison for Racketeering, Extortion, and Fraud Offenses," November 10, 2014, http://www.fbi.gov/losangeles/press-releases /2014/armenian-power-leader-sentenced-to -32-years-in-prison-for-racketeering-extortion -and-fraud-offenses.

134. Louise I. Shelley, "Crime and Corruption: Enduring Problems of Post-Soviet Development," *Demokratizatsiya* 11 (2003): 110–114; James O. Finckenauer and Yuri A. Voronin, *The Threat of Russian Organized Crime* (Washington, DC: National Institute of Justice, 2001).

135. Omar Bartos, "Growth of Russian Organized Crime Poses Serious Threat," *CJ International* 11 (1995): 8–9.

136. FBI, "Italian Organized Crime," https:// www.fbi.gov/about-us/investigate /organizedcrime/italian_mafia/.

137. Bilyana Tsvetkova, "Gangs in the Caribbean," *Harvard International Review*, June 2009, http://hir.harvard.edu/gangs -in-the-caribbean.

138. United States Department of State, "Mexico Travel Warning," April 15, 2016, https:// travel.state.gov/content/passports/en /alertswarnings/mexico-travel-warning .html.

139. This section leans heavily on Finckenauer and Chin, *Asian Transnational Organized Crime and Its Impact on the United States*.

140. National Institute of Justice, "Major Transnational Organized Crime Groups," http://www.nij.gov/topics/crime/organized -crime/pages/major-groups.aspx.

141. 18 U.S.C. 1952 (1976).

142. Public Law 91-452, Title IX, 84 Stat. 922 (1970) (codified at 18 U.S.C. 1961–68, 1976).

143. William Booth, "Mexican Azteca Gang Leader Arrested in Killings of 3 Tied to U.S.," *Washington Post*, March 30, 2010, http://www.washingtonpost.com/wp -dyn/content/article/2010/03/29 /AR2010032903373.html.

144. Angela Kocherga, "Zeta Leader Captured in Mexico," KVUE News, July 4, 2011.

145. Orlando Patterson, "The Other Losing War," *New York Times*, January 13, 2007.

146. White House press release, "Presidential Determination—Major Drug Transit and Drug Producing Countries for FY 2014," http://www.whitehouse.gov/the-press-office

/2013/09/13/presidential-determination -major-drug-transit-and-drug-producing -countri.

147. Belluck, "Prosecutors Say Greed Drove Pharmacist to Dilute Drugs," p. 3.

148. Neal Shover and Peter Grabosky, "White-Collar Crime and the Great Recession," *Criminology and Public Policy* 9 (2010): 429–433. See also, Neal Shover and Andrew Hochstetler, *Choosing White-Collar Crime* (England: Cambridge University Press, 2006).

149. Kathleen Daly, "Gender and Varieties of White-Collar Crime," *Criminology* 27 (1989): 769–793.

150. Mandeep Dhami, "White-Collar Prisoners' Perceptions of Audience Reaction," *Deviant Behavior* 28 (2007): 57–77.

151. Edelhertz and Rogovin, eds., *A National Strategy for Containing White-Collar Crime*, Appendix A, pp. 122–123.

152. Donald Cressey, *Other People's Money: A Study of the Social Psychology of Embezzlement* (Glencoe, IL: Free Press, 1973), p. 96.

153. Rhonda Evans and Dianne Porche, "The Nature and Frequency of Medicare/ Medicaid Fraud and Neutralization Techniques Among Speech, Occupational, and Physical Therapists," *Deviant Behavior* 26 (2005): 253–271.

154. Nicole Leeper Piquero, Stephen Tibbetts, and Michael Blankenship, "Examining the Role of Differential Association and Techniques of Neutralization in Explaining Corporate Crime," *Deviant Behavior* 26 (2005): 159–188.

155. Tom R. Tyler, "Reducing Corporate Criminality: The Role of Values," *American Criminal Law Review* 51 (2014): 267–292.

156. Travis Hirschi and Michael Gottfredson, "Causes of White-Collar Crime," *Criminology* 25 (1987): 949–974.

157. Michael Gottfredson and Travis Hirschi, *A General Theory of Crime* (Stanford, CA: Stanford University Press, 1990), p. 191.

corts
.Com
To You
inutes
V-GIRLS

LEARNING OBJECTIVES

LO1 Clarify the association between law and morality

LO2 Interpret what is meant by the term *social harm*

LO3 Give examples of the activities of moral crusaders

LO4 Describe the various forms of outlawed deviant sexuality

LO5 Summarize the history of prostitution and review what the term means today

LO6 Distinguish between the different types of prostitutes

LO7 Explain what is meant by the terms *obscenity* and *pornography*

LO8 Assess the causes of substance abuse

LO9 Compare and contrast the different methods of drug control

LO10 State the arguments for and against legalizing drugs

14 PUBLIC ORDER CRIME: SEX AND SUBSTANCE ABUSE

Eric Omuro, also known as "Red," of Mountain View, California, pleaded guilty to using a facility of interstate commerce with the intent to facilitate prostitution. During his plea hearing, Omuro admitted that from April 2010 until June 25, 2014, he owned, managed, and operated a website known as MyRedBook. The website hosted advertisements posted by prostitutes containing explicit photos, graphic descriptions of sexual services offered, and rates for the sexual services. The advertisements were searchable by geographic location, including cities throughout California, other U.S. states, and Canada. Members of his website and prostitutes typically used abbreviations for sex acts, which were defined in graphic detail in the website's "Terms and Acronyms" section.

While prostitutes could post advertisements for free, MyRedBook offered additional options for a fee. Prostitutes could pay to have their advertisement featured more prominently on the website. To place a "featured" ad or an "autobump" ad (an ad that stays near/at the top of the page for a limited period of time), the escort had to create an account through the MyRedBook.com website with "ACS, Inc." and pay a fee. Membership fees were paid by credit card, PayPal, money orders, cash, or cashier checks.

Omuro also profited from clients. Though customers could access MyRedBook for free, if they purchased a membership, they obtained early and enhanced access to prostitute reviews posted by other clients, enhanced prostitute review search options, and access to additional VIP forums, among other things. The site turned into a goldmine for Omuro: in the four years before the site was shut down by law enforcement agents, MyRedBook made over $5 million in profit.

In its sentencing recommendation to the court, the government noted that Omuro, through MyRedBook, facilitated unlawful prostitution on a wide scale, encompassing most of the western United States and Canada. Undoubtedly many of the prostitutes who advertised were acting independently, free from coercion and in consensual, though illegal, transactions with customers. Many relied on the reviews of clients that helped keep the sex workers safe; others used the site to be warned of police stings. But government attorneys noted that it is inevitable in the commercial sex industry that many of those advertised on MyRedBook were under the control of pimps, and many were minors. In accepting compensation for advertisements and memberships, Omuro drew no distinction between these very different categories of harm. His motive was clear—facilitating prostitution because it was profitable. The consequences of his actions were acceptable to him so long as the site continued to make millions. The government's conclusion: Omuro's reckless decision to ignore the significant harms facilitated by the site that he created, managed, and administered is exactly the sort of conduct that demands a strong statement of deterrence.[1]

Omuro was sentenced to 13 months behind bars and was forced to forfeit $1.3 million in cash and property. It was the first federal conviction of a website operator for facilitation of prostitution.[2]

Throughout history, tribes, groups, and nation states have banned or limited behaviors believed to run contrary to social norms, customs, and values. These behaviors are often referred to as **public order crimes** or **victimless crimes**, although the latter term can be misleading, as the prosecutors in the Omuro case suggested. While some people engaging in these banned acts may be acting voluntarily, there is no question that others are compelled by people and forces beyond their control. There are real victims in these so-called victimless crimes.

Public order crimes involve acts that interfere with the operations of society and the ability of people to function efficiently. Whereas common-law crimes such as rape or robbery are banned because they cause indisputable **social harm**, public order crimes involve behaviors that are outlawed because they (a) conflict with social policy, prevailing moral rules, and current public opinion and (b) victimize both people and the social order.

Statutes designed to uphold public order usually prohibit the manufacture and distribution of morally questionable goods and services such as erotic material, commercial sex, and mood-altering drugs. They may also ban acts that people who hold political and social power consider morally tinged.

Criminalizing acts because of their perceived immorality is controversial because millions of otherwise law-abiding citizens often engage in these outlawed activities. If apprehended, these citizens can be labeled as criminals.

Public order crimes typically create *boundaries* rather than *bright lines*. For example, it is legal to drink at age 21 but a crime at age 20, even though 20-year-olds can fight for their country and vote in elections. Such boundaries often create confusion and ambivalence: if an act is immoral and illegal, why is it okay for some people to engage in it but not others? How can an act considered a crime in one legal jurisdiction be perfectly legal in another?

This chapter first briefly discusses the relationship between law and morality. Next, the chapter addresses public order crimes of a sexual nature. The chapter concludes by focusing on the abuse of drugs and alcohol.

---

public order crimes Acts that are considered illegal because they threaten the general well-being of society and challenge its accepted moral principles. Prostitution, drug use, and the sale of pornography are considered public order crimes.

victimless crimes Violations of the criminal law without any identifiable evidence of an individual victim who has suffered damage from the crime.

social harm A view that behaviors harmful to other people and society in general must be controlled. These acts are usually outlawed, but some acts that cause enormous amounts of social harm are perfectly legal, such as the consumption of tobacco and alcohol.

Law and Morality

 L01 Clarify the association between law and morality

Legislation of moral issues has continually frustrated lawmakers because many of their constituents see little harm in visiting a prostitute or smoking some pot. When a store is robbed or a child assaulted, it is easy to identify with the victim and condemn the harm done. It is, however, more difficult to sympathize with or even identify the victims of immoral acts, such as pornography or prostitution, where the parties involved may be willing participants. Some porn stars and call girls are paid more for a few days' work than a waitress or a teacher can make in a year. Can we consider them "victims"? People who employ call girls and escorts may be wealthy and powerful men—like conservative Republican Senator David Vitter of Louisiana—who freely and voluntarily spend their money for sexual services.

On July 16, 2007, Vitter publicly apologized after his telephone number showed up in the phone records of Pamela Martin and Associates, the prostitution ring run in the nation's capital by "D.C. Madam" Deborah Jeane Palfrey. "This was a very serious sin in my past for which I am, of course, completely responsible," Vitter said remorsefully. Soon after he issued his statement, Jeanette Maier, a former madam who ran a house of prostitution in New Orleans, claimed Vitter was also a client in her brothel. She told the press: "As far as the girls coming out after seeing David, all they had was nice things to say. It wasn't all about sex. In fact, he just wanted to have somebody listen to him, you know. And I said his wife must not be listening."[3] Vitter asked voters for forgiveness, and his plea must have temporarily worked: he was reelected in 2010.

Frequenting brothels and employing prostitutes is hardly the behavior expected from a married senator known for his strong advocacy of family values; Vitter called marriage "the most important social institution in human history." He also opposes sex education and abortion and has earmarked money for Christian groups who oppose the teaching of evolution.[4] Senator Vitter was not alone in enjoying the services of the D.C. Madam; also on her call list were Randall L. Tobias, who was forced to step down as deputy secretary of state, and Harlan K. Ullman, the military affairs scholar who created the Pentagon's concept known as "shock and awe."[5] With his opponent constantly bringing up the prostitution issue, Vitter lost the governor's race in 2015 and announced he would not run again for the Senate.[6]

Certainly these powerful men are not the "victim" here. If there is no victim, can there be a crime?

To answer this question, we might first consider whether there is actually a victim in "victimless crimes." While some women voluntarily engage in highly paid sex work, others have been pressured into the sex trade; they are therefore true victims. It is common for young runaways and abandoned children to be coerced into a life on the streets, where they are cruelly treated and held as virtual captives. It has been estimated that women involved in street prostitution are 60 to 100 times more likely to be murdered than the average woman and that most of the killings are the result of a dispute over money rather than being sexually motivated.[7] Clearly prostitution carries with it significant professional risk. And while some women may voluntarily perform in adult films critics such as Andrea Dworkin point out that women involved in pornography are "dehumanized—turned into objects and commodities."[8] Is their performance truly voluntary?

Even if public order crimes do not actually harm their participants, perhaps society as a whole should be considered the victim of these crimes. Is the community harmed when a brothel opens down the street? Does this signal that a neighborhood is in decline? Does it teach children that deviance is both tolerated and profitable? If women are degraded and sexualized in adult sex films, does that send a message that it is acceptable to demean and/or harm women?

On January 21, 2015, adult film actress Jillian Janson signs autographs for fans at the AVN Adult Entertainment Expo in Las Vegas. The stars posed for pictures with some of the 25,000 attendees. How can it be said that adult films are depraved or indecent if so many people watch and enjoy them?

AP Images/John Locher

DEBATING MORALITY

In 2011, rising political star Anthony Weiner was forced to resign from office after compromising photos he tweeted to women were posted online. At first, Weiner denied responsibility, telling the media that his account had been hacked and/or that the pictures had possibly been altered. Finally, he admitted on June 6, 2011, that he had sent sexually explicit text messages and photographs to several women, both before and after he got married.[9] Did Weiner's behavior really cause public harm? After all, he never actually met any of the women with whom he carried on a cyber-relationship. All his victims had to do was disconnect or delete his texts, tweets, and emails.

Was Weiner's sexting grossly immoral or merely an example of those harmless human quirks and eccentricities we all possess in some measure? New York City voters were not forgiving: when Weiner tried a political comeback in 2013, his campaign for mayor of New York was shot down. It did not help him when the media found out that he sent additional women explicit photos using the alias "Carlos Danger."

The debate over morality has existed for all of recorded history. As the Bible (Genesis 18:20) tells us, God destroyed the "Cities of the Plain" because "The outcry against Sodom and Gomorrah is so great and their sin so grievous."[10] Though Abraham begs God for mercy, his prayers go unanswered because, despite a posse of angels looking for them, 10 righteous residents could not be found.

Punishing immorality with legal sanctions continues today (though not fire and brimstone). Acts such as pornography, prostitution, and substance abuse are believed to erode the moral fabric of society and are therefore prohibited and punished. They are crimes, according to the great legal scholar Morris Cohen, because "it is one of the functions of the criminal law to give expression to the collective feeling of revulsion toward certain acts, even when they are not very dangerous."[11] In his classic statement on the function of morality in the law, legal scholar Sir Patrick Devlin states,

> Without shared ideas on politics, morals, and ethics no society can exist. . . . If men and women try to create a society in which there is no fundamental agreement about good and evil, they will fail; if having based it on common agreement, the agreement goes, the society will disintegrate. For society is not something that is kept together physically; it is held by the invisible bonds of common thought. If the bonds were too far relaxed, the members would drift apart. A common morality is part of the bondage. The bondage is part of the price of society; and mankind, which needs society, must pay its price.[12]

According to this view, so-called victimless crimes are prohibited because one of the functions of criminal law is to express a shared sense of public morality.[13]

Some influential legal scholars have questioned the propriety of legislating morals. H. L. A. Hart states,

> It is fatally easy to confuse the democratic principle that power should be in the hands of the majority with the utterly different claim that the majority, with power in their hands, need respect no limits. Certainly there is a special risk in a democracy that the majority may dictate how all should live.[14]

Hart may be motivated by the fact that defining morality may be an impossible task: Who defines morality? Are we not punishing differences rather than social harm? As U.S. Supreme Court Justice William O. Douglas once so succinctly put it, "What may be trash to me may be prized by others."[15] After all, many of the great works of Western art depict nude males and females, some quite young. Are the paintings of Rubens or the sculpture of Michelangelo obscene? The nude paintings of Amedeo Modigliani (1884–1920) were considered obscene during his time. A 1917 exhibition in Paris was closed due to public outcry over his sensuous images; in 2015, one of his nudes sold for $170 million.[16] What was once considered obscene is now a highly valued work of art.

Sociologist Joseph Gusfield argues that the purpose of outlawing immoral acts is to show the moral superiority of those who condemn the acts over those who partake of them. The legislation of morality "enhances the social status of groups carrying the affirmed culture and degrades groups carrying that which is condemned as deviant."[17] Research indicates that people who define themselves as liberals are also the most tolerant of sexually explicit material. Demographic attributes such as age, educational attainment, and occupational status may also influence views of pornography: the young and better educated tend to be more tolerant than older, less-educated people.[18] Whose views should prevail? And if a majority of the population chooses to engage in what might objectively be considered immoral or deviant behavior, would it be fair or just to prohibit or control such behavior or render it criminal?

While it's difficult to measure or calculate the visits to porn sites on the Internet, according to Google's DoubleClick advertising tool, which uses a cookie to track users around the Web, dozens of adult destinations populate the top 500 websites; the largest gets 4.4 billion page views per month, three times more than CNN or ESPN. Adult entertainment websites are responsible for 4.41 percent of all desktop visits on the Internet worldwide.[19] Interestingly, the countries with the highest share of adult websites are Iraq, Egypt, Japan, and Peru; the United States does not rank in the top 10! Should all obscenity and pornography be legalized if so many people are active users and wish to enjoy its content? And if the law tried to define or limit objectionable material, might it not eventually inhibit free speech and political dissent? Not so, according to social commentator Irving Kristol:

> If we start censoring pornography and obscenity, shall we not inevitably end up censoring political opinion? A lot of people seem to think this would be the case— which only shows the power of doctrinaire thinking over reality. We had censorship of pornography and obscenity for 150 years, until almost yesterday, and I am not aware that freedom of opinion in this country was in any way diminished as a consequence of this fact.[20]

Cultural clashes may ensue when behavior that is considered normative in one society is deplored by those living in another. The World Health Organization (WHO) estimates that more than 200 million women ages 15 to 49 have undergone female genital mutilation, and 3 million girls suffer the procedure each year.[21] Custom and tradition are by far the most frequently cited reasons for mutilation; there are no health benefits. It is performed on girls ranging in age from newborns to 14-year-olds, and most are cut before age 5. The surgery is done to control virginity, remove sexual sensation, and render the females suitable for marriage; a girl in these societies cannot be considered an adult unless she has undergone genital mutilation. The practice was brought to worldwide attention in the 1990s by American author Alice Walker (*The Color Purple*). Critics consider the procedure to be torture; others argue that this ancient custom should be left to the discretion of the indigenous people who consider it part of their culture. "Torture," counters Walker, "is not culture."

Can an outsider define the morality of another culture?[22] Amnesty International and the United Nations have worked to end the practice. Because of outside pressure, the procedure is now forbidden in Senegal, Egypt, Burkina Faso, the Central African Republic, Djibouti, Ghana, Guinea, and Togo. Other countries, among them Uganda, discourage it. In North Africa, the Egyptian Supreme Court upheld a ban on the practice and also ruled it had no place in Islam.[23] Despite these efforts, millions of girls are still subject to female genital mutilation every day, primarily in Africa and the Middle East but also in other places all over the world. The Centers for Disease Control and Prevention (CDC) reports that 513,000 girls in the United States are at risk for the procedure, a number that has more than tripled in the last 25 years.[24]

SOCIAL HARM

 L02 Interpret what is meant by the term *social harm*

Most societies have long banned or limited behaviors that are believed to run contrary to social norms, customs, and values. Acts that create social harm are made illegal. However, many acts that most of us deem highly immoral and objectionable are not in fact criminal. There are no laws banning *superbia* (hubris/pride), *avaritia* (avarice/greed), *luxuria* (extravagance or lust), *invidia* (envy), *gula* (gluttony), *ira* (wrath), and *acedia* (sloth) even though they are considered the "seven deadly sins." Nor is it a crime to ignore the pleas of a drowning child, even though to do so might be considered callous, coldhearted, and unfeeling. (Of course, some people—lifeguards, paramedics, firemen, police, and the parents—have a legal duty to help save the child.)

While the theory of social harm can explain most criminal acts, it cannot explain them all. Some acts that cause enormous amounts of social harm are perfectly legal, while others that many people consider virtually harmless are outlawed and severely punished.

It is now estimated that more than 500,000 deaths in the United States each year can be linked to the consumption of tobacco and alcohol, yet these "deadly substances" remain legal to produce and sell. Similarly, sports cars and motorcycles that can accelerate to more than 150 miles per hour are perfectly legal to sell and possess even though almost 40,000 people die each year in car accidents, while fewer than 20,000 die from illicit drug overdoses (another 20,000 succumb to prescription drug overdoses).[25] According to the theory of social harm, if more people die each year from alcohol, tobacco, and automobile-related causes than illicit drugs, shouldn't cocaine and heroin be legalized and Corvettes, Johnny Walker, and Marlboros outlawed? But they are not.

MORAL CRUSADES AND CRUSADERS

 LO3 Give examples of the activities of moral crusaders

In the early West, vigilance committees were set up in San Francisco and other boom towns to pursue cattle rustlers and stagecoach robbers and to dissuade undesirables from moving in. These **vigilantes** held a strict standard of morality that, when they caught their prey, resulted in sure and swift justice.

The avenging vigilante has remained part of popular culture. Fictional do-gooders who take it on themselves to enforce the law, battle evil, and personally deal with those whom they consider immoral have become enmeshed in the public consciousness. From the Lone Ranger to Spiderman, the righteous vigilante is expected to go on moral crusades without any authorization from legal authorities. Who actually told Spiderman he can destroy half of New York while fighting Dr. Octopus or the Green Goblin? And what about the Justice League? What gives the Martian Manhunter, Wonder Woman, Plastic Man, and their superhero colleagues the right to fight crime in America? (In contrast, the Avengers—Iron Man, Black Widow, Thor, the Hulk, Captain America, and so on—work for the Strategic Homeland Intervention, Enforcement, and Logistics Division [S.H.I.E.L.D.], so at least they operate under the rule of law.) The assumption that it is okay to take matters into your own hands if the cause is right and the target is immoral is not lost on the younger generation. Gang boys sometimes take

on the street identity of "Batman" or "Superman" so they can battle their rivals with impunity.

Fictional characters are not the only ones who take it upon themselves to fight for moral decency; members of special interest groups are also ready to do battle.[26] Public order crimes often trace their origin to **moral crusaders** who seek to shape the law toward their own way of thinking; Howard Becker calls them **moral entrepreneurs**. These rule creators, argues Becker, operate with an absolute certainty that their way is right and that any means are justified to get their way: "The crusader is fervent and righteous, often self-righteous."[27] Today's moral crusaders take on such issues as prayer in school, gun ownership, same-sex marriage, abortion, and the distribution of sexually explicit books and magazines.

During the 1930s, Harry Anslinger, then head of the Federal Bureau of Narcotics, used magazine articles, public appearances, and public testimony to sway public opinion about the dangers of marijuana, which until that time was legal to use and possess.[28] In testimony before the House Ways and Means Committee, considering passage of the Marijuana Tax Act of 1938, Anslinger stated:

> In Florida a 21-year-old boy under the influence of this drug killed his parents and his brothers and sisters. The evidence showed that he had smoked marihuana. In Chicago recently two boys murdered a policeman while under the influence of marihuana. Not long ago we found a 15-year-old boy going insane because, the doctor told the enforcement officers, he thought the boy was smoking marihuana cigarettes. They traced the sale to some man who had been growing marihuana and selling it to these boys all under 15 years of age, on a playground there.[29]

As a result of Anslinger's efforts, a deviant behavior—marijuana use—became a criminal behavior, and previously law-abiding citizens were defined as criminal offenders.

MORAL CRUSADES TODAY

Moral crusades are sometimes designed to publicize the differences between behaviors that are considered morally

vigilantes Individuals who go on moral crusades without any authorization from legal authorities. The assumption is that it is okay to take matters into your own hands if the cause is right and the target is immoral.

moral crusaders People who strive to stamp out behavior they find objectionable. Typically, moral crusaders are directed at public order crimes, such as drug abuse or pornography.

moral entrepreneurs Interest groups that attempt to control social life and the legal order in such a way as to promote their own personal set of moral values. People who use their influence to shape the legal process in ways they see fit.

acceptable and those that right-thinking people should consider deviant and unacceptable.

Of course, what is right and moral is often in the eye of the beholder. While some moral crusades are aimed at curbing behavior that most of us find objectionable—for instance, animal cruelty or drunk driving—they can also create controversy when they are directed at behaviors engaged in by the majority of citizens. One popular focus for moral crusaders is anti-smut campaigns that target books considered too racy or controversial to be suitable for a public school library. According to the American Library Association, between 2000 and 2009, the *Harry Potter* series topped the yearly list of books challenged by critics who demanded their removal from school library shelves on charges they promoted Satanism and witchcraft. Among the most often challenged books in 2015 were *Looking for Alaska*, by John Green; *Beyond Magenta: Transgender Teens Speak Out*, by Susan Kuklin; *Habibi*, by Craig Thompson; and *Nasreen's Secret School: A True Story from Afghanistan*, by Jeanette Winter.[30] The following are the top books banned or challenged in the last decade:

1. *Harry Potter* series, by J. K. Rowling
2. *Alice* series, by Phyllis Reynolds Naylor
3. *The Chocolate War*, by Robert Cormier
4. *And Tango Makes Three*, by Justin Richardson/Peter Parnell
5. *Of Mice and Men*, by John Steinbeck
6. *I Know Why the Caged Bird Sings*, by Maya Angelou

Are these books actually objectionable? Should librarians accede to the demands of a vocal minority or to the will of the mostly silent majority?

 See the American Library Association's lists of the most frequently challenged books at **http://www.ala.org/bbooks/frequentlychallengedbooks**. **Should racy books be banned from libraries, or should parents instruct their children to avoid them if they object to the content?**

The Same-Sex Marriage Crusade   At one time every state had sodomy laws making it a felony to engage in homosexual relations. This ban on relations between consenting adults set off one of the most heated moral crusades of the past 50 years, with the goal of influencing both public acceptance and the legality of the gay lifestyle. One group of crusaders was determined to prevent the legalization of homosexual behavior, and one of their victories was the Supreme Court's decision in *Bowers v. Hardwick*, a decision that upheld a state's right to criminalize homosexual behavior. In this 1986 case, the Supreme Court said:

The Constitution does not confer a fundamental right upon homosexuals to engage in sodomy. None of the fundamental rights announced in this Court's prior cases involving family relationships, marriage, or procreation bear any resemblance to the right asserted in this case. And any claim that those cases stand for the proposition that any kind of private sexual conduct between consenting adults is constitutionally insulated from state proscription is unsupportable.[31]

The Defense of Marriage Act, which was passed in 1996 and defined marriage for the purposes of federal law as a union of one man and one woman, was another of this group's most significant legal achievements.[32] Opposing them were activists who tirelessly campaigned for the civil rights of gay men and women. One of their most important victories was won in 2003 when the Supreme Court delivered, in *Lawrence et al. v. Texas*, a historic decision that made it impermissible for states to criminalize forms of sex that are not conventionally heterosexual, under statutes prohibiting sodomy, deviant sexuality, or what used to be referred to as "buggery."[33]

After a long, drawn-out tug of moral war between these two opposing groups, the issue of same-sex marriage was resolved in 2015, when the U.S. Supreme Court ruled in *Obergefell v. Hodges* that state-level bans on same-sex marriage are unconstitutional. The Court ruled that the denial of marriage licenses to same-sex couples and the refusal to recognize those marriages performed in other jurisdictions violates the due process and equal protection clauses of the Fourteenth Amendment of the U.S. Constitution.[34] For all intents and purposes, *Obergefell* put an end to the conflict over gay marriage.

The same-sex marriage crusade raised a number of important issues: Is it fair to prevent one group of loyal taxpaying citizens from engaging in a behavior that is allowed for others? Are there objective standards of morality or should society respect people's differences? After all, opponents of same-sex marriage claim, polygamy is banned, and there are age standards for marriage in every state. If same-sex marriage is legal, what about marriage to multiple partners or with underage minors? How far should the law go in curbing human behaviors that do not cause social harm? Who controls the law and should the law be applied to shape morality?

The public order crimes discussed in this chapter are divided into two broad areas. The first relates to what conventional society considers deviant sexual practices. The second area concerns the use of substances that have been outlawed or controlled because of the harm they are alleged to cause: drugs and alcohol.

To read the Supreme Court's opinion in *Obergefell v. Hodges*, go to **http://www.supremecourt.gov/opinions/14pdf/14-556_3204.pdf**. **Should a baker be forced to make a wedding cake for a gay couple even if gay marriage violates his personal religious beliefs?**

Sexually Related Offenses

LO4 Describe the various forms of outlawed deviant sexuality

On August 24, 2009, Phillip Garrido, a long-time sex offender, was placed under arrest for the kidnapping of Jaycee Lee Dugard, a California girl who had been abducted on June 10, 1991, when she was 11 years old. She had been held captive for 18 years and raped repeatedly, bearing him two children. In 2011, Garrido was sentenced to 431 years in prison; his wife received a sentence of 36 to life. The highly regarded 2015 film *Room*, whose lead actress Brie Larson won an Academy Award, is based on the Dugard case.

Unfortunately, the Dugard kidnapping is not unique and numerous other cases have received national attention:

- On October 1, 1993, 12-year-old Polly Klaas was having a slumber party when a man holding a knife entered her bedroom, tied up all the girls, put pillow cases over their heads, and kidnapped the sobbing Polly. Her body was found three months later. Her kidnapper and killer, Richard Allen Davis, is currently on death row in California.
- On June 5, 2002, Elizabeth Smart was abducted from her bedroom in Salt Lake City, Utah, and held captive until found nine months later. Elizabeth had been kidnapped by Brian David Mitchell, who was indicted for her kidnapping and sent to a mental health facility after being ruled mentally unfit to stand trial.[35] After six years in psychiatric custody Mitchell was deemed fit to stand trial. Found guilty of rape and kidnapping, he was sentenced to life in prison on May 25, 2011.
- Between 2002 and 2004, Ariel Castro kidnapped Michelle Knight, Amanda Berry, and Georgina "Gina" DeJesus and held them in his house on Seymour Avenue in Cleveland until May 6, 2013, when Berry was able to shout through a locked door and alert the neighbors. The women had been raped and beaten continually. Knight had become pregnant five times and endured miscarriage brought on by beatings and starvation. Berry had also become pregnant and had a 6-year-old daughter at the time of her rescue. After his

arrest, Castro pleaded guilty to 937 criminal counts of rape, kidnapping, and aggravated murder and was sentenced to life in prison without the chance of parole plus 1,000 years. Castro hanged himself in his prison cell within a month of his incarceration.[36]

While these cases are extreme, each year about 100 children are abducted by strangers and thousands more by family members.[37] In addition, thousands of children are subjected to some form of sexual exploitation, including sexual abuse, prostitution, pornography, and molestation.[38]

Because of these alarming statistics and also because some sexual practices are believed to cause social harm, society has long criminalized what are considered to be deviant sexual practices. Three of the most common offenses, paraphilias, prostitution, and obscenity and pornography, are discussed in some detail here.

Paraphilias

Paraphilias (Greek *para*, "to the side of" and *philos*, "loving") encompasses bizarre or abnormal sexual practices involving recurrent sexual urges focused on (a) nonhuman objects (such as underwear, shoes, or leather), (b) humiliation or

> **paraphilias** Bizarre or abnormal sexual practices that may involve recurrent sexual urges focused on objects, humiliation, or children.

Ariel Castro was sentenced to prison for life on hundreds of charges including kidnapping, rape, and holding captive Amanda Berry, Gina DeJesus, and Michelle Knight for nearly a decade. Castro committed suicide while in prison.

Angelo Merendino/Getty Images

the experience of receiving or giving pain (such as in sado-masochism or bondage), or (c) children or others who cannot grant consent. Such practices are not a modern invention. Buddhist texts more than 2,000 years old contain references to sexually deviant behaviors in monastic communities, including sexual activity with animals and sexual interest in corpses. Richard von Krafft-Ebing's *Psychopathia Sexualis*, published in 1887, was the first Western book to discuss such paraphilias as sadism, bestiality, and incest.[39]

The following are included in this category of sexual behaviors:

- *Pedophilia or paedophilia.* A sexual attraction by an adult or late adolescent to prepubescent children, generally age 11 years or younger.
- *Frotteurism.* Rubbing against or touching a nonconsenting person in a crowd, elevator, or other public area.
- *Voyeurism (peeping Tom).* Obtaining sexual pleasure from spying on a stranger while he or she disrobes or engages in sexual behavior with another.
- *Exhibitionism (flashing).* Deriving sexual pleasure from exposing the genitals to surprise or shock a stranger.
- *Asphyxiophilia.* Self-strangulation that restricts the supply of oxygen or blood to the brain in order to increase sexual intensity.
- *Sadomasochism.* Deriving pleasure from receiving pain or inflicting pain on a willing partner.

Paraphilias are legal if they are not harmful to others, such as wearing clothes normally worn by the opposite sex (transvestite fetishism), or are engaged in by adults in the privacy of their homes. Nonetheless, even these paraphilias can sometimes cause fatal results: such was the case when on June 4, 2009, actor David Carradine (*Kill Bill*) was found dead in a Thailand hotel, the victim of asphyxiophilia gone awry.[40] When paraphilias involve unwilling or underage partners, they are considered legally and socially harmful and subject to criminal penalties—exhibitionism, frotteurism, and voyeurism are therefore illegal and carry criminal penalties. Pedophilia, the most serious form of paraphilia, is discussed in more detail following.

PEDOPHILIA

On February 24, 2005, 9-year-old Jessica Lunsford was reported missing. Known sex offender John Evander Couey, 46, had kidnapped her from her home, keeping her captive and then burying her alive when he believed investigators were closing in. When captured he showed investigators the shallow grave where they found Jessica's body inside two tied plastic garbage bags. Her wrists were bound, but she had managed to poke two fingers through the plastic in an attempt to free herself. In the aftermath of Jessica Lunsford's abduction, Florida passed legislation that requires increased prison sentences, electronic tracking of all convicted sex offenders on probation, and the mandatory use of state databases by all local probation officials so that known sex offenders could not avoid the scrutiny of law enforcement.[41] Couey was sentenced to death but died in prison before the sentence could be carried out.

Couey suffered from **pedophilia**, a psychiatric disorder in which an adult or teen over age 16 is sexually attracted to prepubescent children, generally ages 11 to 13 years or younger. While the causes of pedophilia have not been determined, suspected factors include abnormal brain structure, social maladaption, and neurological dysfunction. The central processing of sexual stimuli in pedophiles may be controlled by a disturbance in the prefrontal networks of the brain.[42] There is also some evidence that pedophilia is heritable and genetic factors are responsible for its development.[43] Other suspected connections range from cognitive distortions to exposure to pornography.[44]

While men are overrepresented in the ranks of sexual predators, women are also involved. In one recent case that made national headlines, former Baltimore Ravens cheerleader Molly Shattuck was sentenced to two years of probation for engaging in a sex act with a 15-year-old boy.[45] At sentencing the prosecutor claimed, "This was not a momentary lapse in judgment. She groomed him, seduced him, supplied him with alcohol, then took advantage of him, all for her own gratification." Shattuck received a suspended 15-year prison sentence and was forced to register as a sex offender and receive therapy. The Shattuck case is far from unique: one study of more than 100 adult female sex offenders found that 23 percent of the cases involved sexual abuse of a child, and in about two-thirds of the cases the women had a male co-offender.[46]

The Church Scandal In 2002, the *Boston Globe's* spotlight team of investigative reporters uncovered serious allegations of child abuse being perpetrated by Roman Catholic priests. Their discovery led to widespread media coverage of the issue in the United States. The Academy Award–winning 2015 film *Spotlight* dramatized these events.

The center of the storm was the Archdiocese of Boston, which was shaken by allegations that a significant number of priests had engaged in sexual relations with minor children. Among the most notorious was Fr. James Porter, who was convicted of molesting at least 200 children of both sexes over a 30-year period. Porter was sentenced to an 18-to-20-year prison term and died of cancer while incarcerated. The archdiocese eventually turned over the names of nearly 100 priests to prosecutors. Cardinal Bernard Law was forced to step down as leader of the diocese. Numerous churches were closed or sold to help raise money for legal fees and victim compensation.

pedophilia A psychosexual disorder in which an adult has sexual fantasies about or engages in sexual acts with an underage minor child.

As the scandal spread, clergy elsewhere in the United States and abroad resigned amid allegations that they had abused children or failed to stop abuse of which they had knowledge. Fr. Lawrence Murphy, who taught at St. John's School for the Deaf in a suburb of Milwaukee from 1950 through 1974, sexually abused about 200 boys.[47] In Ireland, the Most Reverend Brendan Comiskey, the Bishop of Ferns, offered his resignation to the pope for failing in his efforts to stop abuse in his diocese, and an archbishop in Wales was forced to resign because he had ignored complaints about two priests later convicted of sexually abusing children. Thousands of cases have been reported in hundreds of nations around the globe.

Responding to the crisis, Pope John Paul II called a special meeting of American Catholic leaders in April 2002 to create new policies on sex abuse. The pope issued a statement in which he said that there is "no place in the priesthood . . . for those who would harm the young." He added that sexual abuse by the clergy was not only an "appalling sin" but a crime, and he noted that "many are offended at the way in which church leaders are perceived to have acted in this matter."[48] The current pope, Francis, has called the scandal a "grave problem," declaring that "one priest abusing a minor is reason enough to move the Church's whole structure." Pope Francis told clergy that they had "suffered greatly in the not distant past by having to bear the shame of some of your brothers who harmed and scandalized the Church in the most vulnerable of her members."[49]

 To read the most significant report on the pedophilia crisis in the Catholic Church, prepared by researchers at John Jay College of Criminal Justice, go to **http://www.usccb.org/issues-and-action /child-and-youth-protection/upload/The-Causes-and -Context-of-Sexual-Abuse-of-Minors-by-Catholic-Priests -in-the-United-States-1950-2010.pdf.**
Should people convicted of child molestation be punished as criminals or considered as mentally ill and be given treatment?

Prostitution

L05 Summarize the history of prostitution and review what the term means today

Prostitution has existed for thousands of years. The term derives from the Latin *prostituere*, which means "to cause to stand in front of." The prostitute is viewed as publicly offering his or her body for sale. The earliest record of prostitution appears in ancient Mesopotamia, where priests engaged in sex to promote fertility in the community. All women were required to do temple duty, and passing strangers were expected to make donations to the temple after enjoying its services.[50]

Modern commercial sex appears to have its roots in ancient Greece, where Solon established licensed brothels in 500 BCE. The earnings of Greek prostitutes helped pay for the temple of Aphrodite. Famous men openly went to prostitutes to enjoy intellectual, aesthetic, and sexual stimulation; prostitutes, however, were prevented from marrying.[51]

During the Middle Ages, although prostitution was a sin under canon law, it was widely practiced and considered a method of protecting "respectable" women who might otherwise by attacked by young men. In 1358, the Grand Council of Venice declared that prostitution was "absolutely indispensable to the world."[52] Some church leaders such as St. Thomas Aquinas condoned prostitution; St. Augustine wrote, "If you expel prostitution from society, you will unsettle everything on account of lusts."[53] Nonetheless, prostitution was officially condemned, and women were confined to ply their trade in certain areas of the city and required to wear distinctive outfits so they could be easily recognized. Any official tolerance disappeared after the Reformation. Martin Luther advocated abolishing prostitution on moral grounds, and Lutheran doctrine depicted prostitutes as emissaries of the devil who were sent to destroy the faith.[54]

In the early nineteenth century, prostitution was tied to the rise of English breweries: saloons controlled by the companies employed prostitutes to attract patrons and encourage them to drink. This relationship was repeated in major U.S. cities, such as Chicago, until breweries were forbidden to own the outlets that distributed their product.

As the twentieth century began, there was fear over "white slavery" whereby young girls were abducted and turned out on the street as prostitutes. Jane Addams, one of the most famous and influential social reformers of this era, was deeply concerned about the white slave trade.[55] In her 1912 book *A New Conscience and an Ancient Evil*, she described accounts of victims of white slavery during her work at Hull House, a Chicago refuge for the needy.[56] Addams believed that rural American or immigrant girls who became sex workers were victims of sexual slavery and in need of rescue and reform. Though Addams was a vocal opponent of legalized prostitution, her work and writings spurred efforts to regulate prostitution in the United States through medical supervision and the licensing and zoning of brothels in districts outside residential neighborhoods.[57]

During and after World War I, prostitution became associated with disease, and the desire to protect young servicemen from harm helped to end almost all experiments with legalization.[58] Some reformers attempted to paint pimps and procurers as immigrants who used their foreign ways to snare unsuspecting American girls into prostitution. Such fears prompted passage of the federal Mann Act (1925), which prohibited bringing women into the country or transporting them across state lines for the purposes of prostitution. Often called the "white slave act," it carried a $5,000 fine, five years in prison, or both.[59]

PROSTITUTION TODAY

Prostitution is now defined as granting nonmarital sexual access, established by mutual agreement of the prostitute, their client, and their employer (i.e., pimp) for remuneration. This definition is sexually neutral because prostitutes can be straight or gay and male or female.

Prostitutes are referred to by sociologists as "street-level sex workers" whose activities are similar to any other service industry. These conditions are usually present in a commercial sexual transaction:

- *Activity that has sexual significance for the customer.* This includes the entire range of sexual behavior, from sexual intercourse to exhibitionism, sadomasochism, oral sex, and so on.
- *Economic transaction.* Something of economic value, not necessarily money, is exchanged for the activity.
- *Emotional indifference.* The sexual exchange is simply for economic consideration. Although the participants may know each other, their interaction has nothing to do with affection.[60] Clients believe that the lack of involvement makes hiring a prostitute less of a hassle and less trouble than becoming involved in a romantic relationship.[61]

Sociologist Monica Prasad observed these conditions when she interviewed both men and women about their motivation to employ a prostitute. Although their choice was shaped by sexuality, she found that their decision was also influenced by pressure from friends to try something different and exciting, the wish for a sexual exchange free from obligations, and curiosity about the world of prostitution. Prasad found that most customers who became "regulars" began to view prostitution merely as a "service occupation."[62]

INCIDENCE OF PROSTITUTION

The Uniform Crime Report (UCR) indicates that about 47,000 prostitution arrests are made annually, with the gender ratio about 2 to 1 female to male.[63] The number of arrests for prostitution has declined significantly during the past 20 years; in 1995, the UCR recorded 97,000 arrests for prostitution.

How can this decline in arrests for prostitution be explained? The sexual revolution has liberalized sexuality so that people are less likely to use prostitutes because legitimate alternatives for sex are now available. In addition, the prevalence of sexually transmitted diseases has caused many people to avoid visiting prostitutes for fear of irreversible health hazards. While traditional forms of prostitution may be in decline, ehooking, which uses the Internet to shield identities and contact clients, may be responsible

for a resurgence of sex for hire because it promises services with concealment and without the threat of arrest. Ehooking will be discussed more in Chapter 15 in the context of cybercrime.

Despite the decline in the arrest rate, a recent survey by the Urban Institute shows that prostitution still flourishes in major cities. The findings are set out in the Criminology in Action feature "The Sex Trade in Contemporary Society."

PROSTITUTION IN OTHER CULTURES

Prostitution flourishes abroad, and sex trafficking is now an important source of income for transnational criminal syndicates. In some nations, such as Hungary, Switzerland, and the Netherlands, prostitution is legal and regulated by the government, while other countries punish prostitution with the death penalty. An example of the former is Germany, which has a flourishing legal sex trade. In 2002, Germany passed a new law removing the prohibition against prostitution and allowed prostitutes to obtain regular work contracts and receive health insurance. In turn, the prostitutes were required to register with the authorities and pay taxes. The city of Cologne made headlines when it introduced a sex tax that brings in more than a million dollars per year. Each prostitute pays a tax of 150 euros per month, and sex club owners pay 3 euros per 90 square feet of space in their establishments. Some of the larger German brothels offer senior citizen discounts. Many sex establishments are quite lavish and an estimated 400,000 people work in the German sex trade.[64] In contrast, many Islamic countries, including Iran and Saudi Arabia, punish prostitution with death.

There is also a troubling overseas trade in prostitution in which men from wealthy countries frequent semi-regulated sex areas in needy nations such as Thailand in order to procure young girls forced or sold into prostitution—a phenomenon known as *sex tourism*. In addition to sex tours, there has also been a soaring demand for pornography, strip clubs, lap dancing, escorts, and telephone sex in developing countries.[65] To protect children from sex tourism, the Violent Crime Control and Law Enforcement Act of 1994 included a provision, referred to as the Child Sexual Abuse Prevention Act, which made it a criminal offense to travel abroad for the purpose of engaging in sexual activity with a minor.[66] Despite these efforts, prosecuting sex tourists is often tricky due to the difficulty of gathering evidence of crimes that were committed in other countries and that involve minor children.[67]

TYPES OF PROSTITUTES

 Distinguish between the different types of prostitutes

Several different types of prostitutes operate in the United States. As you will see, each group operates in a particular venue.

---

prostitution The granting of nonmarital sexual access for remuneration.

CRIMINOLOGY IN ACTION

The Sex Trade in Contemporary Society

04

Meredith Dank and her colleagues at the Urban Institute conducted a recent study of prostitution in contemporary society, focusing on eight U.S. cities—Atlanta, Dallas, Denver, Kansas City, Miami, Seattle, San Diego, and Washington, D.C. Contemporary prostitution runs the gamut from high-end escort services to high school "sneaker pimps." As a result, the sex trade leaves no demographic unrepresented and circuits almost every major U.S. city. The study found that the underground sex economy's worth to these cities was between $40 million and $290 million. Almost all types of commercial sex venues—massage parlors, brothels, escort services, and street- and Internet-based prostitution—existed in some degree.

Pimps

Profiting from this vast enterprise were pimps and traffickers, who took home between $5,000 and $32,833 a week. Most pimps believed that the media portrayals exaggerated their violence; some saw the term *pimp* as derogatory. They told the research team that they rarely used physical abuse for punishment, but instead relied on frequent use of psychological coercion to maintain control over their employees; they rely on their natural capacity for manipulation more than force and violence. No matter how persuasive they are, pimps are rarely the sole reason a man or woman enters the sex trade. Most sex workers had a history of social problems that began long before they met their pimp. And not all

sex workers had pimps. Some solicited protection from friends and acquaintances, some of whom had exposed them to the sex trade at a young age and influenced their decision to participate.

The Internet Is Changing the Sex Trade

Dank and her associates found that prostitution is decreasing on the street but thriving online. Pimps and sex workers advertise on social media and sites like Backpage.com to attract customers and new employees, and to gauge business opportunities in other cities. An increasing online presence makes it both easier for law enforcement to track activity in the underground sex economy and for an offender to promote and provide access to the trade.

Dank and her colleagues also looked at the distribution of obscene material and found that explicit content involving younger victims is becoming increasingly available and graphic on the Net. Online child pornography communities frequently trade content for free; offenders often consider their participation a "victimless crime."

The Sex Trade Is Low Risk

Pimps, traffickers, and child pornography offenders said that their crimes were low-risk despite some fears of prosecution. Those who got caught for child pornography generally had low technological know-how, and multiple pimp offenders expressed that "no one actually gets locked up for pimping," despite their own incarcerations.

What can be done to reduce or control the incidence of prostitution?

- Cross-train drug, sex, and weapons trade investigators to better understand circuits and overlaps
- Continue using federal and local partnerships to disrupt travel circuits and identify pimps
- Offer law enforcement training for both victim and offender interview techniques, including identifying signs of psychological manipulation
- Increase awareness among school officials and the general public about the realities of sex trafficking to deter victimization and entry into the sex trade
- Consistently enforce the laws for offenders to diminish low-risk perception
- Impose more fines for ad host websites

 CRITICAL THINKING

Rather than control or eliminate prostitution, might we be better off to legalize and regulate it? After all, it's the world's oldest profession, and it seems unlikely that it can be eliminated. What are the drawbacks to legalization?

SOURCE: Meredith Dank, Bilal Khan, P. Mitchell Downey, Cybele Kotonias, Debbie Mayer, Colleen Owens, Laura Pacifici, and Lilly Yu, *Estimating the Size and Structure of the Underground Commercial Sex Economy in Eight Major US Cities* (Washington, DC: Urban Institute, 2014), http://www.urban.org /publications/413047.html (accessed June 2016).

Streetwalkers Prostitutes who work the streets in plain sight of police, citizens, and customers are referred to as *hustlers*, *hookers*, or *streetwalkers*. Although glamorized by the Julia Roberts character in the film *Pretty Woman* (who winds up with a billionaire played by Richard Gere), streetwalkers are considered the least attractive, lowest paid, most vulnerable men and women in the profession. They are most likely to be impoverished members of ethnic or racial minorities.

Many are young runaways who gravitate to major cities to find a new, exciting life and escape from sexual and physical abuse at home.[68] In the United States and abroad, streetwalkers tend to be younger than other prostitutes, start working at a younger age, and have less education. More use money from sex work for drugs and use drugs at work; they are more likely than other prostitutes to be the targets of extreme forms of violence.[69]

Grace Marie, a Los Angeles sex worker and dominatrix, pauses for photos in July 2015. Should prostitution be legalized? In 1999, Sweden legalized prostitution in order to meet two essential objectives. Legalization helps protect the human rights of sex workers, while reducing the demand for paid sex, making commercial sexual exploitation less profitable.

AP Images/Jae C. Hong

Experienced sex workers are able to come up with protective strategies that help them manage the risk of the profession. Most do not randomly accept all clients and eliminate those they consider dangerous or threatening. Sanders found that they develop methods to deal with the emotional strain of the work as well as techniques to maintain their privacy and keep their "occupation" hidden from family and neighbors.[72]

Bar Girls B-girls, as they are also called, spend their time in bars, drinking and waiting to be picked up by customers. Although alcoholism may be a problem, B-girls usually work out an arrangement with the bartender so they are served diluted drinks or water colored with dye or tea, for which the customer is charged an exorbitant price. In some bars, the B-girl is given a credit for each drink she gets the customer to buy. It is common to find B-girls in towns with military bases and large transient populations.[73]

Brothel Prostitutes Also called bordellos, cathouses, sporting houses, and houses of ill repute, **brothels** flourished in the nineteenth and early twentieth centuries. They were large establishments, usually run by madams, that housed several prostitutes. A **madam** is a woman who employs prostitutes, supervises their behavior, and receives a fee for her services; her cut is usually 40 to 60 percent of the prostitute's earnings. The madam's role may include recruiting women into prostitution and socializing them in the trade.[74]

Brothels declined in importance following World War II. The closing of the last brothel in Texas is chronicled in the play and movie *The Best Little Whorehouse in Texas*. Today the most well-known brothels are in Nevada, where prostitution is legal outside large population centers (one, the Mustang Ranch, has an official website that sells souvenirs!). Despite their decline, some madams and their brothels have achieved national prominence.

Call Girls The aristocrats of prostitution are **call girls**. Some charge customers thousands per night and net hundreds of thousands per year. Some gain clients through employment in escort services, and others develop independent customer lists. Many call girls come from middle-class backgrounds and service upper-class customers. Attempting to dispel the notion that their service is simply sex for money, they concentrate on making their clients feel important and attractive. Working exclusively via telephone

Streetwalkers wear bright clothing, makeup, and jewelry to attract customers, and they take their customers to hotels. The term *hooker*, however, is not derived from the ability of streetwalkers to hook clients on their charms. It actually stems from the popular name given women who followed Union General "Fighting Joe" Hooker's army during the Civil War.[70] Because streetwalkers must openly display their occupation, they are likely to be involved with the police.

Research shows that there are a variety of working styles among women involved in street-based prostitution. Some are controlled by pimps who demand and receive a major share of their earnings. Others are independent entrepreneurs interested in building stable groups of steady clients. Another group might manipulate and exploit their customers and may engage in theft and blackmail.[71]

The street life is very dangerous. Teela Sanders's research on the everyday life of British sex workers found that street-level prostitutes use rational decision making and learning experiences to reduce the risk of violent victimization.

brothel A house of prostitution, typically run by a madam who sets prices and handles "business" arrangements.

madam A woman who employs prostitutes, supervises their behavior, and receives a fee for her services.

call girls Prostitutes who make dates via the phone and then service customers in hotel rooms or apartments. Call girls typically have a steady clientele who are repeat customers.

"dates," call girls get their clients by word of mouth or by making arrangements with bellhops, cab drivers, and so on. They either entertain clients in their own apartments or visit clients' hotels and apartments. Upon retiring, a call girl can sell her "date book" listing client names and sexual preferences for thousands of dollars. Despite the lucrative nature of their business, call girls suffer considerable risk by being alone and unprotected with strangers. They often request the business cards of their clients to make sure they are dealing with "upstanding citizens."

Escort Services/Call Houses   Some escort services are fronts for prostitution rings. Both male and female sex workers can be sent out after the client calls a number published in an ad in the Yellow Pages. How common are adult escort services? In 2016, Las Vegas had 114 Yellow Pages listings for escort services; New York City had 175.[75]

A relatively new phenomenon, the call house combines elements of brothels and call girl rings. A madam receives a call from a prospective customer, and if she finds the client acceptable, she arranges a meeting between the caller and a prostitute in her service. The madam maintains a list of prostitutes, who are on call rather than living together in a house. The call house insulates the madam from arrest because she never meets the client or receives direct payment.

Circuit Travelers   Prostitutes known as circuit travelers move around in groups of two or three to lumber, labor, and agricultural camps. They ask the foremen for permission to ply their trade, service the whole crew in an evening, and then move on. Some circuit travelers seek clients at truck stops and rest areas. Sometimes young girls are forced to become circuit travelers by unscrupulous pimps who force them to work as prostitutes in agricultural migrant camps.[76]

Skeezers   Surveys conducted in New York and Chicago have found that a significant portion of female prostitutes have substance abuse problems, and more than half claim that prostitution is how they support their drug habits. On the street, women who barter drugs for sex are called **skeezers**. These women suffer a host of social and psychological problems ranging from homelessness and unemployment to low self-esteem, depression, and anxiety.[77]

Massage Parlors/Photo Studios   Some "working girls" are based in massage parlors and photo studios. Although it is unusual for a masseuse to offer all the services of prostitution, oral sex and manual stimulation are common. Most localities have attempted to limit commercial sex in massage parlors by passing ordinances specifying that the masseuse keep certain parts of her body covered and limiting the areas of the body that can be massaged. Some photo studios allow customers to put body paint on models before the photo sessions start.

WHO BECOMES A PROSTITUTE?

At 38, Lt. Cmdr. Rebecca Dickinson had risen from the enlisted ranks in the navy to its officer corps. She started her navy career in 1986 as an aviation electronics technician, attended Auburn University and the Naval Supply Corps School. After becoming a commissioned officer, Dickinson served on the support ship *Camden*, the supply ship *Santa Barbara*, and the cruiser *Bunker Hill*. She was assigned to the naval academy where she helped teach a leadership course. But faced with money and marital problems, Dickinson contacted the D.C. Madam Deborah Jeane Palfrey (whose client list included Senator David Vitter) and worked as a prostitute for some of the richest and most powerful men in Washington. When asked why she did it, she replied, "I needed the money, yes, I did." This desperate navy officer, whose career was destroyed in the scandal, was paid $130 for a 90-minute session.[78]

Why do people like Lt. Cmdr. Dickinson turn to prostitution? She was a successful career officer (earning over $75,000 per year from the navy) motivated by an immediate financial need. However, her history is certainly not the norm: it is more common for male and female street-level sex workers to come from troubled homes marked by extreme conflict and hostility.[79] Many had experienced sexual trauma at an early age.[80] Future prostitutes were initiated into sex by family members at ages as young as 10 to 12; they have long histories of sexual exploitation and abuse.[81]

Sexual abuse is not the only social problem that is a forerunner to prostitution. Young people who get involved in prostitution also have extensive histories of substance abuse, health problems, posttraumatic stress disorder (PTSD), social stigmatization, and isolation; they experience the kind of strain that has been linked to deviant behavior choices (see Chapter 6).[82] Often having little family support, they turn to equally troubled peers for survival: self-medicating with drugs and alcohol and self-mutilation are the norm.[83] One survey of street-level sex workers in Phoenix, Arizona, found that women engaging in prostitution have limited educational backgrounds; most did not complete high school.[84] Girls who get into the life report conflict with school authorities, poor grades, and an overly regimented school experience; a significant portion have long histories of drug abuse.[85] Young girls who frequently use drugs and begin using at an early age are most at risk for prostitution to support their habits.[86]

Once they get into the life, personal danger begins to escalate. Girls who may be directed toward prostitution because of childhood sexual abuse are also likely to become revictimized as adults.[87] They are hurt when people label and depersonalize them as "whores" or "hookers."[88] Many sex workers struggle with substance use problems, typically

skeezers Prostitutes who trade sex for drugs, usually crack.

involving crack cocaine, cocaine, and/or heroin.[89] STD infections, including HIV, are a daily threat, and while some take precautions, such as using or making their clients use condoms, many sex workers forego protection if pimps and brothel owners forbid it or clients refuse to cooperate.[90] Prostitutes find themselves in a vicious cycle of violence, substance abuse, and AIDS risk.[91]

Considering these dangers, why do women remain on the street? Even when they try to go straight, street prostitutes are stymied by limited education and lack of skills, conditions that make finding employment very difficult. Without means to support themselves and their children, they may think staying on the streets is less risky than leaving prostitution.

Child Prostitution   It was routine for poor young girls to serve as prostitutes in nineteenth-century England.[92] In contemporary society, child prostitution has been linked to sexual trauma experienced at an early age.[93] Many have long histories of sexual exploitation and abuse.[94] The early experiences with sex help teach them that their bodies have value and that sexual encounters can be used to obtain affection, power, or money. Each year in the United States, thousands of children are subjected to some form of sexual exploitation, which often begins with sexual assaults by relatives and acquaintances, such as a teacher, coach, or a neighbor. Abusers are nearly always men, many married with children.

Once they flee an abusive situation at home, kids are vulnerable to life on the streets. Some get hooked up in the sex trade, starting as strippers and lap dancers and drifting into prostitution and pornography. They remain in the trade because they have lost hope and are resigned to their fate.[95] Some meet pimps who quickly turn them to a life of prostitution and beat them if they do not make their daily financial quotas. Others who fled to the streets exchange sex for money, food, and shelter. Some have been traded between prostitution rings, and others are shipped from city to city and even trafficked overseas as prostitutes. In 2014, 580 minors under 18 were arrested on charges of prostitution; of these, about 75 were children age 15 and younger, some under 10 years of age.[96]

One danger of child prostitution is that it leaves permanent damage. The women Jolanda Sallmann interviewed shared stories of feeling permanently altered by their prostitution and substance use. Although the majority of participants were no longer using substances or exchanging sex, they could not escape their past lives. As one, B.T., explained:

B.T.: The damage is done.
Interviewer: And what do you think the damage is?
B.T.: My spirit, my health. Um, my mind, because it's never going to leave me. I'm, you know, even when I'm not selling my body, I was still a prostitute. Before in the past, you know.

Interviewer: What does that mean?
B.T.: Like once a prostitute always a prostitute. I sold my body. For a long time.
Interviewer: So you feel that that is something that doesn't leave you?
B.T.: It doesn't go away.[97]

CONTROLLING PROSTITUTION

Today, prostitution is considered a misdemeanor, punishable by a fine or a short jail sentence. Most states punish both people engaging in prostitution and those who hire people for sexual activities with a small fine; those who are involved with juvenile prostitution face much tougher penalties. Minnesota punishes those hiring prostitutes over age 18 with a fine of $500; the statute setting out punishments for hiring a juvenile for the purposes of prostitution is set out in Exhibit 14.1.

In practice, clients (known generically as johns) are rarely arrested, though some studies show that an arrest can deter future involvement.[98] Most law enforcement is uneven and aims at confining illegal activities to particular areas in the city.[99] Some local police agencies concerned about prostitution have used high-visibility patrols to discourage prostitutes and their customers, undercover work to arrest prostitutes and drug dealers, and collaboration with hotel and motel owners to identify and arrest pimps and drug dealers.[100] One novel approach is "john schools," described in Exhibit 14.2, attended by clients who desire to avoid a criminal label.

LEGALIZE PROSTITUTION?

While most research depicts prostitutes as troubled women who have lived troubled lives, there may be a trend for some young women to enter the sex trade as a rational choice based on economic need. Changing sexual mores help reduce or eliminate the stigma attached to prostitution. There is even evidence that students turn to prostitution to help pay tuition bills.[101] One recent research study conducted in Australia found that the sex industry has become attractive to college students as a way to supplement their income during a time of reduced government aid and increasing educational costs. They view sex work as a "normal" form of employment for students seeking to obtain a higher education.[102] If this more liberal attitude toward prostitution becomes normative, should the practice become legal?

In some countries, especially in the Muslim world, prostitution carries the death penalty. In others, such as Holland, prostitutes pay taxes and belong to a union. Other countries, such as Australia, allow adults to engage in prostitution but regulate their activities, such as requiring that they must get timely health checkups. Still other countries, such as Brazil, allow women to become prostitutes but criminalize earning money from the work of prostitutes—that is,

Penalties for Hiring a Minor to Engage in Prostitution in Minnesota

609.324, Patrons; Prostitutes; Housing Individuals Engaged in Prostitution; Penalties.

Subdivision 1. Engaging in, hiring, or agreeing to hire minor to engage in prostitution; penalties.

(a) Whoever intentionally does any of the following may be sentenced to imprisonment for not more than 20 years or to payment of a fine of not more than $40,000, or both:
  (1) engages in prostitution with an individual under the age of 13 years; or
  (2) hires or offers or agrees to hire an individual under the age of 13 years to engage in sexual penetration or sexual contact.

(b) Whoever intentionally does any of the following may be sentenced to imprisonment for not more than ten years or to payment of a fine of not more than $20,000, or both:
  (1) engages in prostitution with an individual under the age of 16 years but at least 13 years; or
  (2) hires or offers or agrees to hire an individual under the age of 16 years but at least 13 years to engage in sexual penetration or sexual contact.

(c) Whoever intentionally does any of the following may be sentenced to imprisonment for not more than five years or to payment of a fine of not more than $10,000, or both:
  (1) engages in prostitution with an individual under the age of 18 years but at least 16 years;
  (2) hires or offers or agrees to hire an individual under the age of 18 years but at least 16 years to engage in sexual penetration or sexual contact; or
  (3) hires or offers or agrees to hire an individual who the actor reasonably believes to be under the age of 18 years to engage in sexual penetration or sexual contact

SOURCE: Office of the Revisor of Statutes, 2015 Minnesota Statutes, 609.324, Patrons; Prostitutes; Housing Individuals Engaged in Prostitution; Penalties, https://www.revisor.mn.gov/statutes/?id=609.324 (accessed June 2016).

John Schools

John schools focus on clients and attempt through education to steer them away from prostitution. One of the first, called the John Group, is a court-based program located in Grand Rapids, Michigan. The John Group is a court-ordered treatment program that can be required as a condition of probation for men arrested for soliciting prostitutes. The intervention includes four group counseling sessions of about one hour each and one individual session lasting about two hours. The group sessions convey information about prostitution, including legal consequences, health risks, impact on survivors (including testimony from former prostitutes) and communities, sexual addiction, pimping, and healthy relationships. The individual session is where offenders develop plans for addressing how they will meet their needs through more prosocial avenues in the future. In addition, the program includes a mandatory screening for STDs and HIV.

San Francisco's First Offender Prostitution Program (FOPP) is offered to arrestees who are given the choice of paying a fee and attending a one-day class (john school) or being prosecuted. The program is a partnership of the San Francisco district attorney's office, the San Francisco Police Department, and a local nonprofit organization, Standing Against Global Exploitation (SAGE). Client fees support all of the costs of conducting the john school classes, as well as subsidizing police vice operations, the screening and processing of arrestees, and recovery programs for women and girls involved in commercial sex.

Evaluations of the program by an independent research group (Abt Associates) found the program has been effective in substantially reducing recidivism among men arrested for soliciting prostitutes. The program has been successfully replicated in 12 other U.S. sites and adapted in more than 25 additional U.S. sites; many others are considering adopting similar programs.

SOURCE: Michael Shively, Sarah Kuck Jalbert, Ryan Kling, William Rhodes, Peter Finn, Chris Flygare, Laura Tierney, David Squires, Christina Dyous, Kristin Wheeler, and Dana Hunt, *Final Report on the Evaluation of the First Offender Prostitution Program* (Cambridge, MA: Abt Associates, 2008), http://www.abtassociates.com/reports/FOPP_Evaluation_full_report.pdf (accessed June 2016).

serving as a pimp. In the United States, prostitution is illegal in all states, though brothels are legal in a number of counties in Nevada (but not in Las Vegas or Reno).

Some feminists have staked out conflicting views of prostitution. One position is that women must become emancipated from male oppression and reach sexual equality. The *sexual equality view* considers the prostitute a victim of male dominance. In patriarchal societies, male power is predicated on female subjugation, and prostitution is a clear example of this gender exploitation.[103] In contrast, for some feminists, the fight for equality depends on controlling all attempts by men or women to impose their will on women. The *free choice view* is that prostitution, if freely chosen, expresses women's equality and is not a symptom of subjugation.

Advocates of both positions argue that the penalties for prostitution should be reduced (decriminalized); neither side advocates outright legalization. Decriminalization would relieve already desperate women of the additional burden of severe legal punishment. In contrast, legalization might be coupled with regulation by male-dominated justice agencies. Required medical examinations would mean increased governmental control over women's bodies.

Both positions have had significant influence around the world. In Sweden, feminists have succeeded in getting legislation passed that severely restricts prostitution and criminalizes any effort to buy sexual activities.[104] In contrast, Holland legalized brothels in 2001 but ordered that they be run under a strict set of guidelines.[105]

Should prostitution be legalized? In her book *Brothel*, Alexa Albert, a Harvard-trained physician who interviewed young women working at a legal brothel in Nevada, makes a compelling case for legalization. She found that the women remained HIV-free and felt safer working in a secure environment than alone on city streets. Despite long hours and rules that gave too much profit to the owners, the women actually took pride in their work. In addition to the added security, most earned between $300 and $1,500 per day.[106]

Respected criminologist Ronald Weitzer also suggests that prostitution be legalized under strict guidelines. Weitzer believes that using law enforcement and criminal penalties to control prostitution has little effect on sex workers, who will soon return to street life. After evaluating the way prostitution is dealt with around the world, Weitzer presents the argument that getting sex workers off the street by relaxing enforcement against those who work indoors is the best solution to an age-old problem. Those who operate indoors in brothels and other controlled venues are much safer and suffer far less injury from clients, pimps, and other victimizers; they also suffer less psychological hardship than those who work the streets.[107] Not all experts agree. British criminologist Roger Matthews opposes legalizing prostitution. It is foolish, he claims, to view prostitution as "sex work" that should be either legalized and/or tolerated and regulated. An example is Holland's "tolerance zones," where women can engage in prostitution without fear of arrest. After studying street prostitution for more than two decades, Matthew finds that women on the street are extremely desperate, damaged, and disorganized and are at frequent risk for beatings, rape, and other forms of violence. Prostitution is, he concludes, the world's most dangerous occupation. His solution is to treat the women forced into prostitution as victims and the men who purchase their services as the criminals. He applauds Sweden's decision to make buying sexual services a crime, thus criminalizing the johns rather than the women in prostitution. Matthews believes that, sadly, when governments legalize prostitution, it leads to a massive expansion of the trade, both legal and illegal.[108]

pornography Sexually explicit books, magazines, films, or other media intended to provide sexual titillation and excitement for paying customers.

obscenity According to current legal theory, sexually explicit material that lacks a serious purpose and appeals solely to the prurient interest of the viewer. While nudity per se is not usually considered obscene, open sexual behavior, masturbation, and exhibition of the genitals is banned in most communities.

Obscenity and Pornography

L07 Explain what is meant by the terms *obscenity* and *pornography*

Pornography derives from the Greek *porne*, meaning "prostitute," and *graphein*, meaning "to write." Pornography refers to the explicit portrayal of sexual subject matter in media, books, photographs, and magazines for the purpose of sexual arousal. Although material depicting pornography is typically legal, protected by the First Amendment's provision limiting governmental control of speech, most criminal codes prohibit its production, display, and sale when it crosses the line and is considered *obscene*. The term **obscenity**, derived from the Latin *obscaenus*, is defined by Webster's dictionary as "deeply offensive to morality or decency . . . designed to incite to lust or depravity."[109]

There is always controversy over what is obscene and how obscenity is defined. Police and law enforcement officials can legally seize only material that is judged obscene. But who, critics ask, is to judge what is obscene? At one time, such novels as *Tropic of Cancer* by Henry Miller, *Ulysses* by James Joyce, and *Lady Chatterley's Lover* by D. H. Lawrence were prohibited because they were considered obscene; today, they are considered works of great literary value. Thus, what is obscene today may be considered socially acceptable in the future.

Allowing individual judgments on what is obscene makes the Constitution's guarantee of free speech unworkable. Could anti-obscenity statutes also be used to control political and social dissent? The uncertainty surrounding this issue is illustrated by Supreme Court Justice

Former Subway spokesperson Jared Fogle (center) walks out of the courthouse on August 19, 2015, in Indianapolis. Fogle pleaded guilty to federal charges related to child pornography and having sex with minors. He also pleaded guilty to traveling across state lines to engage in illicit sexual conduct with a minor—specifically, from Indiana to New York City, where he was charged with paying to engage in sexual acts with a 17-year-old girl. Fogle received a nearly 16-year sentence for his crimes.

Joey Foley/Getty Images

mood swings, withdrawal, edginess, and nervousness. In cases of extreme, prolonged victimization, children may lock on to the sex group's behavior and become prone to further victimization or even become victimizers themselves.

DOES PORNOGRAPHY CAUSE VIOLENCE?

An issue critical to the debate over pornography is whether viewing it produces sexual violence or assaultive behavior. The evidence is mixed; there is no clear-cut evidence that viewing sexually explicit material has an effect on sexual violence. There seem to be relatively minor differences in sexual aggression between men who report using pornography very frequently and those who said they rarely used it at all.[114] Put simply, if a person has relatively aggressive sexual inclinations resulting from various personal and cultural factors, exposure to pornography may activate and reinforce associated coercive tendencies and behaviors. But even high levels of exposure to pornography do not turn nonaggressive men into sexual predators.

How might we account for this surprisingly moderate association?[115] It is possible that viewing erotic material may act as a safety valve for those whose impulses might otherwise lead them to violence.[116] Viewing prurient material may have the unintended side effect of satisfying erotic impulses that otherwise might result in more sexually aggressive behavior.

Violent Pornography   While the pornography–violence link seems at best modest, there is a much clearer association between pornography with a violent theme and sexual violence. Research shows that:

- Men who are predisposed to violence are more likely to be sexually aggressive toward women if they are exposed to adult material with themes of rape, violence, and/or sadism.[117]
- There is an association between watching violent pornography and engaging in domestic violence.[118]
- Serial killers have been found to collect and watch violent pornography. Some make their own "snuff" films starring their victims.[119]
- Men who are both at high risk for sexual aggression and who are very frequent users of pornography are much more likely to engage in sexual aggression than their counterparts who consume pornography less frequently.[120]

Potter Stewart's famous 1964 statement on how he defined obscenity: "I know it when I see it." Because of this legal and moral ambiguity, a global pornography industry is becoming increasingly mainstream, currently generating many billions of dollars per year in revenue.[110] Nonetheless, while adult material has gone mainstream, courts still hold that the First Amendment was not intended to protect indecency and therefore material considered offensive and obscene can be controlled by the rule of law.[111]

CHILD PORNOGRAPHY

In 2015, former Subway pitchman Jared Fogle agreed to plead guilty to allegations that he paid for sex acts with minors and was in possession of child pornography. The admission destroyed his career with the sandwich shop chain and sent him to prison for 15 years.[112]

While few people are prosecuted for possessing, distributing, or manufacturing pornography involving adults, buying or selling kiddie porn is a totally different matter. Each year more than a million children are believed to be used in pornography or prostitution, many of them runaways whose plight is exploited by adults.[113] Sexual exploitation by child pornography rings can devastate victims, causing them physical problems ranging from headaches and loss of appetite to genital soreness, vomiting, and urinary tract infections, as well as psychological problems including

Though this evidence has been found, it is still not certain if watching violent pornographic material drives people to sexual violence or whether people predisposed to sexual violence are drawn to pornography with a violent theme. It's just as possible that people who have been sexually aggressive toward adult and children later become collectors of violent pornography as it is for frequent pornography users to later be violent and aggressive. So while the association between viewing violent pornography and sexual violence seems apparent, its direction and time order are still uncertain.

PORNOGRAPHY AND THE LAW

All states and the federal government prohibit the sale and production of pornographic material. Under existing federal law, trafficking in obscenity (18 U.S.C. Sec. 1462, 1464, 1466), child pornography (18 U.S.C. Sec. 2252), harassment (18 U.S.C. Sec. 875(c)), illegal solicitation or luring of minors (18 U.S.C. Sec. 2423(b)), and threatening to injure someone (18 U.S.C. Sec. 875(c)) are all felonies punished by long prison sentences.

While these laws are designed to control obscene material, the First Amendment of the U.S. Constitution protects free speech and prohibits police agencies from limiting the public's right of free expression. This legal protection has sent the government along a torturous road in the attempt to define when material is criminally obscene and eligible for legal control. In 1957, the Supreme Court held in the twin cases of *Roth v. United States* and *Alberts v. California* that the First Amendment protects all "ideas with even the slightest redeeming social importance—unorthodox ideas, controversial ideas, even ideas hateful to the prevailing climate of opinion, but implicit in the history of the First Amendment is the rejection of obscenity as utterly without redeeming social importance."[121] In the 1966 case of *Memoirs v. Massachusetts*, the Supreme Court again required that for a work to be considered obscene it must be shown to be "utterly without redeeming social value."[122] These decisions left unclear how obscenity is defined. If a highly erotic movie tells a "moral tale," must it be judged legal even if 95 percent of its content is objectionable? A spate of movies made after the *Roth* decision alleged that they were educational so they could not be said to lack redeeming social importance. Many state obscenity cases were appealed to federal courts so judges could decide whether the films totally lacked redeeming social importance. To rectify the situation, the Supreme Court redefined its concept of obscenity in the case of *Miller v. California*:

> The basic guidelines for the trier of fact must be (a) whether the average person applying contemporary community standards would find that the work taken as a whole appeals to the prurient interest; (b) whether the work depicts or describes, in a patently offensive way, sexual conduct specifically defined by the applicable state law; and (c) whether the work, taken as a whole, lacks serious literary, artistic, political or scientific value.[123]

To convict a person of obscenity under the *Miller* doctrine, the state or local jurisdiction must specifically define obscene conduct in its statute, and the pornographer must engage in that behavior. The Court gave some examples of what is considered obscene: "patently offensive representations or descriptions of masturbation, excretory functions and lewd exhibition of the genitals."

The *Miller* doctrine has been criticized for not spelling out how community standards are to be determined. Obviously, a plebiscite cannot be held to determine the community's attitude for every trial concerning the sale of pornography. Works that are considered obscene in Omaha might be considered routine in New York City, but how can we be sure? There are even differences of opinion on what is considered obscene within individual communities; surveys show that there is little consensus even over the most extreme of pornographic materials.[124] Therefore, it does not seem possible that objective community standards actually exist and that there is a consensus on what material is outlawed and what is acceptable.

To resolve this dilemma, in *Pope v. Illinois* the Supreme Court articulated a reasonableness doctrine: a work is not obscene if a reasonable person applying objective standards would find that the material in question has at least some social value.[125] The Court ruled that the proper jury instruction for the third prong of the *Miller* obscenity test should be whether a reasonable person would find value in the material taken as a whole, not whether an ordinary member of any given community would find serious value in the supposedly obscene material. The work does not have to be accepted by a majority of the community to be protected, and the value of the work does not vary from community to community.

> The proper inquiry is not whether an ordinary member of any given community would find serious value in the allegedly obscene material, but whether a reasonable person would find such value in the material, taken as a whole.[126]

The Law and Child Pornography Because the use of children in pornography is considered so serious, kiddie porn is usually a separate legal category that involves either the creation or reproduction of materials depicting minors engaged in actual or simulated sexual activity ("sexual exploitation of minors") or the publication or distribution of obscene, indecent, or harmful materials to minors.[127]

Computer-generated images and other high-tech innovations now make it possible for pornographers to create and distribute virtual images of a child engaging in sexual activity that is almost impossible to distinguish from an actual child. Fearing the proliferation of kiddie porn over the Internet, Congress enacted the Child Pornography Prevention Act of 1996 (CPPA) that outlawed sexually related material that used or *appeared to use* children under 18 engaging in sexual conduct. In *Ashcroft v. The Free Speech Coalition*, the Supreme Court struck down sections of the CPPA relating to virtual kiddie porn: sexually related material in which an actual child appears is illegal, but possessing "virtual" pornography is legal. The Court reasoned that real children are not harmed with a virtual child.

In response to the Court's decision, Congress passed the PROTECT Act of 2003 (Prosecutorial Remedies and Other Tools to end the Exploitation of Children), which outlawed virtual kiddie porn that makes it almost impossible to distinguish the difference between a real child and a morphed or created image.[128] The Supreme Court reviewed this law in a 2008 case, *United States v. Williams*, which concerned Michael Williams, who was convicted in federal district court of "pandering" (promoting) child pornography under the PROTECT Act. At trial, the district court held that the government can legitimately outlaw the pandering of material as child pornography, even if the images are computer generated, if they were being offered to someone who *thought they were buying images of real children*. The Court noted that offers to engage in illegal transactions are excluded from First Amendment protection, so that the "speech" of an individual claiming to be in possession of child pornography is therefore not protected by the First Amendment. The Court also stated that the law did not violate due process because its requirements were clear and could be understood by courts, juries, and potential violators.[129] In sum, someone who offers to sell child pornography can be found guilty of a crime even if the images they are selling are fake or computer generated. It is the *intent* to sell that is the crime; no images are necessary to be convicted.

CONTROLLING PORNOGRAPHY

Sex for profit predates Western civilization. Considering its longevity, there seems to be little evidence that it can be controlled or eliminated by legal means alone. In 1986, the Attorney General's Commission on Pornography advocated a strict law enforcement policy to control obscenity, directing that "the prosecution of obscene materials that portray sexual violence be treated as a matter of special urgency."[130]

Since then, there has been a concerted effort by the federal government to prosecute the distribution of obscenity. Law enforcement has been so fervent that industry members have filed suit claiming they are the victims of a "moral crusade" by right-wing zealots.[131]

Although politically appealing, controlling sex for profit is difficult because of the public's desire to purchase sexually related material and services. Law enforcement crusades may not necessarily obtain the desired effect. A get-tough policy could make sex-related goods and services scarce, driving up prices and making their sale even more desirable and profitable. Going after national distributors may help decentralize the adult movie and photo business and encourage local rings to expand their activities, by making and marketing videos as well as still photos or distributing them through computer networks.

An alternative approach has been to restrict the sale of pornography within acceptable boundaries. Some municipal governments have tolerated or even established adult entertainment zones in which obscene material can be openly sold.[132] While these efforts are applauded, the Internet has become a favored method of delivering adult material and one that defies easy regulation since distribution can be international in scope. While there is little effort to control adult porn, law enforcement agencies have focused their attention on the use of children in Internet porn. This will be discussed once more in Chapter 15 as a type of cybercrime.

Substance Abuse

The drug-related deaths of such great entertainers as Prince, Michael Jackson, Whitney Houston, Heath Ledger, and Philip Seymour Hoffman are stark reminders of the dangers of substance abuse, a social problem that spans every segment of society. Large urban areas are beset by drug-dealing gangs, drug users who engage in crime to support their habits, and alcohol-related violence. Rural areas are important staging centers for the shipment of drugs around the country and are often the production sites for synthetic drugs and marijuana farming.[133]

Despite the scope of the drug problem, some still view it as another type of victimless public order crime. There is great debate over the legalization of drugs and the control of alcohol. Some consider drug use a private matter and drug control another example of government intrusion into people's private lives. Furthermore, legalization could reduce the profit of selling illegal substances and drive suppliers out of the market.[134] Others see these substances as dangerous, believing that the criminal activity of users makes the term *victimless* nonsensical. Still another position is that the possession and use of all drugs and alcohol should be legalized but that the sale and distribution of drugs should be heavily penalized. This would punish those profiting from drugs and would enable users to be helped without fear of criminal punishment.

The debate over dangerous prescription drug use has been intensified because they are now easily obtained on the Web. Many suppliers do not require prescriptions. For more on this issue, see the discussion in Chapter 15 on obtaining dangerous drugs via the Internet.

ASK YOURSELF . . .

Does the fact that people can easily obtain addicting drugs online negate government efforts to control the drug trade?

WHEN DID DRUG USE BEGIN?

The use of chemical substances to change perception of reality and to provide stimulation, relief, or relaxation has gone on for thousands of years. The opium poppy was first cultivated more than 5,000 years ago and was used by the Persians, Sumerians, Assyrians, Babylonians, and Egyptians. Users discovered the bliss that could be achieved by smoking the extract derived from crushing the seed pods; the poppy yielded a pleasurable, peaceful feeling throughout the body. Known as the Hul Gil or "plant of joy," its use spread quickly around the Fertile Crescent.[135] The ancient Greeks knew and understood the problem of drug use. At the time of the Crusades, the Arabs were using marijuana.

In the Western hemisphere, natives of Mexico and South America chewed coca leaves and used "magic mushrooms" in their religious ceremonies.[136] Drug use was also accepted in Europe well into the twentieth century. Recently uncovered pharmacy records circa 1900 to 1920 showed sales of cocaine and heroin solutions to members of the British royal family; records from 1912 show that Winston Churchill, then a member of Parliament, was sold a cocaine solution while staying in Scotland.[137]

In the early years of the United States, opium and its derivatives were easily obtained. Opium-based drugs were used in various patent medicine cure-alls. Morphine was used extensively to relieve the pain of wounded soldiers in the Civil War. By the turn of the twentieth century, an estimated 1 million U.S. citizens were opiate users.[138]

Several factors precipitated the current stringent U.S. drug laws. The rural religious creeds of the nineteenth century—especially those of the Methodists, Presbyterians, and Baptists—emphasized individual human toil and self-sufficiency while designating the use of intoxicating substances as an unwholesome surrender to the evils of urban morality. Religious leaders were thoroughly opposed to the use and sale of narcotics. The medical literature of the late 1800s began to designate the use of morphine and opium as a vice, a habit, an appetite, and a disease. Nineteenth- and early twentieth-century police literature described drug users as habitual criminals. Moral crusaders in the nineteenth century defined drug use as evil and directed that local and national entities should outlaw the sale and possession of drugs. Some well-publicized research efforts categorized drug use as highly dangerous.[139] Drug use was also associated with the foreign immigrants recruited to work in factories and mines; they brought with them their national drug habits. Early antidrug legislation appears to be tied to prejudice against immigrating ethnic minorities.[140]

After the Spanish-American War of 1898, the United States inherited Spain's opium monopoly in the Philippines. Concern over this international situation, along with the domestic issues just outlined, led the U.S. government to participate in the First International Drug Conference, held in Shanghai in 1908, and a second one at The Hague in 1912. Participants in these two conferences were asked to strongly oppose free trade in drugs. The international pressure, coupled with a growing national concern, led to the passage of the antidrug laws discussed here.

ALCOHOL AND ITS PROHIBITION

The history of alcohol and the law in the United States has also been controversial and dramatic. In the late nineteenth century, a drive was mustered to prohibit the sale of alcohol. This **temperance movement** was fueled by the belief that the purity of the U.S. agrarian culture was being destroyed by the growth of the city. Urbanism was viewed as a threat to the lifestyle of the majority of the nation's population, then living on farms and in villages. The forces behind the temperance movement were such lobbying groups as the Anti-Saloon League led by Carrie Nation, the Women's Christian Temperance Union, and the Protestant clergy of the Baptist, Methodist, and Congregationalist faiths.[141] They viewed the growing city, filled with newly arriving Irish, Italian, and eastern European immigrants, as centers of degradation and wickedness. The propensity of these ethnic people to drink heavily was viewed as the main force behind their degenerate lifestyle. The eventual prohibition of the sale of alcoholic beverages, brought about by ratification of the Eighteenth Amendment in 1919, was viewed as a triumph of the morality of middle- and upper-class Americans over the threat posed to their culture by the "new Americans."[142]

Anti-immigrant sentiment was not the only motivation for temperance. By 1830, the average American over 15 years old consumed about seven gallons of pure alcohol a year—three times as much as we drink today—and alcohol abuse, primarily by men, was destroying the family structure. Women had few legal rights at the time and were hard-pressed to find avenues of support to protect them

temperance movement An effort to prohibit the sale of liquor in the United States that resulted in the passage of the Eighteenth Amendment to the Constitution in 1919, which prohibited the sale of alcoholic beverages.

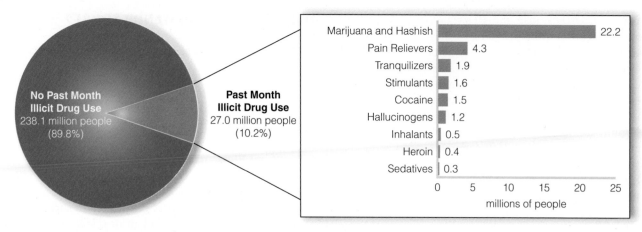

FIGURE 14.1 Numbers of Past Month Illicit Drug Users Among People Ages 12 or Older

SOURCE: Center for Behavioral Health Statistics and Quality, "Behavioral Health Trends in the United States: Results from the 2014 National Survey on Drug Use and Health," http://www.samhsa.gov/data/sites/default/files/NSDUH-FRR1-2014/NSDUH-FRR1-2014.pdf (accessed June 2016).

from the abuse of drunken husbands. Many married women joined the temperance movement as a means of survival.[143]

Prohibition failed. It was enforced by the Volstead Act, which defined intoxicating beverages as those containing one-half of 1 percent, or more, alcohol.[144] What doomed Prohibition? One factor was the use of organized crime to supply illicit liquor. Also, the law made it illegal only to sell alcohol, not to purchase it; this cut into the law's deterrent capability. Finally, despite the work of Eliot Ness and his "Untouchables," law enforcement agencies were inadequate, and officials were likely to be corrupted by wealthy bootleggers.[145] Eventually, in 1933, the Twenty-First Amendment to the Constitution repealed Prohibition, signaling the end of the "noble experiment."

HOW MUCH DRUG USE IS THERE TODAY?

Despite continuing efforts at control, the use of mood-altering substances persists in the United States. What is the extent of the substance abuse problem today?

A number of national surveys attempt to chart trends in drug abuse in the general population. One important source of information on drug use is the annual Monitoring the Future (MTF) self-report survey of drug abuse among high school students conducted by the Institute for Social Research (ISR) at the University of Michigan. This annual survey is based on the self-report responses of approximately 50,000 8th-, 10th-, and 12th-graders and is considered the most important source of data on adolescent drug abuse. MTF survey data indicate that drug use declined from a high point late in the 1970s until 1990, when it once again began to increase, finally stabilizing around 1996. Since then there has been a decline in both lifetime and current usage. In 2014, alcohol use by the nation's teens continued its long-term decline, and students in all three grades showed a decline in the proportion reporting any alcohol use in the prior 12 months. The three grades combined

dropped to 41 percent, down from more than 60 percent in 1997. Of perhaps greater importance, the proportion of teens who report **binge drinking**—consuming five or more drinks in a row at least once in the prior two weeks—fell to 12 percent, down from a high point of 22 percent in 1997. Still, one in five (19 percent) 12th graders report binge drinking at least once in the prior two weeks.

Drug use among teens has also declined significantly, and marijuana—which remains the most popular drug by far—declined in use in 2014 (the last data available) after rising for the past few years. Nonetheless, about 6 percent of all high school students claim to use marijuana every day and about 6 percent of 8th graders, 11 percent of 10th graders, and 16 percent of 12th graders used some other drug such as ecstasy, LSD, or cocaine in the prior 12 months.[146]

The National Household Survey on Drug Abuse and Health, sponsored by the federal government, provides a look at both juvenile and adult drug and alcohol abuse. The most recent data show that in 2014 27 million people ages 12 or older used an illicit drug in the past 30 days, which corresponds to about 1 in 10 Americans. Drug use in 2014 was higher than in every year from 2002 through 2013. As Figure 14.1 shows, of all drug users (27 million people) more than 22 million were current marijuana users (i.e., users in the past 30 days), and 4.3 million people ages 12 or older reported current nonmedical use of prescription pain relievers.[147]

ALCOHOL ABUSE

All data sources agree that alcohol abuse is another significant national problem. According to the National Household

> **binge drinking** Having five or more drinks on the same occasion (that is, at the same time or within a couple of hours of each other) on at least 1 day in the past 30 days.

Survey on Drug Abuse and Health, about 140 million Americans are routine drinkers; of these, 61 million are binge drinkers and 16 million can be classified as heavy alcohol users. In 2014, 23 percent of underage people were current alcohol users, 14 percent were binge alcohol users, and 3 percent were heavy alcohol users. While binge drinking has declined, the survey found that more than one-third of young adults in 2014 were binge alcohol users (and about 1 in 10 were heavy alcohol users).[148]

These data are reinforced by surveys conducted by the National Institute on Alcohol Abuse and Alcoholism, which found almost 90 percent of people ages 18 or older report that they drank alcohol at some point in their lifetime; 71 percent report that they drank in the past year; 56 percent reported that they drank in the past month.[149] While imbibing is not a significant problem per se, binge drinking (having five or more alcoholic drinks on the same occasion) can be, and 25 percent of all people surveyed reported that they engage in binge drinking; 7 percent reported that they binged at least once a week. An estimated 17 million Americans have an alcohol disorder; each year in the United States nearly 80,000 people die from alcohol-related causes.

COSTS OF SUBSTANCE ABUSE

Considering how many people indulge in illicit drug and alcohol abuse, it should not be surprising that the costs of drugs and alcohol are quite significant. The National Institute on Drug Abuse estimates that health and other costs directly related to substance abuse are now $700 billion per year (see Table 14.1).

In addition to these, enforcement costs add additional billions. Research compiled by the Cato Institute, a Washington, D.C., think tank, estimates that legalizing drugs would save roughly $41 billion per year in government enforcement expenditure. State and local governments could save about $25 billion per year; $16 billion would accrue to the federal government.[150] About $9 billion of the savings would result from legalization of marijuana, $20 billion from legalization of cocaine and heroin, and $13 billion from legalization of all other drugs.

TABLE 14.1		
Costs of Drug and Alcohol Abuse		
	HEALTH CARE	OVERALL
Tobacco	$130 billion	$295 billion
Alcohol	$25 billion	$224 billion
Illicit drugs	$11 billion	$193 billion

SOURCE: National Institute on Drug Abuse, 2016, http://www.drugabuse.gov/related-topics/trends-statistics (accessed June 2016).

WHAT CAUSES SUBSTANCE ABUSE?

 L08 Assess the causes of substance abuse

What causes people to abuse substances? Although there are many different views on the causes of drug use, most can be characterized as seeing the onset of an addictive career as being either an environmental or a personal matter.

Subcultural View   Those who view drug abuse as having an environmental basis concentrate on lower-class addiction. Because a disproportionate number of drug abusers are poor, the onset of drug use can be tied to such factors as racial prejudice, devalued identities, low self-esteem, poor socioeconomic status, and the high level of mistrust, negativism, and defiance found in impoverished areas. Residents feel trapped in a cycle of violence, drug abuse, and despair.[151] Youths in these disorganized areas may join peers to learn the techniques of drug use and receive social support for their habit. Research shows that peer influence is a significant predictor of drug careers that actually grow stronger as people mature.[152] Drug use splits some communities into distinct groups of relatively affluent abstainers and desperately poor abusers.[153]

Psychological View   There is evidence linking substance abuse to psychological deficits such as impaired cognitive functioning, personality disturbance, and emotional problems that can strike people in any economic class.[154]

Research on the psychological characteristics of drug abusers does in fact reveal the presence of a significant degree of personal pathology. Studies have found that addicts suffer personality disorders characterized by low frustration tolerance, anxiety, and fantasies of omnipotence. Many addicts exhibit psychopathic or sociopathic behavior characteristics, forming what is called an addiction-prone personality.[155] Statistics from the most recent survey conducted by the Substance Abuse and Mental Health Services Administration (SAMHSA) show that about 44 million Americans age 18 and up experienced some form of mental illness. In the past year, 20 million adults had a substance use disorder. Of these, 8 million people had both a mental disorder and substance use disorder, also known as co-occurring mental and substance use disorders (see Figure 14.2).[156]

What is the connection between psychological disorder and drug abuse? Drugs may help people deal with unconscious needs and impulses and relieve dependence and depression. People may turn to drug abuse as a form of self-medication in order to reduce the emotional turmoil of adolescence, deal with troubling impulses, or cope with traumatic life experiences such as institutional child abuse (kids who were sexually or physically abused in orphanages, mental institutions, juvenile detention centers, day care centers, etc.).[157] Survivors of sexual assault and physical abuse in the home have also been known to turn to drug and alcohol abuse as a coping mechanism.[158] Depressed people may

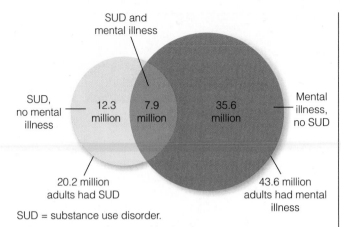

SUD and
mental illness

SUD,
no mental
illness

12.3
million

7.9
million

35.6
million

Mental
illness,
no SUD

20.2 million
adults had SUD

43.6 million
adults had mental
illness

SUD = substance use disorder.

FIGURE 14.2 Past Year Substance Use Disorders and Mental Illness Among Adults Ages 18 or Older

SOURCE: Substance Abuse and Mental Health Services Administration (SAMHSA), "Results from the 2014 National Survey on Drug Use and Health (NSDUH), 2015," http://www.samhsa.gov/data/sites/default/files/NSDUH-FRR1-2014/NSDUH-FRR1-2014.pdf (accessed June 2016).

use drugs as an alternative to more radical solutions to their pain such as suicide.[159] Kids who are self-conscious about their body image or who have poor self-esteem may turn to drugs to ease psychological turmoil.[160]

The Criminology in Action feature "Substance Abuse and Psychosis" looks at the substance abuse involvement of people with severe mental disorders.

Genetic Factors Research shows that substance abuse may have a genetic basis.[161] A number of studies comparing alcoholism among identical twins and fraternal twins have found that the degree of concordance (both siblings behaving identically) is twice as high among the identical twin groups.[162]

Taken as a group, studies of the genetic basis of substance abuse suggest that people whose parents were alcoholic or drug dependent have a greater chance of developing a problem than the children of nonabusers, and this relationship occurs regardless of parenting style or the quality of the parent–child relationship.[163] However, not all children of abusing parents become drug dependent themselves, suggesting that even if drug abuse is heritable, environment and socialization must play some role in the onset of abuse.[164]

Social Learning Social psychologists suggest that drug abuse may also result from observing parental drug use. Parental drug abuse begins to have a damaging effect on children as young as 2 years old, especially when parents manifest drug-related personality problems such as depression or poor impulse control.[165] Children whose parents abuse drugs are more likely to have persistent abuse problems than the children of nonabusers.[166]

People who learn that drugs provide pleasurable sensations may be the most likely to experiment with illegal substances; a habit may develop if the user experiences lower

anxiety, fear, and tension levels.[167] Having a history of family drug and alcohol abuse has been found to be a characteristic of violent teenage sexual abusers.[168] Heroin abusers report an unhappy childhood that included harsh physical punishment and parental neglect and rejection.[169]

Problem Behavior Syndrome (PBS) For many people, substance abuse is just one of many problem behaviors.[170] Longitudinal studies show that drug abusers are maladjusted, alienated, and emotionally distressed and that drug use is only one among many social problems.[171] Having a deviant lifestyle begins early in life and is punctuated with criminal relationships, family history of substance abuse, educational failure, and alienation. Crack cocaine use has been linked to sexual abuse as children and social isolation as adults.[172] There is robust support for the interconnection of problem drinking and drug abuse in adolescence and delinquency, precocious sexual behavior, school failure, running away, homelessness, family conflict, and other similar social problems.[173] In adulthood, people who manifest substance abuse problems also exhibit a wide variety of other social and legal problems.[174]

Rational Choice Not all people who abuse drugs do so because of personal pathology. Some may use drugs and alcohol because they want to enjoy their effects: get high, relax, improve creativity, escape reality, and increase sexual responsiveness. Claire Sterk-Elifson's research on middle-class drug-abusing women shows that most were introduced by friends in the context of "just having some fun."[175]

Substance abuse, then, may be a function of the rational but mistaken belief that drugs can benefit the user. The decision to use drugs involves evaluations of personal consequences (such as addiction, disease, and legal punishment) and the expected benefits of drug use (such as peer approval, positive affective states, heightened awareness, and relaxation). Adolescents may begin using drugs because they believe their peers expect them to do so.[176]

IS THERE A DRUG GATEWAY?

Some experts believe that, regardless of its cause, most people fall into drug abuse slowly, beginning with alcohol and then following with marijuana and more serious drugs as the need for a more powerful high intensifies. A number of research efforts have confirmed this **gateway model**. In a now classic study, James Inciardi, Ruth Horowitz, and Anne Pottieger found a clear pattern of adult involvement in adolescent drug abuse. Kids on crack started their careers with early experimentation with alcohol at age 7, began getting

gateway model An explanation of drug abuse that posits that users begin with a more benign drug (alcohol or marijuana) and progress to more potent drugs.

Substance Abuse and Psychosis

04

Most estimates suggest that people diagnosed with mood or anxiety disorders are about twice as likely as the general population to also suffer from a substance use disorder. Studies exploring the link between substance use disorders and other mental illnesses have typically not included people with severe psychotic illnesses.

In a recent study, 9,142 people diagnosed with schizophrenia, schizoaffective disorder, or bipolar disorder with psychotic features were matched with 10,195 controls according to geographic region. Mental disorder diagnoses were confirmed using the Diagnostic Interview for Psychosis and Affective Disorder (DI-PAD), and the controls were screened to verify the absence of schizophrenia or bipolar disorder in themselves or close family members. The DI-PAD was also used for all participants to determine substance use rates.

Compared to the controls, people with severe mental illness were about 4 times more likely to be heavy alcohol users (four or more drinks per day), 3.5 times more likely to use marijuana regularly (21 times per year), and 4.6 times more likely to use other drugs at least 10 times in their lives. The greatest increases were seen with tobacco, with patients with severe mental illness 5 times more likely to be daily smokers. This is of concern because smoking is the leading cause of preventable death in the United States. The association between mental issues and substance abuse was constant when controlling for gender, age, and race.

Previous research has shown that people with schizophrenia have a shorter life expectancy than the general population, and chronic cigarette smoking has been suggested as a major contributing factor to higher morbidity and mortality from malignancy as well as cardiovascular and respiratory diseases. These new findings indicate that the rates of substance use in people with severe psychosis may be underestimated, highlighting the need to improve the understanding of the association between substance use and psychotic disorders so that both conditions can be treated effectively.

CRITICAL THINKING

What is the connection between psychosis and substance abuse? Is it possible that people with severe mental disorders use drugs and alcohol to self-medicate and relieve their symptoms? What other reasons might there be for the connection?

SOURCE: Sarah M. Hartz, Carlos N. Pato, Helena Medeiros, Patricia Cavazos-Rehg, Janet L. Sobell, James A. Knowles, Laura Bierut, and Michele T. Pato, "Comorbidity of Severe Psychotic Disorders with Measures of Substance Use," *JAMA Psychiatry* 71 (2014): 248-254.

---

drunk at age 8, had alcohol with an adult present by age 9, and became regular drinkers by the time they were 11 years old.[177] Drinking with an adult present, presumably a parent, was a significant precursor of future substance abuse and delinquency. "Adults who gave children alcohol," they argue, "were also giving them a head start in a delinquent career."[178]

Other research efforts support this view when they find that the most serious drug users have a history of recreational drug and alcohol abuse.[179] Kids who begin using alcohol in adolescence become involved in increasing levels of deviant behavior as they mature.[180] Marijuana users are up to five times more likely to escalate their drug abuse and try cocaine and heroin than nonusers.[181] In sum, while most marijuana smokers do not become hard drug users, some do, and the risk of using dangerous substances may be increased by first engaging in recreational drugs.

The drug gateway vision is popular, but not all research efforts find that users progress to ever-more potent drugs, and some show that, surprisingly, many hard-core drug abusers never actually smoked pot or used alcohol.[182] And although many American youths have tried marijuana, few actually progress to crack or heroin abuse.[183]

TYPES OF DRUG USERS AND ABUSERS

The general public often groups all drug users together without recognizing that there are many varieties, ranging from adolescent recreational drug users to adults who run large smuggling operations.[184]

Adolescents Who Distribute Small Amounts of Drugs
Some dealers began their involvement in the drug trade by using and distributing small amounts of drugs; they do not commit any other serious criminal acts. Some start out as "stash dealers" who sell drugs to maintain a consistent access to drugs for their own consumption; their customers are almost always personal acquaintances, including friends and relatives.[185] They are insulated from the legal system because their activities rarely result in apprehension and sanction.

Adolescents Who Frequently Sell Drugs A small number of adolescents, most often multiple-drug users or heroin or cocaine users, are high-rate dealers who bridge the gap between adult drug distributors and the adolescent user. Frequent dealers often have adults who "front" for them—that is, loan them drugs to sell without upfront cash. The teenagers then distribute the drugs to friends and acquaintances, returning most of the proceeds to the supplier while keeping a commission for themselves. Frequent dealers are more likely to sell drugs in public and can be seen in known drug user hangouts in parks, schools, or other public places. Deals are irregular, so the chances of apprehension are slight.

Teenage Drug Dealers Who Commit Other Delinquent Acts

A more serious type of drug-involved youth comprises those who use and distribute multiple substances and also commit both property and violent crimes; many are gang members. Although these youngsters make up about 2 percent of the teenage population, they commit a significant portion of all robberies, assaults, felony thefts, and drug sales.[186]

These youths are frequently hired by older dealers to act as street-level drug runners. Each member of a crew of three to twelve boys will handle small quantities of drugs, perhaps three bags of heroin, which are received on consignment and sold on the street; the supplier receives 50 to 70 percent of the drug's street value. The crew members also act as lookouts, recruiters, and guards. Between drug sales, the young dealers commit robberies, burglaries, and other thefts.[187]

Adolescents Who Cycle In and Out of the Justice System

Some drug-involved youths are failures at both dealing and crime. They do not have the savvy to join gangs or groups and instead begin committing unplanned, opportunistic crimes that increase their chances of arrest. They are heavy drug users, which both increases apprehension risk and decreases their value for organized drug distribution networks. Drug-involved "losers" can earn a living steering customers to a seller in a "copping" area, "touting" drug availability for a dealer, or acting as a lookout. However, they are not considered trustworthy or deft enough to handle drugs or money. They may bungle other criminal acts, which solidifies their reputation as undesirable.

Drug-Involved Youth Who Continue to Commit Crimes as Adults

Although about two-thirds of substance-abusing youths continue to use drugs after they reach adulthood, about half desist from other criminal activities. Those who persist in both substance abuse and crime as adults exhibit a wide variety of social and developmental problems. Some evidence also exists that these drug-using persisters have low nonverbal IQs and poor physical coordination.

Outwardly Respectable Adults Who Are Top-Level Dealers

A few outwardly respectable adult dealers sell large quantities of drugs to support themselves in high-class lifestyles. These dealers are often indistinguishable from other professionals. Upscale dealers seem to drift into dealing from many different walks of life. Some begin as campus dealers who seem just like other students.[188] Frequently they are drawn from professions and occupations that are unstable, have irregular working hours, and accept drug abuse. Some use their business skills and drug profits to get into legitimate enterprises or illegal scams. Others drop out of the drug trade because they are the victims of violent crime committed by competitors or disgruntled customers; a few wind up in jail or prison.

Smugglers

Smugglers import drugs into the United States. They are generally men, middle-aged or older, who have strong organizational skills, established connections, capital to invest, and a willingness to take large business risks. Smugglers are a loosely organized, competitive group of individual entrepreneurs. There is a constant flow in and out of the business as some sources become the target of law enforcement activities, new drug sources become available, older smugglers become dealers, and former dealers become smugglers.

Adult Predatory Drug Users Who Are Frequently Arrested

Many users who begin abusing substances in early adolescence continue in drugs and crime in their adulthood. Getting arrested, doing time, using multiple drugs, and committing predatory crimes are a way of life for them. They have few skills, did poorly in school, and have long criminal records. The threat of conviction and punishment has little effect on their criminal activities. These "losers" have friends and relatives involved in drugs and crime. They specialize in robberies, burglaries, thefts, and drug sales. They filter in and out of the justice system and resume committing crimes as soon as they are released. In some populations, at least one-third of adult males are involved in drug trafficking and other criminal acts well into their adulthood.[189]

If they make a "big score," perhaps through a successful drug deal, they may significantly increase their drug use. Their increased narcotics consumption then destabilizes their lifestyle, destroying family and career ties. When their finances dry up, they may become street junkies, people whose traditional lifestyle has been destroyed, who turn to petty crime to maintain an adequate supply of drugs. Cut off from a stable source of quality heroin, not knowing from where their next fixes or the money to pay for them will come, looking for any opportunity to make a buck, getting sick or "jonesing," being pathetically unkempt and unable to maintain even the most primitive routines of health or hygiene, street junkies live a very difficult existence. Because they are unreliable and likely to become police informants, street junkies pay the highest prices for the poorest quality heroin; lack of availability increases their need to commit habit-supporting crimes.[190]

Adult Predatory Drug Users Who Are Rarely Arrested

Some drug users are "winners." They commit hundreds of crimes each year but are rarely arrested. On the streets, they are known for their calculated violence. Their crimes are carefully planned and coordinated. They often work with partners and use lookouts to carry out the parts of their crimes that have the highest risk of apprehension. These "winners" are more likely to use recreational drugs, such as coke and pot, than the more addicting heroin or opiates. Some become high-frequency users and risk apprehension and punishment. But for the lucky few, their criminal careers can stretch for up to 15 years without interruption by the justice system. These users are sometimes referred to as *stabilized junkies* who have learned the skills needed to purchase and process larger amounts of heroin. Their addiction enables them to maintain normal lifestyles, although they may turn to drug dealing to create contacts with drug suppliers. They are employable, but earning legitimate income does little to reduce their drug use or dealing activities.[191]

Less Predatory Drug-Involved Adult Offenders Most adult drug users are petty criminals who avoid violent crime. These occasional users are people just beginning their addiction, who use small amounts of narcotics, and whose habit can be supported by income from conventional jobs; narcotics have relatively little influence on their lifestyles.[192] They are typically high school graduates and have regular employment that supports their drug use. They usually commit petty thefts or pass bad checks. They stay on the periphery of the drug trade by engaging in such acts as helping addicts shoot up, bagging drugs for dealers, operating shooting galleries, renting needles and syringes, and selling small amounts of drugs. These petty criminal drug users do not have the stomach for a life of hard crime and drug dealing. They violate the law in proportion to the amount and cost of the drugs they are using. Pot smokers have a significantly lower frequency of theft violations than daily heroin users, whose habit is considerably more costly.

Outwardly Respectable Adults Who Are Frequent Users Some drug users continue their activities into their adulthood, while others may initiate drug use as part of a new lifestyle developed in adulthood. These users may be successful college graduates who become caught up in the club scene in major cities and get involved in recreational drug use. Surveys of urban young adults find that almost 40 percent report usage of at least one club drug.[193]

Another element of the outwardly respectable adult drug abuser is that he or she uses illegal substances to enhance their professional careers. The sports world has been rocked by stories of famed athletes who have admitted taking performance-enhancing drugs. Recent research shows that professional ballet dancers, a group not usually suspected of being drug involved, routinely use banned substances to improve performance.[194]

The number of outwardly respectable drug users is expected to rise as the aging baby boomers, who grew up in the drug culture, both live longer and continue to use banned substances. Evidence shows that this group, who may amount to 70 million people by 2030, will continue to use illegal substances in amounts previously unheard of for people of their age and lifestyle.[195]

Drug-Involved Female Offenders Women who are drug-involved offenders constitute a separate type of substance abuser. Although women are far less likely than men to use addictive drugs, research conducted by the National Center on Addiction and Substance Abuse (CASA) at Columbia University found that 15 million girls and women use illicit drugs or abuse controlled prescription drugs, 32 million smoke cigarettes, and 6 million are alcohol abusers and alcoholics. Substance abuse is nondiscriminatory and affects all women—rich, poor, young, old, urban, rural, professional, and homemaker.[196]

Though infrequently violent criminals, women who abuse substances are more likely to get involved in prostitution and low-level drug dealing; a few become top-level dealers. Many are pregnant or are already mothers, and because they share needles, they are at high risk of contracting AIDS and passing the HIV virus to their newborn children. They maintain a high risk of victimization. One study of 171 women using crack cocaine found that since initiating crack use, 62 percent reported suffering a physical attack and 32 percent suffered rape; more than half were forced to seek medical care for their injuries.[197]

DRUGS AND CRIME

One of the main reasons for the criminalization of particular substances is the assumed association between drug abuse and crime. People who use illicit drugs are more likely to engage in criminal activity; people involved in criminal activity are more likely to use drugs. While drug use does not turn people violent, it does increase the frequency of criminal activity.[198] Substance abuse appears to be an important precipitating factor in a variety of criminal acts, especially income-generating crimes such as burglary.[199]

Numerous self-report studies have examined the criminal activity of drug users. As a group, they show that people who take drugs also have extensive involvement in crime.[200] Youths who abuse alcohol are also the most likely to engage in violence during their life course; violent adolescents report histories of alcohol abuse. Adults with long histories of drinking are also more likely to report violent offending patterns.[201]

Arrestee Data ADAM II is a federal data collection program that shows drug use patterns among arrestees in five U.S. cities: Atlanta, Chicago, Denver, New York, and Sacramento. In each of these areas, drug use data on 10 illegal substances are collected from adult male arrestees, through voluntary interviews and drug tests, within 48 hours of arrest. The sample of almost 2,000 people was drawn from all adult males arrested, not just those arrested on drug charges.

What do the data show about the association between drug use and crime? In the most recent survey available (2013), the proportion of arrestees testing positive for any of the 10 drugs ranged from 63 percent in Atlanta to 83 percent in Chicago and Sacramento. Arrestees testing positive for multiple drugs in their system ranged from 12 percent in Atlanta to 50 percent in Sacramento. Marijuana remained the most commonly detected drug, from 34 percent of testing positive in Atlanta to 59 percent in Sacramento. Those who obtained marijuana in the prior 30 days reported little difficulty obtaining the drug, indicating an overall high availability of the drug in all sites. The most disturbing trend in the arrest data is that from 2000 to 2013 the proportion of arrestees testing positive for opiates (e.g., heroin, morphine, synthetic opiates) in their systems at the time of arrest rose significantly in all sites; for example, in Sacramento the rate doubled, from 4 to 8 percent, and in Denver it increased from 3 to 18 percent. On a more positive note, in 2013, cocaine use continued a significant decline in all sites since 2000, including the self-reported use of crack, which has declined more than 50 percent in most places since 2007. Despite these variations and trends, the drug–crime connection is strongly supported by the ADAM II data.[202]

Correctional Surveys   Another indication of a drug–crime connection is found in correctional surveys that disclose that many convicted criminals are lifelong substance abusers.[203] The most recent surveys show that the drug use rate among parolees is double that of the general population. Similarly, about 24 percent of adults on probation reported drug abuse, more than double the rate in the general population.[204]

Researchers at CASA found that approximately 85 percent of current inmates could benefit from drug abuse treatment. CASA estimates that 1.5 million of the current 2.3 million prison inmates meet the clinical criteria for substance abuse or addiction. Another 458,000 inmates have a history of substance abuse and either:

- Were under the influence of alcohol or other drugs at the time of their crime
- Committed their offense to get money to buy drugs
- Were incarcerated for alcohol or drug law violations

The CASA study also found that alcohol and drugs are significant factors in the commission of many crimes. Alcohol and drugs are involved in the following:

- 78 percent of violent crimes
- 83 percent of property crimes
- 77 percent of weapon offenses
- 77 percent of probation or parole violations[205]

These data seem to show a powerful connection between drug abuse, crime, and punishment.

Is There a Drug–Crime Connection?   It is of course possible that most criminals are not actually drug users but that police are more likely to apprehend muddle-headed substance abusers than clear-thinking abstainers. A second, and probably more plausible, interpretation is that most criminals are in fact substance abusers.

Although the drug–crime connection is powerful, the true relationship is still uncertain because many users have had a history of criminal activity before the onset of their substance abuse. It is possible that:

- Chronic criminal offenders begin to abuse drugs and alcohol *after* they have engaged in crime; that is, crime causes drug abuse.
- Substance abusers turn to a life of crime to support their habits; that is, the economics of drug abuse causes crime. Employed drug users don't commit crime, only those who need money to support their habits.
- Drug use and crime co-occur in individuals; that is, both crime and drug abuse are caused by some other common factor. Adolescents who are risk takers may abuse drugs and also commit crime.[206] Individuals with psychotic behavioral disorders may use drugs to self-medicate and are also prone to crime. Psychosis may bring on both drug abuse and criminality; particularly those who also abuse drugs and alcohol tend to engage in higher levels of violence than individuals with other forms of mental illness.[207]
- Drug users engage in activities that involve them with peers who encourage them to commit crime or support their criminal activity.[208] Kids who join gangs are more likely later to abuse substances and commit crime.
- Drug abusers face social problems that lead them to crime. They are more likely to drop out of school, be underemployed, engage in premarital sex, and become unmarried parents.[209] Social problems and not drug use are the cause of crime.

In sum, while there is no conclusive evidence that taking drugs turns otherwise law-abiding citizens into criminals, there are indications that people who commit crime also use drugs significantly more than the average citizen.[210] As addiction levels increase, so too do the frequency and seriousness of criminality. Even if the crime rate of drug users were actually half that reported in the research literature, users would be responsible for a significant portion of the total criminal activity in the United States.

DRUGS AND THE LAW

The federal government first initiated legal action to curtail the use of some drugs early in the twentieth century. In 1906, the Pure Food and Drug Act required manufacturers to list the amounts of habit-forming drugs in products on the labels but did not restrict their use. However, the act prohibited the importation and sale of opiates except for medicinal purposes. In 1914, the Harrison Narcotics Tax Act restricted importation, manufacture, sale, and dispensing of narcotics. It defined *narcotic* as any drug that induces sleep and relieves pain, such as heroin, morphine, and opium. The act was revised in 1922 to allow importation of opium and coca (cocaine) leaves for qualified medical practitioners. The Marihuana Tax Act of 1937 required registration and payment of a tax by all who imported, sold, or manufactured marijuana. Because marijuana was classified as a narcotic, those registering would also be subject to criminal penalty.

In later years, other federal laws were passed to clarify existing drug statutes and revise penalties. The Boggs Act of 1951 provided mandatory sentences for violating federal drug laws. The Durham-Humphrey Act of 1951 made it illegal to dispense barbiturates and amphetamines without a prescription. The Narcotic Control Act of 1956 increased penalties for drug offenders. In 1965, the Drug Abuse Control Act set up stringent guidelines for the legal use and sale of mood-modifying drugs, such as barbiturates, amphetamines, LSD, and any other "dangerous drugs," except narcotics prescribed by doctors and pharmacists. Illegal possession was punished as a misdemeanor and manufacture or sale as a felony. In 1970, the Comprehensive Drug Abuse Prevention and Control Act set up unified categories of illegal drugs and associated penalties with their sale, manufacture, or possession. The law gave the U.S. attorney general discretion to decide in which category to place any new drug.

Since then, various federal laws have attempted to increase penalties imposed on drug smugglers and limit the manufacture and sale of newly developed substances. The 1984 Controlled Substances Act set stringent penalties for drug dealers and created five categories of narcotic and non-narcotic substances subject to federal laws.[211] The Anti-Drug Abuse Act of 1986 again set new standards for minimum and maximum sentences for drug offenders, increased penalties for most offenses, and created a new drug penalty classification for large-scale offenses (such as trafficking in more than 1 kilogram of heroin), for which the penalty for a first offense was 10 years to life in prison.[212] With President George H. W. Bush's endorsement, Congress passed the Anti-Drug Abuse Act of 1988, which created a coordinated national drug policy under a "drug czar," set treatment and prevention priorities, and, symbolizing the government's hardline stance against drug dealing, imposed the death penalty for drug-related killings.[213]

For the most part, state laws mirror federal statutes. Some states now apply extremely heavy penalties for selling or distributing dangerous drugs, involving long prison sentences of up to 25 years. The main disconnect is in the sale and possession of marijuana for personal use, which more than 20 states, including Massachusetts, Colorado, and Washington, have either legalized or significantly decriminalized. In response, the federal government pledged not to enforce laws restricting marijuana in these states.[214]

DRUG CONTROL STRATEGIES

 LO9 Compare and contrast the different methods of drug control

Substance abuse remains a major social problem in the United States. Politicians looking for a safe campaign issue can take advantage of the public's fear of drug addiction by calling for a war on drugs even when drug usage is stable or in decline. Can these efforts pay off? Can illegal drug use be eliminated or controlled?

A number of drug control strategies have been tried with varying degrees of success. Some aim to deter drug use by stopping the flow of drugs into the country, apprehending and punishing dealers, and cracking down on street-level drug deals. Others focus on preventing drug use by educating potential users to the dangers of substance abuse (convincing them to "say no to drugs") and by organizing community groups to work with the at-risk population in their area. Still another approach is to treat known users so they can control their addictions. Some of these efforts are discussed here.

Source Control One approach to drug control is to deter the production, sale, and importation of drugs through the systematic destruction of crops and apprehension of large-volume drug dealers, coupled with the enforcement of strict drug laws that carry heavy penalties. This approach is designed to capture and punish known international drug dealers and deter those who are considering entering the drug trade. A major effort has been made to cut off supplies of drugs by destroying overseas crops and arresting members of drug cartels in Central and South America, Asia, and the Middle East, where many drugs are grown and manufactured. The federal government has been in the vanguard of encouraging exporting nations to step up efforts to destroy drug crops and prosecute dealers.

One approach is to use manual and/or aerial spray to eradicate crops before they can be harvested. Eradication is an important element in the strategy for reducing potential cocaine production in Peru, and aerial spray is an important tool in remote and insecure areas where manual eradication is cost prohibitive or too dangerous. Spraying is not without its danger. The Colombian government reported 32 police, military, and civilian eradicator fatalities and nearly 150 injured personnel as a result of improvised explosive devices, sniper fire, and other attacks during their manual eradication operations in 2010.[215]

But even with such human costs, translating words into deeds is a formidable task. Drug lords are willing and able to fight back through intimidation, violence, and corruption when necessary. Transnational gangs (see Chapter 13) are actively involved in the drug trade and are immune from prosecution because they are active in areas where the United States has little influence.[216] War and terrorism make source control strategies problematic. Despite government efforts, cocaine production has actually risen in Peru's remote tropical valleys, helping it to surpass Colombia as the world's largest exporter of cocaine. Peruvian traffickers now grow about 285 tons of cocaine each year compared to Colombia's 245 tons.[217]

Interdiction Strategies   Law enforcement efforts have also been directed at intercepting drug supplies as they enter the country. Border patrols and military personnel using sophisticated hardware have been involved in massive interdiction efforts; many impressive multimillion-dollar seizures have been made.

While law enforcement efforts are impressive, U.S. borders are so vast and unprotected that total interdiction is impossible. Drug importers have dug cross-border tunnels to evade detection, use go-fast boats and constantly changing trans-shipment points, use an army of "drug mules" to trans-ship narcotics, and may be bribing border guards to look the other way when drug shipments pass through their checkpoints.[218] Take the importation of cocaine, for example. Government sources indicate that despite control efforts the overall flow of cocaine from South America to the United States has remained relatively stable for the past few years. The use of go-fast boats to haul cocaine across the ocean (Figure 14.3) has resulted in decreased seizures, allowing more cocaine than ever to enter U.S. markets. Approximately 480 metric tons of cocaine now enter the country each year.[219]

What would happen if the government was successful and all importation of illegal substances was shut down? It's possible that homegrown marijuana and laboratory-made drugs, such as "ice," LSD, and PCP, could become the drugs of choice. Even now, their easy availability and relatively low cost are increasing their popularity among the at-risk population.

Law Enforcement Strategies
It made headlines around the world when Joaquin "El Chapo" Guzmán, the head of Mexico's Sinaloa cartel, was captured in the beach resort town of Mazatlán in 2014. Convicted and sent to prison, El Chapo was able to escape via an elaborate tunnel only to be recaptured on January 8, 2016.[220] During his recapture by Mexican marines, a shootout occurred in which five gunmen

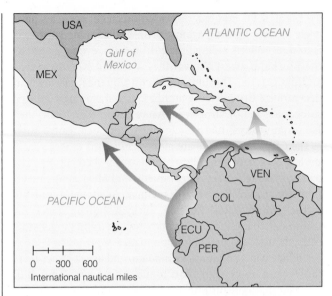

FIGURE 14.3 The Flow of Cocaine from Producing Nations

SOURCE: Office of National Drug Control Policy, "Cocaine Smuggling in 2013," https://www.whitehouse.gov/sites/default/files/ondcp/international-partnerships -content/cocaine_smuggling_in_2013_digital_1505-05221.pdf.

were killed and one marine was wounded. Found on the premises were two armored cars, eight assault rifles, including two sniper rifles, two M16 rifles with grenade launchers, and a loaded rocket-propelled grenade launcher.[221]

On January 8, 2016, Joaquin Guzmán, the world's most-wanted drug trafficker, is escorted by Mexican security forces at a Navy hangar in Mexico City. Guzmán, known as El Chapo, was recaptured by Mexican authorities six months after he escaped from a maximum-security prison by slipping into an elaborate tunnel under his shower, thus humiliating the government that had promised tougher public order.

Bloomberg/Getty Images

Local, state, and federal law enforcement agencies have been actively fighting against drug dealers. One approach is to direct efforts at large-scale drug rings, even though (as the El Chapo arrest shows) they are often heavily armed and dangerous. The long-term consequence has been to decentralize drug dealing and has encouraged new groups to become major suppliers. Asian, Latin American, and Jamaican groups, motorcycle clubs, and local gangs such as the Crips and Bloods are all now involved in large-scale dealing. Colombian syndicates have established cocaine distribution centers on every continent, and Mexican organizations are responsible for large methamphetamine shipments to the United States. Russian, Turkish, Italian, Nigerian, Chinese, Lebanese, and Pakistani heroin trafficking syndicates are now competing for dominance.

Police can also target, intimidate, and arrest street-level dealers and users in an effort to make drug use so much of a hassle that consumption is cut back and the crime rate reduced. Some departments use reverse stings, in which undercover agents pose as dealers to arrest users who approach them for a buy.

In terms of weight and availability, there is still no commodity more lucrative than illegal drugs. They cost relatively little to produce and provide large profit margins to dealers and traffickers. It is difficult for law enforcement agencies to counteract the inducement of drug profits. When large-scale drug busts are made, supplies become scarce and market values increase, encouraging more people to enter the drug trade. There are also suspicions that a displacement effect occurs: stepped-up efforts to curb drug dealing in one area or city simply encourage dealers to seek out friendlier territory.[222]

Punishment Strategies   Even if law enforcement efforts cannot produce a general deterrent effect, the courts may achieve the required result by severely punishing known drug dealers and traffickers. A number of initiatives have made the prosecution and punishment of drug offenders a top priority. State prosecutors have expanded their investigations into drug importation and distribution and created special prosecutors to focus on drug dealers. Once convicted, drug dealers can get very long sentences.

However, these efforts often have their downside. Defense attorneys consider delay tactics to be sound legal maneuvering in drug-related cases. Courts are so backlogged that prosecutors are anxious to plea bargain. The consequence of this legal maneuvering is that more than 25 percent of people convicted on drug charges are granted probation or some other form of community release. Of those incarcerated, about half received a few months of jail time, and the rest, about 34 percent, were sent to prison. Even if incarcerated in prison, the median sentence for drug offenders was about 24 months.[223]

It is unlikely that the public would approve of a drug control strategy that locks up large numbers of traffickers; research indicates that the public already believes drug trafficking penalties are too harsh (while supporting the level of punishment for other crimes).[224] And some critics are disturbed because punishment strategies seem to have a disproportionate effect on minority group members, who face far higher arrest rates despite the fact that their drug use is no greater than members of the white majority.[225]

Community Strategies   Another type of drug control effort relies on the involvement of local community groups to lead the fight against drugs. Representatives of various local government agencies, churches, civic organizations, and similar institutions are being brought together to create drug prevention and awareness programs.

Citizen-sponsored programs attempt to restore a sense of community in drug-infested areas, reduce fear, and promote conventional norms and values.[226] These efforts can be classified into four distinct categories:[227]

- *Law enforcement–type efforts.* These may include block watches, cooperative police–community efforts, and citizen patrols. Some of these citizen groups are nonconfrontational: they simply observe or photograph dealers, write down their license plate numbers, and then notify police. On occasion, telephone hotlines have been set up to take anonymous tips on drug activity. Other groups engage in confrontational tactics that may even include citizens' arrests. Area residents have gone as far as contracting with private security firms to conduct neighborhood patrols.
- *Using the civil justice system to harass offenders.* Landlords have been sued for owning properties that house drug dealers, and neighborhood groups have scrutinized drug houses for building code violations. Information acquired from these various sources is turned over to local authorities, such as police and housing agencies, for more formal action.
- *Community-based treatment efforts.* Some of these programs utilize citizen volunteers who participate in self-help support programs. Some, such as Narcotics Anonymous or Cocaine Anonymous, have more than 1,000 chapters nationally. Other programs provide youths with martial arts training, dancing, and social events as an alternative to the drug life.
- *Enhancing the quality of life, improving interpersonal relationships, and upgrading the neighborhood's physical environment.* Activities might include the creation of drug-free school zones (which encourage police to keep drug dealers away from the vicinity of schools) and consciousness-raising efforts such as demonstrations and marches to publicize the drug problem and build solidarity among participants.

Education Strategies   According to this view, substance abuse would decline if kids could be taught about the dangers of drug use. The most widely known drug education program, Drug Abuse Resistance Education (D.A.R.E.), began as an elementary school course designed to give students the skills for resisting peer pressure to experiment with tobacco, drugs, and alcohol. Research in the 1990s found that D.A.R.E. made only a marginal impact on student drug use and attitudes.[228] These evaluations caused D.A.R.E. to revise its curriculum. It is now a K-12 program primarily aimed at older students and relies more on having them question their assumptions about drug use than on listening to lectures on the subject.

D.A.R.E. is not the only school-based drug abuse prevention program; some of the most widely used are set out in Exhibit 14.3.

EXHIBIT 14.3

Widely Used School-Based Drug Prevention Programs

- *Caring School Community Program (formerly Child Development Project).* This is a universal family-plus-school program to reduce risk and strengthen protective factors among elementary school children. The program focuses on strengthening students' sense of community and connection to school. Research shows that this sense of community has been key to reducing drug use, violence, and mental health problems, while promoting academic motivation and achievement.

- *Classroom-Centered (CC) and Family-School Partnership (FSP) Intervention.* These are universal 1st-grade interventions to reduce later onset of violence and aggressive behavior and to improve academic performance. Program strategies include classroom management and organizational strategies, reading and mathematics curricula, parent–teacher communication, and children's behavior management in the home.

- *Guiding Good Choices (GGC) (formerly Preparing for the Drug-Free Years).* This curriculum was designed to educate parents on how to reduce risk factors and strengthen bonding in their families. In five two-hour sessions, parents are taught skills in family involvement and interaction; setting clear expectations, monitoring behavior, and maintaining discipline; and other family management and bonding approaches.

- *Life Skills Training (LST).* LST is a universal program for middle school students designed to address a wide range of risk and protective factors by teaching general personal and social skills, along with drug resistance skills and education. An elementary school version was recently developed, and the LST booster program for high school students helps to retain the gains of the middle school program.

- *Lions-Quest Skills for Adolescence (SFA).* SFA is a commercially available, universal, life skills education program for middle school students in use in schools nationwide. The focus is on teaching skills for building self-esteem and personal responsibility, communication, decision making, resisting social influences and asserting rights, and increasing drug use knowledge and consequences.

- *Project ALERT.* Project ALERT is a two-year universal program for middle school students, designed to reduce the onset and regular use of drugs among youth. It focuses on preventing the use of alcohol, tobacco, marijuana, and inhalants. Project ALERT Plus, an enhanced version, has added a high school component, which is being tested in 45 rural communities.

- *Project STAR.* Project STAR is a comprehensive drug abuse prevention community program to be used by schools, parents, community organizations, the media, and health policy makers. The middle school portion focuses on social influence and is included in classroom instruction by trained teachers over a two-year timetable. The parent program helps parents work with children on homework, learn family communication skills, and get involved in community action.

- *Promoting Alternative Thinking Strategies (PATHS).* PATHS is a comprehensive program for promoting emotional health and social skills. The program also focuses on reducing aggression and behavior problems in elementary school children, while enhancing the educational process in the classroom.

- *Skills, Opportunity, and Recognition (SOAR).* This universal school-based intervention for grades 1 through 6 seeks to reduce childhood risks for delinquency and drug abuse by enhancing protective factors. The multicomponent intervention combines training for teachers, parents, and children during the elementary grades to promote children's bonding to school, positive school behavior, and academic achievement.

- *Strengthening Families Program: For Parents and Youth 10–14 (SFP 10–14).* This universal evidence-based program offers seven two-hour sessions, each attended by youth and their parents, and is designed to help families have better communication skills, teach peer pressure skills, and prevent teen substance abuse. It has been conducted through partnerships that include state university researchers, cooperative extension staff, local schools, and other community organizations.

- *National Drug and Alcohol Facts Week (NDAFW).* This is a national health observance for teens to promote local events that use the National Institute on Drug Abuse's "NIDA science" to "shatter the myths" about drugs.

SOURCES: National Institute on Drug Abuse, "Preventing Drug Use Among Children and Adolescents," https://www.drugabuse.gov/publications/preventing-drug-abuse-among-children-adolescents/preface; NIDA for Teens, "National Drug and Alcohol Facts Week," https://teens.drugabuse.gov/national-drug-alcohol-facts-week; Melissa H. Stigler, Emily Neusel, and Cheryl L. Perry, "School-Based Programs to Prevent and Reduce Alcohol Use Among Youth," *Alcohol Research and Health* 34 (2012), http://pubs.niaaa.nih.gov/publications/arh342/157-162.htm. (URLs accessed June 2016.)

Drug-Testing Strategies Drug testing of students, private employees, government workers, and criminal offenders is believed to deter substance abuse. In the workplace, employees are tested to enhance on-the-job safety and productivity. In some industries, such as mining and transportation, drug testing is considered essential because abuse can pose a threat to the public.[229] Mandatory drug-testing programs in government and industry have become routine. The federal government requires employee testing in regulated industries such as nuclear energy and defense contracting. About 4 million transportation workers are subject to testing.

Drug testing is also part of the federal government's Drug-Free Workplace Program, which has the goal of improving productivity and safety. Employees most likely to be tested include presidential appointees, law enforcement officers, and people in positions of national security.

Criminal defendants are now routinely tested at all stages of the justice system, from arrest to parole. The goal is to reduce criminal behavior by detecting current users and curbing their abuse. Can such programs reduce criminal activity? Two evaluations of pretrial drug-testing programs found little evidence that monitoring defendants' drug use influenced their behavior.[230]

Schools have adopted drug testing of students and there is some evidence that random tests can reduce drug use among youth. Those who favor student testing believe it may also help improve the learning environment in schools by diminishing the culture of drugs without sacrificing school morale.[231]

Drug Treatment Strategies A number of approaches are taken to treat known users, getting them clean of drugs and alcohol, and thereby reducing the at-risk population. One approach rests on the assumption that each user is an individual, and successful treatment must be geared to the using patterns and personality of the individual offenders in order to build a sense of self.[232] Some programs have placed abusers in regimens of outdoor activities and wilderness training to create self-reliance and a sense of accomplishment.[233] Others focus on problem-solving skills, helping former and current addicts deal with their real-world issues.[234] Providing supportive housing for formerly homeless drug addicts may also lead to better access to medical care, food, and job opportunities—all of which result in lower levels of addiction.[235]

More intensive efforts use group therapy approaches relying on group leaders who have been substance abusers; through such sessions users get the skills and support to help them reject social pressure to use drugs. These programs are based on the Alcoholics Anonymous approach, which holds that users must find within themselves the strength to stay clean and that peer support from those who understand their experiences can help them achieve a drug-free life.

Some detoxification efforts use medical procedures to wean patients from the more addicting drugs to others, such as methadone, that can be more easily regulated. Methadone is a drug similar to heroin, and addicts can be treated at clinics where they receive methadone under controlled conditions. However, methadone programs have been undermined because some users sell their methadone on the black market and others supplement their dosages with illegally obtained heroin. Other programs utilize drugs such as Naxalone, which counter the effects of narcotics and ease the trauma of withdrawal.[236] Others, such as Naltrexone, are used in conjunction with counseling and social support to help people who have already terminated their substance abuse and help them avoid drinking or using drugs. Naltrexone works by blocking the effects of heroin or other opioids at their receptor sites. Medications have also been developed to ease withdrawal symptoms and help the transition to a drug-free life. Other therapeutic programs attempt to deal with the psychological causes of drug use. Hypnosis, aversion therapy (getting users to associate drugs with unpleasant sensations, such as nausea), counseling, biofeedback, and other techniques are often used.

Some treatment programs are delivered on an outpatient basis while others rely on residential care. Which approach is better is still being debated. A stay in a residential program may stigmatize people as addicts and while in treatment they may be introduced to other users with whom they will associate after release. Users do not often enter these programs voluntarily and have little motivation to change.[237]

The best treatment for drug use may be a continuum of care that includes a customized treatment regimen—addressing all aspects of an individual's life, including medical and mental health services—and follow-up options (e.g., community- or family-based recovery support systems) that can be crucial to a person's success in achieving and maintaining a drug-free lifestyle.[238] Exhibit 14.4 covers the most commonly used and relevant treatment strategies. However, relatively few drug-dependent people actually receive the treatment efforts they so desperately need. Many people who need treatment are unaware or in denial. And even those who could be helped soon learn that there are simply more users who need treatment than there are beds in treatment facilities. Many facilities are restricted to users whose health insurance will pay for short-term residential care; when their insurance coverage ends, patients are often released, even though their treatment is incomplete.

Supporters of treatment argue that many addicts are helped by intensive inpatient and outpatient treatment. As one District of Columbia program shows, clients who complete treatment programs are less likely to use drugs than those who drop out.[239] Although such data support treatment strategies, it is also possible that completers are

EXHIBIT 14.4

Effective Treatment Approaches

MEDICATIONS

Medications can be used to help with different aspects of the treatment process.

- *Withdrawal.* Medications offer help in suppressing withdrawal symptoms during detoxification. Patients who go through medically assisted withdrawal but do not receive any further treatment show drug abuse patterns similar to those who were never treated.
- *Treatment.* Medications can be used to help reestablish normal brain function and to prevent relapse and diminish cravings. Medications are now available for treating opioids (heroin, morphine), tobacco (nicotine), and alcohol addiction; others are being developed for treating stimulant (cocaine, methamphetamine) and cannabis (marijuana) addiction. A significant problem: many addicts are polydrug users, requiring multiple medications.

BEHAVIORAL TREATMENTS

Behavioral treatments help patients engage in the treatment process, modify their attitudes and behaviors related to drug abuse, and increase healthy life skills. These treatments can also enhance the effectiveness of medications and help people stay in treatment longer. Outpatient behavioral treatment encompasses a wide variety of programs for patients who visit a clinic at regular intervals. Most of the programs involve individual or group drug counseling. Some programs also offer other forms of behavioral treatment such as:

- *Cognitive-behavioral therapy*, which seeks to help patients recognize, avoid, and cope with the situations in which they are most likely to abuse drugs
- *Multidimensional family therapy*, which was developed for adolescents with drug abuse problems—as well as their families—and addresses a range of influences on their drug abuse patterns and is designed to improve overall family functioning
- *Motivational interviewing*, which capitalizes on the readiness of individuals to change their behavior and enter treatment
- *Motivational incentives* (contingency management), which uses positive reinforcement to encourage abstinence from drugs

Residential treatment programs can also be very effective, especially for those with more severe problems. *Therapeutic communities* (TCs) are highly structured programs in which patients remain at a residence, typically for 6 to 12 months. TCs differ from other treatment approaches principally in their use of the community—treatment staff and those in recovery—as a key agent of change to influence patient attitudes, perceptions, and behaviors associated with drug use.

Patients in TCs may include those with relatively long histories of drug addiction, involvement in serious criminal activities, and seriously impaired social functioning. TCs are now also being designed to accommodate the needs of women who are pregnant or have children. The focus of the TC is on the resocialization of the patient to a drug-free, crime-free lifestyle.

SOURCE: National Institute on Drug Abuse, "DrugFacts: Treatment Approaches for Drug Addiction," http://www.drugabuse.gov/publications/drugfacts /treatment-approaches-drug-addiction (accessed June 2016).

---

motivated individuals who would have stopped using drugs even if they had not been treated.

In order to aid in dispensing treatment, state jurisdictions have developed specialized drug courts. These are described in the Policy and Practice in Criminology feature.

Employment Programs   There have been a number of efforts to provide vocational rehabilitation for drug abusers. One approach is the supported work program, which typically involves job-site training, ongoing assessment, and job-site intervention. Rather than teach work skills in a classroom, support programs rely on helping drug abusers deal with real work settings. Other programs that have merit provide training to overcome barriers to employment and improve work skills, including help with motivation, education, experience, the job market, job-seeking skills, and personal issues.[240]

Does providing work experiences help reduce drug use? In one of the most comprehensive studies of this issue, Christopher Uggen and Sarah Shannon interviewed young adults leaving drug treatment to find out whether finding employment helped reduce their substance abuse levels. They found that while finding employment did not actually reduce subjects' dependence on cocaine and/or heroin, it did correlate favorably with reducing their involvement in crime. The rate of robbery and burglary arrests fell by approximately 46 percent for the users who found meaningful work. The implication is that drugs themselves are not a cause of crime; rather, it's the lack of income experienced by most users that accounts for their involvement in criminal activity.[241]

DRUG LEGALIZATION

 State the arguments for and against legalizing drugs

In terms of weight and availability, there is still no commodity more lucrative than illegal drugs. They cost relatively little to produce and provide large profit margins to dealers and traffickers. At the current average street price

Drug Courts

The mission of drug courts is to stop the abuse of alcohol and other drugs and related criminal activity by offenders. Drug courts handle cases involving drug-addicted offenders through an extensive supervision and treatment program. In exchange for successful completion of the program, the court may dismiss the original charge, reduce or set aside a sentence, offer some lesser penalty, or offer a combination of these. The aim is to place nonviolent first offenders into intensive treatment programs rather than in jail or prison.

The drug court movement began in 1989, when the Dade County (Miami) Circuit Court developed an intensive, community-based treatment, rehabilitation, and supervision program for felony drug defendants designed to reduce recidivism rates. There are now more than 3,400 drug courts in operation with hundreds more being planned or developed.

Drug court diverts nonviolent, substance abusing offenders from prison and jail into treatment. By increasing direct supervision of offenders, coordinating public resources, and expediting case processing, drug courts can help break the cycle of criminal behavior, alcohol and drug use, and incarceration. The most recent research indicates that drug court reduces crime by lowering rearrest and conviction rates, improving substance abuse treatment outcomes, and reuniting families, and also produces measurable cost benefits.

Drug courts address the overlap between the public health threats of drug abuse and crime: crimes are often drug related; drug abusers are frequently involved with the criminal justice system. Drug courts provide an ideal setting to address these problems by linking the justice system with health services and drug treatment providers while easing the burden on the already overtaxed correctional system.

Are Drug Courts Effective?

The U.S. government has a great deal of confidence in drug courts and points to most recent research on programs around the nation, which taken in sum confirms that drug courts are successful. There are numerous success stories. One study of nine adult drug courts in California reported that rearrest rates over a four-year period were 29 percent for drug court clients (and only 17 percent for those completing the program) as compared to 41 percent for similar drug offenders who did not participate in a drug court program. Another study of four adult drug courts in Massachusetts found that drug court participants were 13 percent less likely to be rearrested, 34 percent less likely to be reconvicted, and 24 percent less likely to be reincarcerated than probationers who had been carefully matched to the drug court participants. These evidence-based evaluations support the utility of the drug court concept. The National Institute of Justice's Multisite Adult Drug Court Evaluation found that participants reported less criminal activity and had fewer rearrests than similar offenders processed under traditional court procedures. Drug court participants also reported less drug use (56 percent versus 76 percent) and were less likely to test positive for drug use than those processed in traditional courts. Treatment investment costs were higher for participants but with less recidivism, so drug courts saved an overall average of $5,680 to $6,208 per offender. Drug courts that target offenders with high criminogenic risk and high substance abuse treatment needs yield the most effective interventions and maximize return on investment.

Not Everyone Agrees

While this research is reassuring, drug courts have been criticized by the influential Drug Policy Alliance, a nonprofit organization dedicated to reforming the nation's drug laws. According to the Alliance, drug courts often "cherry pick" people expected to do well anyway, many of whom are in drug court because of a petty drug law violation, including marijuana. As a result, drug courts do not typically divert people from lengthy prison terms. Because they focus on low-level offenses, even positive results for individual participants translate into little public safety benefit to the community. Treatment in the community, whether voluntary or probation-supervised, often produces better results. The Alliance also finds that drug courts leave many people worse off than if they had received drug treatment outside the criminal justice system, had been left alone, or even had been conventionally sentenced. The successes represent only some of those who pass through drug courts and only a tiny fraction of people arrested. One reason is that drug court participants spend more days in jail *while in drug court* than if they had been conventionally sentenced, but participants deemed "failures" may actually face longer sentences than those who did not enter drug court in the first place (often because they lost the opportunity to plead to a lesser charge). The participants, they conclude, who stand the best chance of succeeding in drug courts are those without a drug problem, while those struggling with compulsive drug use are more likely to end up incarcerated.

 CRITICAL THINKING

1. Are drug treatment programs doomed to failure because there are so many different types of drug abusers, with entirely different motivations?
2. Are drug courts inherently coercive? Should drug users be forced to go into treatment?

SOURCES: National Institute of Justice, Bureau of Justice Assistance, Office of Juvenile Justice and Delinquency Prevention, "Drug Courts," May 2016, https://www.ncjrs.gov/pdffiles1 /nij/238527.pdf; Drug Policy Alliance, "Moving Away from Drug Courts: Toward a Health -Centered Approach to Drug Use," http://www .drugpolicy.org/resource/moving-away-drug -courts-toward-health-centered-approach-drug -use. (URLs accessed June 2016.)

of $170 per gram in the United States, a metric ton of pure cocaine is worth more than $150 million; cutting it and reducing purity can double or triple the value.[242] With that kind of profit to be made, can any strategy, whether it be treatment or punishment oriented, reduce the lure of drug trafficking? The futility of drug control efforts is illustrated by the fact that despite massive long-term efforts the price of illegal narcotics such as crack cocaine and heroin has drifted downward as supplies become more plentiful. Considering these problems, some commentators have called for the legalization or decriminalization of restricted drugs.

Despite the massive effort to control drugs through prevention, deterrence, education, and treatment strategies, the fight against substance abuse is always difficult. There are enormous profits involved in the drug trade, and few treatment efforts have been successful. There is no uniform method of drug control; some use enforcement and punishment and others rely on treatment and rehabilitation. While the former approach requires drug users to be secretive and discreet in order to avoid detection, the latter demands openness and receptivity to treatment.[243] Some experts believe that the only effective way to deal with the drug problem is through legalization of most drugs and decriminalization of drug offenses. Legalization is warranted because the use of mood-altering substances is customary in almost all human societies; people have always wanted—and will find ways of obtaining—psychoactive drugs.[244]

The Drug Policy Alliance, a national organization dedicated to ending the war against drugs, cites a number of reasons why the drug war should end and drugs should be decriminalized:

- Since the war on drugs began, the Supreme Court has sent a consistent message that when it comes to fighting drug crime, privacy and personal liberties take a back seat. In most drug-related cases brought before the Court, the majority has favored scaling back constitutional protections, clearing the way for drug policies that infringe on our rights to free speech, religious expression, and protection from unreasonable searches. Police now routinely search individuals without cause, raid homes on flimsy evidence, and engage in racial profiling. Employers, schools, and hospitals may conduct suspicionless drug testing.
- Public health problems like HIV and hepatitis C are all exacerbated by draconian laws that keep users in hiding and restrict their access to clean needles. And when they get caught and go to prison their families suffer: children of inmates are at risk of educational failure, joblessness, addiction, and delinquency. People suffering from cancer, AIDS, and other debilitating illnesses are regularly denied access to their medicine or even arrested and prosecuted for using medical marijuana.
- Policies that exclude and discriminate against people with a conviction are numerous and varied and have

effectively created a permanent second-class status for millions of Americans. Given the systemic racism inherent in the drug war, these lifelong exclusions inequitably affect individuals and communities of color. A drug arrest can result in even a legal resident's deportation.

- A drug arrest can result in denying child custody, voting rights, employment, business loans, trade licensing, student aid, and even public housing and other public assistance. Relative to the crime being committed, the punishments for drug law violations are unjustifiably harsh and cause more harm than the drug itself.
- The drug war creates racial discrimination by law enforcement and disproportionate drug war misery suffered by communities of color. Although rates of drug use and selling are comparable across racial lines, people of color are far more likely to be stopped, searched, arrested, prosecuted, convicted, and incarcerated for drug law violations than are whites. The mass criminalization of people of color, particularly young African American men, is as profound a system of racial control as the Jim Crow laws were in this country until the mid-1960s.
- The drug war is responsible for hundreds of billions of wasted tax dollars and misallocated government spending, as well as devastating human costs that far outweigh the damage caused by drugs alone. The war on drugs has also driven the drug trade underground, creating a violent illicit market that is responsible for far too many lost lives and broken communities. Organized crime, gangs, and drug cartels have the most to gain financially from prohibition, and these profits can easily be funneled into arms smuggling, violence, and corruption. The devastation wrought by Mexican cartels in particular has made it far too costly to continue with a failed prohibition strategy.

The DPA is not the only organization to note the expense created by the so-called war on drugs. According to Cato Institute researchers Jeffrey Miron and Katherine Waldock, drug control is now costing $40 billion a year. Not only would legalization save the government enforcement money, it would yield tax revenue of $46.7 billion annually, assuming legal drugs were taxed at rates comparable to those on alcohol and tobacco. Approximately $8.7 billion of this revenue would result from legalization of marijuana and $38 billion from legalization of other drugs.[245]

If drugs were legalized, the argument goes, price and distribution could be controlled by the government. This would reduce addicts' cash requirements, so crime rates would drop because users would no longer need the same cash flow to support their habits. Drug-related deaths would decline because government control would reduce needle sharing and the spread of AIDS. Legalization would also destroy the drug-importing cartels and gangs.

Because drugs would be bought and sold openly, the government would reap a tax windfall both from taxes on the sale of drugs and from income taxes paid by drug dealers on profits that have been part of the hidden economy. The profits of legalized drugs can already be viewed in states like Washington and Colorado where tax on legalized marijuana is bringing in millions to state coffers. Sales of legal marijuana have reached the billion-dollar mark in Colorado, producing more than $100 million in state taxes.[246] Of course, drug distribution would be regulated, like alcohol, keeping drugs away from adolescents, public servants such as police and airline pilots, and known felons.

The Consequences of Legalization Critics claim the legalization approach might have the short-term effect of reducing the crime rate, but it might also have grave social consequences. Legalization would increase the nation's rate of drug usage, creating an even larger group of non-productive, drug-dependent people who must be cared for by the rest of society.[247] If drugs were legalized and freely available, drug users might significantly increase their daily intake. In countries like Iran and Thailand, where drugs are cheap and readily available, the rate of narcotics use is quite high. Historically, the availability of cheap narcotics has preceded drug-use epidemics, as was the case when British and American merchants sold opium in nineteenth-century China. Furthermore, if the government tried to raise money by taxing legal drugs, as it now does with liquor and cigarettes, that might encourage drug smuggling to avoid tax payments, creating a black market supply chain; these "illegal" drugs might then fall into the hands of adolescents.

There are also health concerns. Because women may more easily become dependent on crack than men, the number of drug-dependent babies could begin to match or exceed the number delivered with fetal alcohol syndrome.[248] Drunk-driving fatalities, which today number about 10,000 per year, might be matched by deaths due to driving under the influence of pot or crack. And although distribution would be regulated, it is likely that adolescents would have the same opportunity to obtain potent drugs as they now have to obtain alcoholic beverages.

The debate over drug legalization rages on. While the Washington and Colorado legalization experiments have produced dividends in terms of tax money for education and other expenses, it is still too early to tell whether applying the policy to other drugs would yield similar benefits. Nor can it be determined what effect an across-the-board drug legalization policy could have on crime and health rates. The answers to these issues have proven elusive.

Concept Summary 14.1 summarizes the various drug control efforts.

CONCEPT SUMMARY 14.1
Drug Control Strategies

CONTROL STRATEGY	MAIN FOCUS	PROBLEMS/ISSUES
Source control	Destroy overseas crops and drug labs	Drug profits hard to resist; drug crops in hostile nations are off limits
Interdiction	Seal borders; arrest drug couriers	Extensive U.S. borders hard to control
Law enforcement	Police investigation and arrest of dealers	New dealers are recruited to replace those in prison
Punishment	Deter dealers with harsh punishments	Crowded prisons promote bargain justice
Community programs	Help community members deal with drug problems on the local level	Relies on community cohesion and efficacy
Drug education	Teach kids about the harm of taking drugs	Evaluations do not show programs are effective
Drug testing	Threaten employees with drug tests to deter use	Evaluations do not show drug testing is effective; people cheat on tests
Treatment	Use of therapy to get people off drugs	Expensive; requires motivation; clients associate with other users
Employment	Provide jobs as an alternative to drugs	Requires that former addicts become steady employees
Legalization	Decriminalize or legalize drugs	Political hot potato; danger of creating more users

LO1 Clarify the association between law and morality

Public order crimes are acts considered illegal because they conflict with social policy, accepted moral rules, and public opinion. There is usually great debate over public order crimes. Some charge that they are not really crimes at all and that it is foolish to legislate morality. Others view such morally tinged acts as prostitution, gambling, and drug abuse as harmful and therefore subject to public control.

LO2 Interpret what is meant by the term *social harm*

According to the theory of social harm, acts become crimes when they cause injury and produce harm to others. However, some dangerous activities are not considered crimes and others that do not appear harmful are criminalized. It is legal to sell cigarettes and alcohol though they may be more dangerous than illicit drugs. Fast sports cars are legal though more people are killed in traffic accidents from drug overdoses.

LO3 Give examples of the activities of moral crusaders

Moral crusaders seek to shape the law toward their own way of thinking. These moral entrepreneurs go on moral crusades to take on such issues as prayer in school, gun ownership, abortion, and the distribution of sexually explicit books and magazines. One such movement, the gay marriage crusade, has resulted in the legalization of same-sex marriage on a national level.

LO4 Describe the various forms of outlawed deviant sexuality

Outlawed sexual behavior, known as paraphilias, include such acts as: frotteurism, rubbing against or touching a nonconsenting person in a crowd, elevator, or other public area; voyeurism, obtaining sexual pleasure from spying on a stranger while he or she disrobes or engages in sexual behavior with another; exhibitionism, deriving sexual pleasure from exposing the genitals to surprise or shock a stranger; sadomasochism, deriving pleasure from receiving pain or inflicting pain on another; and pedophilia, attaining sexual pleasure through sexual activity with prepubescent children.

LO5 Summarize the history of prostitution and review what the term means today

Prostitution has been known for thousands of years. The earliest record of prostitution appears in ancient Mesopotamia, where priests engaged in sex to promote fertility in the community. Modern commercial sex appears to have its roots in ancient Greece. Today, prostitution can be defined as granting nonmarital sexual access, established by mutual agreement of the prostitutes, their clients, and their employers, for remuneration.

LO6 Distinguish between the different types of prostitutes

Prostitutes who work the streets in plain sight of police, citizens, and customers are referred to as hustlers, hookers, or streetwalkers. B-girls spend their time in bars, drinking and waiting to be picked up by customers. Brothel prostitutes live in a house with a madam who employs them, supervises their behavior, and receives a fee for her services. Call girls work via telephone "dates," get their clients by word of mouth or by making arrangements with bellhops, cab drivers, and so on. Some escort services are fronts for prostitution rings. Prostitutes known as circuit travelers move around in groups of two or three to lumber, labor, and agricultural camps. Prostitutes set up personal websites or put listings on web boards that carry personals.

LO7 Explain what is meant by the terms *obscenity* and *pornography*

Pornography involves the production, distribution, and sale of sexually explicit material intended to sexually excite paying customers. The depiction of sex and nudity is not illegal, but it does violate the law when it is judged obscene. *Obscenity* is a legal term that today is defined as material offensive to community standards. Legally, something is considered obscene if the average person applying contemporary community standards would find that the work taken as a whole appeals to the prurient interest; that the work depicts or describes prohibited sexual conduct; and the work, taken as a whole, lacks serious literary, artistic, political, or scientific value. Thus, each local jurisdiction must decide what pornographic material is obscene. A growing problem is the exploitation of children in obscene materials (kiddie porn), which has been expanded through the Internet.

LO8 Assess the causes of substance abuse

The onset of drug use can be tied to such factors as racial prejudice, devalued identities, low self-esteem, poor socioeconomic status, and the high level of mistrust, negativism, and defiance found in impoverished areas. Some experts have linked substance abuse to psychological deficits such as impaired cognitive functioning, personality disturbance, and emotional problems. Substance abuse may have a genetic basis. Social psychologists suggest that drug abuse may also result from observing parental drug use. Substance abuse may be just one of many social problem behaviors. Some may use drugs and alcohol because they want to enjoy their effects: get high, relax, improve creativity, escape reality, and increase sexual responsiveness.

LO9 Compare and contrast the different methods of drug control

A number of different drug control strategies have been tried, with varying degrees of success. Some aim to deter drug use by stopping the flow of drugs into the country, apprehending and punishing dealers, and cracking down on street-level drug deals. Others focus on preventing drug use by educating potential users to the dangers of substance abuse (convincing them to "say no to drugs") and by organizing community groups to work with the at-risk population in their area. Still another approach is to treat known users so they can control their addictions.

L010 State the arguments for and against legalizing drugs

Drugs should be legalized because the money spent on control could be used on education and economic development. People have always wanted, and will find ways of obtaining, psychoactive drugs. The drug war causes many health problems like HIV and hepatitis C because users are in hiding and thus their access to clean needles is restricted. Children of addicts are at risk of educational failure, joblessness, addiction, and delinquency. People suffering from cancer, AIDS, and other debilitating illnesses are arrested and prosecuted for using medical marijuana. Banning drugs creates networks of manufacturers and distributors, many of whom use violence as part of their standard operating procedures. If drugs were legalized, price and distribution could be controlled by the government. Those who oppose legalization fear that it will lead to much more widespread use of dangerous drugs, leading to drug smuggling to avoid tax payments. There are also health concerns. The number of drug-dependent babies could begin to match or exceed the number delivered with fetal alcohol syndrome.

CRITICAL THINKING QUESTIONS

1. Under what circumstances, if any, might the legalization or decriminalization of drugs be beneficial to society?
2. Do you consider alcohol a drug? Should greater control be placed on the sale of alcohol?
3. Do TV shows and films glorify drug usage and encourage youths to enter the drug trade? Should all images on TV of drugs and alcohol be banned?
4. Is prostitution really a crime? Should a man or woman have the right to sell sexual favors if they so choose?
5. Do you believe there should be greater controls placed on the distribution of sexually explicit material on the Internet? Would you approve of the online sale of sexually explicit photos of children if they were artificial images created by computer animation?
6. Which statement is more accurate? (a) Sexually aggressive men are drawn to pornography because it reinforces their preexisting hostile orientation to sexuality. (b) Reading or watching pornography can make men become sexually aggressive.
7. Are there objective standards of morality? Does the existing criminal code reflect contemporary national moral standards? Or are laws banning sexual behaviors and substance abuse the product of a relatively few "moral entrepreneurs" who seek to control other people's behaviors?

KEY TERMS

public order crimes (504)
victimless crimes (504)
social harm (504)
vigilantes (507)
moral crusaders (507)

moral entrepreneurs (507)
paraphilias (509)
pedophilia (510)
prostitution (512)
brothel (514)

madam (514)
call girls (514)
skeezers (515)
pornography (518)
obscenity (518)

temperance movement (522)
binge drinking (523)
gateway model (525)

NOTES

All URLs accessed in 2016.
1. *United States v. Eric Omuro,* https://s3 .amazonaws.com/pacer-documents/N.D. %20Cal.%2014-cr-00336%20dckt%20 000070_000%20filed%202015-05-14.pdf; Tara Burns, "The War on Sex Workers Escalates with FBI Shutdown of MyRedBook" *Vice,* July 17, 2014, https://www.vice.com /read/the-fbi-shut-down-myredbook-and -thats-dangerous-for-sex-workers-717.
2. Ric Steuer, "The Rise and Fall of Redbook, the Site that Sex Workers Couldn't Live Without," *Wired,* February 24, 2015, http:// www.wired.com/2015/02/redbook/.
3. Joel Roberts, "New Woes for Senator Caught in Sex Scandal," CBS News, July 11, 2007, http://www.cbsnews.com/news/new -woes-for-senator-caught-in-sex-scandal/.
4. Adam Nossiter, "A Senator's Moral High Ground Gets A Little Shaky," *New York* *Times,* July 11, 2007, http://www.nytimes .com/2007/07/11/us/11vitter.html.
5. Glen Kessler, "Rice Deputy Quits After Query over Escort Service," *Washington Post,* April 28, 2007, http://www.washingtonpost .com/wp-dyn/content/article/2007/04/27 /AR2007042702497.html.
6. Jazz Shaw, "David Vitter Somehow Manages to Lose the Louisiana Governor's Office," *Hot Air,* November 22, 2015, http://hotair

.com/archives/2015/11/22/david-vitter
-somehow-manages-to-lose-the-louisiana
-governors-office/.

7. C. Gabrielle Salfati, Alison James, and Lynn Ferguson, "Prostitute Homicides: A Descriptive Study," *Journal of Interpersonal Violence* 23 (2008): 505–543.

8. Andrea Dworkin, quoted in "Where Do We Stand on Pornography," *Ms.* (January–February 1994): 34.

9. Raymond Hernandez, "Weiner Resigns in Chaotic Final Scene," *New York Times*, June 16, 2011, http://www.nytimes.com /2011/06/17/nyregion/anthony-d-weiner -tells-friends-he-will-resign.html.

10. The Bible, New International Version, Genesis 18:20.

11. Morris Cohen, "Moral Aspects of the Criminal Law," *Yale Law Journal* 49 (1940): 1017.

12. Sir Patrick Devlin, *The Enforcement of Morals* (New York: Oxford University Press, 1959), p. 20.

13. See Joel Feinberg, *Social Philosophy* (Englewood Cliffs, NJ: Prentice Hall, 1973), Ch. 2, 3.

14. H. L. A. Hart, "Immorality and Treason," *Listener* 62 (1959): 163.

15. *United States v. 12 200-ft Reels of Super 8mm Film*, 413 U.S. 123 (1973) at 137.

16. Robin Pogrebin and Scott Reyburn, "With $170.4 Million Sale at Auction, Modigliani Work Joins Rarefied Nine-Figure Club," *New York Times*, November 9, 2015, http:// www.nytimes.com/2015/11/10/arts/with -170-4-million-sale-at-auction-modigliani -work-joins-rarefied-nine-figure-club.html.

17. Joseph Gusfield, "On Legislating Morals: The Symbolic Process of Designating Deviancy," *California Law Review* 56 (1968): 58–59.

18. John Franks, "The Evaluation of Community Standards," *Journal of Social Psychology* 139 (1999): 253–255.

19. Matthew Hussey, "Who Are the Biggest Consumers of Online Porn?" *TNW News*, http://thenextweb.com/market-intelligence /2015/03/24/who-are-the-biggest-consumers -of-online-porn/; Sebastian Anthony, "Just How Big Are Porn Sites?" *ExtremeTech*, April 4, 2012, http://www.extremetech.com /computing/123929-just-how-big-are-porn -sites.

20. Irving Kristol, "Liberal Censorship and the Common Culture," *Society* 36 (September 1999): 5.

21. World Health Organization, "Female Genital Mutilation (FGM)," May 2016, http://www .who.int/mediacentre/factsheets/fs241/en/; UNICEF, "Female Genital Mutilation/ Cutting: A Global Concern," February 3, 2016, http://data.unicef.org/corecode /uploads/document6/uploaded_pdfs /corecode/FGMC-2016-brochure _250.pdf.

22. David Kaplan, "Is It Torture or Tradition?" *Newsweek*, December 20, 1993, p. 124; see also Alice Walker, *Warrior Marks: Female Genital Mutilation and the Sexual Blinding of Women* (Boston: Harvest Books, 1996).

23. Barbara Crossette, "Senegal Bans Cutting of Genitals of Girls," *New York Times*, January 18, 1999, http://www.nytimes .com/1999/01/18/world/senegal-bans -cutting-of-genitals-of-girls.html.

24. Centers for Disease Control and Prevention, "Female Genital Mutilation/Cutting in the United States," *Public Health Reports*, January 14, 2016, http://www.publichealthreports .org/fgmutilation.cfm.

25. Centers for Disease Control and Prevention, "Opioid Overdose," http://www.cdc.gov /drugoverdose/.

26. Howard Becker, *Outsiders* (New York: Macmillan, 1963), pp. 13–14.

27. Ibid.

28. Edward Brecher, *Licit and Illicit Drugs* (Boston: Little, Brown, 1972), pp. 413–416.

29. Hearings on H.R. 6385, April 27, 28, 29, 30, and May 4, 1937, http://www.hempfarm .org/Papers/Hearing_Transcript_1.html.

30. American Library Association, "Frequently Challenged Books," http://www.ala.org /bbooks/frequentlychallengedbooks.

31. *Bowers v. Hardwick*, 478 U.S. 186 (1986): 190–191.

32. U.S. Code, Title 1 § 7. Definition of "marriage" and "spouse."

33. *Lawrence et al. v. Texas*, No. 02-102, June 26, 2003.

34. *Obergefell v. Hodges*, 576 U.S. ___ (2015).

35. David Gardner, "I Feel Guilty: Girl Held for 18 Years 'Bonded with Kidnapper,'" *London Evening Standard*, August 28, 2009, http:// www.standard.co.uk/news/i-feel-guilty -girl-held-for-18-years-bonded-with -kidnapper-6745223.html.

36. Lateef Mungin and Dave Alsup, "Cleveland Kidnapper Ariel Castro Dead: Commits Suicide in Prison," CNN, September 4, 2013, http://www.cnn.com/2013/09/04/justice /ariel-castro-cleveland-kidnapper-death/.

37. Polly Klass Foundation, National Child Kidnapping Facts, http://www.pollyklaas .org/about/national-child-kidnapping.html.

38. Richard Estes and Neil Alan Weiner, *The Commercial Sexual Exploitation of Children in the U.S., Canada, and Mexico* (Philadelphia: University of Pennsylvania Press, 2001).

39. W. P. de Silva, "Sexual Variations," *British Medical Journal* 318 (1999): 654–655.

40. Associated Press, "David Carradine Found Dead in Thailand Hotel," *Today*, June 4, 2009, http://www.today.com/id/31103217# .U6MIgyhwz74.

41. Curt Anderson, "Death Sentence Endorsed in Lunsford Case," *Washington Post*, March 15, 2007, http://www.washingtonpost.com /wp-dyn/content/article/2007/03/15 /AR2007031500518.html.

42. Boris Schiffer, Thomas Paul, Elke Gizewski, Michael Forsting, Norbert Leygraf, Manfred Schedlowski, and Tillmann H. C. Kruger, "Functional Brain Correlates of Heterosexual Paedophilia," *NeuroImage* 41 (2008): 80–91.

43. Michael Allan and Randolph Grace, "Psychometric Assessment of Dynamic Risk Factors for Child Molesters," *Sexual Abuse: A Journal of Research* 19 (2007): 347–367.

44. For an analysis of this issue, see Theresa Gannon, and Devon Polaschek, "Cognitive Distortions in Child Molesters: A Re-examination of Key Theories and Research," *Clinical Psychology Review* 26 (2006): 1000–1019.

45. Associated Press, "Ex-Baltimore Ravens Cheerleader Molly Shattuck Gets Probation for Raping a 15-Year-Old Boy," *New York Daily News*, August 21, 2015.

46. Miriam Wijkman, Catrien Bijleveld, and Jan Hendriks, "Women Don't Do Such Things! Characteristics of Female Sex Offenders and Offender Types," *Sexual Abuse: A Journal of Research and Treatment* 22 (2010): 135–156.

47. CNN, "Archbishop: Mistakes Made in Priest Sex Abuse Case," March 31, 2010, http:// www.cnn.com/2010/US/03/31/wisconsin .church.abuse/.

48. *Boston Globe* archives, "The Boston Area's First Predator Priest Case," http://www .boston.com/globe/spotlight/abuse/extras /porter_archive.htm.

49. Laurie Goodstein, "After Criticism, Pope Francis Confronts Priestly Sexual Abuse," *New York Times,* September 27, 2015, http:// www.nytimes.com/2015/09/28/us/pope -francis-philadelphia-sexual-abuse.html.

50. See, generally, V. Bullogh, *Sexual Variance in Society and History* (Chicago: University of Chicago Press, 1958), pp. 143–144.

51. Spencer Rathus, *Human Sexuality* (New York: Holt, Rinehart & Winston, 1983), p. 463.

52. Jeffery Richards, *Sex, Dissidence and Damnation: Minority Groups in the Middle Ages* (New York: Routledge, 1994). p. 125.

53. Ibid., p. 118.

54. Annette Jolin, "On the Backs of Working Prostitutes: Feminist Theory and Prostitution Policy," *Crime and Delinquency* 40 (1994): 60–83.

55. Nicole Bromfield, "Sex Slavery and Sex Trafficking of Women in the United States: Historical and Contemporary Parallels, Policies, and Perspectives in Social Work," *Journal of Women and Social Work* 31 (2016): 129–139.

56. Jane Addams, *A New Conscience and an Ancient Evil* (Champaign: University of Illinois Press, 2002).

57. Barbara G. Brents and Kathryn Hausbeck, "State-Sanctioned Sex: Negotiating Formal and Informal Regulatory Practices in Nevada Brothels," *Sociological Perspectives* 44 (2001): 307–335.

58. Ibid.

59. Mara Keire, "The Vice Trust: A Reinterpretation of the White Slavery Scare in the United States, 1907–1917," *Journal of Social History* 35 (2001): 5–42.

60. Charles McCaghy, *Deviant Behavior* (New York: Macmillan, 1976), pp. 348–349.
61. Marian Pitts, Anthony Smith, Jeffrey Grierson, Mary O'Brien, and Sebastian Misson, "Who Pays for Sex and Why? An Analysis of Social and Motivational Factors Associated with Male Clients of Sex Workers," *Archives of Sexual Behavior* 33 (2004): 353–358.
62. Monica Prasad, "The Morality of Market Exchange: Love, Money, and Contractual Justice," *Sociological Perspectives* 42 (1999): 181–187.
63. FBI, "Crime in the United States, 2014," Table 29, https://www.fbi.gov/about-us/cjis/ucr/crime-in-the-u.s/2014/crime-in-the-u.s.-2014/tables/table-29.
64. Mark Landler, "World Cup Brings Little Pleasure to German Brothels," *New York Times*, July 3, 2006, http://www.nytimes.com/2006/07/03/world/europe/03berlin.html.
65. Elizabeth Bernstein, "The Meaning of the Purchase: Desire, Demand, and the Commerce of Sex," *Ethnography* 2 (2001): 389–420.
66. 18 U.S.C. [section] 2423(b) (2000).
67. Sara K. Andrews, "U.S. Domestic Prosecution of the American International Sex Tourist: Efforts to Protect Children from Sexual Exploitation," *Journal of Criminal Law and Criminology* 94 (2004): 415–453.
68. Mark-David Janus, Barbara Scanlon, and Virginia Price, "Youth Prostitution," in *Child Pornography and Sex Rings*, ed. Ann Wolbert Burgess (Lexington, MA: Lexington Books, 1989), pp. 127–146.
69. Teela Sanders and Rosie Campbell, "Designing Out Vulnerability, Building in Respect: Violence, Safety and Sex Work Policy," *British Journal of Sociology* 58 (2007): 1–19.
70. Charles Winick and Paul Kinsie, *The Lively Commerce* (Chicago: Quadrangle Books, 1971), p. 58.
71. Celia Baker, "Women in Street-Based Prostitution: A Typology of their Work Styles," *Qualitative Social Work* 8 (2009): 27–44.
72. Teela Sanders, *Sex Work: A Risky Business* (Devon, England: Willan Publishing, 2005).
73. Winick and Kinsie, *The Lively Commerce*, pp. 172–173.
74. Paul Goldstein, "Occupational Mobility in the World of Prostitution: Becoming a Madam," *Deviant Behavior* 4 (1983): 267–279.
75. Yellow Pages, http://www.yellowpages.com.
76. Mireya Navarro, "Group Forced Illegal Aliens into Prostitution, U.S. Says," *New York Times*, April 24, 1998, p. A10.
77. Jessica Edwards, Carolyn Halpern, and Wendee Wechsberg, "Correlates of Exchanging Sex for Drugs or Money Among Women Who Use Crack Cocaine," *AIDS Education and Prevention* 18 (2006): 420–429; Jan Risser, Sandra Timpson, Sheryl McCurdy, Michael Ross, and Mark Williams, "Psychological Correlates of Trading Sex for Money Among African American Crack Cocaine Smokers," *American Journal of Drug and Alcohol Abuse* 32 (2006): 645–653.
78. Ginger Thompson and Philip Shenon, "Navy Officer Describes Working as a Prostitute," *New York Times*, April 12, 2008, http://www.nytimes.com/2008/04/12/us/12officer.html.
79. Alyson Brown and David Barrett, *Knowledge of Evil: Child Prostitution and Child Sexual Abuse in Twentieth Century England* (Devon, England: Willan, 2002).
80. Jocelyn Brown, Patricia Cohen, Henian Chen, Elizabeth Smailes, and Jeffrey Johnson, "Sexual Trajectories of Abused and Neglected Youths," *Journal of Developmental and Behavioral Pediatrics* 25 (2004): 77–83.
81. Gerald Hotaling and David Finkelhor, *The Sexual Exploitation of Missing Children* (Washington, DC: U.S. Department of Justice, 1988).
82. Joan Reid and Alex Piquero, "Applying General Strain Theory to Youth Commercial Sexual Exploitation," *Crime and Delinquency* 62 (2016): 341–367.
83. Tammy Heilemann and Janaki Santhiveeran, "How Do Female Adolescents Cope and Survive the Hardships of Prostitution? A Content Analysis of Existing Literature," *Journal of Ethnic and Cultural Diversity in Social Work* 20 (2011): 57–76.
84. Lisa Kramer and Ellen Berg, "A Survival Analysis of Timing of Entry into Prostitution: The Differential Impact of Race, Educational Level, and Childhood/Adolescent Risk Factors," *Sociological Inquiry* 73 (2003): 511–529.
85. John Potterat, Richard Rothenberg, Stephen Muth, William Darrow, and Lynanne Phillips-Plummer, "Pathways to Prostitution: The Chronology of Sexual and Drug Abuse Milestones," *Journal of Sex Research* 35 (1998): 333–342.
86. Sheila Royo Maxwell and Christopher Maxwell, "Examining the 'Criminal Careers' of Prostitutes Within the Nexus of Drug Use, Drug Selling, and Other Illicit Activities," *Criminology* 38 (2000): 787–809.
87. Michael Miner, Jill Flitter, and Beatrice Robinson, "Association of Sexual Revictimization with Sexuality and Psychological Function," *Journal of Interpersonal Violence* 21 (2006): 503–524.
88. Jolanda Sallmann, "Living with Stigma: Women's Experiences of Prostitution and Substance Use," *Afillia Journal of Women and Social Work* 25 (2010): 146–159.
89. Mandi Burnette, Emma Lucas, Mark Ilgen, Susan Frayne, Julia Mayo, and Julie Weitlauf, "Prevalence and Health Correlates of Prostitution Among Patients Entering Treatment for Substance Use Disorders," *Archives of General Psychiatry* 65 (2008): 337–344.
90. Michael Rekart, "Sex-Work Harm Reduction," *The Lancet* 366 (2005): 2123–2134.
91. Nancy Romero-Daza, Margaret Weeks, and Merrill Singer, "Nobody Gives a Damn if I Live or Die: Violence, Drugs, and Street-Level Prostitution in Inner-City Hartford, Connecticut," *Medical Anthropology* 22 (2003): 233–259.
92. Brown and Barrett, *Knowledge of Evil: Child Prostitution and Child Sexual Abuse in Twentieth Century England*.
93. Brown, Cohen, Chen, Smailes, and Johnson, "Sexual Trajectories of Abused and Neglected Youths."
94. Hotaling and Finkelhor, *The Sexual Exploitation of Missing Children*.
95. Shu-ling Hwang and Olwen Bedford, "Juveniles' Motivations for Remaining in Prostitution," *Psychology of Women Quarterly* 28 (2004): 136–137.
96. FBI, "Crime in the United States, 2014," Table 41, https://www.fbi.gov/about-us/cjis/ucr/crime-in-the-u.s/2014/crime-in-the-u.s.-2014/tables/table-41.
97. Sallmann, "Living with Stigma: Women's Experiences of Prostitution and Substance Use," 153.
98. Devon Brewer, John Potterat, Stephen Muth, John Roberts, Jr., Jonathan Dudek, and Donald Woodhouse, *Clients of Prostitute Women: Deterrence, Prevalence, Characteristics, and Violence* (Washington, DC: National Institute of Justice, 2007), http://www.ncjrs.gov/pdffiles1/nij/grants/218253.pdf.
99. Ronald Weitzer, "The Politics of Prostitution in America," in *Sex for Sale*, ed. Ronald Weitzer (New York: Routledge, 2000): 159–180.
100. Sherry Plaster Carter, Stanley Carter, and Andrew Dannenberg, "Zoning Out Crime and Improving Community Health in Sarasota, Florida: Crime Prevention Through Environmental Design," *American Journal of Public Health* 93 (2003): 1442–1445.
101. Ron Roberts, Sandra Bergström, and David La Rooy, "UK Students and Sex Work: Current Knowledge and Research Issues," *Journal of Community and Applied Social Psychology* 17 (2007): 141–146.
102. Sarah Lantz, "Students Working in the Melbourne Sex Industry: Education, Human Capital and the Changing Patterns of the Youth Labour Market," *Journal of Youth Studies* 8 (2005): 385–401.
103. Andrea Dworkin, *Pornography* (New York: Dutton, 1989).
104. Arthur Gould, "The Criminalisation of Buying Sex: The Politics of Prostitution in Sweden," *Journal of Social Policy* 30 (2001): 437–438.
105. Suzanne Daley, "New Rights for Dutch Prostitutes, but No Gain," *New York Times*, August 12, 2001, p. A4.
106. Alexa Albert, *Brothel: Mustang Ranch and Its Women* (New York: Random House, 2001).
107. Ronald Weitzer, *Legalizing Prostitution: From Illicit Vice to Lawful Business* (New York: New York University Press, 2011).
108. Roger Matthews, *Prostitution, Politics and Policy* (London, Routledge-Cavendish, 2008).
109. *Merriam-Webster Dictionary* (New York: Pocket Books, 1974), p. 484.

110. Neil Malamuth, Tamara Addison, and Mary Koss, "Pornography and Sexual Aggression: Are There Reliable Effects and Can We Understand Them?" *Annual Review of Sex Research* 11 (2000): 26–94.

111. Lynn Morgan, "Indecency, Pornography, and the Protection of Children," *Georgetown Journal of Gender and the Law* 7 (2006): 701–721.

112. Julie Jargon, "Jared Fogle Sentenced to 15 1/2 Years in Prison, Former Subway Pitchman Pleaded Guilty in Child-Sex Case," *Wall Street Journal*, November 19, 2015, http://www.wsj.com/articles/jared-fogle-to-be-sentenced-thursday-1447942432.

113. Albert Belanger et al., "Typology of Sex Rings Exploiting Children," in *Child Pornography and Sex Rings*, ed. Ann Wolbert Burgess (Lexington, MA: Lexington Books, 1984), pp. 51–81.

114. Malamuth, Addison, and Koss, "Pornography and Sexual Aggression: Are There Reliable Effects and Can We Understand Them?"

115. Berl Kutchinsky, "The Effect of Easy Availability of Pornography on the Incidence of Sex Crimes," *Journal of Social Issues* 29 (1973): 95–112.

116. Michael Goldstein, "Exposure to Erotic Stimuli and Sexual Deviance," *Journal of Social Issues* 29 (1973): 197–219.

117. Michael Seto, Alexandra Maric, and Howard Barbaree, "The Role of Pornography in the Etiology of Sexual Aggression," *Aggression and Violent Behaviour* 6 (2001): 35–53; Joetta Carr and Karen VanDeusen, "Risk Factors for Male Sexual Aggression on College Campuses," *Journal of Family Violence* 19 (2004): 279–289; see Edward Donnerstein, Daniel Linz, and Steven Penrod, *The Question of Pornography* (New York: Free Press, 1987).

118. Catherine Simmons and Peter Shannon Collier-Tenison, "Linking Male Use of the Sex Industry to Controlling Behaviors in Violent Relationships: An Exploratory Analysis," *Violence Against Women* 14 (2008): 406–417.

119. James Alan Fox and Jack Levin, "Multiple Homicide: Patterns of Serial and Mass Murder," in *Crime and Justice: An Annual Edition*, Vol. 23, ed. Michael Tonry (Chicago: University of Chicago Press, 1998): 418–419.

120. Malamuth, Addison, and Koss, "Pornography and Sexual Aggression: Are There Reliable Effects and Can We Understand Them?"

121. *Roth v. United States*, 354 U.S. 476 (1957).

122. *A Book Named "John Cleland's Memoirs of a Woman of Pleasure" v. Attorney General of Massachusetts* 383 U.S. 413 (1966).

123. *Miller v. California*, 413 U.S. 15 (1973).

124. Michael Fix, "A Universal Standard for Obscenity? The Importance of Context and Other Considerations" *Justice System Journal* 37 (2016): 72–88.

125. *Pope v. Illinois*, 481 U.S. 497 (1987).

126. Ibid.

127. "State Laws on Obscenity, Child Pornography, and Harassment," http://www.lorenavedon.com/laws.htm.

128. The Prosecutorial Remedies and Other Tools to End the Exploitation of Children, 18 U.S.C. 1466A (2003).

129. *United States v. Williams*, 553 U.S. 285 (2008).

130. Attorney General's Commission on Pornography, 1986, pp. 376–377.

131. Bob Cohn, "The Trials of Adam and Eve," *Newsweek*, January 7, 1991, p. 48.

132. 427 U.S. 50 (1976).

133. Ralph Weisheit, "Studying Drugs in Rural Areas: Notes from the Field," *Journal of Research in Crime and Delinquency* 30 (1993): 213–232.

134. Arnold Trebach, *The Heroin Solution* (New Haven, CN: Yale University Press, 1982).

135. James Inciardi, *The War on Drugs* (Palo Alto, CA: Mayfield, 1986), p. 2.

136. See, generally, David Pittman, "Drug Addiction and Crime," in *Handbook of Criminology*, ed. D. Glazer (Chicago: Rand McNally, 1974), pp. 209–232; Board of Directors, National Council on Crime and Delinquency, "Drug Addiction: A Medical, Not a Law Enforcement, Problem," *Crime and Delinquency* 20 (1974): 4–9.

137. Associated Press, "Records Detail Royals' Turn-of-Century Drug Use," *Boston Globe*, August 29, 1993, p. 13.

138. See Brecher, *Licit and Illicit Drugs*.

139. James Inciardi, *Reflections on Crime* (New York: Holt, Rinehart & Winston, 1978), p. 15.

140. William Bates and Betty Crowther, "Drug Abuse," in *Deviants: Voluntary Actors in a Hostile World*, ed. E. Sagarin and F. Montanino (New York: Foresman and Co., 1977), p. 269.

141. Inciardi, *Reflections on Crime*, pp. 8–10. See also A. Greeley, William McCready, and Gary Theisen, *Ethnic Drinking Subcultures* (New York: Praeger, 1980).

142. Joseph Gusfield, *Symbolic Crusade* (Urbana: University of Illinois Press, 1963), Ch. 3.

143. Kens Burns, "Roots of Prohibition," http://www.pbs.org/kenburns/prohibition/roots-of-prohibition/.

144. McCaghy, *Deviant Behavior*, p. 280.

145. Ibid.

146. Lloyd Johnston, Patrick O'Malley, Richard Miech, Jerald Bachman, and John Schulenberg, *Monitoring the Future, 2014*, National Institute on Drug Abuse, National Institutes of Health, http://www.monitoringthefuture.org//pubs/monographs/mtf-overview2014.pdf.

147. Center for Behavioral Health Statistics and Quality, "Behavioral Health Trends in the United States: Results from the 2014 National Survey on Drug Use and Health," http://www.samhsa.gov/data/.

148. Ibid.

149. The National Institute on Alcohol Abuse and Alcoholism (NIAAA), "Alcohol Facts and Statistics," http://www.niaaa.nih.gov/alcohol-health/overview-alcohol-consumption/alcohol-facts-and-statistics.

150. Jeffrey Miron and Katherine Waldock, "The Budgetary Impact of Ending Drug Prohibition," Cato Institute (Washington, DC: Cato Institute, 2010), http://www.cato.org/sites/cato.org/files/pubs/pdf/DrugProhibitionWP.pdf.

151. Susan James, Janice Johnson, and Chitra Raghavan, "I Couldn't Go Anywhere," *Violence Against Women* 10 (2004): 991–1015.

152. Marvin Krohn, Alan Lizotte, Terence Thornberry, Carolyn Smith, and David McDowall, "Reciprocal Causal Relationships Among Drug Use, Peers, and Beliefs: A Five-Wave Panel Model," *Journal of Drug Issues* 26 (1996): 205–428.

153. Kellie Barr, Michael Farrell, Grace Barnes, and John Welte, "Race, Class, and Gender Differences in Substance Abuse: Evidence of Middle-Class/Underclass Polarization Among Black Males," *Social Problems* 40 (1993): 314–326.

154. Peter Giancola, "Constructive Thinking, Antisocial Behavior, and Drug Use in Adolescent Boys with and without a Family History of a Substance Use Disorder," *Personality and Individual Differences* 35 (2003): 1315–1331.

155. Jerome J. Platt, *Heroin Addiction and Theory, Research and Treatment: The Addict, the Treatment Process and Social Control* (Melbourne, FL: Krieser Publishing, 1995), p. 127.

156. Center for Behavioral Health Statistics and Quality, "Behavioral Health Trends in the United States: Results from the 2014 National Survey on Drug Use and Health."

157. Alan Carr, Barbara Dooley, Mark Fitzpatrick, Edel Flanagan, Roisin Flanagan-Howard, Kevin Tierney, Megan White, and Margaret Egan, "Adult Adjustment of Survivors of Institutional Child Abuse in Ireland," *Child Abuse and Neglect* 34 (2010): 477–489.

158. Daniel Smith, Joanne Davis, and Adrienne Fricker-Elhai, "How Does Trauma Beget Trauma? Cognitions About Risk in Women with Abuse Histories," *Child Maltreatment* 9 (2004): 292–302.

159. Sean Kidd, "The Walls Were Closing In, and We Were Trapped," *Youth and Society* 36 (2004): 30–55.

160. David Black, Steve Sussman, Jennifer Unger, Pallay Pokhrel, and Ping Sun, "Gender Differences in Body Consciousness and Substance Use Among High-Risk Adolescents," *Substance Use and Misuse* 45 (2010): 1623–1635.

161. Tracy Hampton, "Genes Harbor Clues to Addiction, Recovery," *Journal of the American Medical Association* 292 (2004): 321–323.

162. D. W. Goodwin, "Alcoholism and Genetics," *Archives of General Psychiatry* 42 (1985): 171–174.

163. Martha Vungkhanching, Kenneth Sher, Kristina Jackson, and Gilbert Parra, "Relation of Attachment Style to Family History of Alcoholism and Alcohol Use Disorders in Early Adulthood," *Drug and Alcohol Dependence* 75 (2004): 47–54.

164. For a thorough review of this issue, see John Petraitis, Brian Flay, and Todd Miller, "Reviewing Theories of Adolescent Substance Use: Organizing Pieces in the Puzzle," *Psychological Bulletin* 117 (1995): 67–86.

165. Judith Brooks and Li-Jung Tseng, "Influences of Parental Drug Use, Personality, and Child Rearing on the Toddler's Anger and Negativity," *Genetic, Social and General Psychology Monographs* 122 (1996): 107–128.

166. Thomas Ashby Wills, Donato Vaccaro, Grace McNamara, and A. Elizabeth Hirky, "Escalated Substance Use: A Longitudinal Grouping Analysis from Early to Middle Adolescence," *Journal of Abnormal Psychology* 105 (1996): 166–180.

167. Denise Kandel and Mark Davies, "Friendship Networks, Intimacy, and Illicit Drug Use in Young Adulthood: A Comparison of Two Competing Theories," *Criminology* 29 (1991): 441–471.

168. J. S. Mio, G. Nanjundappa, D. E. Verlur, and M. D. DeRios, "Drug Abuse and the Adolescent Sex Offender: A Preliminary Analysis," *Journal of Psychoactive Drugs* 18 (1986): 65–72.

169. D. Baer and J. Corrado, "Heroin Addict Relationships with Parents During Childhood and Early Adolescent Years," *Journal of Genetic Psychology* 124 (1974): 99–103.

170. Chie Noyori-Corbett and Sung Seek Moon, "Multifaceted Reality of Juvenile Delinquency: An Empirical Analysis of Structural Theories and Literature," *Child and Adolescent Social Work Journal* 27 (2010): 245–268.

171. John Wallace and Jerald Bachman, "Explaining Racial/Ethnic Differences in Adolescent Drug Use: The Impact of Background and Lifestyle," *Social Problems* 38 (1991): 333–357.

172. Amy Young, Carol Boyd, and Amy Hubbell, "Social Isolation and Sexual Abuse Among Women Who Smoke Crack," *Journal of Psychosocial Nursing* 39 (2001): 16–19.

173. Xiaojin Chen, Kimberly Tyler, Les Whitbeck, and Dan Hoyt, "Early Sexual Abuse, Street Adversity, and Drug Use Among Female Homeless and Runaway Adolescents in the Midwest," *Journal of Drug Issues* 34 (2004): 1–20.

174. Michael Hallstone, "Types of Crimes Committed by Repeat DUI Offenders," *Criminal Justice Studies* 27 (2014): 159–171.

175. Claire Sterk-Elifson, "Just for Fun? Cocaine Use Among Middle-Class Women," *Journal of Drug Issues* 26 (1996): 63–76, at 69.

176. Icek Ajzen, *Attitudes, Personality and Behavior* (Homewood, IL: Dorsey Press, 1988).

177. James Inciardi, Ruth Horowitz, and Anne Pottieger, *Street Kids, Street Drugs, Street Crime: An Examination of Drug Use and Serious Delinquency in Miami* (Belmont, CA: Wadsworth, 1993), p. 43.

178. Ibid.

179. Cesar Rebellon and Karen Van Gundy, "Can Social Psychological Delinquency Theory Explain the Link Between Marijuana and Other Illicit Drug Use? A Longitudinal Analysis of the Gateway Hypothesis," *Journal of Drug Issues*, Summer 36 (2006): 515–539; Mary Ellen Mackesy-Amiti, Michael Fendrich, and Paul Goldstein, "Sequence of Drug Use Among Serious Drug Users: Typical vs. Atypical Progression," *Drug and Alcohol Dependence* 45 (1997): 185–196.

180. Bu Huang, Helene White, Rick Kosterman, Richard Catalano, and J. David Hawkins, "Developmental Associations Between Alcohol and Interpersonal Aggression During Adolescence," *Journal of Research in Crime and Delinquency* 38 (2001): 64–83.

181. Rebellon and Van Gundy, "Can Social Psychological Delinquency Theory Explain the Link Between Marijuana and Other Illicit Drug Use?"

182. Andrew Golub and Bruce Johnson, "The Multiple Paths Through Alcohol, Tobacco and Marijuana to Hard Drug Use Among Arrestees," paper presented at the annual meeting of the American Society of Criminology, San Diego, November 1997.

183. Andrew Golub and Bruce D. Johnson, *The Rise of Marijuana as the Drug of Choice Among Youthful Adult Arrestees* (Washington, DC: National Institute of Justice, 2001).

184. These lifestyles are described in Marcia Chaiken and Bruce Johnson, *Characteristics of Different Types of Drug-Involved Offenders* (Washington, DC: National Institute of Justice, 1988).

185. Kenneth Tunnell, "Inside the Drug Trade: Trafficking from the Dealer's Perspective," *Qualitative Sociology* 16 (1993): 361–381.

186. Stephen Tripodi and Kimberly Bender, "Substance Abuse Treatment for Juvenile Offenders: A Review of Quasi-Experimental and Experimental Research," *Journal of Criminal Justice* 39 (2011): 246–279; Douglas Young, Richard Dembo, and Craig Henderson, "A National Survey of Substance Abuse Treatment for Juvenile Offenders," *Journal of Substance Abuse Treatment* 32 (2007): 255–266.

187. National Drug Intelligence Center, "Drugs and Gangs Fast Facts," https://www.justice.gov/archive/ndic/pubs11/13157/13157p.pdf.

188. Richard Tewksbury and Elizabeth Ehrhardt Mustaine, "Lifestyle of the Wheelers and Dealers: Drug Dealing Among American College Students," *Journal of Crime and Justice* 21 (1998): 37.

189. Hilary Saner, Robert MacCoun, and Peter Reuter, "On the Ubiquity of Drug Selling Among Youthful Offenders in Washington, D.C., 1985–1991: Age, Period, or Cohort Effect?" *Journal of Quantitative Criminology* 11 (1995): 362–373.

190. Charles Faupel and Carl Klockars, "Drugs–Crime Connections: Elaborations from the Life Histories of Hard-Core Heroin Addicts," *Social Problems* 34 (1987): 54–68.

191. Charles Faupel, "Heroin Use, Crime and Unemployment Status," *Journal of Drug Issues* 18 (1988): 467–479.

192. Faupel and Klockars, "Drugs–Crime Connections."

193. Jeffrey T. Parsons, Perry N. Halkitis, and David S. Bimbi, "Club Drug Use Among Young Adults Frequenting Dance Clubs and Other Social Venues in New York City," *Journal of Child and Adolescent Substance Abuse* 15 (2006): 1–14.

194. Damir Sekulic, Mia Peric, and Jelena Rodek, "Substance Use and Misuse Among Professional Ballet Dancers," *Substance Use and Misuse* 45 (2010): 1420–1430.

195. David Duncan, Thomas Nicholson, John White, Dana Burr Bradley, and John Bonaguro, "The Baby Boomer Effect: Changing Patterns of Substance Abuse Among Adults Ages 55 and Older," *Journal of Aging and Social Policy* 22 (2010): 237–248.

196. National Center on Addiction and Substance Abuse (CASA), *Women Under the Influence* (Baltimore: The Johns Hopkins University Press, 2006).

197. Russel Falck, Jichuan Wang, and Robert Carlson, "The Epidemiology of Physical Attack and Rape Among Crack-Using Women," *Violence and Victims* 16 (2001): 79–89.

198. Benjamin Nordstrom and Charles Dackis, "Drugs and Crime," *Journal of Psychiatry and Law* 39 (2011): 663–687.

199. Denise Gottfredson, "Substance Use, Drug Treatment, and Crime: An Examination of Intra-Individual Variation in a Drug Court Population," *Journal of Drug Issues* 38 (2008): 601–630.

200. Ibid.

201. Huang, White, Kosterman, Catalano, and Hawkins, "Developmental Associations Between Alcohol and Interpersonal Aggression During Adolescence."

202. Office of National Drug Control Policy, "Fact Sheet: The 2012 Arrestee Drug Abuse Monitoring Program II," May 23, 2013, http://www.whitehouse.gov/sites/default/files/ondcp/Fact_Sheets/adamfactsheet_for_web.pdf.

203. Jerome Cartier, David Farabee, and Michael Prendergast, "Methamphetamine Use, Self-Reported Violent Crime, and Recidivism Among Offenders in California Who Abuse Substances," *Journal of Interpersonal Violence* 21 (2006): 435–445.

204. Bureau of Justice Statistics, "Drugs and Crime Facts," http://bjs.ojp.usdoj.gov/content/dcf/duc.cfm.

205. National Center on Addiction and Substance Abuse (CASA), "Behind Bars II: Substance Abuse and America's Prison Population," February 2010, http://www.casacolumbia

.org/addiction-research/reports/substance-abuse-prison-system-2010.

206. Evelyn Wei, Rolf Loeber, and Helene White, "Teasing Apart the Developmental Associations Between Alcohol and Marijuana Use and Violence," *Journal of Contemporary Criminal Justice* 20 (2004): 166–183.

207. Matt Vogel, "Mental Illness and Criminal Behavior," *Sociology Compass* 8 (2014): 337–347.

208. Susan Martin, Christopher Maxwell, Helene White, and Yan Zhang, "Trends in Alcohol Use, Cocaine Use, and Crime," *Journal of Drug Issues* 34 (2004): 333–360.

209. Marvin Krohn, Alan Lizotte, and Cynthia Perez, "The Interrelationship Between Substance Use and Precocious Transitions to Adult Sexuality," *Journal of Health and Social Behavior* 38 (1997): 87–103, at 88.

210. Arielle Baskin-Sommers and Ira Sommers, "Methamphetamine Use and Violence Among Young Adults," *Journal of Criminal Justice* 34 (2006): 661–674.

211. Controlled Substance Act, 21 U.S.C. 848 (1984).

212. Anti-Drug Abuse Act of 1986, PL 99-570, U.S.C. 841 (1986).

213. Anti-Drug Abuse Act of 1988, PL 100-690; 21 U.S.C. 1501; Subtitle A—Death Penalty, Sec. 7001, Amending the Controlled Substances Abuse Act, 21 U.S.C. 848.

214. "Eric Holder Says DOJ Will Let Washington, Colorado Marijuana Laws Go into Effect," *Huffington Post*, September 3, 2103, http://www.huffingtonpost.com/2013/08/29/eric-holder-marijuana-washington-colorado-doj_n_3837034.html.

215. Office of National Drug Control Policy, "Coca in the Andes," 2016, https://www.whitehouse.gov/ondcp/targeting-cocaine-at-the-source.

216. George Rengert, *The Geography of Illegal Drugs* (Boulder, CO: Westview Press, 1996), p. 2.

217. Office of National Drug Control Policy, "Coca in the Andes."

218. CNN, "Official: Mexican Cartels Use Money, Sex to Bribe U.S. Border Agents," June 9, 2011, http://www.cnn.com/2011/US/06/09/mexico.border.corruption/.

219. Office of National Drug Control Policy, "Cocaine Smuggling in 2013," https://www.whitehouse.gov/sites/default/files/ondcp/international-partnerships-content/cocaine_smuggling_in_2013_digital_1505-05221.pdf.

220. Tracy Wilkinson, "Mexico Drug Lord Guzman's Escape Tunnel Is a Minor Engineering Masterpiece," *Los Angeles Times*, July 12, 2015, http://www.latimes.com/world/mexico-americas/la-fg-drug-lord-escapes-mexico-prison-20150711-story.html.

221. Azam Ahmed, "How El Chapo Was Finally Captured, Again," *New York Times*, January 16, 2016, http://www.nytimes.com/2016/01/17/world/americas/mexico-el-chapo-sinaloa-sean-penn.html.

222. Mark Moore, *Drug Trafficking* (Washington, DC: National Institute of Justice, 1988).

223. Brian Reaves, *Felony Defendants in Large Urban Counties, 2009—Statistical Tables* (Washington, DC: Bureau of Justice Statistics, 2013), http://www.bjs.gov/content/pub/pdf/fdluc09.pdf.

224. Peter Rossi, Richard Berk, and Alec Campbell, "Just Punishments: Guideline Sentences and Normative Consensus," *Journal of Quantitative Criminology* 13 (1997): 267–283.

225. Ojmarrh Mitchell and Michael S. Caudy, "Examining Racial Disparities in Drug Arrests," *Justice Quarterly* 32 (2015): 288–313.

226. Robert Davis, Arthur Lurigio, and Dennis Rosenbaum, eds., *Drugs and the Community* (Springfield, IL: Charles C Thomas, 1993), pp. xii–xv.

227. Saul Weingart, "A Typology of Community Responses to Drugs," in Davis, Lurigio, and Rosenbaum, *Drugs and the Community*, pp. 85–105.

228. Dennis Rosenbaum, Robert Flewelling, Susan Bailey, Chris Ringwalt, and Deanna Wilkinson, "Cops in the Classroom: A Longitudinal Evaluation of Drug Abuse Resistance Education (D.A.R.E.)," *Journal of Research in Crime and Delinquency* 31 (1994): 3–31; Donald R. Lynam, Rich Milich, Rick Zimmerman, Scott Novak, T. K. Logan, Catherine Martin, Carl Leukefeld, and Richard Clayton, "Project D.A.R.E.: No Effects at 10-Year Follow-Up," *Journal of Consulting and Clinical Psychology* 67 (1999): 590–593.

229. Ibid., pp. 115–122.

230. John Goldkamp and Peter Jones, "Pretrial Drug-Testing Experiments in Milwaukee and Prince George's County: The Context of Implementation," *Journal of Research in Crime and Delinquency* 29 (1992): 430–465; Chester Britt, Michael Gottfredson, and John Goldkamp, "Drug Testing and Pretrial Misconduct: An Experiment on the Specific Deterrent Effects of Drug Monitoring Defendants on Pretrial Release," *Journal of Research in Crime and Delinquency* 29 (1992): 62–78.

231. Joseph R. McKinney, "The Effectiveness and Legality of Random Student Drug Testing Programs Revisited," *West's Education Law Reporter* 196 (2006); "Effectiveness of Random Student Drug-Testing Programs, 2005," http://www.studentdrugtesting.org/2005%20McKinney%20survey%20results.pdf.

232. Katherine Theall, Kirk Elifson, Claire Sterk, and Eric Stewart, "Criminality Among Female Drug Users Following an HIV Risk-Reduction Intervention," *Journal of Interpersonal Violence* 22 (2007): 85–107.

233. See, generally, Peter Greenwood and Franklin Zimring, *One More Chance* (Santa Monica, CA: Rand, 1985).

234. Daniel Rosen, Jennifer Morse, and Charles Reynolds, "Adapting Problem-Solving Therapy for Depressed Older Adults in Methadone Maintenance Treatment," *Journal of Substance Abuse Treatment* 40 (2011): 132–141.

235. Audrey Hickert and Mary Jane Taylor, "Supportive Housing for Addicted, Incarcerated Homeless Adults," *Journal of Social Service Research* 37 (2011): 136–151.

236. Tracy Beswick, David David, Jenny Bearn, Michael Gossop, Sian Rees, and John Strang, "The Effectiveness of Combined Naloxone/Lofexidine in Opiate Detoxification: Results from a Double-Blind Randomized and Placebo-Controlled Trial," *American Journal on Addictions* 12 (2003): 295–306.

237. Eli Ginzberg, Howard Berliner, and Miriam Ostrow, *Young People at Risk: Is Prevention Possible?* (Boulder, CO: Westview Press, 1988), p. 99.

238. National Institute on Drug Abuse, "DrugFacts: Treatment Approaches for Drug Addiction," http://www.drugabuse.gov/publications/drugfacts/treatment-approaches-drug-addiction.

239. National Evaluation Data and Technical Assistance Center, *The District of Columbia's Drug Treatment Initiative (DCI)* (Washington, DC: author, February 1998).

240. Celia Lo, "Sociodemographic Factors, Drug Abuse, and Other Crimes: How They Vary Among Male and Female Arrestees," *Journal of Criminal Justice* 32 (2004): 399–409.

241. Christopher Uggen and Sarah Shannon, "Productive Addicts and Harm Reduction: How Work Reduces Crime but Not Drug Use," *Social Problems* 61 (2014): 105–130.

242. United Nations Office on Drugs and Crime, "Cocaine Retail Prices," http://www.unodc.org/unodc/secured/wdr/Cocaine_Heroin_Prices.pdf.

243. Barry Goetz, "Pre-Arrest/Booking Drug Control Strategies: Diversion to Treatment, Harm Reduction and Police Involvement," *Contemporary Drug Problems* 33 (2006): 473–520.

244. Ethan Nadelmann, "An End to Marijuana Prohibition," *National Review*, July 12, 2004; Peter Andreas and Ethan Nadelmann, *Policing the Globe: Criminalization and Crime Control in International Relations* (London: Oxford University Press, 2006).

245. Miron and Waldock, "The Budgetary Impact of Ending Drug Prohibition."

246. Ricardo Baca, "Colorado Marijuana Sales Skyrocket to More than $996 Million in 2015," *The Cannabist*, February 9, 2016, http://www.thecannabist.co/2016/02/09/colorado-marijuana-sales-2015-reach-996-million/47886/; Elizabeth Hernandez, "Colorado Monthly Marijuana Sales Eclipse $100 Million Mark," October 9, 2015, http://www.denverpost.com/2015/10/09/colorado-monthly-marijuana-sales-eclipse-100-million-mark/.

247. David Courtwright, "Should We Legalize Drugs? History Answers No," *American Heritage* (February–March 1993): 43–56.

248. James Inciardi and Duane McBride, "Legalizing Drugs: A Gormless, Naive Idea," *Criminologist* 15 (1990): 1–4.

Request from CEO

Subject: Immediate Wire Transfer

To: Chief Financial Officer

❗ *High Importance*

Please process a wire transfer payment in the amount of $250,000 and code to "admin expenses" by COB today. Wiring instructions below...

LEARNING OBJECTIVES

LO1 Describe the concept of cybercrime and trace its development

LO2 Compare and contrast cybertheft, cyberdeviance, cybervandalism, and cyberwar

LO3 Give some examples of computer fraud

LO4 Distinguish between the different forms of stealing intellectual property

LO5 Define the terms *identity theft* and *phishing*

LO6 Assess how the Internet can facilitate the sale of illegal materials

LO7 Discuss the different types of cybervandalism

LO8 Articulate the extent of cyberbullying and the damage it causes people

LO9 Discuss efforts to control cybercrime

LO10 Examine the concepts of cyberwar and cyberterrorism

15 CRIMES OF THE NEW MILLENNIUM: CYBERCRIME

An accountant working for a U.S. company recently received an email from her chief executive, who was on vacation out of the country, requesting a transfer of funds on a time-sensitive acquisition that required completion by the end of the day. The CEO said a lawyer would contact the accountant to provide further details. It was not unusual for her to receive emails requesting a transfer of funds, so when she was contacted by the lawyer via email, she noted the appropriate letter of authorization—including her CEO's signature over the company's seal—and followed the instructions to wire $737,000 to a bank in China.

The next day, when the CEO happened to call regarding another matter, the accountant mentioned that she had completed the wire transfer the day before. The CEO said he had never sent the email and knew nothing about the alleged acquisition. The accountant immediately reviewed the email thread and noticed the first email's reply address was missing one letter—instead of ".com," it read ".co." On closer inspection, the attachment provided by the phony lawyer revealed that the CEO's signature was forged and the company seal was cut and pasted from the company's public website. Further assisting the perpetrators, the website also listed the company's executive officers and their email addresses and identified specific global media events the CEO would attend during the calendar year so they could gauge when he would be out of town.

The firm had been the victim of a business email compromise, a growing financial fraud that has resulted in actual and attempted losses of more than a billion dollars to businesses worldwide. More than 7,000 U.S. companies have been victimized, with total dollar losses exceeding $740 million. The scammers, believed to be members of organized crime groups from Africa, eastern Europe, and the Middle East, primarily target businesses that work with foreign suppliers or regularly perform wire transfer payments. The scam succeeds by compromising legitimate business email accounts through social engineering (fooling individual people into cooperating) or computer intrusion techniques. Businesses of all sizes are targeted, and the fraud is proliferating. Victim companies have come from all 50 U.S. states and nearly 80 countries abroad. The majority of the fraudulent transfers end up in Chinese banks.

Scammers employ sophisticated techniques such as learning to use language specific to the company they are targeting in order to avoid suspicion, along with dollar amounts that lend legitimacy to the fraud. To make matters worse, the criminals often infiltrate company networks, gaining access to legitimate email threads about billing and invoices they can use to ensure the suspicions of an accountant or financial officer aren't raised when a fraudulent wire transfer is requested. Instead of making a payment to a trusted supplier, the scammers direct payment to their own accounts. Sometimes they succeed at this by switching a trusted bank account number by a single digit. Consequently, when a wire transfer happens, the window of time to identify the fraud and recover the funds before they are moved out of reach is extremely short.[1]

ust a few years ago, complex global incidents involving long distance fraud could not have been contemplated, let alone transacted. Innovation brings change and with it new opportunities to commit crime.

The technological revolution has provided new tools to misappropriate funds, damage property, sell illicit material, or conduct warfare, espionage, and terror. It has created **cybercrime**, a new breed of offenses that can be singular or ongoing, but typically involve the theft and/or destruction of information, resources, or funds utilizing computers, computer networks, and the Internet.

While there is no entirely accurate measure of cybercrime, there is little doubt that offenses number in the

cybercrime The use of modern technology for criminal purposes.

millions. The crime rate for England and Wales doubled to more than 11.6 million offenses in 2015 when cybercrime began to be included in the national crime rate. While common-law crimes continued to decline, the overall crime rate jumped with the inclusion of an estimated 5.1 million online fraud incidents and 2.5 million cybercrime offenses.[2] England and Wales have a population of about 56 million people; the U.S. population is about 320 million. If the ratio is the same, then U.S. citizens may be victimized by more than 40 million cybercrime incidents each year.

Another indication of the extent of cybercrime can be found in the complaints reported to FBI's Internet Crime Complaint Center (IC3).[3] In 2015, the most recent data available, IC3 received 288,000 complaints with an adjusted dollar loss of more than $1 billion. More than 20,000 complaints are now received each month (see Figure 15.1).

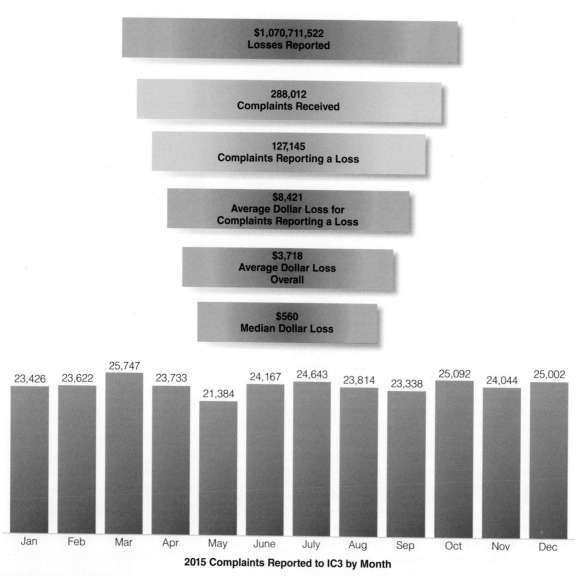

2015 Overall Statistics

$1,070,711,522
Losses Reported

288,012
Complaints Received

127,145
Complaints Reporting a Loss

$8,421
Average Dollar Loss for
Complaints Reporting a Loss

$3,718
Average Dollar Loss
Overall

$560
Median Dollar Loss

23,426 · 23,622 · 25,747 · 23,733 · 21,384 · 24,167 · 24,643 · 23,814 · 23,338 · 25,092 · 24,044 · 25,002

Jan · Feb · Mar · Apr · May · June · July · Aug · Sep · Oct · Nov · Dec

2015 Complaints Reported to IC3 by Month

FIGURE 15.1 Complaints and Losses Reported to the Internet Crime Complaint Center

SOURCE: FBI, Internet Crime Complaint Center, *2015 Internet Crime Report,* https://pdf.ic3.gov/2015_IC3Report.pdf.

In the past five years, the complaint center has received almost 3.5 million complaints of Internet fraud.

These data indicate that the crime drop in America may in fact be a function of criminals switching from common-law crime to cybercrime.[4] Rather than shoplift from Macy's and risk getting caught by security guards, offenders may take the safer route of engaging in etailing fraud. Rather than walking the streets, sex workers have turned to ehooking, where customers are vetted by online companies set up to connect prostitutes with safe clients. Instead of robbing a bank at gunpoint, contemporary thieves find it easier to hack into accounts and transfer funds to offshore banks. And instead of limiting their criminal escapades to the local population, transnational gang members now have a whole world of opportunity.

It is not surprising that cybercrime is a growth industry in which the returns are great and the risks are low. According to Internet security company MacAfee, a conservative estimate of the annual cost to the global economy from cybercrime is more than $400 billion and losses may actually reach $575 billion. This is more than the national income of most countries and governments.[5]

Development of Cybercrime

 L01 Describe the concept of cybercrime and trace its development

The widespread use of computers and the Internet ushered in the age of **information technology (IT)** and made it an intricate part of daily life in most industrialized societies. IT involves computer networking, the Internet, and advanced communications. It is the key to the economic system and will become even more important as major industries continue to shift their manufacturing plants to areas of the world where production is much cheaper. IT is responsible for the **globalization** phenomenon, the process of creating transnational markets, politics, and legal systems—in other words, creating a global economy. The Internet is now the chosen medium to provide a wide range of global services, ranging from entertainment and communication to research and education.

The cyber age has also generated an enormous amount of revenue. Though total spending on IT and telecommunications has been slowing down, it is now around $2.5 trillion per year.[6] More than 3 billion people are on the Net, sending 205 billion emails per day, and more than 8 *trillion* text messages per year.[7] Social media sites like Facebook and Twitter are expanding exponentially; Facebook now has more than 1.5 billion users.[8] Magnifying the importance of the Internet is the fact that many critical infrastructure functions are conducted online, ranging from banking to control of shipping on the Mississippi River.

 To read an article on the implications and direction of the information technology revolution, go to **http://www.federalreserve.gov/pubs/feds /2013/201336/201336pap.pdf**. **Is the IT revolution over? Or are there dramatic transformations still to come?**

THE STAGES OF CYBERCRIME

According to Christopher Donner and his associates, cybercrime has gone through three stages of development:

- The first generation of cybercrime involved deviant acts characterized by the illegal exploitation of mainframe computers and operating systems. These behaviors involved crimes that were in existence before the creation of computers and the Internet, but technological innovations provided another method of commission. They were designed for financial gain or destruction of restricted information.

- The second generation of cybercrime used computer networks and is considered hybrid crime. It involves criminality that was already in existence but has expanded and adapted through the use of the Internet. Hacking and cracking are common forms of this generation, as they were a product of early "phone phreakers." (Phone phreakers dialed around the telephone network to understand how the phone system worked, then used their knowledge to make free long distance calls, wiretap telephones, or steal telephone company equipment.) These crimes were created prior to the creation of the Internet but could now be performed in a more criminally effective manner. Using the Internet made cybercrime more difficult to detect and rendered cybercriminals more immune from prosecution.

- The third generation of cybercrime is identified by the nature of distribution and was solely developed by the creation of the Internet. These crimes would not exist if not for the Internet. Dissemination of malware, such as viruses or Trojan horses, is an example of this generation of cybercrime.[9]

Contemporary Cybercrime

 L02 Compare and contrast cybertheft, cyberdeviance, cybervandalism, and cyberwar

The vast network of mobile and stationary computer networks has become a target for illegal activities and enterprise. Criminals are becoming more technologically

information technology (IT) All forms of technology used to create, store, retrieve, and exchange data in all its various forms, including electronic, voice, and still image.

globalization The process of creating transnational markets, politics, and legal systems in an effort to form and sustain a global economy.

sophisticated, routinely using the Internet to carry out their criminal conspiracies. Some cybercriminals use modern technology to sell illegal goods and services, or conversely, to illegally appropriate legitimate products and services. **Cybertheft** schemes range from illegal copying of copyrighted material to using technology to commit traditional theft-based offenses such as larceny and fraud.

Some cybercriminals engage in **cyberdeviance**, the sale and distribution of morally tainted material and products over the Net. Other cybercriminals are motivated less by profit and more by the urge to commit **cybervandalism** or technological destruction. They aim their malicious attacks at disrupting, defacing, and destroying technology that they find offensive.

A fourth type of cybercrime, **cyberwar**, involves the actions by a nation-state or international organization to attack and attempt to damage another nation's computers or information networks through, for example, computer viruses or distributed denial-of-service attacks (DDoS).[10] One element, **cyberterrorism**, aims to undermine the social, economic, and political system of an enemy nation by destroying its electronic infrastructure and disrupting its economy.

In sum, some cybercriminals are high-tech thieves while others are high-tech vandals; the property they destroy is electronic rather than physical. Some use the Internet to distribute illegal services and material, and some use it to plot and carry out terrorist activities, going as far as to wage cyberwar (see Concept Summary 15.1).

This array of modern crimes presents a compelling challenge for the justice system and law enforcement community because (a) it is rapidly evolving with new schemes being created daily, (b) it is difficult to detect through traditional law enforcement channels, and (c) its control demands that agents of the justice system develop technical skills that match those of the perpetrators.

Cybercrimes also present a significant challenge for criminologists because they defy long-held assumptions about the cause of crime. How can we say that crime is a function of social forces, the social environment, or the social structure, when these contemporary criminals are typically highly educated and technologically sophisticated people who commit their crimes in places far removed from their victims? By their very nature, cybercrimes demand a high degree of self-control and planning, something a truly impulsive or mentally unstable person would have difficulty

---

cybertheft Use of computer networks for criminal profits. Illegal copyright infringement, identity theft, and Internet securities fraud are examples of cybertheft.

cyberdeviance The sale and distribution of morally tainted material and products over the Net.

cybervandalism Malicious attacks aimed at disrupting, defacing, and destroying technology.

cyberwar Using cyberspace for acts of war, including spying and disrupting an enemy's computer network.

cyberterrorism Internet attacks against an enemy nation's technological infrastructure.

CONNECTIONS

Chapter 13 reviewed the concept of enterprise crime and its motivations, and Chapter 14 covered public order crimes. Cybercrime can be viewed as a type of enterprise crime employing sophisticated technology to achieve illegal profits. It can also involve public order crimes such as the online purchase and sale of pornography and controlled substances. The Internet now enables these previously localized crimes to be conducted on a global scale.

ASK YOURSELF . . .

Which theories of crime do you believe best explain cybercrimes? Are cybercriminals impulsive people who lack self-control? If so, how did they attain the technological expertise to devise intricate Internet theft schemes or hack into the computers of financial institutions?

CONCEPT SUMMARY 15.1
Types of Cybercrime

CRIME	DEFINITION	EXAMPLES
Cybertheft	Use of cyberspace to defraud people for quick profits	Illegal copyright infringement, identity theft, Internet securities fraud, warez
Cyberdeviance	Distribution of illegal goods and services	Ehooking; distribution of pornography and drugs
Cybervandalism	Use of cyberspace for revenge, destruction, and to achieve a malicious intent	Website defacement, worms, viruses, cyberstalking, cyberbullying
Cyberwar	An effort by enemy forces to disrupt the intersection where the virtual electronic reality of computers meets the physical world	Logic bombs used to disrupt or destroy "secure" systems or networks, Internet used to communicate covertly with agents around the world

Cybertheft: Cybercrimes for Profit

In 2014, Russian national Aleksandr Andreevich Panin pleaded guilty to a conspiracy charge associated with his role as the primary developer and distributor of malicious software (malware) designed to facilitate online theft from financial institutions. SpyEye infected more than 1.4 million computers and had the ability to detect and copy information stored on those computers and use it to transfer money out of victims' bank accounts and into accounts controlled by criminals. What made this case unusual was that rather than using SpyEye himself, Panin sold the "product" online in criminal forums. He actually advertised the features of the program, bragging that it could be used to obtain credit card information. His 150 clients paid him up to $8,500 for the program and then used it to infect victims' computers. The program collected large amounts of financial and personal information and sent it back to servers under the control of the criminals. They were then able to hack into bank accounts, withdraw funds, create bogus credit cards, and so on. Things were going well until one of Panin's "clients" turned out to be an FBI agent.[12]

It is ironic that technological breakthroughs since the dawn of the Industrial Revolution—such as telephones and automobiles—not only brought with them dramatic improvements for society but also created new opportunities for criminal wrongdoing: criminals use the telephone to place bets or threaten victims; cars can be stolen and sold for big profits.[13] The same pattern is now occurring during the IT revolution. The computer and Internet provide opportunities for socially beneficial endeavors—such as education, research, commerce, and entertainment—while at the same time serving as a tool to facilitate illegal activity. Computer-based technology allows criminals to operate in a more efficient and effective manner. Cyberthieves now have the luxury of remaining anonymous, living in any part of the world, conducting their business during the day or in the evening, working alone or in a group, while at the same time reaching a much wider number of potential victims than ever before. No longer is the con artist or criminal entrepreneur limited to fleecing victims in a particular geographic locale; the whole world can be his or her target. The advent of these international cybercrimes necessitates novel approaches to law enforcement. Take the case of Aleksandr Panin, the

Cybertheft can take many forms. Here, Bryan Caputo (middle) consults with his attorney Reginald Sharpe, with co-defendant Daniel Petryszyn (right), during arraignment proceedings in New York State Supreme Court on July 23, 2014. They are two of six people who were indicted in an international ring that took over more than 1,600 StubHub users' accounts and fraudulently bought tickets to such prime events as Jay-Z and Elton John concerts and Broadway shows like *The Book of Mormon*.

SpyEye program developer. He lived in Russia, beyond the reach of American law. However, he made the mistake of traveling to the Dominican Republic for a vacation, where he was detained by local police. He was then put on a plane to Atlanta, where he was taken into custody by federal agents.

The technology revolution has opened novel methods for cybertheft that heretofore were nonexistent, ranging from the unlawful distribution of software to Internet security fraud. Cyberthieves conspire to use cyberspace to either distribute illegal goods and services or to defraud people for quick profits. Some of the most common methods are discussed here.

COMPUTER FRAUD

L03 Give some examples of computer fraud

In 2016, Tonia Bright pleaded guilty to two counts of obtaining information from a protected computer for a fraudulent purpose. Bright was a civilian employee of the Tampa (Florida) Police Department working as a community service officer. As part of her duties, she took reports from citizens related to incidents not requiring the response of a sworn police officer. In this capacity, she had access to local, state, and federal law enforcement databases, including the National Crime Information Center (NCIC) computerized index. Her use of these databases was restricted to the performance of her authorized duties.

Bright accessed the personally identifiable information (PII) of individuals using a variety of sources, including NCIC, despite having no legitimate law enforcement purpose. She then provided the stolen PII to other conspirators, knowing that the information would be used to commit crimes. Others in the conspiracy used the stolen PII to electronically file fraudulent federal income tax returns claiming tax refunds to which they were not entitled. The fraudulently obtained tax refunds were deposited onto reloadable debit cards issued in the conspirators' names and the names of others, including the victims' names. The debit cards were then used at retail establishments and ATMs to withdraw the illegally obtained funds.[14]

Tonia Bright's crime falls under the general category of computer fraud—not a unique offense, but rather a common-law crime committed using contemporary technology. Many computer crimes are prosecuted under such traditional criminal statutes as larceny or fraud. However, not all computer crimes fall under common-law statutes because the property stolen may be intangible (electronic and/or magnetic impulse). Some of these crimes are listed in Exhibit 15.1.

ATM skimming Using an electronic device on an ATM that copies information from a bank card's magnetic strip whenever a customer uses the machine.

EXHIBIT 15.1

Examples of Computer Fraud

- *Theft of information.* The unauthorized obtaining of information from a computer (hacking), including software that is copied for profit.
- *The "salami" slice.* With this type of fraud, the perpetrator carefully skims small sums from the balances of a large number of accounts in order to bypass internal controls and escape detection.
- *Software theft.* The comparative ease of making copies of computer software has led to a huge illegal market, depriving authors of very significant revenues.
- *Manipulation of accounts/banking systems.* Similar to a "salami" slice but on a much larger and usually more complex scale. Sometimes perpetrated as a "one-off kamikaze" fraud.
- *Corporate espionage.* Trade secrets are stolen by a company's competitors, which can be either domestic or foreign. The goal is to increase the rival company's (or nation's) competitive edge in the global marketplace. Such companies as Anthem Health Care, Primera Blue Cross, Staples, and Home Depot have had their computer systems hacked and the names, Social Security numbers, birthdays, addresses, email, employment information, and income data of current and former customers and employees stolen.

SOURCE: Australian Institute of Criminology, "Nine Types of Computer Crime," http://www.crime.hku.hk/cybercrime.htm; Cross Domain Solutions, "Cyber Crime," http://www.crossdomainsolutions.com/cyber-crime/; Kevin Granville, "9 Recent Cyberattacks Against Big Businesses," *New York Times*, February 5, 2015, http://www.nytimes.com/interactive/2015/02/05/technology/recent-cyberattacks.html. (URLs accessed June 2016.)

These are but a few of the most common examples, and the actual list is as long as the imagination of the criminal mind.

There are a number of recent trends in computer frauds. Internal attacks are now surpassing external attacks at the world's largest financial institutions. A 2016 global security survey of more than 6,000 industry leaders found that about 25 percent had been affected by computer-based attacks on their business enterprise in the prior year. Attacks are so stealthy that almost 20 percent of the CEOs were not sure if they had been attacked. Losses can be heavy: about 50 organizations had suffered losses over $5 million; of these, nearly a third reported computer crime–related losses in excess of $100 million.[15]

THEFT FROM ATMs

Automatic teller machines (ATMs) attract the attention of cybercriminals looking for easy profits.[16] Rather than robbing an ATM user at gunpoint, the cybercriminal relies on stealth and technological skill to commit the crime. Take for instance the case of two brothers from Bulgaria who were charged with attempting to defraud two banks of more than $1 million by engaging in **ATM skimming**: placing an electronic device on an ATM that scoops information from a bank card's magnetic strip whenever a customer uses the machine. Skimmers can then create their own bank cards and steal from customer accounts.[17] ATM skimming now costs U.S. banks hundreds of millions of dollars annually.

Recent (2016) surveys show that skimming attacks on ATMs are increasing rapidly in the United States and Europe. While in the past attacks were aimed at large banks, recent activity is now highest at non-bank ATMs, such as those in convenience stores. And while in the past skimming attacks targeted banks in big cities, they are now spread across the country in small towns and suburban areas.[18]

The devices planted on ATMs are usually undetectable because they blend right in with the ATM's physical structure. Some cybercriminals attach a phony keypad on top of the real keypad which records every keystroke as customers punch in their PINs. These skimming devices are installed for short periods of time—usually just a few hours—so they're often attached to an ATM by nothing more than double-sided tape. They are then removed by the criminals, who download the stolen account information and encode it onto blank cards. The cards are used to make withdrawals from victims' accounts at other ATMs. Some cyberthieves use a realistic-looking card reader placed over the factory-installed card reader. When customers insert their ATM card into the phony reader, their account info is swiped and stored on a small, attached laptop and sent wirelessly to the criminals waiting nearby. Skimmers can also make use of a hidden camera, installed on or near an ATM, to record customers' entry of their PINs into the ATM's keypad.

RANSOMWARE: EXTORTION VIA THE INTERNET

For more than five years, computers around the nation have been attacked by the Reveton virus used by hackers in conjunction with Citadel malware—a software delivery platform that can disseminate various kinds of computer viruses. Unlike many other viruses—which activate when users open a file or attachment—Reveton is a drive-by virus that installs itself when users go to a compromised website; once infected, the victim's computer immediately locks. With the original Reveton virus, the infected computer's monitor displayed an official-looking screen (with an FBI logo) stating there had been a violation of federal law: illegal use of downloaded media, underage porn viewing, or computer-use negligence. It listed fines and penalties for each, and directed victims to pay $200 via a MoneyPak order. Victims were told if the demands were not met, criminal charges would be filed and the computer would remain locked on that screen. Newer variants of Reveton can even turn on computer webcams and display the victim's picture on the frozen screen. Unfortunately for victims, the virus is difficult to resolve and may require professional attention. Even if victims are able to unfreeze their computer, the malware may still operate in the background and gather personal information such as usernames, passwords, and credit card numbers through embedded keystroke logging programs.[19]

Ransomware such as Reveton targets organizations and individual networks in an effort to deny the availability of critical data and/or systems. In 2015, the Internet Crime Complaint Center received 2,453 complaints identified as ransomware, with losses of more than $1.6 million.[20]

Not only have individuals been the victim of ransomware attacks, so have businesses, banks, government agencies, and academic institutions. Once the infection is present, ransomware begins encrypting files and folders on local drives, any attached drives, backup drives, and potentially other computers on the network to which the victim's computer is attached. Users and organizations are generally not aware they have been infected until they can no longer access their data or until they begin to see computer messages advising them of the attack and demands for a ransom payment in exchange for a decryption key.[21]

While some of the earlier ransomware scams involved having victims pay the ransom with prepaid credit cards, victims are now increasingly asked to pay with Bitcoin, a decentralized virtual currency network that attracts criminals because of the anonymity the system offers. A ransomware variant called CryptoWall encrypts files on a computer's hard drive and any external or shared drives to which the computer has access. It directs the user to a personalized victim ransom page that contains the initial ransom amount (anywhere from $500 to $5,000), detailed instructions about how to purchase bitcoins, and typically a countdown clock to notify victims how much time they have before the ransom doubles. Victims are infected with CryptoWall by clicking on links in emails that appear to be from legitimate businesses and through compromised advertisements on popular websites. With the most recent version (CryptoWall 4.0), there is no way to recover the files other than restoring from a backup—or paying the ransom.[22]

Ransomware attacks are not only becoming more frequent, they're becoming more sophisticated. Because email systems are now more adept at filtering out spam, some cybercriminals have turned to spear-phishing with emails that target specific individuals. Others forgo emails in favor of seeding legitimate websites with malicious code, taking advantage of the lack of security on many computers. Sadly, paying the ransom doesn't guarantee an individual victim or organization will get its data back; some never get a decryption key after having paid the ransom. And unfortunately, paying a ransom encourages cyberthieves to expand their activities.

ILLEGAL COPYRIGHT INFRINGEMENT

 L04 Distinguish between the different forms of stealing intellectual property

Groups of individuals work together to illegally obtain software and then "crack" or "rip" its copyright protections, before posting it on the Internet for other members of the group to use; this is called **warez**.

Frequently, these new pirated copies reach the Internet days or weeks before the legitimate product is commercially available. The government has actively pursued members of the warez community, and some have been charged and convicted under the Computer Fraud and Abuse Act (CFAA), which criminalizes accessing computer systems without authorization to obtain information,[23] and the Digital Millennium Copyright Act (DMCA), which makes it a crime to circumvent antipiracy measures built into most commercial software and also outlaws the manufacture, sale, or distribution of code-cracking devices used to illegally copy software.[24]

File Sharing   Another form of illegal copyright infringement involves file-sharing programs that allow Internet users to download music and other copyrighted material without paying the artists and record producers their rightful royalties. Theft through the illegal reproduction and distribution of movies, software, games, and music is estimated to cost U.S. industries more than $20 billion worldwide each year.

---

ransomware Malicious software, usually attached to an email, designed to block access to a computer system until a sum of money is paid.

warez A term computer hackers and software pirates use to describe a game, media, or application that is made available for use on the Internet in violation of its copyright protection.

Although music sharing has become routine with the creation of services such as Pandora and Spotify, criminal copyright infringement still represents a significant economic threat to producers, artists, and programmers. The United States Code provides penalties for a first-time offender of five years incarceration and a fine of $250,000.[25] Other provisions provide for the forfeiture and destruction of infringing copies and all equipment used to make the copies.[26]

INTERNET SECURITIES FRAUD

Fifteen-year-old Jonathan Lebed was charged with securities fraud by the SEC after he repeatedly bought low-cost, thinly traded stocks and then spread hundreds of false and misleading messages concerning them—generally baseless price predictions. After their values were artificially inflated, Lebed sold the securities at an inflated price. His smallest one-day gain was $12,000, and one day he made $74,000. Lebed agreed to findings of fraud but later questioned whether he had done anything wrong; he was forced to hand over his illicit gains, plus interest, which came to $285,000.[27]

Though he might not agree, young Lebed's actions are considered Internet fraud because they involve using the Internet to intentionally manipulate the securities marketplace for profit. There are three major types of Internet securities fraud today:

- *Market manipulation.* Stock market manipulation occurs when an individual tries to control the price of stock by interfering with the natural forces of supply and demand. There are two principal forms of this crime: the "pump and dump" and the "cybersmear." In a pump and dump scheme, erroneous and deceptive information is posted online to get unsuspecting investors interested in a stock while those spreading the information sell previously purchased stock at an inflated price. The cybersmear is a reverse pump and dump: negative information is spread online about a stock, driving down its price and enabling people to buy it at an artificially low price before rebuttals by the company's officers reinflate the price.[28]
- *Fraudulent offerings of securities.* Some cybercriminals create websites specifically designed to fraudulently sell securities. To make the offerings look more attractive than they are, assets may be inflated, expected returns overstated, and risks understated. In these schemes, investors are promised abnormally high profits on their investments. No investment is actually made. Early investors are paid returns with the investment money received from the later investors. The system usually collapses, and the later investors lose their initial investment and do not receive dividends.

- *Illegal touting.* This crime occurs when individuals make securities recommendations and fail to disclose that they are being paid to disseminate their favorable opinions. Section 17(b) of the Securities Act of 1933 requires that paid touters disclose the nature, source, and amount of their compensation. If those who tout stocks fail to disclose their relationship with the company, information misleads investors into believing that the speaker is objective and credible rather than bought and paid for.

IDENTITY THEFT

 L05 Define the terms *identity theft* and *phishing*

Identity theft occurs when a person uses the Internet to steal someone's identity and/or impersonate the victim to open a new credit card account or conduct some other financial transaction. It is a type of cybercrime that has grown at surprising rates over the past few years.[29]

Identity theft can destroy a person's life by manipulating credit records or stealing from their bank accounts. Identity thieves use a variety of techniques to steal information. They may fill out change of address cards at the post office and thus obtain people's credit card bills and bank statements. They may then call the credit card issuer and, pretending to be the victim, ask for a change in address on the account. They can then charge numerous items over the Internet and have the merchandise sent to the new address. It may take months for the victim to realize the fraud because the victim is not getting bills from the credit card company.

What are the most common goals of identity thieves? Opening new lines of credit remains the most frequently occurring use for a victim's identity, followed by using personal information to make charges on stolen credit cards and debit cards, obtaining utilities, applying for bogus personal loans and business loans, and check fraud (personal information is used to access an existing account via theft or the creation of false checks).[30]

How Common Is Identity Theft? According to the most recent government surveys, almost 18 million persons, or about 7 percent of U.S. residents age 16 or older, are victims of at least one incident of identity theft each year. Today, the most common type of identity theft is the unauthorized misuse or attempted misuse of an existing account— experienced by more than 16 million persons. Victims may have experienced multiple types of identity theft. Almost 9 million victims experienced the fraudulent use of a credit card, 8 million experienced the unauthorized use or attempted use of existing bank accounts (checking, savings, or other), and 1.5 million experienced other types of existing account theft, such as misuse or attempted misuse of a phone, Internet, or insurance account.

identity theft Using the Internet to steal someone's identity and/or impersonate the victim in order to conduct illicit transactions such as committing fraud using the victim's name and identity.

Most identity theft victims discover the incident when a financial institution contacts them about suspicious activity or when they notice fraudulent charges on an account. The majority of identity theft victims surveyed did not know how the offender obtained their information, and 90 percent of victims did not know anything about the offender. Victims whose personal information was misused or who had a new account opened in their name experienced greater out-of-pocket financial losses than those who had an existing credit card or bank account compromised; 14 percent lost $1,000 or more. Despite their problems, fewer than 1 in 10 identity theft victims reported the incident to police. The great majority contacted their credit card company or bank to report misuse or attempted misuse of an account or personal information, while 8 percent contacted a credit bureau.[31]

Phishing   Some identity thieves create false emails or websites (there are now nearly 300,000 in operation worldwide) that look legitimate but are designed to gain illegal access to a victim's personal information; this is known as **phishing** (also known as carding or spoofing).[32]

Some phishers send out emails that look like they come from a credit card company or online store telling victims there is a problem with their account credit or balance. To fix the problem and update their account, they are asked to submit their name, address, phone numbers, personal information, credit card account numbers, and Social Security number. Or the email may direct them to a phony website that purports to be a legitimate company or business enterprise. Once victims access the website, they are asked to provide personal information or financial account information so the problem can be fixed. Some phishing schemes involve job offers. Once the unsuspecting victims fill out the "application," answering personal questions and including their Social Security number, the phisher has them in his or her grasp. Another variation of this crime is **spear-phishing**, where cybercriminals target specific victims, sending them emails that contain accurate information about their lives, friends, and activities that was obtained from social networking sites, blogs, or other websites. Personal information makes the message seem legitimate and increases the chances the victims will open the email or go to a tainted website by clicking on a link where malware harvests details such as the victims' usernames and passwords, bank account details, credit card numbers, and other personal information. The criminals can also gain access to private networks and cause disruptions or steal intellectual property and trade secrets.[33] One ingenious scam is referred to as *reshipping* and is discussed in Exhibit 15.2.

Once phishers have a victim's personal information, they can do three things. They can gain access to preexisting accounts, banking, credit cards, and buy things using those accounts. Phishers can use the information to open brand new banking accounts and credit cards without the

EXHIBIT 15.2

Reshipping

The reshipping scheme requires individuals in the United States to receive packages at their residence and subsequently repackage the merchandise for shipment, usually abroad. Reshippers are recruited in various ways but most often through online employment offers and Internet chat rooms.

Unknown entities post help-wanted advertisements at popular Internet job search sites, and respondents quickly reply to the online advertisement. The prospective employee is required to complete an employment application, which requires him or her to divulge sensitive personal information, such as date of birth and Social Security number. The "employer" then uses this information to get a credit card in the victim's name.

The applicant is informed he or she has been hired and will be responsible for forwarding, or reshipping, merchandise purchased in the United States to the company's overseas home office. The packages quickly begin to arrive and, as instructed, the employee dutifully forwards the packages to their overseas destination. The reshipper doesn't realize that the recently received merchandise was purchased with fraudulent credit cards—until the victim is charged for the merchandise he or she just shipped out of the country!

SOURCE: Internet Crime Complaint Center, http://www.ic3.gov /crimeschemes.aspx#item-16 (accessed June 2016).

victim's knowledge. Finally, the phishers can implant viruses into their software that forwards the phishing email to other recipients once one person responds to the original email, thereby luring more potential victims into their net. Some common phishing scams are listed in Exhibit 15.3.

Phishing emails and websites have become even more of a problem now that cybercriminals can easily copy brand names, logos, and corporate personnel insignia directly into the email. The look is so authentic that victims believe the email comes from the advertised company. Most phishers send out spam emails to a large number of recipients knowing that some of those recipients will have accounts with the company they are impersonating.

phishing Sometimes called carding or spoofing, phishing is a scam where the perpetrator sends out emails appearing to come from legitimate web enterprises such as eBay, Amazon, and PayPal in an effort to get the recipient to reveal personal and financial information.

spear-phishing Targeting specific victims, sending them emails that contain accurate information about their lives obtained from social networking sites, and asking them to open an email attachment where malware harvests details such as the victims' usernames and passwords, bank account details, credit card numbers, and other personal information.

EXHIBIT 15.3

Common Phishing Scams

- *Account verification scams.* Individuals purchase domain names that are similar to those of legitimate companies, such as Amazon.Accounts.net. The real company is Amazon, but it does not have *Accounts* in its domain name. These con artists then send out millions of emails asking consumers to verify account information and Social Security numbers. The victim is directed to a bogus website by clicking the legitimate-looking address.
- *Sign-in rosters.* There are some companies and governmental agencies (colleges, EDD, state-sponsored programs) that ask you to put your name and SSN on a sign-in roster. Identity thieves may sign up toward the end of a page so that they can copy and collect personal identifying information.
- *"Help move money from my country," aka Nigerian 419 scam.* A bogus email is sent from an alleged representative of a foreign government asking the victim to help move money from one account to another. Some forms include requests to help a dying woman or free a political prisoner. Some claim that the victim has been the recipient of a legacy or a winning lottery ticket. Nigerian money offers now account for about 12 percent of the scam offers.
- *Canadian/Netherlands lottery.* Originating from the Netherlands and other foreign countries, these scams usually ask for money to hold the prize until the victim can collect in person.
- *"Free credit report."* Almost all "free credit report" emails are scams. Either the person is trying to find out the victim's Social Security number or the victim is billed for services later on.
- *"You have won a free gift."* The victims receive an email about a free gift or prize. They just have to send their credit card info to take care of shipping and handling. Responding may result in hundreds of spams or telemarketing calls.
- *Email chain letters/pyramid schemes.* Victims are sent an official-looking email requesting cooperation by sending a report to five friends or relatives. Those who respond are then contacted for money in order to keep the chain going.
- *"Find out everything on anyone."* This email is trying to solicit money by offering a CD or program that victims can use to find out personal information on another person. However, the information is actually in the public domain and can be easily accessed without the program.
- *Job advertisement scams.* Phishers spoofing legitimate Internet job websites (for instance spoofing Monster.com) contact a victim promising a high-paying job. They solicit personal information, including Social Security numbers.
- *VISA/MasterCard scam.* A VISA or MasterCard "employee" sends an email asking to confirm unusual spending activity and asks the victim for the code on the back of his or her credit card.

SOURCE: Identity Theft Resource Center (ITRC), "Scams and Consumer Alerts," http://www.idtheftcenter.org (accessed June 2016).

Money Mules Once phishers get your personal and financial information through deception and trickery, how do they profit from their account access? One way is to divert money electronically from bank accounts in order to buy high-end merchandise such as precious stones and expensive watches from jewelry stores.[34] The phishers contact these jewelry stores, tell them what they'd like to buy, and promise they will wire the money the next day. A **money mule** goes to the store to pick up the merchandise and either gives the items to the organizers of the scheme or converts them to cash and uses money transfer services to launder the funds.

In many cases, these money mules are willing participants in the criminal scheme. But increasingly they are unsuspecting people hired via "work-at-home" advertisements who end up laundering some of the funds stolen from bank accounts. The criminals email prospective candidates claiming to have seen their résumés on job websites and offer them a job. The hired employees are provided long and seemingly legitimate work contracts and actual websites to log on to for instructions. They're instructed to either open a bank account or use their own bank account in order to receive funds via wire transactions from numerous banks and then use money transfer services to send the money overseas.

Smishing and Vishing Smishing and vishing scams use smart phones and landlines to trick people into providing access information for their bank, checking, and other accounts. Some scammers use the information to impersonate the victim and open new accounts. The word "smishing" is derived from SMS (texting) and phishing, and "vishing" comes from voice and phishing. In these scams, criminals set up an automated dialing system to text or call people in a particular region or area code, sometimes using stolen customer phone numbers from banks or credit unions. The victims receive messages like "There's a problem with your account" or "Your ATM card needs to be reactivated" and are directed to a phone number or website asking for personal information. Armed with that information, criminals can steal from victims' bank accounts, charge purchases on their credit cards, create a phony debit card, and so on. In one case, bank customers received a text saying they needed

money mule Someone who collects and transfers money or goods acquired illegally and then transfers them to a third party.

to reactivate their ATM card. When they called the phone number in the text, they were prompted to provide their ATM card number, PIN, and expiration date. Many victims fell for the ruse and thousands of fraudulent withdrawals followed.[35] If victims log on to one of the tainted websites with a smart phone, they might download malicious software that could give criminals access to anything on the phone.

Combating Phishing and Identity Theft To meet the increasing threat of phishing and identity theft, Congress passed the Identity Theft and Assumption Deterrence Act of 1998 (Identity Theft Act) to make it a federal crime when anyone:

> Knowingly transfers or uses, without lawful authority, a means of identification of another person with the intent to commit, or to aid or abet, any unlawful activity that constitutes a violation of Federal law, or that constitutes a felony under any applicable State or local law.[36]

Violations of the act are investigated by federal investigative agencies such as the U.S. Secret Service, the FBI, and the U.S. Postal Inspection Service. In 2004, the Identity Theft Penalty Enhancement Act was signed into law; the act increases existing penalties for the crime of identity theft, establishes aggravated identity theft as a criminal offense, and establishes mandatory penalties for aggravated identity theft. According to this law, anyone who knowingly "transfers, possesses, or uses, without lawful authority" someone else's identification will be sentenced to an extra prison term of two years with no possibility of probation. Committing identity fraud while engaged in crimes associated with terrorism—such as aircraft destruction, arson, airport violence, or kidnapping top government officials—will receive a mandatory sentence enhancement of five years.[37]

ETAILING FRAUD

New fraud schemes are evolving to reflect the fact that billions of dollars in goods are sold on the Internet each year. **Etailing fraud** can involve both illegally buying and selling merchandise on the Net.

Not only do etail frauds involve selling merchandise, they can also involve buyer fraud. One scam involves purchasing top-of-the-line electronic equipment over the Net and then purchasing a second, similar looking but cheaper model of the same brand. The cheaper item is then returned to the etailer after switching bar codes and boxes with the more expensive unit. Because etail return processing centers don't always check returned goods closely, they may send a refund for the value of the higher priced model. In another tactic, called shoplisting, a person obtains a legitimate receipt from a store either by buying it from a customer or finding it in the trash and then returns to the store and, casually shopping, picks up an identical product. He then takes the product and receipt to the returns department and attempts to return it for cash, store credit, or a gift card. The thief then sells the store credit or gift card on the Internet at a discount for quick cash. Not surprisingly, the underground market for receipts has been growing, as stores have liberalized return policies.[38]

Some of the most common Internet fraud schemes are included in Exhibit 15.4. Before you say, "How could anyone fall for this stuff?" remember that more than 280,000 people file complaints with the government's Internet Crime Complaint Center each year and these scams create more than $1 billion in losses.[39]

> **etailing fraud** Illegally buying and/or selling merchandise on the Internet.

Common Internet Fraud Schemes

AUTO AUCTION FRAUD

This is an Internet auction fraud involving the sale of automobiles. Many of the listings are for vehicles located outside the United States. In most cases the criminal attempts to sell vehicles they do not own. Criminals create attractive deals by advertising vehicles at prices below book value and claim that they must sell the vehicle because they are moving or being relocated for work. Due to the pending move, the criminals often refuse to meet with potential buyers or allow vehicle inspections and ultimately try to rush the sale. In an attempt to make the deal appear legitimate, the criminal often instructs victims to send full or partial payments to third-party agents via wire transfers and to fax their payment receipt to the seller as proof of payment. Once payment is made, the criminal pockets the money and the victim never receives the vehicle.

HITMAN SCAM

The victim receives an email from a member of an organization such as the "Ishmael Ghost Islamic Group." The emailer claims to have been sent to assassinate the victim and the victim's family members. The emailer asserts that the reason for the impending assassination resulted from an alleged offense by the victim against a member of the emailer's gang. In a bizarre twist, the emailer reveals that another member of the gang (purporting to know a member of the victim's extended family) pleaded for the victim's pardon. The emailer alleges that an agreement was reached with the pleading

(Continued)

---

gang member to pardon the victim from assassination if the victim takes some action, such as sending $800 to a receiver in the United Kingdom for the migration of Islamic expatriates from the United States. Victims of this email are typically instructed to send the money via Western Union or MoneyGram. The emailer gives the victim 72 hours to send the money or else pay with his/her life.

ECONOMIC STIMULUS SCAM

Another popular scam involves unsolicited calls offering "government stimulus money." A recorded voice message describes alleged government funds available for those who apply; in one such scam, the voice reportedly sounded very much like President Obama. Victims are warned that the offer is only available for a limited time and are instructed to visit certain websites to receive their money. These sites require victims to enter personal identifying information after which they are directed to a second page to receive notification of eligibility. Upon completion of an online application and payment of small fees, victims are guaranteed to receive a large sum of stimulus money, but they never do.

PET SCAMS

A self-proclaimed breeder posts an online ad (along with a cute picture or even a streaming video) offering to sell a pet. The breeder asks the buyer to send in money, plus a little extra for delivery costs. But the buyer never gets the pet; the scam artist simply takes the money and runs.

SECRET SHOPPERS AND FUNDS TRANSFER SCAMS

Individuals are hired via the Web to rate experiences while shopping or dining. They are paid by check and asked to wire a percentage of the money to a third party. The check they had been sent bounces, and they are out the money they sent to the other party. As part of the scam, the fraudsters often use real logos from legitimate companies.

ADOPTION AND CHARITY FRAUD

A person is sent an email that tugs on his or her heartstrings, asking for a pressing donation to a charity and often using the subject header "Urgent Assistance Is Needed." The name of a real charity is generally used, but the information provided sends the money to a con artist. One set of scams used the name of a legitimate British adoption agency to ask for money for orphaned or abandoned children.

ROMANCE FRAUD

A person encounters someone in an online dating or social networking site who lives far away or in another country. That person strikes up a relationship with him or her and then wants to meet, but needs money to cover travel expenses. Typically, that's just the beginning—the person may claim to

have been taken ill or injured during the journey and asks for money to pay the hospital expenses.

OVERPAYMENT FRAUD

Victims who have advertised some item for sale via the Internet are contacted by "buyers" who remit counterfeit checks in excess of the purchase price as payment. The victim is told to cash the check, deduct any expenses, and return or forward the excess funds to the "buyer," but later discovers the check was counterfeit. Victims in this fraud not only lose the value of the property sold, but they are also indebted to their financial institutions for the funds withdrawn on the counterfeit check.

ADVANCE-FEE FRAUD SCHEMES

A victim is promised a substantial benefit—such as a million-dollar prize, lottery winnings, a substantial inheritance, or some other item of value—but must pay a fee or series of fees before he or she can receive that benefit. While there are almost endless variations on this basic scheme, the following are some of the more frequently used types.

Business Opportunity/Work-at-Home Schemes

Fraudulent schemes often advertise purported business opportunities that supposedly allow individuals to earn thousands of dollars a month in "work-at-home" ventures. These schemes typically require victims to pay anywhere from tens to hundreds of dollars (or more) to get started. The fraudsters then fail to deliver the materials or information needed to make the work-at-home opportunity a potentially viable business.

Credit Card Interest Reduction Schemes

Some fraudulent schemes offer to help individuals lower their credit card interest rates, charging fees without effecting any actual reductions in the cardholders' rates.

Inheritance Schemes

Some fraudulent schemes contact prospective victims by representing that the people contacted are in a position to receive a substantial inheritance from a family member or from an individual who has died without heirs. The person contacted is then subjected to a series of demands for advance payment of various fees before the inheritance can be transferred.

Lottery/Prize/Sweepstakes Schemes

Operating from a growing number of countries, including Costa Rica, the Dominican Republic, Jamaica, the Netherlands, Nigeria, and Spain, these schemes falsely represent that the person contacted has just won a substantial lottery prize or other sweepstakes or prize contest, but must pay what proves to be a growing number of fees or "taxes" before he or she can receive the prize.

SOURCES: FBI, "Mass Marketing Fraud," https://www.fbi.gov/news/stories/2010/june/mass-marketing-fraud; U.S. Department of Justice, "Mass Marketing Fraud," https://www.justice.gov/criminal-fraud/mass-marketing-fraud. (URLs accessed June 2016.)

Cyberdeviance: The Darker Side of the Net

L06 Assess how the Internet can facilitate the sale of illegal materials

Cyberdeviance refers to a range of activities, some considered illegal, others considered amoral, and many considered both. Included within this realm of cybercrime are the distribution of pornography and obscene material, including kiddie porn, online prostitution, and the distribution of dangerous drugs.

The Internet has transformed the accessibility of these banned acts and materials, making it possible for people who sell these illicit goods and services to connect with one another across the globe. Because there are a myriad of people engaging in similar behaviors, someone who heretofore has lurked in the shadows can now find companions who will reinforce and share behaviors they may have previously considered socially and legally unacceptable. Obsessive and irrational individuals are no longer limited by time, position, or space. They can dwell in a virtual world filled with people just like themselves but who may be living on the far side of the planet. Cyberdeviance has no boundaries. It may not have created a new breed of crime but, rather, serves as an efficient delivery system for some traditional types of deviant behavior. What forms of behavior does cyberdeviance take?

DISTRIBUTING PORNOGRAPHY

The IT revolution revitalized the porn industry. The Internet is an ideal venue for selling and distributing obscene material; the computer is an ideal device for storage and viewing. It is difficult to estimate the vast number of websites featuring sexual content, including nude photos, videos, live sex acts, and webcam strip sessions among other forms of "adult entertainment."[40] Adult content is so pervasive and easily obtained that it has driven some adult magazines out of business. In 2015, *Playboy* announced it would no longer feature nudity in the magazine, finding it impossible to compete with what is on the Internet.

There is no conclusive data on the extent of Internet porn sites. Estimates are all over the map. Some estimates calculate that about 5 percent of the top million websites are sex related.[41] That would mean that adult sites get billions of hits each year. Other estimates suggest that by 2017 a quarter of a billion people will be accessing mobile adult content from their phones or tablets, an increase of more than 30 percent from 2013. Mobile adult video chat alone will have a compound annual growth rate of 25 percent.[42] With most porn on the Internet now free and easy to find, the number of adult sites and traffic to them have exploded to an estimated 700 to 800 million individual porn pages. Surveys now show that:

The Internet has changed the adult entertainment industry. In 2015, *Playboy* founder Hugh Hefner announced the magazine would no longer publish pictures of naked women, saying easy access to such images online rendered them "passé." The magazine aimed to become more accessible to the general public as it entered its 63rd year.

AP Images/Ian West

- Every second, 28,258 users are watching pornography on the Internet.
- Every second, $3,075.64 is being spent on pornography on the Internet.
- Every second, 372 people are typing the word *adult* into search engines.
- Forty million American people regularly visit porn sites.
- Thirty-five percent of all Internet downloads are related to pornography.
- Twenty-five percent of all search engine queries are related to pornography, or about 68 million search queries a day.[43]

But these data may undercount the actual number of adult sites: a Google search on the word "porn" returned more than 98 million results, and "xxx" returned more than 216 million. People are often directed to these sites through "porn-napping" and "typosquatted" websites. Porn-nappers buy expired domain names of existing sites and then try to sell adult material to people who stumble upon them while surfing. Typosquat websites are those where a pornographer has deliberately registered names with typos so that people searching online are directed to pornography sites if they misspell a word or put in the wrong keystroke—for example, typing teltubbies.com instead of teletubbies.com.[44] There are also people who access the **darknet** in order to

> **darknet** Computer network that can only be accessed using non-standard communications protocols and ports, with restricted access that can only be opened with specific software configurations.

The Lost Boy Case

The Lost Boy online bulletin board was established to provide a forum for men with a sexual interest in young boys to trade child pornography. Law enforcement in the United States and abroad became aware of the network when Norwegian and Italian authorities discovered that a North Hollywood, California, man was communicating via an Internet site with an Italian national about child pornography and how to engage in child sex tourism in Romania. Further investigation revealed that Lost Boy had 35 members; more than half were U.S. nationals. Other members of the network were located in countries around the world, including Belgium, Brazil, Canada, France, Germany, New Zealand, and the United Kingdom.

To shield themselves from prosecution, the Lost Boy network had developed a thorough vetting process for new members to weed out law enforcement agents. Members were required to post child pornography in order to join the organization and to continue posting child pornography to remain in good standing. Lost Boy members advised one another on techniques to evade detection by law enforcement, which included using screen names to mask identities and encrypting computer data.

As the investigation unfolded, law enforcement agencies identified child molestation suspects in South America, Europe, and New Zealand. Suspects in Romania, France, Brazil, Norway, and the United Kingdom were charged and convicted, receiving long prison sentences. In the United States, offenders were prosecuted under the Adam Walsh Child Protection and Safety Act, a 2006 law with a three-tier system of categorizing sex offenders that mandates lifetime sex offender registration for tier one offenders and more severe criminal penalties when compared to less serious offenders. It also allows judges to levy heavier sentences on child molesters who are engaged in cooperative, sustained criminal efforts with others, such as running the Lost Boy network. Fifteen U.S. Lost Boy defendants have been convicted, one died in custody, and three remain at large. All told, the authorities identified 200 victims as a result of the investigation.

At the time, the Lost Boy indictment was the largest-ever child exploitation enterprise investigation since the signing of the Walsh Act. Because of the sentencing enhancements, some of those prosecuted in the Lost Boy case received sentences of between 20 and 35 years in prison. One man, Jeffrey Greenwell, who produced pornographic images and videos that appeared on the Lost Boy online bulletin board, pleaded guilty to five counts of production of child pornography and was sentenced to a total of 100 years in prison. Since the Lost Boy case was prosecuted, Operation Delego, conducted by the Justice Department and the Department of Homeland Security, resulted in the indictment of 72 defendants for their participation in Dreamboard—a private, members-only, online bulletin board created to promote pedophilia.

The Lost Boy case illustrates the difficulty of controlling Internet pornography. Getting evidence sufficient for prosecution involved the cooperation of law enforcement agencies around the world and the arrests of people in multiple countries, a very expensive and time-consuming activity.

SOURCES: Text of the Adam Walsh Child Protection and Safety Act of 2006, http://www.govtrack.us/congress/bills/109/hr4472/text; U.S. Department of Justice, "Ohio Man Sentenced to 35 Years in Prison for His Participation in an Online Child Pornography Bulletin Board," http://www.fbi.gov/losangeles/press-releases/2012/ohio-man-sentenced-to-35-years-in-prison-for-his-participation-in-an-online-child-pornography-bulletin-board. (URLs accessed June 2016.)

trade in kiddie porn and other illegal material—searches that do not show up in efforts to count visits to porn sites.

How do adult sites operate today? There are a number of different schemes in operation:[45]

- A large firm sells annual subscriptions in exchange for unlimited access to content.
- Password services charge an annual fee to deliver access to hundreds of small sites, which share the subscription revenues.
- Large firms provide free content to smaller affiliate sites. The affiliates post the free content and then try to channel visitors to the large sites, which give the smaller sites a percentage of the fees paid by those who sign up.
- Webmasters forward traffic to another porn site in return for a small per-consumer fee. In many cases, the consumer is sent to the other sites involuntarily, which is known in the industry as mousetrapping. Web surfers who try to close out a window after visiting an adult site are sent to another web page automatically. This can repeat dozens of times, causing users to panic and shut down their computers in order to escape.
- Adult sites cater to niche audiences looking for specific kinds of adult content. While some sites deal in legal sexually related material, others cross the legal border by peddling access to obscene material or even kiddie porn.

Prosecuting Internet Pornography Despite some successful prosecutions, it has been difficult to control Internet pornography. One reason is that offenders are scattered around the world, making identification and arrest challenging. There needs to be significant law enforcement agency cooperation to gather evidence and locate suspects. When there are prosecutions, they are aimed at child pornography, considered a much more serious crime than sale of adult material. Take for instance the Lost Boy case, which resulted in lengthy prison sentences for the principals involved. The Lost Boy case is set out in the Profiles in Crime feature.

EHOOKING

The technological revolution has begun to alter the world of prostitution. Instead of walking the streets or hanging out in a brothel waiting for customers, cyberprostitutes set up personal websites or put listings on web boards, such as Adult FriendFinder, that carry personals. **Ehooking** sites may use loaded phrases such as "looking for generous older man" in their self-descriptions. When contacted, sex workers ask to exchange emails, chat online, or make voice calls with prospective clients. They may exchange pictures. This preliminary contact allows them to select whom they want to be with and avoid clients who may be threatening or dangerous. Some cyberprostitution rings offer customers the opportunity to choose women from their Internet page and then have them flown in from around the country. In Germany, where prostitution is legal, an app called Peppr makes it easy to find a sex worker. A potential client types in his or her location and up pops a list of the nearest prostitutes, along with pictures, prices, and physical characteristics; users can arrange a session for a booking fee that averages $10. Peppr is located in Berlin and has plans to expand to more cities.[46]

In addition to booking dates, online forums allow prostitutes to share tips about how to stay safe and avoid tangling with the law. Services such as Roomservice 2000 (recently renamed RS-AVS) allow customers to pay for a background check to present to sex workers. Both sides benefit since the client can demonstrate trustworthiness without giving credit card details or phone numbers to the prostitute.[47]

DISTRIBUTING DANGEROUS DRUGS

In 2013, Michael Arnold was sentenced to five years in prison for his role as the organizer and leader of the Pitcairn Internet pharmacy. From 2003 through 2007, Pitcairn sold more than 14 million doses of Schedule III and IV controlled substances, earning over $69 million in its four years of operation

on websites such as ezdietpills.net, pillsavings.com, and doctorrefill.net. Arnold laundered Pitcairn's illegal proceeds through accounts in at least eight different countries, including Switzerland, Liechtenstein, the Netherlands, Canada, Panama, the Bahamas, St. Kitts and Nevis, and Curaçao.[48]

The Arnold case, in addition to many others, shows how the Internet has become a prime purveyor of prescription drugs, some of which can be quite dangerous when they are used to excess or fall into the hands of minors. One survey by the National Center on Addiction

ehooking Using the Internet to advertise sexual services and make contact with clients.

The "dark web" is made up of websites that do not show up on regular Internet searches and is an anonymous, virtually untraceable global network. In July 2015, Cei William Owens, shown here, was sentenced to two years in jail after admitting to five drug offenses on the dark web. Owens committed his offenses on the Silk Road 2.0 illicit marketplace, which has since been shut down but was well known for its trade in illegal drugs. Owens was one of five people arrested across the United Kingdom as part of a National Crime Agency (NCA) operation.

AP Images/Legakis/REX Shutterstock

and Substance Abuse at Columbia University uncovered a total of 365 websites that advertised or sold controlled prescription drugs such as Oxycontin, Valium, Xanax, Vicodin, Ritalin, and Adderall. Only two of the sites were certified by the National Association of Boards of Pharmacy as verified Internet pharmacy practice sites, and 85 percent of the sites did not require a prescription from a doctor.[49] Of those that did, about half only required that the original prescription be provided, not a prescription authorizing refills. This allowed buyers to make multiple purchases with a single script. The report also found sites selling online "medical consultations," where doctors see many patients a day to fill or refill prescriptions for controlled drugs without regard for the standards of medical practice.

Children are especially at risk, and millions of children are now feared to be abusing an illegally obtained prescription drug. More teens have abused these drugs than many other illegal drugs, including Ecstasy, cocaine, crack, and methamphetamine. With access to a credit card, they can order opioid-based drugs (e.g., codeine, Demerol, Oxycontin, Percocet, and Darvon), depressants (e.g., Xanax, Librium, and Valium), and stimulants (e.g., Adderall, Dexedrine, and Ritalin).

Cybervandalism: Cybercrime with Malicious Intent

 LO7 Discuss the different types of cybervandalism

Cybervandalism typically involves a cyberattack to achieve a malicious or vengeful intent (such as a denial-of-service attack launched in retaliation for some slight), to hurt and embarrass someone they are angry at, or simply to hurt people because they enjoy being destructive. Cybervandals usually do not profit from their crimes other than to enjoy the havoc and harm they inflict on others; they are vandals in cyberspace.

Cybervandalism ranges from sending destructive viruses and worms to stalking or bullying people using cyberspace as a medium. Cybervandals may want to damage or deface websites or even, as Exhibit 15.5 reveals, pull a virtual fire alarm; they are motivated more by malice than greed:

- Some cybervandals target computers and networks seeking revenge for some perceived wrong.
- Some want to exhibit their technical prowess and superiority.
- Some want to highlight the vulnerability of computer security systems.
- Some want to spy on other people's private financial or personal information (computer voyeurism).
- Some are mean-spirited bullies who want to harm others socially rather than physically.
- Some want to destroy computer security because they believe in a philosophy of open access to all systems and programs.[50]

What forms does cybervandalism take?

DATA BREACHES

In 2015, the online hookup site Ashley Madison was hacked; stolen personal information on 32 million of the site's members, such as email addresses, was posted on the Net. The hackers claimed two motivations: they objected to Ashley Madison's intent of arranging affairs between married individuals, and they objected to its requirement that users pay $19 for the privilege of deleting all their data from the site.[51] The company issued a $500,000 reward for the identity of the hackers.

The Ashley Madison case is not unique. At the close of 2015, 191 million records were uncovered on the Web containing various pieces of personal information related to American citizens registered to vote; no one knows who was responsible for the data theft. In 2015, there were nine similar data breaches in which more than 10 million records were stolen. In all, 429 million people had personal information illegally accessed by hackers, though this may be a conservative estimate since private companies are loath to reveal the extent of breaches. Internet security company Symantec believes that the real number is more than half a billion.[52]

WORMS, VIRUSES, TROJAN HORSES, LOGIC BOMBS, AND SPAM

The most typical use of cyberspace for destructive intent comes in the sending or implanting of disruptive programs, called viruses, worms, Trojan horses, logic bombs, and spam.

Viruses and Worms   Viruses are a type of malicious software program (also called **malware**) that disrupts or destroys existing programs and networks, causing them to perform the task for which the virus was designed.[53] The virus is then spread from one computer to another when a user sends out an infected file through email, a network, or a portable drive. **Computer worms** are similar to viruses but use computer networks or the Internet to self-replicate and send themselves to other users, generally via email, without the aid of the operator.

Trojan Horses   Some hackers introduce a **Trojan horse** program into a computer system. The Trojan horse looks like a benign application but contains illicit codes that can damage the system operations. Sometimes hackers with a sense of irony will install a Trojan horse and claim that it is an antivirus program. When it is opened, it spreads viruses in the computer system. Though Trojan horses do not replicate themselves like viruses, they can be just as destructive.

Logic Bombs   A fourth type of destructive attack that can be launched on a computer system is the **logic bomb**, a program that is secretly attached to a computer system, monitors the network's work output, and waits for a particular signal such as a date to appear. Also called a slag code, it is a type of delayed-action virus that may be set off when a program user makes certain input that sets it in motion. A logic bomb may cause a variety of problems ranging from displaying or printing a spurious message to deleting or corrupting data.

Spam   An unsolicited advertisement or promotional material, spam typically comes in the form of an unwanted email message; spammers use electronic communications to send unsolicited messages in bulk. While email is the most common form of spam, it can also be sent via instant messaging, online newsgroup, and texting, among other media.

Spam can simply be in the form of an unwanted and unwelcome advertisement. For example, it may advertise sexually explicit websites and get into the hands of minors. A more dangerous and malicious form of spam contains a Trojan horse disguised as an email attachment advertising some commodity such as free software or an electronic game. If the recipient downloads or opens the attachment, a virus may be launched that corrupts the victim's computer. The Trojan horse may also be designed to capture important data from the victim's hard drive and send it back to the hacker's email address.

Sending spam can become a crime and even lead to a prison sentence when it causes serious harm to a computer or network.

WEBSITE DEFACEMENT

Cybervandals may aim their attention at the websites of their victims. **Website defacement** is a type of cybervandalism that occurs when a computer hacker intrudes on another owner's website by inserting or substituting codes that expose visitors to the site to misleading or provocative information. Defacement can range from installing humorous graffiti to sabotaging or corrupting the site. In some instances, defacement efforts are not easily apparent or noticeable—for example, when they are designed to give misinformation by substituting or replacing authorized text on a company's web page. The false information may mislead customers and frustrate their efforts to utilize the site or make it difficult for people using search engines to find the site.

---

malware   A malicious software program.

computer worms   Programs that attack computer networks (or the Internet) by self-replicating and sending themselves to other users, generally via email, without the aid of the operator.

Trojan horse   A computer program that looks like a benign application but contains illicit codes that can damage the system operations. Though Trojan horses do not replicate themselves like viruses, they can be just as destructive.

logic bomb   A program that is secretly attached to a computer system, monitors the network's work output, and waits for a particular signal such as a date to appear. Also called a slag code, it is a type of delayed-action virus that may be set off when a program user makes certain input that sets it in motion. A logic bomb may cause a variety of problems ranging from displaying or printing a spurious message to deleting or corrupting data.

website defacement   A type of cybervandalism that occurs when a computer hacker intrudes on another person's website by inserting or substituting codes that expose visitors to the site to misleading or provocative information. Defacement can range from installing humorous graffiti to sabotaging or corrupting the site.

Almost all defacement attacks are designed to vandalize web pages rather than bring profit or gain to the intruders (though some defacers may eventually extort money from their targets). Some defacers are simply trying to impress the hacking community with their skills. Others may target a corporation when they oppose its business practices and policies (such as oil companies, tobacco companies, or defense contractors). Some defacement has political goals such as disrupting the website of a rival political party or fund-raising group.

Website defacement is a major threat to online businesses and government agencies. It can harm the credibility and reputation of the organization and demonstrate that its security measures are inadequate. As a result, clients lose trust and may be reluctant to share information such as credit card numbers and personal information. An etailer may lose business if potential clients believe the site is not secure. Financial institutions, such as web-based banks and brokerage houses, are particularly vulnerable because they rely on security and credibility to protect their clients' accounts.[54]

CYBERSTALKING

In 2012, a scandal rocked the nation when General David Petraeus, head of the Central Intelligence Agency, was forced to resign when word came out that he had a long-term extramarital affair with his biographer, Paula Broadwell. The affair was uncovered when Jill Kelley, a Florida socialite, asked a friend in the FBI to investigate a series of harassing emails she had received from an unknown person.[55] The FBI traced the emails to Broadwell, and found that she was also exchanging intimate messages with an email account belonging to Petraeus. The head of the CIA was brought down because his former girlfriend was cyberstalking a rival!

Cyberstalking refers to the use of the Internet, email, or other electronic communication devices to stalk another person. Traditional stalking involves repeated harassing or threatening behavior, such as following a person, appearing at a person's home or place of business, making harassing phone calls, leaving written messages or objects, or vandalizing a person's property. In the Internet age, stalkers can pursue victims through online chat rooms. Pedophiles can use the Internet to establish a relationship with a child, and later make contact for the purpose of engaging in criminal sexual activities. Internet predators are more likely to meet, develop relationships with at-risk adolescents, and beguile underage teenagers, rather than use coercion and violence.[56] The Profiles in Crime feature "Christopher Gunn, Cyberstalker" reviews the case of a well-known cyberstalker.

Not all cyberstalkers are sexual predators. Some send repeated threatening or harassing messages via email and use programs to automatically send messages at regular or random intervals. A cyberstalker may trick other people into harassing or threatening a victim by impersonating the victim on Internet bulletin boards or chat rooms, posting messages that are provocative, such as "I want to have sex." The stalker then posts the victim's name, phone number, or email address hoping that other chat participants will stalk or hassle the victim without the stalker's personal involvement.

DENIAL-OF-SERVICE ATTACK

Colorado resident David Joseph Rezendes, 27, was sentenced to serve 18 months in federal prison for intentionally damaging a protected computer system. He also had to forfeit equipment he used in the attack, including three desktop computers, three laptops, nine hard drives, two routers, three cable modems, and a magnetic stripe card reader/writer, among other things.

What did he do to deserve such a sentence? Rezendes was responsible for a denial-of-service attack he implemented to retaliate against the Larimer County government. During his attack, he saturated the county's computer network with such an overwhelming amount of traffic and communication requests that county employees were unable to access email or county records. In addition, the public's ability to use county services online was diminished, and thousands of people were unable to access needed information. What motivated the attack? Rezendes was angry about a traffic ticket![57]

A **distributed denial-of-service attack (DDoS)** involves multiple compromised networks infected with a Trojan virus that targets a single system, causing a shutdown. It involves threats or attacks designed to prevent the legitimate operation of the site. In most cases, such as the Rezendes attack, there is no monetary objective and the attack is a type of cybervandalism.

In 2015, an attack against Rutgers University interrupted Internet service for students, faculty, and staff; another attack knocked out all of New York City's email accounts.[58] Some of the most vulnerable targets are online gaming sites. Massive attacks have disrupted service on games such as Blizzard's Battle.net, Riot Games' League of Legends, and the Origin service run by Electronic Arts.[59] Also in 2015, the BBC's entire network of websites and its iPlayer streaming service were the subject of a cyberattack that resulted in users being met with an error message saying there had been an "internal error"; the disruption continued for around an hour before the service was fully restored.[60]

cyberstalking Use of the Internet, email, or other electronic communications devices to stalk another person. Some cyberstalkers pursue minors through online chat rooms; others harass their victims electronically.

distributed denial-of-service attack (DDoS) A type of DoS attack where multiple compromised systems, which are often infected with a virus, are used to target a single system, causing a denial-of-service (DoS) attack.

Christopher Gunn, Cyberstalker

In 2011, Christopher Gunn, 31, pleaded guilty to producing child pornography in connection with an online sextortion scheme that spanned the globe. Over a period of more than two years, Gunn repeatedly used chat rooms and other social media outlets to threaten hundreds of girls ages 9 to 16 and coerce them into sending him sexually suggestive or explicit photos.

The first scheme—dubbed the "new kid ruse"—involved contacting the victims on Facebook and pretending to be a new kid in town looking for friends. Once he had gained their trust through chatting, Gunn would ask the girls a series of personal questions, such as their sexual histories, intimate details about their bodies, and so on. If they divulged that personal information, Gunn would then ask the girls to send him a topless photo. If they refused, he would threaten to email their intimate conversation to the school principal or post it on Facebook for everyone to see. The second scheme—dubbed the "Justin Bieber ruse"—involved pretending to be pop star Justin Bieber, contacting young girls via

video chat services, such as Omegle and Skype, and offering them free concert tickets, backstage passes, or some other fan-related benefits if they would agree to send him a webcam transmission or photo of themselves with their breasts exposed.

For those who complied, Gunn sent further demands and more threatening communications, asking for fully nude photos and then escalating to sexually explicit photos and webcam videos. If any of his demands were not met, Gunn would threaten to publish the compromising images and videos over the Internet. During the sentencing hearing, the assistant U.S. attorney described conversations that occurred over the computer between Gunn and his young victims. During those conversations, the victims begged and pleaded for Gunn to allow them to stop performing degrading, humiliating, and sexually explicit acts. Each time the victims wanted to stop, Gunn threatened to send the pictures to the victim's friends and family. The U.S. attorney also read in court a transcript of a conversation between

Gunn and a 13-year-old victim. The victim told Gunn that she did not want to take her shirt off in front of the webcam. Gunn replied that if she did not, he would click Send. The victim responded that she was only 13 years old and that she had a life: "Please do not ruin it." Gunn responded, "I am sending it now since u won't do what I want." The victim then told Gunn that if he pushed the Send button she would kill herself. Gunn completely disregarded her cry for help and demanded that she take off her top. The victim complied. When Gunn asked the court for mercy, the federal attorney replied that he believed in justice tempered with mercy. However, because Gunn showed no mercy to his young victims his sentence should reflect his cruelty. The judge agreed and gave Gunn 35 years in prison.

SOURCE: U.S. Attorney's Office, Middle District of Alabama, "Child Predator Is Sentenced to 35 Years in Prison for His Massive Online Sextortion Scheme," https://www.fbi.gov/mobile/press-releases/2013/child-predator-is-sentenced-to-35-years-in-prison-for-his-massive-online-sextortion-scheme (accessed June 2016).

 Established in 1988, the CERT® Coordination Center (CERT/CC) is a center of Internet security expertise, located at the Software Engineering Institute, a federally funded research and development center operated by Carnegie Mellon University. Learn more at **http://www.cert.org/**.

Why would someone spend his or her time and energy writing code simply to stop someone or some organization from using their website? Does such defacement really make hackers "feel good"?

In extortion-driven DDoS attacks, the perpetrators flood an Internet site with millions of bogus messages or orders so that its services will be tied up and unable to perform as promised. Unless the site operator pays extortion money, the attackers threaten to keep up the interference until real consumers become frustrated and abandon the site. Even so-called respectable businesspeople have been accused of launching denial-of-service attacks against rival business

interests.[61] Online gambling casinos—a multibillion-dollar-a-year industry—have proven particularly vulnerable to this type of attack. If the attack coincides with a big sporting event such as the Super Bowl, the casinos may give in and make payments rather than lose revenue and fray customer relations.[62]

CYBERBULLYING

 Articulate the extent of cyberbullying and the damage it causes people

Experts define bullying among children as repeated negative acts committed by one or more children against another. These negative acts may be physical or verbal in nature—for example, hitting or kicking, teasing or taunting—or they may involve indirect actions such as manipulating friendships or purposely excluding other children from activities. Implicit in this definition is an imbalance in real or perceived power between the bully and the victim. It may come as no surprise that lesbian, gay, bisexual, and transgender (LGBT) students are subject to a disproportionate amount of bullying:

- Eight in ten LGBT students have been verbally harassed at school.
- Four in ten have been physically harassed at school.
- Six in ten have felt unsafe at school.
- One in five has been the victim of a physical assault at school.[63]

This exposure to violence and bullying takes a toll: more than half of LGBT students (61 percent) were more likely than their non-LGBT peers to feel unsafe or uncomfortable as a result of their sexual orientation. The percentage of gay, lesbian, and bisexual students who did not go to school at least one day during the past 30 because of safety concerns ranged from 11 to 30 percent of gay and lesbian students and 12 to 25 percent of bisexual students.[64]

Studies of bullying suggest that there are short- and long-term consequences for both the perpetrators and the victims of bullying. Students who are chronic victims of bullying experience more physical and psychological problems than their peers who are not harassed by other children, and they tend not to grow out of the role of victim. Young people mistreated by peers may not want to be in school and may thereby miss out on the benefits of school connectedness as well as educational advancement. Longitudinal studies have found that victims of bullying in early grades also reported being bullied several years later.[65] Chronically victimized students may, as adults, be at increased risk for depression, poor self-esteem, and other mental health problems, including schizophrenia.[66]

While bullying is a problem that remains to be solved, it has now morphed from the physical to the virtual. Because of the creation of cyberspace, physical distance is no longer a barrier to the frequency and depth of harm doled out by a bully to his or her victim.[67] **Cyberbullying** is defined as willful and repeated harm inflicted through the medium of online communications. Like their real-world counterparts, cyberbullies are malicious aggressors who seek implicit or explicit pleasure or profit through the mistreatment of other individuals. Although power in traditional bullying might be physical (stature) or social (competency or popularity), online power may simply stem from Net proficiency. Cyberbullies are able to navigate the Net and utilize technology in a way that puts them in a position of power relative to their victim. There are two main formats that bullies employ to harass their victims: (1) a cyberbully can use a computer and send harassing emails or instant messages; post obscene, insulting, and slanderous messages to online bulletin boards or social networking sites;

or develop websites to promote and disseminate defamatory content; (2) a cyberbully can use a cell phone to send harassing text messages and other media to the victim.[68]

Catfishing Some cyberbullies want to stalk victims, and some stalkers want to bully their targets. Take the practice that has become known as *catfishing*, a term that refers to the practice of setting up a fictitious online profile, most often for the purpose of luring another into a fraudulent romantic relationship. According to the Urban Dictionary, a catfish is "someone who pretends to be someone they're not, using Facebook or other social media to create false identities, particularly to pursue deceptive online romances." So, to "catfish" someone is to set up a fake social media profile with the goal of duping that person into falling for the false persona.

While catfishing has been around a while, it became a topic of public interest when 13-year-old Megan Meier began an online relationship with a boy she knew as Josh Evans. For almost a month, Megan corresponded with this boy exclusively online because he said he didn't have a phone and was homeschooled. One day Megan received a message from Josh on her MySpace profile saying, "I don't know if I want to be friends with you any longer because I hear you're not nice to your friends." This was followed by bulletins being posted through MySpace calling Megan "fat" and a "slut." After seeing the messages, Megan became distraught and ran up into her room. A few minutes later, Megan's mother Tina found her daughter hanging in her bedroom closet. Though Tina rushed her to the hospital, Megan died the next day.

Six weeks after their daughter's death, the Meier family learned that the boy with whom Megan had been corresponding never existed. Josh Evans (and his online profile) was created by Lori Drew, a neighbor and the mother of one of Megan's friends. She created the profile as a way to spy on what Megan was saying about her daughter. Drew was charged with violations of the Computer Fraud and Abuse Act (CFAA), though her conviction was later overturned.

How common is cyberbullying? Sameer Hinduja and Justin Patchin, leading experts on cyberbullying, have conducted yearly surveys using large samples of high school youth. Their most recent effort (see Figure 15.2) finds that about 35 percent of the high school and middle school students they surveyed report having been the target of some form of Internet harassment.[69]

Over the last decade, Hinduja and Patchin have conducted eight different surveys with nearly 15,000 middle school and high school students in more than 80 schools throughout the United States. On average, about 25 percent of the students said they have been the victim of cyberbullying at some point in their lifetime, and about 16 percent of the students admitted that they have cyberbullied others at least once. Hinduja and Patchin's most important findings include:

---

cyberbullying Willful and repeated harm inflicted through the medium of online communications.

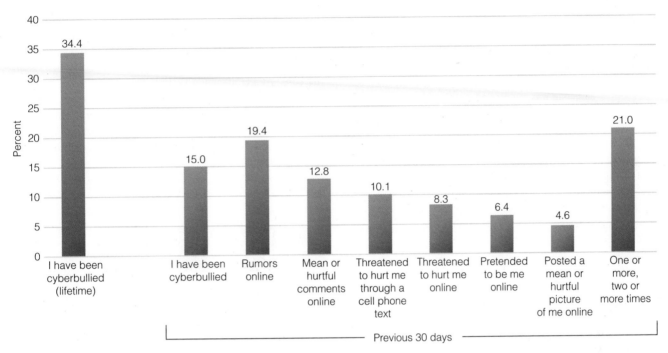

Cyberbullying Victimization
(Random sample from one school in midwestern U.S.–Feb. 2015)

FIGURE 15.2 Cyberbullying Victimization

SOURCE: Sameer Hinduja and Justin Patchin, Cyberbullying Research Center, http://www.cyberbullying.org.

- Adolescent girls are just as likely, if not more likely, than boys to experience cyberbullying (as a victim and/or offender).
- Cyberbullying is related to low self-esteem, suicidal ideation, anger, frustration, and a variety of other emotional and psychological problems.
- Cyberbullying is related to other issues in the real world, including school problems, antisocial behavior, and substance use.
- Traditional bullying is still more common than cyberbullying.
- Traditional bullying and cyberbullying are closely related: those who are bullied at school are bullied online and those who bully at school bully online.

Hinduja and Patchin's research is supported by other survey results. According to the most recent data compiled by the National Center for Education Statistics, about 7 percent of students ages 12 to 18 reported being cyberbullied anywhere during the school year. A higher percentage of female students than of male students reported being victims of cyberbullying overall (9 percent versus 5 percent).[70] Of those who reported cyberbullying, about 27 percent indicated that they were cyberbullied at least once or twice a month; less than a quarter of the victims (23 percent) told an adult what happened to them.

CYBERSPYING

Spyware is a type of software that gathers personal information, including web browser histories, emails, and online purchases. Once information is gathered, it is automatically transmitted to those who installed the software either directly on the computer or when the victim opened an attachment. In some instances, the computer operator gives consent to the spying, which is legal. For example, an employee agrees to have their computer monitored by their employer to make sure they are not web surfing during business hours.

Parents can legally install spyware on their minor child's computer if they are the owners of the machine. If their child is a legal adult, parents must obtain consent. The FlexiSPY Corporation of Wilmington, Delaware, offers software that can capture every Facebook message, email, text, and photo sent from a phone, as well as record phone calls. They also promote the ability to catch cheating spouses by monitoring their cell phone so that the purchaser "will know for sure what your partner is really feeling, saying and doing when you are not there. FlexiSPY will let you read all their cell phone messages . . . and let you know their location at any time, and even let you listen to their cell phone conversations as they happen. It's easy to install and is completely hidden so they will never know." These services are legal only if the person installing the software also owns the device or was given consent by the owner, a warning that the FlexiSPY makes clear on their website.[71]

To learn more about FlexiSPY, go to **http://www.flexispy.com/en/employee-monitoring.htm.** How would you feel if you found out that someone was monitoring your Internet activity with a software app?

Cyberspying becomes illegal when it involves using the Internet to gather information considered private and confidential. Cyberspies have a variety of motivations. Some are people involved in marital disputes who may want to seize the emails of their estranged spouse. Business rivals might hire disgruntled former employees, consultants, or outside contractors to steal information from their competitors. These commercial cyberspies target upcoming bids, customer lists, product designs, software source code, voicemail messages, and confidential email messages.[72] Some of the commercial spying is conducted by foreign competitors who seek to appropriate trade secrets in order to gain a business advantage.[73]

Cyberspying by the Government   While spyware to monitor Internet messages and traffic by spouses, children, employees, and so on has become common, spying by government agencies on U.S. citizens remains quite controversial.

In Chapter 11, Edward Snowden's efforts to warn the public about the National Security Agency's domestic spying program were discussed within the context of espionage. Implemented by President George W. Bush in 2007 as part of the massive increase in homeland security that began shortly after the attacks on September 11, 2001, the program—officially called PRISM—was known in government circles as the "president's surveillance program." The NSA's PRISM program extracts information from the servers of nine major American Internet companies: Microsoft, Yahoo, Google, Facebook, PalTalk, AOL, Skype, YouTube, and Apple. PRISM gives the NSA access to audio, video, photographs, emails, documents, and connection logs for each of these systems. PRISM allows the NSA to track targeted individuals over time, while the online surveillance of search terms gives them insights into their thoughts and intentions. In addition, the government receives records of phone calls they make—across town or across the country—to family members, co-workers, business contacts, and others.

The surveillance was undertaken without a warrant, which some legal scholars claim is in violation of the spirit of federal law and the Constitution.[74] The American Civil Liberties Union filed suit, arguing that the program violates the First Amendment rights of free speech and association as well as the right of privacy protected by the Fourth Amendment. The complaint also charged that the dragnet program exceeds the authority that Congress provided through the Patriot Act.[75] In 2015, a federal court dismissed the case. ACLU attorney Patrick Toomey responded: "The decision turns a blind eye to the fact that the government is tapping into the Internet's backbone to spy on millions of Americans. The dismissal of the lawsuit's claims as 'speculative' is at odds with an overwhelming public record of warrantless surveillance."[76]

THINKING LIKE A CRIMINOLOGIST

An Ethical Dilemma

Big Brother Is Watching You

The president's national security adviser approaches you with a problem. It seems that a tracking device has been developed that can be implanted under the skin that will allow people to be constantly monitored. Implanted at birth, the data surveillance device could potentially cover *everyone*, with a record of every transaction and activity they engage in entered into databases monitored by powerful search engines that would keep them under constant surveillance. The surveillance device would enable the government to keep tabs on their whereabouts as well as monitoring biological activities such as brain waves, heart rate, and so on. The benefits are immense. Once a person becomes a suspect in a crime or is believed to be part of a terrorist cell, he or she can be easily monitored from a distance without danger to any government agent. The suspect cannot hide or escape detection. Physical readings could be made to determine if the suspect is under stress, using banned substances, and so on.

The director wants you to write a paper for the NSA expressing your opinion on this device. You begin by reading what the American Civil Liberties Union has to say: "The United States is at risk of turning into a full-fledged surveillance society. The tremendous explosion in surveillance-enabling technologies, combined with the ongoing weakening in legal restraints that protect our privacy, mean that we are drifting toward a surveillance society. The good news is that it can be stopped. Unfortunately, right now the big picture is grim." Is it worthwhile, considering the threats faced by America from terrorists and criminals, or, as the ACLU suggests, would it be unethical because it violates the personal privacy and freedom of people before they have broken any law?

cyberspying   Illegally using the Internet to gather information that is considered private and confidential.

The Costs of Cybercrime

How common are cybercrimes, and how costly are cybercrimes to American businesses and the general public? The Internet has become a huge engine for illegal profits and criminal entrepreneurs. An accurate accounting of cybercrime will probably never be made because so many offenses go unreported, but there is little doubt that its incidence is growing rapidly.

Though thousands of breaches occur each year, most are not reported to local, state, or federal authorities. Some cybercrime goes unreported because it involves low-visibility acts—such as copying computer software in violation of copyright laws—that simply never get detected. Some businesses choose not to report cybercrime because they fear revealing the weaknesses in their network security systems. However, the information that is available indicates that the profit in cybercrime is vast and continually growing.

Losses due to phishing and identity theft are now in the billions of dollars and rising with the continuing growth of ecommerce. Symantec Corporation (publisher of Norton AntiVirus) conducts an annual Internet security threat report that makes use of data from more than 24,000 security devices deployed in more than 180 countries.[77] According to the most recent survey, attackers trick companies into infecting themselves with Trojan horse software updates to common programs and patiently wait for their targets to download the malware. Once a victim has downloaded the software update, attackers are given unfettered access to the corporate network. Highly targeted spear-phishing attacks are a favorite tactic for infiltrating networks. Attackers use stolen email accounts from one corporate victim to attack other victims higher up the food chain. They are learning to take advantage of companies' management tools and procedures to move stolen intellectual property around the corporate network before exfiltration. In the most recent survey year, there were more than 430 million new pieces of malware created—nearly a million per day. A sizable portion of all software is now being installed without proper licensing, especially in emerging economies, where unlicensed software use is widespread.

Private business enterprise is not the only target that bears the cost of cybercrime. The Internal Revenue Service (IRS) revealed that it has paid refunds to criminals who filed false tax returns, in some cases on behalf of people who had died. By 2017, the IRS is expected to have lost as much as $21 billion in false pay-outs due to identity theft.[78]

Combating Cybercrime

LO9 Discuss efforts to control cybercrime

The proliferation of cybercrime and its cost to the economy have created the need for new laws and enforcement processes specifically aimed at controlling its emerging formulations. Because technology evolves so rapidly, the enforcement challenges are particularly vexing. There are numerous organizations set up to provide training and support for law enforcement agents. In addition, new federal and state laws have been aimed at particular areas of high-tech crimes.

Congress has treated computer-related crime as a distinct federal offense since the passage of the Counterfeit Access Device and Computer Fraud and Abuse Act in 1984.[79] The act protected classified U.S. defense and foreign relations information, financial institution and consumer reporting agency files, and access to computers operated for

The Defense Computer Forensics Laboratory (DCFL) in Linthicum, Maryland—ground zero in the nation's fight against cybercrime—hides in plain sight in a nondescript suburban office building with no government seals or signs. The government now maintains an incident-response venue where computer scientists like the one shown here work to combat an increasing bombardment by thieves, hostile states, and hacktivists.

AP Images/Manuel Balce Ceneta

the government. The act was supplemented in 1996 by the National Information Infrastructure Protection Act (NIIPA), which significantly broadens the scope of the law.[80]

Because cybercrime is relatively new, existing laws sometimes are inadequate to address the problem. Therefore new legislation has been drafted to protect the public from the cybercriminal. For example, before October 30, 1998, when the Identity Theft and Assumption Act of 1998 became law, there was no federal statute that made identity theft a crime. Today, federal prosecutors are making substantial use of the statute and are actively prosecuting cases of identity theft.[81]

In the wake of the 9/11 attacks, the NIIPA has been amended by sections of the USA Patriot Act to make it easier to enforce laws against crimes by terrorists and other organized enemies against the nation's computer systems. Subsection 1030(a)(5)(A)(i) of the act criminalizes knowingly causing the transmission of a program, code, or command that intentionally causes damage to a protected computer. This section applies regardless of whether the user had authorization to access the protected computer; company insiders and authorized users can be culpable for intentional damage to a protected computer. The act also prohibits intentional access without authorization that results in damage but does not require intent to damage; the attacker can merely be negligent or reckless.

In addition to these main acts, computer-related crimes can also be charged under at least 40 different federal statutes. These include the Digital Millennium Copyright Act, the National Stolen Property Act, the mail and wire fraud statutes, the Electronic Communications Privacy Act, the Communications Decency Act of 1996, the Child Online Protection Act, the Child Pornography Prevention Act of 1996, and the Internet False Identification Prevention Act of 2000.[82] Movie pirates who use the Internet to sell illegally copied films have led the federal government to create the Family Entertainment and Copyright Act of 2005. One part of that statute, known as the ART Act (Artists' Rights and Theft Prevention Act of 2005), criminalizes the use of recording equipment to make copies of films while in movie theaters. The statute also makes it illegal to make a copy of a work in production and put it on the Internet so it will be accessible to members of the public when the individual making the copy knew or should have known the work was intended for commercial distribution.[83]

CYBERCRIME ENFORCEMENT AGENCIES

To enforce these laws, the federal government is now operating a number of organizations to control cybercrime. One approach is to create working groups that coordinate the activities of agencies involved in investigating cybercrime. For example, the International Cyber Crime Coordination Cell (IC4) pools the resources of major cybercrime investigators from the United States, Australia, Germany, and the United Kingdom.

In one recent case, IC4 agents coordinated with the Dutch National High Tech Crime Unit, Europol's European Cybercrime Centre (EC3) and Joint Cybercrime Action Taskforce (J-CAT), and private sector partners to take down Beebone, a botnet that installed malicious software on victims' computers without their consent or knowledge. Beebone's software stole banking logins and passwords, as well as fraudulent antivirus software and ransomware.[84]

Specialized investigative agencies have also been created. For example, the Internet Crime Complaint Center (IC3) is run by the FBI and the National White Collar Crime Center. Its mission is to provide the public with a reliable and convenient reporting mechanism to submit information to the FBI concerning suspected Internet-facilitated criminal activity and to develop effective alliances with law enforcement and industry partners. Information is analyzed and disseminated for investigative and intelligence purposes to law enforcement and for public awareness.

The IC3 receives more than 280,000 complaints each year, spanning the spectrum of cybercrime, including online fraud, intellectual property rights matters, hacking, economic espionage such as theft of trade secrets, online extortion, international money laundering, and identity theft. It analyzes the complaints to find distinct patterns, develop information on particular cases, and send investigative packages to law enforcement authorities in the jurisdiction that appears likely to have the greatest interest in the matter.

The U.S. Secret Service maintains electronic crimes task forces (ECTFs), which focus on identifying and locating international cybercriminals connected to cyber intrusions, bank fraud, data breaches, and other computer-related crimes. One of the most successful of these efforts is the New York–New Jersey Electronic Crimes Task Force (NYECTF), a partnership between the Secret Service and a host of other public safety agencies and private corporations. The task force consists of more than 250 individual members representing federal, state, and local law enforcement; the private sector; and computer science specialists from 18 universities. It has trained more than 60,000 law enforcement personnel, prosecutors, and private industry representatives in cybercrime prevention. Its success has prompted similar electronic crime task forces to be set up in Boston, Miami, Charlotte, Chicago, Las Vegas, San Francisco, Los Angeles, and Washington, D.C.[85] To give a hint at the scope of these investigations, in one fiscal year (2013), the Secret Service arrested more than 1,000 individuals for cybercrime violations, who were responsible for more than $235 million in fraud losses and had the potential to cause more than $1 billion in fraud losses.[86]

INTERNATIONAL TREATIES

Because cybercrime is essentially global, international cooperation is required for its control. The Convention on Cybercrime, ratified by the U.S. Senate in August 2006, is the first international treaty that addresses the definition and enforcement of cybercrime. Now signed by 49 nations, it focuses on improving investigative techniques and increasing cooperation among nations. The convention includes a list of crimes that each signatory state must incorporate into its own law, including such cyber offenses as hacking, distribution of child pornography, and protection of intellectual property rights. It also allows law enforcement agencies new powers, including the ability to require that an Internet service provider monitor a person's online viewing and search choices in real time. The convention also requires signatory states to cooperate whenever possible in the investigations and prosecution of cybercriminals. The vision is that a common legal framework will eliminate jurisdictional hurdles to facilitate the law enforcement of borderless cybercrimes.[87]

Carrying out this mandate may be difficult to achieve given the legal rights afforded U.S. citizens that may not be realized by residents of other nations. For example, First Amendment protections that restrict the definition of pornography and obscenity in this country may not apply overseas. It is not surprising that watchdog institutions such as the ACLU have condemned the treaty and campaigned against U.S. participation.[88]

Cyberwar: Politically Motivated Cybercrime

L010 Examine the concepts of cyberwar and cyberterrorism

It is now generally accepted and understood that the developed world is totally dependent upon electronic communication and data storage for its survival. Protecting a nation's critical technological infrastructure has been raised in priority so that it is now considered by many countries alongside the traditional aspects of national defense.

It is routine for defense agencies around the world to employ units to conduct cyberattacks on enemy nations. Cyberwar enables the forces of one nation-state to penetrate another nation's computers or networks for the purposes of causing damage or disruption. Computer systems may be compromised so that vital war material is misdirected or even destroyed. Ground attacks are facilitated by destroying command systems and compromising air defenses. Instead of blowing up air defense radar systems and giving up the element of surprise before hitting targets, in the age of cyberwar the computers controlling air defense are put out of action.

CYBERESPIONAGE

Intelligence agencies are now able to penetrate computer networks of an enemy nation's most sensitive military bases, defense contractors, and aerospace companies in order to steal important data or to damage their infrastructure; a practice known as **cyberespionage**. In 2014, the Justice Department filed charges against five Chinese military officers, all hackers in an international cyberespionage case. These Chinese hackers worked directly for the government and were trained at universities run by the People's Liberation Army. In addition to hackers who work for the government or military, some are mercenaries who sell their skills to state-owned and private companies.

CYBERATTACKS

In addition to espionage and the theft of military intelligence, cyberwar can also involve attacks on an enemy's defense industry, compromising their ability to wage war. As a response to such a cyberattack that occurred on November 23, 2010, Iran was forced to shut down its main uranium enrichment plant at Natanz for seven days after it was targeted by the Stuxnet computer worm. Experts believe that Stuxnet was specifically designed to attack systems at the plant that control the speed at which the enrichment centrifuges spin.[89]

Cyberwar can also involve attacks designed to compromise an enemy's command and control structure by hacking into computer systems to disrupt missile targeting systems, rendering them ineffective during attacks. Israeli cyberunits have "blinded" Syrian antiaircraft installations guarding a secret nuclear plant that was being constructed for Syria by North Korea. While the exact methodology remains classified, Syrian computers that controlled their missile defenses were reprogrammed so that the attacking Israeli aircraft did not show up on radar screens. Israel was able to penetrate a sophisticated defense system without losing a single aircraft.[90] U.S. cyberwar agents infiltrated the Iraqi "closed-loop" private, secure military network before the start of the second Gulf War. The agents sent email to thousands of Iraqi military officers on the Iraqi Defense Ministry email system telling them they would not be harmed if they left their tanks and weapons parked on the side of the road and went home; many complied.

The United States and Israel are not alone in perfecting cyberwar capability. In 2012, Iran launched a major cyberattack on Saudi Arabia's state-owned oil company, Aramco, releasing a virus named AMED that replicated itself across 30,000 computers and took almost two weeks to remove. In March 2015, South Korea formally accused North Korea of cyberattacks on its nuclear reactor operations.[91] The Chinese government has established an online warfare team to beef up the defense capabilities of the People's Liberation Army (PLA). These hackers may have penetrated the U.S. Office of Personnel Management, using a phishing email to first breach a private contractor and then crack the agency's network, exposing the records of more than

cyberespionage Efforts by intelligence agencies to penetrate computer networks of an enemy nation in order to steal important data.

21 million people. Though China denies involvement in such attacks, its army has divisions devoted to cyberattacks.[92] The cyberwar competition between the U.S. and China has gotten so fierce that the two countries have reached a limited agreement not to conduct certain types of cyberattacks against each other, such as intrusions that steal foreign corporate information and then pass it along to their own domestic companies.

Other nations practicing cyberwar include rivals Pakistan and India, while others such as Estonia and Belarus are racing to build cybershields to counter Russia. Denmark and the Netherlands have begun programs to develop offensive computer weapons, as have Argentina and France.[93]

CYBERTERRORISM

Cyberterrorism is an element of cyberwar that involves an effort by covert forces to disrupt the intersection where the virtual electronic reality of computers meets the physical world.[94] Cyberspace is a handy battlefield for the terrorist because an attack can strike directly at a target that bombs won't affect: the economy. Because technological change plays a significant role in the development of critical infrastructures, they are particularly vulnerable to attack. And because of rapid technological change, and the interdependence of systems, it is difficult to defend against efforts to disrupt services.[95]

Cyberterrorists have many advantages. There are no borders of legal control, making it difficult for prosecutors to apply laws to some crimes. Criminals can operate from countries where cyber laws barely exist, making them almost untouchable. Cyberterrorists can also use the Internet and hacking tools to gather information on targets.[96] There is no loss of life because there is no need to infiltrate enemy territory. Terrorists can commit crimes from anyplace in the world, and the costs are minimal. Nor do terror organizations lack for skilled labor to mount cyberattacks. There are a growing number of highly skilled computer experts in developing countries who are available at reasonable costs. Cyberterrorism may result in a battered economy in which the government is forced to spend more on the military and cut back on social programs and education. These outcomes can weaken the terrorists' target and undermine its resolve to continue to resist.

Recruitment and Fund-Raising Terrorist organizations are now using cyberspace in a number of different operational areas. They use the Internet to recruit new members and disseminate information. For example, radical Islamic militant organizations use the Internet to broadcast anti-Western slogans and information. An organization's charter and political philosophy can be displayed on its website, which can also be used to solicit funds. The Policy and Practice in Criminology feature discusses this phenomenon further.

Terrorist groups use the Internet to raise funds to buy arms and carry out operations. One method of funding is through fraudulent charitable organizations claiming to support a particular cause such as disaster relief or food services. Charitable organizations in the United States raise more than $350 billion per year. Using bogus charities to raise money is particularly attractive to cyberterrorists because they face far less scrutiny from the government than for-profit corporations and individuals. They may also qualify for financial assistance from government-sponsored grant programs.[97] One such bogus group, Holy Land Foundation for Relief and Development (HLFRD), provided more than $12 million to the terrorist group Hamas; in total, HLFRD raised more than $57 million but only reported $36.2 million to the IRS.[98]

Bogus companies have also been used by terrorist groups to receive and distribute money. These shell companies may engage in legitimate activities to establish a positive reputation in the business community but produce bills for nonexistent products that are "paid" by another party with profits from illegal activities, such as insurance fraud or identity theft. If a shell company generates revenues, funds can be distributed by altering financial statements to hide profits and then depositing the profits in accounts that are used directly or indirectly to support terrorist activities.[99]

Cyberterror Attacks Cyberspace is used by terrorist groups to remain connected and communicate covertly with agents around the world. Networks are a cost-effective tool for planning and striking. They enable terror groups to plan and carry out a variety of Internet-related attacks. Here are some possible scenarios:

- Logic bombs are implanted in an enemy's computer. They can go undetected for years until they are instructed through the Internet to overwhelm the computer system.
- Programs are used to allow terrorists to enter secure systems and disrupt or destroy the network.
- Using conventional weapons, terrorists overload a network's electrical system, thereby threatening computer security.
- The computer system of a corporation whose welfare is vital to national security—such as Boeing or Raytheon—is breached and disrupted.
- Internet-based systems used to manage basic infrastructure needs—such as an oil pipeline's flow or water levels in dams—are attacked and disrupted, posing a danger of loss of life and interruption of services.

One attack method is to release a *botnet* or software robot, also known as a zombie or drone, that allows an unauthorized user to remotely take control of a host computer without the victim's knowledge or permission. Infected computers can be used to launch denial-of-service attacks, send spam and spyware, or commit cyber extortion. In one attack, a global telecommunications company with a business unit in Central America experienced several unusual problems, including multiple network outages—some

Terrorism on the Net

Shannon Conley was an isolated high school dropout who, desperate for attention, met a suitor online who persuaded her to travel to Syria, where she planned to fight alongside him or serve as a battlefield nurse for ISIL. FBI agents became aware of her interest in jihad after she discussed it with members of her suburban Denver church, and they arrested her in April 2014 as she was boarding a plane on her way to Syria. Though she later claimed she was misled while converting to Islam, she was sentenced to four years in prison.

The Islamic State of Iraq and the Levant (ISIL) is now actively using the Internet to recruit Westerners like Conley and to solicit and raise funds. ISIL has used the Internet and social media to recruit at least 30,000 foreign fighters from more than 100 countries to fight in Syria and Iraq. In almost every American case, social media played some part in recruitment and/or radicalization. One online video tells potential recruits, "I am your brother in Islam here in Syria. We have safety here for your family and children." ISIL has its own multilingual media arm, al-Hayat, which produces videos using American-made GoPro action cameras. ISIL has released videos featuring foreign fighters who speak Western languages and who encourage others to come to Syria to wage violent jihad or help the caliphate in some other way.

The Internet is only one part of the use of cyberspace to wage jihad. One study found at least 46,000 Twitter accounts that support ISIL currently in use. Twitter has suspended the accounts of ISIL supporters in large numbers, but users create new accounts and return.

ISIL recruiters also use the Net to groom potential recruits. Recruiters monitor online communities trolling for receptive individuals and making themselves available to curiosity seekers. In some instances, ISIL agents seek out targets, while in others they respond to people who are seeking out the Islamic State. Once contact is made with a highly motivated recruit, teams keep in constant contact in order to shape his or her worldview and encourage direct action in support of ISIL. Agents try to insulate potential recruits against outside influences. Trips may be arranged to receive training. Online interventions are most common in countries where there are few opportunities to meet with ISIL agents in a face-to-face setting. While Americans have been recruited, there is considerably more activity in France, the United Kingdom, Belgium, and other European countries.

In addition to recruiting, ISIL uses the Internet to instill fear and threaten reprisals. ISIL has issued public statements confirming the terrorist organization's determination and dedication to global terrorism. The videos ISIL released online depicting the beheadings of American hostages James Foley and Steven Sotloff were aimed at sowing terror in the U.S. population. The message is that ISIL may continue to capture American hostages in an attempt to force the U.S. government and people into making concessions that would only strengthen ISIL recruiting and further its terrorist operations.

ISIL is not the only group using the Internet. Al-Qaeda in the Arabian Peninsula (AQAP) publishes an online English language magazine called *Inspire*, in which the group advocates simple and inexpensive lone-wolf attacks against the U.S. and other Western targets. The first issue of *Inspire*, released in the summer of 2010, provided specific instructions on how to build a pipe bomb. In another issue, AQAP further expanded upon these instructions to include building a pressure cooker bomb similar to the one used in the Boston Marathon bombing.

Given the scope of the cyber threat, agencies across the federal government are making cyber security a top priority. The Department of Justice, including the FBI, the Department of Homeland Security, the National Security Agency, and other U.S. intelligence community and law enforcement agencies are cooperating to combat the cyber threat. The U.S. military's Cyber Command has launched a new campaign to disrupt the spread of ISIL's message, impeding their ability to attract new recruits, and prevent commanders from carrying out day-to-day functions, like circulating orders or paying its fighters. Though the work is top secret, it is known that U.S. commanders can now imitate ISIL leaders and send false and damaging messages to fighters, sending them to areas where they are vulnerable to drone strikes.

 CRITICAL THINKING

Given the use of the Net by terror groups to recruit fighters and spread propaganda, would you advocate greater government control over Internet content, granting agencies a free hand to shut down websites? What problems could develop from such a policy?

SOURCES: David E. Sanger, "U.S. Cyberattacks Target ISIS in a New Line of Combat," *New York Times*, April 24, 2016, http://www.nytimes.com/2016/04/25/us/politics/us-directs-cyberweapons-at-isis-for-first-time.html; United Nations Radio, "Internet, Social Media Help ISIL Recruit 30,000 fighters," December 17, 2015; http://www.unmultimedia.org/radio/english/2015/12/internet-social-media-help-isil-recruit-30000-fighters/; CBS News, "ISIS Recruits Fighters Through Powerful Online Campaign," August 29, 2014; http://www.cbsnews.com/news/isis-uses-social-media-to-recruit-western-allies/; James B. Comey, Director, Federal Bureau of Investigation, "Statement Before the House Homeland Security Committee, Washington, D.C.," September 17, 2014, https://www.fbi.gov/news/testimony/worldwide-threats-to-the-homeland. (URLs accessed July 2016.)

lasting up to six hours—which disrupted businesses and national connectivity, and took automated teller machines offline for extended periods of time. A botnet-based distributed denial-of-service attack had crippled the country's infrastructure. The Center for Strategic and International Studies has uncovered cyberterror attacks on the National Security Agency, the Pentagon, and a nuclear weapons laboratory; operations were disrupted at all of these sites.[100]

Financial System Attacks   In ever-increasing numbers people are spending and investing their money electronically, using online banking, credit card payment, and online brokerage services. The banking/financial system transacts billions of dollars each day through a complex network of institutions and systems. A cyberattack can disrupt these transactions and interfere with the nation's economic well-being.

The financial service sector is a prime target and has been victimized by information warfare. In 2013, a massive cyberattack was directed at some of the nation's largest banks, including JPMorgan Chase, Bank of America, and Citigroup, by a hacker group calling itself Izz ad-Din al-Qassam Cyber Fighters. What made this different was that the traffic came from data centers around the world that had been infected with malware designed to evade detection by antivirus solutions. The bank attackers used those infected servers to simultaneously fire traffic at each banking site until it slowed or collapsed. The purpose of the attack: to punish the American financial system in retaliation for a film insulting to Muslims.[101]

COMBATING CYBERWAR

There are a number of government agencies assigned the task of countering cyberwar and cyberterror. The military has formed the United States Cyber Command (USCYBER-COM), a division that "plans, coordinates, integrates, synchronizes and conducts activities to: direct the operations and defense of specified Department of Defense information networks and; prepare to, and when directed, conduct full spectrum military cyberspace operations in order to enable actions in all domains, ensure U.S./Allied freedom of action in cyberspace and deny the same to our adversaries."[102] USCYBERCOM ties together the cyberwarfare arms of the various service branches:

The National Security Agency/Central Security Service (NSA/CSS) encompasses both signals intelligence (SIGINT) and information assurance (IA) programs. The NSA's information assurance mission is to prevent foreign adversaries from gaining access to sensitive or classified national security information. Their signals intelligence mission collects, processes, and disseminates intelligence information from foreign signals for intelligence and counterintelligence purposes and to support military operations.[103]

SUMMARY

 Describe the concept of cybercrime and trace its development

Cybercrime is a new breed of offenses that involve the theft and/or destruction of information, resources, or funds utilizing computers, computer networks, and the Internet. Cybercrime presents a challenge for the justice system because it is rapidly evolving, it is difficult to detect through traditional law enforcement channels, and its control demands that agents of the justice system develop technical skills that match those of the perpetrators. Cybercrime has grown because information technology (IT) has become part of daily life in industrialized societies. The new globalization age has encouraged the development of cybercrime that can be committed at any time in any place on the planet. Illegal goods produced in one country can be easily distributed in another on deals made over the Internet.

 Compare and contrast cybertheft, cyberdeviance, cybervandalism, and cyberwar

Some cybercrimes use modern technology to accumulate goods and services (cybertheft). Cyberdeviance includes the sale and distribution of morally tainted material and products over the Net. Cybervandalism involves malicious attacks aimed at disrupting, defacing, and destroying technology that the attackers find offensive. Cyberwar is aimed at undermining the social, economic, and political system of an enemy nation by destroying its electronic infrastructure and disrupting its economy. A significant aspect of modern cyberwarfare is the use of the Internet by terrorists to plan operations, raise funds, and attack computer networks.

 Give some examples of computer fraud

Computer fraud involves compromising a computer system in order to steal property or use the system for personal gain. Theft from an ATM machine, reprogramming a computer to send funds illegally, illegally obtaining information from a computer, manipulating accounts, and corporate espionage would all be considered computer fraud.

L04 **Distinguish between the different forms of stealing intellectual property**

Warez are illegally obtained software acquired by groups of individuals who work together to "crack" or "rip" its copyright protections before posting it on the Internet for other members of the group to use. Another type of illegal copyright infringement involves file-sharing programs that allow Internet users to distrbute copyrighted material without paying the artists or producers their rightful royalties.

L05 Define the terms *identity theft* and *phishing*

Identity theft occurs when a person uses the Internet to steal someone's identity and/or impersonate the victim to open a new credit card account or conduct some other financial transaction. Identity theft can destroy a person's life by manipulating credit records or stealing from their bank accounts. Phishing involves the creation of false emails and/or websites that look legitimate but are designed to gain illegal access to a victim's personal information. Vishing is a form of phishing utilizing Internet phone protocols.

L06 Assess how the Internet can facilitate the sale of illegal materials

The Internet has become an important source for selling and distributing pornography. While some sites cater to legal sexually related material, others cross the legal border by peddling access to obscene material or kiddie porn. It is unlikely that any law enforcement efforts will put a dent in the Internet porn industry. It is also possible to obtain drugs via the Net without a prescription or with bogus prescriptions.

L07 Discuss the different types of cybervandalism

Cybervandalism ranges from sending destructive viruses and worms to hacker attacks designed to destroy important computer networks. A computer virus is one type of malicious software program that disrupts or destroys existing programs and networks, causing them to perform the task for which the virus was designed. Computer worms are similar to viruses but use computer networks or the Internet to self-replicate and send themselves to other users, generally via email, without the aid of the operator. A Trojan horse looks like a benign application but contains illicit codes that can damage the system operations. A logic bomb is a program that is secretly attached to a computer system, monitors the network's work output, and waits for a particular signal such as a date to appear.

L08 Articulate the extent of cyberbullying and the damage it causes people

Cyberbullying is defined as the willful and repeated harm inflicted through the medium of online communications. Cyberbullies are malicious aggressors who seek implicit or explicit pleasure or profit through the mistreatment of other individuals. About 35 percent of the high school and middle school students surveyed reported having been the target of some form of Internet harassment. Adolescent girls are just as likely, if not more likely, than boys to experience cyberbullying (both as victim and offender). Victims of bullying suffer long-term consequences and mental health issues. There are well-known cases where kids who were cyberbullied have taken their own lives.

L09 Discuss efforts to control cybercrime

Because cybercrime is relatively new, existing laws sometimes are inadequate to address the problem. Therefore new legislation has been drafted to protect the public from this new breed of criminal. The growth of cybercrime and its cost to the economy have created the need for enforcement processes specifically aimed at controlling its emerging formulations. Specialized enforcement agencies have been created to crack down on cybercriminals. Congress has treated computer-related crime as a distinct federal offense since passage of the Counterfeit Access Device and Computer Fraud and Abuse Act in 1984.

L010 Examine the concepts of cyberwar and cyberterrorism

Cyberwar enables the forces of one nation-state to penetrate another nation's defense networks for the purposes of causing damage or disruption. Computer systems may be compromised so that vital war material is misdirected or even destroyed. Attacks are facilitated by destroying command systems and compromising air defenses. Cyberterrorism can be viewed as an effort by covert forces to disrupt the intersection where the virtual electronic reality of computers meets the physical world.

CRITICAL THINKING QUESTIONS

1. Which theories of criminal behavior best explain the actions of cybercriminals, and which ones do you believe fail to explain cybercrime?
2. How would you punish a web page defacer who placed an antiwar message on a government site? Prison? Fine?
3. What guidelines would you recommend for the use of IT in law enforcement?
4. Are we creating a "Big Brother" society? Is the loss of personal privacy worth the price of safety?
5. How can cyberbullies be convinced of the harmfulness of their acts? Would it be ethical to create a web page mocking them as punishment?

KEY TERMS

cybercrime (548)

information technology (IT) (549)

globalization (549)

cybertheft (550)

cyberdeviance (550)

cybervandalism (550)

cyberwar (550)

cyberterrorism (550)

ATM skimming (552)

ransomware (553)

warez (553)

identity theft (554)

phishing (555)

spear-fishing (555)

money mule (556)

etailing fraud (557)

darknet (559)

ehooking (561)

malware (563)

computer worms (563)

Trojan horse (563)

logic bomb (563)

website defacement (563)

cyberstalking (564)

distributed denial-of-service attack (DDoS) (564)

cyberbullying (566)

cyberspying (568)

cyberespionage (571)

NOTES

All URLs accessed in 2016.

1. FBI, "Business E-Mail Compromise: An Emerging Global Threat," August 28, 2015, https://www.fbi.gov/news/stories/2015/august/business-e-mail-compromise/business-e-mail-compromise.

2. Alan Travis, "Crime Rate in England and Wales Soars as Cybercrime Is Included for First Time," *The Guardian*, October 15, 2015, https://www.theguardian.com/uk-news/2015/oct/15/rate-in-england-and-wales-soars-as-cybercrime-included-for-first-time.

3. FBI, Internet Crime Complaint Center, *2015 Internet Crime Report*, https://pdf.ic3.gov/2015_IC3Report.pdf.

4. Maria Tcherni, Andrew Davies, Giza Lopes, and Alan Lizotte, "The Dark Figure of Online Property Crime: Is Cyberspace Hiding a Crime Wave?" *Justice Quarterly*, published online January 8, 2015.

5. McAfee, "Net Losses: Estimating the Global Cost of Cybercrime," Center for Strategic and International Studies, June 2014, http://www.mcafee.com/us/resources/reports/rp-economic-impact-cybercrime2.pdf.

6. Gartner, Inc., press release, "Gartner Says Worldwide IT Spending to Decline 5.5 Percent in 2015," http://www.gartner.com/newsroom/id/3084817; "Gartner Worldwide IT Spending Forecast," 2016, http://www.gartner.com/technology/research/it-spending-forecast/.

7. Radicati Group, "Email Statistics Report, 2015–2019," http://www.radicati.com/wp/wp-content/uploads/2015/02/Email-Statistics-Report-2015-2019-Executive-Summary.pdf.

8. Rose Troup Buchanan, "Facebook Used by Half the World's Internet Users," *The Independent*, July 30, 2015, http://www.independent.co.uk/life-style/gadgets-and-tech/facebook-used-by-half-the-worlds-internet-users-10426003.html.

9. Christopher M. Donner, Catherine Marcum, Wesley Jennings, George E. Higgins, and Jerry Banfield, "Low Self-Control and Cybercrime: Exploring the Utility of the General Theory of Crime Beyond Digital Piracy," *Computers in Human Behavior* 34 (2014): 165–172.

10. Rand Corporation, "Cyber Warfare," http://www.rand.org/topics/cyber-warfare.html.

11. Majid Yar, *Cybercrime and Society* (Thousand Oaks, CA: Sage Publications, 2006), p. 19.

12. FBI, "Botnet Bust: SpyEye Malware Mastermind Pleads Guilty," January 28, 2014, http://www.fbi.gov/news/stories/2014/january/spyeye-malware-mastermind-pleads-guilty/spyeye-malware-mastermind-pleads-guilty.

13. The President's Working Group on Unlawful Conduct on the Internet, "The Electronic Frontier: The Challenge of Unlawful Conduct Involving the Use of the Internet," 2000, http://www.politechbot.com/docs/unlawfulconduct.txt.

14. Department of Justice, U.S. Attorney's Office, Middle District of Florida, "Former Police Department Employee Pleads Guilty to Computer Intrusion," February 5, 2016, https://www.justice.gov/usao-mdfl/pr/former-police-department-employee-pleads-guilty-computer-intrusion.

15. PWC Global, *Global Economic Crime Survey 2016*, http://www.pwc.com/gx/en/services/advisory/consulting/forensics/economic-crime-survey.html.

16. Brian Krebs, "ATM Skimmer," *Krebs on Security*, http://krebsonsecurity.com/tag/atm-skimmer/.

17. FBI, "Taking a Trip to the ATM? Beware of 'Skimmers,'" July 14, 2011, http://www.fbi.gov/news/stories/2011/july/atm_071411.

18. Krebs on Security, "A Dramatic Rise in ATM Skimming Attacks," April 29, 2016, http://krebsonsecurity.com/2016/04/a-dramatic-rise-in-atm-skimming-attacks/.

19. FBI, "Incidents of Ransomware on the Rise: Protect Yourself and Your Organization," April 29, 2016, https://www.fbi.gov/news/stories/2016/april/incidents-of-ransomware-on-the-rise/incidents-of-ransomware-on-the-rise.

20. FBI, *2015 Internet Crime Report*.

21. FBI, "Incidents of Ransomware on the Rise: Protect Yourself and Your Organization."

22. FBI, "Ransomware on the Rise: FBI and Partners Working to Combat this Cyber Threat," January 20, 2015, http://www.fbi.gov/news/stories/2015/january/ransomware-on-the-rise/ransomware-on-the-rise.

23. The Computer Fraud and Abuse Act (CFAA), 18 U.S.C. §1030 (1998).

24. The Digital Millennium Copyright Act, Public Law 105–304 (1998).

25. Title 18, United States Code, Section 2319.

26. Title 17, United States Code, Section 506.

27. This section is based on Richard Walker and David M. Levine, "'You've Got Jail': Current Trends in Civil and Criminal Enforcement of Internet Securities Fraud," *American Criminal Law Review* 38 (2001): 405–430.

28. Jim Wolf, "Internet Scams Targeted in Sweep: A 10-Day Crackdown Leads to 62 Arrests and 88 Indictments," *Boston Globe*, May 22, 2001, p. A2.

29. These sections rely on APWG, "Phishing Activity Trends Report, Q1 2016," https://docs.apwg.org/reports/apwg_trends_report_q1_2016.pdf.

30. Matt Cullina, Eva Velasquez, Paul Bond, Susan Grant, Mike Cook, Julie Fergerson, and James Lee, "Identity Theft: The Aftermath 2014," Identity Theft Resource Center, http://www.idtheftcenter.org/images/surveys_studies/Aftermath2014FINAL.pdf.

31. Erika Harrell, "Victims of Identity Theft, 2014," Bureau of Justice Statistics, 2015, http://www.bjs.gov/index.cfm?ty=pbdetail&iid=5410.

32. APWG, "Phishing Activity Trends Report, Q1 2016."

33. FBI, "Cyber Criminals Continue to Use Spear-Phishing Attacks to Compromise Computer Networks," June 25, 2013, https://www.ic3.gov/media/2013/130625.aspx.

34. FBI, "Malware Targets Bank Accounts: 'Gameover' Delivered via Phishing E-Mails," January 6, 2012, http://www.fbi.gov/news /stories/2012/january/malware_010612 /malware_010612.

35. FBI, "Smishing and Vishing," November 24, 2010, https://www.fbi.gov/news/stories /2010/november/cyber_112410/cyber _112410.

36. Identity Theft and Assumption Deterrence Act, as amended by Public Law 105–318, 112 Stat. 3007 (October 30, 1998).

37. Public Law 108–275 (2004).

38. Elizabeth Woyke and Dan Beucke, "Many Not-So-Happy Returns," Business Week, August 15, 2005, p. 10.

39. FBI, 2015 Internet Crime Report.

40. Andreas Philaretou, "Sexuality and the Internet," Journal of Sex Research 42 (2005): 180–181.

41. Julie Ruvolo, "How Much of the Internet Is Actually for Porn," Forbes, September 7, 2011, http://www.forbes.com/sites /julieruvolo/2011/09/07/how-much-of -the-internet-is-actually-for-porn/.

42. "Naked Capitalism: The Internet Blew the Porn Industry's Business Model Apart. Its Response Holds Lessons for Other Media Firms," The Economist, http://www .economist.com/news/international /21666114-internet-blew-porn-industrys -business-model-apart-its-response-holds -lessons.

43. Webroot, "Internet Pornography by the Numbers; a Significant Threat to Society," http://www.webroot.com/us/en/home /resources/tips/digital-family-life/internet -pornography-by-the-numbers.

44. Marie-Helen Maras, Computer Forensics: Cybercriminals, Laws, and Evidence (Sudbury, MA: Jones and Bartlett, 2011).

45. Jeordan Legon, "Sex Sells, Especially to Web Surfers: Internet Porn a Booming, Billion-Dollar Industry," CNN, December 11, 2003, http://www.cnn.com/2003/TECH /internet/12/10/porn.business/.

46. "More Bang for Your Buck," The Economist, August 9, 2014, http://www.economist .com/news/briefing/21611074-how-new -technology-shaking-up-oldest-business -more-bang-your-buck.

47. Ibid.; the RS-AVS site is located at https:// www.rs2kmembership.com/rs2k-membership .htm.

48. U.S. Attorney's Office, Northern District of California, "Nine Sentenced for Illegally Distributing Controlled Substances over the Internet," March 27, 2013, https://www .justice.gov/usao-ndca/pr/nine-sentenced -illegally-distributing-controlled-substances -over-internet.

49. National Center on Addiction and Substance Abuse, Columbia University, "'You've Got Drugs!' V: Prescription Drug Pushers on the Internet," 2008, http://www .casacolumbia.org/addiction-research /reports/youve-got-drugs-perscription -drug-pushers-internet-2008.

50. Anne Branscomb, "Rogue Computer Programs and Computer Rogues: Tailoring Punishment to Fit the Crime," Rutgers Computer and Technology Law Journal 16 (1990): 24–26.

51. Robert Hackett, "What to Know About the Ashley Madison Hack," Fortune, August 26, 2015, http://fortune.com/2015/08/26/ashley -madison-hack/.

52. Symantec, Internet Security Threat Report, Vol. 21, 2016, https://www.symantec.com /content/dam/symantec/docs/reports/istr -21-2016-en.pdf.

53. Heather Jacobson and Rebecca Green, "Computer Crimes," American Criminal Law Review 39 (2002): 272–326.

54. Yona Hollander, "Prevent Web Page Defacement," Internet Security Advisor 2 (2000): 1–4.

55. Peter Foster, "David Petraeus Scandal: Jill Kelley Issues Legal Letters," The Telegraph, November 28, 2012, http://www.telegraph .co.uk/news/worldnews/northamerica /usa/9709972/David-Petraeus-scandal-Jill -Kelley-issues-legal-letters.html.

56. Janis Wolak, David Finkelhor, Kimberly Mitchell, and Michele Ybarra, "Online 'Predators' and Their Victims: Myths, Realities, and Implications for Prevention and Treatment," American Psychologist 63 (2008): 111–128.

57. U.S. Attorney's Office, District of Colorado, "Former Fort Collins Resident Sentenced for Denial of Service Attack on Larimer County Government Computers," June 6, 2013, https://www.fbi.gov/denver/press -releases/2013/former-fort-collins-resident -sentenced-for-denial-of-service-attack-on -larimer-county-government-computers.

58. Top Tech News, "Rutgers Suffers Foreign DDoS Attack," March 30, 2015, http:// www.toptechnews.com/article/index .php?story_id=1320044NONV0.

59. John Callaham, "Steam and Other Online Gaming Services Hit by DDoS Attacks," January 3, 2014, Neowin, http://www .neowin.net/news/steam-and-other-online -gaming-services-hit-by-ddos-attacks.

60. Lexi Finnigan and Mark Molloy, "BBC's Network of Websites and iPlayer Service Suffers DDoS attack," Telegraph, December 31, 2015, http://www.telegraph.co.uk/news /bbc/12075679/BBC-website-crashes -and-Twitter-goes-into-meltdown.html.

61. Saul Hansell, "U.S. Tally in Online-Crime Sweep: 150 Charged," New York Times, August 27, 2004, p. C1.

62. Stephen Baker and Brian Grow, "Gambling Sites, This Is a Holdup," BusinessWeek, August 9, 2004, pp. 60–62.

63. Centers for Disease Control and Prevention, "Lesbian, Gay, Bisexual and Transgender Health," http://www.cdc.gov/lgbthealth /youth.htm (accessed March 2016).

64. Ibid.

65. Jane Ireland and Rachel Monaghan, "Behaviors Indicative of Bullying Among Young and Juvenile Male Offenders: A Study of Perpetrator and Victim Characteristics," Aggressive Behavior 32 (2006): 172–180.

66. Dan Olweus, "A Useful Evaluation Design, and Effects of the Olweus Bullying Prevention Program," Psychology, Crime and Law 11 (2005): 389–402.

67. This section leans heavily on Justin Patchin and Sameer Hinduja, "Bullies Move Beyond the Schoolyard: A Preliminary Look at Cyberbullying," Youth Violence and Juvenile Justice 4 (2006): 148–169.

68. Sameer Hinduja and Justin Patchin, "Cyberbullying: An Exploratory Analysis of Factors Related to Offending and Victimization," Deviant Behavior 29 (2008): 129–156.

69. Cyberbullying Research Center, http:// cyberbullying.org/2015-data.

70. National Center for Education Statistics, "Indicators of School Crime and Safety: 2014," http://nces.ed.gov/pubs2015 /2015072.pdf.

71. FlexiSPY, Inc., http://www.flexispy.com/en /catch-cheating-spouse-cell-phone.htm.

72. Tom Yager, "Cyberspying: No Longer a Crime for Geeks Only," InfoWorld 22 (2000): 62.

73. Nathan Vardi, "Chinese Take Out," Forbes 176 (2005).

74. CBS News, "NSA Surveillance Exposed," http://www.cbsnews.com/feature/nsa -surveillance-exposed/.

75. American Civil Liberties Union, "ACLU Files Lawsuit Challenging Constitutionality of NSA Phone Spying Program," June 11, 2013, https://www.aclu.org/news/aclu-files -lawsuit-challenging-constitutionality-nsa -phone-spying-program.

76. ACLU, "Court Dismisses ACLU Challenge to NSA Internet Surveillance," https://www .aclu.org/news/court-dismisses-aclu -challenge-nsa-internet-surveillance.

77. Symantec, Internet Security Threat Report.

78. Jeremy Kirk, "Identity Theft May Cost IRS $21 Billion over Next Five Years," PC World, August 3, 2012, http://www.pcworld.idg .com.au/article/432584/identity_theft _may_cost_irs_21_billion_over_next _five_years/.

79. Public Law 98-473, Title H, Chapter XXI, [sections] 2102(a), 98 Stat. 1837, 2190 (1984).

80. Public Law 104-294, Title II, [sections] 201, 110 Stat. 3488, 3491–3494 (1996).

81. Heather Jacobson and Rebecca Green, "Computer Crime," American Criminal Law Review 39 (2002): 273–326; Identity Theft and Assumption Act of 1998 (18 U.S.C. S 1028(a)(7)).

82. Comprehensive Crime Control Act of 1984, PL 98–473, 2101–03, 98 Stat. 1837, 2190

(1984), Adding 18 USC 1030 (1984); Counterfeit Active Device and Computer Fraud and Abuse Act, Amended by PL 99–474, 100 Stat. 1213 (1986), Codified at 18 U.S.C. 1030 (Supp. V 1987); Computer Abuse Amendments Act 18 U.S.C. Section 1030 (1994); Copyright Infringement Act 17 U.S.C. Section 506(a) 1994; Electronic Communications Privacy Act of 1986 18 U.S.C. 2510–2520 (1988 and Supp. II 1990).

83. Family Entertainment and Copyright Act of 2005, Title 18 United States Code Section 2319B.

84. FBI, "FBI Works with Foreign Partners to Target Botnet," April 9, 2015, https://www .fbi.gov/news/pressrel/press-releases/fbi -works-with-foreign-partners-to-target -botnet; "FBI Creates the International Cyber Crime Coordination Cell, May 5, 2016, https://www.fbi.gov/news/podcasts /thisweek/fbi-creates-the-international -cyber-crime-coordination-cell.mp3/view.

85. United States Secret Service, Electronic Crimes Task Force, 2016, https://www.dhs .gov/sites/default/files/publications/USSS %20Electronic%20Crimes%20Task%20 Force.pdf.

86. George I. Seffers, "Ramping Up the Cyber Criminal Hunt," Signal, March 1, 2014, http://www.afcea.org/content/?q=ramping -cyber-criminal-hunt.

87. Council of Europe Convention on Cybercrime, CETS No. 185, http://www .coe.int/en/web/conventions/full-list /-/conventions/treaty/185.

88. "ACLU Memo on the Council of Europe Convention on Cybercrime," June 16, 2004, https://www.aclu.org/aclu-memo -council-europe-convention-cybercrime ?redirect=technology-and-liberty/aclu -memo-council-europe-convention -cybercrime.

89. Kim Zetter, Countdown to Zero Day: Stuxnet and the Launch of the World's First Digital Weapon (New York: Broadway Books, 2015); William J. Broad, John Markoff, and David E. Sanger, "Israeli Test on Worm Called Crucial in Iran Nuclear Delay," New York Times, January 15, 2011, http://www .nytimes.com/2011/01/16/world/middleeast /16stuxnet.html.

90. Richard A. Clarke and Rob Knake, Cyber War: The Next Threat to National Security and What to Do About It (New York: HarperCollins, 2012).

91. Fergus Hanson, "Norms of Cyberwar in Peacetime," Brookings Institute, November 17, 2015, http://www.brookings .edu/blogs/markaz/posts/2015/11/17 -norms-of-cyberwar-peacetime-hanson.

92. Damian Paletta, Danny Yadron, and Jennifer Valentino-Devries, "Cyberwar Ignites a New Arms Race," Wall Street Journal, October 11, 2015, http://www.wsj .com/articles/cyberwar-ignites-a-new-arms -race-1444611128.

93. Ibid.

94. Barry C. Collin, "The Future of CyberTerrorism: Where the Physical and Virtual Worlds Converge," Institute for Security and Intelligence, http://www .crime-research.org/library/Cyberter.htm.

95. Tomas Hellström, "Critical Infrastructure and Systemic Vulnerability: Towards a Planning Framework," Safety Science 45 (2007): 415–430.

96. Mathieu Gorge, "Cyberterrorism: Hype or Reality?" Computer Fraud and Security 2 (2007): 9–12.

97. See, generally, U.S. Department of the Treasury, "Protecting Charitable Organizations," 2016, https://www.treasury .gov/resource-center/terrorist-illicit-finance /Pages/protecting-index.aspx.

98. United States v. Holy Land Foundation for Relief and Development, http://scholar .google.com/scholar_case?case =4324794569509460028.

99. Loretta Napoleoni, Modern Jihad: Tracing the Dollars Behind the Terror Networks (Sterling, VA: Pluto Press, 2003).

100. Center for Strategic and International Studies, https://www.csis.org/.

101. Nicole Perlroth, "U.S. Banks Again Hit by Wave of Cyberattacks," New York Times, January 4, 2013, http://bits.blogs.nytimes .com/2013/01/04/u-s-banks-again-hit-by -wave-of-cyberattacks/.

102. U.S. Army Cyber Command, http://www .arcyber.army.mil/ (accessed March 2016).

103. National Security Agency, "Signals Intelligence FAQs," https://www.nsa.gov /about/faqs/sigint-faqs.shtml; NSA, "Information Assurance," https://www.nsa .gov/what-we-do/information-assurance/.

acquaintance rape Forcible sex in which offender and victim are acquainted with each other.

acquaintance robbery Robbers who focus their thefts on people they know.

active precipitation The view that the source of many criminal incidents is the aggressive or provocative behavior of victims.

active shooter incident A term used by law enforcement to describe a situation in which a mass shooting is in progress when police and law enforcement agents arrive at the scene.

adolescent-limited offender Offender who follows the most common criminal trajectory, in which antisocial behavior peaks in adolescence and then diminishes.

age-graded theory A developmental theory that posits that (a) individual traits and childhood experiences are important to understand the onset of delinquent and criminal behavior; (b) experiences in young adulthood and beyond can redirect criminal trajectories or paths; (c) serious problems in adolescence undermine life chances; (d) positive life experiences and relationships can help a person knife off from a criminal career path; (e) positive life experiences such as gaining employment, getting married, or joining the military create informal social control mechanisms that limit criminal behavior opportunities; (f) former criminals may choose to desist from crime because they find more conventional paths more beneficial and rewarding.

aggravated rape Rape involving multiple offenders, weapons, and victim injuries.

aging out The process by which individuals reduce the frequency of their offending behavior as they age. It is also known as spontaneous remission because people are believed to spontaneously reduce the rate of their criminal behavior as they mature. Aging out is thought to occur among all groups of offenders.

alexithymia A deficit in emotional cognition that prevents people from being aware of their feelings or being able to understand or talk about their thoughts and emotions; they seem robotic and emotionally dead.

al-Qaeda (Arabic for "the base") An international fundamentalist Islamist organization comprising independent and collaborative cells, whose goal is reducing Western influence upon Islamic affairs. Also spelled al-Qa'ida.

American Dream The goal of accumulating material goods and wealth through individual competition; the process of being socialized to pursue material success and to believe it is achievable.

anal stage In Freud's schema, the second and third years of life, when the focus of sexual attention is on the elimination of bodily wastes.

androgens Male sex hormones.

anomie According to Durkheim, an anomic society is one in which rules of behavior (i.e., values, customs, and norms) have broken down or become inoperative during periods of rapid social change or social crisis.

antithesis An opposing argument.

arousal theory A view of crime suggesting that people who have a high arousal level seek powerful stimuli in their environment to maintain an optimal level of arousal. These stimuli are often associated with violence and aggression. Sociopaths may need greater than average stimulation to bring them up to comfortable levels of living; this need explains their criminal tendencies.

arson for profit People looking to collect insurance money, but who are afraid or unable to set the fire themselves, hire professional arsonists. These professionals have acquired the skills to set fires and yet make the cause seem accidental.

arson fraud A business owner burns his or her property, or hires someone to do it, to escape financial problems.

atavistic anomalies According to Lombroso, the physical characteristics that distinguish born criminals from the general population and are throwbacks to animals or primitive people.

ATM skimming Using an electronic device or camera on an ATM that copies information from a bank card's magnetic strip whenever a customer uses the machine or photographs their key strokes.

at-risk Children and adults who lack the education and skills needed to be effectively in demand in modern society.

attachment theory The belief that the ability to form attachments—that is, emotionally bond to another person—has important lasting psychological implications that follow people across the life span.

attention deficit hyperactivity disorder (ADHD) A psychological disorder in which a child shows developmentally inappropriate impulsivity, hyperactivity, and lack of attention.

authority conflict pathway The path to a criminal career that begins with early stubborn behavior and defiance of parents.

behaviorism The branch of psychology concerned with the study of observable behavior rather than unconscious motives. It focuses on the relationship between particular stimuli and people's responses to them.

behavior modeling Process of learning behavior (notably aggression) by observing others. Aggressive models may be parents, criminals in the neighborhood, or characters on television or in video games and movies.

binge drinking Having five or more drinks on the same occasion (that is, at the same time or within a couple of hours of each other) on at least 1 day in the past 30 days.

biological determinism A belief that criminogenic traits can be acquired through indirect heredity from a degenerate family whose members suffered from such ills as insanity, syphilis, and alcoholism, or through direct heredity—being related to a family of criminals.

biophobia A view held by sociologists that no serious consideration should be given to biological factors when attempting to understand human nature.

biosocial theory An approach to criminology that focuses on the interaction between biological and social factors as they relate to crime.

bipolar disorder An emotional disturbance in which moods alternate between periods of wild elation and deep depression.

blameworthy Basing punishment solely on whether a person is responsible for wrongdoing and deserving of censure or blame.

booster box Device with a false bottom that can be opened and closed by a professional shoplifter, lined with metal or some other substance to prevent security tags from setting off alarms, placed over merchandise.

boosters Professional shoplifters who steal with the intention of reselling stolen merchandise.

brothel A house of prostitution, typically run by a madam who sets prices and handles "business" arrangements.

California Personality Inventory (CPI) A frequently administered personality test used to distinguish deviant groups from nondeviant groups.

call girls Prostitutes who make dates via the phone and then service customers in hotel rooms or apartments. Call girls typically have a steady clientele who are repeat customers.

capable guardians Effective deterrents to crime, such as police or watchful neighbors.

capitalist bourgeoisie The owners of the means of production.

career criminal A person who repeatedly violates the law and organizes his or her lifestyle around criminality.

carjacking Theft of a car by force or threat of force.

cerebral allergies A physical condition that causes brain malfunction due to exposure to some environmental or biochemical irritant.

chemical restraints or chemical straitjackets Antipsychotic drugs such as Haldol, Stelazine, Prolixin, and Risperdal, which help control levels of neurotransmitters (such as serotonin/dopamine), that are used to treat violence-prone people.

child abuse Any physical, emotional, or sexual trauma to a child for which no reasonable explanation, such as an accident, can be found. Child abuse can also be a function of neglecting to give proper care and attention to a young child.

chiseling Crimes that involve using illegal means to cheat an organization, its consumers, or both on a regular basis.

chivalry hypothesis The idea that low female crime and delinquency rates are a reflection of the leniency with which police treat female offenders.

chronic offender According to Wolfgang, a delinquent offender who is arrested five or more times before he or she is 18 stands a good chance of becoming an adult criminal; such offenders are responsible for more than half of all serious crimes.

chronic victimization Those who have been crime victims maintain a significantly higher chance of future victimization than people who have remained nonvictims. Most repeat victimizations occur soon after a previous crime has occurred, suggesting that repeat victims share some personal characteristic that makes them a magnet for predators.

civil law The set of rules governing relations between private parties, including both individuals and organizations (such as business enterprises and/or corporations). The civil law is used to resolve, control, and shape such personal interactions as contracts, wills and trusts, property ownership, and commerce.

classical criminology Eighteenth-century social thinkers believed that criminals choose to commit crime and that crime can be controlled by judicious punishment.

cleared crimes Crimes are cleared in two ways: when at least one person is arrested, charged, and turned over to the court for prosecution; or by exceptional means, when some element beyond police control precludes the physical arrest of an offender (for example, the offender leaves the country).

closure A term used by Lemert to describe people from a middle-class background who have little identification with a criminal subculture but cash bad checks because of a financial crisis that demands an immediate resolution.

cognitive theory The study of the perception of reality and of the mental processes required to understand the world in which we live.

cohort A sample of subjects whose behavior is followed over a period of time.

collective efficacy Social control exerted by cohesive communities, based on mutual trust, including intervention in the supervision of children and maintenance of public order.

college boy A disadvantaged youth who embraces the cultural and social values of the middle class and actively strives to be successful by those standards. This type of youth is embarking on an almost hopeless path because he is ill-equipped academically, socially, and linguistically to achieve the rewards of middle-class life.

commitment to conformity A strong personal investment in conventional institutions, individuals, and processes that prevents people from engaging in behavior that might jeopardize their reputation and achievements.

common law Early English law, developed by judges, that incorporated Anglo-Saxon tribal custom, feudal rules and practices, and the everyday rules of behavior of local villages. Common law became the standardized law of the land in England and eventually formed the basis of the criminal law in the United States.

Communist Manifesto In this document, Marx focused his attention on the economic conditions perpetuated by the capitalist system. He stated that its development had turned workers into a dehumanized mass who lived an existence that was at the mercy of their capitalist employers.

computer worms Programs that attack computer networks (or the Internet) by self-replicating and sending themselves to other users, generally via email, without the aid of the operator.

concentration effect Working- and middle-class families flee inner-city poverty areas, resulting in the most disadvantaged population being consolidated in the most disorganized urban neighborhoods.

conduct disorder (CD) A pattern of repetitive behavior in which the rights of others or social norms are violated.

conduct norms Behaviors expected of social group members. If group norms conflict with those of the general culture, members of the group may find themselves described as outcasts or criminals.

confidence (con) game A swindle, usually involving a get-rich-quick scheme, often with illegal overtones, so that the victim will be afraid or embarrassed to call the police.

conflict view The view that human behavior is shaped by interpersonal conflict and that those who maintain social power will use it to further their own needs.

conscience One of two parts of the superego; it distinguishes between what is right and wrong.

consensus view of crime The belief that the majority of citizens in a society share common ideals and work toward a common good and that crimes are acts that are outlawed because they conflict with the rules of the majority and are harmful to society.

consent In prosecuting rape cases, it is essential to prove that the attack was forced and that the victim did not give voluntary consent to her attacker. In a sense, the burden of proof is on the victim to show that her character is beyond question and that she in no way encouraged, enticed, or misled the accused rapist. Proving victim dissent is not a requirement in any other violent crime.

constructive possession In the crime of larceny, willingly giving up temporary physical possession of property but retaining legal ownership.

contagion effect Genetic predispositions and early experiences make some people, including twins, susceptible to deviant behavior, which is transmitted by the presence of antisocial siblings in the household.

containment theory The idea that a strong self-image insulates a youth from the pressures and pulls of criminogenic influences in the environment.

continuity of crime The view that crime begins early in life and continues throughout the life course. Thus, the best predictor of future criminality is past criminality.

corner boy According to Cohen, a role in the lower-class culture in which young men remain in their birth neighborhood, acquire families and menial jobs, and adjust to the demands of their environment.

corporate crime White-collar crime involving a legal violation by a corporate entity, such as price fixing, restraint of trade, or hazardous waste dumping.

covert pathway A path to a criminal career that begins with minor underhanded behavior and progresses to fire starting and theft.

crackdowns The concentration of police resources on particular problem areas, such as street-level drug dealing, to eradicate or displace criminal activity.

crime discouragers Discouragers can be grouped into three categories: guardians, who monitor targets (such as store security guards); handlers, who monitor potential offenders (such as parole officers and parents); and managers, who monitor places (such as homeowners and doorway attendants).

crime typology The study of criminal behavior involving research on the links between different types of crime and criminals. Because people often disagree about types of crimes and criminal motivation, no standard exists within the field. Some typologies focus on the criminal, suggesting the existence of offender groups, such as professional criminals, psychotic criminals, occasional criminals, and so on. Others focus on the crimes, clustering them into categories such as property crimes, sex crimes, and so on.

criminal anthropology Early efforts to discover a biological basis of crime through measurement of physical and mental processes.

criminality A personal trait of the individual as distinct from a "crime," which is an event.

criminal justice The field of study that focuses on law enforcement, the legal system, corrections, and other agencies of justice involved in the apprehension, prosecution, defense, sentencing, incarceration, and supervision of those suspected of or charged with criminal offenses.

criminogenic knowledge structure (CKS) The view that negative life events are connected and produce a hostile view of people and relationships, preference for immediate rewards, and a cynical view of conventional norms.

criminologists Researchers who use scientific methods to study the nature, extent, cause, and control of criminal behavior.

criminology The scientific study of the nature, extent, cause, and control of criminal behavior.

criminology in action Efforts of criminologists to use their knowledge, training, insight, and experience to understand human behavior and predict its occurrence.

crisis intervention Emergency counseling for crime victims.

critical criminologists Researchers who view crime as a function of the capitalist mode of production and not the social conflict that might occur in any society regardless of its economic system.

critical criminology The view that capitalism produces haves and have-nots, each engaging in a particular branch of criminality. The mode of production shapes social life. Because economic competitiveness is the essence of capitalism, conflict increases and eventually destabilizes social institutions and the individuals within them.

critical feminism An area of scholarship whose focus is on the effects of gender inequality and the unequal power of men and women in a capitalist society.

cross-sectional survey Survey data derived from all age, race, gender, and income segments of the population measured simultaneously. Because people from every age group are represented, age-specific crime rates can be determined. Proponents believe this is a sufficient substitute for the more expensive longitudinal approach that follows a group of subjects over time to measure crime rate changes.

crusted over Children who have been victims of or witnesses to violence and do not let people inside, nor do they express their feelings. They exploit others and in turn are exploited by those older and stronger; as a result, they develop a sense of hopelessness.

cultural deviance theory Branch of social structure theory that sees strain and social disorganization together resulting in a unique lower-class culture that conflicts with conventional social norms.

culture conflict According to Sellin, a condition brought about when the rules and norms of an individual's subcultural affiliation conflict with the role demands of conventional society.

culture of poverty The view that people in the lower class of society form a separate culture with its own values and norms that are in conflict with conventional society; the culture is self-maintaining and ongoing.

cumulative disadvantage A condition in which repeated negative experiences in adolescence undermine life chances and reduce employability and social relations. People who increase their cumulative disadvantage risk continued offending.

cyberbullying Willful and repeated harm inflicted through the medium of online communications.

cybercrime The use of modern technology for criminal purposes.

cyberdeviance The sale and distribution of morally tainted material and products over the Net.

cyberespionage Efforts by intelligence agencies to penetrate computer networks of an enemy nation in order to steal important data.

cyberspying Illegally using the Internet to gather information that is considered private and confidential.

cyberstalking Use of the Internet, email, or other electronic communications devices to stalk another person. Some cyberstalkers pursue minors through online chat rooms; others harass their victims electronically.

cyberterrorism Internet attacks against an enemy nation's technological infrastructure.

cybertheft Use of computer networks for criminal profits. Illegal copyright infringement, identity theft, and Internet securities fraud are examples of cybertheft.

cybervandalism Malicious attacks aimed at disrupting, defacing, and destroying technology.

cyberwar Using cyberspace for acts of war, including spying and disrupting an enemy's computer network.

cycle of violence A hypothesis that suggests that a childhood history of physical abuse predisposes survivors to becoming violent themselves in later years.

darknet Computer network that can only be accessed using nonstandard communications protocols and ports, with restricted access that can only be opened with specific software configurations.

date rape Forcible sex during a courting relationship.

defective intelligence Traits such as feeblemindedness, epilepsy, insanity, and defective social instinct, which Goring believed had a significant relationship to criminal behavior.

defensible space The principle that crime prevention can be achieved through modifying the physical environment to reduce the opportunity individuals have to commit crime.

deliberation Planning a homicide after careful thought, however brief, rather than acting on sudden impulse.

delinquent boy A youth who adopts a set of norms and principles in direct opposition to middle-class values, engaging in short-run hedonism, living for today and letting tomorrow take care of itself.

demystify To unmask the true purpose of law, justice, or other social institutions.

Department of Homeland Security (DHS) An agency of the federal government charged with preventing terrorist attacks within the United States, reducing America's vulnerability to terrorism, and minimizing the damage and aiding recovery from attacks that do occur.

deterrence theory The view that if the probability of arrest, conviction, and sanctioning increases, crime rates should decline.

developmental criminology A view of criminal behavior that places emphasis on the changes people go through over the life course. It presents a criminal career as a dynamic process involving onset, continuity, persistence, acceleration, and eventual desistance from criminal behavior, controlled by individual level traits and conditions.

deviant behavior Behavior that departs from the social norm.

deviant place theory People become victims because they reside in socially disorganized, high-crime areas where they have the greatest risk of coming into contact with criminal offenders.

dialectic method For every idea, or thesis, there exists an opposing argument, or antithesis. Because neither position can ever be truly accepted, the result is a merger of the two ideas, a synthesis. Marx adapted this analytic method for his study of class struggle.

differential association theory According to Sutherland, the principle that criminal acts are related to a person's exposure to an excess amount of antisocial attitudes and values.

differential opportunity The view that lower-class youths, whose legitimate opportunities are limited, join gangs and pursue criminal careers as alternative means to achieve universal success goals.

differential reinforcement Behavior is reinforced by being either rewarded or punished while interacting with others; also called direct conditioning.

differential reinforcement theory An attempt to explain crime as a type of learned behavior. First proposed by Akers in collaboration with Burgess in 1966, it is a version of the social learning view that employs differential association concepts as well as elements of psychological learning theory.

differential susceptibility model The belief that there is an indirect association between traits and crime.

diffusion of benefits Efforts to prevent one crime help prevent another; in other instances, crime control efforts in one locale reduce crime in another area.

direct conditioning Behavior is reinforced by being either rewarded or punished while interacting with others; also called differential reinforcement.

Director of National Intelligence (DNI) Government official charged with coordinating data from the nation's primary intelligence-gathering agencies.

discouragement Crime control efforts targeting a particular locale help reduce crime in surrounding areas and populations.

disorders Any type of psychological problems (formerly labeled neuroses or psychoses), such as anxiety disorders, mood disorders, and conduct disorders.

displacement A program that helps lower crime rates at specific locations or neighborhoods may be redirecting offenders to alternative targets.

disputatiousness Behavior within culturally defined conflict situations in which an individual who has been offended by a negative outcome in a dispute seeks reparations through violent means.

distributed denial-of-service attack (DDoS) A type of DoS attack where multiple compromised systems, which are often infected with a virus, are used to target a single system, causing a denial-of-service (DoS) attack.

diversion programs Programs of rehabilitation that remove offenders from the normal channels of the criminal justice system, thus avoiding the stigma of a criminal label.

dramatization of evil As the negative feedback of law enforcement agencies, parents, friends, teachers, and other figures amplifies the force of the original label, stigmatized offenders may begin to reevaluate their own identities. The person becomes the thing he is described as being.

drift According to Matza, the view that youths move in and out of delinquency and that their lifestyles can embrace both conventional and deviant values.

dropout factories High schools in which the completion rate is consistently 40 percent or less.

early onset A term that refers to the assumption that a criminal career begins early in life and that people who are deviant at a very young age are the ones most likely to persist in crime.

economic crime An act in violation of the criminal law that is designed to bring financial gain to the offender.

edgework The excitement or exhilaration of successfully executing illegal activities in dangerous situations.

egalitarian families Families in which spouses share similar positions of power at home and in the workplace.

ego The part of the personality, developed in early childhood, that helps control the id and keep people's actions within the boundaries of social convention.

ego ideal Part of the superego; directs the individual into morally acceptable and responsible behaviors, which may not be pleasurable.

ehooking Using the Internet to advertise sexual services and make contact with clients.

elder abuse A disturbing form of domestic violence by children and other relatives with whom elderly people live.

eldercide The murder of a senior citizen.

election fraud Illegal interference with the process of an election. Acts of fraud tend to involve affecting vote counts to bring about a desired election outcome, whether by increasing the vote share of the favored candidate, depressing the vote share of the rival candidates, or both. Varieties of election fraud include intimidation, disruption of polling places, distribution of misinformation such as the wrong election date, registration fraud, and vote buying.

Electra complex A stage of development when girls begin to have sexual feelings for their fathers.

electroencephalograph (EEG) A device that can record the electronic impulses given off by the brain, commonly called brain waves.

embezzlement A type of larceny that involves taking the possessions of another (fraudulent conversion) that have been placed in the thief's lawful possession for safekeeping, such as a bank teller misappropriating deposits or a stockbroker making off with a customer's account.

Enlightenment A philosophical, intellectual, and cultural movement of the seventeenth and eighteenth centuries that stressed reason, logic, criticism, education, and freedom of thought over dogma and superstition.

enterprise crimes Ongoing illegal activities by an individual or a group of individuals involved in commerce that either violate the laws regulating legitimate business or whose acknowledged purpose is profit through illegitimate commercial enterprise.

eros The instinct to preserve and create life, a basic human drive present at birth.

espionage The practice of obtaining information about a government, organization, or society that is considered secret or confidential without the permission of the holder of the information. Commonly called spying.

etailing fraud Illegally buying and/or selling merchandise on the Internet.

exploitation Forcing victims to pay for services to which they have a clear right.

expressive crimes Crimes that have no purpose except to accomplish the behavior at hand, such as shooting someone.

expressive violence Violence that is designed not for profit or gain but to vent rage, anger, or frustration.

failed state A nation whose government has lost control of its own territory, is unable to provide public services and protection, and lacks the ability to interact with other states as a full member of the international community.

false pretenses (fraud) Misrepresenting a fact in a way that causes a deceived victim to give money or property to the offender.

felony A serious offense, such as rape, murder, robbery, or burglary, that is punishable by a prison sentence or, in the case of first-degree murder, by capital punishment.

felony murder A homicide in the context of another felony, such as robbery or rape; legally defined as first-degree murder.

fence A buyer and seller of stolen merchandise.

feticide Endangering or killing an unborn fetus.

filicide The murder of one's own child.

first-degree murder Unlawful killing that is both willful and premeditated, committed after planning or "lying in wait" for the victim.

fixated An adult who exhibits behavior traits characteristic of those encountered during infantile sexual development.

flash houses Public meeting places in England, often taverns, that served as headquarters for gangs.

focal concerns According to Miller, the value orientations of lower-class cultures; features include the needs for excitement, trouble, smartness, and personal autonomy.

focused deterrence A policy that relies on pulling every deterrent "lever" available to reduce crime in the targeted problem.

gang rape Forcible sex involving multiple attackers.

gateway model An explanation of drug abuse that posits that users begin with a more benign drug (alcohol or marijuana) and progress to more potent drugs.

general deterrence A crime control policy that depends on the fear of criminal penalties. General deterrence measures, such as long prison sentences for violent crimes, are aimed at convincing the potential law violator that the pains associated with crime outweigh its benefits.

general strain theory (GST) According to Agnew, the view that multiple sources of strain interact with an individual's emotional traits and responses to produce criminality.

General Theory of Crime (GTC) According to Gottfredson and Hirschi, a developmental theory that modifies social control theory by integrating concepts from biosocial, psychological, routine activities, and rational choice theories.

gentrification A residential renewal stage in which obsolete housing is replaced and upgraded; areas undergoing such change seem to experience an increase in their crime rates.

globalization The process of creating transnational markets, politics, and legal systems in an effort to form and sustain a global economy.

good burglar Professional burglars use this title to characterize colleagues who have distinguished themselves as burglars. Characteristics of the good burglar include technical competence, maintenance of personal integrity, specialization in burglary, financial success, and the ability to avoid prison sentences.

grand larceny Theft of money or property of substantial value, punished as a felony.

green crime Acts involving illegal environmental harm that violate environmental laws and regulations.

guerilla The term means "little war" and developed out of the Spanish rebellion against French troops after Napoleon's 1808 invasion of the Iberian Peninsula. Today the term is used interchangeably with the term *terrorist*.

hate crimes Acts of violence or intimidation designed to terrorize or frighten people considered undesirable because of their race, religion, ethnic origin, or sexual orientation.

human agency A person's ability to intentionally make choices based on free will.

humanistic psychology A branch of psychology that stresses self-awareness and "getting in touch with feelings."

hypoglycemia A condition that occurs when glucose (sugar) levels in the blood fall below the necessary level for normal and efficient brain functioning.

id The primitive part of people's mental makeup, present at birth, that represents unconscious biological drives for food, sex, and other life-sustaining necessities. The id seeks instant gratification without concern for the rights of others.

identity crisis A psychological state, identified by Erikson, in which youth face inner turmoil and uncertainty about life roles.

identity theft Using the Internet to steal someone's identity and/or impersonate the victim in order to conduct illicit transactions such as committing fraud using the victim's name and identity.

incapacitation effect The idea that keeping offenders in confinement will eliminate the risk of their committing further offenses.

incivilities Rude and uncivil behavior; behavior that indicates little caring for the feelings of others.

income inequality The unequal distribution of household or individual income across the various participants in an economy.

index crimes The eight crimes that, because of their seriousness and frequency, the FBI reports the incidence of in the annual Uniform Crime Report. Index crimes include murder, rape, assault, robbery, burglary, arson, larceny, and motor vehicle theft.

individual vulnerability model Assumes there is a direct link between traits and crime; some people are vulnerable to crime from birth.

industrial espionage Activities designed to gain illegal competitive advantage over a business rival, such as bribing employees to reveal trade secrets and product formulas.

infanticide The murder of a newborn or very young baby.

inferiority complex People who have feelings of inferiority and compensate for them with a drive for superiority.

influence peddling Using an institutional position to grant favors and sell information to which their co-conspirators are not entitled.

informal sanctions Disapproval, stigma, or anger directed toward an offender by significant others (parents, peers, neighbors, teachers), resulting in shame, embarrassment, and loss of respect.

information processing A branch of cognitive psychology that focuses on the way people process, store, encode, retrieve, and manipulate information to make decisions and solve problems.

information technology (IT) All forms of technology used to create, store, retrieve, and exchange data in all its various forms, including electronic, voice, and still image.

inheritance school Advocates of this view trace the activities of several generations of families believed to have an especially large number of criminal members.

insider trading Illegal buying of stock in a company based on information provided by someone who has a fiduciary interest in the company, such as an employee or an attorney or accountant retained by the firm. Federal laws and the rules of the Securities and Exchange Commission require that all profits from such trading be returned and provide for both fines and a prison sentence.

institutional anomie theory The view that anomie pervades U.S. culture because the drive for material wealth dominates and undermines social and community values.

instrumental crimes Offenses designed to improve the financial or social position of the criminal.

instrumental theory The view that criminal law and the criminal justice system are capitalist instruments for controlling the lower class.

instrumental violence Violence used in an attempt to improve the financial or social position of the criminal.

insurgent The typical goal of an insurgency is to confront the existing government for control of all or a portion of its territory, or force political concessions in sharing political power. While terrorists may operate in small bands with a narrow focus, insurgents represent a popular movement and may also seek external support from other nations to bring pressure on the government.

integrated theories Models of crime causation that weave social and individual variables into a complex explanatory chain.

intelligence A person's ability to reason, think abstractly, understand complex ideas, learn from experience, and discover solutions to complex problems.

interactionist view The view that one's perception of reality is significantly influenced by one's interpretations of the reactions of others to similar events and stimuli.

involuntary or negligent manslaughter A homicide that occurs as a result of acts that are negligent and without regard for the harm they may cause others, such as driving under the influence of alcohol or drugs.

Islamic State of Iraq and the Levant (ISIL) A jihadist militant group that follows an Islamic fundamentalist version of Sunni Islam. Their objective is to create an independent caliphate in lands seized from Syria and Iraq. Also known as ISIS and Daesh.

just desert The philosophy of justice that asserts that those who violate the rights of others deserve to be punished. The severity of punishment should be commensurate with the seriousness of the crime.

justice The quality of being fair under the law. Justice is defined by the relationship that exists between the individual and the state; justice demands that the state treats every person as equally as possible without regard to their gender, religion, race, or any other personal status.

latency A developmental stage that begins at age 6. During this period, feelings of sexuality are repressed until the genital stage begins at puberty; this marks the beginning of adult sexuality.

latent delinquency A psychological predisposition to commit antisocial acts because of an id-dominated personality that renders an individual incapable of controlling impulsive, pleasure-seeking drives.

latent trait A stable feature, characteristic, property, or condition, present at birth or soon after, that makes some people crime prone over the life course.

latent trait theories Theoretical views that criminal behavior is controlled by a master trait, present at birth or soon after, that remains stable and unchanging throughout a person's lifetime.

learning disability (LD) A disorder in one or more of the basic psychological processes involved in understanding or using spoken or written languages.

left realism An approach that views crime as a function of relative deprivation under capitalism and that favors pragmatic, community-based crime prevention and control.

liberal feminist theory Theory suggesting that the traditionally lower crime rate for women can be explained by their second-class economic and social position. As women's social roles have changed and their lifestyles have become more like those of men, it is believed that their crime rates will converge.

life course persister One of the small group of offenders whose criminal career continues well into adulthood.

life course theories Theoretical views studying changes in criminal offending patterns over a person's entire life.

lifestyle theory People may become crime victims because their lifestyle increases their exposure to criminal offenders.

logic bomb A program that is secretly attached to a computer system, monitors the network's work output, and waits for a particular signal such as a date to appear. Also called a slag code, it is a type of delayed-action virus that may be set off when a program user makes certain input that sets it in motion. A logic bomb may cause a variety of problems ranging from displaying or printing a spurious message to deleting or corrupting data.

lumpen proletariat The fringe members at the bottom of society who produce nothing and live, parasitically, off the work of others.

madam A woman who employs prostitutes, supervises their behavior, and receives a fee for her services.

mala in se Acts that are outlawed because they violate basic moral values, such as rape, murder, assault, and robbery.

mala prohibitum Acts that are outlawed because they clash with current norms and public opinion, such as tax, traffic, and drug laws.

malware A malicious software program.

manslaughter A homicide without malice.

marginal deterrence The concept that a penalty for a crime may prompt commission of a marginally more severe crime because that crime receives the same magnitude of punishment as the original one.

marginalization Displacement of workers, pushing them outside the economic and social mainstream.

marital exemption The practice of prohibiting the prosecution of husbands for the rape of their wives.

marital rape Forcible sex between people who are legally married to each other.

mark The target of a con man or woman.

masculinity hypothesis The view that women who commit crimes have biological and psychological traits similar to those of men.

mass murder The killing of a large number of people in a single incident by an offender who typically does not seek concealment or escape.

mechanical solidarity A characteristic of a preindustrial society, which is held together by traditions, shared values, and unquestioned beliefs.

meta-analysis A research technique that uses the grouped data from several different studies.

middle-class measuring rods According to Cohen, the standards by which teachers and other representatives of state authority evaluate lower-class youths. Because they cannot live up to middle-class standards, lower-class youths are bound for failure, which gives rise to frustration and anger at conventional society.

minimal brain dysfunction (MBD) An abruptly appearing, maladaptive behavior that interrupts an individual's lifestyle and life flow. In its most serious form, MBD has been linked to serious antisocial acts, an imbalance in the urge-control mechanisms of the brain, and chemical abnormality.

Minnesota Multiphasic Personality Inventory (MMPI) A widely used psychological test that has subscales designed to measure many different personality traits, including psychopathic deviation (Pd scale), schizophrenia (Sc scale), and hypomania (Ma scale).

misdemeanor A minor or petty crime, typically punished by a fine, community sentence, or a jail term.

mission hate crimes Violent crimes committed by disturbed individuals who see it as their duty to rid the world of evil.

money mule Someone who collects and transfers money or goods acquired illegally and then transfers them to a third party.

moral crusaders People who strive to stamp out behavior they find objectionable. Typically, moral crusaders are directed at public order crimes, such as drug abuse or pornography.

moral development The way people morally represent and reason about the world.

moral entrepreneurs Interest groups that attempt to control social life and the legal order in such a way as to promote their own personal set of moral values. People who use their influence to shape the legal process in ways they see fit.

motivated offenders The potential offenders in a population. According to rational choice theory, crime rates will vary according to the number of motivated offenders.

Multidimensional Personality Questionnaire (MPQ) A test that allows researchers to assess such personality traits as control, aggression, alienation,

and well-being. Evaluations using this scale indicate that adolescent offenders who are crime prone maintain negative emotionality, a tendency to experience aversive affective states such as anger, anxiety, and irritability.

murder The unlawful killing of a human being (homicide) with malicious intent.

naive check forgers Amateurs who cash bad checks because of some financial crisis but have little identification with a criminal subculture.

narcissistic personality disorder A condition marked by a persistent pattern of self-importance, need for admiration, lack of empathy, and preoccupation with fantasies of unlimited success, power, brilliance, beauty, or ideal love.

National Crime Victimization Survey (NCVS) The ongoing victimization study conducted jointly by the Justice Department and the U.S. Census Bureau that surveys victims about their experiences with law violation.

National Incident-Based Reporting System (NIBRS) A program that requires local police agencies to provide a brief account of each incident and arrest within 22 crime patterns, including incident, victim, and offender information.

nature theory The view that intelligence is largely determined genetically and that low intelligence is linked to criminal behavior.

negative affective states According to Agnew, anger, depression, disappointment, fear, and other adverse emotions that derive from strain.

negative reinforcement Using either negative stimuli (punishment) or loss of reward (negative punishment) to curtail unwanted behaviors.

neglect Not providing a child with the care and shelter to which he or she is entitled.

neocortex A part of the human brain; the left side of the neocortex controls sympathetic feelings toward others.

networks When referring to terrorist organizations, networks are loosely organized groups located in different parts of the city, state, or country (or world) that share a common theme or purpose, but have a diverse leadership and command structure and are only in intermittent communication with one another.

neuroallergies Allergies that affect the nervous system and cause the allergic person to produce enzymes that attack wholesome foods as if they were dangerous to the body. They may also cause swelling of the brain and produce sensitivity in the central nervous system—conditions that are linked to mental, emotional, and behavioral problems.

neurophysiology The study of brain activity.

neutralization theory Neutralization theory holds that offenders adhere to conventional values while "drifting" into periods of illegal behavior. In order to drift, people must first overcome (neutralize) legal and moral values.

nurture theory The view that intelligence is not inherited but is largely a product of environment. Low IQ scores do not cause crime but may result from the same environmental factors.

obscenity According to current legal theory, sexually explicit material that lacks a serious purpose and appeals solely to the prurient interest of the viewer. While nudity per se is not usually considered obscene, open sexual behavior, masturbation, and exhibition of the genitals is banned in most communities.

obsessive-compulsive disorder An extreme preoccupation with certain thoughts and compulsive performance of certain behaviors.

occasional criminals Offenders who do not define themselves by a criminal role or view themselves as committed career criminals.

Oedipus complex A stage of development when males begin to have sexual feelings for their mothers.

offender-specific crime The idea that offenders evaluate their skills, motives, needs, and fears before deciding to commit crime.

offense-specific crime The idea that offenders react selectively to the characteristics of particular crimes.

oral stage In Freud's schema, the first year of life, when a child attains pleasure by sucking and biting.

organic solidarity Postindustrial social systems, which are highly developed and dependent upon the division of labor; people are connected by their interdependent needs for one another's services and production.

overt pathway Pathway to a criminal career that begins with minor aggression, leads to physical fighting, and eventually escalates to violent crime.

paraphilias Bizarre or abnormal sexual practices that may involve recurrent sexual urges focused on objects, humiliation, or children.

parental efficacy Parenting that is supportive, effective, and noncoercive.

Part I crimes Another term for index crimes; eight categories of serious, frequent crimes.

Part II crimes All crimes other than index and minor traffic offenses. The FBI records annual arrest information for Part II offenses.

passive precipitation The view that some people become victims because of personal and social characteristics that make them attractive targets for predatory criminals.

paternalistic families Traditional family model in which fathers assume the role of breadwinners, while mothers tend to have menial jobs or remain at home to supervise domestic matters.

patriarchy A society in which men dominate public, social, economic, and political affairs.

peacemaking An approach that considers punitive crime control strategies to be counterproductive and favors the use of humanistic conflict resolution to prevent and control crime.

pedophilia A psychosexual disorder in which an adult has sexual fantasies about or engages in sexual acts with an underage minor child.

perceptual deterrence The theory that the perceived certainty, severity, and celerity of punishment are inversely related to the decisions by would-be offenders to commit crime, regardless of the actual likelihood of being apprehended and punished. People who believe they will be punished will be deterred even if the actual likelihood of punishment is insignificant.

permeable neighborhood Areas with a greater than usual number of access streets from traffic arteries into the neighborhood.

persistence The idea that those who started their delinquent careers early and who committed serious violent crimes throughout adolescence are the most likely to persist as adults.

personality The reasonably stable patterns of behavior, including thoughts and emotions, that distinguish one person from another.

petit (petty) larceny Theft of a small amount of money or property, punished as a misdemeanor.

phallic stage In Freud's schema, the third year, when children focus their attention on their genitals.

phishing Sometimes called carding or brand spoofing, phishing is a scam where the perpetrator sends out emails appearing to come from legitimate web enterprises such as eBay, Amazon, and PayPal in an effort to get the recipient to reveal personal and financial information.

pigeon drop A con game in which a package or wallet containing money is "found" by a con man or woman, and the victims are bilked out of money they are asked to put up as collateral.

pink slime A substance made by gathering waste trimmings, cooking them so the fat separates easily from the muscle, and using a centrifuge to complete the separation.

pleasure principle According to Freud, a theory in which id-dominated people are driven to increase their personal pleasure without regard to consequences.

poachers Early English thieves who typically lived in the country and supplemented their diet and income with game that belonged to a landlord.

political crime Illegal acts that are designed to undermine an existing government and threaten its survival. Political crimes can include both violent and nonviolent acts and range in seriousness from dissent, treason, and espionage to violent acts such as terrorism or assassination.

Ponzi scheme An investment fraud that involves the payment of purported returns to existing investors from funds contributed by new investors.

population All people who share a particular personal characteristic, such as all high school students or all police officers.

population heterogeneity The view that the propensity of an individual to participate in antisocial behavior is a relatively stable trait, unchanging over their life course.

pornography Sexually explicit books, magazines, films, or other media intended to provide sexual titillation and excitement for paying customers.

positivism The branch of social science that uses the scientific method of the natural sciences and suggests that human behavior is a product of social, biological, psychological, or economic forces.

posttraumatic stress disorder (PTSD) Psychological reaction to a highly stressful event; symptoms may include depression, anxiety, flashbacks, and recurring nightmares.

power–control theory The view that gender differences in crime are a function of economic power (class position, one-earner versus two-earner families) and parental control (paternalistic versus egalitarian families).

predictive policing A technique that relies on data mining's ability to predict future crime using large data sets and geospatial technologies.

preemptive deterrence Efforts to prevent crime through community organization and youth involvement.

premeditation Consideration of a homicide before it occurs.

premenstrual syndrome (PMS) The stereotype that several days prior to and during menstruation females are beset by irritability and poor judgment as a result of hormonal changes.

primary deviance According to Lemert, deviant acts that do not help redefine the self-image and public image of the offender.

primary prevention programs Treatment programs that seek to correct or remedy personal problems before they manifest themselves as crime.

problem behavior syndrome (PBS) A cluster of antisocial behaviors that may include family dysfunction, substance abuse, smoking, precocious sexuality and early pregnancy, educational underachievement, suicide attempts, sensation seeking, and unemployment, as well as crime.

procedural criminal law Those laws that set out the basic rules of practice in the criminal justice system. Some elements of the law of criminal procedure are the rules of evidence, the law of arrest, the law of search and seizure, questions of appeal, jury selection, and the right to counsel.

productive forces Technology, energy sources, and material resources.

productive relations The relationships that exist among the people producing goods and services.

professional criminals Offenders who make a significant portion of their income from crime.

proletariat A term used by Marx to refer to the working class members of society who produce goods and services but who do not own the means of production.

propensity An inclination or tendency to behave in a particular way.

prostitution The granting of nonmarital sexual access for remuneration.

psychoanalytic or psychodynamic perspective Branch of psychology holding that the human personality is controlled by unconscious mental processes developed early in childhood.

psychopath People who have an antisocial personality that is a product of a defect or aberration within themselves.

psychopathic personality A personality characterized by a lack of warmth and feeling, inappropriate behavior responses, and an inability to learn from experience. Some psychologists view psychopathy as a result of childhood trauma; others see it as a result of biological abnormality.

psychosis A mental state in which the perception of reality is distorted. People experiencing psychosis hallucinate, have paranoid or delusional beliefs, change personality, exhibit disorganized thinking, and engage in unusual or bizarre behavior.

public (or administrative) law The branch of law that deals with the government and its relationships with individuals or other governments. It governs the administration and regulation of city, county, state, and federal government agencies.

public order crimes Acts that are considered illegal because they threaten the general well-being of society and challenge its accepted moral principles. Prostitution, drug use, and the sale of pornography are considered public order crimes.

racial profiling Selecting suspects on the basis of their ethnic or racial background.

racial threat hypothesis The belief that as the percentage of minorities in the population increases, so too does the amount of social control that police direct at minority group members.

Racketeer Influenced and Corrupt Organizations (RICO) Act Federal legislation that enables prosecutors to bring additional criminal or civil charges against people whose multiple criminal acts constitute a conspiracy. RICO features monetary penalties that allow the government to confiscate all profits derived from criminal activities. Originally intended to be used against organized criminals, RICO has also been used against white-collar criminals.

ransomware Malicious software, usually attached to an email, designed to block access to a computer system until a sum of money is paid.

rational choice theory The view that crime is a function of a decision-making process in which the potential offender weighs the potential costs and benefits of an illegal act.

reaction formation According to Cohen, rejecting goals and standards that seem impossible to achieve. Because a boy cannot hope to get into college, for example, he considers higher education a waste of time.

reactive (defensive) hate crimes Perpetrators believe they are taking a defensive stand against outsiders whom they believe threaten their community or way of life.

reality principle According to Freud, the ability to learn about the consequences of one's actions through experience.

reasoning criminal According to the rational choice approach, law-violating behavior occurs when an offender decides to risk breaking the law after considering both personal factors (such as the need for money, revenge, thrills, and entertainment) and situational factors (how well a target is protected and the efficiency of the local police force).

reciprocal altruism According to sociobiology, acts that are outwardly designed to help others but that have at their core benefits to the self.

reflected appraisals When parents are alienated from their children, their negative labeling reduces their children's self-image and increases delinquency.

Reign of Terror The origin of the term *terrorism*, the French Revolution's Reign of Terror began in 1793 and was initiated by the revolutionary government during which agents of the Committee of Public Safety and the National Convention were referred to as terrorists.

reintegrative shaming A method of correction that encourages offenders to confront their misdeeds, experience shame because of the harm they caused, and then be reincluded in society.

relational aggression Psychological and emotional abuse that involves the spreading of smears, rumors, and private information in order to harm their partner.

relative deprivation The condition that exists when people of wealth and poverty live in close proximity to one another. Some criminologists attribute crime rate differentials to relative deprivation.

restitution agreements Conditions of probation in which the offenders repay society or the victims of crime for the trouble the offenders caused. Monetary restitution involves a direct payment to the victim as a form of compensation. Community service restitution may be used in victimless crimes and involves work in the community in lieu of more severe criminal penalties.

restorative justice Using humanistic, nonpunitive strategies to right wrongs and restore social harmony.

restrictive deterrence Convincing criminals that committing a serious crime is too risky and that other less-dangerous crimes or actions might be a better choice.

retaliatory hate crimes A hate crime motivated by revenge for another hate crime, either real or imaginary, which may spark further retaliation.

retributive terrorists Terror groups who refrain from tying specific acts to direct demands for change. They want to instead redirect the balance between what they believe is good and evil. They see their revolution as existing on a spiritual plane; their mission is to exact retribution against sinners.

retrospective cohort study A study that uses an intact cohort of known offenders and looks back into their early life experiences by checking their educational, family, police, and hospital records.

retrospective reading The reassessment of a person's past to fit a current generalized label.

road rage A term used to describe motorists who assault each other.

role exit behaviors In order to escape from a stifling life in male-dominated families, girls may try to break away by running away and or even attempting suicide.

routine activities theory The view that the volume and distribution of predatory crime are closely related to the interaction of suitable targets, motivated offenders, and capable guardians.

sadistic personality disorder A repeating pattern of cruel and demeaning behavior. People suffering from this type of extreme personality disturbance seem prone to engage in serious violent attacks, including homicides motivated by sexual sadism.

sampling Selecting a limited number of people for study as representative of a larger group.

schizophrenia A type of psychosis often marked by bizarre behavior, hallucinations, loss of thought control, and inappropriate emotional responses. Schizophrenic types include catatonic, which characteristically involves impairment of motor activity; paranoid, which is characterized by delusions of persecution; and hebephrenic, which is characterized by immature behavior and giddiness.

scientific method Using verifiable principles and procedures for the systematic acquisition of knowledge; typically involves formulating a problem, creating a hypothesis, and collecting data through observation and experiment to verify the hypothesis.

secondary deviance According to Lemert, accepting deviant labels as a personal identity. Acts become secondary when they form a basis for self-concept, as when a drug experimenter becomes an addict.

secondary prevention programs Treatment programs aimed at helping offenders after they have been identified.

second-degree murder A homicide with malice but not premeditation or deliberation, as when a desire to inflict serious bodily harm and a wanton disregard for life result in the victim's death.

self-control A strong moral sense that renders a person incapable of hurting others or violating social norms.

self-control theory According to Gottfredson and Hirschi, the view that the cause of delinquent behavior is an impulsive personality. Kids who are impulsive may find that their bond to society is weak.

self-report survey A research approach that requires subjects to reveal their own participation in delinquent or criminal acts.

sentencing circle A peacemaking technique in which offenders, victims, and other community members are brought together in an effort to formulate a sanction that addresses the needs of all.

serial killer The killing of a large number of people over time by an offender who seeks to escape detection.

serial rape Multiple rapes committed by one person over time.

sexual abuse Exploitation of a child through rape, incest, or molestation by a parent or other adult.

shame The feeling we get when we don't meet the standards we have set for ourselves or that significant others have set for us.

Sherman Antitrust Act Law that subjects to criminal or civil sanctions any person "who shall make any contract or engage in any combination or conspiracy" in restraint of interstate commerce.

shield laws Laws designed to protect rape victims by prohibiting the defense attorney from inquiring about their previous sexual relationships.

shoplifting The taking of goods from retail stores.

siege mentality Residents who become so suspicious of authority that they consider the outside world to be the enemy out to destroy the neighborhood.

situational crime prevention A method of crime prevention that stresses tactics and strategies to eliminate or reduce particular crimes in narrow settings, such as reducing burglaries in a housing project by increasing lighting and installing security alarms.

situational inducement Short-term influence on a person's behavior, such as financial problems or peer pressure, that increases risk taking.

skeezers Prostitutes who trade sex for drugs, usually crack.

skilled thieves Thieves who typically work in the larger cities, such as London and Paris. This group includes pickpockets, forgers, and counterfeiters, who operate freely.

smugglers Thieves who move freely in sparsely populated areas and transport goods, such as spirits, gems, gold, and spices, without bothering to pay tax or duty.

snitches Amateur shoplifters who do not self-identify as thieves but who systematically steal merchandise for personal use.

social bond Ties a person has to the institutions and processes of society. According to Hirschi, elements of the social bond include attachment, commitment, involvement, and belief.

social capital Positive relations with individuals and institutions that are life sustaining.

social class Segment of the population whose members are at a relatively similar economic level and who share attitudes, values, norms, and an identifiable lifestyle.

social control theory The view that people commit crime when the forces that bind them to society are weakened or broken.

social disorganization theory Branch of social structure theory that focuses on the breakdown of institutions such as the family, school, and employment in inner-city neighborhoods.

social harm A view that behaviors harmful to other people and society in general must be controlled. These acts are usually outlawed, but some acts that cause enormous amounts of social harm are perfectly legal, such as the consumption of tobacco and alcohol.

socialization The interactions people have with various organizations, institutions, and processes of society.

social learning theory The view that human behavior is modeled through observation of human social interactions, either directly from observing those who are close and from intimate contact or indirectly through the media. Interactions that are rewarded are copied, while those that are punished are avoided.

socially disorganized Communities where social institutions are incapable of functioning as expected and as a result their ability to create social control is nullified.

social process or socialization theory The view that criminality is a function of people's interactions with various organizations, institutions, and processes in society.

social reaction theory (labeling theory) The view that people become criminals when significant members of society label them as such and they accept those labels as a personal identity.

social schemas Cognitive frameworks that help people quickly process and sort through information.

social structure theory The view that disadvantaged economic class position is a primary cause of crime.

sociobiology The scientific study of the determinants of social behavior, based on the view that such behavior is influenced by both the individual's genetic makeup and interactions with the environment.

sociological social psychology The study of human interactions and relationships, emphasizing such issues as group dynamics and socialization.

sociopath Personality disorder characterized by superficial charm and glibness, a lack of empathy for others, amoral conduct, and lack of shame, guilt, or remorse for antisocial behavior. The term may be used interchangeably with psychopath, but both terms have been replaced by antisocial behavior disorder.

somatotype A system developed for categorizing people on the basis of their body build.

spear-phishing Targeting specific victims, sending them emails that contain accurate information about their lives obtained from social networking sites, and asking them to open an email attachment where malware harvests details such as the victims' usernames and passwords, bank account details, credit card numbers, and other personal information.

specific deterrence The view that if experienced punishment is severe enough, convicted offenders will be deterred from repeating their criminal activity.

stalking A pattern of behavior directed at a specific person that includes repeated physical or visual proximity, unwanted communications, and/or threats sufficient to cause fear in a reasonable person.

stalking statutes Laws that prohibit "the willful, malicious, and repeated following and harassing of another person."

state dependence The propensity to commit crime profoundly and permanently disrupts normal socialization. Early rule breaking strengthens criminal motivation and increases the probability of future rule breaking.

state political crime Political crime that arises from the efforts of the state to either maintain governmental power or to uphold the race, class, and gender advantages of those who support the government. It is possible to divide state political crimes into five varieties: (1) political corruption, (2) illegal domestic surveillance, (3) human rights violations, (4) state violence such as torture, illegal imprisonment, police violence and use of deadly force, and (5) state corporate crime committed by individuals who abuse their state authority or who fail to exercise it when working with people and organizations in the private sector.

state-organized crime Acts defined by law as criminal and committed by state officials, either elected or appointed, in pursuit of their jobs as government representatives.

state-sponsored terrorism Terrorism that occurs when a repressive government regime forces its citizens into obedience, oppresses minorities, and stifles political dissent.

status frustration A form of culture conflict experienced by lower-class youths because social conditions prevent them from achieving success as defined by the larger society.

statutory rape Sexual relations between an underage individual and an adult; though not coerced, an underage partner is considered incapable of giving informed consent.

stigma An enduring label that taints a person's identity and changes him or her in the eyes of others.

strain The emotional turmoil and conflict caused when people believe they cannot achieve their desires and goals through legitimate means. Members of the lower class might feel strain because they are denied access to adequate educational opportunities and social support.

strain theory Branch of social structure theory that sees crime as a function of the conflict between people's goals and the means available to obtain them.

stratified society A social structure that places people along a status-based hierarchy. In the United States, status is based primarily on wealth, power, and prestige.

street efficacy A concept in which more cohesive communities with high levels of social control and social integration foster the ability for kids to use their wits to avoid violent confrontations and to feel safe in their own neighborhood. Adolescents with high levels of street efficacy are less likely to resort to violence themselves or to associate with delinquent peers.

structural theory The view that criminal law and the criminal justice system are means of defending and preserving the capitalist system.

subculture of violence Norms and customs that, in contrast to society's dominant value system, legitimize and expect the use of violence to resolve social conflicts.

subcultures Groups that are loosely part of the dominant culture but maintain a unique set of values, beliefs, and traditions.

substantive criminal law The branch of the law that defines crimes and their punishment. It involves such issues as the mental and physical elements of crime, crime categories, and criminal defenses.

subterranean values Morally tinged influences that have become entrenched in the culture but are publicly condemned. They exist side by side with conventional values and while condemned in public may be admired or practiced in private.

sufferance The aggrieved party does nothing to rectify a conflict situation; over time, the unresolved conflict may be compounded by other events that cause an eventual eruption.

suitable target According to routine activities theory, a target for crime that is relatively valuable, easily transportable, and not capably guarded.

superego Incorporation within the personality of the moral standards and values of parents, community, and significant others.

supranational criminology The study of war crimes, crimes against humanity, and the supranational penal system in which such crimes are prosecuted and tried.

surplus value The Marxist view that the laboring classes produce wealth that far exceeds their wages and goes to the capitalist class as profits.

symbolic interaction theory The sociological view that people communicate through symbols. People interpret symbolic communication and incorporate it within their personality. A person's view of reality, then, depends on his or her interpretation of symbolic gestures.

synthesis A merger of two opposing ideas.

systematic forgers Professionals who make a living by passing bad checks.

systematic review A research technique that involves collecting the findings from previously conducted studies, appraising and synthesizing the evidence, and using the collective evidence to address a particular scientific question.

target hardening Making one's home or business crime proof through the use of locks, bars, alarms, and other devices.

target removal strategies Displaying dummy or disabled goods as a means of preventing shoplifting.

temperance movement An effort to prohibit the sale of liquor in the United States that resulted in the passage of the Eighteenth Amendment to the Constitution in 1919, which prohibited the sale of alcoholic beverages.

terror cells Divisions of terrorist group affiliates, each of which may be functionally independent so that each member has little knowledge of other cells, their members, locations, and so on. The number of cells and their composition depend on the size of the terrorist group. Local or national groups will have fewer cells than international terrorist groups that may operate in several countries, such as the al-Qaeda group.

terrorism The illegal use of force against innocent people to achieve a political objective.

tertiary prevention programs Crime control and prevention programs that may be a requirement of a probation order, part of a diversionary sentence, or aftercare at the end of a prison sentence.

testosterone The principal male steroid hormone. Testosterone levels decline during the life cycle and may explain why violence rates diminish over time.

thanatos According to Freud, the instinctual drive toward aggression and violence.

theory of anomie A modified version of the concept of anomie developed by Merton to fit social, economic, and cultural conditions found in modern U.S. society. He found that two elements of culture interact to produce potentially anomic conditions: culturally defined goals and socially approved means for obtaining them.

thesis In the philosophy of Hegel, an original idea or thought.

three strikes Policies whereby people convicted of three felony offenses receive a mandatory life sentence.

thrill-seeking hate crimes Acts by hatemongers who join forces to have fun by bashing minorities or destroying property; inflicting pain on others gives them a sadistic thrill.

ticking bomb scenario A scenario that some experts argue in which torture can perhaps be justified if the government discovers that a captured terrorist knows the whereabouts of a dangerous explosive device that is set to go off and kill thousands of innocent people.

tipping point The minimum amount of expected punishment necessary to produce a significant reduction in crime rates.

torture An act that causes severe pain or suffering, whether physical or mental, that is intentionally inflicted on a person for such purposes as obtaining a confession, punishing them for a crime they may have committed, or intimidating or coercing them into a desired action.

trait theory The view that criminality is a product of abnormal biological and/or psychological traits.

trajectory theory A view of criminal career formation that holds there are multiple paths to crime.

transitional neighborhood Areas undergoing a shift in population and structure, usually from middle-class residential to lower-class mixed use.

transnational organized crime A criminal enterprise that involves the planning and execution of the distribution of illicit materials or services by groups or networks of individuals working in more than one country.

treason An act of disloyalty to one's nation or state.

Trojan horse A computer program that looks like a benign application but contains illicit codes that can damage the system operations. Though Trojan horses do not replicate themselves like viruses, they can be just as destructive.

turning points According to Laub and Sampson, the life events that alter the development of a criminal career.

underclass The lowest social stratum in any country, whose members lack the education and skills needed to function successfully in modern society.

Uniform Crime Report (UCR) Large database, compiled by the Federal Bureau of Investigation, of crimes reported and arrests made each year throughout the United States.

USA Patriot Act (USAPA) Legislation giving U.S. law enforcement agencies a freer hand to investigate and apprehend suspected terrorists.

victim compensation The victim ordinarily receives compensation from the state to pay for damages associated with the crime. Rarely are two compensation schemes alike, however, and many state programs suffer from lack of both adequate funding and proper organization within the criminal justice system. Compensation may be made for medical bills, loss of wages, loss of future earnings, and counseling. In the case of death, the victim's survivors can receive burial expenses and aid for loss of support.

victimization (by the justice system) While the crime is still fresh in their minds, victims may find that the police interrogation following the crime is handled callously, with innuendos or insinuations that they were somehow at fault. Victims have difficulty learning what is going on in the case; property is often kept for a long time as evidence and may never be returned. Some rape victims report that the treatment they receive from legal, medical, and mental health services is so destructive that they cannot help but feel "re-raped."

victimless crimes Violations of the criminal law without any identifiable evidence of an individual victim who has suffered damage from the crime.

victimologists People who study the victim's role in criminal transactions.

victim precipitation theory The idea that the victim's behavior was the spark that ignited the subsequent offense, as when the victim abused the offender verbally or physically.

victim-witness assistance programs Government programs that help crime victims and witnesses; may include compensation, court services, and/or crisis intervention.

vigilantes Individuals who go on moral crusades without any authorization from legal authorities. The assumption is that it is okay to take matters into your own hands if the cause is right and the target is immoral.

violentization process According to Lonnie Athens, the process by which abused children are turned into aggressive adults. This process takes violent youths full circle from being the victims of aggression to being its initiators; they are now the same person they grew up despising, ready to begin the process with their own children.

virility mystique The belief that males must separate their sexual feelings from needs for love, respect, and affection.

voluntary or nonnegligent manslaughter A homicide committed in the heat of passion or during a sudden quarrel; although intent may be present, malice is not; also called voluntary manslaughter.

warez A term computer hackers and software pirates use to describe a game, media, or application that is made available for use on the Internet in violation of its copyright protection.

website defacement A type of cybervandalism that occurs when a computer hacker intrudes on another person's website by inserting or substituting codes that expose visitors to the site to misleading or provocative information. Defacement can range from installing humorous graffiti to sabotaging or corrupting the site.

white-collar swindle A crime in which people use an ongoing business enterprise to fraudulently expropriate money from unsuspecting victims.

workplace violence Irate employees or former employees attack coworkers or sabotage machinery and production lines; now considered the third leading cause of occupational injury or death.

zealot The original Zealots were Hebrew warrior groups active during the Roman occupation of Palestine during the first century BCE. Today the term commonly refers to a fanatical or over-idealistic follower of a political or religious cause.

CASE INDEX

NAME INDEX

Campa, Mary, 336n54
Campbell, Alec, 545n224
Campbell, Anne, 65n106; 339n137
Campbell, Doris, 374
Campbell, Jacquelyn, 374
Campbell, Luther, 16
Campbell, Rebecca, 96n146
Campbell, Rosie, 542n69
Campo-Flores, Arian, 225n3
Cancino, Jeffrey Michael, 64n79; 227n104
Canela-Cacho, Jose, 136n199
Canfield, Richard, 179nn81, 90
Cannon, Martha Patricia "Patty," 367
Cannon, Robert, 330
Cantor, David, 387n113
Cao, Liqun, 386n60
Capaldi, Deborah, 265n65; 336n30; 385n32
Caplan, Joel, 88; 96n156; 136n197
Capone, Al, 485
Capowich, George E., 228n124; 229n191
Caputo, Bryan, 551
Caputo, Gail A., 458nn48, 49
Carano, Gina, 325
Carbone-Lopez, Kristin, 94n60; 336n55
Cardoso, Maria R.A., 179n83
Cardwell, Stephanie, 184n287
Carey, Gregory, 181n146, 167
Caringella-MacDonald, Susan, 302n108
Carlen, Pat, 301n88
Carlo, Philip, 171
Carlock, Arna, 63n34
Carlson, Robert, 544n197
Carr, Alan, 543n157
Carr, James, 101
Carr, Joetta, 543n117
Carradine, David, 510
Carrano, Jennifer, 264n35
Carrington, Frank, 90; 97n170
Carroa, Mark, 264n15
Carroll, Douglas, 185n296
Carroll, Leo, 66n122
Carrotte, Elise, 25n8
Carson, Ann, 132n17
Carson, D., 180n129
Carson, Jennifer Varriale, 135n147
Carson, Mark, 115
Carter, Lisa, 178n46
Carter, Sherry Plaster, 542n100
Carter, Stanley, 542n100
Cartier, Jerome, 544n203
Cartwright, Desmond, 266n125
Caspi, Avshalom, 181n163; 182nn192, 200;
    184n277; 335n18; 336n29; 337n64;
    341nn208, 215, 216
Castillo, Anjelica, 362
Castillo, Melissa, 316
Castro, Ariel, 509
Catalano, Richard, 312; 341n218; 544n180
Catan, Thomas, 484
Cauce, Mari, 95n94
Caudy, Michael S., 269n211; 336n44; 545n225
Cauffman, Elizabeth, 65n109; 183nn221, 239
Cavanagh, Kevin, 179n87
Cavazos-Rehg, Patricia, 526
Cecil, Joe, 25n46
Cederblad, Marianne, 185n298
Cernkovich, Stephen, 63n30; 209; 229n168;
    267n160; 335n21; 341n217
Cerruto, Michael John, 303n162
Chafetz, Janet Saltzman, 301nn94, 95

Chaiken, Marcia, 544n184
Chalk, Peter, 428n58
Chambliss, William, 277; 300n16; 434
Chamlin, Mitchell, 66n124; 135n144; 459n98
Chan, Raymond, 180n111
Chan, Tony, 177n29
Chancer, Lynn, 301n86
Chaplin, Terry, 459n117
Chapman, Jane Roberts, 301n99
Chappell, Duncan, 63n14
Charlebois, P., 67n170
Charnigo, Richard, 389nn189, 192
Chayet, Ellen, 136n185
Chazan, Guy, 484
Chen, C.Y., 227n81
Chen, Frances R., 181n141; 339n135
Chen, Henian, 542n80
Chen, Jieming, 266n90
Chen, Jieru, 391n304
Chen, Wan-Yi, 386n42
Chen, Xiaojin, 340n190; 544n173
Cheng, Zhongqi, 177n37
Chepke, Lindsey, 126
Cherbonneau, Michael, 112; 113; 377; 391n272
Cherlin, Andrew, 192
Chermak, Steven, 66n137; 389n186; 415
Chesney-Lind, Meda, 289; 290; 301nn88, 90,
    93; 302nn108, 113, 115, 117
Cheuk, D.K.L., 177n36
Chibnall, Susan, 387n113
Chien-Peng, Chung, 428n56
Chilcoat, Howard, 336n47
Chin, Ko-lin, 500nn124, 139
Chiricos, Ted, 64n84; 135n158; 136n172;
    227n88; 269n208; 301n67
Chmelka, Mary, 180n133
Cho, Adrian, 499n48
Cho, Seung-Hui, 369
Choi, Tiffany, 228n128
Chon, Don, 386n69
Chothia, Farouk, 412; 428n59
Choudhury, Muhtashem, 498n29
Choy, Olivia, 181n142
Christenson, Cornelia, 388n140
Christenson, R.L., 265n51
Christodoulou, G., 180n136
Chronis, Andrea, 264n31
Chung, Ick-Joong, 340nn182, 192
Church, Wesley, II, 266n93
Ciavarella, Mark, 470
Cicchetti, Dante, 183n245; 264n39
Cirillo, Kathleen, 184nn255; 185n297
Clapper, James R., 420
Clark, Jamar, 208
Clark, James, 389nn189, 192
Clark, Patterson, 500n103
Clark, Richard D., 136n162
Clark-Daniels, Carolyn, 135n152
Clarke, Gregory N., 182n213
Clarke, Richard A., 578n90
Clarke, Ronald V., 97n164; 116; 132n19;
    133n36; 134nn108, 109, 111, 134;
    135n132; 458nn47, 73; 459n97
Clarke-Stewart, K. Alison, 177n29
Clason, Dennis L., 266n115
Classen, Gabriele, 229nn162, 163
Clay-Warner, Jody, 387n93
Clayton, Richard, 545nn228, 229
Clear, Todd, 388n164
Cleary, Hayley, 136n168

Cleveland, H. Harrington, 184n280; 340n175
Clinard, Marshall, 499n45
Clines, Francis X., 390n233
Clingempeel, Glenn, 336nn53, 54
Clinkinbeard, Samantha, 180n120
Clinton, Hillary Rodham, 256
Clinton, Monique, 385n25
Clooney, George, 432
Close, Billy, 65n119
Cloward, Richard, 218; 219; 220; 221;
    230nn231-237
Cochran, John, 132n26; 134n100; 267n151;
    339n139; 374
Cochran, Joshua, 185n295
Cohen, Albert, 216; 218; 220; 228n156;
    230nn222-225, 227-229
Cohen, Jacqueline, 25n5; 63n40; 95n103;
    133n63; 136n199
Cohen, Lawrence, 81; 82; 96nn118, 129;
    181n172
Cohen, Mark, 70; 71; 93n4
Cohen, Morris, 505; 541n11
Cohen, Patricia, 542n80
Cohen, Robert, 95n107; 265n71
Cohen, Youssef, 20
Cohen-Bendahan, Celina, 178n66
Cohen-Kettenis, Peggy, 178n66
Cohn, Ellen, 48; 64nn61, 66; 68
Colby, Reggy, 49
Cole, Christopher, 500n111
Cole, David, 137n204
Coley, Rebekah Levine, 228n122
Colletti, Patrick, 179n96
Collier, Kevin, 165
Collier-Tenison, Peter Shannon, 543n118
Collin, Barry, 578n94
Collins, James, 385n24
Collins, Mark, 337n82
Collins, Randall, 348
Colvin, Mark, 321
Colwell, Brian, 184n255; 185n297
Colwell, Lori, 63n26
Comer, James, 66n142
Comey, James B., 573
Comiskey, Brendan, 511
Comstock, George, 165
Comte, Auguste, 140
Conahan, Michael, 470
Conger, Katherine, 263n10
Conger, Rand D., 235; 263nn7, 10; 268n190;
    315; 338n96; 385n37; 386n49
Conklin, John, 178nn73, 74; 376
Conley, Shannon, 573
Connolly, Eric J., 181n148; 182n175; 184n288
Connolly, Jennifer, 165
Conoscenti, Lauren M., 387n91
Conwell, Chic, 435; 457nn17-19
Cook, Kimberly, 282
Cook, Mike, 576n30
Cook, Philip J., 48; 64n73; 135n129; 137n203;
    389n184
Cook, Sarah, 387n90
Cooley, Charles Horton, 13; 253; 254;
    268nn175, 176
Cooley, John, 182n210
Coomer, Brandi Wilson, 63n39
Cooper, Alison, 178n43
Cooper, Cary, 64n67; 178n68
Cooper, Chris, 401
Cooper, Helene, 484

Cooper, Janet R., 391n295
Cooper, Michael, 428n39
Copes, Heith, 266n92; 377; 391n272
Cordella, Peter, 181n140
Corill, Dean, 369
Corman, Hope, 135n140
Cormier, Robert, 508
Cornejo, Eduardo, 470
Cornish, Derek, 132n19; 133n36; 134n111
Corrado, J., 544n169
Corrigan, Patrick, 268n187
Corrigan, Rose, 95n85
Corsianos, Marilyn, 25n9
Cortese, Samuele, 177n33
Corvo, Kenneth, 386n42
Cory-Slechta, Deborah A., 179n90
Costanzo, Michael, 133n60
Costello, Jane, 183n222
Cota-Robles, Sonia, 264n33
Couch, Ethan, 233; 234
Couch, Tonya, 233
Couey, John Evander, 510
Coupe, Richard Timothy, 96n125
Coupe, Timothy, 459n94
Courey, Michael, 340n169
Courtney, Robert, 467; 494
Courtwright, David, 352; 386n71; 545n247
Coutts, Holly, 165
Covington, Jeanette, 227n88; 228n152
Cowen, Richard, 458n69
Cox, Louis, 104; 132n12
Coyne, Sarah, 165
Cragin, Kim, 428n58
Craig, Jessica M., 265n75
Craig, Wendy, 165
Crane, D. Russell, 263n10
Crane, Jonathan, 226n47
Crawford, Charles, 301n67
Creamer, Vicki, 265n83
Cresap, Wayne G., 470
Cressey, Donald, 4; 12; 25n2, 18; 240; 241;
    265n82; 500nn122, 152
Creswell, Julie, 498n14
Cretacci, Michael, 267n153
Crews, F.T., 177n32
Crinella, Francis, 177n29
Croisdale, Tim, 67n166
Cromwell, Paul, 133nn58, 59, 75; 348n44; 440;
    454; 457n27; 458n44; 459n113
Crosby, L., 337n57
Crosby, Rick, 336n32
Crosnoe, Robert, 267n141
Crossette, Barbara, 541n23
Crouch, Ben, 136n198
Crow, Matthew, 55; 66n135
Crowder, Kyle, 226n65
Crowe, R.R., 181n171
Crowley, Thomas, 180n113
Crowther, Betty, 543n140
Cruise, Keith, 385n8
Crumpler, Debbie, 178n43
Cui, Ming, 263n7
Cullen, Francis T., 65nn87, 106; 94n44;
    95nn78, 99, 100; 133n79; 143; 177n21;
    179n82; 183n219; 229n190, 199;
    230n203; 263n7; 264nn15, 29; 265nn74,
    86; 267n145; 268nn163, 184; 303n169;
    337n69; 339n162; 340n189; 387n103,
    111; 391n306; 499nn74, 75
Cullina, Matt, 576n30

Culpan, Tim, 427n26
Cummings, Andrea, 387n101
Cundiff, Patrick, 388n150
Cunliffe, Christina, 95n85
Cunningham-Niederer, Michele, 500n119
Cuola-Kern, Amy, 302n114
Currie, Janet, 386n44
Curry, G. David, 226n72; 227n90
Curry, Mary Ann, 374
Curry, Sheree, 93n7
Cuvelier, Steven, 133n79
Czaja, Ronald, 63n36

D

Dabney, Dean, 458n56
Dackis, Charles, 544n198
Dadds, Mark, 459n119
Dafeamekpor, Denise Spriggs, 388n153
Dahl, Julia, 366
Dahrendorf, Ralf, 275; 276
Daigle, Leah E., 94n44; 95n78; 265n86;
    341n210; 387n103, 111
Dalen, Lindy, 178n43
D'Alessio, Stewart, 25n32; 65n98; 66n126; 253;
    268n162; 459n92
Daley, Suzanne, 542n105
Dalton, Katharina, 146; 178n70
Dalwani, Manish, 180n113
Daly, Kathleen, 301nn88, 93, 97; 302n108;
    303n142; 501n149
Daly, Martin, 95n86; 156; 182nn177, 178,
    183–185; 227n85; 228n149; 229n173;
    390n241
Daly, Sara A., 428n58
Danhach, Sameh Khaled, 439
Daniels, R. Steven, 135n152
Danielson, Melissa, 180nn123, 124, 126
Dank, Meredith, 513
Dannefer, Dale, 65n115
Dannenberg, Andrew, 542n100
Dantzler, Joyce, 388n153
D'Aquino, Iva Ikuko Toguri ("Tokyo Rose"), 400
Darbinyan, Mher ("Hollywood Mike"), 490
Darrow, William, 542n85
Darwin, Charles, 140
Darwish, Dania, 251
Das, Shyamal, 178n61
Davey, Monica, 64n55; 498n36
David, David, 545n236
Davidson, Laura, 65n86
Davies, Andrew, 576n4
Davies, Garth, 226n48; 340n177
Davies, Mark, 266nn97, 101; 268n161; 544n167
Davies, Susan, 336n32
Davies-Netley, Sally, 93n26
Davis, Joanne, 543n158
Davis, John, 177n29
Davis, Michael, 228n131
Davis, Richard Allen, 19; 509
Davis, Robert C., 94n40; 96nn138, 155; 97n165;
    545n226
Davis, Roy, 388n127
Davis-Frenzel, Erika, 387n105; 388n155
Davison, Elizabeth, 134n90
Dawes, Chris, 180n138
Dawson, Jim, 134n114
D.C. Madam (pseudonym), 504; 515
De Coster, Stacy, 226n59; 229n182
De Li, Spencer, 265n77; 337n80
de Silva, W.P., 541n39

De Vries, Reinout E., 340n168
Dean, Charles, 335n27; 341n210
Dean, K., 183n227
Deane, Glenn, 63n10; 336n42; 385n20; 386n56
Deaton, Raelynn, 182n186; 341n213
DeBaryshe, Barbara, 335n23
Deboutte, Dirk, 264n34
Decker, Scott H., 65n99; 66n125; 134n93;
    268n164; 376; 391n266; 453; 459n109
Deckman, Timothy, 178n48
Defoe, Ivy, 180n133
DeFronzo, James, 228n138; 230n246
DeGruchy, John W., 303n163
DeHart, Erica, 93n16
DeJesus, Georgina "Gina," 509
Dejong, Christina, 136n179, 183, 186;
    269n210
DeKeseredy, Walter S., 25n9; 301nn84, 87;
    302n104; 388nn135, 143
Delaema, Wesam al-, 422
DeLamatre, Mary, 95n103
deLara, Ellen, 386n42
DeLisi, Matt, 179n99; 181n149; 183n240;
    184nn252, 261, 287; 266n92; 337n59;
    339nn143, 144
Deluca, Stefanie, 227n98
Dembo, Richard, 544n186
DeMuth, Phil, 225n18
Demuth, Stephen, 55; 66nn136, 138; 301nn60,
    68
DeNavas-Walt, Carmen, 194
DeNevi, Don, 457n8
Dengate, Sue, 177n34
Denney, Robert, 95n109
Denno, Deborah, 179nn89, 95, 101; 182nn189,
    190
Densley, James A., 112; 113; 133n80
DePadilla, Lara, 337n72
Deptula, Daneen, 95n107; 265n71
DeRios, M.D., 544n168
Derksen, Jan, 184n269
Dershowitz, Alan M., 404; 427n33
Derzon, James, 336n31
Desai, Manisha, 179n91
Desilets, Christian, 498nn9–11
DeSilver, Drew, 225n18
Deutsch, Joseph, 133n62
Devine, Paul Shin, 470
Devlin, Patrick, 505; 541n12
DeWall, Nathan, 145; 178n48
Dhami, Mandeep, 501n150
Diamond, Brie, 339n151
DiCaprio, Leonardo, 13
Dickinson, Rebecca, 515
DiClemente, Ralph, 336n32
Dietz, Tracy, 94n66
DiLalla, David, 181n146
Dinitz, Simon, 267n137
Dinos, Sokratis, 95n85
Dishion, Thomas, 265n65
Dobash, R. Emerson, 390nn251, 254
Dobash, Russell, 390nn251, 254
Dobrin, Adam, 94n44; 95n103; 226n72
Dodge, K.A., 183n236
Dodge, Kenneth, 227n115; 264n17; 264nn36,
    38; 337n65; 385n36
Doerner, Jill, 55; 66n136
Dogan, Shannon J., 263n10
Doherty, Elaine Eggleston, 316; 338nn95, 103
Dohrenwend, Bruce, 268n184

Dollar, Cindy Brooks, 45
Dolling, Dieter, 135n149
Domonoske, Camila, 427n1
Donker, Andrea, 341n211
Donnellan, M. Brent, 263n10
Donner, Christopher M., 549; 576n9
Donnerstein, Edward, 388n145; 543n117
Donohue, John J., 44; 45; 122; 123
Doob, Anthony, 135n157
Dooley, Barbara, 543n157
Dorahy, Martin, 93n23
Doran, Michael Scott, 428n70
Doraz, Walter, 178n45
Dorn, Richard, 161; 183n218
Douglas, Emily M., 390n244
Douglas, William O., 506
Downey, Douglas, 225nn23, 34
Downey, P. Mitchell, 513
Downs, Daniel M., 135n130
Downs, William, 93n26; 268n191
Doyle, Daniel, 386n58
Drabick, Deborah, 184n268
Drake, Francis, 408
Drake, J.J.P., 178n75
Drass, Kriss, 228n152; 389n181
Dressler, Joshua, 25n30
Drew, Christopher, 390n233
Drew, Lori, 566
Drewitz, Ed, 285
Driver, Edwin, 182n194
Drugge, Jeff, 388n141
Drury, Alan, 337n59
Du, Yiping, 180n113
Dudek, Jonathan, 542n98
Dugan, Andrew, 62n2
Dugan, Laura, 418; 458n56
Dugard, Jaycee Lee, 509
Dugdale, Richard, 142; 177n13
Dunaway, R. Gregory, 65nn87, 106; 265n74; 268n163
Duncan, David, 544n195
Duncan, Greg J., 225nn27, 28; 227nn98, 99; 265n62
Dunford, Franklyn, 126
D'Unger, Amy, 340nn183, 185
Dunkel, Curtis, 428nn83–85
Dunn, Melissa, 302n113
Dunning, Nancy, 17
Durkheim, Émile, 189; 190; 206; 225nn11, 12
Durlauf, Steven, 135n146
Durrant, Lynne, 341n220
Duwe, Grant, 390n227
Dworkin, Andrea, 541n8
Dworkin, Andrew, 542n103
Dyous, Christina, 517
Dyson, Laronistine, 93n10

E

Earls, Felton J., 67n171; 227n111; 228nn140, 144; 351; 386nn53, 54
Earnest, Terri, 226n77
Eaves, Lindon, 180n138
Ebeling, Hann, 180n133
Ebright, Olsen, 427n9
Eccles, Jacquelynne, 178n63
Eck, John, 118; 134nn120, 121
Eckenrode, John, 336n54
Eckert, Mary, 83
Edelhertz, Herbert, 498n13; 499n73; 501n150
Edelson, Jeffrey I., 366

Edwards, Jessica, 542n77
Egan, Margaret, 543n157
Egelko, Bob, 389n175
Egger, Steven, 390n225
Egley, Arlen, Jr., 225n5
Eichenwald, Kurt, 499n52
Einat, Amela, 150; 180n122
Einat, Tomer, 150; 180n122
Eisenberg, Jesse, 432
Eisenberg, Nancy, 181n145
Eisner, Manuel, 95n89
Eitle, David, 66n126; 302n130; 459n93
Eitle, Tamela McNulty, 302n130
Eitzen, D. Stanley, 499n76
El Chapo (pseudonym), 531; 532
El-Magd, Nadia Abou, 427n32
Elber, Lynn, 388n138
Elder, Glen, 267n152
Eley, Thalia, 181n168
Elifson, Kirk, 337n72; 545n232
Elis, Lori, 324
Elizabeth I (Queen of England), 408
Elkind, Peter, 499n52
Ellingworth, Dan, 94n72
Elliott, Amanda, 228n137
Elliott, Delbert, 65n115; 126; 226n73; 228n137; 269n203; 339nn149, 163
Ellis, Lee, 146; 177n19; 178nn58, 61; 180nn137, 139, 140; 182n181; 338n114; 388n131
Ellwood, Charles, 142
Elonheimo, Henrik, 263n11
Elstein, Sharon, 388n127
Emerson, Robert M., 391n301
Emmert, Amanda, 63n34
Emmett, Pauline, 177n29
Endresen, Inger, 266n108
Engel, Robin Shepard, 65n121; 66n131
Engel, Stephanie M., 179n81
Engels, Friedrich, 274; 275; 300nn8, 12
Engels, Rutger, 183n235
Engen, Rodney, 269n208
Ennett, Susan, 66n148
Ensminger, Margaret E., 338n95
Entorf, Horst, 135n149
Epstein, Gil, 133n62
Erdman, Shelby Lin, 366
Erdogan, Recep Tayyip, 394
Erez, Edna, 96n155
Erickson, Kai, 254; 268n178
Erickson, Maynard, 135n158
Erickson, Rosemary, 25n10
Ericson, Jonathon, 177n29
Ericsson, Kjersti, 302n112
Erikson, Erik, 159
Erkanli, Alaattin, 183n222
Ernst, Frederick, 384n5
Erwin, Brigette, 94n49
Esagian, Gkaro, 384n5
Esbensen, Finn-Aage, 94n52; 217; 227n96; 230n238; 269n219; 335n16
Esmail, Aneez, 389n210
Espelage, Dorothy, 65n109; 183n221
Estabrook, Arthur, 142; 177n13
Estes, Richard, 541n38
Estrada, Felipe, 64n74
Estrich, Susan, 388n162
Eterno, John, 31; 63n17
Evans, Jeff, 179n88
Evans, Josh, 566
Evans, Mary, 180n120

Evans, Michelle, 229nn188, 198
Evans, Rhonda, 501n153
Evans, Spencer, 182n210
Evans, T. David, 65nn87, 106; 229n190; 265n74; 268n163
Eve, Raymond, 65n112
Ewell, Patrick, 165
Exline, Julie Juola, 135n161
Eysenck, Hans, 169; 184n258; 306; 307; 335n2
Eysenck, M.W., 184n258
Ezell, Michael, 95n103

F

Factor-Litvak, Pamela, 177n37; 179n91
Fader, James, 66n164
Fagan, Abigail A., 181n160; 267n147; 386nn45, 46
Fagan, Jeffrey, 122; 123; 135n150; 217; 226n48; 230nn221, 241
Fahim, Kareem, 412; 428n46
Fairweather, David, 388n141
Falck, Russel, 544n197
Falco, Christi, 229n166
Fang, Hai, 93n5
Fantz, Ashley, 387n112
Farabee, David, 544n203
Farah, Adnan Abdihamid, 416
Farah, Mohamed Abdihamid, 416
Faraone, Stephen, 180n132
Fargeon, Samantha, 180n134
Farley, Reynolds, 66n153
Farnworth, Margaret, 312
Farook, Syed Rizwan, 2; 3; 4; 369
Farrall, Stephen, 336n56; 337n66
Farrell, Amanda L., 389n212; 390nn215, 216, 218
Farrell, Graham, 95nn74, 75, 77; 459nn92, 96, 106
Farrell, Michael, 264n18; 543n153
Farrell, Stephen, 427n5
Farrington, David P., 32; 39; 63nn38, 41, 46; 66n162; 93n9; 95n103; 96n124; 134nn123, 125; 135n138; 180n133; 181nn154, 156, 157, 158; 235; 264nn22–25; 321; 327; 335n25; 336nn31, 35, 48, 54; 337n61; 338n131; 340nn174, 186, 187, 188, 202; 364; 385n11; 386n66; 389n185
Farrooque, Rokeya, 384n5
Fass, Simon, 457n23
Fassbender, Pantaleon, 184n263
Fastow, Andrew, 471
Fata, Farid, 471
Faupel, Charles, 544nn190–192
Fay-Ramirez, Suzanna, 228n142
Fazel, Seena, 385n28
Fazlullah, Mullah, 419
Fearn, Noelle E., 265n86
Fears, Darryl, 500n103
Feeha, Jennifer, 132n2
Fein, Robert, 389n204
Feinberg, Joel, 541n13
Feingold, Alan, 339n158
Feldmeyer, Ben, 386n51
Felson, Marcus, 81; 82; 83; 96nn118, 129; 117; 134nn110, 120; 376; 391n269
Felson, Richard B., 45; 63n10; 96nn128, 133; 114; 133nn83, 85; 134n94; 230n220; 336n43; 359; 377; 386n61; 388nn149, 150; 389nn194, 195; 391nn273–275

Fendrich, Michael, 63n35; 544n179
Ferdinand, Archduke Franz, 408
Fergerson, Julie, 576n30
Ferguson, Lynn, 541n7
Fergusson, David, 336nn37, 39; 337n65
Ferracuti, Franco, 6; 25n3; 351; 386n57
Ferrell, Jeff, 132n25; 134n101
Ferri, Enrico, 141; 142; 177n12
Ferris, Kerry O., 391n301
Feucht, Thomas, 389n203
Fiedler, Mora, 226n76
Fienberg, Stephen, 179n89
Figert, Anne E., 178n69
Figlio, Robert M., 58; 59; 62; 65n116; 66n158;
    67n167; 133n60; 335n8
Finckenauer, James O., 25n47; 500nn124, 134,
    139
Finkelhor, David, 77; 93n20; 94nn61, 63;
    95n76; 387n122; 390nn244, 245;
    542nn81, 94; 577n56
Finn, Peter, 96n140; 97nn159, 160; 517
Finnigan, Lexi, 577n60
Firman, John, 282
Fischer, Mariellen, 180n128
Fishbein, Diana, 146; 178nn49, 73, 74; 179n102
Fisher, Bonnie S., 80; 94n59; 95nn78, 79, 91,
    99, 100; 387nn90, 94, 103, 111, 113;
    391n306
Fishman, Shira, 428n73
Fite, Paula, 182n210
Fitzpatrick, Mark, 543n157
Fix, Michael, 543n124
Flaherty, Austin, 97n161
Flaherty, Claire, 385n8; 389n213
Flaherty, Sara, 97n161
Flaming, Karl, 226n76
Flanagan, Edel, 543n157
Flanagan, Vester, 139; 380
Flanagan-Howard, Roisin, 543n157
Flannery, Daniel, 65n112; 338n115
Flay, Brian, 133n78; 544n164
Fleming, Charles, 267n142
Fletcher, Jason, 151; 180n130
Fletcher, Kara, 182n207
Fletcher, Kenneth, 180n128
Flewelling, Robert, 66n148; 545nn228, 229
Flexon, Jamie, 266n99; 338n127
Flitter, Jill, 542n87
Flitter, Jill Klotz, 93n28
Flygare, Chris, 517
Flynn, Kevin, 390n236
Flynt, Larry, 371
Foer, Jonathan, 480
Fogel, C.A., 179n94
Fogle, Jared, 519
Foglia, Wanda, 136nn172, 173
Foley, Tracy, 400
Fong, Grace, 179n107
Forbes, Gordon, 387n104
Forde, David, 338n124
Formby, William, 135n152
Formoso, Diana, 263n6
Fornango, Robert, 45; 64n83; 391n264
Forrest, Walter, 339n167
Forsting, Michael, 541n42
Forsythe, Lubica, 459n108
Foster, Holly, 302n123; 335n22
Foster, Jodie, 164
Foster, Peter, 577n55
Fowler, Tom, 181n147

Fowles, Richard, 229n179
Fox, James Alan, 367; 369; 371; 389n211;
    390nn222, 225, 229; 391nn291, 297;
    543n119
Fox, Kathleen, 95n90; 340n170
Fox, Kristan, 66n134
Francis, Janice, 457n23
Francis (pope), 511
Frank, David John, 388n168
Frank, Guido, 149
Frank, Nancy, 498n4; 499n65
Franklin, Benjamin, 394
Franklin, Joseph Paul, 371
Franklin, Lonnie David, 361
Franks, John, 541n18
Frase, Richard, 130; 137nn212, 213
Fraser, Jennifer, 459n119
Frayne, Susan, 542n89
Frazee, Sharon Glave, 134n90
Fream, Anne, 266n97
Frederick, Tyler, 94n43
Freeman, Naomi J., 135n128
Freeman-Gallant, Adrienne, 181n158; 266n89
Freilich, Joshua, 389n186; 415
Freisthler, Bridget, 227n95
French, Michael T., 93n5
Freng, Adrienne, 66n132; 217
Frenken, J., 387n99
Freud, Sigmund, 142; 157; 158; 159; 347;
    385n15
Frey, William, 66n153
Fricker-Elhai, Adrienne, 543n158
Friday, Paul, 265n58
Fried, Gabriela, 428n64
Friedland, Justin, 445
Friedlander, Laura, 165
Friedlander, Robert, 428nn44, 49
Friedrichs, David, 300nn37, 39, 40
Friedrichs, Jessica, 300nn39, 40
Frisell, Thomas, 181n153; 385n22
Fritch, April, 301n100
Fritsch, Eric, 134n116
Frost, S.S., 178n42
Fry, Richard, 225n17
Frye, Victoria, 374; 389n188
Fuchs, Siegmund Fred, 386n75
Fuentes, Angel Ilarraza, 391n302
Fukurai, Hiroshi, 268n198
Fulton, Betsy, 303n169

G

Gabbidon, Shaun, 458n53
Gacy, John Wayne, 367; 368; 369
Gadd, David, 336n56
Gaddafi, Muammar, 272; 394; 411
Gaffney, Michael, 227n104
Gagnon, C., 67n170
Gagnon, John, 388n140
Gailliot, Matthew, 178n48
Gainey, Randy, 228n123; 269n208
Gale, Nathan, 133n60
Gall, Fran Joseph, 141
Gamble, Thomas J., 302n114
Gamble, Wendy, 264n33
Gannon, Theresa, 541n44
Gao, Yu, 181n142
Garcia, Luis, 227n117; 391n288
Garcia, Michelle, 391nn305, 307
Gardner, Carol Brooks, 391n301
Gardner, David, 335n1; 541n35

Garfinkel, Robin, 179n82
Garner, Connie Chenoweth, 267n145
Garnier, Helen, 267n147
Garofalo, James, 96n112; 97n158
Garofalo, Raffaele, 141; 142; 177n11
Garrido, Phillip, 509
Gartner, Rosemary, 95n88
Gary, Faye, 374
Gasper, Joseph, 265n49
Gates, Bill, 209
Gatzke-Kopp, Lisa M., 177n31
Gau, Jacinta M., 265n86
Gault-Sherman, Martha, 264n44
Gaylor, Rita, 183n217
Ge, Xiaojia, 65n89
Geberth, Vernon J., 389n196
Gebhard, Paul, 388n140
Geis, G., 499n50
Geis, Gilbert, 63n14; 457n16
Geller, Susan Rose, 341n219
Gelles, Richard J., 374; 390nn240; 256
George, David, 179n107
Georges-Abeyie, Daniel, 66n140
Gere, Richard, 513
Gershman, Jacob, 268nn182, 183
Gertz, Marc, 48; 64n72; 97n168; 134n88;
    227n88
Gialopsos, Brooke Miller, 94n71
Giancola, Peter, 543n154
Gibbons, Donald, 184n257; 458n66
Gibbons, Frederick X., 177n26; 180n135;
    181n147; 182n206
Gibbs, Benjamin, 229n165
Gibbs, Carole, 500n110
Gibbs, Jack, 135n158; 269n221; 301n72;
    428n43
Gibbs, Jennifer, 287
Gibbs, John, 65n106; 133n77
Gibbs, Natalie, 387n101
Gibson, Chris, 93n11; 181n150; 227n104;
    336n28; 338n128; 339n154
Gidycz, Christine, 387n90
Gifford, Robert, 459n114
Giffords, Gabby, 124
Gilbert, Michael, 427n11
Gilchrist, Lewayne, 340n182
Gill, Charlotte, 228n131
Gill, James, 389n197
Gillars, Mildred Elizabeth ("Axis Sally"), 400
Gillis, A.R., 302n122
Gillman, Matthew W., 179n92
Gino, Francesca, 178n56
Ginsburg, Ruth, 8
Ginzberg, Eli, 545n237
Giordano, Peggy, 63n30; 229n168; 266nn88, 95;
    267n160; 268n167; 311; 335n21; 337n62;
    339n165; 341n217; 458n65
Giroux, Bruce, 340n203
Gitter, Seth, 165
Gizewski, Elke, 541n42
Gjeruldsen, Susanne Rogne, 385n28
Glaberson, William, 25n38
Glass, Laura, 184n289
Glass, Nancy, 374
Glaze, Lauren, 136n191
Glazer, Daniel, 177n27; 457n16; 543n136
Glueck, Eleanor, 169; 184n258; 263n5; 306;
    307; 313; 317; 318; 333; 335nn4, 5
Glueck, Sheldon, 169; 184n258; 263n5; 306;
    307; 313; 317; 318; 333; 335nn4, 5

Goddard, Henry H., 142; 172; 177n13
Goetz, Barry, 545n243
Goffman, Alice, 56; 57
Gold, Martin, 65n112
Golding, Jean, 177n29
Goldkamp, John, 545n230
Goldman, Ron, 71
Goldsmith, Eric, 305
Goldstein, Michael, 543n116
Goldstein, Paul, 385n21; 542n74; 544n179
Golinelli, Daniela, 132n17
Golub, Andrew, 544nn182, 183
Gonzales, Nancy, 263n6
Gonzalez, M. Liliana, 66n122
González, Nazario Moreno, 494
Gooch, Erik, 390n217
Goodman, Robert, 182n211
Goodman, Sam, 436
Goodstein, Laurie, 541n49
Goodwill, Alasdair, 389n207
Goodwin, D.W., 543n162
Gootman, Elissa, 390n231
Gordon, Dave, 500n94
Gordon, Kristina Coop, 93n32
Gordon, Rachel, 386n66
Gordon, Robert, 266n125
Gorge, Mathieu, 578n96
Goring, Charles, 141; 157; 182n193
Gorr, Wilpen, 25n5
Gorton, Nathaniel, 345
Gossop, Michael, 545n236
Gottfredson, Denise, 95n96; 96n121; 228n121; 544nn199, 200
Gottfredson, Gary, 95n96; 228n121
Gottfredson, Michael, 51; 63n22; 65n88; 111; 133n37; 134n102; 152; 320; 321; 322; 323; 324; 325; 326; 334; 338nn120–122, 125, 126; 339nn136, 148, 161; 496; 501nn156, 157; 545n230
Gottfredson, Stephen, 133n70
Gould, Arthur, 542n104
Gould, Jon, 282
Gould, Leroy, 65n114
Gould, Stephen Jay, 177n14
Gove, Walter, 132n26; 134n100; 178n55
Grabosky, Peter, 495; 501n148
Grace, Randolph, 541n43
Grady, Melissa D., 182n206
Graham, Vincent, 5
Graif, Corina, 226n64
Grandison, Terry, 93n10
Grandjean, P., 177n33
Grann, Martin, 385n28
Grant, Susan, 576n30
Grasmick, Harold G., 135nn144, 159; 228n135; 339nn139, 146, 152, 159
Gray, Louis N., 132n20; 183n244
Gray-Ray, Phyllis, 268n186
Graziano, Joseph, 177n37; 179n91
Greeley, A., 543n141
Green, Aisa, 179n108
Green, Donald, 135n158; 230n251
Green, John, 508
Green, Lorraine, 135n133
Green, Rebecca, 577nn53, 81
Green, Stuart, 476
Green, Stuart P., 499n77
Green, William, 386n72, 79
Greenall, Paul V., 389nn198, 199
Greenbaum, Robert, 384n2

Greenberg, David, 301n70
Greene, Michael, 386n55
Greenfeld, Lawrence, 95n81; 136n181
Greenhouse, Joel, 179n89
Greening, Leilani, 184n249
Greenwell, Jeffrey, 560
Greenwood, Peter, 545n233
Gregg, Heather S., 428n58
Gregory, Alice, 181n168
Grierson, Jeffrey, 542n61
Griffin, Alaine, 335n1
Griffiths, Curt Taylor, 303n160
Grimm, Mica, 208
Grimshaw, Kate, 178n43
Grinc, Randolph, 230n250
Griswold, D., 268n169
Groff, Elizabeth, 135n137; 458n91
Gross, Samuel, 8; 11; 25nn12, 15
Grossman, Leigh, 95n110
Grosso, Catherine, 123
Groth, A. Nicholas, 354; 359; 387n98; 388n144
Grove, H., 499n50
Grove, Louise, 459n106
Groves, W. Byron, 227n121; 299n4; 300nn8, 21, 26
Grow, Brian, 577n62
Grubesic, Tony, 385n18
Grubstein, Lori, 66n164
Gruenewald, Jeff, 134n103; 389n200; 415
Gruenewald, Paul, 227n95
Grus, Catherine, 93n20
Gu, Joann, 391n288
Guadagno, Rosanna, 165
Guerry, André-Michel, 189
Guess, Teresa, 301n71
Guevara, Miguel, 187
Gulley, Bill, 181n161
Gumz, Edward, 303n170
Gunn, Christopher, 565
Gunter, Tracy, 180n131
Gunther, Wanda M.R., 179n83
Guo, Guang, 265n62
Guryev, Lydia, 401
Guryev, Vladimir, 401
Gusfield, Joseph, 506; 541n16; 543n142
Gutierrez, Carmen, 64n53
Gutner, Cassidy, 96n135
Guzmán, Joaquin ("El Chapo"), 531; 532
Gwlasda, Victoria, 93n12

H

Haapanen, Rudy, 67n165; 340nn173, 180
Haas, Ain, 229n200
Haberman, Cory, 64n62; 135n137
Habermann, Niels, 179n98; 184nn264, 265
Hackett, Robert, 577n51
Hackler, James, 459n120
Haden, Sara Chiara, 93n17
Hafemeister, Thomas, 76
Hafen, Christopher, 265n68
Hagan, John, 94n43; 132n23; 225n40; 229nn162, 163; 290; 291; 301n59; 302nn121–123; 335n22
Hagelstam, Camilla, 185n291
Haikkanen, Helina, 459n119
Hakim, Simon, 97n166; 133nn60, 76; 459nn99, 100
Hakkanen, Heliná, 185n291
Hale, Matthew, 356
Halkitis, Perry N., 544n193

Hall, Jerome, 458n87
Hall, Joseph S., 499n67
Halleck, Seymour, 182n201
Haller, Mark, 498n3
Hallett, Michael, 300n22
Hallstone, Michael, 544n174
Halperin, William, 133n60
Halpern, Carolyn, 542n77
Haltigan, John, 302n114
Halvorsen, Jessica, 387n92
Hamby, Sherry, 94n61
Hamdan, Salim, 423
Hamdi, Yaser, 423
Hamilton, Alexander, 400
Hamilton, Thomas, 346
Hamlin, John, 267n129
Hamm, Mark, 413; 414; 428nn66, 68
Hammock, Georgina, 96n122
Hammond, Karen, 95n85
Hammond, Rodney, 389n203
Hammurabi, 15
Hampton, Ashley, 184n268
Hampton, Tracy, 543n161
Hanks, Chris, 179n108
Hanks, Tom, 488
Hanna-Attisha, Mona, 178n79
Hansell, Saul, 577n61
Hansen, Ellen Beate, 458n45
Hansen, Ronald D., 181n148
Hanslmaier, Michael, 226n79
Hanson, Fergus, 578n91
Hanssen, Robert, 401
Hansson, Kjell, 185n298
Harden, Philip, 179n95
Harding, Alan, 132n3
Harding, David, 265n70
Hardinge, Tara, 388n168
Hardy, Margaret, 386n48
Harper-Mercer, Chris, 139; 140; 144
Harrell, Erika, 391n298; 576n31
Harries, Keith, 226n57; 390n235
Harrington, Kathy, 336n32
Harris, Andrew, 9
Harris, Angela P., 302n103
Harris, Casey T., 386n51
Harris, Chris, 458n69
Harris, Danielle, 449
Harris, Judith Rich, 264n16; 265n59
Harris, Kamala, 494
Harris, Mark, 66n141; 228n126
Harris, Meena, 225n5
Harris, Nathan, 303n150
Harris, Patricia, 458n73
Harris, Philip, 66n164
Harris, Richard J., 64n73
Harrison, Marissa, 385n8; 389n213
Harrrendorf, Stefan, 64n54
Harry, Joseph, 136n172
Hart, C., 183n227
Hart, Daniel, 181n145
Hart, H.L.A., 505–506; 541n13
Hart, Timothy, 64n58
Hartjen, Clayton, 266n100
Hartnagel, Timothy, 268n170
Hartsfield, Jennifer, 229n189
Hartstone, Eliot, 230n241
Hartwig, Holly, 302nn115, 116; 337n63
Hartz, Sarah M., 5226
Hasan, Nidal Malik, 415
Hasday, Jill Elaine, 388n125

Hatemi, Peter, 180n138
Hathaway, Jeanne E., 391n259
Hathaway, R. Starke, 184nn267, 275
Hausbeck, Kathryn, 541nn57, 58
Haveman, Roelof, 277; 300nn24, 25
Haviland, Amelia M., 64n82
Hawk, Shila René, 227n97
Hawke-Petit, Jennifer, 305
Hawkins, Darnell, 386n56
Hawkins, David, 264n42; 267n147
Hawkins, Gordon, 64n70
Hawkins, J. David, 312; 336n48; 340n182;
    341n218; 544n180
Hawkins, John, 408
Hawkins, Keith, 499n78
Hay, Carter, 229nn188, 197; 264n32; 268n193;
    303n152; 338n127; 339n167
Hay, Dale, 184n253; 385n31
Hayden, Michael Edison, 427n1
Hayes, Hennessey, 303n162
Hayes, Read, 135n130
Hayes, Steven, 305; 306
Haynie, Dana, 181n162; 226nn63, 72; 266n95;
    339n165; 389n180
Hays, Kristen, 484
Hazelwood, Robert, 387n101
He, J., 177n32
Heald, E.P., 180n115
Healy, Jack, 176n1
Healy, William, 172; 184n279
Heath, Nicole, 301n100
Heathfield, Donald, 400
Heaton, Tim B., 263n10
Hecker, Jeffrey, 183n246
Hefler, Gerd, 229nn162, 163
Hegel, Georg, 275
Heide, Kathleen, 389n214
Heilemann, Tammy, 542n83
Heimer, Karen, 226n59; 228n197
Heiskanen, Markku, 64n54
Hektner, Joel, 266n97
Helenius, Hans, 263n11
Hellard, Margaret, 25n8
Hellstrom, Tomas, 578n95
Helmer, Karen, 134n99
Hemenway, David, 178n47
Henderson, Charles R., Jr., 179n90
Henderson, Craig, 93n18; 387n95; 544n186
Henderson, Russell, 379
Hendrick, C., 387n107
Hendriks, Jan, 541n46
Henggeler, Scott, 183nn233, 235,
    336nn53, 54
Henigsberg, Neven, 93n19
Henley, Wayne, Jr., 369
Hennard, George, 369
Hennessy, James, 179nn97, 106
Hennigan, Karen, 135n147
Henning, Peter, 135n145
Henry II (King of England), 15
Hensley, Christopher, 385n11
Henslin, James, 63n14
Henson, Trudy Knicely, 458n65
Hepburn, John, 457n12
Herba, Catherine, 180n112
Herbig, F.J.W., 500n92
Hermann, Christopher, 228n128
Hermann, Dieter, 135n149
Hernandez, Daphne, 228n122
Hernandez, Elizabeth, 545n246

Hernandez, Raymond, 541n9
Herrenkohl, Todd I., 94n48; 264n42; 267n142;
    336n48; 385nn30, 38
Herrnstein, Richard, 22; 25n45; 65nn93, 94;
    136n177; 172; 184n286; 185n292;
    230n243; 320; 334; 338nn117–119
Herve, Huues, 388n141
Hetu, Celine, 458n46
Hibbeln, Joseph, 177n29
Hickert, Audrey, 545n235
Hickey, Eric, 134n95
Hickey, J., 183n232
Hickman-Barlow, Melissa, 300n31
Hicks, Craig, 378
Hidaym, Virginia, 183n224
Higgins, George E., 184n252; 340n172; 576n9
Hilbert, Richard, 228nn154, 155
Hill, Andreas, 179n98; 184nn264, 265
Hill, D., 178n50
Hill, Karl G., 340n182
Hill, Rodney, 489
Hillyard, Paddy, 500n94
Hinckley, John, 164
Hindelang, Michael, 25n44; 65n112; 172;
    184nn275, 283, 284; 253; 267n126;
    268n168; 458n50
Hinduja, Sameer, 266n109; 566; 567; 577nn67,
    68
Hinshaw, Stephen, 180n134
Hipp, John R., 64n79; 66n130; 225n41;
    226nn61, 78; 227n110; 228n146
Hippchen, Leonard, 177nn27, 28; 178n76
Hirky, A. Elizabeth, 544n166
Hirschi, Travis, 25n44; 51; 63n22; 65n88; 115;
    133n37; 134n102; 152; 172; 184nn283,
    284; 238; 240; 249; 250; 251; 252; 253;
    259; 262; 265n76; 266n106; 267nn138,
    139, 143; 320; 321; 322; 323; 324; 325;
    326; 334; 338nn120–122, 125; 126;
    339nn136, 148, 161; 496; 501nn156, 157
Hirtenlehner, Helmut, 302n130
Hirvikoski, Tatja, 178n56
Hitchcock, Alfred, 140
Hitler, Adolf, 409
Ho, Ching-hua, 182n216
Ho, Lavinia, 385n8; 389n213
Hobbes, Thomas, 103
Hobbs, David, 16
Hoberman, Harry M., 9
Hochstetler, Andy, 96n127; 132n24; 266n92;
    377; 391n272; 501n148
Hodge, Carole, 268n185
Hodge, Jessica P., 302n119
Hoek, Hans, 183n217
Hoepner, Lori, 179n82
Hoffman, John, 229n196; 230n209
Hoffman, Philip Seymour, 111; 521
Hogan, Michael, 227n88
Hoge, Robert, 337n83
Hogg, J., 183n227; 185nn293, 294
Hoheimer, Francis, 451
Hoheimer, Frank, 459n95
Holand, Ashleigh, 181n150
Holcomb, Jefferson, 66n138
Holland, A.J., 180n129
Hollander, Yona, 577n54
Holleran, David, 360; 388n161
Hollinger, Richard, 458n56
Holmes, James, 347; 369
Holmes, Malcolm, 66n132; 267n146

Holmes, Oliver Wendell, 18; 25n29
Holmes, Ronald, 389n208; 390nn221, 222
Holmes, Stephen, 389n208; 390nn221, 222
Holmqvist, Rolf, 184n272
Holsinger, Alexander, 264n39
Holsinger, Kristi, 264n39; 302nn113, 119
Homant, Robert, 458n52
Homel, Ross, 134n111
Homes, Malcolm, 301n66
Hommer, Daniel, 179n107
Hong, Rachelle, 96n154
Hook, Edward, III, 336n32
Hooker, "Fighting Joe," 514
Hooton, Earnest, 141
Hope, Tim, 94n72
Horgan, John, 25n14
Horney, Julie, 63n37; 178n72; 386n61
Horowitz, Ruth, 525; 544nn177, 178
Horwood, L. John, 336nn37, 39; 337n65
Hosein, Vanessa, 389n188
Hoskin, Anthony, 63n10; 180n139
Hotaling, Gerald, 542nn81, 94
Hough, Richard, 93n26
House, James, 338n93
Houston, Whitney, 521
Howard, C. Vyvyan, 178n42
Howard, Gregory, 134n92
Howard, L.M., 183n227
Howell, James, 67n169; 95n106; 134n92; 225n5
Hoyt, Dan, 95n94; 387n108; 544n173
Hoza, Betsy, 95n108; 265n66
Hrabac, Pero, 93n19
Hribal, Alex, 167
Hu, Howard, 179n92
Huang, Bu, 94n48; 385n30; 544nn180, 201
Hubbard, Ben, 412; 428n46
Hubbell, Amy, 544n172
Huberty, James, 369
Huebner, Beth, 225n42; 226n75
Huff, Rodney, 498nn9–11
Hughes, Lorine, 45; 229n165; 263n8; 268n166;
    339n155; 386n68
Huh, David, 237; 264n43
Huie, S.A., 228n151
Huizinga, David, 65n115; 126; 132n29; 227n96;
    228n137; 230n238
Hummer, R.A., 228n151
Humphries, Drew, 302n108
Hunt, Dana, 517
Hunter, Denis, 25n35
Hunter, Jeremy, 330
Hunter, Jerome, 330
Hunter, John, 268n185
Hureau, David M., 135n134; 137n206
Hurlburt, Michael, 93n26
Hurley, Jimmy, 93n17
Hurley, Robert S., 184n255; 185n297
Hurtado, Patricia, 498n27
Hurtig, Tuula, 180n133
Hussein, Saddam, 283
Hussey, Matthew, 541n19
Husted, David, 336n33
Hwang, Shu-ling, 542n95
Hyde, Janet Shibley, 65n106

I

Ialongo, Nicholas, 336n47
Ikram, Khawaja, 442
Ilgen, Mark, 542n89
Ilonen, Noora, 93n21

Immarigeon, Russ, 303n142
Inciardi, James, 457n13; 525; 543nn135, 139, 141; 544nn177, 178; 545n248
Inglis, Ruth, 390n242
Ingram, Jason, 266n109
Ingram, Philip, 300n46
Innes, Christopher, 95n81
Iovanni, Leeann, 258; 269n225
Ireland, Jane, 577n65
Ireland, Timothy, 94n46
Irwin, John, 132n18
Izaguirre, Ainhoa, 63n43

J

Jackson, Dylan, 268n193
Jackson, Jennifer, 387n92
Jackson, Jesse L., Jr., 398
Jackson, Kenneth, 269n210
Jackson, Kristina, 543n163
Jackson, Linda, 268n185
Jackson, Lori, 385n6
Jackson, Michael, 112; 521
Jackson, Patrick, 63n16
Jackson, Shelley, 76
Jackson, Toby, 301n73
Jacobs, Bruce A., 109; 110; 111; 112; 113; 123; 133nn50–55, 68; 136nn166, 189; 177n23; 225n35; 376; 385n29; 391n265; 458n71
Jacobs, David, 264n133, 146; 301nn56, 62
Jacobs, K.J., 178n78
Jacobson, Heather, 577nn53, 81
Jacobson, Michael, 301n86
Jacoby, Kristen, 25n12
Jacques, Scott, 113; 133n86; 391nn270, 271
Jaffe, Pater, 96n150
Jaffee, Sara, 181n163
Jaki, Thomas, 267n147
Jalbert, Sarah Kuck, 517
James, Alison, 541n7
James, J.E., 178n42
James, Susan, 543n151
James, William, 166
Janes, Nicole, 500n111
Jang, Hyunseok, 263n15
Jang, Sung Joon, 265n77
Janis, Irving, 265nn53, 54
Jansen, Robert, 134n89; 375; 391n261
Janson, Jillian, 505
Janus, Mark-David, 542n68
Jargon, Julie, 543n112
Jargowsky, Paul, 226nn66, 69
Jarjoura, G. Roger, 229n186; 265n51
Jeanmard, Matthew, 388n156
Jeffery, C. Ray, 116; 134n106
Jenkins, Brian Michael, 424; 425
Jennings, J. Richard, 181n141; 339n135
Jennings, Wesley, 9; 327; 340nn181, 187, 200; 576n9
Jensen, Gary, 65nn112, 114; 95n97; 266n118; 268n169; 302n127
Jensen, Vickie, 386n60
Jesilow, Paul, 303n159
Jin, Ellie Shuo, 178n56
Joe, Karen Ann, 109; 133n49
John Paul II (Pope), 511
Johnson, Brian, 66n128; 337n73
Johnson, Bruce D., 544nn182–184
Johnson, Byron, 265n77
Johnson, Carrie, 499n52
Johnson, David, 123; 498n29

Johnson, Dawn, 93n32
Johnson, Holly, 182n184
Johnson, Janice, 543n151
Johnson, Jeffrey, 542n80
Johnson, Joseph, 225n38
Johnson, Kathrine, 55; 66n135
Johnson, L. Clark, 136n187
Johnson, Lee Michael, 268n190
Johnson, Mark, 63n48
Johnson, Matthew, 340n190
Johnson, Norman, 183n218
Johnson, Richard, 388nn147, 148
Johnson, Robert, 268n198; 269n212
Johnson, S., 183n227
Johnson, Shane D., 133n84
Johnson, W. Wesley, 300n31
Johnson, Wendell, 93n12
Johnson, Wendi, 337n62
Johnston, David, 427n38
Johnston, Lloyd, 63nn27, 28; 64n52; 543n146
Johnstone, J., 230n230
Jokinen, Jussi, 178n56
Jolin, Annette, 541n54
Jolliffe, Darrick, 335n25; 338n131
Jon, Nina, 302n112
Jones, Adrian, 339n154
Jones, Alice, 180n112
Jones, Donald, 154; 181nn169, 170; 337n60
Jones, Heather, 264n31
Jones, Lisa, 390nn244, 245
Jones, Marshall, 154; 181nn169, 170; 337n60
Jones, Michael R., 362
Jones, Peter, 66n164; 545n230
Jones, Shayne, 227n114; 338n128
Jones, Willard Leonard, 448
Jonzon, Eva, 390n246
Jordan, Carol E., 389nn189, 192; 391n311
Jordan, Lamar, 94n64
Jorgensen, Jenel S., 182n213
Jorgensen, P.J., 177n33
Josephs, Robert, 178n56
Joyce, James, 518
Juarez, Conrado, 362
Julius Caesar, 407
Jung, Helen, 458n55
Jung, Hyunzee, 385n38
Junger, Marianne, 267n156
Junger-Tas, Josine, 267n156
Jusko, Todd A., 179n90

K

Kadleck, Colleen, 134n122
Kaeble, Danielle, 136n191
Kageyama, Yuri, 386n80
Kahler, Christopher, 93n32
Kahn, Arnold, 387n92
Kakoulidis, Christos, 384n5
Kalb, Larry, 335n25; 338n131
Kaloupek, Danny, 94n49
Kaltiala-Heino, Rittakerttu, 182n214
Kandel, Denise, 266nn97, 101; 268n161; 544n167
Kandel, Elizabeth, 179n94
Kandel, Jason, 427n9
Kane, John, 498nn9–11
Kane, Robert J., 228n134; 386n63
Kanka, Maureen, 90
Kanka, Megan, 8; 20; 90; 91
Kanka, Richard, 90
Kaplan, David, 541n22

Kaplan, Howard, 229n180; 268nn198, 199; 269n212
Karasik, Theodore W., 428n58
Karch, Debra, 389n196
Karimi, Faith, 225n19
Karmaus, Wilfried, 179n87
Karmen, Andrew, 63n12; 96n152; 388n166
Karp, David R., 303n158
Kassin, Saul, 63n26
Kasza, Kristen, 177n30
Kates, Don, 133n66
Katsiyannis, Antonis, 182n212
Katz, Charles M., 227n108
Katz, Jack, 109
Kauffman, K., 183n232
Kaufman, Jeanne, 93n24
Kaufman, Joanne, 66n144; 229n193; 389n203
Kauzlarich, David, 300n37
Kavanaugh, Philip, 289; 302n107
Kavish, Daniel Ryan, 268n194
Kawai, Eriko, 386n66
Kaysen, Debra, 65n110; 95n101
Kayslett-McCall, Karen L., 182n205
Kazemian, Lila, 63n38; 67n165
Keckler, Charles N.W., 136n165
Keeler, Gordon, 183n222
Keels, Micere, 227n98
Keen, Bradley, 66n133
Keenan, Kate, 265n63; 340n203
Keeney, Belea, 389n214
Keire, Mara, 541n59
Keith, Bruce, 264n19
Keith, H., 500n108
Kellam, Sheppard, 336n47
Kelley, Jill, 564
Kelley, Thomas, 458n52
Kelling, George, 200; 226n60
Kellogg, Michael, 409; 428n50
Kelly, Kathryn, 182n196
Kelly, Mark, 124
Kelman, Jonathan H.C., 300n43
Kempe, C. Henry, 390n238
Kempe, Ruth S., 390n238
Kemper, Rick, 134n109
Kempf, Kimberly, 267n158
Kempf-Leonard, Kimberly, 60; 65n101; 67nn168, 169; 136n180; 302n114
Kempner, Michael, 256
Kennedy, Daniel, 458n52
Kennedy, Leslie, 97n163; 338n124
Kenney, T.J., 180n115
Keppelm, Robert D., 389n212; 390nn215, 216, 218
Kerbs, Jodi, 183n217
Kerich, Michael, 179n107
Kerner, Hans-Jürgen, 265n58; 341n207
Kerns, Suzanne, 336n51
Kerr, Margaret, 265n68; 340n196
Kershaw, Sarah, 390n231
Kessler, Daniel, 121; 135n156
Kessler, Glen, 540n5
Kethineni, Sesha, 268n163
Keys, David, 301n71
Khalifeh, H., 183n227
Khan, A.Q., 420
Khan, Bilal, 513
Khan, Haji Juma, 422
Khomeini, Aytolah Ruhollah, 407
Kidd, Sean, 543n159
Kilewer, Wendy, 226n80

Kilias, Martin, 45
Killip, Steve, 96n150
Kilpatrick, Dean G., 93n20; 94nn35, 36; 385n24; 386n77; 387n91
Kilpatrick, Kwame, 398
Kim, D., 177n32
Kim, Euikyung, 165
Kim, Julia Yun Soo, 63n35
Kim, KiDeuk, 136n164
Kim, Min Jung, 94n48
Kinard, Griffin, 316
King, Anna, 458nn48, 49
King, Harry, 434; 457n14
King, Ryan, 65n95; 115; 134n98; 264n26
Kingery, Paul M., 184n255; 185n297
Kingree, J.B., 182n216
Kingsworth, Rodney, 388n159
Kinkade, Patrick, 391n302
Kinlock, Timothy, 336n46
Kinney, Linda, 388n153
Kinsey, Richard, 301n83
Kinsie, Paul, 542nn70, 73
Kinsman, Erica, 80
Kipp, Heidi, 264n31
Kirby, Ronald, 17
Kircheimer, Otto, 275
Kirk, David, 64n53; 337n85; 386n48
Kirk, Jeremy, 577n78
Kirschel, David, 126
Kitchin, Elizabeth, 178n43
Kivivuori, Janne, 25n4; 64n81; 93n15; 94n37; 182n214; 458n43
Kjelsberg, Ellen, 182n209
Klaas, Polly, 19; 509
Klaus, Patsy, 375; 458nn70, 72
Kleck, Gary, 48; 64nn71, 72, 84; 89; 97n168, 169; 133n66; 134n88; 301n67
Klein, Andrew, 126
Klein, Brent R., 134n103
Klein, Uwe, 184n263
Kleinman, Ken P., 179n92
Klenowski, Paul M., 247
Klika, Bart, 385n38
Kline, Jennie, 177n37
Kling, Kristen, 65n106
Kling, Ryan, 517
Klinger, David, 228n132
Klockars, Carl, 301n75; 436; 457n22; 544nn190, 192
Kluding, Paula, 471–472
Knake, Rob, 578n90
Knight, Michelle, 509
Knight, Raymond A., 184n271; 387n99; 449
Knight, Zelda, 390n219
Knoller, Marjorie, 362
Knott, Jason, 499n51
Knottnerus, G. Mark, 179n87
Knowles, James A., 526
Kobrin, Solomon, 221; 227nn102, 103; 230n247
Kochel, Tammy Rinehart, 54; 66n123; 228n130; 301n65
Kocherga, Angela, 500n144
Kochka, Rakesh, 225n17
Koeppel, Maria D.H., 72; 93n29; 339n157
Kohlberg, Lawrence, 166; 183nn230, 231
Kohn, Robert, 93n32
Koltfreter, Kristy, 339n141
Komisarjevsky, Joshua, 305; 306
Konchalovsky, Andrei, 325
Konofal, Eric, 177nn33, 37

Koons, Barbara, 226n58
Koops, Willem, 183n246
Koper, Christopher, 135n136
Kopie, Kathy, 390n245
Korchevsky, Vitaly, 322
Kornhauser, Ruth, 226n45; 230n239
Koroloff, Nancy, 183n217
Kort-Butler, Lisa, 229n182; 267n155
Koss, Mary, 355; 387nn90, 106; 543nn110, 114, 120
Kosterman, Rick, 264n42; 336n48; 341n218; 544n180
Kotonias, Cybele, 513
Kovandzic, Tomislav, 123; 229n176
Koziol-McLain, Jane, 374
Kozlowski, L. Dennnis, 471
Krabill, Jennifer, 65n91
Krafft-Ebing, Richard von, 510
Krahé, Barbara, 165; 386n74; 388n154
Krahn, Harvey, 268n170
Krajewski, Andrea, 459n98
Kramer, Lisa, 542n84
Kramer, Ronald C., 300n37; 499nn83, 84
Kranidioti, Maria, 265n55
Kranish, Michael, 428n70
Krause, Christina, 165
Krauss, Clifford, 498n14
Kreager, Derek, 65nn90, 97; 132n29
Krebs, Brian, 576n16
Kristjansson, A.L., 178n42
Kristof, Nicholas, 366
Kristol, Irving, 541n20
Krivo, Lauren, 66n141; 193; 195; 225nn35, 37; 228nn126, 128
Krohn, Marvin D., 63n34; 65n114; 134n92; 181n158; 264n28; 265n65; 266nn89, 103, 111, 112, 114; 268nn171, 189, 195, 196, 200; 269n220; 312; 335nn13, 26; 336n34; 337n61; 338n94; 388n149; 543n152; 545n209
Krstic, Sonja, 184n271
Krueger, Freddy, 368
Krueger, P.M., 228n151
Krueger, Robert, 182n200; 184n277
Kruger, Tillmann H.C., 541n42
Kruglanski, Arie, 428n73
Kruttschnitt, Candace, 337n87
Ku, Simon, 96n126
Kubik, Elizabeth, 183n246
Kubrin, Charis, 45; 94n53; 226nn62, 63; 351; 386n62
Kuhl, Danielle, 93n31; 94n68
Kuklin, Susan, 508
Kuklinski, Barbara, 171
Kuklinski, Richard, 171
Kulkarni, Madhur, 96n134
Kully, Christine, 387n92
Kumpulkinen, Kirsti, 263n11
Kunarac, Dragoljub, 353
Kurlychek, Megan, 269n223
Kurniawan, Rudy, 446
Kurtz, Ellen, 226n58
Kurz, Gwen, 59; 66n163
Kutateladze, Besiki, 66n128; 337n73
Kutchinsky, Berl, 543n115

L

La Fave, Wayne, 389n174; 457nn30, 31; 458nn78, 88, 89
La Fon, Dana, 63n26

La Rooy, David, 542n101
La Vigne, Nancy, 458n91
Labrum, Travis, 385n8
Lacasse, Lori, 179n96; 180nn110, 118
Lacerte-Lamontagne, Celine, 458n46
Lacey, Marc, 387n83
LaChance, Jenny, 178n79
Ladd, Jessica, 80
LaFraniere, Sharon, 386n70
LaFree, Gary, 57; 66nn149, 154; 132n35; 134n99; 228n152; 388n163; 418
LaGrange, Teresa, 96n119; 230n213; 267n157
Lahey, Benjamin, 264n31; 386n66
Laird, Robert, 337n65
Lamb, Stanton Richard, 471
Lambert, Sharon, 336n47
Lammers, Marre, 95n73
Lamontagne, Yves, 458n46
Land, Kenneth, 45; 96n129; 97n162; 227n82; 340nn183, 185
Landler, Mark, 542n64
Landwehr, Patricia, 388n156
Lane, Jodi, 95n90; 227n89
Lane, T.J., 160
Langley, Kate, 181n147
Långström, Niklas, 181n153; 385n22
Langton, Lynn, 63n8; 64n51; 93n2; 94n56; 387nn88, 115; 390n237; 457n2
Lanier, Mark, 258; 269n224
Lankford, Adam, 370
Lanphear, Bruce P., 179n90
Lansford, Jennifer, 264nn36, 38; 385n36
Lansky, Meyer, 485; 486
Lantz, Sarah, 542n102
Lanza, Adam, 75; 161; 162; 365; 369
Lanza, Nancy, 162
Lanza, Peter, 162
Lanza, Ryan, 162
Lanza-Kaduce, Lonn, 65n114; 136n172; 266nn111, 112
LaPrairie, Carol, 303n156
Laqueur, Hannah, 65n96
Laqueur, Walter, 428n48
Larivee, S., 67n170
Larson, Brie, 509
Larson, David, 265n77
Larson, Matthew, 229n184; 338nn100, 102
Larson, Reed, 95n111; 96n113
Lascala, Elizabeth, 227n95
Lasley, James, 268n173
Lattimore, Pamela, 385n30
Lau, Karen, 178n42
Laub, John, 177n18; 181n152; 268n202; 269nn216, 217; 306; 312; 313; 314; 315; 317; 318; 319; 333; 334; 335nn6, 7, 24; 337nn67–69, 88
Laufer, Bill, 267n158
Laufer, William, 228n157
Laughon, Kathryn, 374
Laurens, Kristin, 180n112
Lauritsen, Janet, 63n15; 94nn60, 70; 133n56; 386n61
Laursen, Brett, 265n68
Lavater, J.K., 141
Law, Bernard, 510
Lawrence, D.H., 518
Lawrence, Frederick M., 379; 391nn283–287
Lawton, Brian, 45; 94n34
Lay, Kenneth, 571
Layton, Allison, 461; 462; 464

Lazoritz, Martin, 336n33
Lea, John, 286; 301nn79, 80, 83
Leach, Amy-May, 63n26
Leaf, Philip, 336n47
Leal, Wanda, 65n92
LeBeau, James, 387n102
Lebed, Jonathan, 554
Lebel, Thomas, 269n226
LeBlanc, Marc, 67nn165, 170; 307; 333; 335n9; 336nn48, 54; 339n139; 340n177
Lecendreux, Michel, 177nn33, 37
LeClerc, Benoit, 134nn96, 97
Lecter, Hannibal, 368
Ledger, Heath, 111; 521
Lee, Beverly, 96n140
Lee, Daniel, 226n72
Lee, Felicia, 391n282
Lee, Gang, 266n117
Lee, Hyunshik, 387n113
Lee, James, 576n30
Lee, Joca Julia, 178n56
Lee, Joongyeup, 263n15
Lee, Jungeun, 385n38
Lee, Matthew, 93n16; 226nn62, 63, 77; 385n18
Lee, Yan, 227n101
Lefforge, Noelle, 263n9
Legon, Jeordan, 577n45
Lei, Man-Kit, 177n26; 180n135; 181n147; 338n111
Leiber, Michael, 66n134; 225n38; 300n32; 302n129
Leigh-Perrot, Jane, 440
Leitgoeb, Heinz, 302n130
Lejuez, Carl, 180n113
Lemert, Edwin, 240; 257; 262; 269nn206, 207; 442; 457n20; 458n58
Lencz, Todd, 179n96
Lengua, Liliana, 336n48
Lenza, Michael, 301n71
Leo, Richard, 63n26
Leon, Chrysanthi, 290; 302n120
Leonard, Kimberly Kempf, 268n164
Leopold, Nathan, 39
Leschied, Alan, 337n83
Lester, David, 428n75
Letourneau, Elizabeth, 9
Leukefeld, Carl, 545nn228, 229
Levenson, Jill S., 9; 134n115; 182n206
Levi-Minzi, Micòl E., 391nn292, 294, 299
Levin, Jack, 367; 369; 371; 378; 379; 389n211; 390nn222, 225, 229, 391nn276, 278, 291, 297; 543n119
Levine, David M., 576n27
Levine, Murray, 302n127
Levitt, Justin, 427n10
Levitt, Steven D., 44; 45; 64n57; 121; 125; 127; 135n156; 136nn175, 194; 340n171
Levitz, Jennifer, 357
Levrant, Sharon, 303n169
Levs, Josh, 428n60
Levy, Diane, 177n37
Lewis, Dorothy Otnow, 346; 385nn6, 7
Lewis, John, 63n37
Lewis, Oscar, 191; 192; 225n21
Lewis, S.A., 179n105
Leygraf, Norbert, 541n42
Li, Fuzhong, 265n65
Li, Yi, 265n62
Lichtenstein, Paul, 181n153; 385n22
Lim, Megan, 25n8

Limon, Alexandra, 225n2
Lin, Peter, 389n197
Lind, Bronwyn, 96n126
Lindblad, Frank, 390n246
Lindblad, M.R., 227n108
Lindegaard, Marie Rosenkrantz, 133n86; 391n270
Linder, Douglas, 427n18
Linderman, Juliet, 388n152
Lindh, John Walker, 398–399
Lindsay, Mark, 428n75
Lindsay, W.R., 180n129
Link, Bruce, 183n219; 268n184
Linster, Richard, 385n30
Linz, Daniel, 388n145; 543n117
Lipinski, Karol, 69
Lipscomb, Jane A., 391n295
Lipsey, Mark, 336n31
Lipton, D., 184n250
Liska, Alan E., 268n174
Liska, Allen, 228n123
Listokin, Yair, 136n163
Littleton, Heather, 93n18; 387n95
Liu, Jianhong, 178n44; 228n123
Liu, Xiaoru, 229n180
Liu, Xinhua, 177n37
Livaditis, Miltos, 384n5
Livingston, Jennifer, 387nn92, 97
Lizotte, Alan J., 63n34; 95n107; 134n92; 181n158; 264n28; 266n89; 268n195; 301n60; 312; 335nn13, 26; 336n34; 338n94; 386n65; 543n152; 545n209; 576n4
Llakatura, Besnik, 469
Lo, Celia, 545n240
Lochman, J.E., 183n246
Lodato, Ruthanne, 17
Loeber, Rolf, 67n170; 95nn103–105; 177n30; 180n133; 181n141; 182n208; 183n217; 184n253; 264n47; 265n63; 267n150; 307; 328; 329; 333; 335nn9, 14, 25; 336nn31, 48, 54; 337nn65, 70, 75; 338n131; 339nn135, 141, 150; 340n203; 341n208; 385nn11, 31; 386n66; 389n185; 545n206
Lofland, John, 269n204
Loftus, Margaret, 457n36
Logan, T.K., 391n311; 545nn228, 229
Logio, Kim, 93n22
Lok, Kris, 178n43
Lolacono, Nancy J., 177n37
Lombroso, Cesare, 52; 65n102; 141; 142; 143; 174
Lonardo, Robert, 266nn88, 96
Loncar, Mladen, 93n19
Lonczk, Heather, 341n218
Longmire, Dennis, 94n34
Longmore, Monica, 266nn88, 95; 268n167; 337n62; 339n165
Loomis, Dana, 391n300
Looney, Zyontae, 147
Lopes, Giza, 268n195; 338n94; 576n4
Lorenz, Konrad, 347; 348; 385n16
Losel, Fredrich, 178n60
Lough, Richard, 428n61
Loughner, Jared, 124
Loughran, Thomas A., 63n32; 135nn150, 151
Loveless, Peggy, 180n131
Lovell, David, 136n187
Lovett, Ian, 176n1
Lovrich, Nicholas, 227n104

Lowenstein, George, 136n170
Loya, Rebecca, 37; 63n42
Lu, Chunmeng, 95n99
Lucas, Emma, 542n89
Luciano, Charles "Lucky," 485; 486
Luckenbill, David, 365; 386n58; 389n201
Ludwig, Jens, 64n73; 135n129; 137n203; 389n184
Luebbers, Stefan, 183n228
Lueck, Monika, 385n10
Lunde, Donald, 388n169
Lundholm, Lena, 385n22
Lundrigan, Samantha, 387n89
Lunsford, Jessica, 510
Luque, Luis, 388n156
Lurigio, Arthur J., 93n3; 94n40; 97n165; 136n167; 545n226
Lussier, Patrick, 336nn48, 54; 340n177
Luther, Martin, 511
Luukkaala, Tiina, 182n214
Lykken, David, 136n169; 176n6; 184n260
Lynam, Donald R., 179n94; 182n192; 183n241; 184n285; 227n114; 336n49; 337n65; 340nn176, 199; 341n208; 545nn228, 229
Lynch, James, 137n202
Lynch, Kathleen Bodisch, 341n219
Lynch, Michael J., 179n85; 182n180; 282; 299nn4, 5; 300nn8, 10, 13, 26, 32, 51; 483; 498n4; 499n65; 499n90; 500nn114, 116
Lynch, Shannon, 301n100
Lyngstad, Torkild Hovde, 338n105
Lyon, Matthew, 25n40
Lysiak, Matthew, 162

M

Ma, Po Chieng, 447
Maakestad, William, 499nn74, 75
Maas, Carl, 267n142
MacCoun, Robert, 544n189
MacDonald, John M., 64n81; 94n44; 316; 338n99
MacDonald, Julia, 459n114
Mace, David E., 182n213
Machon, Ricardo, 179n94
MacIntosh, Randall, 388n159
Mack, Kristin, 302n129
MacKenzie, Doris Layton, 339n151
Mackesy-Amiti, Mary Ellen, 544n179
Maclean, Donald, 401
MacMillan, Ross, 65n95; 337n87
Madan, Anjana, 165
Maddan, Sean, 135n127
Madensen, Tamara D., 133n71; 265n86
Madoff, Bernard, 465
Maercker, Andreas, 94n51; 96n149
Maetti, Mark, 300n45
Maggs, Jennifer, 340n201
Maguin, Eugene, 264n47
Maguire, Brendan, 303n153
Maguire, Kathleen, 230n245
Maher, Dennis, 360
Mahoney, Margaret, 340n172
Maier, Jeanette, 504
Maier-Katkin, Daniel, 230n211
Makarios, Matthew, 136n195
Malachek, Richard, 181n172
Malamuth, Neil, 388n146; 543nn110, 114, 120

Malby, Steven, 64n54
Maldonado-Molina, Mildred, 340n200
Malik, Tashfeen, 2; 3; 4; 369
Malinowski, Sean, 63n48
Mallouk, Mohammed, 47
Malvo, John, 371
Manasse, Michelle, 230n205
Manchester, Julia, 427n37
Mancini, Christina, 94n45
Mandela, Nelson, 296–297
Manganello, Jennifer, 374
Mannheim, Hermann, 176–177n7
Manning, Chelsea Elizabeth (Bradley Manning), 400
Manning, Wendy, 266nn88, 95; 268n167; 337n62; 339n165
Manturuk, K.R., 227n108
Maples, Michelle, 269n226
Maras, Marie-Helen, 577n44
Marchak, Patricia, 418–419; 428nn87–89
Marcotte, Dave, 385n12
Marcum, Catherine D., 340n172; 576n9
Maricd, Alexandra, 543n117
Marini, Margaret Mooney, 65n106
Markianos, M., 180n136
Markoff, John, 578n89
Markowitz, Fred, 228n123; 230n220
Markowitz, Sara, 385n12
Marquart, James, 133n79; 136n198
Marques, Antonio F., 179n83
Marshall, Ineke Haen, 267n156
Marshall, John, 400
Marshall, Paul, 178n77
Marshall, Stephen, 391n300
Marshall, W.L., 387n99
Martel, Michelle, 179n87
Martens, Frederick, 500n119
Martin, Catherine, 545nn228, 229
Martin, David, 267n155
Martin, Douglas, 171
Martin, Monica J., 263n10
Martin, Susan, 545n208
Martin, Trayvon, 89
Martines, Laura, 390n252
Martinez, Amos, 267n130
Martinez, Jason, 446
Martinez, Ramiro, Jr., 45; 58; 64n79; 66n156; 385n18
Martinez, Servando Gómez, 494
Martinson, Robert, 104; 132n11
Martoma, Mathew, 468
Maruna, Shadd, 183n242; 269n226
Marvell, Thomas, 136n194
Marx, Karl, 274; 275; 276; 279; 298; 300nn8, 9, 11
Marziano, Vincent, 184n251
Maschi, Tina, 184n254
Maser, Jack, 265n65
Mason, Alex, 180n133; 264n42
Mason, Patrick L., 65n119
Mason, W. Alex, 336nn48, 51, 54
Massey, James, 266n114; 268n171
Massoglia, Michael, 65n95
Mastrofski, Stephen, 66n123; 301n65
Mastromarino, Michael, 438
Masunaga, Samantha, 300n36
Mateen, Omar, 369; 393; 394; 414
Matejkowski, Jason, 183n220
Mathers, Richard, 267n145
Matheson, Daniel, 25n12

Matsuda, Kristy N., 135n147; 217
Matsueda, Ross, 132n29; 134n99; 268nn192, 197
Matsuko, Jacqueline, 385n26
Matsumoto, Atsushi, 95n101
Matthews, Roger, 518; 542n108
Matthews, Shelley Keith, 265n72
Mattos, Manoel, 283
Matza, David, 240; 244; 245; 248; 262; 266nn120–123
Maudsley, Henry, 142
Mauer, Marc, 137nn204, 207
Maughan, Barbara, 340n203
Maume, Michael, 226nn62, 63
Mawson, A.R., 178n78
Maxson, Cheryl L., 135n147
Maxwell, Christopher, 341n204; 542n86; 545n208
Maxwell, John, 487
Maxwell, Sheila Royo, 341n204; 542n86
Maxwell, William, 487
Mayer, Debbie, 513
Mayo, Julia, 542n89
Mazerolle, Lorraine Green, 66n130; 134n122; 227n110
Mazerolle, Paul, 183n221; 229nn190, 191; 335nn20, 27; 340nn173, 180; 341n210
Mazzetti, Mark, 395
McAuslan, Pam, 385n25
McBride, Duane, 545n248
McCaghy, Charles, 25n19; 458nn65, 82; 499n49; 542n60; 543nn144, 145
McCain, John, 404
McCall, Andrew, 457nn3, 4
McCall, Patricia L., 45; 66n145; 340nn183, 185
McCann, Donna, 178n43
McCarthy, Bill, 94n43; 95n88; 132n23; 136n176; 265nn84, 85; 302n123
McCauley, Clark, 415
McCauley, Elizabeth, 336n48
McCauley, Jenna, 386n77; 387n91
McClanahan, Bill, 302n141
McClelland, Gary, 25n17
McCluskey, John, 225n42
McCollister, Kathryn, 71; 93n5
McCord, Joan, 335n19
McCready, William, 543n141
McCullough, Jack, 362
McCurdy, Sheryl, 542n77
McDermott, Rose, 180n138
McDevitt, Jack, 378; 391nn276, 277, 288
McDonel, E.C., 184n250
McDowall, David, 93n14; 96n114; 543n152
McElrath, Suzy, 264n27
McFall, R., 184n250
McFarland, Christine, 179n89
McFarlane, Judith, 374
McGahey, Richard, 226n72
McGarrell, Edmund F., 500n110
McGee, Rob, 182n200
McGee, Tara Renae, 303n162
McGloin, Jean Marie, 38; 133nn40–42; 183n238; 265n56; 336nn43–45; 339nn141, 142, 164
McGuire, Stryker, 384n3
Mchugh, Suzanne, 181n162
McKay, Henry D., 198–201; 205; 223; 226nn49, 51, 52
McKenzie, Roderick, 189; 225nn15, 16
McKibben, André, 134n97
McKinney, Aaron, 379

McKinney, Joseph R., 545n231
McLaughlin, Eliott, 391n290
McLean, Anthony, 180n121
McLean, Bethany, 499n52
McLean, W. Graham, 178n42
McLendon, Michael, 371
McLeod, Maureen, 97n158
McMackin, Robert, 94n49
McMahon-Howard, Jennifer, 387n93
McMillan, Richard, 64n80; 96n130; 226n70
McMorris, Barbara J., 337n87
McMurray, Scott, 498n31
McNamara, Grace, 544n166
McNeill, Richard, 228n121
McNulty, Thomas, 228n141; 229n187
McPhaul, Kathleen M., 391n295
McVeigh, Timothy, 19
Mdzinarishvili, A., 177n32
Mead, George Herbert, 13; 253; 268n175
Meade, Benjamin, 136n195
Meade, Christina, 390n249
Mears, Daniel, 65n108; 185n295; 266nn104, 105
Measelle, Jeffrey, 181n163
Medeiros, Helena, 526
Medina, Justin, 227n113
Medlicott, Sandra, 324
Mednick, S.A., 179nn94, 100; 182n191
Mednick, Sarnoff, 66n160; 177n27; 178n44; 179nn94, 100, 105; 181nn143, 144; 182nn190, 191; 185n296; 385n33
Meehan, Albert, 301n64
Meeker, James, 227n89
Meesters, Cor, 180n128
Megargee, Edward, 184n276
Mehsud, Hakimullah, 419
Meier, Megan, 566
Meier, Robert, 96n132; 226n44; 263n4
Meier, Tina, 566
Meissner, Christian, 63n26
Melde, Chris, 94n52; 217
Meldrum, Ryan, 266n99; 338nn127, 129
Melgen, Salomon, 398
Melke, Chris, 335n16
Mellingen, Kjetil, 178n44
Meloy, Reid, 390n217; 391n309
Meltzer, Howard, 182n211
Menard, Scott, 226n73; 339nn149, 163; 340n190
Mendelson, Tamar, 183n226
Mendenhall, Ruby, 227n98
Mendes, Silvia, 135n141
Mendoza, Frank, 381; 382
Menendez, Robert, 398
Menting, Barbara, 95n73
Mercy, James, 389n191
Merkens, Hans, 229nn162, 163
Merrick, Melissa, 391n304
Merton, Robert, 207; 208; 224; 228n153
Merva, Mary, 229n179
Meseck-Bushey, Sylvia, 181nn146, 161
Messer, Julie, 182n211
Messerschmidt, James, 288; 289; 301nn96, 102
Messerschmidt, Pamela, 385n24
Messner, Steven F., 63n10; 64n80; 83; 96n130; 107; 133n85; 134n94; 208; 209; 225n6; 226n70, 71; 227n118; 228nn158, 159; 229nn164, 167, 178; 230n204; 385n20; 386nn56, 64

Michalowski, Raymond, 300n37; 499nn83, 84
Michelson, N., 179n94
Mick, Eric, 180n132
Mickelson, Phil, 468
Miech, Richard, 336n29; 543n146
Mier, Carrie, 65n92
Miethe, Terance, 64n58; 96nn114, 132; 301n60; 389n181
Mikulich-Gilbertson, Susan, 180n113
Milan, Stephanie, 335n15
Miles, William, 63n31
Mileusnic, Darinka, 25n17
Milich, Rich, 545nn228, 229
Miller, Bobbi Viegas, 95n111; 96n113
Miller, Brenda, 93n26
Miller, Henry, 518
Miller, J. Mitchell, 94n55; 336n28
Miller, Jody, 109; 110; 133n53; 336n55; 376; 391nn267, 268
Miller, Joshua, 183n241
Miller, Kirk, 63n36
Miller, Lawrence, 388nn132, 133; 428nn62, 63
Miller, Lisa, 228n147
Miller, Martin, 428n65
Miller, Robert, 177n11
Miller, Ted, 93n4
Miller, Todd, 133n78; 544n164
Miller, Walter, 215; 216; 220; 230n218, 219; 265n79
Mills, Breyan, 488
Mills, Patricia, 401
Milman, Harold, 177n35
Milner, Trudie, 135n160
Milton, Jeffrey, 230n205
Miner, Michael, 93n28; 542n87
Minhas, Rashid, 466
Minor, M. William, 136n172; 266n125
Minter, Adam, 500n109
Minter, Mallory, 337n62
Minton, Todd, 136n191
Mio, J.S., 544n168
Miodovnik, Amir, 179n81
Miron, Jeffrey, 537; 543n150; 545n245
Mirowsky, John, 227n92
Misson, Sebastian, 542n61
Mitchell, Brian David, 509
Mitchell, Derek, 184nn270, 274
Mitchell, Kimberly, 577n56
Mitchell, Nick, 269n226
Mitchell, Ojmarrh, 269n211; 369n151; 545n225
Mocan, Naci, 135n140
Modigliani, Amedeo, 506
Modzeleski, William, 389nn203, 204
Moffitt, Terrie E., 67n171; 179nn93, 94, 105; 181n163; 182nn176, 190, 192; 184nn262, 277, 285; 185n296; 328; 330; 331; 335n18; 336nn29, 49; 337nn58, 64, 65; 340nn175, 176, 186, 188, 189, 199; 341nn206–208, 215, 216
Mohler, G.O., 63n48
Moilanen, Irma, 263n11
Mokherjee, Jessica, 229n170
Möller, Ingrid, 165
Molloy, Mark, 577n60
Momenan, Reza, 179n107
Monachesi, Elio, 184nn267, 275
Monoghan, Rachel, 577n65
Monroe, Laura, 388n153
Monroe, R.R., 180n116

Monson, Candice, 96n135
Montada, Leo, 94n51
Montanino, F., 543n140
Montgomery, Nicholas, 25n12
Montgomery, Paul, 177n38
Montolio, Daniel, 64n69
Monuteaux, Michael, 180n132
Moody, Carlisle, 136n194
Moon, Sung Seek, 544n170
Moore, Charles, 301n60
Moore, Elizabeth, 339n145
Moore, Kristin, 264n35; 267n155
Moore, Mark, 498n13; 545n222
Moore, Matthew, 337n84
Moore, Melanie, 265n51
Moore, Simon, 178n46
Moore, Todd M., 93n32
Moore-Bridger, Benedict, 384n4
Morales, Elliot, 115
Moran, P., 183n227
Morash, Merry, 230n241; 301n90; 302n117
Morenoff, Jeffrey, 226n68; 227n111; 228nn140, 144; 229n171
Morgan, Lynn, 543n111
Morgan, Patricia, 109; 133n49
Morgan, Rachel, 94n58
Morgan, Stephen J., 428n71
Moroney, Dennis, 69
Morris, Jodi Eileen, 228n122
Morris, Miranda, 65n110
Morris, Norval, 177n27; 300n18; 301n74; 335n9
Morris, Robert G., 265n60; 266n113; 269n218; 289; 339n151
Morris, Sarah, 301n101
Morris, Zara, 93n11
Morrissey, Carlo, 94n49
Morse, Jennifer, 545n234
Morselli, Carlo, 132n28; 133nn44, 61; 265nn84, 85
Moses (Bible), 15
Moshalenko, Sophia, 415
Mossakowski, Krysia, 336nn38, 40
Moule, Richard, Jr., 217
Mouren, Marie-Christine, 177nn33, 37
Mousain-Bosc, M., 177n41
Mowen, Thomas, 340n179
Moy, Ernest, 385n6
Mrug, Sylvie, 95n108; 165; 265n66
Mubarak, Hosni, 394; 407
Mucci, Lorelai A., 391n259
Mueller-Johnson, Katrin, 387n89
Mufti, Lisa, 228n160
Muhammad, John Allen, 371
Mullen, Paul, 183n228
Mullings, Janet, 136n198
Mullins, Christopher W., 268n194; 300n37; 450
Mulvey, Edward, 63n37; 135n150
Mungin, Lateef, 541n36
Muñoz, Ed, 66n132
Murata, K., 177n33
Muris, Peter, 180n128
Murphy, Cynthia, 401
Murphy, Erin, 385n8; 389n213
Murphy, Lawrence, 511
Murphy, Megan, 387n90
Murphy, Richard, 401
Murray, Andy, 346
Murray, Charles, 22; 25n45; 104; 132n12; 172; 184n286; 185n292
Murray, Ellen, 267n137

Murray, Joseph, 93n9; 264nn20, 25; 337nn70, 75
Murry, Velma McBride, 182n206
Mustaine, Elizabeth Ehrhardt, 133n67; 391n263; 544n188
Musu-Gillette, Lauren, 94n58
Muth, Stephen, 542nn85, 98
Myers, Jane, 302nn115, 116; 337n63
Myers, Wade, 390n217
Myrdal, Gunnar, 191; 225n22
Myrvang, Bjørn, 385n28

N

Nachshon, Israel, 176n3; 182n190
Nadelmann, Ethan, 545n244
Nagin, Daniel S., 64n82; 135nn139, 146, 155, 158; 136nn170, 184; 137n205; 336n50; 337nn65, 71, 77; 339n140; 340nn182, 183, 185, 186
Naik, Bharati, 387n85
Najdowski, Cynthia, 136n168
Najman, Jake, 181n160
Nalla, Mahesh, 300n32
Nanjundappa, G., 544n168
Naozuka, Juliana, 179n83
Napoleoni, Loretta, 578n99
Nas, Coralijn, 183n246
Nasheri, Hedieh, 427n27
Nasr, Osama Hassan Mustafa, 403
Nation, Carrie, 522
Natsuaki, Misaki, 65n89
Navarro, Mireya, 542n76
Naylor, Reynolds, 508
Nedelec, Joseph L., 181n148; 182nn175, 187, 188; 184nn272, 288
Nee, C., 459n114
Needleman, Herbert, 179n89
Neeson, Liam, 488
Negroponte, John, 420
Neller, Daniel, 95n109
Neppl, Tricia K., 263n10
Ness, Elliot, 523
Ness, Roberta, 179n89
Neufeld, Peter, 282
Nevin, Rick, 148; 179n86
Newell, Richard, 123
Newman, Elana, 94n49
Newman, Graeme, 300n21
Newman, Oscar, 116; 134n105
Newton, Huey, 410
Neziroglu, F., 178n52
Ngo, Fawn T., 94n38; 229n201
Nguyen, Holly, 38; 133n42
Nicewander, W. Alan, 318; 338n113
Nicholson, Harold, 401
Nicholson, Thomas, 544n195
Niedrist, Fallon, 302n130
Nielsen, Arnie, 385n18
Nielsen, Mark, 165
Nielsen, Matthew Amie, 45
Niemela, Solja, 263n11
Nieuwbeerta, Paul, 94n70; 96n123; 134n91; 264n20; 336n36; 338n101; 459n110
Nigg, Joel, 179n87
Nijman, Henk, 177n39
Nikolas, Molly, 179n87
Nilsonne, Åsa, 178n56
Nilsson, Anders, 64n74
Nisbet, Robert, 225n8
Nixon, K., 177n32

No, Ynkyung, 165
Nobiling, Tracy, 301n69
Nobles, Matt, 134n115; 340n170
Noel, Robert, 362
Nofziger, Stacey, 339n138
Nolasco, Amaury, 325
Nordstrom, Anna-Lena, 178n56
Nordstrom, Benjamin, 544n198
Nordstrom, Peter, 178n56
Nordström, Tanja, 180n133
Normore, Anthony, 489
Nossiter, Adam, 540n4
Novak, Kenneth, 66n124
Novak, Scott, 545nn228, 229
Nowacki, Jeffrey, 217
Noyori-Corbett, Chie, 544n170
Nurco, David, 336n46
Nutton, Jennifer, 182n207
Nuutila, Art-Matti, 263n11
Nye, F. Ivan, 64n76

O

Oakes, Jeannie, 265n48
Obama, Barack, 423; 469; 558
Obradovic, Jelena, 339n150
O'Brien, G., 180n129
O'Brien, Kevin A., 428n58
O'Brien, Mary, 542n61
O'Brien, Robert, 66n154
O'Callaghan, Mark, 185n296
O'Connor, Anne-Marie, 366
O'Connor, Brendan, 427n8
Odiah, Chuk, 385n9
O'Donovan, Michael, 181n147
O'Faolain, Julia, 390n252
Offenhauer, Priscilla, 390n258
Ogilvie, James, 180n111
Ogle, Robin, 230n211
Ogloff, James, 170; 183n228
O'Hare, Thomas, 183n225
O'Hear, Michael M., 96n139; 499n91
Ohlin, Lloyd, 63n41; 218; 219; 220; 221;
    230nn231–237
Oken, Emily, 179n92
O'Leary, Cecilia, 300nn7, 23
O'Leary, K. Daniel, 94n33
Oliveira, Andrew, 500n111
Oliveira, Pedro V., 179n83
Olligschlaeger, Andreas, 25n5
Olson, James, 133nn58, 59, 75; 454; 457n27;
    459n113
Olson, Lynn, 93n12
Olsson, Martin, 185n298
Olweus, Dan, 266n108; 577n66
Olympio, Kelly P.K., 179n83
O'Malley, Patrick, 63nn27, 28; 64n52; 543n146
Omuro, Eric, 503
O'Neil, John, 498n36
Ong, Bao, 498n19
Opjordsmoen, Stein, 385n28
Opler, Mark, 179n91
Oranen, Mikko, 93n21
Orbuch, Terri, 338n93
O'Reilly-Fleming, Thomas, 390n225
Orlebeke, Jacob, 178n66
Ormrod, Richard, 93n20; 94n63
Orobio de Castro, Bram, 183n246
Orth, Ulrich, 94n51; 96n149
Osborn, Andrew, 283
Osborn, D., 183n227

Osborn, Denise, 94n72
Osgood, D. Wayne, 63n28; 65n105; 94n54;
    133n38; 178nn57, 59; 318; 338n92, 113
Osman, Suzanne, 388n134
Ostermann, Michael, 136n197; 183n220
Ostresh, Erik, 267n146
Ostrow, Miriam, 545n237
Ostrowsky, Michael, 230n204
Ouimet, Marc, 339n139; 386n69
Ouimette, Paige Crosby, 182n199
Ousey, Graham C., 45; 94nn55, 79; 226nn62,
    63; 301n63; 341n214
Owen, David, 427n23
Owen, Michael, 181n147
Owens, Cei Williams, 561
Owens, Coleen, 513
Owens, Elizabeth, 180n134
Owens, Jennifer Gatewood, 340n192; 382;
    391n308
Özdemir, Metin, 340n196
Özbay, Özden, 267n144
Özcan, Yusuf Ziya, 267n144

P

Pacifici, Laura, 513
Pahlavi, Mohammad Reza, 407
Paige, Karen, 178n74
Painter-Davis, Noah, 388n150
Palast, Greg, 300n42
Paletta, Damian, 578nn92, 93
Palfrey, Deborah Jeane ("D.C. Madam"), 504;
    515
Pallone, Nathaniel, 179nn97, 106
Palmer, Kimberly, 458n61
Pamer, Melissa, 427n9
Pan, En-Ling, 264n18
Panfil, Vanessa, 301n90
Panin, Aledsandr Andreevich, 551
Pantazis, Christina, 500n94
Papachristos, Andrew, 81; 95n110; 135n134;
    137n206; 351; 386n67
Papillo, Angela Romano, 267n155
Paquette, Mark, 5
Paradis, Emily, 93n30
Paramore, Vickie, 302n113
Pardini, Dustin, 181n141; 337nn70, 75;
    339nn135, 150
Pare, Paul-Philippe, 340n169
Park, Robert E., 189; 190; 198; 225nn13, 15, 16
Park, Yoonhwan, 226nn66, 69
Parker, Alison, 139; 380
Parker, Karen F., 45; 66nn126, 145; 225n36;
    316; 338n99
Parkin, William, 389n186
Parnell, Peter, 508
Parra, Gilbert, 543n163
Parrot, A., 387n121
Parrott, Caroline, 176n2
Parrott, Scott, 176n2
Parsons, Deborah, 303n159
Parsons, Jeffrey T., 544n193
Parsons, Patrick J., 179n90
Partikainen, Pekka, 64n81
Parvez, Faruque, 177n37
Paschall, Mallie, 66n148
Pasko, Lisa, 290; 302n118
Pastore, Ann, 230n245
Patchin, Justin, 225n42; 566; 567; 577nn67, 68
Paternoster, Raymond, 38; 63n32; 64n82;
    65n113; 94n38; 135n158; 136nn164, 170,

172; 229n201; 258; 265n51; 269n225;
    300n34; 301n88; 335nn11, 12, 27;
    336n52; 337nn71, 77, 79, 91; 338n116;
    340n194; 341n210
Patil, Sujata, 25n12
Pato, Carlos N., 526
Pato, Michele T., 526
Patrick, Patricia, 458n53
Pattavina, April, 227n117
Patterson, Gerald R., 335n23; 336n30; 337n57;
    385n32
Patterson, Orlando, 500n145
Pattison, Philippa, 184n251
Paul, Thomas, 541n42
Pauloi, Len, 389n203
Pauwels, Lieven, 133n39
Pawitan, Yudi, 181n153
Payne, Allison Ann, 267n149
Payne, Ed, 62n2
Payne, Gary, 229n190; 268n163
Payne, Monique, 225n40
Pearce, Matt, 62n1
Pearson-Nelson, Benjamin, 385n20
Pease, Ken, 95n77; 135n135; 459n96
Peck, Mitchell, 229n189
Pedneault, Amélie, 449
Peete, Thomas, 135n160
Pein, Liliana, 133n44
Pelham, Molina, Jr., 180n128
Pelham, William, Jr., 264n31
Peltonen, Kirsi, 93n21
Pelullo, Salvatore, 487
Pendleton, Hadiya, 215
Penrod, Steven, 388n145; 543n117
Pepinsky, Harold, 302n139
Pepler, Debra, 165
Perales, Angel, 397
Perea, Ignacio, 362
Perera, Frederica, 179n82
Perez, Cynthia, 335n13; 336n34; 545n209
Perez, Evan, 427n12
Peric, Mia, 544n194
Perkins, Elizabeth, 459n97
Perkins, Molly, 337n72
Perlmutter, M., 183n236
Perlroth, Nicole, 578n101
Persico, Nicola, 65n120
Persky, Aaron, 355
Peterson, Dana, 301n90
Peterson, David, 267n154
Peterson, Ruth, 66n141; 193; 195; 225nn35, 37;
    228nn126, 129
Petit, Hayley, 305
Petit, Jennifer, 305
Petit, Michaela, 305
Petit, William, Jr., 305
Petraeus, David, 564
Petraitis, John, 133n78; 544n164
Petras, Hanno, 336n47
Petras, Tricia, 384n2
Petrocelli, Matthew, 301nn76, 77
Petrosino, Anthony, 25n47; 303n148
Petrosino, Carolyn, 303n148
Petrossian, Gohar A., 134n109
Petryszyn, Daniel, 551
Pettit, Gregory, 227n115; 264n17; 264nn36, 38;
    337n65; 385n36
Petts, Richard, 238; 265n78
Phenix, Amy, 9
Philaretou, Andreas, 577n40

Philby, Kim, 401
Philibert, Robert A., 177n26; 180n135; 181n147
Philip, Michael, 66n140
Phillips, Coretta, 95n77; 459n96
Phillips, Julie A., 66n151; 225n41
Phillips, Matthew D., 264n28; 335n26
Phillips, Monte, 179n107
Phillips, Scott, 385n26
Phillips, Susan, 183n222
Phillips, Tim, 227n83
Phillips-Plummer, Lynanne, 542n85
Pi, Yijun, 229n200
Piaget, Jean, 166; 183n230
Pick, Lawrence, 387n114
Pickett, Kate, 177n30; 229n170
Piehl, Anne Morrison, 66n155
Pietz, Christina, 95n109
Piha, Jorma, 263n11
Pihl, Robert, 179n95
Piispa, Minna, 93n21
Piliavin, Irving, 249; 267nn132, 135
Pinckney, Clementa, 27
Pinderhughes, Ellen, 335n15
Pinel, Philippe, 141
Pinker, Steven, 347; 385n14
Piquero, Alex R., 63n33; 94n44; 135n150; 136nn174, 189; 178n64; 183nn221, 239; 184n287; 229nn190–192; 265n75; 269n218; 301nn76, 77; 302n 131; 316; 327; 335nn10, 27; 336nn35, 36, 43, 45; 338nn99, 100, 123, 128; 339nn141, 151; 340nn173, 174, 176, 180, 186, 187, 188, 199; 341nn205, 210; 542n82
Piquero, Nicole Leeper, 229n192; 230n212; 265n75; 267n128; 337n58; 340n175; 341n210; 501n154
Pitt, Brad, 432
Pittaro, Michael, 489
Pittman, David, 543n136
Pitts, Marian, 542n61
Piza, Eric, 95n110
Planells-Struse, Simón, 64n69
Planty, Michael, 63n8
Platt, Alyssa, 126
Platt, Anthony, 226n50; 300nn7, 23; 301n78
Platt, Jerome J., 543n155
Ploeger, Matthew, 65n108; 266nn97, 104, 105
Plomin, Robert, 181n168; 184n262
Plushnick-Masti, Ramit, 263n1
Podolsky, E., 178n51
Pogarsky, Greg, 135nn139, 140, 148, 155; 136nn164, 190; 339n140
Pogrebin, Mark, 267n130
Pogrebin, Robin, 541n16
Pokhrel, Pallay, 543n160
Pol Pot, 404
Polaschek, Devon, 541n44
Pole, Nnamdi, 96n134
Polge, A., 177n41
Polk, Kenneth, 230n244
Pollack, Harold A., 64n73
Pollack, Otto, 65n103
Pomeroy, Wardell, 388n140
Ponder, Michael, 301n64
Ponischil, Kristina, 73
Ponzi, Charles, 465
Poole, Eric, 267nn126, 130
Popkin, Susan, 93n12
Porat, Daniela, 386n70
Porche, Dianne, 501n153

Porteous, Lucy, 178n43
Porter, James, 510
Porter, Lauren, 264n26
Porter, Stephen, 388n141
Portnoy, Jill, 181nn141, 142; 339n135
Posick, Chad, 228n125; 337n91
Post, Charles, 180n119
Post, Jerrold M., 417; 428n79
Potter, Lloyd, 389n203
Potterat, John, 542nn85, 98
Pottieger, Anne, 525; 544nn177, 178
Poussin, Nicolas, 352
Powell, Andrea, 226n57
Powell, Michael, 457n29
Powers, Ráchael, 97n167
Pradai-Prat, D., 177n41
Pranis, Kay, 303n155
Prasad, Monica, 512; 542n62
Pratt, Travis C., 94n50; 95nn80, 93; 183n238; 265n86; 336n43; 339n141
Prendergast, Michael, 544n203
Presser, Lois, 303n167
Pribesh, Shana, 227n92
Price, Aubrey Lee, 466; 467
Price, Jamie, 226n72
Price, Virginia, 542n68
Pridemore, William Alex, 385n18
Prince (entertainer), 112; 521
Prince, Emily, 178n43
Prinz, Ronald, 177n40; 336n51
Pritchard, Adam, 389nn189, 192
Priyadarsini, S., 266n100
Proctor, Bernadette, 194
Proctor, Keith, 134n124
Proffitt, Fiona, 428n53
Prokupecz, Shimon, 427n12
Prom-Wormley, Elizabeth, 180n138
Propp, Jennifer, 386n42
Proulx, Jean, 134n97; 336nn48, 54
Pruitt, B.E., 184n255; 185n297
Pruitt, Matthew, 225n36
Prunella, Jill, 179n108
Puanghera, Jim, 300n36
Pugh, M.D., 267n160
Pugh, Meredith, 63n30
Pullmann, Michael, 183n217
Punter, Helen, 303n162
Putin, Vladimir, 283
Pyrooz, David, 335n17

Q

Qaiser, Saba, 366
Quercia, R.G., 227n108
Quetelet, L.A.J., 189; 223; 225nn9, 10
Quinet, Kenna Davis, 94n70; 389n211
Quinney, Richard, 277; 300n17; 301nn57, 58; 302nn139, 140; 498n23
Quinsey, Vernon, 459n117
Qureshi, Babar, 442

R

Raaijmakers, Quinten, 183n235
Rabasa, Angel, 428n58; 429n111
Rada, Richard, 388n140
Rader, Dennis, 367; 368
Radosevich, Marcia, 65n114; 266nn111, 112
Radosh, Polly, 303n153
Raffalovich, Lawrence, 64n80; 96n130; 226n70
Rafter, Nicole, 176nn4, 5; 177nn9, 10; 335n3
Raghavan, Chitra, 543n151

Raine, Adrian, 145; 148; 152; 174; 177n28; 178n44; 179nn96, 100; 180nn109, 110, 118; 181nn141–144; 182n191; 183n237; 184n256; 339n135; 341n208; 385n33
Raitt, F.E., 178n71
Raj, Anita, 391n259
Raley, R. Kelly, 66n150
Ramey, David, 255; 268n188
Ramsey, Elizabeth, 335n23
Ramsey, Susan, 93n32
Randa, Ryan, 63n11
Randall, Susan, 386n73
Range, Lillian, 93n26
Rangel, Charles, 260
Rankin, Bruce, 228n137
Rankin, Joseph, 63n25
Rapin, J., 177n41
Rapp, Geoffrey, 123
Rappley, Marsha D., 179n87
Ratahus, Spencer, 265n50
Ratchford, Marie, 338nn132, 134
Ratcliffe, Jerry, 64nn49, 62; 135n137
Rath, Saroj Kumar, 428n78
Rathouz, Paul, 264n31
Rathus, Spencer, 184n275; 267n127; 541n51
Raudenbush, Stephen W., 226n68; 227n105; 229n171
Rauh, Virginia, 148; 179n82
Rawlings, Robert, 179n107
Ray, James V., 336n44
Ray, Melvin, 268nn186, 191
Raymond, Kristen, 180n113
Reagan, Ronald, 84; 164
Realmuto, George, 265n96
Reaves, Brian, 545n223
Rebellon, Cesar, 229nn185, 192, 193; 263n14; 265n73; 268n171; 386n41; 544nn179, 181
Reboussin, Roland, 387n101
Rebovich, Donald, 135n138
Reckdenwald, Amy, 94n45
Recker, Nicholas, 337n84
Reckless, Walter, 189; 249; 267nn136, 137
Reddy, Marisa, 389n204
Reed, Elizabeth, 95n101
Reed, M.D., 268n174
Rees, Carter, 265n57
Rees, Stan, 545n236
Regnerus, Mark, 267n152
Regoeci, Wendy, 389n181
Regoli, Robert, 267n126
Reid, Joan, 337nn70, 76; 542n82
Reiman, Jeffery, 300n27
Reingle, Jennifer, 340nn181, 200
Reisig, Michael, 95n93; 227n94; 339n141
Reiss, Albert, Jr., 133n70; 226n72; 227n84; 249; 267n134; 499n78
Reitzel, Deborah, 96n150
Rekart, Michael, 542n90
Rell, M. Jodi, 305
Remy, Nicholas, 102
Ren, Xin, 265n58
Renauer, Brian, 230n249
Rengert, George, 97n166; 132n34; 133nn57, 60, 76; 136n174; 545n216
Rengifo, Andres, 45; 228n128
Renk, Kimberly, 302n109
Renner, Lynette, 264n40
Rennison, Callie Marie, 63n24; 117; 134n112; 459n104
Reno brothers, 433

Renzetti, Claire M., 366
Resick, Patricia, 65n110; 96n135
Resnick, Heidi, 94nn35, 36; 385n24; 386n77; 387n91
Restifo, Nicholas, 385n6
Restivo, Emily, 258; 269n224
Reuter, Peter, 544n189
Reyburn, Scott, 541n16
Reynolds, B.J., 180n115
Reynolds, Charles, 545n234
Reynolds, Matthew, 388n153
Reynolds, Morgan, 132n19
Reyns, Bradford W., 63n11
Reyos, Frank, 219
Rezendes, David Joseph, 564
Rheingold, Alyssa, 94nn35, 36
Rhodes, William, 517
Riach, James Clayton, 280
Ribaud, Denis, 95n89
Rice, Frances, 181n147
Rice, Leslie, 178n56
Rice, Stephen, 66n126; 338n127
Rich-Edwards, Janet W., 179n92
Rich, Karen, 96n145
Richards, Jeffery, 541nn52, 53
Richards, Maryse, 95n111; 96n113
Richardson, Alexandra, 177n38
Richardson, Clare, 389n199
Richardson, Deborah, 96n122
Richardson, Justin, 508
Richardson, Samuel, 352
Richman, Kimberly, 63n26
Richmond, F. Lynn, 230n244
Richter, Linda, 132n21
Ricketts, Melissa L., 340n172
Ridde, James, 338n107
Ridder, Elizabeth, 336nn37, 39
Riddle, David, 177n40
Rideout, Greta, 356
Rideout, John, 356
Ridulph, Maria, 362
Riess, Julie, 179n89
Riggs, Shelley, 182n204
Rijsdijk, Fruhling, 181n163
Rimland, Bernard, 177n22
Rimpelä, Matti, 182n214
Ringwalt, Chris, 545nn228, 229
Rinne, Thomas, 183n217
Risen, James, 395; 427n38
Risser, Jan, 542n77
Ritakallio, Minna, 182n214
Rivera, Craig, 268nn189, 196
Rizvi, Shireen, 65n110; 96n135
Robers, Simone, 94n58
Roberts, Aki, 64n75; 229n177
Roberts, Albert, 96nn141, 142
Roberts, Eric, 325
Roberts, Jennifer, 63n37
Roberts, Joel, 540n3
Roberts, John, Jr., 542n98
Roberts, Julia, 513
Roberts, Kathleen, 338n134
Roberts, M., 268n169
Roberts, Ron, 542n101
Robertson, Alison, 459n118
Robertson, Carrie A., 184n271
Robertson, Craig, 268n186
Robertson, Richard T., 177n29
Robespierre, Maximilien, 408
Robin, D.R., 180n115

Robin, Gerald, 388n158
Robin Hood, 432
Robins, Lee, 67n171
Robinson, Alexander, 241
Robinson, Beatrice, 93n28; 542n87
Robinson, James Wesley, 241
Robinson, Matthew, 133n74; 459n102
Robinson, Veronica, 147
Robinson, Zachary, 241
Roccato, Michele, 226n80
Roche, Declan, 303n168
Roche, M., 177n41
Rockefeller, John D., 474
Rocque, Michael, 174; 184n256; 300n34; 337n91
Rodek, Jelena, 544n194
Rodriguez, Nancy, 65n99
Roehl, Jan, 134n122
Roettger, Michael, 264n20; 337nn70, 74
Rogan, Dennis, 267n133
Rogers, Imogen, 177n29
Rogers, Joseph, 181nn146, 161
Rogers, Joseph Lee, 184n280
Rogers, Richard G., 228n151; 385n8
Rogosch, Fred, 264n39
Rogovin, Charles, 498n13; 499n73; 500n151
Rohde, Paul, 182n213
Rojek, Jeff, 66n125
Romano, Stephen, 391nn292, 294, 299
Romero-Daza, Nancy, 542n91
Roof, Dylann, 27; 28; 396
Roosevelt, Franklin, 10
Rose, Vicki McNickle, 386n73
Rosen, Andy, 357
Rosen, Daniel, 545n234
Rosenau, William, 428n58
Rosenbaum, Dennis P., 93n12; 97n165; 545nn226, 228, 229
Rosenbaum, James, 227n98
Rosenbaum, Jill Leslie, 268n172
Rosenberg, Charles, 390n253
Rosenfeld, Richard, 45; 63n40; 64n83; 66n125; 133n56; 208; 209; 225n6; 227n118; 228nn152, 158, 159; 229n164
Rosenmerkel, Sean, 499n88
Rosenthal, Lawrence, 227n91
Roshier, Bob, 132n10
Ross, Catherine E., 227n92
Ross, Edward Alsworth, 462; 474; 498n5
Ross, Jeffrey Ian, 300nn37, 44, 52; 427n2
Ross, Mark, 16
Ross, Michael, 542n77
Rossi, Peter, 114; 134n87; 545n224
Roth, Byron, 156; 182n182
Roth, Gerhard, 385n10
Roth, Loren, 177n27
Roth, Randolph, 10
Rothe, Dawn L., 300n37
Rothenberg, Richard, 542n85
Rotton, James, 48; 64n68
Rountree, Meredith Martin, 123
Rountree, Pamela Wilcox, 94n39; 97n162; 227n82
Rowe, Alan, 135n153
Rowe, David, 65n112; 179n103; 181nn146, 161, 164, 165; 184n280; 318; 338nn113, 115
Rowe, Richard, 182n211
Rowland, Meghan, 184n272
Rowling, J.K., 508
Royer, Marie-Noele, 132n28; 133n61

Ruben, Alan, 177n34
Rubenfeld, Jed, 388n128
Rubens, Sonia, 182n210
Ruby, Charles, 428n74
Ruchkin, Vladislav, 264n34
Rucklidge, Julia, 180n121
Rudo-Hutt, Anna, 181n142
Rudolph, Jennifer, 229n168; 335n21
Rugala, Eugene A., 391nn292, 294, 299
Ruggiero, Kenneth J., 385n24; 386n77; 387n91
Ruiter, Stijn, 95n73; 133nn39, 84
Rupp, Thomas, 135n149
Ruppert, Carol, 267n127
Rusche, George, 275
Rush, Benjamin, 142
Rushton, J. Philippe, 155; 182n179; 185n290
Russell, Diana, 358; 373; 387n121; 388nn136, 137, 145; 390n243
Russo, Silvia, 226n80
Rutter, Michael, 337n64
Ruvolo, Julie, 577n41
Ryan, George, 389n203; 469
Ryan, Joseph, 184n289
Ryan, Kimberly, 95n94
Ryan, Patrick, 385n21

S

Sabol, William, 137n202
Sachs, Carolyn, 374
Sadd, Susan, 230n250
Sadler, Richard Casey, 178n79
Sagarin, E., 543n140
Sageman, Marc, 417; 428nn80, 82
Said, Yaser Abdel, 366
Sakheim, George, 459n116
Salahaydn, Salah, 69
Salas, Michael, 330
Salekin, Randall, 385n8
Salfati, C. Gabrielle, 541n7
Salihovic, Selma, 340nn178, 196
Sallmann, Jolanda, 516; 542nn88, 97
Saltafi, Gabrielle, 390n223
Saltzman, Linda, 136n172; 389n191
Samaha, Joel, 25n30
Samakouri, Maria, 384n5
Sami, Nilofar, 180n134
Sample, Barry, 66n140
Sample, Lisa, 302n114
Sampson, Robert J., 133n63; 177n18; 181n152; 226nn54, 68; 227nn104, 111, 121; 228nn135, 137, 140, 144, 152; 229n171; 230n240; 268n202; 269nn216, 217; 306; 312; 313; 314; 315; 317; 318; 319; 333; 334; 335nn6, 7, 24; 337nn67–69, 88; 386n59
Samuelson, Leslie, 268n170
Sanborn, Josh, 498n22
Sanchez, Ray, 62n2
Sanders, Bernie, 271
Sanders, Teela, 514; 542nn69, 72
Saner, Hilary, 544n189
Sanger, David E., 573; 578n89
Sansone, Lori, 93n26
Sansone, Randy, 93n26
Santhiveeran, Janaki, 542n83
Santora, Marc, 428n39
Santtila, Pekka, 459n119
Sarat, Austin, 427n16
Sargent, W., 178n50
Sarkar, N.N., 93n25

Sarkar, Rina, 93n25
Saunders, Benjamin, 93n20; 385n24
Savage, Charlie, 300n45; 395
Savolainen, Jukka, 180n133; 229n169; 263n12; 338n104
Scanlon, Barbara, 542n68
Scarfo, Nicodemo "Nicky", Jr., 487
Scarpa, Angela, 93n17
Scarpitti, Frank, 267n137
Schackelford, Todd, 181n148
Schaefer, Catherine, 179n91
Schaefer, David R., 65n99
Schaefer, Diane, 303n157
Schaeffer, Cindy, 336n47
Schaeffer, Rebecca, 19
Schafer, Joseph, 226n75
Schafer, Stephen, 11; 63n14; 78; 95n82; 427n6
Schafer, Walter, 230n244
Schaible, Lonnie, 229n165; 386n68
Scharf, P., 183n232
Scheck, Barry, 282
Schedlowski, Manfred, 541n42
Scheinberger-Olwig, Renate, 386n74
Schenck, Christopher, 500n111
Scheuerman, Leo, 227nn102, 103
Schiffer, Boris, 541n42
Schiller, Lawrence, 427n25
Schlaupitz, Sheila, 302n124
Schlegel, Alexander, 184n263
Schlegel, Kip, 498n8; 499n82
Schlesinger, Traci, 66nn127, 134
Schmid, Alex, 405
Schmidt, Janell, 267n133
Schmidt, Melinda G., 341n219
Schmidt, Nicole M., 268n195; 335n26; 338n94
Schmucker, Martin, 178n60
Schmutte, Pamela, 184n277
Schnapp, Patrick, 66n157
Schnebly, Stephen M., 227n108
Schneider, Jacqueline, 336n41
Schnepp, Allison Champney, 178n79
Schoenthaler, Stephen, 178n45
Schofield, Thomas J., 263n10
Schollenberger, Janet, 374
Schrag, Clarence, 64n50; 230n226
Schreck, Christopher, 94nn54, 55; 95n91
Schroeder, Ryan, 338n106; 340n179
Schubert, Carol, 63n33
Schulenberg, John, 338n92; 543n146
Schumacher, Michael, 59; 66n163
Schur, Edwin, 268n179
Schutt, Russell, 65n115
Schwab-Stone, Mary, 264n34
Schwartz, Joseph A., 181n148; 182n175; 184nn272, 288
Schwartz, Martin D., 301nn84, 87; 302n104; 388nn135, 143, 164
Schwartz, Seth, 428nn83–85
Schwendinger, Herman, 63n45; 301nn89, 96
Schwendinger, Julia, 63n45; 301nn89, 96
Schworm, Peter, 357
Sciutto, Jim, 427n37
Scott, Austin, 389n174; 457nn30, 31; 458nn78, 88, 89
Scott, Peter, 176n7
Seale, Bobby, 410
Sealock, Miriam, 65n117; 230n212
Seddig, Daniel, 264n46
Seeley, John R., 182n213
Seffers, George I., 578n86

Seffrin, Patrick, 96n145; 268n167
Segal, David, 457n29
Segal, Nancy, 181n164
Seguin, Jean, 179n95
Seidel, Jon, 498n18
Seidman, Robert, 277; 300n16
Sekulic, Damir, 544n194
Sellars, James, 25n35
Sellers, Christine S., 265n86; 266n115; 302n124; 374
Sellers, Courtenay, 183n225
Sellin, Thorsten, 58; 59; 62; 66nn158, 159; 215; 230nn214–217; 335n8
Selyukh, Alina, 499n46
Sepper, Elizabeth, 427n35
Serra, Susan, 385n6
Seto, Michael, 543n117
Severance, Charles, 17
Sevigny, Eric, 349; 385n27
Sewell, Kenneth, 385n8
Shachmurove, Yochanan, 459nn99, 100
Shackelford, Todd, 389nn182, 183
Shadid, Anthony, 427n5; 428n70
Shah, Saleem, 177n27
Shahin, Emad El-Din, 283
Shakespeare, William, 352
Shallwani, Pervaiz, 429n101
Shane, Jon, 119; 135n131; 183n225
Shane, Scott, 427n38
Shannon, Lyle, 66n161
Shannon, Sarah, 535; 545n241
Shapira, Nathan, 336n33
Sharkey, Patrick, 228n143
Sharp, Susan, 229n189
Sharpe, Reginald, 551
Sharps, Phyllis, 374
Shattuck, Molly, 510
Shatz, Naomi, 389n190
Shatz, Steven, 389n190
Shavers, Trendon, 464
Shaw, Clifford R., 189; 198–201; 205; 221; 223; 226nn49, 51, 52
Shaw, Daniel, 264n21; 266n87
Shaw, Jazz, 540n6
Shdaimah, Corey S., 290; 302n120
Shedd, Carla, 225n40
Sheikh, Pervaze A., 500nn100, 105
Shelden, Randall, 302n115
Sheldon, William, 141; 142–143; 177n15
Shelley, Louise I., 280; 300n41; 500n134
Shelly, Peggy, 133n77
Shen, Aril Chiung-Tao, 390n248
Shen, Ce, 183n225
Shenon, Philip, 542n78
Shepard, Matthew, 379
Shepherd, Joanna, 123
Shepherd, Jonathan, 336n35
Sheppard, David, 95n107
Sher, Kenneth, 543n163
Sherman, Lawrence W., 126; 129; 267n133; 303n164
Sherman, William, 457n29
Shermer, Lauren O'Neill, 339n164
Sherrer, Margaret, 183n225
Shevlin, Mark, 93n23
Shields, Ian, 266n125
Shields, Ryan, 9
Shifley, Rick, 303n154
Shihadeh, Edward S., 226n67
Shipley, Bernard, 136n182

Shipman, Harold Frederick, 367
Shirazi, Ali Memar Mortazavi, 280
Shively, Michael, 517
Shoesmith, Gary L., 44; 45
Shoichet, Catherine, 391n290
Short, James, 64n76; 263n8; 266n125
Short, M.B., 63n48
Short, Tamsin B.R., 183n228
Shotland, R. Lance, 387n107
Shover, Neal, 133n48; 452; 453; 457nn8–10; 459n107; 495; 501n148
Showers, Carolin, 65n106
Shrout, Patrick, 268n184
Shteir, Rachel, 348n39
Shubert, Atika, 387n85
Shum, David, 180n111
Shutt, J. Eagle, 338n134
Sieder, Jill Jordan, 458n51
Siegel, Jane, 93n27; 390n247
Siegel, Larry, 63n14; 181n140; 184n275; 267n127
Sieleni, Bruce, 180n131
Sieler, DeDe, 183n217
Siennick, Sonja E., 264n45; 338n92; 340n201
Sigfusdottir, I.D., 178n42
Silbereisen, Ranier, 340n198
Silberman, Matthew, 135n158
Silke, Andrew, 399; 428nn47, 72
Sillanmäki, Lauri, 263n11
Silva, David, 397
Silva, Julie, 180n132
Silva, Manori, 179n81
Silva, Phil, 67n171; 179n94; 182nn192, 200; 184n277; 335n18; 336nn29, 49; 337n64; 341nn215, 216
Silver, Clayton, 263n9
Silver, Eric, 183n223; 228nn142, 147
Silver, Sheldon, 398; 469
Silverman, Eli B., 31; 63n17
Silverman, Jay G., 391n259
Silverman, Jenna, 263n9
Silverman, Robert, 267n157
Silverman, Teresa, 230n213
Simi, Pete, 180n120
Simister, John, 64n67; 178n68
Simmons, Catherine, 543n118
Simmons, Keith Franklin, 464–465
Simon, David, 499n76
Simon, Lenore, 63n29
Simon, Leonore M.J., 180n127; 337n78
Simon, Rita, 25n10; 65n111
Simon, Thomas, 389n203
Simons, Leslie Gordon, 182n206; 339n166
Simons, Marlise, 386n82
Simons, Ronald L., 155; 177n26; 180n135; 181n147; 182n206; 217; 268n190; 317; 318; 337nn90, 91; 338n108–112; 339nn153, 155, 166; 385n37; 386n49
Simos, Alexander, 385n6
Simpson, John, 302n122
Simpson, M.K., 185nn293, 294
Simpson, Murray, 185nn293, 294
Simpson, Nicole Brown, 71
Simpson, O.J., 71; 282
Simpson, Sally, 65n117; 230n206
Sims, Barbara, 300nn19, 29
Sinai, Cave, 178nn56, 67
Singer, Jane, 459n115
Singer, Merrill, 542n91
Singer, Simon, 302n127

Tait, David, 388nn135, 143
Tajima, Emiko, 94n48; 385n30
Talbot, Margaret, 299n2
Tallichet, Suzanne, 385n11
Tamminen, Tuulk, 263n11
Tan, Jo-Pei, 229n197
Tandon, Darius, 183n226
Tang, Deliang, 179n82
Tannenbaum, Frank, 256; 269n205
Tanner-Smith, Emily, 95n103
Tarde, Gabriel, 157; 182n195
Tardiff, Kenneth, 226n71; 386n64
Tark, Jongyeon, 89; 97n169
Tatchell, Renny, 341n220
Tatchell, Thomas, 341n220
Taub, Richard, 195
Taub, Robert, 469
Taylor, Alan, 181n163
Taylor, Bruce, 94n40; 135n136
Taylor, Ian, 276; 286; 300n14; 301nn81, 82
Taylor, J.L., 180n129
Taylor, John, 459n118
Taylor, Julie, 266n93
Taylor, M., 459n114
Taylor, Mark Lewis, 293; 303n144
Taylor, Mary Jane, 545n235
Taylor, Natalie, 498n12
Taylor, Ralph, 133n70; 226n58; 227nn88, 116, 152
Taylor, Robert, 134n116
Taylor, Terrance, 94n52; 217; 265n58
Taylor, Wendy, 134nn104, 118
Tcherni, Maria, 576n4
Teaar, Morgan, 165
Tekin, Erdal, 386n44
Telep, Cody, 45
Templer, Donald I., 185n290
Teplin, Linda, 25n17
Terrill, William, 227n94
Testa, Maria, 387nn92, 97, 110
Tewksbury, Richard, 9; 133n67; 391n263; 544n188
Thapar, Anita, 181n147
Thatcher, Robert, 179n102
Thaxton, Sherod, 229nn192, 193
Theall, Katherine, 545n232
Theerathorn, Pochara, 134n107
Theisen, Gary, 543n141
Theobald, Delphine, 340n174
Thomas, Gail, 387n113
Thomas, John M., 499n78
Thomas, Kyle J., 38; 63n32; 265n61; 339nn142, 146
Thomas, Melvin, 66n147
Thomas, Stuart, 183n228
Thomas, Suzie Dod, 302n104
Thomas, W.I., 13; 190
Thomlinson, R. Paul, 95n109
Thompson, Craig, 508
Thompson, Ginger, 542n78
Thompson, Kevin, 302nn127, 128
Thompson, Martie, 182n216
Thompson, Melissa, 109; 132n31; 133nn43, 46
Thompson, Rebecca, 459n106
Thornberry, Terence P., 63n31; 65n116; 67n167; 181n158; 230n203; 264nn28, 37; 265nn51, 52, 65; 266nn89, 103; 269n216; 312; 337n61; 543n152
Thorne, Ian, 459n118
Thornton, Omar, 380

Thrasher, Frederick, 189; 190; 225n13
Thurman, Quint, 440; 457n27; 458n44
Tibbetts, Stephen, 267n128; 338n123; 341n210; 501n154
Tierney, Kevin, 543n157
Tierney, Laura, 517
Tifft, Larry, 291; 302nn135, 136, 138
Tilley, Nick, 459n106
Tillyer, Marie Skubak, 51; 65n100; 74; 77; 94nn47, 57, 59, 71; 95n90; 133n71
Tillyer, Rob, 51; 65nn100, 118; 74; 94n57
Timko, Christine, 96n134
Timmendequas, Jesse, 8; 20; 90; 91
Timpson, Sandra, 542n77
Tita, George, 63n48; 95n103; 384n2
Titchener, Edward, 166
Titterington, Victoria B., 94n62; 302n111; 389n212; 390nn215, 216, 218
Tittle, Charles R., 64n77; 135n153; 226n44; 230n242; 263n4; 265n55; 269nn215, 222; 321; 339nn139, 146, 152, 159
Tjaden, Patricia, 391n301
Tobias, J.J., 457nn5, 6
Tobias, Randall L., 504
Tobin, Kimberly, 134n92
Tobin, Michael, 179n89
Tobin, Terri, 126
Tobler, Nancy, 341n221
Toby, Jackson, 301n73
Toch, Hans, 183n229
Todd, Petra, 65n120
"Tokyo Rose" (pseudonym), 400
Tolar, Melinda, 471
Tomaskovic-Devey, Donald, 63n36
Tomasovic, Elizabeth, 385n26
Tombs, Steve, 500n94
Tompson, Lisa, 64n60
Tonry, Michael, 71; 93n8; 132n16; 133n70; 177n27; 182n177; 226n72; 227n84; 264n47; 300n18; 301n74; 319; 335n9; 390n225; 543n119
Tontodonato, Pamela, 96n155
Toomey, Patrick, 568
Topalli, Volkan, 248; 391nn264, 271; 458nn56, 71
Towns-Miranda, Luz, 459n116
Townsend, Reanne, 387n113
Townsley, Michael, 133n84
Tracy, Paul, 60; 65nn101, 116; 67nn168, 169; 136n180
Tracyjan, Marc, 95n98
Travis, Alan, 576n2
Travis, Lawrence, 136n195
Trebach, Arnold, 543n134
Treiber, Kyle, 228n145
Trejo, Danny, 325
Tremblay, Pierre, 133n44; 265nn84, 85
Tremblay, Richard, 67n170; 179n95; 336n50; 337n65; 339n139
Treno, Andrew, 227n95
Trickett, Alan, 94n72
Triplett, Ruth, 228n123; 269n213
Tripodi, Stephen, 544n186
Tristan, Jennifer, 264n43
Truman, Jennifer L., 63n8; 64n51; 93n2; 94n56; 387n88; 390n237; 457n2
Trumbetta, Susan, 387n101
Trump, Donald, 209; 271; 299n1; 404
Tsarnaev, Dzhokar, 4; 413–414; 415; 418
Tsarnaev, Tamerlan, 4; 413–414; 415; 418

Tseloni, Andromachi, 459n106
Tseng, Li-Jung, 544n165
Tsetkova, Bilyana, 500n137
Tsoutis, Anastasios, 136n191
Tuch, Steven, 66n139
Tunnell, Kenneth, 133n64; 242; 266n102; 544n185
Turanovic, Jillian J., 94n50; 95nn80, 93
Turic, Darko, 181n147
Turner, Alezandria, 183n226
Turner, Brock, 355
Turner, Heather, 93n20; 94nn61, 63
Turner, Michael G., 65n113; 95n100; 181n150; 387n111; 391n306
Turpin-Petrosino, Carolyn, 25n47
Tyler, Kimberly, 79; 95n95; 387n108; 544n173
Tyler, Tom R., 501n155
Tzavaras, Nikos, 384n5
Tzoumakis, Stacy, 340n177

U

Uchida, Craig, 226n77
Uggen, Christopher, 109; 132n31; 133nn43, 46; 264n27; 302nn126, 131; 337n89; 535; 545n241
Ullman, Harlan K., 504
Ullman, Sarah, 387n100
Ulman, Arina, 373; 390n250
Ulmer, Jeffery T., 386n51; 457n24
Ulrich, Yvonne, 374
Umhau, John, 179n107
Unfold, Douglas, 459n117
Unger, Jennifer, 543n160
Unnever, James, 263n7; 301n63; 339n162
Urban, Lynn, 184n289

V

Vaccaro, Donato, 544n166
Vader Ven, Thomas, 264n15
Vaillant, George, 319
Valentino-Devries, Jennifer, 578nn92, 93
Valiente, Carlos, 181n145
Valier, Claire, 226n53
Van Daele, Stijn, 459n105
van de Rakt, Marieke, 264n20
van den Bergle, Pierre, 177n17
Van den Bree, Marianne, 181n147
van den Oord, Edwin, 184n280
van der Geest, Victor, 340n195
van der Laan, Peter, 341n211
van der Staak, Cees, 177n39
van Dijk, Mirjam, 388n142
van Dongen, Josanne, D.M., 340nn184, 197
van Dusen, Katherine Teilmann, 66n160
van Geen, Alexander, 177n37
van Gelder, Jean-Louis, 95n89; 340n168
Van Goozen, Stephanie, 178nn46, 66
van Gundy, Karen, 268n171; 386n41; 544nn179, 181
Van Hasselt, Vincent, 391nn292, 294, 299
Van Hentig, Hans, 78
van Hoof, Anne, 183n235
Van Horn, M. Lee, 267n147
van Kammen, Wemoet, 265n63; 340n203
Van Koppen, Peter, 391n261
van Koppen, Peter J., 375
van Marle, Hjalmar J.C., 340nn184, 197
van Schellen, Marieke, 338n101
van Voorhis, Patricia, 267nn145, 148; 303n167
van Wormer, Katherine, 385n9

Vander Beken, Tom, 459n105
Vander Ven, Thomas, 264n15; 267n159
VanDeusen, Karen, 543n117
Vandeviver, Christophe, 459n105
VanEseltine, Matthew, 338n92
Vanzile-Tamsen, Carol, 387nn92, 97
Varano, Sean, 225n42; 226n77
Vardi, Nathan, 577n73
Vargas, Elizabeth, 379
Vashista, Anish, 498n29
Vasquez, Bob Edward, 135n127
Vaughn, Michael, 181n150; 184nn252, 261; 339nn143, 144
Vavilova, Yelena, 400
Vazsonyi, Alexander, 65n112; 338n115
Veach-White, Ernie, 183n217
Velasquez, Eva, 576n30
Velez, Maria, 225n35; 228nn127, 129
Venables, Peter, 178n44; 181n144; 183n237
Veneziano, Carol, 183n234
Veneziano, Louis, 183n234
Venkatesh, Sudhir Alladi, 125; 136n175; 340n171
Verhulst, Frank, 341n211
Verlur, D.E., 544n168
Vermeiren, Robert, 264n34; 341n210
Vermeule, Adrian, 123; 130; 137n209
Veysey, Bonita, 183n225
Victor, Timothy, 25n46
Victorino, Troy, 330
Viding, Essi, 180n112; 184n262
Vieno, Alessio, 226n80
Vieraitis, Lynne, 123; 229n176; 289; 301n101
Villaume, Alfred, 303n145
Villemez, Wayne, 64n77
Vinkers, David, 183n217
Virkkunen, Matti, 178n53; 179n94
Visher, Christy, 385n30
Visser, Susanna, 180nn123, 124, 126
Vitaro, Frank, 337n65
Vitter, David, 504; 515
Vogel, Matt, 545n207
Volavka, Jan, 177n27; 179n105; 183n218
Vold, George, 275; 276
von Hentig, Hans, 11; 25n16; 78; 95n82
von Hirsch, Andrew, 130; 137nn210, 211
von Koppen, Peter, 134n89
Voronin, Yuri A., 500n134
Voss, Harwin, 65n114
Vossekuil, Bryan, 389n204
Vowell, Paul, 266n90
Vuchinich, S., 337n57
Vugkhanching, Martha, 543n163

W

Wachtveitl, Jerad, 372
Wade, Emily, 264n43
Wade, Terry, 484
Wadsworth, Tim, 45
Wager, Laura, 264nn36, 38; 385n36
Wagner, Charles, 459n116
Wagner, H. Ryan, 183n224
Wahlberg, Mark, 432
Waite, Phillip, 341n220
Wakschlag, Lauren, 177n30
Waldo, Gordon, 135n158; 136n172
Waldock, Katherine, 537; 543n150; 545n245
Walfield, Scott, 9
Walker, Alice, 506; 541n22
Walker, Jeffery T., 135n127

Walker, Richard, 576n27
Walker, Robert, 391n311
Walker-Rodriguez, Amanda, 489
Wall, Johnny Brickman, 77
Wallace, Cameron, 294
Wallace, Danielle, 226n80
Wallace, Harry, 135n161
Wallace, John, 544n171
Wallace, Johnny, 294
Wallace, Rodrick, 226n47
Wallerstedt, John, 136n196
Walsh, Anthony, 177n24; 178nn62, 65; 229n195; 388n131
Walsh, Marilyn, 457nn7, 21, 22, 25
Waltermaurer, Eve, 389n188
Walters, Billy, 468
Walters, Glenn, 181n173; 183n240; 266n91; 337n58
Walters, Mikel, 391n304
Walton, Paul, 276; 300n14
Walz, Liz, 302n133
Wang, Hongyu, 265n62
Wang, Jichuan, 544n197
Wang, Morgan, 64n64
Wanson, Jeffrey, 183n224
Ward, Adam, 139; 380
Ward, Clifford, 388n170
Ward, David A., 132n20; 183n244; 339n159
Ward, Jeffrey, 95n90; 340n170
Ward, Tony, 183n243; 184n251
Waring, Elin, 136n185; 499n87
Warner, Barbara, 63n39; 225n24; 227n97; 386n52
Warner, David, 93n31; 94n68
Warner, John O., 178n43
Warner, Tara, 93n31
Warr, Mark, 65n108; 265n67; 266nn98, 104, 105; 316; 338nn97, 98; 387n96
Warren, Janet, 387n101
Washington, George, 394
Wasilchick, John, 132n34; 133n57
Wasserman, Gail, 177n37
Waterman, Alan, 428nn83–85
Watts, Stephen, 229n187
Weatherburn, Don, 96n126; 337n82; 459n108
Weaver, John, 25n24
Webb, Nancy, 459n116
Weber, Eugen, 132n4
Webster, Cheryl Marie, 135n157
Webster, Daniel, 374
Webster, Pamela, 338n93
Wechsberg, Wendee, 542n77
Weekes-Shackelford, Viviana, 389nn182, 183
Weeks, Margaret, 542n91
Weerman, Frank, 133n39; 265n73
Wei, Evelyn, 545n206
Weihe, P., 177n33
Weiner, Anthony, 256; 505
Weiner, Neil Alan, 541n38
Weingart, Saul, 545n226
Weis, Joseph, 184n275
Weisburd, David, 45; 64n59; 118; 134n120; 135nn132, 133; 136n185; 228n131; 498n8; 499n87
Weiser, Benjamin, 458n83
Weisheit, Ralph, 543n133
Weiss, Alexander, 66n137
Weiss, P., 458n77
Weist, Mark, 388n153
Weitekamp, Elmar, 265n58; 341n207

Weitlauf, Julie, 542n89
Weitzer, Ronald, 66n139; 94n53; 351; 386n62; 518; 542nn99, 107
Welch, Brandon, 63n46
Welch, Michael, 135n160
Welchans, Sarah, 25n39
Wells, L. Edward, 63n25
Wellsmith, Melanie, 96nn120, 131; 132n27
Welsh, Brandon C., 39; 96n124; 134nn123, 125; 135n138; 174; 184n256; 228n125
Welte, John, 543n153
Wenk, Ernst, 65n89
Wentworth, Jennifer, 388n159
Wesselman, Kristina, 362
West, Donald J., 66n162; 181nn154, 155; 264n22
West, Valerie, 301n70
Western, Bruce, 269n208
Westervelt, Saundra, 282
Westmoreland, Patricia, 151; 180n131
Whaley, Rachel Bridges, 388n139
Wharton, Tracy, 266n93
Whatley, Mark, 388n155
Wheeler, J.R., 180n129
Wheeler, Kristin, 517
Wheeler, Stanton, 499n87
Whichard, Corey, 340n201
Whipple, Diane, 362
Whitbeck, Les, 387n108; 544n173
White, Garland, 133nn72, 73
White, Gentry, 133n84
White, Helene, 544n180; 545nn206, 208
White, Jennifer, 67n171
White, John, 544n195
White, Megan, 543n157
White, Norman, 267n150; 339n141
White, Rob, 300n28; 478; 498n2; 500nn93, 104
Whitehall, George, 266n125
Whitehead, Ralph, 179n82
Whitman, Charles, 369
Whitman, Terry, 390n220
Whitney, Stephen, 385n30
Whittinger, Naureen, 181n147
Whyatt, Robin, 179n82
Whyte, Carrie, 459n119
Whyte, Laurence, 459n119
Whyte, William F., 38; 63n44
Wiatrowski, M., 268n169
Wickes, Rebecca, 66n130; 227n110
Widaman, Keith F., 263n10
Widom, Cathy Spatz, 93n24; 94nn45, 46; 264n41; 349; 350; 385n39; 386n40
Wiederman, Michael, 93n26
Wiersema, Brian, 93n4
Wiesner, Margit, 337n58; 340n198
Wijkman, Miriam, 541n46
Wikstrom, Per-Olof H., 228n145; 341n209
Wilbur, Del Quentin, 429n103
Wilcox, Pamela, 94nn59, 71, 79; 133n71; 341n214
Wilczak, Andrew, 94n68
Wild, Jack, 433
Wilens, Timothy, 180n132
Wiley, Stephanie Ann, 258; 269n219
Wilkes, Nicole, 387nn116, 117
Wilkinson, Deanna, 545nn228, 229
Wilkinson, Paul, 428n42
Wilkinson, Richard, 229n170
Wilkinson, Tracy, 545n220

Williams, Bryce, 380
Williams, Cathy, 177n29
Williams, Dominic P., 178n42
Williams, Kirk, 389n193
Williams, Linda, 93n27; 366; 390n247
Williams, Marian, 66n138
Williams, Mark, 183n237; 542n77
Williams, Michael, 521
Williams, Stephanie, 267n155
Williams, Stephanie Hall, 264n31
Williams, Wendol, 179n107
Willis, Katie, 375; 376
Willits, Dale, 64n75; 229n177
Wills, Thomas Ashby, 544n166
Wilson, David, 66n123; 301n65
Wilson, Edmund O., 143; 174; 177n20
Wilson, James Q., 63n41; 65nn93, 94; 104; 105;
    130; 132nn14, 15, 26; 134n100; 136n177;
    146; 178n54; 200; 226n60; 230n243; 320;
    334; 338nn117–119
Wilson, Margo, 95n86; 156; 182nn177, 178,
    183–185; 227n85; 228n149; 229n171;
    390n241
Wilson, William Julius, 81; 96n117; 194; 195;
    200; 228n137; 386n59
Wilt, Susan, 374; 389n188
Wilzek, Alexander, 178n56
Windle, Michael, 337n58
Winehouse, Amy, 111
Winfree, L. Thomas, Jr., 265n86; 266n115
Wingood, Gina, 336n32
Winick, Charles, 542nn70, 73
Winston, Jameis, 80
Winston, Kenyatta, 219
Winter, Jeanette, 508
Wirth, Louis, 190; 225n13
Wish, Eric, 267n131
Wislar, Joseph S., 63n35
Wissow, Lawrence, 264n39; 385n34
Wittebrood, Karin, 94n70; 96n123
Wittrock, Stacy, 226n59
Wofford, Sharon, 339n149
Wolak, Janis, 577n56
Wolf, Jim, 576n28
Wolfe, Barbara, 151; 180n130
Wolfe, Scott, 339n141
Wolfendale, Jessica, 427n35
Wolfers, Justin, 122; 123
Wolff, Mary, 179n81
Wolfgang, Marvin E., 6; 9; 25nn3, 13; 37; 58;
    59; 62; 65n116; 66nn158–160; 67n167;
    95n83; 132n9; 306; 307; 327; 333; 335n8;
    351; 386n57
Wolfner, G.D., 390n240
Wolraich, Mark, 180nn123, 124, 126
Won, Christopher Wong, 16
Wong, Stephen, 170
Wong, Virginia, 177n36
Wood, Eric, 182n204
Wood, Peter, 132n26; 134n100; 136n188;
    339n139
Wooden, Wayne, 454; 459n120

Woodhouse, Donald, 542n98
Woods, Daniel, 135n136
Woods, Jordan Blair, 301n90
Woods, Katherine, 66n146
Woodworth, George, 123
Woolford, Andrew, 300n6
Wooton, Barbara, 181n152
Wormith, J. Stephen, 184n257
Worrall, John, 228n139; 459n112
Wortham, Thomas, III, 48
Wortham, Thomas, IV, 48
Wortley, Richard, 134n96
Wosick-Correa, Kassia, 388n168
Woyke, Elizabeth, 577n38
Wozniak, John F., 302n134; 303n169
Wright, Alexis, 108
Wright, Bradley E., 265n77; 331; 335n18;
    336n29; 341nn215, 216
Wright, Cynthia Pfaff, 63n36
Wright, Emily M., 94n47; 386n45, 46
Wright, James, 94n66; 114; 134n87
Wright, John Paul, 143; 177n21; 179n99;
    181n149; 182n175; 184n289; 229n199;
    230n203; 264nn15, 29; 337n69; 338n133;
    340n189
Wright, Michelle, 389n198
Wright, Rex, 165
Wright, Richard, 111; 133nn56, 68, 81; 376;
    391nn264, 266, 271; 450; 453; 458n71;
    459n109
Wright, Robert O., 179n92
Wrightsman, Lawrence S., 387nn109, 120, 123
Wu, Lawrence, 229n194
Wunderlich, Ray, 178n76
Wundt, Wilhelm, 166
Wung, Phen, 340n203
Wuornos, Aileen, 368
Wyckoff, Laura, 134n109
Wyler, Liana Sun, 500nn100, 105
Wymer, Michael, 101; 102

X

Xie, Min, 63n9; 93n14
Xu, Xiao, 374

Y

Yadron, Danny, 578nn92, 93
Yager, Tom, 577n72
Yamamoto, T., 179n104
Yan, Holly, 428n60
Yang, Bijou, 428n75
Yang, Yaling, 179n96
Yanukovych, Viktor, 283
Yar, Majid, 576n11
Yaryura-Tobias, J.A., 178n52
Ybarra, Michele, 577n56
Ye, Fei, 403
Yeager, Peter, 499n45
Yeisley, Mark, 229n176
Yeudall, L.T., 180n117
Yeung, W. Jean, 225n28
Yildirim, Baris, 184n269

Yili, Xu, 226n76
Yllo, K., 387n122
Yodanis, Carrie, 302n110
You, Sukkyung, 165
Young, Amy, 544n172
Young, Douglas, 544n186
Young, Jacob, 265n73; 338n127
Young, Jock, 276; 286; 300n14; 301nn79, 80, 83
Young, Kimball, 184n282
Young, Lawrence, 184n275
Younts, Wesley, 266n94
Youstin, Tasha, 134n115
Yu, Lilly, 513

Z

Zaalberg, Ap, 177n39
Zaff, Jonathan, 267n155
Zahnow, Renee, 66n130; 227n110
Zalman, Marvin, 25n35
Zara, Georgia, 340n202
Zarqawi, Abu Musab al-, 412
Zarroli, Jim, 458n63
Zatz, Marjorie, 269n209
Zavala, Egbert, 386n41
Zawacki, Tina, 385n25
Zayed, Z.A., 179n105
Zaykoswki, Heather, 63n13
Zedong, Mao, 492
Zeedyk, M.S., 178n71
Zehr, Howard, 292; 293; 303n143
Zenko, Micah, 300nn37, 44, 52; 427n3
Zetter, Kim, 578n89
Zgoba, Kristen, 8; 9
Zhang, Anlan, 94n58
Zhang, Dake, 182n212
Zhang, Dalun, 182n212
Zhang, Lening, 269n214
Zhang, Quanwu, 265n63
Zhang, Yan, 545n208
Zhao, Jihong Solomon, 94n34; 227n104
Zheng, Wei, 179n91
Zheng, Yan, 177n37
Zheng, Yao, 340n175
Zhong, Ming, 403
Zhu, Chenbo, 179n81
Zielinski, David, 336n54
Ziff, John, 427n16
Zimmerman, George, 89
Zimmerman, Gregory M., 225n7; 228n125; 326;
    339nn155, 156; 386n50
Zimmerman, Rick, 545nn228, 229
Zimmermann, Gregoire, 182n215
Zimring, Franklin, 64n70; 65n96; 123; 135n157;
    545n233
Zinzow, Heidi, 386n77
Zlotnick, Caron, 93n32
Zorbaugh, Harvey, 190; 225n13
Zottoli, Michael, 401
Zuberi, Daniyal, 183n223
Zuckerberg, Mark, 209
Zurbriggen, Eileen, 353; 387n86
Zweig, Phillip L., 498n14

SUBJECT INDEX

A

Abortion, trends in crime and, 44
Abortion providers, murder of, 410
Abu Ghraib (prison), 413
Abuse. *See* Child abuse; Elder abuse; Intimate partner violence; Rape; Sexual abuse; Sexual assault
Abuse of office, 398
Abused women. *See* Intimate partner violence; Rape; Sexual assault; Violence against women
Account verification scams, 556
ACLU. *See* American Civil Liberties Union
Acquaintance murder, 364, 383
Acquaintance rape, 355
Acquaintance robbery, 377
ACTIC. *See* Arizona Counter Terrorism Information Center
Active precipitation, 79
Active shooter incidents, 369
Actus reus, 18, 19, 24
ADAM II (data collection program), 528–529
Adam Walsh Child Protection and Safety Act (2006), 560
AddHealth study, 151
ADHD. *See* Attention deficit hyperactivity disorder
Administrative law, 16, 24
Adolescence, life influences in, 309
Adolescent-limited offenders, 330
Adolescents
  aggressive behavior in, 149
  aging out of crime, 51, 61, 246, 320
  antisocial behavior in, 105–106, 149
  buying drugs online, 562
  choosing crime, 105–106, 108–110
  crime rate and, 41–42, 46, 47, 51, 75–76
  cyberbullying, 566–567, 575
  as drug dealers, 526–527
  drug use by, 523, 526
  gangs and, 310
  identity crisis in, 159
  international trends in crime, 43
  mood disorders in, 160–161
  parents with criminal record, 314
  peer relations and, 38, 51, 108, 237–238
  problem behavior syndrome (PBS), 310, 525
  social control and, 205
  strain, sources of, 212
  victimization of, 72, 79, 80
Adoption fraud, 558
Adoption studies, 154
Adult entertainment, 506
Adult escort services, 515, 539
Adult films, 505
Advance fee fraud, 466, 558
Advertising, false claims, 475

Advocates for victims, 86–87, 90–91, 92
"Affluenza" drunk driving case, 233–234
Afghanistan, 406, 419, 423, 494
African Americans. *See* Race and ethnicity
Aftermath: Violence and the Remaking of a Self (Brison), 73
Age
  age of onset, 311, 334
  aging out, 51, 61, 246, 320
  trends in crime and, 44, 51, 75–76
  victimization and, 77
Age-graded theory, 312, 313–317, 334
  marriage and, 315–316
  summary of, 332
  testing, 315
  validity of, 316–317
Age-Graded Theory of Informal Social Control (Sampson and Laub), 313
Age of onset, 311, 334
Aggravated assault, as Part I crime, 28, 29
Aggravated rape, 360
Aggressive behavior
  attention deficit hyperactivity disorder (ADHD) and, 151, 160
  gender differences in, 52–53
  lead ingestion and, 147, 148
Aging out, 51, 61, 246, 320
Air loans, 473
Air pollution laws, 479
Air quality standards, 483
AK Steel Corp., 479
al-Qaeda, 394, 399, 409, 413, 415, 419, 424, 573
al-Shabaab (terror group), 411, 419
Alabama, 6, 87, 371
Alcohol abuse
  causes of, 524–525, 539
  costs of, 524
  genetics and, 525
  incidence of, 523–524
Alcohol consumption
  among adolescents, 523
  binge drinking, 523
  crime and, 118, 144–145, 529
  gateway model of substance abuse, 525–526
  incidence of abuse, 523–524
  Prohibition, 522–523
  temperance movement, 522
  violence and, 349
  Volstead Act, 523
Alexithymia, 161
ALF. *See* Animal Liberation Front
Alienation view, of terrorism, 417–418
All God's Children: The Bosket Family and the American Tradition of Violence (Butterfield), 55
Altered checks, 442

Amateur receivers, 437
Amateur thieves, 434, 456
AMED virus, 571
American Civil Liberties Union (ACLU), 568, 571
American Dream, 208–209
American Homicide (Roth), 10
American Humane Association, 479
Amnesty International, 413, 506
Amphetamines, drug use statistics, 43
Anal stage, 158
Androgens, behavior and, 146, 152, 175
Anger rape, 354
Animal Liberation Front (ALF), 410
Animals
  animal rights, 479, 480
  endangered species, 480
  illegal fishing, 481–482
  wildlife contraband, 480–481
Annie E. Casey Foundation, 193
Anomie, 206–208, 214, 224
ANS. *See* Autonomic nervous system
Ansar al-Shari'a (organization), 411
Ansar Bayt al-Maqdis (organization), 411
Anti-Drug Abuse Acts (1986 and 1988), 530
Anti-Saloon League, 522
Anti-stalking statutes, 19, 20, 382
Antigua, 464
Antigua and Barbuda, 361
Antipsychotic drugs, 152
Antisocial behavior
  in adolescents, 105–106, 149
  allergies and, 147
  arousal theory, 152
  attention deficit hyperactivity disorder (ADHD) and, 151, 160
  contagion, 311
  damaged identity and, 253, 256, 258
  emotional abuse and, 349
  environmental contaminants and, 147, 148
  Eysenck on, 306
  gangs and, 309
  inheritance of, 153–155
  labeling and, 255
  lead ingestion and, 147, 148
  life influences and, 309
  minimal brain dysfunction (MBD) and, 150
  mood disorders and, 161
  neurological disorders and, 148, 149
  parenting and, 322
  peer relations and, 237–238
  personality and, 169
  problem behavior syndrome (PBS) and, 310, 525
  psychodynamics of, 159, 168, 175
  strain and, 210
  twin studies of, 154

Brothel (Albert), 518
Brothels, 512, 514, 539
  See also Prostitution
Brown shooting (Ferguson, MO), 46
Brutalization stage, of violentization process, 350
BTK Killer, 365
"Buggery," 508
Bullying
  cyberbullying, 565–567, 575
  emotional toll on victim, 72, 565–566
Bureau of Justice Statistics website, 28
Burglars on the Job (Wright and Decker), 453
Burglary, 17, 111, 448–454
  careers in burglary, 452–454
  commercial burglary, 452
  defined, 448
  fences, 432, 435–437, 441, 453, 456
  gender differences in, 450, 456
  "good burglar," 452–453, 456
  nature and extent of, 449–450
  as Part I crime, 28, 29
  repeat burglary, 451
  residential burglaries, 451–452
  sexual burglary, 448, 456
Business email compromise, 547
Business opportunity scams, 558
Business-related bribery, 470

C

Calabrian Mafia, 491
Cali cartel, 492
California, 19, 21, 58, 59, 127, 251, 361, 369, 397, 410, 454, 469, 483, 490, 494, 509, 517
California Personality Inventory (CPI), 171
Call girls, 514–515
Call houses, 515
Cambodia, 492
Cambridge Five (spies), 401
Cambridge Study in Delinquent Development (CSDD), 153, 235, 311
Camorra (crime group), 491
Campus rape, 80, 289, 355–356, 357
Canada, 561
Canadian lottery scam, 556
Capable guardians, 82
CAPI. *See* Computer-assisted personal interviewing
Capital punishment
  constitutional limits on, 17
  as crime deterrent, 122–123
  deterrent effect of, 129–130
  DNA evidence and, 11
  as ethical issue, 105, 121
  research on, 11
  social science evidence used in capital cases, 8
  wrongful conviction in capital cases, 8, 11
Capitalism, Patriarchy, and Crime (Messerschmidt), 288
Capitalist bourgeoisie, 274
Captain Phillips (movie), 488
Car cloning, 445
Car theft. *See* Auto theft
Career criminals, 58
Caregiver stress view, of elder abuse, 76
Cargo thieves, 437–438
Caring-compelled profile, 415
Caring School Community Program, 533
Carjacking, 375, 377, 444, 445
Cartographic school of criminology, 189

"Castle doctrine," 89
Catfishing, 566–567
Catholic Church scandal, 510–511
Causes of Delinquency (Hirschi), 249
CCTV. *See* Closed-circuit television
CD. *See* Conduct disorder
Ceasefire group (Boston), 129
Cell phones
  criminal acts involving, 21
  illegal dumping of, 482
Center for Restorative Justice (CRJ), 296–297
Central European Working Group, 493
Cerebral allergies, 147
CERT Coordination Center, 565
CFAA. *See* Computer Fraud and Abuse Act
Charitable organizations, fund-raising by, 572
Charity fraud, 558
Charleston killings, 27, 28
Charlie Hebdo attack, 405
Cheater theory, 155–156
Chechnya, Russian invasion of, 283
Check forgery, 472
Check fraud schemes, 442
Check kiting, 442, 472
Chemical countermeasures, in the U.S., 421
Chemical restraints (chemical straitjackets), 152
Chemicals, behavior and, 145
Chicago, 199, 202, 351, 486
Chicago Area Project, 221
Chicago School, 190, 198
Chicken farming, green crime, 480
Child abuse, 372–373
  Catholic church scandal, 510–511
  causes of, 373, 383
  child molestation, 115, 560
  crime and, 237
  help for victims, 87
  international trends, 43
  pedophilia, 510–511, 539
  violence and, 349
Child Development Project, 533
Child molestation, 115, 560
Child Online Protection Act, 570
Child pornography, 519, 521, 560, 565, 575
Child Pornography Prevention Act of 1996 (CPPA), 521, 570
Child poverty, 193
Child prostitution, 516
Child Protection Act (1990), 88
Child Sexual Abuse Prevention Act, 412
Children
  allergies in, 147
  as arsonists, 454–455
  at-risk children, 191
  attachment theory, 160
  attention deficit hyperactivity disorder (ADHD), 148–151, 160
  child pornography, 519, 521, 560, 565, 575
  Child Pornography Prevention Act of 1996 (CPPA), 521
  child poverty, 193
  child prostitution, 516
  chronic offenders, 60–61
  cognitive differences and gender, 53
  conduct disorder (CD), 149
  continuity of crime, 60
  crusted over children, 351
  developmental interventions for, 331–333
  early onset criminals, 311
  exposure to violence, 350–351

female genital mutilation, 506
infanticide, 364
Internet pharmacies, 562
juvenile fire starter, 454–455
learning disabilities in, 150
maltreatment of, 237
molestation of, 115, 560
mood disorders in, 161
neurological disorders and, 148
pedophilia, 510–511, 539
poverty of, 193
PROTECT Act (2003), 52
psychosexual stages of development, 158–159
sex tourism, 512
sexual stigmatization of girls, 290
sexually related offenses against, 509
socialization and development and gender, 52–53
socialization of, 311
substance abuse by, 523, 525–526
trafficking in, 43
victimization in childhood, 72
as witnesses, 87
  See also Adolescents; Child abuse
China, 279, 281, 401, 411, 470, 482, 571, 572
Chiseling, 466–468, 496
Chivalry effect, 364
Chivalry hypothesis, 52
Chloropyrifos, behavior and, 148
Chop shop, 101
Chronic offenders, 58–61, 327
Chronic victimization, 77, 92
Chronicity, early onset of, 59–60
Church scandal, 510–511
Circle of Support and Accountability (COSA), 297
Circuit travelers, 515, 539
CITES. *See* Convention on International Trade in Endangered Species of Wild Fauna and Flora
Citizen groups against green crime, 483
Citizen-sponsored programs, for drug control, 532
Civil law, 16, 24
CKS. *See* Criminogenic knowledge structure
Clarissa (Richardson), 352
Class
  Marxist theory of, 274
  See also Social class
Classical criminology, 103–104
Classroom Centered (CC) Intervention, 533
Clean Water Act (1972), 478, 482
Clearance rate, 30
Cleared crimes, 30
Clergy, Catholic church scandal, 510–511
Cleveland, 509
Client fraud, 471–474, 496
Climate, crime rate and, 46–47
Closed account check fraud, 442
Closed-circuit television (CCTV), 118
Closure, 442
CLP. *See* Community Liaison Program
Co-offending, 51–52
Cocaine, 43, 522, 531
Code of Hammurabi, 15
"Code of the streets," 217
Coercion, 321
Cognitive deficits, 168
Cognitive factors, in life course theories, 312
Cognitive processing, 167, 175

cyberstalking, 564, 565
data breaches, 562–563
denial-of-service attack, 564–565, 572
distributed denial-of-service attack
    (DDoS), 564
logic bombs, 563, 572, 575
spam, 563, 572
swatting, 562
viruses and worms, 549, 563, 575
website defacement, 563–564
Cyberwar, 550, 571–574, 575
combatting, 574
cyberespionage, 571–572
cyberterrorism, 550, 572–574, 575
Cycle of violence, 73–74, 91, 349

D

Damaged identity, 253, 256, 258
D.A.R.E. *See* Drug Abuse Resistance Education
Darfur, 353
Darknet, 559–560, 561
Data fraud, 21
Data mining, 39–40
Data theft, 21
Date rape, 355–356, 357, 374
Dating violence, 374–375
DBD. *See* Disruptive behavior disorder
DC snipers, 371
DDoS. *See* Distributed denial-of-service attack
Death penalty. *See* Capital punishment
Death squads, 282–283
Decent values, 217
Deceptive pricing, 475
Declaration of the Rights of Man (France), 104
Deepwater Horizon explosion, 483, 484
Defective intelligence, 157
Defense of Marriage Act (1996), 408
Defenses. *See* Criminal defenses
Defensible space, 116
Defensive hate crimes, 378
Defiance, in control/balance theory, 321
Delinquency and Opportunity (Cloward and
    Ohlin), 218
Delinquency in a Birth Cohort (Wolfgang, Figlio,
    & Sellin), 58
"Delinquent boy," 218
Delinquent Boys (Cohen), 216
"Delinquent" fire setter, 455
Delinquent subcultures, 216–218, 219
Delinquents
    desistance and, 318
    social bond theory and, 252
Demystify, 284
Denial-of-service attack, 564–565, 572
Denmark, 572
Denver, 529
Department of Homeland Security (DHS),
    421–422, 426
Desistance, 311–312, 318
Deterrence, 120–121
    capital punishment and, 129–130
    compulsion of offenders and, 124
    of domestic violence, 126
    focused deterrence, 129
    general deterrence, 120–125, 128, 131
    greed of offenders and, 124–125
    incapacitation strategies, 126–128, 131

marginal deterrence, 103
perceptual deterrence, 120
policing and, 129
preemptive deterrence, 286
restrictive/partial deterrence, 122–123
sentencing and, 129–130
severity of punishment and, 121
shame and humiliation as deterrent, 118,
    121, 166
situational crime prevention, 116–120,
    128, 131
specific deterrence, 125, 126, 128, 131
speed (celerity) of punishment and, 121–122
white-collar crime, 477, 496
See also Crime prevention
Deterrence theory, 120–121, 124
Detoxification, drug abuse, 534
Detroit, 398
Developmental criminology, 306
Developmental theories, 305–334
    early onset criminals, 311
    elements of, 308
    evaluating, 331
    foundations of, 302–309, 333
    General Theory of Crime (GTC), 51, 320–
        327, 332, 334, 496
    General Theory of Crime and Delinquency
        (GTCD), 332
    latent trait theories, 307–308, 318–321, 332,
        333
    life course theories, 307, 308, 312–317, 331,
        332, 333, 334
    persistence and desistance, 311–312, 318
    population heterogeneity, 308–309
    propensity, 319, 327, 334
    public policy implications of, 331–333
    social schematic theory (SST), 317–318
    state dependence, 309
    summary of, 332
    trajectory theories, 308, 327–329, 332, 333
Deviance
    defined, 254
    deviant sexuality, 509–510
    family deviance, 235–236
    primary deviance, 257
    secondary deviance, 257
    See also Cyberdeviance
Deviant behavior
    in adolescents, 106
    crime and, 5–6, 23, 81
    defined, 5, 6
Deviant place theory of victimization, 81, 84, 92
DHS. *See* Department of Homeland Security
Dialectic method, 275
Diet
    behavior and, 145
    lead exposure in, 148
Differential association, principles of, 240–241
Differential association theory, 240–243, 262
    analysis of, 243
    cultural deviance critique, 243
    summary of, 259
    testing of, 242
Differential coercion theory, 321, 332
Differential law enforcement, 257–258
Differential opportunity, 218–220
Differential reinforcement, 243, 244
Differential reinforcement theory, 243–244, 259
Differential susceptibility model, 144
Diffusion of benefits, 119

Digital Millennium Copyright Act (DMCA),
    553, 570
Direct conditioning, 243
Direct Referral Reparative Program, 297
Director of National Intelligence (DNI), 420, 426
Disabled people. *See* Persons with disabilities
Disconnected-disordered profile, 415
Discouragement, 119
Disorders, 159
Disorganized area, 196, 204
    See also Social disorganization theory
Displacement, 119
Disputatiousness, 351
Disruption, in election fraud, 397
Disruptive behavior disorder (DBD), 160–161
Distributed denial-of-service attack (DDoS), 564
District of Columbia. *See* Washington, D.C.
Disturbing the peace, 17
Divergent Social Worlds (Peterson and Krivo), 195
Diversion programs, 261, 296
The Division of Labor in Society (Durkheim), 190
Division of markets, 475
Divorce, crime and, 77, 235, 316
Dizygotic twins, 154
DMCA. *See* Digital Millennium Copyright Act
DNA evidence, 117
DNI. *See* Director of National Intelligence
"Doing gender," 289
Doing Justice (Von Hirsch), 130
DOMA. *See* Defense of Marriage Act
Domestic terrorists, 409–410
Domestic violence
    deterrence of, 126
    gender and, 75
    murders, 364
    See also Intimate partner violence; Marital
        rape; Spousal abuse
Donetsk People's Republic, 419
Double agents, 401, 402
Double marginality, 288
Dramatization of evil, 256–257
Drift, 245
Drinking. *See* Alcohol consumption
Drive down auto accident fraud, 447
"Driving while black" (DWB), 35, 54
Drone (software), 572
Dropout factories, 279
Dropouts, 237
Drug abuse
    causes of, 524–525, 539
    detoxification, 534
    as deviant behavior, 5
    drug control strategies, 530–535, 539–540
    gateway model, 525–526
    psychosis and, 526
    skeezers, 515
    treatment strategies, 534–535, 538
    types of drug users and abusers, 526–528
    violence and, 348–349
    See also Substance abuse
Drug Abuse Control Act (1965), 530
Drug Abuse Resistance Education (D.A.R.E.),
    532–533
Drug cartels, 492
Drug control strategies, 530–535, 538, 539–540
    drug-testing strategies, 534, 538
    drug treatment strategies, 534–535, 538
    education strategies, 532–533, 538
    employment programs, 535, 538
    interdiction strategies, 531, 538

Medications
  behavior and, 145
  for drug treatment, 534, 535
Mega-gangs, 490
Megan's laws, 8–9, 20, 90, 118
Men
  burglary and, 450, 456
  hypermasculinity, 351, 353
  intimate partner murder, 364
  male socialization and rape, 358
  masculinity hypothesis, 52, 289, 299
  rape of, 353
  as serial killers, 367–369
  as spousal abuse victims, 374
  virility mystique, 358
Mens rea, 18, 19, 24
Menstruation, behavior and, 146–147
Mental disorders
  crime and, 160–162, 163
  serial killers, 368
  substance abuse and, 526
  terrorists, 417
  violence and, 346–347
Mental impairment, as defense, 19, 24
Mentally challenged people, hate crimes against, 378
Merchant privilege laws, 441
Merton's theory of anomie, 207–208, 214
Mesomorphs, 142
Meta-analysis, 39
Methadone, 534
Mexican drug cartels, 492
Mexican Mafia, 490
Mexico, 493
Miami, 536
Michigan, 101, 478, 485, 517
Microchip technology, for credit cards, 443
Middle-class measuring rods, 218
Migrant smuggling, 489
Military Commissions Acts (2006 and 2009), 423
Military service, spousal abuse and, 374
Militia extremists, 409–410
Miller doctrine, 520
Miller's lower-class focal concerns, 216, 220
Minerals, behavior and, 145
Minimal brain dysfunction (MBD), 150
Minnesota, 126, 517
Minnesota Multiphasic Personality Inventory (MMPI), 170–171
Minnesota Twin Family Study, 154
Minorities. *See* Race and ethnicity
Miracles Egg Donation case, 461
Misdemeanors, 17
Misinformation, in election fraud, 397
"Missing cases" phenomenon, 35
Mission hate crimes, 378
Mission killers, 367
Missouri, 351, 376, 467
"Mistake-of-age" defense, 358
Mistrust, fear and, 202
MMPI. *See* Minnesota Multiphasic Personality Inventory
Money mules, 556
Monitoring the Future (MTF) study, 45, 523
Monoamine oxidase (MAO), 152
Monozygotic twins, 154
Mood disorders, 159, 160–161
Moon rocks, theft of, 470
Moral belief, in social bond theory, 251, 252, 262

Moral crusades, 507–508, 522, 539
Moral development, 166
Moral development theory, 166
Moral entrepreneurs, 14, 254, 507
Morality
  criminal law expressing, 18
  legislation of, 505–506, 539
  moral crusades, 507–508, 522, 539
  social harm, 12, 479, 480, 504, 506–507, 539
More than Just Race: Being Black and Poor in the Inner City (Wilson), 195
Morphine, 522, 529
Mortgages, bank fraud involving, 473
Mosaic Code, 15
Motivated offenders, 82
Motor vehicle theft. *See* Auto theft
Movie pirates, 570
MPQ. *See* Multidimensional Personality Questionnaire
MTF study. *See* Monitoring the Future (MTF) study
Muckrakers, 474
Mujahideen, 399, 416
Multidimensional Personality Questionnaire (MPQ), 171
Murder, 17, 361–371
  acquaintance murder, 364, 383
  active shooter incidents, 369
  cult killers, 371
  defined, 361
  degrees of, 362–363, 383
  deliberation in, 362
  economic cost of, 71
  eldercide, 364
  felony murder, 362
  feticide, 363
  gang killings, 371
  honor killing, 366
  infanticide, 364
  intimate partner murder, 364
  legal criteria for, 362
  love killers, 371
  mass murder, 139, 140, 369–371, 383
  medical treatment of victims and crime rate, 45
  nature and extent of, 363–364
  neighborhoods and, 74, 82
  as Part I crime, 28, 29
  premeditation, 362
  profit killers, 371
  rational choice theory, 114
  revenge killers, 371
  school murders, 365
  sentencing and race, 55
  serial murder, 367–369
  sexually based murders, 364–365
  social theory and, 10
  spree killers, 371, 383
  statute of limitations on, 361–362
  stranger murder, 365, 367, 383
  terrorist killers, 371
  victim impact statements, 88
  workplace violence, 380–381, 383–384
  See also Homicide
Murderers, neurological disorders and, 148
Music industry, payola, 470
Music sharing, illegal, 554
Muslim Order of the Assassins (zealots), 408
Mustang Ranch (brothel), 514
Myanmar, 494

MyRedBook (website), 503

N

NACP. *See* National Advocate Credentialing Program
Naive check forgers, 442
Naltrexone, 534
Narcissistic personality disorder, 359
Narcotic Control Act (1956), 530
Narcotics, 19, 530
  See also Drug abuse; Drug crime; Drug trafficking; Drug use; Substance abuse
National Advocate Credentialing Program (NACP), 73
National Association of Fraud Investigators, 463
National Center for Victims of Crime, 73
National Commission on Terrorist Attacks Upon the United States, 420
National Counterproliferation Center, 420
National Counterterrorism Center (NCTC), 420, 421, 426
National Crime Victimization Survey (NCVS), 33–34, 35–36, 61
National Cybersecurity and Communications Integration Center, 421
National Deviancy Conference (NDC), 276
National Drug and Alcohol Facts Week (NDAFW), 533
National Household Survey on Drug Abuse and Health, 523
National Incident-Based Reporting System (NIBRS), 31–32, 61
National Longitudinal Study of Adolescent Health, 151
National Mental Health Association (NMHA), 162
National Minimum Drinking Age Act (1984), 254
National Organization for Victim Assistance, 73
National security, 568
National Security Agency (NSA), 281, 395, 424, 568, 574
National Stolen Property Act, 570
National Whistleblowers Center, 475
National White Collar Crime Center, 570
Nationalist terrorism, 410–411, 416, 426
Nature theory, 172
Navy Yard shootings, 369
Nazis, 419
NCTC. *See* National Counterterrorism Center
NCVS. *See* National Crime Victimization Survey
NDAFW. *See* National Drug and Alcohol Facts Week
NDC. *See* National Deviancy Conference
'Ndrangheta (crime group), 491
Neapolitan Mafia, 491
Necessity, as defense, 19
Negative affective states, 210–211, 224
Negative labeling, 254, 257, 262
Negative life events, 309
Negative reinforcement, 244
Negative stimuli, 211
Neglect (child abuse), 372
Negligent tort, 16
Neighborhood hustlers, 437
Neighborhood patrols, 89
Neighborhoods
  broken windows, 200
  Chicago School on, 190, 198
  collective efficacy, 203–205, 223

Phoenix (AZ), 515
Phone phreakers, 549
Photo studios, prostitution through, 515
Phrenology, 141
Phthalates, behavior and, 147
Physically challenged people. *See* Persons with disabilities
Physician-assisted suicide, 20
Physicians, medical billing fraud, 472
Physiognomy, 141
Pigeon drop, 446
PII. *See* Personally identifiable information
Pilferage, 470–471
Pimps, 513
"Pink slime," 467
Pinkerton Detective Agency, 433
Piracy
    illegal file sharing, 553, 570
    maritime piracy, 488–489
    software piracy, 21
Pitcairn Internet pharmacy, 561
Playboy (magazine), 559
"Playing with matches" fire setter, 454
Pleasure principle, 158
PLO. *See* Palestine Liberation Organization
PMS. *See* Premenstrual syndrome
Poachers, 433
Pocket-picking, 434
Poland, 470
Police
    crime reduction by adding more police, 45
    deterrent effect of, 129
    drug control by, 532
    influence peddling in, 470
    payoffs, 469
    restorative justice and, 295
    victim advocates, 86
Police corruption, 470
Police guardianship, victimization and, 82
Policing
    community policing, 222–223
    crackdowns, 129
    deterrence and, 129
    predictive policing, 39
    "pulling levers policing," 129
    social control by, 204
Political crime, 394–404
    abuse of office, 398
    becoming a political criminal, 396
    causes of, 425
    defined, 425
    election fraud, 397–398
    espionage, 400–403, 425
    goals of, 395–396
    public corruption, 398
    state political crime, 403, 425
    torture, 283, 403–404, 413, 425
    treason, 398–400, 425
    types of, 397–404
    See also Terrorism
Political detainees, torture of, 283, 403–404, 413, 425
Political prisoners, 413
Political terrorism, 409–410, 416, 426
Politically motivated cybercrime. *See* Cyberwar
Pollution, 479, 482
    BP oil spill, 484
    Exxon Valdez oil spill, 483
Polychlorinated biphenyls (PCBs), behavior and, 147

Polycyclic aromatic hydrocarbons (PAHs), behavior and, 147
Ponzi schemes, 461, 464, 465
Population, 32
Population heterogeneity, 308–309
"Porn-napping," 559
Pornography, 518–521
    child pornography, 519, 521, 560, 565
    controlling, 521
    defined, 518
    Internet porn, 559–561, 575
    law enforcement and, 521
    legislation, 520–521
    morality of, 506
    sociology of law and, 7–8
    violence and, 518–520
    See also Obscenity
Positive stimuli, removal of, 211
Positivism, 140, 141–142
Positron emission tomography (PET), 149, 150
Posse Comitatus, 409
Posttraumatic stress disorder (PTSD), 72, 74, 84, 349, 356
Poultry industry, green crime, 480
Poverty
    child poverty, 193
    concentration effect, 200
    culture of poverty, 191
    inner-city poverty, 195
    minority group poverty, 193–195
    poverty line, 191
    social disorganization theory, 198, 210, 223
    "War on Poverty," 221
Power and control view, of elder abuse, 76
Power-control theory, 290–291, 292
Power rape, 354
Powerlessness, 202, 289
Predation, in control/balance theory, 321
Predictive policing, 39
Preemptive deterrence, 286
Pregnancy
    diet and crime, 144
    environmental contaminants during, 144, 148
    feticide, 363
    lead exposure in, 148
Premeditation, murder, 362
Premenstrual syndrome (PMS), behavior and, 146–147
Preparing for the Drug-Free Years, 533
Presidential primary campaign (2016), 271, 272
Pretty Woman (movie), 513
Price fixing, 463, 474–475
Primary deviance, 257
Primary prevention programs, 173
Prime bank investment swindles, 466
Princeton University Survey Research Center, 32
Principles of Criminology (Sutherland), 240
PRISM program, 568
Prisons
    1980's crime control, 105
    as crime deterrent, 127–128
    supermax prisons, 125
    See also Incarceration
Privacy and Civil Liberties Board, 420
Prize/sweepstakes schemes, 558
Problem behavior syndrome (PBS), 310, 525
Procedural criminal law, 16, 23–24
Productive forces, 274
Productive relations, 274
Professional car thieves, 444–445

Professional cargo thieves, 437–438
Professional chiseling, 467
Professional criminals, 434
Professional shoplifters, 440–441, 456
The Professional Thief (Sutherland), 435
Professional thieves, 434–435, 456
Profit, political crime for, 396
Profit killers, 371
Prohibition (of alcohol use), 522–523
Project ALERT, 533
Project COPE, 222
Project STAR, 533
Proletariat, 274
Promoting Alternative Thinking Strategies (PATHS), 533
Propensity, 319, 327, 334
Property crime, 431–457
    arson, 28, 29, 454–455
    burglary, 17, 28, 29, 111, 448–454
    larceny/theft, 17, 28, 29, 438–448, 456
    reporting of, 30
    theft, 432–438
    trends in, 41, 42
Prosecutorial Remedies and Other Tools to end the Exploitation of Children (PROTECT Act) (2003), 52
Prostitutes
    types of, 512–515, 539
    who becomes a prostitute, 515–516
Prostitution, 511–518
    brothels, 512, 514, 539
    child prostitution, 516
    controlling, 516
    defined, 512, 539
    ehooking, 561
    free choice view, 517
    history of, 511, 539
    incidence of, 512
    "john" schools, 517
    legalization of, 512, 514, 516–518
    Omuro case, 503
    in other cultures, 512, 516
    pimps, 513
    sex tourism, 512
    sex trade, 513
    sexual equality view, 517
    types of prostitutes, 512–515, 539
    as victimless crime, 504
PROTECT Act (2003), 52
Pseudo-conviction, political crime for, 396
Psycho (movie), 140
Psychoanalytic perspective, 157
Psychodynamic theory, 157–159, 168, 175
Psychological disorders
    rape and, 358–359
    substance abuse and, 524–525
Psychological learning theories, 243
Psychological sociology, 234
Psychological trait theories, 157–168
    attachment theory, 160
    behavioral theory, 162–166, 168, 175
    cognitive theory, 157, 166–168, 175
    mental disorders and crime, 160–162, 163
    psychodynamic theory, 157–159, 168, 175
Psychological treatment, 173
Psychological view
    of substance abuse, 524–525
    of terrorism, 417
Psychopath, 170
Psychopathia Sexualis (Krafft-Ebing), 510

on genetics and crime, 154–155
on intimate partner murder, 364
objectivity of, 22
observational and interview research, 37–38
on personality, 170–171
on professional thieves, 436
on psychopaths, 170
quasi-experimental design, 37
retrospective cohort study, 36–37
on school murder, 365
on sexually related homicide, 365
on social reaction theory, 257, 262
on terrorism, 10
on violent behavior in gangs, 351
Reshipping, 555
Residential burglaries, 451–452
Restitution, 18, 88, 261
Restoration, 294–297
Restoration programs, 295
Restorative justice, 292–293, 297–298, 299, 381
Restorative Justice (Sullivan and Tifft), 291
Restraint of trade, 474–475
Restrictive/partial deterrence, 122–123
Retaliatory hate crimes, 378–379
Retreatism, 207
Retreatist gangs, 220
Retributive terrorism, 411–413, 416
Retrospective cohort study, 36–37
Retrospective reading, 256
Revenge, 17, 74, 91
Revenge killers, 371
Revolution, 396, 407
Revolutionaries, 407
Revolutionary terrorists, 409, 416, 426
Rezendes attack, 564
Rhinoceros, poachers, 481
Rhode Island, 40
RICO Act. *See* Racketeer Influenced and Corrupt Organization Act
Right-wing political groups, as terrorists, 49–410
Ritualism, 207
Road rage, 371
Robbery, 375–377, 383
    acquaintance robbery, 377
    armed robbery, 156, 375, 376
    carjacking, 375, 377, 444, 445
    characteristics of robbers, 375–377
    commercial robbery, 375
    economic cost of, 71
    as Part I crime, 28, 29
    rational choice theory, 111, 114
    rationality of, 114
    types of, 375, 376
Rochester Youth Development Study (RYDS), 153
Role exit behavior, 290
Roman Catholic Church scandal, 510–511
Romance fraud, 558
"Romeo and Juliet provisions," 357–358
Room (movie), 509
Roomservice (online service), 561
Roseburg (Oregon) community college massacre, 139
Roth decision, 520
Routine activities theory, 81–83, 84, 92, 110
RS-AVS (online service), 561
Russia, 283, 407, 408–409, 419, 490, 491, 493, 572
Russian crime groups, 491
Russian Revolution, 407
RYDS. *See* Rochester Youth Development Study

S

SAC Capital, 468
Sacra Corona Unita (crime group), 491
Sacramento, 529
Sadistic personality disorder, 169
Sadistic rape, 354
Sadists, 367
Sadomasochism, 510, 539
Safecracking, 433–434
Safety regulations, 19
Salami cyberfraud, 552
Same-sex marriage crusade, 508
Sampling, 32
Sampson and Laub's age-graded theory, 312, 313–317, 334
    marriage and, 315–316
    summary of, 332
    testing, 315
    validity of, 316–317
San Bernardino attack, 2–4, 369
San Francisco, 517
San Francisco dog attack case, 362
Sandy Hook school shootings, 75, 124, 162, 369
Sarbanes-Oxley Act (2002), 477
Saudi Arabia, 424, 466
Schizophrenia, 161
School dropouts, 237
Schools
    murder in, 365
    victims and victimization and, 74–75
    See also Education
Sciari (terrorists), 408
Scientific method, 4, 9, 140–141
SDM. *See* Social development model
SDS. *See* Students for a Democratic Society
Search warrants, Patriot Act and, 277, 423–424, 568, 570
Seasons, crime rate and, 46–47
Second Chance for Ex-Offenders Act (2011), 260
Second-degree murder, 362, 383
Second International Drug Congress, 522
Secondary prevention programs, 173
Secret shoppers (cyberfraud), 558
Securities
    chiseling, 468
    fraud on the Internet, 554
    fraudulent offerings of, 554
    illegal touting, 554
Securities Act (1933), 554
Securities and Exchange Commission (SEC), 477
Security cameras, illegal domestic surveillance, 281
Security systems, victimization and, 82
Sedition, 18
Seductions of Crime (Katz), 109
Self-control, 321, 324
Self-control theory, 324
Self-defense, as defense, 19
Self-image, 249, 255
Self-protection by victims, 89–90
Self-report surveys, 34–35, 36, 41–42
Sentencing
    1980's crime control, 105
    deterrent effect of, 129–130
    fairness, 130
    just desert, 130
    race and, 55
    sentencing circle, 295
Sentencing circle, 295
Serbia, 353, 408

Serial killers, 367–369, 383
    rational choice theory, 114–115
    "Son of Sam," 161
Serial rape, 354–355
Serotonin, 161
17th Judicial District Crime Victim Compensation Program, 86
"Severely disturbed" fire setter, 455
Sex crimes. *See* Sexually related offenses
Sex offender registration, 8–9, 20, 91, 117, 293, 560
Sex offenders
    Megan's laws, 8–9, 20, 90, 118, 293
    recidivism of, 9
    registration of, 8–9, 20, 91, 117, 293, 560
Sex tourism, 512
Sex trade, 513
Sex trafficking, 512, 516
Sex workers, 561
    See also Prostitutes
"Sexting," 256, 505
"Sextortion," 565
Sexual abuse, 373
    Catholic church scandal, 510–511
    of children, 43, 237, 373
    international trends, 43
Sexual assault, 352
    "blaming the victim," 359
    campus rape, 80
    of college women, 80
    in colleges, 289
    economic cost of, 71
    economic impact of, 37
    gender and, 75
    international trends, 43
    posttraumatic stress disorder (PTSD) following, 72, 84
    time of day and, 74
    victim advocates, 86
    victim impact statements, 88
    See also Rape
Sexual burglary, 448, 456
Sexual exploitation, 43
    child pornography, 519, 521, 560, 565, 575
Sexual initiation, forces, 43
Sexual predators, 19, 509, 510
Sexual violence, 43
    status of women and, 289
    virility mystique, 358
Sexuality, deviant sexuality, 509–510
Sexually based murders, 364–365
Sexually related offenses, 509–521
    cyberdeviance, 550, 559–562, 574
    obscenity, 7–8, 16–17, 506, 518, 575
    paraphilias, 509–510, 539
    as Part II crimes, 29
    pedophilia, 510–511, 539
    pornography, 7–8, 506, 518–521, 575
    prostitution, 503, 504, 511–518
    rationality of perpetrators, 115
    sexually oriented contact burglaries, 449, 456
    See also Sexual abuse; Sexual assault; Sexual exploitation; Sexual violence
SFA. *See* Skills for Adolescence
SFP. *See* Strengthening Families Program
Shame
    as crime deterrent, 118, 121, 166, 293–294
    defined, 293
    reintegrative shaming, 293–294
Shark fins, illegal fishing for, 481

Commerce Clause, 21, 475
cruel and unusual punishment, 17, 104
Eighteenth Amendment, 486, 522
First Amendment, 520, 521, 568
Fourth Amendment, 568
free speech, 520
on hate crimes and free speech clause, 380
limits on criminal law, 17, 24
militia extremists on, 409–410
obscenity and, 520
pornography and, 520–521
Prohibition, 522–523
Twenty-First Amendment, 523
U.S. Foreign Intelligence Surveillance Court, 424
U.S. Secret Service, 570
USA Freedom Act, 424
USA Patriot Act (USAPA), 277, 423–424, 568, 570
USCYBERCOM. *See* United States Cyber Command
Utah, 509
Utilitarian calculus, 103
Uyghur separatists, 411

V

Vandalism, 245
appeal of, 109
cybervandalism, 550, 562–568, 574, 575
as Part II crimes, 29
Vehicle theft. *See* Auto theft
Vermont, 296–297
Versatile contact burglary, 449, 456
Viagra, behavior and, 145
VICAP. *See* Violent Criminal Apprehension Program
Vicarious fear, 71–72
Victim. *See* Victims
Victim advocates, 86–87
Victim blaming, 359
Victim compensation, 18, 84–86, 92
Victim impact statements, 88
Victim Offender Reconciliation Program (VORP), 88
Victim-offender reconciliation programs, 88
Victim precipitation theory of victimization, 78–79, 84, 92
Victim-witness advocates, 86–87
Victim-witness assistance programs, 85, 92
Victimization, 69–91
of adolescents, 72, 79, 80
age and, 77
in childhood, 72
chronic victimization, 77, 92
community organizations and, 89
costs associated with, 70–73
crime and, 74
criminal lifestyle and, 81
cycle of violence, 73–74, 91
elder abuse, 76
of the elderly, 76
emotional costs of victimization, 71–73
fears of victims, 72–73
gang lifestyle and, 81
gender and, 289
of girls, 289
governmental response to, 84–88
marital status and, 77
National Crime Victimization Survey (NCVS), 33–34, 35–36, 61
nature of, 74–78

neighborhood and, 46, 74, 82, 89, 111
of persons with disabilities, 79
posttraumatic stress disorder (PTSD), 72, 74, 84
of prostitutes, 513, 514
race and ethnicity and, 77
rational choice theory, 110–111
repeat victimization, 77–78, 92
school and, 74–75
social ecology of, 74–75, 91
in suburbia, 83
theories of, 78–84, 92
trends in, 41
victim personality and, 79
See also Victims
Victimization theories, 78–84, 92
deviant place theory, 81, 84, 92
lifestyle theory, 79–81, 84, 92
routine activities theory, 81–83, 84, 92
victim precipitation theory, 78–79, 84, 92
Victimless crimes, 12, 504, 505, 521
See also Public order crimes
Victimologists, 70
Victims, 9, 11, 69–91
adolescents and children, 72
age of, 44, 51, 75–76
caring for, 84–91, 92
characteristics of, 78, 91–92
chronic victimization, 77, 92
compensation of, 18, 84–86, 92
costs associated with victimization, 70–73, 91
crisis intervention, 88
cycle of violence, 73–74, 91
denying the victim, 245
economic costs of victimization to, 70–71
emotional costs of victimization, 71–73
fears of, 72–73
fighting back, 89
gender of, 52–53, 75
household of, 75, 91
injury resulting from crime, 74, 75
justice system handling of, 70
marital status of, 77
medical treatment of, 45
personality and victimization risk, 79
posttraumatic stress disorder (PTSD), 72, 74, 84
public education about assistance, 87–88
race and ethnicity of, 77
relationship stress following, 72
repeat victimization, 77–78, 92
reporting crimes, 30
restitution programs for, 18, 88
revenge by, 17, 74, 91
self-protection, 89–90
social status of, 76–77
stress of, 72–73
victim advocates, 86–87
victim impact statements, 88
victim-offender reconciliation programs, 88
victim surveys, 33
victim-witness assistance programs, 85, 92
victims' rights, 90–91, 92
See also Victimization
Victims' Bill of Rights, 90–91
Victims of Child Abuse Act (1990), 87
Victims of Crime Act of 1984 (VOCA), 80, 85, 86
Victims' rights, 90–91, 92
Vigilantes, 507

VINshield program, 445
Violence, 346
androgens and, 146, 152, 175
causes of, 346–352, 383
child abuse and, 349
contemporary black violence, 55
cycle of violence, 73–74, 91, 349
dating violence, 374–375
evolution and, 156, 175
exposure to, effect of, 350–351
expressive violence, 346
human instinct and, 347–348
instrumental violence, 346
intimate partner violence (IPV), 38
mental disorders and, 161, 163
national values and, 351–352
parenting and, 349–350
pornography and, 518–520
psychological/biological abnormality and, 346–347
rape, 352–361
rationality of, 113–115
in schools, 365
social learning and, 164–165
socialization and, 349–350
state violence, 282–283
subculture of violence, 351
substance abuse and, 348–349
violentization process, 350, 383
workplace violence, 380–381, 383–384
See also Interpersonal violence; Terrorism; Violent crimes
Violence: A Microsociological Theory (Collins), 348
Violence against women, international trends, 43
The Violence of Hate (Levin), 379
Violent Crime Control and Law Enforcement Act (1994), 512
Violent crimes
causes of, 346–352, 383
drug use and, 45
mental disorders and, 161, 163
reporting of, 30
trends in, 41, 42
victim impact statements, 88
violent media and, 45, 164–165
See also Violence
Violent Criminal Apprehension Program (VICAP), 369
Violent performance stage, of violentization process, 350
Violent pornography, 519–520
Violentization process, 350, 383
Virginia, 21, 380
Virginia reporter murders, 139, 380
Virginia Tech mass murder, 369
Virility mystique, 358
Virtual pornography, 521
Virulency stage, of violentization process, 350
Viruses, 549, 563, 575
VISA scams, 556
Vishing (cybertheft), 556–557
VOCA. *See* Victims of Crime Act of 1984
Volstead Act, 523
Voluntary manslaughter, 363, 383
VORP. *See* Victim Offender Reconciliation Program
Vote buying, 397
Voter IDs, 398
Voting fraud. *See* Election fraud
Voyeurism, 449, 510, 539